APA Handbook of

Research Methods in Psychology

APA Handbooks in Psychology

APA Handbook of
Research Methods in Psychology

VOLUME 3

Data Analysis and Research Publication

Harris Cooper, *Editor-in-Chief*
Paul M. Camic, Debra L. Long, A. T. Panter,
David Rindskopf, and Kenneth J. Sher, *Associate Editors*

American Psychological Association • Washington, DC

Published by
American Psychological Association
750 First Street, NE
Washington, DC 20002-4242
www.apa.org

To order
APA Order Department
P.O. Box 92984
Washington, DC 20090-2984
Tel: (800) 374-2721; Direct: (202) 336-5510
Fax: (202) 336-5502; TDD/TTY: (202) 336-6123
Online: www.apa.org/pubs/books/
E-mail: order@apa.org

In the U.K., Europe, Africa, and the Middle East, copies may be ordered from
American Psychological Association
3 Henrietta Street
Covent Garden, London
WC2E 8LU England

AMERICAN PSYCHOLOGICAL ASSOCIATION STAFF
Gary R. VandenBos, PhD, *Publisher*
Julia Frank-McNeil, *Senior Director, APA Books*
Theodore J. Baroody, *Director, Reference, APA Books*
Kristen Knight, *Project Editor, APA Books*

Typeset in Berkeley by Cenveo Publisher Services, Columbia, MD

Printer: Maple-Vail Book Manufacturing Group, York, PA
Cover Designer: Naylor Design, Washington, DC

Library of Congress Cataloging-in-Publication Data

APA handbook of research methods in psychology / Harris Cooper,
editor-in-chief.
       v. cm.
    Includes bibliographical references and index.
    Contents: v. 1. Foundations, planning, measures, and psychometrics—
v. 2. Research designs : quantitative, qualitative, neuropsychological,
and biological—v. 3. Data analysis and research publication.
    ISBN-13: 978-1-4338-1003-9
    ISBN-10: 1-4338-1003-4
    1. Psychology—Research—Methodology—Handbooks, manuals, etc. 2.
Psychology—Research—Handbooks, manuals, etc. I. Cooper, Harris M. II.
American Psychological Association. III. Title: Handbook of research
methods in psychology.
    BF76.5.A73 2012
    150.72′1—dc23
                            2011045200

British Library Cataloguing-in-Publication Data
A CIP record is available from the British Library.

Printed in the United States of America
First Edition

DOI: 10.1037/13621-000

Contents

Editorial Board

PART I
QUANTITATIVE DATA ANALYSIS

Section I

Preparing Data for Analysis

METHODS FOR DETECTING BADLY BEHAVED DATA: DISTRIBUTIONS, LINEAR MODELS, AND BEYOND

Robert Andersen

We often make assumptions about the distributions to which statistical methods are applied. For example, the mean is an appropriate measure of center only when the variable has a symmetric and unimodal distribution. The same conditions pertain to the use of the standard deviation as a measure of spread. Similarly, the use of linear regression makes sense only when the relationship between variables can be adequately summarized by a straight line. Just as important, classical statistical inference rests on assumptions regarding sampling distributions and underlying population distributions. The inspection of distributions is thus an important step in statistical analysis. Failure to detect and remedy so-called badly behaved data can lead to erroneous conclusions. Reflecting the importance of distributions to statistical analysis, this chapter has two main goals: (a) it explores various methods for examining and transforming the distributions of quantitative variables, and (b) it demonstrates related methods for diagnosing problems in linear models. Although many of the diagnostics procedures that are discussed can be extended to generalized linear models and other related methods, they are mentioned only briefly because of space constraints.

DISTRIBUTIONS

Normal Distributions and Statistical Inference

The first step in statistical analysis is to explore the distributions of the variables to be analyzed. Attention should be given to the general spread; the center, the mode, and the length of the tails; and whether there are outliers. Because of its importance to many statistical methods, including classical statistical inference, we often use the normal distribution as a benchmark to which we compare the distributions of observed variables or the residuals from regression models. Below I provide a brief description of normal distributions (for greater detail see Krishnamoorthy, 2006).

Normal distributions are symmetric, single-peaked, bell-shaped, and can be entirely described by their mean μ and standard deviation σ. Commonly noted by $N(\mu, \sigma^2)$, the probability density function of a normal distribution is given by

$$f\left(x \mid \mu, \sigma\right) = \frac{1}{\sigma\sqrt{2\pi}} \exp\left[-\frac{\left(x - \mu\right)^2}{2\sigma^2}\right]. \quad (1)$$

Normal curves follow the 68–95–99.7 rule where approximately 68% of cases fall within one σ of the mean, 95% fall within two σ, and 99.7% of cases fall within three σ of the mean. Often we make comparisons to the *standard normal distribution*, which has a mean of 0 and standard deviation of 1. If a variable is approximately normally distributed, we can calculate *standardized values*, z (called z scores) for each observation:

$$z = \frac{x_i - \mu}{\sigma}. \quad (2)$$

The z score tells how many standard deviations the observation falls from the mean. Negative values indicate that the observation is smaller than the mean; positive values indicate that it is larger than

DOI: 10.1037/13621-001
APA Handbook of Research Methods in Psychology: Vol. 3. Data Analysis and Research Publication, H. Cooper (Editor-in-Chief)

the mean. Normal distributions, and standardized scores, play a particularly important role in statistical inference.

Statistical inference provides us with methods for drawing conclusions from data that are from a *random sample* or a *randomized experiment*. Using probability theory, we can take chance variation into account when making judgments about the trustworthiness of a statistic. Statistical inference does not tell us whether our statistics are correct but rather how they perform on average. Classical statistical inference, otherwise known as the frequentist approach, is formed on the basis of the idea of repeated random sampling from a population (Neyman, 1937). The sampling distribution of a statistic (e.g., the sample mean $\bar{x}$) pertains to the distribution of the statistic ($\bar{x}$) for all possible samples of a given size. Statistical theory tells us three important things about the sampling distribution of a sample statistic ($\bar{x}$):

1. It is close to normally distributed;
2. the mean of all the statistics (i.e., the mean of $\bar{x}$) equals the population parameter μ (in other words, the statistic is *unbiased*); and
3. the standard deviation of the sampling distribution gets smaller as the sample gets larger, $s_{\bar{x}} = \sigma / \sqrt{n}$.

These conclusions are made on the basis of the *central limit theorem* and the *law of large numbers*. The central limit theorem states that, with repeated sampling, the shape of the sampling distribution becomes normal with the population parameter at its center regardless of the shape of the sample distribution. The law of large numbers holds that if we repeat a random phenomenon many times, the average value will get closer and closer to the population parameter. The larger the sample, the more likely a statistic represents the true population parameter (for more details, see Kish 1965; Sudman 1976)

The fact that statistics from random samples have definite sampling distributions allows a more careful estimate of how trustworthy a statistic is as an estimate of a population parameter. Variability is described by the spread of its sampling distribution, which is determined by the sampling design and the size of the sample. The larger the sample, the

smaller the spread. As long as the population is at least 10 times larger than the sample, the spread of the sampling distribution is approximately the same regardless of the population size. These facts allow us to make claims about a population by constructing confidence intervals and hypothesis tests.

When the probability of obtaining a particular value of a statistic is very small (called the *p* value), we say that the result is statistically significant. More specifically, a statistic is considered statistically significant when it is so large that it would rarely occur by chance alone. Statistical significance tests test whether an observed sample statistic differs from some specified value. Confidence intervals give a range around that parameter estimate (i.e., the statistic) that indicates how precisely the estimate has been measured, and a confidence level, which states the probability that the method used to calculate the interval will contain the population parameter.

Assume that we unrealistically know the standard deviation in the population σ, we could then easily standardize our observed value of $\bar{x}$ relative to the sampling distribution of all possible values of $\bar{x}$ from repeated samples of the same size:

$$z = \frac{\bar{x} - \mu}{\sigma / \sqrt{n}}. \tag{3}$$

We call this a one-sample *z* statistic. The value of *z* tells us how far the observed sample mean $\bar{x}$ is from the population parameter μ in the units of the standard deviation of $\bar{x}$. Because $\bar{x}$ is normally distributed, *z* is $N(0,1)$.

In the real world, we typically do not know the population standard deviation σ (and thus we also do not know the standard deviation of the sampling distribution), so we estimate it using the sample standard deviation *s*. We thus estimate the standard deviation of the sampling distribution with the standard error, $SE_{\bar{x}} = s / \sqrt{n}$. These added estimates increase the uncertainty of our estimate of μ. With this in mind, the *t*-statistic adjusts for the uncertainty by taking into account the sample size

$$t = \frac{\bar{x} - \mu}{s / \sqrt{n}}. \tag{4}$$

The *t* statistic has a different degrees of freedom ($n - 1$) for each sample size. The *t* distributions are similar in shape to the normal distribution—they are symmetric, have a mean of zero, are single peaked and bell-shaped—but have larger spread than the normal distribution. Reflecting the fact that we have less certainty in estimates from small samples, the spread of the *t*-distribution gets smaller as the sample size grows until it is identical to the *z* statistic for very large samples sizes.

We can use the *t*-distributions to test the null hypothesis that μ equals a specified hypothesized value, μ_0, such that $H_0: \mu = \mu_0$. Depending on the research question, we specify one of three different possibilities for the alternative hypothesis:

1. The population mean μ is greater than the null hypothesized value, $H_a: \mu > \mu_0$;
2. The population mean μ is less than the null hypothesized value, $H_a: \mu < \mu_0$; or
3. The population mean μ is not equal to the null hypothesized value, $H_a: \mu \neq \mu_0$

We then calculate the *t* statistic for our sample statistic on the basis of the notion that the null hypothesis is true:

$$t = \frac{\bar{x} - \mu_0}{s/\sqrt{n}}. \tag{5}$$

The corresponding *p* value for the *t* statistic is used to determine whether or not we should reject the null hypothesis (i.e., whether the *t* statistic is statistically significant). Very small *p* values suggest that the result we have observed is unlikely to occur by chance alone. That is, the observed $\bar{x}$ is so different from μ_0 that it is unlikely that the true population parameter μ is the null hypothesized value. As a result, we reject the null hypothesis, and by implication, accept the alternative hypothesis. Conventionally a test is considered statistically significant if its *p* value is less than $\alpha = .05$, $\alpha = .01$, or $\alpha = .001$.

Rearranging the equation for the *t*-statistic, we can also estimate a confidence interval for μ:

$$\begin{aligned} \mu &= \bar{x} \pm t^* SE_{\bar{x}} \\ &= \bar{x} \pm t^* \frac{s}{\sqrt{n}}, \end{aligned} \tag{6}$$

where t^* is the upper $(1 - C)/2$ critical value for the $t(n - 1)$ distribution that corresponds to the desired level of confidence C for the sample size under investigation. For example, for a 95% confidence interval, we require the value of t^* that encloses the middle 95% of the *t* distribution (for more details, see Moore, 2004).

Departure From Normality

Distributions are never exactly normally distributed but well-behaved data can be characterized as having distributions that are symmetric, unimodal, and free of extremely long tails or outliers. Severe departures from normality can cause trouble for many statistical methods (for a classic illustration, see Tukey, 1960). For example, the mean and standard deviation can be severely pulled toward a skew or outliers. As another example, regression slopes are considerably less efficient if the error distribution is skewed or has outliers. Badly behaved data, then, suffer from kurtosis, suffer from skewness, have many modes, or have significant outliers. Some of these problems are depicted in Figure 1.1. Figure 1.1b demonstrates a *bimodal* distribution. Distributions such as this suggest that the data can be divided into groups. As Figure 1.1c indicates, the term *leptokurtosis* describes distributions that have short tails and elevated peaks. In contrast, *platykurtosis* refers to distributions that have flat peaks and heavy tails as shown in Figure 1.1d. *Skewness* refers to an asymmetry in the tails of the distribution. A negative skew shown in Figure 1.1e is characterized by a stretched tail at low values of the distribution, whereas a positive skew given in Figure 1.1f is indicated by a stretched tail at high values (for more details, see Krishnamoorthy, 2006). *Outliers* are observations that stand apart from the bulk of the data (i.e., individual departures from the general pattern of the data). Although outliers and skews can have similar practical effects for many statistics—especially in terms of their effect on efficiency—they are conceptually quite different and are typically rectified using different methods (see Andersen, 2008).

Histograms

Histograms are useful for assessing the general shape of a distribution, especially its mode and tails. A histogram is a two-dimensional plot of a quantitative distribution that dissects the range of the data into bins of equal width along the horizontal axis.

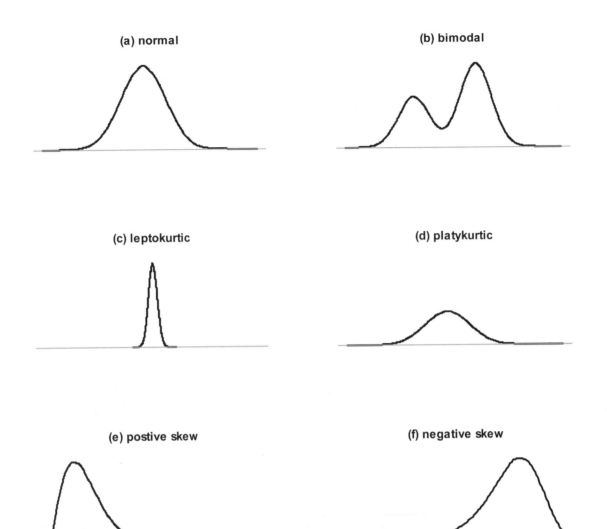

FIGURE 1.1. Describing distributions.

The vertical axis represents the frequency counts (or percentages or proportions). Vertical bars are used to represent the counts. Reflecting the continuous nature of the data, the bars are plotted side by side without space between them (in contrast to a bar graph used for a categorical variable).

Given that histograms are used to describe the distributions of quantitative variables—that is, the variables do not have discrete categories—we must decide the number of bins to be employed. A general guideline for small data sets ($n = 100$ or less) is to use # of bins $= 2\sqrt{n}$. On the other hand, for larger data sets, Freedman and Diaconis (1981) have recommended using the following formula:

$$\text{\# of bins} = \left[\frac{n^{1/3}\left(\max - \min\right)}{2\left(Q_3 - Q_1\right)} \right], \qquad (7)$$

where max is the maximum value, min is the minimum value, and Q_3 and Q_1 are the third and first quartiles, respectively (i.e., $Q_3 - Q_1$ is the interquartile range or hinge-spread). There is a trade-off between smoothness and the level of detail displayed in the histogram. The greater the number of bins employed, the smoother the histogram. Ideally, the plot will preserve as much detail as possible without being too jagged. Concern over jaggedness is especially important for sample data, for which jaggedness is more likely to reflect sampling variability rather than a true feature of the population distribution.

Nonparametric Density Estimation
Nonparametric density estimation overcomes the problem of determining the number of bins that are

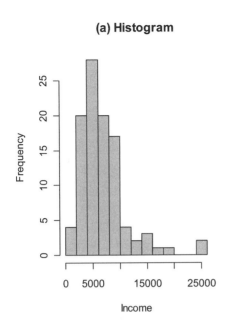
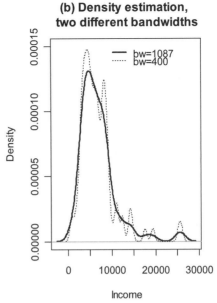

FIGURE 1.2.   Histogram and density estimation showing the distribution of income in the 1997 Canadian Election Survey.

associated with histograms by estimating the probability density function for the distribution (Bowman & Azzalini, 1997). Less formally, density estimation can be thought of as a smoothed histogram. In other words, density estimation is essentially a sophisticated form of locally weighted averaging of the distribution.

Reflecting that a density function encloses an area of one, we start by rescaling the histogram so that its total area (i.e., the area within the bins) equals one. This rescaling results in points on the density curve representing the proportion of cases—rather than the frequency counts—at particular values. A kernel density function, such as the standard normal density function, is used to weight observations to ensure the total area under the curve equals 1:

$$\hat{p}(x) = \frac{1}{n \times bw} \sum_{i=1}^{n} K\left(\frac{x - X_i}{bw}\right), \qquad (8)$$

where K is the kernel density function, x is the point at which the density is estimated, X_i is the center of the interval, and bw is the bandwidth (or window half-width).

Although the problem of setting the number of bins has been solved, the bandwidth bw must now be selected. We can decide on the bandwidth visually by simply increasing it to the point at which the estimated curve is no longer jagged or we can rely on statistical theory, which suggests the formula $bw = 0.9\sigma n^{-1/5}$, where σ is the unknown population standard deviation and n is the sample size (see Fox, 2008). Because σ is unknown, we replace it with an adaptive estimator of spread (the sample standard deviation s can be inflated if the underlying density is not normal):

$$A = \min\left(s, \frac{Q_3 - Q_1}{1.349}\right), \qquad (9)$$

where 1.349 is the interquartile range of the standard normal distribution. The bandwidth is then determined by $bw = 0.9An^{-1/5}$.

Figure 1.2 displays a histogram and density estimates for the distribution of income from the 1997 Canadian Election Survey.[1] Both plots suggest that income is positively skewed. Figure 1.2b further demonstrates that if the underlying density distribution is

[1]Data from the 1997 Canadian Election Survey were provided by the Institute for Social Research, York University, Toronto, Ontario, Canada. The survey was funded by the Social Sciences and Humanities Research Council of Canada (SSHRC) Grant 412-96-0007 and was completed for the 1997 Canadian Election Team of André Blais (Université de Montréal), Elisabeth Gidengil (McGill University), Richard Nadeau (Université de Montréal), and Neil Nevitte (University of Toronto). Neither the Institute for Social Research, the SSHRC, nor the Canadian Election Survey Team are responsible for the analyses and interpretations presented here.

substantially nonnormal, $bw = 0.9An^{-1/5}$ can produce a bandwidth that is too wide (i.e., the line is too rough). As the bandwidth increases, the density curve becomes smoother. Ideally we want a smooth curve. In this case, we required a significantly larger bandwidth ($bw = 1,087$). Nevertheless, this formula usually provides a good starting point.

Quantile Comparison Plots

Quantile comparison plots (Q-Q plots) are useful for examining the tails of the distribution, including the detection of outliers. Unlike histograms and density functions, Q-Q plots do not require arbitrary bins or smoothing parameters and thus preserve the continuous nature of the data. They do so by comparing the sample distribution to a theoretical cumulative distribution function, such as the normal distribution. The plot is constructed as follows (see Fox, 2008):

1. Order the observations from lowest to highest value: $x_{(1)}, x_{(2)}, x_{(n)}$.
2. Calculate the cumulative proportion before each $x_{(i)}$:

$$P_i = \frac{i - \frac{1}{2}}{n}. \tag{10}$$

3. Calculate z_i values that correspond to the cumulative probability P_i from the inverse of the cumulative distribution function:

$$z_i = P^{-1}\left(\frac{i - \frac{1}{2}}{n}\right). \tag{11}$$

4. Plot the z_i values on the horizontal axis and the $x_{(i)}$ on the vertical axis, drawing a line that connects the hinges (Q_1 and Q_3).
5. A 95% confidence envelope can be constructed using the formula $\hat{x}_{(i)} = \pm 1.96 \times \hat{S}E(x_i)$, where

$$\hat{S}E(x_{(i)}) = \frac{\hat{\sigma}}{p(z_i)}\sqrt{\frac{P_i(1 - P_i)}{n}} \text{ and } \hat{\sigma} \text{ is estimated}$$

from $\dfrac{Q_3 - Q_1}{1.349}$. Alternatively, bootstrapped confidence envelopes can be employed.

Figure 1.3 displays Q-Q plots for similar distributions to those shown in Figure 1.1. Interpretation of the Q-Q plot is relatively straightforward. If x is

normally distributed, $x_{(i)} = z_i$. In other words, the plot should be approximately linear as in Figure 1.3a, where the data points lie along the reference line connecting the hinges. Figure 1.3b displays the same bimodal distribution shown in Figure 1.1b. Here we see that the Q-Q plot is less capable of uncovering features of the center of the distribution compared to the histogram. That is, the Q-Q plot gives little indication that the distribution has two modes. Figure 1.3c indicates a light-tailed distribution (i.e., *leptokurtosis*), in which case observations fall below the confidence envelope at high values and above the confidence envelope for low values. As Figure 1.3d demonstrates, platykurtosis is indicated by the opposite pattern—that is, the highest values lie above the confidence envelope and lowest values lie below the confidence envelope. Figure 1.3e illustrates a positive skew, which is indicated by points above the line on both ends. A negative skew, on the other hand, is indicated by points below the line on both ends (see Figure 1.3f). Finally, the axes of the plots differ because of the nature of the distributions. Although the x-axis and y-axis are identical when the distribution is normal, they can differ drastically when the distribution is nonnormal. In summary, Q-Q plots are very useful for exploring the tails of a distribution but tell us little about its center.

Boxplots

Attributed to Tukey (1977), boxplots explicitly display the center, spread, and outliers of a distribution. Boxplots are particularly useful for rough comparisons of the distributions of many variables or subsets of the same variable. Construction of the boxplot is as follows:

1. Typically the vertical axis of the plot represents the range of the variable (although the plot can be reversed so that the horizontal axis is used instead).
2. A box is drawn to represent the hinge spread, with a horizontal line representing the median being drawn through the box.
3. Observations a distance of more than 1.5 hinge spread (Q_3 to Q_1) from the median are typically marked individually as outliers.
4. *Whiskers* connect the box to the most extreme nonoutlying observation.

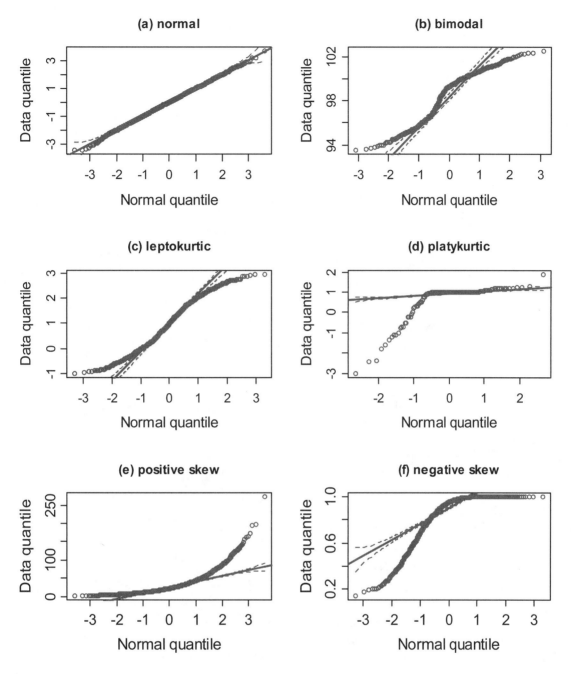

FIGURE 1.3.   Quantile comparison plots.

Figure 1.4 displays the distribution of the average incomes for three different types of occupation—blue collar, professional, and nonprofessional white collar—from Canadian occupational prestige data (Fox, 1997). We can see that professional jobs not only have a much higher median income but also much more variability in income than the other two occupation groups. We also see a positive skew and two outliers—noted by the two points at the top of the plot—for professional occupations. Aside from the median, boxplots provide no other information about the shape of a distribution in its middle. In other words, although the boxplots for blue-collar occupations and white-collar occupations are more symmetric than the boxplot for professional jobs, this does not necessarily mean that the distributions are more symmetric.

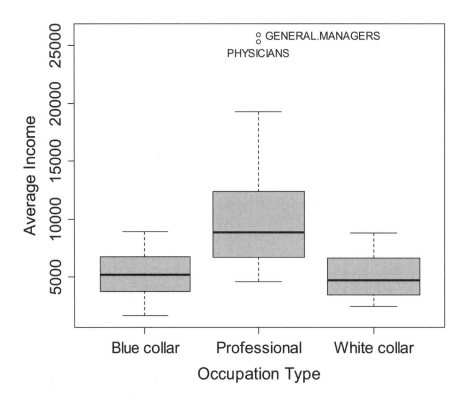

FIGURE 1.4. Side-by-side boxplots showing the distribution of average incomes by occupation type, Canadian Prestige data.

Numerical Tests for Univariate Distributions

Although many statistical procedures are based on the assumption that the data are normally distributed, this assumption is never met in reality. As a result, we are usually satisfied if distributions are close to normal. As a result, graphic analysis typically provides all the information about distributions that one needs to assess whether particular statistics can be employed. For example, histograms and density estimation are usually sufficient for uncovering the general shape of distributions. Similarly, Q-Q plots are usually adequate for assessing problems at the tails of the distribution. Numerical tests are also available, however.

The *coefficient of skewness* measures the skew of a distribution relative to the normal distribution (Krishnamoorthy, 2006). The formula is as follows:

$$\text{skewness} = \frac{\sum_{i=1}^{n}\left(x_i - \bar{x}\right)^3}{\left(n-1\right)s^3}. \tag{12}$$

The normal distribution has a coefficient of skewness equal to zero. Negative values indicate that the

distribution is skewed to the left; positive values indicate a skew to the right. The coefficient of kurtosis is defined by the following:

$$\text{kurtosis} = \frac{\sum_{i=1}^{n}\left(x_i - \bar{x}\right)^4}{\left(n-1\right)s^4}. \tag{13}$$

Like the coefficient of skewness, the normal distribution has a value of 0 for the coefficient of kurtosis. If the coefficient of kurtosis is less than 3, the distribution is considered to be platykurtic; if it is greater than 3, the distribution is leptokurtic (Krishnamoorthy, 2006).

Goodness-of-fit tests for data with respect to the normal distribution include the Kolmogorov–Smirnov test and the D'Agostino–Pearson test. Although the Kolmogorov–Smirnov test is widely used and generally considered effective (Conover, 1999; Hollander & Wolfe 1999; Sprent, 1993), D'Agostino, Belanger, and D'Agostino (1990) claimed that the D'Agostino–Pearson test is more powerful. For more detailed descriptions of these and other related tests, see Sheskin (2004).

There are several simple tests for univariate outliers (see Barnett & Lewis 1994; Tietjen, 1986). The most basic of these is *Grubbs' test*, which is based on the assumption of normality and extends directly from z-scores for the normal distribution

$$G = \frac{|x_i - \bar{x}|}{s}. \tag{14}$$

The null hypothesis that there are no outliers in the data is rejected if G is larger than the critical value of the t-distribution for the sample size and desired significance level. As with t tests for means and regression slopes, one-sided or two-sided tests can be performed.

Transformations

Many statistical methods assume that the variables being analyzed take on particular distributional shapes. Most common is the assumption that a variable is approximately normally distributed. Given that variables often deviate from this assumption, it is often desirable to change the shape of their distributions using a transformation. Although there are an infinite number of functions $f(x)$ that can be used to transform a distribution, in practice, a relatively small

number are regularly used. For quantitative variables, one can usually rely on the "family" of powers and roots, $x \rightarrow x^p$, where p is the transformation. Descending the ladder of powers and roots compresses the large values of x and spreads out the small values. As p moves away from one in either direction, the transformation becomes more powerful. When p is negative, the transformation is an inverse power. For example, $x^{-1} = 1/x$, $x^{-2} = 1/x^2$, and $x^{-3} = 1/x^3$. When p is a fraction, the transformation represents a root. For example, $x^{1/2} = \sqrt{x}$ and $x^{-1/2} = 1/\sqrt{x}$.

It makes no sense to use a power transformation of $p = 0$ because it changes all values to one (i.e., it makes the variable a constant). Still, we often use x^0 as a shorthand to represent the log transformation $\log_e x$, where $e = 2.718$ is the base of the natural logarithm. Similar to going down the ladder of powers, log transformations can be effective for rectifying a positive skew. In terms of result, changing the base is equivalent to multiplying by a constant, so other values for the base will give the same substantive result.

Figure 1.5 demonstrates the use of a $\log_{10}$ transformation to correct a positive skew. Density esti-

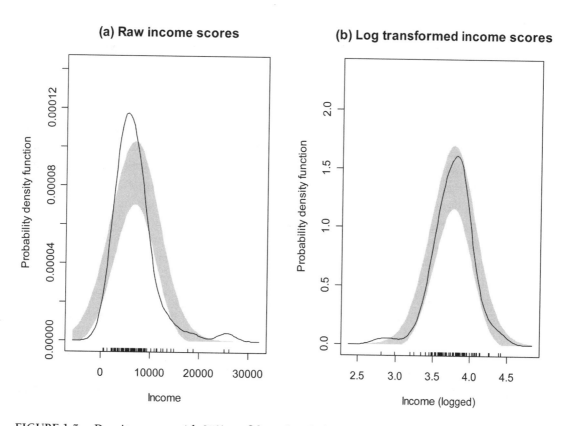

(a) Raw income scores

(b) Log transformed income scores

FIGURE 1.5.   Density curves with 95% confidence bands for the normal distribution.

mates for the raw scores for the average income of occupations in the Canadian occupational prestige data are shown in Figure 1.5a; Figure 1.5b shows the density estimate for the transformed incomes. The shaded lines surrounding the density curves represent the 95% confidence envelope for the normal distribution. We see quite clearly that the log transformation removed the positive skew.

There are some important caveats with respect to power transformations. First, they are sensible only when all the *x* values are positive. Some transformations (e.g., the log and roots) are undefined for zero and negative numbers. Other power transformations can change the order of the data if there are negative values. The problem of negative values can often be rectified with a positive start—that is, adding a constant to each value so that the lowest value is greater than zero. Power transformations are only effective if the ratio of the largest data value to the smallest data value is large. If the ratio is very close to one, the transformation will have little effect. This problem can usually be fixed with a negative start.

Finally, power transformations do not work on proportions (including percentages and rates) if the data values approach the boundaries of zero and one. More effective for highly skewed proportion distributions are the *logit* and *probit* transformations. The logit transformation takes the following form:

$$\text{logit}(P) = \log_e \frac{P}{1-P}, \tag{15}$$

where *P* is the observed proportion. This transformation: (a) removes the boundaries of the scale, (b) spreads out the tails of the distribution, and (c) makes the distribution symmetric about zero. The probit transformation, $\text{probit}(P) = \Phi^{-1}(P)$, where Φ^{-1} is the inverse distribution function of the normal distribution, is similarly effective (Fox, 2008). In fact, if their scales are equated, the probit transformation and logit transformation are practically indistinguishable (logit $\approx \left(\pi/\sqrt{3}\right) \times$ probit).

Examining Relationships

Figure 1.6 displays the relationship between variables in four data sets contrived by Anscombe's (1973) to show the importance of using graphs in regression analysis. Although displaying quite

different patterns, the data in the four plots yield exactly the same correlation coefficient, and linear regression output, including the standard deviation of the residuals, the regression coefficients, and their standard errors. Nevertheless, it is clear that the linear regression adequately summarizes only the pattern in Figure 1.5a. Applying linear regression to the data in the other three plots, without first rectifying the notable problems, would miss important features of the data. Without graphing the data, these failures would likely go unnoticed.

Scatterplots

A sensible way to begin analyzing patterns in the data is to use scatterplots. A scatterplot summarizes the relationship between two quantitative variables. Each observation is represented by a point on the graph, with the explanatory variable being placed on the horizontal axis and the response variable placed on the vertical axis. The scatterplot can be augmented in several ways. For example, nonparametric regression curves (see Andersen, 2009) and linear regression lines can help assess linearity. Moreover, if the variables take on relatively few values and thus the data are overplotted—that is, data points lie on top of each other, making it difficult to see how many there are—it can be helpful to *jitter* the data (i.e., add a random component to each value), so that they separate from each other. The benefits of jittering are shown in Figure 1.7, which plots the relationship between age and conservative attitudes in a large survey data set. In Figure 1.7a, we cannot discern any pattern in the data because of the discrete nature of the two variables. On the other hand, Figure 1.7b, which jitters the two variables, demonstrates a clear relationship between them.

It can be helpful to distinguish between categories of a categorical control variable with different symbols. Figure 1.8 displays the relationship between the country-level income inequality (measured by the Gini coefficient) and average attitudes toward income inequality, distinguishing democracies from nondemocracies, for 49 countries surveyed in the World Value Survey (more details of the data can be seen in Weakliem, Andersen, & Heath, 2005). The contrasting slopes for the two groups

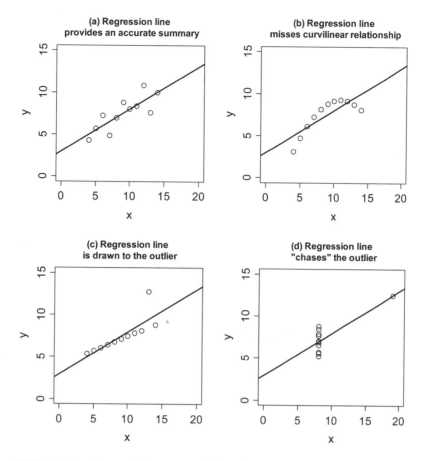

FIGURE 1.6.   Anscombe's contrived data showing four quite different data scenarios that all produce the same summary measures for a regression analysis. From "Graphs in Statistical Analysis," by F. J. Anscombe, 1973, *The American Statistician, 27*, pp. 19–20. Copyright 1973 by the American Statistical Association. All rights reserved. Adapted with permission.

suggest an interaction between democracy and income inequality in their effects on attitudes.

Known as a scatterplot matrix, it is often useful to include several scatterplots in the same figure. We must keep in mind, however, that scatterplots display only *marginal bivariate relationships* (i.e., they do not control for other variables), which limits their utility for multivariate analyses. Still, they are useful as a preliminary measure to uncover features of the data that might cause problems later in the analysis.

Conditioning Plots

Conditioning plots improve on standard scatterplots by displaying *partial relationship* between two variables. That is, they show the relationship between two quantitative variables conditional on values of other variables. As an example, returning to data

from the 1997 Canadian election study, Figure 1.9 displays the relationship between age and attitudes, controlling for gender and race. We see a similar pattern in each of the plots: As age increases so too does conservatism. Had we observed different patterns, it would indicate that the predictors interact with each other in their effects on attitudes. These plots are useful when using large data sets with relatively few independent variables, but if the sample is small and the number of predictors is large, the number of observations included in each scatterplot becomes too sparse to facilitate sound judgments about the patterns in the data.

Multivariate Density Estimates

The kernel smoothing method used for histograms can be easily extended to the joint distribution of

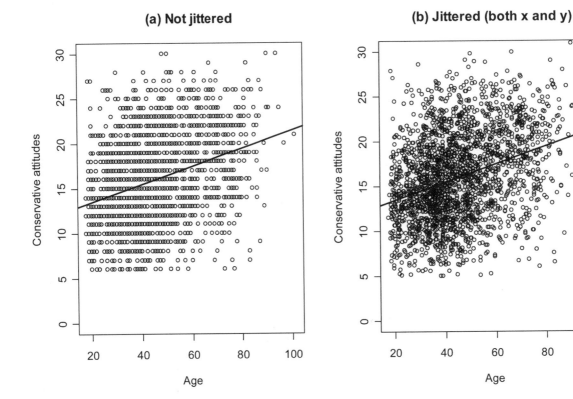

FIGURE 1.7. Jittering scatterplots.

two or three random continuous variables. As in the univariate case, these plots of multivariate density estimates are helpful for assessing clustering of the data. In contrast to univariate densities, which are associated with the *area* under the density curve, probabilities for multivariate estimates are associated with the *volume* under the density contours.

The bivariate density function takes the following form:

$$\hat{p}(x_1, x_2) = \frac{1}{n \times bw_1 \times bw_2}$$

$$\times \sum_{i=1}^{n} K\left(\frac{x_1 - X_{1i}}{bw_1}\right) K\left(\frac{x_2 - X_{2i}}{bw_2}\right), \quad (16)$$

where K is the kernel function and bw_1 and bw_2 are the joint smoothing parameters (Bowman & Azzalini, 1997). Three types of bivariate density plots can be considered: perspective plots, image plots, and contour plots. *Perspective plots* display the joint distribution as a three-dimensional plot, where height is used to show the level of density. *Image plots* show density using different heat shades to represent intensity (i.e., the number of observations). *Contour plots* (also known as *slice*

plots) trace paths of constant levels of density in the same way that a geographic contour map depicts elevation. As an example, Figure 1.10 displays the relationship between age and conservative attitudes as uncovered by the three types of density plots. In all three plots, we see that the greatest density has both average age and average attitudes. The fact that the greatest density—that is, the greatest number of observations—lies along the diagonal from bottom left to top right in the plots indicates a positive relationship between the two variables. Three-dimensional density estimates extend simply from the bivariate case:

$$\hat{p}(x_1, x_2, x_3) = \frac{1}{n \times bw_1 \times bw_2 \times bw_3} \sum_{i=1}^{n} K\left(\frac{x_1 - X_{1i}}{bw_1}\right)$$

$$\times K\left(\frac{x_2 - X_{2i}}{bw_2}\right) K\left(\frac{x_3 - X_{3i}}{bw_3}\right), \quad (17)$$

where K is the kernel function and bw_1, bw_2, and bw_3 are the joint smoothing parameters. When we plot these densities, the contours take the form of *closed surfaces*, which are typically illustrated in the form of wire mesh. It is common practice to show shadowing

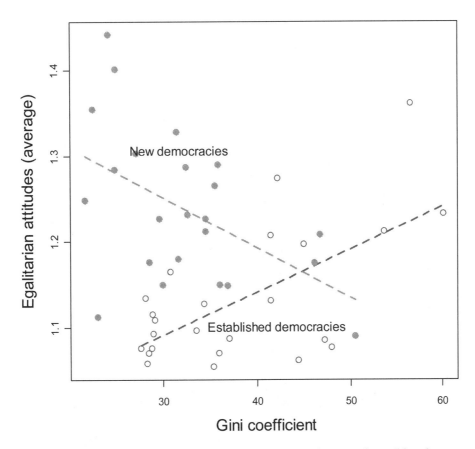

FIGURE 1.8.   Using symbols to distinguish categories of a control variable. The scatterplot shows the relationship between Income inequality (measured by the Gini coefficient) and attitudes toward income for both new democracies and established democracies.

in the plot to facilitate where the data lie in the three-dimensional space. Returning to the cross-national public opinion data, Figure 1.11 displays three-dimensional density estimates for the relationship among gross domestic product (GDP) per capita, the Gini coefficient for income inequality, and public opinion toward pay equality in 49 countries. The fact that there are two distinct spheres in the figure indicates clustering of the data. Such clustering suggests the possible omission of an important categorical variable (e.g., new vs. old democracies).

REGRESSION DIAGNOSTICS

Thus far we have explored various ways of assessing the distributional shape of variables and the relationships among them. Exploring the data with these methods before applying more sophisticated statistical methods is important because it can often uncover

characteristics of the data that could be problematic later. Nevertheless, some problems cannot be uncovered until after fitting statistical models. With this in mind, we now turn to various methods for detecting badly behaved data in regression analysis. If the relationship between the dependent variable and its predictors cannot be adequately summarized by a straight line, linear regression can give misleading results. Unusual observations can also have undue influence on the regression estimates. Moreover, heteroskedasticity and nonnormally distributed errors can cause problems for standard errors. Many of these problems can be diagnosed by adapting the general methods described thus far and applying them to the residuals from the regression model.

Nonlinearity

Use of linear regression is predicated on the assumption that the expected value of y is a linear function

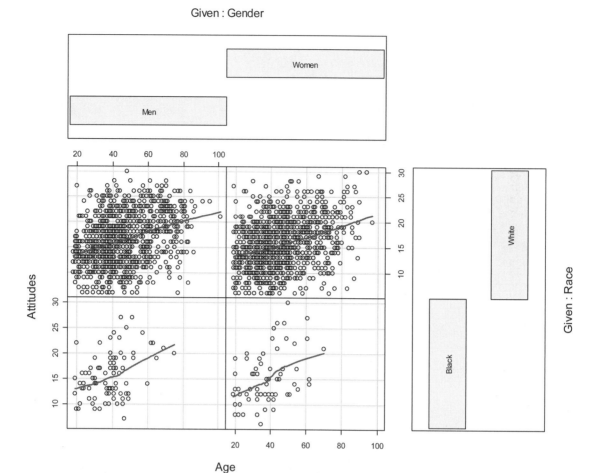

FIGURE 1.9. Conditioning plots showing the relationship between age and attitudes, controlling for gender and race.

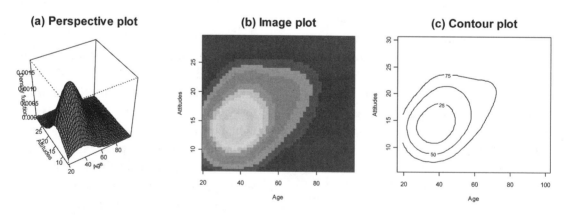

FIGURE 1.10. Three bivariate density plots showing the relationship between age and attitudes.

of the *x*s. Simply put, the relationship between *y* and the *x*s should be adequately characterized by a straight line. Put another way, we must assume that the average value of the errors given *x* is equal to zero. It is thus very important to ensure that the data

exhibit a linear relationship before using linear regression. A scatterplot does a suitable job of describing the relationship between two variables in the simple regression case. Typically we are interested in more than one predictor, however, in which

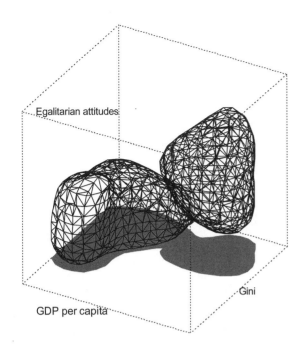

FIGURE 1.11. Three-dimensional density estimates for gross domestic product (GDP) per capita, income inequality (the Gini coefficient), and attitudes toward pay equality.

case a simple scatterplot does not necessarily give an adequate description of the partial relationship between two variables controlling for others. On the other hand, because their estimates pertain to partial relationships (i.e., they are conditional on values of the other predictors), *partial residual plots* (also called component-plus-residual plots) are more effective for assessing linearity in multiple regression.

The partial residuals $e_i^{(j)}$ for the *j*th independent variable are simply the linear component of the partial regression of *y* on x_j added to the least squares residuals e_i from the multiple regression, $e_i^{(j)} = e_i + b_j x_{ij}$. Plotting the $e_i^{(j)}$ against x_j allows us to assess linearity in the same manner as the scatterplot for simple regression. The slope of $e_i^{(j)}$ regressed on x_j is the partial regression slope from the multiple regression b_j. If the pattern of the data does not follow reasonably along this line, we can conclude that there is a nonlinear relationship between *y* and x_j. The plot can be augmented with a nonparametric smooth, which relies on the data to determine the functional form of the relationship between the two variables.

Continuing with the cross-national public opinion data, we fit a model regressing average attitudes on GDP per capita and the Gini coefficient for

income inequality for each country. Partial residual plots for this model are displayed in Figure 1.12. Aside from evidence of outliers, the partial relationship between public opinion and GDP appears to be adequately summarized by a straight line. On the other hand, there appears to be a curvilinear relationship between public opinion and the Gini coefficient. A standard linear regression would fail to adequately represent the trend in the data. In this case, where the relationship is simple but not monotone (more about this later), a polynomial regression would work well. Alternatively, as suggested by the previous graphs we have explored (Figures 1.8 to 1.11), specifying an interaction between length of democracy (established vs. new) and the Gini coefficient linearizes the relationship between Gini and public opinion.

Once discovering a nonlinearity problem, we must decide on how to cope with it. The appropriate method depends on the nature of the nonlinearity. More specifically, we must assess the number of bends in the relationship and whether the direction is monotone. A *simple* trend implies that the curvature does not change—that is, there is only one bend in the relationship. We consider the relationship to be *monotone* if the curve is always positive or always negative. If the trend is both simple and monotone, a transformation of *x*, *y*, or both variables will usually straighten the relationship between them. If the pattern of nonlinearity is not monotone but relatively simple, polynomial regression tends to work well. If there is a single bend in the relationship, a quadratic regression can be considered. Polynomial regression also tends to work well if there are two bends in the relationship, in which case a cubic regression could be employed. For more complicated patterns of nonlinearity, however, nonparametric regression and generalized additive models should be considered (see Andersen, 2009).

Mosteller and Tukey's (1977) bulging rule provides a good starting point for possible transformations to correct nonlinearity. Positive relationships with upward curvature in the middle of the data can often be rectified by a transformation of *y* up the family of powers or a transformation of *x* down the family of powers (e.g., square root or log). The opposite—that is, transformation of *y* down the family of powers or of *x* up the family of powers—is

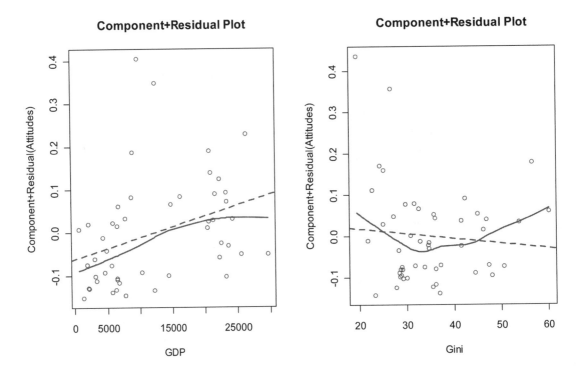

FIGURE 1.12. Partial regression plots showing the partial relationships of egalitarian attitudes with gross domestic product (GDP) per capita and income inequality.

required to rectify a positive relationships that bulges downward in the middle of the data. On the other hand, a transformation of either *x* or *y* up the ladder of powers can help linearize a negative relationship characterized by an upward bulge. In contrast, a negative relationship with a downward bulge requires a transformation down the ladder of powers and roots of *y* or *x* or both. Normally, a transformation of the explanatory variables is most desirable because transforming the response variable will affect the relationship of *y* with all *x*s, rather than just the *x* with the nonlinear relationship. Still, it is often sensible to transform the response variable if it is highly skewed.

Adapted from Fox (2008), Figure 1.13 provides an example of how transformations can effectively linearize a nonlinear relationship. The data represent the GDP per capita and infant mortality rates (per 1,000 births) for 193 nations. Figure 1.13a shows the relationship between these two variables before any transformations. The nonparametric regression indicates serious nonlinearity. Because the bulge in the data is down and to the right, the *bulging rule* suggests that the relationship can be straightened by transforming one or both of the

variables down the ladder of powers. Guided by the *bulging rule*, then, I chose the log transformation for both income and infant mortality. As we see from Figure 1.13b, the transformations effectively straighten the relationship between the two variables, making the use of linear regression sensible.

Although the above ad hoc methods for determining transformations typically work well, more sophisticated methods based on maximum likelihood estimation are also available. Two commonly used methods are the Box–Tidwell transformation of the independent variables (see Box & Tidwell, 1962) and the Box–Cox transformation of the dependent variable (Box & Cox, 1964). These techniques embed the usual multiple-regression model in a more general nonlinear model that further contains estimates of parameters for appropriate transformations. A good summary of these methods is given in Cook and Weisberg (1999) and Fox (2008).

Outliers and Influential Cases

It is important to distinguish among four types of unusual cases: univariate outliers, regression outliers, observations with high leverage, and influential observations. A univariate *outlier* is an observation

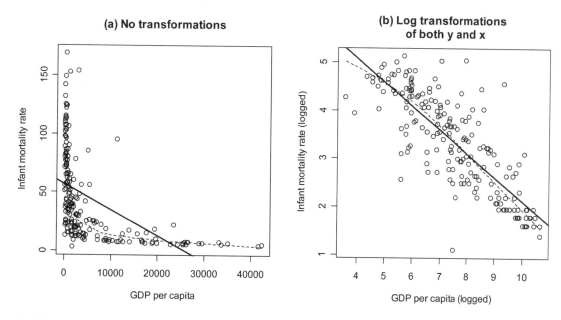

FIGURE 1.13. Using log transformations to linearize the relationship between gross domestic product (GDP) and infant mortality rate.

that has an unusual value for a single variable. *Regression outliers*, on the other hand, are observations that have an unusual value of y given their value of x. A high *leverage observation* is an observation with an unusual value of x. Most important, an *influential observation* is one that unduly influences the fit of the regression line. To have influence, an observation must be both a regression outlier and have high leverage.

The standard way to measure leverage is by the hat values h_i, which capture the extent to which the observed values of y_i affect the predicted values $\hat{y}_i$:

$$\hat{y}_i = h_{ij}y_1 + h_{2j}y_2 + \ldots + h_{nj}y_n. \tag{18}$$

In simple regression, the h_i measures distance from $\bar{x}$:

$$h_i = \frac{1}{n} + \frac{\left(x_i - \bar{x}\right)^2}{\sum_{j=1}^{n}\left(x_j - \bar{x}\right)^2}. \tag{19}$$

In multiple regression, the hat values measure distance from the centroid point (i.e., the point of means) of all of the xs. If an h_{ij} value is large, the ith observation has a substantial impact on the jth fitted value. The average hat value is given by $\bar{h} = (k + 1)/n$, where k is the number of terms in the model.

In the simple regression case, regression outliers can be easily detected using a scatterplot. In multiple regression, regression outliers can be detected by

exploring the residuals from the model. A first diagnostic is the same Q-Q plot of the studentized residuals as seen earlier. The studentized residuals are calculated by the following:

$$e_i^* = \frac{e_i}{S_{e(-i)}\sqrt{1 - h_i}}, \tag{20}$$

where $Se_{(-1)}$ is the variance of the residuals with the observation of interest removed, and h_i is the observation's hat value. Observations that stray outside of the 95% confidence bands have residuals much larger than one would expect if the residuals were normally distributed.

A related formal test for a single outlying observation is the *mean shift* regression model, which simply includes a dummy variable coded one for the unusual observation and zero for all other cases. If the coefficient for the dummy variable is statistically significant, the observation significantly deviates from the bulk of the data. A Bonferroni adjustment to the p-value accounts for the fact that we intentionally select the observation with the largest residual despite that the t-test assumes the observation to be randomly selected. The Bonferroni p value for the largest outlier is $p = 2np^*$, where p^* is the unadjusted p value from a t test with $n - k - 2$ degrees of freedom. Standard practice is to consider hat values more than twice the average as noteworthy.

A straightforward measure to assess the influence of a particular observation on any one particular regression slope is the *DFBeta* (or D_{ij}). The D_{ij} are determined by the difference in the slope estimates when an observation of interest is removed, $D_{ij} = B_j - B_{j(-i)}$. This measure is useful for detecting observations that stand clearly apart from the bulk of the data for one explanatory variable, but it does not provide a measure of overall influence on the regression surface. It is possible, for example, that an observation does not have an obviously strong effect on any one particular coefficient, but its combined influence on many slopes is high.

The most commonly used diagnostic for overall influence on the regression surface is Cook's Distance (or, more simply, Cook's D). Cook's D takes into account both the size of the residual and the leverage of the observations:

$$D_i = \frac{e_i^{*2}}{k+1} \times \frac{h_i}{1-h_i}. \tag{21}$$

Although there is no test of statistical significance for Cook's D, an observation is typically considered influential if it has a Cook's D larger than $4/(n - k - 1)$. Still, there is no substitute for examining the relative size of the Cook's Ds. Particularly useful is Fox's (1991) influence plot (or bubble plot), which plots the hat values, studentized residuals, and Cook's D on a single graph.

Figure 1.14 displays an influence plot for a model predicting public opinion toward pay equality from GDP per capita and the Gini coefficient for 49 countries. The hat values for each country are shown on the horizontal axis and the studentized residuals are displayed on the vertical axis. The area of the circles depicting each observation is proportional to its Cook's D. We see quite clearly from this plot that Slovakia, the Czech Republic, and Chile have much larger influence than the other countries on the regression surface.

The DFBetas and Cook's D usually do a good job of detecting influence, but they can fail if several observations are jointly influential. *Added-variable plots* (also called *partial regression plots*) overcome this problem. These plots essentially show the

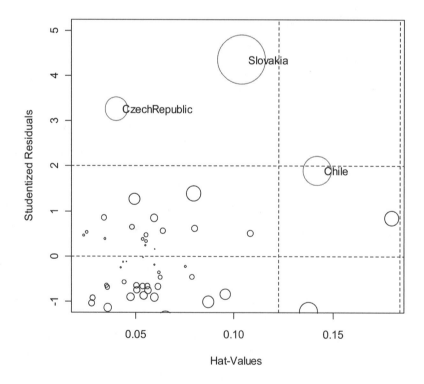

FIGURE 1.14. Influence plots showing the roles of discrepancy in terms of *y*-value (measured by the studentized residual) and leverage (measured by the hat-value) in determining influence (measured by Cook's D). The areas of the circles representing the observations are proportional to the observations' Cook's D.

partial relationships between y and each of the xs. The plot is constructed as follows:

1. Let $y_i^{(1)}$ represent the residuals from the least-squares regression of y on all of the xs except for x_1:

$$y_i = a^{(1)} + b_2^{(1)} x_{i2} + b_3^{(1)} x_{i3} + \ldots + b_k^{(1)} x_{ik} + y_i^{(1)}. \quad (22)$$

2. Similarly, $x_i^{(1)}$ are the residuals from the regression of x_1 on all other xs:

$$x_{i1} = c^{(1)} + d_2^{(1)} x_{i2} + d_3^{(1)} x_{i3} + \ldots + d_k^{(1)} x_{ik} + x_i^{(1)}. \quad (23)$$

3. Plot $y_i^{(1)}$ against $x_i^{(1)}$.

The residuals from these two regressions, $y_i^{(1)}$ and $x_i^{(1)}$, represent the variation in y and x_1 that remains after removing the effects of the other xs. As a result, the variation of $x^{(1)}$ is the conditional variance of x_1 holding the other xs constant, and the slope of the regression of $y^{(1)}$ on $x^{(1)}$ is the least squares slope b_1 from the full multiple regression.

Continuing with the cross-national public opinion example, Figure 1.15 displays the partial regression plots for GDP per capita and the Gini coefficients from the linear model predicting public opinion

toward pay equality. Consistent with the story told by the Cook's Ds, the Czech Republic and Slovakia stand apart from the bulk of the data for both predictors. They appear to be most problematic for the Gini coefficient, however, in that they pull the regression line toward them. If they are excluded from the model, the regression slope changes from negative to positive (and statistically significant at conventional levels).

Unusual observations may reflect miscoding, in which case the coding can be fixed or the observations simply deleted. Often, an outlier is of substantive interest, however, so we may decide to deal with it separately from the rest of the analysis. The presence of many outliers may indicate that an important explanatory variable is missing from the model. If there are no strong reasons to remove outliers, but we still desire to limit their influence, robust regression, which downweights outliers, can be used in place of regular regression methods (see Andersen, 2008).

Nonnormality

We now turn to ways of assessing the normality assumption. In this regard, the assumption of

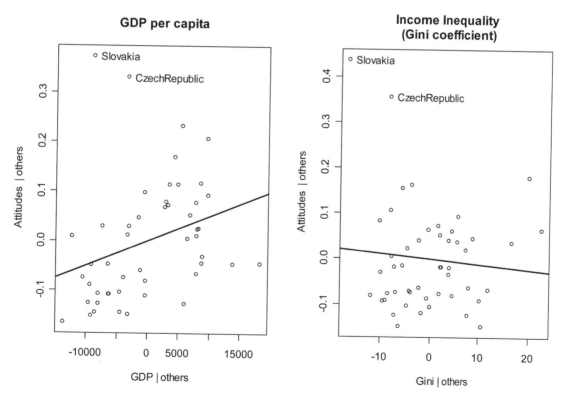

FIGURE 1.15. Partial regression plots for relationships between egalitarian attitudes and gross domestic product (GDP) per capita and income inequality.

normality in linear regression applies to the errors and not to the individual variables in the model. Although we do not know the error distribution in the population, we can look to the sample residuals for an indication of how it might appear. A histogram or density estimate of the distribution of the residuals is useful for exploring the general shape of the errors. In particular, these plots are useful for uncovering multimodal error distributions, which suggest the absence of an important control variable. The tails of the distribution can be effectively assessed using a Q-Q plot of the studentized residuals e_i^* against the quantiles of the corresponding t distribution. If the error distribution has normal tails, the relationship should be roughly linear. In other words, observations at the tails of the distribution should remain within the 95% confidence envelope. Skewed distributions can often be remedied by a transformation of y.

Heteroskedasticity

The assumption of constant error variance, also known as homoskedasticity, holds that the variance of the errors is the same regardless of the value of y. Heteroskedasticity (i.e., nonconstant error variance) can be detected by plotting the residuals e_i (or studentized residuals, e_i^*) against the predicted values from the model, $\hat{y}_i$. If the values of the predicted values are all positive, we can use a spread-level plot, which plots $\log \left| e_i^* \right|$ (called the *log spread*) against $\log \hat{y}_i$ (called the *log level*). The slope b of the regression line fit to the spread-level plot suggests a variance-stabilizing power transformation p for y, with $p = 1 - b$. Other solutions for heteroskedasticity include adding an omitted independent variable, weighted least squares (which can be effective if the residual variance increases with y), or the use of robust standard errors for an unknown pattern of heteroskedasticity.

Figure 1.16 displays a spread-level plot for the cross-national public opinion model that predicts attitudes from GDP per capita and the Gini coefficient for income inequality. Given that we see no apparent trend in the variance of the residuals as the fitted values change, we conclude that heteroskedasticity is not a problem for this model. Nevertheless,

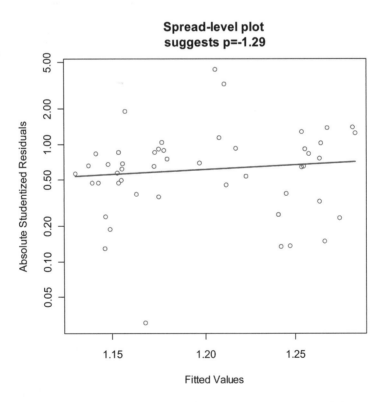

FIGURE 1.16. Spread-level plot for a linear regression model predicting average egalitarian attitudes from gross domestic product per capita and the Gini coefficient for income inequality.

for illustrative purposes, it is interesting to note that the slope of the spread-level plot suggests a variance stabilizing transformation for y of $p = -1.29$.

Diagnostics for Generalized Linear Models

The generalized linear model (GLM) extends from the linear model to accommodate a wide variety of nonnormal and noninterval dependent variables (for more information, see Gill, 2001; McCullagh & Nelder, 1983). Some commonly employed GLMs are the logit and probit models for binary dependent variables and Poisson regression models for count data. As in the GLM, the influence of the explanatory variables in GLMs remains linear, $\eta = \Sigma x_j b_j$, where η is the *linear predictor*. The relationship between η and the modeled mean μ is generalized from the linear case of $\mu_i = \eta_i$ to $g(\mu)_i = \eta_i$, where g is the link function that maps the response to the linear predictor through a transformation. Finally, the assumption that the errors are normally distributed is relaxed to a less restrictive assumption that the errors follow a specified exponential family distribution. GLMs are fitted using maximum likelihood and iterative reweighted least squares (IWLS).

Compared with a linear model, it is more difficult to assess how variations in the data affect the fit of a GLM. Still, some diagnostic tools extend straightforwardly and effectively from the linear case. For example, nonlinearity can be detected using partial residual plots, although in the case of GLMs, linearity pertains to the relationship between the xs and the linear predictor η, rather than y itself. Moreover, unusual and influential observations can be detected by exploring the residuals, hat values, DFBetas, Cook's D, and partial regression plots. Although residuals for GLMs can be defined in several ways, the so-called working residuals, which are the residuals from the final WLS fit, are typically employed for these diagnostics. Hat values, which have the same interpretation as for linear models, are taken directly from the final IWLS fit. Again, following directly from the case of the linear model, heteroskedasticity can be detected by plotting the residuals e_i (or studentized residuals, e_i^*) against the predicted values on the scale of the linear predictor $\hat{\eta}$. For a more extensive discussion of diagnostics for GLMs see Fox (2008).

CONCLUSION

This chapter has focused on exploring and describing distributions. It underscores the importance of detecting badly behaved data before carrying out even simple statistical analyses. Non-normality and outliers in univariate distributions often signal problems that may be encountered in statistical analyses further down the line, for example, in regression analysis. Given that many statistical procedures make assumptions about normality, either with respect to the distribution of the variables themselves of sampling distributions, the normal distribution is often used as a benchmark. Data are seldom perfectly normally distributed, however, and thus we are typically satisfied with distributions that are roughly normal—that is, they are fairly symmetric, have a single mode, and have no obvious outliers. As a result, although there are formal tests for departures from normality, graphic analysis typically will tell us all we need to know.

Many statistical methods require that significant deviations from normality be rectified. A skewed distribution can typically be fixed with a power transformation or by removing outliers. If there are several outliers, this may indicate that the data are clustered according to categories of an omitted explanatory variable. Often single outliers can be removed because they have been miscoded or more generally that they simply do not fit the pattern in the bulk of the data.

This chapter also has demonstrated the importance of detecting badly behaved data in regression analysis. In this regard, we can adapt many of the methods used for univariate distributions. Particular emphasis was placed on the problems of nonlinearity and influential observations. It makes no sense to impose a linear trend on the data when the pattern is clearly nonlinear. With this in mind, it is important to detect and carefully examine the nature of nonlinear relationships. In the simple regression case, scatterplots do the job well. In multiple regression, however, nonlinear patterns are best detected using partial residual plots (component-plus-residual plots) and generalized additive models. Outliers in simple regression are also easily detected in scatterplots, though the DFbetas and

Cook's Ds can provide more detailed information. For multiple regression, DFBetas, Cook's Ds and partial regression plots aid in the detection of influential observations that unduly pull the regression surface toward them. Heteroskedasticity and nonnormality can be effectively assessed using various residual plots. Finally, many of these diagnostics can also be adapted for use on generalized linear models and other related methods.

References

Andersen, R. (2008). *Modern methods for robust regression* (Sage University Papers Series: Quantitative Applications in the Social Sciences, No. 07-152). Thousand Oaks, CA: Sage.

Andersen, R. (2009). Nonparametric methods for modelling nonlinearity in regression analysis. *Annual Review of Sociology, 35,* 67–85. doi:10.1146/annurev.soc.34.040507.134631

Anscombe, F. J. (1973). Graphs in statistical analysis. *The American Statistician, 27,* 17–21. doi:10.2307/2682899

Barnett, A., & Lewis, T. (1994). *Outliers in statistical data* (3rd ed.). New York, NY: Wiley.

Bowman, A. W., & Azzalini, A. (1997). *Applied smoothing techniques for data analysis: The Kernel approach with S-Plus illustrations.* Oxford, England: Clarendon Press.

Box, G. E. P., & Cox, D. R. (1964). An analysis of transformations. *Journal of the Royal Statistical Society, Series B: Methodological, 25,* 211–252.

Box, G. E. P., & Tidwell, P. W. (1962). Transformation of the independent variables. *Technometrics, 4,* 531–550. doi:10.2307/1266288

Conover, W. J. (1999). *Practical nonparametric statistics* (3rd ed.). New York, NY: Wiley.

Cook, R. D., & Weisberg, S. (1999). *Applied regression including computing and graphics.* New York, NY: Wiley.

D'Agostino, R. B., Belanger, A., & D'Agostino, R. B., Jr. (1990). A suggestion for using powerful and informative tests of normality. *The American Statistician, 44,* 316–321. doi:10.2307/2684359

Fox, J. (1991). *Regression diagnostics: An introduction.* Newbury Park, CA: Sage.

Fox, J. (1997). *Applied regression, linear models, and related methods.* Newbury Park, CA: Sage.

Fox, J. (2008). *Applied regression analysis and generalized linear models* (2nd ed.). Thousand Oaks, CA: Sage.

Freedman, D. A., & Diaconis, P. (1981). On the histogram as a density estimator. *Zeitschrift fur Wahrscheinlicheitstheorie und verwandte Gebiete, 87,* 453–476.

Gill, J. (2001). *Generalized linear models. A unified approach.* Sage University Papers Series: Quantitative Applications in the Social Sciences, no. 07-134. Thousand Oaks, CA: Sage.

Hollander, M., & Wolfe, D. A. (1999). *Nonparametric statistical methods.* New York, NY: Wiley.

Kish, L. T. (1965). *Survey sampling.* New York, NY: Wiley.

Krishnamoorthy, K. (2006). *Handbook of statistical distributions with applications.* New York, NY: Chapman & Hall.

McCullagh, P., & Nelder, J. A. (1983). *Generalized linear models.* New York, NY: Chapman & Hall.

Moore, D. S. (2004). *The basic practice of statistics.* New York, NY: Freeman.

Mosteller, F., & Tukey, J. W. (1977). *Data analysis and regression: A second course in statistics.* Reading, MA: Addison-Wesley.

Neyman, J. (1937). Outline of a theory of statistical estimation based on the classical theory of probability. *Philosophical Transactions of the Royal Society of London, Series A: Mathematical and Physical Sciences, 236,* 333–380. doi:10.1098/rsta.1937.0005

Sheskin, D. J. (2004). *Handbook of parametric and nonparametric statistical procedures* (3rd ed.). New York, NY: Chapman & Hall.

Sprent, P. (1993). *Applied nonparametric statistical methods* (2nd ed.). London, England: Chapman & Hall.

Sudman, S. (1976). *Applied sampling.* San Diego, CA: Academic Press.

Tietjen, G. L. (1986). The analysis and detection of outliers. In R. B. D'Agostino & M. A. Stephens (Eds.), *Goodness-of-fit techniques* (pp. 497–522). New York, NY: Marcel Dekker.

Tukey, J. W. (1960). A survey of sampling from contaminated normal distributions. In I. Olkin, S. Ghurye, W. Hoeffding, W. Madow, & H. Mann (Eds.), *Contributions to probability and statistics* (pp. 448–485). Stanford, CA: Stanford University Press.

Tukey, J. W. (1977). *Exploratory data analysis.* Reading, MA: Addison-Wesley.

Weakliem, D., Andersen, R., & Heath, A. (2005). By popular demand: The effect of public opinion on income inequality. *Comparative Sociology, 4,* 261–284. doi:10.1163/156913305775010124

## CHAPTER 2

WHAT TO DO ABOUT MISSING VALUES

Alan C. Acock

Missing values are almost unavoidable in psychological research. The ethical imperative that participation in studies is voluntary means that participants are free to skip individual questions as well as to withdraw from a study whenever they wish. Furthermore, as longitudinal designs become more common, missing values have become more serious. There are many reasons why particular values are missing for an item, a participant, or a wave of data collection. For example, the following situations have occurred:

- The participant became frustrated after answering 20 items about depression and did not answer any subsequent items on that scale.
- The person entering data accidentally skipped entering an answer.
- The participant lacked knowledge or interest in an issue and skipped to the next section of the questionnaire.
- A participant decided she really wanted to smoke cigarettes and withdrew from the intervention on healthy behaviors.
- A participant decided she had successfully quit smoking halfway through the intervention and saw no reason to continue.
- A student was absent when data were collected for Wave 3 of a seven-wave study.

It is clear that issues related to missing values are common.

GOALS WHEN WORKING WITH MISSING VALUES

In the presence of missing values, a researcher has three goals, and these goals provide the standard for evaluating alternative strategies:

1. Maximize the information used in the analysis;
2. Minimize the bias in estimating model parameters; and
3. Minimize the bias in estimating standard errors by correctly reflecting the degree of uncertainty associated with parameter estimates.

The goal of using all available information may seem apparent, but the default method of dealing with missing values in standard software packages has been listwise deletion. This default throws out information. For example, with multiple data collection points, it is quite possible that many study participants will have missing values on all the variables at one or more of the waves (wavewise missing). A student may be sick, an employee may be on vacation, or an adolescent may be in detention during the data collection for the wave. The goal is to keep all the information on such people so that the analysis can be conducted as closely as possible on the basis of all the available data. As another example, missing data on variables related to age, weight, or income are particularly common because many people consider these private matters. Yet, these participants may have useful data on all the other variables in the study.

I thank Brian Flay, Peter Lachenbruch, Megan McClelland, Sara Schmidt, and Frank Snyder for comments on an earlier version of this chapter.

DOI: 10.1037/13621-002

Depending on the source of missing values, meeting the second goal of unbiased parameter estimates may or may not be difficult. For example, if data were collected on intercity adolescents by sampling high school students, there will be substantial missing data because of school dropouts. This exclusion of a substantial subset of participants will greatly bias the estimates of parameters. Researchers need to clearly define the limits of their sample design by acknowledging design-based missing data and not generalize parameter estimates to all intercity adolescents. The estimates would likely be biased.

The third goal in working with missing values is to produce unbiased standard errors that correctly reflect the degree of uncertainty associated with parameter estimates. In this chapter, I review some traditional ways of handling missing values that yield unbiased estimates of the parameters and seriously underestimate the uncertainty of these estimates. The standard errors will be too small, and this results in erroneous statistical significance, that is, a Type 2 error. Unbiased estimates of the standard error must reflect two key elements: (a) the gain in certainty that is obtained by using all available information, and (b) the loss in certainty obtained depending on how missing values are handled.

AN IMPORTANT ASSUMPTION WHEN WORKING WITH MISSING VALUES

When working with missing values, the first question to answer is why values are missing. Perhaps values are missing completely at random (MCAR). The MCAR assumption can be defined as the probability that a missing value on a variable is unrelated to a person's score on any other variable, whether the other variable is observed or unobserved. That is, whether a person answers or skips an item is unrelated to how the person answers any other item.

This assumption may be reasonable when missing values are missing by design (Graham, 2009; Graham, Taylor, Olchowski, & Cumsille, 2006). Suppose a team of researchers identifies 100 items to ask young children in order to measure 10 conceptual variables. Because the quality of the responses they would get from young children answering such a long survey may be poor, it is necessary to reduce

the number of items they ask. A pilot study determines that they cannot use more than 40 items. The researchers have at least three options. If each conceptual variable is based on a 10-item scale, the researchers could eliminate six of the 10 conceptual variables. Most researchers would find this solution unacceptable. The second alternative would be to ask just four of the 10 items used to measure each of the conceptual variables. This solution, however, would make it difficult to tap the full domain of each of the conceptual variables. A third approach is the use of a computer-based interview that randomly samples 40 of the original 100 items. Each child would get an individualized subset of 40 of the 100 items with the 60 dropped items dropped completely at random. This third approach involving missing by design illustrates the idea of MCAR: There would be a massive amount of missing values, but the "missingness" would be completely at random, and thus, less problematic.

Another example of missing values in cases in which the MCAR assumption is reasonable involves longitudinal models that focus on the growth of an outcome variable over age without regard to the year that the variable was measured. Table 2.1 illustrates a hypothetical study design in which data were initially collected in 2007 for children who were between the ages of 10 and 13 at the time. Subsequent waves were conducted in 2008, 2009, 2010, and 2012. There was no survey in 2011 for this hypothetical study. Suppose a researcher is interested in changes in attitudes regarding drinking as this changes from age 10 to age 18. With five waves of data collection, there are data on children as they age from 10 years to 18 years. As seen in Table 2.1, the blank areas have 100% missing values. Table 2.1 shows that 10-year-olds, born in 1997, were interviewed 10 years later in 2007, in 2008 at age 11, in 2009 at age 12, and in 2010 at age 13, and they will be interviewed again in 2012 at age 15. However, these study participants will not be interviewed when they are 14, 16, 17, or 18 and they will have missing values at those ages on the basis of the sample design. The table shows that another cohort of children were 13-year-olds when they were interviewed in 2007 with follow-up interviews in 2008, 2009, 2010, and 2012. However, no data are

TABLE 2.1

MCAR in Longitudinal Analysis Showing Years Each Birth Cohort Was Interviewed

Birth cohort	Age								
	10	**11**	**12**	**13**	**14**	**15**	**16**	**17**	**18**
1994				2007	2008	2009	2010		2012
1995			2007	2008	2009	2010		2012	
1996		2007	2008	2009	2010		2012		
1997	2007	2008	2009	2010		2012			

Note. The blank cells of the table have 100% missing values. MCAR = missing completely at random.

available for this group of children when they were ages 10 through 12, and data will not be available when they will be 17.

Because the missing values are missing by design, researchers can treat them as MCAR unless they are concerned about a cohort or historical effect— assuming that the children born in 1997 would be comparable from ages 14 to 18 to the children born earlier or later. One way to analyze these data keeping all available information, obtaining unbiased parameter estimates, and obtaining unbiased standard errors is to use the Mplus program (Muthén & Muthén, 2009). Mplus has a set of commands to rearrange the data and then can estimate a growth curve for the outcome variable from ages 10 to 18, even though only five waves of data are collected.

Consider how MCAR relates to the three goals mentioned thus far regarding maximizing the use of available information, minimizing biases in estimating parameters and their standard errors, and maximizing the use of available information. Two modern approaches, multiple imputation (MI) and full information maximum-likelihood (ML) estimation, are effective methods of dealing with data that are MCAR. These modern approaches have less power than if no data were missing. This is because of the uncertainty introduced when using MI or ML estimation. However, both approaches yield unbiased parameter estimates and standard errors (Schafer, 1997). There is no problem with the second goal because the MCAR assumption means that scores of missing values are completely consistent with scores of observed values. Given that missing values are MCAR, the resulting parameter estimates will have no more bias than they would have had with no missing data.

The MCAR assumption is an unreasonable assumption in most studies because missing values in a data set are usually related to other variables such as gender or education. Thus, a second model for dealing with missing values assumes that values are missing at random (MAR), which is a less stringent requirement (Rubin, 1987). Although the MAR name may suggest the same thing as MCAR, there is a crucial difference. Under the MAR assumption, the fact that a person has no score on a variable, say depression, does not depend on how the person actually would score on that variable after controlling for all other observed variables. MAR assumes that the variables that explain missingness are either included in the *analysis model*, as independent or dependent variables, or they are added as auxiliary variables, additional variables that predict whether a value is missing or not, when imputing missing values or using ML estimation.

To evaluate the MAR assumption, researchers can create an indicator variable for each analysis variable that has missing values. The indicator is coded zero if a person has a score on a variable and one if the person has a missing value. Next, a researcher can conduct a logistic regression that includes a number of variables that predict missingness on the indicator variable. This will quickly identify a set of variables that help explain missingness (e.g., gender, education, ethnicity, income, age). These variables that explain missingness (called auxiliary variables) can then be added to the *imputation model* using the MI approach or integrated into the ML approach.

The imputation model is on the left in Figure 2.1. The auxiliary variables and the variables used in the analysis are all included in the imputation model that is applied to a single data set that has missing values. Thus, any variable that predicts missingness in the logistic regression represents a mechanism that explains why some values are missing. Once a researcher controls for the independent and dependent variables used in the analysis and the additional auxiliary variables, the residual pattern of missingness is more likely to be random. On the right side of Figure 2.1 is the analysis model. Here the relationship between the independent and dependent variables is analyzed on a set of 20 or more imputed complete data sets. The 20 or more complete data sets are produced when the imputation model is applied to the single incomplete data set.

There is no test of the MAR assumption, and it is hard to imagine developing one. Even if a large number of auxiliary variables were specified, an unobserved variable may still be excluded from the specification that accounts for missing values. Thus, it is never possible to know that all appropriate variables have been included. Fortunately, many data sets include key auxiliary variables that predict who will and who will not be as likely to answer individual items. For example, gender, race or ethnicity, and education are often related to missingness, and many studies include measures of these variables.

Men are less likely to answer most items than are women, people of color are less likely to answer certain types of questions, and people who have low education are likely to skip some questions because of limited language skills (Collins, Schafer, & Kam, 2001). By simply including some key auxiliary variables like these, researchers can go a long way toward meeting the MAR assumption.

INTERPRETATIVE ISSUES WITH DIFFERENT ASSUMPTIONS ABOUT MISSING DATA

Although MAR is less restrictive than MCAR, many researchers still feel that it is a difficult assumption to justify. This concern may be exaggerated because researchers confuse the name MAR with MCAR. For example, imagine an exercise program designed to reduce obesity. There are three conditions: a high-intensity running program, a low-intensity walking and jogging program, and a control group. Some participants who were randomly assigned to the low-intensity walking or jogging program may soon quit because the program is not vigorous enough to challenge them. Some participants who were randomly assigned to the high-intensity running condition may give up because they are unable or unwilling to

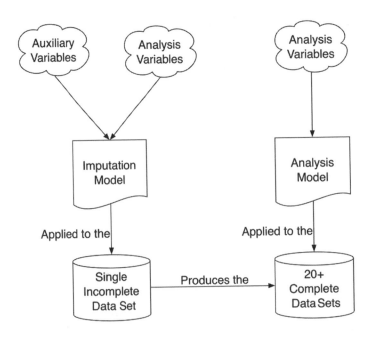

FIGURE 2.1.   Multiple imputation model for data analysis.

exercise at that level. Certainly, the dropouts are not MCAR. They are MAR, however, because the reason they have missing data (the intensity of the intervention) is a variable that is included in the imputation model.

An argument can be made that there is no certainty in justifying the MAR assumption because it is always possible that some unobserved variable helps explain missingness. This concern does not "justify" going with a traditional approach such as listwise deletion (Graham, 2009). Although it is not possible to be certain that the MAR assumption has been met, the MI or ML approaches will always be at least as good as listwise deletion, and usually better. This is extremely important because listwise deletion is not a safe and conservative approach as assumed. In contrast, listwise deletion is only unbiased when data are MCAR, and so it is singularly inappropriate to use it when there is concern about data being MAR (Schafer, 1997).

Modern methods are not really making up new data. Consider MI, which is a process in which multiple complete data sets are created that have imputed values for the values that are missing. The imputed values for variables with missing values are simply consistent placeholders allowing for the preservation of the observed data. This allows researchers to use all available information in their analysis. Thus, the assumption of MAR is important because, if it is reasonable, then making missing values consistent with observed data will not introduce any bias in the analysis.

TRADITIONAL APPROACHES FOR WORKING WITH MISSING VALUES

The limitations of traditional approaches working with missing values have been well-documented (Acock, 2005; Allison, 2001). Standard traditional practices include listwise (casewise) deletion, mean substitution, and pairwise deletion. *Listwise* or *casewise* deletion drops any participant who does not answer every item used in a study. Listwise deletion clearly violates the first goal of using all available information. When several variables have missing values, but for different participants, the pooled effect drops a lot of cases. In political science, which

relies heavily on survey research, listwise deletion often results in 50% of the cases being dropped because the cases have missing values on at least one of the variables (King, Honaker, & Scheva, 2001). In addition, listwise deletion assumes that missing data are exactly like the nonmissing data, that is, missing completely at random (MCAR). Listwise deletion reduces the effective sample size and thus is likely to overestimate standard errors and reduce the power of the analysis.

It is difficult to reconstruct the historical reasoning why standard statistical packages use listwise deletion as the default (Mplus is a notable exception). Perhaps it was the easiest solution when computers from earlier generations were much slower. If listwise deletion drops a small percentage of participants, it may not introduce a serious loss of information or biased estimates. This argument made more sense when MI and ML were difficult to implement, but it holds little credence today.

A second traditional approach is *mean substitution*. This keeps all observed data. However, mean substitution fails on both the second and the third goals (minimizing bias in parameter estimates and standard errors). There are two problems. First, the variance is reduced because people will be assigned the identical score. Second, the mean may not be a reasonable value. When data are not MCAR, the mean may be a poor guess. Consider missing values on income. Who is mostly likely to have a missing value? A person with average income? Or a person who is either very wealthy or very poor? More than likely, people with extremely high or low incomes will be reluctant to share this information. Some researchers have improved on mean substitution by using the mean of a subgroup, such as the mean income of never married mothers, as the impute values (Acock & Demo, 1994). Although this approach is superior to the grand mean, it still has the problem of introducing considerable error and results in biased estimates.

A third traditional method for dealing with missing data is *pairwise deletion*. Many parametric statistical applications can be estimated from a covariance matrix or a covariance matrix and vector of means. Pairwise deletion calculates each covariance using all observations that have a score on both variables in any pair and can yield unbiased parameter estimates if the MCAR assumption is realistic and can do reasonably well even with MAR assumptions (Acock, 2005).

Pairwise deletion has two limitations. Because there is no single sample on which all the moments are estimated, this can result in a covariance matrix that could not exist for any single population. Mathematically, this situation can also result in a matrix that is not positive definite (hence, the matrix cannot be inverted) and is not useable for parameter estimation. The second problem is that the third goal of minimizing unbiased standard errors becomes challenging. Even if the standard errors are acceptable, the degrees of freedom used to evaluate significance tests are ambiguous. Because each covariance reflects a potentially different sample, there is no defensible way to calculate the degrees of freedom. Using the covariance that has the fewest observations will reduce the statistical power drastically, and there is no statistical rationale for using the average N, minimum N, or maximum N.

In addition to these three traditional approaches for dealing with missing values, there are many specialized imputation approaches, such as last observation carried forward or hot deck imputation. These approaches will not be reviewed here because they offer no significant advantages over ML or MI.

Because missing values are ubiquitous, it is interesting that more research has not been done to develop optimal solutions until fairly recently. It was not until the late 1970s that statistical theory developed the capabilities of MI (Dempster, Laird, & Rubin, 1977; Little & Rubin, 1987; Rubin, 1976, 1987). Researchers were slow to implement modern techniques because easily accessible software was unavailable and computers were extremely slow by 21st-century standards. Today, most statistical packages have some way to do either MI or full information ML estimation.

MODERN APPROACHES TO WORKING WITH MISSING VALUES

There are several modern methods for working with missing values, and for the most part, these all produce similar results when the MAR assumption

is reasonable (Collins et al., 2001; Schafer & Olsen, 1998). I describe ML estimation with missing values and MI. I do not describe all the variations of these broad approaches.

ML Estimation

How does ML work? The ML approach is sometimes referred to as *full information maximum-likelihood* (FIML) or as *direct maximum-likelihood* estimation (Enders, 2006). There is not sufficient space in this chapter to explicate everything that ML involves, but a basic understanding of these concepts is useful. An analysis begins with a vector of parameters being estimated, θ. This vector might be quite long, including parameters estimates for measurement errors, loadings of observed variables on latent variables, paths from one latent variable to another, intercepts and means, and residual variances and covariances. All parameters are estimated simultaneously. A log likelihood function is calculated for different sets of solutions. After a number of iterations, a single set of estimates for all the parameters is obtained that maximizes the log likelihood function. At this point of convergence, the values in the vector, θ, provides the solution.

Without going into the details of the likelihood function, a key component is called the *Mahalanobis distance*, $(y_i - \mu_i) \sum_i^{-1} (y_i - \mu_i)$ (Peugh & Enders, 2004), where y_i is a score on a variable and μ_i is the mean on the variable. Suppose a researcher had four variables: depression, education, income, and stress. If the first observation had no missing data on any of these variables, the Mahalanobis distance portion of the likelihood function would be as follows:

$$\left[\begin{pmatrix} y_{dep} \\ y_{edu} \\ y_{inc} \\ y_{str} \end{pmatrix} - \begin{pmatrix} \mu_{dep} \\ \mu_{edu} \\ \mu_{inc} \\ \mu_{str} \end{pmatrix} \right] \begin{pmatrix} \sigma^2_{dep} & & & \\ \sigma_{edu,dep} & \sigma^2_{edu} & & \\ \sigma_{inc,dep} & \sigma_{inc,edu} & \sigma^2_{inc} & \\ \sigma_{str,dep} & \sigma_{str,dep} & \sigma_{str,inc} & \sigma^2_{str} \end{pmatrix}^{-1} \left[\begin{pmatrix} y_{dep} \\ y_{edu} \\ y_{inc} \\ y_{str} \end{pmatrix} - \begin{pmatrix} \mu_{dep} \\ \mu_{edu} \\ \mu_{inc} \\ \mu_{str} \end{pmatrix} \right]. \quad (1)$$

Equation 1 has three parts. On the left side is the difference of each score on each variable from its mean. On the right side is the same matrix repeated. The central matrix is the covariance of all the variables. For example, $\sigma_{edu,dep}$ is the covariance of education with depression. What happens when there is a missing value on income for the second observation? Researchers can still use all available information they have on the second observation. Because there is no information on y_{inc} for the second observation, the variance of y_{inc} and its covariances are not estimated. The Mahalanobis distance portion of the likelihood function for the second observation reduces to the following:

$$\left[\begin{pmatrix} y_{dep} \\ y_{edu} \\ y_{str} \end{pmatrix} - \begin{pmatrix} \mu_{dep} \\ \mu_{edu} \\ \mu_{str} \end{pmatrix}\right] \begin{bmatrix} \sigma^2_{dep} & & \\ \sigma_{edu,dep} & \sigma^2_{edu} & \\ \sigma_{str,dep} & \sigma_{str,edu} & \sigma^2_{str} \end{bmatrix}^{-1}$$
$$\left[\begin{pmatrix} y_{dep} \\ y_{edu} \\ y_{str} \end{pmatrix} - \begin{pmatrix} \mu_{dep} \\ \mu_{edu} \\ \mu_{str} \end{pmatrix}\right]. \tag{2}$$

The ML approach discards no information. This is why it is sometimes called an FIML estimate. It is important to note that the ML approach imputes no values for missing data but instead uses all available variances and covariances. ML or FIML estimation is estimated by all of the major structural equation modeling programs (LISREL, Mplus, EQS, AMOS). However, one limitation of many studies that have used ML is that they do not incorporate auxiliary variables needed to strengthen the MAR assumption. The Mplus package has an option (Muthén & Muthén, 2009) that simplifies the inclusion of auxiliary variables. There might, for instance, be three auxiliary variables labeled X_1, X_2, and X_3 that help explain missingness (gender would be an example of one of these if males were less likely than females to answer items). Then, there may be two additional auxiliary variables (X_4 and X_5) that help predict a person's score on a variable that has a missing value (education would help predict missing values on income). These additional auxiliary variables (X_4 and X_5) may not predict whether a person answers or skips an item, but these additional auxiliary variables help predict a person's score on a variable. In Mplus, these five variables can be included, even though they are not part of the analysis model.

Although structural equation modeling packages were designed to work with latent variables, they work well when all variables are observable. For example, a researcher could estimate traditional multiple regression models using the Mplus program. These could be estimated as easily as they could be estimated using Stata, SAS, or SPSS.

MI

Although the ML approach is effective in many applications, the use of MI is now widely available. SAS and Stata have two MI approaches, including a multivariate normal-based MI, *proc mi* in SAS, and *mi mvn* in Stata. This approach works best with continuous variables assuming multivariate normality. SAS and Stata also offer an implementation of IVEware that does the imputations through a sequence of multiple regressions in which the variables are imputed one at a time but taking each other into account through a process called chained equations. Stata offers this approach using the mi impute chained, which is adapted from the R command, multivariate imputation by chained equations (MICE). This approach uses regression, logistic regression, ordinal logistic regression, or multinomial logistic regression depending on the type of variable being imputed. As this is written, the SPSS's manual is not clear on its approach, but it appears to be similar that is offered by IVEware.

MI begins with a single imputation and involves an iterative process. One approach is to use regression to obtain a predicted value for each missing value. This is a simple way to impute predicted values to substitute for missing values; however, the variance of a variable will be reduced when the predicted values are substituted for the missing values. This is because all of the predicted values fall exactly on the hyperplane. Because all the imputed values would fall on this plane, the variance about the plane is lost. One solution to the attenuation of the variance is to randomly select a value from the residual vector $(X_i - \hat{X})$ where i refers to a case that has a missing value. This value is then added to the predicted value of X_i. This maintains the variance of

X_i (Schafer, 1997). If the model does a poor job of predicting X_i, the elements in the residual vector will be large, and this uncertainty in the prediction will be reflected in the imputed values and ultimately in the standard errors of the estimated parameters.

This first iteration in MI produces a data set that has no missing values. Some of the values in this data set will be observed scores whereas the rest will be imputed scores. One way to evaluate this imputed complete data set is to generate a covariance matrix for the imputed data set and compare it with the covariance matrix for the original data set that has missing values. If there is more than a trivial difference, the imputed data set is considered useful because the new covariance matrix used more information when it estimated values to substitute for the missing values.

The second iteration repeats this process. However, this series of regressions takes advantage of the values that were imputed for missing data in the first iteration. Once the regressions are done, it again adds an element from the residual vector to each imputed value. To evaluate the second imputed data set, its covariance matrix is calculated and compared with the covariance matrix for the first iteration. If there is a difference, it is assumed that the second iteration was an improvement, because it used more information than the first iteration. This iterative process is repeated until a subsequent data set generates a covariance matrix that is so close to the prior matrix that there is no meaningful improvement. When this point is reached, the process stops with a final complete data set that has no missing values. A number of data sets may have been iteratively imputed before reaching this point, but the final result is a single imputed complete data set, hence the name single imputation.

Single imputation yields biased (underestimated) standard errors and hence fails to meet the third goal. The underestimated standard errors will inflate t-values and misrepresent the level of significance increasing the likelihood of a Type 2 error. That is, a researcher will be more likely to find a statistically significant effect when none actually exists. MI simply repeats the entire imputation process from five to 100 or more times generating from five to 100 or more new, complete data sets, each of which has no missing values. By estimating the model on each of the imputed data sets, the parameter estimates and standard errors can be pooled across analyses as well as allowing appropriate adjustments in the degrees of freedom. MI, like ML, responds successfully to all three of the goals.

The analysis stage is illustrated on the right side of Figure 2.1. The analysis model is applied to each of the imputed complete data sets. The parameter estimates are simply the average of the estimates over however many data sets were generated. This pooling uses what are referred to as Rubin's rules (named after person who originally derived them; Rubin, 1976, 1987):

$$\bar{Q} = \frac{\sum_{i=1}^{m} \hat{Q}_i}{m},$$ (3)

where $\bar{Q}$ is the pooled parameter estimate and $\hat{Q}_i$ is the estimate of the parameter for each of the m data sets.

Estimates of the unstandardized regression coefficient, B, for a child's educational performance regressed on maternal depression might have $B = 1.2$ in the first imputed data set, 2.1 in the second data set, 1.7 in the third data set, 1.9 in the fourth data set, and 1.4 in the fifth data set. The estimated B is the mean over the five data sets, or 1.66. The estimated Bs may or may not vary this much across the five data sets. With very large samples and relatively few missing values, the Bs will be quite similar; however, with small samples and substantial missing values the Bs can vary widely. One advantage of using MI rather than single imputation is that random fluctuations average out. A single imputation gives an unbiased estimate of the parameter, but inspecting the values of the parameter estimates across data sets often shows quite a bit of variability.

Pooling the standard errors using Rubin's rules (Rubin, 1976, 1987) is only slightly more complex. There are two components. The first term below, $\bar{U}$, is the mean of the m standard errors squared. For regression parameters the $\bar{U}$ is as follows:

$$\bar{U} = \frac{\sum_{i=1}^{m} se_i^2}{m}.$$ (4)

We add to this the between-solution variance in the parameter estimate (Graham, Olchowski, & Gilreath, 2007). This addition reflects the variance in the estimates:

$$B = \frac{\sum_{i=1}^{m}\left(\hat{Q}_i - \bar{Q}\right)^2}{m-1}. \tag{5}$$

The pooled standard error of the parameter estimate is the square root of the sum of these two variance estimates with an adjustment for the number of imputations, m, that have been used.

$$se = \sqrt{\bar{U} + \left(1 + \frac{1}{m}\right)B}. \tag{6}$$

The number of imputed data sets was traditionally recommended to be three to five, but there are benefits, although decreasing marginal benefits, to using more imputed data sets. Graham et al. (2007) pointed out that when trying to estimate small effect sizes, far more imputed complete data sets are needed, and they recommend imputing 40. Using a larger number of imputed data sets improves the stability of the results as reflected in the $1 + 1/m$ part of Equation 6. In Equation 6, the between solution variance of the parameter estimates, B, would be multiplied by 1.2 using $m = 5$, and this reduces to 1.01 using $m = 100$.

The degrees of freedom are defined as follows:

$$df = (m-1)\left[1 + \left(\frac{m\bar{U}}{(m+1)B}\right)\right]^2. \tag{7}$$

A 95% confidence interval for a parameter, θ, is as follows:

$$\theta \pm t_{df,\alpha/2}se. \tag{8}$$

The estimation of the degrees of freedom was derived assuming infinite sample size. For small samples, an alternative estimator is available from Reiter (2007). Rubin (1987; see also Graham et al., 2007) has also shown how the relative efficiency of the estimates depends on both the number of imputed data sets and the percentage of values that are missing:

$$\text{Relative Efficiency} = \left(1 + \frac{\gamma}{m}\right)^{-1}. \tag{9}$$

In Equation 9, γ is the proportion of values that are missing for the parameter being estimated and m is the number of imputed data sets. Stata, for example, provides a separate relative efficiency of each parameter being estimated. With $m = 5$ and 10% missing values, the relative efficiency is 98%. By comparison, with $m = 20$ and 10% missing values the relative efficiency is approximately 99.5%. With modern procedures, it is no more difficult to have $m = 20$ than it is to have $m = 5$. With 50% of the values missing and assuming MAR, the relative efficiency of $m = 5$ drops to 90.9%, whereas the relative efficiency of $m = 20$ is 97.6% and with $m = 100$ the relative efficiency is 99.5%. When values are missing by design, such as when each child answers only half of the items, using a large value of m regains most of the power that a researcher would have had by asking the children all of the questions. The formula only considers the amount of missing values and the number of imputations. The complexity of the analysis is also important. Research suggests that stable results require an m of 50 or more in complex analyses (Horton & Lipsitz, 2001; Kenward & Carpenter, 2007; Stata, 2011).

WHAT AUXILIARY VARIABLES SHOULD BE INCLUDED?

Whether researchers use ML or MI to handle missing values, there are two criteria to use when selecting auxiliary variables. The first criterion is designed to help justify the MAR assumption. In this case, education and gender may provide the mechanism for explaining the missingness for a given variable. By including variables that predict who will and who will not answer items, any remaining missingness, after controlling for these variables, is reasonably thought of as being random (i.e., MAR).

The second criterion includes auxiliary variables that predict the score on variables that have missing values. A number of simulation studies (e.g., Collins et al., 2001) are designed to determine which of these types of auxiliary values is most important. If there are missing data and the MAR assumption is reasonable, then adding auxiliary variables to help explain why some people have missing values will not be valuable. In these cases, adding variables that help predict the score for a missing value will be much more important. Conversely, if the data used in the analysis model are clearly not MAR, but the mechanism is understood to be because certain auxiliary variables explain the missingness, then adding those variables to the imputation model is important. The ideal auxiliary variable is a variable that meets both criteria. That is, a variable such as education that not only predicts who will answer and who will skip questions but also predicts how they would have scored on many of these questions had they answered them.

This section has been deliberately vague about how many auxiliary variables should be included. Some researchers add a few auxiliary variables and others try to add 100 or more. Although there is a risk in leaving out an important auxiliary variable, adding a very large number can also be problematic. First, it is doubtful that all 100+ auxiliary variables are helpful because there is likely a great deal of multicolinearity. If many of the auxiliary variables contain missing values themselves, as is almost certain, they are likely to add noise (i.e., error) to the process. Second, as shown in Equation 1, there are $j(j+1)/2$ elements in the covariance matrix, plus the j means where j is the number of variables. In the four-variable example illustrated in Equation 1, there were 14 parameters. Imagine having 20 variables in the analysis model plus 100 auxiliary variables. The number of parameters in Equation 1 mushrooms to 7,381 parameters, that is, $120(121)/2 + 120$, which would be a most ambitious analysis, even with a large sample size.

WHAT HAPPENS WITH A SMALL SAMPLE?

Both MI and ML procedures are large-sample procedures, and all the assumptions of ML estimation apply. If variables are highly skewed, for example, a large sample can mitigate the problem ensuring that the sampling distributions will be approximately normal. A small sample cannot do this, and MI will not help make skewed variables normal.

These observations are often problematic because many psychological studies rely on small samples. In such cases, the question is whether a researcher is better off using MI/ML or using a traditional

approach such as listwise deletion. Graham and Schafer (1999) showed that MI performs reasonably well on samples as small as $N = 50$ and with as much as 50% missing values. One strategy with skewed variables is to transform variables before doing the imputations and then reverse these transformations.

These comments, however, should not be taken to mean that small samples are acceptable for complex analyses. A power analysis will show that running a complex structural equation model or even a large multiple regression model on a sample with 50 observations will have unacceptably low power. The point is simply that doing ML or MI to handle missing values will work as well or better in such a situation as using listwise deletion.

WHAT HAPPENS WHEN THERE ARE MISSING VALUES ON THE OUTCOME VARIABLE?

When people initially use a modern approach to missing values, they may be reluctant to include the observations that have missing values on an outcome variable, Y. ML must include the outcome variable because there is no imputation of data. When using MI, it is important to include the outcome variable when running the multiple imputation model (see Figure 2.1) because leaving out any of the analysis variables introduces bias. When not including the outcome variable, researchers are implicitly assuming that Y is unrelated to the values they impute (von Hippel, 2007). Imputing values in a predictor variable, X_i, without including Y, means that those imputed values are estimated without recognizing the covariance between Y and X_i.

In spite of the importance of including Y in MI for the imputation model, there are special circumstances in which imputing Y is not necessary. When all the X_i variables are complete and the only missing values are on Y, then imputing the missing values on Y adds no information to the estimation of Y from X_i. This situation can happen in a longitudinal intervention in which the Xs involve observed variables, but there is some participant dropout and hence some missing values on the outcome variable Y (Little, 1992; von Hippel, 2007). However, if auxiliary variables that are related to Y and X_i are included, then some additional information may be gained by imputing scores on Y.

In addition, von Hippel (2007) has suggested a modification of the MI approach when there are missing values on the outcome variables. He suggested proceeding with the MI in the imputation model including the outcome variables, but then, before estimating the analysis model, he recommended dropping the observations that have an imputed value on the outcome variables. He has called this *multiple imputation, then delete* (MID), where *then delete* means to drop the observations that had a missing value on the outcome variable but only after the imputation stage has been completed. This may give a small gain in the quality of the standard errors by removing the uncertainty in the imputed outcome variables. The imputed Ys will add nothing other than noise because of the uncertainty of the estimated values. This slight advantage of the MID approach can become substantial when there are many missing values on the outcome variable, such as when there is a very high attrition rate. Importantly, von Hippel acknowledged that when there is an important set of auxiliary variables, the imputed Ys will contain additional information gained from the relationship that the Y variables have to the auxiliary variables. In this case, keeping the observations with missing values on the outcome is reasonable. Following is a set of recommendations for handling missing values on Y:

1. If there are no missing values on any of the X_i variables, just missing values on Y, then do listwise deletion of the observations that are missing a score on Y. There is no information gain from MI or ML procedures. ML or MI will not introduce bias estimates and will use all available information, but may have slightly larger standard errors than listwise deletion of observations missing on Y.
2. If there are missing values on the X_i variables, then do the MI including the Y variable as a first step in the imputation model and then drop the observations with imputed values on Y as a second step before doing the analysis model. It would seem reasonable to do it this way and to repeat it without dropping the cases and picking

whichever approach minimizes the confidence interval widths because no bias is introduced in the parameter estimates either way.
3. If there is a strong set of auxiliary variables that provide information for imputing Y, then dropping the cases with imputed values on Y is a mistake.

WORKING WITH CATEGORICAL VARIABLES, OUT OF RANGE IMPUTATIONS, AND INTERACTIONS

Most packaged solutions for working with missing values (*proc mi* in SAS and *mi mvn* in Stata) are designed to work with quantitative variables making a multivariate normal assumption of the variables, rather than with categorical variables (although MICE using R, mi impute chained using Stata, and IVEware using SAS, and SPSS are notable exceptions: Horton & Kleinman, 2007; Royston, 2007). When values are imputed for a categorical variable using a multivariate approach, they are not restricted to be the values of the categorical variables. If gender has been coded zero for men and one for women, an imputed value might be –0.2 or 1.3. These imputed values are consistent with the observed data, but researchers often round the imputed value to the nearest legitimate coded value, recoding the –0.2 as a 0 and the 1.3 as a 1. Such recoding rarely has substantive consequences, but it violates the basic idea of not adding new information (Horton, Lipsitz, & Parzen, 2003). The –0.2 or 1.3 are the values that are most consistent with the observed data and should be left at these fractional values. Recoding such values adds ad hoc information that is inconsistent with the observed information.

This same issue happens with continuous variables where there is an out-of-range prediction. The imputed score of –2 or a 7.4 on a scale that ranges from zero to five seems worrisome. Multivariate normal imputation models do not recognize these restrictions. Although these are impossible values, they are the values that are consistent with the observed data and should not be adjusted.

A similarly perplexing result occurs when there is an interaction term, X_1X_2. If there is a missing value on either main effect, then there will also be a missing value on the product. When imputation is done entering the three variables, X_1, X_2, and X_1X_2 in the imputation model, there is no reason to assume that X_1X_2 will be the product of $X_1 \times X_2$. For example, imputed values for X_1, X_2, and X_1X_2 might be 2.1, 3.2, and 8.4, respectively. Some packages have options to impute only the main effects and then to passively impute their product to eliminate such inconsistencies. Although eliminating the numerical inconsistency, these restrictions result in ad hoc changes that are inconsistent with the observed data.

A choice needs to be made. Should researchers impute values that are consistent with the observed data even if some of these values (categorical variables, interactions, out of range) are impossible? Or, should they override the imputation process and adjust imputed values? Some software appears to favor the recoding and passive calculation. The missing values module available as an add-on since SPSS Version 17 appears to favor recoding. SPSS offers a menu for constraining imputations. The following statement is from the SPSS (2009) manual regarding constraints:

> Some variables may be used as scale, but have values that are naturally further restricted; for instance, the number of people in a household must be integer, and the amount spent during a visit to the grocery store cannot have fractional cents. (p. 28)

Similarly, Stata has the option of passive imputation, that is, impute only the main effects and then generate the interaction as the product of those imputed values, of an interaction term (Royston, 2005).

Both Allison (2002) and von Hippel (2009) have been very critical of this approach. von Hippel presented the most systematic argument against adjusting imputed values. The key to understanding this argument is to recognize that there are two models, the imputation model and the analysis model as was shown in Figure 2.1. To maintain compatibility between the two models, all variables such as interaction terms and squared terms (X_i^2) that are in the analysis model are also included in the imputation model.

Compatibility does not require that an imputed value, $X^{(m)}$, be identical to the true score of X for the missing value. Indeed, von Hippel (2009) shows that the correlation between X and the imputed value $X^{(m)}$ will be less than one and possibly much less than one. Thus, although X and $X^{(m)}$ fit the same regression equation, "we should not expect them to have much more than that in common" (von Hippel 2009, p. 268). All that is necessary is that the imputed data set has the same mean vector and covariance matrix as the complete data set. If they have the same mean vector and covariance matrix, they will produce equivalent results in the analysis stage even when the values on any variable may differ. Thus, a participant imputed to have a score on gender of 1.1 is not a problem. Ad hoc adjustments in values will cause the mean vector and covariance matrix to be different from the true values, resulting in biased estimates of parameters (Shih, 2002).

The assumption of multivariate normality is problematic when data include categorical variables. The IVEware implemented in SAS and ice implemented in Stata use a series of regressions using chained equations. This iterative approach imputes one variable at a time and is conditional on the other variables. When a researcher has a number of categorical variables, especially when there are variables with more than two possible outcome categories, these approaches may have an advantage. They use regression, logistic regression, ordinal logistic regression, and multinomial logistic regression depending on the measurement level of the variable being imputed. Although these approaches have a weaker theoretical justification and are more prone to convergence problems, they may be more reasonable than the multivariate normal imputation, when working with a large number of categorical variables.

When a researcher has more than two possible outcomes on a variable, special care is needed. Using the multivariate approach, a researcher would need to generate $k - 1$ dummy/indicator variables for the imputation stage. If a sample consists of Protestant, Catholic, Muslim, Jewish, and Hindu participants, then four dummy variables would be generated. The researcher might have a few participants imputed to have values close to one on more than one category. With IVEware, the researcher would impute religion using multinomial logistic regression. With a large number of variables, these alternatives to the multivariate normal approach can have convergence problems.

WHAT SHOULD BE DONE WITH A BINARY DEPENDENT VARIABLE?

Even with a binary outcome variable, an argument can be made to use a multivariate imputation approach. When a binary variable is imputed using the multivariate approach, it can be argued that there is an underlying continuous latent variable. If an individual is above a certain threshold value, then they are a one. If they are below this threshold value, they are a zero (Long, 1997; Long & Freese, 2006). If this view is convincing, then standard regression analyses can be used. If a researcher is predicting a particular behavior, whether it is condom use or smoking cessation, it is possible to conceptualize an underlying latent variable and use standard regression procedures.

In many applications, however, the binary nature of the outcome is essential and a logistic analysis model is required. This occurs with a discrete outcome, such as divorce, birth of first child, or use of illegal drug, where researchers and readers expect a logistic (or probit) analysis model. In this case, researchers may want to use a multivariate imputation and then round the outcome variable or chose a program that does logistic regression in the imputation stage, such as MICE with R, mi impute chained with Stata, SPSS, or IVEware with SAS.

DO WE IMPUTE SCALE SCORES OR SCORES ON INDIVIDUAL ITEMS?

In many research settings there are many variables, each with a scale score and a huge number of individual items used to measure the set of variables. This is where the art of compromise can be important. Ideally, missing values would be imputed on all individual items in all scales used in the analysis stage. If there are 10 scales and each has 20 items, this results in 200 variables before even thinking about adding any auxiliary variables. When it is practical to do the imputations at the item level for all the items used in all of the scales in the analysis

stage, this is the best choice. Given the limitations of current software and computer performance, this may not be practical.

Some researchers may decide to impute missing values for each variable separately. This is a mistake. If one does the MI separately for the 20 items that are measuring depression and then separately for the 20 items that are measuring stress, then the covariances of the full set of 50 items will be ignored. As a result, the imputed values on depression will not be consistent with the imputed values on stress and vice versa. Only partial information will be used.

There are reasonable solutions. As Graham (2009) noted, when coefficient alpha is high, it is reasonable to assume that the scale items are interchangeable. The correlation matrix should show items are consistently intercorrelated to further justify interchangeability. Additional evidence of interchangeability is obtained if a factor analysis produces a single factor with similar loadings on all items. These results indicate that any item is the equivalent to any other item and any subset of items will be equivalent to any other subset of the items. If a person answered at least 70% of the items and the alpha was more than 0.80, then it may be reasonable to assign the person the average of the items they answered. This assumes that the items they skipped are neither more nor less discriminating than the items they answered and that all of the items for each scale reflect a single dimension. If this is done, then the 200 items going into the 10 scales used in the analysis model are just 10 variables in the imputation model to go with the 10 variables in the analysis model.

Although this is a reasonable solution, a researcher needs to be careful about generating scale scores when some items are missing. In standard statistical packages, the commands to generate a sum or total score assigns a value of zero to missing values. It is safest to generate a mean score because programs calculate the mean of however many items are answered.

MONOTONE MISSING VALUES IN LONGITUDINAL RESEARCH

Most missing values conform to what is called a *nonmonotone pattern* of missingness, but a *monotone pattern* is sometimes observed in longitudinal studies. In a monotone pattern all observations have complete data up to the point at which they drop out of the study. Unfortunately, many of the people who drop out of a study have some missing values before that time. With a monotone missing values pattern, the imputation process gains considerable flexibility (Rubin, 1987). A strictly monotone pattern rarely occurs, and space does not permit coverage of the resulting flexibility. A detailed discussion is available in Stata (2011).

POWER ANALYSIS WITH MISSING VALUES

When designing a study, it is always important to do a power analysis because there is little sense in starting a study that lacks sufficient power to demonstrate significant results, and there is little justification for including more participants than needed to have adequate power. One way to estimate power is to use a conventional rule of so many observations per variable or per parameter being estimated (Kline, 2010). It is also possible, but somewhat statistically demanding, to do a power analysis even when there are missing values. Doing such an individualized power analysis requires making a series of assumptions and then doing a simulation. Because the assumptions are sometimes difficult to justify, it is also useful to try several alternative sets of assumptions.

Davey and Savia (2010) have produced an accessible and comprehensive treatment of how to perform a power analysis when there are missing values. They rely on a structural equation modeling approach, but their methods apply quite broadly. They illustrate a series of applications using LISREL, Mplus, Amos, Stata, SAS, and SPSS.

The first step in Davey and Savia's (2010) approach is to specify the model and include reasonable values for all parameters for at least two alternatives. The first alternative is the model that is similar to what the researcher thinks of as a null hypothesis. The second alternative is the model with the results that would be considered conceptually important. For example, one model may assume there is no growth by fixing the mean of the latent slope growth factor at zero and the other might fix the slope at whatever

minimum growth would be considered important. Once alternative models are specified, it is possible to generate data (often only needing a covariance matrix and vector of means) that are consistent with the specifications. These data are treated as the population data. Davey and Savia then showed how to change these models to reflect different assumptions about missing values, such as the amount of missing data and whether the data are MCAR or MAR.

By drawing a large number of samples from the model-implied population data, it is possible to empirically show what proportion of the samples produce a significant result for the parameter or parameters of interest. This proportion is the power. Although power analysis can be difficult to execute, Davey and Savia (2010) have provided step-by-step procedures using standard software programs.

SOFTWARE

The software available for working with missing values is developing at a rapid pace. The best practice at the time this is written will be superseded by future software developments. Horton and Lipsitz (2001) and Horton and Kleinman (2007) reviewed popular software solutions and have an online appendix to their 2007 article showing the code for a wide variety of software, including Amelia, HMisc package in R, ice in Stata, IVEware in SAS, LogXact, MICE in R, SAS *proc mi*, and the S-Plus missing data library.

In addition, UCLA has an online tutorial for working with missing values using both Stata and SAS and covering both the multivariate model and the chained equation approaches (UCLA Academic Technology Services, 2009a, 2009b, 2010a, 2010b). Both of these provide carefully annotated code and output. SPSS (2009) also has a manual that clearly illustrates how to use its single imputation program (although this method is not recommended) and the SPSS MI program.

A WORKED EXAMPLE

This example applies Stata's multivariate normal approach that is comparable to SAS in its capabilities. Stata is used because of the simple command structure and because it illustrates a comprehensive suite of the aspects of the output that need to interpreted regardless of software being used. The focus is on appropriate decision making and interpretations. The data for this example were collected by Day et al. (2009). These data have virtually no missing values on the variables being used and after listwise deletion, these data are used as the complete data set. Missing values were generated on all but one of the variables. The missing values are related to a small set of auxiliary variables that will be used to illustrate their used in the imputation model.

The model to be estimated is a regression predicting a child's engagement in school at age 11. The predictors include the child's report of positive peer influence, prosocial behavior, hopefulness, parental conflict, parent–child conflict, and gender. The analysis model was selected to illustrate multiple imputation not as an important theoretical model. The model is first estimated using a complete data set (no missing values). This solution is the gold standard for evaluating alternative treatments of missing values.

Although Stata offers a menu system for doing evaluating alternatives, the code in Stata is much simpler than most other software packages so only the code will be reported. This code will be useful for people who use SAS or SPSS because this code will explain the choices for running the imputation model, the analysis model, and how to interpret the results. School engagement is *sch_engaged*, peer influence is *peer*, prosocial behavior is *prosocial*, hopefulness is *hope*, parental conflict is *parcon*, parent–child conflict is *conflict*, and gender is *male*. The auxiliary variables are mother's age, *mom_age*, percentage of neighborhood in poverty, *poverty*, percent of neighborhood married with children under 18, *neighbor_mar*, self-reported health, *health*, health risks, *healthrisk*, and religiosity, *religiosity*.

A Stata user-written command, *misschk* (Long & Freese, 2006), was first run with the results as shown in Exhibit 2.1. The first panel shows that there are no missing values on gender, and parent–child conflict has the most missing values (70 or 15.7%). The second panel shows the different patterns of missing values in cases in which the variables are numbered from one to seven as in the first table. The last entry has a dash for each variable,

---

Exhibit 2.1
The misschk Command to Explore Missing Values

```
. misschk scheng peers prosocial hope
    parcon conflict male, gen(ind)
    dummy
```

Variables examined for missing values

#	Variable	# Missing	% Missing
1	sch_engaged	38	8.5
2	peers	46	10.3
3	prosocial	57	12.8
4	hope	73	16.4
5	parcon	47	10.5
6	conflict	70	15.7
7	male	0	0.0

Missing for which variables?	Freq.	Percent	Cum.
1234_ 6_	1	0.22	0.22
123__ 6_	1	0.22	0.45
12_45 6_	1	0.22	0.67
12__5 6_	1	0.22	0.90
12___ __	1	0.22	1.12
1_34_ 6_	1	0.22	1.35
1_3__ __	8	1.79	3.14
omitted results here			
_____ __	249	55.83	100.00
Total	446	100.00	

Missing for how many variables?	Freq.	Percent	Cum.
0	249	55.83	55.83
1	99	22.20	78.03
2	74	16.59	94.62
3	14	3.14	97.76
4	8	1.79	99.55
5	2	0.45	100.00
Total	446	100.00	

Note. sch_engaged = school engagement; peers = peer influence; prosocial = the amount of pro social behavior; hope = the level of hope for the future; parcon conflict = represents the level of parental conflict; male = gender; Freq. = frequency; Cum. = cumulative.

---

indicating there are no missing values on any of the variables for 249 observations. Using listwise deletion, the *N* is just 249 representing only 55.8% of the 446 observations in the full data set. The final panel shows how many observations have missing values on zero to five variables.

A nice feature of the misschk command is that it generates an indicator/dummy variable for each variable that has missing values. Each generated variable is coded 1 if an observation has a missing value on the variable and zero if it is present. To locate possible auxiliary variables, a series of logistic regressions were run using each of the six generated indicator variables for the six variables that have missing values. An example of how Stata does logistic regression for one of these variables is the command, logit sch_engagedM mom_age poverty neighbor_mar health healthrisk religiosity, or, where sch_engagedM is the indicator variable for a missing value on school engagement. Table 2.2 shows the results. The religiosity variable does not provide a mechanism for explaining missing values on any of the variables, so religiosity can be dropped as a possible auxiliary variable.

There are no missing values on male, so a logistic regression for gender was not run. For parcon, 10.5% of the observations were missing and none of the six auxiliary variable candidates have a significant effect. This result demonstrates that nothing explains the missingness on parental conflict. Unless we can assume the missing values on parental conflict are missing in a purely random fashion, further analyses should be completed to explore additional auxiliary variables to justify the MAR assumption with respect to parental conflict. Table 2.2 shows that the mother's age (mom_age), the two variables about the neighborhood (poverty, neighbor_mar), and the two health variables provide mechanisms for missingness for at least one analysis variable. This justifies their inclusion in the MI imputation model.

Stata offers a sequence of commands to do the MI. Here are the commands:

- `mi set mlong`
- `set seed 1259`
- `mi register imputed sch_engaged peers prosocial hope parcon conflict male mom_age poverty neighbor_mar health healthrisk`
- `mi impute mvn sch_engaged peers prosocial hope parcon conflict male mom_age poverty neighbor_ mar health healthrisk, add(20)`
- `mi impute mvn scheng peers prosocial hope parcon conflict male mom_age poverty neighbor_mar health healthrisk, add(20)`

Stata wants to know how to arrange the new data sets. The mlong option creates a very long (tall) file in which the data sets will be vertically stacked. Setting the seed insures that the same result will be obtained if the analysis is replicated. Any value may be entered. The third command registers the variables to be imputed including both the analysis variables and the auxiliary variables selected after doing the logistic regression.

The command that does the MI is as follows:

```
mi impute mvn scheng peers
prosocial hope parcon conflict
male mom_age poverty neighbor_
mar health healthrisk,
add(20)
```

TABLE 2.2

Significant Predictors of Missing Values on the Basis of a Series of Logistic Regressions

Variable	sch_engaged	peers	prosocial	hope	parcon	conflict	male
mom_age	—	—	✓	—	—	—	—
poverty	—	✓	✓	—	—	✓	—
neighbor_mar	✓	✓	—	✓	—	—	—
health	—	—	✓	—	—	—	—
healthrisk	—	✓	—	✓	—	✓	—
religiosity	—	—	—	—	—	—	—

The command mi impute mvn specifies a multivariate normal imputation. This is followed by a list of the six analysis variables and the five auxiliary variables. All variables including the outcome variable and male (that has no missing values) are included. After the comma, there is the option of adding 20 new complete data sets. It takes little time to generate many complete data sets unless there are a very large number of variables. Imputing 20 complete data sets took 10 seconds and generating 100 complete data sets took less than a minute on a Macintosh computer with several other programs running concurrently. Other software may take considerably longer because of the way Stata manages memory.

The final pair of commands specifies the analysis model. A regression is shown but many other commands can be used. Here are the commands:

```
. mi estimate, dftable vartable:
    regress scheng peers prosocial
    hope parcon conflict male
. mibeta scheng peers prosocial hope
    parcon conflict male
```

Before the colon in the first command, the code tells Stata to run the analysis on each of the imputed data sets. The *mi estimate, dftable vartable* is a prefix command in Stata. The *dftable* option and the *variable* option provide additional tables that are interpreted below. The regression command appears after the colon. The second command, *mibeta*, is a userwritten command that was created by Marchenko (2010), who also directed the development of the multivariate normal command in Stata. This command provides output that many psychologists prefer, including R^2 and standardized β weights. Other software may not provide this information, so the researcher should check each solution and calculate the R^2 and β weights as the average of each value in all of the corresponding solutions. This would be quite tedious with many imputed data sets.

Exhibit 2.2 presents the results. The first panel has information about the imputations. Using 20 imputed data sets has between 98.6% and 99.1% of the efficiency achieved with an infinite number of imputations. Had there been 100 imputed data sets, then all relative efficiencies would have exceeded

99% for all estimates. The within- and between-group variance columns indicate how much of the variance was part of the sample (within) and how much from the uncertainty associated with MI (between sample differences). There appears to be very little between-group variance for any of the parameter estimates for the 20 solutions being pooled. The RVI is the relative variance increase (error) because of the nonresponse.

The second set of output in Exhibit 2.2 provides standard regression results. Notice that there are 446 observations in each of the 20 imputed data sets. Stata uses a small sample equation to estimate the degrees of freedom (Reiter, 2007), although this small sample equation can be overridden. With no missing values, there would have been 439 degrees of freedom. With missing values using the pooled estimates of the standard errors there are between 149 and 219 degrees of freedom for each parameter estimate. The overall $F(6, 367.8) = 23.09$; $p < .001$ indicates the model is highly significant. The coefficients are the unstandardized regression coefficients, B.

The *mibeta* command shows standardized coefficients and R^2. The column labeled mean reports the standardized β weight. Notice that the β = .199 for the influence of positive peers on school engagement. The value of β will vary from one imputed complete data set to another. For the imputed data set with the smallest value for the influence of positive peers, the β = .117 and for the largest value, the β = .252. This variation shows the importance of having a reasonable number of imputed complete data sets. For example, before version 17, SPSS could only impute a single complete data set. The β = .199 when averaged across 20 data sets is better than reporting the result for a single imputed complete data set. If the median value of a β weight differs markedly from its mean, the sampling distribution is not normal and increasing the number of imputed data sets is advisable. The R^2 = .287 indicates that, on average, 28.7% of the variance in school engagement is explained across the 20 imputed complete data sets.

Table 2.3 compares the analysis models for three imputation models and the complete data set (no missing values). Both the third and fourth results were estimated using a multivariate normal imputation model, $N = 446$.

Exhibit 2.2
The Analysis Model

Imputations (20)
Multiple-imputation estimates   Imputations   =   20
Variance information

| | Imputation variance | | | | | Relative efficiency |
	Within	Between	Total	RVI	FMI	
peers	.000678	.000227	.000917	.352023	.265589	.986895
prosocial	.000945	.000218	.001173	.241927	.197997	.990197
hope	.000961	.000238	.001211	.26038	.210129	.989603
parcon	.000767	.00018	.000956	.246905	.201304	.990035
conflict	.000926	.000313	.001255	.355362	.267471	.986803
male	.001171	.000249	.001432	.22349	.185522	.990809
_cons	.026078	.008123	.034608	.327061	.251227	.987594

Linear regression

	Number of obs = 446	
	Average RVI = 0.2476	
	Complete DF = 439	
DF adjustment: Small sample	DF: min = 148.82	
	avg = 183.40	
	max = 219.50	
Model F test: Equal FMI	F(6, 367.8) = 23.09	
Within VCE type: OLS	Prob > F = 0.0000	

scheng_	Coef.	Std. Err.	t	P>|t|	DF	% Increase Std. Err.
peers	.1102389	.0302862	3.64	0.000	150.1	16.28
prosocial	.1201695	.0342506	3.51	0.001	206.7	11.44
hope	−.1657666	.0347975	−4.76	0.000	194.9	12.27
parcon	−.0031542	.0309227	−0.10	0.919	203.4	11.66
conflict	−.0793242	.0354239	−2.24	0.027	148.8	16.42
male	−.0562899	.0378459	−1.49	0.138	219.5	10.61
_cons	3.271537	.1860313	17.59	0.000	160.4	15.20

. mibeta scheng_ peers prosocial hope parcon conflict male

Standardized coefficients and R-squared
Summary statistics over 20 imputations

	mean	min	p25	median	p75	max
peers	.1986562	.117	.1893918	.2068778	.2140895	.252
prosocial	.1975532	.145	.1878171	.1973794	.2120342	.237
hope	−.2451571	−.297	−.2529118	−.2465516	−.2246981	−.2
parcon	−.0049676	−.0429	−.020385	−.0016605	.0059775	.0312
conflict	−.1116102	−.148	−.126576	−.1158565	−.0950978	−.0658
male	−.0668147	−.097	−.080679	−.0689141	−.0493133	−.0393
R-square	.2874377	.267	.2787939	.2840081	.2961681	.314
Adj R-square	.2776988	.257	.2689369	.2742223	.2865486	.304

Note. RVI = relative variance increase; FMI = largest fraction of missing information, P>|t| = the two-tail probability for the corresponding *t* test; p25 = the value corresponding to the 25th percentile; p75 = the value corresponding the the 75th percentile; min = the smallest value; max = the maximum value.

TABLE 2.3

A Comparison of Three Approaches to Missing Values

Variable	Estimate	No missing—complete N = 446	Listwise deletion N = 249	MI MVN N = 446	MI MVN with auxiliary N = 446
Peers	B	0.105	0.107	0.104	0.110
	SE	0.025	0.034	0.031	0.030
	t	4.240	3.160	3.400	3.640
Prosocial	B	0.143	0.088	0.126	0.120
	SE	0.030	0.041	0.035	0.034
	t	4.740	2.170	3.600	3.510
Hope	B	−0.143	−0.174	−0.160	−0.166
	SE	0.030	0.041	0.035	0.035
	t	−4.740	−4.190	−4.560	−4.760
Parent conflict	B	−0.008	0.011	−0.011	−0.003
	SE	0.027	0.036	0.034	0.031
	t	−0.029	0.031	−0.350	−0.010
Parent–child conflict	B	−0.069	−0.074	−0.800	−0.079
	SE	0.300	0.040	0.034	0.035
	t	−2.320	−1.840	−2.340	−2.240
Gender (male)	B	−0.059	−0.112	−0.059	−0.056
	SE	0.034	0.045	0.037	0.038
	t	−1.730	−2.510	−1.620	−1.490
Constant	B	3.150	3.369	3.274	3.271
	SE	0.156	0.216	0.191	0.186
	t	20.180	15.610	17.17	17.590

Note. MI = multiple imputation; MVN = multivariate normal.

With a couple exceptions, the MI analysis models performed better than the listwise analysis model by estimating values that were closer to the complete data set. If the results from the listwise deletion were used, the researcher would have decided that the parent–child conflict was not statistically significant, when it was significant for the complete data set and for both of the MI analyses. Thus, listwise deletion resulted in a Type 2 error. On the other hand, using the listwise deletion, the researcher would have decided that there was a significant gender difference when the complete data set and both of the MI analyses showed that gender was not significant. Thus, the listwise deletion resulted in a Type 1 error. The biggest difference between the complete data set, and the MI analyses is that although the *t* values are closer than they were for the listwise deletion, the MI analyses produce *t* values that are a bit smaller in absolute size than the *t* values for the complete data set. This reflects the uncertainty that is inherent with imputation.

In this example adding the auxiliary variables makes the MAR assumption more reasonable. It is an empirical question, however, whether the parameter estimates and *t* values perform better when the auxiliary variables were included in the MI model. The MI with auxiliary variables is closer in three cases, and the MI without the auxiliary variables is closer in two cases. None of the differences affect a decision in interpreting the results. Both MI with and without using auxiliary variables identified all parameter estimates that were significant in the complete data set and all parameter estimates that were nonsignificant in the complete data set. Overall, results from this example suggest that the MI models produced results that were remarkably similar to the complete data set, even though almost half of the observations had missing values on at least one variable.

RECOMMENDATIONS ABOUT MODELS AND REPORTING MISSING DATA ANALYSES

This chapter has reviewed approaches to missing values and many of the issues surrounding choices. A series of practical recommendations may be useful. However, it is essential to acknowledge that methods for working with missing values are under constant development. These recommendations may be thought of as a list of useful guidelines at the time this chapter was written. These reflect the three guiding goals that form the foundation of this chapter: (a) maximize the information used in the analysis, (b) minimize the possible bias in estimating parameters, and (c) minimize the possible bias in estimating standard errors by correctly reflecting the degree of uncertainty associated with the parameter estimates.

1. *Is it important to use a modern approach?* Yes, even when the MAR assumption is violated, MI and ML are superior to listwise deletion that assumes MCAR and loses power. Perhaps more software should follow Mplus and drop listwise deletion as the default.

2. *Does it matter whether I use ML or MI?* For most applications, the ML and the MI alternatives yield similar results. They are asymptotically equivalent. Some of the diagnostic information available with MI is not available with ML. Whichever approach is more accessible may be the best way to make a choice.

3. *What software package should I use?* This choice matters less and less because of the rapidly improving software market. The single imputation approach in SPSS before Version 17 should be avoided. Most structural equation modeling software offers ML and can properly analyze MI data sets that have been produced by other software. The standard statistical packages, SAS, Stata, and SPSS, now offer some form of MI. SAS and Stata both offer a multivariate normal model and a chained equations approach that allow for logistic, multinomial logistic, and ordered logistic estimators of categorical variables. SPSS offers only the chained equation approach as an optional module.

4. *Does it matter whether I use a multivariate imputation model or the chained equation model?* The multivariate approach has stronger statistical theory behind it and is robust to violations of normality. The use of chained equations has produced similar results in many applications. It appears that both models are currently acceptable.

5. *How can I meet the assumptions about missingness, and how do I select auxiliary variables?* The MCAR assumption is probably only going to be reasonable if the values are missing by design. The MAR is more reasonable and it can be justified, but not tested, by including auxiliary variables. Including a large number of auxiliary variables, especially if they have substantial missing data themselves, can add more in uncertainty and may not be justified. There are two types of auxiliary variables to consider. First, it may be a variable that explains missingness, that is, who answers and who does not answer an item. Second, it may be a variable that predicts the score for missing values. Ideally, a researcher would have a few auxiliary variables that do both of these: help predict missing values and help explain missingness. In the example presented in Table 2.2, the inclusion of auxiliary variables on the basis of the logistic regressions helped justify the MAR assumption, but did not substantially improve the estimated parameters or their standard errors.

6. *When doing MI, how many imputations are recommended?* At least 20 imputed complete data sets is a reasonable minimum. A relative efficiency for each parameter being estimated of .99 is a possible standard. If the relative efficiency for each parameter being estimated is below this, impute more data sets. If small effect sizes are being estimated, then use at least 40 imputed complete data sets, regardless of the relative efficiency index. With large data sets, drop all variables that are not being used to control the size of the file that has so many data sets stacked on top of each other and take advantage of other formats. For example, Stata can show only those observations that had missing values in each imputed data set since the observations with complete data are already known. The example presented did not use this option, and when 100 complete data

sets were imputed, the 446 records ballooned to 44,600 plus the original 446.

7. *Should outcome variables be included in the imputation model?* Yes, failure to include the outcome variable in the imputation model means that the imputed values for missing values on the predictor variables will have a different covariance with the outcome variable than the observed values have with the outcome variables. This is why the outcome variable normally should be included in the imputation model. In the analysis model, a researcher may want to drop observations that have imputed values on the outcome variables, but dropping them or keeping them does not make much difference. This is because the imputed values add no new information but are simply consistent with the observed variables and the relationship among the observed variables. If there are missing values on the outcome but on none of the predictors, then nothing is gained by imputation and listwise deletion would be appropriate.

8. *Should skewed variables be transformed?* Perhaps, but transformations of skewed variables may make interpreting output difficult. One approach is to transform variables prior to their use in the imputation model. Then, it might be useful to reverse the transformed values before estimating the analysis model. It is essential to have the reversals apply to all of the imputed complete data sets. Stata, for example, has an option that does this automatically.

9. *How are categorical variables, out of range imputations, and interactions handled?* If ML is being used, there is no issue because there are no values being imputed. If MI is being used, however, people are bothered by imputed values that are "impossible." There may be a score for gender of 1.2 or an imputed interaction product (X_iX_j) that is not equal to $X_i \times X_j$. There may be a family that has an imputed –0.89 children. However, these "impossible" imputed values are, nonetheless, consistent with the observed values on the set of variables. Remember, it is not necessary for the imputed values to be identical to the true values, only that the covariance matrix and the vector of means are the same. If a researcher

changes values to the nearest "possible" value, this involves an ad hoc adjustment that has no theoretical justification. Leaving the imputed values as is (without rounding) does slightly better in some simulations than rounding or even than using alternatives, such as logistic regression in the imputation model with IVEware (von Hippel, 2009).

10. *What do we tell our readers?* Although the chapter suggests that all of the modern approaches work reasonably well, it is important to tell readers what has been done and to provide some diagnostic information on the process. For example, if imputed values are on scales rather than items, then the researcher needs to explain how missing values on individual items were treated. The description should include how many values were missing and where they were missing (e.g., just on one variable or a small subset of variables). If auxiliary variables that explain missingness are included, explain to readers how these were located and what variables were used. If auxiliary variables that predict scores that were missing are included, explain to reader that they were moderately to strongly correlated with the variables that had missing values. Specify whether ML or an MI was used and, if MI was used, indicate the software used and whether it used multivariate imputation model or chained equations. It is important to specify the number of data sets that were imputed as well as the relative efficiency for each variable. Reporting that the relative efficiency was at least .99 for each variable reassures readers that there are a sufficient number of imputed complete data sets. If reporting β weights, it would be helpful to report the high and low values as well as the mean value.

CONCLUSION

Missing values have always been a serious problem in psychological research. As the research has become more sophisticated, the problems caused by missing values have become even more serious. Traditional approaches, such as listwise deletion or mean substitution, may not introduce serious bias when there are few missing values. With more missing values, however, the bias and loss of information can lead to incorrect inferences. Until fairly recently, the lack of integrated software applications in major statistical packages has been a disincentive to widespread use of modern methods. This is no longer a barrier, and all major statistical packages now provide an effective approach for working with missing values.

Another possible barrier to the adoption of modern techniques has been the mistaken notion that modern methods, such as multiple imputation, create new data where none existed. A key to understanding the modern approaches is to recognize the difference between the analysis model and the imputation model. When estimating the multiple imputation model, the imputed values are consistent with the observed values. They do not add any new information but allow all the information that is present in the data to be used. Because of the inherent uncertainty in any imputation process, the imputed values incorporate a stochastic error component and adjust the degrees of freedom reflecting the prevalence of missing values. The fact that no new information is created is even clearer in the case of maximum likelihood solutions in cases in which there are no imputed values. Instead, a covariance matrix is generated that is optimally consistent with the observed data. Multiple imputation and maximum likelihood solutions are more powerful than listwise deletion because they do not ignore available information, and they almost certainly produce less biased results.

The assumption that data are missing at random has been posed as a barrier by some researchers who chose to use listwise deletion because they do not feel they can justify the MAR assumption. The present chapter demonstrates that the unfortunate result of this action has been more biased results precisely because listwise deletion assumes missing values are missing completely at random. The MCAR assumption can rarely be justified outside of planned missing research designs. Even when the MAR assumption is doubtful, the multiple imputation approach will be less biased than listwise deletion. The present chapter also introduced the use of auxiliary variables in the imputation model as an effective way of justifying the MAR assumption. Adding auxiliary variables is quite manageable with multiple

imputation and can be used with maximum likelihood estimation.

Approaches to working with missing values have been under development since the 1980s and rapid development since the 1990s. The approaches presently available may prove to be less than ideal as new techniques are developed. One area that needs to be strengthened is work with mixed models either where observations are grouped at one or more levels or in longitudinal models. There have been some developments (Goldstein, Carpenter, Kenward, & Levin, 2009; Rabe-Hesketh & Skrondal, 2008; Spiegelhalter, Thomas, & Best, 1999) that show promise in working with missing values that involve multilevel models. Future work in this area and its implementation in standard software packages is a high priority. Although we wait for these future developments, however, current methods establish far greater isomorphism between the analysis model and the data than has been possible in the past.

References

Acock, A. C. (2005). Working with missing values. *Journal of Marriage and Family, 67,* 1012–1028. doi:10.1111/j.1741-3737.2005.00191.x

Acock, A. C., & Demo, D. (1994). *Family diversity and well-being.* Thousand Oaks, CA: Sage.

Allison, P. D. (2001). *Missing data.* Thousand Oaks, CA: Sage.

Allison, P. D. (2002, April). *Imputation of categorical variables with PROC MI.* Paper presented at the 30th Meeting of the SAS UsersGroup, Philadelphia, PA. Retrieved from http://www2.sas.com/proceedings/sugi30/113–30.pdf

Collins, L. M., Schafer, J. L., & Kam, C. M. (2001). A comparison of inclusive and restrictive strategies in modern missing data procedures. *Psychological Methods, 6,* 330–351. doi:10.1037/1082-989X.6.4.330

Davey, A., & Savia, J. (2010). *Statistical power analysis with missing data: A structural equation modeling approach.* New York, NY: Routledge.

Day, R. D., Bean, R., Harper, J., Miller, R., Walker, L., & Yorgason, J. (2009). *Flourishing Families Project: A study of family life and child well-being.* Provo, UT: Department of Family Studies, Brigham Young University.

Dempster, A. P., Laird, N. M., & Rubin, D. B. (1977). Maximum likelihood from incomplete data via the EM algorithm. *Journal of the Royal Statistical Society Series B. Methodological, 39,* 1–38.

Enders, C. K. (2006). A primer on the use of modern missing-data methods in psychosomatic medicine research. *Psychosomatic Medicine, 68,* 427–436. doi:10.1097/01.psy.0000221275.75056.d8

Goldstein, H., Carpenter, J., Kenward, M. G., & Levin, K. (2009). Multilevel models with multivariate mixed response types. *Statistical Modelling, 9,* 173–197. doi:10.1177/1471082X0800900301

Graham, J. W. (2009). Missing data analysis: Making it work in the real world. *Annual Review of Psychology, 60,* 549–576. doi:10.1146/annurev.psych.58.110405.085530

Graham, J. W., Olchowski, A. E., & Gilreath, T. D. (2007). How many imputations are really needed: Some practical clarifications of multiple imputation theory. *Prevention Science, 8,* 206–213. doi:10.1007/s11121-007-0070-9

Graham, J. W., & Schafer, J. L. (1999). On the performance of multiple imputation for multivariate data with small sample size. In R. Hoyle (Ed.), *Statistical strategies for small sample research* (pp. 1–29). Thousand Oaks, CA: Sage.

Graham, J. W., Taylor, B. J., Olchowski, A. E., & Cumsille, P. E. (2006). Planned missing data designs in psychological research. *Psychological Methods, 11,* 323–343. doi:10.1037/1082-989X.11.4.323

Horton, N. J., & Kleinman, K. P. (2007). Much ado about nothing: A comparison of missing data methods and software to fit incomplete data regression models. *The American Statistician, 61,* 79–90. doi:10.1198/000313007X172556

Horton, N. J., & Lipsitz, S. R. (2001). Multiple imputation in practice: Comparison of software packages for regression models with missing variables. *The American Statistician, 55,* 244–254. doi:10.1198/000313001317098266

Horton, N. J., Lipsitz, S. R., & Parzen, M. (2003). A potential for bias when rounding in multiple imputation. *The American Statistician, 57,* 229–232. doi:10.1198/0003130032314

Kenward, M. G., & Carpenter, J. R. (2007). Multiple imputation: Current perspectives. *Statistical Methods in Medical Research, 16,* 199–218. doi:10.1177/0962280206075304

King, G., Honaker, J., & Scheva, K. (2001). Analyzing incomplete political science data: An alternative algorithm for multiple imputation. *American Political Science Review, 95,* 46–69.

Kline, R. B. (2010). *Principles and practice of structural equation modeling* (3rd ed.). New York, NY: Guilford Press.

Little, R. (1992). Regression with missing X's: A review. *Journal of the American Statistical Association, 87,* 1227–1237. doi:10.2307/2290664

Little, R., & Rubin, D. B. (1987). *Statistical analysis with missing data.* New York, NY: Wiley.

Long, J. S. (1997). *Regression models for categorical and limited dependent variables.* Thousand Oaks, CA: Sage.

Long, J. S., & Freese, J. (2006). *Regression models for categorical dependent variables using Stata* (2nd ed.). College Station, TX: Stata Press.

Marchenko, Y. (2010). *mibeta: Stata module for estimating Betas using multiple imputation.* Retrieved from http://www.stata.com/users/ymarchenko

Muthén, L., & Muthén, B. (2009). Version 5.1: Mplus Language Addendum [Computer software]. Retrieved from http://www.statmodel.com/download/language1.pdf

Peugh, J. L., & Enders, C. K. (2004). Missing data in educational research. *Review of Educational Research, 74,* 525–556. doi:10.3102/00346543074004525

Rabe-Hesketh, S., & Skrondal, A. (2008). *Multilevel and longitudinal modeling using Stata* (2nd ed.). College Station, TX: Stata Press.

Reiter, J. P. (2007). Small-sample degrees of freedom for multi-component significance tests with multiple imputation for missing data. *Biometrika, 94,* 502–508. doi:10.1093/biomet/asm028

Royston, P. (2005). Multiple imputation of missing values: Update. *The Stata Journal, 5,* 1–14.

Royston, P. (2007). Multiple imputation of missing values: Further update of ice with an emphasis on interval censoring. *The Stata Journal, 7,* 445–464.

Rubin, D. B. (1976). Inference and missing data. *Biometrika, 63,* 581–592. doi:10.1093/biomet/63.3.581

Rubin, D. B. (1987). *Multiple imputation for nonresponse in surveys.* New York, NY: Wiley.

Schafer, J. L. (1997). *Analysis of incomplete multivariate data.* London, England: Chapman & Hall.

Schafer, J. L., & Olsen, M. K. (1998). Multiple imputation for multivariate missing-data problems: A data analyst's perspective. *Multivariate Behavioral Research, 33,* 545–571. doi:10.1207/s15327906mbr3304_5

Shih, W. (2002). Problems in dealing with missing data and informative censoring in clinical trials. *Current Controlled Trials in Cardiovascular Medicine, 3*(4). doi:10.1186/1468-6708-3-4

Spiegelhalter, D. J., Thomas, A., & Best, N. G. (1999). *WINBUGS Version 1.2, user manual.* Cambridge, MA: MRC Biostatistics Unit.

SPSS. (2009). *SPSS missing values 17.0.* Chicago, IL: SPSS.

Stata. (2011). *Stata multiple imputation reference manual: Release 12.* College Station, TX: Stata Press.

UCLA Academic Technology Services. (2009a). *Multiple imputation in Stata, Part 1.* Retrieved from http://www.ats.ucla.edu/stat/seminars

UCLA Academic Technology Services. (2009b). *Multiple imputation in Stata, Part 2.* Retrieved from http://www.ats.ucla.edu/stat/seminars

UCLA Academic Technology Services. (2010a). *Multiple imputation in SAS, Part 1.* Retrieved from http://www.ats.ucla.edu/stat/seminars

UCLA Academic Technology Services. (2010b). *Multiple imputation in SAS, Part 2.* Retrieved from http://www.ats.ucla.edu/stat/seminars

von Hippel, P. T. (2007). Regression with missing Y's: An improved strategy for analyzing multiple imputed data. *Sociological Methodology, 37,* 83–117. doi:10.1111/j.1467-9531.2007.00180.x

von Hippel, P. T. (2009). How to impute interactions, squares, and other transformed variables. *Sociological Methodology, 39,* 265–291. doi:10.1111/j.1467-9531.2009.01215.x

## CHAPTER 3

EXPLORATORY DATA ANALYSIS

Paul F. Velleman and David C. Hoaglin

Exploratory data analysis (EDA), pioneered by John W. Tukey (1915–2000), introduces a variety of innovative techniques and combines them with five important principles of data analysis: display, re-expression, residuals, resistance, and iteration. Many of the techniques that Tukey pioneered have become familiar: stem-and-leaf display, five-number summary, boxplot, and a rule for flagging potential outliers in batches of data. Computing methods have extended EDA to larger data sets and higher dimensions, and diagnostic statistics have extended the EDA approach to include more traditional statistical methods.

Although its innovative methods have received much attention, the principal contribution of EDA is philosophical. EDA advocates exploring data for patterns and relationships without requiring prior hypotheses. The principle of *resistance* calls for identifying extraordinary cases and then setting them aside or downweighting them. *Re-expression* uses mathematical transformations to simplify patterns in data. EDA suggests that analyses are more scientifically useful and productive when data have been transformed to agree better with basic assumptions. *Residuals* come from summarizing the patterns found so far and subtracting that summary from the data, to reveal departures and additional patterns. EDA often works with residuals to refine or extend models fitted to data. Frequent use of graphical *displays* maintains contact with data, residuals, and summaries, and it often reveals unexpected behavior. EDA approaches do not terminate with a hypothesis test. Effective data analysis is *iterative*, finding and summarizing patterns and then probing more deeply.

These approaches stand in contrast to the formalistic scientific method paradigm of first stating a hypothesis based on prior theory, then collecting data, and finally applying a statistical test of the hypothesis. Proponents of the EDA philosophy maintain that the EDA approach is more likely to discover new and interesting patterns and relationships, in much the same way that science has traditionally made progress. Exploratory analyses can incorporate methods of statistical inference, but use them more as indicators of the strength of a relationship or the fit of a model than as confirmation of a hypothesis.

In this chapter, we elucidate the EDA approach, illustrating it with examples. We hope to convince the reader that this approach should be a standard part of anyone's analysis of data. For many experienced data analysts, an EDA approach forms the main ingredient of their analyses, with only the occasional "seasoning" of formal hypothesis testing.

WOES OF TRADITIONAL STATISTICS

The discipline of statistics offers a wide variety of ways to formulate and test hypotheses. But all rely on assumptions about the pattern of behavior in the data and about the distribution of variations around that pattern. For example, fitting a simple regression line is appropriate when the relation of y to x

The authors are grateful to Gloria Gogola for permission to use the data on functional dexterity trials and to Katherine Freier for preparing Figure 3.17.

DOI: 10.1037/13621-003

resembles a straight line and the fluctuations around a line all have the same variance. Methods that compare groups may require that the groups share the same variance. The basic model in a two-factor analysis of variance (ANOVA) expresses the response as an additive combination of the contributions of the two factors and assumes that the error variance is the same for all treatment levels. In logistic regression, the individual outcomes are usually assumed to follow binomial distributions, whose success probabilities (in the logit scale) follow the pattern specified in the linear predictor. Virtually every standard method makes the tacit assumption that the underlying data are homogeneous—that is, that they are all consistent measurements of the same things about the same kinds of individuals for whom the same model, analysis, or comparison is appropriate.

These assumptions are frequently violated by otherwise perfectly ordinary data. Often, to check, we need only make an appropriate display. As the famous philosopher (and baseball Hall of Famer) Yogi Berra said, "You can learn a lot by looking."

Ironically, although statistics software makes displaying data simple, it also abets the tendency to rush to a hypothesis test without pausing for displays. The traditional approach to statistics has an even more fundamental weakness. By focusing on testing hypotheses, we fail to ask the far more fundamental and important question of our data: "Is anything going on that I didn't expect?" Isaac Asimov is commonly credited[1] with saying,

> The most exciting phrase to hear in science, the one that heralds new discoveries, is not "Eureka!" but "That's funny . . ."

EDA increases our chance of a "That's funny . . ." insight about our data—and those are the events that lead to new theories and breakthroughs. For example, Leonard Mlodinow, in his 2008 book *The Drunkard's Walk,* tells the story of the "That's funny . . ." moment that led Daniel Kahneman to begin his revolutionary research with Amos Tversky into the psychology of how humans misperceive random events—work that led to his 2002 Nobel Prize in Economics. As a junior professor of

psychology at Hebrew University, Kahneman was lecturing to a group of flight trainers. The trainers insisted that when they chastised a flyer for a poor maneuver, the flyer improved, but when they complimented a good one, the flyer usually did worse the next time. The trainers had concluded that negative reinforcement worked and positive reinforcement did not. Kahneman knew that psychology had shown otherwise. Rather than ignoring this observation as just a strange aberration, he searched for the explanation. His insight that the often-counterintuitive result known as *regression to the mean* was responsible for the trainers' misperception started him on his research path.

Exploratory data analyses incorporate techniques, such as boxplots and stem-and-leaf displays, and also commonly use such traditional methods as least squares regression, ANOVA, analysis of covariance (ANOCOV), and logistic regression. So EDA should be viewed primarily as an enhancement of, rather than a replacement for, traditional methods. By using both wisely, you will learn more from your data.

EXPLORING

The tradition of the scientific method requires researchers to follow a straight and narrow path: theory first, then hypothesis, then data collection, and finally statistical tests of the stated hypothesis (and no others).

Exploring often requires that we leave the beaten path. But it does not require us to travel without a compass—or a GPS. The challenge is less to know where we are than to see where we are going. In this chapter, we present guidelines and best practices to help you make progress without wandering aimlessly. Our guiding principles are display, re-expression, resistance, residuals, and iteration.

Lacking a map, we need to take frequent sightings. We make many displays of the data, and we continue to do so all along the way. We are not trying—or even hoping—to confirm that the required assumptions for a hypothesis test have been met. We are looking for new territory to explore. Like all explorers, we are seeking—and expecting—the unexpected. Fortunately, displays

---

[1]This is commonly, and plausibly, credited to Asimov, but we have not found a reference.

are particularly good tools for this task. Appropriate displays readily show outliers, unexpected clumps and clusters, and relationship patterns that we might not have anticipated.

Nor are we obliged to follow steep or thorny paths when gentler, clearer ones are available. We re-express data to make it easier to summarize and compare them and to fit models that describe relationships. It is easier and more scientifically useful to fit a simple linear model to the logarithm of a variable than to fit an exponential model to the original data. Speed (reciprocal time) is often a more useful variable than duration.

Resistant methods protect against undue influence by outlying cases or even small clusters of cases. Some statistics, such as the median, are inherently resistant. Others, such as least squares regression, can be made resistant by diagnostics that identify potentially influential cases so they can be dealt with separately.

Whenever we fit a model to data, it is wise to examine the residuals—the differences between the model and the data. EDA suggests displays such as quantile–quantile plots, partial regression plots, and partial boxplots that are particularly well suited to understanding what residuals tell us about our data and models. In the names of these displays, *partial* refers to the removal (*partialing out*) of the contributions of the other predictors or factors.

EDA anticipates that what we learn from examining the residuals will lead us to improve our understanding and our models. We may decide to re-express variables to mitigate violations of assumptions revealed only in the residuals, set aside outliers identified in the residuals, or introduce additional variables suggested by the residuals.

DISPLAYS AND SOME OF WHAT THEY REVEAL

Every data analysis should begin with graphs. Of course, this idea is not unique to EDA. Every introductory statistics text starts with data displays (see Chapter 4 of this volume). But often, displays of the data appear only in the introductory chapters, and the figures in the chapters on statistical inference show only normal or *t*-distribution curves. EDA teaches that we should make graphs early and often.

Some data displays are taught in every statistics class. We look at histograms to get a picture of how the data are distributed and to check for multiple modes and outliers. We look at scatterplots to see how one variable changes in relation to another, focusing on the direction, form, and strength of that relationship.

To illustrate, consider a standard test of manual dexterity, which records the time it takes subjects to invert 16 cylinders with one hand (Aaron & Jansen, 2003). This test can form the basis for studying crossover training: whether training one limb can benefit the other and what underlying mental processes might support the benefit. Gogola, Lacy, Morse, Aaron, and Velleman (2010) studied the performance of 175 subjects ranging in age from 4 to 16. A histogram of their times (see Figure 3.1) is skewed to the right and suggests that two subjects had unusually long times.

Modes

Histograms such as the one in Figure 3.1 may be the most common display for examining the distribution of a variable. Exploratory analyses often start with histograms. But EDA teaches that histograms can be a call to action. Histograms offer the opportunity to detect *inhomogeneity* in the data. All statistical methods make the tacit assumption that the data are homogeneous—that is, that we are dealing with measurements of the same thing made on members of a coherent population. Without homogeneity, it is difficult to imagine what—or whom—a summary of the data would be about.

One clue that the data may not be homogeneous is the presence of two or more modes in a histogram.

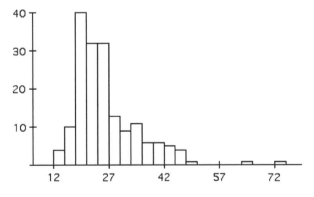

FIGURE 3.1.   Histogram of the times of 175 subjects on a test of manual dexterity.

For example, the same researchers also measured the dexterity of patients who had had surgery, using a variety of measures. One of these measures, the Jebsen Large Heavy Object Test (Jebsen, Taylor, Trieschmann, Trotter, & Howard, 1969), records the time (in seconds) to lift and move a weighted can. In the histogram of the times for 34 subjects, shown in Figure 3.2, the mode around 9 s consists of patients who had had surgery on both limbs, who may differ from other patients in important ways.

Outliers

A related issue is the identification and treatment of outliers. Values that stray far from the rest of the data, or that stand apart from important patterns in the data, demand our attention. They may be particularly informative by clarifying the limits of our data or pointing out special cases, or they may be errors in need of correction or removal. Regardless of the reason, they should not be allowed to distort subsequent analyses of the data. EDA teaches that if we cannot correct an outlier, we should set it aside or use methods that are immune to its effects.

The argument that outliers should be prevented from subverting a data analysis reflects the philosophical foundations of EDA. Some analysts are reluctant to set aside any legitimately recorded values, fearing that doing so could bias subsequent analyses. But standard statistical methods are notoriously sensitive to outlying values and are likely to be invalid when applied to data that include outliers. Data containing outliers are, almost by definition,

not homogeneous. So statistical models intended for homogeneous data are likely to strike a clumsy compromise between the outliers and the rest of the data rather than describe patterns and relationships in the bulk of the data.

Boxplots

One tool that can be helpful in nominating extreme values for consideration as outliers is the boxplot, introduced by John Tukey in his pathbreaking 1977 book *Exploratory Data Analysis*. The standard boxplot uses a rule to identify possible outliers (as *outside* or, if extreme enough, *far outside*) and plot them individually. Hoaglin, Iglewicz, and Tukey (1986) studied the rule's performance, and Hoaglin and Iglewicz (1987) refined it.

A boxplot of the task times for the 175 normal subjects, shown in Figure 3.3, identifies five task times as outside and two as far out. The records for these subjects should be examined for possible explanations of their particularly slow performance.

The boxplot's outlier nomination rules should not be taken as a *definition* of outliers. The decision to treat a case as an outlier is a judgment call

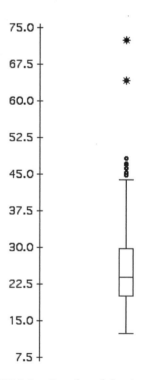

FIGURE 3.3. Boxplot of the times (in seconds) of the 175 normal subjects on the test of manual dexterity.

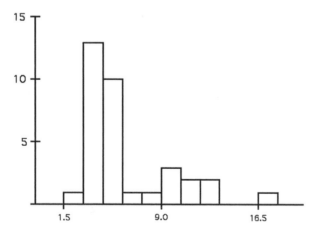

FIGURE 3.2. Times (in seconds) on the Jebsen Large Heavy Object Test for 34 subjects who had had surgery.

that the data analyst must make. But boxplots can help by directing attention to cases that deserve consideration as outliers. The standard boxplot calls attention to outside observations fairly often. Hoaglin et al. (1986) found that in well-behaved (i.e., Gaussian) data the percentage of samples that contain one or more outside observations varies between 33% and 14% for $5 \leq n \leq 20$. The corresponding percentage for far outside lies between 1% and 5%.

Boxplots are also helpful for comparing groups. Because they show the median and quartiles of each group, they make it easy to compare centers and spreads (as interquartile ranges) among groups. Because they suppress details of the distributions, they minimize distractions that can make it difficult to compare several histograms.

Figure 3.4 shows the results of repeated dexterity trials by the same 175 subjects. Except for a few high values, times decreased from Trial 1 to Trial 3 as subjects practiced the task, but times stabilized after Trial 3. Because boxplots isolate outliers, we can more easily ignore their influence when judging the performance pattern of most of the subjects.

Stem-and-Leaf Displays

Another display introduced by John Tukey (in the late 1960s) is the stem-and-leaf display, which offers a histogram's view of distribution shape while preserving the individual data values. Each digit to the right of the vertical line represents a data value (e.g.,

12 s and 14 s on the first line). A stem-and-leaf display of some of the dexterity times (Figure 3.5) shows individual values as well as the overall distribution shape. Stem-and-leaf displays are particularly useful as pencil-and-paper tools for a quick look at modest collections of data values.

Two-Variable Relationships

The EDA approach guides the consideration of relationships between pairs of variables. Of course, we start with a display. Now we look at the overall *direction*, *shape*, and *strength* of the relationship. The scatterplot of dexterity task time versus age in Figure 3.6 shows a negative direction with older subjects taking less time, a curved shape, and a reasonably consistent pattern.

Because exploratory analyses rely on displays, they often push common methods a bit farther. For example, points in scatterplots can be assigned

```
1|24
1|67888999999
2|0000111123344
2|555555666677889
3|0023333
3|5567889
4|0012
4|57
5|
5|
6|4
6|
7|2
```

FIGURE 3.5.   Stem-and-leaf display of the task times (in seconds) for 63 subjects.

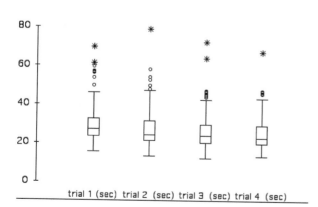

FIGURE 3.4.   Boxplots of the times (in seconds) of the 175 normal subjects on four consecutive dexterity tests.

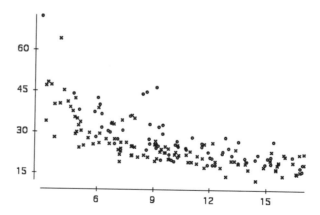

FIGURE 3.6.   Scatterplot of task time (in seconds) versus age (in years). The plotting symbol distinguishes the dominant hand (x) from the nondominant hand (o).

colors or symbols according to values of a third categorical variable. The symbols in Figure 3.6 record whether the tested hand was the subject's dominant (×) or nondominant (o) hand.

If the form of the relationship were straight, then lines fitted separately to each group could be compared. That is not feasible with a curved plot such as this one. Modern statistics software often supports the ability to "touch" a point in a plot to ask for its identity—a valuable tool for identifying and understanding outliers and subgroups in the data.

Other Displays

Other displays and display methods are less common or depend on computers. Normal probability plots provide a better way to compare a variable's distribution with the normal than does a histogram with a normal curve overlaid. One drawback of such histograms is related to Winsor's Principle: All distributions are normal in the middle (Tukey, 1960). Although the principle is clearly not universally true, it does correctly—and memorably—advise us to focus attention on the tails of a distribution.

A scatterplot matrix (called a SPLOM by some programs) is an array of scatterplots laid out in the same pattern as correlations in a correlation table. *Plot brushing* highlights the same cases in each plot simultaneously as the viewer passes a rectangular "brush" over any one of them, so that relationships among several variables can been seen. An alternative approach to displaying three variables together is an animated *rotating plot*, offered in several statistics programs. Some programs, such as Data Desk (Velleman, 2004), can display data that have up to nine dimensions.

Another approach to displaying high-dimensional data is a parallel-coordinate plot (Inselberg, 2009). Figure 3.7 shows the four trials of the dexterity experiment seen in the boxplots of Figure 3.4. In a parallel-coordinate plot, lines connect the times for each subject. Here we can trace the performance of individual subjects—for example, to see that the outlying slow performances were by the same subjects.

RE-EXPRESSION

One of the most versatile techniques in the data analyst's toolkit, re-expression applies the same

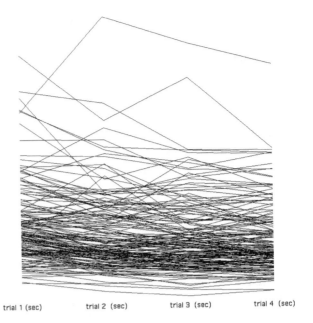

| trial 1 (sec) | trial 2 (sec) | trial 3 (sec) | trial 4 (sec) |

FIGURE 3.7. Parallel-coordinate plot of the times (in seconds) of the 175 normal subjects on four consecutive dexterity trials.

mathematical function (such as the logarithm or the square root) to each data value of a variable. This transformation smoothly changes the relative positions of the data, with the aim of simplifying the analysis.

Some researchers mistakenly believe that transforming the data is wrong, that the analysis must work with the data in their original scale. Those who hold this view often fail to find important features of their data. In fact, many measures in science and social science involve a transformation. Some of these are familiar in everyday experience (Hoaglin, 1988).

Reports of earthquakes usually give the magnitude on the Richter scale, which expresses the strength of the earthquake's motion in logarithmic units (base 10).

Measurements of the intensity of sounds customarily produce results in decibels. The fundamental quantity actually measured, however, is sound pressure (in dynes per square centimeter, e.g.), and the "sound pressure level" (in decibels) is related logarithmically to sound pressure.

Although ratings of automobiles' fuel economy are usually given in miles per gallon in the United States, these often come from measurements that determine the number of gallons used on a standard test course. Thus, the familiar miles-per-gallon figures result from a reciprocal transformation. In fact, throughout the rest of the world, fuel efficiency is reported in units of liters per 100 km—the reciprocal (gasoline volume per distance) of miles per gallon. (The constant multiple needed to convert from metric to old British units does not affect the distribution.)

EDA teaches that we should always consider whether an alternative form of a variable might allow a simpler model or description. This aspect of EDA draws on more than 70 years of work in statistics (Bartlett, 1947; Tukey, 1957; Box & Cox, 1964; Kruskal, 1968; Emerson, 1983; Emerson & Stoto, 1983). This work has identified a variety of benefits of a wisely chosen re-expression:

1. The distribution of data and residuals can be made more symmetric and more nearly normal.
2. The variances of several groups to be compared can be made more nearly equal.
3. The relationship between two variables can be made more nearly linear.
4. The variation of points around a regression line can be made more nearly equal across the span of the data.
5. A linear relationship between two variables can be made more nearly parallel for groups of values in the data.
6. The appropriateness of an additive model for two or more factors can be improved (and the need for interaction terms reduced or removed).

In traditional terms, the symmetry achieved by Benefit 1 is necessary for the mean to summarize the center of the distribution. Normality is expected for *t* tests, and normal fluctuations are assumed for linear models such as regression and ANOVA. The equality of variance among groups (Benefit 2) is assumed by ANOVA and ANOCOV models as well as for a pooled *t* test. Linearity (Benefit 3) is fundamental to regression methods, which also require the residuals to have constant variance everywhere (Benefit 4) for common inference methods. Both the use of dummy variables in regression and the generalization of that idea to

ANOCOVs require that linear models for subgroups be parallel (Benefit 5). And the ANOVA model calls for additivity (Benefit 6).

One remarkable insight noted by the authors is that re-expressions that improve one aspect of the data often improve several—or even all—of the others.

A Re-Expression Example

The dexterity experiment offers a good example. Many task-based measures of performance record the time for a subject to complete a task. These include the classic mouse-running maze tasks as well as cognitive function tests, such as the Trail Making Test (Reitan, 1958) and the Stroop Test (Stroop, 1935).

Thinking about re-expression encourages us to consider constraints on the distribution of the data values. For *time per task*, it is not possible to get a value below some lower limit—certainly not less than zero. But there is no upper limit. Indeed, some subjects may not be able to complete some tasks at all. (The dexterity measure is used in cognitive-based training of postsurgery patients who have suffered severe hand or arm injuries, some of whom cannot complete the task in any reasonable amount of time. In addition, mice under sufficiently stressful conditions may give up on solving a maze.) These constraints introduce two problems for data analysis. First, the distribution of values is almost certain to be skewed to the high end—and the stem-and-leaf, histogram, and boxplot in Figures 3.5, 3.1, 3.3, and 3.4 show the expected skewness. And, second, we must cope with *infinities* for subjects who do not complete the task at all.

Researchers have often ignored skewness, hoping it would not be severe enough to invalidate statistics applied to the data. A variety of ad hoc methods have been suggested for the infinities, including just substituting "some large value" and omitting them from the data. Neither ignoring the data nor assigning some large value is suitable, because either approach can severely distort statistical analyses. Some authors have suggested that nonparametric methods would be more appropriate because they are insensitive to both skewness and outlier problems. But these methods often restrict what we can see in the data.

Exploratory data analysis suggests that, by reconsidering the way the data are recorded, we may gain additional insights and understanding. And, along the way, we can obtain simpler models for how the data behave. For the dexterity results, EDA-trained analysts would immediately think of looking at the *reciprocal* of the recorded times. These values have units of *tasks per second*—a measure of speed rather than duration. To make the units easier to deal with, we might multiply by 60 to obtain *tasks per minute*. A scale change or a shift in values from adding or subtracting a constant has no effect on the pattern of the values.

The reciprocal addresses both of the problems we noted. Infinities are now dealt with rationally as a speed of zero tasks per second. And re-expressing data as $1/x$ has the effect of pulling in the high tail relative to the low one. For example, Figure 3.8 shows the histogram and boxplot of the speeds that correspond to the durations in Figures 3.1 and 3.3. The boxplot looks much more symmetric, and one data value is outside at the upper end—a 14-year-old whose speed was 5 tasks per min.

As most discussions of re-expression have noted, appropriate re-expression can improve the relationships among variables as well as their individual distributions. Figure 3.9 shows the scatterplot of speed versus age, with symbols assigned according to hand as in Figure 3.6.

Now the relationship is nicely linear—suitable for a regression model. The slope has changed from

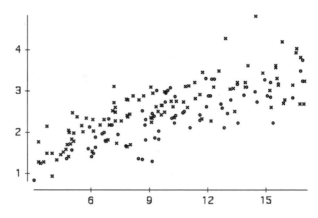

FIGURE 3.9. Scatterplot of speed (in reciprocal seconds) versus age (in years). The plotting symbol distinguishes the dominant hand (×) from the nondominant hand (o).

negative to positive, corresponding to the change in the meaning of the response variable. Durations are shorter for older subjects, so speed improves with age. The variation in speed is roughly constant across the age range.

Occam

William of Occam (c. 1288–c. 1348) is known for asserting that the simpler explanation that accounts for the facts is generally better. Years of experience in consulting and data analysis, along with the advice of prominent statisticians who have amassed far more experience, have convinced us that this is excellent guidance for analyzing data. Simpler models are not only easier to understand and explain; they are more likely to lead to future advances.

We often choose a re-expression such as the logarithm or square root because it works to simplify the analysis. Appropriate re-expression has merit for this reason alone. Models built to fit appropriately re-expressed data are both easier to understand and more likely to lead to further advances.

The cynical (but quite correct) view is that proper re-expression and data exploration are more likely to answer the most important question a researcher can ask: "What should my next grant proposal be about?" For the clinician, an analysis of appropriately re-expressed data is likely to give simpler diagnostic rules and guidelines.

For example, in Figure 3.10 the original scale (time) does not make it easy to summarize the effect of dominant versus nondominant hand. In the

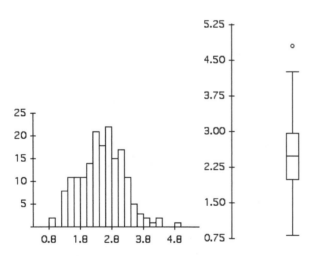

FIGURE 3.8. Histogram and boxplot of the speeds (in reciprocal seconds) of the 175 normal subjects on the test of manual dexterity.

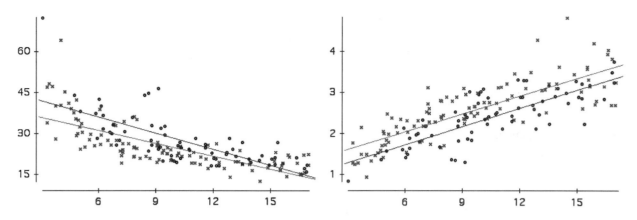

FIGURE 3.10.   Scatterplots with separate regression lines for dominant (x) and nondominant (o) hands. (a) Time (in seconds) versus age (in years). (b) Speed (in reciprocal seconds) versus age (in years). The dominant hand takes less time (lower line in the left plot) and is, correspondingly, faster (upper line in the right plot).

reciprocal scale (speed), the patterns for the two hands are linear and parallel, offering the summary that the dominant hand is about 0.3 tasks per minute faster at any of the ages studied.

EXTENDING THE ANALYSIS

One purpose of the dexterity trials was to investigate the phenomenon of crossover training. As we have seen, subjects improve with training up to about the third session. Researchers wanted to investigate whether performance in one hand is improved by training the *other* hand. The question is of importance to cognitive researchers because it addresses issues of how learning takes place. It is of clinical importance to therapists, who do not want to tire out an injured limb by training and wonder whether training the other, uninjured limb would be an appropriate protocol.

In Figure 3.11 the boxplots show that, overall, training the opposite hand does lead to improvement. A parallel-coordinate plot of the speeds in the tested hand before and after training the other hand shows the individual improvements and would support investigating, for example, whether handedness matters.

DATA ANALYSIS ETHICS

We set outliers aside for special consideration and re-express to improve the ability of models to fit the data. Both of these practices can improve the *p*-values of hypothesis tests. Are we cheating?

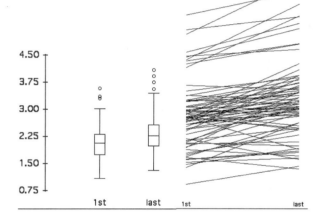

FIGURE 3.11.   Boxplots and parallel-coordinate plot of speeds (in reciprocal seconds) before and after training the opposite hand.

This question cuts to the core of the difference in philosophy between EDA and the way traditional statistical inference is often used in psychology. Those who look to statistical methods to guard against the misuse of data may be scandalized by our proposal that a scientist should be free to seek the most appropriate re-expression and should focus on modeling the main body of the data and not the occasional extraordinary case. We reject the idea that statistical methods can or should serve as enforcers of honest data analysis. The goal should be truth about the world. Truth is, of course, a challenging goal, and one that we may rarely, if ever, attain. Nevertheless, it should be our guiding principle. (Philosophers call such a goal a *regulative ideal*.)

Methods alone can never approach this ideal. It requires the honest efforts of the scientists and social scientists who do the research and analysis. In short, if a researcher wants to cheat, no amount of standardized statistical practice can stop it. Indeed, it may be easier to hide misconduct by following so-called standard practice and reporting only the usual summary statistics. We should not constrain honest researchers in an attempt to restrain less honest ones. Moreover, we should teach the ethics of honest research as a fundamental part of the education of researchers in all fields (Velleman, 2008).

Even honest researchers share the well-known human tendency to imagine patterns in data. In a provocative essay, Diaconis (1985) examined this aspect of EDA and discussed a variety of remedies:

- Publish without *p*-values
- Try to quantify and correct for the distortion
- Try it out on fresh data
- Borrow strength[2]
- Cross-validate
- Bootstrap the exploration.

He placed EDA in the context of theories of data analysis and concluded that "the new exploratory techniques seem to be a mandatory supplement to more classical statistical procedures" (p. 32).

MEASUREMENT SCALES

One tradition in psychology categorizes measurement scales as nominal, ordinal, interval, or ratio. The work in measurement arose from a debate about whether psychology could be a true science when many measurements made by psychologists were not comparable to those made by physicists. Although the argument for psychology as a science has largely been won, it has led some to suggest that the measurement scale of a variable should constrain the appropriate analysis methods. Often, for example, this line of reasoning has been used to argue in favor of nonparametric methods.

But this approach misunderstands measurement scales in many situations. Velleman and Wilkinson (1993), for example, noted that the measurement scale of a variable is not a property of the variable itself, but rather a property of how it is used. They offer a number of examples of common variables that may be viewed as having one measurement scale in one context and a different scale in another.

A little thought reveals many common examples. Playing card suits appear to be nominal, but are ordered in bridge. Playing card values can be ratio scaled in some games (casino), ordinal in others (poker), and nominal in still others (Go Fish). Velleman and Wilkinson (1993) offered the example of the consecutive numbers on tickets for a door prize handed out as attendees arrive at a meeting. These are nominal when selecting the winner but could be used (in interval scale) to count the number of attendees or (in ordinal scale) to record the order of their arrival.

We approach measurement scales by exploring data without any assumptions but then asking whether the best models and descriptions found for the data can be supported by the ways in which the data were measured. Surprisingly often, we have discovered a richness in data that was not evident at first. In short, exploratory data analyses deemphasize measurement scales—at least, until the final summary of the analysis.

Kinds of Data

Although it rejects measurement scale as a constraint, EDA does categorize data by types to offer guidance for re-expression. Mosteller and Tukey (1977, Chapter 5) suggested the categories and recommended re-expressions in Table 3.1.

REGRESSION

The EDA approach extends beyond elementary data summaries. Analyses that use multiple regression or ANOVA should consider the benefits of re-expression and of removing outliers.

Most statistics programs compute diagnostic statistics that can help identify both influential cases

---

[2]Borrowing strength is a general term that refers to seeking support for estimating values and, especially, variances from other parts of the data or other sources. When we fit a regression, we borrow strength from all the data (and the assumption that a linear model is appropriate) to enable more precise estimates and predictions for individual values.

TABLE 3.1

Summary of Re-Expressions Suggested for Various Types of Data

Type of data	Suggested re-expressions
Amounts	Nonnegative real values. Logarithms are a good first guess. Natural and base-10 logs differ only by a constant multiplier, but base-10 logs are usually easier to interpret. (Times and rates are examples of amounts although, as we have noted, rates—because they are ratios—often benefit from a reciprocal transformation.)
Counts	Nonnegative integer values whose units are "number of. . . ." Square roots and logs are a good place to start.
Balances	Real values that may be positive or negative. Often these arise as a difference between two amounts (and then re-expressing those amounts may be helpful). Balances often need no re-expression.
Counted fractions	Fractions of a whole such as percentages (100 × number counted in a group/total group size). Special re-expressions that acknowledge the boundaries of these data at both ends, such as the logit, may be helpful.
Ranks	Integer values recording order. Treat like a counted fraction.
Grades	Ordered groups such as Freshman/First-Year, Sophomore, Junior, Senior. Little need to re-express.
Names	Nominal data. If the data simply name individuals, re-expression offers no advantage.

and unexpected patterns. We recommend examining the following:

- Leverage. The leverage of any case in a simple or multiple regression is the amount by which that case's predicted value would change if the dependent value of the case were changed by one unit and the regression recomputed. Cases with particularly large leverage can dominate the fitting of a regression model.
- Studentized Residuals. The standard deviation of the sampling distribution of a regression residual depends on the case's leverage. Cases near the multivariate mean of the x's have smaller variance than those far from the center of the data. Studentized residuals adjust for this. A scatterplot of the studentized residuals versus the predicted values has had the linear effects of the predictors removed and is adjusted for differences in the underlying variation of the prediction errors. Consequently, it displays any underlying patterns more clearly and vividly. This makes it an effective tool for assessing whether the relationship of the response variable to the predictors is linear (and, thus, whether the regression model is appropriate).
- DFFITS. The DFFITS statistic for each case shows the impact of omitting that case on the corresponding predicted value. This leave-out-one diagnostic combines leverage and studentized residual in a single measure.

- DFBETAS. When the *coefficients* of predictor variables are of interest, the DFBETAS statistics provide a suitably scaled measure of the change in each coefficient associated with omitting each case.

Most statistics packages have options to report all four of these statistics for a regression analysis. Each can be used to identify cases that may deserve special attention because of their undue influence on the regression model or because they deviate sharply from the pattern fitted by the regression model.

Diagnostic plots can be especially helpful for exploring multiple-regression models. Displays of residuals are commonly offered by all statistics software and should be examined for the same features that one would look for in a single variable.

In a multiple regression, it is common to make a scatterplot of the residuals against the predicted values. Displays of studentized residuals are more useful because of their stabilized standard deviations.

When a coefficient is of interest, it is important to interpret it correctly: The coefficient for a particular predictor indicates how the dependent variable changes in response to change in that predictor after adjusting for the linear effects of the other predictor variables (in the data at hand). In general, no simpler language is satisfactory. We often read (even in textbooks) that a regression coefficient estimates the amount of change in the dependent variable when its predictor changes by one unit and all other predictors are held fixed. It is straightforward to show mathematically that such an interpretation is incorrect—unless the data have been collected in a way that explicitly holds the other predictors fixed (e.g., in a well-controlled experiment, to which we turn next). More important, EDA offers displays that help to interpret regression coefficients correctly.

One particularly useful exploratory display, offered by most modern statistics programs, is the *partial regression plot*. This scatterplot displays the relationship between the response variable and any selected predictor variable after adjusting for simultaneous linear change in the other predictor variables. The plot thus displays exactly what the coefficient of the selected predictor means. Specifically, the plot has a least squares slope equal to the coefficient of the selected predictor in the multiple regression model, and it has the same least squares residuals as the full multiple regression. It is an excellent tool for understanding how consistently the selected predictor fits the response (by judging the variation in the residuals) and for diagnosing unusual behavior in the data that may affect that particular coefficient (Cook & Weisberg, 1982; Velleman & Welsch, 1981).

ANALYSIS OF VARIANCE

The term *analysis of variance* customarily describes analyses of data that involve two or more factors and have one or more observations for each possible combination of the levels (or versions) of all the factors. Beyond such *factorial designs*, a wide variety of designs use balanced subsets of the possible combinations.

EDA emphasizes analyzing the data first and only later summarizing the contributions of various sources of variability (Hoaglin, Mosteller, & Tukey, 1991). Natural initial steps include looking at the data and considering the possibility of re-expression. We illustrate these ideas in the context of a classical set of data from a difference limen experiment for

which a variety of illustrative analyses have been published on several occasions (Green & Tukey, 1960; E. G. Johnson & Tukey, 1987; P. O. Johnson, 1946; P. O. Johnson & Tsao, 1944).

The experiment involved eight subjects, "two persons in each cell of a 2 × 2 design for male versus female and sighted versus [congenitally] blind." Subjects were asked to detect a change in the weight pulling on a ring. The controlled treatments consisted of "two *Dates* (1, 2), four *Rates* (50, 100, 150, and 200 grams per 30 seconds), and seven (initial) *Weights* (100, 150, 200, 250, 300, 350, and 400 grams). The experimental procedure involved attaching a pail by a lever system to a ring on the subject's finger. One of the seven initial *Weights* was placed into the pail, and then water was allowed to flow into the pail at one of four constant *Rates* until the subject reported a change in pull on the finger. The intended response, the difference limen (*DL*), was measured by the amount of water added [up to the] time of report. Five determinations were made for each of the 28 *Rate* × *Weight* combinations, and the average of these values was used as the response. The entire experiment was conducted, for each person, at each of two *Dates*, one week apart" (E. G. Johnson & Tukey, 1987, p. 174).[3] The design calls for an analysis predicting *DL* from *Date*, *Rate*, *Weight*, *Sight*, *Sex*, and *Subject* (nested within the combination of *Sight* and *Sex*). That ANOVA is shown in Table 3.2.[4]

EDA teaches that we should *always* examine the residuals in an analysis because subtracting a summary of the patterns found so far is likely to reveal additional patterns or further evidence about the current summary. Plotting the residuals from the ANOVA of Table 3.2 against the predicted values (Figure 3.12) reveals that *DL* as originally measured does not satisfy the assumptions of ANOVA. In particular, it is clear that the variance of the response is not constant across the values of the factors studied. The pattern resembles a

---

[3]In this quotation, we have added italics and initial capitals to names of factors for consistency with usage in this chapter.

[4]Our results do not exactly match those of P. O. Johnson and Tsao (1944) or those of Green and Tukey (1960). P. O. Johnson (1946) used these data to illustrate complex ANOVA calculations and found a model with all interaction terms but without a *Subject* term. Green and Tukey followed a path closer to the one we are about to discuss. All of the previous authors had to perform these rather daunting calculations by hand, so errors may have crept in.

TABLE 3.2

Analysis of Variance Table for Difference Limen (DL)

Source	DF	Sum of squares	Mean square	F-ratio	p-value
Const	1	276799	276799	46.296	0.0024
Date	1	115.629	115.629	1.6582	0.1985
Rate	3	51077.6	17025.9	244.16	≤ 0.0001
Weight	6	1913.63	318.939	4.5737	0.0002
Sight	1	11816.3	11816.3	1.9763	0.2325
Sex	1	31543.7	31543.7	5.2758	0.0832
Subject (Sight × Sex)	4	23915.6	5978.89	85.740	≤ 0.0001
Sight × Sex	1	14136.8	14136.8	2.3644	0.1989
Error	430	29985.3	69.7332		
Total	447	164504			

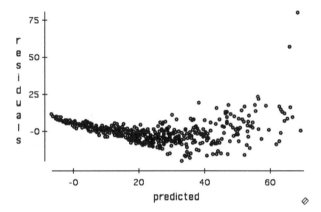

FIGURE 3.12. Residuals from the analysis of variance for *DL* on *Date*, *Weight*, *Rate*, *Sight*, *Sex*, and *Subject* (*Sight × Sex*) show nonlinearity and a fan shape that calls for re-expression or reformulation.

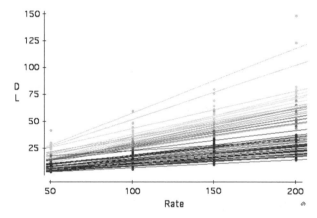

FIGURE 3.13. *Difference Limen* plotted against *Rate*. Lines are least squares fits for each *Subject × Weight × Date* combination.

fan, opening to the right (larger residuals tend to belong to larger predicted values), and also shows some curvature.

Green and Tukey (1960) discussed the importance of the scale used for the response variable:

> We want to choose a scale that will yield the simplest relations with the independent variables. By simplest relations we mean, for example, fewer important interactions, and larger main effects relative to the error variance. A change of variable that nearly removes a particular main effect also usually leads to very revealing results. Secondarily, we would like the dependent variable to have approximately homogeneous variance within cells of the design. (p. 128)

When variance increases with predicted value (as in Figure 3.12), functions such as the square root, logarithm, and reciprocal are likely to help. For these data, the units of the variables suggest an alternative way to address the first goal mentioned by Green and Tukey. The *Difference Limen* is measured in grams. The *Rate* factor is measured in grams per 30 sec. If we plot the *DL* against *Rate* and add lines to the plot for each *Subject × Weight × Date* combination, we obtain Figure 3.13.

But if we reformulate *Rate* as *Time* (in seconds) until the subject declares a felt change, we obtain Figure 3.14. (The calculation is *Seconds* =

(*DL/Rate*) × 30.) The fact that response *Time* is virtually constant for the four rates of increase (for each combination of *Subject*, *Weight*, and *Date*) suggests that one can get whatever difference limen one wants by choosing the *Rate* appropriately. That observation argues strongly that converting the average *DL* to an average *Time* (in seconds) will produce a simpler analysis. P. O. Johnson and Tsao (1944) found this relation (as an interaction in their analysis of average *DL*). Green and Tukey found it and made the argument for using *Time* as the response that we recount here. Technically, this type of change is sometimes called *reformulation* rather than re-expression because it does not involve applying a simple mathematical function to each data value. When available, it is another useful technique in the analyst's toolkit.

Although the summary is simpler for the data in seconds, the residual plot in Figure 3.15 still shows a bend, increasing spread from left to right, and possible subgroups. An analysis of *Log₁₀ Seconds* yields the residual plot in Figure 3.16. This pattern is more like what we hope for: roughly flat, with similar variation in the residuals across the range of predicted values and no bends. The overall pattern in Figure 3.16 is horizontal and homoskedastic. The residuals form clusters. Further checking shows that each subject is a cluster, although some subjects' clusters overlap. The ANOVA table presented in Table 3.3 shows significant effects for *Date* and *Weight*. Because this ANOVA treats *Subject* as a random factor (and the other factors as fixed), we do

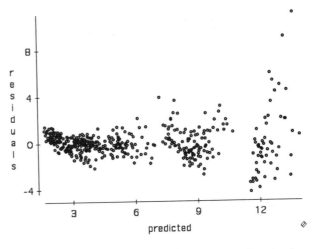

FIGURE 3.15. Plot of residuals versus predicted values for the ANOVA of *Seconds* on *Date*, *Weight*, *Rate*, *Sight*, *Sex*, and *Subject* (within *Sight* × *Sex*).

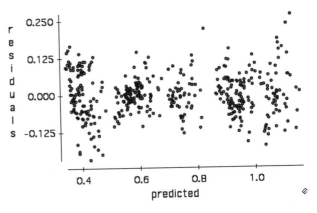

FIGURE 3.16. Plot of residuals versus predicted values for the ANOVA of *Log₁₀Seconds* on *Date*, *Weight*, *Rate*, *Sight*, *Sex*, and *Subject* (within *Sight* × *Sex*).

not focus on the significance of the effects for the individual subjects; the *p* value for *Subject* arises from comparing the *Subject* mean square against the residual mean square. Although they have much larger mean squares than *Date* and *Weight* (and *Rate*), *Sight*, *Sex*, and *Sight* × *Sex* are far from significant because the denominator for their *F* ratios is the *Subject* (*Sight* × *Sex*) mean square. Green and Tukey (1960) discussed choices between fixed and random for the various factors and the reasons for them.

From an EDA perspective, the analysis does not end with an ANOVA table. The customary next step examines the individual values for each line in the table: the main effects for *Date*, *Rate*, *Weight*, *Sight*, and *Sex*; the interaction effects for *Sight* × *Sex*; the

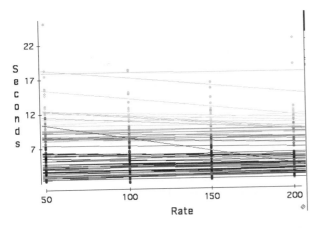

FIGURE 3.14. Response in seconds is almost constant versus *Rate* for each *Subject* × *Weight* × *Date* combination.

TABLE 3.3

Analysis of Variance Table for *Log₁₀ Seconds*

Source	DF	Sum of squares	Mean square	F-ratio	p-value
Const	1	223.836	223.836	80.238	0.0009
Date	1	0.093378	0.093378	17.592	≤ 0.0001
Rate	3	0.012418	0.004139	0.77983	0.5057
Weight	6	0.332250	0.055375	10.433	≤ 0.0001
Sight	1	3.79149	3.79149	1.3591	0.3085
Sex	1	7.70730	7.70730	2.7628	0.1718
Subject(Sight × Sex)	4	11.1586	2.78964	525.56	≤ 0.0001
Sight × Sex	1	3.40870	3.40870	1.2219	0.3310
Error	430	2.28240	0.005308		
Total	447	28.7865			

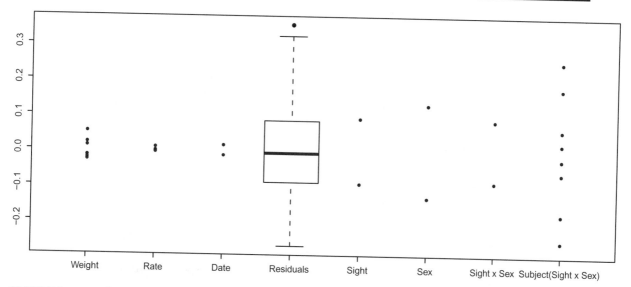

FIGURE 3.17. Effects and residuals for the ANOVA of *Log₁₀ Seconds* on *Date, Weight, Rate, Sight, Sex,* and *Subject* (within *Sight × Sex*).

effects for *Subject* (nested within *Sight × Sex*); and the residuals. Figure 3.17 shows dot plots of the various effects and a boxplot of the residuals; we chose the order because the residuals provide the denominator for *Weight, Rate,* and *Date* and the *Subject* effects provide the denominator for *Sight, Sex,* and *Sight × Sex*. Because each set of effects sums to zero (in two ways for *Sight × Sex*), the effects for the lines other than *Weight* and *Rate* consist of positive and negative values with the same magnitude. Such a display makes it easy to compare the sizes of the effects for the various parts of the model.

The variation among the residuals and among the *Subject* effects dominates the display. The effects for *Date* appear small alongside the residu-

als, but each of those effects represents a mean of 224 observations. On the other hand, the effects for *Sight, Sex,* and *Sight × Sex* do not seem much smaller than the *Subject* effects, but each *Subject* effect represents a mean of 56 observations. Relative to the variation in the *Subject* effects, the effects for *Sight, Sex,* and *Sight × Sex* are not large enough to reach significance.

Of the two experimental factors, different *Weights* have noticeable effects, although they are not very large compared with the variation in the residuals. By contrast, differing *Rates* have little effect at all.

As Figure 3.18 shows, the effects for *Weight* are systematically related to the level of weight. Subjects were able to more quickly discern a change when

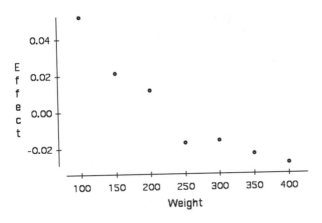

FIGURE 3.18. The effects of *Weight* generally fall consistently with increasing weight.

the initial weight was small than when it was larger—a result consistent with Weber's law but not a particularly exciting outcome for so complex an experiment.

Exploratory ANOVA can go further (Hoaglin et al., 1991), but we stop here for this chapter. The choice to reformulate the response as seconds and then re-express it as log-seconds may seem specific to this analysis and difficult to generalize, but other analyses present similar opportunities. And for re-expression, EDA has specific techniques for letting the data guide the choice (Emerson, 1983; Emerson & Stoto, 1983).

THE EDA PROCESS

Data exploration is a diagnostic procedure. The data analyst attempts to detect and characterize any aspect of the data that may help in understanding the underlying pathologies. Diagnosis requires an open mind and a willingness to expect the unexpected. Checklists have proved helpful in clinical medicine (e.g., Gawande, 2010). In that spirit, we offer a data exploration and diagnosis checklist. As with many checklists for complex processes, this one is divided into shorter, focused checklists for each of the large steps of analysis.

Checklist I: Display the Data
A. **Look at the distributions of the variables with a stem-and-leaf display, histogram, or dot plot.**
 1. Be alert for multiple modes
  a) Consider splitting data into subgroups

2. Be alert for outliers
  a) Identify, understand, correct (if possible), or set aside
3. Check for skewness
  a) Consider re-expression to improve symmetry
B. **Compare groups with boxplots.**
 1. Check for skewness within groups
  a) Consider re-expression to improve symmetry
 2. Check that groups have similar spreads
  a) Consider re-expression to promote constant spread (spread-vs.-level plot)
 3. Check for outliers
  a) Identify, understand, correct (if possible), or set aside
C. **Consider bivariate relationships with scatterplots.**
 1. Check for approximate straightness
  a) Consider re-expression to improve straightness
  b) Usually re-expressing *y* is preferred, as it is likely also to make the variability of *y* more nearly constant across the range of *x*
 2. Check for constant variance of *y* for all *x* values (homoskedasticity)
  a) Consider re-expressing *y*, especially if larger values of *y* are more variable
 3. Check for local clusters, parallel trends, or other evidence of subgroups
  a) Consider splitting the data into subgroups
 4. Check for outliers
  a) Consider both *y*-direction outliers and *x*-direction high-leverage points
   i) The influence of a case depends on both
   ii) Identify, understand, correct (if appropriate), or consider setting aside or treating specially
D. **Consider multivariate relationships with scatterplot matrices and rotating plots.**
 1. Check for approximate straightness
  a) Consider re-expression to improve linearity
  b) Scatterplot matrices make it easy to notice variables that would benefit from

re-expression in several bivariate relationships; re-express those variables first

2. Check for local clusters, parallel trends, or other evidence of subgroups
   a) In rotating plots, rotate so that the main trend is perpendicular to the screen to look for subgroups
   b) In scatterplot matrices, use plot brushing to identify clusters in one scatterplot and check whether they stand out in other scatterplots
   c) Consider splitting the data into subgroups
3. Check for outliers
   a) In scatterplot matrices, select points that stand away from the other data to see whether they may be unusual in other scatterplots; they may be outliers in a multivariate sense
   b) Be alert for points that may be multivariate outliers but are not unusual on any univariate or bivariate display
      i) Diagnostic statistics are available to help with this (see discussion of regression)

If the exploratory displays in the first checklist suggest that it is appropriate to summarize variables or model their behavior, then use Checklists II through V, depending on the number and structure of the variables.

Checklist II: Summarize and Describe Individual Variables

A. **Summarize individual variables with resistant measures.**
   1. Median
   2. Quartiles
      a) Several definitions of quartiles are in use, but it matters little which you use
   3. Q-spread (interquartile range [IQR])
   4. Extremes (minimum and maximum)
B. **Summarize individual variables with traditional maximum-likelihood methods.**
   1. Mean
   2. Standard deviation
   3. Confidence interval
      a) But check displays to be sure assumptions are plausible

Checklist III: Compare Multiple Groups

A. **Use ANOVA to compare group means.**
   1. Consider the form of the response variable
      a) Use spread-vs.-level plot to check for need to re-express
      b) Plot residuals against predicted values and look for violations of homoskedasticity and for curvature
   2. Check residuals for outliers

Checklist IV: Summarize and Describe Relationships Between Pairs of Quantitative Variables

A. **Use resistant smoothing to reveal general trends.**
B. **Fit linear models with least squares regression and check diagnostic displays and statistics.**
   1. Plot studentized residuals vs. predicted values; check for the following:
      a) Curvature
         i) If so, go back to Checklist I.D.1, consider re-expression, and fit again
      b) Subgroups, especially parallel patterns
         i) Parallel patterns suggest an analysis of covariance approach or the introduction of indicator variables and a multiple regression
      c) Outliers and high-leverage points
         i) Consider correcting, omitting, or treating specially; one possibility is introducing an indicator variable for each errant case

Checklist V: Summarize Multivariate Relationships Involving a Single Quantitative Response Variable and Multiple Potential Quantitative Predictors

A. **Fit a least squares multiple regression and compute and examine the residuals.**
   1. Plot studentized residuals against predicted values
      a) Look for bends—consider re-expressing y
      b) Look for heteroskedasticity—consider re-expressing y
      c) Look for parallel patterns—consider indicator variables for groups

d) Look for outliers—consider correcting, setting aside, or treating specially (e.g., with an indicator variable for each)
2. Examine leverage and influence measures; identify influential cases
   a) Histograms and stem-and-leaf displays help to identify extreme values; boxplots can do that conveniently for large numbers of values; leverages are not likely to be normally distributed because they are bounded by zero and one
   b) Set aside influential cases and repeat the analysis to assess their true influence on your conclusions
3. Examine partial regression plots—especially for coefficients that are of particular interest
   a) Check as for simple regressions in Checklist IV

Regression model building is an exploration of several aspects at once. We simultaneously seek effective functional forms to model the data and appropriate variables with which to build our models. Along the way, we identify extraordinary cases and prevent them from dominating our decisions. There is no fixed path. You may choose to examine a response variable plotted against each factor or predictor before moving on to models with multiple factors and predictors. The most important aspect of the EDA approach is that the human analyst is intimately involved at each step, using discipline-based knowledge to guide decisions. For example, one path for building a multiple regression model might go according to Checklist VI.

Checklist VI: Build a Multiple Regression Model With Interactive Steps

A. Choose a promising predictor variable and fit a simple (y vs. x) regression. Look at plots and diagnostics as in Checklist V. Use the information from displays of this relationship to reconsider the form of the model, possible re-expressions of the variables, isolation of possible outliers, and whether the selected predictor should be replaced with an alternative predictor.

B. Consider the relationships between the residuals and remaining available predictors. Be alert to opportunities for re-expression and the possibility that other cases should be isolated as outliers. Select one or more of the available predictors (after possible re-expression and outlier deletion) to add to the model. Diagnose as in Checklist V.
   1. Isolate extraordinary cases by assigning individual indicator variables to them and including those in the model

C. Iterate. At each iteration it may be appropriate to proceed stepwise—that is, introduce one predictor at a time or introduce collections of conceptually related predictors together. The most important idea is to continually monitor and diagnose the developing model, exploring for unanticipated relationships, clusters, outliers, and violations of assumptions.

Designed experiments are likely sources of data with a quantitative response and two categorical factors. In such cases the factors are defined and controlled. However, this form of data can also arise from observational studies, in which case the factors may be observed and not under control.

Checklist VII: Summarize Multivariate Relationships of a Single Quantitative Response Variable and Two Categorical Factors

A. Median polish.
B. Look for re-expressions to improve additivity.
   1. Use the diagnostic plot for a two-way table to suggest a function for re-expression[5]
C. Plot residuals. If they are reasonably symmetric and not heavy-tailed, consider fitting the ANOVA model (i.e., summarize by means).
   1. Diagnose ANOVA residuals as in Checklist VI; check for heteroskedasticity and curvature
   2. Diagnose possible outliers

---

[5]Emerson and Hoaglin (1983) and Emerson (1983) discussed the diagnostic plot for a two-way table and its background. The plot is a graphical descendant of Tukey's one degree of freedom for nonadditivity (ODOFFNA; Tukey, 1949).

Checklist VIII: Summarize Multivariate Relationships of a Single Quantitative Response Variable and Multiple Categorical Factors

A. **If data come from a designed experiment, explore the ANOVA corresponding to the design.**
   1. Examine boxplots of the residuals at each level of each factor and possibly for combinations of factors
       a) Look for outliers—treat them as before
       b) Look for skewness—consider re-expressing *y*
   2. Explore for evidence of nonadditivity

B. **Data from designed experiments can be explored in much the same way as for multiple regression. EDA supports the idea that factors and interactions can be included or removed from a developing model. At each step, the residuals should be checked, and unanticipated clusters, outliers, nonlinearity, or (for analyses of covariances) lack of parallelism should be addressed.**

These EDA principles and approaches extend naturally to more complex situations. The general rules are to make displays of individual variables first and deal with any special issues. Then check any models for the data by similarly examining residuals to see whether they reveal anything worthy of special attention. Always be alert to the opportunity to re-express variables to simplify the models or to better satisfy model assumptions. Be willing to isolate outliers and influential cases by setting them aside or by fitting special terms just for them.

COMPETING MODELS

When we explore data with many variables, it is often productive to entertain multiple, competing models, developing each, comparing results, and learning from one to inform the others. This strategy might lead simply to offering multiple alternative models for the data. Or it might develop into a Darwinian competition among the models, with those that develop into less useful or successful forms being abandoned in favor of the more successful models—a "Survival of the Best Fit."

When researchers apply statistics primarily to test hypotheses, they often have a sense of completion. We have stated and tested the hypotheses, reached conclusions about them, and can move on to other topics. EDA does not adopt that attitude. There is never a natural stopping place. As with the larger corpus of science, an exploratory data analysis is never done. There is always the possibility that new data or new understanding can lead us to modify or develop an analysis further. Of course, you can reach a point at which everyone involved agrees that there is little gain from doing more with the data you have. But experience has shown that, even then, a new idea or suggestion can reopen the question.

References

Aaron, D. H., & Jansen, C. W. S. (2003). Development of the Functional Dexterity Test (FDT). *Journal of Hand Therapy, 16*, 12–21. doi:10.1016/S0894-1130(03)80019-4

Bartlett, M. S. (1947). The use of transformations. *Biometrics, 3*, 39–52. doi:10.2307/3001536

Box, G. E. P., & Cox, D. R. (1964). An analysis of transformations. *Journal of the Royal Statistical Society Series B, 26*, 211–252.

Cook, R. D., & Weisberg, S. (1982). *Residuals and influence in regression.* New York, NY: Chapman & Hall.

Diaconis, P. (1985). Theories of data analysis: From magical thinking through classical statistics. In D. C. Hoaglin, F. Mosteller, & J. W. Tukey (Eds.), *Exploring data tables, trends, and shapes* (pp. 1–36). New York, NY: Wiley.

Emerson, J. D. (1983). Mathematical aspects of transformation. In D. C. Hoaglin, F. Mosteller, & J. W. Tukey (Eds.), *Understanding robust and exploratory data analysis* (pp. 247–282). New York, NY: Wiley.

Emerson, J. D., & Hoaglin, D. C. (1983). Analysis of two-way tables by medians. In D. C. Hoaglin, F. Mosteller, & J. W. Tukey (Eds.), *Understanding robust and exploratory data analysis* (pp. 166–210). New York, NY: Wiley.

Emerson, J. D., & Stoto, M. A. (1983). Transforming data. In D. C. Hoaglin, F. Mosteller, & J. W. Tukey (Eds.), *Understanding robust and exploratory data analysis* (pp. 97–128). New York, NY: Wiley.

Gawande, A. (2010). *The checklist manifesto.* New York, NY: Metropolitan Books.

Gogola, G. R., Lacy, B., Morse, A., Aaron, D., & Velleman, P. F. (2010, June). *Hand dexterity values for 3 to 17 year-old typically developing children.* Paper presented at the Eighth Triennial Congress of the International Federation of Societies for Hand Therapy, Orlando, FL.

Green, B. F., & Tukey, J. W. (1960). Complex analyses of variance: General problems. *Psychometrika, 25,* 127–152. doi:10.1007/BF02288577

Hoaglin, D. C. (1988). Transformations in everyday experience. *CHANCE, 1*(4), 40–45.

Hoaglin, D. C., & Iglewicz, B. (1987). Fine-tuning some resistant rules for outlier labeling. *Journal of the American Statistical Association, 82,* 1147–1149. doi:10.2307/2289392

Hoaglin, D. C., Iglewicz, B., & Tukey, J. W. (1986). Performance of some resistant rules for outlier labeling. *Journal of the American Statistical Association, 81,* 991–999. doi:10.2307/2289073

Hoaglin, D. C., Mosteller, F., & Tukey, J. W. (Eds.). (1991). *Fundamentals of exploratory analysis of variance.* New York, NY: Wiley.

Inselberg, A. (2009). *Parallel coordinates: Visual multidimensional geometry and its applications.* New York, NY: Springer.

Jebsen, R. H., Taylor, N., Trieschmann, R. B., Trotter, M. H., & Howard, L. A. (1969). An objective and standardized test of hand function. *Archives of Physical Medicine and Rehabilitation, 50,* 311–319.

Johnson, E. G., & Tukey, J. W. (1987). Graphical exploratory analysis of variance illustrated on a splitting of the Johnson and Tsao data. In C. L. Mallows (Ed.), *Design, data, and analysis by some friends of Cuthbert Daniel* (pp. 171–244). New York, NY: Wiley.

Johnson, P. O. (1946). *Statistical methods in research.* New York, NY: Prentice Hall.

Johnson, P. O., & Tsao, F. (1944). Factorial design in the determination of differential limen values. *Psychometrika, 9,* 107–144. doi:10.1007/BF02288717

Kruskal, J. B. (1968). Statistical analysis: Transformations of data. In D. L. Sills (Ed.), *International encyclopedia of the social sciences* (Vol. 15, pp. 182–193). Chicago, IL: Macmillan & The Free Press.

Mlodinow, L. (2008). *The drunkard's walk.* New York, NY: Pantheon Books.

Mosteller, F., & Tukey, J. W. (1977). *Data analysis and regression.* Reading, MA: Addison-Wesley.

Reitan, R. M. (1958). Validity of the Trail Making Test as an indicator of organic brain damage. *Perceptual and Motor Skills, 8,* 271–276. doi:10.2466/PMS.8.7.271-276

Stroop, J. R. (1935). Studies of interference in serial verbal reactions. *Journal of Experimental Psychology, 18,* 643–662. doi:10.1037/h0054651

Tukey, J. W. (1949). One degree of freedom for non-additivity. *Biometrics, 5,* 232–242. doi:10.2307/3001938

Tukey, J. W. (1957). On the comparative anatomy of transformations. *Annals of Mathematical Statistics, 28,* 602–632. doi:10.1214/aoms/1177706875

Tukey, J. W. (1960). A survey of sampling from contaminated distributions. In I. Olkin, S. G. Ghurye, W. Hoeffding, W. G. Madow, & H. B. Mann (Eds.), *Contributions to probability and statistics: Essays in honor of Harold Hotelling* (pp. 448–485). Stanford, CA: Stanford University Press.

Tukey, J. W. (1977). *Exploratory data analysis.* Reading, MA: Addison-Wesley.

Velleman, P. F. (2004). *Data Desk.* Ithaca, NY: Data Description.

Velleman, P. F. (2008). Truth, damn truth, and statistics. *Journal of Statistics Education, 16*(2). Retrieved from http://www.amstat.org/publications/jse/v16n2/velleman.html

Velleman, P. F., & Welsch, R. E. (1981). Efficient computing of regression diagnostics. *The American Statistician, 35,* 234–242. doi:10.2307/2683296

Velleman, P. F., & Wilkinson, L. (1993). Nominal, ordinal, interval, and ratio typologies are misleading. *The American Statistician, 47,* 65–72. doi:10.2307/2684788

Describing Data

CHAPTER 4

GRAPHIC DISPLAYS OF DATA

Leland Wilkinson

Figure 4.1 shows the results of a survey by Cleveland (1984) on the use of graphics in scientific articles. The horizontal axis represents the percentage of total page area devoted to graphics in 47 articles sampled from the 1980–1981 volumes of selected science journals. The circles represent Cleveland's individual measurements, and the box-and-whisker schematics divide each set of circles into quartiles. There are significant differences among disciplines in the use of graphs. Moreover, as Cleveland noted, the substantial differences among disciplines remain when the measure is number of graphs per article instead of page area.

This pattern of graphics usage appears not to have changed in the decades following Cleveland's study. Best, Smith, and Stubbs (2001) found similar results in a more recent survey. Furthermore, they found differences in graphics usage among subdisciplines of psychology, with the hard scientists using more graphics than the soft scientists. These results appear paradoxical. Why would soft scientists, who eschew mathematics, tend to avoid graphics (even simple charts, illustrations, or diagrams)? Why would hard scientists turn to graphs when equations, algorithms, and tables are sufficient support for their findings?

We might speculate that social scientists have always had an aversion toward graphics. On the contrary, Beniger and Robyn (1978), Collins (1993), Fienberg (1979), Funkhouser (1937), Stigler (1983), Tufte (1983, 1990, 1997), Wainer (1997, 2009), Wainer and Spence (1997), and Wainer and Velleman (2001) demonstrated that social scientists were among the earliest, most enthusiastic, and most inventive users of graphics in scientific publications. If anything, hard scientists were latecomers to the graphics field. The beautiful reproductions in Playfair (1786/2005) reveal, in a wealth of figures, probably the first instances of bar, line, pie, and stacked area charts.

We might also imagine that social scientists think the use of graphics is evidence of sloppy thinking: Numbers are precise, and graphics are fuzzy. It is no easier to lie with graphics than with statistics, however (Huff, 1954; Monmonier, 1996). And it is a simple calculation to show that the typical printed journal figure (assuming a width of 3 inches) permits approximately four digits of precision in its resolution—more than typical data analyzed by psychologists. And if social scientists are prejudiced against graphics, why do they use them so often in their talks?

We might also think that software to make the kind of graphics needed by social scientists (as opposed to business people) is lacking. On the contrary, there is a plethora of such software. As we shall see, almost every major statistics package has comprehensive graphics capabilities, and there are several good charting packages to produce the kind of technical graphics featured in this chapter.

Because I have taught in the past 40 years in graduate departments of psychology, statistics, and computer science, I have been exposed to developments in each field that affect practices in the others. I have also witnessed the isolation in these communities; few researchers have the time to read the literature outside their fields. This chapter is an attempt to call on all three disciplines.

DOI: 10.1037/13621-004
APA Handbook of Research Methods in Psychology: Vol. 3. Data Analysis and Research Publication, H. Cooper (Editor-in-Chief)

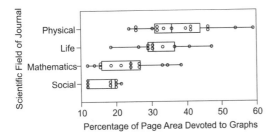

FIGURE 4.1. Dot–boxplot of results in Cleveland (1984) on the use of graphics in scientific journals. The horizontal axis represents the percentage of total page area devoted to graphics in 47 articles sampled from the 1980–1981 volumes of selected science journals.

We might also think that publishers make the use of graphics in articles inordinately expensive. Unfortunately, there is some truth to this assumption. Some journal publishers (especially in the social sciences and humanities) have failed to keep up with new technology and continue to imagine that embedding graphics in articles is more expensive than setting type. These publishers still require authors to submit double-spaced, plain-text manuscripts, with figures separated from the text. This manuscript format dates from the time of manual typewriters, when production assistants used rubber cement to lay out figures for photo-offset printing. Publishers used a simple formula to calculate book and journal prices; they multiplied cost-of-goods-sold by 7. Today, although publishers have automated their production process (using software like Quark Express or Adobe PageMaker), they continue to use the multiply-by-7 rule. Consequently, the publisher's expense of arranging figures and text by hand in Quark or Adobe is multiplied by a factor of 7. This is why some publishers ask authors to keep figures to a minimum. Other publishers, using different tools, welcome figures and do not charge extra for them. I discuss these technologies later in this chapter.

In this chapter, I advocate new policies and present new ideas rather than summarize conventional thinking about graphics usage. The reason for this approach is simple: Much conventional wisdom on the production and usage of graphics in scientific publications is wrong. I support this assertion through citations to the psychological and statistical literature and to commercial production technology. Moreover, I try to expose the subjectivity in popular writing on graphics usage as well as the long-standing tendency of graphics gurus to ignore scientific research on graphic communication. There is nothing wrong with aesthetic prescriptions that are based on reasonable rules and clean design, as long as these opinions are not disguised as facts.

The point of view in this chapter differs somewhat from other chapters in this handbook. Some of the assertions in this chapter are subjective, so I use the first person to prevent a false impression of scientific objectivity. More important, I am trying to influence four groups in this chapter: (a) researchers who are publishing, (b) editors and reviewers, (c) publishers, and (d) software developers.

The remainder of this chapter consists of three parts. The next section presents guidelines on the basis of aesthetics and cognitive science. The third section offers exemplars—suggested graphics for displaying one or more variables embedded in models frequently employed by psychologists and other researchers. The brief final section surveys software for producing scientific graphics on computers.

GUIDELINES

Charts are maps of abstract worlds. The word *chart* and the word *cartography* have the same root (Latin *charta*, a piece of paper or papyrus). We map the globe to orient ourselves in the world. Graphic worlds transcend geography. We graph abstractions to orient ourselves in abstract worlds. As Pinker (1997) argued, abstract reasoning is built on metaphors for reality. We manipulate abstractions by making them analogous to concrete objects.

Thus, many useful guidelines for making charts and scientific graphics understandable can be derived from the regularities of the perceived physical world. As with computer interfaces, well-designed graphics are generally consistent with these perceived regularities. Dense objects (mountains or histograms) rest on a base. Members of a group (birds in a flock or points in a cloud) are near each other. Paths through space (geographic or abstract) are connected. Violating commonsense reasoning leads to confusion. We think of images as having a natural orientation, with a top and a bottom. We interpret red as hot and blue as cool. We perceive pale-blue objects as more distant than bright-green ones. The designer who ignores these regularities interferes with the primary purpose of a graphic: to convey veridically a structured message through the visual system.

Regularity in the physical world is not the same as perceived regularity of the physical world. In some cases, graphics can compensate for our biases. For example, Stevens (1985) and others demonstrated that our psychometric function for stimulus intensity is nonlinear. If we wish to convey magnitude via certain stimulus modes (area, volume, brightness, etc.), we might want to arrange for a nonlinear mapping from the data to the representation—similar to the way engineers design nonlinear inputs to controls that pilots expect to process linearly.

In proposing guidelines for chart construction, we must remember our communication goals. Popular writers frequently overlook this caveat when they develop their lists of design rules. Over the centuries of their history, various charts have emphasized *communication* (e.g., Snow's map of cholera deaths in London, reproduced in Tufte, 1983), *persuasion* (Fletcher's map of the distribution of ignorance in 19th-century England and Wales, reproduced in Wainer, 1997), and artistic *design* (e.g., Playfair's chart of imports and exports of England to and from North America, reproduced in Tufte, 1983). These criteria are not exclusive, of course. Some charts incorporate all three (e.g., Minard's famous map–chart of Napoleon's troop losses in the Russian campaign, reproduced in Tufte, 1983).

Not surprisingly, modern critics of graphics have tended to align themselves along these same dimensions. Communicators (e.g., William S. Cleveland and Stephen Kosslyn) have conducted experiments to determine rules that improve the transfer of information from chart-maker to chart-viewer. Persuaders (e.g., Holmes, 1991) have evaluated charts on the basis of their emotional impact. Designers (e.g., Herdeg, 1981) have looked for elegance and simplicity. Others (e.g., Tufte, 1983) have adopted the criteria of the communicator and the methods of the designer. None of these approaches can claim exclusive validity. Because scientists are more interested

in rules that foster accurate communication of replicable results, however, I focus on communication.

Evaluating graphic communication has been the province of psychology in the subdisciplines of human factors, ergonomics, and applied cognitive science. For almost a century, human factors psychologists have developed methods and criteria for evaluating graphics. Military psychologists, for example, have conducted randomized experiments to test the effectiveness of aircraft cockpit displays.

Psychologists gave less attention to the perception of statistical graphics until a statistician, William Cleveland, published a series of experiments designed to identify aspects of charts that helped or hindered accurate decoding of quantitative data (Cleveland & McGill, 1984). Beniger and Robyn (1978) cited a number of statisticians' informal studies of the effectiveness of popular charts in the 1920s, but this research did not induce many psychologists to study the topic more formally.

Cleveland used paper-and-pencil tests containing simple graphic elements—points, lines, angles, areas, colors—generated randomly by a computer. His subjects gave magnitude estimates of the values generating the instances of each element. From these estimates, he derived and analyzed error rates. One can quibble with his methodology, but the results are intriguing and stimulated subsequent studies by psychologists to test them further.

Figure 4.2 summarizes the main result of Cleveland's experiments. The top of the figure (*BEST*) represents elements that resulted in fewer errors and the bottom (*WORST*) represents those with more.

Cleveland's hierarchy gives us a start in designing effective displays. There are exceptions to these rules, however. A chart is more than the sum of its parts; elements interact in the perceptual mix of a chart. These interactions can suppress or enhance errors. Thus, it is dangerous to extrapolate from Cleveland's findings to the evaluation of complex charts.

Interactions in the perceptual mix immediately suggest Gestalt effects. There is reasonable evidence that similarity, proximity, closure, figure ground, and configural effects apply to the perception of statistical graphics (Coren & Girgus, 1978; Garner, 1981; Klippel, Knuf, Hommel, & Freksa, 2004). For

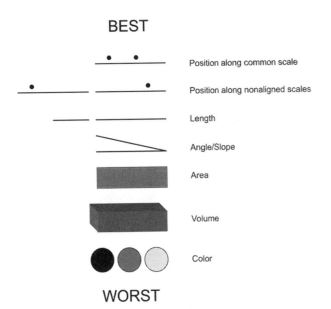

BEST

Position along common scale

Position along nonaligned scales

Length

Angle/Slope

Area

Volume

Color

WORST

FIGURE 4.2. Hierarchy of graphic elements derived from Cleveland and McGill (1984) and other studies by Cleveland.

example, Cleveland, Diaconis, and McGill (1982) found that the relation between the size of a scatterplot cloud and the size of a surrounding frame affects the judgment of correlation by both novice and expert viewers. Their result is most likely due to a figure–ground effect: Small clouds surrounded by large, white frames are perceived as more correlated. There is a confound in this study, however. The size of the plotting symbols was allowed to vary with the size of the cloud. In unpublished research with a graduate student, I found that the effect disappears when the darkness of the cloud is attenuated by reducing the size of the plotting symbols. The conclusion of Cleveland et al. should be modified to say that small, *dark* clouds surrounded by large, white frames are perceived as more correlated. This modified result is consistent with Gestalt principles of figure ground and proximity. Doherty and Anderson (2009) discussed this and other effects in the perception of correlation in scatterplots.

Another caution against generalizing from Cleveland's findings arises from the absence of consideration of cognitive processes in the derivation of the hierarchy. Cleveland deliberately ignored cognition in his studies, preferring instead to concentrate on perception. Because his methods are consistent with those of psychophysical scaling and his stimuli are

similar to ones used by the psychophysicists, his results are fairly consistent with the psychophysical literature on power-function exponents for graphic stimuli (Stevens, 1961). If we remove annotation, text, legends, and axes from a graph, leaving only a single type of element (e.g., points, lines, areas), then Cleveland's hierarchy would probably be consistent with the patterns of responding.

Cognition introduces strong biases. Images, icons, text, and other symbolic aspects of a graphic affect higher level visual processing in strange ways. For example, features such as physical or political boundaries drawn as lines between two cities on a map can cause overestimation of Euclidean distance between them when viewing the map (Tversky, 1993; Tversky, Zacks, Lee, & Heiser, 2000). Similarly, connecting paths drawn between two cities can induce underestimation of distance (Klippel et al., 2004). The Cleveland rules are too simple for capturing these contextual effects. Kosslyn (1994); Heiser, Tversky, Agrawala, and Hanrahan (2003); Tversky (2005); and Tversky et al. (2007) are good sources for understanding how these processes affect graphic information processing in general.

Another important and frequently ignored role of cognition involves memory for graphs. Wilkinson and McConathy (1990) found that the Cleveland hierarchy is not always consistent in accounting for subjects' errors in magnitude estimation of the Cleveland elements under recall. This result is consistent with the finding that graphic elements are not stored as photographic images (Kosslyn, 1994). Line elements, for example, are encoded through simple prototypes (mountains, camel humps, snakes) that can distort global shape. For thematic elements in maps, Tversky (1981) and McNamara, Ratcliff, and McKoon (1984) found substantial distortions in memory when judging distance and other relations.

Many writers have prescribed general rules for effective graphic communication. The following guidelines are derived from Bertin (1967/1983, 1981), Cleveland (1993, 1994, 1995), Few (2009), Kosslyn (1994), Lewandowsky (1999), Lewandowsky and Spence (1989), Robbins (2005), Tufte (1983), and Ware (2008). Some guidelines are formed on the basis of my opinions; I will make clear when I disagree with the other writers.

Although I am a strong believer in the use of color in scientific graphics (see Wilkinson, 2005), all the graphics in this article are in black and white because publishing requirements restricted my examples to monochrome. Nevertheless, this restriction has forced me to examine more closely the many issues involved in producing black-and-white graphics. For clear scientific communication, lack of color is not as much of a handicap as it first seems. In many cases, it is an asset.

I will use the term *gurus* to denote those who write books, blogs, or other informal publications on graphics usage. I use the term without pejorative implication. I intend this term to be more inclusive than the term *experts* because gurus include writers who have no formal training or expertise in psychology, statistics, or design; these writers nevertheless express strong opinions on proper usage. I will paraphrase gurus in italics without attribution because these ubiquitous statements share forms derived from common but unknown sources (analogous to the *Q* unknown common source for the Synoptic Gospels). The following prescriptions are not ordered by importance.

Avoid Clutter

Do not clutter the data region inside the plotting frame delimited by axes. Tufte (1983) informally defined a data–ink ratio and urged us to maximize it by removing irrelevant detail. At the limit, this exhortation is nonsense, of course: The ultimate graph would contain no ink. And some of Tufte's examples (reducing Tukey's boxplot to a dot and two lines) are extreme. But this exhortation has value as long as we do not remove redundant features that can reinforce an accurate perception. Most writers agree that one should avoid ornate textures (especially stripes and screens), gratuitous colors, excessive tick marks and grid lines, ornate fonts, and unnecessary embellishment.

The use of gratuitous clutter has been termed *chartjunk* (Tufte, 1983). Graphics gurus like to lampoon chartjunk:

- "Markings and visual elements are chartjunk if they go beyond the minimum set of visuals necessary to communicate the information."

The scientific evidence suggests the gurus are wrong. Carswell (1992) and Gillan and Richman (1994) found mixed results for the relation of the data–ink ratio to performance. Gillan and Sorensen (2009) found that decorative backgrounds in charts can actually *enhance* processing. And it is not clear that viewers prefer lower data–ink ratios (Inbar, Tractinsky, & Meyer, 2007; Norman, 2007).

So, the case against chartjunk has to rest on aesthetics. My opinion is to avoid it because it is unnecessary and incompatible with the look and feel of a scientific journal. Claims that chartjunk graphs in *USA Today* (or other popular media) are misleading, however, have relatively little scientific support.

Exploit Redundancy

Redundancy is not clutter. Although worthless from a game theory point of view, redundancy aids selective attention in a viewing task by providing a richer relevant feature set. And although irrelevant (orthogonal to signal) cues indeed interfere with reaction times and accuracy (Stroop, 1935), redundant relevant cues (coincident with signal) do not generally hurt performance (Backs & Walrath, 1995). Mapping a variable to both color and shape, for example, is not necessarily a bad idea. Placing numbers on bars to denote their magnitude is not a bad thing, despite the admonitions of gurus. If the exact magnitude of a line slope is focal to the research context (as in psychophysical response functions), it can help to place a number indicating its value next to the line. Such annotations inside the frame of a graphic, if used sparingly, can improve communication.

Use Three-Dimensional Graphs Sparingly

In most applications, the use of one or more panels of two-dimensional (2D) graphs is preferable to one panel of three-dimensional (3D) graphs. Psychologists are accustomed to this practice because they conventionally represent two-way analysis of variance (ANOVA) interactions with several lines in a single frame rather than attempting a 3D plot of the response surface. The exception to this 3D proscription is (a) when a surface is relatively coherent, (b) the audience is accustomed to reading surface graphs, and (c) 2D paneling would create a messy

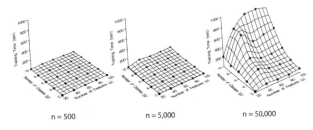

n = 500   n = 5,000   n = 50,000

FIGURE 4.3. 3D plot of classifier performance derived from a figure in Wilkinson (in press).

graph. Figure 4.3 is an example derived from Wilkinson, Anand, and Dang (in press). This graphic depicts the time performance of a statistical classifier. The point of the figure is to show that for higher levels of *n* (number of cases), the surface based on two other variables is not exponentially increasing. It would be difficult to convey this structure in separate 2D plots because the contours would be messy. 3D plots can work well for smooth functional surfaces. Needless to say, 3D bar and pie graphics have no place in a scientific journal (Rangecroft, 2003).

There is considerable controversy over pseudo-3D (2.5D) and drop-shadow effects. Gurus tend to lampoon those who use it, saying it interferes with veridical perception:

- "My pet peeve is adding shading to figures."
- "Creating charts with drop shadows or pseudo 3D is a bad idea."
- "These gimmicks ruin the clarity of the chart."

The research record does not support this contention. Spence (1990, 2004) drew a distinction between *apparent* and *effective* dimensionality and found that properly drawn pseudo-3D bar charts (apparent dimensionality of 3D and effective dimensionality of 2D) do not impair processing. As with chartjunk, however, my opinion is to avoid these embellishments because they are aesthetically inappropriate for a scientific journal.

Avoid Visual Illusions

One reason to avoid 3D graphics is because the projections used to display them in 2D can lead to visual illusions. Black-and-white perspective projections lack texture and color depth cues and thus tend to flatten images. Isometric (axis–parallel) projections, used in front-top-side engineering drawings, are used

in some graphing software. These projections lead to illusions such as the Necker cube. Psychologists are well aware of this topic. Readers also can consult Coren and Girgus (1978) and Gregory (2009).

Limit Categories

When I designed the new graphics system in SPSS, I ran into trouble with the marketing department. The marketers insisted on placing no limit on the number of categories allowed in a legend. Against my advice, the programmers were forced to devise a multicolumn legend to accommodate larger numbers of categories. When they ran out of colors and textures, the programmers were forced to cycle through the same set more than once. I mentioned Miller's (1956) magic number seven but to no avail. In fact, the number of colors or textures or shapes easily processed in a graph is somewhat less than seven. There is a large literature relevant to this area. The aspects that determine processing involve Miller's estimate of working-memory chunking capacity, the discriminability of an ordered set of colors or shapes in the visual system, and the psychophysical power function for the stimulus dimension (color or shape). The relations are complex, but the result is simple: A graphic that uses many more than four categories of a color or shape is unlikely to be processed accurately.

If you need to represent a large number of categories, do not try to do it with symbols or colors. Instead consider using a position on an axis (sorted on a reasonable feature dimension) to order the categories (see Figure 4.13 for an example). If you have no choice but to represent categories in a scatterplot, consider aggregating categories into a manageable number. Wasting legend space on rarely occurring categories means that viewers will ignore them or be unable to locate them in the first place.

Transform

When I programmed the graphics system in SYSTAT, I made a simple rule for determining default frame limits: Set each axis range to an interval that encloses *all* values of the variable plotted. For example, imagine superimposing a scatterplot on top of a bar chart of the same variables. In SYSTAT, the default axis chosen for each plot is the same, so the points fall appropriately on top of the bars that summarize them.

I soon heard from a few users that they did not like this feature. Upon closer examination, I discovered that they were creating bar charts on the means of variables within groups and the tops of their bars fell near the bottom of the frame. They did not like seeing all the white space above the bars.

The left panel of Figure 4.4 shows what was happening. The plot shows the number of McDonald's restaurants in each of 57 countries as of 1990. I have superimposed the data to show where the means of the raw data (represented by the tops of the bars) fall. In effect, users making this type of plot are computing means on highly skewed distributions—not a good idea. As an alternative, the middle panel shows the graphic after a log transformation of the counts. Now the bars fall in the middle of the frame, and the means of the logs are a reasonable summary of the counts in each group. Correcting the statistics solves the aesthetic problem. In Wilkinson (2005), I discussed this problem in more detail, providing examples in which supposed outliers in a graph are not outliers when the data are appropriately transformed.

Interestingly, we usually use square-root counts (to symmetrize Poisson distributions). The highly skewed distribution of McDonald's restaurants responds better to logging. There is a remaining issue, however. Most people have difficulty comprehending the magnitudes of decimal logs. They fail to understand, for example, that a unit increase on the Richter scale indicates an earthquake with a tenfold increase in energy. Or, they do not realize that decibels increase by a factor of 10. For many, doublings are easier to understand. The right panel of Figure 4.4 shows the same plot computed on a base-two log scale. An added benefit is that base-two logs produce more tick marks, yielding a finer description of the distribution. Finally, the middle and right plots are identical except for the scale. This congruence highlights the fact that statistics (*t* tests, *F* tests, etc.) do not care which base we use for logs.

Sort

Sorting a categorical variable is an inescapable step toward creating a statistical graphic. It is inescapable because any ordering of categorical axis or legend implies a sort. Bertin (1967/1983) used numerous examples to show the value of simple and multivariate data sorts. Some gurus advise against sorting alphabetically. This is nonsense. Sorting alphabetically is meaningful if the organizing principle is alphabetical (words, names, brands, etc.) and viewers need to look up individual items rather than detect trends. In cases in which this is disputable, a good compromise is to panel two or more graphics with different sort orders on the same categories. Figure 4.5 contains two panels showing confusions among Morse Code signals using data in Rothkopf (1957).

There are several types of sorts relevant to graphics. A *lexical* sort uses a lexical ordering of strings ("0," "1," "10," "2," "3," "4," "5," "6," "7," "8," "9"). A *numerical* sort uses a numerical ordering ("0," "1," "2," "3," "4," "5," "6," "7," "8," "9," "10"). Most computer languages have a default lexical sort order, so users must take care when sorting categories denoted by numerals. A *nested* sort orders multiple variables (A, B within A, C within B within A). Nested sorts can use lexical or some other ordering. An example of a lexical nested sort for two variables is ({"Female," "Young"}, {"Male," "Old"}, {"Male," "Young"}).

A useful type of sort for graphics is to order categories by frequency or by some other numerical

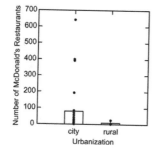
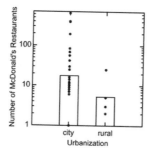
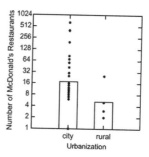

FIGURE 4.4. The effect of transformations on the height of bars. Data are based on the number of McDonald's restaurants in each of 57 countries as of 1990.

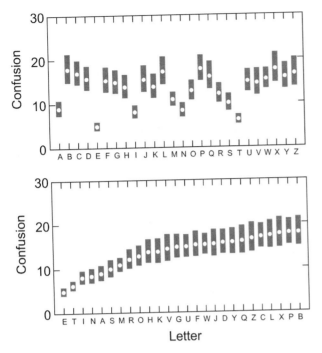

FIGURE 4.5. Confusions among Morse code signals using data in Rothkopf (1957).

variable. The classic example of this type of ordering is the so-called Pareto chart (Juran, 1951). Sorting benefits many types of multivariate graphics, including icons, parallel coordinate plots, and scatterplot matrixes (SPLOMs). There are many published papers in the informational visualization community on this topic (particularly IEEE InfoVis conference papers). Almost all of these papers use a simple ordering algorithm: Compute the principal components on a correlation matrix of the variables and order the variables according to their loadings on the first principal component. Alternatively, one can use MDS to determine a nonlinear seriation.

Orient

We are accustomed to seeing graphics in a canonical orientation (bottom–top, left–right). There are exceptions (e.g., Hebrew and Mandarin speakers), but the following simple rule should be followed in English language journals: Order categories from top to bottom and continua from bottom to top. This ordering is followed almost universally for tables (top to bottom, left to right) and for *XY* plots (bottom to top, left to right). The rare exceptions are notable for their obtuseness. For example, computer pixel displays index top to bottom and left to right;

this indexing scheme was devised to allow simple linear addressing of raster-scan frame buffers, but it has caused graphics programmers endless grief navigating from graphics world to display world. The mathematical transformation is trivial, but the mental transformation is counterintuitive.

Anchor

Graphics need an origin and other reference points to anchor absolute and comparative judgments. The origin of a graph frame is conventionally in the lower left corner (unless axes are crossed). For paneled graphics, the global origin is at the bottom left of all the panes, and local origins for each pane are at its bottom left. This overall structure allows panes to be nested within panes. Tufte (1983, 1990, 1997) called paneled graphics *small multiples*, but this is too flat a description. Paneled graphics are *nested tables* of graphics.

The *trellis* plot (Becker, Cleveland, & Shyu, 1996) is close to Tufte's idea. The visual distinction between a one-way layout and a multiway layout is embedded in the strip labels attached to the cells; a one-way table has one strip label per cell and multiway tables have more. Figure 4.6 compares this design to an alternative that is based on the classic ANOVA table. The two panels contain plots of the miles per gallon of selected cars versus their weights. The scatterplots are arranged in a two-way table of number of gears by number of cylinders. The top panel was produced using the trellis facility in the R Lattice package. The bottom panel was produced by SYSTAT. The strip labels in the trellis plot steal the plotting area from the scatterplots (forcing them to be nonsquare) and add complexity. The scales and tick labels are arranged in an alternating pattern around the trellis panel, making it difficult to decode values.

The SYSTAT panel, called a *multiplot*, employs a simple scheme for arranging axes. Tabular variables go on the left and top, just as they do in conventional table layouts. Continuous variables go on the right and bottom, with a smaller typeface to distinguish them from the tabular variables. The continuous variable axis labels are repeated to facilitate lookup; repetition also helps the viewer to see that these are not one big axis. I also made the tabular

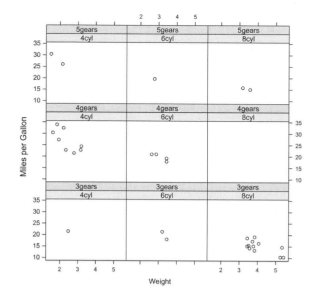

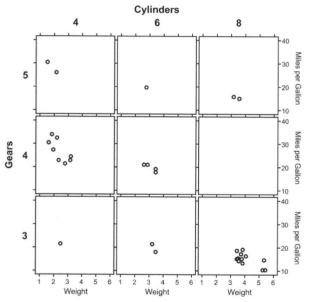

FIGURE 4.6. Trellis plot and multiplot for car data.

variables boldface to emphasize this distinction. This layout scheme allows us to display higher order factorials and nested designs that are not easily discernible in a trellis layout. Visually decoding the design is assisted by anchoring the factorial structure at the margins of the table, exactly the way ANOVA tables are conventionally arranged.

There are advantages to both displays. The trellis facilitates a bottom-up scan of its graphic contents; after a remarkable cell is located, the viewer discerns the values of the table (factor) variables by looking at the strip labels. The multiplot facilitates a top-

down scan; the viewer looks for trends across factors, and after locating simple or interaction effects, she examines individual cells for deviations from expected effects. The success of trellis indicates that different people have different scanning strategies. Overall, neither form can be considered superior for all purposes. I should mention that the SYSTAT design can be implemented in R with some custom programming. I urge R developers to produce a macro for this plot design so that psychologists can use R to make a display more in keeping with the customary ANOVA layout used in journals.

A second type of anchoring is important for decoding values in a frame. Figure 4.7 illustrates two ways of displaying tick marks on an axis. The panel on the left was produced by the default tick mark algorithm in R and does not include a full-width interval on either end of the scale. The panel on the right was produced by SYSTAT. The floating ticks in the left panel impair positional judgments because the frame cannot be used to anchor the scales at round numbers; positions of the elements have to be referenced against individual tick marks.

The motivation for floating ticks was the finding by Cleveland et al. (1982) that I discussed earlier. To keep the frame filled, the designers picked a frame size to minimize white space and then added tick marks wherever round values occur. By contrast, the ticking algorithm on the right panel draws a compromise between filling the frame and anchoring nice numbers at the corners. By enlarging the set of nice numbers for scale values, it is possible to fill the frame and anchor the corners at the same time. This algorithm is more consistent with tick spacing in graphics produced by psychologists, engineers, scientists, and mathematicians. The R project needs to fix this defect as soon as possible.

A third type of anchoring is facilitated by grid lines. As Tufte (1983, 1990, 1997) and others have argued, grid lines—especially dashed grid lines—can clutter a graphic. Carr (1994) developed a solution to this problem. Instead of drawing grid lines as black dashes against a white background, Carr drew white gridlines against a light gray frame background. Figure 4.8 shows an example. There is a bonus in this approach: Frames stand out from the rest of an article's text and white space. I would

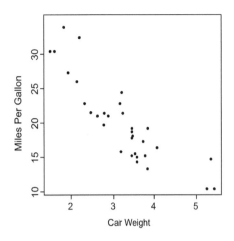

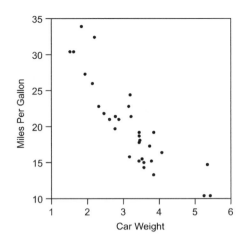

FIGURE 4.7.   Tick mark placement in R and SYSTAT.

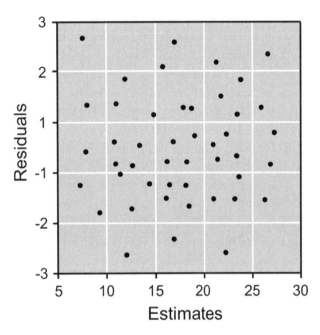

FIGURE 4.8.   Residual plot with gray background and white gridlines.

advocate a faint gray background as a default mode for published statistical graphics in the future, whether or not grid lines are used.

Annotate

Captions, titles, legends, and other annotations help make a graphic communicate a message without dependence on the article text. Authors need to keep in mind that readers will sometimes skip text (and even abstracts) and look at figures to decide whether to read in more detail. One detail that is often overlooked, however, involves legends. Computer programs routinely produce legends, but it is sometimes

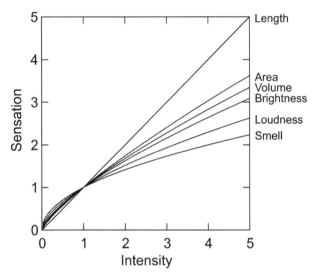

FIGURE 4.9.   Psychophysical power functions with annotation next to curves as an alternative to a legend.

better to annotate directly on graphic elements. Figure 4.9 shows an example. A conventional legend would distinguish each curve in this plot by using different types of dashed lines or lines of different colors. Much simpler and more easily decodable is to label each line with its own annotation, as in Figure 4.9. When there is room in a frame, try to consider this type of annotation rather than a separate legend, which forces scanning from two different locations.

EXEMPLARS

We now turn to examples for specific problems. This section is organized by type of model (univariate, multivariate) and type of variable (continuous, categorical). I discuss specific problems researchers encounter in graphing scientific data, such as huge data sets. As with other figures in this chapter, I include only what I regard as the best approach to the problem. It is easier to lampoon poorly designed graphics and harder to offer exemplars. When offering exemplars, however, I do not mean to imply that there are no examples that might be better.

One Variable

The simplest graphics involve only one variable. These graphics are often omitted in articles, perhaps because scientists want to get to models as quickly as possible. The distributions of variables affect models, however, so a well-documented article should provide a simple display of the data. For multivariate analyses, the one-dimensional plots in this section can be paneled in a space-conserving display.

Categorical variable. Figure 4.10 shows a simple display representing values on one categorical variable. The data are from 1,606 respondents to the 1993 General Social Survey (Davis, Smith, & Marsden, 1993). Respondents were asked, "How many sex partners have you had in the last 12 months?" Those reporting more than four partners (some reported up to 100) were consolidated into the last category. There were 1,466 responses in the resulting six categories.

This bar graphic is conventional and appropriate for these data. Bars are most suited for displaying either magnitudes referenced against zero (anchored bars, as in this figure) or a range of values on a continuous scale (range bars, as in Figure 4.12). I have omitted a bounding box from the frame of this plot; it is optional and not harmful. The plot might be improved by using a bounding box and gray background with white grid lines so that the heights of the bars are easier to assess.

Much has been made of the requirement that bars be anchored at zero. There is no canon law requiring this, but it is probably a good idea. If the data are not on a so-called absolute scale, it is probably better to consider a dot plot, as in Figure 4.13. If our goal is to represent counts or incomes or reaction times, however, a bar is a reasonable graphic element.

Suppose we want to represent the proportion of each subgroup in our total sample. Figure 4.11 shows how to do this: a pie chart. Gurus wax apoplectic over pie charts:

- "Pie charts are bad! They are ugly and provide the reader no visual assistance in comparing categories."

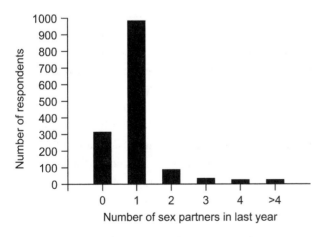

FIGURE 4.10. Bar graphic of data from the General Social Survey. The variable is the reported number of sexual partners in the past year.

FIGURE 4.11. Pie chart of the same data used in Figure 4.10, but displayed as proportions of total responses found within each category.

- "We all know that pie charts are bad."
- "Pie charts are hopeless."
- "Warning! Pie charts are generally not recommended for visualizing information!"

The scientific evidence to the contrary is unambiguous, however. Pie charts are better than bar charts for representing proportions of wholes (Simkin & Hastie, 1987; Spence 2005; Spence & Lewandowsky, 1991). The gurus' animosity toward pie charts may be based on pie charts' ubiquity and frequent abuses (3D pies, pies of means or medians). Unfortunately, gurus have been given a boost by Cleveland's hierarchy (see Figure 4.2). Gurus mistakenly assume that the perception of pie slices involves a judgment of angle, which is low on Cleveland's hierarchy. As the research shows, however, the process is more complex; both angle and area interact to overcome the bias of each. Gurus sometimes construct straw-man examples to show that a bar chart with nearly equal-height bars can reveal

slight differences that a pie chart with nearly equal-area slices conceals. This misses the point, however; comparative and absolute judgment are not the same thing; bars are good for one, pies for the other.

So, what are the real pitfalls in using pies? First of all, pie slices are usually colored. Unfortunately, colors, particularly bright colors, affect judgments of area. Coloring a slice red, for example, will tend to make the slice appear larger (Cleveland & McGill, 1983). I have ameliorated this bias in Figure 4.11 by choosing two alternating shades of light gray to increase the contrast between adjacent slices.

Second, pies are not good for representing many categories—whether sorted or unsorted—because the eye resolves tiny angles downward toward zero. In such a case, it is probably better to revert to a bar chart with a percentage scale, sorting the bars by percentage. Figure 4.12 shows the gold medal counts for various countries in the 2004 Summer Olympics. The data are sorted by proportions with a range-bar format originally from Juran (1951). This is a good substitute for a pie when there are many categories. Unlike a divided bar graph (which is really a pie chart in rectangular coordinates), this range-bar form allows one to see both the cumulative distribution and the contributions to the whole for each category.

My general advice on pies is this: Do not be bullied out of using a pie chart for proportion-of-whole data with a few categories. Cite the references I mentioned if an editor or reviewer argues with you.

There is another alternative to bars for categorical data: dot plots. Anchoring bars at zero can sacrifice resolution when no data values exist near zero; this creates tall bars of nearly equal height even when data vary significantly across bars (Chambers, Cleveland, Kleiner, & Tukey, 1983). Also, there are times when we need to display confidence intervals or standard errors. The bar chart with error bars, used in many scientific journals, is not a good way to handle the problem. Solid bars cover the lower half of error bars. Hollow bars allow us to see the error bars, but this type of graphic pairs a symmetric element (error bar) with an asymmetric element (anchored bar), in an awkward display.

Dots are preferable to bars in such cases. Figure 4.13 shows an example using the Olympic data. The

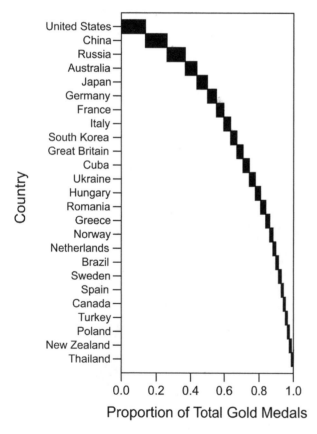

FIGURE 4.12.   Gold medal counts for various countries in the 2004 Summer Olympics.

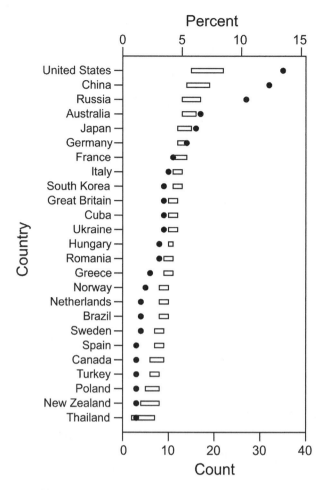

FIGURE 4.13. Modified Pareto chart of gold medal counts used in Figure 4.12. Bars are used to represent confidence intervals.

dots are sorted by frequency and confidence intervals are shown for each country using an algorithm in Wilkinson (2006).

Some users and computer programs apply line or area elements to categorical variables. Popular examples are line graphics of means in ANOVA, or area graphics of profiles across categories. These elements should generally be avoided with categorical data. Spacings between categories (even ordered categories) are not fixed, so slopes of line segments or profiles between categories are meaningless.

Continuous variable. Figure 4.14 shows five ways of representing a continuous variable. None of these is preferable to the other; each has a particular purpose. The data are per capita consumption of spirits for each of the 50 U.S. states (Bureau of the Census, 1986). The two graphics on the left are traditional

densities. On the top is a histogram. Histogram bars look like ordinary bars, but they measure areas rather than intervals, and they rest on a continuous scale rather than on a set of categories.

Most histogram programs and statistical textbooks produce incorrect or suboptimal histograms. The problems with them are as follows. (a) They use the wrong number of bars. The statistical literature provides clear guidelines on this, but they have been largely ignored by software developers (Scott, 1979; Wand, 1997). (b) They do not deal properly with integer or granular data. Instead of detecting granularity, programs tend to use a formula that is based on sample size for determining the number of bars. They should also be paying attention to the number of discrete values in the data. For much psychological data, where values fall on Likert scales, ordinary histogram programs are inadequate; users have to fiddle with sensitive parameters to get nice-looking histograms. (c) They do not locate bars at appropriate tick marks on the base scale. A primary purpose of a histogram is to assess the density of data within meaningful subregions of the range of a variable. If a computer program locates the limits of a bar at fractional values on a Likert-scale variable, this purpose is defeated. (d) They place tick marks in the middle of bars. This is nonsensical. Histogram bars partition a scale into intervals; tick marks need to demarcate these intervals by locating the endpoints.

The histogram in Figure 4.14 is a kernel density. In contrast to histograms in which we wish to inspect density within discrete intervals, we use a kernel density to estimate the shape of a population density. Silverman (1986) and Scott (1992) explained the details. Kernel densities overcome a serious flaw in histograms—they do not depend on a choice of cutpoints. If the intervals of a histogram are shifted to the left or right on the base scale, the shape of that histogram can change dramatically. Kernel densities *are* relatively sensitive to a parameter called *bandwidth* (analogous to the width of histogram bars), but there is well-understood statistical theory for dealing with this problem, and some simple guidelines that work quite well. Kernel density software generally uses these guidelines for its default settings.

The scale for the kernel density and the histogram are identical in Figure 4.13. That is not

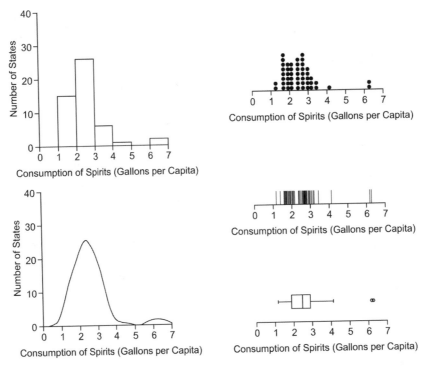

FIGURE 4.14. Five ways of representing a density. Data are per capita consumption of spirits for each of the 50 U.S. states.

coincidental. SYSTAT uses the histogram algorithm to determine the tick marks and scale for kernel densities and all other densities, including the ones on the right panels of Figure 4.13. This makes it easy to overlay densities, including mathematical densities such as the normal curve or chi-square. Constructing a density scale this way should be the default for any statistical graphics program.

Histograms are more useful than kernels when we are interested in displaying frequencies within intervals, especially when the intervals themselves are bounded by meaningful, round units. We see from the histogram in Figure 4.14 that 26 states have an average spirits consumption between 2 and 3 gallons a year. Kernels are more useful than histograms when we are looking for a smooth estimate of a continuous distribution. We see from the kernel density in Figure 4.14 that the distribution is bimodal, with a few states having extremely high consumption. We do notice that in the histogram as well but need to remember that other cutpoints and locations could mask that feature in a histogram. It is a well-known defect of the ordinary histogram that its shape changes when bar locations (centers of bars) are moved on the scale.

The densities on the right panel are useful for displaying distributions in less space. Each can be embedded in a Categorical × Continuous variable display, as in Figure 4.1. On the top right is a dot histogram (Wilkinson, 2005). This display represents each observation with a dot located at its scale value. If several values coincide on the scale, the dots are stacked vertically. This display is most suited for small samples, when each value is to be displayed. It is not well suited for large samples; consider a histogram or kernel density instead. Many programs for dot plots compute them incorrectly. They simply create a histogram and replace the bars with dots stacked to the heights of the bars. The whole point of a dot plot is to place each dot (or tower of dots) at the location given by its data value (or neighborhood value). Placing dots at the center of intervals defeats its purpose and makes the data appear granular instead of appropriately irregular.

The next lower graphic is a stripe plot (Chambers et al., 1983). A vertical stripe occurs at each data value. This display can handle more cases than the dot plot, although it is not suitable for large data sets.

The bottom graphic on the right of Figure 4.14 is a boxplot, or schematic plot (Tukey, 1977). As Tufte

(1983) noted, Tukey's plot is based on an earlier display that represented the quartiles of a distribution. In that earlier plot, the whiskers cover the range, and the box covers the midrange. Tukey improved on this design by scaling the whiskers to allow for outliers. The display in Figure 4.14 shows how important this feature can be. Two states (Nevada and New Hampshire) have unusually large values, possibly due to gambling and cheap liquor in one convenient location.

Recall that Figure 4.1 combines dot and boxplots in one frame. This combination is felicitous for small samples because the dots reveal bimodality and local features, whereas the boxes reveal the quartiles. This so-called dot–boxplot can be produced by a single command in SYSTAT or by overlaying multiple plots in a package such as R.

Two Variables

This section covers categorical and continuous variables in their various combinations. I will cover each combination in a separate subsection.

Categorical variables. Figure 4.15 shows five ways of representing two categorical variables crossed with each other. The data are from the 1993 General Social Survey (Davis et al., 1993) used in Figure 4.10. The additional variable is general happiness, as measured by the response to the question, "Taken all together, how would you say things are these days— would you say that you are very happy, pretty happy, or not too happy?"

The upper left plot shows a heatmap of happiness against number of sexual partners. The darkness scale represents the proportion of respondents within each happiness category. This plot is simply a table. In the lower panel of the figure is another table containing the actual cell counts. I have conditioned the darkness of the numerals on the row totals. This usage is potentially misleading unless the dependency on row totals is made clear in the caption. This is always an issue with displaying tables of percentages or proportions (of row, column, or total counts). I have provided this example to show that tables of numerals are in fact graphics. With modern publishing capabilities, we can use shading to represent the magnitude of residuals, probabilities, or other statistics.

The graphic at the top right is a mosaic plot (Friendly, 1994, 2002; Hartigan & Kleiner, 1981), a close relative of the treemap (Shneiderman, 1992). This graphic uses area to indicate the relative frequency of each category combination. As Cleveland's research and Figure 4.9 show, however, the judgment of area involves a psychometric function with an exponent considerably less than one. More problematic is the judgment of *rectangle* areas; there is a large literature in psychology showing that rectangle judgments are multidimensional. Mosaics are also potentially confusing because the rows and columns do not align as they do in an ordinary table. Despite the passionate following mosaics and treemaps have among some statistical computing and visualization experts, the rest of the world appears to find them confusing. When they are in color, as is the custom, the potential for confusion is even greater.

The graphic in the middle row of Figure 4.15 features confidence intervals on the percentages within each happiness group. There is no need to use area or brightness to represent additional variables. The correlation in partner patterns across the happiness levels is readily apparent. This plot also illustrates another point. Confidence intervals on proportions or percentages are asymmetric. There is no need to display the actual cell percent. The intervals keep our eyes from focusing on points and encourages us to think of ranges. I have argued elsewhere that confidence intervals should be primary and point estimates secondary in many statistical summaries (Wilkinson & Task Force on Statistical Inference, 1999).

The bottom panel shows a multiple divided bar chart. This layout has the same problems as the single divided bar chart, which is worse than the pie chart for most applications. It is a popular display, but I do not recommend it.

Continuous variables. Figure 4.16 shows the usual way of representing two continuous variables crossed with each other: the scatterplot. The data are per capita consumption of spirits for each of the 50 U.S. states, which were used in Figure 4.14 (Bureau of the Census, 1986). The additional variable is number of deaths from chronic liver disease and cirrhosis per 100,000 people by state. I have enhanced

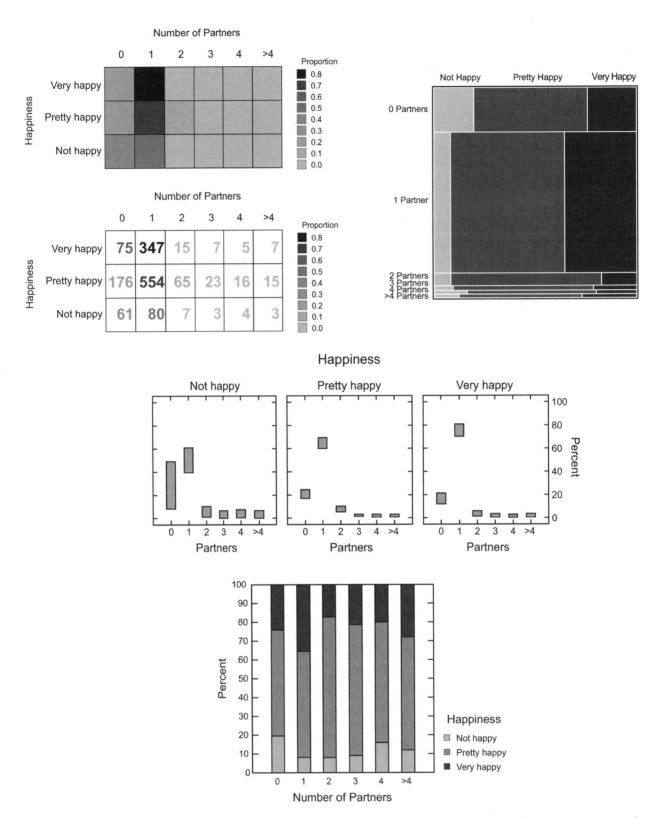

FIGURE 4.15.   Five ways to represent the crossing of two categorical variables. The data are from the 1993 General Social Survey used in Figure 4.10. The additional variable is general happiness, as measured by the response to the question, "Taken all together, how would you say things are these days—would you say that you are very happy, pretty happy, or not too happy?"

this scatterplot in a number of ways. The bordering boxplots help us to assess the marginal distributions of the variables and highlight the Nevada and New Hampshire outliers; there are outliers for consumption but not for deaths. The smoother shows the conditional mode of deaths (estimated mode of deaths given consumption). This was computed through kernel regression (Scott, 1992). This smoother limits itself to areas that have a concentration of points, so it provides a conservative estimate of trend. We can see a suggestion of a positive relationship between aggregate consumption and deaths.

Time-series data require special treatment. Figure 4.17 shows four examples. The data are numbers of U.S. patents issued in the century from 1880 to 1980 (Wilkinson, Blank, & Gruber, 1996). The top panel shows a line element. Lines are most useful when a series is relatively smooth. The next panel shows a point element with a superimposed *loess* smooth (Cleveland & Devlin, 1988). Points are best when supplemented with a smoother; they tend to obscure time order if used alone, unless the series is especially smooth. The third panel contains spikes. These are vertical lines used to reveal deviation from a constant

level. Here they are used to display the residuals from the loess smooth. The lowest panel shows an area chart for the raw series. This highlights trend but prevents the use of confidence intervals and other enhancements to the plot. Cleveland's (1994) landmark book discussed other graphic representations for time-series data and is still the best reference for learning how to plot time series.

Figure 4.18 shows four ways of representing a categorical variable crossed with a continuous variable. The data are based on 80 graduate students over a 10-year period in a U.S. psychology department (Wilkinson, 2005). Graduate Record Examination Advanced Psychology Test scores are plotted against whether the students eventually received their doctorate.

The upper left graphic employs a dot for the mean and a range bar to represent a 95% confidence interval on the mean. The bars do not overlap, which suggests that the advanced test can identify

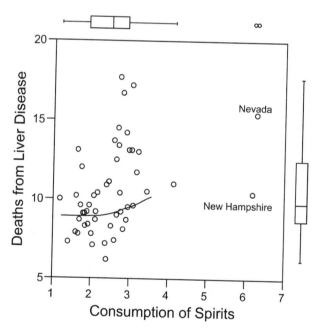

FIGURE 4.16.   Scatterplot with bordered boxplots. The data are per capita consumption of spirits for each of the 50 U.S. states, used in Figure 4.14. The additional variable is number of deaths from chronic liver disease and cirrhosis per 100,000 people by state.

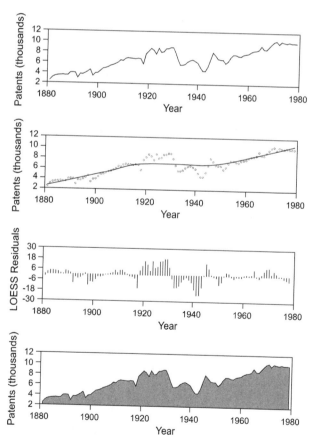

FIGURE 4.17.   Four types of display of time series. The data are numbers of U.S. patents issued in the century from 1880 to 1980.

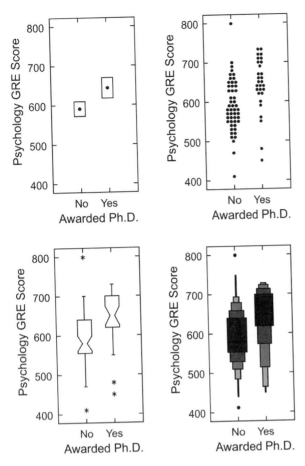

FIGURE 4.18. Four ways of representing a categorical variable crossed with a continuous variable. The data are based on 80 graduate students over a 10-year period in a U.S. psychology department. Graduate Record Examination Advanced Psychology Test scores are plotted against whether the students eventually received their doctorate.

those who achieve a doctorate. (Interestingly, neither the verbal nor quantitative test scores predicted graduation in this sample.)

The lower left graphic is a notched boxplot (McGill, Tukey, & Larsen, 1978). This variation on the boxplot not only conveys more of the important data landmarks than the classic confidence interval plot but also provides an approximate confidence interval of its own. If the data are independent samples from identically distributed populations that are lumpy in the middle (approximately normal in their interquartile range), then comparing the notches yields an approximate 95 percent test of the null hypothesis that the true medians in the population are equal. In this example, the notches do not overlap, reinforcing what we concluded from the

confidence intervals on the means. Because it relies on the median instead of the mean, the notched boxplot procedure is more robust against outliers. Note also that the boxplot highlights outliers in both groups. The other two types of display do not.

The lower right graphic is a letter-value boxplot (Hofmann, Kafadar, & Wickham, 2006). This is a variation on the boxplot that uses more of the letter values (successive splits of the data batch). The boxplot uses two letter values (*median* and *hinge*), whereas this plot uses many more. The letter-value boxplot is useful for large samples, in cases in which there is more information to be mined in the tails of the distribution.

The upper right graphic is a dot plot (Wilkinson, 1999). Used frequently in the medical literature, this plot shows every data point. In a small sample (e.g., clinical case study), a dot plot can be useful for readers who wish to consider every data value. It is of little use in making graphic inferences on group differences, however. It is best to think of dot plots as one-dimensional scatterplots.

Three Variables

Figure 4.19 shows a triple crossing of categorical variables. The data are from the 1993 General Social Survey (Davis et al., 1993) used in Figure 4.3 and Figure 4.5. The additional variable is gender (observed by the interviewer, not reported by the respondent). We ask whether the relationship between reported happiness and number of sexual partners differs by gender.

The top plot in the figure shows a paneled graphic. The format is similar to a trellis display (Becker et al., 1996), but the labeling of the paneling variables (happiness and gender) is placed outside the plotting area to improve readability.

The middle plot collapses happiness into a legend to reduce the number of panels. This is a popular method for saving space, particularly when representing factorial layouts in ANOVA and other designs. It is a favorite of statistical computer programs as well, but it has several problems. First, the line segments used to highlight trends have slopes that depend on the particular spacing and arrangement of partner categories. Unless we employ an external scaling procedure to determine the spacing of the partners

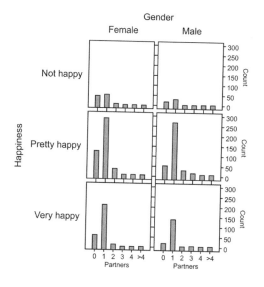

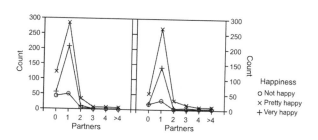

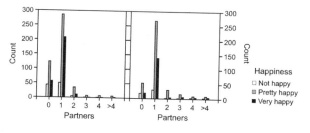

FIGURE 4.19. Different ways to handle a triple crossing of categorical variables. The data are from the 1993 General Social Survey used in Figure 4.3 and Figure 4.5. The additional variable is gender.

categories, we have scant justification for using these lines. Second, the collapsing introduces a symbol choice problem. It is difficult to find symbols that are easily distinguishable for more than a few categories. The symbols collide, as well, at the upper end of the horizontal scales. Using different types of dashed lines does not ameliorate the problem; we have the same dearth of choices as for symbols.

The bottom plot introduces an even less attractive alternative. Clustered bar charts are used widely, but they have several defects. First, it is difficult to discern separate patterns for the categories. One needs

to focus on one set of bars to do this, but there is visual interference from the other bars in each cluster. Second, these bars can become quite thin with more than a few categories. Decoding this graphic is problematic. Some programs do this type of interleaving for multiple-group histograms. That practice is even worse, however, because densities are misleadingly segmented. A graphic using back-to-back histograms or bars (as in an age–sex pyramid) is useful for two categories, but it is not easily extended to more.

Three continuous variables usually force us into 3D (see Figure 4.3), but we have alternatives. One alternative is to contour. Figure 4.20 shows a graphic of death rates against birth rates per 100,000 population for 27 selected countries in a 1990 United Nations data bank (Wilkinson, 1999). The third dimension is the kernel density estimate. The plot reveals two concentrations of countries. Industrial countries, to the left, have relatively low death rates and moderate birth rates. Developing countries, toward the upper right, have high death rates and extraordinarily high birth rates. The curve in the middle of the contours (a loess smooth) shows that the overall relation between death and birth rates is curvilinear. This is one of my favorite data sets because it elicits thinking about several issues: (a) the proper scaling of the axes (a 2-to-1 aspect ratio because of the common rate scale), (b) the need for a nonlinear smoother (linear regression would be inappropriate for this distribution), (c) the use of annotation (the zero population growth line divides the frame into two meaningful regions), and (d) the use of contours (the kernel density estimate highlights the nonnormality of the joint distribution and emphasizes the bimodal clusters). Plotting this data set with default values in the typical statistical package would generate visual nonsense.

Many Variables

There is no single effective way to display many variables, but there are several methods, including projection and paneling, that work fairly well. Some of the best methods are the simplest, including the examples in this section. One relatively simple approach is to project from higher dimensional space into a 2D space via principal components or

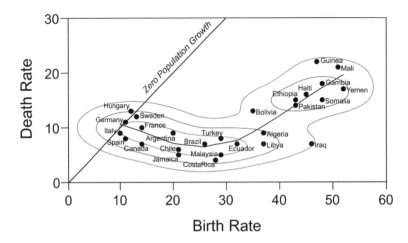

FIGURE 4.20. Plot of death rates against birth rates per 100,000 population for 27 selected countries in a 1990 United Nations data bank. Contours represent level curves of a kernel density.

multidimensional scaling. Psychologists have done this for decades, when they graph the first two dimensions of a factor or components analysis.

One paneling method, invented by Hartigan (1975), has many uses. Figure 4.21 shows a scatterplot matrix (SPLOM) of five continuous and categorical variables. The data are from Chartrand (1997), based on a national survey of attitudes toward psychological counseling. There were 3035 respondents to the survey. The variables in the SPLOM are age, gender, income, number of children, and number of years with one's partner in a current relationship.

This SPLOM pairs every variable against every other. Usually, SPLOMs are symmetric like this one, so only half of the panels are displayed. Rectangular SPLOMs plot one set of variables against another. Scales are usually unnecessary because the display is intended to show joint distributions rather than specific values. This is especially true when more than a few variables are displayed.

SPLOMs usually involve only continuous variables. This example shows why this limitation is unnecessary. By using dot plots on the diagonals and scatterplots off the diagonals, we are able to discern the distributions of categories as well as continua. We see several anomalies, including the single value at the bottom of the children-age panel and the group of extreme values (missing value codes) at the high end of the age scale. One anomaly is more subtle, but the graphic leads us to it. The

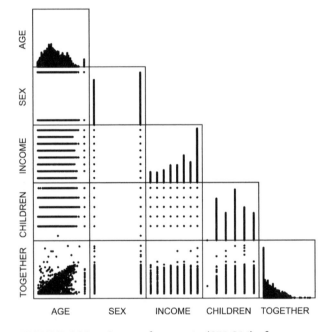

FIGURE 4.21. Scatterplot matrix (SPLOM) of survey data from Chartrand (1997) measuring attitudes toward psychological counseling.

together-age plot at the lower left corner has an unusual shape.

A clean triangular bivariate distribution like this suggests a logical implication. In this case, we would expect the reported duration of a relationship to be less than the age of the respondent. There appear to be some respondents above the main diagonal in this panel who are ghosts or, alternatively, have made a serious error in judging their age or the duration of their relationship (assuming both scales are the same). This curiosity was not detected in the preliminary data cleaning performed by the polling organization. Sometimes we need graphic methods to reveal anomalies.

Sometimes, also, we need different coordinate systems to represent a table and reveal graphic patterns. *The Grammar of Graphics* (Wilkinson, 2005) includes examples of tables in various coordinate systems in the chapter "Coordinates" and in the chapter "Facets." In those chapters, I have shown why Tufte's small multiples terminology is too limited. I use the term *facets* to indicate that a table is formally a product of sets (an idea borrowed from Louis Guttman). The layout of a table can be performed in rectangular, polar, or other coordinate systems. Figure 4.22 provides an example. There are two facets in this graphic—the month of the year and the compass orientation. Each is intrinsically circular, so the display naturally requires a nested polar layout. The elements inside the circular frames are histograms of wind direction (sometimes called *wind roses*) in a 24-hour period. A similar table might be used to represent circadian rhythms in an organism over a single year or a circumplex nested within a circumplex (Wiggins, 1982).

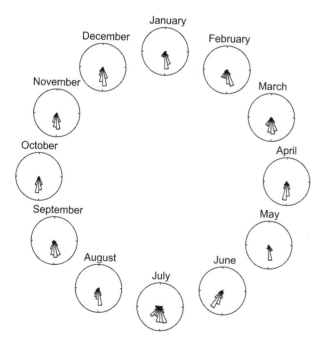

FIGURE 4.22. Circular plot of wind roses from geophysical data.

Nonrectangular Data Sets

I have covered rectangular data sets (cases by variables) in all the examples so far. Recently, there has been an explosion of interest in other forms of data. This trend has been facilitated by computer programs designed to analyze social network, text, weblink, and other relational data. Some of the most beautiful examples of network graphics have been produced in Katy Börner's lab at Indiana University (http://ella.slis.indiana.edu/ katy/gallery/index. html), Tamara Munzner's lab at the University of British Columbia (http://www.cs.ubc.ca/ tmm/ papers.html), Stephen North's lab at AT&T Research (http://www.research.att.com/people/ North_Stephen_C), the Marcotte LGL project at the University of Texas–Austin (http://lgl.sourceforge. net/#gallery), the Tree of Life project at Berkeley (http://ucjeps.berkeley.edu/TreeofLife), and Graham Wills's group at IBM (http://www.willsfamily.org/ gwills/index.html).

The algorithms used to lay out vertex-edge graphs are largely ad hoc. The most widely used ones are based on a derivation of the multidimensional scaling (MDS) algorithm, invented by psychologists in the 1960s and reinvented by engineers 25 years later. The so-called *force-directed* (Fruchterman & Reingold, 1991) or *springs* (Kamada & Kawai, 1989) methods have well-known drawbacks, but they are widely available in open-source software and frequently produce attractive results. As Newman (2003) noted, however, "We have no special reason to suppose that this very simple algorithm would reveal anything particularly useful about the network" (p. 17).

Graph layouts are often cluttered, with edges and nodes filling the display frame. The result is often described as a *hairball*. An alternative approach is to use MDS directly and display only nodes. Figure 4.23 presents a *word cloud* of the top 50 words in *Moby Dick*. I filtered stop words (*a, the, and, . . .*) from the text and computed a node-edge graph of the 50 most frequent words. Edges in this graph were assigned to any pair of words if both occurred within a sliding window (*n*-gram) of seven words. From this graph, I computed a 50 × 50 matrix of the pairwise geodesic distances (shortest paths through the *n*-gram graph) between words.

I computed the MDS on this geodesic distance matrix. In Figure 4.23, the sizes of the words are proportional to their frequency in the novel. To display more than 50 words, one can use transparency to keep words from obscuring other words.

Until recently, there have been few ways to visualize relations between sets of objects. The Venn diagram is more than a century old, but computing one on sets of real data has been problematic. Recently, I developed a statistical method for fitting Venn and Euler (more than three sets) diagrams (Wilkinson, in press). A package for producing them, called venneuler(), is available in R (CRAN). Figure 4.24 shows a Venn diagram of the shared words in *Ulysses*, *Moby Dick*, and the King James translation of the Bible. The sizes of the circles are proportional to the number of unique words (omitting stop words) in each book. The algorithm devised to fit this model is similar to MDS, but it is designed on the basis of the areas of $2n$ possible circle intersections rather than the distances between $n(n-1)/2$ objects. This algorithm has applications in psychology and bioinformatics. For example, it can be used to fit a Venn–Euler diagram to the correlation matrix of regression coefficient estimates in linear or logistic regression to reveal multicolinearity—a common textbook example (Cohen, Cohen, West, & Aiken, 2003).

Uncertainty

There are two chief methods for representing error in a graphic. The first is sharp: Error bounds are represented by clear edges, points, or lines. The second is fuzzy: Error is represented by blurring an estimate. Figure 4.25 shows a conventional sharp way of representing error in a graphic. The data are from the 1993 General Social Survey (Davis et al., 1993) used in Figure 4.3. The additional variable is feelings about the Bible, as measured by the response to the question, "Which of these statements comes closest to describing your feelings about the Bible?" The responses coded are 1 (Word of God), 2 (Inspired Word), and 3 (Book of Fables). We assume that the dependent variable is continuous (biblical absolutism vs. relativism) even though the responses are integers.

The upper plot shows error bars representing 95% confidence intervals on the means by category. Error bars are also used to represent 1 standard deviation or 1 standard error. It is important to

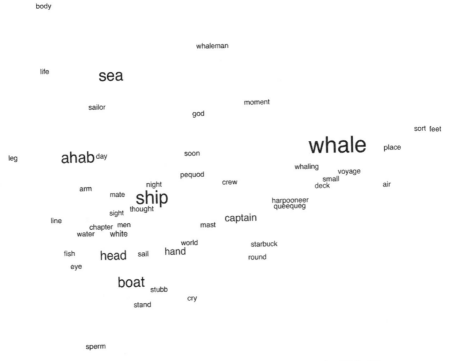

FIGURE 4.23. Multidimensional scaling of words from *Moby Dick*. Distances were computed from cooccurrences in a seven-word window moving through the text.

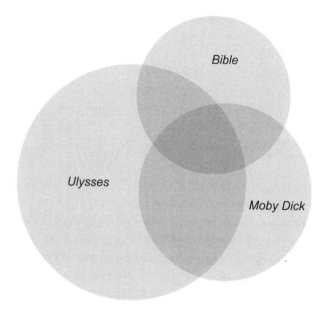

FIGURE 4.24. Venn diagram of shared words in three different books—James Joyce's *Ulysses*, the King James translation of the Bible, and *Moby Dick*. Size of circles is proportional to count of unique words in each work.

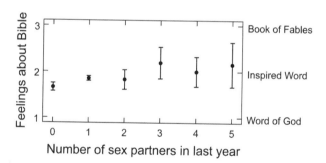

FIGURE 4.25. Plot of 95% confidence intervals. The data are from the 1993 General Social Survey used in Figure 4.3. The additional variable is feelings about the Bible, as measured by the response to the question, "Which of these statements comes closest to describing your feelings about the Bible?" The responses coded are 1 (Word of God), 2 (inspired word), and 3 (book of fables).

make clear in accompanying titles or notes which type is used.

Figure 4.26 shows one way to represent error by fuzziness. The data are from Gonnelli et al. (1996). They represent concentration of bone alkaline phosphatase (BAP) in a sample of women of different ages. The authors fit a linear regression (shown in the upper left panel) to argue that BAP levels increase with age.

A modal regression in the upper right panel indicates that there is a discontinuity in this relationship

at age 45 or so, corresponding most likely to the onset of menopause. Accordingly, I fit separate linear regressions to the two subgroups split at age 45 (third panel). These regressions appear to be sensitive to outliers, however, so I fit linear models using robust regression with t weighting (fourth panel). This fit indicates that a plausible model for predicting BAP from age involves level differences but no slope differences.

It is not easy to compute confidence intervals on the robust linear fits, so I resorted to bootstrapping to provide an estimate of error. The bottom panel shows the result of 20 bootstrap robust fits displayed as faint dashed lines. The nonoverlapping envelopes of the fits indicate that the level-change model is reasonable. I show many more examples of representing error in the chapter called "Uncertainty" in *The Grammar of Graphics* (Wilkinson, 2005).

SOFTWARE

The graphic software field changes so rapidly that I will not provide published references to packages. To learn more about them, search for the names of these packages on Google or Bing.

Programming Systems

Sophisticated graphics require programming systems. The best programmable graphics systems are SAS, SPSS, SYSTAT, Stata, R, and Python Graphics. The last two open-source packages are free. Some of these packages have menus for drawing graphics, but one must use their scripting capabilities to produce many of the graphics in this article. The R system is growing more rapidly in this area than the others. The R Lattice package is needed for trellises. Wickham (2009) has produced an R package, based on *The Grammar of Graphics* (Wilkinson, 2005), called ggplot2. This package greatly simplifies the production of tabular and complex graphics. The graphics in this chapter were produced using SYSTAT and A Second Opinion (an analytic and graphics program I wrote in Java).

For Java programmers, Prefuse is a library of graphing classes that can be used to do a wide range of visualizations (http://prefuse.org). Its author, Jeffrey Heer, has teamed with another developer at Stanford, Mike Bostock, to build another system

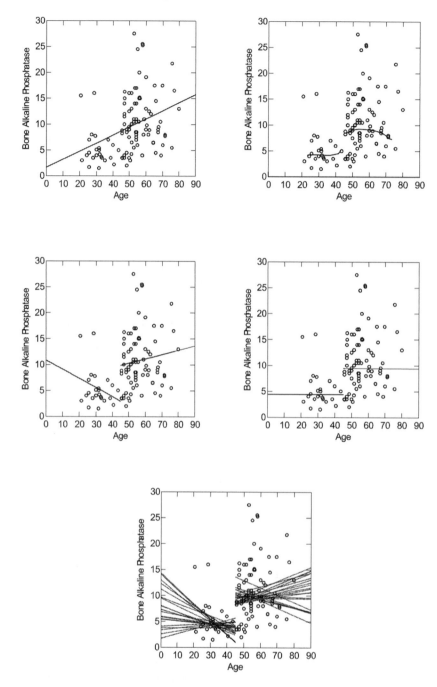

FIGURE 4.26. Using fuzziness to depict error. The data are from Gonnelli et al. (1996). They represent concentration of bone alkaline phosphatase in a sample of women of different ages.

called Protovis (http://mbostock.github.com/protovis). This system, based on *The Grammar of Graphics* (Wilkinson, 2005), facilitates the development of web-based visualizations in Javascript.

Menu Systems

The best menu-driven graphics systems for producing the type of graphics featured in this chapter are SigmaPlot and Origin. Tableau Software offers a menu-driven business graphing system. Because its architecture is based on *The Grammar of Graphics* (Wilkinson, 2005), it is capable of producing an enormous number of different graphics, including many in this article. Some of the most significant people in the visualization field, such as Pat Hanrahan and Jock Mackinlay, are involved with Tableau.

PRODUCTION

For layout and final production of graphics files, I recommend Adobe Illustrator. I have used it for some minor editing of the graphics in this chapter. There have been other editing packages that are easier to use, but they have gone out of business, unfortunately. The primary advantage of Illustrator is its graphics file processing capability. Adobe is one of the few, if only, programs that can handle transparency in encapsulated postscript files (EPS). Because Adobe is the originator of PDF and EPS files, it maintains control over file standards. In my experience, Illustrator handles different variants of Windows metafiles (WMF) and extended Windows metafiles (EMF) more flexibly than Microsoft's own applications.

All of the graphics files for this chapter were printed from vector (as opposed to bitmap) files. Vector files are resolution independent, so they can be typeset at the highest resolution of printers' Linotronic machines (more than 2,500 dots per inch). I used EPS, but some publishers have switched to PDF for graphics files because it is more portable and supports transparency. Web publishers are increasingly turning to another vector format, scalable vector graphics (SVG), because those files can be printed or displayed on the web at maximum resolution.

Never use bitmap file formats such as TIFF, PNG, JPEG, GIF, PCT, or BMP for production publishing. Doing so will make your typefaces and graphics look like you photocopied them through a screen door. If you try to make the resolution of bitmap files fine enough for hard-copy publication, they will balloon into tens of megabytes for each graphic, even after file compression.

For typesetting, I recommend learning LaTeX if a journal allows it. LaTeX is free and supports indexing, citations, bibliographies, and cross-referencing—all things that are difficult to do in Word or other word processors. For APA publications, use Microsoft Word. I used Open Office (Neo Office on the Macintosh) to process the original manuscript.

References

Backs, R. W., & Walrath, L. C. (1995). Ocular measures of redundancy gain during visual search of colour symbolic displays. *Ergonomics, 38,* 1831–1840. doi:10.1080/00140139508925230

Becker, R. A., Cleveland, W. S., & Shyu, M.-J. (1996). The design and control of trellis display. *Journal of Computational and Graphical Statistics, 5,* 123–155. doi:10.2307/1390777

Beniger, J. R., & Robyn, D. L. (1978). Quantitative graphics in statistics: A brief history. *The American Statistician, 32,* 1–11. doi:10.2307/2683467

Bertin, J. (1981). *Graphics and graphic information–processing* (W. J. Berg & P. Scott, Trans.). New York, NY: Walter de Gruyter.

Bertin, J. (1983). *Semiologie graphique* [Semiology of graphics] (W. J. Berg & H. Wainer, Trans.). Madison: University of Wisconsin Press. (Original work published 1967)

Best, L. A., Smith, L. D., & Stubbs, A. (2001). Graph use in psychology and other sciences. *Behavioural Processes, 54,* 155–165. doi:10.1016/S0376-6357(01)00156-5

Bureau of the Census. (1986). *State and metropolitan area data book.* Washington, DC: U.S. Government Printing Office.

Carr, D. B. (1994). Using gray in plots. *Statistical Computing and Statistical Graphics Newsletter, 5,* 11–14.

Carswell, C. M. (1992). Choosing specifiers: An evaluation of the basic tasks model of graphical perception. *Human Factors, 34,* 535–554.

Chambers, J. M., Cleveland, W. S., Kleiner, B., & Tukey, P. A. (1983). *Graphical methods for data analysis.* Monterey, CA: Wadsworth.

Chartrand, J. M. (1997). *National sample survey.* Unpublished raw data.

Cleveland, W. S. (1984). Graphs in scientific publications. *The American Statistician, 38,* 261–269. doi:10.2307/2683400

Cleveland, W. S. (1993). A model for studying display methods of statistical graphics (with discussion). *Journal of Computational and Graphical Statistics, 2,* 323–343. doi:10.2307/1390686

Cleveland, W. S. (1994). *The elements of graphing data* (Rev. ed.). Summit, NJ: Hobart Press.

Cleveland, W. S. (1995). *Visualizing data.* Summit, NJ: Hobart Press.

Cleveland, W. S., & Devlin, S. (1988). Locally weighted regression analysis by local fitting. *Journal of the American Statistical Association, 83,* 596–640. doi:10.2307/2289282

Cleveland, W. S., Diaconis, P., & McGill, R. (1982). Variables on scatterplots look more highly correlated when the scales are increased. *Science, 216,* 1138–1141. doi:10.1126/science.216.4550.1138

Cleveland, W. S., & McGill, R. (1983). A color-caused optical illusion on a statistical graph. *The American Statistician, 37*, 101–105. doi:10.2307/2685868

Cleveland, W. S., & McGill, R. (1984). Graphical perception: Theory, experimentation, and application to the development of graphical methods. *Journal of the American Statistical Association, 79*, 531–554. doi:10.2307/2288400

Cohen, J., Cohen, P., West, S., & Aiken, L. S. (2003). *Applied multiple regression/correlation analysis for the behavioral sciences.* Hillsdale, NJ: Erlbaum.

Collins, B. M. (1993). Data visualization: Has it all been seen before? In R. A. Earnshaw & D. Watson (Eds.), *Animation and scientific visualization: Tools and applications* (pp. 3–28). New York, NY: Academic Press.

Coren, S., & Girgus, J. S. (1978). *Seeing is deceiving: The psychology of visual illusions.* Hillsdale, NJ: Erlbaum.

Davis, J. A., Smith, T. W., & Marsden, P. V. (1993). *The general social survey.* Chicago, IL: National Opinion Research Center.

Doherty, M. E., & Anderson, R. B. (2009). Variation in scatterplot displays. *Behavior Research Methods, 41*, 55–60. doi:10.3758/BRM.41.1.55

Few, S. (2009). *Now you see it: Simple visualization techniques for quantitative analysis.* Oakland, CA: Analytics Press.

Fienberg, S. (1979). Graphical methods in statistics. *The American Statistician, 33*, 165–178. doi:10.2307/2683729

Friendly, M. (1994). Mosaic displays for n-way contingency tables. *Journal of the American Statistical Association, 89*, 190–200. doi:10.2307/2291215

Friendly, M. (2002). A brief history of the mosaic display. *Journal of Computational and Graphical Statistics, 11*, 89–107. doi:10.1198/106186002317375631

Fruchterman, T. M. J., & Reingold, E. M. (1991). Graph Drawing by Force-Directed Placement. *Software, Practice and Experience, 21*, 1129–1164. doi:10.1002/spe.4380211102

Funkhouser, H. G. (1937). Historical development of the graphical representation of statistical data. *Osiris, 3*, 269–404. doi:10.1086/368480

Garner, W. R. (1981). The analysis of unanalyzed perceptions. In M. Kubovy & J. R. Pomerantz (Eds.), *Perceptual organization* (pp. 119–139). Hillsdale, NJ: Erlbaum.

Gillan, D. J., & Richman, E. H. (1994). Minimalism and the syntax of graphs. *Human Factors, 36*, 619–644.

Gillan, D. J., & Sorensen, D. (2009). Effects of graph backgrounds on visual search. In *Proceedings of the HFES 53rd Annual Meeting* (pp. 1096–1100). Santa Monica, CA: Human Factors and Ergonomics Society.

Gonnelli, S., Cepollaro, C., Montagnani, A., Monaci, G., Campagna, M. S., Franci, M. B., & Gennari, C. (1996). Bone alkaline phosphatase measured with a new immunoradiometric assay in patients with metabolic bone diseases. *European Journal of Clinical Investigation, 26*, 391–396. doi:10.1046/j.1365-2362.1996.142304.x

Gregory, R. L. (2009). *Seeing through illusions.* Oxford, England: Oxford University Press.

Hartigan, J. A. (1975). Printer graphics for clustering. *Journal of Statistical Computation and Simulation, 4*, 187–213. doi:10.1080/00949657508810123

Hartigan, J. A., & Kleiner, B. (1981). Mosaics for contingency tables. In K. W. Heiner, R. S. Sacher, & J. W. Wilkinson (Eds.), *Computer science and statistics: Proceedings of the 13th Symposium on the Interface* (pp. 268–273). New York, NY: Springer-Verlag.

Heiser, J. Tversky, B., Agrawala, M., & Hanrahan, P. (2003). Cognitive design principles for visualizations: Revealing and instantiating. In R. Alterman & D. Kirsh (Eds.), *Proceedings of the Cognitive Science Society Meetings* (pp. 545–550). Boston, MA: Cognitive Science Society.

Herdeg, W. (1981). *Graphis diagrams: The graphic visualization of abstract data.* Zurich, Switzerland: Graphis Press.

Hofmann, H., Kafadar, K., & Wickham, H. (2006). *Letter-value box plots—Adjusting box plots for large data sets.* Iowa City: Department of Statistics, Iowa State University.

Holmes, N. (1991). *Designer's guide to creating charts and diagrams.* New York, NY: Watson-Guptill.

Huff, D. (1954). *How to lie with statistics.* New York, NY: Norton.

Inbar, O., Tractinsky, N., & Meyer, J. (2007). Minimalism in information visualization: Attitudes towards maximizing the data-ink ratio. In *Proceedings of the 14th European Conference on Cognitive Ergonomics* (pp. 185–188). New York, NY: ACM Press.

Juran, J. M. (1951). The economics of quality. In J. M. Juran (Ed.), *Quality control handbook* (pp. 1–41). New York, NY: McGraw-Hill.

Kamada, T., & Kawai, S. (1989). An algorithm for drawing general undirected graphs. *Information Processing Letters, 31*, 7–15. doi:10.1016/0020-0190(89)90102-6

Klippel, A., Knuf, L., Hommel, B., & Freksa, C. (2004). Perceptually induced distortions in cognitive maps. In C. Freksa, M. Knauff, B. Krieg-Brückner, B. Nebel, & T. Barkowsky (Eds.), *Spatial cognition* (pp. 204–213). Berlin, Germany: Springer-Verlag.

Kosslyn, S. M. (1994). *Elements of graph design.* New York, NY: Freeman.

Lewandowsky, S. (1999). Statistical graphs and maps: Higher level cognitive processes. In M. G. Sirken, D. J. Herrmann, S. Schechter, N. Schwarz, J. M. Tanur, & R. Tourangeau (Eds.), *Cognition and survey research* (pp. 349–362). New York, NY: Wiley.

Lewandowsky, S., & Spence, I. (1989). The perception of statistical graphs. *Sociological Methods and Research, 18,* 200–242. doi:10.1177/0049124189018002002

McGill, R., Tukey, J. W., & Larsen, W. A. (1978). Variations of box plots. *The American Statistician, 32,* 12–16. doi:10.2307/2683468

McNamara, T. P., Ratcliff, R., & McKoon, G. (1984). The mental representation of knowledge acquired from maps. *Journal of Experimental Psychology: Learning, Memory, and Cognition, 10,* 723–732. doi:10.1037/0278-7393.10.4.723

Miller, G. A. (1956). The magical number seven, plus or minus two: Some limits on our capacity for processing information. *Psychological Review, 63,* 81–97. doi:10.1037/h0043158

Monmonier, M. (1996). *How to lie with maps.* Chicago, IL: University of Chicago Press.

Newman, M. E. J. (2003). The structure and function of complex networks. *SIAM Review, 45,* 167–256. doi:10.1137/S003614450342480

Norman, D. A. (2007). Simplicity is highly overrated. *Interaction, 14,* 40–41. doi:10.1145/1229863.1229885

Pinker, S. (1997). *How the mind works.* New York, NY: Norton.

Playfair, W. (2005). *The commercial and political atlas and statistical breviary.* H. Wainer & I. Spence (Eds.). Cambridge, England: Cambridge University Press. (Original work published 1786)

Rangecroft, M. (2003). As easy as pie. *Behaviour and Information Technology, 22,* 421–426. doi:10.1080/01 449290310001615437

Robbins, N. B. (2005). *Creating more effective graphs.* Hoboken, NJ: Wiley.

Rothkopf, E. Z. (1957). A measure of stimulus similarity and errors in some paired associate learning tasks. *Journal of Experimental Psychology, 53,* 94–101. doi:10.1037/h0041867

Scott, D. W. (1979). On optimal and data-based histograms. *Biometrika, 66,* 605–610. doi:10.1093/biomet/66.3.605

Scott, D. W. (1992). *Multivariate density estimation: Theory, practice, and visualization.* New York, NY: Wiley.

Shneiderman, B. (1992). Tree visualization with tree-maps: A 2-d space-filling approach. *ACM Transactions on Graphics, 11,* 92–99. doi:10.1145/102377.115768

Silverman, B. W. (1986). *Density estimation for statistics and data analysis.* New York, NY: Chapman & Hall.

Simkin, D., & Hastie, R. (1987). An information processing analysis of graph perception. *Journal of the American Statistical Association, 82,* 454–465. doi:10.2307/2289447

Spence, I. (1990). Visual psychophysics of simple graphical elements. *Journal of Experimental Psychology: Human Perception and Performance, 16,* 683–692. doi:10.1037/0096-1523.16.4.683

Spence, I. (2004). The apparent and effective dimensionality of representations of objects. *Human Factors, 46,* 738–747. doi:10.1518/hfes.46.4.738.56809

Spence, I. (2005). No humble pie: The origins and usage of a statistical chart. *Journal of Educational and Behavioral Statistics, 30,* 353–368. doi:10.3102/10769986030004353

Spence, I., & Lewandowsky, S. (1991). Displaying proportions and percentages. *Applied Cognitive Psychology, 5,* 61–77. doi:10.1002/acp.2350050106

Stevens, S. S. (1961). To honor Fechner and repeal his law. *Science, 133,* 80–86. doi:10.1126/science.133.3446.80

Stevens, S. S. (1985). *Psychophysics: Introduction to its perceptual, neural, and social prospects.* New Brunswick, NJ: Transaction Books.

Stigler, S. (1983). *The history of statistics.* Cambridge, MA: Harvard University Press.

Stroop, J. R. (1935). Studies of interference in serial verbal reactions. *Journal of Experimental Psychology, 18,* 643–662. doi:10.1037/h0054651

Tufte, E. R. (1983). *The visual display of quantitative information.* Cheshire, CT: Graphics Press.

Tufte, E. R. (1990). *Envisioning data.* Cheshire, CT: Graphics Press.

Tufte, E. R. (1997). *Visual explanations.* Cheshire, CT: Graphics Press.

Tukey, J. W. (1977). *Exploratory data analysis.* Reading, MA: Addison-Wesley.

Tversky, B. (1981). Distortions in memory for maps. *Cognitive Psychology, 13,* 407–433. doi:10.1016/0010-0285(81)90016-5

Tversky, B. (1993). Cognitive maps, cognitive collages, and spatial mental models. In U. A. Frank & I. Campari (Eds.), *Spatial information theory: A theoretical basis for GIS—Proceedings of COSIT '93.* (pp. 14–24). Berlin, Germany: Springer-Verlag.

Tversky, B. (2005). Prolegomenon to scientific visualization. In J. K. Gilbert (Ed.), *Visualization in science education* (pp. 29–42). Dordrecht, the Netherlands: Springer.

Tversky, B., Agrawala, M., Heiser, J., Lee, P. U., Hanrahan, P., Phan, D., & Daniele, M.-P. (2007).

Cognitive design principles for generating visualizations. In G. Allen (Ed.), *Applied spatial cognition: From research to cognitive technology* (pp. 53–73). Mahwah, NJ: Erlbaum.

Tversky, B., Zacks, J., Lee, P. U., & Heiser, J. (2000). Lines, blobs, crosses, and arrows: Diagrammatic communication with schematic figures. In M. Anderson, P. Cheng, & V. Haarslev (Eds.), *Theory and application of diagrams* (pp. 221–230). Berlin, Germany: Springer-Verlag. doi:10.1007/3-540-44590-0_21

Wainer, H. (1997). *Visual revelations: Graphical tales of fate and deception from Napoleon Bonaparte to Ross Perot.* New York, NY: Springer-Verlag.

Wainer, H. (2009). *Picturing the uncertain world.* Princeton, NJ: Princeton University Press.

Wainer, H., & Spence, I. (1997). Who was Playfair? *Chance, 10*, 35–37.

Wainer, H., & Velleman, P. F. (2001). Statistical graphs: Mapping the pathways of science. *Annual Review of Psychology, 52*, 305–335. doi:10.1146/annurev.psych.52.1.305

Wand, M. P. (1997). Data-based choice of histogram bin width. *The American Statistician, 51*, 59–64. doi:10.2307/2684697

Ware, C. (2008). *Visual thinking for design.* Burlington, MA: Morgan Kaufman.

Wickham, H. (2009). *ggplot2: Elegant graphics for data analysis.* New York, NY: Springer.

Wiggins, J. S. (1982). Circumplex models of interpersonal behavior in clinical psychology. In P. C.

Kendall & J. N. Butcher (Eds.), *Handbook of research methods in clinical psychology* (pp. 183–221). New York, NY: Wiley.

Wilkinson, L. (1999). Dot plots. *The American Statistician, 53*, 276–281. doi:10.2307/2686111

Wilkinson, L. (2005). *The grammar of graphics* (2nd ed.). New York, NY: Springer-Verlag.

Wilkinson, L. (2006). Revising the Pareto chart. *The American Statistician, 60*, 332–334. doi:10.1198/000313006X152243

Wilkinson, L. (in press). Exact and approximate area-proportional circular Venn and Euler diagrams. *IEEE Transactions on Visualization and Computer Graphics.*

Wilkinson, L., Anand, A., & Dang, T. N. (in press). Substantial improvements in the set-covering projection classifier CHIRP (Composite Hypercubes on Iterated Random Projections). *ACM Transactions on Knowledge Discovery From Data.*

Wilkinson, L., Blank, G., & Gruber, C. (1996). *Desktop data analysis with SYSTAT.* Upper Saddle River, NJ: Prentice-Hall.

Wilkinson, L., & McConathy, D. (1990). Memory for graphs. In *Proceedings of the Section on Statistical Graphics of the American Statistical Association* (pp. 25–32). Alexandria, VA: American Statistical Association.

Wilkinson, L., & Task Force on Statistical Inference. (1999). Statistical methods in psychology journals: Guidelines and explanations. *American Psychologist, 54*, 594–604. doi:10.1037/0003-066X.54.8.594

## Chapter 5

ESTIMATING AND GRAPHING INTERACTIONS

Leona S. Aiken, Stephen G. West, Maike Luhmann, Amanda Baraldi, and Stefany J. Coxe

Interactions are defined as the unique effects of combinations of independent variables that contribute over and above the effects of each variable taken separately (i.e., the average effects of individual variables). Interactions, also termed *moderator effects*, are among the most interesting effects we have in psychology. They reflect nuances of the relationship between an independent variable and an outcome variable, characterizing how such a relationship is modified by or moderated by another variable. Interactions are at the heart of theorizing in many areas of psychology. In personality and social psychology, we consider Person × Situation interactions, with questions about how personality traits modify individuals' reactions to particular situations. In treatment outcome research, we explore the characteristics of individuals (e.g., gender, level of health risk) for whom particular psychological interventions are more (or less) likely to be effective. In industrial–organizational psychology, we examine how the level of control of work activities modifies the impact of responsibility for productivity on work stress.

When we characterize interactions, we typically think of the relationship of a focal independent variable to an outcome variable and examine how that relationship is altered by another variable, termed the moderator variable. In treatment outcome research, the type of treatment (e.g., psychotherapy; control) would typically be the focal predictor of a treatment outcome such as level of depression. In such research, the level of depression before treatment might be expected to be a moderator that

alters the extent to which treatment is subsequently effective, an effect referred to as a *Baseline × Treatment interaction* (Morgan-Lopez & MacKinnon, 2006). In this case, prior level of depression is the variable that alters the effectiveness of treatment on the outcome.

Historically, the consideration of interactions in psychology began in the context of analysis of variance (ANOVA), developed in now-classic texts (e.g., Kirk, 1968; McNemar, 1962; Winer, 1962). This initial consideration was universally of interactions between *categorical* variables. When all variables are truly categorical (e.g., treatment condition, gender), ANOVA provides appropriate estimates of all effects and prescriptions for characterizing, testing, and post hoc probing of interactions. When underlying variables were continuous, however, these variables were historically coarsely categorized (e.g., low intelligence, high intelligence groups) to permit the familiar machinery of ANOVA to be utilized. Only later did we learn that such practices decrease the statistical power of the tests and often introduce bias, potentially leading to incorrect answers (e.g., Cohen, 1983; Maxwell & Delaney, 1993). Cohen's (1968) *Psychological Bulletin* article alerted the field to the fact that multiple regression was a general statistical methodology that largely subsumed ANOVA. A decade later, Cohen's (1978) *Psychological Bulletin* article elucidated the characterization of interactions between continuous variables in multiple regression. Aiken and West's (1991) text, *Multiple Regression: Testing and*

Stephen G. West was supported by a Forschungspreis from the Alexander von Humboldt Foundation during the writing of this chapter.

DOI: 10.1037/13621-005
APA Handbook of Research Methods in Psychology: Vol. 3. Data Analysis and Research Publication, H. Cooper (Editor-in-Chief)

Interpreting Interactions, specified a broad approach to testing and interpreting interactions between continuous variables and between continuous and categorical variables in multiple regression. This approach generalized well-established strategies in the ANOVA framework for characterizing, testing, and post hoc probing of interactions to multiple regression with continuous independent variables.

Research in psychology has historically emphasized the evaluation of a priori hypotheses using data. This confirmatory approach has much to recommend it; we can test whether estimated effects differ in the expected direction (positive or negative) from zero using a significance test and interpret the magnitude of these effects using confidence intervals and effect size measures. Graphic displays depict the results of the statistical model. This confirmatory approach can provide evidence to support our hypothesized statistical model. The machinery of this approach is widely available in standard textbooks (e.g., for interactions in multiple regression, see Aiken & West, 1991; for multiple regression, Cohen, Cohen, West, & Aiken, 2003; for ANOVA, Maxwell & Delaney, 2004), to which we refer in this chapter. What is typically forgotten in this approach is that the hypothesized model may *not* provide a particularly good account of the data—there may be other models that appear to provide equally good or even better accounts. In this chapter, we emphasize exploratory data analysis procedures that forcefully reveal patterns in the data to the researcher. Such procedures have great ability to identify problems with hypothesized models and offer potential improvements. As the great statistician John Tukey (1977) noted, "Today, exploratory and confirmatory can—and should—proceed side by side" (p. vii). Our chapter attempts to remedy the imbalance that has developed in psychology: Too much attention is given to the *p* values of hypothesis tests and not enough to what the data themselves are saying.

In this chapter, we examine the treatment of interactions first in multiple regression and then in ANOVA. Our rationale for focusing first and more intensively on multiple regression is that, although there are almost five decades of writing on the treatment of interactions in ANOVA, strategies for characterizing interactions in multiple regression

are more recent and less widely disseminated. We provide an integrative framework that brings together strategies for characterization and analysis of interactions. Throughout the chapter, our focus will be on the interplay between data and statistical models. We emphasize the use of exploratory graphic procedures to inform the relationship between the data on the one hand and the statistical models we employ to represent the data and to test hypotheses on the other. The researchers' hope is that the hypothesized model can provide an adequate fit to the data and lead to statistically significant predicted relationships between variables. Researchers also hope that they have developed a statistical model that represents the data well at best and does not distort or give an inaccurate representation of the data at worst. Exploratory graphic methods provide tools for probing these latter, often neglected issues.

In illustrating exploration of data, we have prepared graphs in three statistical packages: SPSS, SAS, and R. We also have generated graphs in Excel. The caption of each figure indicates the package used to produce the figure.

INTERACTIONS IN MULTIPLE REGRESSION

Consider that we have measured a focal independent variable X and an outcome variable Y. In addition, we have assessed a second independent variable Z that we believe may potentially moderate the relationship of X to Y; in other words we predict an interaction between X and Z. All three variables are continuous. The regression model that represents our prediction is as follows:

$$\hat{Y} = b_1 X + b_2 Z + b_3 XZ + b_0. \qquad (1)$$

The first two terms represent approximately the average effects of the two predictors (so long as the predictors are centered, i.e., scaled in deviation form; more about this later). The third term $b_3 XZ$ represents the Linear × Linear interaction between X and Z, that is, an interaction in which the relationship of X to Y is linear at every value of Z and the converse. The XZ term is the product of the scores on predictors X and Z.

To provide an applied context for our presentation, assume that that we have two independent variables and one outcome variable, each measured on a 15-point scale. *X* is a measure of a married individual's desire to lose weight, ranging from 1= *no desire to lose weight* to 15 = *great desire for weight loss* (*DESIRE*). The moderator *Z* is the view of the spouse (*SPOUSE*) about the individual's desire to lose weight, ranging from 1 = *complete indifference* ("Do what you want to do.") to 15 = *a strong positive view* ("I fully support your losing weight.") The outcome variable *Y* is the individual's emotional reaction to the spouse's input (*REACTION*), again ranging from 1 = *a negative reaction* ("My spouse doesn't care about my own goals.") to 15 = *a very positive reaction* ("My spouse really supports me."). We rewrite the regression equation in terms of Equation 2:

$$REACT_{predicted} = b_1\ DESIRE + b_2\ SPOUSE$$
$$+ b_3\ DESIRE * SPOUSE + b_0 . \qquad (2)$$

The Starting Point: Graphic Explorations of the Data

Normally, researchers dive into the data analysis, fit Equation 1 to the data, and report the results. Here, we proceed in parallel with an exploratory data analysis, by carefully examining the actual data both without consideration of the model and by fitting models and examining if there are other potential effects that may be present. We begin by examining the distribution of each of these variables on the basis of a simulated data set.

Single variables. Figure 5.1 displays the distributions of the variables using two types of graphs. The three panels across the top are histograms with kernel density functions overlaid. Kernel density functions are the curved lines that estimate the shape of the distribution in the population. They are based on smoothing functions that use a weighted average of many segments of the data to represent the height of the curve at each point. These lines

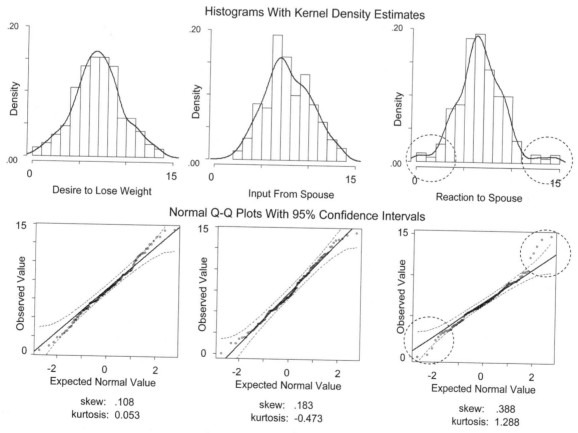

FIGURE 5.1. Distribution of each predictor (*DESIRE, SPOUSE*) and the criterion (*REACT*) illustrated by histograms with kernel density estimates and with quantile–quantile (Q-Q) plots with 95% confidence intervals. Histograms and Q-Q plots were made in R. Similar graphics are available in SPSS and SAS.

do not impose a standard statistical distribution such as a normal or chi-square distribution; rather, they display the actual distribution of the data. The three panels at the bottom of the page are quantile–quantile (also called *q-q*) plots with 95% confidence intervals. Such q-q plots are extremely useful plots for displaying deviations from a specified statistical distribution, here a normal distribution. All of the data points would fall on the diagonal line if the variable were perfectly normally distributed. Points that deviate from the line, particularly outside the 95% confidence interval, reflect deviations from normality (for further explanation of Kernel density plots, see Cohen et al., 2003, pp. 105–109; for q-q plots, see pp. 137–140). We note from inspecting the two sets of graphs that the predictors *DESIRE* and *SPOUSE* are very close to normally distributed; however, the dependent variable *REACTION* has both an upper tail and a lower tail (both circled) that deviate from normality. If the dependent variable *REACT* were predicted only from the two normally distributed predictor variables *DESIRE* and *SPOUSE*, then *REACT* would necessarily be normally distributed.[1] However, the fact that deviations do occur provides a clue that there may be some form of nonlinear effect in the data.

Predictors in relation to the criterion. Figures 5.2a and 5.2b portray the relationship of each predictor to the outcome variable. Panels A and B are two-dimensional enhanced scatterplots of these relationships. Each point represents the value of one of the predictors and the criterion for a single individual. Each graph also contains two overlaid lines. The straight line (Fit) is the linear fit line from a linear regression analysis predicting the outcome from the single predictor. The second curved line is a lowess nonparametric smooth. The lowess nonparametric smooth tracks the relationships between pairs of variables as they actually exist; again, no statistical model is imposed on the relationship. If the form of the relationship is linear, the lowess line will look like a child's freehand drawing of a straight line. In Figure 5.2a, we note that the lowess lines are bowed, suggestive of curvilinear relationships. Given this

suggestion of curvilinearity, it is well to realize that an interaction introduces curvilinearity by warping the regression surface. A simple conception of how an interaction introduces curvilinearity is as follows. Think of a flat sheet on a bed; now pick up one corner and hold it up to your nose. The surface of the sheet curves like the surface of a tent. The raised corner and associated upwardly curving surface would represent a synergistic interaction, that is, a combination of two variables that produces a greater outcome than merely the sum of the two predictors making up the interaction.

In Panels A and B of Figure 5.2a, we see that there is also more variability of the points around the lowess line at the ends compared with the middle of the predictor variables. This pattern of variability is termed *butterfly heteroskedasticity*, often reflecting the presence of an interaction. Panels C and D of Figure 5.2a provide two perspectives (vantage points) on a three-dimensional representation of the data points with *DESIRE* and *SPOUSE* as two axes and *REACTION* as the vertical axis. Overlaid on the graph in each panel is a lowess surface that illustrates the simultaneous relationship of the two predictors to the criterion. Panel C shows that the surface is twisting. The relationship of *DESIRE* to lose weight to the criterion *REACTION* is positive for some portion of the data. However, the twisting of the surface suggests that there might be no relationship of *DESIRE* to *REACTION* or even a negative relationship for other portions of the data.

Figure 5.2b provides additional three-dimensional graphic displays using an alternative nonparametric spline interpolation. The symbols *D+,S+* and *D–,S–* have been imposed on the existing graph. *D+,S+* indicates the highest desire to lose weight and the highest positive support from the spouse. *D–,S–* indicates the lowest desire and the lowest support for losing weight from the spouse. These graphs make even more vivid the metaphor of lifting the corner of a sheet to produce an interaction—now think of yourself as standing at the corner of the bed representing *D+,S+* and your friend standing at the corner representing *D–,S–*. At the same time, you raise your corners of the sheet. You have

---

[1] The predicted scores for *REACT* on the basis of *DESIRE* and *SPOUSE* will be normally distributed. Normal distributions having the same mean and variance (as is the case for predicted scores) exhibit reproducibility: The sum of the normally distributed variables is itself normally distributed.

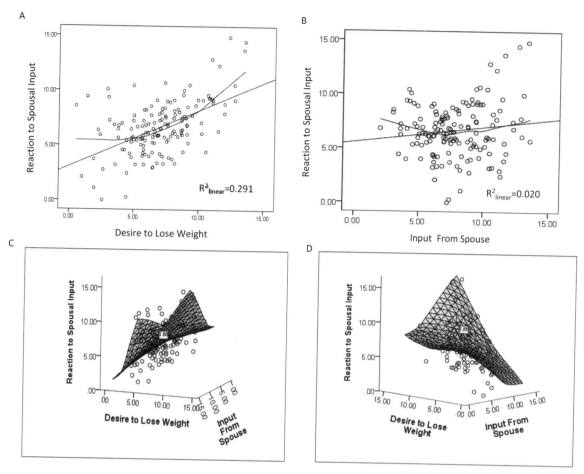

FIGURE 5.2a.   Scatterplots of relationships of predictors to criterion. (A) *REACT* as a function of *DESIRE* to lose weight. (B) *REACT* as a function of input from *SPOUSE*. (C) and (D) Three-dimensional scatterplot representations of the relationships of both predictors to the criterion from different perspectives (horizontal perspective 140°; 350°; vertical perspective 10°). All plots produced in SPSS.

produced a *synergistic* interaction, the two predictors, working in the same direction on the emotional reaction combine together in a more than additive way to produce an even stronger response. We note that this is an interactive effect, but it does produce curvature of the regression surface.

Regression surfaces of various regression models. At this point, we summarize the clues on the basis of our observations of Figures 5.2a and 5.2b. In Figure 5.2a, the lowess lines in the graphs of Panels A and B suggest curvilinear relationships of both predictors to the criterion. The twisted shape of the three-dimensional lowess surfaces in graphs of Panels C and D suggests an interaction. In Figure 5.2b, the twisting of the regression surface because of the synergistic interaction is clearly apparent. To place these clues in context, let us compare the nonparametric

lowess and spline surfaces to the regression surfaces that would result from three different regression models that we might apply to the data. First is a simple linear regression model:

$$REACT_{predicted} = b_1 \; DESIRE + b_2 \; SPOUSE + b_0. \quad (3)$$

This model is shown in Panel A of Figure 5.3. The regression surface is completely flat, with linear relationships of both predictors to the outcome. This graph shows the surface on which all predicted scores would fall, the Linear × Linear regression plane. This linear regression plane clearly does not resemble the twisted surface representing the data presented in Figures 5.2a and 5.2b.

We now fit a model in which a quadratic relationship of each predictor to the outcome is built into the model by including the square of *DESIRE*

D

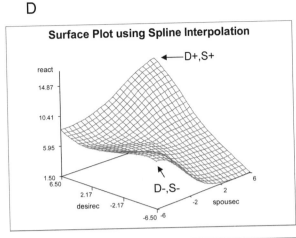

E

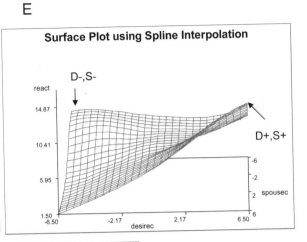

F

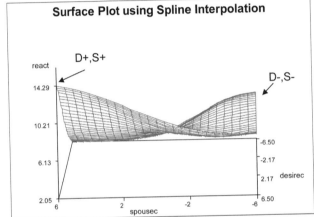

FIGURE 5.2b. Three views of a spline interpolation of the surface of the data. All three graphs have the same vertical perspective; however, each has a different horizontal perspective: (D) from the corner representing low desire and spouse input; (E) from *DESIREC*, and (F) from *SPOUSEC*. The symbols *D+,S+* and *D–,S–* have been added to the existing graphs. *D+,S+* indicates the highest desire to lose weight and the highest positive support from the spouse. *D–,S–* indicates the lowest desire and the lowest support for losing weight from the spouse. These graphs were produced in SAS 9.2 (the first SAS version to have this graphics capability).

and the square of *SPOUSE* as two additional predictors:

$$REACT_{predicted} = b_1\ DESIRE + b_2\ SPOUSE$$
$$+ b_3\ DESIRE^2 + b_4\ SPOUSE^2 + b_0 .\ (4)$$

Panel B of Figure 5.3 shows that the regression surface corresponding to Equation 4 looks like a hammock, bearing no resemblance to the twisted regression surface representing the data.

Finally, we fit the regression model (Equation 2), repeated here, containing the interaction between the two predictors:

$$REACT_{predicted} = b_1\ DESIRE + b_2\ SPOUSE$$
$$+ b_3\ DESIRE * SPOUSE + b_0 .\ (2)$$

The resulting regression surface based on Equation 2, which is shown in Figure 5.3C, closely resembles the twisted surface of the data.

There is a key difference between the three-dimensional graphs in Figures 5.2a, 5.2b, and 5.3. Those in Figures 5.2a and 5.2b were *not* generated from a statistical model; rather they were generated from plotting the three variables and fitting a nonparametric lowess surface or spline interpolation surface through the data. These three-dimensional graphs are exploratory; they let the data speak for themselves. The graphs of Figure 5.3 were generated from statistical models, specifically Equations 3 (linear), 4 (quadratic), and 2 (interactive), respectively. These surfaces represent predicted scores from regression models. Each of these surfaces may or

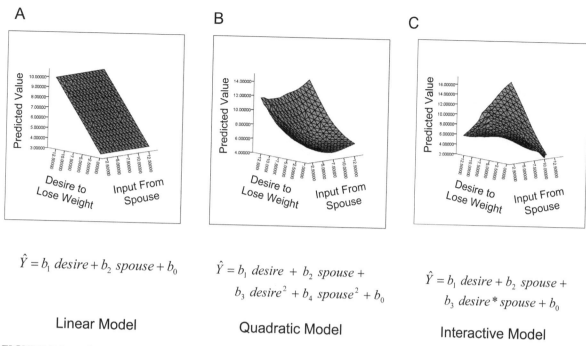

FIGURE 5.3.   Three-dimensional displays of a linear model, a quadratic model, and an interactive model. These plots display the predictions from each of the regression models, not the data. All graphs were produced in SPSS.

may not provide a good representation of the data themselves.

Conditioning plots to explore possible moderators. The twisting of the lowess surface in the three-dimensional representation presented in Figures 5.2a and 5.2b can sometimes be depicted more clearly in two dimensions using a graphical technique known as *slicing* (also called *conditioning plots*). A series of small ranges of the data (slices) on one independent variable is selected, and the relationship of the second independent variable to the outcome is studied. In Figure 5.4 the data have been divided into fifths (lowest 20% of scores, next 20%, etc.) on the basis of the putative moderator variable SPOUSE. The five graphs in Figure 5.4 show the regression of *REACT* on *DESIRE* in the five slices, each representing 20% of the data. The lowess lines approximate the linear fit lines. The relationship between *DESIRE* and *RESPONSE* is slightly negative at very low values of *SPOUSE* input and increases in a regular manner across the slices to be strongly positive at very high positive values of *SPOUSE* input. More complex nonlinear forms of interactions will appear as curved lines or nonlinear changes in the slopes of the lines (e.g., increasing to a maximum slope,

then decreasing across the slices; such interactions are treated in detail in Aiken & West, 1991, Chapter 6). Irregular patterns of data that can produce a statistically significant interaction (e.g., a few outliers in some of the slices) can also be detected. In the present example, the results of the slicing are consistent with a linear interaction between *SPOUSE* and *DESIRE*. Figure 5.4 was produced in SPSS by actually selecting each fifth of the scores and developing the associated scatterplot. Figure 5.5 shows a representation of the same five conditioning plots generated in a single trellis plot in the R software package. A *trellis plot* is a plot that stacks together a series of conditioning plots.

Summarizing the explorations.   Our exploratory graphic work thus far has focused on the raw data. We have seen several clues that there may be a nonlinear or interactive relationship in the data. Even though the two predictors *DESIRE* and *SPOUSE* are normally distributed, the dependent variable *REACT* shows evidence of non-normality in the tails. The two-dimensional scatterplots display butterfly heteroskedasticity, hinting that an interaction may be present. The comparison of the lowess surface to plots of linear, curvilinear, and interactive

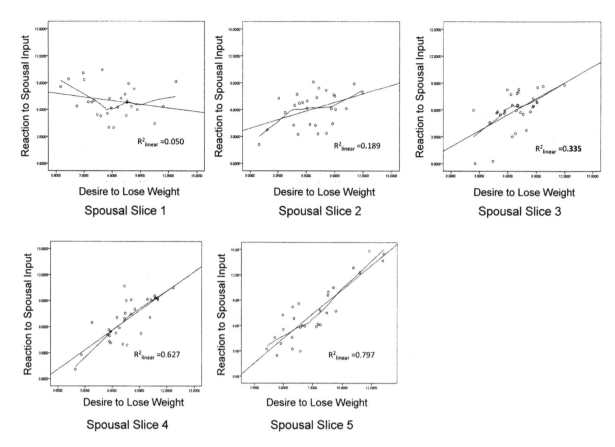

FIGURE 5.4. Conditioning plots showing the regression of *REACT* on *DESIRE* to lose weight within five slices of data based on the values on *SPOUSE* input. Each slice represents one fifth of the data points. The value of *SPOUSE* increases from graph (1) to graph (5), as does the magnitude of the positive relationship of *DESIRE* to *REACT*. The straight line in each graph is the linear regression line; the slightly curved lines are lowess nonparametric smooths that track the relationship in the data. All graphs were produced in SPSS.

regression surfaces again suggested that the interactive statistical model most closely resembles the data. Finally, the slicing graph illustrating how the relationship of *DESIRE* to *REACT* changes across five ordered segments of *SPOUSE* input was highly consistent with the hypothesis that *SPOUSE* moderates the relationship of *DESIRE* to *REACT*.

STATISTICAL MODELING

A second exploratory way to learn about data is to fit a variety of statistical models to the data and to carefully study the fit of the models and the residuals. The residuals are of special importance: They amplify any remaining systematic information left in the data after the model is fit, making it easier to detect nonhypothesized effects. Tables 5.1 and 5.2 present simple descriptive information about the data. Our original variables *DESIRE*, *SPOUSE*, and

REACT are all measured on 15-point scales. We have created additional terms in Tables 5.1 and 5.2. *DESIREC* is the *DESIRE* variable in *centered* or deviation form, and *SPOUSEC* is *SPOUSE* in centered form.

$$DESIREC = DESIRE - MEAN_{DESIRE}. \qquad (5)$$

$$SPOUSEC = SPOUSE - MEAN_{SPOUSE}. \qquad (6)$$

DESIRESPOUSEC is the product of *DESIREC* with *SPOUSEC*; this variable carries the interaction between *SPOUSE* and *DESIRE* in the regression equation.

$$DESIRESPOUSEC = DESIREC * SPOUSEC. \qquad (7)$$

These computed variables serve as predictors in the regression analysis. We will see in the section Why Center Predictors? that centering has advantages for the interpretation of the results of the regression analysis.

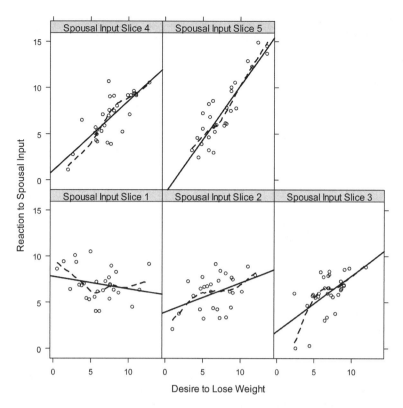

FIGURE 5.5.   A trellis plot of the five conditioning plots of the regression of *REACTION* on *DESIRE* to lose weight within five slices of data
based on the values on *SPOUSE* input. Each slice represents one fifth of
the data points. The straight line in each graph is the linear regression line;
the slightly curved lines are lowess nonparametric smooths. Note that the
slope of the linear regression lines increases from Slice 1 (lowest *SPOUSE*
support) to Slice 5 (highest *SPOUSE* support). This figure, generated in a
single graphic in the R software package, corresponds to Figure 5.4, generated in five separate graphs in SPSS. The placement of the five slices on the
graph is as generated by the R software, to be read from the bottom row,
left to right, then the top row, left to right, to correspond to Figure 5.4.

TABLE 5.1

Descriptive Summary of the Data: Distributions of All Variables

| | | | | | | Skewness | | Kurtosis | |
Variable	*N*	Minimum	Maximum	*M*	*SD*	Statistic	*SE*	Statistic	*SE*
DESIRE	150	0.489	13.518	7.000	2.596	0.108	0.198	0.053	0.394
SPOUSE	150	2.014	13.576	7.800	2.469	0.183	0.198	−0.473	0.394
REACT	150	0.008	14.850	6.664	2.454	0.388	0.198	1.288	0.394
DESIREC	150	−6.511	6.518	0.000	2.596	0.108	0.198	0.053	0.394
SPOUSEC	150	−5.786	5.776	0.000	2.469	0.183	0.198	−0.473	0.394
DESIRESPOUSEC	150	−18.592	31.664	1.623	7.220	1.555	0.198	5.335	0.394
Valid *N* (listwise)	150								

Note. DESIRE = desire to lose weight (15-point scale) from low to high desire; SPOUSE = spousal input (15-point scale) from
low to high support for losing weight; REACT = emotional reaction of the potential dieter to the spousal input (15-point scale
from negative to positive emotional reaction); DESIREC = desire in centered form (deviations from the mean); SPOUSEC =
spouse in centered form (deviations from the mean); DESIRESPOUSEC = cross-product of DESIREC with SPOUSEC.

TABLE 5.2

Descriptive Summary of the Data: Correlations Among All Variables[a]

Variable	DESIRE	SPOUSE	REACT	DESIREC	SPOUSEC	DESIRESPOUSEC
DESIRE						
Pearson corr.	1	.255	.539	1.000	.255	−.043
Sig. (2-tailed)		.002	.000	.000	.002	.598
SPOUSE						
Pearson corr.	.255	1	.140	.255	1.000	.010
Sig. (2-tailed)	.002		.087	.002	.000	.900
REACT						
Pearson corr.	.539	.140	1	.539	.140	.479
Sig. (2-tailed)	.000	.087		.000	.087	.000
DESIREC						
Pearson corr.	1.000	.255	.539	1	.255	−.043
Sig. (2-tailed)	.000	.002	.000		.002	.598
SPOUSEC						
Pearson corr.	.255	1.000	.140	.255	1	.010
Sig. (2-tailed)	.002	.000	.087	.002		.900
DESIRESPOUSEC						
Pearson corr.	−.043	.010	.479	−.043	.010	1
Sig. (2-tailed)	.598	.900	.000	.598	.900	

Note. DESIRE = desire to lose weight (15-point scale) from low to high desire; SPOUSE = spousal input (15-point scale) from low to high support for losing weight; REACT = emotional reaction of the potential dieter to the spousal input (15-point scale from negative to positive emotional reaction); DESIREC = desire in centered form (deviations from the mean); SPOUSEC = spouse in centered form (deviations from the mean); DESIRESPOUSEC = cross-product of DESIREC with SPOUSEC; corr. = correlation.

[a]N = 150.

From Table 5.1 we see that centering *DESIRE* and *SPOUSE* has *no effect whatever* on the shape of their distributions. The standard deviation, skew, and kurtosis of a variable are unchanged by centering. From Table 5.2 we see that correlations with the criterion *REACTION* are not affected by centering. *DESIRE* and *SPOUSE* are moderately positively correlated ($r = .255$); *DESIRE* is strongly correlated with *REACT* ($r = .539$), but *SPOUSE* is only weakly correlated with *REACT* ($r = .140$).

Regression Model I: Linear Regression

We begin by estimating a linear regression model with no interaction, $\hat{Y} = b_1\ DESIREC + b_2\ SPOUSEC + b_0$; results are summarized in Table 5.3, Panel A. The overall variance accounted for, $R^2_{multiple,\ linear} = .291$, is substantial; *DESIREC* is a significant positive predictor of *REACT*, but *SPOUSEC* is not significant. We have used the centered predictors; had we used predictors in the original raw score form, the only value

that would have changed is the intercept. The intercept $b_0 = \bar{Y} - b_1\ \bar{X}_1 - b_2\ \bar{Z}$ is a function of the means of the predictors and of the outcome variable. Centering makes the means of both predictors equal to zero, so that the intercept equals the mean of the outcome variable REACT = 6.664.

Plot of residuals as a function of predicted scores. Our first step in considering model adequacy is to examine a plot of residuals from the analysis (observed Y minus predicted Y) as a function of predicted scores. This plot is given in Figure 5.6A. Three lines are overlaid on the data. First is the *zero-line* (a line of zero slope intersecting the y-axis at zero, the arithmetic mean of the residuals), which represents the target for a line fitting the residuals for a properly specified regression model. This line has slope zero because the linear regression has fitted any linear trends in the data; only the residuals remain after these linear trends have been removed.

TABLE 5.3

Regression Models

Model	Unstandardized coefficients		Standardized coefficients			
	b	SE	b*	SE	t	Sig.
A. Linear regression with no interaction—centered predictors						
$\hat{Y} = b_1\ desirec + b_2\ spousec + b_0$						
$R^2_{multiple,\ linear} = .291$, $F(2, 147) = 30.144$, $p < .001$						
(constant)	6.664	0.170			39.234	.000
DESIREC	0.509	0.068	0.538	0.072	7.497	.000
SPOUSEC	0.003	0.071	0.003	0.072	0.043	.966
B. Regression model with interaction—centered predictors						
$\hat{Y} = b_1\ desirec + b_2\ spousec + b_3\ desirespousec + b_0$						
$R^2_{multiple,\ interactive} = .544$, $F(3, 146) = 57.994$, $p < .001$						
$R^2_{gain} = R^2_{multiple,\ interactive} - R^2_{multiple,\ linear} = .253$; $F_{gain}(1,146) = 80.916$						
(constant)	6.386	0.140			45.568	.000
DESIREC	0.532	0.055	0.563	0.058	9.733	.000
SPOUSEC	–0.008	0.057	–0.008	0.058	–0.146	.884
DESIRESPOUSEC	0.171	0.019	0.503	0.056	8.995	.000
C. Regression model with interaction—uncentered predictors						
$\hat{Y} = b_1\ desire + b_2\ spouse + b_3\ desirespouse + b_0$						
$R^2_{multiple,\ interactive} = .544$, $F(3, 146) = 57.994$, $p < .001$						
$R^2_{gain} = R^2_{multiple,\ interactive} - R^2_{multiple,\ linear} = .253$; $F_{gain}(1,146) = 80.916$						
(constant)	12.067	1.130			10.678	.000
DESIRE	–0.802	0.156	–0.849	0.165	–5.154	.000
SPOUSE	–1.206	0.146	–1.214	0.147	–8.251	.000
DESIRESPOUSE	0.171	0.019	2.126	0.236	8.995	.000

Note. The dependent variable is REACT. b = unstandardized regression coefficient; $b*$ = standardized regression coefficient; Sig. = significance.

Second is a solid line from fitting a quadratic model to the regression of the residuals to the predicted scores. More than 10% of the variation in the residuals is accounted for by this curvilinear relationship, indicating that there is systematic relationship remaining in the data not accounted for by the linear regression model. Third is a dashed nonparametric lowess line that closely matches the quadratic fit. Overall, this graph tells us that the linear model is not appropriate; there is systematic nonlinearity remaining in the data. Moreover, butterfly heteroskedasticity remains, possibly suggesting an interaction.

Partial regression leverage plots (also called *added variable plots*). Figures 5.6B and 5.6C are partial regression leverage plots. In contrast to Figures 5.2a and 5.2bm which illustrate the relationship of each predictor taken separately to the criterion, Figures 5.6B and 5.6C illustrate the relationships between each predictor and the outcome when other predictors are held constant. Figure 5.6B depicts the regression of REACT on DESIREC with SPOUSEC partialed out of both DESIREC and REACT. Both a linear regression line (solid) and a lowess fit are illustrated. The substantial positive slope ($b_1 = 0.509$) of the linear regression line in Figure 5.6B equals the

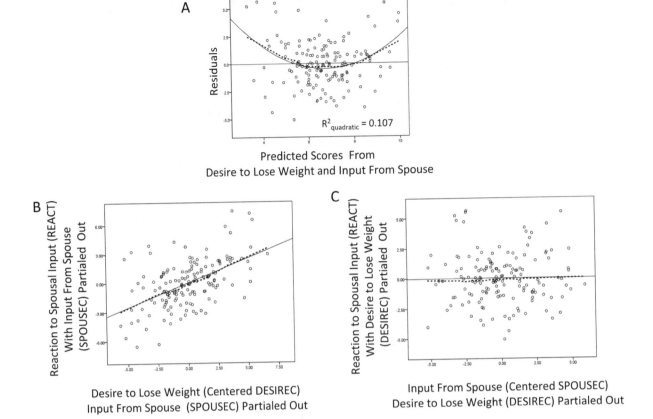

B-C: Partial Regression Leverage Plots

FIGURE 5.6. On the basis of the linear regression model $\hat{Y} = b_1\ desirec + b_2\ spousec + b_0$, the relationship of residual scores to predicted scores (A), and partial regression leverage plots of the criterion on each predictor with the other predictor partialed out (B, C). The dashed line in each graph is the lowess smooth. All graphs produced in SPSS.

unstandardized regression coefficient for the predictor *DESIRE* in the linear regression model, reported in Table 5.3, Panel A. The close match of the nonparametric lowess line and the linear regression line suggests that a linear relationship between *DESIRE* and *REACT* is appropriate. Figure 5.6C depicts the regression of *REACT* on *SPOUSEC* with *DESIREC* partialed out of both *REACT* and *SPOUSEC*. The slope of the linear regression line in Figure 5.6C equals the unstandardized regression coefficient ($b_2 = 0.003$) for the predictor *SPOUSEC* in the linear regression model, reported in Table 5.3, Panel A. Again, the nonparametric lowess fit indicates a linear relationship is appropriate. If one of the predictors had had a curvilinear relationship to *REACT*, then the lowess line for that predictor would show the curvilinearity. Partial regression plots provide

informative diagnostic information about which predictor(s) may be contributing nonlinearity. Here, neither *DESIRE* nor *SPOUSE* appears to be doing so.

Regression Model II: Interaction Model

We now turn to the interaction model given the multiple clues from our exploratory analyses that this is an important candidate model. We also note that the interaction model has a special status in our example: It is the a priori model that was hypothesized by the researchers. Nothing in our exploratory analyses has strongly suggested that the interaction model is inappropriate for these data. The interaction model (Equation 2), repeated here, is as follows:

$$REACT_{predicted} = b_1\ DESIRE + b_2\ SPOUSE$$
$$+ b_3\ DESIRE * SPOUSE + b_0. \qquad (2)$$

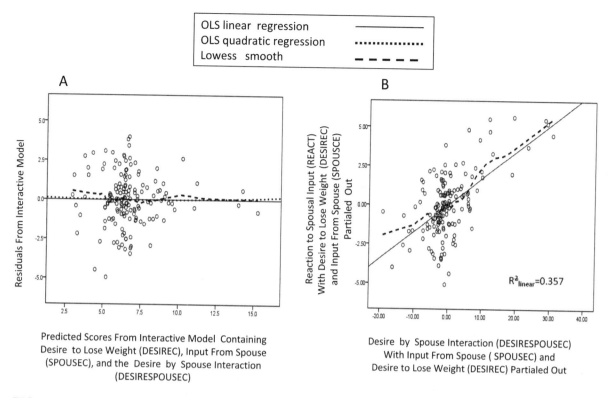

OLS linear regression	——————
OLS quadratic regression	··················
Lowess smooth	— — — —

A

Residuals From Interactive Model (y-axis)

Predicted Scores From Interactive Model Containing Desire to Lose Weight (DESIREC), Input From Spouse (SPOUSEC), and the Desire by Spouse Interaction (DESIRESPOUSEC)

B

Reaction to Spousal Input (REACT) With Desire to Lose Weight (DESIREC) and Input From Spouse (SPOUSCE) Partialed Out (y-axis)

$R^2_{linear} = 0.357$

Desire by Spouse Interaction (DESIRESPOUSEC) With Input From Spouse (SPOUSEC) and Desire to Lose Weight (DESIREC) Partialed Out

FIGURE 5.7. Regression of residuals from interactive model on predicted scores with three lines: the linear zero-line, a quadratic model, and a lowess smooth (A), and partial regression leverage plot of *REACT* on cross-product term (B), created on the basis of the interactive regression model. Both graphs produced in SPSS. OLS = ordinary least squares.

The results of the regression analysis including the interaction are given in Table 5.3, Panel B. The squared multiple correlation has increased from .291 for the linear model to .544 for the interactive model, a substantial, statistically significant increase, with the interaction accounting for an additional 25% of the variation in *REACT*, a large effect size in these simulated data. Figure 5.7A depicts the relationship between the residuals and the predicted scores. An ordinary least squares (OLS) linear fit (solid line with slope zero), an OLS quadratic fit (finely dotted line that curves upward very slightly from the linear fit at the right and left ends of the graph), and a lowess fit (dashed line that jiggles along) are overlaid. That the three lines are extremely close together tells us that the model has been properly specified and accurately reproduces the relationships in the data. Figure 5.7B gives the partial regression leverage plot for the regression of *REACT* on the interaction term *DESIRESPOUSEC* with both *DESIREC* and *SPOUSEC* partialed out of *REACT* and

DESIRESPOUSEC. The relationship is approximately linear. How can this be? When we apply linear regression to the modeling of nonlinear relationships like interactions, the strategy for representing the nonlinearity in a linear model is to create a predictor that is a nonlinear function of the original predictors, here *DESIRESPOUSEC*, that carries the nonlinear relationship. If we have successfully captured the nonlinear relationship, the created nonlinear predictor term will properly represent the true nonlinear relationship in the data, and the nonlinear predictor will be linearly related to the outcome variable after the other independent variables have been partialed out.

Quadratic Versus Interaction Models: Can They Be Distinguished?

The simulated data used in the present example were generated to have an interaction and not quadratic relationships. Yet we have seen evidence of curvilinearity in the data, even though we know all nonlinearity was produced by the interaction. Recall

Equation 4, repeated here, for the quadratic regression surface of which is plotted in Figure 5.3:

$$REACT_{predicted} = b_1\ DESIRE + b_2\ SPOUSE$$
$$+ b_3\ DESIRE^2 + b_4\ SPOUSE^2 + b_0\ (4)$$

Fitting this incorrect regression model to the data after centering DESIRE and SPOUSE yields significant positive curvilinear coefficients for both desire and spouse, indicative of U-shaped relationships of both predictors to the criterion. The R^2 for this quadratic model is .410, with a statistically significant gain in prediction from the addition of the two quadratic terms to the linear model (i.e., $R^2_{gain} = R^2_{multiple, quadratic} - R^2_{multiple, linear} = .410 - .291 = .119$). This increment in prediction is smaller than from the addition of the interaction term, but it still represents a moderate effect size (Cohen, 1988). Fitting the quadratic model without doing the exploratory analyses might well have led us to accept the quadratic model as appropriate. This observation raises the classic question of whether we can properly distinguish a curvilinear relationship from an interaction relationship through the use of statistical testing alone. This is a challenging problem. Successfully distinguishing the two classes of models is far more likely in data sets in which the correlation between predictor variables is low, the reliability of predictor variables is high, the distributions of the predictor variables have high tails, that is, there are numerous high and low values, and sample size is large. As we have seen, exploratory graphic methods provide useful evidence for this decision; however, they do not provide a formal hypothesis test. Diverse perspectives on this issue are provided by Ganzach (1997), Kromrey and Foster-Johnson (1999), Ma (2010), and MacCallum and Mar (1995).

Why Center Predictors?

When a regression equation contains higher order terms (e.g., XZ, X^2), the regression coefficients of the lower order terms that make up the higher order term are *conditional*. A conditional regression coefficient gives the regression of Y on a predictor only at a single specific value of the other predictor(s) in the regression equation. In the interactive regression equation, each lower order coefficient (b_1 and b_2) is conditional on the value of the other predictor. Examine the regression surfaces for the interactive and quadratic models in Figure 5.3. No single value of a regression coefficient for either predictor can characterize the change in the criterion as a function of the predictor across the full range of the other predictor. Inspection of the conditioning plots in Figure 5.4, which show the regression of REACT on DESIRE in different ranges of the SPOUSE predictor, clarifies that no one value of the coefficient for the regression of REACT on DESIRE can characterize this relationship. Aiken and West (1991, Chapter 3) provides a full explication of centering.

In the interactive regression equation, Equation 1, the b_1 coefficient is the regression of Y on X *only* at the value $Z = 0$. The b_2 coefficient is the regression of Y on Z *only* at the value $X = 0$. Table 5.1 shows for our numerical example there is no value of zero within the observed range of either predictor DESIRE or SPOUSE. Therefore, the b_1 and b_2 coefficients in the interactive model with uncentered predictors would produce coefficients that have no clear interpretation. In contrast, when predictors are centered, the arithmetic mean of each centered predictor is defined as zero. Thus the b_1 and b_2 coefficients in the interactive model with centered data have a clear interpretation. In our example, the b_1 regression coefficient for uncentered DESIRE is –.802 (Table 5.3, Panel C), whereas the regression coefficient for centered DESIREC is .532 (Table 5.3, Panel B). The value .532 from the centered regression equation is the regression of REACT on DESIREC at the arithmetic mean of the whole sample on centered SPOUSEC. Figure 5.4 shows us that for the most part the regression of REACT on DESIRE is positive. In Figure 5.4, only in Spousal Slice 1 is there a negative relationship of SPOUSEC to REACT. Recall that Slice 1 of Figure 5.4 includes the 20% of cases with the lowest scores on the SPOUSE variable; in this slice, the regression coefficient is slightly negative at –.135. What, then, is the source of the large negative value of –.802 for the regression of REACT on DESIRE in the uncentered regression equation? The –.802 is the regression of REACT on DESIRE beyond the edge of the warped interaction surface, at uncentered

SPOUSE = 0, a value that does not exist on the *SPOUSE* scale. The value −.802 has no meaning for this data set. Similar issues arise in the interpretation of the b_2 regression coefficient; $b_2 = -1.206$ for uncentered *SPOUSE* compared with the b_2 regression coefficient = −.008 for centered *SPOUSE*. Clear interpretation of the lower order regression coefficients in equations containing interactions requires centering predictors.

There is a final key point about centering— centering has no effect whatever on the highest order term in the regression equation, here the interaction term *XZ*. The regression coefficients, standard errors, and significance tests for the interaction term in the centered analysis (Table 5.3, Panel B) are identical to the corresponding values in the uncentered analysis (Table 5.3, Panel C). The reason that there is no effect of centering on the highest order regression coefficient is that the highest order term represents the warped shape of the regression surface, which does not change with centering predictors.

Interpreting the Interaction Between Two Continuous Variables

The interpretation of an interaction between two continuous variables proceeds by examining *simple slopes*, calculated from the overall regression equation containing the interaction. Simple slopes (also called *conditional slopes*) represent the value of the regression coefficient of the outcome variable on the focal predictor at a series of specific single values of the moderator. The slicing procedure presented in Figure 5.4 produces an approximation of the simple slopes using data for a narrow range of the moderator *Z*. However, the slicing procedure is nonparametric so no model is imposed. The nonparametric lowess fit permits other nonlinear forms of the relationship between the focal predictor and the outcome variable in the slice to be detected. With slicing, cases in which outliers (a few unusual data points) are producing the interaction can be detected. Slicing is used to explore the data; simple slopes are used to interpret the results of the regression model.

To understand simple slopes, we rearrange the interactive regression equation $\hat{Y} = b_1 X + b_2 Z + b_3 XZ + b_0$

into a simple regression equation that shows the regression of *Y* on *X* at specific values of *Z*:

$$\hat{Y} = (b_1 + b_3 Z) X + b_2 Z + b_0. \tag{8}$$

Rearranging the overall interactive regression makes clear that the regression of *Y* on *X* is different for every value of *Z*, so long as the b_3 coefficient for the interaction is nonzero. The term $(b_1 + b_3 Z)$ is the *simple slope*, the regression coefficient for the regression of *Y* on *X* at one specific value of *Z*. For the numerical example, the simple regression equation is as follows:

$$REACT_{predicted} = (b_1 + b_3 SPOUSEC) DESIREC \\ + (b_2 SPOUSEC + b_0). \tag{9}$$

The value $(b_1 + b_3 SPOUSEC)$ is the simple slope for the regression of *REACT* on *DESIREC*, which is different for every value of *SPOUSEC*. The value $(b_2 SPOUSEC + b_0)$ is the simple intercept.

When there is a clear metric for the moderator variable, specific interesting values are chosen. For example, in a study of young children in the age range 1 to 5 years, we might chose 1, 3, and 5 years as the values. If the moderator were scores on the revised Beck Depression Inventory–II (BDI-II; Beck, Steer, & Brown, 2006), with defined ranges of 0 to 13 for minimal depression, 14 to 19 for mild depression, 20 to 28 for moderate depression, and 29 to 36 for severe depression, we might choose 14, 20, and 29 as the cutpoints between categories. In the absence of a clear metric, a long-standing convention (Aiken & West, 1991; Cohen & Cohen, 1983) is to plot three simple regression lines to illustrate the interaction: the regression of *Y* on *X* 1 standard deviation above the mean of *Z*, at the mean of *Z*, and 1 standard deviation below the mean of *Z*. A plot of the interaction between *DESIREC* and *SPOUSEC* is given in Figure 5.8, showing the regression of *REACT* on *DESIREC* at these specific values of *SPOUSE*. Panels A and B depict the same graph created in two different software packages. We have added an additional simple regression line to this graph at 2 standard deviations below the mean of *SPOUSEC* for pedagogical purposes; we do *not* recommend inclusion of this line in most data sets.

A

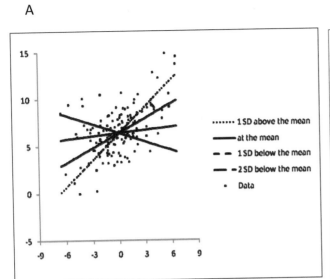

B

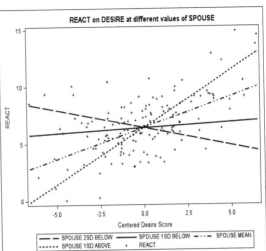

FIGURE 5.8.   Two representations of the simple regression lines for the regression of *REACT* on *DESIRE* at particular values of *SPOUSE*. As *SPOUSE* support increases, the relationship of *DESIRE* to *REACT* becomes more positive. Panel A produced in Excel; Panel B produced in SAS 9.2.

This additional line is included to show a location on the regression surface at which the surface has twisted from a positive relationship of *DESIREC* to *REACT* to a negative relationship (as we saw in Figures 5.4 and 5.5 in the conditioning graphs). The approach of plotting simple regression equations preserves the continuous nature of the variables in plotting the surface on the basis of the regression model. But, note that the small black dots in the figure are the actual data points. It is important to examine the simple regression lines in the context of the data to ensure that the simple regression lines fall within the range of the data. On the basis of the model, the simple regression of *REACT* on *DESIREC* 3 standard deviations below the mean of *SPOUSEC* can be computed. But, there are no cases located 3 standard deviations below the mean of *SPOUSEC*. The data are quite sparse at even 2 standard deviations below the mean of *SPOUSEC*, so that there do not appear to be sufficient cases to provide clear support for an interpretation of this negative simple slope. We strongly encourage researchers to compare the actual data with the specific values of the moderator at which they would like to interpret the moderator effect to ensure that there are sufficient cases to support the interpretation. In fact, there are only two cases more extreme than 2 standard deviations below the mean. Thus, one would be unwise

to render any interpretation of this negative relationship at 2 standard deviations below the mean, except perhaps to say that collecting data on individuals with extremely unsupportive spouses might reveal an interesting relationship. We are seeing an important distinction between the data themselves and the statistical models we apply to the data. Regression surfaces theoretically range from minus to plus infinity in all directions; the data do not. Interpretations must be confined to the actual range of the data. This is why Cohen and Cohen (1975) originally recommended using values of plus and minus 1 standard deviation from the mean, values at which there are sufficient data in most actual data sets. Occasionally, with highly skewed moderators, even this convention may fail so that the range of the data on the moderator should always be examined to ensure that interactions are interpreted within the range of the data.

Statistical tests of the significance of simple slopes have been developed. The development is fully explicated in Aiken and West (1991) and also explained in Cohen et al. (2003, Chapter 7). Aiken and West provided the SPSS syntax for generating simple regression lines, including the standard errors of simple regression slopes and *t* tests for their significance. A number of websites have also provided software for probing interactions with the

		TABLE 5.4		

Simple Regression Analyses to Probe the DESIRE × SPOUSE Interaction

Relation to mean of moderator	Simple regression line	$t(1,146)$	p
A. Simple Regression of REACT on DESIREC at particular values of SPOUSEC			
In general: $\hat{Y} = (.532 + .171\ SPOUSEC) + (-.008\ SPOUSEC + 6.386)$			
1 *SD* above mean of SPOUSEC	$\hat{Y} = 1.003\ DESIREC + 6.41$	12.94	.001
At the mean of SPOUSEC	$\hat{Y} = 0.548\ DESIREC + 6.39$	9.73	.001
1 *SD* below mean of SPOUSEC	$\hat{Y} = 0.094\ DESIREC + 6.37$	1.56	ns
2 *SD* below mean of SPOUSEC	$\hat{Y} = -0.313\ DESIREC + 6.42$	-2.94	.01
B. Simple Regression of REACT on SPOUSEC at particular values of DESIREC			
In general: $\hat{Y} = (-.008 + .171\ DESIREC) + (.532\ SPOUSEC + 6.386)$			
1 *SD* above mean of DESIREC	$\hat{Y} = 0.436\ SPOUSEC + 7.77$	5.82	.001
At the mean of DESIREC	$\hat{Y} = -0.008\ SPOUSEC + 6.39$	-0.15	ns
1 *SD* below mean of DESIREC	$\hat{Y} = -0.452\ SPOUSEC + 5.00$	-5.00	.001

Aiken and West procedure. Table 5.4, Panel A, provides the results of the simple regression analysis, including simple regression equations and tests of significance of simple slopes. At the mean of *SPOUSEC* and at 1 standard deviation above the mean of *SPOUSEC*, there is a significant positive regression of *REACT* on *DESIREC*; at 1 standard deviation below the mean of *SPOUSE*, there is no relation of *DESIREC* to *REACT*; at 2 standard deviations below, there is a significant negative relationship, a finding that should be interpreted cautiously given the sparseness of the data.

In some cases, additional perspective on the interaction can be gained by reversing the focal and moderator variables. In our example, we would examine the regression of the individual's reaction to the spouse's input, that is, *REACT* on *SPOUSEC* support, at levels of *DESIREC* to lose weight. The results of this analysis are shown in Table 5.4, Panel B. At 1 standard deviation above the mean of *DESIREC* to lose to lose weight, the relationship is significantly positive; at the mean of *DESIREC*, the relation is nonsignificant. At 1 standard deviation below the mean of *DESIREC*, the relationship is significantly negative. This finding illustrates the how the same behavior on the part of the spouse can appear to function as positive social support versus negative social control depending on the desires of

the wife (see Ranby, 2009, for an empirical example of this phenomenon).

A final note about the simple slope analysis is that it was carried out here with centered predictors. If it had been carried out with uncentered predictors, the simple slopes would be identical—the shape of the warped regression surface does not change with centering. Centering does not affect the interpretation of the interaction, whereas it contributes to meaningful interpretation of the of the lower order coefficients.

Linear × Linear and More Complex Interactions

The interaction model we have considered in depth includes only a Linear × Linear interaction—that is, the regression of Y on X is linear at every value of Z, and the regression of Y on Z is linear at every value of X. The simple regression equations in Table 5.4 are all linear regression equations. Other more complex forms of interaction are possible, for example, a Curvilinear × Linear interaction modeled by the following equation:

$$\hat{Y} = b_1 X + b_2 X^2 + b_3 Z + b_4 XZ + b_5 X^2 Z + b_0. \quad (10)$$

Such an interaction is one in which there is a curvilinear relationship of X to Y with the degree of curvature varying as a function of the value of Z. This and other more complex interaction models are fully developed in Aiken and West (1991).

Summary

In this section of the chapter, we have presented the exploratory examination of interactions between continuous variables. We have strongly emphasized the use of exploratory graphics as a complement to testing a priori hypotheses. The consistent theme has been to look first with exploratory graphics and then to analyze, and having analyzed, look again with graphics to examine model adequacy. At no point have we taken findings from the output of statistical analyses at face value; at every point we have looked graphically. In the present case, our exploratory data analysis has not identified other candidate models that may provide a better account of the data than our hypothesized linear interaction model.

In other cases, exploratory data analysis may surface one or more alternative models that provide an equally good or better account of the data. These models provide alternative potential explanations of the results and weaken the evidence base for the hypothesized model. At the same time, the a priori model has a special status: It was hypothesized without looking at the data so that its findings may be directly interpreted. In contrast, models derived from exploratory data analyses may capitalize on chance findings that are unique to the single data set under consideration. The goal of developing the regression model is to characterize the relationships that exist in the entire population. Consequently, new models developed from exploratory data analysis should be treated as tentative models. Ideally, the results need to be replicated in a new data set before they are interpreted as supporting the new model. Alternatively, computer-intensive procedures that repeatedly sample part of the data for estimating the model and another part for replicating it can be used to provide stronger evidence that the model is likely to hold in the population. Diaconis (1985) and West (2006) provided discussions of these issues. For more information about computer-intensive resampling techniques, see Volume 2, Chapter 22, this handbook; for information about the design of simulations, see Volume 2, Chapter 23, this handbook.

CATEGORICAL × CONTINUOUS VARIABLE INTERACTIONS

Not infrequently we encounter data sets in which a categorical variable interacts with a continuous variable, for example, gender interacting with age to predict verbal achievement in children, and intervention conditions interacting with baseline severity of depression to predict the posttreatment level of depression. The major change in the regression analysis of the hypothesized model is that a coding scheme must be used to represent these categories. For example, imagine a clinical trial in which one of three treatment conditions is delivered to depressed patients: (a) placebo only, (b) psychotherapy plus placebo, (c) psychotherapy plus drug. G-1 code variables, here 2, must be used to represent the G treatment groups. Depending on the researcher's hypothesis, different coding schemes can be used. For example, code variable 1 could be placebo = –2/3, psychotherapy plus placebo = +1/3, and psychotherapy plus drug = +1/3. Code variable 2 could be placebo = 0, psychotherapy plus placebo = –1/2, psychotherapy plus drug = +1/2. This coding scheme tests the average of the two active treatment conditions against the placebo and then compares the two active treatment conditions. Equation 11 is the regression model representing these hypotheses, with G_1 and G_2 being the group code variables 1 and 2, respectively, and X_C representing the centered value of baseline depression.

$$\hat{Y} = b_1 X_C + b_2 G_1 + b_3 G_2 + b_4 X_C G_1 + b_5 X_C G_2 + b_0. \quad (11)$$

The specification of code variables is described in Cohen et al. (2003, Chapter 8), and the interpretation of the results of the regression analysis including two-dimensional and three-dimensional graphs is presented in West, Aiken, and Krull (1996). Of importance, all that has been illustrated about the analysis of interactions—specification of the regression equation, centering of predictors, simple regression analysis, and examination of simple slopes in each group—applies. The value of exploratory data analysis in closely examining the hypothesized model and potentially examining alternative models also applies.

A new feature is that a special statistical procedure, the Johnson–Neyman procedure, can be used to identify the values on the moderator variable at which the differences between two treatment conditions are statistically significant. As an illustration, we have created a categorical spouse variable *SPOUSECAT*. We do not recommend categorizing continuous variables because doing so attenuates parameter estimates (MacCallum, Zhang, Preacher, & Rucker, 2002) and reduces the statistical power to detect interactions (Maxwell & Delaney, 1993). We do so here only for pedagogical purposes to provide an illustration using the same example data set. The highest third of cases in the *SPOUSE* distribution are categorized as Strong Support for weight loss (*n* = 50) and the lowest third of cases in the *SPOUSE* distribution are categorized as Weak Support for weight loss (*n* = 50). For this analysis comparing two groups, the Strong versus Weak Support groups, one contrast code is created (+.5, –.5, for Strong Support and Weak Support, respectively). We create a second centered *DESIRE* variable *DESIRECC* on the basis of the 100 cases in the analysis

(we use the *CC* to denote that *DESIRE* has been centered again for just the 100 cases in this example). The outcome variable *REACT* remains the same. Given that there is only one code variable, the regression equation is as follows:

$$\hat{Y} = b_1 X_C + b_2 G_1 + b_3 X_C G_1 + b_0. \tag{12}$$

The results of the regression analysis are provided in Table 5.5. There is a significant positive relationship of *DESIRECC* to *REACT*, and a significant interaction between *DESIRECC* and *SPOUSECAT*. In Figure 5.9 and Table 5.5, we see that for potential dieters with spouses in the Weak Support category, the potential dieters' desire to lose weight has little relationship to *REACT*: The simple regression line is flat. For potential dieters whose spouses are in Strong Support category, the regression line indicates there is a very strong relationship between *DESIRECC* and *REACT*. Considering the difference between the lines, when desire to lose weight is low (–3), spouses in the Strong Support category engender low scores on REACT compared with those in the Weak Support category. When one does not want to lose

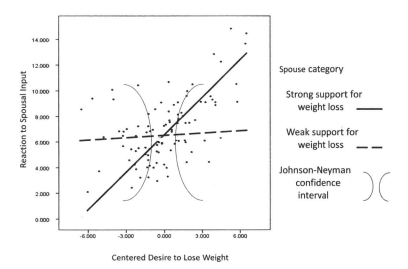

FIGURE 5.9.   Categorical × Continuous variable interaction between continuously measured desire to lose weight and two categories of spouse input: Weak support for losing weight (heavy dashed line); strong support for losing weight (solid line). The two vertical curved lines represent the Potthoff cutoffs of the simultaneous confidence intervals in the extension of the Johnson Neyman procedure. To the left of the left curved line, reaction is significantly more negative when spouses offer strong support. To the right of the right curved line, reaction is significantly more positive when spouses offer strong positive support. This graph was produced in SPSS; simple regression lines enhanced and confidence intervals overlaid in Powerpoint.

TABLE 5.5

Analysis of a Categorical × Continuous Variable Interaction

	A. Overall regression analysis					
	Unstandardized coefficients		**Standardized coefficients**			
Model	*b*	*SE*	*b**	*SE*	*t*	**Sig.**
1 (constant)	6.589	0.188			34.973	.000
DESIRECC	0.523	0.070	0.558	0.075	7.475	.000
SPOUSECAT	0.078	0.377	0.015	0.074	0.206	.837
SPOUSECATDESIRE	0.940	0.140	0.480	0.072	6.713	.000

B. Simple regression analysis of REACT on DESIRECC for each group of spouses,(i.e. each category of SPOUSECAT)

In general: $\hat{Y} = (.523 + .940 \text{ SPOUSECAT}) + (.078 \text{ SPOUSECAT} + 6.589)$

Level of spouse support	Simple regression line	*t*(1,146)	*p*
At Strong spouse support	$\hat{Y} = .993 \text{ DESIRECC} + 6.628$	10.44	.001
At Weak spouse support	$\hat{Y} = .053 \text{ DESIRECC} + 6.550$	0.52	*ns*

Note. A: DESIRECC remains a continuous predictor. The SPOUSEC variable is transformed into a categorical variable SPOUSECAT with the top third (*n* = 50) of the SPOUSEC distribution categorized as strong positive support for weight loss and the bottom third (*n* = 50) of the SPOUSEC distribution categorized as weak support for weight loss (coded +.5 and −.5, respectively). B: DESIRECC is the centered score on DESIREC, centered again at the mean of the 100 cases from the distribution of DESIREC (50 in the high third, 50 in the low third). The dependent variable is REACT. *b* = unstandardized regression coefficient; *b** = standardized regression coefficient; Sig. = significance.

weight and one's spouse is expressing support for losing weight, a negative emotional reaction is the response. When desire to lose weight is high (+3), the findings are reversed: Spouses in the Strong Support Category engender high scores on *REACT* compared with those in the Weak Support Category.

The Johnson–Neyman procedure examines the difference in elevation between the regression lines for two groups at specific individual points on a continuous variable and identifies the point or points at which the difference in elevation become significant; see the classic writing by Huitema (1980, Chapter 13) and a recent overview by Hayes and Matthes (2009). The Potthoff generalization of the Johnson–Neyman procedure extends the Johnson–Neyman procedure to provide a simultaneous confidence interval that specifies the range or ranges of values on the focal predictor (here *DESIRECC*) for which the elevations of the two lines differ. Hayes and Matthes have provided both SPSS and SAS macros for implementing the Johnson–Neyman procedure (see also http://www.comm.ohio-state.edu/ahayes/SPSS%20programs/modprobe.htm); we applied the macro here.

In the example, there are two regions of difference, indicated by the two vertical curved lines on Figure 5.9. According to the Potthoff generalization, at values of *DESIRECC* below −1.179, reaction to the spouse is significantly more negative when spouses offer strong support than when they offer weak support. At values of *DESIRECC* above .971, reaction is significantly more positive when spouses offer strong positive support than when they offer weak support. Between the two curved lines is a range of values of desire to diet in which the emotional reaction to the spouse does not differ when spouses offer Strong Support versus Weak Support. Again we find that a graphic display produces an easily grasped communication of the outcome of the Categorical × Continuous variable interaction.

INTERACTIONS IN ANALYSIS OF VARIANCE

For the sake of pedagogical simplicity, we present graphics for the exploration of interactions in ANOVA with the same example. We retain the same a priori hypothesis, that *DESIRE* and

SPOUSE interact or that *SPOUSE* moderates the relationship of *DESIRE* to *REACT*, the reaction to spouse input. To render the data amenable to treatment in ANOVA, we take a step backward in time and in quality from the perspective of statistical analysis and divide continuous *DESIRE* to lose weight into thirds representing three levels of a factor *DESIRE3* (Low, Moderate, and High). We do the same for *SPOUSE*, yielding a factor *SPOUSE3* with three levels (Low, Moderate, and High) of support for losing weight. We append the number 3 to the names of these variables to indicate their new status as factors with three levels each. We repeat what we have said before—we do *not* endorse or recommend such an approach in practice. As we have pointed out, cutting variables loses information, diminishing statistical power. Cutting variables also introduces measurement error and may produce spurious lower order effects when the independent variables are correlated, as they are here (Maxwell & Delaney, 1993). Finally, the outcome variable *REACT*, the reaction to spouse input, is the same as before; these scores are unchanged.

The Starting Point: Graphic Explorations of the Data

Table 5.6 provides information on the nine cells of the 3 × 3 factorial design of *DESIRE3* × *SPOUSE3*, including means, standard deviations, standard errors, 95% confidence intervals, and sample sizes. We see that the sample sizes are unequal because of the correlation between *DESIRE3* and *SPOUSE3*. We see that the mean of the high–high cell, for high *DESIRE3* to lose weight and high support from the *SPOUSE3* is exceptionally elevated, compared with all the remaining cells—there is a synergy between wanting to lose weight and having a spouse who supports this. Table 5.6 provides substantial information about the cells, but this information is not easily discerned and can be much more easily conveyed graphically.

Side-by-side boxplots. Figure 5.10 is a side-by-side boxplot (or box and whiskers plot) of the nine cells in the design. The boxplot is a fine example of the exploratory graphs developed by Tukey (1977) in his monumental contribution to the field of

---

TABLE 5.6

Cell Statistics for Analysis of Variance of Reaction as a Function of DESIRE TO LOSE WEIGHT (Low, Moderate, High) and SPOUSAL INPUT (Low Support, Moderate Support, High Support)

Desire to lose weight	Spousal input		
	Low support	Moderate support	High support
Low			
M	6.408	4.668	4.987
SD	2.271	2.387	1.638
SE	.441	.505	.560
95% CI	[5.537, 7.279]	[3.670, 5.666]	[3.880, 6.094]
n	21	16	13
Moderate			
M	6.424	6.327	6.048
SD	1.714	1.824	1.881
SE	.490	.476	.521
95% CI	[5.456, 7.393]	[5.387, 7.268]	[5.017, 7.079]
n	17	18	15
High			
M	6.807	7.255	9.723
SD	1.583	1.536	2.564
SE	.583	.505	.431
95% CI	[5.655, 7.960]	[6.257, 8.253]	[8.872, 10.574]
n	12	16	22

Note. These standard errors are as reported in SPSS. Each is taken from the $MS_{within\ cell}$ from the whole design, that is the pooled within cell variance from across all cells in the design. For these data, $MS_{within\ cell}$ = 4.078, and $\sqrt{MS_{within\ cell}}$ = 2.019. The standard error for cell $_{j,k}$ is given as $SE_{j,k} = \sqrt{MS_{within\ cell}} / \sqrt{n_{j,k}}$. In sum, a pooled estimate from the whole of the sampling error associated with each cell is employed in estimating the standard error. *SD* = standard deviation within the cell; *SE* = standard error of the cell mean; 95% CI = 95% confidence interval on the cell mean; *n* = number of cases in the cell.

---

exploratory data analysis. A boxplot provides a graphic representation of Tukey's five-number summary—the median or 50th percentile, the 25th and 75th percentiles, and the most extreme high and low scores. The same graph is depicted here in R and in SPSS. In each figure, the cells are organized into three clusters of three cells each. These clusters are arranged such that the three cells in each cluster represent the three levels of *DESIRE3* at one level of *SPOUSE3*. This layout permits visualization of the hypothesized interaction, an examination of the

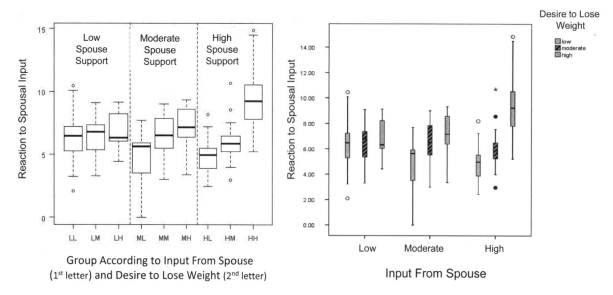

FIGURE 5.10. Side-by-side boxplots of the distribution of scores within each cell of the design. The same figure is produced in R (left figure) and in SPSS (right figure). For each cell, the box represents the middle 50% of all scores in the cell, the heavy horizontal bar within the box is the median; the vertical whiskers emanating from the box represent the distance to the extreme scores. SPSS can provide the case numbers of these extreme points on the graph (the numbers were deleted here). In SPSS, points beyond three IQRs from the end of the box are noted with an asterisk (*), those between 1.5 and 3 IQRs are noted with a circle (whether the circle is open or filled depends on the editing of the graphic in SPSS, shown in high spousal support above, and not on the location of the point).

relationship of *DESIRE3* to *REACT* at each of the three levels of *SPOUSE3*. Seeing these plots side by side illustrates important trends in central tendency, from inspection of the medians. Furthermore, we have a clear visualization of variability and of skew of the distribution within each cell. We also see any outliers, because it is conventional to plot extreme scores separately. Figure 5.10 strongly suggests the presence of the *DESIRE3* × *SPOUSE3* interaction—the pattern of medians differs across the three clusters of boxplots.

Trellis plots of Kernel density functions in individual cells. Figure 5.11 complements Figure 5.10. Figure 5.11 is a trellis plot of the distribution of the dependent variable *REACT* in each of the nine cells of the 3 × 3 factorial design of *DESIRE3* × *SPOUSE3*. A kernel density smooth of the frequency histogram in each cell is illustrated. This plot gives us more of an impression of the distribution in each cell than we obtain from the boxplot. We look for ceiling and floor effects and see none. The distributions are close to normal in form. There are no severely bimodal distributions

or severely skewed distributions. We look for evidence of nonconstant variance. The variability of the scores appears similar across cells, although slightly smaller in the cell in row 1, column 2 (high desire, moderate spouse support). The smoothness of kernel density functions is controlled by a parameter that can be changed to decrease or increase the smoothness of a function. To the right of the trellis plot are displayed three levels of smoothing on one cell (high desire, moderate support). In generating these graphs, the analyst typically examines a range of smoothing levels, searching for a graph that is not too lumpy but that captures the main features of the distribution.

Means with error bars. Figure 5.12 is more familiar than the previous two figures and is often presented in journal articles. However, this graph is often *grossly misunderstood and ill communicated* (Belia, Fidler, Williams, & Cumming, 2005). We take this opportunity to clarify the meaning of the two graphs in Figure 5.12. Figure 5.12A shows the means of the nine cells with the vertical bars representing *margins of error* (MEs) of the 95%

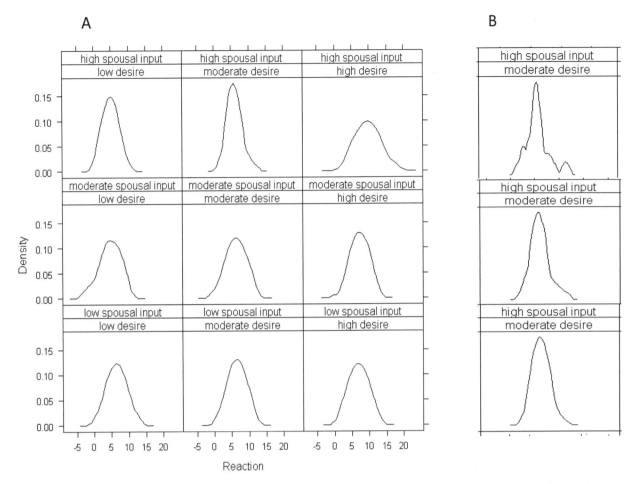

FIGURE 5.11. Trellis plot (A) of the distribution of scores within each of the nine cells of the 3 × 3 factorial design. Distributions are illustrated with Kernel density functions. Single cell with three levels of smoothing (B). Graph produced in R.

confidence intervals around the means (these same confidence intervals are reported in Table 5.6). To review, the confidence interval around a single mean is given as follows:

$$C[(\bar{X} - ME) \leq \mu \leq (\bar{X} + ME)] = 1 - \alpha,$$
$$\text{where } ME = t_{1-\alpha/2} SE_{\bar{X}}. \tag{13}$$

The value $(1 - \alpha)$ is the level of confidence, for example, 95%. The ME is composed of two values: the value of some test statistic and the value of a standard error of the mean. The value $t_{1-\alpha/2}$ is that value of the t-distribution, which leads to coverage of the middle $(1 - \alpha)$ proportion of scores. The

value $SE_{\bar{X}}$ is the estimate of the standard error of the mean.[2] For 95% confidence, the value $t_{.975}$ is employed because it cuts off the top .025 and bottom .025 of the distribution, leaving the central .95 of all scores. For example, with $(n - 1) = 15$ degrees of freedom for a cell mean, $t_{.975} = 2.131$, or slightly over two standard errors of the mean. The values $(\bar{X} - ME)$ and $(\bar{X} + ME)$ are the lower limit and upper limit of the confidence interval, respectively, what we see as the top and bottom ends of the confidence intervals in Figure 5.12A.

Figure 5.12B shows the same means; however, vertical bars are now only *one* standard error on

---

[2]In general, the expression for the estimate of the standard error of the mean is $s_X / \sqrt{n}$, that is, the standard deviation in the cell divided by the square root of the sample size. In nonrepeated measures ANOVA, the typical calculation of the standard error of each cell mean in software packages (e.g., SPSS, SAS) is computed using $\sqrt{MS_{within\ cell}}$ from the whole design in lieu of the specific standard deviation in each individual cell. This is so for the standard errors reported in Table 5.6, as explained in more detail in the footnote of Table 5.6. Put another way, in nonrepeated measures ANOVA, a pooled estimate from the whole of the sampling error of all cell means is employed in estimating the standard error of the mean in each cell.

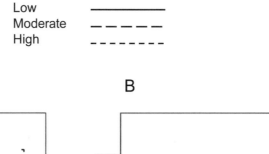

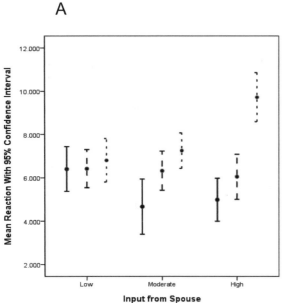
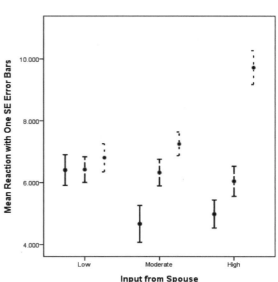

FIGURE 5.12.   Cell means with error bars of two types. Clusters of three cells show the means at three levels of *DESIRE*3 within a single level of *SPOUSE*3. Panel A displays a 95% confidence interval around each mean, that is, *margin of error* bars. Panel B displays one standard error on each side of the mean, that is, *standard error* bars.

either side of the mean. The bars are about half the length of the bars in Figure 5.12A. The bars in Figure 5.12A are referred to as *margin of error bars*; those in Figure 5.12B as *standard error* bars. It is absolutely critical that one report which bars are actually represented in graphs like those Figure 5.12; in Figure 5.12, we have indicated the specific nature of the nature of the bars in the y-axis label.

The two graphs in Figure 5.12 are similar to the box plot graphs of Figure 5.10. However, there are important differences. Figure 5.12 displays means; Figure 5.10 displays medians. The high-desire, high-spouse cell appears more extreme when the means are illustrated in Figure 5.12 than when the medians are exhibited in Figure 5.10. The reason is straightforward—there is a very high outlier that is drawing the mean upward; the outlier is easily seen in Figure 5.10 as the single point above the upper whisker in the boxplot of that cell. Of course, the mean, but not the median, is affected by extreme scores.

In Figure 5.10, each central box covers the middle 50% of scores. The measure of variability is based on the interquartile range (IQR; i.e., the distance between the 25th and 75th percentiles of the distribution). In contrast, in Figure 5.12a, the measure of spread is the standard deviation; for a normal distribution, the 95% confidence intervals represented in the bars cover the middle 95% of scores. In Figure 5.12b, the error bars, one standard error on either side of the mean, capture the middle 68% of scores in a normal distribution.

When we inspect graphs like those in Figure 5.12, it seems natural to look for cells with bars that do not overlap. The standard conception (often wrong) is to conclude that two means are statistically significantly different only if their bars do not overlap. It is true that if the error bars represent one standard error on either side of the mean, as in Figure 5.12B, then the two means with error bars that do not overlap are significantly different from one another. If the error bars are confidence intervals, however, as in Figure 5.12A, the story is quite different. In fact, 95% confidence intervals may overlap between two cells when the two cells are significantly different from one another at Type I error of $\alpha = .05$. Cumming and Finch (2005) provided an extended discussion of graphing of means with error bars versus margins of error and provided guidelines (not rules) for interpretation.

ANOVA and Displays of Means

We have provided visualization of the data through boxplots, trellis plots of cell kernel densities, and plots of means with margin of error or standard error bars. We have gained a strong idea of the behavior of

our data with regard to statistical assumptions and also a strong idea of whether the pattern of the data is consistent with hypotheses. Now we move to the ANOVA. A series of three ANOVA summary tables is provided in Table 5.7. The first ANOVA summary table given in Table 5.7, Panel A, is a main effects model, with no interaction included. We are accustomed in ANOVA to run the default of a complete factorial model including all main effects and interactions. Here we begin by examining a main effects only model, parallel to the first order effects only regression model in Table 5.3, Panel A. We note in Table 5.7, Panel A, that the variation accounted for by the main effects model is $R^2_{multiple,\ main\ effects} = .253$, which is less than the variation accounted for by the

---

TABLE 5.7

Analysis of Variance Summary Table and Simple Effects Analyses

Source	Type III sum of squares	df	MS	F	Sig.	Partial η^2
A. Main effects only analysis of variance[a]						
Between cell	227.118[a]	4	56.779	12.289	.000	.253
DESIRE3	183.335	2	91.667	19.841	.000	.215
SPOUSE3	26.553	2	13.227	2.874	.060	.038
Within cell	669.928	145	4.620			
Total	897.046	149				
B. Full factorial analysis of variance[b]						
Between cell	322.092[b]	8	40.282	9.874	.000	.359
DESIRE3	161.862	2	80.931	19.847	.000	.220
SPOUSE3	17.108	2	8.554	2.098	.127	.029
DESIREC*SPOUSEC	94.974	4	23.744	5.823	.000	.142
Within cell	574.954	141	4.078			
Total	897.046	149				

C. Simple main effects of DESIRE3 on REACT at three levels of SPOUSE3						
Spouse support	Sum of squares	df	MS	F	Sig.	Partial η^2
Low						
Contrast	1.403	2	0.702	0.172	.842	.002
Within cell	574.954	141	4.078			
Moderate						
Contrast	55.074	2	27.537	6.753	.002	.087
Within cell	574.954	141	4.078			
High						
Contrast	221.831	2	110.916	27.201	.000	.278
Within cell	574.954	141	4.078			

Note. The dependent variable: REACT. DESIRE3 is the three-level desire factor. SPOUSE3 is the three-level spouse factor. [a]For the main effects only model, $R^2 = .253$ (Adj. $R^2 = .233$). [b]For the full factorial model with interaction, $R^2 = .359$ (Adj. $R^2 = .323$).

linear regression, first order effects model in Table 5.3, Panel A, where $R^2_{multiple, linear} = .291$. The loss in variance accounted for is due to our having categorized the continuous variables for the ANOVA. Table 5.7, Panel B, gives the ANOVA summary table for standard full factorial design with the two main effects and the interaction, parallel to the full interactive regression model in Table 5.3, Panel B. In the full factorial ANOVA model in Table 5.7, Panel B, the variation accounted for by the main effects plus interaction is $R^2_{multiple, main effects plus interaction} = .359$. This is notably less than the variation accounted for by the full regression model with interaction in Table 5.3, Panel B, where $R^2_{multiple, main effects plus interaction} = .544$. In the ANOVA, the gain in variance accounted for by the interaction is $R^2_{gain} = R^2_{multiple, main effects plus interaction} - R^2_{multiple, main effects} = .359 - .253$, or $R^2_{gain} = .106$, again less than the gain from the interaction in multiple regression, $R^2_{gain} = .253$. The building up of an ANOVA model from main effects only to full factorial is precisely the same operation as building up regression models. This way of approaching ANOVA as a series of models is consistent with modern treatments of ANOVA (e.g., Maxwell & Delaney, 2004).

Here we introduce a new model, a pure interaction model from which the main effects have been removed. Recall the often-stated definition of an interaction in the context of ANOVA, that is, that part of an outcome that is over and above the main effects because of the unique combination of a level of each factor, for example, the combination of high desire to lose weight combined with high spouse support. For each cell mean $\overline{AB}_{ij}$ in the design, we compute the difference of the cell mean from the grand mean $\overline{G}$. This *between-cell* difference $(\overline{AB}_{ij} - \overline{G})$ contains the influence of the individual factors (main effects) and the interaction. From this difference we subtract the portion of the difference attributable to the main effect of the first factor, factor A; we also subtract the portion of the difference attributable to the main effect of the second factor, factor B. The computation is as follows:

$$\text{Between-cell residual} = (\overline{AB}_{ij} - \overline{G}) - (\overline{A}_i - \overline{G}) - (\overline{B}_j - \overline{G}), \quad (14)$$

where $\overline{A}_i$ and $\overline{B}_j$ are the means of the levels of factor A and B, respectively.

The between-cell residual reflects only the pure effect of the interaction between the two variables (along with any random error in all the means, of course). A graphic display of the between-cell residuals in each cell shows us the true nature of the interaction, unconfounded by main effects. Each value in such a graph is a positive or negative residual that shows by how much and in what direction the cell mean is changed by the interaction away from the cell mean one would expect on the basis of main effects only. Such a graph illustrates vividly the role of the interaction in producing the outcome. Rosnow and Rosenthal (1989, 1991) argued strongly that an understanding of the interaction was best accomplished by examining between-cell residuals. We do so here graphically.

Figure 5.13 provides three graphs. In each graph, a single line connects the cell means representing reaction to spousal input at three levels of desire to lose weight. Each line is confined to one level of spousal support (the solid line for low support, the large dashes line for moderate support, and the small dashes line for high support). These lines are the familiar simple main effect lines from post hoc probing in ANOVA. Each line addresses the effect of desire to lose weight at one level of spousal support. These lines are the analogs of simple regression lines in multiple regression with interactions. Figure 5.13A shows the profiles that result from a model containing only main effects. Figure 5.13B shows the cell means from the full factorial design. Figure 5.13C shows the between cell residuals, that is, the impact of the interaction between *DESIRE3* and *SPOUSE3* on the value of each cell mean. Note first that the y-axis values in Figure 5.13C range from negative to positive—these are residuals, the differences between each cell mean and the predicted means from the main effects only model. Figure 5.13C is literally the figure that results if you subtract the means in Figure 5.13B from corresponding means in Figure 5.13A. Figure 5.13C powerfully displays the crossover interaction. If a spouse is not supportive (the solid line), then increasing desire to lose weight is associated with an increasingly negative reaction to the unsupportive spouse.

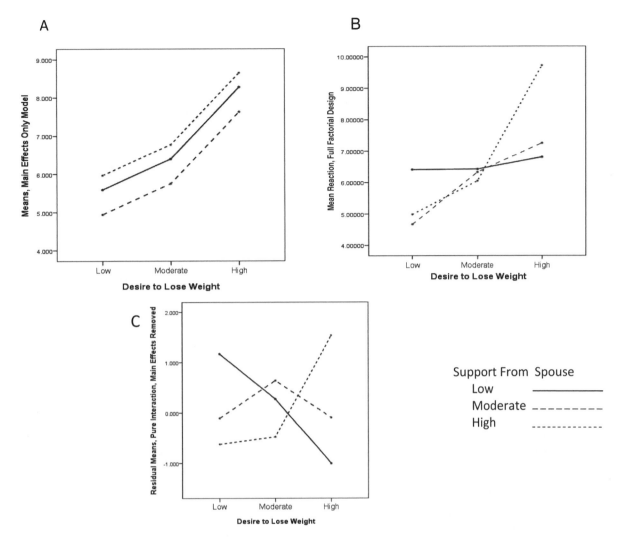

FIGURE 5.13.   Profiles of mean *REACT* as a function of level of desire to lose weight, at each of three levels of spousal support. Panel A shows the profiles that result from a model containing only main effects, ignoring the interaction. Panel B shows the cell means from the full factorial design. Panel C shows the between-cell residuals, that is, the impact of the interaction between *DESIRE*3 and *SPOUSE*3 on the value of each cell mean. Panel C clarifies the interaction effect, that if a spouse is not supportive, increasing desire to lose weight is associated with an increasingly negative reaction. If a spouse is highly supportive, then increasing desire to lose weight is associated with an increasingly positive reaction.

If a spouse is highly supportive (the small dashes line), then increasing desire to lose weight is associated with an increasingly positive reaction to the spouse. Only in the pure interaction Figure 5.13C is the full nature of the interaction, the effect over and above the two main effects, revealed.

For completeness we provide the simple main effects summary in Table 5.7, Panel C. What is apparent from the plots of cell means with error bars (Figure 5.10) and the cell means (Figure 5.13B) is borne out in the simple effects table. There is no significant difference among the mean reaction scores

as a function of *DESIRE*3 at low *SPOUSE*3 support, and a significant difference among the means at moderate and high *SPOUSE*3 support.

Summary of graphic explorations in ANOVA.
Rather than racing forward to the ANOVA summary table and tests of simple main effects (i.e., post hoc tests), we explored the data with graphics that focused on the distribution of data within the cells and the visual comparison of cell means. These graphic displays revealed a great deal about the data. The ANOVA was almost an afterthought,

permitting us to associate significance levels with what we observed through graphic displays. Once again, the exploratory graphic displays informed us about the behavior of our data and about the nature of the interaction in the data. The between-cell residual plot, a novel plot in the ANOVA framework, vividly illustrated the synergistic interaction between the desire to lose weight, the support received from the spouse, and the emotional reaction to spousal input.

CONCLUSION

Modern graphic approaches to data display provide a rich understanding of our data. These approaches bring us far closer to our data than tables of descriptive statistics and tables of the outcomes of statistical tests. The immediate application of complex statistical methodologies to data as soon as the data are available is not wise. Such an approach separates us from the true nature of our data. It may hide subtle signals about theoretically important and novel relationships in our data that may be obscured when, from force of habit or familiarity, we ignore data exploration. It may fail to alert us when important assumptions about the nature of the data, necessary for proper statistical analyses, are violated. Modern graphic displays go far beyond what we have introduced here; they represent a highly refined set of lenses through which we can detect the rich messages in our data.

References

Aiken, L. S., & West, S. G. (1991). *Multiple regression: Testing and interpreting interactions.* Newbury Park, CA: Sage.

Beck, A. T., Steer, R. A., & Brown, G. K. (2006). *Beck Depression Inventory* (2nd ed.). Resource Centers for Minority Aging Research Measurement Tools. Retrieved from http://www.musc.edu/dfm/RCMAR/Beck.html

Belia, S., Fidler, F., Williams, J., & Cumming, G. (2005). Researchers misunderstand confidence intervals and standard error bars. *Psychological Methods, 10,* 389–396. doi:10.1037/1082-989X.10.4.389

Cohen, J. (1968). Multiple regression as a general data-analytic system. *Psychological Bulletin, 70,* 426–443. doi:10.1037/h0026714

Cohen, J. (1978). Partialed products are interactions; partialed powers are curve components. *Psychological Bulletin, 85,* 858–866. doi:10.1037/0033-2909.85.4.858

Cohen, J. (1983). The cost of dichotomization. *Applied Psychological Measurement, 7,* 249–253. doi:10.1177/014662168300700301

Cohen, J. (1988). *Statistical power analysis for the behavioral sciences* (2nd ed.). Mahwah, NJ: Erlbaum.

Cohen, J., & Cohen, P. (1975). *Applied multiple regression/correlation analysis for the behavioral sciences.* Hillsdale, NJ: Erlbaum.

Cohen, J., & Cohen, P. (1983). *Applied multiple regression/correlation analysis for the behavioral sciences* (2nd ed.). Hillsdale, NJ: Erlbaum.

Cohen, J., Cohen, P., West, S., & Aiken, L. (2003). *Applied multiple regression/correlation analysis for the behavioral sciences* (3rd ed.). Mahwah, NJ: Erlbaum.

Cumming, G., & Finch, S. (2005). Inference by eye: Confidence intervals, and how to read pictures of data. *American Psychologist, 60,* 170–180. doi:10.1037/0003-066X.60.2.170

Diaconis, P. (1985). Theories of data analysis: From magical thinking through classical statistics. In D. C. Hoaglin, F. Mosteller, & J. Tukey (Eds.), *Exploring data tables, trends, and shapes* (pp. 1–36). New York, NY: Wiley.

Ganzach, Y. (1997). Misleading interaction and curvilinear terms. *Psychological Methods, 2,* 235–247. doi:10.1037/1082-989X.2.3.235

Hayes, A. F., & Matthes, J. (2009). Computational procedures for probing interactions in OLS and logistic regression: SPSS and SAS implementations. *Behavior Research Methods, 41,* 924–936. doi:10.3758/BRM.41.3.924

Huitema, B. E. (1980). *Analysis of covariance and alternatives.* New York, NY: Wiley.

Kirk, R. E. (1968). *Experimental design.* Belmont, CA: Brooks/Cole.

Kromrey, J. D., & Foster-Johnson, L. F. (1999). Statistically differentiating between interaction and nonlinearity in multiple regression analysis: A Monte Carlo investigation of a recommended strategy. *Educational and Psychological Measurement, 59,* 392–413. doi:10.1177/00131649921969947

Ma, Y. (2010). *Comparison of statistical power for resting interactive versus quadratic effects* (Unpublished doctoral dissertation). Arizona State University, Tempe.

MacCallum, R. C., & Mar, C. M. (1995). Distinguishing between moderator and quadratic effects in multiple regression. *Psychological Bulletin, 118,* 405–421. doi:10.1037/0033-2909.118.3.405

MacCallum, R. C., Zhang, S., Preacher, K. J., & Rucker, D. D. (2002). On the practice of dichotomization of quantitative variables. *Psychological Methods, 7,* 19–40. doi:10.1037/1082-989X.7.1.19

Maxwell, S. E., & Delaney, H. D. (1993). Bivariate median-splits and spurious statistical significance. *Psychological Bulletin, 113,* 181–190. doi:10.1037/0033-2909.113.1.181

Maxwell, S. E., & Delaney, H. D. (2004). *Designing experiments and analyzing data: A model comparison perspective.* Mahwah, NJ: Erlbaum.

McNemar, Q. (1962). *Psychological statistics* (3rd ed.). New York, NY: Wiley.

Morgan-Lopez, A. A., & MacKinnon, D. P. (2006). Demonstration and evaluation of a method to assess mediated moderation. *Behavior Research Methods, 38,* 77–87. doi:10.3758/BF03192752

Ranby, K. (2009). *Spousal influences on physical activity among adult women: An expansion of the health action process approach* (Unpublished doctoral dissertation). Arizona State University, Tempe.

Rosnow, R., & Rosenthal, R. (1989). Definition and interpretation of interaction effects. *Psychological Bulletin, 105,* 143–146. doi:10.1037/0033-2909.105.1.143

Rosnow, R., & Rosenthal, R. (1991). If you're looking at the cell means, you're not looking at *only* the interaction (unless all main effects are zero). *Psychological Bulletin, 110,* 574–576. doi:10.1037/0033-2909.110.3.574

Tukey, J. W. (1977). *Exploratory data analysis.* Reading, MA: Addison-Wesley.

West, S. G. (2006). Seeing your data: Using modern statistical graphics to display and detect relationships. In R. R. Bootzin & P. E. McKnight (Eds.), *Strengthening research methodology: Psychological measurement and evaluation* (pp. 159–182). Washington, DC: American Psychological Association.

West, S. G., Aiken, L. S., & Krull, J. (1996). Experimental personality designs: Analyzing categorical by continuous variable interactions. *Journal of Personality, 64,* 1–48. doi:10.1111/j.1467-6494.1996.tb00813.x

Winer, B. J. (1962). *Statistical principles in experimental design.* New York, NY: McGraw Hill. doi:10.1037/11774-000

## CHAPTER 6

EFFECT SIZE ESTIMATION

Michael Borenstein

An *effect size* is a value that reflects the magnitude of the relationship between two variables. It captures the substantive finding that the research is intended to address, and it does so using a metric that is meaningful and intuitive.

For example, the impact of a coaching program on SAT scores might be reported as a *raw difference* of 50 points. Or, the impact of a program to keep recovering alcoholics from drinking might be reported as a *risk ratio* of 0.50, meaning that the program reduced the risk of drinking by 50%. Similarly, the relationship between an aptitude test score and students' actual performance in a class might be reported as a *correlation* of .80. In each case, the metric is meaningful—people working in education will understand the substantive impact of a 50-point increase in SAT scores, and how this compares with the impact of other interventions. The same holds true for the risk ratio of 0.50 and the correlation of .80.

The effect size reported in a *study* serves as an estimate of the effect size in the *population*, and for that reason, the study effect size is reported with a confidence interval that reflects its precision. For example, a mean difference might be reported as 50 points with a 95% confidence interval of 40 to 60. This indicates that the mean difference in the study is 50 points and the true (population) mean difference probably falls in the range of 40 to 60.[1] Taken together, the effect size and its confidence interval summarize the core findings of the research—"How large is the effect?" and "How precise is our estimate?"

In this chapter I introduce the idea of an effect size and show why the effect size is generally a more appropriate index than the *p* value for summarizing the results of a study. Then, I introduce some common effect size indexes. Other effect size indexes are discussed briefly toward the end of the chapter.

EFFECT SIZE VERSUS TREATMENT EFFECT

The term *effect size* refers to the relationship between any two variables. When one of the variables is a deliberate intervention, then the effect size may also be called a *treatment effect*. For example, the difference in test scores for coached versus control groups may be called either an *effect size* or a *treatment effect*. By contrast, the difference in test scores for males versus females is an *effect size* but is not a *treatment effect* because we are not dealing with a treatment.

Thus, the difference between an *effect size* and a *treatment effect* depends on the nature of the variables, and not on the index itself. Any index, such as the standardized mean difference, the risk ratio, or any other, could be called an *effect size* in one study

---

This work was funded in part by the following grants from the National Institutes of Health: "Combining Data Types in Meta-Analysis" (AG021360) from the National Institute on Aging under the direction of Sidney Stahl, and "Power Analysis for Meta-Analysis" (DA022799) under the direction of Augusto Diana. My thanks to Larry Hedges, Julian Higgins, and Hannah Rothstein for their assistance in clarifying some of the issues discussed in this chapter.

[1]Formally, it means that if we perform an infinite number of studies and compute a confidence interval for each one, 95% of these intervals will include the true effect size.

DOI: 10.1037/13621-006
APA Handbook of Research Methods in Psychology: Vol. 3. Data Analysis and Research Publication, H. Cooper (Editor-in-Chief)

and a *treatment effect* in another, depending on the context. In this chapter I use the more general term, *effect size*, but the distinction between an *effect size* and a *treatment effect* is one of nomenclature only. The same computational formulas apply to both.

PARAMETERS, STATISTICS, AND PRECISION

Studies work with samples, and the effect size in the sample (the *statistic*) is intended to estimate the effect size in the larger population (the *parameter*). Because the sample effect size serves as an estimate of the population effect size, any time we report a sample effect size, we also need to report how precise that estimate is (American Psychological Association [APA], 2010, p. 34). The formula for precision varies from one effect size index to the next, but an important factor in all of these formulas is the size of the sample, with larger samples yielding more precise estimates.

Consider Figure 6.1, which uses the raw mean difference to display the impact of four different interventions on SAT scores. Assume that a mean difference of less than 20 points between the treated (i.e., coached) and control groups is considered trivial and a difference of more than 40 points is considered large. In Studies A and B, the *observed* effect size is large (50 points). In Study A, however, the *true* effect size is known precisely, whereas in Study B the *true* effect size could fall anywhere in the range of –12 points (the intervention is actually harmful) to +112 points. In Studies C and D, the *observed* effect size is trivial (10 points). In Study C, however, the *true* effect size is known precisely, whereas in

Study D the *true* effect size could fall anywhere in the range of –52 points to +72 points.

The effect size and precision, taken together, summarize the key findings—that the treatment effect is large (Study A), that the effect is trivial (Study C), or that we cannot estimate the effect size precisely enough to say whether it is large or trivial (Studies B and D). As such, these are generally the values that should be highlighted in the analysis and drive the discussion section—"How large (or small) is the effect?" "How precise is our estimate?" and "What are the implications for theory and practice?"

EFFECT SIZES AND *p* VALUES

Some readers will be more familiar with the idea of *p* values than with the idea of effect sizes. It is important to understand how the two are related to each other and where they differ. The purpose of the *p* value is to test the null hypothesis. The *p* value combines information about the size of the effect and its precision (or sample size) because it is the combination of these that speaks to the viability of the null. By contrast, the purpose of the effect size is to reflect the magnitude of the effect, whereas the precision addresses its accuracy. For this purpose, we report the effect size and its precision (or confidence interval) as two distinct values.

The *Publication Manual of the American Psychological Association* (APA, 2010) points out that the two approaches (the *p* value on the one hand, and the effect size with confidence interval on the other) are complementary in the sense that the *p* value will generally fall under 0.05 if, and only if, the 95% confidence interval does not include the null. Therefore,

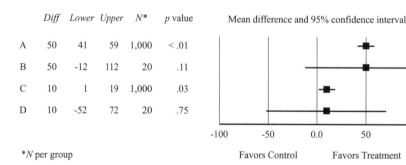

	Diff	Lower	Upper	N*	p value
A	50	41	59	1,000	< .01
B	50	-12	112	20	.11
C	10	1	19	1,000	.03
D	10	-52	72	20	.75

*N per group

Mean difference and 95% confidence interval

-100   -50   0.0   50   100

Favors Control   Favors Treatment

FIGURE 6.1. Effect size (Diff) and confidence intervals (Lower, Upper) for four fictional studies

the researcher may elect to report both. It is important to understand that the *p* value and the effect size address different questions. The *p* value addresses the question, "Can we conclude that the true effect size is not zero?" By contrast, the effect size addresses the questions, "What is the magnitude of the relationship?" or "What is the substantive impact of the intervention?"

There are some situations in which we really do care about the first question. For example, if we anticipate that homeopathic remedies will have no impact at all on a disease, we would expect the impact of these remedies to be precisely zero. Therefore, it would be appropriate for the analysis to focus on the test of significance. These kinds of situations are relatively rare in social science, however.

Rather, in the vast majority of cases, it is the second question that we really care about. For example, if we perform a study to assess the impact of coaching on test scores, we probably assume that the impact of the coaching program is not precisely zero, and therefore we have little (if any) interest in testing the null hypothesis. What we really care about is the *size* of the effect—whether the coaching increases the mean score by 20 points, 50 points, or 100 points—because this is the information that tells us whether the program is practically useful and whether it is better than other alternatives (see Chapter 7 of this volume).

Because researchers care about the magnitude of the effect, when a study reports a *p* value and fails to report an effect size, the *p* value is often pressed into service as a surrogate for effect size. The researcher may report that the *p* value is 0.75 and then proceed to discuss the "fact" that the treatment is not effective. Or, the researcher may report that the *p* value is <.01 and then proceed to discuss the "large" impact of the intervention. In fact, however, these conclusions are not justified. A nonsignificant *p* value tells us only that we cannot reject the null hypothesis. This could be because the effect size is small, but it also could be because the sample size is small (even if the effect size is large)—see Studies D and B, respectively, in Figure 6.1. Conversely, a significant *p* value tells us *only* that we can reject the null. This could be because the effect size is large, but it also could be because the sample size is large (whereas the effect size is small)—see Studies A and C, respectively, in Figure 6.1.

Still, the practice of using the *p* value as a surrogate for effect size is difficult to extinguish. For example, suppose you are told that one study had a *p* value of .03 whereas another had a *p* value of 0.11. Most people would assume that the effect size was larger in the first study, even if they had recently read the previous paragraph (Tversky & Kahneman, 1971). It is entirely possible, however, that the effect size was substantially larger (albeit less precise) in the second study—see studies C and B, respectively, in Figure 6.1.

In sum, the *p* value combines information about the size of the effect *and* the size of the sample because both are relevant to its function, which is to assess the viability of the null hypothesis. By contrast, when we report the effect size and its confidence interval, we are reporting two distinct items of information. First, the effect size is small or large. Second, the estimate is precise or imprecise. For the studies in Figure 6.1, the key distinction should be between Studies A and B (where the effect is large) versus Studies C and D (where the effect is small). This is the distinction that is captured by the effect size. At the same time, we need to distinguish between Study A (where the effect is known precisely) and Study B (where it is not). Similarly, we need to distinguish between Study C (where the effect is known precisely) and Study D (where it is not). These are the distinctions that are captured by confidence interval. (For a more extensive discussion of this issue, see Borenstein, 1994, 2000; Borenstein, Hedges, Higgins, & Rothstein, 2009.)

META-ANALYSIS

Meta-analysis refers to the process of synthesizing data from a series of studies (Cooper, 2010; Borenstein et al., 2009). The meta-analysis tells us if the effect size is consistent or if it varies from study to study. If the effect size is consistent, the meta-analysis allows us to report that the effect size is robust across the studies included in the analysis and to estimate the true common effect size more precisely than is possible with any single study. If the effect sizes vary across studies, then the meta-analysis will yield a picture of how the effect size varies, and in some cases, it will allow us to identify the factors associated with the variation.

The same effect sizes that we have been discussing for the individual study also serve as the unit of currency in the meta-analysis—it is these effect sizes that we compare, combine, and contrast to perform the synthesis. Thus, in addition to providing the key summary points for the individual study, the effect size allows the study results to be used in a meta-analysis as part of the larger research endeavor. In this process, the precision that we have been reporting for the individual study helps determine how much weight to assign to each study in the meta-analysis, with more weight being assigned to the more precise studies.

CHOOSING AN EFFECT SIZE INDEX

The process of choosing an effect size index for a given study consists of two steps. First, we narrow the selection of effect sizes on the basis of the kinds of data reported in the study. For example, there is one set of effect size indexes for studies that report means, another for studies that report proportions, and so on. Then, within each set, we select the effect size index that matches the study goals. For example, one effect size index might be based on a *difference* in proportions whereas another is based on the *ratio* of the proportions. In the next section, I introduce some of the more common effect size indexes for studies that report means, proportions, or the relationship between continuous variables.

EFFECT SIZE INDEXES BASED ON MEANS

Consider a study in which students are randomly assigned to either of two groups, *treated* or *control* (200 per group). Those in the former are provided with coaching intended to improve their scores on the SAT (a college-admissions test), and those in the latter are be provided with a standard curriculum. The mean SAT scores for the two groups are 450 versus 400, with a standard deviation of 100 in each group.

In a variant of this example, consider a study in which 200 students are tested on the SAT (the

pretest), spend 2 weeks being coached, and then take the actual SAT (the posttest). The mean pretest score is 400, the mean posttest score is 450, the standard deviation within either time-point is 100, and the correlation between the pretest scores and the posttest scores is 0.70. (For the present purposes, I ignore potential problems of internal validity with this design.)

The most common effect size indexes for these kinds of studies are the *raw* mean difference and the *standardized* mean difference. The *raw* mean difference is simply the difference in means. The *standardized* mean difference is also based on the difference in means, but rather than being reported on the raw scale, it is reported on a scale that has been standardized to have a standard deviation of 1.0 within-groups.

The *raw* mean difference can serve as the effect size index when the outcome is based on a scale that is widely used (such as SAT scores in the United States) or that is inherently meaningful (such as blood pressure or weight). When this condition is met, the raw mean difference has the advantage of being transparent and intuitive (we *understand* the practical implications of a 50-point difference on the SAT or a 20-pound difference in weight).

By contrast, when the outcome is reported on a relatively obscure scale, the raw mean difference has less to recommend it. If the reader is not familiar with the *XYZ* scale, then a report that the intervention increased the mean score by 10 points will have no real meaning (if scores on this scale range from 0 to 1,000, then 10 points may be a small difference, but if scores range from 0 to 100, then 10 points may be a very large difference). In this case, the standardized mean difference is a better option. A standardized mean difference (sometimes called *d* or Hedges' *g*) simply transforms the raw difference to a scale with a standard deviation of 1.0 within-groups. On this scale, a difference of 0.50 indicates that the mean for one group was one half a standard deviation higher than the mean for the other group. As such, this effect size index is meaningful even if the reader is not familiar with the original scale.

Another reason for using the standardized mean difference rather than the raw mean difference is to facilitate the synthesis of effect sizes across studies. If all the studies used the same scale, then the synthesis can be based on either the raw mean difference or the standardized mean difference. If the scale varies from study to study, however, then the synthesis cannot be based on the raw mean difference—for example, it makes no sense to compute an average of SAT scores (on a scale of 200 to 800) and American College Testing (ACT) scores (on a scale of 2 to 36). Therefore, if we intend to compare the effect across studies, then the standardized mean difference, which puts all effects onto the same scale, is a better option. Here, I show how to compute the raw mean difference and the standardized mean difference—first, working with data from two independent groups, and then, working with pre–post scores in one group.

THE RAW MEAN DIFFERENCE

If the true (population) means in the two groups are denoted by μ_1 and μ_2, then the true (population) mean difference, *delta* (Δ) is defined as follows:

$$\Delta = \mu_1 - \mu_2. \tag{1}$$

Computing *D* From Studies That Use Independent Groups

To estimate the raw mean difference from two independent groups, we apply the formula for Δ, but replace the true (population) means with the estimated (sample) means.[2] If the sample means in the two groups are denoted by $\overline{Y}_1$ and $\overline{Y}_2$, then the sample estimate, *D*, is given by the following:

$$D = \overline{Y}_1 - \overline{Y}_2. \tag{2}$$

Let S_1^2 and S_2^2 be the sample variances of the two groups, and n_1 and n_2 be the sample sizes in the two groups. If we assume that the two population variances are the same (as we do in most parametric data analysis techniques), so that $\sigma_1^2 = \sigma_2^2 = \sigma^2$, we pool the sample values S_1^2 and S_2^2 to obtain a more accurate estimate of the common value,

$$S_{Pooled}^2 = \frac{(n_1-1)S_1^2 + (n_2-1)S_2^2}{n_1 + n_2 - 2}. \tag{3}$$

Then, the variance, standard error, and 95% confidence limits for *D* are given by

$$v_D = \frac{n_1 + n_2}{n_1 n_2} S_{Pooled}^2, \tag{4}$$

$$SE_D = \sqrt{v_D}, \tag{5}$$

$$LL_D = D - t_{df,1-\alpha/2} \times SE_D, \tag{6}$$

and

$$UL_D = D + t_{df,1-\alpha/2} \times SE_D. \tag{7}$$

The *t*-value in these formulas ($t_{df,1-\alpha/2}$) is the *t*-value for the relevant degrees of freedom ($n_1 + n_2 - 2$) and the desired confidence level ($1 - \alpha/2$). For a large sample and 95% confidence interval, this *t*-value will approach 1.96. We use *t* (rather than *Z*) to compute the confidence interval for the *raw* mean difference because this interval depends on S_{Pooled}, and this value is *estimated* from the sample.

These formulas can be applied to the SAT example for two independent groups. The raw mean difference, *D*, is given by

$$D = 450 - 400 = 50. \tag{8}$$

If we assume that $\sigma_1^2 = \sigma_2^2$, then the pooled within-groups standard deviation is

$$S_{Pooled} = \sqrt{\frac{(200-1)\times 100^2 + (200-1)\times 100^2}{200+200-2}} = 100. \tag{9}$$

The variance, standard error, and 95% confidence limits for *D* are given by

$$v_D = \frac{200+200}{200\times 200} \times 100^2 = 100, \tag{10}$$

$$SE_D = \sqrt{100} = 10. \tag{11}$$

$$LL_D = 50 - 1.966 \times 10 = 30.341, \tag{12}$$

and

$$UL_D = 50 + 1.966 \times 10 = 69.659, \tag{13}$$

where 1.966 corresponds to the t-value for 95% confidence and 398 degrees of freedom.

In words, *D* in the study is 50 points, and the true raw mean difference (Δ) probably falls in the range of 30.341 points to 69.659 points.

---

[2]Following common practice, I use Greek letters to represent population values and Roman letters to represent sample values.

Computing *D* From Studies That Use Pre–Post Scores or Matched Groups

To estimate the raw mean difference from a study that reported pretest scores and posttest scores, we again apply the formula for Δ, and replace the true (population) means with the estimated (sample) means. If the pretest and posttest means are denoted by $\bar{Y}_{Pre}$ and $\bar{Y}_{Post}$, then the sample estimate *D* is

$$D = \bar{Y}_{Post} - \bar{Y}_{Pre}. \tag{14}$$

The effect size, *D*, is now based on the difference from pretest scores to posttest scores (rather than the difference between independent groups), but it has the same substantive meaning. (The direction of the difference is arbitrary, and we use post minus pre to yield the same direction of effect as when we used treated minus control.) The difference between using independent groups or the pre–post design is not in the estimate of the effect size but rather in the precision of the estimate. The pre–post design tends to yield a more precise estimate of the effect because the correlation between the two sets of scores typically reduces the standard error of the effect size.

To compute the standard error of *D* for the pre–post design, we first compute standard deviation of the difference,

$$S_{Difference} = \sqrt{S_{Pre}^2 + S_{Post}^2 - 2 \times r \times S_{Pre} \times S_{Post}}, \tag{15}$$

where S_{Pre}^2 and S_{Post}^2 are the variance of the pretest scores and posttest scores, *r* is the correlation between the pretest scores and posttest scores, and S_{Pre} and S_{Post} are the standard deviation of the pretest scores and posttest scores. Then, the variance of *D* is given by

$$v_D = \frac{S_{Difference}^2}{n}, \tag{16}$$

where *n* is the number of pairs. Finally, the standard error of *D* and 95% confidence limits are given by

$$SE_D = \sqrt{v_D}, \tag{17}$$

$$LL_D = D - t_{df,1-\alpha/2} \times SE_D, \tag{18}$$

and

$$UL_D = D + t_{df,1-\alpha/2} \times SE_D, \tag{19}$$

where the *t* value is for $n - 1$ degrees of freedom.

These formulas can be applied to the SAT example for a study with pretest scores and posttest scores. The raw mean difference, *D*, is given by

$$D = 450 - 400 = 50. \tag{20}$$

The standard error of the difference (assuming a pretest, posttest correlation of $r = .70$) is given by

$$S_{Difference} = \sqrt{100^2 + 100^2 - 2 \times 0.70 \times 100 \times 100}$$
$$= 77.460. \tag{21}$$

The variance, standard error, and 95% confidence limits for *D* are given by

$$v_D = \frac{77.460^2}{200} = 30.000, \tag{22}$$

$$SE_D = \sqrt{30.00} = 5.477, \tag{23}$$

$$LL_D = 50 - 1.972 \times 5.477 = 39.199, \tag{24}$$

and

$$UL_D = 50 + 1.972 \times 5.477 = 60.801, \tag{25}$$

where 1.972 corresponds to the *t* value for 95% confidence with 199 degrees of freedom. In words, *D* in the study is 50, and the true raw mean difference (Δ) probably falls in the range of 39.199 to 60.801.

The formulas to compute *D* for a pre–post design can also be used for a matched design. In the SAT study, for example, this would mean that each subject was *paired* with a classmate who had a similar ranking in the class. In the formulas, the pretest scores and posttest scores become the two students' SAT scores, and the pre–post correlation is replaced with the correlation of scores for the two sets of students. As is true for the pre–post design, the use of matching tends to yield a more precise estimate of *D* as compared with the same number of independent observations.

THE STANDARDIZED MEAN DIFFERENCE

We now turn from the raw mean difference (in the metric of the outcome scale) to the standardized mean difference (for which the difference is reported on a scale with a standard deviation of 1.0 within-groups). This effect size index can be used for any study that reports mean differences, but it is especially useful when the outcome scale is obscure (in which case the raw mean difference is a poor choice) or when we want to compare effects based on different scales (in which case the raw mean difference is not an option).

We need to distinguish among three terms—δ, d, and Hedges' g—which are used to represent the standardized mean difference (Borenstein et al., 2009; Cohen, 1977; Hedges, 1981). *Delta* (δ) is the population parameter, the true mean difference divided by the true standard deviation, and is the value we intend to estimate. By contrast, d and Hedges' g are both sample estimates of δ. The statistic d, which is often used as the estimate of δ, is simply the sample mean difference divided by the sample standard deviation. However, d has a slight bias and tends to overestimate δ, especially in small samples. To remove this bias, we multiply d by a factor (called J) to yield an estimate called Hedges' g (Hedges, 1981).

In sum, d and Hedges' g are both intended to estimate the same parameter (δ), but the former is biased and the latter is not. It follows that we should always report Hedges' g rather than d. Nevertheless, we include d in this discussion because it is widely used. Fortunately, the difference between d and g is usually too small to have any practical implications (Hedges, 1981).

The standardized mean difference in the population, delta (δ) is defined as the raw mean difference divided by the within-group standard deviation,

$$\delta = \frac{\mu_1 - \mu_2}{\sigma}. \tag{26}$$

Computing *d* and *g* From Studies That Use Independent Groups

To estimate the standardized mean difference from the data, we apply the formula for δ, but replace the true (population) means with the estimated (sample) means. If the sample means in the two groups are $\bar{Y}_1$ and $\bar{Y}_2$, then the standardized mean difference d is computed as

$$d = \frac{\bar{Y}_1 - \bar{Y}_2}{S_{Pooled}}. \tag{27}$$

In the denominator, S_{Pooled} is the within-groups standard deviation, pooled across groups,

$$S_{Pooled} = \sqrt{\frac{(n_1 - 1)S_1^2 + (n_2 - 1)S_2^2}{n_1 + n_2 - 2}}, \tag{28}$$

where n_1, n_2 are the sample size in the two groups, and S_1, S_2 are the standard deviations in the two groups.

The variance, standard error, and 95% confidence limits for d are given (to a very good approximation) by

$$v_d = \frac{n_1 + n_2}{n_1 n_2} + \frac{d^2}{2(n_1 + n_2)}, \tag{29}$$

$$SE_d = \sqrt{v_d}, \tag{30}$$

$$LL_d = d - Z_{1-\alpha/2} \times SE_d, \tag{31}$$

and

$$UL_d = d + Z_{1-\alpha/2} \times SE_d, \tag{32}$$

where $Z_{1-\alpha/2}$ is the standardized normal critical value at level $\alpha/2$ (e.g., for 95% confidence intervals, $\alpha = 0.05$ and $Z_{1-\alpha/2} = 1.96$).

As explained, d has a slight bias, tending to overestimate the absolute value of δ in small samples. To remove this bias we compute a correction factor, J, where

$$J(df) = 1 - \frac{3}{4df - 1}. \tag{33}$$

In this expression, df is the degrees of freedom used to estimate S_{Pooled}, which for two independent groups is $n_1 + n_2 - 2$. Then, Hedges' g, its variance, standard error, and confidence limits are given by

$$g = J(df)d, \tag{34}$$

$$v_g = [J(df)]^2 v_d, \tag{35}$$

$$SE_g = \sqrt{v_g}, \tag{36}$$

$$LL_g = g - Z_{1-\alpha/2} \times SE_g, \tag{37}$$

and

$$UL_g = g + Z_{1-\alpha/2} \times SE_g. \tag{38}$$

The SAT example for independent groups, presented earlier for the raw mean difference, serves here as well. Recall that the sample means are $\overline{Y}_1 = 450$, $\overline{Y}_2 = 400$, sample standard deviations $S_1 = 100$, $S_2 = 100$, and sample sizes $n_1 = n_2 = 200$. The pooled within-groups standard deviation is

$$S_{Pooled} = \sqrt{\frac{(200-1)\times100^2+(200-1)\times100^2}{200+200-2}} = 100. \quad (39)$$

Then,

$$d = \frac{450-400}{100} = 0.500, \quad (40)$$

$$v_d = \frac{200+200}{200\times200} + \frac{0.500^2}{2(200+200)} = 0.010, \quad (41)$$

$$SE_d = \sqrt{0.010} = 0.102, \quad (42)$$

$$LL_d = 0.50 - 1.96 \times 0.102 = 0.301, \quad (43)$$

and

$$UL_d = 0.50 + 1.96 \times 0.102 = 0.699. \quad (44)$$

In words, d in the study is 0.500, and the true standardized mean difference (δ) probably falls in the range of 0.301 to 0.699.

The correction factor J is as follows:

$$J(200+200-2) = 1 - \frac{3}{4\times398-1} = 0.998. \quad (45)$$

We multiply J by d to yield Hedges' g, and we multiply J^2 by the variance of d to yield the variance of g. Thus,

$$g = 0.998 \times 0.500 = 0.499, \quad (46)$$

$$v_g = 0.998^2 \times 0.010 = 0.010. \quad (47)$$

Then, the standard error and confidence limits for g are computed as

$$SE_g = \sqrt{0.010} = 0.102, \quad (48)$$

$$LL_g = 0.499 - 1.96 \times 0.102 = 0.300, \quad (49)$$

and

$$UL_g = 0.499 + 1.96 \times 0.102 = 0.698. \quad (50)$$

In words, Hedges' g in the study was 0.499, and the true standardized mean difference (δ) probably falls in the range of 0.300 to 0.698.

Computing *d* and *g* From Studies That Use Pre–Post Scores or Matched Groups

We can estimate the standardized mean difference (δ) from studies that used pre–post scores in one group or matched groups. The formula for the sample estimate of d is

$$d = \frac{\overline{Y}_{Post} - \overline{Y}_{Pre}}{S_{Pooled}}. \quad (51)$$

This is analogous to the formula for the standardized mean differences based on independent groups. There is, however, an important difference in the mechanism used to compute S_{Pooled}. When we are working with independent groups, the natural unit of deviation is the standard deviation within-groups. Therefore, this value is typically reported or easily computed from the data that *are* reported. By contrast, when we are working with pretest scores and posttest scores, the situation is more complicated. Now, there are three standard deviations involved. One is the standard deviation of the pretest scores, and one is the standard deviation of the posttest scores (which are analogous to the standard deviations within Groups 1 and 2 when the groups are independent). The third is the standard deviation of the difference scores.

To compute S_{Pooled}, we need the standard deviation within-groups. Therefore, if we have the standard deviation of the pretest scores and the standard deviation of the posttest scores, we can compute the standard deviation pooled within-groups using

$$S_{Pooled} = \sqrt{\frac{S_{Pre}^2 + S_{Post}^2}{2}}, \quad (52)$$

where S_{Pre} and S_{Post} are the standard deviations of the pretest scores and posttest scores. Some studies do not report these values, however, and report instead the standard deviation of the difference scores. In this case, we can compute the standard deviation pooled within-groups using

$$S_{Pooled} = \frac{S_{Difference}}{\sqrt{2(1-r)}}, \quad (53)$$

where r is the correlation between pairs of observations (e.g., the correlation between pre and post). Then we can apply this estimate to compute d.

(Because the correlation between pretest scores and posttest scores is required for this computation, we must assume that this correlation is known or can be estimated with high precision.)

The variance of d is given by

$$v_d = \left(\frac{1}{n} + \frac{d^2}{2n}\right) 2(1-r), \tag{54}$$

where n is the number of pairs. The standard error of d and the 95% confidence limits are given by

$$SE_d = \sqrt{v_d}, \tag{55}$$

$$LL_d = d - Z_{1-\alpha/2} \times SE_d, \tag{56}$$

and

$$UL_d = d + Z_{1-\alpha/2} \times SE_d. \tag{57}$$

As explained above, d has a slight bias, tending to overestimate the absolute value of δ in small samples. To remove this bias, we compute a correction factor, J, where

$$J(df) = 1 - \frac{3}{4df - 1}. \tag{58}$$

The df for computing J is $n - 1$, where n is the number of pairs. Then, Hedges' g, its variance, standard error, and 95% confidence limits are computed using

$$g = J(df) \times d, \tag{59}$$

$$v_g = [J(df)]^2 \times v_d, \tag{60}$$

$$SE_g = \sqrt{v_g}, \tag{61}$$

$$LL_g = g - Z_{1-\alpha/2} \times SE_g, \tag{62}$$

and

$$UL_g = g + Z_{1-\alpha/2} \times SE_g, \tag{63}$$

The SAT example for a pre–post design, presented earlier for raw mean differences, serves here as well. Recall that the sample size is 200, the pretest mean is 400, the posttest mean is 450, the standard deviation within either time-point is 100, and the correlation between pretest scores and posttest scores is 0.70.

If we start with the standard deviation of the pretest scores and the standard deviation of the posttest scores, S_{Pooled} is given by

$$S_{Pooled} = \sqrt{\frac{100^2 + 100^2}{2}} = 100. \tag{64}$$

Alternatively, if we start with the standard deviation of the difference, then S_{Pooled} can be estimated by

$$S_{Pooled} = \frac{77.460}{\sqrt{2(1-0.7)}} = 100. \tag{65}$$

These two approaches will yield the same value when the sample pretest and posttest standard deviations are identical.

In either case, d, its variance, standard error, and 95% confidence limits are computed as

$$d = \frac{450 - 400}{100} = 0.500, \tag{66}$$

$$v_d = \left(\frac{1}{200} + \frac{0.500^2}{2 \times 200}\right)(2(1-0.7)) = 0.003, \tag{67}$$

$$SE_d = \sqrt{0.003} = 0.058, \tag{68}$$

$$LL_d = 0.50 - 1.96 \times 0.058 = 0.386, \tag{69}$$

and

$$UL_d = 0.50 + 1.96 \times 0.058 = 0.614. \tag{70}$$

In words, d in the study is 0.500, and the true standardized mean difference (δ) probably falls in the range of 0.386 to 0.614.

Finally, the correction factor J is computed as

$$J(200 - 1) = 1 - \frac{3}{4 \times 199 - 1} = 0.996, \tag{71}$$

and Hedges' g, its variance, standard error and confidence limits are given by

$$g = 0.996 \times 0.500 = 0.498, \tag{72}$$

$$v_g = 0.996^2 \times 0.003 = 0.003, \tag{73}$$

$$SE_g = \sqrt{0.003} = 0.058, \tag{74}$$

$$LL_g = 0.498 - 1.96 \times 0.058 = 0.385, \tag{75}$$

and

$$UL_g = 0.498 + 1.96 \times 0.058 = 0.612. \qquad (76)$$

In words, Hedges' g in the study is 0.498, and the true standardized mean difference (δ) probably falls in the range of 0.385 to 0.612. As discussed earlier (for D), the formulas for a pre–post design can be applied also for a matched design.

EFFECT SIZE INDEXES FOR BINARY DATA

In the previous section, I discussed effect size indexes based on the difference in means, which are employed when outcomes are reported on a continuous scale. Now, I turn to effect size indexes based on binary data—for which the outcome for each subject is the presence or absence of a characteristic or event. For example, a study might assign students to two groups and report the proportion in each group that passes a test, or a study might assign patients to two groups and report the proportion in each group that relapses. Although the event being recorded may be either a success (pass a test) or failure (relapse), in keeping with common practice, I use the term *risk* to refer to the proportion of subjects with the event. These data are usually presented as a 2 × 2 table such as in Table 6.1. The rows represent the groups, the columns represent the outcomes, and each subject falls into one of the four cells.

Table 6.2 shows how to convert the cell counts in Table 6.1 into proportions. For Group 1, the proportion with the event (or characteristic) is denoted p_1, and defined as A/n_1. The proportion without the

TABLE 6.1

A 2 × 2 Table of Cell Counts for a Prospective Study With a Binary Outcome

	Events	Nonevents	Total
Group 1	A	B	n_1
Group 2	C	D	n_2

Note. We classify a specific outcome as the "Event," and all study participants are classified as either "Event" or "Nonevent." In a study of college admissions these might be "Accepted" or "Rejected," and in a study of a medical intervention these might be "Dead" or "Alive." The outcome classified as the "Event" may be the preferred outcome (Accepted) or the alternate outcome (Rejected).

TABLE 6.2

A 2 × 2 Table of Proportions Derived From Table 6.1

	Events	Nonevents	Total
Group 1	$P_1 = A/n_1$	$1 - P_1 = B/n_1$	1.0
Group 2	$P_2 = C/n_2$	$1 - P_2 = D/n_2$	1.0

Note. This table shows how to use the data in Table 6.1 to compute the proportion of events (P) and nonevents ($1 - P$) in each group.

event is denoted $1 - p_1$, and defined as B/n_1. Similarly, for Group 2, the proportion with the event is denoted p_2, and defined as C/n_2. The proportion without the event is denoted $1 - p_2$, and defined as D/n_2.

Three effect size indexes commonly are used to report this kind of data (binary outcomes in two groups). One is the risk difference, which is simply the difference in risks, analogous to the raw difference in means for continuous data. The second is the risk ratio, which is ratio of the risks, rather than the difference in risks. The third is the odds ratio, which is discussed in a later section.

The risk difference reflects the absolute difference in risk between the two groups. As such, it is analogous to the raw difference in means for continuous data. The risk difference is an intuitive index, but the substantive implications may depend on the absolute risks—a 10-point drop from 20% to 10% has a different substantive meaning than a 10-point drop from 80% to 70%.

The main distinction between the risk difference and the risk ratio is that the former is an absolute measure whereas the latter is a relative measure. For example, consider one study in which the treatment reduces the risk of relapse from 2% to 1%, and another study in which the treatment reduces the risk of relapse from 80% to 40%. In both studies, the risk ratio is the same (50%). But the risk difference is 1 percentage point in the first case and 40 percentage points in the second. If we are dealing with a case in which the treatment is expected to always cut the risk in half, then the risk ratio is the index that captures this expectation. By contrast, if we want to know the likely impact of the treatment for a given patient, then the risk difference is the index that addresses this question. In one case, the patient's risk drops by 1 percentage point, and in the other, risk drops by 40 percentage points.

If we elect to work with a ratio, then in addition to the risk ratio we also have the option of reporting the odds ratio. Where the *risk ratio* is the ratio of the two risks, the *odds ratio* is the ratio of the two odds (the odds in each group is the ratio of the risk of events to the risk of nonevents in that group). The risk ratio is more intuitive than the odds ratio, but the odds ratio has some useful mathematical properties that lead to its being preferred in some fields (Deeks, 2002).

Often, people in a specific field will tend to favor one index over the others, which can help a researcher decide among the options. Also, it is possible to present more than one index, because the indexes provide complementary views of the effect. The relative merits of these three indexes are discussed in Deeks (2002), Fleiss and Berlin (2009), and Higgins and Green (2008).

Consider a study in which recovering alcoholics are assigned to either of two groups, treated (intensive support) or control (standard support). Outcome is defined by the presence or absence of relapse within the study period. The results are shown in Table 6.3. The risk of relapse is 20/100 (20%) in the treated group, and 40/100 (40%) in the control group. This study serves as an example in the sections that follow.

Risk Difference

The risk difference delta (Δ) is defined as the difference in probabilities (or risks) in the two groups. If the risk for Groups 1 and 2 in the population are denoted by π_1 and π_2, then the risk difference (Δ) is defined as the difference in risks,

$$\Delta = \pi_1 - \pi_2. \tag{77}$$

A risk difference of zero indicates that the two risks are equal. In the relapse example (where

TABLE 6.3

Events × Treatment in a Fictional Study

	Relapse	Stable	Total
Treated	20	80	100
Control	40	60	100

Group 1 is treated and Group 2 is control), risk differences above zero indicate that the risk of relapse is higher for treated group, whereas risk differences below zero indicate that the risk of relapse is higher for the control group.

To estimate the risk difference from the study data, we apply the formula for Δ, but replace the true (population) risks (π_1 and π_2) with the estimates (sample) risks (p_1 and p_2). Using the notation in Tables 6.1 and 6.2, the risk difference is computed as

$$RD = p_1 - p_2 = A/n_1 - C/n_2. \tag{78}$$

The approximate variance, standard error, and 95% confidence limits are given by

$$V_{RD} = \frac{AB}{n_1^3} + \frac{CD}{n_2^3}, \tag{79}$$

$$SE_{RD} = \sqrt{V_{RD}}, \tag{80}$$

$$LL_{RD} = RD - Z_{1-\alpha/2} \times SE_{RD}, \tag{81}$$

and

$$UL_{RD} = RD + Z_{1-\alpha/2} \times SE_{RD}. \tag{82}$$

Applying these formulas to the example of relapse prevention in alcoholics, we compute the risk difference, variance, standard error, and confidence limits as

$$RD = 0.200 - 0.400 = -0.200. \tag{83}$$

$$V_{RD} = \frac{20 \times 80}{100^3} + \frac{40 \times 60}{100^3} = 0.004, \tag{84}$$

$$SE_{RD} = \sqrt{0.004} = 0.063, \tag{85}$$

$$LL_{RD} = -0.20 - 1.96 \times 0.063 = -0.324, \tag{86}$$

and

$$UL_{RD} = -0.20 + 1.96 \times 0.063 = -0.076, \tag{87}$$

In words, the risk difference in the study is –0.200, and the true risk difference (Δ) probably falls in the range of –0.324 to –0.076.

Risk Ratio

The risk ratio, theta (θ), is the ratio of the risks in the two groups. If the risk for Groups 1 and 2 in the population are denoted by π_1 and π_2, then the risk ratio (θ), often called the *relative risk*, is defined as the *ratio* of the risks,

$$\theta = \frac{\pi_1}{\pi_2}. \tag{88}$$

A risk ratio of 1.0 would indicate that the risks are equal in the two groups. In the relapse example (where Group 1 is treated and Group 2 is control), a risk ratio of less than 1.0 would indicate that the risk of relapse was lower in the treated group, whereas a risk ratio of more than 1.0 would indicate that the risk of relapse was higher in the treated group.

To estimate the risk ratio from the study data, we apply the formula for θ, but replace the true (population) risks (π_1 and π_2) with the estimates (sample) risks (p_1 and p_2). Using the notation in Tables 6.1 and 6.2, the risk ratio is computed as

$$RR = \frac{p_1}{p_2} = \frac{A/n_1}{C/n_2}. \tag{89}$$

It might seem that we could compute the standard error of the *RR* and then build a confidence interval using *RR* plus or minus this standard error times 1.96. However, the distribution of the risk ratio is skewed, and a more accurate confidence interval can be obtained from the log of the risk ratio. Therefore, rather than work directly with the *RR*, we work with the natural log of the *RR* (*lnRR*), compute the confidence limits in log units, and then convert these values back to the *RR* scale.

The log of the risk ratio, *ln(RR)*, is denoted *lnRR*. Then, in log units, the approximate variance, standard error, and confidence limits are

$$V_{lnRR} = \frac{1}{A} - \frac{1}{n_1} + \frac{1}{C} - \frac{1}{n_2}, \tag{90}$$

$$SE_{lnRR} = \sqrt{V_{lnRR}}, \tag{91}$$

$$LL_{lnRR} = lnRR - Z_{1-\alpha/2} \times SE_{lnRR}, \tag{92}$$

and

$$UL_{lnRR} = lnRR + Z_{1-\alpha/2} \times SE_{lnRR}. \tag{93}$$

We then convert the confidence limits back to the original scale using

$$LL_{RR} = \exp(LL_{lnRR}) \tag{94}$$

and

$$UL_{RR} = \exp(UL_{lnRR}). \tag{95}$$

Working with the data in Table 6.3 and applying the formulas above,

$$RR = \frac{20/100}{40/100} = \frac{.200}{.400} = 0.500. \tag{96}$$

In log units,

$$lnRR = \ln(0.500) = -0.693, \tag{97}$$

$$V_{lnRR} = \frac{1}{20} - \frac{1}{100} + \frac{1}{40} - \frac{1}{100} = 0.055, \tag{98}$$

$$SE_{lnRR} = \sqrt{0.055} = 0.235, \tag{99}$$

$$LL_{lnRR} = -0.693 - 1.96 \times 0.235 = -1.153, \tag{100}$$

and

$$UL_{lnRR} = -0.693 + 1.96 \times 0.235 = -0.233. \tag{101}$$

We then convert the confidence limits back to the original scale using

$$LL_{RR} = \exp(-1.153) = 0.316 \tag{102}$$

and

$$UL_{RR} = \exp(-0.233) = 0.792. \tag{103}$$

In words, the risk ratio in the study is 0.500, and the true risk ratio (θ) probably falls in the range of 0.316 to 0.792.

Odds Ratio

The odds ratio, omega (ω), is the ratio of the odds in the two groups. If the risk of the event for Group 1 in the population is denoted by π_1, then the odds of the event in Group 1 are given by $\pi_1/(1-\pi_1)$. Similarly, if the risk of the event for Group 2 in the population is denoted by π_2, then the odds of the event in Group 2 are given by $\pi_2/(1-\pi_2)$. The odds ratio is the ratio of these two odds,

$$\omega = \frac{\pi_1/(1-\pi_1)}{\pi_2/(1-\pi_2)} = \frac{\pi_1(1-\pi_2)}{\pi_2(1-\pi_1)}. \tag{104}$$

An odds ratio of 1.0 would indicate that the risks are equal in the two groups. In the relapse example (where Group 1 is treated and Group 2 is control), an odds ratio of less than 1.0 would indicate that the risk of relapse was lower in the treated group, whereas an odds ratio of more than 1.0 would indicate that the risk of relapse was higher in the treated group.

To estimate the odds ratio from the study data, we apply the formula for ω, but replace the true (population) risks (π_1 and π_2) with the estimates (sample) risks (P_1 and P_2). Using the notation in Tables 6.1 and 6.2, the odds ratio (OR) is

$$OR = \frac{P_1\left(1-P_2\right)}{P_2\left(1-P_1\right)} = \frac{AD}{BC}. \tag{105}$$

As was true for the risk ratio, we compute the confidence limits in log units because of the asymmetry of confidence intervals and then convert these values to the original scale. The log of the odds ratio, $ln(OR)$, is denoted $lnOR$. Then, in log units, the approximate variance, standard error, and confidence limits are

$$V_{lnOR} = \frac{1}{A}+\frac{1}{B}+\frac{1}{C}+\frac{1}{D}, \tag{106}$$

$$SE_{lnOR} = \sqrt{V_{lnOR}}, \tag{107}$$

$$LL_{lnOR} = lnOR - Z_{1-\alpha/2} \times SE_{lnOR}, \tag{108}$$

and

$$UL_{lnOR} = lnOR - Z_{1-\alpha/2} \times SE_{lnOR}. \tag{109}$$

We convert the confidence limits back to the original scale using

$$LL_{OR} = \exp(LL_{lnOR}) \tag{110}$$

and

$$UL_{OR} = \exp(UL_{lnOR}). \tag{111}$$

Applying these formulas to the relapse example, the odds ratio is

$$OR = \frac{20 \times 60}{80 \times 40} = 0.375. \tag{112}$$

In log units, the odds ratio, variance, standard error and confidence limits are

$$lnOR = \ln(0.375) = -0.981, \tag{113}$$

$$V_{lnOR} = \frac{1}{20}+\frac{1}{80}+\frac{1}{40}+\frac{1}{60} = 0.104, \tag{114}$$

$$SE_{lnOR} = \sqrt{0.104} = 0.323. \tag{115}$$

$$LL_{lnOR} = -0.981 - 1.96 \times 0.323 = -1.613, \tag{116}$$

and

$$UL_{lnOR} = -0.981 + 1.96 \times 0.323 = -0.348. \tag{117}$$

Finally, we convert the confidence limits back to the original metric,

$$LL_{OR} = \exp(-1.613) = 0.199 \tag{118}$$

and

$$UL_{OR} = \exp(-0.348) = 0.706. \tag{119}$$

In words, the odds ratio in the study is 0.375, and the true odds ratio (ω) probably falls in the range of 0.199 to 0.706.

Notes for Binary Data

Dealing with studies in which no people possess the characteristic in question or in which there are zero events. For the risk difference, if either or both groups have zero events, we add 0.5 to each cell (A, B, C, D in Table 6.1) to compute the variance. For the risk ratio and the odds ratio, if one group has zero events, some people add 0.5 to each cell to compute the effect size and its variance. If both groups have zero events, then the risk ratio and the odds ratio are undefined.

Events versus nonevents. For the risk difference we can select either outcome (for example, "Dead" or "Alive") to serve as the "Event" (cells A and C in Table 6.1). If the risk difference for "Dead" is –0.20, then the risk difference for "Alive" is + 0.20, which has the same meaning. The same holds true for the odds ratio—if the odds ratio for "Dead" is 0.50 then the odds ratio for "Alive" is 2.0 (i.e., the inverse of 0.50). Again, the substantive meaning is the same (we halve the odds by using the treatment, or double the odds by withholding it). However, the situation is different for the risk ratio. Suppose that 98/100 people are alive in one group versus 99/100 in the other. If we choose "Alive" as the event, then the impact of the treatment appears to be relatively small (risks of 0.98 vs. 0.99 translate to a risk ratio near 1.0). By contrast, if we choose "Dead" as the event, then the impact of the treatment appears to be relatively large (risks of 0.01 vs. 0.02 translate to a risk ratio of 0.50). Therefore, the decision to select one outcome or the other as the "Event" should reflect the logic of the study and not exaggerate small risks.

EFFECT SIZE INDEXES BASED ON THE RELATION BETWEEN TWO CONTINUOUS VARIABLES

To this point I have presented effect size indexes for analyses that compare two means, and for analyses that compare two proportions. Now, I turn to analyses that assess the relationship between two sets of continuous data, that is, the kind of analysis typically reported as a correlation.

When working with means or proportions, we needed to create an effect size index that started with two values (such as means or proportions) and compare them in some way (e.g., by computing a difference or ratio). By contrast, when we are working with the relation between two continuous variables, the correlation coefficient can serve as the effect size index. The correlation is a pure measure of effect size (not affected by the sample size). Additionally, the correlation is an intuitive measure (people who work with correlations have a sense of what a given correlation means), and it is reported on a standardized scale.

Consider a study in which students who enroll in a computer-programming course are given an aptitude test on the first day of class and a final exam on the last day. The study goal is to determine the correlation between the two scores. The correlation is reported as 0.80 on the basis of a sample size of 100 students.

The true (population) value of the correlation is called rho (ρ). The sample statistic (the observed effect) is denoted by r. The sample estimate of ρ is simply the sample correlation coefficient, r. The variance of r is approximately

$$v_r = \frac{(1-r^2)^2}{n-1}, \quad (120)$$

where n is the sample size.

It might seem that we could compute the standard error of r and then build a confidence interval using r plus or minus this standard error times 1.96. However, the distribution of r is skewed. Therefore, rather than work directly with r, we convert r to another metric, Fisher's z score, compute the confidence limits in the Fisher's z metric, and then convert these values back to the r scale. We use the notation Fisher's z to avoid confusion with the (unrelated) normal curve Z.

The transformation from r to Fisher's z score is given by the following:

$$Fisher's\, z = 0.500 \times \ln\left(\frac{1+r}{1-r}\right). \quad (121)$$

The variance, standard error, and 95% confidence limits in the Fisher's z metric are (to an excellent approximation)

$$V_{Fisher's\ z} = \frac{1}{n-3}, \quad (122)$$

$$SE_{Fisher's\ z} = \sqrt{V_{Fisher's\ z}}, \quad (123)$$

$$LL_{Fisher's\ z} = Fisher's\ z - Z \times SE_{Fisher's\ z}, \quad (124)$$

and

$$UL_{Fisher's\ z} = Fisher's\ z + Z \times SE_{Fisher's\ z}. \quad (125)$$

Finally, the lower and upper limits are converted back to the original metric using

$$LL_r = \frac{e^{2LL_{Fisher's\ z}} - 1}{e^{2LL_{FisherZ}} + 1} \quad (126)$$

and

$$UL_r = \frac{e^{2UL_{Fisher's\ z}} - 1}{e^{2UL_{Fisher's\ z}} + 1}. \quad (127)$$

We can apply these formulas to the study that reported the correlation between an aptitude test and performance in a computer programming class. The effect size r is simply 0.80. The transformation from r to Fisher's z score is given by

$$Fisher's\ z = 0.500 \times \ln\left(\frac{1+0.800}{1-0.800}\right) = 1.099. \quad (128)$$

In Fisher's z score units, the variance, standard error, and confidence limits are computed as

$$v_{Fisher's\ z} = \frac{1}{100-3} = 0.010, \quad (129)$$

$$SE_{Fisher's\ z} = \sqrt{0.010} = 0.102, \quad (130)$$

$$LL_{Fisher's\ z} = 1.099 - 1.96 \times 0.102 = 0.900, \quad (131)$$

and

$$UL_{Fisher's\ z} = 1.099 + 1.96 \times 0.1012 = 1.298. \quad (132)$$

To convert the Fisher's *z* score values back to a correlation, we use

$$LL_r = \frac{e^{2(0.900)}-1}{e^{2(0.900)}+1} = 0.716 \qquad (133)$$

and

$$UL_r = \frac{e^{2(1.298)}-1}{e^{2(1.298)}+1} = 0.861. \qquad (134)$$

In words, the correlation in the study is 0.80, and the true correlation (ρ) probably falls in the range of 0.716 to 0.861.

CONVERTING EFFECT SIZES FROM ONE INDEX TO ANOTHER

In general, we choose from among one set of effect size indexes for data presented as means, from another set for data presented as proportions, and from another set for correlational data. However, there are formulas that can be used to convert among effect size indices. For example, after we use means to compute a standardized mean difference, it is possible to convert that effect size to an odds ratio or a correlation. This approach is useful if we know the treatment effect for one intervention as (say) a standardized mean difference and want to see how this compares with the treatment effect for another intervention which was reported as an odds ratio or a correlation. It is also useful if we want to include different studies in a meta-analysis, and the studies reported the effects using different indices of effect size. The formulas, worked examples, and the limitations of this approach, are discussed in Borenstein et al. (2009) and Borenstein, Hedges, Higgins, and Rothstein (in press).

The examples in this chapter show how to compute effect sizes and confidence intervals for some of the more common study designs, such as a design that employs two independent groups or a pre–post design. Borenstein et al. (in press) extended the discussion to include additional designs (such as cluster-randomized trials). They also showed how to compute effect sizes when a study fails to report all full set of summary statistics (such as the means, standard deviations, and sample sizes) and reports (e.g.) only the *p* value and sample size.

The effect size indexes introduced in this chapter are among the most widely used, but many others are used as well. Effect size indexes for means include not only the raw mean difference and standardized mean difference but also the response ratio (the ratio of means). Effect size indexes for proportions include not only the risk difference, risk ratio, and odds ratio but also such indexes as the *number needed to treat* (NNT), which is the number of people we need to treat to prevent one event. Similarly, this chapter was limited to effect size indexes based on means, proportions, or correlations, but analogous effect size indexes have been developed for other kinds of data. For example, the comparison of survival times in two groups may be captured by the difference in hazard rates of the ratio of hazard rates, analogous to the risk difference or risk ratio.

Borenstein et al.'s (in press) book is dedicated entirely to the computation of effect sizes. Other references are Borenstein (2009); Borenstein et al. (2009); Fleiss and Berlin (2009); Hedges and Olkin (1985); Lipsey and Wilson (2001); and Rosenthal, Rosnow, and Rubin (2000).

CONCLUSION

According to the *Publication Manual of the American Psychological Association* (APA, 2010), reporting an effect size with confidence intervals can be an effective way of communicating results. In this chapter I have tried to explain why this is so.

Almost invariably, the goal of a research study is to assess the strength of a relationship or the impact of an intervention. These are the issues that are addressed by an effect size and its confidence interval, and for this reason, it is these values that should be highlighted in the analysis and serve as the basis for the discussion. Effect sizes also enhance the larger research endeavor because they can be used to compare and synthesize estimates of effects across studies.

References

American Psychological Association. (2010). *Publication manual of the American Psychological Association* (6th ed.). Washington, DC: Author.

Borenstein, M. (1994). The case for confidence intervals in controlled clinical trials. *Controlled Clinical Trials, 15*, 411–428. doi:10.1016/0197-2456(94)90036-1

Borenstein, M. (2000). The shift from significance testing to effect size estimation. In A. S. Bellack & M. Herson (Eds.), *Comprehensive clinical psychology* (pp. 313–349). New York, NY: Pergamon.

Borenstein, M. (2009). Effect sizes for continuous data. In H. Cooper, L. V. Hedges, & J. C. Valentine (Eds.), *The handbook of research synthesis and meta-analysis* (2nd ed., pp. 221–235). New York, NY: Russell Sage Foundation.

Borenstein, M., Hedges, L. V., Higgins, J., & Rothstein, H. R. (2009). *Introduction to meta-analysis*. Chichester, England: Wiley. doi:10.1002/9780470743386

Borenstein, M., Hedges, L. V., Higgins, J., & Rothstein, H. R. (in press). *Computing effect sizes for meta-analysis*. Chichester, England: Wiley.

Cohen, J. (1977). *Statistical power analysis for the behavioral sciences* (2nd ed.). New York, NY: Academic Press.

Cooper, H. (2010). *Research synthesis and meta-analysis— A step-by-step approach* (4th ed.). Thousand Oaks, CA: Sage.

Deeks, J. J. (2002). Issues in the selection of a summary statistic for meta-analysis of clinical trials with binary outcomes. *Statistics in Medicine, 21,* 1575–1600. doi:10.1002/sim.1188

Fleiss, J. L., & Berlin, J. A. (2009). Effect sizes for dichotomous data. In H. Cooper, L. V. Hedges, & J. C. Valentine (Eds.), *The handbook of research synthesis and meta-analysis* (2nd ed., pp. 237–253). New York, NY: Russell Sage Foundation.

Hedges, L. (1981). Distribution theory for Glass's estimator of effect size and related estimators. *Journal of Educational Statistics, 6,* 107–128. doi:10.2307/1164588

Hedges, L. V., & Olkin, I. (1985). *Statistical models for meta-analysis.* New York, NY: Academic Press.

Higgins, J. P. T., & Green, S. (Eds.). (2008). *Cochrane Handbook for Systematic Reviews of Interventions.* Chichester, England: Wiley. doi:10.1002/9780470712184

Lipsey, M. W., & Wilson, D. B. (2001). *Practical meta-analysis.* Thousand Oaks, CA: Sage.

Rosenthal, R., Rosnow, R. L., & Rubin, D. B. (2000). *Contrasts and effect sizes in behavioral research: A correlational approach.* Cambridge, England: Cambridge University Press.

Tversky, A., & Kahneman, D. (1971). Belief in the law of small numbers. *Psychological Bulletin, 76,* 105–110. doi:10.1037/h0031322

## CHAPTER 7

MEASURES OF CLINICALLY SIGNIFICANT CHANGE

Michael J. Lambert and Russell J. Bailey

Clinical research employs several statistics to estimate whether mental health treatment works. Side-by-side comparisons of treatments in clinical trials use estimates of statistical significance, effect size, and clinical significance. Each type of statistic can be used to determine whether a given difference in scores is meaningful and consequently whether the given mental health treatment has resulted in meaningful change. Although each statistic offers information to address the question of meaningful change resulting from treatment, each operates from a different rationale and communicates unique information to address the question. It is therefore necessary to illustrate how these statistics offer distinctly different information. In this chapter, the different purposes of the aforementioned statistics are discussed, followed by a focus on clinical significance as an index of the individual patient's treatment response. The variety of ways that clinical significance has been conceptualized is presented followed by statistical formulations of these concepts. Near the end of the chapter the advantages and limitations of methods for estimating clinical significance are highlighted.

TRADITIONAL METHODS OF ASSESSING CHANGE DUE TO TREATMENT

When *statistical significance* is reported in measurements of change, the mean difference between groups exceeds what would be expected by chance alone. A staple for psychological research, finding group differences (or changes in the functioning of a group of patients in response to an intervention) to be statistically significant reduces the likelihood of *chance* findings being reported as reliable change. Differences between groups found by this method may not sufficiently address the question of whether such differences reflect practical or clinically meaningful change. For example, consider a weight loss treatment that is compared with a control group. One hundred individuals who are at extreme risk for detrimental physical consequences related to their obesity are selected to participate in the study. After 2 months, those receiving treatment have lost an average of 8 pounds. The comparison group has lost no weight during the time that elapsed. The statistical test reveals a statistically significant finding in favor of the treatment group compared with the control group. These statistical effects suggest that the differences between the groups are important as opposed to differences that are unreliable. With an average of 8 pounds of weight loss, some individuals who received treatment may have lost 16 pounds, whereas others who received treatment lost no weight or even gained weight. Even though the 50 treated individuals lost an average of 8 pounds, many, if not all of them, remain extremely overweight or classified as obese and are likely to experience the physical consequences of obesity despite treatment. In a pragmatic or clinical sense, the treatment and control groups may be considered identical (with regard to meaningful change) after 2 months of treatment. The magnitude, or amount of change, must be taken into account if one wishes to understand the meaning of change.

DOI: 10.1037/13621-007
APA Handbook of Research Methods in Psychology: Vol. 3. Data Analysis and Research Publication, H. Cooper (Editor-in-Chief)

The *effect size* statistic addresses this issue—the relative importance of the amount of change (for a more complete discussion, see Chapter 6 of this volume). By standardizing group means, one can use an effect size to communicate the group's mean change score in standard deviation units. Interpreting these statistics is straightforward, as the effect size reflects the degree of change relative to overall group variability. Small effect sizes indicate smaller effects resulting from treatment, and larger effect sizes indicate larger effects. *Meta-analyses* (quantitative research summaries; see Chapter 25 of this volume) use effect sizes from groups of studies because this allows one to combine change scores under a standard metric and thus estimate an average amount of change in treatment groups from a body of primary studies simultaneously. However, effect sizes still do not communicate variation within the group and do not address the clinical relevance of change. By way of illustration, an effect size of 0.8 for a treatment group indicates that the average change from baseline for all clients in the treatment group was 0.8 standard deviation units (based on baseline standard deviation; generally considered a large effect because the effect size demonstrates that the proportion of controls have a success rate of 31%, whereas the experimental group's success rate is 69%). Although meaningful in its own right, the 0.8 effect size does not communicate whether the treatment group patients met a clinically relevant criterion, such as remission of depressive symptoms. The 0.8 effect size masks variation within the group by arithmetically combining the individual client with 2.0 standard deviation units of change, as well as the client with –0.5 standard deviation units of change, with the rest of the group. Although effect sizes may be applied to the individual, in general, effect sizes are used for between-*group* estimates of change or within-*group* estimates of change.

THE CONCEPT OF CLINICAL SIGNIFICANCE

The concept of *clinical significance* arose to address the issue of clinical relevance of change scores (Jacobson, Follette, & Revenstorf, 1984). To speak to *clinical* relevance, researchers and clinicians are interested in whether an intervention results in a change in clinical status of the individual patient. Criteria for clinically relevant change might include a patient moving from major depression to subthreshold symptoms, from dysfunctional to functional, or from resembling the patient group to resembling the community nonpatient group. One central question in the methods of determining clinically significant change includes whether to use estimates that consider change at the level of the individual rather than the level of the group.

To address clinical relevance, the concept of clinical significance typically speaks to *individual* change more than it does group change. Statistics of clinical significance give the additional benefit of individual-level information, which effect sizes, statistical significance tests, and other group-level statistics do not. In this way, researchers and clinicians can make inferences about individual patients (e.g., decisions regarding alterations to treatment such as termination, stepping up treatment intensity, determining recovery or deterioration) as well as about the impact of treatments on groups of individuals (e.g., what percentage of individual patients in a treatment group recovered or deteriorated).

Clinical significance as an outcome construct can differ from remission of symptoms, although both are qualitative descriptions of clinically meaningful improvement. As presented by McGlinchey, Zimmerman, and Atkins (2008), remission focuses on the "absence of features that originally warranted the diagnosis of a condition" (p. 26), in keeping with a more biomedical understanding of psychiatric disorders. Of note, remission criteria typically involve diagnostic considerations, but they do not necessarily entail complete absence of symptoms. Although this chapter focuses on other methods of evaluating clinical significance, the consideration of remission in medical literature and methods for determining remission may further inform methods of determining clinical significance.

Beutler and Moleiro (2001) illustrated the difference between statistical and clinical significance and emphasized two aspects of clinical significance: reliable change and clinically meaningful change. *Reliable change*, based on the work of Jacobson et al.

(1984), refers to whether a change score drawn from a specific measure exceeds the level of change that may be present simply due to measurement error and unreliability in the outcome measure. *Clinically meaningful change* implies significant change in clinical status. Beutler and Moleiro (2001) cited equivalence testing (Sheldrick, Kendall, & Heimberg, 2001) as one method to support the presence of clinically meaningful change. By comparing treatment groups with a normative nonpatient sample, one can test the hypothesis whether the treatment group is equivalent to nonpatients. Equivalence testing has a different focus compared with most methods of clinical significance in that group change is measured and tested rather than individual change.

It appears that considerations of clinical significance may temper the optimism of researchers in claiming high effectiveness for interventions. Not all patients respond positively to treatment, with many patients' outcomes remaining unchanged, and a small percentage of patients (about 5%–10%) deteriorating rather than improving in therapy (Lambert & Ogles, 2004). Hansen, Lambert, and Forman (2002) found an average of 58% of patients in clinical trials (from a sample of 28 trials with 2,109 patients) experienced clinically significant change. In routine care, however, the percentage of patients experiencing clinically significant change was about 14%, and the deterioration rate was about 8%.

Another example of moderating claims of effectiveness is provided by examination of clinically significant change in data from the National Institute of Health Collaborative Depression Project (Ogles, Lambert, & Sawyer, 1995). This multisite study of two psychotherapies, antidepressant medication, and a medication placebo showed all the treatments were effective, with a surprisingly good showing for the medication placebo (with a manualized method of clinical management). Ultimately, the active treatments (cognitive behavior therapy [CBT], interpersonal psychotherapy [IPT], and Imipramine) distinguished themselves from placebo only with the most severely disturbed cases. The outcomes of treatment as measured by the Beck Depression Inventory showed clinically significant improvement; the number of patients going from the depressed range to the

nondepressed range after 12 weeks of treatment was 50% for CBT, 64% for IPT, 66% for Imipramine, and 46% for placebo with clinical management. All the treatments were a long way from being perfectly effective, and clinical significance ratings calculated for each patient made this quite clear.

EMPHASIS ON INDIVIDUAL CHANGE

Historically, the study of individual change has been the province of behaviorist research and methodology. The stimulus–response paradigm led to logically parsimonious methods of measuring baseline responses and determining changes in responses at the level of an individual organism after pairing stimuli or reinforcing behavior. Behavior therapy has therefore been consistently interested in measuring individual change, as the methods are conducive to such measurement (Ulrich, Stachnik, & Mabry, 1966).

Social validity was a term adopted in the 1970s by behaviorists (specifically, applied behavior analysis) to attempt external confirmation of subject change, such as confirming change with other sources in contact with the subject or comparing the subject's new behavior to that of the subject's peers. Wolf (1978) argued for establishing methods of asking society whether the effects of behavioral interventions are important to society. Behavior change that meets socially acceptable levels as determined by a functional population would be considered clinically important (Kazdin, 1977). In addition to questions of social validity, the discussion of external validity has resulted in consideration of ways to advance the generality and relevance of findings (Kazdin, 2003). Contrived laboratory conditions may not be relevant to daily experience and real-world functioning. External validity speaks to the question of how research studies reflect the real world.

In the 1980s, Jacobson worked to address clinical significance statistically and introduced a formula that is most common for calculating clinical significance. Jacobson et al. (1984) based the method not only on the rational concept of clinical significance (as has been discussed here) but also on the empirical concept of statistical reliability. Because change scores require the calculation of the difference between two measurements, the potential exists for compounding measurement error (Cohen & Swerdlink, 1999). Such potential for error underscores the necessity of selecting highly reliable measures when designing a study's methodology. Jacobson's method attempted, however, to account statistically for possible measurement error by using parameters that are specific to the measure used to assess client functioning, thus taking into account the measure's reliability.

Jacobson and Truax (1991) created a method to identify change scores that are both statistically reliable and clinically significant. As is discussed in the section Jacobson–Truax Method, the statistical method that they initially proposed has been debated, and several alternative methods of calculating clinical significance have been proposed. Several other methods follow a rationale similar to that of the original measure, requiring two essential criteria for determining clinically significant change over the course of treatment: (a) The change score for the patient reflects change that is statistically reliable, and (b) the patient more closely represents the functional population than the nonfunctional population, usually determined by data collected from normal and patient samples (Jacobson & Truax, 1991; also see the column "Clinical cutoff" in Table 7.1).

Although not universally accepted and used, the Jacobson–Truax (JT) method offers criteria that can be thought of as necessary conditions for establishing clinically significant change. Neither is a sufficient condition, but it is notable that most methods of estimating clinical significance include one or both of these criteria in principle. It may well be that other conditions may be developed in the future that are necessary to establish clinical significance, but these two conditions give a logical framework for most methods of determining the clinical relevance of change.

Before discussing the JT method and related methods in detail, however, it is important to note certain aspects of other methods, which attempt to establish clinical significance. These methods are briefly described in Table 7.1. In the study by Eisen, Ranganathan, Seal, and Spiro (2007), the authors used the standard error of measurement (SEM) to evaluate meaningful change according to the recommendations of McHorney and Tarlow (1995). Because the SEM is, in theory, the standard deviation of an

individual score, the strategy for using it as a statistical threshold suggests that a change at the level of 1 SEM reflects a "minimal clinically important intraindividual change" (Eisen et al., 2007, p. 274).

Equivalence testing does not test individual-level change but rather attempts to test the clinical meaningfulness of group-level change. Other methods use fairly standard statistics applied to individual change scores to estimate clinical significance.

Normative comparisons (Kendall, Marrs-Garcia, Nath, & Sheldrick, 1999) are a useful tool in determining whether "end-state functioning . . . falls within a normative range on important measures" (p. 285). Conceptually similar to equivalence testing, normative comparisons combine statistical significance tests with equivalence tests to compare treated to nondisturbed populations (Kendall & Grove, 1988).

Blanchard and colleagues (Blanchard et al., 1990; Blanchard & Schwarz, 1988) devised a straightforward scheme to determine clinically significant change with headache. Change scores were converted to a percentage change from baseline, with a 50% improvement indicating a noticeable change. This method has some utility and is often seen in medical research, but it fails to index entry into a range of normal functioning. Nevertheless, it allows researchers to classify specific patients as having met a criterion or not.

JACOBSON–TRUAX METHOD

The JT method (see also Jacobson, Roberts, Berns, & McGlinchey, 1999) is in many ways definitive for establishing clinical significance, also serving as the logical basis for other methods that followed. The JT method is composed of two essential steps: (a) determine whether the pre–post score reflects a statistically reliable change, that is, the score exceeds the difference due to measurement error or other sources of error and thus represents actual change; and (b) estimate a cutoff score to separate functional and dysfunctional populations, such that a client must move from the dysfunctional to the functional population to be considered recovered. The first step necessitates determining the reliability (r_{xx}) of the outcome measure used—often, the internal

TABLE 7.1

List of Strategies for Determining Clinically Significant Change

Strategy	Relevant citation	Within-group change[a]	Clinical cutoff	Reliable change	Brief description
Effect size	Cohen, 1988	Yes, No	No	No	Change score rendered into standard deviation units, typically calculated as group effect size, but individual effect sizes can also be used.
Standard error of measurement (SEM)	McHorney & Tarlow, 1995	Yes	No	Yes	The standard deviation of an individual score, it is estimated using the sample reliability coefficient and can be used as a threshold for reliable change.
Equivalence testing	Kendall, Marrs-Garcia, Nath, & Sheldrick, 1999	No	Yes	No	Typically a *t* test or other statistical significance test of group means, testing whether the posttreatment group is equivalent to functional, nontreated sample.
Normative comparison	Kendall & Grove, 1988	No	Yes	No	Combines clinical equivalence test with statistical significance test to determine whether group mean reflects clinically meaningful change.
Blanchard's method	Blanchard & Schwarz, 1988	Yes	No	No	Prescore minus postscore divided by prescore, calculated as a percentage, with 50% change as a cutoff. More common in health-related outcome literature.
Jacobson–Truax (JT)	Jacobson & Truax, 1991	Yes	Yes	Yes	Two criteria required, including passing a reliable change index (change exceeds expectation due to measurement error) and moving past a clinical cutoff demarking the boundary between functional and dysfunctional populations.
Variations on JT method					
Gulliksen–Lord–Novick (GLN)	Hsu, 1989	Yes	Yes	Yes	First major revision to JT method accounting for change scores' regression toward the mean.
Edwards–Nunnally (EN)	Speer, 1992	Yes	Yes	Yes	Attempts to account for regression to the mean by creating confidence intervals around change scores.
Hageman–Arrindell (HA)	Hageman & Arrindell, 1999	Yes	Yes	Yes	Amends the reliable change index and clinical cutoff, with the aim of reducing the risk of misclassification.
Hierarchical linear model (HLM)	Speer & Greenbaum, 1995	Yes	Yes	Yes	Using growth curve modeling, takes into account change occurring between pre- and posttest measurements.

[a]This column indicates whether the strategy accounts for within-group variability of change scores.

consistency reliability, Cronbach's alpha (Cronbach, 1951) is used instead of test–retest reliability—to calculate the SEM (S_E):

$$S_E = SD\sqrt{1 - r_{xx}}. \qquad (1)$$

The standard deviation of the pretreatment scores is used here, although alternative methods advocate using a normative population standard deviation. The SEM can then be used to calculate the standard error of the difference, thus describing the distribution of change scores that would exist had no real change occurred:

$$S_{diff} = \sqrt{2S_E^{\,2}}. \qquad (2)$$

Dividing the difference in scores from pretest to posttest by the standard error of the differences will result in the reliable change index (RCI):

$$\text{RCI} = \frac{\left(x_{post} - x_{pre}\right)}{S_{diff}}. \qquad (3)$$

If the RCI is greater than 1.96, then it is unlikely ($p < .05$) that the change score can be accounted for by chance alone and therefore represents real change. In this manner, the change score can be considered statistically reliable and not due to measurement error or other source of unreliability. The greater the reliability (r) of the outcome measure, the smaller the standard error, the smaller the standard error of the differences, and therefore smaller change scores are more likely to be statistically reliable, thus meeting the first of the JT criteria.

The second step involves using an established cutoff point between functional and dysfunctional populations, with recovered patients not only achieving statistically reliable change but also moving into the functional population (although Jacobson & Truax, 1991, proposed two other possible cutoff points, A and B, when two contrasting groups were not available). When normative data are available for *patients* and *nonpatients* and there is overlap between these populations, then *cutoff C* is the weighted midpoint between the means of these populations; the calculation must also consider the size of the distribution of scores around the mean of each population:

$$Cutoff \ C = \frac{\left(SD_{patient}M_{nonpatient}\right)+\left(SD_{nonpatient}M_{patient}\right)}{\left(SD_{patient}+SD_{nonpatient}\right)}. \quad (4)$$

These two steps establish criteria for categorizing patients into groups according to their level of clinically significant change, as shown in Table 7.2. If both criteria are passed, the patient is classified as

recovered. If the first criterion (RCI) is passed in the positive direction but the second criterion is failed, the patient is classified as *improved.* If RCI is passed in the negative direction, the patient is classified as *deteriorated*, being reliably worse than at pretreatment (in addition, such patients do not pass the criterion of moving from the dysfunctional to the functional population). If the first criterion is failed, the patient is classified as *unchanged.*

Less criticism has been applied to the logical premises of the JT method than to the method of determining statistical reliability of change scores, such that a number of alternative formulas have been proposed. Particular attention has been paid to the issue of possible regression of change scores to the mean (Hsu, 1999). Several alternative methods have been proposed, with studies such as Bauer, Lambert, and Nielsen (2004) comparing these methods. Ogles, Lunnen, and Bonesteel (2001) found the JT method to be most common in the outcome literature, although the JT method is not applied uniformly across studies. This issue is addressed later in this chapter. Several alternative methods are briefly described conceptually, and in the subsequent section, findings from the comparative studies based on these alternative methods are noted.

ADAPTATIONS OF THE JT METHOD

Gulliksen–Lord–Novick Method

Hsu (1989, 1996, 1999) noted the problem of failing to account for regression to the mean in the original JT method and proposed an alternative method. The crux of the regression to the mean problem is that more extreme scores (i.e., scores that fall far from the mean) are more likely on repeated assessments to become less extreme (i.e., fall closer to, or regress toward, the mean). Although the JT method was designed to account for measurement error, the criticism is that with two-wave data (i.e., pre- and posttest data), change scores may be reliable statistically and represent change above what is expected due to measurement error; however, inferring that the change is therefore due to psychotherapy ignores the internal validity consideration of regression toward the mean. Hsu advocated using a hypothetical population mean and standard deviation toward

---

	TABLE 7.2	

Criteria for Categorization of Patients' Change by Jacobson–Truax Method

Patient status	First criterion (RCI)	Second criterion (cutoff)
Recovered	Pass	Pass
Improved	Pass	Fail
Deteriorated	Pass (negative direction)	Fail
Unchanged	Fail	Fail

Note. RCI = reliable change index.

which scores are expected to regress. Ideally, these population parameters would be those of the group from which the sample was selected, but in most cases, this population information is unknown. Hsu recommended using the parameters of the pretreatment scores (e.g., M_{pre} and SD_{pre}) when the population parameters are unknown. The RCI by the Gulliksen–Lord–Novick (GLN) method is as follows:

$$RCI = \frac{\left(x_{post} - M_{pre}\right) - r_{xx}\left(x_{pre} - M_{pre}\right)}{SD_{pre}\sqrt{1 - r_{xx}^{\;2}}}. \quad (5)$$

The formula relies on the mean of a normative sample to reference twice in calculating the numerator.

Edwards–Nunnally Method

Speer (1992) used a rationale that is similar to, yet distinguishable from, that of JT. By this method, as implemented in the Edwards–Nunnally (EN) method, confidence intervals around pretreatment scores are created to minimize the effect of regression toward the mean. Using the reliability of the outcome measure, the pretreatment score is adjusted to an estimated true score at the center of a confidence interval. Posttreatment scores falling 2 S_E (SEM) units away from the adjusted score are considered statistically reliable. RCI by the EN method is given as

$$RCI = \left[r_{xx}\left(x_{pre} - M_{pre}\right) + M_{pre}\right] \pm 2SD_{pre}\sqrt{1 - r_{xx}}. \quad (6)$$

Hageman–Arrindell Method

The Hageman–Arrindell (HA) method represents a more pronounced departure from the JT method, with Hageman and Arrindell (1999) employing the strategy of Cronbach and Gleser (1959) to minimize φ (phi) or face "the risk of misclassification." Their version, the RC_{INDIV}, is purported to be both more precise and more sensitive to detecting true change. The index introduces the reliability of difference scores (r_{dd}) to account for the relationship between pre- and posttest scores. The RCI by the HA method is as follows:

$$RC_{INDIV} = \frac{\left(x_{post} - x_{pre}\right)\left(r_{dd}\right) + \left(M_{post} - M_{pre}\right)\left(1 - r_{dd}\right)}{\sqrt{r_{dd}}\sqrt{2S_E^{\;2}}}. \quad (7)$$

The r_{dd} by the HA method is as follows:

$$r_{dd} = \frac{SD_{pre}^{\;2} r_{xx(pre)} + SD_{post}^{\;2} r_{xx(post)} - 2SD_{pre}SD_{post}r_{pre*post}}{SD_{pre}^{\;2} + SD_{post}^{\;2} - 2SD_{pre}SD_{post}r_{pre*post}}. \quad (8)$$

In addition to amending the RCI for precision and to account for regression toward the mean, Hageman and Arrindell (1999) also amended the second JT method criterion, the clinical cutoff score. Following the same strategy to minimize the risk of misclassification, they determined a more conservative strategy to establishing a cutoff. Also note a new term is used in their formula, TRC, which stands for the *true reliable change* score. To explain their rationale for the TRC, Hageman and Arrindell pointed out that rather than using means and standard deviations of observed scores to calculate cutoff scores (as posited by the JT method), by the logic of classical test theory one can calculate true score equivalents of cutoff scores. Because the mean of true scores equals the mean of observed scores, the observed means are not transformed in the formula for the TRC. Because the standard deviation of true scores equals the standard deviation of the observed scores multiplied by the square root of the appropriate reliability index, the formula for the TRC is altered accordingly. (For a more complete description of this rationale, see Hageman & Arrindell, 1999, pp. 1176–1178.)

The individual clinical significance index calculated by the HA method is given as:

$$CS_{INDIV} = \frac{M_{post} + \left(x_{post} - M_{post}\right)\left(r_{xx(post)}\right) - TRC}{\sqrt{r_{xx(post)}}S_E} \quad (9)$$

and

$$TRC = \frac{SD_{norm}\sqrt{r_{xx(norm)}}M_{pre} + SD_{pre}\sqrt{r_{xx(pre)}}M_{norm}}{SD_{norm}\sqrt{r_{xx(norm)}} + SD_{pre}\sqrt{r_{xx(pre)}}}. \quad (10)$$

Hierarchical Linear Model

The benefit of using the hierarchical linear model (HLM), as given by Speer and Greenbaum (1995), lies in the ability of this statistical method to take into account multiple data points collected from patients during the entire course of treatment (for further elaboration, see Chapter 11 of this volume).

Estimating change with this additional information purports to capture more precisely the change that occurs between initial and final assessment. According to proponents, two-wave data, or pre–post change, may not render as precise an estimate of overall change as the use of additional information from multiwave data. In addition to the parameter estimation based on multiwave data, further advantages of HLM include the use of empirical Bayes estimates, which are weighted estimates that combine information from the individual and the sample as a whole, and the ability to handle missing data. The HLM approach calculated improvement rates using the z ratio formed by each client's empirical Bayes-estimated linear slope coefficient divided by the sample-estimated posterior standard error of the slope.

COMPARATIVE STUDIES

Several studies (Atkins, Bedics, McGlinchey, & Beauchaine, 2005; Bauer et al., 2004; Speer & Greenbaum, 1995) have examined the various methods empirically (with simulated data as well as with real patient data) to determine how each method classifies patients. Each of these has focused on the JT method and adaptations to this method.

In the first study of its kind, Speer and Greenbaum (1995) tested four of the five methods discussed in this chapter (they did not include the HA method). Their original conclusions favored the HLM method, but they later favored the JT method because of ease of calculation and wide acceptance among researchers (Speer & Greenbaum, 2002). The rates of improvement for HLM and the EN method were similar, with high sensitivity to change and classifying more patients as improved. Favoring a method because it provides higher rates for improvement cannot be considered a sign of accuracy because there is no known gold standard with which to compare any of the methods. Findings related to the JT method showed that it was more moderate in its classification, whereas the GLN method was an outlier from other methods in that it was conservative, classifying about half of patients as unchanged. Average agreement among methods' classification of patients was lowest for the GLN

method, with general agreement among the other four methods notably high.

Atkins et al. (2005), noting the lack of systematic guidance in choosing which method to use to determine clinical significance, simulated data that varied along key parameters important to clinical significance. These parameters included reliability of measurement, effect size, and correlation between pre- and posttest scores. These simulated data resulted in marked agreement among methods at high levels of reliability, especially when reliability was .90 or greater, a routine reliability level for outcome measures generally used in studies. The EN method tended to classify definitively, classifying patients as either having definitely recovered or definitely deteriorated rather than classifying them as unchanged. The original JT method and the GLN method yielded similar results in spite of differing formulae. The HA method appeared to be the most conservative in classifying patients as recovered, but when certain conditions existed (low reliability, high pre–post correlations), the R_{dd} was invalid, suggesting that this method may not be useful under these conditions. The HLM method was not included in this investigation. Overall, the researchers concurred with Maassen (2000) that the JT method may be preferred because of ease of computation and because the different methods are virtually indistinguishable.

Bauer et al. (2004) used empirical data from 386 patients to compare the same methods as Atkins et al. (2005) but included the HLM method. One advantage in this study was that the outcome measure (OQ-45; Lambert et al., 2004) was administered at each therapy session, allowing HLM to be used. Another major advantage was the presence of normative data for the outcome measure, with established clinical cutoffs for the functional versus the dysfunctional populations. Bauer et al. found that the JT, GLN, and HLM methods provided comparable results, whereas the EN and HA methods differed from these three. The EN method was more likely to classify patients as improved or recovered, and the HA method was more likely to conservatively classify patients as unchanged. Overall, the JT method was found again to be moderate in its classification of patient change, especially related to the two more extreme methods (EN and HA methods).

Ogles et al. (2001) identified 74 studies using clinical significance in the *Journal of Consulting and Clinical Psychology* over the period from 1990 to 1998. Of the 74 total studies using clinical significance methods, 26 (35%) used some variation of the JT method (which has varied slightly over the years). As a close second, 21 studies (28%) used normative comparisons or clinical cutoffs without using an estimate for the RCI. It is of interest that many used the Jacobson two-criteria method to establish the clinical cutoff but did not use Jacobson's RCI. A total of 19 (26%) studies used Kendall and Grove's (1988) method of using social validation comparisons. Only two studies used the RCI by itself, and six of the 74 studies used Blanchard's method (Blanchard & Schwarz, 1988). The JT method has been the most commonly used method, and it is advantageous for outcome research to account for both criteria of clinically significant change.

In a more recent study, Eisen, Ranganathan, Seal, and Spiro (2007) examined a large number of patients ($N = 2,248$ inpatients and outpatients) and compared three methods for addressing the statistical reliability of change but did not compare the clinical cutoff of the JT method. When the HA method for calculating the RCI was compared with individual effect sizes and the SEM, the HA method was the most conservative. Interestingly, however, Eisen et al. found that the SEM was highly concordant with estimates of positive change (including changes in clinician-rated Global Assessment of Functioning Scale scores). Their support of the SEM as a method of establishing change may merit examination by other researchers because of this concordance.

Overall, these studies suggested that differences exist in the use of the various methods. The JT method, however, was consistently moderate in its classification of patients, that is, it provided neither the highest or lowest estimates of proportion of patients who changed. Individuals who conducted validation studies recommended the JT method in relation to the alternatives studied. On the basis of this evidence and the fact that this method is preferable in many ways because of logical parsimony and ease of calculation, the generally recommended method for outcome researchers is to report findings

with, at least, this format, although other methods can also be included.

ADVANTAGES OF CLINICAL SIGNIFICANCE

Outcome research studies need to include estimates of clinical significance (preferably following the JT method explicitly) to establish the clinical relevance of psychotherapy change. The advantages to using clinical significance—and particularly the JT method—are numerous and extend beyond the establishment of clinical relevance. Inclusion of clinical significance requires different language about psychotherapy change. Rather than using the language of statistical significance, effect sizes, and likelihood of change on the basis of group membership, individual patients can be classified as improved, recovered, deteriorated, or unchanged. Not only is the language specific to individuals within the group but also the categorization gives face-valid terms that are clinically relevant.

Limiting statistics to traditional tests of statistical significance and effect sizes fails to examine (and therefore ignores) the importance of within-group variability (which is typically not unremarkable). With regard to this limitation, the JT method and related methods are far superior, classifying each patient individually. However, several methods of determining clinical significance described in this chapter operate on the basis of between-group comparisons rather than within-group variations. Effect sizes, equivalence testing, and normative comparisons undoubtedly have value as clinically relevant information reported in outcome literature. Normative comparisons are especially relevant to determine the clinical cutoff criterion, in a manner not unlike the JT method. However, capturing within-group variation enables the researcher to determine the clinical significance of individual change. Individual treatment response can be measured over time, and much has been learned about the effectiveness of therapist feedback of treatment response data throughout the course of treatment (Harmon et al., 2007; Lambert et al., 2003; Lutz et al., 2006; Slade, Lambert, Harmon, Smart, & Bailey, 2008).

Clinical significance methods that classify individual patient treatment response have been helpful not only in making decisions about when a patient may be ready to terminate treatment (that they have reliably changed and are no more disturbed than other members of their community) but also in contributing information relevant to policy decisions, such as how many treatment sessions will be needed to return individuals to a state of normal functioning. In recent years psychotherapy outcome research has addressed this question using survival analysis or related techniques to identify at what point in therapy a clinically significant change occurs for most patients (Anderson & Lambert, 2001; Hansen et al., 2002; Kopta, Howard, Lowry, & Beutler, 1994). The results from these studies suggest a range of 11 to 18 sessions as the number of sessions needed to achieve clinically significant change for *half* of the sample starting therapy. Such information is dependent on the classification of each patient's treatment response. Perhaps most important, reporting clinical significance estimates reduces the likelihood of outcome research overestimating the benefit of mental health treatments. Taking the corpus of psychotherapy literature into account, it appears that psychotherapy is generally effective in spite of specific treatments showing variability in degree of effectiveness (Lambert & Ogles, 2004). Although group mean change scores may demonstrate statistically significant differences over control groups, the degree of change may be clinically nonsignificant. Furthermore, large numbers of patients in a clinical trial may in fact deteriorate in a treatment group, whereas simultaneously the group mean shows change in the therapeutic direction. Clinical significance adds a level of precision to estimating the benefits of treatment, especially when the dual criteria of the JT method are required to define *recover*. Greater precision in determining outcomes can lead to greater confidence in practitioners and outcome researchers with regards to the validity of a treatment effect.

Finally, clinical significance (by definition) gives information that is clinically relevant. A treatment that results in clinically significant improvement for a majority of patients undergoing the treatment provides a higher standard being met by that treatment. Clinical significance can also be used to narrow the gap between research and practice by indicating benchmarks for treatment response. As cited, progress feedback to clinicians is one application of clinical significance to practice that has been shown to be effective (i.e., resulting in clinically significant change for a large number of patients).

LIMITATIONS OF CLINICAL SIGNIFICANCE

Methods of determining clinical significance are not without limitations. Several limitations are discussed here as they have been discussed in the outcome literature. Important limitations include the plurality of methods, the lack of uniformity in applying these methods, categorization and validity problems, and the limits of the functional distribution for cutoffs. Hsu (1999) and others have spelled out the weakness of the JT method in not taking into account regression toward the mean as an alternative explanation for the difference between pre- and post-scores. This limitation has been treated in the section Gulliksen–Lord–Novick Method, and on the basis of comparative studies, it represents less of a threat than previously thought, with the JT method showing high agreement with other methods and also to be moderate in its classification of patients.

The most obvious of the limitations, as demonstrated by the content of this chapter, is the diversity of methods and the failure by the field to adopt a single common metric. Multiple sources have pointed to this need for a common method. McGlinchey et al. (2008) argued for standardized, empirically derived cutoffs to simplify comparison across outcome studies. Lambert has argued persuasively for the use of the JT method—if not used by itself, then at least reported in addition to the results of other methods—on the basis of an explicitly pragmatic rationale (Lambert & Ogles, 2009). Reasons for this recommendation include allaying confusion about classification of recovered and deteriorated patients, the absence of evidence that the alternative methods are superior, the fact that newer methods require often-unavailable population data, the relative ease of computation of the JT method, and the simple fact, as found in Ogles et al. (2001), that it is the most commonly used method in outcome research.

The discussion of different methods takes for granted the fact that the methods are uniformly applied. Ogles et al. (2001) noted high variability in the application of methods, particularly the question of which norms are most appropriate for calculating the RCI. Although about 35% of studies they found examining clinically significant change used the JT method, many of these included some variation of the method. Hsu (1999) commented that researchers choosing between sample-specific norms or general population norms, or other parameters such as standard deviations and reliability coefficients, base their choices on a judgment about which norms are most realistic. However, no consensus exists on which norms to use. Recommended norms include the use of internal consistency reliability estimates when calculating the standard error of the difference and the use of normative data to establish the clinical cutoff (Lambert & Ogles, 2009).

An additional limitation of clinical significance methods is the problem common to all methods of categorization. Cutoff scores run the risk of misclassifying those persons scoring closest to the cutoff, which creates discrete boundaries from a continuous variable. Strategies for determining the cutoff have been discussed, but the very nature of a cutoff score runs the risk of misclassification (see also Volume 1, Chapter 37, this handbook). Following the statistical strategies of clinical significance and reliable change indexes greatly reduces this risk, but this limitation concerns the *validity* of the classifications of recovered versus no change versus deteriorated. Newnham, Harwood, and Page (2007) found evidence to support the validity of the JT method, indicating that patients who were classified by the method on the basis of a self-reported symptom measure (SF-36 Health Survey, classified as improved, recovered, no change, deteriorated) also showed differing levels of self-reported quality of life and clinician-rated symptom distress. Such studies show promise in demonstrating convergent validity, but more validity studies are certainly needed (see Lambert & Ogles, 2009).

Using a functional distribution cutoff presents yet another limitation based on the opposing ends of the distribution of initial symptom severity scores. Inpatient populations, for example, are likely to

meet the reliable change criterion by discharge, but they may not meet the clinical cutoff criterion, as they typically continue to improve after discharge. Newnham et al. (2007), for example, argued that for the inpatient population entering a normal range of functioning may be too high a benchmark for relatively brief inpatient stays. Tingey, Lambert, Burlingame, and Hansen (1996) made a similar point but suggested this problem could be overcome by using gradations of normal–abnormal functioning as the goal of treatment. They argued that a return to normal functioning may be an unrealistic goal for highly disturbed individuals. For example, the patient who is severely disturbed and who receives brief inpatient treatment may only return to a level of functioning that is still within the clinical range. The use of multiple functioning cutoff points would allow their change to be classified as clinically significant. One may legitimately question whether recovery necessitates a return to the nonclinical range of functioning.

At the opposite end of the spectrum, a large minority of patients enter treatment already in the normal range, and their scores and their functioning remain in this range throughout treatment. Defining clinically significant change for this population may demand different criteria, as the clinical cutoff is a less meaningful criterion for such cases. Floor effect responses for patients presenting for treatment are neither typical nor unheard of, but both recovery and reliable change criteria would be difficult to meet under these circumstances. Yet, denial of psychiatric symptoms by a patient who presents for treatment while depressed has diagnostic implications and clinical utility, and the one-size-fits-all approach for defining meaningful change may not be suitable.

CONCLUSION

Establishing the relevance of changes made in psychological treatments necessitates the establishment of not only statistically significant change but also clinically significant change. Necessary conditions for determining clinical significance include two criteria: (a) the change score exceeding a difference score that would be expected with measurement error, and (b) the movement from a dysfunctional to a functional population. The importance of clinical significance in addressing within-group variation has been noted. The advantages to using clinical significance estimates include not only establishing clinical relevance beyond statistical significance but also limiting the probability that treatment effects are overestimated.

Many methods have been proposed and described in this chapter, with the JT method being the most commonly used, the most parsimonious for calculation, and the one showing high agreement with methods attempted to revise it. Because a common limitation for clinical significance methods is the lack of a common index to report, we recommend the use of the JT method (alone or in combination with other methods) in all outcome studies to enable researchers to compare the results of studies using a common metric. The parameters for calculating the JT method should be commonly applied, including the use of internal consistency reliability estimates to calculate the standard error of the difference and the use of measure-specific normative data (i.e., for patient and nonpatient populations; see Beckstead et al., 2003) for establishing clinical cutoff scores. Following these recommendations would enable the comparison of research studies, with the goal of illuminating the effects of psychotherapy for patients.

As perhaps every study in psychological literature (or even all scientific literature) recommends, we recommend more research. Specifically, future studies need to address the validity of the categorization of clinically significant categories. The predictive validity in particular of these categories has not been studied. The question of different raters of clinically significant change also needs additional study. Furthermore, the concordance of clinical significance as given by different outcome measures may continue to be studied with great benefit to the outcome literature. In summary, outcome research literature must continually address the vital question of the clinical relevance of change.

References

Anderson, E. M., & Lambert, M. J. (2001). A survival analysis of clinically significant change in outpatient psychotherapy. *Journal of Clinical Psychology, 57*, 875–888. doi:10.1002/jclp.1056

Atkins, D. C., Bedics, J. D., McGlinchey, J. B., & Beauchaine, T. P. (2005). Assessing clinical significance: Does it matter which method we use? *Journal of Consulting and Clinical Psychology, 73*, 982–989. doi:10.1037/0022-006X.73.5.982

Bauer, S., Lambert, M. J., & Nielsen, S. L. (2004). Clinical significance methods: A comparison of statistical techniques. *Journal of Personality Assessment, 82*, 60–70. doi:10.1207/s15327752jpa8201_11

Beckstead, D. J., Hatch, A. L., Lambert, M. J., Eggett, D. L., Vermeersch, D. A., & Goates, M. K. (2003). Clinical significance of the Outcome Questionnaire (OQ-45.2). *Behavior Analyst Today, 4*, 74–90.

Beutler, L. E., & Moleiro, C. (2001). Clinical versus reliable and significant change. *Clinical Psychology: Science and Practice, 8*, 441–445. doi:10.1093/clipsy.8.4.441

Blanchard, E. B., Appelbaum, K. A., Radnitz, C. L., Michultka, D., Morrill, B., Kirsch, C., . . . Dentinger, M. P. (1990). Placebo controlled evaluation of abbreviated progressive muscle relaxation and of relaxation combined with cognitive therapy in the treatment of tension headache. *Journal of Consulting and Clinical Psychology, 58*, 210–215. doi:10.1037/0022-006X.58.2.210

Blanchard, E. B., & Schwarz, S. P. (1988). Clinically significant changes in behavioral medicine. *Behavioral Assessment, 10*, 171–188.

Cohen, J. (1988). *Statistical power analysis for the behavioral sciences* (2nd ed.). Hillsdale, NJ: Erlbaum.

Cohen, R. J., & Swerdlink, M. E. (1999). *Psychological testing and assessment.* Mountain View, CA: Mayfield.

Cronbach, L. J. (1951). Coefficient alpha and the internal structure of tests. *Psychometrika, 16*, 297–334. doi:10.1007/BF02310555

Cronbach, L. J., & Gleser, G. C. (1959). Interpretation of reliability and validity coefficients: Remarks on a paper by Lord. *Journal of Educational Psychology, 50*, 230–237. doi:10.1037/h0042848

Eisen, S. V., Ranganathan, G., Seal, P., & Spiro, A. (2007). Measuring clinically meaningful change following mental health treatment. *Journal of Behavioral Health Services and Research, 34*, 272–289. doi:10.1007/s11414-007-9066-2

Hageman, W. J., & Arrindell, W. A. (1999). Establishing clinically significant change: Increment of precision between individual and group level of analysis. *Behaviour Research and Therapy, 37*, 1169–1193.

Hansen, N. B., Lambert, M. J., & Forman, E. M. (2002). The psychotherapy dose-response effect and its implications for treatment delivery services. *Clinical Psychology: Science and Practice, 9*, 329–343. doi:10.1093/clipsy.9.3.329

Harmon, S. C., Lambert, M. J., Smart, D. M., Hawkins, E., Nielsen, S. L., Slade, K., & Lutz, W. (2007).

Enhancing outcome for potential treatment failures: Therapist-client feedback and clinical support tools. *Psychotherapy Research, 17,* 379–392. doi:10.1080/10503300600702331

Hsu, L. M. (1989). Reliable changes in psychotherapy: Taking into account regression toward the mean. *Behavioral Assessment, 11,* 459–467.

Hsu, L. M. (1996). On the identification of clinically significant client changes: Reinterpretation of Jacobson's cut scores. *Journal of Psychopathology and Behavioral Assessment, 18,* 371–385. doi:10.1007/BF02229141

Hsu, L. M. (1999). Caveats concerning comparisons of change rates obtained with five methods of identifying significant client changes: Comment on Speer and Greenbaum (1995). *Journal of Consulting and Clinical Psychology, 67,* 594–598. doi:10.1037/0022-006X.67.4.594

Jacobson, N. S., Follette, W. C., & Revenstorf, D. (1984). Psychotherapy outcome research: Methods for reporting variability and evaluating clinical significance. *Behavior Therapy, 15,* 336–352. doi:10.1016/S0005-7894(84)80002-7

Jacobson, N. S., Roberts, L. J., Berns, S. B., & McGlinchey, J. B. (1999). Method for defining and determining the clinical significance of treatment effects: Description, application, and alternatives. *Journal of Consulting and Clinical Psychology, 67,* 300–307. doi:10.1037/0022-006X.67.3.300

Jacobson, N. S., & Truax, P. (1991). Clinical significance: A statistical approach to defining meaningful change in psychotherapy research. *Journal of Consulting and Clinical Psychology, 59,* 12–19. doi:10.1037/0022-006X.59.1.12

Kazdin, A. E. (1977). Assessing the clinical or applied importance of behavior change through social validation. *Behavior Modification, 1,* 427–452. doi:10.1177/014544557714001

Kazdin, A. E. (2003). *Research design in clinical psychology* (4th ed.). Boston, MA: Allyn & Bacon.

Kendall, P. C., & Grove, W. M. (1988). Normative comparisons in therapy outcome. *Behavioral Assessment, 10,* 147–158.

Kendall, P. C., Marrs-Garcia, A., Nath, S. R., & Sheldrick, R. C. (1999). Normative comparisons for the evaluation of clinical significance. *Journal of Consulting and Clinical Psychology, 67,* 285–299. doi:10.1037/0022-006X.67.3.285

Kopta, S. M., Howard, K. I., Lowry, J. L., & Beutler, L. E. (1994). Patterns of symptomatic recovery in psychotherapy. *Journal of Consulting and Clinical Psychology, 62,* 1009–1016. doi:10.1037/0022-006X.62.5.1009

Lambert, M. J., Morton, J. J., Hatfield, D., Harmon, C., Hamilton, S., Reid, R. C., . . . Burlingame, G. M.

(2004). *Administration and scoring manual for the OQ-45.2.* Salt Lake City, UT: OQMeasures.

Lambert, M. J., & Ogles, B. M. (2004). The efficacy and effectiveness of psychotherapy. In M. J. Lambert (Ed.), *Bergin and Garfield's handbook of psychotherapy and behavior change* (5th ed., pp. 139–193). New York, NY: Wiley.

Lambert, M. J., & Ogles, B. M. (2009). Using clinical significance in psychotherapy outcome research: The need for a common procedure and validity data. *Psychotherapy Research, 19,* 493–501. doi:10.1080/10503300902849483

Lambert, M. J., Whipple, J. L., Hawkins, E. J., Vermeersch, D. A., Nielsen, S. L., & Smart, D. W. (2003). Is it time for clinicians to routinely track patient outcome? A meta-analysis. *Clinical Psychology: Science and Practice, 10,* 288–301. doi:10.1093/clipsy.bpg025

Lutz, W., Lambert, M. J., Harmon, S. C., Tschitsaz, A., Schurch, E., & Stulz, N. (2006). The probability of treatment success, failure and duration—What can be learned from empirical data to support decision making in clinical practice? *Clinical Psychology and Psychotherapy, 13,* 223–232. doi:10.1002/cpp.496

Maassen, G. H. (2000). Principles of defining reliable change indices. *Journal of Clinical and Experimental Neuropsychology, 22,* 622–632. doi:10.1076/1380-3395(200010)22:5;1-9;FT622

McGlinchey, J. B., Zimmerman, M., & Atkins, D. C. (2008). Clinical significance and remission in treating major depressive disorder: Parallels between related outcome constructs. *Harvard Review of Psychiatry, 16,* 25–34. doi:10.1080/10673220701885815

McHorney, C. A., & Tarlow, A. R. (1995). Individual-patient monitoring in clinical practice: Are available health status surveys adequate? *Quality of Life Research, 4,* 293–307. doi:10.1007/BF01593882

Newnham, E. A., Harwood, K. E., & Page, A. C. (2007). Evaluating the clinical significance of responses by psychiatric inpatients to the mental health subscales of the SF-36. *Journal of Affective Disorders, 98,* 91–97. doi:10.1016/j.jad.2006.07.001

Ogles, B. M., Lambert, M. J., & Sawyer, J. D. (1995). Clinical significance of the National Institute of Mental Health Treatment of Depression Collaborative Research Program data. *Journal of Consulting and Clinical Psychology, 63,* 321–326. doi:10.1037/0022-006X.63.2.321

Ogles, B. M., Lunnen, K. M., & Bonesteel, K. (2001). Clinical significance: History, application, and current practice. *Clinical Psychology Review, 21,* 421–446. doi:10.1016/S0272-7358(99)00058-6

Sheldrick, R. C., Kendall, P. C., & Heimberg, R. G. (2001). The clinical significance of treatments: A comparison of three treatments for conduct disordered children. *Clinical Psychology: Science and Practice, 8,* 418–430. doi:10.1093/clipsy.8.4.418

Slade, K., Lambert, M. J., Harmon, S. C., Smart, D. W., & Bailey, R. J. (2008). Improving psychotherapy outcome: The use of immediate electronic feedback and revised clinical support tools. *Clinical Psychology and Psychotherapy, 15,* 287–303. doi:10.1002/cpp.594

Speer, D. C. (1992). Clinically significant change: Jacobson & Truax (1991) revisited. *Journal of Consulting and Clinical Psychology, 60,* 402–408. doi:10.1037/0022-006X.60.3.402

Speer, D. C., & Greenbaum, P. E. (1995). Five methods for computing significant individual client change and improvement rates: Support for an individual growth curve approach. *Journal of Consulting and Clinical Psychology, 63,* 1044–1048. doi:10.1037/0022-006X.63.6.1044

Speer, D. C., & Greenbaum, P. E. (2002). Correction to Speer and Greenbaum (1995). *Journal of Consulting and Clinical Psychology, 70,* 1239. doi:10.1037/0022-006X.70.6.1239

Tingey, R. C., Lambert, M. J., Burlingame, G. M., & Hansen, N. B. (1996). Assessing clinical significance: Proposed extensions to method. *Psychotherapy Research, 6,* 109–123. doi:10.1080/10503309612331331638

Ulrich, R., Stachnik, T., & Mabry, J. (1966). *Control of human behavior* (Vol. 1). Glenview, IL: Scott, Foresman.

Wolf, M. M. (1978). Social validity: The case for subjective measurement or how applied behavior analysis is finding its heart. *Journal of Applied Behavior Analysis, 11,* 203–214. doi:10.1901/jaba.1978.11-203

Methods With Single Outcomes

## CHAPTER 8

ANALYSIS OF VARIANCE AND THE GENERAL LINEAR MODEL

James Jaccard and Kim Daniloski

Analysis of variance (ANOVA) and the general linear model (multiple regression) are probably the most widely used methods of analysis in the social sciences. Traditional ANOVA is a special case of multiple regression in the sense that any statistical contrast performed in ANOVA can be replicated using multiple regression. Despite this, the two approaches have evolved from different research traditions, and hence, we treat them separately.

We begin by discussing key concepts in statistical modeling and the analysis of mean differences. We then discuss ANOVA and multiple regression separately. For each topic, we describe the statistical model that motivates common applications of the approach. We then discuss a range of topics that are frequently misunderstood or that need to be reinforced in scientific practice. We refrain from developing the technical foundations of the methods because these, as well as relevant computational formulas, are available elsewhere (e.g., Judd, McClelland, & Ryan, 2009; Kirk, 1995; Maxwell & Delaney, 2004). Instead, we opt for a more informal approach to the interpretation of relevant statistics to underscore their intuitive and conceptual underpinnings.

In practice, researchers typically think about multiple regression using a mind-set of statistical modeling. The outcome variable is expressed as a linear function of a set of explanatory variables, and researchers seek to determine the accuracy with which one can predict the outcome from the predictors (using the squared multiple correlation) and interpret the coefficients associated with each predictor in the linear equation. Researchers often are concerned with the percent of variation that each predictor accounts for in the outcome, both alone and independent of the other predictors. ANOVA, by contrast, is often associated with a mind-set of analyzing mean differences. Researchers evaluate how means differ as a function of different variables, or *factors*, and pass judgment on the theoretical and practical implications of those mean differences. In point of fact, both multiple regression and ANOVA accommodate both mind-sets. That is, one can readily think of multiple regression as analyzing mean differences and how means vary as a function of variables, and one can readily think of ANOVA in terms of expressing the outcome variable as a function of a set of predictors and how well one is able to account for that outcome on the basis of the predictors. We characterize ANOVA and multiple regression from both perspectives, but we emphasize the mind-sets that dominate practical applications of the respective frameworks.

KEY CONCEPTS IN MODEL-BASED ANALYSIS

In this section, we highlight selected concepts relevant to model-based analysis in both the ANOVA and multiple regression frameworks.

Model Predictions and Errors in Prediction

Suppose we wish to characterize the annual income of assistant professors at universities in the United

DOI: 10.1037/13621-008
APA Handbook of Research Methods in Psychology: Vol. 3. Data Analysis and Research Publication, H. Cooper (Editor-in-Chief)

States. If we obtain data on annual income for the entire population of such individuals, we might construct a model that *explains* the different scores on this variable. A simple but obviously incorrect model is one that predicts that every individual has a score equal to the mean of all the scores. This model can be written as

$$\hat{Y}_i = \mu, \tag{1}$$

where μ is the grand mean calculated across all individuals and $\hat{Y}$ is the predicted annual income for individual i.[1] For example, if the (grand) mean is $48,348, the model states that everyone has an annual income of $48,348. We define the errors in prediction as the difference between the observed and predicted scores:

$$\varepsilon_i = Y_i - \hat{Y}_i, \tag{2}$$

where ε is the error score for individual i. On the basis of Equations 1 and 2, we can specify a model that completely accounts for the population scores as follows:

$$Y_i = \hat{Y}_i + \varepsilon_i, \tag{3}$$

where the annual income, Y, is said to equal the predicted annual income on the basis of our model ($\hat{Y}$) plus errors in prediction (ε). Equation 3 is a general expression for representing statistical models, namely, observed scores are a function of model-based predicted scores plus error. For the present case, because $\hat{Y}_i = \mu$, Equation 3 can be rewritten substituting μ for $\hat{Y}_i$, yielding

$$Y_i = \mu + \varepsilon_i. \tag{4}$$

Indexes of the Magnitude of Errors

When working with models, we want to index how far off model predictions are, that is, the magnitude of the errors. The average of the error scores across individuals is not a useful index because the positive errors cancel the negative errors during summation and produce an average error of zero. A better index is a positive square root average of the error scores. We first calculate the average squared error:

$$\sum_{i=1}^{N} \varepsilon_i^2 / N$$

and then calculate the square root of this result to return the index to its original Y metric:

$$\sqrt{\sum_{i=1}^{N} \varepsilon_i^2 / N}. \tag{5}$$

This index of average error is called the *standard error of estimate* and is often symbolized by σ_ε or by $\sigma_{Y-\hat{Y}}$. In our example, if the standard error of estimate is $3,012, this means that the predicted scores for the model were off, on average, by $3,012. The smaller the standard error of estimate, the better the model's predictions. Note that one must take into account the metric of Y when interpreting the standard error of estimate. If Y is the number of children married couples have in their family, then a standard error of estimate that equals 3.0 for a model is considerable, indicating that predictions are off, on average, by 3 children. If Y is annual income in units of dollars, however, then a standard error of estimate that equals 3.0 for a model is small because predicted scores are off, on average, by only $3.00. The standard error of estimate is an informative statistic, but it is rarely reported in social science research. Other indexes of the magnitude of error that are similar to the standard error of estimate but that rely on indexes that are less affected by extreme errors are discussed in Wilcox (2005a).

The most popular index of prediction errors is the squared correlation between the observed (Y) and predicted ($\hat{Y}$) scores. In the ANOVA literature, this index is often called eta squared, and in multiple regression it is called the squared multiple correlation. It is based on the concept of explaining variability in the outcome measure. Specifically, variability on Y can be decomposed into two parts: (a) that which can be accounted for by the model and (b) that which represents errors in prediction. The squared multiple correlation is the proportion of variability of Y that can be explained by the model, and one minus the squared multiple correlation is the proportion that is due to errors in prediction.

Modeling and Conditional Predictions

The model we used to predict the annual income of new assistant professors on the basis of the grand

---

[1] We use Greek symbols for parameters that are based on scores for the entire population.

mean was simplistic. More complex explanatory models make predictions using additional information about each individual in the population. For example, we might hypothesize that males, on average, are paid more than females and that the gender of an individual therefore should be taken into account when making predictions. For this model, the predicted scores are based on the grand mean and then are further conditioned on a person being male or female, with different scores being predicted depending on a person's gender. Models differ in the amount of conditional information they use and how that information is combined to make predictions.

Model Comparisons

Model comparison is a popular practice in the social sciences (Judd et al., 2009; Maxwell & Delaney, 2004; Rodgers, 2010). In this approach, one formally documents the improvement in prediction errors as a result of adding information to a simpler model. For example, in the model discussed in the previous section, the predicted annual income of assistant professors was initially based on a model that asserted the annual income of each individual is the mean income of all individuals in the population. A more complex model that built on this model also predicts that the annual income is equal to this mean but that income is further conditionalized on other pieces of information about individuals in the population, such as gender. The extent to which errors in prediction are reduced by considering these additional pieces of information is indexed quantitatively by documenting the change in the standard error of estimate or the change in the squared multiple correlation. If the more complex model does not meaningfully reduce the errors in prediction, the simpler model is preferred.

Model Population Parameters and Sample Estimates of Those Parameters

Although models are posited to represent the state of affairs in a population, we seldom have access to population data. Instead, we obtain what are conceptualized as random samples from the population and then make inferences about the values of the population model using indexes from the sample

data. In so doing, we recognize that sampling error is operative and this must be taken into account when characterizing model parameters from sample data. We elaborate on sampling error later.

KEY CONCEPTS FOR ANALYZING MEAN DIFFERENCES

Model-based frameworks approach data in terms of estimating model parameters used to generate predicted scores, documenting the magnitude of prediction errors, and determining the reduction in prediction errors that result by adding information to the model. A different mind-set that some researchers invoke when analyzing data is not to think in terms models but instead to think of group means and ask whether those means, or some combination of them, are different from one another. For example, a researcher might ask whether the population mean annual income of assistant professors for males, μ_M, is different from the population mean for females, μ_F, and then seek to test the hypothesis that the two means are not equal. The parameter of interest is the difference between the two means:

$$\delta = \mu_M - \mu_F, \tag{6}$$

and researchers seek to (a) determine whether the hypothesis that δ is not zero is viable relative to the null hypothesis that δ is zero and (b) estimate the magnitude of δ. In this mind-set, the dominant concepts are population–sample means and sampling error, which we now discuss.

Sampling Error

Estimates of a population mean on the basis of sample data are invariably accompanied by sampling error. For example, the true annual income for assistant professors in the population might be $\mu = \$48,348$. The researcher, constrained by the inability to obtain data on the entire population, obtains a random sample of 100 assistant professors from the population and calculates the sample mean, M. The calculated sample mean likely will not exactly equal the population mean, and the discrepancy between the sample mean and the population mean, $M - \mu$, represents *sampling error*. Suppose the sample mean is $47,144. The amount of sampling error is $47,144 – $48,348 = –$1,208. In practice, we cannot know how much sampling error is operating in a given study because, to do so, we would need to know the value of the population mean.

Although we can never know exactly how much sampling error is operating in a given study, statisticians have derived indexes that estimate the typical amount of sampling error that occurs if the same study were to be replicated many times using the same sample size but with a new random sample from the population each time. This estimate is called the *estimated standard error* of the parameter of interest (not to be confused with the standard error of estimate, described earlier). We use the notation *SE* to refer to an estimated standard error in conjunction with a Greek subscript to reflect the population parameter to which it refers. For example, SE_μ is the estimated standard error of a mean, and $SE_{\mu 1 - \mu 2}$ is the estimated standard error of the difference between two means. As an example, if a researcher reports that the sample mean for $N = 100$ is $47,144 and that the estimated standard error for the mean is $1,502, this suggests that sample means that are based on random samples of $N = 100$ deviate, on average, about $1,502 from the true population mean. The estimated standard error of a parameter tells us, in essence, how much confidence we can have in the accuracy of a sample mean, with smaller values leading to increased confidence. If, for example, the estimated standard error of the mean annual income of assistant professors is $12.00, then we would have a great deal of confidence in the accuracy of the sample mean we observe because, on average, sample means deviate only $12.00 from the true population mean. But if the estimated standard error of the mean income is $12,000, we would not have as much confidence in the accuracy of the sample mean. Estimated standard errors must be interpreted with caution because they are only *estimates* of the typical amount of sampling error and are, themselves, subject to sampling error. Despite this caution, they can be viewed as indicators of sampling error and are

useful in statistical theory and applications of that theory.

Margins of Error

In political polls in the popular media, it is customary to report an estimate of a population parameter in conjunction with a margin of error (MOE). We might be told, for example, that the percentage of people who prefer Candidate A to Candidate B is 30%, with an MOE equal to plus or minus 5%. The MOE is a recognition of sampling error, and, like the estimated standard error, it provides us with a sense of the amount of sampling error operating. We have more confidence in a poll, for example, with a small MOE (e.g., ±5%) than one with a large MOE (e.g., ±25%). It is surprising that most research in the social sciences fails to report MOEs when reporting means, percentages, or correlations. Reporting MOEs should be standard practice.

One way to define MOEs is to use the upper and lower limit of the 95% confidence interval (CI) of the statistic.[2] For example, a researcher might state that the mean annual income for assistant professors is $47,144, with an MOE of ±$300. This MOE is derived from the 95% CI, which was $46,844 to $47,444. It is the width of the CI divided by two (in this example, ($47,444 – $46,844)/2 = $300). In some cases, the CI will not be symmetrical about the statistic, so one will need to report the lower and upper levels of error separately. When planning a study, most researchers make sample size decisions to maximize statistical power relative to practical constraints. We suggest that researchers also make sample size decisions to minimize MOEs relative to practical constraints. Methods for determining sample sizes that yield a priori desired levels of MOE are described by Maxwell, Kelley, and Rausch (2008). Not surprisingly, MOEs are systematically related to estimated standard errors, as both reflect sampling error.

Critical Ratios for Mean Differences

In null hypothesis testing frameworks that evaluate mean differences, we seek to determine whether we can reject the null hypothesis of equal population

---

[2]Alternatively, one can define MOE using credibility intervals in the context of Bayesian statistics (Carlin & Louis, 2000), an approach we find preferable. Technically, a CI should not be interpreted as an MOE in the way a lay person might think of it but rather in terms of the formal statistical theory underlying CIs.

means in favor of an alternative hypothesis of unequal population means. For the case of two means, the null and alternative hypotheses are

$$H_0: \mu_M - \mu_F = \delta = 0 \text{ and}$$

$$H_1: \mu_M - \mu_F = \delta \neq 0.$$

An informal way of thinking about a standard error of mean differences is that it reflects the average absolute amount of sampling error that operates in studies like the one being analyzed. For example, assume the estimated standard error of the mean difference is $2,000 for samples of 100 per group when comparing male and female means for annual income. This would mean (roughly) that the absolute amount of sampling error tends to be about $2,000 in studies like the one being analyzed. Some errors would be larger than this, some would be smaller, and some would be close to zero. But the average discrepancy (more technically, the root-mean-square average) of the sample mean difference from the true mean difference across repeated replications of the study would be about $2,000.

We can form a ratio that compares the sample mean difference we obtain in a given study relative to our index of sampling error:

$$\text{Critical Ratio} = \frac{\text{Observed mean difference}}{\text{Estimated standard error of mean difference}}. \quad (7)$$

If we obtain a critical ratio of 2.0, this means that the observed mean difference is twice as large as what we would expect on the basis of sampling error. If we obtain a critical ratio of 3.0, this means that the observed mean difference is three times as large as what we would expect on the basis of sampling error. Although there is much more to the underlying logic than this, t ratios and F ratios from ANOVA can be interpreted (roughly and descriptively) as such critical ratios. A value of 1.0 means the observed sample difference is the same as what one would expect on the basis of sampling error, given the null hypothesis of no mean difference is true. Values larger than 1.0 indicate the observed mean difference is larger than what we would expect by chance. If the critical ratio is large enough, we conclude that the null hypothesis is unlikely to be true (i.e., that the observed mean differences are too

large relative to what we expect by chance given a true null hypothesis).

With this background, we can now discuss model-based and mean-based conceptualizations of ANOVA and multiple regression.

THE ANOVA FRAMEWORK

A Model-Based Perspective on ANOVA

As noted, models make predictions about scores on outcome variables conditioned on information about individuals in the target population. A popular representation of ANOVA is called an *effects model* in which the conditioned information is represented as deviations from the grand mean.

Returning to our example on the annual income of new assistant professors, we might hypothesize that males are paid more than females, on average, and that the gender of the individual should therefore be taken into account when making predictions. We define the effect of being *male* as the difference between the mean annual income for males relative to the grand mean (i.e., the typical score for everyone):

$$\tau_M = \mu_M - \mu, \quad (8)$$

where τ_M is the *treatment effect*, or the effect of being treated as a male, and μ_M is the mean annual income for all males in the population. If the mean male annual income is $50,350 and the grand mean is $48,348, then the effect of being male is to increase annual income, on average, by $50,350 − $48,348 = $2,002 over the typical income as indexed by the grand mean. We can define a similar effect for females as the female mean minus the grand mean:

$$\tau_F = \mu_F - \mu, \quad (9)$$

where τ_F is the treatment effect of being female, and μ_F is the mean annual income for all females in the population. If the mean female annual income is $46,346, then the effect of being female is to decrease annual income, on average, by $46,346 − $48,348 = −$2,002.

We can incorporate the effect of gender into the initial model of predicted scores as follows:

$$\hat{Y}_i = \mu + \tau_j, \quad (10)$$

where τ is the treatment effect for the group j that the person i is a member of (either male or female). The complete model of observed scores is then

$$Y_i = \hat{Y}_i + \varepsilon_i = \mu + \tau_j + \varepsilon_i. \tag{11}$$

The effects-based ANOVA model uses the logic that a predicted score is an additive function of the grand mean plus treatment effects associated with one or more factors (independent variables) or the interaction between those factors. For multifactor studies, rather than making predictions conditional on one piece of information (e.g., gender), we make predictions conditional on multiple pieces of information. For example, the effect-based model for a two factor design is

$$Y_i = \hat{Y}_i + \varepsilon_i = \mu + \tau_{A_j} + \tau_{B_k} + \tau_{AB_{jk}} + \varepsilon_i, \tag{12}$$

where τ_{A_j} is the treatment effect for the group j that the individual is in on factor A, τ_{B_k} is the treatment effect for the group k that the individual is in on factor B, and $\tau_{AB_{jk}}$ is the (residualized) interaction for factors A and B.

The Cell Means Approach

If researchers were to use the model in Equation 12 in practice, they would estimate and directly interpret the different parameters in the model (i.e., μ, τ_{A_j}, τ_{B_k}, and $\tau_{AB_{jk}}$) while also seeking to gain some sense of how large the errors in prediction for the model are by estimating $\sigma_{Y-\hat{Y}}$ or the squared multiple correlation between predicted and observed scores. However, even a casual inspection of research literature reveals that few investigators focus on these parameters. It is far more common for researchers to focus on group means, or combinations of them, and frame questions about those means. To be sure, researchers do focus on t ratios and F ratios that map directly onto t ratios and F ratios in the effects model of ANOVA. But technically, the focus is on parameters that directly reflect mean differences between groups, not μ and τ. Kirk (1995) referred to this focus as a *cell means approach* and provided statistical details of the method. Given its prominence, it garners most of our attention.

The central role of contrasts in the cell mean approach. When comparing means, it is common

practice for researchers to first conduct an omnibus F test for each factor in the design and then pursue follow-up contrasts that test mean differences dependent on the results of the omnibus tests. The questions addressed by omnibus tests alone usually are not focused sufficiently, so, invariably, the analyst pursues specific contrasts focused on more specific mean differences given a statistically significant omnibus test. These contrasts are the heart of making substantive conclusions in ANOVA. Interestingly, most of the more popular follow-up contrast strategies (e.g., the Tukey HSD test, Bonferroni tests, the Games-Howell test) were developed without an omnibus F test serving as a screen to decide whether more specific contrasts should be pursued. Studies suggest that using an omnibus F test as a screen unnecessarily lessens the statistical power of these methods (Bernhardson, 1975), so there is good reason not to use them in conjunction with omnibus tests. Some researchers believe that a two-step strategy that uses an omnibus F test in conjunction with pooled variance follow-up t tests controls for inflated Type I error rates that result from conducting multiple follow-up tests. This is only true for certain, however, if a factor has exactly three levels (Levin, Serlin, & Seaman, 1994). Given the above points, we recommend that analysts generally forgo omnibus tests and move directly to the specific contrasts of interest. If it is desired to control for inflated error rates from conducting multiple contrasts, then one should use an appropriate method for doing so, and this often will not involve using results of an omnibus test. If one is interested in evaluating the omnibus effect for a factor in its own right, then an omnibus test is appropriate. But more often than not, the omnibus test will play a subsidiary role to more focused questions addressed by contrasts.

Given the central role that contrasts have in the cell means approach, an important question is whether there are certain kinds of contrasts that capture the interest of researchers more so than others. Rosenthal and Rosnow (1985) suggested there are and referred to these as contrasts that are conceptually "wired in" to most factorial designs. Three types of contrasts are far and away the most popular. To make these contrasts explicit, we consider a numerical example using a between-subjects factorial design. The study is a hypothetical experiment in which 120 participants read a transcript of a trial and then made a judgment on whether the accused was guilty on a 0-to-10 scale, with higher scores implying a higher likelihood of guilt. A 0 was labeled as definitely not guilty, a 10 as definitely guilty, and a five as 50–50. The investigator went to great lengths to ensure the scale points were interpreted like probabilities and divided the responses by 10 to yield an outcome metric ranging from zero to one, which reflected *subjective probability* units. All participants read identical transcripts, except that half were told the accused was African American (Level 1 of Factor *A*) and the other half were told the accused was European American (Level 2 of Factor *A*). One third of the participants in the study were European American (Level 1 of Factor *B*), one third were African Americans (Level 2 of Factor *B*), and one third were Latino (Level 3 of Factor *B*). Thus, the design was a 2 × 3 factorial in which the two factors were the ethnicity of the accused and the ethnicity of the juror, both of which were between-subjects and fixed in nature. Table 8.1 presents sample means and standard deviations for the factorial design on the basis of a sample size of 20 participants per cell.

The first type of contrast that captures the interest of many researchers is the difference between marginal means representing the main effect of each factor. For the juror study, these are contrasts comparing mean probability judgments of guilt for the ethnicity of the accused person collapsing across the ethnicity of the juror as well as contrasts comparing mean probability judgments of guilt for the ethnicity of the juror collapsing across the ethnicity of the accused.

A second type of contrast that often is of interest is typically associated with interaction effects, so we digress briefly into how interaction effects are usually conceptualized in the cell means approach. Interaction effects can be parameterized in many ways (see Jaccard, 1998; Judd et al., 2009; Maxwell & Delaney, 2004), but the most common way in the literature invokes the concept of moderation. An interaction effect is said to exist when the effect of an independent variable on a dependent variable

TABLE 8.1

Factorial Analysis of Variance Example

(a) Cell Means

Ethnicity of juror (Factor *B*)

Ethnicity of accused (Factor *A*)	EA	AA	L	Marginal mean
AA	.77	.60	.60	.66
EA	.50	.45	.50	.49
Marginal mean	.64	.52	.55	

(b) Simple Main Effects (SME)

Ethnicity of juror (Factor *B*)

Ethnicity of accused (Factor *A*)	EA	AA	L
AA	.77	.60	.60
EA	.50	.45	.50
SME mean difference	.27	.15	.10

(c) Interaction Contrasts

	EA	AA
AA	.77	.60
EA	.50	.45

(.77 − .50) − (.60 − .45) = .12;

	EA	L
AA	.77	.60
EA	.50	.50

(.77 − .50) − (.60 − 50) = .17;

	AA	L
AA	.60	.60
EA	.45	.50

(.60 − .45) − (.60 − .50) = .05.

Note. EA = European American; AA = African American; L = Latino.

differs depending on the value of a third variable, called a *moderator variable*. Researchers first identify the factor they want to treat as the moderator variable and the factor that is to be the focal independent variable. In some studies, the choice is theoretically obvious, such as when one wants to evaluate the effect of a cognitive behavior therapy (CBT) versus a control group (the focal independent variable) on anxiety and wants to test whether the effectiveness of CBT varies as a function of the gender of the respondent (the moderator variable). In other cases, such as the juror study in Table 8.1, the choice is not so obvious. One could reasonably ask whether the effect of ethnicity of the accused on guilt judgments varies as a function of the ethnicity of the juror, or one could ask whether the effect of the ethnicity of the juror on guilt judgments varies as a function of the ethnicity of the accused. In such cases, the designation of the moderator variable should follow from how the researcher wants to frame the interaction conceptually. Statistically, it is of little consequence as to which variable is chosen to be the moderator variable. In our example, we will use ethnicity of the juror as the moderator variable. The second type of contrast that often captures the interest of researchers is whether the independent variable affects the outcome variable at a given level of the moderator variable. For example, is there an effect of ethnicity of the accused on guilt judgments for just European American jurors? Is there an effect of ethnicity of the accused on guilt judgments for just African American jurors? Is there an effect for just Latino jurors? These contrasts are called *simple main effects* (see Table 8.1).

The third type of contrast that often is of interest is an interaction contrast. These contrasts test whether one simple main effect is different in magnitude from another simple main effect. Table 8.1 presents three interaction contrasts for the juror study. As an example, the estimated effect of the ethnicity of the accused for just European Americans is $M_{A1B1} - M_{A2B1} = .77 - .50 = .27$. The estimated effect for just African Americans is $M_{A1B2} - M_{A2B2} = .60 - .45 = .15$. The difference between these effects is $[M_{A1B1} - M_{A2B1}] - [M_{A1B2} - M_{A2B2}] = .12$. If the value of this interaction contrast is zero, then the effect of the independent variable on the outcome variable is the same for the two groups in question as defined on the moderator variable. An interaction contrast essentially focuses on a 2 × 2 subtable and is the difference between mean differences. We discuss

strategies for testing the statistical significance of interaction contrasts shortly.

In sum, researchers using factorial designs who adopt a cell means perceptive are typically interested in three types of contrasts: (a) contrasts for differences between the marginal means associated with a main effect, (b) simple main effect contrasts to determine whether an independent variable affects an outcome variable at a given level of the moderator variable, and (c) interaction contrasts that determine whether the effect of the independent variable on the outcome variable shifts from one level of the moderator variable to another level. These contrasts, of course, do not exhaust the possibilities. Ultimately, the contrasts that a researcher pursues are determined by the theory and questions one wants to address.

The cell means approach to contrasts. We can now specify a general formulation for the cell means approach in one-way and factorial designs. Specifically, we show how to pursue contrasts of the three types noted thus far. We begin by defining a parameter, called a contrast value, ψ, as being a linear function of the cell means of the different groups in the experiment. For the juror example, the design has six cell means and any given contrast value can be represented as

$$\psi_m = c_1\,\mu_{A1B1} + c_2\,\mu_{A2B1} + c_3\,\mu_{A1B2} + c_4\,\mu_{A2B2} + c_5\,\mu_{A1B3} + c_6\,\mu_{A2B3}, \qquad (13)$$

where ψ_m is the mth contrast value (an investigator can pursue more than one contrast), μ_{AjBk} is the cell mean for factor A at level j crossed with factor B at level k, and the cs are contrast coefficients that are assigned numerical values by the researcher to isolate a theoretically interesting contrast. For example, suppose a researcher desires to examine a contrast that focuses just on European Americans (level 1 of factor B) and that compares the mean when the accused is African American with the mean when the accused is European American (a simple main effect contrast). This is accomplished using the following contrast values:

$$\psi_1 = (1)\,\mu_{A1B1} + (-1)\,\mu_{A2B1} + (0)\,\mu_{A1B2} + (0)\,\mu_{A2B2} + (0)\,\mu_{A1B3} + (0)\,\mu_{A2B3}. \qquad (14)$$

The terms with contrast coefficient values of zero drop out of the equation because a mean times zero is zero, leaving us with

$$\psi_1 = (1)\ \mu_{A1B1} + (-1)\ \mu_{A2B1} = \mu_{A1B1} - \mu_{A2B1}, \qquad (15)$$

which is the contrast of interest to the researcher. So, a researcher interested in this contrast would use the contrast coefficients of 1, −1, 0, 0, 0, 0 in Equation 13.

Suppose instead, we desired to examine a contrast for the main effect of factor *A* where we compare the marginal mean for all cases in which the accused is African American with the corresponding marginal mean where the accused is European American. The contrast coefficients that accomplish this are

$$\psi_2 = (1/3)\ \mu_{A1B1} + (-1/3)\ \mu_{A2B1} + (1/3)\ \mu_{A1B2}$$
$$+ (-1/3)\ \mu_{A2B2} + (1/3)\ \mu_{A1B3}$$
$$+ (-1/3)\ \mu_{A2B3}. \qquad (16)$$

Note that the three means for the accused African American are each weighted by 1/3 and summed (which yields the average for the accused African American across levels of factor *B*), and the three means for the accused European American are each weighted by −1/3 and summed (which yields the average for the accused European American across levels of factor *B*, signed negatively). With rearrangement of terms, this yields

$$\psi_2 = [(1/3)\ \mu_{A1B1} + (1/3)\ \mu_{A1B2} + (1/3)\ \mu_{A1B3}]$$
$$- [(1/3)\ \mu_{A2B1} + (1/3)\ \mu_{A2B2} + (1/3)\ \mu_{A2B3}], \quad (17)$$

which yields

$$\psi_2 = [(\mu_{A1B1} + \mu_{A1B2} + \mu_{A1B3})/3]$$
$$- [(\mu_{A2B1} + \mu_{A2B2} + \mu_{A2B3})/3], \qquad (18)$$

which is the contrast of interest. So, a researcher interested in comparing these two main effect means would use the contrast coefficients of 1/3, −1/3, 1/3, −1/3, 1/3, −1/3 in Equation 13.

Finally, suppose we were interested in the first interaction contrast in Table 8.1. This contrast focuses on the difference between mean differences (i.e., $[\mu_{A1B1} - \mu_{A2B1}] - [\mu_{A1B2} - \mu_{A2B2}]$). The coefficients that accomplish this contrast are 1, −1, −1, 1, 0, 0. The contrast coefficients for the second interaction

contrast in Table 8.1 are 1, −1, 0, 0, −1, 1 and for the third interaction contrast they are 0, 0, 1, −1, −1, 1. The common feature of all these contrasts is that each is a (linear) function of the individual cell means in the design, hence the term *cell means approach*.

Sampling error and critical ratios for contrasts. In practice, the contrasts of interest are performed on sample data. When applied to samples, the sample contrast value, CV_m, serves as an estimate of its population counterpart, ψ_m. An index of sampling error can be obtained for any sample-based contrast in the form of an estimated standard error for that contrast, $SE\psi_m$, and a critical ratio is defined, per Equation 3, as

$$\text{Critical Ratio} = CV_m\ /\ SE\psi_m. \qquad (19)$$

In traditional ANOVA, this critical ratio is distributed as a *t*-distribution with degrees of freedom equal to the degrees of freedom associated with $SE\psi_m$. The *p* value associated with the contrast is the *p* value associated with the t ratio. Statistical software generates these *p* values, $SE\psi_m$, and a 95% CI for the contrast, allowing one to also report an MOE for the contrast. It is statistically convenient if a restriction is placed on the various *c*s within a given contrast so that they sum to zero. This restriction rarely limits the ability of the researcher to pursue contrasts that are of theoretical interest. Because the critical ratio is evaluated relative to a *t*-distribution, the contrasts are often called *single degree of freedom contrasts*.

The formulas for calculating $SE\psi$ and the degrees of freedom associated with it can be complex and vary depending on design features (e.g., within-subject vs. between-subject factors, fixed vs. random effects, nesting, the presence of covariates, equal or unequal *n* per cell), how the investigator chooses to act on design features (e.g., whether one desires the CV for marginal means to reflect weighted or unweighted composites of the cell means in the face of unequal sample sizes), and the nature of the population data itself (e.g., whether one assumes variance homogeneity in each group). Computer software simplifies much of this work for us. Indeed, the software does not even require that researchers explicitly generate contrast coefficients, instead generating them implicitly on the basis of either contrasts that are common or purely statistical grounds (e.g., orthogonal contrasts).

Most of us are familiar with contrasts in ANOVA paradigms under the guise of follow-up tests, post hoc tests (e.g., Tukey's HSD test), a priori contrasts, or multiple comparisons. Researchers often do not appreciate that the data of a factorial design can be expressed as a set of cell means and then combined via Equation 13 to yield perspectives on main effects, simple main effects, or interaction effects. In the final analysis, the vast majority of research that uses ANOVA eventually zeros in on one or more single degrees of freedom contrasts that are of theoretical interest and that represent the combination of cell means per Equation 13.

In principle, an infinite number of contrasts can be performed. However, some contrasts have redundant or overlapping information value. For example, for three means (μ_1, μ_2, and μ_3), if we conduct the three pairwise contrasts $\psi_1 = \mu_1 - \mu_2$, $\psi_2 = \mu_1 - \mu_3$, and $\psi_3 = \mu_2 - \mu_3$, one can easily show algebraically that $\psi_3 = \psi_2 - \psi_1$. In other words, there is a linear dependency between the contrasts because one of them can be expressed as a linear function of the others. Such redundancy motivates some researchers to pursue only sets of contrasts that are nonredundant, such as the well-known case in which contrasts are orthogonal. The problem with this logic is that sometimes orthogonal contrasts make no theoretical sense or fail to address the questions that are of primary interest to the investigator. In such cases, theory should prevail as the guide to contrasts.

In sum, two models of ANOVA are common. In the statistical literature, it is common to find ANOVA framed using an effects model that emphasizes the grand mean (μ) and treatment effects (τ_{Aj}, τ_{Bk}, τ_{ABjk}) relative to that mean. In the actual research literature, however, one is much more likely to find the cell means approach with its emphasis on mean contrasts. This is not to say that applications that use the effects model and its parameters are nonexistent or inappropriate. They just occur with much less frequency.

ISSUES IN THE APPLICATION OF ANOVA

In this section, we consider issues and controversies in the application of ANOVA. We discuss five topics: (a) outliers and the violation of model assumptions, (b) family-wise error rates, (c) the analysis of interactions, (d) indexes of effect size, and (e) asserting mean equivalence. To set the stage for this section, we describe the typical approach one would encounter in the literature for analyzing the data in Table 8.1. An investigator likely would conduct a 3 × 2 factorial ANOVA on the outcome variable. *F* ratios are examined for the main effects and the interaction effect. If the *F* ratio for a main effect is statistically nonsignificant, then no further analyses for that effect are pursued and the researcher fails to reject the null hypothesis of no mean differences for that factor. If the *F* test for a main effect with more than two levels is statistically significant, then follow-up analyses are pursued to determine which of the group means are statistically significantly different from one another. This analysis often takes the form of statistical comparisons between all possible pairs of means for the factor. Because multiple follow-up tests are performed when executing these contrasts, a procedure is invoked to control the family-wise error rate across the pairwise contrasts. The choice of method to accomplish this varies, but the most popular methods are the Tukey HSD method and Bonferroni-based procedures. If a statistically significant *F* ratio for the interaction is observed, then follow-up analyses are performed to elucidate the nature of the interaction effect. The most common strategy is to apply simple main effects analysis.

This analytic strategy is fraught with controversy, and we have alluded to one such controversy, namely, the use of omnibus *F* tests as a screen before conducting tests of contrasts. The remainder of this section considers additional controversies and issues.

Outliers and Violations of Model Assumptions

An important issue that analysts must address is whether outliers are present and whether the distributional assumptions of the relevant inferential tests are met to a satisfactory degree. When comparing means using traditional F and t tests, two key population assumptions are (a) the within-cell scores on the outcome variable are normally distributed (called the *normality* assumption), and (b) the within-cell variances of the outcome variable are equal (called the *homogeneity of variance* assumption). There are other assumptions made in ANOVA, but we focus on these two assumptions because of the attention they have garnered in the statistical literature. For a discussion of additional assumptions, see Maxwell and Delaney (2004).[3]

We will make reference to the robustness of a test to violations of these assumptions. A statistical test is said to be robust to violations of assumptions if (a) the nominal Type I error rate (alpha level) set by the investigator a priori (usually 0.05) is maintained in the face of assumption violations and (b) the statistical power of the test is relatively unaffected by assumption violations. For a more technical and nuanced discussion of robustness, see Wilcox (2005a).

The assumptions of homogeneity of variance and normality.

A common perception of many researchers is that the F tests of ANOVA are quite robust to violations of normality and homogeneity of variance. This is not necessarily the case. Keselman et al. (1998) have noted that ratios of largest to smallest variances of 8:1 are not uncommon in the social sciences and that such ratios can have deleterious effects on traditional t tests and F tests. Variance heterogeneity can be particularly problematic when paired with unequal sample sizes (for detailed discussions, see Maxwell & Delaney, 2004; Wilcox, 2005a). In repeated measure designs, the variance homogeneity assumption takes a special form. As an example, if there are three repeated measures for a factor (Y_1, Y_2, and Y_3), there are three possible pairs of difference scores ($Y_1 - Y_2$, $Y_1 - Y_3$, and $Y_2 - Y_3$). The homogeneity of variance assumption is that the population variances of these difference scores are equal. This is also called *sphericity*. In general, omnibus F-tests are not robust to violations of sphericity, and pooled variance estimates for contrasts that are based on this assumption also are problematic (Maxwell & Delaney, 2004).

For the normality assumption, Cressie and Whitford (1986) and Westfall and Young (1993) have raised concerns about the adverse effects of skewness on Type I errors. Wilcox (1998, 2001, 2003) described the harmful effects that skewness has on Type II errors when comparing means. Wilcox (2005a) noted that although the F tests and t tests that compare means often are robust to violations of nonnormality, this is not the case when the distributions within the various experimental groups differ. For example, if the population data are normal in one condition but skewed in another condition, then the robustness of the F test can be compromised. Prudent data analysis should not simply assume F tests in ANOVA are robust to violations of variance homogeneity and normality.

Strategies for dealing with violations of homogeneity of variance and normality.

A common strategy for dealing with assumption violations is to perform a preliminary test of the viability of the assumption in question and, if the test suggests a problem, perform a metric transformation or revert to a robust analytic alternative. The use of this two-step strategy has been found to be problematic for several reasons. First, many preliminary tests lack power without large sample sizes and yield nonsignificant results for testing an assumption violation even when the violation is problematic (Wilcox, 2003; Wilcox, Charlin, & Thompson, 1986). Second, the crucial issue is not whether the null hypothesis of normality or variance homogeneity can be rejected, but instead estimating the *degree* to which the assumption is violated and making a decision as to whether the degree of violation is consequential. This requires documenting the *magnitude* of the assumption violation in the sample data and then using MOEs to take sampling error into account when making decisions. For example, we might find that a variance ratio comparing the variances of two groups is 4.0 with an MOE of plus or minus 3.0. The MOE suggests that the variance could be as large as 7.0 and hence this could be problematic. Unfortunately, it is rare for researchers to take MOEs into account when evaluating preliminary tests. Indeed, many preliminary tests of assumptions

---

[3]The assumption of independent errors also is central to ANOVA, but we do not discuss it here (see Maxwell & Delaney, 2004).

are not amenable to analyses of the magnitude of assumption violation, permitting only the evaluation of the viability of a null hypothesis of normality or homoskedasticity. Third, many tests of non-normality are based on asymptotic theory and perform only adequately with large sample sizes (Shapiro & Wilk, 1965). With large N, however, such tests tend to detect minor departures from normality that may be of little consequence. In addition, normality tests can be differentially sensitive to different types of non-normality. Some tests are sensitive mostly to skew whereas others are sensitive mostly to kurtosis. Fourth, the preliminary tests often make assumptions in their own right and may perform poorly when their assumptions are violated. For example, many tests of variance homogeneity assume the population data are normally distributed (Carroll & Schneider, 1985; Keyes & Levy, 1997; Parra-Frutos, 2009). If the population data are non-normal, than the preliminary test of variance homogeneity may be invalid. Fifth, using preliminary tests as a screen can change the sampling distribution of F tests and t tests in unpredictable ways. Although it seems reasonable, the strategy of conducting preliminary tests of model assumptions has numerous challenges and is not straightforward.

Transformation strategies for dealing with assumption violations have also been criticized. For example, Budescu and Appelbaum (1981) found that transformations to address variance heterogeneity can create more problems than they solve in inferential tests because they can adversely affect normality (see also Blaylock, Salathe, & Green, 1980; Doksum & Milligan, 1987; Wilcox, 1996, 1998; Wong, 1983). Transformed variables often are difficult to interpret (e.g., the mean log of annual income is not easily interpreted). In complex ANOVAs with covariates, transformations of the dependent variable can create specification error that undermines covariate control because it alters the relationships between the outcome variable and covariates. Years ago, before high-speed computers were widespread, analysts had little choice but to use transformations to make measures conform to the assumptions of the limited number of parametric statistical models available. Indeed, researchers were sometimes forced to impose transformations to make measures follow a normal distribution even though they knew the constructs being measured were not normally distributed in the general population (e.g., depression). Such practices are rarely needed in the 21st century given the array of modern methods of analysis that are available.

A growing number of statisticians recommend that analysts simply abandon the more traditional F-tests and t-tests of ANOVA unless they are confident in assumption viability on the basis of theory or extant research. Instead, analysts should routinely use modern-day robust methods of analysis or, at the very least, routinely supplement traditional methods with modern robust methods (Keselman, Algina, Lix, Wilcox, & Deering, 2008; Wilcox, 2005a). These scientists recognize that cases may occur in which defaulting to robust analytic strategies will result in some loss of statistical power and inaccurate probability coverage of CIs. In the long run, however, they argue that the use of robust methods will result in better Type I error protection, increased power to detect effects, and CIs that more accurately reflect the desired probability coverage (Wilcox, 1998). It is always important to explore the metrics of measurements, shapes of distributions, dispersions of data, and outliers. The recommendation is to view traditional tests of model assumptions and remedial strategies that are based on transformations with caution, deferring instead to the use of more modern robust analytic methods.

Outliers.   *Outliers* are unusually small or large scores that distort basic trends in the data. For example, for the scores 2, 3, 4, 5, 6, 7, 8, 9, 10, and 50, the last score is an outlier that distorts the mean and makes the use of the mean suspect as a way to characterize the central tendency of the data. Simple methods for outlier detection compare the results of an analysis when the case is included versus the results of an analysis when the case is deleted. Such approaches, however, can be nondiagnostic when multiple outliers are present. For example, if there are two individuals in an analysis who distort a mean upward, deleting only one of them may not reveal an outlier effect as long as the second outlier is still included in the data. Only when both outliers are removed is their distorting character revealed.

Outlier identification in ANOVA is a complex enterprise, with some of the most sophisticated work being pursued in the literature on robust statistics (for elaboration, see Wilcox, 2003, 2005a).

Sometimes, a theory-driven decision rule emerges from outlier analysis that permits outliers to be validly eliminated from an analysis on the basis of substantive criteria. For example, in studies of sexual behavior in college students, outliers might correspond with older, married students who have returned to college after many years. Their patterns of sexual activity may be so distinct as to distort the more fundamental trends that are evident in young, unmarried students. The decision might be made in this case to eliminate all married students (which may result in eliminating both outliers and some nonoutliers) and then to restrict inferences to nonmarried students only. Such outlier elimination strategies are appropriate.

Wilcox (1998, 2006) objected to applying traditional inferential methods to data that have eliminated outliers on the basis of simple outlier detection methods. He argued that doing so invalidates the statistical theory on which the *F*-tests and *t*-tests are based because of dependencies that outlier elimination creates. Others recommend conducting analyses with and without outliers to determine whether conclusions change. If conclusions do change, then one moves forward with any conclusions on a tentative basis. We tend to agree with Wilcox that applying traditional inferential methods after outliers have been eliminated on nonsubstantive grounds is suspect and that better approaches to dealing with outliers are available.

Probably the most effective strategy for dealing with outliers is to focus on measures of central tendency that are resistant to outliers. The best known outlier-resistant measure of central tendency is the median, but it has been found to have several undesirable statistical properties (Wilcox, 2005a). An alternative to the median is a 20% trimmed mean. To calculate a trimmed mean, one places observations in ascending order and then trims away scores from the upper and lower ends of the distribution, calculating the arithmetic mean on the remaining scores. A 10% trimmed mean strips away the 10% most extreme scores from each tail of the distribution, a 20% trimmed mean strips away the 20% most extreme scores, and so on. Trimming is conducted separately for each cell of the experimental design.

An objection to the use of trimmed means is that one throws away data, but this is not the case. *All* of the data are used to order the scores initially. Hence, all of the data are used in the calculations. In fact, a median is based on stripping away 50% of the data above and below the midpoint of the distribution and working with the single or few data values that occur in the middle of the distribution. A large amount of research has shown that a 20% trimmed mean has many desirable statistical properties and, as such, it is widely used in robust statistics (Wilcox, 2005a).

Another approach to dealing with outliers is to trim only the outliers and then use methods for estimating standard errors and *p*-values that take this into account. This approach is taken for a robust measure of central tendency on the basis of *M* estimation (Wilcox, 2005a). Keselman, Wilcox, Lix, Algina, and Fradette (2007) suggested a method of customized trimming on the basis of the nature of the skewness in the data. Their approach can lead to trimming different amounts from the upper and lower ends of the distribution, such as trimming 20% of the largest observations but none of the smaller observations.

In sum, an effective way of dealing with outliers in ANOVA is to shift attention to outlier-resistant robust estimators of central tendency, such as trimmed means or *M* estimators.

Robust alternatives to ANOVA. There is an extensive statistical literature on analyzing trimmed means and other robust indexes of central tendency (Wilcox, 2005a). These methods not only use outlier-resistant indexes of central tendency but also use approaches that tend to be robust to violations of normality and variance homogeneity. The tests often have more statistical power than traditional *F* tests and *t* tests (Wilcox, 1998). Technically, when one focuses on a robust measure of central tendency in sample data, the population parameter being estimated is the counterpart of the sample statistic. For example, when calculating a trimmed mean in sample data, the parameter that is being estimated is the trimmed mean in the population. The majority of statistical analyses pursued in ANOVA have a robust counterpart for analyzing trimmed means and other robust measures of central tendency. This includes the contrast strategies that are based on the cell means approach as well as omnibus tests for one-way and complex factorial designs. Wilcox (2005a) has written a suite of programs available as freeware in R that can be used to execute the analyses. Researchers should be using these approaches more often.

An interesting robust approach to comparing groups is based on the analysis of quantiles (Wilcox, 2005a). This strategy allows researchers to address group differences at various points in the distribution of the outcome variable. For example, to compare groups on the median of the outcome variable (which will equal the mean for symmetric distributions), one would focus on the 0.50 quantile. To compare groups on the upper portion of the distribution, one might focus on the 0.75 or 0.90 quantile, and to compare groups on the lower portion of the distribution, one might focus on the 0.25 or 0.10 quantile. Wilcox (2005a) presents a single degree of freedom contrast algorithm that permits application of the quantile approach to a wide range of contexts. This approach is useful because social scientists have tended to focus only on group differences in central tendency rather than more fine-grained features of the outcome distribution.

Controlling Family-Wise Error Rates

It is typical for researchers to pursue multiple contrasts in a single study. Statisticians distinguish between two types of error rates. The first type is a *per comparison error rate*, which refers to the probability of falsely rejecting the null hypothesis for a single significance test. The probability of a Type I error for a given comparison is the alpha level, traditionally 0.05. The second error rate is called the *family-wise error rate* (although it goes by other names as well) and refers to the error rate across multiple contrasts. For example, if we conduct five contrasts, then the rate at which at least one chance effect occurs across the five comparisons is the family-wise error rate. Even if the per comparison error rate

is 0.05, the family-wise error rate across the multiple comparisons will be larger than 0.05.

Consider a simple coin flipping analogy. If we flip a coin, two possible outcomes can occur, one of which is a "head." The likelihood of observing a head on a given coin toss is 1/2 = 0.50. If we flip a coin twice, four possible outcomes can occur: (a) a head on the first flip followed by a head on the second flip, (b) a head on the first flip followed by a "tail" on the second flip, (c) a tail on the first flip followed by a head on the second flip, and (d) a tail on the first flip followed by a tail on the second flip. Note that a head occurs on three of the four flips, so the probability of a head occurring on at least one of the flips is 3/4 = 0.75. Even though the probability of a head is 0.50 on a given flip, the probability of observing at least one head across two flips is 0.75. The same type of dynamic operates for making errors across multiple contrasts. Social scientists traditionally desire to invoke analytic methods that will maintain a 0.05 error rate across multiple contrasts.

The choice of a method for controlling family-wise error rates across a set of contrasts in factorial designs is complex and we dare not attack this issue here. Interested readers are referred to Kirk (1995); Maxwell and Delaney (2004); Toothaker (1993); Westfall, Tobias, Rom, Wolfinger, and Hochberg (1999); and Wilcox (1996). More than 30 such procedures have been proposed in the statistical literature. Appendix 8.1 presents a modified Bonferroni method that has widespread applicability and has much to offer as a general approach to controlling family-wise error rates. It is preferable to the traditional Bonferroni method in that it has more statistical power yet maintains the family-wise error rate at the desired level. Tests with somewhat more statistical power are available, however, depending on the analytic situation.

Many investigators feel that controls for inflated error rates should be invoked whenever multiple contrasts are performed. However, using such controls reduces statistical power for a given comparison, which results in the possibility of an unacceptably high rate of Type II errors. In research areas in which sample sizes tend to be small because of practical constraints, the issue is germane because statistical power is low to begin with. In such situations, one might decide not to invoke family-wise controls because the effect on statistical power is too severe. It gives too much weight to avoiding Type I errors at the cost of making Type II errors.

Given a large number of contrasts, researchers seek to balance the need for statistical power with the need to control the error rate for multiple contrasts. A common strategy is to define different "families" of contrasts in which the error rate for multiple contrasts is controlled within a family but not across families. Tradition for factorial ANOVA is to let each factor define a family of contrasts. In the juror example, the main effect for the ethnicity of the juror represents one family and controls for multiple contrasts for the main effect means would be invoked within that family. The main effect for the ethnicity of the accused is a second family, but it consists of a single contrast, and hence no controls for family-wise error rates are used. The interaction effect is a third family, but it is typically broken into two separate families: (a) those involving simple main effects and (b) those involving interaction contrasts.

A common misperception among researchers is that the error rates for multiple contrasts do not inflate as long as the contrasts are orthogonal. This is not the case. The rate at which the error rate inflates is different for orthogonal versus nonorthogonal contrasts, but inflation occurs in both cases. Another common belief is that if contrasts are specified a priori, one need not control for error rates for multiple contrasts. Stating a priori that one wants to examine, say, four contrasts does not change the fact that the error rate will inflate across these contrasts. The crucial issue is not so much whether contrasts are stated a priori as whether one wants to control the error rate.

Post hoc contrasts are contrasts that are conducted on the basis of the examination of the data. For example, an investigator who conducts an experiment using a one-way design with four groups may examine the means and decide that only two of the groups exhibit a large discrepancy from each other and then proceed to conduct this contrast, ignoring all other contrasts. In some respects, the researcher has conducted analyses of all possible contrasts using a subjective criterion ("This difference looks large to me, but this difference does not") rather than a formal statistical criterion. Corrections for family-wise errors in such post hoc cases can be invoked by the well known Scheffé method (Maxwell & Delaney, 2004). However, the Scheffé method usually lacks power relative to its alternatives in settings other than this post hoc scenario and should not be used. We believe that researchers usually have a good sense of the contrasts they want to explore, and it is rarely the case that they engage in purely post hoc analyses on the basis of examination of means after the fact. As such, the Scheffé method should rarely be used because there are more powerful alternatives to it.

In sum, analysts must address how to deal with inflated error rates across multiple contrasts. Contrasts are partitioned into separate families and specialized procedures to maintain the family-wise error rate at a prespecified alpha level are invoked. In the case of small sample sizes and low statistical power, some statisticians recommend performing contrasts both with and without family-wise controls. If a given conclusion holds across both scenarios, one moves forward with that conclusion with more confidence. If conclusions differ, one moves forward tentatively.

Interaction Analysis

The most common strategy that investigators use to explore interaction effects are contrasts focused on simple main effects. Ironically, such contrasts do not capture the essence of interactions. Simple main effects address the question of whether an independent variable affects a dependent variable at a given level of a moderator variable. For example, we might ask whether the ethnicity of the accused affects judgments of the probability of guilt for European American jurors. We might also ask whether this is the case for just African American jurors or whether it is the case for just Latino jurors. These are meaningful questions. However, they do not bear on an interaction effect. As noted, an interaction asks whether the effect of an independent variable on a dependent variable in one group is different from that effect *for another group*. A simple main effect focuses on only one group, so it cannot address this question. Only a formal interaction contrast does. To illustrate, suppose that the mean difference in salary for a sample of Latino male and female assistant professors is $1,243 and the gender difference is $1,096 for a sample of African American assistant professors. Suppose that the mean difference is statistically significant for males ($p < .05$) but not for females ($p > .05$). These significance tests are simple main effect tests. Can we conclude from these data that the mean gender difference for Latinos is larger than that for African Americans? Certainly not. Even though the mean difference was statistically significant in one group but not in the other, we can only say that there are ethnic differences in gender disparities if we directly test the difference between the two ethnicities. This is an interaction contrast. Thus, to probe interactions, researchers should use interaction contrasts. Such contrasts can be pursued using appropriately defined contrast coefficients either in traditional ANOVA or with robust measures of central tendency (Wilcox, 2005a).

Indexes of Effect Size

Traditional null hypothesis testing in ANOVA allows one to address the question of whether a mean difference exists in the population. However, the approach says little about the magnitude of the effect. The American Psychological Association's Task Force on Statistical Inference has encouraged the reporting of effect sizes that capture the magnitude of an effect (Wilkinson, 1999). More than 60 different indexes of effect size have been suggested, and there is no consensus about which one is preferable (for reviews, see Kirk, 1995; Olejnik & Algina, 2000; see also Chapter 6 of this volume). Most (but not all) of the measures can be classified into two classes: (a) standardized indexes of effect size and (b) unstandardized indexes of effect size. Unstandardized indexes are expressed in the raw metric of the outcome measure, such as the actual mean difference between two groups. Standardized indexes are expressed in a transformed metric that is thought to have intuitive and interpretational appeal. The most commonly reported standardized effect size for ANOVA designs are Cohen's *d* (or variants of it) and indexes that reflect the percent of variance accounted for (e.g., omega squared, eta

squared, epsilon squared). Because effect sizes are discussed in depth in other chapters of this handbook, we do not discuss them further here. However, we encourage researchers to routinely report effect size indexes. Our own preference is for the use of unstandardized rather than standardized effect size indexes because standardized indexes can be easily misinterpreted and misleading (Prentice & Miller, 1992; Rosenthal, 1995; Yeaton & Sechrest, 1981)

Asserting Equivalence Between Groups

A common mistake that researchers make when applying ANOVA is to accept the null hypothesis after a test of a contrast. The null hypothesis when comparing means traditionally states that the difference between population means is exactly zero. We can never know the exact value of the true population difference on the basis of sample data because of sampling error. If the mean difference between an experimental and control group in sample data is zero, this does not mean that the population mean difference is zero. If a statistically nonsignificant difference is observed in a sample, we cannot conclude that the mean difference in the population is zero. All we can say is that the data do not allow us to confidently say that the means are different.

The literature is replete with cases in which, on the basis of a statistically nonsignificant interaction effect, researchers conclude that an effect of an independent variable on an outcome variable holds at each level of a potential moderator variable and that the effect is reflected in the main effect mean difference. This is tantamount to accepting the null hypothesis for the interaction effect. Researchers need to exercise caution in their conclusions, being careful not to phrase their conclusions in a way that accepts the null hypothesis (e.g., "there was no difference between the groups"). In the case of a statistically nonsignificant interaction effect, researchers should state that "we cannot confidently conclude that the effect varies across levels of the moderator variable," rather than stating that the effect is the same at all levels of the moderator variable.

Asserting group equivalence has received considerable attention in epidemiology under the rubric of equivalence testing. Most of this work evolved from pharmaceutical research that was designed to establish treatment equivalence of new medications to existing medications. Space constraints limit our ability to explain these methods, but they represent a viable approach to asserting group equivalence. Interested readers are referred to Weller (2002).

CONCLUDING COMMENTS ON ANOVA

There are many topics in ANOVA that we have not touched upon, including the analysis of covariance, fixed versus random effects, multilevel analysis, strategies for analyzing data with unequal sample sizes, trend analysis, complex nesting, higher order interactions, and repeated measures. For excellent discussions of these matters, see Kirk (1995) and Maxwell and Delaney (2004). For a detailed discussion of single degree of freedom contrast strategies in ANOVA, see Jaccard (1998) and Rosenthal and Rosnow (1985). For an excellent introduction to robust methods of analysis, see Wilcox (2005a). For a discussion of model comparison approaches, see Judd et al. (2009) and Maxwell and Delaney (2004).

THE MULTIPLE REGRESSION FRAMEWORK AND THE GENERAL LINEAR MODEL

Multiple regression examines the relationship between a continuous outcome and several predictor variables. Whereas ANOVA is typically associated with studies that use factorial designs with explanatory variables that are categorical (or discrete quantitative with few values), multiple regression embraces explanatory variables that usually are continuous in nature, but they also can be categorical. Traditional multiple regression focuses on the case in which the mean Y in a population is expressed as a linear function of a set predictors, in accord with the following equation:

$$\mu_j = \alpha + \beta_1 X_1 + \beta_2 X_2 \ldots + \beta_k X_k, \qquad (20)$$

where μ_j is the population mean for a given profile of predictor scores (such as the case where $X_1 = 1$, $X_2 = 3$, through $X_k = 0$), k is the number of predictor variables, α is a numerical constant that represents an intercept, and the various βs are numerical constants

or linear coefficients that reflect how much change in μ_j will result from a one-unit change in the X variable associated with a given β, holding all other X variables constant. The various βs are often called unstandardized regression coefficients or regression coefficients for short. μ_j is assumed to be a linear function of the Xs. The intercept is the predicted mean of Y when all predictors equal zero. For individuals, the predicted value of the outcome variable, $\hat{Y}_i$ is the mean response associated with the predictor profile that characterizes that individual (i.e., $\hat{Y}_i = \mu_j$). As in the model-based view of ANOVA, there is variability around each mean associated with a specific predictor profile, and this represents errors in prediction, so that $Y_i = \hat{Y}_i + \varepsilon_i$. The traditional multiple regression model for individuals is thus

$$Y_i = \alpha + \beta_1 X_{1i} + \beta_2 X_{2i} \ldots + \beta_k X_{ki} + \varepsilon_i, \qquad (21)$$

where i signifies an individual's standing on a given variable and $\hat{Y}_i = \alpha + \beta_1 X_{1i} + \beta_2 X_{2i} \ldots + \beta_k X_{ki}$.

In practice, we do not have access to population data and must estimate the population coefficients in Equation 21 from sample data. The dominant strategy for doing so is to use ordinary least squares (OLS) methods that derive sample values of the different β so as to minimize the sum of the squared error scores in the sample data. We use the letter B to represent a sample estimate of a β. As with any sample estimate, there is sampling error associated with B. Statisticians have developed indexes of the extent to which sampling error impacts our sample estimates, and these are reflected in estimated standard errors for each β, which we symbolize as SE_β. Of interest to researchers is whether the value of a β is zero because, if it is, the X variable associated with it contributes nothing to the prediction of Y. As such, researchers test the viability of the alternative hypothesis that a given β is not zero by forming a critical ratio, defined as B/SE_β. This critical ratio is essentially a single degree of freedom contrast that follows a t distribution (given model assumptions are satisfied), from which p-values, confidence intervals, and MOEs can be derived. The critical ratio and SE_β have analogous interpretations to those described for the ANOVA model, but the focus is on a β rather than a mean difference.

An excellent introduction to multiple regression analysis is provided in Cohen, Cohen, West, and Aiken (2003). The multiple regression model is often referred to as the *general linear model* (not to be confused with the *generalized linear model*; see Chapter 9 of this volume) because it is linear in form and because it can be adapted to test a wide variety of research questions, including all of those described earlier for ANOVA. For example, it is possible to include categorical variables or factors in the model by using dummy variables as predictors. A dummy variable is a variable that the researcher creates to represent the different groups of the categorical variable in which individuals are assigned scores on the basis of an a priori coding scheme. The form of dummy coding used is dictated by the types of contrasts that one wants to pursue, per the cell means model described in a previous section. For a discussion of the different coding schemes and what they accomplish, see Cohen et al. For continuous variables, interaction effects can be introduced through the use of product terms (discussed in the section Interaction Analysis).

As with ANOVA, we do not focus on the statistical mechanics or intricacies of conducting multiple regression in this chapter, as these are covered in depth elsewhere (Cohen et al., 2003; Judd et al., 2009). Rather, we focus on more general issues that benefit from commentary given research practice. We address seven topics, many of which parallel those in the ANOVA section: (a) outliers and violation of model assumptions, (b) family-wise error rates, (c) the analysis of interactions, (d) indexes of predictor importance, (e) the use of covariates, (f) nonlinear regression, and (g) model-based perspectives.

ISSUES IN THE APPLICATION OF MULTIPLE REGRESSION

The major assumptions for ANOVA, homogeneity of variance of errors and normality of errors, apply to multiple regression analysis as well. A common misperception about assumptions in multiple regression is that they are made about the distributions of variables in the analysis. As typically applied in the research literature, the assumptions do not pertain to the criterion and predictor variables. Rather, the assumptions are about the behavior of the errors, namely the e.

Outliers and Violations of Model Assumptions

An additional assumption, called the *assumption of a correctly specified model*, also applies to ANOVA; however, we deferred discussion until now because it is easier to discuss in the context of multiple regression. The assumption of a correctly specified model reflects on two matters: (a) the accuracy of the assumed functional form relating the predictor variables to the outcome variable as well as each other and (b) left out variable error (also called LOVE). When predictors are continuous, multiple regression assumes that there is a linear relationship between the scores on the predictors and the mean of the outcome as a function of those scores. If the relationship is nonlinear, the model is misspecified. If the predictor variables do not combine in an additive fashion per Equation 20 but combine multiplicatively, for example, the model is misspecified. We discuss methods for dealing with nonlinear and multiplicative functions in the section Interaction Analysis.

LOVE refers to the assumption that all variables that directly affect the outcome relative to the other predictors have been included in the equation. If a key determinant of Y has been omitted, then one commits LOVE and the fitted model is misspecified. LOVE can create bias in coefficients and invalidate significance tests and confidence intervals. In most social science research, LOVE is inevitable. The question is not so much whether LOVE exists (because it almost always does) but whether it is of a sufficient size and nature that we will be misled in our conclusions. LOVE problems are minimized if the omitted variable has a modest correlation (technically a zero correlation) with the other predictors in the equation, although it can still inflate Type II errors in such cases. If the omitted variable's impact on Y is completely mediated by the predictors already in the equation, LOVE is minimized. LOVE is most likely to introduce problems if the omitted variable is moderately correlated with other predictors and has a nontrivial, independent impact on Y. In ANOVA, random assignment to groups will cause omitted variables to be uncorrelated with the factors involved in the random assignment. For an in-depth discussion of LOVE, see Mauro (1990).

The same issues we discussed for robustness for ANOVA apply with equal vigor to multiple regression. Many researchers believe that multiple regression analysis is robust to assumption violations, but this is not necessarily the case. Wilcox (1998, 2005a) has discussed the limitations of traditional OLS regression in depth. Applications of preliminary tests for assumption violations have the same problems in multiple regression as they do in ANOVA. Transformations are more problematic because a transformation of a given predictor can affect its correlation with all other predictors as well as the outcome, thereby producing specification error. Outliers also are problematic for regression analysis and outlier detection is even more complex than it is in simple ANOVA designs. Many traditional methods of outlier detection discussed in texts on multiple regression have limitations, but promising outlier detection methods are being pursued in the field of robust statistics (Wilcox, 2005a).

As with ANOVA, methods of analysis have evolved that permit the use of robust regression methods in a wide range of situations that can greatly improve on OLS regression in the face of outliers or possible assumption violations. Wilcox (2005a) provides an introduction to these methods as well as freeware to implement them. As with ANOVA, some analysts argue for the adoption of these methods over OLS strategies. Many robust regression methods focus on the modeling of trimmed means or on another index of central tendency, called *M* estimators. A useful variant of these methods is called *quantile regression*, which models different quantiles of a distribution rather than a mean (see Wilcox, 2005a).

Controlling Family-Wise Error Rates

The significance test for each coefficient in a regression equation represents a single degree of freedom test–contrast. In ANOVA, we noted the misconception that using an omnibus test as a screen generally controls the family-wise error rate for the various single degree of freedom contrasts pursued in the analysis. This also is the case for the omnibus test

for the overall squared multiple correlation in multiple regression analysis. If one wants to control for family-wise error rates in multiple regression, it is better to use methods such as those in Appendix 8.1 rather than relying on omnibus tests of the squared multiple correlation.

One rarely finds investigators invoking controls for family-wise error rates in multiple regression analysis. This is because, like ANOVA, it is traditional to treat each variable or predictor as a separate family of contrasts. If multiple contrasts are pursued within a variable (such as when dummy variables are used for a categorical predictor), then family-wise error rate controls can be invoked using the method in Appendix 8.1 or some other method reviewed earlier in this chapter. This also is true for interaction analysis and simple effects analysis in which multiple single degree of freedom contrasts are the focus of the interaction or simple main effects. Again, as with ANOVA, the strategy is to find an optimal balance between Type I and Type II error rates.

Interaction Analysis

Moderated relationships can be tested in multiple regression in a more flexible way than in traditional ANOVA because of the ability to analyze continuous moderators and continuous focal independent variables. We consider here the case in which all variables involved in the interaction are continuous. Like ANOVA, interaction effects are usually parameterized using the framework of moderator variables, although there are other ways to parameterize them. In the three variable case, there is an outcome variable (Y), an independent variable (X_1), and a moderator variable (X_2). The independent variable is thought to affect the outcome variable and that impact is indexed by the regression coefficient associated with it (i.e., β_{X1}). The value of β_{X1} is said to vary depending on the value of the moderator variable. For example, when X_2 is small, the value of β_{X1} (reflecting the effect of X_1 on Y) might be smaller or larger than when X_2 is large . The choice of which variable X_1 or X_2 takes the role of the moderator is dictated by theory and how the investigator wants to frame the interaction. The choice from a statistical standpoint is arbitrary (Jaccard & Turrisi, 2003).

It is customary, but not necessary, to mean center continuous predictors. Mean centering converts the raw scores to deviation scores by subtracting the mean of the variable from the individual variable. So, $X_{1C} = X_1 - M_{X1}$ and $X_{2C} = X_2 - M_{X2}$. The mean of the transformed scores X_{1C} and X_{2C} are both zero. Mean centering makes the intercept and the regression coefficients more interpretable, a point that will become more apparent shortly.

The transformed focal independent variable and the transformed moderator variable are multiplied by each other and then the component parts and their product term are used as predictors:

$$Y_i = a + b_1 X_{1Ci} + b_2 X_{2Ci} + b_3 X_{1Ci} X_{2Ci} + \varepsilon_i. \quad (22)$$

The presence of the product term changes the traditional interpretation of b_1. Specifically, b_1 no longer represents a main effect but now represents a simple main effect. It is the effect of X_{1C} on Y when the other variable in the product term, in this case X_{2C}, equals zero. Because a score of zero on X_{2C} corresponds to the mean of the original X_2 variable, b_1 estimates the effect of X_1 on Y when X_2 is at its mean value. Variable b_3 is a single degree of freedom interaction contrast and is of primary interest in interaction analysis. It reflects the number of units that b_1 is predicted to change every time the moderator variable increases by one unit. For example, if X_2 increases by one unit relative to its mean, then the estimated effect of X_1 on Y is $b_1 + b_3$. If X_2 increases by two units relative to its mean, then the estimated effect of X_1 on Y is $b_1 + 2 b_3$. The mechanics of interaction analysis in multiple regression are straightforward but too involved to consider in depth here. Interested readers are referred to Jaccard and Turrisi (2003) for a wide range of applications in multiple regression contexts, including the case of categorical and continuous predictors. We focus here on points that are important to keep in mind as one pursues interaction analysis in multiple regression.

Median splits. It is not uncommon for researchers who have a small number of continuous predictors to pursue interaction analysis by using ANOVA instead of multiple regression, presumably because they are more familiar with the ANOVA approach to interaction analysis. Such researchers categorize the predictors into a small number of groups, usually by performing a median split on each one. The continuous predictor variable, in essence, is reduced to a 2-point scale of *low* (at or below the median) and *high* scorers, and then the data are analyzed as if they come from a factorial design. Statisticians have argued against such median split strategies for more than 20 years, and the limitations of the approach are well documented (e.g., Maxwell & Delaney, 1993). Despite this, the practice continues to be popular.

Without delving into technical matters, consider how a median split ignores valuable information. Suppose a researcher performs a median split on the Wechsler Intelligence Scale for Children (WISC) by dividing individuals into low and high groups on the basis of whether they score above or below the median score of 100. In doing so, the researcher has usurped a scale that distinguishes many gradations of intelligence and reduced it to a crude, 2-point scale. The researcher treats someone who has an IQ score of 55 as being exactly the same as someone who has an IQ score of 99 because both are in the low group. At the same time that the researcher is willing to overlook this 44-point difference in IQ, the researcher treats someone who has an IQ score of 99 as being lower in intelligence than a person who has an IQ score of 101 because the former is in the low group and the latter is in the high group. Just as damaging, the researcher acts as if the difference in IQ between someone who has a score of 99 versus someone who has a score of 101 is exactly the same as someone who has an IQ score of 60 versus someone who has an IQ score of 140. Surely, we can do better than this when pursuing interaction analysis. Multiple regression analysis allows us to do so.

The form of the interaction. When a continuous variable is part of an interaction analysis in multiple regression, it is important to keep in mind that the classic product term approach to interaction analysis tests only for an interaction that has a specific form that is called a *bilinear interaction*. Other forms of interaction may be operating. If X_1 is the focal independent variable and X_2 is the moderator variable, the product term approach models the coefficient for X_1 as being a linear function of X_2. It is possible, however, that the coefficient for X_1 changes as a nonlinear function of X_2 and, if this is the case, the product term approach represents a misspecified model. As such, it is important for researchers to explore alternative forms of interactions when pursuing interaction analysis in multiple regression in case the form of the interaction is not bilinear. For details on how to do this, see Jaccard and Turrisi (2003).

Confounds with curvilinearity. Ganzach (1997) has noted that interaction effects can be observed in models in which no interaction is present but in which the relationship between a predictor and outcome variable is nonlinear in form. The application of an interaction model in such cases represents a misspecified model and can lead the theorist astray. See Ganzach (1997) and Jaccard and Turrisi (2003) for analytic solutions to this problem.

Exclusion of component terms. It is sometimes stated that the product term in a regression equation represents an interaction effect. Technically, the product term reflects an amalgamation of main effects and interactions. In general, it is only when the component parts of the product term are included in the equation with the product term that interactions of the form social scientists typically study are isolated. Excluding the component parts of the product term places strong measurement demands on the analysis, as the measures must then be ratio in nature. In a multiplicative model that excludes the component parts, the squared multiple correlation and the significance test of the regression coefficient that derives from regressing Y onto the product term changes with simple rescaling of the measures of the component parts. Although there are exceptions, it is generally good practice to include the component parts of the product term in the regression equation with the product term (see Blanton & Jaccard, 2006b; Jaccard & Turrisi, 2003).

Regions of significance for simple main effects. In ANOVA, we often conduct simple main effects analysis to identify at which levels of the moderator variable we can confidently conclude that the focal independent variable affects the outcome variable.

With a continuous moderator variable, this task is challenging because there are as many levels of the moderator as the measure is precise. Potthoff (1964) developed a method, on the basis of the classic work of Johnson and Neyman (1936), that establishes *regions of significance* for the case of a continuous moderator and a dichotomous focal independent variable. The technique defines a range of scores on the moderator variable at which the population means of the two groups defined by the dichotomous focal independent variable are not expected to differ. Jaccard, Daniloski, and Brinberg (2012) extended the method to the case of all continuous variables as well as categorical independent variables with more than two levels, making simple main effects analysis with continuous moderator variables straightforward.

In sum, interaction analysis with continuous predictors can be pursued in multiple regression analysis, but there are complications that need to be taken into account. These include the restrictive form of the interaction being tested and confounds with curvilinearity, among others (for consideration of additional issues, see Jaccard & Turrisi, 2003). Forming median splits is a bad strategy for interaction analysis, as is omitting the component parts of the product term from the equation. Simple main effects analyses with continuous variables can be conducted in multiple regression using the Jaccard et al. (2012) extension of the regions-of-significance strategy.

Indices of Predictor Importance

An issue often addressed when using multiple regression is identifying the relative importance of different predictors. The intent is to identify the most and least important predictors in an equation. Numerous strategies have been used for this purpose. One global strategy focuses on significance tests of the coefficients and declares variables that fail to yield statistically significant regression coefficients as *unimportant* and those that yield statistically significant coefficients as *important*. As straightforward as this appears, the approach can be problematic. The most obvious problem is if the study has low statistical power, leading to Type II errors. This problem is more insidious than most scientists realize. Maxwell (2000) reported that the typical correlation between variables in psychological research is about 0.30. If five predictors in a population are each correlated 0.30 with the criterion, as well as 0.30 with each other, then the percent of unique explained variance in Y for each predictor is 1.5%, and the population regression coefficient for each predictor is nonzero. The sample size necessary to obtain statistical power of 0.80 for a significance test of a regression coefficient in this scenario is about 420. Maxwell (2000) reported a simulation study in which a multiple regression analysis was conducted in this scenario using a sample size of 100. Maxwell found that the most frequently occurring pattern of results, occurring 45% of the time, was the case in which one predictor had a statistically significant regression coefficient, but the other four did not. The next most common pattern, occurring 32% of the time, was that two of the predictors had statistically significant regression coefficients, but three did not. Thus, in such situations, there is a high probability that one or two of the predictors will show statistical significance and three or four of the predictors will not. Which predictors show a significant coefficient among the five predictors is random. Results such as these should give theorists using small sample sizes (e.g., less than 100) some pause about declaring a variable *unimportant* if it receives a statistically nonsignificant regression coefficient.

A second strategy that researchers sometimes use to identify important variables is based on stepwise regression. The predictor variables act as a pool of potential variables to include in the final regression equation. Stepwise algorithms are invoked to enter variables into the equation sequentially on the basis of how much they augment the squared multiple correlation relative to predictors already in the equation (for a description of the algorithms, see Cohen et al., 2003). Adding variables to the equation ceases when the increase in model fit is no longer statistically significant. The variables that enter the equation are deemed the most important predictors and the order in which they enter the equation further discriminates their importance.

Numerous objections to this approach have been raised, including the misleading nature of the *p* values

and significance tests (Altman & Andersen, 1989), bias in the regression coefficients (Tibshirani, 1996), and a general failure to accurately identify the variables in the true generating equation (Derksen & Keselman, 1992; Mantel, 1970). To elaborate on one example, the first predictor that enters the equation in a stepwise analysis is the predictor that has the highest zero order correlation with the criterion. At the second step, all remaining variables are considered for inclusion relative to that first variable. Only variables that add significant unique explained variance relative to it are candidates for inclusion at the second step. Suppose X_1 has a sample correlation of 0.30 with the criterion and X_2 has a sample correlation of 0.29 and the two variables are correlated 0.80. X_1 will enter the equation first, even though its correlation with the criterion is only larger by a miniscule amount relative to X_2. X_2 will not enter the equation at later steps because its explained variance in Y is redundant with X_1. It might be the case that the correlation between X_2 and Y is larger in the population than the correlation between X_1 and Y, and the reversal of rank order in the sample data reflects nothing but sampling error. Despite this, X_1 will be given theoretical priority and enter the equation first. In this case, a relatively small amount of sampling error alters the variables that enter the equation and that ultimately are deemed as *important*. Judd and McClelland (1989) captured current thinking when they stated that

> it seems unwise to let an automatic algorithm determine the questions we do and do not ask about our data. It is our experience and strong belief that better models and a better understanding of one's data result from focused data analysis, guided by substantive theory. (p. 204)

Another popular approach for determining predictor importance is to compare predictors in terms of their standardized regression coefficients. Standardized coefficients are based on a multiple regression analysis in which the metric of each variable has been converted to a standard score, thereby allegedly placing all measures on a common metric. Those predictors with larger standardized coefficients are deemed as being more important than those with smaller standardized coefficients. This strategy is problematic because differences in the coefficients could reflect sampling error. One needs to conduct formal significance tests of their difference (for such methods, see Cohen et al., 2003). In addition, the common view that standardization places the variables on a common metric is debatable (see Blanton & Jaccard, 2006a; Judd et al., 2009). Reliance on standardized coefficients requires the assumption that the variance of a predictor is constant at each combination of the other predictors. This assumption is often unrealistic (Bring, 1994). In addition, removing the variable with the smallest standardized coefficient does not necessarily result in the smallest reduction in the squared multiple correlation (Bring, 1994). Darlington (1968) has noted several other pitfalls with this strategy as well as an analogous strategy that is based on the squared semipart correlation associated with a predictor.

The most sophisticated approaches to evaluating variable importance derive from dominance analysis (Azen & Budescu, 2003, 2006) and orthogonal transformation analysis (also called epsilon analysis; Johnson & LeBreton, 2004). These approaches document the extent to which a predictor contributes to the overall squared multiple correlation considering both its zero order correlation with the criterion and its relationship to other predictors in the equation. Dominance analysis uses an index of importance that is based on the average increase in R^2 associated with a variable across submodels, on the basis of strategically defined reduced predictor variables. In the transformation method, predictors are transformed to orthogonal components using least squares orthogonalization methods. The components are then used to predict the outcome; the relative weight of the predictor is the sum across the orthogonal components of the proportion of variance that each component accounts for in explaining the criterion multiplied by the squared correlation between the predictor and the component. A relative importance index is this weight divided by the sum of the weights across predictors, multiplied by 100. The indexes in dominance analysis and the transformation method tend to converge with one another (Johnson & LeBreton, 2004).

The Use of Covariates

A frequent use of multiple regression is to gain perspectives on the effects of a variable on an outcome while controlling for covariates included in the regression equation. Covariates usually are not of theoretical interest but researchers include them in the prediction equation to protect against LOVE. Meehl (1971) objected to what he calls atheoretical partialing of covariates. In atheoretical partialing, covariates are added to the equation simply because they might be relevant. The most common example of this is the inclusion of demographic variables, such as gender, age, and social class, in an equation without careful justification. One simply includes these variables because they are commonly used as covariates. Problems associated with atheoretical partialing were noted more than 30 years ago in a thoughtful discussion by Meehl (1971). Atheoretical partialing can increase Type II errors and can bias parameter estimates for the causal conclusions researchers seek to make (for the statistical basis, see Jaccard, Guilamo-Ramos, Johansson, & Bouris, 2006). An egregious form of atheoretical partialing occurs when a researcher classifies potential predictor variables into broad categories, such as demographic predictors, family predictors, social predictors, and personality predictors, and then includes variables from all of the categories in one large regression equation. If the coefficient associated with a given predictor is statistically nonsignificant, the variable is deemed noncausally relevant to the outcome variable. In such cases, the predictor in question may indeed be causally relevant, but the regression coefficient may not reflect this depending on the causal dynamics operating among the predictors. For example, if one of the predictors partially or completely mediates the effect of another predictor, then the regression coefficient for the target predictor will understate its causal impact on the outcome as any mediated effect of the predictor is partialed out.

Another example of atheoretical partialing occurs when a researcher unwittingly uses a covariate that is a defining part of the phenomenon being studied. For example, one might examine the impact of self-esteem on social anxiety holding constant a measure of social desirability response tendencies. However, an integral part of having low self-esteem is being defensive about admitting one's weaknesses and controlling one's self-presentation. By including social desirability as a covariate, the researcher partials out a defining feature of self-esteem.

Decisions about controlling covariates require careful thought. Researchers must consider the possible causal relations between predictor variables and covariates and then judiciously control for covariates in accord with the presumed causal dynamics. In general, a variable should be statistically controlled for if (a) doing so increases statistical power in a low power situation (such as including a baseline measure of the outcome as a covariate in a randomized clinical trial), (b) it removes misspecification caused by LOVE, (c) it is not a second indicator of another construct already included in the prediction equation, (d) it is not a defining feature of another predictor or the outcome, and (e) it is theoretically meaningful to include the covariate. There will be instances in longitudinal research in which researchers include lagged outcome variables as covariates, but this is typically because theory or the question being investigated dictates this should be so.

Nonlinear Regression

Relationships between predictors and outcomes may be nonlinear, in which case applying traditional multiple regression represents application of a misspecified model. Most researchers who seek to deal with nonlinearity in the applied literature prefer to stay within the familiar confines of the general linear model when doing so. One such approach is to use polynomial regression in which additional predictors are added to the linear equation that reflect power polynomials of the target predictor. The addition of a squared predictor models a quadratic function between the predictor and the outcome and the further addition of a cubed term models a cubic function. Cohen et al. (2003) described polynomial regression in depth. A problem with polynomial regression is that it uses a relatively small class of nonlinear functions that may not adequately capture the nature of the nonlinearity in question. For example, if the relationship between X and Y is logarithmic, then the polynomial approach may not adequately model the nonlinear dynamics.

Another approach to dealing with nonlinear relationships while retaining the linear model is the use of variable transformations. For example, if Y is a logarithmic function of X, then the relationship between the log of X and Y should be linear. Y can be predicted from the log of X in the general linear model. Transformations to linearize relationships are discussed by Box and Cox (1964) and Mosteller and Tukey (1977)—see also the useful summary in Cohen et al. (2003). A problem with the transformation approach is that the metrics of the transformed variables often are nonintuitive (e.g., log income). Also, it is usually not appropriate to back-transform the coefficient associated with a transformed variable to its original metric because the back-transformed coefficient does not minimize the relevant squared error (although there are some exceptions). Finally, transforming the metric of a predictor not only changes the relationship between the predictor and the criterion but also changes the relationship between the transformed predictor and the other predictors in the equation. This can result in specification error.

Yet another approach to dealing with nonlinearity while staying within the comfort of the linear model is spline regression (Marsh & Cormier, 2001). Spline regression divides a curve into segments so that the relationship between X and Y is approximately linear within a segment but not necessarily across segments. Estimates of the slope within each segment are derived using OLS regression in conjunction with predictors that represent spline knots. Spline knots are points on the X continuum that define the segments. Formal tests of slope differences between segments are possible, and slope differences are expected given nonlinearity.

Finally, recent work on nonlinear regression has used methods based on smoothers and the generalized additive model (Wilcox, 2005a). In this approach, a measure of location of Y is assumed to be some function of the predictors, $m(X_1, X_2, \ldots, X_k)$, but the exact function is unknown. The location measure can be a mean, a median, a trimmed mean, or an M estimator and the function, m, is estimated nonparametrically. Estimation for a point of interest typically is based on the X continua using a small number of neighboring data points or, more technically, a weighted average of Y values, with the weights being a function of how close the vector of predictor values is to the point of interest. These methods offer a great deal of promise for nonlinear modeling in the social sciences. See Wilcox (2005a, 2005b) for an excellent introduction.

Model Testing Perspectives on Multiple Regression

As noted, researchers tend to adopt a mind-set of model fitting when using multiple regression. Thus, it is common to find explicit recognition of the use of the linear model, reports of statistics related to the coefficients in the linear model, and reports of the magnitude of error scores (in the form of squared multiple correlations). More informative fit indexes could routinely be reported, such as the standard error of estimate. Model comparisons are also common in the form of hierarchical regression, in which case one formally compares simpler models with more complex models that add predictors. Researchers often fail to appreciate that multiple regression is a method for analyzing mean outcome values and how these values vary as a function of predictor variable profiles. In this sense, its concern with means is similar to ANOVA.

CONCLUDING COMMENTS ON MULTIPLE REGRESSION AND THE GENERAL LINEAR MODEL

As with ANOVA, there are many issues we have not addressed, including commonality analysis, cross-validation, dichotomous, count, and categorical outcomes, fixed versus random variables, hierarchical regression, latent variable regression, longitudinal regression models, measurement error, issues of metrics (use of ordinal vs. interval measures), missing data, regression-based mixture models, multicolinearity, multilevel regression, power analysis, development of prediction models, reciprocal causation models, and regression-based time-series analysis, to name a few. These topics are discussed in Cohen et al. (2003), Draper and Smith (1998), and Fox (1997). A model comparison approach to multiple regression analysis is presented by Judd et al. (2009). For robust regression, see Wilcox (2005a).

CONCLUSION

ANOVA is a special case of multiple regression in that all of the analyses of ANOVA can ultimately be conducted using the general linear model. The general linear model, in turn, is a special case of a broader modeling perspective on the basis of generalized linear models (see Chapter 9 of this volume). Generalized linear models are a special case of an even broader approach to analysis that is based on systems of linear equations, called structural equation modeling (SEM; see Volume 2, Chapter 19, this handbook; see also Muthén, 2004). Each of these frameworks has in common its focus on linear equations and, as such, the material in this chapter is fundamental to all of them. Some of the most exciting developments in linear modeling are occurring in the field of robust statistics, which is freeing analysts from the constraints of the assumptions of normally distributed data and other parametric assumptions. Robust methods are also being developed and applied to factor analysis, which ultimately should allow us to use them for latent variable regression and more advanced latent variable SEM models. Indeed, the promising methods discussed in Wilcox (2005a) can currently be applied to many forms of SEM using limited information methods that partition a causal model into a set of linear equations and then estimate the coefficients of the equations separately rather than in a simultaneous, full information sense. The usual advantage of more efficient estimation on the basis of full information strategies may be offset by the use of efficient robust estimation methods as well as the compartmentalization of specification error that typifies limited information approaches. The linear model and the emerging robust methods surrounding it have a bright future in data analysis.

APPENDIX 8.1: MODIFIED BONFERRONI METHODS

Holm (1979; see also Holland & Copenhaver, 1988; Seaman, Levin, & Serlin, 1991) has suggested a modified Bonferroni method that is more powerful than the traditional Bonferroni-based approach but adequately maintains family-wise error rates at the desired alpha level.

First, a *p* value is obtained for each contrast in the family of contrasts. The *p* values are then ordered from smallest to largest. If two *p* values are identical, they are ordered arbitrarily or using theoretical criteria. The contrast with the smallest *p* value is evaluated against an alpha of $0.05/k$, where k is the total number of contrasts in the family. If this leads to rejection of the corresponding null hypothesis (because the observed *p* value is less than the adjusted α), the next smallest *p* value is tested against an alpha level of $0.05/(k - 1)$, where $k - 1$ is the remaining number of contrasts. If this test leads to null hypothesis rejection, the next smallest *p* value is tested against an alpha level of $0.05/(k - 2)$. The process continues until a nonsignificant difference is observed. Once a nonsignificant difference is observed, all remaining contrasts are declared nonsignificant.

The Holm method is a *step-down* method in that one adjusts the critical value for the smallest *p* value, then the second smallest, and so on until the largest one is reached and evaluated against an alpha level of 0.05. An alternative approach is to use a *step-up* procedure, such as that suggested by Hochberg (1988). The Hochberg approach is identical to the Holm (1979) procedure, but it works in the reverse direction, from the largest *p* value to the smallest. If the largest *p* value in the family of contrasts is less than 0.05, all contrasts are declared statistically significant. If the largest *p* value is greater than 0.05, but the next largest one is less than 0.05/4, then the contrast in question and all those with smaller *p* values are declared statistically significant. The Hochberg method has slightly more statistical power than the Holm method and, hence, may be preferable. However, it does not control family-wise error rates as well as the Holm method under some error structures (see Westfall et al., 1999).

References

Altman, D. G., & Andersen, P. (1989). Bootstrap investigation of the stability of a Cox regression model. *Statistics in Medicine, 8,* 771–783. doi:10.1002/sim.4780080702

Azen, R., & Budescu, D. (2003). The dominance analysis approach for comparing predictors in multiple regression. *Psychological Methods, 8,* 129–148. doi:10.1037/1082-989X.8.2.129

Azen, R., & Budescu, D. (2006). Comparing predictors in multivariate regression models: An extension of dominance analysis. *Journal of Educational and Behavioral Statistics, 31,* 157–180. doi:10.3102/10769986031002157

Bernhardson, C. S. (1975). Type I error rates when multiple comparison procedures follow a significant *F* test of ANOVA. *Biometrics, 31,* 229–232. doi:10.2307/2529724

Blanton, H., & Jaccard, J. (2006a). Arbitrary metrics in psychology. *American Psychologist, 61,* 27–41. doi:10.1037/0003-066X.61.1.27

Blanton, H., & Jaccard, J. (2006b). Tests of multiplicative models in psychology: A case study using the unified theory of implicit attitudes, stereotypes, self esteem and self concept. *Psychological Review, 113,* 155–166. doi:10.1037/0033-295X.113.1.155

Blaylock, J., Salathe, L., & Green, R. (1980). A note on the Box–Cox transformation under heteroskedasticity. *Western Journal of Agricultural Economics, 45,* 129–135.

Box, G. E. P., & Cox, D. R. (1964). An analysis of transformations (with discussion). *Journal of the Royal Statistical Society, Series B: Methodological, 26,* 211–246.

Bring, J. (1994). How to standardize regression coefficients. *The American Statistician, 48,* 209–213. doi:10.2307/2684719

Budescu, D., & Appelbaum, M. (1981). Variance stabilizing transformations and the power of the F test. *Journal of Educational Statistics, 6,* 55–74. doi:10.3102/10769986006001055

Carlin, B. P., & Louis, T. A. (2000). *Bayes and empirical Bayes methods for data analysis* (2nd ed.). Tampa, FL: Chapman & Hall.

Carroll, R. J., & Schneider, H. (1985). A note on Levene's test for equality of variances. *Statistics and Probability Letters, 3,* 191–194. doi:10.1016/0167-7152(85)90016-1

Cohen, J., Cohen, P., West, S. G., & Aiken, L. S. (2003). *Applied multiple regression/correlation analysis for the behavioral sciences* (3rd ed.). Mahwah, NJ: Erlbaum.

Cressie, N. A. C., & Whitford, H. J. (1986). How to use the two sample *t*-test. *Biometrical Journal, 28,* 131–148. doi:10.1002/bimj.4710280202

Darlington, R. (1968). Multiple regression in psychological research and practice. *Psychological Bulletin, 69,* 161–182. doi:10.1037/h0025471

Derksen, S., & Keselman, H. (1992). Backward, forward and stepwise automated subset selection algorithms: Frequency of obtaining authentic and noise variables. *British Journal of Mathematical and Statistical Psychology, 45,* 265–282.

Doksum, K. A., & Wong, C. (1983). Statistical tests based on transformed data. *Journal of the American Statistical Association, 78*, 411–417. doi:10.2307/2288649

Draper, N., & Smith, H. (1998). *Applied regression analysis.* New York, NY: Wiley.

Fox, J. (1997). *Applied regression analysis, linear models, and related methods.* Thousand Oaks, CA: Sage.

Ganzach, Y. (1997). Misleading interaction and curvilinear terms. *Psychological Methods, 2*, 235–247. doi:10.1037/1082-989X.2.3.235

Hochberg, Y. (1988). A sharper Bonferroni procedure for multiple tests of significance. *Biometrika, 75*, 800–802. doi:10.1093/biomet/75.4.800

Holland, B. S., & Copenhaver, M. (1988). Improved Bonferroni-type multiple testing procedures. *Psychological Bulletin, 104*, 145–149. doi:10.1037/0033-2909.104.1.145

Holm, S. (1979). A simple sequentially rejective multiple test procedure. *Scandinavian Journal of Statistics, 6*, 65–70.

Jaccard, J. (1998). *Interaction effects in factorial analysis of variance.* Newbury Park, CA: Sage.

Jaccard, J., Daniloski, K., & Brinberg, D. (2012). *Extending the Newman-Johnson method for interaction analysis to complex interactions.* Unpublished manuscript, Department of Psychology, Florida International University, Miami.

Jaccard, J., Guilamo-Ramos, V., Johansson, M., & Bouris, A. (2006). Multiple regression analyses in clinical child and adolescent psychology. *Journal of Clinical Child and Adolescent Psychology, 35*, 456–479. doi:10.1207/s15374424jccp3503_11

Jaccard, J., & Turrisi, R. (2003). *Interaction effects in multiple regression.* Newbury Park, CA: Sage.

Johnson, J., & LeBreton, J. (2004). History and use of relative importance indices in organizational research. *Organizational Research Methods, 7*, 238–257. doi:10.1177/1094428104266510

Johnson, P. O., & Neyman, J. (1936). Tests of certain linear hypotheses and their application to some educational problems. *Statistical Research Memoirs, 1*, 57–93.

Judd, C., & McClelland, G. (1989). *Data analysis: A model comparison approach.* New York, NY: Harcourt Brace Jovanovich.

Judd, C. M., McClelland, G. H., & Ryan, C. S. (2009). *Data analysis: A model comparison approach.* New York, NY: Routledge.

Keselman, H., Algina, J., Lix, L., Wilcox, R., & Deering, K. (2008). A generally robust approach for testing hypotheses and setting confidence intervals for effect sizes. *Psychological Methods, 13*, 110–129. doi:10.1037/1082-989X.13.2.110

Keselman, H. J., Huberty, C. J., Lix, L. M., Olejnik, S., Cribbie, R., Donahue, B., . . . Levin, J. R. (1998). Statistical practices of educational researchers: An analysis of their ANOVA, MANOVA, and ANCOVA analyses. *Review of Educational Research, 68*, 350–386. doi:10.3102/00346543068003350

Keselman, H. J., Wilcox, R. R., Lix, L. M., Algina, J., & Fradette, B. A. (2007). Adaptive robust estimation and testing. *British Journal of Mathematical and Statistical Psychology, 60*, 267–293. doi:10.1348/000711005X63755

Keyes, T., & Levy, M. S. (1997). Analysis of Levene's test under design imbalance. *Journal of Educational and Behavioral Statistics, 22*, 227–236.

Kirk, R. (1995). *Experimental design: Procedures for the behavioral sciences.* Pacific Grove, CA: Brooks-Cole.

Levin, J., Serlin, R., & Seaman, M. (1994). A controlled, powerful multiple comparison strategy for several situations. *Psychological Bulletin, 115*, 153–159. doi:10.1037/0033-2909.115.1.153

Mantel, N. (1970). Why stepdown procedures in variable selection. *Technometrics, 12*, 621–625. doi:10.2307/1267207

Marsh, L., & Cormier, D. (2001). *Spline regression models.* Newbury Park, CA: Sage.

Mauro, R. (1990). Understanding LOVE (left out variables error): A method for estimating the effects of omitted variables. *Psychological Bulletin, 108*, 314–329. doi:10.1037/0033-2909.108.2.314

Maxwell, S. (2000). Sample size and multiple regression analysis. *Psychological Methods, 5*, 434–458. doi:10.1037/1082-989X.5.4.434

Maxwell, S., & Delaney, H. (1993). Bivariate median splits and spurious statistical significance. *Psychological Bulletin, 113*, 181–190. doi:10.1037/0033-2909.113.1.181

Maxwell, S. E., & Delaney, H. D. (2004). *Designing experiments and analyzing data: A model comparison perspective.* Mahwah, NJ: Erlbaum.

Maxwell, S. E., Kelley, K., & Rausch, J. (2008). Sample size planning for statistical power and accuracy in parameter estimation. *Annual Review of Psychology, 59*, 537–563. doi:10.1146/annurev.psych.59.103006.093735

Meehl, P. (1971). High school yearbooks: A reply to Schwarz. *Journal of Abnormal Psychology, 77*, 143–148. doi:10.1037/h0030750

Milligan, G. (1987). The use of the arc-sine transformation in the analysis of variance. *Educational and Psychological Measurement, 47*, 563–573. doi:10.1177/001316448704700303

Mosteller, F., & Tukey, J. (1977). *Data analysis and regression.* Reading, MA: Addison-Wesley.

Muthén, B. O. (2004). *Mplus technical appendices.* Los Angeles, CA: Muthén & Muthén.

Olejnik, S., & Algina, J. (2000). Measures of effect size for comparative studies: Applications, interpretations, and limitations. *Contemporary Educational Psychology, 25,* 241–286. doi:10.1006/ceps.2000.1040

Parra-Frutos, I. (2009). The behaviour of the modified Levene's test when data are not normally distributed. *Computational Statistics, 24,* 671–693. doi:10.1007/s00180-009-0154-z

Potthoff, R. F. (1964). On the Johnson–Neyman technique and some extensions thereof. *Psychometrika, 29,* 241–256. doi:10.1007/BF02289721

Prentice, D. A., & Miller, D. T. (1992). When small effects are impressive. *Psychological Bulletin, 112,* 160–164. doi:10.1037/0033-2909.112.1.160

Rodgers, J. L. (2010). The epistemology of mathematical and statistical modeling: A quiet methodological revolution. *American Psychologist, 65,* 1–12. doi:10.1037/a0018326

Rosenthal, R. (1995). Methodology. In A. Tesser (Ed.), *Advanced social psychology* (pp. 17–50). New York, NY: McGraw-Hill.

Rosenthal, R., & Rosnow, R. L. (1985). *Contrast analysis: Focused comparisons in the analysis of variance.* Cambridge, England: Cambridge University Press.

Seaman, M. A., Levin, K. R., & Serlin, R. C. (1991). New developments in pairwise multiple comparisons: Some powerful and practicable procedures. *Psychological Bulletin, 110,* 577–586. doi:10.1037/0033-2909.110.3.577

Shapiro, S. S., & Wilk, M. B. (1965). An analysis of variance test for normality (complete samples). *Biometrika, 52,* 591–611.

Tibshirani, R. (1996). Regression shrinkage and selection via the lasso. *Journal of the Royal Statistical Society, Series B: Methodological, 58,* 267–288.

Toothaker, L. E. (1993). *Multiple comparison procedures.* Newbury Park, CA: Sage.

Weller, S. (2002). *Testing statistical hypotheses of equivalence.* New York, NY: Chapman.

Westfall, P., Tobias, R., Rom, D., Wolfinger, R., & Hochberg, Y. (1999). *Multiple comparisons and multiple tests: Using the SAS system.* Cary, NC: SAS Institute.

Westfall, P. H. & Young, S. S. (1993). *Resampling based multiple testing.* New York, NY: Wiley.

Wilcox, R. R. (1996). *Statistics for the social sciences.* New York, NY: Academic Press.

Wilcox, R. R. (1998). How many discoveries have been lost by ignoring modern statistical methods. *American Psychologist, 53,* 300–314. doi:10.1037/0003-066-X.53.3.300

Wilcox, R. R. (2001). *Fundamentals of modern statistical methods: Substantially improving power and accuracy.* New York, NY: Springer.

Wilcox, R. R. (2003). *Applying contemporary statistical techniques.* San Diego, CA: Academic Press.

Wilcox, R. R. (2005a). *Introduction to robust estimation and hypothesis testing* (2nd ed.). San Diego, CA: Academic Press.

Wilcox, R. R. (2005b). New methods for comparing group: Strategies for increasing the probability of detecting true differences. *Current Directions in Psychological Science, 14,* 272–275. doi:10.1111/j.0963-7214.2005.00379.x

Wilcox, R. R. (2006). Graphical methods for assessing effect size: Some alternatives to Cohen's d. *Journal of Experimental Education, 74,* 351–367. doi:10.3200/JEXE.74.4.351-367

Wilcox, R. R., Charlin, V. L., & Thompson, K. (1986). New Monte Carlo results on the robustness of the ANOVA F, W, and F* statistics. *Communications in Statistics Simulation and Computation, 15,* 933–944

Wilkinson, L. (1999). Statistical methods in psychology journals: Guidelines and explanations. *American Psychologist, 54,* 594–604. doi:10.1037/0003-066X.54.8.594

Yeaton, W. H., & Sechrest, L. (1981). Meaningful measures of effect. *Journal of Consulting and Clinical Psychology, 49,* 766–767. doi:10.1037/0022-006X.49.5.766

## CHAPTER 9

GENERALIZED LINEAR MODELS

David Rindskopf

Most social scientists are now acquainted with the general linear model, which allows one statistical method (regression) to be used to analyze data from a number of different research designs. Multiple regression can be used for the standard case with one or more continuous predictors as well as for the equivalent of a two-group *t* test, multiple group analysis of variance (ANOVA), analysis of covariance (ANCOVA), and many more designs. The usual multiple regression, however, still has some major limitations for the data many social scientists analyze: (a) Dependent (predicted, or outcome) variables in the social sciences are not always continuous, (b) the residuals (observed minus predicted values) do not always have a normal distribution, and (c) the relationships between independent and dependent variables are not always linear.

In some cases, a simple transformation (such as a logarithm, square root, or inverse) of the dependent variable helps solve one or more of the problems. But eventually statisticians developed techniques that were correct for some of these situations—for example, log-linear models when all variables were categorical, logit models when one or more of the categorical variables were dependent and others are independent (predictor) variables, and logistic regression for binary (two-category) dependent variables (and extensions to ordered outcomes and multiple category outcomes).

Statisticians eventually realized that a large number of these models could be put into one general framework, which they named the *generalized linear*

model (GLM; note the difference between *generalized* and *general*). The key initial works in this area are Nelder and Wedderburn (1972) and McCullagh and Nelder (1989). In all of the models, there is a linear function connecting the predictors (independent variables) to an outcome that is not always directly observed. This (unobserved) outcome is connected to the expected observed outcome using a transformation called a link function. Finally, various probability distributions are available to describe the random component of the model, which connects the observed dependent variable to the expected value in the model.

In this chapter I show some of the most common GLMs and give examples of how they are conceptualized, fit, tested, and interpreted. I primarily use small, artificial data sets to make it possible for readers to reproduce these results on any computer package that fits GLMs. I demonstrate using the glm function in the R software package and also discuss some of the other software available for fitting GLMs. Finally, I discuss various extensions of GLM to handle additional complexities that are common in social science data. I assume familiarity with the usual analyses outside the context of GLM (e.g., logistic regression, loglinear models), although some explanatory context is provided.

Many of the steps of analysis using GLM are the same as for other methods of data analysis. As usual, begin with calculations of descriptive statistics and plots of relevant quantities. Next, decide on a strategy for building the linear part of the model. For example,

The detailed comments of Harris Cooper and A. T. Panter were most helpful in preparing the revision of this chapter.

DOI: 10.1037/13621-009
APA Handbook of Research Methods in Psychology: Vol. 3. Data Analysis and Research Publication, H. Cooper (Editor-in-Chief)

how will the categorical predictors be coded? Should any predictors be centered or otherwise transformed? Will polynomial terms for continuous variables likely be needed? Interactions? Consider the possible choices for a link function and distribution; as will be seen, for some types of dependent variables there are several reasonable choices. Estimate the initial model, check the fit, and revise as necessary. Finally, interpret the results, do any needed auxiliary calculations and plots, and write about findings.

LOGLINEAR AND LOGIT MODELS

In some cases, all variables are categorical. Consider a study of middle-school students that assesses the student's gender (male/female), race–ethnicity (Black, Hispanic, White), and whether the student is classified as learning disabled. The data from such a study are usually displayed in a cross-tabulation such as that shown (for fictional data) in Table 9.1.

There is quite a bit of variability among the six groups in the proportion who are learning disabled. The proportion for Hispanic males appears to be about the same as for Hispanic females, whereas in the other two race–ethnicity groups the rate is higher among males. Some of this variability might be just sampling variability, and the statistical analysis will attempt to disentangle real differences from those caused by sampling.

This data set can be approached in at least two related ways. From one perspective, the three variables are treated equally, and we look for which relationships are and are not present among them; this is the loglinear model perspective. Another perspective treats one variable (learning disability) as dependent, with the other two as explanatory (independent); this is the logit model. Both fit into the GLM framework. We begin with the logit model because it can be represented and interpreted most simply.

Logit Model

Most researchers would find it natural to express the outcome in terms of the proportion who are learning disabled in each group in the 2 (sex) × 3 (race–ethnicity) design. One would want to determine whether this proportion is related to the main effect of sex, the main effect of race–ethnicity, and whether there is an interaction between sex and race–ethnicity such that differences between males and females in the proportion of those who are learning disabled differ across race–ethnic groups. But a proportion has many flaws as a dependent variable, not the least of which is that with a linear model one can predict proportions less than zero or greater than one. Statisticians therefore look at transformations that do not have this flaw. The most common one first transforms a *proportion* π into an *odds*, $\pi/(1-\pi)$. Although a proportion is bounded between zero and one, an odds can range from zero to infinity. Then, taking the natural (base e) logarithm of the odds, that is, $\ln[\pi/(1-\pi)]$, gives what is called a *logit transformation*. The *logit* can vary over the whole real number range, so that as a dependent variable, it has no values outside an allowable range as the proportion does. Another advantage of the logit transformation is symmetry: A proportion of .2 (for example) has the same logit (except for sign) as the proportion .8 = 1 – .2.

In GLM, the logit is called the *link function* and connects (links) the logit that we are modeling to the proportion that we observe. The usual logit model formulation for the systematic part of the model can therefore be expressed as

$$\ln\left(\frac{\pi}{1-\pi}\right) = \beta_0 + \beta_1 Sex + \beta_2 Black + \beta_3 Hisp$$
$$+ \beta_4 Sex * Black + \beta_5 Sex * Hisp, \quad (1)$$

TABLE 9.1

The Relationship Among Learning Disability, Gender, and Race–Ethnicity: Observed Frequencies and Proportion Learning Disabled

Gender	Race	Learning disabled? Yes	Learning disabled? No	Proportion (yes)
Male	Black	13	27	.325
	Hispanic	14	66	.175
	White	49	151	.245
Female	Black	8	32	.200
	Hispanic	13	67	.163
	White	32	168	.160

where π is the expected probability of being learning disabled, the two predictor variables (Sex, Race–Ethnicity) are coded using either dummy or effect coding, as in any linear model, and, as before, ln() is the natural logarithm function. In the more general notation for GLM, we would write the model in two parts. The first part is for the linear predictor, η (eta):

$$\eta = \beta_0 + \beta_1 Sex + \beta_2 Black + \beta_3 Hisp$$
$$+ \beta_4 Sex * Black + \beta_5 Sex * Hisp. \qquad (2)$$

The second part of the specification is the link function, which in this case is the logit: $\eta = \ln\left(\dfrac{\pi}{1-\pi}\right)$. By writing the model this way, we allow for a simple change in the specification of the model by changing the link function, and at the same time, we emphasize that the linear part of the model is in the form familiar to most researchers.

The probability model connecting the expected values to the observed is the *binomial distribution*. The probability model is the nonsystematic, or random, part of the GLM. The estimated values of π for each group predict the proportion who are learning disabled, and the actual number who are and are not learning disabled arise from a binomial distribution with parameters π and n, where n is the number of people in the group. In this form, the model is saturated; that is, with six groups, there are five degrees of freedom available, and Equation 2 uses all five degrees of freedom estimating five parameters (slopes only; the intercept, β_0, is not counted). One approach under these circumstances is to estimate the parameters of this model, test each parameter for significance, and drop nonsignificant parameters from the model in order, starting with highest level interactions. Another approach is to start with a simpler model, such as a main effects only model, and see whether the model fits sufficiently well that interactions are not needed. Here I take the latter approach; the relevant output for this model is in Exhibit 9.1. In the analysis, sex is coded 0 for males, 1 for females; Black and Hispanic are also dummy coded (and are thus implicitly compared with the remaining category, White).

The output indicates that sex is significant; the negative coefficient indicates that those with a value of 1 (females) are lower than those with a value of 0

Exhibit 9.1
Output for Logit Model Predicting Probability of Learning Disability

```
Coefficients:
              Estimate Std.Error z-value  Pr(>|z|)
(Intercept)   -1.1597     0.1520   -7.629  2.37e-14***
sex           -0.4526     0.2001   -2.261    0.0237*
black          0.3408     0.2843    1.199    0.2306
hisp          -0.2255     0.2459   -0.917    0.3592

Signif. codes:  0 '***' 0.001 '**' 0.01 '*' 0.05
   '.' 0.1 ' ' 1

      Null deviance: 9.01827 on 5 degrees of freedom
Residual deviance: 0.98965 on 2 degrees of freedom
```

Note. Model includes main effects for sex and ethnicity. This model was fit using the glm function in R.

(males), meaning that females are less likely to be learning disabled in this population. Neither coefficient for race–ethnicity is significant, meaning that there are no significant relationships between race–ethnic group and learning disability. Is there an interaction between sex and race–ethnic group? The *residual deviance*, which in this case has a chi-square distribution, is so small (.99 with 2 degrees of freedom) that it would be impossible for an interaction term to reduce it by anywhere near a significant amount (3.84, the critical value of chi-square with 1 degree of freedom and $p = .05$). Therefore, we conclude that the only clear effect in the data is the main effect of sex, with males having a higher learning disability rate than females. (This is actually in accord with the way the data were generated; with a simulation, you can know what the right answer is.)

In discussing the fit of the model, it was noted that the residual deviance has a chi-square distribution if the model is correct. This is true for grouped data such as those we analyzed in this example but not for individual-level data. That is, here we are predicting proportions for whole groups of people; in other cases (such as the logistic regression model described in the section Logistic Regression and Its Extensions), we would be predicting the behavior of each individual, and the residuals would pertain to the individuals, not the groups. Even in that case, the deviance can help assess model fit: If the deviance is about equal to the residual degrees of freedom, the model fits reasonably well. If the deviance is much greater than the degrees of freedom (with *much greater* not being precisely defined), then the model does not fit well. For some models, this relatively large deviance may be due to obvious random sources of heterogeneity, such as large variation among subjects within groups, and the model can be extended by including a parameter for overdispersion. Examples later in this chapter illustrate this procedure.

In some cases, residuals can be used to assess the fit of the model. The meaning of these residuals and their utility depend on the nature of the data. In this example the data are grouped, so the residuals essentially test whether the set of omitted terms (all of which are interactions) are zero. In other cases, in which the observations are made at the individual level (such as in the logistic regression example to be discussed later), the residuals refer to a prediction of the behavior of the individual, not a group; this use of residuals is more analogous to the use of residuals in ordinary regression situations. But many times the residuals for GLM are not expected to behave in quite the same way as in the linear regression case. For example, if each individual is observed only to be in one of two states, a large residual means that we predict a high probability of being in one state, but the person actually is in the other. For example, a person with a high school grade point average (GPA) of 1.3 might be predicted to have a low probability of graduating from college but nonetheless might do so. This result does not necessarily indicate that the model (or that observation) is problematic.

In many cases, the logit transform of the proportion discussed in this section will be satisfactory, but other transforms are also part of the GLM framework. One alternative viewpoint is that the unobserved dependent variable η has a normal distribution, and the observed dichotomous variable is 0 (or failure) unless η exceeds a threshold value, in which case the outcome is 1 (or success). The probability of success is therefore related to the area under the normal curve, and the transform is called a *probit*. In practice, the probit and logit models are so close that if one model fits the data well, the other usually also will do so;

when scaled comparably, the predicted probabilities will differ by no more than .01. For other transformations, this is not true. For example, the complementary log–log function, $\ln[-\ln(\pi)]$, is qualitatively different from both the logit and probit. The ability to discern differences among these models generally occurs only in data with one or more continuous predictors.

Loglinear Model

The logit model is appropriate when there is a dependent variable, such as learning disability in the previous example. When there is no obvious dependent variable, or when one wishes to treat all variables symmetrically and model all relationships among them, loglinear models are used. In this section I use the same data set to illustrate, even though logit models seem most appropriate for these data.

Using loglinear models, the dependent variable is the cell frequency in the full contingency table, for our example, of $2 \times 3 \times 2 = 12$ cells. The terms in the model represent relationships among the variables. The most common example is the usual test for independence in a two-way cross-tabulation; in that case, the model is that the two variables (call them *A* and *B*) are independent. In the loglinear model framework, a model of independence means that only main effects for A and B are included, but not their interaction (relationship).

Frequencies are nonnegative, and the logarithm of a frequency can be any real number, so the logarithm is commonly used as the link function in the GLM framework. For a loglinear model that is equivalent to the main-effects logit model we fit, the GLM can be written as

$$\begin{aligned} \ln(F) = \beta_0 &+ \beta_1 Sex + \beta_2 Blk + \beta_3 Hisp + \beta_4 LD \\ &+ \beta_5 Sex * Blk + \beta_6 Sex * Hisp + \beta_7 Sex * LD \\ &+ \beta_8 Blk * LD + \beta_9 Hisp * LD, \end{aligned} \qquad (3)$$

where *LD* represents the variable *learning disabled*, *Blk* represents a dummy variable for Black, and *Hisp* is a dummy variable for Hispanic. The interactions between *LD* and the variables *Sex*, *Blk*, and *Hisp* are comparable to the main effects in the logit model. That is, in the logit model these terms are the effects of independent on dependent variables, but in the loglinear model they merely specify relationships (in a symmetric sense, like a correlation, rather than asymmetric as in regression). For example, the *Sex * LD* term in the loglinear model allows a relationship between *Sex* and *LD*; in a logit model this would be a main effect of *Sex* (on *LD*).

I have specified the linear part of the model and that the link is the logarithm; the final aspect of the model is specifying the probability distribution. The usual distribution for the loglinear model is the *Poisson*; thus, the cell frequencies each have a Poisson distribution with means equal to the expected values given by the systematic part of the model. The Poisson is the simplest distribution for variables that represent counts (or, in general, variables that are nonnegative integers). I also discuss the Poisson distribution as it applies in other contexts later in this chapter.

The results of fitting the data in Table 9.1 using the loglinear version of the model are contained in Exhibit 9.2. The residual deviance for the loglinear model is the same as the residual deviance for the comparable logit model, indicating that the fit of the two models is identical. Next, notice that the significance levels of $LD \times Sex$, $LD \times Blk$, and $LD \times$

Exhibit 9.2

Output From the glm Package in R for a Loglinear Model Fit to the Learning Disability Data

---

```
Coefficients:
            Estimate Std. Error z value  Pr(>|z|)
(Intercept)  5.02555    0.07948  63.231  < 2e-16***
blk         -1.70196    0.19246  -8.843  < 2e-16***
ld          -1.15967    0.15201  -7.629  2.37e-14***
his         -0.86690    0.14213  -6.099  1.06e-09***
fe           0.09091    0.10792   0.842  0.3995
blk:ld       0.34078    0.28429   1.199  0.2306
ld:his      -0.22548    0.24593  -0.917  0.3592
ld:fe       -0.45260    0.20014  -2.261  0.0237*
blk:fe       0.02719    0.24642   0.110  0.9122
his:fe      -0.01525    0.18789  -0.081  0.9353

Signif. codes: 0 '***' 0.001 '**' 0.01 '*' 0.05
   '.' 0.1 ' ' 1

  Null deviance: 506.86470 on 11 degrees of freedom
Residual deviance:   0.98965 on  2 degrees of freedom
```

Note. The colon (:) is used by this program to represent an interaction; the more usual notation is * or x. The terms in bold are equivalent to terms in the logit model discussed in the text. blk = Black; ld = learning disabled; his = Hispanic; fe = female.

Hisp in the loglinear model are the same as for the effects of *Sex*, *Blk*, and *Hisp* in the logit model. (In the R output, interactions are represented with a colon instead of the more typical asterisk.) In this case, the parameter estimates and standard errors are the same because of the coding methods used, but they will not always be. The ratio of the parameter to the standard error, called the *z* value in the output, will be the same, however, as will the significance level.

When would the loglinear model be used instead of the logit model? If there is no clear dependent variable, then the logit model would not be appropriate. In other cases, in which the data or the model are nonstandard (e.g., the data set is not a rectangular table), then the generality of loglinear models is useful; for details, see Rindskopf (1990).

LOGISTIC REGRESSION AND ITS EXTENSIONS

In some cases, each individual in a sample is measured on a binary (dichotomous) outcome. This outcome variable might be success or failure on some task, or that one decision rather than another is made (e.g., acquiring some postsecondary education vs. not), or that one opinion is favored over another. No matter what the context, when two choices are available, one is arbitrarily called a success (even if it represents an event with an undesirable outcome, such as cheating on a test) and the other outcome is called a failure (e.g., not cheating on a test). The goal is to model the probability of success as a function of one or more independent variables, which may be continuous, categorical, or a mixture of these types of variables. Outside the context of GLM, this is called logistic regression, and the link function is usually the log(odds), or logit, as discussed. The primary difference from the logit model is that in logistic regression, typically at least one predictor variable is (quasi-)continuous, so that a linear relationship (on some scaling of the outcome) is expected, and modeling group frequencies is not practical because of the fineness of the scaling of the continuous variable.

As an example, we consider a (fictional) study by an industrial–organizational psychologist who is trying to determine the relationship between cognitive load and the probability of a major safety error by air traffic controllers. She simulates various amounts of traffic (on a scale from 1 to 20), measuring one air traffic controller in each condition, and assesses whether they make a potentially dangerous error (e.g., allowing planes to get too close). Suppose that the results, using 0 for no error and 1 for a major error, for amounts of traffic (in order from one to 20, with spacing to help count the corresponding amount of traffic) are as follows:

00000 00001 00111 11111

For lower amounts of traffic, controllers do not seem to make errors; for high amounts of traffic, controllers seem very likely to make an error; the transition seems to be somewhere between 10 and 12 on the complexity scale. The transition also seems to be fairly abrupt, evidenced by the long beginning string of zeros and the long ending string of ones. This abrupt transition from zeros to ones will cause some puzzling results.

The model looks similar to that for a logit model:

$$\ln\left(\frac{\pi}{1-\pi}\right) = \beta_0 + \beta_1 Traffic, \qquad (4)$$

where π is the probability of making a dangerous error, and $Traffic$ is the amount of traffic (here it varies from one to 20). In terms of the GLM formulation, the link function is the logit (logarithm of the odds), and the distribution is *Bernoulli* (which can be thought of as a *binomial with one trial*). Selected parts of the output from fitting this model to the data are included in Exhibit 9.3, and a plot of the data along with the fitted response curve is in Figure 9.1. The results demonstrate a possible inconsistency between the results of two tests that often are equivalent but that in some cases will diverge. The usual test for significance of the effect of amount of traffic is the parameter estimate divided by the standard error; here this ratio is 1.888, which is not significant. Another test of whether the slope for amount of traffic is significant is to compare the null model (i.e., the model that does not have a predictor) with the model that includes the predictor. The difference in the deviance values for that comparison is 27.53 – 7.18 = 20.35, with 19 – 18 = 1 degree of freedom, which is clearly significant, because 20.35 is

---

Exhibit 9.3
Output for Logistic Regression Predicting, From Amount of Air Traffic, Whether a Major Error Was Made on an Air Traffic Control Task

```
glm(formula = y ~ traffic, family = binomial(link =
    logit))
Coefficients:
            Estimate  Std. Error  z value  Pr(>|z|)
(Intercept) -10.5309     5.6594    -1.861    0.0628
traffic       0.9157     0.4851     1.888    0.0591

    Null deviance: 27.5256 on 19 degrees of freedom
Residual deviance:  7.1786 on 18 degrees of freedom
```

Note. The variable "y" is the dependent variable, coded 1 if a serious error was made and 0 if not; the variable "traffic" is the amount of air traffic in the simulation.

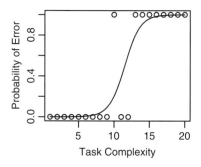

FIGURE 9.1. Plot of data on serious judgment errors by air traffic controllers as a function of task complexity. Open circles are raw data; solid line is the fit of a logistic regression model.

---

much greater than 3.84, the critical value of the chi-square distribution with 1 degree of freedom. The difference between these two tests is due to prediction being too good; this makes both the slope and its standard error large, and when this happens, their ratio is no longer a valid test of significance (nor are confidence intervals accurate). Normally, one would not think of .92 as being a large slope, but it represents the change caused by a difference of only one more unit of traffic on a scale going from 1 to 20; this means that the odds of a dangerous error change by exp(.92), or about 2.5, for each increase of one unit on the traffic scale, which is quite a large amount. (To understand this, remember that the slope is the change in the logarithm of the odds; to go back to the scale of the odds, we need the inverse of the logarithm, which is exponentiation.)

As is evident from this example, it is not always easy to detect such a problem by examining the estimate of the slope or its standard error; a more reliable method is to examine the deviance statistics. For these data, three interrelated pieces of information suggest there is a problem: First, the deviance for the null model is much greater than the degrees of freedom. The deviance does not have a chi-square distribution, so we cannot test the hypothesis of lack of fit when the predictor is omitted. Second, the deviance for the model with the predictor has a deviance well below the degrees of freedom, indicating an excellent fit. Finally, as noted, the direct test of significance for the slope using the difference in deviance values (which does have a chi-square distribution under the null hypothesis) is significant.

Extensions of the basic logistic regression model are available when the outcome variable is categorical but not dichotomous. I will describe the most typical models for unordered (nominal) and ordered outcome variables.

Nominal Response Scales

Not all categorical outcomes are dichotomous; nominal responses (unordered categorical responses) may have three, four, or more categories. Although sophisticated methods exist to model such variables (e.g., see Agresti, 2002; Fox, 2008; Long, 1997), a simple approach often suffices: With k categories, the researcher forms $k - 1$ dichotomies and uses logistic regression on each outcome. For example, suppose the possible outcomes on a measure of music preference are jazz, country, rock, and classical. One might first create a dichotomy for classical versus all others. Then, for those who do not favor classical, one might create another dichotomy of jazz versus country or rock. Finally, for those who chose either country or rock, create a dichotomy contrasting these two categories. Then, three analyses are done, using the appropriate subset of people for each analysis. Naturally, this choice of dichotomies is not unique; other choices might be made depending on the hypotheses of the study. For example, a different researcher might first compare those who like jazz or classical (more serious music) with those who like country or rock. Then among those who chose either jazz or classical, she would predict which one

they liked; similarly, among those who liked either country or rock, an analysis would try to differentiate their preference. Thus, dichotomies need not merely take one category at a time compared with the remaining categories. (Those familiar with orthogonal contrasts in ANOVA contexts will notice the connection to these two examples.)

Ordinal Data

When the outcome variable is ordered, an extension of the logistic regression model provides a natural framework for the analysis. Consider the case of a college that wants to validate the use of a mathematics placement test for determining whether students should be allowed to register for a particular course. It has data for 20 students who took the placement test before taking the course and the grade those students earned in the course. The test scores range from 1 to 20, with one student having achieved each score; the corresponding grades (in order of increasing test score) for those students are as follows:

$$0\ 0\ 0\ 0\ 2 \quad 1\ 1\ 0\ 1\ 2 \quad 2\ 2\ 3\ 2\ 3 \quad 4\ 4\ 2\ 4\ 3,$$

where 0 represents a grade of F and 4 represents a grade of A. The course grades rise as the test scores increase, but the relationship is not perfect: One of the students with the lowest test score earned a C in the course, as did one of the highest-scoring students.

To understand the most common model for such data, consider that one could dichotomize the course grades in four ways, by considering grades of D or higher versus not (F), C or higher versus not (D or F), B or higher versus not (C, D, or F), and A versus not (B, C, D, or F). Then one could use the usual logistic regression model to predict high or low grade (using each of the four possible dichotomizations that preserve ordering) from the placement test score. The usual ordinal data model does this but with a restriction that the slope (effect of test score on the logit) is equal across the four dichotomizations. This model, called the *proportional odds model*, guarantees that the results are logically consistent: If the lines were not parallel, but were allowed to cross, then for some test score the probability of (for example) earning a B or better would be greater than the probability of earning a C or better. If the slopes differed only a little, this might occur outside the usual range of test scores, but it nonetheless represents a potential logical problem.

To fit these data, I used an extension of the glm function called polr (proportional odds logistic regression) in the MASS library for R. The results are contained in Exhibit 9.4. The predictor *test*, which is the score on the placement test, is clearly useful because its *t* value (coefficient divided by standard error) is 3.60.

To interpret the output, some reconceptualization is needed. In this context, it seems natural to want to model the (logit of the) probability of receiving a certain grade or higher; the statistical model, on the other hand, is set up to model the probability of receiving a certain grade or lower. (One can trick the program into doing it the other way by reversing the coding, using 0 for an A, and so on down to 4 for an F. It is mostly a matter of personal preference for coding and interpretation.) The general form of the model, using zeta (ζ_i) to represent the intercept for category *i*, and η to represent the systematic (linear) part of the model except for the intercept, is written as follows:

$$\text{logit}[\text{Probability(category } i \text{ or lower)}] = \zeta_i - \eta. \quad (5)$$

The change of sign is due to the conceptualization as the probability of category *i* or lower, rather than higher.

To take an example, the logit of the probability of getting a grade of C or lower is 8.5164 – .5825 * *test*, where *test* is the score on the placement test. (The reversal of sign on the slope to become negative is correct; it indicates that the higher the test score, the lower the probability of receiving a grade of C or lower.) Thus, for a person with a test score of 10, the logit would be 8.5164 – 5.825 = 2.6914, the odds would be exp(2.6914) = 14.75, and the probability of a C or lower would then be 14.75/15.75 = .94. So we predict a student with a score of 10 would likely not do well in the course. On the other hand, with a score of 15 a student's logit would be 8.5164 – .5825(15) = 8.5164 – 8.7375 = –.22, the odds would be exp(–.22) = .80, and the probability of a C or below would be .80/1.80 = .45, which is much better.

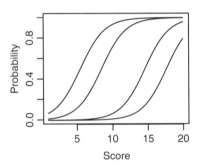

FIGURE 9.2. Probability plot for ordinal logistic model. The left-most curve is the probability of attaining a grade of at least D; the right-most curve the probability of attaining an A.

Often the most useful way to present the results of an ordinal analysis is in the form of a plot, such as that contained in Figure 9.2. The four lines indicate the conditional probability of receiving a particular grade or higher, given the person's placement test score. The curve on the left, which rises first, is the probability of receiving at least a D (that is, passing the course); the curve on the far right, which rises last, is the probability of receiving an A. Using these curves, decision makers can easily determine the effect of making different choices for the cutpoint to allow a student into this course. For example, if it is desired to admit only students who have at least an 80% chance of getting a C or better, a cutscore of about 11 will work. (This can be read reasonably accurately from the plot but can also be calculated exactly from the parameter estimates if such precision is desired.)

PREDICTING A COUNT VARIABLE

Suppose that we want to determine whether a particular psychological treatment can reduce the incidence of acting out in the classroom among third graders. (Assume that the behavior of each child does not affect the behavior of other children in the study, perhaps because they are in different classrooms.) We randomly assign five children to the treatment condition and another five to the control condition. After the treatment has been implemented, we count the number of times (during a 30-min observation) that each child acts out. The counts are displayed in Exhibit 9.5.

Because the outcome is a (relatively small) count, there is good reason to doubt whether the distribution (within each group) has approximately a normal distribution. Even more serious, it seems that the variance of acting out may be greater in the control group than in the experimental group. If there were a covariate (such as baseline measures of acting out), we would probably also have to deal with some nonlinearity in the relationship between pretest and posttest. For all of these reasons, the usual linear model would be inappropriate, and we turn to a GLM. In this case, the Poisson distribution is the simplest to use, and in many cases, it will be sufficient. (This model is similar to that for loglinear models, where the Poisson distribution is also used.) The link function is the logarithm—that is, we will model as the dependent variable the logarithm of the expected counts,

$$\ln(Y_i) = \beta_0 + \beta_1 X_i, \tag{6}$$

where X is a dummy variable taking the value 1 for the treatment group and 0 for the control group.

Partial output from the R function glm is contained in Exhibit 9.6. The coefficient estimates produce a prediction equation: $\ln(y) = 1.5686 - 1.2321$ *Group*. The logarithm of the expected number of disruptive acts for the control group (Group = 0) is 1.5686, and the comparable value for a person in the treatment group (Group = 1) is $1.5686 - 1.2321 = .3365$. To find the predicted number of disruptive acts, we exponentiate to get $\exp(1.5686) = 4.80$ for the control group and $\exp(.3365) = 1.40$ for the experimental group. This difference between groups is large, but is it significant? We test the significance of the difference by examining the ratio of the parameter for Group to its standard error: $-1.2321/.4296 = -2.868$ ($p = .004$), which is strong evidence for an effect.

Exhibit 9.6
Output From Fitting Poisson Regression to Data on Children Acting Out, Using R Function glm

```
Coefficients:
             Estimate Std. Error  z value  Pr(>|z|)
(Intercept)    1.5686     0.2041    7.685  1.53e-14***
group         -1.2321     0.4296   -2.868  0.00413**

Signif. codes:  0 '***' 0.001 '**' 0.01 '*' 0.05
   '.' 0.1 ' ' 1

    Null deviance: 17.9765 on 9 degrees of freedom
Residual deviance:  8.1193 on 8 degrees of freedom
```

Note. The variable "group" is coded 0 for control, 1 for experimental.

Exhibit 9.5
Number of Times Each Child Acted Out During a 30-Min Observation Session

Treatment	1	1	1	1	1	0	0	0	0	0
Acting out	1	2	3	0	1	7	7	3	4	3

Note. Artificial data generated from a Poisson model. 0 = control condition, 1 = experimental condition.

Another test of the same effect would compare the residual deviance statistics for the null model (i.e., the model without predictors) and the model we fit; the difference ($17.9765 – 8.1193 = 9.8572$) has a chi-square distribution with degrees of freedom equal to the difference between the degrees of freedom for the two models ($9 – 8 = 1$ degree of freedom). This value is clearly significant, as the critical value of chi square at the .01 level is 6.64, well below the observed value of nearly 10. In this case, the two methods of testing the effect give similar results, but (as seen in the logistic regression example) this convergence of results may not always occur; when they differ, the chi-square difference test will typically be more accurate.

Offsets

In some cases we might not observe each person for the same length of time. In this case, we would model the *rate* of problem behaviors, which is the expected count (Y) divided by observation time (T). The model then becomes

$$\ln(Y_i / T_i) = \beta_0 + \beta_1 X_i. \tag{7}$$

Expanding the left-hand side gives

$$\ln(Y_i) - \ln(T_i) = \beta_0 + \beta_1 X_i. \tag{8}$$

Rearranging this produces

$$\ln(Y_i) = \ln(T_i) + \beta_0 + \beta_1 X_i. \tag{9}$$

On the right-hand side, it appears that the logarithm of observation time is a predictor (similar to X), but with a coefficient of one (i.e., the regression coefficient is fixed, not estimated). In the GLM literature, this is known as an *offset*, and most software for GLM can easily incorporate these offsets into models. The same procedure is also used in discrete–time survival models, in which the counts are the number of observed events (deaths, failures, or other events being counted), and the offset is the logarithm of the total period of observation of an individual or group.

OVERDISPERSION AND THE NEGATIVE BINOMIAL MODEL

Another extension might be required if the Poisson model is too simple. If the ratio of the model deviance to degrees of freedom is larger than one, overdispersion is indicated. This can occur for two general types of reasons: A fixed effect is missing, or a random effect is missing. An example of the former would be a useful covariate that is omitted. Of course, one cannot always know which variables might be useful predictors, and even then it is sometimes impossible to measure the desired variables.

The other possibility is that variability among units either cannot be explained or is too complicated to explain—for example, people within groups often differ for many more reasons than we could possibly know or measure. In this case, a negative binomial distribution might provide a better fit to the data. Although the negative binomial has a sensible interpretation in its own right in certain contexts, it is equivalent to another distribution that has a more useful interpretation in the context of overdispersion, the gamma-mixed Poisson distribution. In this interpretation, individuals with the same values on the predictor variables (here, group) would not have a constant probability of misbehaving, but their rates would vary (in the shape of a gamma distribution, to be technical). In general, this is more likely when the units of observation are individuals, such as the case here, rather than groups. In our context, it is very likely that children within each group vary in their rate of acting out, even though all are considered to do so at a high enough rate to be considered in need of treatment. (Another common context is the rate of accidents, in which people may vary in their rate of accident-proneness.)

Many software packages for GLM will allow overdispersion; for count data, the most usual distribution is the negative binomial (gamma-mixed Poisson). (In the R package I have used for all examples in this chapter, the glm.nb function in the MASS library extends the glm function to include the negative binomial distribution.)

To demonstrate fitting the negative binomial model, consider the data in Exhibit 9.7, which are similar to those in Exhibit 9.5 but with extra variation within each of the two groups. (Technical note for readers who are curious: For this example, the extra variation was created by generating data from a gamma distribution with means of one for the treatment group and four for the control group, and

---

Exhibit 9.7
Negative Binomial (Gamma-Mixed Poisson) Model: Number of Times Each Child Acted Out During a 30-Min Observation Session

Treatment	1	1	1	1	1	0	0	0	0	0
Acting out	0	4	0	0	1	4	2	0	5	4

Note. 0 = control condition, 1 = experimental condition.

Exhibit 9.8
Output for Poisson Model Fit to Data That Are Generated Using a Gamma-Mixed Poisson Distribution

```
Coefficients:
            Estimate Std. Error  z value Pr(>|z|)
(Intercept)   1.0986     0.2582    4.255 2.09e-05***
group        -1.0986     0.5164   -2.127   0.0334*

Signif. codes: 0 '***' 0.001 '**' 0.01 '*' 0.05
    '.' 0.1 ' ' 1
    Null deviance: 24.412 on 9 degrees of freedom
Residual deviance: 19.180 on 8 degrees of freedom
```

Note. The variable "group" is coded 0 for control, 1 for experimental.

Exhibit 9.9
Output for Negative Binomial Model Fit to Data Generated From a Negative Binomial (Gamma-Mixed Poisson) Model

```
Coefficients:
            Estimate  Std. Error  z value Pr(>|z|)
(Intercept)   1.0986      0.3978    2.762  0.00575**
group        -1.0986      0.6707   -1.638  0.10143

Signif. codes: 0 '***' 0.001 '**' 0.01 '*' 0.05
    '.' 0.1 ' ' 1
(Dispersion parameter for Negative Binomial
    (2.1835) family taken to be 1)

    Null deviance: 15.245 on 9 degrees of freedom
Residual deviance: 12.427 on 8 degrees of freedom

      Theta: 2.18
   Std. Err.: 3.00
```

Note. The variable "group" is coded 0 for the control group, 1 for the experimental group.

---

then sampling from a Poisson distribution to generate each number of disruptive acts.) Comparing the two tables, it is easy to see the increased variation in Exhibit 9.7 compared with Exhibit 9.5.

First, we fit the usual Poisson model to see whether the lack of fit is detected. The results are contained in Exhibit 9.7. If this model fits well, the residual deviance should be close to the degrees of freedom; the ratio of deviance to degrees of freedom is often used as a measure of overdispersion. The large residual deviance we observe in this case (compared with the degrees of freedom) indicates that the model does not fit well; we will see what effect this has on the results when we compare these results to those obtained using the negative binomial model.

The output from the negative binomial model is contained in Exhibit 9.9. The residual deviance is much lower for this model than for the Poisson model (19.180 – 12.427 = 6.753), which, with

1 degree of freedom difference between the models, is clearly significant. The direct comparison of the fit of these models is possible because the usual Poisson model is a restricted version (special case) of the negative binomial model in which overdispersion does not occur, so the parameter value is fixed instead of estimated. We conclude that there is overdispersion and that the negative binomial model provides a better fit than the simpler Poisson model.

Now we turn to the comparison of the two results and the interpretation. The Poisson model gives the same parameter estimates as the negative binomial model, but the Poisson results have smaller standard errors, larger z values (ratio of parameter divided by standard error), and smaller p values (significance level). In fact, if we believed the

Poisson results, the group effect would be significant, but the negative binomial results would not be. Using the correct model for the research situation results in a loss of power, much to the disappointment of researchers (and analogous to what usually happens in multilevel models). Why? The extra variability within groups is extra noise, which makes detecting the signal (group differences) more difficult. Fitting the Poisson model pretends this variability does not exist and produces results that are too liberal (too significant) when the assumption of no overdispersion is false.

BINOMIAL DATA WITH OVERDISPERSION

As with the count data illustrated in the previous section, binomial data can be generated for each person in a study. For example, one might count how many items testing a concept are answered correctly. Under conditions in which such data are well behaved, one can merely get a total score and ignore the binomial nature of the constituent items; this is what is done when total test scores are used as if they represent a continuous normally distributed quantity in a regression or ANOVA. If many scores are at or near zero (e.g., a very difficult test) or are at or near the maximum (e.g., a very easy test), then the distribution will be decidedly nonnormal, and other analytic methods must be used.

Several possible methods of analysis are available. One, which uses simple methodology, is to transform the proportion right and then use the usual ANOVA or regression methods. For example, the arcsine of the square root of proportions is well-known in certain fields and the logit in others. In each case, one must either have the same number of

trials for each individual or use weighting to properly account for variation in number of trials. Another possibility is to use methods for nested (multilevel) data and have trials nested within individuals. In this section, I will illustrate a method that falls between these in terms of complexity.

To put the model in context, consider a study in which 10 people are randomly assigned to one of two groups. Each person is given a 10-item test at the end of the study, with one group having received a treatment (or new treatment) and the other group receiving nothing (or an old treatment). As with the example for count data, we expect that people might vary within groups for reasons additional to sampling variability in the binomial distribution of outcomes of each trial. To account for this heterogeneity in a GLM, we can allow for overdispersion in a similar manner to the situation with count data.

Simulated data are contained in Exhibit 9.10 for one such study as described. Note that the number right varies quite widely for those in control group (Group = 0), which is due to the overdispersion. For the treatment group (Group = 1), this is not evident because these people are all performing at a high level; the ceiling effect disguises the heterogeneity.

Results for fitting two models are presented in Table 9.2. The first model does not account for the variation among people, except for sampling variability in the binomial distribution. That is, the underlying probability of a correct response is the same for all people in the control group as well as for the experimental group (although this probability differs for the two groups). Any difference in the number of items answered correctly is assumed to be due to differences in the treatment or sampling

---

Exhibit 9.10
Data for an Overdispersed Binomial Example

Person	1	2	3	4	5	6	7	8	9	10
Group	0	0	0	0	0	1	1	1	1	1
Number right	0	7	5	4	0	8	9	7	7	8

Note. Data for each person are the group into which they were placed (0 = control; 1 = treatment), and the number of trials (out of 10) on which they responded correctly.

TABLE 9.2

GLM Results for a Model Without (Binomial) and With (Quasi-Binomial) Overdispersion

Parameter	Binomial	Quasi-binomial
Treatment	−2.0194	−2.0194
SE	0.4566	0.7121
t = param/*SE*	−4.423	−2.836
Significance	0.000001	0.0220

Note. The deviance for the binomial model was 24.885 with 8 degrees of freedom; the ratio of these is 24.885/8 = 3.111. The estimate of the dispersion parameter (param) for the quasi-binomial model was 2.43.

variability. For the second model this is not true; people within the same group are allowed to differ in their probability of answering correctly.

The first model, without overdispersion, evidently does not fit the data well; the deviance is much larger than the degrees of freedom; in fact their ratio is greater than three. The results for the model with overdispersion differ in a predictable way from those for the model without overdispersion. The parameter estimate is unchanged, but the standard error is larger, correctly reflecting the additional source of variability among people. Because the standard error is larger, the z ratio is smaller, and therefore the significance level is much larger. Here, the effect of group is still significant, but in many cases, the (incorrect) model without overdispersion would indicate a significant effect but the (correct) model with overdispersion would not. (As noted, this effect also occurs in multilevel models.)

TIME TO AN EVENT (SURVIVAL MODELS)

Researchers often are interested in the amount of time people spend on various activities and in the ways that that amount of time might be increased or decreased. An educational psychologist, for example, would like to increase the amount of time students spend studying. One problem with laboratory studies in this case is that there is a limit to the amount of time one can spend observing people, so the data are often censored; that is, the person may be willing to spend more time doing some activity, but the researcher is not and thus ends the research session. Another problem is that such time lengths usually will not be normally distributed, and the variance will typically depend on the mean, violating the assumptions for the typical regression model. All of these issues are addressed by *survival analysis* (as it is called in the medical literature; other terms are *event history* and *failure time*, from sociology and reliability.)

For concreteness, we suppose that 10 students have been randomly assigned to one of two methods of increasing motivation to read, and after the treatment, each is given a period of up to 60 min to read. If the student is still reading after 60 min, the experimental session is ended. Simulated data from Group 1 might be: 2, 5, 8, 19, 60* min, where the data are ordered from smallest to largest, and an asterisk (*) indicates censoring; comparable data from Group 2 might be: 10, 20, 60*, 60*, 60*. It appears that the second group is reading more than the first; this is evident both in the larger times and in the fact that only one student reads the maximal amount in Group 1, but three students read the maximal amount in Group 2.

Several possible distributions are commonly used for continuous–time survival data. The simplest is the exponential distribution, which was used to generate the data for this example. More complex distributions (which include the exponential as a special case) are the gamma and the Weibull. Although some survival models can be fit using GLM programs that employ certain tricks, in practice it is more straightforward to use special functions that are written for survival models. This is one case in which the generality of the model does not currently seem worth the price paid in lack of interpretability.

In some cases, time is not continuous but a small count (e.g., the number of semesters to graduate from college). In this case, a model similar to that used in Poisson regression for counts is often used.

EXTENSIONS TO THE ORIGINAL GLM FORMULATION

One extension of GLM is to explicitly model nesting of data. One situation that can be represented as a nested model involves repeated measures data, in which observations are considered to be nested within individuals. Another common situation occurs when individuals are nested within groups; examples include students within classes (and classes within schools, etc.), voters nested in election districts, people nested within neighborhoods, and employees nested within work groups. Models for nested (hierarchical) data are treated in more detail in Chapter 11 of this volume as well as in many textbooks and reference works.

A large number of latent variable models, including exploratory and confirmatory factor analysis and structural equation models, were originally conceptualized for continuous observed and latent variables. As with models for observed variables, special cases were treated individually; these include models in which the latent variable is categorical, but the observed variables are continuous (finite mixture models and cluster models); the observed variables are categorical, but the latent variables are continuous (item response theory); and both observed and latent variables are categorical (latent class analysis). Most of these models have been put into a general framework as an extension of GLMs by Skrondal and Rabe-Hesketh (2004).

One extension of the GLM involving latent variables is especially useful for some missing data problems: the use of composite link functions, as developed by Thompson and Baker (1981). In this extension, the GLM is written to apply to unobserved variables, which are then combined (summed through the composite link) to produce the observed variables. One variation of this approach can be used to fit all examples of missing categorical data discussed in Little and Rubin (2002) as well as many additional models such as latent class models and even latent class models with missing data (for details, see Rindskopf, 1992).

SOFTWARE TO FIT GLMS

Most large statistical packages commonly used by psychologists have at least some facility to fit GLMs; these packages include SAS, SPSS/PASW, Statistica, and Stata. Even packages that do not explicitly include the full range of GLMs often include some separate components, such as logistic regression and loglinear models. The free software package R (http://www.r-project.org) and its commercial equivalent Splus

(http://spotfire.tibco.com/Products/S-Plus-Overview.aspx) have extensive capabilities for fitting GLMs; R has been used to illustrate examples in this chapter. Several GLMs for nested data can be fit using the HLM (http://www.scientificsoftware.com) and MLWiN (http://www.cmm.bristol.ac.uk/MLwiN) packages and with add-on functions in R and Splus. For Bayesian versions of generalized linear models, the WinBUGS (http://www.mrc-bsu.cam.ac.uk/bugs) package is available as well as its successor OpenBUGS (http://www.openbugs.info/w). An Excel interface, BUGSXLA (http://www.axrf86.dsl.pipex.com), simplifies the fitting of many Bayesian GLMs by keeping the WinBUGS package in the background.

FURTHER READING

For those wishing an introduction to GLM, several books are available, including Dobson and Barnett (2008), Gill (2000), and Hoffmann (2004). More advanced books include Fahrmeir and Tutz (2001) and Hardin and Hilbe (2007). Books covering GLM in whole or in part, but oriented toward a particular software package, include Aitkin, Francis, Hinde, and Darnell (2009) for R; Chambers and Hastie (1992) for S; and Venables and Ripley (2002) for R and Splus. For details on the GLM as originally conceptualized, the original article introducing the topic is Nelder and Wedderburn (1972), and the current authoritative source is McCullagh and Nelder (1989). Germán Rodríguez maintains an excellent website (http://data.princeton.edu/wws509) on GLMs; included are detailed lecture notes and data sets. Extensions and related models include generalized additive models (Hastie & Tibshirani, 1990), models for nested or longitudinal data (Lee & Nelder, 2001; Liang & Zeger, 1986; McCulloch, Searle, & Neuhaus, 2008; Pinheiro & Bates, 2000; Zeger & Liang, 1986), and models that include latent variables (Skrondal & Rabe-Hesketh, 2004).

Many regression texts now include material on GLM, and some are devoted mostly to the topic. An example of the former is the text by Fox (2008) and of the latter is one by Faraway (2006). Some specialized books emphasize specific aspects of generalized linear models: Hilbe (2007) concentrated on negative binomial models, Cameron and Trivedi (1998) concentrated on count data; Agresti (2002), Long (1997), and Long and Freese (2006) dealt with categorical data; Hosmer and Lemeshow (2000) dealt with logistic regression; Cox and Oakes (1984) and Singer and Willett (2003) dealt with survival data.

A few specialized technical references include Lawless (1987), who discussed negative binomial and mixed Poisson regression; McCullagh (1983), who provided the theory for quasi-likelihood functions; and Pierce and Schafer (1986), Pregibon (1981), and Williams (1987), who all dealt with residuals and outlier detection.

CONCLUSION

Most psychologists are familiar with linear models in the form of regression and ANOVA. Such models are useful as long as the dependent variable is continuous, the relationship is linear, and the residuals are normally distributed and of constant variance. Many situations require a broader class of models, however. For example, the dependent variable may be dichotomous (e.g., success–failure), unordered categorical (Republican, Democrat, independent), ordered categorical (dislike, neutral, like), or counts (number of times a student is disruptive during class). A continuous dependent variable may not be normally distributed (e.g., waiting times might be exponentially distributed, among other possibilities). Survival analysis, both discrete and continuous versions, also require methods outside the usual regression model. GLMs include a generalization of the usual linear model to take into account many of these issues; they do this primarily by allowing different error distributions and various transformations of the dependent variable. This chapter has described and illustrated applications of the GLM, including special cases such as logistic regression, logit models, loglinear models, and Poisson regression.

References

Agresti, A. (2002). *Categorical data analysis* (2nd ed.). New York, NY: Wiley. doi:10.1002/0471249688

Aitkin, M., Francis, B., Hinde, J., & Darnell, R. (2009). *Statistical modelling in R*. New York, NY: Oxford University Press.

Cameron, A. C., & Trivedi, P. K. (1998). *Regression analysis of count data*. Cambridge, England: Cambridge University Press.

Chambers, J. M., & Hastie, T. J. (1992). *Statistical models in S*. Pacific Grove, CA: Wadsworth & Brooks/Cole.

Cox, D. R., & Oakes, D. (1984). *Analysis of survival data*. London, England: Chapman and Hall.

Dobson, A. J., & Barnett, A. (2008). *An introduction to generalized linear models* (3rd ed.). London, England: Chapman & Hall.

Fahrmeir, L., & Tutz, G. (2001). *Multivariate statistical modeling based on generalized linear models* (2nd ed.). New York, NY: Springer-Verlag.

Faraway, J. J. (2006). *Extending the linear model with R: Generalized linear, mixed effects and nonparametric regression*. London, England: Chapman & Hall.

Fox, J. (2008). *Applied regression analysis and generalized linear models* (2nd ed.). Thousand Oaks, CA: Sage.

Gill, J. (2000). *Generalized linear models: A unified approach*. Thousand Oaks, CA: Sage.

Hardin, J. W., & Hilbe, J. W. (2007). *Generalized linear models and extensions* (2nd ed.). College Station, TX: Stata Press.

Hastie, T. J., & Tibshirani, R. J. (1990). *Generalized additive models*. New York, NY: Chapman & Hall.

Hilbe, J. M. (2007). *Negative binomial regression*. Cambridge, England: Cambridge University Press.

Hoffmann, J. P. (2004). *Generalized linear models: An applied approach*. Boston, MA: Pearson, Allyn, & Bacon.

Hosmer, D. W., & Lemeshow, S. (2000). *Applied logistic regression*. New York, NY: Wiley. doi:10.1002/0471722146

Lawless, J. E. (1987). Negative binomial and mixed Poisson regression. *Canadian Journal of Statistics, 15*, 209–225. doi:10.2307/3314912

Lee, Y., & Nelder, J. A. (2001). Hierarchical generalized linear models: A synthesis of generalized linear models, random effect models and structured dispersions. *Biometrika, 88*, 987–1006. doi:10.1093/biomet/88.4.987

Liang, K. Y., & Zeger, S. L. (1986). Longitudinal data analysis using generalized linear models. *Biometrika, 73*, 13–22. doi:10.1093/biomet/73.1.13

Little, R. J. A., & Rubin, D. B. (2002). *Statistical analysis with missing data* (2nd ed.). New York, NY: Wiley.

Long, J. S. (1997). *Regression models for categorical and limited dependent variables*. Thousand Oaks, CA: Sage.

Long, J. S., & Freese, J. (2006). *Regression models for categorical dependent variables using Stata* (2nd ed.). College Station, TX: Stata Press.

McCullagh, P. (1983). Quasi-likelihood functions. *Annals of Statistics, 11*, 59–67. doi:10.1214/aos/1176346056

McCullagh, P., & Nelder, J. A. (1989). *Generalized linear models* (2nd ed.). London, England: Chapman & Hall.

McCulloch, C. E., Searle, S. R., & Neuhaus, J. M. (2008). *Generalized, linear, and mixed models.* New York, NY: Wiley.

Nelder, J. A., & Wedderburn, R. W. M. (1972). Generalized linear models. *Journal of the Royal Statistical Society Series A (General), 135*, 370–384. doi:10.2307/2344614

Pierce, D. A., & Schafer, D. W. (1986). Residuals in generalized linear models. *Journal of the American Statistical Association, 81*, 977–986. doi:10.2307/2289071

Pinheiro, J. C., & Bates, D. M. (2000). *Mixed-effects models in S and S-PLUS.* New York, NY: Springer-Verlag.

Pregibon, D. (1981). Logistic regression diagnostics. *Annals of Statistics, 9*, 705–724. doi:10.1214/aos/1176345513

Rindskopf, D. (1990). Nonstandard log-linear models. *Psychological Bulletin, 108*, 150–162. doi:10.1037/0033-2909.108.1.150

Rindskopf, D. (1992). A general approach to categorical data analysis with missing data, using generalized linear models with composite links. *Psychometrika, 57*, 29–42. doi:10.1007/BF02294657

Singer, J. D., & Willett, J. B. (2003). *Applied longitudinal data analysis: Modeling change and event occurrence.* New York, NY: Oxford University Press.

Skrondal, A., & Rabe-Hesketh, S. (2004). *Generalized latent variable modeling: Multilevel, longitudinal and structural equation models.* Boca Raton, FL: Chapman & Hall/CRC.

Thompson, R., & Baker, R. J. (1981). Composite link functions in generalized linear models. *Journal of the Royal Statistical Society, Series C, 30*, 125–131.

Venables, W. N., & Ripley, B. D. (2002). *Modern applied statistics with S* (4th ed.). New York, NY: Springer.

Williams, D. A. (1987). Generalized linear models diagnostics using the deviance and single case deletions. *Applied Statistics, 36*, 181–191. doi:10.2307/2347550

Zeger, S. L., & Liang, K. Y. (1986). Longitudinal data analysis for discrete and continuous outcomes. *Biometrics, 42*, 121–130. doi:10.2307/2531248

## CHAPTER 10

TAXOMETRICS: CONCEPTUAL AND APPLIED ASPECTS

William M. Grove and Scott I. Vrieze

Taxometrics is directly useful in clinical and counseling psychology. The aim of taxometric procedures is to test a psychological theory positing the existence of a discrete class of individuals, such as individuals afflicted by a disease. In clinical psychology, the existence of discrete mental diseases has long been discussed and debated, and taxometrics was initially developed to test a theory that schizophrenia was a discrete disease caused by a dominant gene (Meehl, 1992). Indeed, whether to characterize various mental illnesses as categorical or dimensional is currently being debated by members of the *Diagnostic and Statistical Manual of Mental Disorders* task force of the American Psychiatric Association (First, 2010), the body that develops highly influential diagnostic criteria used in hospitals and clinics nationwide.

Diseases need not be categorical—hypertension is a good medical example of a *dimensional* disease, in which everyone in the population is hypertensive to some degree, and there is no natural bright line that distinguishes those who are hypertensive from those who are nonhypertensives (Murphy, 1964). Height is another example. Height is a dimensional entity because people vary from the tall to the short and everywhere in between. There exist taxa within the height dimension, however. Dwarfism is not simply the lower end of the height spectrum, but rather it represents a class of individuals suffering from one of many diseases (e.g., achondroplasia) that cause extremely short stature. The possibility of categorical structure is not limited to disease but also arises in other areas of social science: industrial–organization

(possibility of distinct patterns of vocational interests), social (possibility of different types of social interaction patterns), and personality (e.g., Jung's theory of types [Jung, 1934–1954/1981] vs. the Big Five factors of personality [Norman, 1963]). In sum, taxometric approaches are applicable whenever one is confronted with a theory positing the existence of class structure. It is applicable in any case in which other class-based statistical methods are used, such as latent class and latent profile analysis (Heinen, 1996) or mixture models (McLachlan & Peel, 2000).

Taxometrics can be distinguished from other forms of finite mixture model such as latent class analysis and other parametric mixture models. The major differing features between taxometrics and parametric mixture models are that (a) taxometrics makes weaker statistical assumptions of the data than does a parametric mixture model, and (b) taxometric procedures include a number of tests of model validity, collectively called *consistency tests*. (We discuss consistency tests for various taxometric procedures in the section Example Application.) Parametric finite mixture models have no consistency tests to make theory testing as rigorous as possible and to provide evidence for or against taxonicity. Instead, fit statistics such as the Bayesian information criterion (Schwarz, 1978) and others are used to determine whether the data are categorical or dimensional (e.g., for applications, see Krueger, Markon, Patrick, & Iacono, 2005; Kuo, Aggen, Prescott, Kendler, & Neale, 2008; Muthén, 2006).

Why should one care to have an answer to the question, "Do these data contain a taxon and its

DOI: 10.1037/13621-010
APA Handbook of Research Methods in Psychology: Vol. 3. Data Analysis and Research Publication, H. Cooper (Editor-in-Chief)

complement class, or do these data instead fit a dimensional model?" There are three reasons to seek answers to this question. The first is *truth-seeking*, that is, we wish to have valid statements in our theory about the latent structure of the domain. The second reason is *assessment*, that is, the clinical or actuarial reasoning processes for finding out whether a given observation comes from a categorical set-up or instead represents an example of data following a dimensional model (e.g., factor analysis). The third reason *causal*, in that there are intuitive causal frameworks that naturally give rise to taxa. Taxometric method is designed to test psychological theories that posit such causes contributing to individual differences (Meehl, 1977). For example, there is a gene for early-onset Alzheimer's disease on chromosome 21; there is an allele at that locus that quite substantially increases the risk of early-onset Alzheimer's (Rovelet-Lecrux et al., 2006). Biological sex is taxonic as a rule, with quite a number of measures reliably differentiating men from women. In psychiatry, Rett's disorder (National Institute for Neurological Disorders and Stroke, 2010) appears to be strongly taxonic. Alzheimer's disease, biological sex, and Rett's syndrome, among many others, are noteworthy objects of assessment, in which case a taxonic structure, when it is correctly identified, is primarily caused by a categorical etiological agent.

Use of taxometric procedures is rising. We scanned the Social Science Citation Index for articles with *taxon* or *taxometric* in the title from 1975 to 2009 and found 158 articles. Papers before 1975 did not have online versions of articles, so we chose to look only at the post-1974 era. The rise in use is plotted in Figure 10.1. Although it is unclear why taxometrics is being used more often, it is clear that the method is coming into wide use, with no sign of leveling off. (For further reading, see the partial list of taxometric studies compiled in Ruscio, 2011.)

HOW TAXOMETRICS FITS INTO RESEARCH PROGRAMS BY PROVIDING RISKY THEORY TESTS

The problem taxometrics tries to solve is to give a strong test (high power to falsify) to theories that

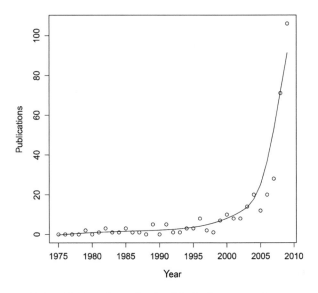

FIGURE 10.1. Growth of published taxometric articles over time.

postulate either a taxonic latent structure or a dimensional one. Several people, including the founder of taxometric method, Paul Meehl, have contributed to the current repertoire of taxometric procedures (e.g., MAXCOV, MAMBAC, and MAXSLOPE, all described in detail in this chapter; see Grove, 2004; Ruscio, Haslam, & Ruscio, 2006; Waller & Meehl, 1998). At present, eight taxometric procedures are discussed in the literature; numerous consistency tests are used within each procedure to attempt to falsify the categorical hypothesis.

Meehl (1978, 1990) was a neo-Popperian in his philosophy of science, emphasizing theory falsification. According to this view, it is more important for a researcher to try (and, one hopes, fail) to find evidence contrary to one's theory than to find evidence that is consistent with a theory. When no such evidence can be found, the theory is relatively well corroborated. When contrary evidence is found, the theory is falsified (at least partially) and must be amended to conform to the contrary evidence. If no amendments can be made to explain the negative falsifying results, the theory is considered falsified.

In this vein, Meehl (1992) valued consistency tests greatly. Consistency tests are a strong way of putting the falsifiability criterion to work. In essence, one attempts to obtain, through as diverse methods as possible, multiple estimates of each parameter for a given model. If all estimates agree within an acceptable range, the parameter is considered to represent something stable about nature, even if that stable aspect of nature remains to be elucidated.[1]

TAXOMETRIC PROCEDURES

In this section we briefly catalogue many of the present taxometric procedures. Computer code for each procedure can be obtained from Grove or from Ruscio (2011). All analyses described are taken from Ruscio's code, which is readily available and well described in his book (Ruscio et al., 2006) and modified for present purpose.

The easiest way, we think, to approach a nontechnical introduction to taxometric procedures is to pursue an analogy (for technical introductions, see Ruscio et al., 2006; Waller & Meehl, 1998). The analogy likens certain taxometric procedures to the analysis of variance (ANOVA) for two groups and (at least) three variables, X, Y, and Z. In ANOVA, one partitions the total sum of squares into one or two components measuring within-class variability on X, Y, or Z, and the other component measuring between-class variability on the same variable. Taking X as the variable of interest, in taxometric language we have

$$SS_{XT} = (n_t/N)\, SS_{Xwt} + (n_c/N)\, SS_{Xwc}$$
$$+ (n_t n_c/N^2)\, (\mu_{Xt} - \mu_{Xc})^2. \qquad (1)$$

Here, SS_{XT} is the total population sum of squares, SS_{Xwt} is the population within-taxon sum of squares on X, and SS_{Xwc} is the population within-complement-class sum of squares. μ_{Xt} is the taxon mean on X, and μ_{Xc} is the corresponding complement class mean in the population. n_t is the number of sample observations in the taxon, n_c the corresponding n for the complement class, and N

the total number of observations. Using $P = (n_t/N)$ and $Q = (n_c/N)$ as abbreviations for the population values, P is the taxon base rate and $Q = 1 - P$ is the complement class base rate. Rearranging, one obtains, with a few simple algebraic manipulations the following:

$$SS_{XT}/N = \sigma^2_{XT} = P\, \sigma^2_{Xwt} + Q\, \sigma^2_{Xwc}$$
$$+ PQ\, (\mu_{Xt} - \mu_{Xc})^2. \qquad (2)$$

Equation 2 is valid in the whole population. It partitions the total covariance between two variables in a population, or a sample from that population, including samples defined by having observations' scores on a third variable fall within a certain interval.

Now consider calculating the variance of X conditional on the value of Z, assuming that X, Y, and Z all discriminate the taxon from the complement class by a nontrivial amount; Z orders the conditional variances on the local, intermediate value of P, namely, p_k where k indexes the kth subinterval on Z. Common widths for these intervals are $z_{k+1} - z_k = (1/4)\sigma^2_z$ giving constant-width intervals. Sliding windows of constant size would also be applicable in place of constant-width nonoverlapping intervals. Because Z discriminates taxon from complement class, as Z goes up so does the local probability of taxon membership, p_k, the base rate of taxon membership in the kth window. If Z has adequate range, and adequately discriminates taxon from complement class, p_k will approximate zero at the low end of Z and one at the high end.

Now consider a direct analogy to Equation 2, substituting for variance terms the covariance between X and Y, both overall and in intervals on Z, for the variance. One obtains

$$\sigma_{XY} = P\, \sigma_{XYt} + Q\, \sigma_{XYc} + PQ\, (\mu_{Xt} - \mu_{Xc})(\mu_{Yt} - \mu_{Yc}). \qquad (3)$$

---

[1]As the most popular and illustrative example of a strong consistency test, consider the quantification of *Avogadro's number*, the number of molecules in a mole of a gas at standard temperature and pressure. There are at present more than a dozen mathematically and empirically distinguishable ways to estimate this constant (Perrin, 1919/1990). All of these methods give values of about 4 to 6 × 10²³. When Perrin (1919/1990) found that he could, by several of these different methods, arrive at highly similar estimates, it was enough to make him adopt the theory that atoms are real. The reasoning proceeds approximately as follows: One can either conclude that a natural law is taking place, which results in the similar numbers, or that the results are coincidental. As more and more different consistency tests are obtained and are mutually supportive, it becomes less rational to attribute the similarities to coincidence. The fact that these starkly different methods yield very similar values of Avogadro's number (in relation to the size of the figure being estimated) is a powerful support in the form of a consistency test. Taxometricians regard different taxometric procedures as analogues to the various ways of estimating Avogadro's number.

Equation 3 underlies the original taxometric procedure developed by Meehl (Meehl & Yonce, 1996), MAXCOV standing for MAXimizing the COVariance. One graphs the total covariance of X and Y as a function of Z. One travels along Z from lower to higher intervals, until a peak of XY-covariance is reached and the covariance is about to decline. The peak-covariance interval is what Meehl called the *hitmax cut*. This value refers to the fact that if one cuts the Z-distribution at the point of maximum covariance, classifying higher observations into the taxon and lower observations into the complement class, a researcher can define a maximum classification accuracy on the basis of Z. One then replaces, say, X with Z, and graphs the YZ-covariance as a function of X, followed by Y being the new Z, graphing the XZ-covariance. Each one of these furnishes us with a new optimal cutscore for each new variable combination. If there are more than three variables, one cycles through all possible triplets, where one variable takes the role of Z, and two others have their covariance graphed against the Z variable. Covariance$(X, Y \mid Z)$ is the same as Covariance$(Y, X \mid Z)$, so only one graph is generated for both triplets. The size of the covariance in the hitmax interval allows estimation of the taxon base rate P. Substitution of this derived value into the total covariance formula—with X, Y as the covarying variables and Z as the third variable—and then proceeding to generate all other distinct triplets in turn yields a set of simultaneous equations that can be solved to yield estimates of means for the taxon and complement class on each of the variables X, Y, and Z (in our notation this corresponds to μ_{Xt}, μ_{Xc}, μ_{Yt}, μ_{Yc}, and μ_{Zt}, μ_{Zc}. Subtraction of estimated PQ $(\mu_{Xt} - \mu_{Xc})(\mu_{Yt} - \mu_{Yc})$ from σ^2_T and substitution of P and $Q = 1 - P$ obtains estimates of the within-class covariances. These multiple estimates can be then compared and represent one of many possible consistency tests.

A consistency test is a way to subject a substantive hypothesis to a rigorous test by deducing as many mathematically independently derived point or interval-valued predictions of the taxon base rate P as well as within-taxon and within-complement-class means and covariances for the indicator variables X, Y, and Z. In short, one can calculate independent estimates of model parameters (such as the base rate) and then see whether those different estimates agree. If they do agree, it is up to the researcher to conclude whether that agreement is merely by chance or arises because the taxonic model has fit. The closer the agreement, the harder it is to justify it as chance occurrence. To take the simplest example of a consistency test, we expect three estimates of P from MAXCOV, one for each of X, Y, and Z, to be close to each other if a taxon really exists. Other consistency tests involve comparing parameter estimates across procedures. For example, MAMBAC and MAXCOV, two independent taxometric procedures, yield estimates of means and standard deviations (SDs) of the taxon and complement class for all indicator variables (e.g., X, Y, and Z). If these estimates agree across MAMBAC and MAXCOV, the taxonic hypothesis is further corroborated; if they disagree, the hypothesis is falsified. The main consistency test, however, is graphical. In the presence of a taxon, the MAXCOV curve is bell-shaped. In the absence of a taxon, the bell-shaped curve is not obtained. Instead, the curve is expected to be flat.[2]

Niels Waller, one of Meehl's students, cowrote a book with Meehl on taxometric method (Waller & Meehl, 1998). In that book, two new procedures are introduced. The first is called MAXEIG, standing for MAXimum EIGenvalue, which is essentially a multivariate generalization of MAXCOV. A set of $K - 1$ variables are analyzed by principal components in intervals on the Kth variable, and the value on the Kth variable that maximizes the first eigenvalue of the matrix containing all other $K - 1$ l variables is found. This in turn allows estimation of all model parameters.

MAMBAC (Meehl & Yonce, 1994), the next-developed procedure after MAXCOV, is a consistency test for MAXCOV that was later treated as an

---

[2]Specifically, if a symmetric unmixed distribution is present, one expects a flat graph. If a right-skewed unmixed distribution is present (e.g., an appropriately parameterized gamma distribution, or chi square with low degrees of freedom), one expects something between the right limb of a quadratic curve, on the one hand, and a curve that resembles a hyperbola on the other hand. (Meehl in his writings derived, and simulated, findings for admixed or dimensional normal distributions and so did not report the nonflat graphs obtainable from nonnormal dimensional data, e.g., X, Y, and Z being a function of a single common factor that is gamma distributed.)

independently valid taxometric procedure (Meehl, 1965). MAMBAC stands for Mean above Minus [Mean] Below a Cut, and this acronym outlines the essential feature of the procedure. MAMBAC works with just two taxon-versus-complement class discriminating variables, X and Y. In MAMBAC, a cut is moved along Y, and the observations are classified into the low category (complement class) if the Y-score is below the cut and into the high category (taxon) if the Y-score is higher than the cut. One plots the difference in mean of X between the high and low observations on X, as a function of increasing Y-score. If a taxon is present and X and Y nontrivially discriminate taxon from complement class, then the MAMBAC graph will form a "sombrero" shape fairly similar to a taxonic MAXCOV curve.

Grove (2004) and Grove and Meehl (1993) contributed a regression-based taxometric procedure, dubbed MAXSLOPE, to denote the search for the maximum slope of the smoothed, interpolated Y-on-X nonlinear regression. A nonparametric curve smoother is applied to the regression to regularize and interpolate the regression; the derivative of the regression slope is then estimated by finite differences. The point is to obtain (if there is a taxon) a peaked sombrero shape (visually similar, but not identical, to either MAXCOV or MAMBAC curves) and a linear regression otherwise.

The analysis of these numerous curves is visual rather than statistical. Although seemingly crude, Meehl and Yonce (1996) reported that individuals familiar with taxometrics can distinguish between taxonic and dimensional MAXCOV and MAMBAC curves, with accuracy greater than 99%. Mechanizing curve inspection is one challenge facing taxometrics.

TO WHAT TYPES OF DATA MAY TAXOMETRIC METHOD BE APPLIED?

For examples of taxometric applications, see the list compiled by Ruscio (2011). The interested reader can find many empirical applications and methodological articles to guide in data set construction (for simulated–data methodological explorations) and programs that implement taxometric procedures.

The requirements of suitable data differ by taxometric procedure. MAXCOV and MAXEIG require at least three quasi-continuous or ordinal indicators (e.g., at least seven distinct scores on each variable, with more possible scores providing a big plus, for this allows the MAXCOV and other curves to be traced in detail). MAMBAC and MAXSLOPE require at least two quasi-continuous variables. Ordered categorical (polychoric) variables will generally also work, although rating scales with less than 20 values should be avoided. Variables should be selected to be as valid and theoretically justified as possible. There is in principle no limit to the number of observed variables, and the R code Ruscio has written, along with our own R code, for performing taxometric analyses allows truly gigantic numbers of variables (e.g., the only restriction is that the data matrix must be less than 2 gigabytes). In general, the more variables the better because with more variables more consistency tests can be performed (i.e., more independent parameter estimates can be derived). Here, however, is an important caveat: Poorly validated observed variables should not be used just to increase the number of variables available.

Sample sizes should be large (e.g., > 500) for the taxometric method to be used because the equations that get solved in various methods equate sample values to population values, mostly ignoring sampling error. Sample sizes of 1,000 to 2,000 have been used, and the more is merrier because larger samples make smoothed MAXCOV and other curves more "lump free" ($N = 500$ is near the point at which the sample would be labeled as barely sufficient). Ruscio et al. (2006) dealt with the sampling error issue by bootstrapping the taxometric analysis.[3] Ruscio also used bootstrapping to generate data samples of the same size, mean, and variance to evaluate under what conditions (taxonic or continuous) the root-mean-square error between the generated sample and the actual data sample are as small as possible.

---

[3]*Bootstrapping* is a statistical technique involving numerous, for example, $B = 1,000$, repeated samplings with replacement from the data sample, calculating a given statistical analysis for each sample and averaging the parameter estimates across bootstrap samples (for more detail, see Volume 2, Chapter 22, this handbook).

This procedure is considered to be a consistency test; that is, in the presence of a taxon, simulated taxonic data should produce procedure curves (e.g., MAXCOV curves) more similar than simulated dimensional (unifactorial) data MAXCOV curves.

We prefer a MAXCOV or MAMBAC analysis that is based on variables with at least 25 possible scores, spelling out our meaning of *quasi-continuous*. In this way, fine-grained curve shapes can be obtained for inspection.

The biggest single desideratum for taxometric method is a substantive theory that makes both the taxonic and dimensional analyses flow as predictions from the theory. MAXCOV, MAMBAC, and other taxometric approaches are not exploratory data analysis techniques but rather are ways of testing the predictions about a categorical theory (Meehl, 1992).

EXAMPLE APPLICATION

To illustrate the methodology, we illustrate MAXCOV and MAMBAC with a simplistic, short, and concrete example. Assume that clinical depression is a taxon, and three measures exist that discriminate to some extent between depressed and nondepressed patients (e.g., scores on three widely used depression inventories). Call the measures X, Y, and Z to be consistent with the technical descriptions used in this chapter. Each of these fictitious measures ranges in score from 0 to 10, and each has been extensively validated. Depressed patients score on average a 6, with a standard deviation of 2. The distributions of depressed patients' scores appear approximately normal. Community controls score on average 4, with a standard deviation of 2. Thus, for each measure, there is a standardized mean separation of 1 standard deviation. It is unknown, however, whether depression is a taxon. It may be that depressed patients score higher than community controls simply because they are selected for depression, and thus people with high dysphoria make up the patient population, whereas few with sufficiently high dysphoria to be diagnosable as patients exist in the community control population.

A picture of one of the generated test-score distributions is given in Figure 10.2. The test scores are plotted as smoothed histograms for ease of visualization.

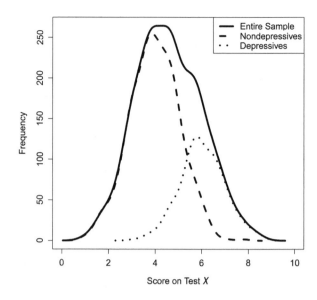

FIGURE 10.2. Smoothed histograms for simulated taxonic data.

Note that three distributions are plotted. First, the admixed distribution, the distribution of the entire sample without regard for taxonicity, is displayed. Notice that it appears normally distributed (perhaps somewhat skewed and platykurtic) with a small hump on the right-hand side at approximately $X = 5$. Also depicted are the depressed patients in our community sample (30%) and the nondepressed patients (70%). This explains why the nondepressed distribution is so much larger (because it is composed of 700 individuals), whereas the depressed distribution smaller (it is composed of 300 individuals). Thus, the base rate of depression in this fictional community sample is 30%.

An application of MAXCOV would proceed in the following way. A researcher would obtain data on a large number of individuals. A good sample size might be 1,000, as in our simulated data. If possible, data from a community-representative sample would be best, assuming that base rates of taxon membership (if a taxon exists—in general this is not known with certainty, but here we have the luxury of having assumed it at the outset) are sufficiently high in the community, which may not be the case. Choose one of the depression measures, say Z. Sort the data set from low to high on Z. Take the lowest, say, 50 individuals on Z (this number may vary depending on the sample size). Calculate the covariance between X and Y for these 50 individuals.

Plot this covariance as a function of Z (with Z values on the *x*-axis and covariance on the *y*-axis). Move up one observation, so the window on Z consists of the second through the 51st individual on sorted Z. Calculate the covariance. Plot the covariance. Repeat until the window on Z has moved as high as possible (i.e., observation 950 to 1,000 on sorted Z). A MAXCOV plot for our taxonic simulated data is displayed on the right-hand side of Figure 10.3.

Note the peakedness of the curve. It is not entirely bell-shaped because of the 30% base rate. This causes the hitmax cut (i.e., the cutscore on the input-observed variable that results in the greatest fraction of correct classifications—located at the peak of the MAXCOV curve) to be shifted rightward, and the MAXCOV curve does not have a chance to descend to zero covariance. With smaller base rates, the peak would be shifted even further right. For low base rates (e.g., 5%), taxometrics is not applicable, unless the mean separation between the taxon and complement class is quite large (e.g., 4 standard deviations). It is entirely possible to fail to find a taxon in taxometrics (e.g., by curve shape or consistency test failure) not because the data are continuous but rather because the taxon is too small to be

detectable. For example, if *N* = 500 and the base rate is .01, we would only expect five individuals in the taxon. This low number will be subject to extreme sampling error, and because taxometric procedures are in general windowed approaches, the number of individuals in the taxon within a particular window may be even less than five. In this case, the base rate would be prohibitively low to conduct taxometrics.

MAXCOV is not the only taxometric procedure applicable to our depression data. An available consistency test is simple: Use another taxometric procedure—if results for the other procedure are the same as the original procedure, then conclusions can be drawn with even more confidence. Here we also apply MAMBAC to the data to observe consistency between MAMBAC and MAXCOV. A sample MAMBAC curve for our taxonic data is depicted on the right-hand side of Figure 10.4. Here we notice again the peakedness. The peak for the MAMBAC curve is shifted far to the right, however, to the extent at which it never really descends.

Even in this example, with high base rate and a reasonable mean separation between taxon and complement class (1 standard deviation), the taxometric graphs do not always give clear-cut tests of

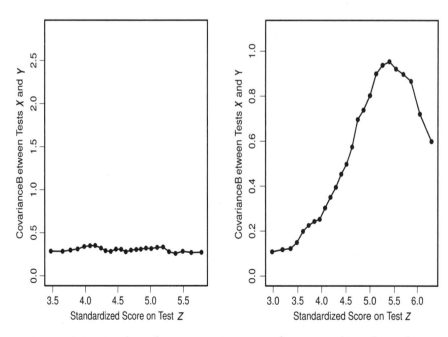

FIGURE 10.3. On the right is a MAXCOV curve for taxonic data. The peak is shifted rightward because the base rate is .30, less than .50. On the left is a MAXCOV curve for dimensional data. This is a flat graph as expected when the data arise from a common factor model. Note the difference in scaling on the *y*-axes—this does not affect interpretation.

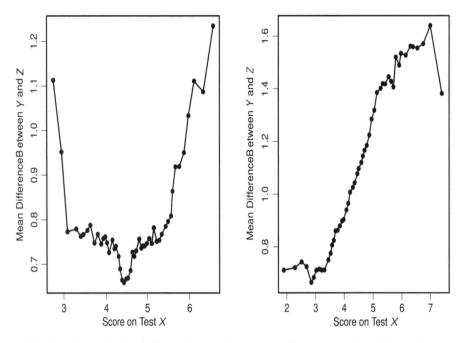

FIGURE 10.4. On the right is the MAMBAC curve for taxonic data. The peak is shifted rightward because the base rate is .30, less than .50. This curve is not strongly suggestive for taxonicity, despite the presence of a sizable taxon in the simulated data. On the left is the MAMBAC curve for dimensional data. This is a flat graph as expected when the data conform to a common factor model. Note the difference in scaling on the *y*-axes—this does not affect interpretation.

taxometric hypotheses. This is one reason to use other consistency tests (such as base rate, mean, and variance estimates) for each complement class and taxon. For example, MAXCOV produced three estimates of the base rate for the taxonic data of .23, .27, and .23 (with true value = .3), estimated complement class means of 4.1, 4.1, and 4.1 (with true value = 4), and estimated taxon means of 6.2, 6.2, and 6.2 (with true value = 6). MAMBAC produced multiple estimates similarly close to the true values. Thus, even though the MAMBAC curve shape is ambiguous, the parameter estimates all agree and support the conclusion that the curve would be shifted rightward (because of the low estimated base rate), and the taxonic hypothesis is corroborated in this simulated data set. The basic rationale is that if all the parameter estimates agree, then the underlying model (i.e., of an admixed distribution of taxon members and complement class members) is verisimilar in an important way. In short, the parameter estimates all agree because they are estimating something real that actually exists. If, on the other hand, the MAMBAC curve suggested dimensionality

(i.e., was U-shaped, as opposed to being ambiguous on the point), then conclusions would be more tentative. One can begin to see the attractiveness of having multiple consistency tests in hand to check model assumptions and provide mutual support for or against the taxonic hypothesis. Model assumption checking often includes ensuring that the estimated base rate is large enough for taxometrics to work (e.g., > 5%). In MAXCOV, an assumption that may require checking is whether within-taxon and within-complement class correlations between all pairwise sets of indicator variables are close to zero, as required by the traditional MAXCOV method (note that the generalized MAXCOV [Meehl & Yonce, 1996] does not have this assumption).

Using the means, standard deviations, and correlations of our taxonic data, we also constructed a dimensional data set. This data set was multivariate normal with no admixture. In this case, one expects a flat graph from MAXCOV (left-hand side of Figure 10.3) and a U-shaped graph from MAMBAC (left-hand side of Figure 10.4). They are indeed flat and U-shaped, respectively.

For more examples of curve shapes, consistency tests, and their interpretations, see Ruscio et al. (2006); Meehl and Yonce (1994, 1996); and Waller and Meehl (1998).

DATA SUITED FOR TAXOMETRIC ANALYSIS

We will explore this issue by looking at the MAXCOV–HITMAX taxometric procedure. Most other procedures have requirements that are quite similar.

First, let us point out that the "requirements" discussed here are chiefly desiderata and not requirements in the strict sense of the term. A strict requirement for MAXCOV, MAMBAC, and MAXSLOPE is that for each variable, the taxon and complement class distributions are unimodal and cross only once. Other desiderata for taxometric analyses include the following items.

1. Because the whole distribution contributes information to the question of taxonicity (existence of a taxon vs. a complement class), the total sample N is important. We have not established a critical threshold N, but we would have misgivings about analyzing a data set with less than 500 observations, with the N desired for analysis going up as the difference between taxon and complement class means decreases. $N > 1,000$ is ideal.
2. Consider potential values of the conditioning variable Z as z_1, z_2, z_3. Rank these from low to high. There should be a minimum number of distinct potential values. We have performed successful analyses with as few as seven to 10 possible values, but we would be concerned about lower values than these.
3. Each potential z value has a certain number of observations on X, Y, for each value of Z. If one printed a histogram of Z, the height of a particular histogram bar would be equal to this number, differing from bar to bar. We would recommend 50 or more observations per bar, recognizing that in some data sets the *tail* bars may have fewer observations than this, even if the total N is high. If one programs, for example, MAXCOV by sliding a moving window of width 50 from the bottom of the Z distribution to the 50 highest

observations (in terms of value on Z), this criterion will automatically be satisfied.
4. If the data are not quasi-continuous as outlined above (e.g., 1–7 ratings), then another mixture model such as latent class analysis should be considered instead of Meehlian taxometrics. (For latent class analysis, one would dichotomize the variables if they are, e.g., 1–7 ratings.)
5. Mean separation between the two latent categories should be as great as possible. We have successfully performed analyses with X- and Y-separations between group means as low as 2 within-class standard deviations, but ideal results come forth when the separations exceed 3 standard deviations at least for some variables.
6. *Nuisance* correlations (within-class correlations between all pairwise sets of indicator variables) should not be large. We recommend rs less than .35 (e.g., $r(X,Y)$ for complement class members only), to the extent that one can preliminarily put the observations into latent classes and then estimate the within-class correlations.

CRITICISMS OF TAXOMETRIC PROCEDURES

We now address four objections to taxometrics that have been raised in the literature or in conversation with the authors.

1. Taxometrics, in particular MAXCOV and MAMBAC, is based on assumptions that are insufficiently strong to derive the empirical results, which, in turn, are used as evidence that a data set contains a taxon–complement class admixture (Maraun & Slaney, 2005).
2. Using taxometric procedures results throws away valuable information because the parameter estimates generated are not statistically sufficient.
3. Taxometric procedures do not provide maximum-likelihood estimates (MLEs) for their corresponding parameters, violating the likelihood principle. Instead, taxometrics can be seen as a semiparametric estimation method. This is because assumptions underlying the different procedures do not require a particular parametric latent or error distribution.

4. In substantive applications, the primary evidence garnered for support of a taxonic hypothesis is from a curve shape. These curves must be eye-balled, and despite some evidence that eyeballs work well for this purpose, there is no way objectively to determine fit or lack thereof.

The first criticism is highly technical and requires mathematical proofs to controvert, but we note that Grove, Waller, and Vrieze (2010) have shown that an assumption set defensibly attributable to Meehl does suffice to derive the predicted taxonic and dimensional curve shapes Meehl portrayed. In sum, this discussion is about what mathematical assumptions are required to make taxometrics work. Grove et al. contended that the assumption set is semiparametric, whereas Maraun and Slaney (2005) contended that an assumption that indicators variables are normally distributed is required.

The next two objections are that taxometric procedures MAXCOV and MAMBAC do not produce MLEs of the relevant distributional parameters. They can be answered together. Relative efficiency (essentially, precision) is unproven for Meehl's procedures, but Meehl had theory–inference tests other than sufficient statistics to offer: the consistency tests. Our answer to the likelihood argument is that we consider the taxometrics approach to be a semi-parametric mixture model. Meehl was willing to give up some efficiency (precision) of parameter estimates such as means and base rates in trade for having a procedure that works with a wide array of mixture distributions, not just normal mixtures or gamma mixtures, and so on. To get MLEs, one must have the (unknown) probability density function (e.g., normal) of both taxon and complement class. Indeed, parameter estimates, and their associated confidence intervals, are interpretable only if the true model family is under consideration (e.g., that the taxon and complement class distributions are normal in a Gaussian mixture model). We conjecture that the true parametric model is never under consideration in all but the most trivial applied psychological problems. To quote an eminent statistician: "The idea that complex physical, biological, or sociological systems can be exactly described by a few formulae is patently absurd" (Cox, 1995, p. 456).

A mixture of normals is exactly one such simple formula, and psychological phenomena are assuredly complex systems. Hence, although a parametric statistical model's confidence interval may appear narrow, the true coverage is unknown and inestimable. Any observed confidence interval from a statistical model should be viewed as quite conservative because the model is never actually correct, and confidence intervals depend on the model.

The next issue is related to finding false positives and discriminating between taxonic and dimensional curves. Discovering automated ways to quantify curve fit is an important next step in developing taxometric method. Currently, all curve discrimination is conducted visually. Some may obtain good classification of taxonic and dimensional data (e.g., the 96%–99% rates discussed in the section Taxometric Procedures); however, even if good visual discrimination is possible, it does not lend itself to Monte Carlo simulation, the bread and butter of taxometric validation studies.

The small semiparametric assumption set required for MAXCOV, for example, makes the issue of curve shape complex. That is, MAXCOV and MAMBAC curve shapes depend on the underlying mixture distributions. A mixture of normals will result in different MAXCOV curves than a mixture of skewed distributions. An analytically derived curve shape would be an impossible task because sufficient statistics for each parametric family are different, and the curve shape depends on those sufficient statistics (e.g., sufficient statistics for multivariate normals are a mean vector and covariance matrix). A large number of distributional admixtures can be handled by MAXCOV and will result in widely different, but valid, peaked MAXCOV graphs. Even within a particular distributional family, say a normal admixture, the variety of parameters (e.g., mean, variance, base rate) and range of values they can assume will affect the MAXCOV curve in many ways. For this reason, we conjecture that a tractable analytical formula for the expected MAXCOV graph shape will never be found. Advances in machine-learning techniques, such as neural nets (Bishop, 2005) and random forests (Hastie, Tibshirani, & Friedman, 2009), can be used to discriminate between taxonic and dimensional MAXCOV curves in a training data set. Then a new, theretofore unseen, graph can be presented to the algorithm, which attempts to classify it as dimensional or taxonic on the basis of the training runs. Major advances have been made in the field of handwritten letter identification, which is likely more difficult to decipher than MAXCOV or MAMBAC curves. The machine-learning algorithm (e.g., neural net), once properly trained, can then be applied in simulation studies to automatically classify a curve as taxonic or dimensional. This approach would allow researchers to conduct gigantic simulation studies and quantify the results quickly, easily, and replicably. Applied taxometricians could use the machine-learning algorithm in their applied work, with full knowledge of its expected classification error.

CONCLUSION

Taxometric research has exploded in the past decade. Much of taxometrics remains to be developed, however, especially quantifying graphs and formal test statistics for consistency tests (which as of now must be subjectively interpreted). We have offered an overview of the methodological research to date for graduate students and other researchers who are unfamiliar MAXCOV and MAMBAC, the two most popular taxometric procedures. We emphasized the importance of consistency tests, a weak spot in most applied taxometrics papers submitted for publication. We have indicated, finally and briefly, some future directions for taxometrics research.

References

Bishop, C. M. (2005). *Neural networks for pattern recognition.* New York, NY: Oxford University Press.

Cox, D. R. (1995). Model uncertainty, data mining, and statistical inference [Discussion]. *Journal of the Royal Statistical Society Series A (General), 158,* 419–466.

First, M. B. (2010). *Dimensional aspects of psychiatric diagnosis (July 26–28, 2006).* Retrieved from http://www.dsm5.org/Research/Pages/DimensionalAspectsofPsychiatricDiagnosis(July 26–28,2006).aspx

Grove, W. M. (2004). The MAXSLOPE taxometric procedure: Mathematical derivation, parameter estimation, consistency tests. *Psychological Reports, 95,* 517–550.

Grove, W. M., & Meehl, P. E. (1993). Simple regression-based procedures for taxometric investigations. *Psychological Reports, 73*(Suppl. 1), 707–737.

Grove, W. M., Waller, N. G., & Vrieze, S. I. (2010). *The minimal necessary conditions for the validity of the MAXCOV taxometric procedure.* Manuscript in preparation.

Hastie, T., Tibshirani, R., & Friedman, J. (2009). *The elements of statistical learning: Data mining, inference, and prediction.* New York, NY: Springer.

Heinen, T. (1996). *Latent class and discrete latent trait models: Similarities and differences.* Thousand Oaks, CA: Sage.

Jung, C. G. (1981). *Collected works: Vol. 9. The archetypes and the collective unconscious* (2nd ed.). Princeton, NJ: Bollingen. (Original work published 1934–1954)

Krueger, R. F., Markon, K. E., Patrick, C. J., & Iacono, W. G. (2005). Externalizing psychopathology in adulthood: A dimensional-spectrum conceptualization and its implications for *DSM–V. Journal of Abnormal Psychology, 114,* 537–550. doi:10.1037/0021-843X.114.4.537

Kuo, P. H., Aggen, S. H., Prescott, C. A., Kendler, K. S., & Neale, M. C. (2008). Using a factor mixture modeling approach in alcohol dependence in a general population sample. *Drug and Alcohol Dependence, 98,* 105–114. doi:10.1016/j.drugalcdep.2008.04.018

Maraun, M., & Slaney, K. (2005). An analysis of Meehl's MAXCOV-HITMAX procedure for the case of continuous indicators. *Multivariate Behavioral Research, 40,* 489–518. doi:10.1207/s15327906mbr4004_5

McLachlan, G., & Peel, D. (2000). *Finite mixture models.* New York, NY: Wiley-Interscience.

Meehl, P. E. (1965). *Detecting latent clinical taxa by fallible quantitative indicators lacking an accepted criterion* [Technical report]. University of Minnesota. Research Laboratories of the Department of Psychiatry, Minneapolis.

Meehl, P. E. (1977). Specific etiology and other forms of strong influence: Some quantitative meanings. *Journal of Medicine and Philosophy, 2,* 33–53.

Meehl, P. E. (1978). Theoretical risks and tabular asterisks: Sir Karl, Sir Ronald, and the slow progress of soft psychology. *Journal of Consulting and Clinical Psychology, 46,* 806–834. doi:10.1037/0022-006X.46.4.806

Meehl, P. E. (1990). Appraising and amending theories: The strategy of Lakatosian defense and two principles that warrant using it. *Psychological Inquiry, 1,* 108–141. doi:10.1207/s15327965pli0102_1

Meehl, P. E. (1992). Factors and taxa, traits and types, differences of degree and differences in kind. *Journal of Personality, 60,* 117–174. doi:10.1111/j.1467-6494.1992.tb00269.x

Meehl, P. E., & Yonce, L. J. (1994). Taxometric analysis: I. Detecting taxonicity with two quantitative indicators using means and below a sliding cut (MAMBAC procedure). *Psychological Reports, 74,* 1059–1274.

Meehl, P. E., & Yonce, L. (1996). Taxometric analysis: II. Detecting taxonicity using covariance of two quantitative indicators in successful intervals of a third indicator (MAXCOV procedure). *Psychological Reports, 78,* 1091–1227.

Murphy, E. A. (1964). One cause? Many causes? The argument from the bimodal distribution. *Journal of Chronic Diseases, 17,* 301–324. doi:10.1016/0021-9681(64)90073-6

Muthén, B. (2006). Should substance use disorders be considered as categorical or dimensional? *Addiction, 101,* 6–16. doi:10.1111/j.1360-0443.2006.01583.x

National Institute for Neurological Disorders and Stroke. (2010). *Rett syndrome fact sheet.* Retrieved from http://www.ninds.nih.gov/disorders/rett/detail_rett.htm

Norman, W. T. (1963). Toward an adequate taxonomy of personality attributes: Replicated factor structure in peer-nominated personality ratings. *Journal of Abnormal and Social Psychology, 66,* 574–583. doi:10.1037/h0040291

Perrin, J. (1990). *Atoms* (D. Hammick, Trans.). Woodbridge, CT: Ox Bow Press. (Original work published 1919)

Rovelet-Lecrux, A., Hannequin, D., Raux, G., Le Meur, N., Laquerriere, A., Vital, A., . . . Campion, D. (2006). APP locus duplication causes autosomal dominant early-onset Alzheimer disease with cerebral amyloid angiopathy. *Nature Genetics, 38,* 24–26. doi:10.1038/ng1718

Ruscio, J. (2011). *Taxometrics references.* Retrieved from http://www.tcnj.edu/~ruscio/Taxometrics%20References.pdf

Ruscio, J., Haslam, N., & Ruscio, A. M. (2006). *Introduction to the taxometric method: A practical guide.* Mahwah, NJ: Erlbaum.

Schwarz, G. E. (1978). Estimating the dimension of a model. *Annals of Statistics, 6,* 461–464. doi:10.1214/aos/1176344136

Waller, N. G., & Meehl, P. E. (1998). *Multivariate taxometric procedures: Distinguishing types from continua.* Thousand Oaks, CA: Sage.

## CHAPTER 11

MULTILEVEL MODELING FOR PSYCHOLOGISTS

John B. Nezlek

Multilevel analyses have become increasingly common in psychological research, although unfortunately, many researchers' understanding of multilevel analysis has lagged behind this increased interest and use. Many researchers have heard of and are curious about multilevel modeling (MLM), but they are unfamiliar with it, perhaps so unfamiliar that they do not know where to start. This unfamiliarity is probably due in part to the fact that many graduate programs in psychology do not offer (or have not offered) courses in multilevel analysis. This chapter is an attempt to meet this need by familiarizing readers with MLM as it pertains to psychological research broadly defined.

In writing this chapter, I had two goals in mind. First, I wanted readers to learn the basics of multilevel analysis. Second, I wanted to increase readers' awareness of the multilevel perspective so that they might recognize the multilevel features of the data they have collected and would be able to be formulate more clearly research questions that might involve multilevel data. As Kreft and de Leeuw (1998) noted, "Once you know that hierarchies exist you see them everywhere" (p. 1). Conversely, if you do not know how to conceptualize a multilevel data structure and the accompanying analyses, you may not see or recognize hierarchies anywhere.

In this chapter, I provide a rationale for MLM: why it is necessary, its advantages over other techniques, and so forth. I describe the basic structure of univariate multilevel analyses: the nature of the models and the types of parameters they can estimate and how to conduct multilevel analyses,

including different aspects of analyses such as centering, modeling error, weighted analyses, and categorical independent and dependent measures. I also offer suggestions about how to interpret the results of analyses and how to report results in papers. Finally, although they are in flux, I discuss software options.

This chapter is intended as an introduction for those who are not familiar with MLM. When writing this chapter, the only statistical training I assumed readers would have was an understanding of basic ordinary least squares (OLS) regression. Analysts who are familiar with the basics of MLM may find some value in my treatment, but advanced topics are not covered. Other chapters in this handbook cover some of these topics, such as Chapters 18, 19, and 20 of this volume.

DEFINING MULTILEVEL ANALYSIS

What Is Meant by *Multilevel*?

A multilevel data structure is one in which observations at one level of analysis are nested (or clustered or grouped) within observations at another level of analysis. Sometimes, multilevel data structures are described simply as *nested* or as *hierarchically nested*. The critical, defining feature of such multilevel data is that observations at one level of analysis are not independent of each other—there is an interdependence among the data that needs to be taken into account. In this chapter, I focus on two-level data structures, but the framework and logic I use to describe two-level structures are readily applicable

DOI: 10.1037/13621-011
APA Handbook of Research Methods in Psychology: Vol. 3. Data Analysis and Research Publication, H. Cooper (Editor-in-Chief)

to data structures with more than two levels. I discuss how to conceptualize the levels of a model in a separate section later in this chapter.

The lack of independence among observations is exemplified in studies of groups (e.g., students in classes or workers in work groups). Individuals in the same group all share the characteristics associated with their group, whereas they differ from each other in terms of individual-level characteristics. In addition, group-level characteristics such as teacher experience or the style of group leaders are likely to vary across groups. Therefore, individual differences such as performance can be examined in terms of explanatory variables at two levels of analysis—the individual (skill, motivation, etc.) and the group (e.g., teacher characteristics)—and members of different groups may vary in terms of measures at both levels of analysis.

The question is how to disentangle relationships between an outcome of interest and measures at multiple levels of analysis. For example, why are Mary's test scores higher than Jane's? Is this because Mary is smarter or works harder than Jane (an individual-level relationship), or is it because Mary's teacher is better than Jane's and so the students in Mary's class tend to have higher grades on average (a group-level relationship), or is it both? Moreover, it is possible that the individual-level relationship between how intelligent a student is and her grades varies across classes. The relationship may be stronger in some classes than in others, and it may be of interest to understand (model) the differences between classes in such relationships.

When addressing such questions it is critical to recognize that relationships at different levels of analysis are mathematically independent. In a study in which persons are nested within groups, relationships at the between-group level tell us nothing about relationships at the within-group level, and vice versa. This independence is illustrated by the data in Tables 11.1 and 11.2. In Table 11.1, the within-group relationships are positive and the between-group relationships are negative, and in Table 11.2, the within-group relationships are negative and the between-group relationships are positive.

Moreover, these two examples do not exhaust the possible combinations. Relationships at the within-group level might vary across groups; some could be

TABLE 11.1

Relationships: Positive at Within-Group Level and Negative at Between-Group Level

	Group 1		Group 2		Group 3	
	X	Y	X	Y	X	Y
	26	31	29	29	31	26
	27	32	30	30	32	27
	28	33	31	31	33	28
	29	34	32	32	34	29
	30	35	33	33	35	30
Mean	28	33	31	31	33	28

TABLE 11.2

Relationships: Negative at Within-Group Level and Positive at Between-Group Level

	Group 1		Group 2		Group 3	
	X	Y	X	Y	X	Y
	11	18	19	23	19	28
	12	17	20	22	20	27
	13	16	21	21	21	26
	14	15	22	20	22	25
	15	14	23	19	23	24
Mean	13	16	21	21	21	26

positive and some could be negative. Seeing data such as these, one might ask, "Which one is correct?" The answer is that neither is correct. If an analyst is interested in constructs defined at the between-group level, then the between-group relationships are correct. Correspondingly, if the interest is in constructs defined at the within-group level, then the within-group relationships are correct, with the caveat that these relationships may not be consistent across groups.

In MLM the term *group* refers to an organizing unit or cluster. For studies of actual groups (e.g., work groups) this creates no confusion; however, for other types of nesting (e.g., observations within person, such as in a diary study), the term *group* can be confusing. So when observations are nested within people, a person constitutes a group. In a cross-cultural study, cultures might be the groups; in a community psychology study, communities might be the groups, and so forth. Using the term *group* in this way is a tradition in MLM, and as confusing as it may be for those unfamiliar with MLM, I follow this tradition.

Analytic Strategies for Analyzing Multilevel Data

Before describing multilevel random coefficient modeling, which is the currently accepted "gold standard" for analyzing multilevel data sets, I briefly review other methods, in part to highlight some of the strengths of the MLM techniques I consider in detail. One way to distinguish such methods is to distinguish *aggregation* versus *disaggregation* methods. In aggregation methods, within-group summary statistics are calculated (e.g., means) and then analyzed. For example, a researcher might calculate for each U.S. state means for two variables (literacy and percentage of immigrants) and then calculate a correlation at the state level. Such relationships are perfectly acceptable providing one does not commit what is called the *ecological fallacy* (Robinson, 1950), which occurs when it is assumed that the between-group relationships exist at the within-group level. Using the 1930 U.S. Census data, in a classic paper, Robinson found a positive correlation between literacy and percentage of residents who were foreign born at the between-state level but found that the within-state relationship was negative. The panels of data presented in Tables 11.1 and 11.2 illustrate the potential for such ecological fallacies.

In disaggregation analyses, analyses are done at only Level 1 (e.g., the individual level when persons are nested within groups), and relationships between outcomes and Level-2 measures are examined by assigning Level-2 measures to the corresponding Level-1 observations. For example, in a study of work groups, a group-level measure such as the leadership style of the group leader would be assigned to each member of a group. In such analyses, a least-squared dummy variable (LSDV; e.g., Cohen & Cohen, 1983) is often used to control for Level-2 differences in Level-1 measures. In LSDV analyses, a set of $k - 1$ dummy variables are added to the model, where k is the number of Level-2 units. Although such analyses achieve this control, they are fundamentally flawed in at least two ways. First,

they assume that relationships between the outcome and the predictors are identical in all groups, an untenable assumption, and second, they do not model error properly. Even if interaction terms between the dummy variables and the predictors are included (which can be unwieldy with many groups and multiple predictors), the two sources of error are not modeled properly.

In a two-level multilevel data structure, there are two sources of error: one associated with sampling Level-1 observations, and the other associated with sampling Level-2 observations. For example, in a diary study in which observations are nested within persons, there is error associated with sampling persons and with sampling days. The error associated with sampling persons is well understood, but a coefficient representing the within-person relationship between daily stress and daily anxiety for an individual also has a sampling error. A coefficient that is based on the 2 weeks a study was conducted will probably be similar to, but not the same as, a coefficient based on another 2-week period. Moreover, the unreliability of such a coefficient (how much it might vary across a series of two periods) needs to be incorporated into significance tests of between-person effects. Studies in which people are nested within groups can be understood in the same way. Most analysts would recognize that students in classes constitute a sample that is meant to represent the population of students. In parallel, the classes in which those students are nested also need to be considered as samples representing the population of classes. It is including these two sources of error simultaneously (the Level-1 error and the Level-2 error) that renders OLS analyses inappropriate. Because of the mathematics involved, OLS analyses can estimate only one error term at a time. Estimating multiple unknowns (simultaneous errors) requires maximum-likelihood estimators, which are the basis for the algorithms used by all MLM programs.

For multilevel data, the maximum-likelihood-based procedures that I discuss in this chapter provide more accurate parameter estimates than comparable OLS analyses, such as using OLS regression to estimate coefficients for individual Level-2 units of analysis and using those coefficients in a single-level analysis between Level-2 units. The greater accuracy of MLM using maximum-likelihood estimators is not hypothetical. It is a demonstrated fact on the basis of the results of Monte Carlo studies in which samples have been drawn from populations with known parameters. The sample statistics that are based on maximum-likelihood procedures are more accurate estimates of such population parameters than the sample statistic based on comparable OLS analyses.

A more detailed discussion of the statistical background of MLM is well beyond the scope of this chapter. A somewhat more detailed discussion of the rationale for MLM can be found in Nezlek (2001), but the truly curious reader is advised to consult a formal text such as Goldstein (2003) or Raudenbush and Bryk (2002). A list of suggested readings is presented at the end of this chapter.

The Basic Models

Consistent with the explanatory framework initially offered by Bryk and Raudenbush (1992), I present the equations for each level of a model separately. Nevertheless, all coefficients at all levels of analysis are estimated simultaneously, so the underlying model is represented by an equation in which the outcome (y) is predicted by the intercepts at each level of analysis, the predictors that are included at each level, and the error terms.

In the standard nomenclature, Level-1 coefficients are represented with βs, (subscripted 0 for the intercept, 1 for the first coefficient, 2 for the second, etc.), and the basic Level-1 model is as follows:

$$y_{ij} = \beta_{0j} + r_{ij}. \tag{1}$$

In this model, there are i Level-1 observations for j Level-2 groups of a continuous variable y. The Level-1 observations are modeled as a function of the intercept for each group (β_{0j}, the mean of y in group j) and error (r_{ij}, which is the deviation of each score in a group from the group mean), and the variance of r_{ij} is the Level-1 error variance.

Each Level-1 coefficient is then modeled at Level 2, and Level-2 coefficients are represented by γs. There is a separate Level-2 equation for each Level-1 coefficient. The basic Level-2 model is as follows:

$$\beta_{0j} = \gamma_{00} + \mu_{0j}. \tag{2}$$

In this equation, the mean of y for each of j Level-2 units of analysis (β_{0j}) is modeled as a function of the grand mean (γ_{00} – the mean of means) and error (μ_{0j}), and the variance of μ_{0j} is the Level-2 variance. When these two basic models are combined, this is referred to as totally unconditional or null because there are no predictors at any level of analysis. The value of unconditional models is discussed in the section Building a Model.

Predictors can be added to this basic model at either level of analysis. Assume a study in which students are nested within classes, and the outcome measure is a test score. At the within-class (individual) level, the relationship between test scores and hours of study could be examined with the following model:

$$y_{ij} = \beta_{0j} + \beta_{1j} (Study_{ij}) + r_{ij}. \tag{3}$$

$$\beta_{0j} = \gamma_{00} + \mu_{0j}. \tag{4}$$

$$\beta_{1j} = \gamma_{10} + \mu_{1j}. \tag{5}$$

In this model, the intercept of y (β_{0j}) for each of j Level-2 classes is modeled as a function of the mean intercept (γ_{00}) and error (μ_{0j}), and the slope (β_{1j}) representing the within-class relationship between scores and studying for each of j classes is modeled as a function of the mean slope (γ_{10} – the average relationship across all classes) and error (μ_{1j}).

In MLM, coefficients are tested for significance against zero, and in this model, the significance test of the mean slope (is the mean slope significantly different from zero?) is made at Level 2, via the γ_{10} coefficient. If the γ_{10} coefficient is significantly different from zero, then the null hypothesis is rejected. The intercept is also tested for significance via the γ_{00} coefficient—that is, is the mean intercept significantly different from zero? The meaning of these tests, that is, what the coefficients represent, will vary as a function of the measures themselves, and most important, the meaning of the intercept will vary as a function of how the Level-1 predictors are centered, a topic discussed in a separate section.

In MLM, the random error terms for Level-1 coefficients (the variances of μ_{0j} and μ_{1j}) are also tested for significance, and such significance tests can be used to make decisions about including or excluding random error terms from models. When an error term for a coefficient is included in a model, the coefficient is referred to as a *random coefficient*, and when an error term is not included, the coefficient is referred to as a *fixed coefficient*. This topic is discussed in more detail in the section Modeling Random Error.

Predictors can also be added at Level 2. Continuing the example, at the between-class level, the relationship between test scores and teacher experience could be examined with the following model:

$$y_{ij} = \beta_{0j} + r_{ij}. \tag{6}$$

$$\beta_{0j} = \gamma_{00} + \gamma_{01} (\text{Experience}_j) + \mu_{0j}. \tag{7}$$

In this model, the mean score for a class (the β_{0j} brought up from Level 1) is being modeled as a function of the intercept and the experience of a teacher. If the γ_{01} coefficient is significantly different from zero, then there is a relationship between a teacher's experience and the average score for students in his or her class. Once again, what these Level-2 coefficients represent will vary as a function of how the Level-2 predictors are centered.

Predictors can be added at both levels of analysis simultaneously. Relationships between test scores and hours of study could be examined at the individual level, and in turn, classroom-level differences in these relationships could be modeled at the between-class level as a function of teacher experience. Analyses examining such relationships are sometimes called *slopes-as-outcomes* analyses because a slope from a lower level (e.g., Level 1) becomes an outcome at an upper level (e.g., Level 2).

$$y_{ij} = \beta_{0j} + \beta_{1j} (\text{Study}_{ij}) + r_{ij}. \tag{8}$$

$$\beta_{0j} = \gamma_{00} + \gamma_{01} (\text{Experience}_j) + \mu_{0j}. \tag{9}$$

$$\beta_{1j} = \gamma_{10} + \gamma_{11} (\text{Experience}_j) + \mu_{1j}. \tag{10}$$

In this model, the slope for each class (β_{1j}) is brought up from Level 1 and is modeled as a function of the intercept and the experience of a teacher. If the γ_{11} coefficient is significantly different from zero, then the relationship between test scores and studying varies as a function of teacher experience. Note that *Experience* is included in both Level-2 equations, a topic discussed in the section Building a Model.

Although there is no absolute standard nomenclature, traditionally, in a two-level model, Level-1

coefficients are represented by βs and are analyzed at Level 2 as γs. In a three-level model, Level-1 coefficients are represented by πs and then βs and γs for Levels 2 and 3, respectively. In the popular HLM program, the nomenclature was recently changed to distinguish models in which persons are nested within groups from models in which observations are nested within persons. The traditional βs and γs are used when people are nested within groups, but πs and βs are used when observations are nested within people. (In these systems, people are always represented by βs.) The models and the results of analyses do not vary as a function of which sets of letters are used. The distinction is purely terminological.

Similar to OLS regression, these multilevel models are simply templates that can be applied to various types of data structure. In a study of therapeutic outcomes, clients could be nested within therapists or clinics. In diary-style studies, observations (days or certain types of events such as social interactions) could be nested within persons. In studies relying on reaction times, responses can be treated as nested within persons and experimental conditions can be modeled at the person level. Such applications are limited only by the insight of researchers and their ability to collect the necessary data.

CONDUCTING MULTILEVEL ANALYSES

Building a Model

The first model that should be run is a model that has no predictors at any level of analysis. These are called *unconditional* or *null* models, and in some cases, *variance component* models. Such unconditional models provide the basic descriptive statistics for a multilevel analysis. Although unconditional models typically do not test hypotheses, they provide valuable information about how the total variance of a measure is distributed across the levels of a model. Understanding the distribution of variance can also provide some ideas about how productive analyses at different levels of a model might be. For example, if most of the variance of a measure is at Level 1, it may be difficult to analyze differences in Level-1 means (intercepts) at Level 2. The fact that it may be difficult does not imply that it will not be possible. Small amounts of variance at any level of analysis may still provide a sufficient basis for further analyses at that level. Most multilevel modelers agree that Level-1 models should be finalized before Level-2 differences in Level-1 coefficients are examined. In this instance, *finalized* refers to the selection of predictors and the specification of the error structure. Specifying error structures is discussed in the next section.

Another important recommendation for model building is to forward step rather than backward step models, particularly at Level 1. *Forward stepping* refers to a process that begins with the simplest model to which predictors are added one by one (or in small numbers), with tests of significance at each step. Predictors that are not statistically significant are removed from the model before new predictors are added. *Backward stepping* refers to a process in which all possible predictors are added at the outset and predictors that are not statistically significant are removed sequentially.

Although backward-stepping procedures may be fairly common in OLS regression analyses, because MLM analyses estimate more parameters than seemingly comparable OLS regressions, backward-stepping procedures may stretch what statisticians refer to as the *carrying capacity* of the data. In MLM, the number of parameters that are estimated increases nonlinearly as a function of the number of predictors. For example, in the basic Level-1 model, $y_{ij} = \beta_{0j} + r_{ij}$, three parameters are estimated: a Level-1 variance, and fixed and random effect for the intercept. If a predictor is added, $y_{ij} = \beta_{0j} + \beta_{1j}(x) + r_{ij}$, six parameters are estimated: the Level-1 variance, a fixed and random effect for both the intercept and the slope (four parameters), and the covariance between the two random effects (one parameter). If a second predictor is added, $y_{ij} = \beta_{0j} + \beta_{1j}(x_1) + \beta_{2j}(x_2) + r_{ij}$, 10 parameters are estimated: the Level-1 variance, a fixed and random effect for the intercept and the two slopes (six parameters), and the covariances between the three random effects (three parameters).

When adding predictors at Level 2, the norm is to have (initially) the same Level-2 predictors for each Level-1 coefficient. For example, if a Level-1 model had two predictors, $y_{ij} = \beta_{0j} + \beta_{1j}(x_1) + \beta_{2j}$

$(x_2) + r_{ij}$, then three coefficients, the intercept and two slopes, would be brought up to Level 2. If a Level-2 variable, Z, is used to model the intercept, $\beta_{0j} = \gamma_{00} + \gamma_{01}(Z) + \mu_{0j}$, then the other coefficients (the two slopes) should also be modeled as a function of Z, for example, $\beta_{1j} = \gamma_{10} + \gamma_{11}(Z) + \mu_{1j}$ and $\beta_{2j} = \gamma_{20} + \gamma_{21}(Z) + \mu_{2j}$. One reason for doing this is that if Z is not included as a predictor for a coefficient, it is assumed that there is no relationship between that coefficient and Z. Because all coefficients in a model are being estimated simultaneously (including the covariances between coefficients), the failure to include a relationship between Z and a Level-1 coefficient may lead to a misspecified model.

This discussion of model building has focused on the technical aspects of MLM. Of course, exactly how an analyst chooses to build a model needs to reflect the substantive questions at hand. Nevertheless, these guidelines reflect the knowledge and experience of accomplished multilevel modelers (e.g., Kreft & de Leeuw, 1998; Raudenbush & Bryk, 2002).

Modeling Random Error

As discussed, for each coefficient in a model, MLM can estimate a fixed and a random error term. The fixed term is the focus of most hypotheses. It is an estimate of the relationship between a predictor and the outcome. Is the coefficient significantly different from zero? The random error term reflects the ability of the algorithm to separate true and random error, and a coefficient for which a reliable random error term can be estimated is described as *randomly varying*. Although random errors are usually not the focus of hypotheses per se, it is important to estimate random errors properly because in MLM all coefficients are estimated simultaneously. An improperly specified random error structure can lead to inaccurate estimates of the fixed effects, or in more formal terms, a misspecified model.

For those not familiar with techniques such as structural equation modeling (SEM), in which error structures need to be described by the analyst, specifying error terms in MLM may be challenging. In OLS analyses, there is one error term in a model, whereas in MLM, each Level-1 coefficient can have its own error term. In a two-level model with a single predictor at Level 1, there is an error term for both the intercept and the slope. The simultaneous estimation of such errors is part of the reason MLM provides more accurate parameter estimates and significance tests of coefficients than comparable OLS techniques.

Researchers vary in terms of how much they model error structures, and the guidelines I discuss here may not be normative in all disciplines. Nevertheless, this description should provide a good starting point. At the basic level, I recommend deleting from a model error terms that are not statistically significant. Statistical significance in this case refers to the results of a test in which the null hypothesis is that the random error is zero. For most statistical tests, an α level of $p < .05$ is used, but for decisions about the inclusion or exclusion of error terms, most modelers recommend a more relaxed standard such as $p < .10$. This more relaxed standard reflects the fact that, in most cases, the coefficients are theoretically random, and they should be modeled as such if possible. If a random error term cannot be estimated at all reliably to be different from zero ($p > .20$), then it should be deleted from the model so that the information contained in the data can be used to estimate other parameters.

When a random error term is not modeled for a coefficient, the coefficient is described as having been *fixed*. Most important, analysts need to determine whether the inclusion or exclusion of a random error term makes a difference in the coefficients that are the focus of the model—which is usually the fixed effects. Perhaps most important, such differences can include changes in the results of significance tests of the fixed effects. Finally, the addition of Level-2 variables may change the statistical significance of random error terms of the coefficients being brought up from Level 1, and when this happens, analysts need to determine why this occurred. For example, including a Level-2 predictor for a Level-1 slope may account for sufficient variance in that slope to render nonsignificant a random error term that was statistically significant without the Level-2 predictor.

There is considerable confusion about what a nonsignificant random error term means. In the truest sense, it means that there is not sufficient information in the data to separate true (fixed) variability from random variability. It does not mean that a coefficient does not vary at all. It means that the random variability cannot be modeled. This confusion is increased by the fact that when a coefficient is fixed, the estimated (fitted) values for that coefficient will all be the same because no residual estimate has been estimated for that coefficient, and it is such estimates that represent random effects.

Regardless, it is possible (and completely acceptable statistically) to model differences in fixed coefficients. The inability to model random variability does not limit one's ability to model fixed variability. If the random error term associated with a Level-1 coefficient is not significant, the error term can be dropped from the model, but this does not preclude adding a Level-2 predictor to that part of the model. When the variability in a fixed coefficient is modeled in this way, the coefficient is described as *nonrandomly varying*.

Curious readers can conduct two analyses and examine what are called *residual files* to understand this further. The specific content of residual files may vary from program to program, but such files typically contain various estimated values such as fitted values and residual estimates. These data provide a basis for understanding the impact of modeling effects as randomly or nonrandomly varying. As discussed, for fixed coefficients that are not modeled at Level 2, the fitted values will not vary, whereas if a Level-2 predictor is included, the fitted values will vary. The ability to model variability in fixed coefficients reflects the fact that the information provided by the Level-2 predictor provides a basis to allow this. Admittedly, there are differences between nonrandomly varying coefficients and randomly varying coefficients whose variability is modeled at Level 2, but for many purposes, these differences are not relevant.

Centering

Centering refers to the reference value used to estimate a slope for a predictor. For analysts whose primary experience is with OLS regression, centering can be a bit difficult to understand. In most OLS analyses, predictor variables are centered around the sample mean, and the intercept represents the expected value for an observation that is at the sample mean on all the predictors in a model. In contrast, within the multilevel framework, different types of centering options are available, and choosing among these options is far from automatic. A more detailed discussion of this topic and recommendations for choosing among different options can be found in Enders and Tofighi (2007).

At the upper level of analysis in a model (e.g., Level 2 in a two-level model and Level 3 in a three-level model), predictors can be centered in one of two ways: grand mean centered and zero centered (sometimes referred to as *uncentered*). Grand mean centering is similar to the type of centering represented by the standardized coefficients in most OLS regression analyses. Coefficients reflect relationships on the basis of deviations from the total sample means of predictors, and the intercept represents the expected value for an observation at the total sample mean of a predictor or set of predictors.

When a Level-2 predictor is entered uncentered, coefficients reflect relationships on the basis of deviations from scores of zero on the predictors, and the intercept represents the expected value for an observation that has a score of zero on a predictor. Returning to the students within classes example, if sex of teacher was included at Level 2 by using a dummy-coded variable *Male* (coded one for men, zero for women, $\beta_{0j} = \gamma_{00} + \gamma_{01} (Male) + \mu_{0j}$), and *Male* was entered uncentered, then the Level-2 intercept of intercepts (γ_{00}) would represent the expected average score for a class with a female teacher (i.e., a teacher for which *Male* = 0).

At lower levels of analysis (e.g., Level 1 in a two-level model and Levels 1 and 2 in a three-level model), there is a third option: predictors can be group mean centered (sometimes referred to as *centered within clusters*, or CWC). When a predictor is group mean centered, coefficients reflect relationships on the basis of deviations from the group mean of a predictor, and the intercept represents the expected value for an observation at the group mean of a predictor or set of predictors. In this instance, the term *group* refers to a Level-2 unit of analysis (in a two-level model). Some use the term CWC to reduce the confusion that may occur because Level-2 units may not be groups.

Centering is a critical aspect of a multilevel model, because the meaning of intercepts and slopes can change dramatically as a function of changes in centering. In some senses, centering is more critical for Level-1 predictors than for Level-2 predictors (in a two-level model) because when considering centering at Level 1, the fact that Level-1 coefficients are *passed up* to Level 2 must be kept in mind. For example, assume a study of student achievement (y) in which boys and girls are nested within classrooms with the following Level-1 model. In this model, *Male* is a dummy-coded variable coded one for boys and zero for girls:

$$y_{ij} = \beta_{0j} + \beta_{1j} (Male) + r_{ij}. \qquad (11)$$

If *Male* is entered as an uncentered predictor, the intercept represents the expected score for girls in a classroom (i.e., when *Male* = 0). If *Male* is entered grand mean centered, the intercept now represents the classroom mean for achievement adjusted for between-class differences in the distribution of boys and girls. If *Male* is entered group mean centered, then the intercept simply represents the mean for each class unadjusted for differences in sex distributions of classes. Enders and Tofighi (2007, p. 138) provided an algebraic explanation of this.

Regarding recommendations for when to use what type of centering, Bryk and Raudenbush (1992) noted that "no single rule covers all cases" (p. 27), so analysts will need to decide how to center predictors on the basis of the data they have and the hypotheses of interest. Nevertheless, a few broad recommendations are possible. Generally, at Level 2, continuous predictors should be entered grand mean centered. If a continuous measure is entered uncentered, then the intercept represents the expected outcome for a Level-2 unit that has a score of zero on a predictor, something that may not make much sense if a scale does not have a zero point. If on the other hand, a Level-2 predictor has a valid zero point (or can be transformed so that it does, for example, standardizing a measure across all Level-2 observations), entering it uncentered makes more sense. Categorical predictors (dummy or contrast–effect codes) should usually be entered uncentered to maintain the interpretability of the intercept. In general, how predictors behave at Level 2 can be thought of in the same way that one would think of predictors within the context of OLS regression.

Deciding how to center at Level 1 (and at Levels 1 and 2 in three-level model) is somewhat more complex because the coefficients from Level 1 will be brought up to Level 2. If an analyst is interested in what would be the multilevel equivalent of conducting a regression analysis for each Level-2 unit and using the resulting coefficients as dependent measures in another analysis, then Level-1 predictors should be group mean centered. Such analyses take out of the model Level-2 differences in Level-1 predictors. For example, in a study of work groups in which individual-level productivity was modeled as a function of individual differences in job satisfaction, group-level differences in job satisfaction would not contribute to parameter estimates.

Some researchers (e.g., Kreft & de Leeuw, 1998) have suggested that when predictors are group mean centered such differences should be reintroduced in the model by including the means of Level-1 predictors as predictors at Level 2. In contrast, others (e.g., Enders & Tofighi, 2007; Raudenbush & Bryk, 2002) have not seen the need to include such means at Level 2. Regardless, it is important to note that when Level-1 predictors are group mean centered, Level-2 differences in these Level-1 predictors are eliminated from the model, whereas when Level-1 predictors are grand mean centered or uncentered, Level-2 differences in Level-1 predictors are part of the model. Group mean centering holds constant Level-2 means in Level-1 predictors. At present, it is difficult to provide a clear recommendation regarding this, although it is worth noting that most analysts in personality and social psychology (the types of analyses with which I am more familiar) do not enter the means of group mean centered predictors at Level 2. Whether this norm is observed in all disciplines is another matter. Regardless, analysts who are concerned about this should run models with and without these means included to determine what impact their inclusion or exclusion has on their models, with particular attention paid to the impact on the substantive questions at hand.

Grand mean centering predictors at Level 1 adjusts the intercept for each group for group-level differences in predictors. At times such adjustments make considerable sense. For example, assume a school administrator wants to reward teacher performance as defined by their students' success on a math test. Further assume that on average boys are better than girls in math and that the number of boys and girls is not equal across classes. Such a combination would mean that teachers who had more boys in their classes would have higher average math scores than teachers who had fewer boys, assuming that all teachers were equally competent (i.e., that teacher characteristics were not related to math achievement). If some type of coded variable representing student sex was entered grand mean centered at Level 1, the average score in each class (the intercept) would then be adjusted for differences between classes in the number of boys and girls, allowing our administrator to have an estimate of student performance that was not confounded by differences in the gender composition of classes.

When Level-1 predictors are grand mean centered, it is incorrect to use reductions in error variances to make judgments about the strength of Level-1 relationships. When Level-1 predictors are grand mean centered, between group (Level-2) variance is introduced into the Level-1 model, meaning that relationships at Level 1 reflect a mix of variances at both levels of analysis. Finally, Level-1 predictors can be entered uncentered causing the intercept to represent the expected value in each group for an observation with a value of zero on the predictor. This is analogous to how centering effects the intercept in Level-2 models.

Interactions

Within the multilevel framework, interactions can occur either between or within levels. Between-level interactions (sometimes referred to as cross-level interactions or cross-level moderation) occur when a relationship at a lower level of analysis varies as a function of a measure at a level of analysis above it. In a diary study, a Level-1 (within-person) relationship might vary as a function of a Level-2 (person level) variable, such as a personality characteristic. Different programs have different procedures to conduct such slopes-as-outcomes analyses, but assuming the same model is being tested, different programs will provide the same results. Such cross-level interactions were discussed in the section on basic models.

Testing interactions among predictors at the top level of a model is pretty much the same as testing interactions within OLS regression, and analysts are advised to consult Aiken and West (1991). In such cases, the dependent measure is simply a coefficient brought up from a lower level of analysis.

Testing interactions among predictors that are all at the same lower level of analysis (e.g., all at Level 1 in a two-level model) is conceptually similar to testing interactions at the top level of analysis, but there are important procedural differences. Consistent with the recommendations of Aiken and West (1991), for categorical predictors, I recommend simply multiplying them and entering the product uncentered into the model. This can help clarify the results because the intercept remains the expected value for an observation with a value of zero on the predictors.

Aiken and West (1991) recommended centering continuous measures before multiplying them to create interaction terms. Consistent with this, my recommendation is to center continuous Level-1 measures *within* their corresponding Level-2 unit. If they are not centered at all, problems can arise (e.g., in the multilevel setting, colinearity among error terms). If they are grand mean centered, then Level-2 variability in the Level-1 predictors is introduced into the Level-1 interaction term.

The procedures for creating such interaction terms varies from program to program. For example, in HLM, within-level interaction terms (within any level of analysis) need to be created outside of the HLM program and read into the data file the program uses for analysis. When interaction terms involving such centered continuous measures are entered into an analysis, I recommend entering them *uncentered* because the centering has already taken place. Moreover, entering variables representing interactions uncentered, when combined with group mean centered predictors, simplifies the calculation of predicted values. An example of testing within-level interactions using these guidelines can be found in Nezlek and Plesko (2003).

Testing within-level interactions within the multilevel framework has not received that much attention in the literature, but the recommendations I provide here are consistent with what many

consider to be good practice. Norms about best practice may vary across disciplines, but the issues I address here should provide, at the least, a good starting point.

Model Diagnostics and Model Fits

Occasionally, models will not converge. Similar to SEM and other techniques that estimate solutions, the maximum-likelihood estimation algorithms that are at the heart of MLM programs fit a model (a set of estimated coefficients and parameters) and then change these estimates to improve the fit of the model—to get the model to fit the data more closely. When improvements of a certain size are reached, the algorithm stops. The size of the improvement that stops the algorithm is known as the convergence criterion. Sometimes, this convergence criterion cannot be reached, and an analysis will keep running until a certain number of iterations are reached. Virtually all programs allow the user to specify the convergence criterion and the number of iterations. Although there is no hard and fast rule, solid models will often converge in a few hundred iterations or less.

My experience is that problems with model convergence invariably reflect some type of problem with estimating error terms, most often, error terms that cannot be estimated reliably. What occurs is that the program is trying to make improvements when improvement is not possible, and it gets caught in a loop (sometimes a local minimum). Occasionally (but not commonly), convergence problems are due to very high correlations between error terms. Although each of a pair of error terms might be able to be estimated reliably, if the correlation between them is too high, the algorithm will get stuck. In my experience, such problematic correlations are very high, .98 and higher.

When convergence problems are due to a bad error term, error terms than cannot be estimated reliably can be dropped from the model. The remedy is not so straightforward when convergence problems are due to an inestimable error covariance and both the error terms involved in the problematic covariance are significant. Some programs (e.g., MlwiN) allow the fixing of specific error covariances, and fixing a covariance would solve such a problem. If an analyst does not want to fix a covariance, then one of the error terms creating the problem can be dropped. Deciding which term to drop can be done on the basis of the impact dropping the term has on the model—less impact being more desirable than more impact. At times, such problems can be due to differences in scales (e.g., some scales have very large variances compared with other) or colinearity between scales.

Although the advent of high-speed computing means that even models that require thousands of iterations to converge will run fairly quickly (a matter of minutes at most), analysts may want to terminate an analysis before convergence and examine the output to determine why a model is having problems converging. My experience has been that premature termination has virtually no effect on the fixed effects in a model when convergence problems are due to problems with the error structure. For example, the fixed effects may be virtually identical for models that have run through 500 and 2,500 iterations, and so "early" models can be examined for problems with error structures.

Models may also not work because of problems with the fixed effects. Such problems are not estimation problems per se; rather they are more structural. Similar to OLS regression, if predictors are linearly dependent, a model will not converge. For example, a model will not run if a dependent measure, y, is predicted by x, z, and $x + z$. Most analysts will be experienced enough to avoid problems caused by the colinearity resulting from using linear combinations of variables in an analysis, but analysts may encounter such problems when they retain the intercept in what is meant to be a *zero-intercept* model. When fitting zero-intercept models, analysts need to be certain to delete the intercept—hence the other term for such models, *no-intercept*. Some applications of zero-intercept models can be found in Nezlek (2003, 2007b).

Although MLM analyses provide measures of overall model fit (a deviance statistic), unlike within the SEM tradition, fit indexes do not figure prominently in the evaluation of MLM results. In MLM, the emphasis is less on the overall fit of the model (i.e., how well a model captures all of the hypothesized relationships among a set of measures) than it

is on specific coefficients—for example, is the relationship between two Level-1 variables significant, does it vary as a function of a Level-2 variable, and so forth? There are situations in which the fits of different models need to be compared (e.g., to compare error structures), and deviance statistics can be used when this is necessary, but a discussion of such possibilities is well beyond the scope of this chapter. See Raudenbush and Bryk (2002) for a discussion of the questions that can be addressed by comparing the fits of different models.

SELECTED TOPICS

Missing Data

In terms of the practicalities of setting up data files and models, different programs treat missing data in somewhat different fashions. For example, in the program HLM, when creating the system file that is used for analyses (the MDM file) missing data are allowed at Level 1 of two- and three-level models but are not allowed at Level 2 of a two-level model or at Levels 2 and 3 of three-level models. It is possible to include level units of analysis in the system file that have missing data at Level 1, and such units will be excluded from any analysis in which that measure is included. For example, assume a study in which workers are nested within work groups with four measures for each worker. If one of these measures is missing, that worker can be included in analyses that do not include that missing measure. Earlier versions of the HLM program had an option to use all possible pairs of a set of observations, but that option has been removed from more recent versions. In HLM, it is also possible to eliminate from the system file cases that have any missing data, which will ensure that all results are based on exactly the same data. In HLM, at upper levels of a model, missing data are not allowed, and units of analysis that have missing data are not included in the system file.

In contrast, in MLwiN, cases with missing data are excluded on an analysis-by-analysis basis. Cases that have missing values are excluded from an analysis in which the variable that is missing is included. Most important, if a Level-2 unit has a missing value on a variable that is included in a model, all the

Level-1 cases associated with that Level-2 unit are eliminated from the analysis. Analysts are encouraged to determine exactly how the software they are using treat missing data.

Regardless of how a program treats missing data, analysts may want to estimate missing data to maximize the number of observations that are included in an analysis. Such estimation is particularly important when data are missing for units of analysis at upper levels in a model (e.g., at the person level in a two-level analysis of diary data) because when an upper level unit is excluded, all the lower level units underneath that upper level unit are excluded. (For a discussion of estimating missing data, see Chapter 2 of this volume.)

Irrespective of the software being used, it is important to recognize that missing data within the multilevel context are not missing units of analysis, even though within other analytic frameworks missing units of analysis might be treated as missing data. For example, in a diary study in which participants are asked to provide data for 14 days, within the MLM framework, a participant who provided only 10 days of data would not be considered to have 4 days of missing data. Just as classes might have different numbers of students, individuals can have different numbers of diary entries (days, interactions, etc.). The available Level-1 observations are simply nested within the corresponding Level-2 observations.

Perhaps most important in terms of missing data is understanding why observations are missing. For example, are people who provide only 10 of 14 days of data in a diary study different from (in some meaningful way) people who provide 14 days of data? In this specific instance, a person-level (Level-2) variable could be included in a model and it could be determined whether the absence of data was related to coefficients of interest. Handling missing data is a complex topic, and for present purposes, it will need to suffice to recognize that simply because MLM can accommodate differences in the numbers of Level-1 observations that are nested within Level-2 units does not mean that such differences can be ignored.

Standardization

By design, MLM analyses produce *unstandardized* estimates of coefficients. As far as I know, no program has the option to produce standardized estimates. Moreover, although procedures to standardize coefficients have been proposed (e.g., dividing a coefficient by some type of variance estimate), such procedures are probably, at best, at the edge of being justified statistically. Nevertheless, there are ways to reduce the influence on parameter estimates of differences in the variances of measures, which makes coefficient more readily comparable.

Standardizing Level-2 variables is fairly straightforward and puts all continuous Level-2 measures on the same metric. In studies when observations are nested within persons (e.g., diary studies), this could entail standardizing trait measures such as the FFM, and the same type of standardization could be used when Level-2 units are not persons (e.g., clinics, schools, or work groups). Analysts will need to make such decisions about such matters on the basis of what makes sense within their home disciplines. For example, standardizing measures of personality at Level 2 is probably easily understood by personality psychologists who may be accustomed to interpreting regression analyses by estimating predicted values +/−1 standard deviation (*SD*) from the mean. One of the advantages of standardization at Level 2 is that coefficients for Level-2 predictors represent the change in a Level-1 coefficient associated with a 1-*SD* increase in the Level-2 predictor. Another advantage to standardizing Level-2 measures is that differences in the variances of Level-2 predictors do not contribute to significance tests of differences between Level-2 coefficients.

Standardizing Level-1 variables is not quite so straightforward. Simply standardizing in terms of the total population equates the total variances of different predictors; however, it does not equate the distribution of these variances. Moreover, analysts need to be mindful of the fact that when measures are standardized in terms of the total sample, entering a predictor uncentered is equivalent to entering it grand mean centered. Analysts are advised to avoid standardizing Level-1 variables within Level-2 units. For example, if students were nested within schools, it would not be appropriate to standardize scores within each school. The reason for this is that standardizing in this fashion eliminates from the model differences between Level-2 units in Level-1 measures, and such differences can be important sources of information. In general, covariance modelers prefer to work with raw data rather than standardized data because raw data have more information.

Weighted Analyses

Although assigning weights to observations is not common practice for many psychological researchers, it is a necessity for some. If a researcher is interested in making inferences about populations from which nonrandom samples have been intentionally drawn (e.g., certain groups have been intentionally oversampled), the fact that the sample is intentionally nonrepresentative may need to be taken into account. Within the multilevel framework, such a possibility can exist at each level of analysis. For example, in a study of schools, private schools may be oversampled relative to public schools to provide an adequate basis for drawing inferences about private schools. At the individual level, members of minority groups (defined in various ways such as ethnically, those with a specific diagnosis, etc.) may be oversampled to provide a basis for inference. The weights that are assigned to units at one level of analysis have nothing to do with the weights that are assigned to units at another level of analysis. Analysts who want to weight observations will need to specify weights when they analyze their data. Exactly how to do this will vary from program to program, but the results of the analyses from different programs will be the same because this is a well-understood aspect of MLM.

Power Analysis

Despite the growth in popularity of multilevel models, estimating the power of multilevel data structures is still poorly understood. Certainly, the rule that more observations provide more power holds, but questions remain about how many Level-1 and Level-2 units are needed to test different types of hypotheses. This lack of understanding is primarily due to the fact that MLM analyses estimate so many different parameters that it has been difficult to determine how the power to detect each of these parameters varies as function of the design. Moreover, some discussions of power concern the cost-to-benefit ratios associated with increasing observations at Level 1 versus increasing observations at Level 2, and cost is literally measured monetarily. Such discussions may not be particularly valuable to those for whom such monetary considerations are not important. For those interested in more specific recommendations, I recommend Richter (2006) and Scherbaum and Ferreter (2009), who provided cogent summaries of various rules of thumb, with Scherbaum and Ferreter covering the topic more thoroughly than Richter because their article focuses solely on power.

Given the lack of consensus regarding this matter, I offer the following informal recommendations. When thinking of the power of a multilevel design, keep in mind that as a general rule, intercepts are invariably more reliable than slopes, making them easier to model, particularly when there are cross-level effects. Next, start by thinking about power within a comparable single-level design. How many observations would you need to find a medium or small effect? Within this framework, think of the Level-1 slope in terms of a correlation of a certain size—with smaller, less reliable coefficients corresponding to smaller correlations, and larger, more reliable coefficients corresponding to larger correlations. In terms of examining cross-level interactions, note that two criteria are used to evaluate how easy it will be to model differences in slopes—how large a slope is and how reliable it is. It is such complexity that makes it difficult to provide unambiguous guidelines about power. If you are interested solely in Level-1 relationships, the fact that you may have numerous Level-1 observations nested within Level-2 observations will provide a good basis to estimate some parameters, but a lack of Level-2 units will interfere with your ability to estimate the random effects associated with the Level-1 coefficients and may provide weaker tests of fixed effects.

Effect Size Estimation

Often, researchers want to describe their results in terms of what are commonly called *effect sizes*, which, in the OLS framework, are based on variance estimates. For example, a correlation of .5 can also be explained in terms of the fact that two measures share 25% of their variance. Within the OLS framework, estimating effect sizes using such shared variances or reductions in variance from one model to another is well understood and not particularly controversial.

In contrast, within the multilevel context, estimating effect sizes through the use of shared variances or reductions in variance is neither straightforward nor noncontroversial. To provide a context for this, discussion, I will quote Kreft and de Leeuw (1998) who noted that "in general, we suggest not setting too much store by the calculation of RB2 [Level-2 variance] or RW2 [Level-1 variance]" (p. 119). Part of the difficulty in relying on random error terms to estimate effect sizes is that an additional significant predictor can be added to a model and the Level-1 random error term may not change. In unusual cases, it could increase.

Within the OLS framework, such a situation is not possible. For OLS analyses, significance tests are based on reductions in residual variances, and if a predictor is statistically significant, some reduction in residual variance needs to be associated with the inclusion of this predictor in a model. Within the multilevel framework, significance tests of the fixed effects and estimates of random errors are calculated in separate (albeit related) algorithms. So, it is entirely possible for a Level-1 predictor to have a significant fixed effect but whose inclusion in the model is not associated with any decrease in random error.

Despite the possible problems with estimating effect sizes using random error terms, researchers may still want to do so. In such cases, I urge analysts to be cautious and to remain aware of the problems discussed thus far. Moreover, when estimating effect sizes for Level-1 models, predictors should be entered *group mean centered* (e.g., Kreft & de Leeuw, 1998). If predictors are entered grand mean centered or uncentered, Level-2 differences in the predictors will contribute to the Level-1 variance estimates.

Estimating effect sizes in MLM uses calculations that are similar to those used in OLS analyses. A reduction in variance between two models is calculated, and the difference is divided by the variance in the first (presumably larger) model. This needs to be done separately at each level of analysis, and if multiple coefficients are brought up from a lower level of analysis, such estimates need to be made for each

coefficient. If a Level-1 coefficient is modeled as fixed (i.e., no random error terms are estimated for it), effect sizes cannot be estimated using variance reductions because there is no variance to reduce.

Using Coefficients Estimated by MLM in Other Analyses

Most MLM programs allow analysts to save the estimated coefficients from analyses, providing the opportunity to use these coefficients in other analyses, for example, a cluster analysis to identify clusters of Level-2 units on the basis of coefficients. Although technically possible, such analyses may not be optimal because when estimated coefficients are used outside of the multilevel framework this does not take advantage of, or take into account, the sampling error at all levels of analysis. There may be instances in which such uses are unavoidable, that is, there may not be a way to examine the hypotheses of interest within the multilevel framework. Nevertheless, analysts are encouraged to find ways to examine their questions of interest within the multilevel framework.

Nonlinear Analyses

Thus far, MLM has been discussed in terms of continuous, linear dependent measures, and continuous, linear measures are probably the most common type of outcome with which psychologists are concerned. Nevertheless, there are many instances in which outcomes of interest are nonlinear. They could be categorical, for example, recidivism (yes or no), or they could be continuous but not normally distributed, for example, count data such as peer nominations of students in classrooms.

Analyses of nonlinear outcomes require special techniques that take into account the fact that such outcomes violate a critical assumption of MLM—the independence of means and variances. For example, the variance of a binomial outcome is Npq, where N is the number of observations, p is the probability of the event, and q is $1 - p$. Other types of nonlinear outcomes (e.g., multinomial outcomes) also violate this assumption. In terms of MLM, this means that the variance of a Level-1 outcome for a Level-2 unit will vary as a function of the mean outcome within each Level-2 unit.

Similar to the need to conduct logistic regression for nonlinear outcomes in single-level data structures, MLM analyses of nonlinear outcomes require techniques that eliminate the relationships between means and variances. The underlying logic of modeling nonlinear outcomes is the same as that for liner outcomes, but the algorithms differ, and the specific algorithms vary as a function of the type of outcome. For example, analyzing a dichotomous outcome requires the following (Bernoulli) model at Level 1:

$$\text{Prob}(y = 1|\beta_{0j}) = \Phi. \tag{12}$$

In this model, a coefficient, representing the probability of y is then converted to an expected log-odds ($\text{Log}[\Phi/(1 - \Phi)]$), and an expected log-odds is estimated for each Level-2 unit. These log-odds are then analyzed at Level 2 just as coefficients are for continuous measures, and similar to the analyses of continuous measures, predictors can be added at all levels of analysis.

Unfinished Business

A chapter such as this cannot cover all aspects of MLM, and I offer brief comments about a few topics that we could not cover in detail. Moderation within the multilevel framework can be understood within the previous discussion of interactions. Mediation is a much more complex topic, and at present, the best source for advice about how to do this is Bauer, Preacher, and Gil (2006). Understanding how to estimate the item-level reliability of measures administered within the multilevel context is poorly understood. Reliability estimates can be wildly inaccurate unless the nested nature of the data is taken into account. For example, when measurement occasions are nested within persons, it is not appropriate to estimate reliabilities on the basis of means aggregated across occasions because this confounds within- and between-person variances. It is also not appropriate to calculate the reliability for each day of a study and then average the reliability coefficients because this assumes that days can be matched across people, when a basic underlying assumption of the model is that days are randomly sampled. The appropriate method is to conduct a multivariate MLM in which the items for a scale are nested within occasions that are nested within people. The reliability of the Level-1 intercept is the item-level reliability. This topic is discussed in Nezlek (2007b).

In MLM, it is possible to compare any coefficients (or sets of coefficients) using what are called tests of fixed effects, which are basically tests of constraints on a model. For example, assume a Level-1 model with two predictors, $y_{ij} = \beta_{0j} + \beta_{1j}(x_1) + \beta_{2j}(x_2) + r_{ij}$. The strength of the relationship between y and x_1 can be compared with the strength of the $y - x_2$ relationship by examining the impact on the fit of a model of constraining these coefficients (γ_{10} and γ_{20}) to be equal. If the constraint significantly reduces the fit, then the coefficients are not equal. Such comparisons are influenced by the scales (variances) of the predictors, that is, they are not standardized. When predictors have meaningfully different variances, analysts may want to transform them to reduce differences in variances. Such tests can also be used in conjunction with dummy- and contrast-codes combined with different types of centering options to examine differences across the different categories of a categorical predictor. A discussion of a few ways of doing this is provided in Nezlek (2003).

DETERMINING THE MULTILEVEL STRUCTURE OF A DATA SET

How Many Levels?

In most instances, deciding about the multilevel structure of a data set should be fairly straightforward. Studies of students nested within classrooms, or days nested within persons, or clients nested within clinics are all straightforward two-level models. But what if classrooms are also nested within schools, persons are also nested within groups of some kind (e.g., culture), and clinics are also nested within counties? Should each of these be conceptualized as a three-level model? Unfortunately in terms of simplicity's sake, the answer is "perhaps."

There are two important factors that need to be considered when deciding whether to treat observations as nested. First, is there a reason to believe that there is some dependency among observations? For example, does the county in which a clinic is located really matter in terms of how measures might vary or covary? If it does, then county-level effects should be considered. Second, how many units of analysis are there at each level of analysis? When considering this question, it is important to keep in mind that within a multilevel model, each level of analysis represents a sample from a population. If we have clinics nested within counties, before deciding whether to include county as a level of analysis, we need to consider whether the number of counties we have constitutes a sample that can be used to make an inference to the population of counties. Even if county was conceptually a random variable, two counties would not provide a basis to model the random effect of county, whereas 10 might. Such decisions need to be made on a case-by-case basis.

There are ways to examine differences across units of analysis even if there are not enough units to constitute a level of analysis. In some cases, this may mean conducting analyses that are not formal MLM but that do take into account the possibility that relationships between measures vary across units of analysis. For example, if a cross-culturalist has data from 100 people in two cultures, there are not enough cultures to conduct MLM with people nested within cultures, but other types of analyses can be done—see section Other Types of Multilevel Analyses.

In other cases, levels of analysis that one might want to distinguish but for which there are not enough observations can be represented in another level of analysis. For example, in Nezlek et al. (2008), we collected daily diary data for people in four cultural groups. The planned analyses were three-level models, days nested within people who were nested within cultures. Unfortunately, the four cultures we had did not provide a sufficient basis to estimate random effects for culture for the coefficients of interest. In other words, we did not have enough cultures to generalize to the population of cultures. In light of this, culture was represented as an individual-level variable with a series of dummy codes, and we were then able to compare various coefficients across cultures using tests of fixed effects.

The substantive difference between the analyses we did and the planned (three-level) model is that in the two-level model, country was treated as a fixed effect. Technically speaking, this meant that the inference space of our analyses was limited to the four groups from which we obtained data. Although we were able to compare coefficients for these groups, we could not model (i.e., predict) such differences in a formal way. We were able to establish the fact that the cultural groups differed, but we could not explain (statistically) the variability among the groups.

When deciding about the structure of an analysis, it is important to keep in mind that at least two lower level observations are needed for each upper level unit. For example, in a two-level group study, a group needs at least two people, in a diary study, people need to provide at least 2 days of data, and so forth. If an upper level unit of analysis has only one lower level observation nested within it, there is no nesting—there is no way to separate relationships at the different levels of analysis because the sampling is confounded. Level-2 units that have only one Level-1 observation will be included in an analysis, but they will not contribute to estimates of variances. If an analyst has a data set in which a meaningful majority of Level-2 units have only one Level-1 observation, it might be appropriate to consider whether an MLM is appropriate.

Decisions about how many levels of analysis to use often reflect the tension between the law of parsimony (less is more), and the need to account for dependencies among observations. In the previous clinics within counties example, if I had 15 or 20 counties, I would probably nest clinics within counties simply to take into account any dependency that might exist. On the other hand, sometimes more levels provides no advantage. The data presented in Nezlek and Gable (2001) were originally conceptualized as a three-level multivariate MLM (items for different measures nested within days nested within persons), but we presented the results of two-level univariate MLMs because the results of the simpler two-level models were functionally equivalent to the results of the more complicated three-level multivariate models.

It is not possible to provide rules that cover all cases. In most cases, the number of levels that should be used will be obvious. When it is not, researchers will need to make decisions on the basis of previous practice, their knowledge of the subject matter, and perhaps preliminary analyses describing how important it is to take into account different sources (levels) of variance.

At What Level Should a Construct Be Represented?

In most cases, deciding the level of analysis at which a measure should be placed is straightforward. For example, if workers are nested within groups, then worker-level variables such as time on the job would be Level-1 variables, and group-level measures such as group size would be Level-2 variables. In a daily diary study, day-level data such as daily stressors would be Level-1 data, and person-level data such as personality traits would be Level-2 data.

There may be times when assigning a measure to a level of analysis is not so straightforward. For example, in a study in which students are nested within classes, at what level should student sex be included? If classes have both boys and girls, then student sex is a Level-1 variable. In contrast, if classes are sexually segregated, then student sex would be a Level-2 (or classroom-level) variable.

The critical issue is the extent to which a measure varies within a Level-2 unit of analysis. If it does not vary, it is de facto, a Level-2 variable. Although sex is an individual characteristic, if classes are sexually segregated, then for statistical purposes, sex is a classroom-level characteristic, similar to variables measuring the teacher of a class. Just as all the students in a particular classroom have the same teacher (part of the dependency captured by MLM), if all the students in a class are of the same sex, then sex becomes a classroom-level variable.

The situation becomes a bit more complicated when some classes are single sex and some are mixed sex. In such cases, sexual composition can still be used as a Level-2 predictor (e.g., all male, all female, mixed) but not always in combination with a Level-1 variable representing student sex (e.g., a dummy code for males). If sexual composition is coded as a continuous variable at Level 2 (e.g., percent of males), then a Level-1 variable representing student sex can be included in the same model.

In contrast, if sexual composition is coded as a categorical variable at Level 2 (e.g., all male or not), then a Level-1 variable representing student sex cannot be included in the same model because it will create a linear dependence between the Level-1 and Level-2 predictors.

Similarly, measures that represent some type of aggregation of Level-1 measures are treated as Level-2 measures. For example, if a measure of group cohesion that is based on the similarity of scores of the individuals within a group is calculated for each group, then such a cohesion measure is a Level-2 measure—it is the same for all members of a group. The measure that served as the basis for the measure of cohesion is still treated as a Level-1 variable because there is within-group variability.

CROSS-CLASSIFIED AND MULTIPLE MEMBERSHIP ANALYSES

So far, this chapter has concerned nested data structures in which the nesting is straightforward and consistent. Students have been treated as nested within a classroom or a school, clients as nested within a therapist or clinic, and so forth. Nevertheless, students can change schools, and clients can change therapists. Within MLM, when the Level-2 unit within which a Level-1 observation is nested changes, this is called multiple membership. In contrast, cross-classification occurs when a Level-1 unit cannot be uniquely classified into two different classification schemes. The classic example of this is when students are treated as nested within schools and schools are treated as nested within neighborhoods, but some schools have children from different neighborhoods. There are modeling techniques that are appropriate for cross-classified and multiple membership data, and the details of how to conduct and interpret such analyses are beyond the scope of an introduction such as this. Interested readers are encouraged to consult Raudenbush and Bryk (2002) and Rasbash, Steele, Browne, and Goldstein (2009) for details.

Nevertheless, when the number of cross-classified or multiple membership cases is very small it may be appropriate to drop such cases to simplify the analyses. Such a procedure should be followed cautiously, however, and disclosed fully in any description of the analyses of the data in question. For example, multiple membership may be a meaningful datum in and of itself. Dissatisfied clients may be more likely to switch therapists than satisfied clients. If such is the case, analyses that did not include multiple membership clients could provide biased parameter estimates. The extent of such a bias would depend on the number of cases that were dropped.

WHEN TO USE AND NOT TO USE MLM: RELYING ON INTRACLASS CORRELATIONS

Among some scholars (particularly it seems, those concerned with organizational psychology and related topics) there is an active debate about when to use MLM on the basis of the intraclass correlations (ICC) for a set of measures. The ICC is a ratio of the between-unit variance (Level-2 variance) to the total variance (Levels 1 and 2 combined). The argument (more or less) is that if there is not enough between-group variance (i.e., the ICC is low) for a measure or set of measures, then the grouped structure of the data can and should be ignored.

My advice regarding when to use multilevel analyses is quite simple and contrasts sharply with this position. Multilevel analyses should be used when a researcher has a multilevel (or nested) data structure of some kind. Full stop. Although apparently sensible, recommendations about when to use MLM on the basis of ICCs are not made on the basis of sound statistical practice or theory.

First, and perhaps foremost, ICCs provide no indication about how relationships between variables might vary across groups. Such a possibility is represented in the data presented in Table 11.3. Assume six groups of individuals, each measured on two variables, X and Y. In the data presented in the table, the ICC for both measures is zero. There is no between-group variability in either measure, and the mean for both variables is 15 in all groups. If you ignore the nested structure of the data and treat the observations as individual observations, the correlation between X and Y is zero. Moreover, if you add a dummy-coded variable representing group membership—the LSDV approach described in the

TABLE 11.3

Intraclass Correlations and Within-Group Relationships

Group 1		Group 2		Group 3	
X	Y	X	Y	X	Y
13	17	13	17	13	17
14	16	14	16	14	16
15	15	15	15	15	15
16	14	16	14	16	14
17	13	17	13	17	13

Group 4		Group 5		Group 6	
X	Y	X	Y	X	Y
13	13	13	13	13	13
14	14	14	14	14	14
15	15	15	15	15	15
16	16	16	16	16	16
17	17	17	17	17	17

section Analytic Strategies for Analyzing Multilevel Data—the estimated relationship is still zero.

Nonetheless, inspection of these data reveals that the relationship between X and Y is not zero. It is perfectly negative in Groups 1, 2, and 3, and perfectly positive in Groups 4, 5, and 6. Admittedly, such variability in relationships could be captured by including interaction terms between each of the predictors (we can assume the variable X in this case) and each of the dummy variables. Aside from the awkwardness of such procedures (imagine the model generated with a study of 12 groups with three predictors), such analyses are flawed because they do not take into account the sampling error inherent in a study in which units of analysis are sampled from two populations simultaneously—for example, the group and individual levels.

In addition, it is important to keep in mind that ICCs represent ratios of variances. Even when an ICC is low, there may still be meaningful (absolute) variance at the group level for a data set. Finally, what should the cutoff be for deciding when to use MLM: .20, .15, .30? Any cutoff is arbitrary and is difficult to justify statistically. No doubt, recommendations to ignore the grouped structure of a data set when ICCs are low are well intended. Why use a more sophisticated technique such as MLM when a more familiar and more accessible technique such as OLS regression will suffice? Although such advice may have been appropriate at one time, given the growing familiarity with MLM and the increased accessibility of programs that can conduct MLM, researchers should use MLM to analyze their data whenever possible. I discuss in the next section other ways to analyze nested data structures when it is not appropriate to use MLM.

ANALYZING MULTILEVEL DATA STRUCTURES WHEN MLM MAY NOT BE APPROPRIATE

Although I am a strong advocate of using MLM to analyze nested data structures, there are times when data are nested and it is not possible to conduct the types of multilevel analyses this chapter concerns. For example, assume a researcher collects data at the individual level in three cultural groups. Technically, such a data structure would call for a two-level model in which individuals were nested within cultures. Although an MLM might be able to be fitted to the data (i.e., an MLM program might be able to analyze the data), MLM would not be appropriate for such a data set because there are not enough Level-2 observations (cultures). Recall that we considered the fact that in a multilevel data structure, observations are simultaneously sampled from two populations: the population represented by the Level-1 sampling (people in this example), and the population represented by the Level-2 sampling (cultures in this example). Three cultures is simply not enough to provide a reasonable basis for making inferences about differences among the population of cultures. Admittedly, differences among the specific countries involved can be examined as fixed effects, but no generalization to cultures per se can be made. How many observations is enough to provide a basis for making an inference about the population of cultures? It is not possible to set hard and fast rules for such matters, but researchers can rely on their general knowledge of statistics and inference. Aside from studies that rely on intensive repeated measures from restricted samples (e.g., single-case studies), most researchers would probably assume that 10 or so observations would be the minimum.

Aside from commonsense notions about what constitutes a reasonable basis for drawing inferences to a population, another way to tell whether MLM is not appropriate for a particular data set is to consider how well the data can estimate random effects. Assuming that coefficients are theoretically random, if there is not enough information in a data set to estimate any random error terms, then there might not be enough observations to provide the information needed to estimate random effects. For most psychologists, such problems will consist of an insufficient number of Level-2 observations (cultures, classrooms, clinics, etc.). When deciding not to use MLM when using MLM is dictated by the logic of a data structure, researchers should note the following. The inability to estimate random error terms reliably can and should be used as a justification only when the number of cases is small, for example, when the number of Level-2 units is small (certainly fewer than 10). Random error terms (particularly for slopes) may be difficult to estimate even when there are many observations at both levels of analysis, and in such cases, MLM would be appropriate.

If a researcher decides that MLM is not appropriate for a nested data structure, there are reasonable alternatives. The critically important feature of the recommendations I provide for such alternatives is that they allow for the possibility that relationships among Level-1 measures vary across Level-2 units of analysis. Returning to our three culture example, one way of analyzing these data in a single level would be to conduct what is called a *regression by groups* analysis. A regression equation is estimated for each group (each culture in our example), and the similarity of these equations is compared with an *F* ratio. Alternatively, dummy or contrast codes representing the interaction of culture and various predictors could be entered into an OLS regression. More simply, correlations can be calculated for each culture and compared with a Fisher's *r*-to-*z* transform, and means could be compared with a one-way analysis of variance.

Although such procedures can provide significance tests of differences between groups, and significance tests of within-group relationships, it is essential to recognize their limitations. Most important, the inference of such analyses is limited to the specific groups being studied. Assume we have collected data from Spain, Greece, and the United States. A regression by groups analysis would allow us to conclude whether coefficients from the Spanish sample were different from coefficients from the Greek or U.S. samples, and so forth. We could not make any inferences beyond these samples, and we could not model the differences across the samples—country-level differences that might map onto the differences we found between the three groups. Explaining the differences between the cultures could not be done statistically because three cultures would not constitute a sufficient basis for making inferences about cultures in general.

SOME PRACTICAL MATTERS

Preparing Papers for Publication

Norms vary widely about the details of analyses that should be reported, and the following guidelines need to be considered in that light:

1. Structure of the data—The nesting of the data (what was nested in what) should be described explicitly. This description should include the numbers of observations at each Level of analysis, and for lower levels of analysis (e.g., Level 1 in a two-level model) some indication of the distribution of the number of Level-1 observations for Level-2 units (e.g., the *SD*).

2. Centering—The type of centering used for each predictor should be described explicitly. Coefficients (and the relationships they represent) cannot be understood without knowing how predictors were centered.

3. Error terms—The basis used to include or exclude error terms should be described explicitly. A clear justification should be provided if coefficients are fixed on other than statistical grounds. Nonetheless, extended discussions of error structures are often unnecessary. Unless hypotheses explicitly concern or involve some aspects of the error structure, which may more likely be the case with longitudinal data, extended discussion may distract more than it clarifies.

4. Summary statistics—The mean and variance estimates provided by unconditional analyses are the basic descriptive statistics for MLM analyses. These should be provided for both dependent and independent measures to provide a context for readers to understand the results.

5. Model equations—At present, I think the equations representing the models that were run should be presented. Perhaps after more people become more familiar with MLM, this will not be necessary. Moreover, in keeping with Bryk and Raudenbush (1992), I recommend presenting the equations for each level of an analysis separately. This clarifies what was done, particularly for readers who not are modelers.

6. Statistics—I encourage authors to be lean and mean in terms of the statistics they describe in articles and chapters. For example, the significance of the gamma (Level-2) coefficients that are typically the focus of hypotheses in two-level models are tested with an approximate *t* ratio. This *t* ratio is calculated by dividing an estimate of a fixed effect (gamma) by a standard error. This means that there is no reason to present the gamma, the *t* ratio, and the standard error. Any two will do. I recommend the gamma and the *t* ratio, with an accompanying *p* value.

7. Predicted values—Many MLM analysts recommend interpreting results in terms of predicted values. For categorical predictors, estimated values can be calculated for different groups. For continuous predictors, coefficients can be estimated for units +/–1 *SD*. Keep in mind that the *SD* for a Level-1 measure is *not* the *SD* of that measure from a single-level analysis. The Level-1 *SD* of a measure is the square root of the variance as estimated by an unconditional model. Finally, using predicted values can make real the implications of centering.

8. Indexes of model fits and sequential models—Rarely do I see a justification for presenting indexes of model fits. The fixed effects are the focus of most multilevel hypotheses, and fit indexes include both the fixed and random components. Moreover, comparing models that have different fixed effects requires using full (vs. restricted) maximum likelihood estimators,

and full maximum likelihood estimators are not as accurate as restricted maximum likelihood estimators under many conditions. Sequential comparisons of models frequently provide little information above what is available from final models. When they provide additional insights, they are certainly valuable. When they do not, they distract more than they inform.

Authors should carefully consider just how relevant certain aspects of an analysis are to the substantive questions at hand. Certainly, different disciplines may have different norms (with good reasons) regarding the details of different types of analyses, and authors will need to recognize the importance of presenting the types of details their readers require.

Software Options

The number of programs that can perform MLM has grown meaningfully over the past 10 to 15 years. Different programs provide the same results assuming the same models—including, among other aspects, type of estimation algorithm—are specified. The computational algorithms underlying MLM analyses are well understood, and there is broad agreement about their application. MLM software falls into two broad categories: general-purpose programs that can do all sorts of analyses including MLM (e.g., SAS), and single purpose programs that can do only MLM (e.g., HLM [see Raudenbush, Bryk, & Congdon, 2004]; and MlwiN [see Rasbash, Charlton, Browne, Healy, & Cameron, 2005]).

For those who are unfamiliar with MLM (or with modeling covariances in general), I recommend starting with a single-purpose program such as HLM. This recommendation reflects the fact that setting up models and interpreting the output is generally more straightforward in single-purpose programs than in general-purpose programs. Single-purpose programs were designed to do only MLM and so the user interface is tailored to MLM analyses. HLM is particularly accessible in terms of model set-up and output. In all-purpose programs, the commands for and results of MLM analyses are just one of many possibilities, and so the user interface is not tailored for MLM.

As analysts and their questions become more sophisticated, they may want to consider using MLM modules within a general-purpose program such as SAS. For example, by combining PROC MIXED with other procedures, analysts can perform advanced analyses such as *mixture models* in which similarities among error structures are used as a basis for categorical analyses. Moreover, for analysts interested in error structures that are more complex than the *standard model* (i.e., covariances between all error terms are estimated), programs such as SAS provide more alternatives. Note that MLwiN, a single-purpose program, also provides the opportunity to model some fairly sophisticated error structures.

When discussing software options with analysts, my primary concern is that they fully understand all the parts of the output of their programs. I have spoken with reasonably experienced analysts who have misinterpreted or misunderstood sometimes critical parts of their outputs. Moreover, such confusion seems to be more common with general-purpose programs such as SAS than it is for single-purpose programs such as HLM. Because they involve multiple levels of analysis, multilevel analyses are more complex than single-level analyses, and analysts are advised to proceed cautiously as they add sophisticated options and to master basic techniques before proceeding to more advanced modeling options.

SUGGESTED READINGS

I recommend the following for those who are interested in learning more about the hows and whys of MLM. For overviews, Raudenbush and Bryk (2002), which is the revision of the first edition by Bryk and Raudenbush (1992); Goldstein (2003); Hox (2002); Kreft and de Leeuw (1998); and Snijders and Bosker (1999) all provide good coverage of MLM, with Raudenbush and Bryk and Goldstein being perhaps being the most complete. Moreover, Raudenbush and Bryk was written to accompany the HLM software, so readers can conduct analyses and read about the same analyses in the book. Those who are interested in using SAS to conduct MLM should start with Singer (1998), and those interested in more advanced aspects of random coefficient modeling per se should consult Littell, Milliken, Stroup, and Wolfinger (1996). Moreover, web-based resources about MLM are constantly evolving and expanding. Any decent search engine should point you in the right direction.

In terms of applying MLM to various substantive areas, I have a written a series of articles and chapters that were intended for social and personality psychologists (Nezlek, 2001, 2003, 2007a, 2007b, 2008), and one that is intended for cross-cultural psychologists (Nezlek, 2010). Moreover, detailed, step-by-step descriptions of how to use MLM to analyze these types of data are presented in Nezlek (2011). Although the content of these articles overlaps with each other and with the content of this chapter, each emphasizes different aspects or applications of MLM. A nice discussion of using MLM to analyze reaction time data is provided by Richter (2006), and although Richter discussed MLM in terms of reading comprehension studies, the extension to other substantive areas that rely on reaction times is fairly straightforward. Clinicians (and others) might want to consult Affleck, Zautra, Tennen, and Armeli (1999) for a discussion of the importance of separating relationships at different levels of analysis.

References

Affleck, G., Zautra, A., Tennen, H., & Armeli, S. (1999). Multilevel daily process designs for consulting and clinical psychology: A preface for the perplexed. *Journal of Consulting and Clinical Psychology, 67,* 746–754. doi:10.1037/0022-006X.67.5.746

Aiken, L. S., & West, S. G. (1991). *Multiple regression: Testing and interpreting interactions.* Newbury Park, CA: Sage.

Bauer, D. J., Preacher, K. J., & Gil, K. M. (2006). Conceptualizing and testing random indirect effects and moderated mediation in multilevel models: New procedures and recommendations. *Psychological Methods, 11,* 142–163. doi:10.1037/1082-989-X.11.2.142

Bryk, A. S., & Raudenbush, S. W. (1992). *Hierarchical linear models.* Newbury Park, CA: Sage.

Cohen, J., & Cohen, P. (1983). *Applied multiple regression correlation analysis for the behavioral sciences.* Hillsdale, NJ: Erlbaum.

Enders, C. K., & Tofighi, D. (2007). Centering predictor variables in cross-sectional multilevel models: A new look at an old issue. *Psychological Methods, 12,* 121–138. doi:10.1037/1082-989X.12.2.121

Goldstein, H. I. (2003). *Multilevel statistical models* (3rd ed.). London, England: Edward Arnold.

Hox, J. (2002). *Multilevel analysis: Techniques and applications.* Mahwah, NJ: Erlbaum.

Kreft, I. G. G., & de Leeuw, J. (1998). *Introducing multilevel modeling.* Newbury Park, CA: Sage.

Littell, R. C., Milliken, G. A., Stroup, W. W., & Wolfinger, R. D. (1996). *SAS system for mixed models.* Cary, NC: SAS Institute.

Nezlek, J. B. (2001). Multilevel random coefficient analyses of event and interval contingent data in social and personality psychology research. *Personality and Social Psychology Bulletin, 27,* 771–785. doi:10.1177/0146167201277001

Nezlek, J. B. (2003). Using multilevel random coefficient modeling to analyze social interaction diary data. *Journal of Social and Personal Relationships, 20,* 437–469. doi:10.1177/02654075030204002

Nezlek, J. B. (2007a). A multilevel framework for understanding relationships among traits, states, situations, and behaviors. *European Journal of Personality, 21,* 789–810. doi:10.1002/per.640

Nezlek, J. B. (2007b). Multilevel modeling in research on personality. In R. Robins, R. C. Fraley, & R. Krueger (Eds.), *Handbook of research methods in personality psychology* (pp. 502–523). New York, NY: Guilford Press.

Nezlek, J. B. (2008). An introduction to multilevel modeling for social and personality psychology. *Social and Personality Psychology Compass, 2,* 842–860. doi:10.1111/j.1751-9004.2007.00059.x

Nezlek, J. B. (2010). Multilevel modeling and cross-cultural research. In D. Matsumoto & A. J. R. van de Vijver (Eds.), *Cross-cultural research methods in psychology* (pp. 299–347). Oxford, England: Oxford University Press.

Nezlek, J. B. (2011). *Multilevel modeling for social and personality psychology.* London, England: Sage.

Nezlek, J. B., & Gable, S. L. (2001). Depression as a moderator of relationships between positive daily events and day-to-day psychological adjustment. *Personality and Social Psychology Bulletin, 27,* 1692–1704. doi:10.1177/01461672012712012

Nezlek, J. B., & Plesko, R. M. (2003). Affect- and self-based models of relationships between daily events and daily well-being. *Personality and Social Psychology Bulletin, 29,* 584–596. doi:10.1177/0146167203029005004

Nezlek, J. B., Sorrentino, R. M., Yasunaga, S., Otsubo, Y., Allen, M., Kouhara, S., & Shuper, P. (2008). Cross-cultural differences in reactions to daily events as indicators of cross-cultural differences in self-construction and affect. *Journal of Cross-Cultural Psychology, 39,* 685–702. doi:10.1177/0022022108323785

Rasbash, J., Charlton, C., Browne, W. J., Healy, M., & Cameron, B. (2005). MLwiN version 2.02 [Computer software]. Bristol, England: Centre for Multilevel Modelling, University of Bristol.

Rasbash, J., Steele, F., Browne, W. J., & Goldstein, H. (2009). *A user's guide to MlwiN, Version 2.10.* Bristol, England: Centre for Multilevel Modelling, University of Bristol.

Raudenbush, S. W., Bryk, A. S., & Congdon, R. (2004). HLM 6 for Windows [Computer software]. Lincolnwood, IL: Scientific Software.

Raudenbush, S. W., & Bryk, A. S. (2002). *Hierarchical linear models* (2nd ed.). Newbury Park, CA: Sage.

Richter, T. (2006). What is wrong with ANOVA and multiple regression? Analyzing sentence reading times with hierarchical linear models. *Discourse Processes, 41,* 221–250.

Robinson, W. S. (1950). Ecological correlations and the behavior of individuals. *American Sociological Review, 15,* 351–357. doi:10.2307/2087176

Scherbaum, C. M., & Ferreter, J. M. (2009). Estimating statistical power and required sample sizes for organizational research using multilevel modeling. *Organizational Research Methods, 12,* 347–367.

Singer, J. D. (1998). Using SAS PROC MIXED to fit multilevel models, hierarchical models, and individual growth models. *Journal of Educational and Behavioral Statistics, 23,* 323–355.

Snijders, T., & Bosker, R. (1999). *Multilevel analysis.* London, England: Sage.

Methods With Outcomes Measured Over Time

## CHAPTER 12

LONGITUDINAL DATA ANALYSIS

Michael Windle

No man ever steps in the same river twice, for it's not the same river and he's not the same man.

—*Heraclitus*

The study of stability and change in behavior and the identification of predictors of change are perennial issues in the behavioral and health sciences. For example, changes in cognitive functioning (e.g., intellectual growth, cognitive decline, and reorganization) have been intensively studied in developmental and educational psychology with the ultimate goal of identifying critical periods when changes occur and predictors of those changes that may be targeted for interventions to affect the rate of change and optimal level of cognitive functioning. Similarly, longitudinal models have also been used with experimental designs (e.g., interventions) to make group comparisons between treatment and control groups and to examine mediators of interventions (Lochman & Wells, 2002). Longitudinal models are also being used in neuroimaging studies to evaluate changes in structure and function of various regions and systems of the developing brain (Almli, Rivkin, & McKinstry, 2007; Giedd et al., 1999). The focus of yet other studies is on the occurrence and timing of an event (e.g., age of first use of alcohol) or a repeated event (e.g., interval between first and second heart failure). Modeling these *time-to-event* data and predictors of these events also requires a longitudinal perspective with regard to modeling the occurrence of events, and predictors of these events, across time.

Longitudinal quantitative models and research applications using these models have mushroomed in the past 40 years or so, in no small part facilitated by the computational speed and memory size of computers (e.g., for large matrix manipulations, for multiple iterative estimation algorithms). Many substantive issues surrounding change phenomena and the need for more sophisticated quantitative models of change preceded the advent of modern computers (Harris, 1963; Wohlwill, 1973); the technological advancement of computers and the subsequent development of user-friendly statistical software enabled the major expansion of longitudinal quantitative models of greater complexity to be used by a substantially larger number of users. Numerous continuous and categorical variable longitudinal models have been generated, and Table 12.1 provides a representation of some of the more commonly used models and a brief description of their typical use. Other chapters in this volume focus more intensively and extensively on many of these models and their extensions as well as applications to substantive issues. The more modest goal here is to provide a big picture view of some of the models that are referred to in this chapter. A structural equation modeling (SEM) framework is most often used in this chapter to illustrate longitudinal methodological issues. For some applications, however, such as growth modeling, a multilevel approach may be

This chapter was supported by National Institute on Alcoholism and Alcohol Abuse Grant R01-AA07861 awarded to Michael Windle.

DOI: 10.1037/13621-012

TABLE 12.1

Longitudinal Data Analytic Techniques and Models

Model	Use
Autoregressive models (Markov simplex models)	Useful to measure rank-order stability of repeatedly measured manifest or latent variables by regressing $t+1$ score on score at t, and allows for the modeling of measurement error and correlated residuals (Curran & Bollen, 2001)
Latent growth models	Useful to measure intraindividual change trajectories for repeatedly measured data in which individuals may vary in terms of initial levels, rate of change, and final level (Chapter 15 of this volume; Duncan et al., 2006; Meredith & Tisak, 1990)
Multilevel models	Useful to analyze hierarchically structured data with lower level observations nested, or clustered, within higher levels (e.g., repeatedly measured observations nested within individuals; Hox, 2010; Raudenbush, 2001)
Latent growth mixture models	Useful to identify subgroups within a population that manifest distinctive change trajectories (Nagin, 2005)
Latent state–trait models	Useful to decompose covariance relations of repeatedly measured manifest or latent variables into components representing across-time common trait variance, time-specific state variance, and error variance (Chapter 14 of this volume)
Latent transition analysis	Useful for analyzing categorical manifest variables and discrete latent variables to test stage-sequential models of individual growth (Collins, 2002)
Event history models	Useful for analyzing longitudinal data regarding the occurrence and timing of discrete repeatable and nonrepeatable events (Chapter 13 of this volume; Singer & Willett, 2003)
Time-series models	Useful for analyzing longitudinal data typically with many occasions of measurement (e.g., 80 consecutive days of daily reports) to model time trends in a sequence of observations via both autoregressive and moving average processes (Box & Jenkins, 1970; Hershberger, Molenaar, & Corneal, 1996)

used as well as the SEM latent-growth model approach to address issues about intraindividual change trajectories (see Stoel & Garre, 2011, for a comparison of these approaches).

The primary goal of this chapter on longitudinal data analyses is to provide an overview of critical issues related to research design and statistical analyses to facilitate an appreciation of repeated measures data. To accomplish this objective, a range of conceptual and methodological issues common to different longitudinal models is presented with the intent of orienting readers toward significant issues in planning, implementing, and interpreting longitudinal research. These issues are foundational and enhance or constrain the ability of a specific longitudinal design and associated statistical model to address specific research questions. When appropriate, any unique features associated with a particular model of change (e.g., latent-growth model) are provided. Also, this chapter will focus principally on longitudinal models for which n (i.e., number of subjects) is substantially larger than t (i.e., number of waves of

measurement). Therefore, this chapter does not specifically focus on single-subject designs or longitudinal quantitative models (e.g., time series) where $t > n$ (or where t is very large), although many of the principles enumerated in this chapter are also applicable to these designs and applications.

RESEARCH DESIGN ISSUES COMMON TO DIFFERENT LONGITUDINAL QUANTITATIVE MODELS

In conducting longitudinal research, a range of issues related to internal and external validity (Campbell & Stanley, 1966) that are essential to interpret longitudinal findings need to be addressed in the planning stages of a study. *Internal validity* refers to various design characteristics of a study (e.g., use of control group, matching subjects on baseline characteristics) that facilitate excluding alternative methodological explanations for study findings. For example, nonrandom assignment of subjects to treatment and control groups could threaten the internal validity of study findings that may be affected by initial (nonrandom) systematic differences between the groups. *External validity* refers to the generalizability of study findings to samples and populations beyond those used in a given study. For example, research findings of an intervention study designed to reduce sexual behavior among White adolescents may not be applicable (i.e., generalize) to non-White adolescents because there may be systematic differences between racial–ethnic groups with regard to the onset, prevalence, and causes of sexual behavior.

In any study there are a range of potential threats to internal and external validity that may operate singly or collectively to limit the integrity of study findings. Many of these threats to internal and external validity are particularly prominent in longitudinal research (e.g., subject attrition, cohort effects, maturation effects) and bear elaboration. Six issues of particular relevance to longitudinal research designs are now discussed. (For a more general and extensive discussion of threats to internal and external validity, see Baltes, Reese, & Nesselroade, 1977; Campbell & Stanley, 1966.) These six issues are (a) sample selection and generalizability of findings; (b) attrition and selectivity bias; (c) issues related to the repeated application of measures (e.g., response familiarity and learning and habituation); (d) selection of an appropriate longitudinal statistical model to address substantive research questions; (e) model specification under uncertainty of hypothesized developmental process; and (f) longitudinal coverage validity.

Sample Selection and Generalizability of Findings

The judicious choice of a sample is inextricably associated with research questions of interest and is consequential with regard to the ability to draw statistical and substantive inferences for other populations. There are numerous situations when randomly selected, population-based representative samples are desirable to address some research questions (e.g., to derive national, population-based estimates of the prevalence of psychiatric disorders). There are also many situations in which it is not necessary to use a randomly selected population-based

sampling strategy either because the research question does not necessitate such sampling (e.g., the study of rare diseases) or it may not be feasible (e.g., because of limited financial resources). There is a range of different sampling designs (e.g., simple random sampling, unequal probability sampling, stratified sampling, cluster sampling) to accommodate sampling for different research purposes. A discussion of these alternative sampling designs and associated benefits and costs are beyond the scope of this chapter (see Volume 2, Chapter 14, this handbook). It is important, however, to recognize that sample selection serves as a critical feature in planning a study and in interpreting the data because of the limits that it places on generalizing the findings to other populations. Hence, even if other features of a longitudinal study are well executed (e.g., high reliability measures, high sample retention), the generalizability of the findings could be restricted to a narrow band of the population. By contrast, careful consideration of the selection of the sample can enhance the value and generalizability of findings that can serve as a springboard for subsequent research and associated applications.

In longitudinal research applications, it is imperative that sampling considerations are viewed within the context of changes that may vary according to the sample selected and thereby may affect the generalizability of findings across time. For example, a repeated measures school intervention study to delay the onset of substance use among children using a random sampling of schools within an ethnically homogeneous school district may not be optimal for generalizing findings beyond the ethnically homogenous schools (and students) used in the study. If the intervention focused on predominantly Black children who were ages 13 and 14, the findings of the intervention may not generalize to White children because the age of onset for substances typically occurs earlier for White than Black students (Johnston, O'Malley, Bachman, & Schulenberg, 2009). Hence, the intervention would not be targeting the same critical period across Black and White children because of differences in average age of onset; many of the White children would have already initiated substance use and therefore an intervention focused on delaying onset would be implemented after, rather than before, the critical period of onset for White students. Similarly, for research questions about developmental processes, it is important to consider age-related issues that may influence the sampling of different age groups. There should be a strong correspondence between the age groups selected for study, temporal design features (e.g., number and spacing of intervals of measurement), and the age-appropriate adequacy of selected measures to investigate the developmental processes of interest.

Attrition and Selectivity Bias

A major concern in longitudinal research is the role of attrition and selective dropout on resulting parameter estimates and quantitative models of change (e.g., estimated mean levels and changes in mean levels across time; range restrictions on variables across time that could affect standard errors of measurement and confidence intervals). With regard to attrition, if participants drop out (i.e., do not continue to participate in a longitudinal study) completely at random across the sample (Little & Rubin, 1987), then a *primary* loss with regard to statistical inference is one of statistical power (i.e., a smaller sample size to conduct statistical tests of hypotheses). Attrition of this sort is of concern and substantial investment should be made to retain the larger sample size; however, assuming that the number of missing values is not large, the impact may be minimal and missing values may be estimated to retain the larger sample size for hypothesis testing. In addition, during the planning stages of a study, one could plan to sample an initial larger sample with anticipated attrition so that attrition does not adversely affect statistical power. Completely at random dropout is the exception rather than the rule in most longitudinal applications, however, and a more common concern is the possibility of selective attrition (or dropout) that may bias estimated parameters and model fit statistics.

For example, in long-term (multiyear) longitudinal studies of childhood and adolescent problem behaviors (e.g., alcohol and substance use, delinquent activity), those participants with higher levels of problem behaviors often drop out at higher rates than those participants lower on problem behaviors

(Wolke et al., 2009). Similarly, in longitudinal studies of older adults, differential mortality may occur across time such that those who are unhealthier die earlier, resulting in a more restricted, healthier sample for the prospective study. Differential attrition (or dropout) may introduce selectivity bias into statistical models that affect critical parameter estimates (e.g., mean scores, variance estimates) that are used in statistical models (e.g., parameters associated with intercepts and slopes in the latent-growth model) and thereby influence statistical and substantive inferences. For instance, if none of the adolescents at the higher end of delinquency participated at follow-up waves of measurement after Wave 1 in a longitudinal study of delinquency (e.g., because of dropping out of school), then mean level estimates of delinquency are likely to be substantially lower and variance estimates are likely to be restricted (i.e., a smaller range of scores). Likewise, in a prospective study of changes in cognitive functioning among older adults, differential mortality may disproportionately eliminate those with lower cognitive functioning (e.g., because of vascular difficulties or dementia), thereby affecting critical parameters of change associated with cognitive abilities because of right censoring of the age distribution.

Investigators can implement a number of procedures to maximize the retention of subjects in longitudinal studies. These include activities such as maintaining contact information (e.g., names, addresses, and telephone numbers of close relatives or friends of participant), obtaining more personally sensitive information (e.g., driver's license number; date and place of birth) to facilitate the use of online tracking databases, and escalating levels of incentives across waves of measurement or a bonus incentive if subjects participate at all waves of a study (Farrington, Gallagher, Morley, St. Ledger, & West, 1990; Ribisl et al., 1996). Planning for, and implementing, procedures to retain participants across time in longitudinal studies is a critical step in conducting prospective research and is difficult to achieve if intensive planning does not occur.

Despite one's best efforts, however, some level of attrition is probable in most longitudinal studies. There are a number of data analytic methods used to identify the extent of attrition effects and potential selectivity bias. Briefly, researchers typically perform a series of statistical tests between those who continued (C) to participate in the study and those who dropped out (D) on variables measured at a common wave of assessment (e.g., baseline or Wave 1 assessment). For instance, in a simple two-wave design, group comparisons between C and D would be made on variables assessed at Wave 1. The kinds of analyses could include univariate tests (e.g., chi-square tests for sex differences in the proportion of those who dropped out; one-way analysis of variance models for continuous dependent variables with group as the independent variable) or multivariate tests (e.g., multiple dependent variables by groups C and D). Another more rigorous test would be to specify a simultaneous, two-group (groups C & D) SEM to evaluate the omnibus hypothesis of the equality of variance–covariance matrixes across groups (Vandenberg & Lance, 2000).

It is also important to recognize that making statistical comparisons between groups C and D on Wave 1 variables does not provide a comprehensive method of analysis with regard to drawing inferences about the relative equality of the two samples. First, it is possible that not all of the important variables that could have distinguished groups C and D were included in the Wave 1 comparisons. Therefore, selection bias could occur because of heterogeneity across groups C and D on nonmeasured (omitted) Wave 1 variables. Second, and perhaps more important, without data beyond Wave 1 for group D, one does not know the developmental trajectories and predictors of those trajectories for these individuals that may distinguish them from group C across time. There could be small differences between groups C and D at Wave 1 or omitted variables that exacerbate group differences across time to differentially influence developmental trajectories. Let us take an example in which a longitudinal study was conducted on adolescent delinquency and group differences were not indicated between C and D on Wave 1 variables. Let us assume, however, that we did not assess intelligence at Wave 1 in which low scores predicted not only dropping out of the study but also dropping out of school and contributing to across-time trajectories marked by fewer

higher wage opportunities and social drift downward. In this case, an unmeasured (omitted) Wave 1 variable (intelligence) that distinguished groups C and D had long-term impacts developmentally on upstream factors (e.g., education attainment; higher wage job opportunities) that would have contributed to diverging developmental trajectories of growth for groups C and D. Although often difficult to implement, when possible, a long-term follow-up of at least a subset of the D group on critical variables is one method of attempting to examine the level of selective bias introduced by the D group. In many instances, however, this is not possible and it is important to bear in mind how selective dropout may temper statistical inferences and substantive conclusions about study findings (also see the section Missing Data Estimation With Longitudinal Data).

Confounds Associated With the Repeated Application of Measures

The selection of measures in longitudinal versus cross-sectional research designs is especially important because there must be greater sensitivity to a range of possible inadvertent (confounding) effects associated with repeated measurement that may undermine the validity and interpretation of longitudinal research findings. For example, there may be reactivity effects associated with measures that affect not only measurement at time t but also time $t + n$ (Baltes et al., 1977). For instance, poor performance on a cognitive measure at initial measurement may influence levels of motivation (i.e., decrease it) and increase levels of test anxiety at subsequent assessment points such that performance scores decrease systematically contingent on initial differences in, and ongoing influences of, reactivity effects. These reactivity effects may confound the interpretation of changes on the cognitive measure because they confound maturational change with individual differences in reactivity to the task. As a second example, suppose 50% of a sample is assigned to a treatment condition to reduce weight and 50% to a control condition. Hypothetically, let us assume that the treatment involves taking a pill that is supposed to reduce feelings of hunger. Knowledge of assignment to the treatment condition may foster reactions such that participants also engage in better eating habits and increased physical activity that may affect across-time measures of weight reduction, whereas the control group may not engage in these healthier activities. Thus, initial reactivity effects associated with knowledge of treatment group assignment may introduce confounds with regard to understanding across-time changes in the dependent variable of interest—weight reduction. One might find a statistically significant group difference, but the intervention (the pill) may have had little or nothing to do with the observed change across time because it may have been the better diet and increased physical activity of participants rather than the pill that produced the greater weight reduction.

Response learning and habituation in repeated measures designs are also concerns (Baltes et al., 1977). For example, the repeated assessment of neurocognitive performance measures may yield statistically significant mean-level changes across time indicative of the participants' learning better how to perform the tasks (i.e., reflecting individual differences in task-specific learning) rather than true changes in underlying abilities. Likewise, the repeated administration of neurocognitive measures may produce habituation, whereby response systems (e.g., level of attention, biological arousal to new stimuli) may be attenuated because of the repetitive nature of the task, although lengthier intervals between measurement occasions may minimize the impact of habituation. Another example is that the repeated measurement of survey and questionnaire items could contribute to habituation in the willingness of participants to expend energy in reading and responding to items rather than just responding in the manner that they recall (correctly or incorrectly) they did on a previous measurement occasion. Such learning and habituation responses would introduce systematic bias in repeatedly measured response variables that may limit or undermine inferences about changes in the phenomena of interest—these changes may be artifacts of response learning or habituation.

There have been some alternative ways to address issues related to the repeated application of measures in longitudinal research, although the list is short and the number of applications in practice even shorter (Baltes et al., 1977). For example, utilizing the concept of alternative forms across

measurement occasions could be quite helpful. That is, if there is more than one measure that assesses the same underlying construct, it may be advantageous to use alternate, equivalent forms across waves of assessment to minimize confounding effects associated with learning and habituation. If alternative forms are used, however, it is necessary to equate the different measures to a common metric across time (or age levels), or it may be difficult, if not impossible, to make comparisons to address major longitudinal issues like the mean level changes, rate of growth, shape of growth, and so on.

Selection of an Appropriate Longitudinal Statistical Model

A positive aspect of the relatively recent development of longitudinal models is their range and flexibility in addressing a seemingly infinite number of research questions. This increased power and flexibility in longitudinal models places demands on researchers to be aware of, and select, which statistical models are best able to address the research questions of interest. Furthermore, although the nature of the data available and the research question posed often constrain the selection of a statistical model (e.g., continuous or categorical response variables, interest in mean-level changes vs. autoregressive effects, time-to-event modeling), in practice, there are often multiple research questions and more than one statistical model that is appropriate. There are occasions when it is advantageous to use more than one model to analyze research questions or to use hybrid models that address multiple change issues simultaneously. For example, Curran and Bollen (2001) combined simplex (autoregressive) and latent curve models to facilitate research applications that focus on both continuous latent trajectories and time-specific (e.g., cross-lagged) influences of variables across time.

Model Specification Under Uncertainty of Hypothesized Developmental Process

Model specification involves the clear delineation of the statistical model in terms of variables and their interrelationships (e.g., independent and dependent variables, mediators, measurement error structures, residual covariance relations) that correspond to a testable, hypothesized model (O. D. Duncan, 1975; Rogosa, 1979). For example, a linear regression model could be specified such that it was hypothesized that stressful life events and social support predict depression. This model could then be tested and evaluated; however, as part of the evaluation, one might argue that the model was misspecified because it did not include the two-way interaction term of stressful life events by social support to evaluate the stress-buffering hypothesis (Cohen & Wills, 1985). Basically, the model specification demonstrates one's conceptual or theoretical expectation of the interrelationships among a set of variables with regard both to the internal structure of measures and to the hypothesized structural relationships among variables. Importantly, the exclusion of important variables in the model, referred to as omitted variables, may constrain the validity of the findings. For example, the beta weights associated with the main effects of stressful life events and social support in the example cited previously may be altered by the inclusion of the interaction term or other omitted variables (e.g., socioeconomic status, sex, coping skills, attributional style) relevant to the causal processes predicting depression. Furthermore, omitted variables excluded from the equations could alter beta weights such that they could change from statistically significant to nonsignificant or could reverse direction from positive to negative in terms of the direction of the beta weight (Bentler, 1996).

In longitudinal research, the issue of model specification (and misspecification) becomes increasingly complex because there is often uncertainty with regard to specifying models of change for several reasons. First, it is often unknown what the time course is for various developmental phenomena and the extent of individual variation in intraindividual change across which time periods (e.g., infancy, adolescence). For example, the full range of biological processes associated with pubertal development span a wide age range (e.g., 8–15 years), and there is considerable individual variation in onset and rate of growth features across sex groups, racial and ethnic groups, and so on. Modeling how these individual differences in intraindividual change interrelate with other behaviors (e.g.,

symptoms of depression, cognitive growth) is challenging. Second, it is typically not known a priori which predictors, assessed when, and how (e.g., self-report, behavioral observations) are optimal in moving toward the explanation of developmental processes and outcomes. Third, at present, for many fields of study we do not know enough about the developmental processes under investigation to know how frequently we should be assessing individuals, or how often and for how long we should conduct follow-ups for intervention research applications. Prior research, including pilot studies, theoretical expectations, and critical thinking (e.g., developing a clear rationale that can be implemented and evaluated) is often our best tool in guiding longitudinal model specification. Furthermore, this process is likely to be iterative in that feedback from an initial model specification and evaluation is likely to be revised on the basis of empirical findings and retested and reevaluated again and, quite likely, again.

Longitudinal Coverage Validity

By *longitudinal coverage validity*, I am referring to the relative adequacy of a proposed longitudinal design in terms of the number and spacing of assessment time points, and the duration of the study, to capture the change phenomena related to the research question under investigation. Alternatively, this could be described as *temporal design validity*. As described previously, constraints on the validity and interpretation of longitudinal findings related to subjects (e.g., selective dropout) and to variables (e.g., response habituation; age appropriateness of measures) have been discussed frequently in the literature on longitudinal research designs (Baltes et al., 1977). Equally important, however, are constraints on the validity and interpretation of longitudinal findings related to the structure of the repeated measures design (i.e., the frequency, density, and duration of assessments across time) to address the phenomena under investigation. The concept does not imply a formal statistical test, but rather it is a heuristic to facilitate critical thinking about not only sample and measures selection, which have a long history in formal statistics and psychometric theory, respectively, but also the relative strengths and

251

limitations of various temporal design issues to address prospective questions.

For instance, a four-wave longitudinal research design focused on changes in intellectual development that assessed children every 5 years may have relatively weak longitudinal coverage validity. Changes in intellectual development occur much more rapidly than what would be obtained in an every 5-year assessment, and individual differences in intraindividual change (i.e., individuals changing at different rates) would be masked with a 5-year interval research design (Sternberg & Berg, 1992). Likewise, daily recordings of alcohol use for the past 30 days may provide useful information to address some research questions (e.g., how much daily variation there is in alcohol consumption), but it would be quite limited in addressing research questions about the long-term health consequences of alcohol use (e.g., alcohol use and liver cirrhosis).

Recent advances in longitudinal models enable investigators to address research questions in a more powerful and flexible manner than models in the past. Because of these advances, the temporal (time) dimension and the selection of waves of measurement merit comparable scrutiny in the planning and interpretation of longitudinal research as do characteristics of subjects and measures.

THE NUMBER OF WAVES OF MEASUREMENT AND INTERVALS BETWEEN OCCASIONS

Seemingly straightforward questions regarding longitudinal research designs are how many waves of data should be collected (e.g., two waves, 10 waves) and what time intervals should be used between occasions of measurement (e.g., daily, monthly, annually). The simple answers to these questions are that you need a sufficient number of waves of data, and intervals between waves of measurement, to capture the purported causal processes under investigation and address the research questions and hypotheses that have been posed. Unfortunately, in research applications, these answers are typically unknown and involve critical decisions in conceptualization, design, and data analyses plans (Collins, 2006; Windle & Davies, 1999). Furthermore, all

longitudinal studies are constrained in their interpretation of findings on the basis of these critical decisions. For example, if a research question focused on stability and change of alcohol use across adolescence (measured with reference to use in the past 30 days) and the longitudinal design consisted of only two waves of data collection (e.g., at ages 14 and 18), it is likely that substantial information on individual differences in intraindividual change (i.e., within-person change across time) would not be assessed. Likewise, if the research question focused on the identification of predictors of relapse following drug abuse treatment, a 1-year follow-up period would be inadequate to address the research question because the majority of the sample who will relapse is likely to have already relapsed (Brown, Myers, Mott, & Vik, 1994). Hence, a 1-year, longitudinal follow-up design would be severely limited with regard to addressing the research question and would be unable to capture the underlying change processes associated with relapse outcomes.

Collins and Graham (2002) discussed the issue of the effect of timing and spacing of observations in longitudinal studies with regard to applications in tobacco and other drug use, although the principles extend to other longitudinal applications. They demonstrated, for example, how long intervals between measurement occasions may contribute to inaccurate inferences about the shape of a growth curve (see Figure 12.1). In Figure 12.1, if only three time points had been selected (Times 1, 5, and 9), the statistical and substantive conclusion would have been that the growth curve was linear. By contrast, if nine time points had been selected, as illustrated in the figure, the statistical and substantive conclusion following analyses would have been that an S-shaped curve characterized the phenomena. Furthermore, the selection of the number and timing of observations can have an impact not only in growth model applications but also in a range of other longitudinal models. For example, the accuracy of capturing change processes associated with gateway substance use patterns (e.g., from alcohol use only; to alcohol and cigarette use only; to alcohol, cigarette, and marijuana use) using latent transition analysis would be compromised if the intervals selected for measurement skipped the time

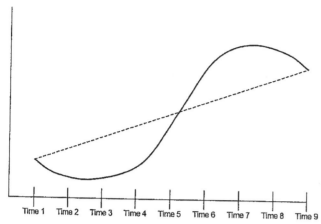

FIGURE 12.1. The solid line represents growth as a function of time. The dashed line represents the growth curve that would be fit if observations took place only at Times 1, 5, 9. From "The Effect of the Timing and Temporal Spacing of Observations in Longitudinal Studies of Tobacco and Other Drug Use: Temporal Design Considerations," by L. M. Collins and J. W. Graham, 2002, *Drug and Alcohol Dependence*, *68*, p. 91. Copyright 2002 by Elsevier. Reprinted with permission.

interval of one of the stages (e.g., skipped the time period when there was a transition to alcohol and cigarette use only). Under these conditions of a skipped time interval, the conclusion would be that there was no intervening gateway stage characterize by alcohol and cigarette use only.

Sher and Wood (1997) also provided a clear illustration of how the timing of assessments can influence not only the statistical significance but also the directionality of influences among variables. Using four-wave data (with 1-year intervals) of alcohol involvement and reasons for drinking with a college sample, they first showed that with a 1- or 2-year follow-up (from baseline to Wave 2 or Wave 3), alcohol use predicted reasons for drinking. However, if the interval selected was 3 years (i.e., from Wave 1 to Wave 4), reasons for drinking predicted alcohol use. Hence, different substantive conclusions about the direction of effects between alcohol involvement and reasons for drinking were contingent on which waves of assessment were included in a specified model. Jackson and Sher (2006) used a similar approach in evaluating the number and timing of assessments in a latent-growth mixture model application with six-wave data on 489 young adults. They specified a model in which all six waves of data were available and then a series of models that

excluded early, middle, or later waves of the study; then they examined the impact of the inclusion or exclusion of waves of measurement on aspects of the resulting growth trajectories (e.g., shapes of trajectories, probability of class membership). They reported that across models, there was a relatively small loss in the overall classification accuracy; hence, the findings were relatively robust to the inclusion or exclusion of early, middle, or later waves of the study on classification accuracy. However, there were influences on the shapes of some of the trajectories and the prevalence of participants within trajectory groups. Not surprisingly, the exclusion of later waves of the study affected the identification of later onset trajectories. This study, using latent-growth trajectory analyses, further demonstrates the importance of the number and spacing of intervals of assessment and their statistical and substantive impact on research questions and findings.

Another set of variables influenced by the timing of measurement relates to the timing of presumed causal lagged effects for predictors (Gollob & Reichardt, 1987). If, for example, one used a conditional latent-growth model (i.e., a latent-growth model with predictors; see T. E. Duncan, Duncan, & Stryker, 2006; Windle, 2000) and hypothesized that a variable such as parental monitoring, measured at Wave 1, influenced changes in adolescent delinquency that was measured across four annual waves of measurement, a number of assumptions could be made that have substantive and statistical consequences. In this case, three assumptions of importance to highlight are that (a) parental monitoring is not changing in its impact on delinquency across time and therefore the need to model this change in parental monitoring via a dual-growth model or time-varying predictors is unnecessary; (b) the strength of the relationship between parental monitoring and delinquency does not decay or decrease across time because of different time lags between the predictor and the length of time to delinquency—that is, the effects are more proximal and decrease with time; and (c) the direction of the effect is unidirectional in that parental monitoring is hypothesized to predict changes in delinquency, but changes in delinquency are not hypothesized to predict changes in parenting monitoring.

In this relatively straightforward example of the influence of parental monitoring on adolescent delinquency, it is clear that quite different conclusions might be drawn from alternative models that treat predictors (e.g., parental monitoring) as static, distal variables, time-varying predictors, or bidirectional influences. Contingent on the modeling approach used, quite different findings may be indicated because the estimates associated with the predictors may range from nonstatistically significant to statistically significant with small to large effect sizes. The upshot of this example is to demonstrate that consideration of the causal time lag and nature of interrelationships between predictor and outcome in specified models are important in evaluating the adequacy to which the research question posed can be answered and to identify assumptions and constraints about findings from specified models.

Although there are no universal truths regarding the number of waves of measurement needed in a longitudinal research designs, there exists knowledge both with regard to some general principles of multiwave designs and influential factors to consider. Singer and Willett (2003) have demonstrated that more waves of measurement ($t + n$) relative to (t), where t = number of times of measurement, and n = additional measurement points, results in increased reliability of measurement for growth parameters related to the shape and rate of change. Raudenbush and Chan (1993) also reported for a given example that the reduction of the number of waves of measurement from five to four resulted in a decrease in the reliability of change from .53 to .36 for the slope parameter. Although these findings do not provide a direct answer to the number of waves question, they do inform critical thinking and decisions about the number of waves that are required to affect the reliable assessment of change for a variable(s) of interest.

Another factor that may influence the selection of the number of waves of measurement is the proposed, or potential, shape of change of the variable(s) of interest. For example, across the course of adolescence, delinquency has been hypothesized to manifest an inverse quadratic shape, with lower levels in early adolescence, increases in middle adolescence, and decreases in late adolescence or early adulthood

(Windle, 2000). A two-wave design (i.e., two time points) would only facilitate the assessment of a linear shape (slope) rather than a quadratic shape. Furthermore, for many longitudinal models such as latent-growth curve modeling, at least four waves of data collection are desirable to facilitate the testing of a range of hypotheses about parameters related to initial status, shape, rate of growth, and alternative covariance error structures without needing to impose constraints to appropriately identify the model (T. E. Duncan et al., 2006; Windle, 2000).

The selection of the interval between waves of assessment is also a topic of interest in longitudinal quantitative modeling. Many longitudinal applications include what is referred to as a *fixed-interval format* in which the intervals between occasions of measurement are the same for everyone (e.g., repeated annual assessments). The fixed interval can assume two forms. First, one could repeatedly measure everyone at a fixed follow-up time interval (e.g., annually). Second, one could repeatedly measure everyone at the same intervals, but the interval lengths between assessment occasions could vary (e.g., follow-ups at 3 months, 6 months, and then annually for 2 years). An alternative to the fixed-interval format is the variable interval format. For the variable interval format, the interval lengths between assessment occasions can vary across individuals (e.g., baseline assessment at the same time for all participants but a follow-up period when a specific event occurs, such as being arrested, becoming pregnant, or having a second heart attack).

The fixed-interval format is most commonly used in longitudinal research and therefore priority issues arise regarding the number of assessments over what intervals and for what duration. However, there are currently issues about the relative trade-offs of fixed-point follow-ups (e.g., annually) versus variable-interval follow-ups on the basis of substantive findings. For example, Jackson and Sher (2006) suggested that the assessment of alcohol use during the college years may occur at longer intervals between waves of measurement because drinking behavior is relatively stable across this time interval. However, more frequent assessments at shorter intervals should occur during the mid–young adult years when drinking behavior is variably altered because of situational influences (e.g., assuming new roles associated with marriage, becoming a parent, career entry and development). Similarly, the selection of unequal intervals for follow-up assessments for interventions may be valuable in evaluating short- and long-term consequences. For instance, short-term assessments may focus on targeted components of an intervention (e.g., immediate increases in prosocial skills and constructive problem solving) and long-term assessments may focus on aggressive encounters at school or involvement in the juvenile justice system. As discussed, the selection of temporal design features (i.e., number and spacing of assessments, overall duration of assessment) should be guided by the presumed causal processes affecting the research question and phenomena of interest.

Another issue that arises in the modeling of longitudinal data with samples that vary in age is whether to model the data by wave of assessment or by age. For instance, if a sample at Wave 1 was ages 10 to 12 years in a four–annual wave design, modeling by wave would yield four time points in which age at each wave was averaged (e.g., age at Wave 1 would be 11 years, at Wave 2 twelve years, etc.). By contrast, modeling by age would result in an accelerated, or cohort-sequential, design (for description, see next section) in which age levels would be treated as continuous units and the time scale would range from ages 10 to 16; hence, seven time points instead of four would be modeled to evaluate change. For many research applications when there is variation in age that may be associated with the processes under investigation, it is substantively advantageous to model the longitudinal data by age rather than wave.

ACCELERATED OR COHORT-SEQUENTIAL LONGITUDINAL DESIGNS

Common laments about longitudinal research are that it takes a long time to collect such data for issues that may be pressing, the costs of such projects are difficult to sustain across time, and there are thorny methodological issues such as attrition and cumulative testing effects that are difficult to address. For example, to address issue about annual

changes in alcohol use from childhood through adolescence and early young adulthood could take 11 years if one were to study a single birth cohort from ages 10 to 20 years. Bell (1953) proposed the notion of *convergence* to resolve the limitations of standard (single cohort) longitudinal designs and cross-sectional designs that were limited to inferences about age differences rather than age changes. The approach proposed by Bell involved limited repeated measurement occasions for independent age cohorts such that across time there was overlap among some of the age groups. This conceptual and methodological approach has been widely adopted in the developmental sciences literature under the title of cohort-sequential design and by others as an accelerated research design (T. E. Duncan et al. 2006; Glen, 2005).

An illustration of an accelerated research design is provided in Table 12.2, Panel A. In this figure, six birth cohorts (ages 10–15 years at Wave 1) are assessed annually at six waves of measurement (i.e., six longitudinal sequences). Note the overlap of different age cohorts across the six waves of measurement. For example, all six birth cohorts would be measured at age 15 years, but at different waves of assessment. Germane to our previous discussion about measuring annual change in alcohol use from childhood to adolescence to early adulthood, a standard single birth cohort longitudinal design would have required 11 years to collect these data. Using the accelerated design presented in Table 12.2, Panel A, this could be accomplished in 6 years. Furthermore, because multiple birth cohorts are being utilized, it is possible to address substantive and statistical issues about birth cohort effects (Glen, 2005; Rogosa, 1979). For instance, new punitive drinking and driving laws related to driving permits for adolescents may reduce alcohol consumption for birth cohorts following the implementation of the law, but they may not affect alcohol consumption among those who were adolescents before the implementation of the law.

The accelerated longitudinal design presented in Table 12.2, Panel A, provides an example of this flexible research design approach. Table 12.2, Panel B, provides a less expansive design, with three birth cohorts across two waves of assessment

TABLE 12.2

Accelerated Longitudinal Design

Birth cohort year	W1	W2	W3	W4	W5	W6
A: Six birth cohorts[a]						
2000	10	11	12	13	14	15
1999	11	12	13	14	15	16
1998	12	13	14	15	16	17
1997	13	14	15	16	17	18
1996	14	15	16	17	18	19
1995	15	16	17	18	19	20
B: Three birth cohorts[b]						
2000	10	11				
1999	11	12				
1998	12	13				

Note. W = wave.
[a]Measured as six occasions of measurement to cover an age span from 10 to 20 years. [b]Measured as two occasions of measurement to cover an age span from 10 to 13 years.

to span growth from ages 10 to 13 (i.e., span 4 years with a two–annual wave design). In other ongoing research examples, the National Institutes of Health's magnetic resonance imaging study of normal brain development (Almli et al., 2007) is using repeated-measures sequences for newborns, infants, toddlers, and preschoolers as well as children and adolescents to age 18 years. Focusing just on the newborn-to-preschool samples, 11 age cohorts were selected (ages in years. months: newborn, 0.3, 0.6, 0.9, 1.0, 1.3, 1.6, 2.0, 2.6, 3.0, and 4.0). The time-varying intervals of measurement in this accelerated design were guided by extant knowledge of developmental periods when brain growth and structural change are proposed as most rapid. The research plan is to eventually merge (or link) data from the newborn-to-preschool samples (ages span from newborn to 4 years, 5 months) with those from an older accelerated cohort sample to provide a developmental function of normal brain change from ages newborn to 18 years. Although the analyses of data from an accelerated longitudinal

design may initially appear daunting, a relatively straightforward approach to analyzing data from an accelerated design for latent-growth models has been provided by T. E. Duncan et al. (2006). For a hierarchical modeling approach to accelerated longitudinal data, see Raudenbush and Chan (1993).

The major advantages of the accelerated research design include the shorter duration of the longitudinal period required, and therefore the opportunity for more rapid results, and reductions in some longitudinal methodological problems (e.g., attrition, cumulative testing effects). The previous example that showed a reduction from 11 years to 6 years to investigate annual changes in alcohol use from ages 10 to 20 illustrates the potential power of accelerated designs. Nevertheless, there are some limitations associated with accelerated designs (T. E. Duncan et al., 2006; Raudenbush & Chan, 1993). A major limitation is that because different birth cohorts are studied over shorter durations (e.g., 6 years relative to 11 years in a standard longitudinal design), within-individual sequences and intraindividual change are restricted for each birth cohort, which could affect the investigation of continuity and change and predictors of change across the full interval of interest (e.g., ages 10–20 years for the example regarding changes in alcohol use). Also, major events may affect birth cohorts at the same age differently and thereby challenge the feasibility of pooling across birth cohorts for specific age groups to form a common curve across time. For example, new social policies or laws that affect the variable of interest (e.g., new or modified drinking age laws in the study of alcohol use) could occur after a given age (e.g., 18 years) for one birth cohort but before this age for another birth cohort. To the extent that the new or modified law affected 18-year-olds, it would have differentially influenced alcohol use for different birth cohorts. Similarly, in a study of aging and cognitive abilities, new medications to improve cognitive abilities could affect the variable of interest such that the new medications could have appeared on the market after a given age (e.g., 70 years) for one birth cohort but before this age for another birth cohort. If the medication was successful in improving cognitive abilities, it could have differentially influenced cognitive performance for different birth cohorts and cast doubt on pooling across birth cohorts (Glen, 2005).

Although some major historical events (e.g., changes in laws and governing policies, wars, national financial crises) may be known to the investigator and can be modeled statistically to facilitate appropriate statistical and substantive inferences, often this is not the case. Furthermore, a major historical event may not be required to differentially influence different birth cohorts at the same age, but rather there may be a number of smaller events that collectively result in the same findings that challenge pooling across birth cohorts at the same age level. Some statistical modeling procedures have been proposed to evaluate the plausibility of pooling across age groups for different birth cohorts (Raudenbush & Chan, 1993), and they typically involve some form of constrained model comparison between the combined or pooled group model and the model of a single birth cohort for comparable age ranges. Such a comparison might involve constraining parameter estimates across cohorts for intercept and slope factors in a latent-growth model to equivalence. If the resulting test statistics indicated that the groups did not differ regarding these parameters, the longitudinal curve from the combined, multiple birth cohorts would be accepted as providing a good fit for the multicohort data. If birth cohort effects were indicated, it would be advantageous to identify specific source(s) of differences (e.g., for which birth cohorts at what ages) and to consider potential explanations of such differences. If data were available on some potential sources of these differences (e.g., the identification of instrumental variables), one could then model these to examine whether the birth cohort differences decreased significantly or disappeared. Alternatively, one might need to identify this limitation of the data in drawing statistical and substantive inferences across birth cohorts for the longitudinal curve from the combined, multiple birth cohorts model.

STRATEGIES AND OPTIONS IN LONGITUDINAL RESEARCH

Exploratory Versus Confirmatory Modeling in Longitudinal Research

An important concept in longitudinal modeling of observational data is that of exploratory versus confirmatory modeling. Exploratory modeling is viewed as preliminary and in need of confirmation before strong substantive inferences may be drawn; confirmatory research is typically viewed as hypotheses driven and necessary to draw explanatory inferences. In practice, however, this dichotomy is better viewed as a continuum because much research in SEM falls somewhere between these two extremes. In some research applications, theory or prior components of a larger model may provide a basis for specifying and evaluating a hypothesized model or models without prior exploratory analyses. Likewise, sometimes competing, or alternative, models are specified to evaluate the plausibility of different theoretical models (Chassin, Pillow, Curran, Molina, & Barrera, 1993)—exploratory research of components of the alternative theoretical models may guide model specification, but a fully exploratory model does not necessarily precede the specification of a confirmatory model.

Even more common in practice is that modifications are made to initially specified models. For example, in confirmatory factor analytic model applications, fit statistics associated with the initial model specification sometime indicate poor fit. In such circumstances, on the basis of output features such as modification indexes provided by statistical software programs, models are then modified (e.g., correlated errors among selected items that had been fixed to zero are freed and allowed to correlate; some items are allowed to "load" on more than one factor, i.e., a *double* loading) and reevaluated for adequacy of fit. In many applications, there are several iterations of this process of freeing additional parameters (i.e., estimating parameters that had previously been fixed to zero or constrained to equivalence) to achieve satisfactory model fit. This model modification process may be even more common in longitudinal studies because often the measurement structure of latent variables across time has not been evaluated, and appropriate lagged effects or fully or partially mediated influences across time for structural portions of the model (e.g., predictor, mediator and moderator effects) have not been tested. There is no reason to despair over the model modification process because in many instances this is the state of the knowledge regarding hypothesized longitudinal processes. However, it is important to be aware that specified models are often somewhere along the exploratory-to-confirmatory continuum, rather than one end or the other, and to report in the text of publications the sequence of modifications made to a model to provide the readership with a sense of where to locate model findings along this continuum (MacCallum, Roznowski, & Necowitz, 1992).

Assessing Model Fit and Equivalent Models

Global model fit for an SEM refers to the adequacy of an implied (or hypothesized) covariance structure (or mean and covariance structure) to reproduce the estimated population covariance matrix. Because neither the implied covariance matrix nor the population covariance matrix is known, sample data are used to estimate parameters for these covariance matrixes in specified models. A major goal in specifying a model or a hypothesized structure is to minimize the discrepancy between the estimated population-based covariance matrix and the covariance structure estimated via the specified model. A major difference in fit between these two matrixes would suggest poor fit of the specified model to the observed data, whereas good fit would suggest that the specified model adequately reproduces the observed data (Bentler, 1996; Hu & Bentler, 1999).

The determination of the adequacy of model fit often is not straightforward. For example, the use of the chi-square test statistic for goodness of model fit provides one method of assessing model fit and is evaluated by comparing discrepancies between logs of a likelihood function for the estimated population covariance matrix and the estimated covariance matrix associated with the specified model. When the natural logarithm of the likelihood ratio is multiplied by –2, it is distributed as a chi-square variate. The fitting function associated with the minimized

maximum likelihood (ML) ratio is multiplied by the quantity $N - 1$ with degrees of freedom (df) equal to $1/2 \, (q)(q + 1) - t$, where q equals the number of observed variables in the covariance matrix, and t equals the number of freely estimated parameters. Critical to the discussion here is that the minimized ML ratio is multiplied by $N - 1$ and therefore the size of the resulting chi-square model fit statistic is dependent on sample size. To provide a hypothetical example, suppose that for a model with 10 df, the sample size was 100 and the minimized ML ratio was .15. The resulting chi-square test statistic would be 14.85 (i.e., the product of 99 × .15) with 10 df, and the null hypothesis of no statistically significant difference between the observed and hypothesized covariance matrixes would be supported—hence, this would reflect good fit. However, for the same minimized ML ratio and df, if the sample size was 1,000, the resulting chi-square test statistic would be 149.85, which would be highly statistically significant (i.e., $p < .001$) and suggest that there are statistically significant differences between the observed and hypothesized covariance matrixes—hence, this would reflect poor fit. The major point of this example is to illustrate that model fit statistics can be affected by other parameters, in this instance sample size, to influence very different conclusions about the adequacy of model fit.

There are a large number of model fit indicators that have been developed to evaluate adequacy of fit. More in-depth articles describing different model fit indexes and their relative advantages and disadvantages exist and merit study (Marsh, Hau, & Grayson, 2005; Wu & West, 2010). Moreover, simulation studies comparing alternative fit indexes under different experimental conditions (e.g., varying sample size, varying the number of manifest variables associated with latent variables, varying the nonnormality of variables) represent a vibrant and ongoing area of study regarding strengths and limitations of fit indexes under different conditions. Given the array of longitudinal models that have been generated and the potential impact of associated influential conditions, simulation studies will continue to be valuable in addressing issues related to the functioning of alternative model fit indexes.

Given that there are a number of alternative model fit indexes, a common practice has been to scrutinize multiple model fit indexes in an attempt to identify consistency across indexes when comparing alternative models. This is often a useful but not necessarily definitive strategy for selecting the "best-fitting" model for (at least) three reasons. First, as simulation studies are proceeding, it is evident that alternative model fit indexes may vary in their adequacy to measure model fit contingent on the specific model tested and variation in associated conditions (e.g., sample size, linear vs. nonlinear shape for growth); hence, consistency of alternative fit indexes may vary as function of model characteristics and contributors to this variation are currently not fully known.

Second, there are differences of opinion as to what constitutes acceptable model fit for alternative fit indicators. For example, Hu and Bentler (1999) conducted simulation studies across a number of model fit indexes and provided criteria (i.e., cutpoints) to determine adequacy of model fit. These criteria have been widely accepted and often cited in the SEM literature. Marsh, Hau, and Wen (2004), however, identified limitations of the simulation study of Hu and Bentler, which was based on a six-item, two-factor model, and suggested that with other more complicated models these criteria might *overfit* a given model. By overfit, reference is made to the common practice of freeing parameters on the basis of modification indexes until the goodness of model fit criteria are met. Problems with this strategy of freeing parameters until model fit is achieved are that the most parsimonious model to account for the data may not be recognized, and replication of the model may be difficult to achieve because sample-specific fluctuations may have affected some of the parameter estimates freed during the model modification process. Therefore, overfitting a model can undermine two important tenets of science—model parsimony and replication of findings.

Yet a third related issue to consider when evaluating model fit indexes is the notion of equivalent models. As described previously, a central concept in evaluating model fit is to minimize the discrepancy between the estimated population-based covariance matrix and the estimated covariance matrix on the basis of the model specified. Another way of understanding this is to ask how adequately the covariance matrix estimated on the basis of a specified model maps onto the estimated population covariance matrix. In specifying a given model, the alternative fit indexes provide information on adequacy of this mapping; however, it is possible that more than one model specification may provide an equally good, or acceptable, fit on the basis of model fit criteria. Hence, more than one specified model may provide an equally good fit to an estimated population-based covariance matrix. A more extensive discussion of equivalent models is provided elsewhere (see MacCallum, Wegener, Uchino, & Fabrigar, 1993; Raykov, 1997; Tomarken & Waller, 2005). Of importance here is to recognize that equivalent models may be identified to characterize the same covariance data. Therefore, support for a model specification via alternative model fit indexes is important in fostering the plausibility of a specified model; however, such support would not necessarily exclude the possibility of an equally good fit for other specified models. A useful strategy to buttress the viability of one's model is to test alternative models to rule out the plausibility of alternative models (Chassin et al., 1993). Although such an approach may not be exhaustive with regard to other model specifications, it can greatly strengthen the credibility of one's proposed model.

Tests of Invariance Across Time

Powerful applications in longitudinal data analyses stem from the flexibility of testing for invariant relations among variables across time. For example, suppose one wanted to evaluate change of a given attribute (e.g., sensation seeking, spatial ability) across time. To accomplish this it would be essential to provide support that the same attribute is being measured across time (e.g., that sensation seeking or spatial ability are assessing the same constructs at, say, ages 10, 15, and 20) or comparisons across time would be meaningless (e.g., you could be comparing mean differences across time between apples and oranges). The investigation of the degree of similarity in the measurement of constructs across time (and samples or groups) provides an example of studying invariance across time with respect to the measurement properties of constructs. As formalized in SEM, *invariance* refers to the equivalence, or nonstatistically significant differences, of parameter estimates for the same variables measured across time. Tests for invariance could include constraining parameter estimates corresponding to factor loadings of a latent variable across time to equivalence and then comparing the statistical model fit of the invariance model to the statistical model fit when constraints associated with the equivalence of parameter estimates are relaxed and the associated parameters are freely estimated (Widaman, Ferrer, & Conger, 2010). One would then conduct a *chi-square difference test* by subtracting the chi-square statistic and *df* of the invariance model from the chi-square statistic and *df* of the freely estimated model. If the resulting chi-square difference test was significant, this would suggest that the parameters associated with the factor loadings are not invariant across time. If the resulting chi-square difference test was not significant, this would suggest that the parameters associated with the factor loadings are invariant across time and this would be one criterion for establishing that the same construct is being measured across the two occasions of measurement.

With regard to the measurement model of latent variables (e.g., a confirmatory factor analytic model) with repeated measures data, alternative sequences of invariance hypotheses have been proposed to satisfy different conditions regarding the equivalence of measurement (Meredith, 1993; Vandenberg & Lance, 2000; Widaman et al., 2010). Collectively, these approaches have suggested a sequence of hypotheses for evaluating invariance relations for confirmatory factor analytic measurement models that include a series of nested tests with increasing degrees of invariance that could be used to describe the degree if invariance. These models are described as follows:

1. Configural invariance: Similarity of the factor-loading pattern across time or groups (i.e., the same items loaded on the same factor across time or groups).
2. Weak factorial invariance: Equivalence of parameter estimates corresponding to factor loadings across time or groups (i.e., not only do items load on the same factor across time or groups, but parameter estimates for the respective

loadings across time or groups can be constrained to equivalence).
3. Strong factorial invariance: Equivalence of parameter estimates corresponding to factor loadings and intercepts (mean levels) across time or groups (i.e., parameter estimates for the respective loadings and intercepts across time or groups can be constrained to equivalence). It is often suggested that strong factorial invariance implies comparability of measures across times of measurement or groups.
4. Additional, more stringent tests of invariance: (a) equivalence of parameter estimates corresponding to factor loadings, intercepts (mean levels), and error parameter estimates for items across time or groups (i.e., parameter estimates for the respective loadings, intercepts, and error terms across time or groups can be constrained to equivalence); (b) equivalence of parameter estimates corresponding to factor loadings, intercepts (mean levels), error parameter estimates for items, and factor means across time or groups (i.e., parameter estimates for the respective loadings, intercepts, error terms, and factor means across time or groups can be constrained to equivalence); and (c) equivalence of parameter estimates corresponding to factor covariances (correlations), in addition to tests of strong factorial invariance (i.e., the equivalence of parameters corresponding to factor loadings and intercepts). Tests of the invariance of factor covariances can be conducted when there are multiple factors and such factor covariances are substantively important (e.g., the factor intercorrelations among cognitive abilities in adulthood and aging is an important substantive issue, and findings on the basis of invariance hypotheses across time would be a high priority).

These alternative tests of invariance related to the measurement model are critical in longitudinal applications to ensure the comparability of measures across time. If the measurement structure of latent variables is changing across time, then it is difficult to draw conclusions about mean-level comparisons that may be scaled differently or even assessing different phenomena across time. In the discussion in the preceding paragraphs, the focus was on hierarchically nested models and tests for invariance using a confirmatory factor analytic model orientation. This orientation is most consistent with measurement approaches that have stemmed from the general SEM literature (Vandenberg & Lance, 2000; Widaman et al., 2010).

An additional valuable approach to studying invariant relations of measures across time (or groups) is item response theory (IRT; Meade, Lautenschlager, & Hecht, 2005; Millsap, 2010; Reise & Waller, 2009). Whereas confirmatory factor analytic models typically use a linear scale to describe relationships between items and traits (or factors), IRT models typically use nonlinear monotonic models to represent the relationships between items and the underlying latent trait with regard to the probability of a specific response given the level of the trait. In longitudinal applications, IRT models can be used to address questions about how the item response function may vary across occasions (e.g., is there a shortening or lengthening of intervals between scale points for items?) or if the item response functions are invariant. Therefore, the goals of studying invariant relations of measurement properties in longitudinal (or multiple group) applications across standard confirmatory factor analytic approaches and IRT methods are similar. Furthermore, some models within each of these approaches, specifically the binary factor analysis models and the two-parameter IRT models, can be parameterized to be virtually identical following appropriate transformations (Kamata & Bauer, 2008). Nevertheless, many of the evaluation features associated with IRT methods (person ability parameters, item and test information functions) can be useful supplements to traditional confirmatory factor analytic measurement methods to optimize the evaluation of possible changes in measures across time and, importantly, to identify the locus and extent (or seriousness) of such changes.

In addition to the study of invariance relations for measurement models, there are many other longitudinal applications that include tests of invariant relations. For example, in a longitudinal study of academic performance, one could constrain autoregressive parameters from adjacent waves of measurement (e.g., W1:W2; W2:W3; W3:W4) to examine whether the stability coefficients are equal (homogenous) across adjacent waves of measurement or whether they vary in a systematic way that may be substantively meaningful (e.g., lower stability in academic performance across a critical transition point such as the transition from elementary to middle school for early adolescents). Similarly, in a comparison of longitudinal predictors (e.g., parental monitoring, deviant peers) in change (growth) in delinquency across adolescence, one could constrain parameters corresponding to the predictors of the intercept and slope factors of delinquency to equivalence across males and females or different ethnic groups to evaluate whether the predictors differ significantly for the respective subgroups. In this kind of group-comparison application, one is evaluating the potential moderating effect of group membership (e.g., male or female) on predictors of delinquency growth (see Windle et al., 2010).

Missing Data Estimation With Longitudinal Data

Given the attrition problem in longitudinal research, investigators are confronted with the issue of missing data. Historically, the easiest ways to address this issue involved a range of ad hoc procedures such as eliminating the data of participants with missing data (e.g., listwise or pairwise deletion) or using mean imputation (i.e., replacing the missing value with the mean score of the sample that did participate). The limitations of these ad hoc methods are well-known and are not recommended because they can contribute to biased and inefficient parameter estimates, incorrect standard errors and confidence intervals, and inaccurate test statistics associated with hypothesis testing (Graham, 2009).

Fortunately, there have been major advances in missing data estimation to replace the preceding ad hoc methods and to accommodate longitudinal model applications (Enders, 2010; Graham, 2009). Central to this evolution has been the seminal work of Little and Rubin (1987), who articulated three different models of missingness. If the data are missing completely at random (MCAR), then the use of missing value estimation procedures (discussed subsequently) would not introduce bias into parameter estimates and would minimize difficulties with other statistical features (e.g., would provide more efficient estimates than prior missing value methods). Similarly, if data were missing at random (MAR), other data within the data set could be used to derive estimates for the missing values and parameter estimates would not be biased, nor would other elements of interest (e.g., standard errors). If the data are missing in a nonrandom (systematic) manner, then the model is one of missing not at random (MNAR), and available missing value estimation procedures may produce estimates that are biased and may influence other relevant statistical elements (e.g., standard errors, width of confidence intervals).

Concomitant with the development of different models of missingness was the development of different approaches and algorithms to estimate missing values. Although several different missing value data estimation procedures have been developed, perhaps the most widely used are those that rely on full information maximum likelihood (FIML) estimates and multiple imputation (MI). Reviews of these methods are provided elsewhere (Graham, 2009; Schafer & Olsen, 1998) but central here is to note that an extensive literature exists regarding the usefulness of these missing value estimation methods (i.e., FIML and MI) to provide relatively unbiased parameter estimates and to increase the precision of other statistical elements (e.g., standard errors) for MCAR and MAR models. There is also evidence that these methods will improve parameter estimates and other statistical elements for MNAR models, although the precision is not as good as for MCAR and MAR models. Furthermore, other approaches are being developed to better address missingness issues for MNAR models, including using auxiliary variables and collecting follow-up data on a subset of those participants who dropped out of the study (Graham, 2009). For those involved in longitudinal research, it is important to be aware of the options and models available for missing value data estimation. Fortunately, missing value estimation methods are rapidly migrating from stand-alone software programs written in specific languages to widely available, user-friendly programs. This should facilitate their widespread use and strengthen longitudinal findings.

Time-Invariant and Time-Varying Predictors

It is common in many instances to measure relevant predictors at Wave 1 that presumably influence variation in initial levels and rate of change of the dependent variable across time. For example, in studying changes in adolescent alcohol use across time, common Wave 1 predictors could include family income, family history of alcoholism, peer alcohol use, and parental alcohol use. If measured at Wave 1 only, these would be described as *time-invariant predictors*, that is, predictors that are not changing across time or not changing in a manner that would affect changes in adolescent alcohol use. It is clear that barring extreme measures (e.g., sex-change operation), some variables such as sex, ethnicity, and birth weight are time invariant. However, for most other variables and for the variables provided in the previous example, change may occur in each of the variables across time that could affect changes in adolescent alcohol use. For instance, changes in adolescent alcohol use could be influenced by changes in family income associated with job loss, the onset of an alcohol disorder for a parent could occur to change family history from negative to positive, alcohol use by parents or peers could change, and so on. It is possible that changes in these predictors may have time-specific (proximal) or $t - 1$ lagged influences on adolescent alcohol use. These potential time-dependent (or time-specific) changes in predictors that influence the time course of adolescent alcohol use are referred to as *time-varying predictors* (i.e., they change across time and the new values that they obtain may influence proximal aspects of the time-ordered processes associated with adolescent alcohol use).

The vast majority of longitudinal applications model predictors as time invariant. Part of the reason for this is related to historical traditions in regression analysis in which time-invariant predictors were commonly used, and part is related to prior computational difficulties associated with the estimation of time-varying covariates. However, current technology has largely overcome the computational challenges of modeling time-varying covariates, and conceptual and longitudinal statistical models are increasingly incorporating both time-invariant and time-varying predictors in research applications. For example, Hussong et al. (2008) compared alternative longitudinal models to predict changes in children's internalizing symptoms from ages 12 to 17 years by different model specifications that included time-invariant predictors (e.g., family history of alcoholism) and time-varying predictor (e.g., time-dependent parental alcohol problems). The role of time-varying predictors may also be especially beneficial in event history models in which proximal influences may be highly significant in the prediction of event occurrences (e.g., stress levels before a heart attack; see Chapter 13 of this volume). The central message of this brief presentation is to encourage consideration of both time-invariant and time-varying predictors in the modeling of longitudinal data to best capture the change phenomena of interest. Furthermore, as illustrated by Hussong et al. with regard to predictors of changes in children's internalizing symptoms, alternative testable models may be formulated regarding presumed distal and proximal influences on the variable of interest.

Single and Multiple Indicator Models

In conducting longitudinal research, a fundamental measurement issue arises as to whether to use single or multiple manifest variable indicators across time to assess important constructs. If the variables used in the longitudinal analyses are conceptualized as latent variables or as containing measurement error, as are most variables in behavioral and health science applications, it is preferable to use multiple manifest variables to provide more reliable and valid measures of the latent variables (constructs) of interest as well as to provide more robust estimates of predictive relationships among latent variables. Bentler (1996) has demonstrated that failing to model measurement errors statistically in a regression model can result in a change of direction for beta coefficients in a regression equation from positive to negative. Findings such as this were instrumental in fostering the development of multiple indicator latent variables in which measurement error was removed (or statistically accounted for) so as not to bias regression or regression-like (structural) parameter estimates. Using multiple indicator latent variables also potentially enables the use of

multi-informant data (e.g., mother, father, child regarding externalizing problems) or multimethod data (e.g., self-reports, significant other reports, behavioral observations) to facilitate tests of relationships among constructs rather than possible method biases (e.g., there may be a significant relationship between two variables across time because of monomethod bias, i.e., the same person reporting on both variables; see Wothke, 1996).

In longitudinal applications, there are more waves of data collected and often more variables than cross-sectional studies. Therefore, measurement errors associated with single manifest indicators measured across time can be compounded and influence critical parameters related to the evaluation of change processes. Similarly, possible monomethod biases may also be compounded across time and undermine the evaluation of change processes. And the combination of single manifest variable indicators with measurement errors and monomethod bias may act jointly (either additively or synergistically) across time to adversely affect the validity of parameter estimates and undermine the hypothesis testing of change phenomena. Hence, it is preferable in longitudinal applications to use multiple indicator measurement models to increase the reliability and validity of research findings. Furthermore, these measurement models facilitate the modeling of correlated errors among the same manifest indicators across time to reduce biases in parameter estimates and foster higher reliability.

CONCLUSION

There have been major advances in quantitative longitudinal models in recent years that provide unparalleled opportunities to pursue research questions about the stability and change of behaviors as well as about the predictors of such change. New continuous and categorical longitudinal models and statistical estimation procedures have been developed to accommodate the assessment of a broad range of possible changes in behaviors across time. More detailed information and examples of some of these models are provided in subsequent chapters of this volume. This chapter has attempted to provide some of the nuts-and-bolts considerations for those designing longitudinal research studies, analyzing extant data (e.g., via secondary data analysis), or critically reading and evaluating the literature. Threats to internal and external validity abound in research applications in the behavioral and health sciences, and they are compounded in longitudinal studies because of across-time change issues that are central to interpreting prospective findings. Furthermore, longitudinal studies are often concerned with the prediction of not only single time-point variables (e.g., baseline measures of dependent variables) but also changes in the dependent variable(s) across time. A focus on such changes requires more rigorous conceptual, measurement, and structural models to account for the dynamic, time-ordered relationships among variables that unfold across time. In addition, as has been demonstrated in growth mixture modeling (Muthén, 2008; Nagin, 2005), there may be subpopulations of growth curves that correspond with different rates (e.g., rapid vs. slow) or shapes (e.g., linear quadratic, decreasing, increasing) of change. Despite the rapid advances that have been made in longitudinal modeling, there remain broad areas of research to be addressed within the longitudinal modeling area itself (e.g., simulation studies on the behavior of model fit indexes under different conditions; nonlinear growth models) as well as a need for expansions in research applications to more adequately capture developmental (change) processes. Hence, although a rapid rate of growth has occurred in longitudinal modeling in recent years, the slope remains steep with regard to attaining any final level, thereby providing numerous opportunities for those who are so inclined.

References

Almli, C. R., Rivkin, M. J., & McKinstry, R. C. (2007). The NIH MRI study of normal brain development (Objective-2): Newborns, infants, toddlers, and preschoolers. *NeuroImage, 35*, 308–325. doi:10.1016/j.neuroimage.2006.08.058

Baltes, P. B., Reese, H. W., & Nesselroade, J. R. (1977). *Life-span developmental psychology: Introduction to research methods.* Belmont, CA: Wadsworth.

Bell, R. Q. (1953). Convergence: An accelerated longitudinal approach. *Child Development, 24*, 145–152. doi:10.2307/1126345

Bentler, P. M. (1996). Covariance structure analysis: Statistical practice, theory, and directions. *Annual Review of Psychology, 47*, 563–592. doi:10.1146/annurev.psych.47.1.563

Box, G. E. P., & Jenkins, G. M. (1970). *Time-series analysis: Forecasting and control.* San Francisco, CA: Holden-Day.

Brown, S. A., Myers, M. G., Mott, M. A., & Vik, P. W. (1994). Correlates of success following treatment for adolescent substance abuse. *Applied and Preventive Psychology, 3*, 61–73. doi:10.1016/S0962-1849(05)80139-8

Campbell, D. T., & Stanley, J. C. (1966). *Experimental and quasi-experimental designs for research.* Chicago, IL: Rand McNally.

Chassin, L., Pillow, D. R., Curran, P. J., Molina, B. S. G., & Barrera, M. (1993). Relation of parental alcoholism to early adolescent substance use: A test of three mediating mechanisms. *Journal of Abnormal Psychology, 102*, 3–19. doi:10.1037/0021-843X.102.1.3

Cohen, S., & Wills, T. A. (1985). Stress, social support, and the buffering hypothesis. *Psychological Bulletin, 98*, 310–357. doi:10.1037/0033-2909.98.2.310

Collins, L. M. (2002). Using latent transition analysis to examine the gateway hypothesis. In D. Kandel & M. Chase (Eds.), *Examining the gateway hypothesis: Stages and pathways of drug involvement* (pp. 254–269). Cambridge, England: Cambridge University Press. doi:10.1017/CBO9780511499777.013

Collins, L. M. (2006). Analysis of longitudinal data: The integration of theoretical model, temporal design and statistical model. *Annual Review of Psychology, 57*, 505–528. doi:10.1146/annurev.psych.57.102904.190146

Collins, L. M., & Graham, J. W. (2002). The effect of the timing and temporal spacing of observations in longitudinal studies of tobacco and other drug use: Temporal design considerations. *Drug and Alcohol Dependence, 68*, 85–96. doi:10.1016/S0376-8716(02)00217-X

Curran, P. T., & Bollen, K. A. (2001). The best of both worlds: Combining autoregressive and latent curve models. In L. M. Collins & A. G. Sayer (Eds.), *New methods for the analysis of change* (pp. 107–135). Washington, DC: American Psychological Association. doi:10.1037/10409-004

Duncan, O. D. (1975). *Introduction to structural equation models.* New York, NY: Academic Press.

Duncan, T. E., Duncan, S. C., & Stryker, L. A. (Eds.). (2006). *Latent variable growth curve modeling: Concepts, issues, and applications* (2nd ed.). Mahwah, NJ: Erlbaum.

Enders, C. K. (2010). *Applied missing data analysis.* New York, NY: Guilford Press.

Farrington, D., Gallagher, B., Morley, L., St. Ledger, R., & West, D. (1990). Minimizing attrition in longitudinal research: Methods of tracing and securing cooperation in a 24-year follow-up study. In D. Magnusson & L. Bergman (Eds.), *Data quality in longitudinal research* (pp. 122–147). Cambridge, England: Cambridge University Press.

Giedd, J. N., Blumenthal, J., Jeffries, N. O., Castellanos, F. X., Liu, H., Zijdenbos, A., . . . Rapaport, J. L. (1999). Brain development during childhood and adolescence: A longitudinal MRI study. *Nature Neuroscience, 2*, 861–863. doi:10.1038/13158

Glen, N. D. (2005). *Cohort analysis* (2nd ed.). Thousand Oaks, CA: Sage.

Gollob, H. F., & Reichardt, C. S. (1987). Taking account of time lags in causal models. *Child Development, 58*, 80–92. doi:10.2307/1130293

Graham, J. W. (2009). Missing data analysis: Making it work in the real world. *Annual Review of Psychology, 60*, 549–576. doi:10.1146/annurev.psych.58.110405.085530

Harris, C. W. (Ed.). (1963). *Problems in measuring change.* Madison: University of Wisconsin Press.

Hershberger, S. L., Molenaar, P. C. M., & Corneal, S. E. (1996). A hierarchy of univariate and multivariate structural time series models. In G. A. Marcoulides & R. E. Schumacker (Eds.), *Advanced structural equation modeling: Issues and techniques* (pp. 159–194). Hillside, NJ: Erlbaum.

Hox, J. J. (2010). *Multilevel analysis: Techniques and applications* (2nd ed.). New York, NY: Routledge.

Hu, L., & Bentler, P. M. (1999). Cutoff criteria for fit indexes in covariance structure analysis: Conventional criteria versus new alternatives. *Structural Equation Modeling, 6*, 1–55. doi:10.1080/10705519909540118

Hussong, A. M., Cai, L., Curran, P. J., Flora, D. B., Chassin, L. A., & Zucker, R. A. (2008). Disaggregating the distal, proximal, and time-varying effects of parental alcoholism on children's internalizing symptoms. *Journal of Abnormal Child Psychology, 36*, 335–346. doi:10.1007/s10802-007-9181-9

Jackson, K. M., & Sher, K. J. (2006). Comparison of longitudinal phenotypes based on number and timing of assessments: A systematic comparison of trajectory approaches II. *Psychology of Addictive Behaviors, 20*, 373–384. doi:10.1037/0893-164X.20.4.373

Johnston, L. D., O'Malley, P. M., Bachman, J. G., & Schulenberg, J. E. (2009). *Monitoring the Future national survey results on drug use, 1975–2008: Vol. I. Secondary school students* (NIH Publication No. 09–7402). Bethesda, MD: National Institute on Drug Abuse.

Kamata, A., & Bauer, D. J. (2008). A note on the relation between factor analytic and item response theory models. *Structural Equation Modeling, 15*, 136–153.

Little, R. J. A., & Rubin, D. B. (1987). *Statistical analysis with missing data.* New York, NY: Wiley.

Lochman, J. E., & Wells, K. C. (2002). Contextual social–cognitive mediators and child outcome: A test of the theoretical model in the Coping Power program. *Development and Psychopathology, 14*, 945–967. doi:10.1017/S0954579402004157

MacCallum, R. C., Roznowski, M., & Necowitz, L. B. (1992). Model modifications in covariance structure analysis: The problem of chance capitalization. *Psychological Bulletin, 111*, 490–504. doi:10.1037/0033-2909.111.3.490

MacCallum, R. C., Wegener, D. T., Uchino, B. N., & Fabrigar, L. R. (1993). The problem of equivalent models in the application of covariance structure models. *Psychological Bulletin, 114*, 185–199. doi:10.1037/0033-2909.114.1.185

Marsh, H. W., Hau, K. T., & Grayson, D. (2005). Goodness of fit in structural equation models. In A. Maydeu-Olivares & J. J. McArdle (Eds.), *Contemporary psychometrics: A Festschrift for Roderick P. McDonald* (pp. 275–340). Mahwah, NJ: Erlbaum.

Marsh, H. W., Hau, K.-T., & Wen, Z. (2004). In search of golden rules: Comment on hypothesis-testing approaches to setting cutoff values for fit indexes and dangers in overgeneralizing Hu and Bentler's findings. *Structural Equation Modeling, 11*, 320–341. doi:10.1207/s15328007sem1103_2

Meade, A. W., Lautenschlager, G. J., & Hecht, J. E. (2005). Establishing measurement equivalence and invariance in longitudinal data with item response theory. *International Journal of Testing, 5*, 279–300. doi:10.1207/s15327574ijt0503_6

Meredith, W. (1993). Measurement invariance, factor analysis, and factorial invariance. *Psychometrika, 58*, 525–543. doi:10.1007/BF02294825

Meredith, W., & Tisak, J. (1990). Latent curve analysis. *Psychometrika, 55*, 107–122. doi:10.1007/BF02294746

Millsap, R. E. (2010). Testing measurement invariance using item response theory in longitudinal data: An introduction. *Child Development Perspectives, 4*, 5–9. doi:10.1111/j.1750-8606.2009.00109.x

Muthén, B. (2008). Latent variable hybrids: Overview of old and new models. In G. R. Hancock & K. M. Samuelsen (Eds.), *Advances in latent variable mixture models* (pp. 1–24). Charlotte, NC: Information Age.

Nagin, D. S. (2005). *Group-based modeling of development.* Cambridge, MA: Harvard University Press.

Raudenbush, S. W. (2001). Comparing personal trajectories and drawing causal inferences from longitudinal data. *Annual Review of Psychology, 52*, 501–525. doi:10.1146/annurev.psych.52.1.501

Raudenbush, S. W., & Chan, W. S. (1993). Application of a hierarchical linear model to study adolescent deviance in an overlapping cohort design. *Journal of Consulting and Clinical Psychology, 61*, 941–951. doi:10.1037/0022-006X.61.6.941

Raykov, T. (1997). Equivalent structural equation models and group equality constraints. *Multivariate Behavioral Research, 32*, 95–104. doi:10.1207/s15327906mbr3202_1

Reise, S. P., & Waller, N. G. (2009). Item response theory and clinical measurement. *Annual Review of Clinical Psychology, 5*, 27–48. doi:10.1146/annurev.clinpsy.032408.153553

Ribisl, K. M., Walton, M. A., Mowbray, C. T., Luke, D. A., Davidson, W. S., & Bootsmiller, B. J. (1996). Minimizing participant attrition in panel studies through the use of effective retention and tracking strategies: Review and recommendations. *Evaluation and Program Planning, 19*, 1–25. doi:10.1016/0149-7189(95)00037-2

Rogosa, D. (1979). Causal models in longitudinal research: Rationale, formulation, and interpretation. In J. R. Nesselroade & P. B. Baltes (Eds.), *Longitudinal research in the study of behavior and development* (pp. 263–302). New York, NY: Academic Press.

Schafer, J. L., & Olsen, M. K. (1998). Multiple imputation for multivariate missing data problems: A data analyst's perspective. *Multivariate Behavioral Research, 33*, 545–571. doi:10.1207/s15327906mbr3304_5

Sher, K. J., & Wood, P. K. (1997). Methodological issues in conducting prospective research on alcohol-related behavior: A report from the field. In K. J. Bryant, M. Windle, & S. G. West (Eds.), *The science of prevention: Methodological advances from alcohol and substance abuse research* (pp. 3–41). Washington, DC: American Psychological Association. doi:10.1037/10222-001

Singer, J. D., & Willett, J. (2003). *Applied longitudinal data analysis.* New York, NY: Oxford University Press. doi:10.1093/acprof:oso/9780195152968.001.0001

Sternberg, R. J., & Berg, C. A. (Eds.). (1992). *Intellectual development.* Cambridge, England: Cambridge University Press.

Stoel, R. D., & Garre, F. G. (2011). Growth curve analysis using multilevel regression and structural equation modeling. In J. J. Hox & J. K. Roberts (Eds.),

Handbook of advanced multilevel analysis (pp. 97–111). New York, NY: Routledge.

Tomarken, A. J., & Waller, N. J. (2005). Structural equation modeling: Strengths, limitations, and misconceptions. *Annual Review of Clinical Psychology, 1*, 31–65. doi:10.1146/annurev.clinpsy.1.102803.144239

Vandenberg, R. J., & Lance, C. E. (2000). A review and synthesis of the measurement invariance literature: Suggestions, practices, and recommendations for organizational research. *Organizational Research Methods, 3*, 4–69. doi:10.1177/109442810031002

Widaman, K. F., Ferrer, E., & Conger, R. D. (2010). Factorial invariance within longitudinal structural equation models: Measuring the same construct across time. *Child Development Perspectives, 4*, 10–18. doi:10.1111/j.1750-8606.2009.00110.x

Windle, M. (2000). A latent growth curve model of delinquent activity among adolescents. *Applied Developmental Science, 4*, 193–207. doi:10.1207/S1532480XADS0404_2

Windle, M., Brener, N. D., Cuccaro, P., Dittus, P. J., Kanouse, D. E., Murray, N., . . . Schuster, M. A. (2010). Parenting predictors of early adolescent's health behaviors: Simultaneous group comparisons across sex and ethnic groups. *Journal of Youth and Adolescence, 39*, 594–606. doi:10.1007/s10964-009-9414-z

Windle, M., & Davies, P. T. (1999). Developmental research and theory. In K. E. Leonard & H. T. Blane (Eds.), *Psychological theories of drinking and alcoholism* (pp. 164–202). New York, NY: Guilford Press.

Wohlwill, J. F. (1973). *The study of behavioral development.* New York, NY: Academic Press.

Wolke, D., Waylen, A., Samara, M., Steer, C., Goodman, R., Ford, T., & Lamberts, K. (2009). Selective dropout in longitudinal studies and non-biased prediction of behavior disorders. *British Journal of Psychiatry, 195*, 249–256. doi:10.1192/bjp.bp.108.053751

Wothke, W. (1996). Models for multitrait-multimethod analysis. In G. A. Marcoulides & R. E. Schumacker (Eds.), *Advanced structural equation modeling: Issues and techniques* (pp. 7–56). Hillside, NJ: Erlbaum.

Wu, W., & West, S. G. (2010). Sensitivity of fit indices to misspecification in growth curve models. *Multivariate Behavioral Research, 45*, 420–452. doi:10.1080/00273171.2010.483378

Chapter 13

EVENT HISTORY ANALYSIS

Fetene B. Tekle and Jeroen K. Vermunt

In social and behavioral sciences in general and in psychology in particular, researchers are often interested in the occurrence of events such as the formation or ending of formal and informal relationships (e.g. marital unions, friendships, love relationships), the onset of and recovery from mental disorders, the entry into and exit from a job, the experience of stressful and pleasant life events (accidents, the death of a parent, being in love for the first time), and the transition across developmental stages. Mortality may also be the event of interest, although that is the more typical event in biomedical studies. Data on the occurrence of the event(s) of interest can either be collected using retrospective or prospective study designs, and these data will contain information on whether the event(s) of interest occurred to the individuals in the sample, and if so, on the time of occurrence. In addition to information on the timing of the event(s) of interest, there will usually also be information on sociodemographic covariates, risk factors, and the treatment or intervention received if there is any.

Event history data makes it possible to determine at what time periods the event of interest is most likely to occur as well as to determine why some individuals experience the event earlier than others and why some do not experience the event of interest at all during the study period. Although event history data gives opportunities to answer such questions, they also pose certain challenges that cannot be dealt with using standard data analysis methods such as linear and logistic regression analysis (Allison, 1982; Tuma & Hannan, 1979; Willett &

Singer, 1993). More specifically, simple linear and logistic regression methods are not suited for dealing with two distinctive features of event history data—that is, with censoring and time-varying covariates. Censoring is a specific kind of missing data problem, namely, that for some individuals it is not known when the event occurs because they did not experience the event during the observation period. Linear regression analysis of such censored data yields biased results and logistic regression analysis yields loss of information. Moreover, standard regression models lack a way to incorporate time-varying covariates, covariates that may change their value over time. To deal with censoring and time-varying covariates, we need special regression techniques that are known as event history models, hazard models, survival models, failure time models, and duration models.

The main distinction made in the field of event history analysis is between continuous-time methods (when the event time can take on any nonnegative value) and discrete-time methods (when the event time can take on a finite set of values). In this chapter, we focus on discrete-time techniques as a part of a course for graduate-level students or as a reference for applied researchers. Although continuous-time methods are predominant in the statistical literature (Blossfeld & Rohwer, 1995; Collett, 2003; Vermunt, 1997), discrete-time methods are more commonly used in psychological research as well as in other social and behavioral sciences, not only because they are conceptually simpler but also because one will seldom have real continuous-time data. Sometimes

DOI: 10.1037/13621-013
APA Handbook of Research Methods in Psychology: Vol. 3. Data Analysis and Research Publication, H. Cooper (Editor-in-Chief)

events can only occur at regular discrete time-points (e.g., weekly, monthly, or yearly), whereas in other situations events can occur in continuous time, but the measurement yields discrete-time data—for example, when a survey asks the age or year of the formation of a relationship, marriage, or divorce instead of the exact date. In both situations, it is more appropriate to use discrete-time methods instead of methods that are developed for continuous event time. Even if the measurement scale of the event time is continuous, discrete-time techniques can be used to approximate the results that would be obtained with continuous-time methods (Vermunt, 1997; Yamaguchi, 1991). Additionally, discrete-time techniques are computationally and conceptually simpler and thus easier to understand by social and behavioral scientists, and they can serve as a good starting point for understanding the more advanced continuous-time methods.

The remainder of this chapter is organized as follows. First, an empirical example that is used throughout this chapter is introduced. Some basic terminologies of event history analysis are presented next. The following section explains why special regression techniques are needed for event history analysis. Then we present the statistical concepts used for describing event time distributions—the hazard and survival functions—and show how a grouped-data method similar to the actuarial method can be used to estimate these functions. Finally, we discuss regression models for discrete-time event history data in which the hazard rate—or the probability of event occurrence at a particular time-point—is related to covariates. Concluding remarks are given in the final section.

AN EMPIRICAL EXAMPLE: ADOLESCENTS' RELATIONSHIPS

Throughout this chapter, a real-life example is used to illustrate the concepts and modeling approaches for event history data.

This example is about adolescents' first experiences with relationships. The data are taken from a small-scale survey of 145 adolescents in the Netherlands (Vinken, 1998). Vermunt (2002) used latent class analysis to construct a typology on the basis of four events related to adolescents' first experience with relationships: *sleeping with someone*, *going out*, *having a steady friend*, and *being very much in love*. Here, we use the event *sleeping with someone for the first time* to illustrate the methods of event history analysis discussed in this chapter. In addition to information on the occurrence of the four events, binary time-constant (i.e., fixed) covariates, youth centrism (*YC*), gender (*G*), and education (*E*) are available. *YC* is a measure for the extent to which young people perceive their peers as a positive valued in-group and perceive adults as a negatively valued out-group. The dichotomous *YC* scale that is used here was constructed by Vinken (1998).

STATE, EVENT, RISK PERIOD, RISK SET, AND CENSORING

To understand the nature of event history data and the purpose of event history analysis, it is important to understand the following concepts: state, event, risk period, risk set, and censoring (Yamaguchi, 1991). These concepts are illustrated in the following paragraphs using the example introduced in the previous section.

The first step in an event history analysis is to define the discrete states that one wishes to distinguish. *States* are the categories of the variable, the dynamics of which one wishes to explain. At every particular point in time, each person occupies exactly one state. In our first experience with relationships example, each adolescent is either in the state *never slept with someone* or *has slept with someone*. An *event* is a transition from one state to another, that is, from an origin state to a destination state. In our example, the event sleeping with someone for the first time is the transition from the state *never slept with someone* to the state *has slept with someone*. In our application, the event of interest can occur only once because it is not possible to exit the destination state (this is called an *absorbing state*). In other applications, the event(s) of interest may occur several times (this is called a *recurrent event*), such as the recovery from a depression, which is the transition between the states depressed and nondepressed.

Another important concept is the risk period. Clearly, not all persons can experience each of the events under study at every point in time. To be able to experience a particular event, one must first occupy the original state, that is, one must be at risk of the event concerned. The period that someone is at risk of a particular event—or exposed to a particular risk—is called the *risk period*. Usually it is straightforward to identify the persons at risk of the event, such as in our relationships example in which adolescents that have never slept with someone at a particular age are at risk of experiencing the event of sleeping with someone for the first time at that age. The risk period(s) for a recovery from depression are the period(s) that a subject stayed in the original state depressed. A strongly related concept is the *risk set*. The risk set at a particular point in time is formed by all subjects who are at risk of experiencing the event concerned at that point in time.

Using these concepts, event history analysis can be defined as the analysis of the duration of the non-occurrence of an event during the risk period. When the event of interest is *sleeping with someone for the first time*, the analysis concerns the duration of non-occurrence of the experience of sleeping with someone, in other words, the time that adolescents remained in the state *never slept with someone*. In practice, as will be demonstrated, the dependent variable in an event history model is not duration or time itself but a transition probability or hazard rate. Therefore, event history modeling can also be defined as the analysis of the probability (or rate) of occurrence of the event of interest during the risk period. In the relationships example, this concerns an adolescent's probability of sleeping with someone given that this has not yet happened.

As was indicated, an issue that always receives a great amount of attention in discussions on event history analysis is *censoring*, in which a distinction should be made between *left* and *right censoring*. These two forms of censoring refer to missing information on the time of nonoccurrence of the event of interest *before* and *after* the observation (or follow-up) period, respectively. Here, we consider only the more common right-censoring problem, and we refer interested readers to Kalbfleisch and Prentice

(2002), Tuma and Hannan (1979), and Yamaguchi (1991) for discussions of alternative censoring mechanisms and their implications.

An observation is called right-censored if it is known that the participant did not experience the event of interest during a certain amount of time (during a follow-up period), but the exact time at which he or she experienced the event is unknown. In the recovery from depression example, a censored observation would be when an individual was in the depressed state at the end of the study or dropped out from the study without recovery. For such a person, we know the duration of the depression until that moment, but we do not know whether or when he or she will recover from depression, which means that the duration of nonoccurrence of recovery is only partially observed for such a person. In the relationships example, a censored observation would be an adolescent who has not experienced the event *sleeping with someone* before the age at which the survey took place. This partial information is called the *censoring time*.

More formally, let T be the event time and U the censoring time. The duration of nonoccurrence of an event that can actually be observed is $Y = \min(T, U)$; that is, we observe the true event time when it is smaller than the censoring time and vice versa. Methods for event history analysis define a model for the dependent variable Y (and thus not for T). However, because it is also relevant to make a distinction between event and censoring times, an event indicator variable has to be defined. For right-censored event data, the event indicator for ith person is defined as

$$Event_i = \begin{cases} 1 & \text{if } T_i \leq U_i \\ 0 & \text{if } T_i > U_i \end{cases}. \tag{1}$$

In other words, $Event_i$ equals 1 if we observe the event time and 0 if the observation is censored.

Although traditional regression methodology such as linear or logistic regression analysis does not provide a way to simultaneously analyze observed and censored event times, as we will show later, event history analysis methodology provides a way of considering both simultaneously. In the next section, we will explain when these event history analysis methods are more appealing in relation to research problems in practice.

WHEN TO USE EVENT HISTORY ANALYSIS

To determine whether the method of event history analysis is applicable in a specific situation, one has to examine the research problem or question and a study's methodological features. A research's method of analysis calls for event history analysis if the research's question is centered on whether events occur and, if so, when they occur. Data can be collected prospectively or retrospectively, over a short or a long period of time, in an experiment or an observational study. The beginning time, which is an initial starting point at which no one under study has yet experienced the target event but everybody is in the risk set, has to be identified. The time of a target event whose occurrence is being studied can be measured in years, months, days, or minutes; however, a meaningful scale needs to be chosen. For example, in the relationships example, the research question is when young adolescents have their first experience of sleeping with someone and whether predictors affect the timing of this event. Clearly, the target event is the transition to sleeping with someone for the first time. The beginning time is the time at which none of the subjects under study has experienced the event and all of the subjects are in the risk set of the event *sleeping with someone*. Because data are collected retrospectively, it is not practical to precisely measure the time of the first experience of sleeping with someone in months, days, or smaller grids of time. During the data collection, subjects may recall the period of the event in terms of the age at which the event happened. Thus, it is logical to consider age in years as the unit of scale for event period in the relationships data example.

DESCRIBING EVENT TIME DISTRIBUTION

Discrete Versus Continuous Time

The manner in which the basic statistical concepts of event history analysis are defined depends on whether the time variable T, indicating the duration of nonoccurrence of an event, is assumed to be continuous or discrete. Of course, it seems logical to assume T to be a continuous variable in the sense that the event of interest may occur literally at any time defined on $(0, \infty)$. In many situations, however, this assumption is not realistic for two reasons. First, in many cases, T is not measured accurately enough to be treated as strictly continuous. Respondents can usually give dates and times only in ranges or round numbers, even if encouraged by interviewers to be more precise. Second, the events of interest can sometimes only occur at finite particular points in time that are discrete (taking a finite set of values, e.g., $t_1, t_2, \ldots, t_L$).

Regardless of the assumption whether T is a discrete or continuous variable, the main aim of event history analysis is to characterize the probability distribution of the random variable T, the duration of nonoccurrence of an event. An additional objective is typically to gain an understanding on how risk factors and covariates affect the event times. This second objective can be addressed by modeling the probability distribution of T in terms of potentially explanatory variables. Even though these objectives are common to any event history analysis, the way the statistical methods are formulated depends on whether the measurement of the time variable is assumed to be discrete or continuous. The methods and discussions considered below in this chapter assume time is measured on discrete scale. We describe in the next subsection possible ways of characterizing the probability distribution of T and give modeling strategies of the probability distribution of T in terms of possible explanatory variables in the section Discrete-Time Event History Models.

Discrete Event Time Distributions

Let T be a discrete random variable indicating the event time, and t_l the lth discrete time-point, with $l = 1, 2, \ldots$ and $0 < t_1 < t_2 < \ldots$. There are three equivalent ways to characterize the probability distribution of the event time T. The simplest is as $f(t_l) = \Pr(T = t_l)$, or as the probability of experiencing an event at $T = t_l$. Another possibility is via the survival function $S(t_l)$, which is the probability of not having the event occur before and in time interval t_l or, equivalently, the probability of having the event occur after t_l. It is defined as follows:

$$S(t_l) = \Pr(T > t_l) = 1 - \Pr(T \le t_l), \quad l = 1, 2, \ldots \quad (2)$$

Another option is to use the discrete-time hazard probability $h(t_l)$, which is the conditional probability that the event occurs at $T = t_l$ given that it did not occur before $T = t_l$ (given $S(t_{l-1})$). Mathematically, the hazard is given as

$$h(t_l) = \Pr(T = t_l \mid T \geq t_l) = \Pr(T = t_l \mid T > t_{l-1})$$
$$= \frac{\Pr(T = t_l)}{\Pr(T > t_{l-1})} = \frac{f(t_l)}{S(t_{l-1})}. \tag{3}$$

What is important is that both $f(t_l)$ and $S(t_l)$ can be expressed in terms of $h(t_l)$. Using the fact that $f(t_l) = S(t_{l-1}) - S(t_l)$, Equation 3 can be rewritten as

$$h(t_l) = \frac{S(t_{l-1}) - S(t_l)}{S(t_{l-1})} = 1 - \frac{S(t_l)}{S(t_{l-1})}. \tag{4}$$

By rearranging Equation 4, we obtain

$$S(t_l) = S(t_{l-1})[1 - h(t_l)]. \tag{5}$$

Using $S(t_0) = 1$, no individual experienced an event before and in $T = t_0$, Equation 5 leads to the required expression that

$$S(t_l) = \prod_{k=1}^{l}[1 - h(t_k)], \tag{6}$$

where Π is a product sign and the term in brackets is a complementary term of the hazard function, which is the conditional probability that the event occurs at time t_k given that it did not occur before t_k. Equation 6 implies that the survival probability to the end of *l*th time is the product of survival probabilities at each of the earlier time-points.

By using Equations 3 and 5, the following expression is also obtained for the probability of experiencing an event at time t_l, $f(t_l)$:

$$f(t_l) = h(t_l)\prod_{k=1}^{l-1}[1 - h(t_k)]. \tag{7}$$

Estimating Event Time Distribution

The grouped-data or life-table method (Cox, 1972; Merrell, 1947) and the Kaplan–Meier (Kaplan & Meier, 1958) estimator are two descriptive methods for estimating the event time distribution from a sample. In the next subsection, we discuss the grouped-data method for discrete event times.

Grouped-Data or Life-Table Method for Discrete Event Times

The most straightforward way to describe the event history in a sample is to construct grouped data by merging event times in groups or intervals. This method is more commonly known as the *life-table* method. The life-table method enables the computation of nonparametric estimates of the survival and hazard functions in separate intervals over time. The distribution of event times is divided into a certain number of intervals. For each interval we can then identify the number of subjects entering the respective interval without having experienced the event, the number of cases that experienced the event in the respective interval, and the number of cases that were lost or censored in the respective interval. On the basis of those numbers, several additional statistics can be computed. Some of these statistics are as follows:

- **Number of cases at risk (risk set r_l):** This is the number of subjects who are at risk of experiencing the event of interest within the specific interval. This number is the number of cases that entered the respective interval.
- **Proportion of cases that experience the event (hazard h_l):** This proportion is computed as the ratio of the number of cases experiencing the event within the interval divided by the number of cases at risk in the interval.
- **Cumulative proportion surviving (survival function S_l):** This is the cumulative proportion of cases surviving up to the end of respective interval.
- **Median survival time:** This is the survival time at which the cumulative survival function is equal to 0.5.

Example: Life-Table Method for Adolescents' Relationship Example

Table 13.1 shows a life table for the data on adolescents' first experiences sleeping with someone introduced in the section An Empirical Example. For 142 cases, we have information on whether the event sleeping with someone had happened (yes or no) and, if yes, when it happened. Results show that 90.1% of these adolescents experienced the event before the time of data collection.

TABLE 13.1

Life Table Describing the Ages at Sleeping With Someone for the First Time for a Sample of 142 Adolescents

		Number		Proportion	
Age interval[a]	Entering interval	Withdrawing during interval (censored)	"Slept with someone for the first time" during interval	"Slept with someone for the first time" during interval (hazard)	Has not slept with someone at the end of the interval (survival function)
[11, 12)	142	0			1.0000
[12, 13)	142	0	1	0.0070	0.9930
[13, 14)	141	0	0	0.0000	0.9930
[14, 15)	141	0	2	0.0142	0.9789
[15, 16)	139	0	11	0.0791	0.9014
[16, 17)	128	0	19	0.1484	0.7676
[17, 18)	109	0	23	0.2110	0.6056
[18, 19)	86	0	21	0.2442	0.4577
[19, 20)	65	0	11	0.1692	0.3803
[20, 21)	54	0	20	0.3704	0.2394
[21, 22)	34	0	11	0.3235	0.1620
[22, 23)	23	0	3	0.1304	0.1408
[23, 24)	20	6	3	0.1500	0.1190
[24, 25)	11	8	3	0.2727	0.0865

[a] Square brackets are used before the initial time to indicate each interval's initial time is included in the interval; parentheses are used after the end time to indicate the end time is not part of the interval.

A natural definition of the beginning time (t_0) for an analysis of this data set is an age at which none of the adolescents experienced the event of interested, or equivalently, an age at which all subjects are at risk of experiencing the event. It does not, however, make sense to start at age 0 because the youngest age at which the event happened is 12, which means that the hazard rate is 0 and the survival probability is 1 for all ages before 12. Without loss of information, we can therefore use age 11 as the beginning time for the event history analysis. By dividing the data into a series of rows indexing the age intervals (column 1), a life table for the relationships example in Table 13.1 contains information on the number of adolescents who (a) entered the age interval (column 2), (b) censored during the age interval (column 3), and (c) experienced the event *sleeping with someone* during the age interval (column 4). The age intervals in Table 13.1 partition the times of the event occurrence in such a way that each interval contains a range of ages that include the initial time and excludes the concluding time. The width of the intervals is set to 1 year for ease of presentation. Conventional mathematical notation [square brackets] denotes inclusions and (parentheses) denote exclusions. Thus, square brackets are used before each interval's initial time, and parentheses are used after the concluding time. In total there are 14 age intervals of 1 year each: [11, 12), [12, 13), . . ., [24, 25). In general, the time intervals of a life table should be defined on the basis of a relevant time unit and respect the way events occur. Data whose time unit is days, weeks, or months may require wider intervals compared with data whose time unit is years, but the grouping should always be such that it yields a series of time intervals $[t_0, t_1), [t_1, t_2), . . ., [t_{l-1}, t_l), [t_l, t_{l+1}), . . .$, and so on. No events occur during the 0th interval, which begins at time t_0 and ends just before t_1. This interval represents what is called the beginning of time. Any event occurring at t_1 or later but before t_2, is classified as an event happening during the first time interval $[t_1, t_2)$. The lth time interval, $[t_l, t_{l+1})$, begins immediately at time t_l and ends just before time t_{l+1}.

The next column in the life table contains the number of adolescents who enter each successive age interval without experiencing the event or censoring in the previous intervals. This number is the risk set for the discrete-time life-table description. As shown in Table 13.1, column 3, censoring happens for some cases in the last two age-groups. For these cases, the event sleeping with someone has not happened before the time of data collection. The only known information is that those adolescents have not experienced the event until age 24 (in the age interval [23, 24)) and 25 (in the age interval [24, 25)), respectively. Column 4 contains the number of events that occurred in each age interval. As can be seen, the risk set or the number in column 2 for each interval is the risk set of the previous interval minus the sum of the numbers in column 3 and 4 of the previous interval.

Table 13.1, column 5, shows the proportion of each interval's risk set that experiences the event during the interval. Thus, these are conditional probabilities (or hazards) that the event occurs to an individual in lth interval given that the event did not occur to that person before the lth interval. In fact, the proportions in column 5 are maximum likelihood estimates of the discrete-time hazard given in Equation 3 (Singer & Willett, 1993, 2003). That means we estimate the discrete-time hazard for each interval in the life table by the proportion of the risk set that experiences the event within the interval. These proportions are mathematically obtained by dividing the numbers in column 4 by the numbers in column 2, that is,

$$\hat{h}(t_1) = \frac{\text{number of events in interval } l}{\text{number at risk in interval } l}, \qquad (8)$$

where $\hat{h}(t_l)$ is an estimate of the discrete hazard probability at time t in interval l.

Hence the estimate of hazard is $\hat{h}(t_1) = 0.0070$ for a time in the first interval; 0 for the second interval because none of the adolescents experienced the event in the second interval, $\hat{h}(t_3) = 0.0142$; and so on. Note that the discrete-time hazard is a probability, which implies that its value always lies between 0 and 1. A helpful way of examining the time-dependence of the hazard probabilities is to graph their values over time. The top panel of Figure 13.1 plots the estimated hazard function on the basis of the proportions in Table 13.1, column 5. The risk of event occurrence (sleeping with someone for the

first time) among the adolescents at ages below 16 is small. The risk in general increases with time starting from age 16 until age 19 at which point it drops suddenly. It again increases in the interval [20, 21) and starts to decrease thereafter. Finally, there is an increase in risk starting from age 23. In general the risky time periods for experiencing the event are from age 16 with a high peak at age 20. The estimated hazard probabilities at each time interval describe the distribution of event occurrence for a random sample of individuals from a homogenous population. In the section Discrete-Time Event History Models, we show how individual difference in the hazard probabilities can be investigated using regression models including predictor variables (e.g., gender and education level).

The proportion of adolescents who have not slept with someone until the end of each time interval (who survived) is shown in Table 13.1, column 6. This proportion is an estimate of the survival function given in Equation 5. Because no one has experienced the event before age 12, the estimate of survival function for the 0th interval, $\hat{S}(t_0)$, is 1.0000. The estimate for the first interval is then the product of the survival function of the 0th interval and the probability of surviving (not having the event) during the first interval. This latter probability is just the complement of the hazard probability in the first interval, $1 - \hat{h}(t_1) = 1 - 0.0070$. Thus, the estimate of the survival function for the first interval is $\hat{S}(t_1) = \hat{S}(t_0)[1 - \hat{h}(t_1)] = 1 \times [1 - 0.0070] = 0.9930$, implying that 99.3% of the adolescents did not experience the event until the end of the first interval. In general the estimate of the hazard function for lth interval is

$$\hat{S}(t_l) = \hat{S}(t_{l-1})[1 - \hat{h}(t_l)]. \qquad (9)$$

In general, the survivor function over time declines to zero, which is the lower bound for the survival probability. A useful way to examine the survival function is again to graph the estimates of survival function over time. The bottom panel of Figure 13.1 graphs the survival function on the basis of the estimates in Table 13.1, column 6. Unlike the hazard function, which can increase, decrease, or remain constant over time, the survivor function never increases. For intervals with no events occurring

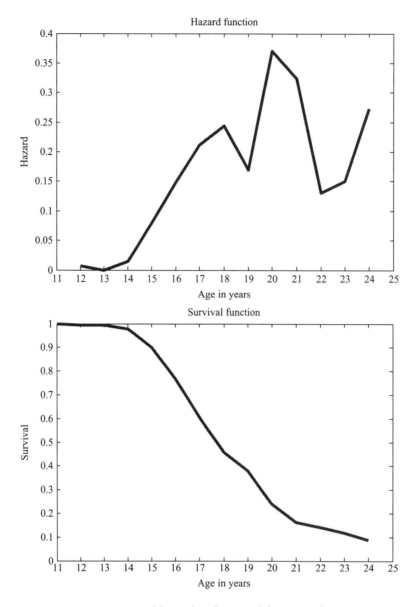

FIGURE 13.1.   Estimated hazard and survival functions for 142 adolescents' experiences with sleeping with someone for the first time.

(e.g., interval [13, 14)), the survivor function remains steady at the value of previous interval. The survivor function drops rapidly in those periods in which the hazard is high and the survivor function declines slowly at the time periods with low hazard.

The life-table estimates of the discrete-time hazard and survival functions yield two alternative descriptions of the event time's distribution. The interest is usually also on the summary statistics or center of the distribution. If there was no censoring, the center of the event time distribution could be estimated using sample mean. Because of censoring, however, the event time is not known for all

individuals and the sample mean cannot be used as an estimate of the center of the distribution. Instead, another measure of central tendency is often used in event history analysis: the median survival time. As a measure of center of the distribution, the estimated median survival time is the value of time (here age) for which the value of the estimated survival function is 0.5. In general, the median survival time, or the 50th percentile for the survival function, is not necessarily the same as the point in time up to which 50% of the sample survived without the event. The median survival time corresponds to the point in time up to which

50% of the sample survived without the event only if there were no censored observations before this time (which is the case in the adolescents' relationship example).

A closer look at the estimate of the survival function in Table 13.1, column 6, shows that 0.6056 of the adolescents survived to the end of the interval [17, 18) and the proportion drops below 0.5 to 0.4577 in the interval [18, 19). Thus, the median survival time could be reported as age between 17 and 18. If needed, the estimate of median survival time can be more accurately obtained by interpolation between the two intervals that have survival estimates close to 0.5 on both sides above 0.5 and below 0.5. In the current adolescents' relationship example, the two intervals are [17, 18) and [18, 19). Let t_m be the initial time for the interval when the sample survivor function is just above 0.5 (in our example, age 17), let $\hat{S}(t_m)$ represent the value of the sample survivor function of that interval, let t_{m+1} and $\hat{S}(t_{m+1})$ be the initial time and sample survivor function, respectively, for the following interval (when the survivor function is just below 0.5). Then, following linear interpolation, the estimated median survival time is

$$M\hat{d}n = t_m + \left[\frac{\hat{S}(t_m) - 0.5}{\hat{S}(t_m) - \hat{S}(t_{m+1})} \right](t_{m+1} - t_m). \quad (10)$$

For the current example the interpolation is illustrated using the following simple sketch.

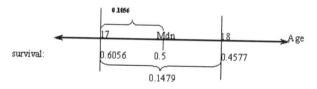

In our application, there are no censored cases for the intervals before [18, 19), which contains the median survival time. As a result, the median survival time 17.7 is also the age at which 50% of the sample units experienced the event.

Hazard functions are the most useful tools in describing patterns of event occurrence because they are sensitive to the unique risk associated with each time period, whereas the survivor functions accumulate information across time periods. Thus, by examining the variation over time in the magnitude

of the hazard function, we identify when events are likely, or unlikely, to occur. The median survival time identifies the center of the distribution and it tells little about the distribution of event times. It is an average event time but relatively less sensitive to the extreme values.

The life-table method for estimating hazard and survival functions using discrete-time event data is similar to the actuarial method for estimating these functions using continuous-time event data. These methods differ only in the assumption about the occurrence of events and censorings within intervals. The discrete-time method assumes events and censorings occur at the endpoint of the time interval, which means that all those who entered the interval are in the risk set throughout the interval. The actuarial method, however, assumes that both events and censorings are distributed equally throughout the interval, which means that the risk set changes during an interval. In the actuarial method, the risk set is estimated as the average number of person at risk during the interval, which leads to slight modifications of Equations 8 and 9 for this method. More details about the actuarial method have been given elsewhere (Cutler & Ederer, 1958; Mould, 1976; Singer & Willett, 2003, p. 480; among others).

The description and estimation of the event time distributions discussed so far assumes a single homogeneous group of subjects. In practice, however, researchers are also interested in identifying factors that affect the occurrence and timing of the event of interest. For example, in intervention or experimental studies, the interest is to estimate the effects of the intervention on the probability of occurrence of the event over time. Therefore, we move from the discussion of method for describing event time distribution to regression models that allow for such predictors as sociodemographic covariates and experimental conditions. The objective is to determine the relationship between those predictors and the likelihood of event occurrence. The specific modeling approach again depends on whether the event time is treated as discrete or continuous. Thus, we pursue the discussion that follows with the assumption of discrete event times, and we refer readers to Blossfeld and Rohwer

(1995), Collett (2003), and Vermunt (1997), among others, for well-developed methodologies on continuous event time models. Regression models for discrete event time data are better known in literature as *discrete-time survival models* (DTSM). Even though discrete- and continuous-time models originally were formulated separately by Cox (1972), asymptotically the two models are equivalent. That is, as the discrete-time interval gets smaller and smaller, a DTSM becomes more and more similar to a continuous-time model (Allison, 1982; D'Agostino et al., 1990; Petersen, 1991; Thompson, 1977; Yamaguchi, 1991).

DISCRETE-TIME EVENT HISTORY MODELS

Cox (1972) was the first to propose models for censored data. He proposed discrete-time models for tied event data alongside his formulation of proportional hazard modeling for continuous-time data. A *tie* refers to the situation in which several subjects experience the event at the same specific time, which is something that in a strict continuous-time framework should not occur. When there are many ties in the data, a discrete-time model is more appropriate. The discrete-time modeling approach involves using a logistic regression model for a person–period data set. For all time-points until a person either experiences the event or is censored, the dependent variable is an indicator of whether or not an individual experienced the event at that time-point (Allison, 1982; Singer & Willett, 1993).

As discussed in the previous section, in contrast to the other distributions for event history data, the hazard function is the most important element in event history analysis for at least three reasons. First, it shows the risk of event occurrence at each time period, that is, it tells us whether and when an event is likely to occur. Second, the event history analysis is able to deal with censored cases because the hazard always includes both censored and non-censored cases. Third, the sample survival function cannot be computed directly for a given time-point when there is censoring, but the survival function can be estimated indirectly from the hazard function. In general, the mathematical relationships described earlier between the distributions of event history data can be used to obtain estimates of other distributions ($S(t_l)$ and $f(t_l)$) if the estimate of hazard is known. By using the hazard $h(t_l)$ as the left-hand side variable in a regression model, one can relate hazard distribution to the covariates of interest. Because hazards are (conditional) probabilities bounded by zero and one, they can be transformed using logit link function so that the transformed hazard is unbounded and can easily be regressed on covariates and time variables. That means instead of modeling the hazard probability directly the logit of the hazard probability is used as the left-hand side variable in a (generalized) linear model. The logit hazard at time $T = t_l$ for a person with covariate value X is given by

$$\text{logit}[h_X(t_l)] = Log_e\left[\frac{h_X(t_l)}{1 - h_X(t_l)}\right] = \alpha_l D_l + \beta X, \quad (11)$$

where $Log_e[c]$ is the natural logarithm of c, $h_X(t_l)$ is the hazard or conditional event probability at time t_l for a person with covariate value X, D_l is a dummy variable indicating the time period ($D_l = 1$, if $T = t_l$ and zero otherwise), α_l is the intercept parameter at time-point $T = t_l$ representing the logit hazard when $X = 0$ (baseline logit hazard at time t_l), and β is the slope parameter that shows the effect of the covariate X on the logit hazard. When there are more covariates, Equation 11 can be extended by including the covariates and corresponding β parameters at the right-hand side of the equation. That means for a person with covariate values $X_1, X_2, \ldots, X_p$ the logit hazard is

$$\text{logit}[h_{X_p}(t_l)] = Log_e\left[\frac{h_{X_p}(t_l)}{1 - h_{X_p}(t_l)}\right]$$
$$= \alpha_l D_l + \beta_1 X_1 + \beta_2 X_2 + \ldots + \beta_p X_p$$
$$= \alpha_l + \Sigma_{k=1}^{p}\beta_k X_k, \quad (12)$$

where $h_{X_p}(t_l)$ is the hazard or conditional probability at time t_l for a person with p covariate values $X_1, X_2, \ldots, X_p$ and β_k is the parameter that shows the effect of the covariate X_k on the logit hazard controlling for other covariates in the model, $k = 1, \ldots, p$.

Equation 12 is a discrete-time event history model or DTSM. When the value of all covariates equals, the logit hazard in Equation 12 reduces to the baseline logit hazard

$$logit[h_0(t_l)] = Log_e\left[\frac{h_0(t_l)}{1-h_0(t_l)}\right] = \alpha_l D_l, \quad (13)$$

where $h_0(t_l)$ is the baseline hazard or conditional probability with covariate values equal to zero at time t_l.

Note that $\dfrac{h_{X_p}(t_l)}{1-h_{X_p}(t_l)}$ is the odds of event occurrence at time t_l and the model in Equation 12 represents the log-odds of event occurrence as a function of time period and covariates. By using an inverse function of the natural logarithm, exponential function, in Equation 12 the odds of an event can be expressed as

$$\frac{h_{X_p}(t_l)}{1-h_{X_p}(t_l)} = \exp(\alpha_l D_l)\exp\left(\Sigma_{k=1}^p \beta_k X_k\right). \quad (14)$$

By using Equation 13, Equation 14 can be rewritten as

$$\frac{h_{X_p}(t_l)}{1-h_{X_p}(t_l)} = \frac{h_0(t_l)}{1-h_0(t_l)}\exp\left(\Sigma_{k=1}^p \beta_k X_k\right). \quad (15)$$

Thus, the discrete-time event history model implies that the odds of having the event at each discrete time-point are $\exp\left(\Sigma_{k=1}^p \beta_k X_k\right)$ times for subjects characterized by covariate values $X_1, X_2, \ldots, X_p$ compared with subjects in the baseline group (subjects characterized by covariate values $X_1 = 0, X_2 = 0, \ldots, X_p = 0$). The model also implies that, controlling for other covariates, an increase in one unit of X_k increases (or decreases depending on the sign of β_k) the odds of having the event $\exp(\beta_k)$ times. When the covariate effects are time-independent (i.e., when there are no time-covariate interactions), the model is a proportional odds model. That means the ratio of odds of having an event among a group characterized by particular covariate values and the baseline group, $\dfrac{h_{X_p}(t_l)}{1-h_{X_p}(t_l)} / \dfrac{h_0(t_l)}{1-h_0(t_l)}$, is constant over time. The proportional odds model is similar to the Cox (1972) proportional hazards model for continuous event times with respect to this property. Although the ratio of odds is time-constant for the proportional odds model, the ratio of hazard rates is time-constant for Cox's

proportional hazards model. As discussed in more detail in the section Proportionality Assumption of the Discrete Event Time Models, the proportional odds assumption can be tested and relaxed by including interaction effects of time and covariates in the model.

An advantage of the discrete-time event history model compared with the continuous time event history model is that we can use the usual logistic regression options of most available computer programs for the estimation of the parameters. The structure of the input data, however, differs between the usual logistic regression analysis and the use of logistic regression for discrete-time event history analysis. Although the former uses one observation for each sample subject, the latter uses multiple observations for each subject. Accordingly, the event history data for the logistic regression must be arranged in a specific way as described in the next subsection.

Construction of Input Data

The discrete-event time model uses a logistic regression approach. Unlike standard logistic regression analysis, such an analysis it is not based on a person-oriented data set, it instead requires a person–period data set in which each person may have a different number of records depending on the duration or stay in the risk set. In a typical person-oriented data set, each person has one record (case) of data. Because researchers often keep event history data in a person-oriented data set format, conversion to a person–period data set that contains for each person as many records as the time (period) he or she stays in the risk set without experiencing the event or censoring is needed. Table 13.2 illustrates such a conversion using three subjects from the adolescents' relationship data. The smallest event time for the adolescents' relationship data is 12 and the maximum is 24. Among the three adolescents whose data on some of the variables are shown in Table 13.2, the event times are known for the first and third (ID 2 and 12 reported event time at age 15). An adolescent with ID 9 is censored, that is, the event has not occurred during data collection and his age is 24. In the converted person–period data set, subjects have different number of records

TABLE 13.2

Conversion of a Person-Oriented Data Set Into a Person–Period Data Set for Adolescents' Relationships Data Example

Original data set (person-oriented data set)			
ID	Time	Censor	Gender
2	15	No	Female
9	24	Yes	Male
12	15	No	Male

Converted person-period data set															
ID	Period	D_{12}	D_{13}	D_{14}	D_{15}	D_{16}	D_{17}	D_{18}	D_{19}	D_{20}	D_{21}	D_{22}	D_{23}	D_{24}	Sleeping with someone (event)	Gender
2	12	1	0	0	0	0	0	0	0	0	0	0	0	0	0	Female
2	13	0	1	0	0	0	0	0	0	0	0	0	0	0	0	Female
2	14	0	0	1	0	0	0	0	0	0	0	0	0	0	0	Female
2	15	0	0	0	1	0	0	0	0	0	0	0	0	0	1	Female
9	12	1	0	0	0	0	0	0	0	0	0	0	0	0	0	Male
9	13	0	1	0	0	0	0	0	0	0	0	0	0	0	0	Male
9	14	0	0	1	0	0	0	0	0	0	0	0	0	0	0	Male
9	15	0	0	0	1	0	0	0	0	0	0	0	0	0	0	Male
9	16	0	0	0	0	1	0	0	0	0	0	0	0	0	0	Male
9	17	0	0	0	0	0	1	0	0	0	0	0	0	0	0	Male
9	18	0	0	0	0	0	0	1	0	0	0	0	0	0	0	Male
9	19	0	0	0	0	0	0	0	1	0	0	0	0	0	0	Male
9	20	0	0	0	0	0	0	0	0	1	0	0	0	0	0	Male
9	21	0	0	0	0	0	0	0	0	0	1	0	0	0	0	Male
9	22	0	0	0	0	0	0	0	0	0	0	1	0	0	0	Male
9	23	0	0	0	0	0	0	0	0	0	0	0	1	0	0	Male
9	24	0	0	0	0	0	0	0	0	0	0	0	0	1	0	Male
12	12	1	0	0	0	0	0	0	0	0	0	0	0	0	0	Male
12	13	0	1	0	0	0	0	0	0	0	0	0	0	0	0	Male
12	14	0	0	1	0	0	0	0	0	0	0	0	0	0	0	Male
12	15	0	0	0	1	0	0	0	0	0	0	0	0	0	1	Male

depending on how long they stay in the risk set before they experience the event or censoring. The period variable is included in the data set to indicate the time to which the corresponding record refers for each adolescent from age 12 and above. Because the first event occurs in the data set at age 12, interest on event history is restricted to ages 12 and above. The period variable takes on the values 12, 13, 14, and 15 for each of adolescent with ID 2 and 12, to indicate that these four records describe their corresponding status in the periods from age 12

until the occurrence of the event at age 15. For the adolescent with ID 9, the variable period takes on the values 12 through 24, to indicate that those are the ages represented in the 13 records. The set of dummy variables D_{12} through D_{24} are also created to represent each time period in the logistic regression model for the discrete-time event history model. The dummy variable $D_l = 1$, if period $= t_l$ and 0 otherwise. A dichotomous event indicator is created for the occurrence of *sleeping with someone for the first time* to indicate whether a person experiences the event during the time period concerned (0 = *no event*, 1 = *event*). For each individual, the event indicator is zero in every record except the last. Noncensored adolescents experience the event in their last period, so the variable event takes on the value one in that last period as shown for ID 2 and ID 12. Censored adolescents never experience at the periods shown in the data, so the variable event remains zero throughout the records as shown for ID 9. Values of the time-constant covariates are repeated in each time period. Only values for the covariate *G* are shown in Table 13.2 because of space limitation. SPSS and SAS syntaxes to convert the person-oriented data set to person–period data set are given in Appendix 13.1.

The person–period data set contains all information on survival time, including the information for censored observations. Once a person–period data set is created, existing procedures in general statistical packages can be directly used for event history analysis without any modifications for censoring. As a descriptive analysis, a cross-tabulation of the variables period and event, which can be obtained using CROSSTABS procedure of SPSS (PASAW statistics) or SAS procedure FREQ (SAS Institute, 2009), gives estimates of hazard or conditional probability at each time period as shown in Table 13.1, column 5.

Maximum Likelihood Estimates

The likelihood function (Myung, 2003) for the discrete event time model expresses the probability that we would observe the specific pattern of event occurrence actually observed over time. The likelihood function is composed of as many terms as there are records in the person–period data set. The probability that *i*th individual experiences the event at time period t_l, given that the event has not occurred before, is $h_i(t_l)$. During the time period when individual i experiences the event (the variable event = 1 in the person–period data set), he or she contributes $h_i(t_l)$ to the likelihood function. The probability that *i*th individual does not experience the event in time period t_l, given that the event has not occurred before, is $[1 - h_i(t_l)]$. During the time periods when individual i does not experience the event (when the variable event = 0), he or she contributes $[1 - h_i(t_l)]$ to the likelihood function. The

contributions are mathematically expressed using the likelihood function as

$$\text{Likelihood} = \prod_{i=1}^{v} \prod_{l=1}^{L} h_i(t_l)^{event_{il}} [1 - h_i(t_l)]^{(1-event_{il})}, \quad (16)$$

where Π is a product sign, n is the total number of subjects (sample size), L_i is the number of records for *i*th person in the person–period data set, and $event_{il}$ is the value on the variable event (either zero or one) for *i*th person at *l*th period. The two product signs ensure that the likelihood function multiplies the contributions of each record in the person–period data set across all individuals via the first product sign and across all time periods for each individual via the second product sign. Because event is coded with either zero or one, only one of the two terms ($h_i(t_l)$ or $[1 - h_i(t_l)]$) contributes to the likelihood function at each record in the person–period data set. During the time period in which the event does occur, only the first term remains, whereas the second term becomes one. During time periods in which the event does not occur, only the second term remains, whereas the first term becomes one.

By using the notation $h_{x_p}(t_l)$ for the conditional probability of an *i*th individual with p covariates from Equation 12 in Equation 16 instead of $h_i(t_l)$, the likelihood function can be written as a function of unknown parameters αs for the baseline hazards and βs for the effects of the covariates. The objective of maximum likelihood estimation is to find estimates of the parameters that maximize the likelihood function. In practice, the logarithm of the likelihood (log-likelihood) function is used as it is mathematically more tractable. Thus, the values of αs and βs that maximize the log-likelihood function should be obtained. In fact the routines for logistic regression model available in most standard statistical packages (e.g., SPSS, SAS, Stata, and so on) provide estimates of the parameters of the discrete event time model that maximize the log-likelihood function when a proper person–period data set is used. Thus, statistical routines of logistic regression to regress the event indicator variable on the dummy variables for time indicators and the selected p covariates in the person–period data set can be used to obtain the maximum likelihood estimates of the parameters in the discrete event time model.

Example: Discrete Event Time Model for Adolescents' Relationship Data

To illustrate the procedures of fitting, interpreting, and testing statistical statements (hypothesis) for the discrete event time model, we use the adolescents' relationship data example. The person–period data set with 1,093 records for the event of *sleeping with someone* for the first time and the covariates YC, G, E, and dummy variable D_l as indicator of time period t_l (see the section Construction of Input Data) is used to fit the following models:

Model 1: $\text{logit}(h_0(t_l)) = \alpha_l D_l$

Model 2: $\text{logit}(h_X(t_l)) = \alpha_l D_l + \beta_1 YC$

Model 3: $\text{logit}(h_X(t_l)) = \alpha_l D_l + \beta_2 G + \beta_3 E$

Model 4: $\text{logit}(h_X(t_l)) = \alpha_l D_l + \beta_1 YC + \beta_2 G + \beta_3 E$

Model 1 contains only the time periods, and it describes the hazard profile over time. The model is estimated using the dummy variables for time with a no intercept option of logistic model in standard software. Model 1 helps to find the risk of event occurrence at each time period and identifies the important periods (ages) during which the event is common among the adolescents. The parameters αs for each time period are the logit of the hazard (log odds). From these parameters, the odds of event occurrence can be obtained by exponentiation of the parameters. The conditional probabilities or hazards of event occurrence can be obtained from the parameter estimates using

$$h(t_l) = \frac{1}{1 + \exp[-(\alpha_l)]}. \tag{17}$$

The estimates of the parameters of discrete event time model and the corresponding hazards for the baseline or reference group (when covariate values YC, G, and E equal zero) under each of the four models fitted for the adolescents' relationship data are shown in Table 13.3. An increase in hazard shows higher risk of event occurrence. A closer look at hazards (on the basis estimates of parameters) in Model 1 shows that this baseline model (a model without a covariate) gives exactly the result on hazard probability of a life-table analysis we have in Table 13.1. Thus, using the baseline model, the hazard at each time period computed in life table can be obtained.

The baseline model estimates the overall population profile of the risk across time and indicates when events are more likely to occur. To know whether the hazard profile is different for adolescents with different values on the covariate YC, the dummy variable YC ($YC = 1$ if youth centric and $YC = 0$ if not youth centric) is considered in addition to the time period variables as given in Model 2. The parameter estimates are given under Model 2 in Table 13.3. The estimates of the parameters $\alpha_{12}, \alpha_{13}, \ldots, \alpha_{23}, \alpha_{24}$ under Model 2 represent the baseline log odds of the hazard profile at each of the time periods for the non-YC group of adolescents (a reference group with $YC = 0$). The parameter β_1 is a shift parameter that displaces the baseline log odds of hazard profile for the YC group ($YC = 1$). The estimated log odds for YC is 0.310 with corresponding odds ratio of 1.363 ($\exp(0.310)$). This indicates that YC adolescents are about 1.4 times more likely than non-YC adolescents to experience the event *sleeping with someone for the first time* (if at risk).

Model 3 contains the covariates G and E in addition to the time period dummy variables. The baseline (or reference group) contains subjects with value zero for G and E, that is, low educated female adolescents. The estimates of the parameters αs for the reference group is shown as log odds under model 3 in Table 13.3. The corresponding hazard (probability) of event occurrence at each time for the reference group is also shown in Table 13.3 under the column for model 3. The parameter β_2 in Model 3 is a shift parameter that displaces the baseline log odds of hazard profile for male adolescents ($G = 1$) keeping the values of education constant. The estimated log odds for gender in Model 3 is –0.542 with the corresponding odds ratio of 0.581 ($\exp(-0.542)$), controlling for E. Similarly, the parameter β_3 in Model 3 is a shift parameter that displaces the baseline log odds of hazard profile for highly educated adolescents ($E = 1$) keeping gender constant. The estimated log odds for education is –0.112 with the corresponding odds ratio of 0.894 ($\exp(-0.112)$), controlling for G.

Model 4 includes the covariates YC, G, and E in addition to the time period dummy variables. The baseline (or reference group) consists of subjects with value zero for YC, G, and E, that is, non-YC

TABLE 13.3

Parameter Estimates and Goodness-of-Fit Statistic for the Discrete Event Time Models Fitted to Adolescents' Relationship Data

Covariate	Parameter	Model 1 Log odds (estimates)	Model 1 Baseline hazard	Model 2 Log odds (estimates)	Model 2 Baseline hazard	Model 3 Log odds (estimates)	Model 3 Baseline hazard	Model 4 Log odds (estimates)	Model 4 Baseline hazard
D_{12}	α_{12}	−4.949	0.0070	−5.062	0.0063	−4.780	0.0083	−4.872	0.0076
D_{13}	α_{13}	−21.203	0.0000	−21.312	0.0000	−21.053	0.0000	−21.135	0.0000
D_{14}	α_{14}	−4.241	0.0142	−4.353	0.0127	−4.071	0.0168	−4.158	0.0157
D_{15}	α_{15}	−2.454	0.0791	−2.566	0.0714	−2.274	0.0933	−2.360	0.0863
D_{16}	α_{16}	−1.747	0.1484	−1.851	0.1358	−1.552	0.1748	−1.625	0.1645
D_{17}	α_{17}	−1.319	0.2110	−1.421	0.1945	−1.165	0.2378	−1.236	0.2251
D_{18}	α_{18}	−1.130	0.2442	−1.232	0.2258	−0.978	0.2733	−1.043	0.2606
D_{19}	α_{19}	−1.591	0.1692	−1.683	0.1567	−1.363	0.2038	−1.418	0.1950
D_{20}	α_{20}	−0.531	0.3703	−0.625	0.3486	−0.318	0.4212	−0.364	0.4100
D_{21}	α_{21}	−0.738	0.3234	−0.823	0.3051	−0.417	0.3972	−0.447	0.3901
D_{22}	α_{22}	−1.897	0.1304	−1.956	0.1239	−1.564	0.1731	−1.543	0.1761
D_{23}	α_{23}	−1.735	0.1500	−1.785	0.1437	−1.389	0.1996	−1.360	0.2042
D_{24}	α_{24}	−0.981	0.2727	−1.011	0.2668	−0.670	0.3385	−0.656	0.3416
Youth centrism (*YC*, yes = 1)	β_1			0.310				0.483	
Gender (*G*) (male = 1)	β_2					−0.542		−0.592	
Education (*E*) (high = 1)	β_3					−0.112		−0.059	
−2LL		645.979		643.933		623.299		619.356	

Note. −2LL = −2 log likelihood.

low-educated female adolescent. The estimates of the parameters αs for the reference group is shown as log odds under Model 4 in Table 13.3. The corresponding hazard (probability) of event occurrence at each time for the reference group is shown in the last columns of Table 13.3. The parameter β_1 in Model 4 is a shift parameter that displaces the baseline log odds of hazard profile for the *YC* group (*YC* = 1) keeping *G* and *E* constant. The estimated log odds for *YC* is 0.483 with the corresponding odds ratio of 1.620 (exp(0.483)), controlling for *G* and *E*. Similarly, the parameter β_2 in model 4 is a shift parameter that displaces the baseline log odds of hazard profile for male adolescents (*G* = 1) keeping the values of *YC* and *E* constant. The estimated log odds for gender is −0.592

with the corresponding odds ratio of 0.553 (exp(−0.592)), controlling for *YC* and *E*. Thus, the odds of *sleeping with someone for the first time* for boys is 0.553 times that for girls. The estimate of β_3 is interpreted in a similar fashion for education by keeping *YC* and *G* constant.

The likelihood ratio test (e.g., Rao, 1973) is used to test the significance of the effects of the covariates in each of the models. The −2 log likelihood (−2LL) statistic, which is often displayed in outputs from commonly used statistical software (e.g., SPSS) for logistic regression routine, is the deviance statistic for the discrete event history models. A deviance statistic is always greater than zero, and the smaller the deviance the better the fit of the model to the observed data. The last row of Table 13.3 shows the deviance statistics for the four models we fit for the adolescents' relationship data.

A likelihood ratio test compares deviance statistics for the comparison of two nested models. Two models are called nested when both contain the same parameters and one of the models has at least one additional parameter. That is, one is obtained by having a constraint on the additional parameters in the other model. In the current example, model 1 can be obtained from all other models by imposing constraints that the parameters corresponding to the covariates YC, G, and E are set to zero. Thus, Model 1 is nested within all other models. Model 4 contains all parameters involved in other models. Thus, Model 4 is the biggest model with all parameters of interest. For the likelihood ratio test, the difference in deviance statistics for two nested models will asymptotically have a chi-square distribution on k degrees of freedom (df), where k is the number of additional parameters in a bigger model in terms of parameters. When the difference in deviance statistic is larger than the critical value for chi-square distribution, we reject the null hypothesis of the model with fewer parameters (reduced model) and conclude that some of the additional covariates in the model with more parameters (full model) have significant effect on the log odds of event occurrence. When the difference in the deviance statistic is small, we fail to reject the reduced parsimonious model, and we conclude that the reduced model is as good as the full model. In the current example, the difference between deviance statistics for Model 1 and Model 2 is 2.046 (= 645.979 − 643.933), which is smaller than the critical value of chi-square distribution with $df = 1$ at 5% level of significance ($\chi^2_{1(0.05)} = 3.84$). Thus, Model 2 is not statistically better than Model 1 and the covariate YC alone has no effect on the log odds of event occurrence. The covariate YC, indeed, has an effect after the variables G and E are controlled. The difference in deviance statistics between Model 1 and Model 3 is 22.680 (= 645.979 − 623.299). Because there are two more parameters in Model 3 compared with Model 1 (βs for G and E), the df for the chi square is now 2. Because the difference in deviance, 22.680 is greater than the chi-square value ($\chi^2_{2(0.05)} = 5.99$), we reject the reduced model (Model 1) and conclude that

Model 3 gives a better fit of the data in such a way that at least one of the covariates involved in the model (G and E) has a significant effect on the log odds of event occurrence. Having Model 3, which contains G and E, we may be interested to know the effect of YC given that G and E are controlled. We can compare Models 3 and 4 for that purpose. Comparison between Models 1 and 2 gives the effect of YC without controlling the variables G and E. The comparison between Models 3 and 4 helps to test whether YC has an effect on hazard probabilities after controlling the covariates G and E.

The difference in deviance statistics between Model 3 and Model 4 is 3.943 (= 623.299 − 619.356). Because there is only one more parameter in Model 4 compared with Model 3 (β_1 for YC), the df for the chi-square is 1. Because the difference in deviance, 3.943, is slightly greater than the chi-square value ($\chi^2_{1(0.05)} = 3.84$), we conclude that YC has significant effect after controlling the covariates G and E.

Polynomial Specification of Time Period

The dummy variable for time period that is included in the discrete event time model helps to maintain the shape of the baseline logit hazard function. The use of $T_1, T_2 ..., T_L$ as a representation of the L discrete time-points in the model puts no specification on the shape of the hazard functions and further makes the interpretation of the parameters in the discrete event history model easier. Each of the coefficients of the dummy variables for time periods, α_l, is interpreted as the population value of logit hazard in time period l for the baseline group, for $l = 1$, 2, . . ., L. The use of dummy variable representation for time periods in the model is encouraged because it does not put any constraint on the shape of the baseline model and facilitates interpretation of the coefficients. However, when there are many discrete time periods, L is large; the model needs the inclusion of many dummy variable representations for the time periods. This leads the model to be overparameterized and to lack of parsimony (Efron, 1988; Fahrmeir & Wagenpfeil, 1996; Singer & Willett, 2003, p. 408). Thus, using an alternative approach for the representation of time periods in the discrete event time model is required when the there are many time-points. The option of considering the time periods as if they are continuous covariates and a specification of a polynomial model for the baseline logit hazard function gives a more parsimonious model provided that the fit of the model to the data is not compromised (Mantel & Hankey, 1978; Singer & Willett, 2003). The variable period in person–period data set whose values represent the time period that the record describes, as shown in Table 13.2, can easily be used as a continuous covariate in polynomial representation of time in the discrete event time models. The polynomial representation could be linear, quadratic, cubic, or higher degree polynomials. The choice could also be a logarithmic transformation of time or any other kind of function of time depending on the theoretical or practical motivation for such functions. In situations in which the polynomial Model is not prespecified, search for the appropriate polynomial model can begin from the most simple one to the more complex models guided by statistical tests for model comparison. As outlined by Singer and Willett (2003, p. 410), a formal goodness-of-fit test should confirm that the selected polynomial fits the data as good as the model with dummy variable representation of time period (*general* model). That means a likelihood ratio test should confirm that there is no statistically significance difference between a polynomial model representation of time period for the baseline logit hazard and Model 1, for example, in the adolescents' relationship data example. Table 13.4 displays the deviance statistics and the differences in deviance statistics for the likelihood ratio test to identify an appropriate polynomial representation of time periods for the adolescents' relationship data. The *df* for the test is the difference in the number of parameters in the models to be compared. The difference in deviance statistics between the linear and the general model, 58.988, is greater than the chi-square value ($\chi^2_{11(0.05)} = 19.68$). Thus, the fit of the linear model is not as good as the general model. The next candidate model is the quadratic model. The difference in deviance statistics between quadratic and general models, 17.312, is less than the chi-square value ($\chi^2_{10(0.05)} = 18.31$). Thus, the fit of the quadratic model is as good as the general model. We found the same result for cubic model. However, a comparison between the quadratic and

cubic models shows that the cubic model is not significantly better than the quadratic model (the difference in deviances, 2.581, is less than the chi-square value $\chi^2_{1(0.05)} = 3.84$. Thus, quadratic polynomial representation of the time periods is parsimonious in its number of parameters when it fits the data as good as the general model for the discrete event time models for the adolescents' relationship data.

The parameters in the polynomial models are estimated using the same procedure as earlier using maximum likelihood method. The logistic regression model routines in the commonly used software can be used with a little modification of the data set. First, a new variable needs to be formed from the variable period within the person–period data set. Then, depending on the degree of the polynomial that we want to fit, a series of additional variables should be recomputed from the new variable to represent each polynomial term in the model. For example, in the current data example, a new variable (*period* – 12) is first computed from the variable period and then the representation of the quadratic term (*period* – 12)^2 is recomputed. In general, the new variable can be obtained by subtracting a constant *c* from period (*period* – *c*) and then other series of variables can be obtained by taking the power of this variable to represent each polynomial term in the model. The choice of the constant *c* is arbitrary, however; *c* should be within the range of the observed event time periods. The constant *c* is in fact the time period at which the estimated logit hazard (probability) of event occurrence for the baseline group is the estimate of the intercept in the polynomial model. For example, the estimate of the parameter a_0 for the current example is the sample estimate of the logit hazard of event occurrence for the baseline group at time period (age) 12.

In general, for the linear model, the intercept parameter a_0 represents the value of the logit hazard when the covariate is zero. The covariate in the current linear models is (*period* – *c*). Thus, a_0 represents the value of the logit hazard when the period is equal to *c*. The slope parameter, b_1, is unaffected by the subtraction of constant *c* from the time period, and it represents the increase (or decrease) in logit hazard per unit increase in time. For the quadratic

TABLE 13.4

Polynomial Representations for Time Period in a Baseline Discrete Event Time Model for Adolescents' Relationships Data

Polynomial model for the baseline logit hazard		Number of parameters	−2LL	Difference in −2LL in comparison with	
				Previous model	General model
Linear	$\text{logit}(h_0(t_l)) = a_0 + b_1(period_l - 12)$	2	704.967		58.988
Quadratic	$\text{logit}(h_0(t_l)) = a_0 + b_1(period_l - 12)$ $+ b_2(period_l - 12)^2$	3	663.291	41.676	17.312
Cubic	$\text{logit}(h_0(t_l)) = a_0 + b_1(period_l - 12)$ $+ b_2(period_l - 12)^2$ $+ b_3(period_l - 12)^3$	4	660.710	2.581	14.731
General	$\text{logit}(h_0(t_l)) = a_{12}T_{12} + \ldots + a_{24}T_{24}$	13	645.979		

Note. −2LL = −2 log likelihood.

model, the intercept still represents the value of the logit hazard in time period c. The slope parameter, too, still measures the increase (or decrease) in logit hazard per unit increase in time but now only at one particular instant, time period c. The curvature parameter, b_2, in the quadratic model specifies whether the logit hazard function is convex with a trough (U shape) or concave with a peak (∩ shape). If b_2 is positive, the hazard function is convex, and if it is negative, the shape is concave. The time period at which the hazard function reaches its peak or trough is given by $[c - \frac{1}{2}(\frac{b_1}{b_2})]$.

For example, the estimates of the parameters a_0, b_1, and b_2 for the quadratic model of the adolescents' relationship data are −5.551, 1.191, and −0.075, respectively, that is, the quadratic model for the baseline group is $\text{logit}(h_0(t_l) = -5.551 + 1.191 (period - 12) - 0.075(period - 12)^2$. This implies that the estimate of the logit hazard at age 12 for the baseline is −5.551 (compared with the result in Table 13.3) and the instantaneous rate of change in logit hazard at age 12 is 1.191. Because the estimate for b_2, <minus0.075, is negative, the hazard function is concave reaching its peak at time period (age) $[12 - \frac{1}{2}(\frac{1.191}{(-0.075)})] = 19.94$. The peak of the hazard function is after age 19 and close to age 20, implying that the risk of the event, *sleeping with someone for the first time*, is highest at age 20.

Time-Varying Covariates

In previous sections, we considered covariates that have constant values with time. The values of some covariates for each person may change over time in practice. With a little modification, it is possible to relate the occurrence of the event of interest to covariates that change their values with time using the discrete event history model. One of the advantages of using a person–period data set is that it naturally allows a time-varying covariate simply to take on its appropriate value for each person in each record or period. In the adolescents' relationship example, we focus in this chapter on the event of sleeping with someone for the first time and discussed the effect of time-constant covariates *YC*, *G*, and *E*. As mentioned in the section An Empirical Example, the survey had also collected the time at which the adolescents experienced the events *going out*, *having a steady friend*, and *being very much in love* for the first time. It may be hypothesized that the occurrence of these events could have an effect on the timing of our event of interest, *sleeping with someone for the first time*. For simplicity and ease of presentation, we consider only the effect of going out on the timing of sleeping with someone for the first time. The value on the covariate going out (*OUT*) for each person at period *l* will be 0 if the person did not go out for the first time until period *l*. The value changes to 1 when a person goes out for the first time at period l. Thus, the covariate *OUT* is time-varying binary covariate in this example as its value changes with time. More technically, the covariate is defined as

$$OUT_l = \begin{cases} 0, & \text{if a person did not go out at time } l \\ 1, & \text{if a person gone out at time } l \text{ or before} \end{cases} . \quad (18)$$

The data values can easily be appended in the person–period data set, for example, next to the last column of Table 13.2.

Considering the quadratic model specification for the baseline group, the model with both a time-constant and time-varying covariate is given by

$$\begin{aligned} \text{logit}(h_X(t_l)) = & a_0 + b_1(period_l - 12) \\ & + b_2(period_l - 12)^2 + \beta_1 YC \\ & + \beta_2 G + \beta_3 E + \beta_4 OUT_l. \end{aligned} \quad (19)$$

The time-constant covariates *YC*, *G*, and *E* do not have the subscript l, whereas the time-varying covariate *OUT* has a subscript l to indicate that the data values for the variable *OUT* can be different values at different time periods for the same person. The parameter β_4 represents the difference in risk of the event sleeping with someone for the first time among adolescents who recently or previously experienced going out and those who still have not experienced going out, controlling for other covariates. Because the covariate *OUT* is time varying, its effect does not contrast a static group but rather adolescents who differ by unit value on the covariate *OUT* at each point in time, that is, individuals can switch group membership and the adolescents who constitute the comparison group differ in each time period even if we are comparing two groups: those who have experienced going out and who have not. Thus, the interpretation of the time-varying covariate's effect must be attached to each point in the time period. In contrast, for the time-constant covariates, we need not to attach a time-point in the interpretation of the covariate's effect because the group members to be compared and data values of the covariate at each time period are constant. As the last model in Equation 19 assumes, the effects of both time-invariant and time-varying covariates do

not vary with time. That is, the effects of the covariates on logit hazard are constant over the time periods. Although the values of the time-varying covariate and the members of the groups to be compared may vary over time periods, the difference between the logit hazard functions for the two groups to be compared in this example is constant and identical in every time period.

By fitting the model in Equation 19 for the adolescents' relationship data, we get

$$\begin{aligned} \text{logit}[h_X(t_l)] = & -6.544 + 0.734(period_l - 12) \\ & -0.043(period_l - 12)^2 + 0.508YC \\ & -0.549G + 0.054E + 2.629OUT_l. \end{aligned} \quad (20)$$

Comparison of the model that excludes the time-varying covariate *OUT* and Equation 20 using deviance statistic shows that the time-varying covariate is statistically significant, controlling for the effect of the other covariates. The estimates of the parameters for the time-constant covariates are interpreted in a similar way as we did in the section Example: Discrete Event Time Model for Adolescents' Relationship Data. For example, the estimate of the parameter β_2, -0.549, for gender could be interpreted as odds ratio by taking the exponent of the estimate, that is, controlling for the effect of other covariates in the model, the odds of sleeping with someone for the first time for boys is 0.578 (exp(-0.549)) multiplied by that of female adolescents. In another words, the odds of sleeping with someone for the first time are 1.73 ($= 1/0.578$) times for girls. In a similar way, by taking the exponent of the estimate of the parameter β_4, (exp (2.629) = 13.866), at every age from 12 to 24 years, the odds of sleeping with someone for the first time are about 14 times higher for adolescents who experienced the event of going out earlier and subsequent times compared with those who remain without the experience of going out, controlling for the effect of the other covariates in the model. The risk of sleeping with someone increases only in those time periods concurrent with, or subsequent to, the event of going out. Before the event going out occurs, those adolescents who are later at greater risk of sleeping with someone are not different from other adolescents who stay at risk without the event of going out.

Proportionality Assumption of the Discrete Event Time Models

The models we have considered so far assume that the covariates have an identical effect in every time period under the study which is known as the proportionality assumption. The assumption is crucial for the estimation procedure of most parametric hazard models for continuous time data. However, in the discrete-time event history models presented in this chapter, apart from simplification of the models, there is no such requirement in the estimation procedure. In some practical situations, this assumption is restrictive and can be relaxed by including an interaction term between the covariates and the time period. An inclusion of an interaction term between a covariate and time period allows the effects of the covariate to depend on time instead of being constant at all time periods. The interaction term with the covariate of interest can be made using the dummy variable representation of time period or the alternative polynomial representation. For the current example, the interaction terms are constructed by multiplying each of the covariates *YC*, *G*, *E*, and *OUT* by the variable (*period* – 12), the linear term of the polynomial representation. The nonproportional discrete event time model is estimated in each case by including the interaction term in Equation 19. One can test whether an effect of a covariate depends on time by comparing the model with proportionality assumption and the model that includes an interaction term between the covariate and time period. As explained, comparison of the deviance statistics helps to make the comparison of the models. Because none of the differences in deviance statistics between Equation 19 and the models that include the interaction terms showed a statistical significance for the current example, the detailed results are not shown here. Thus, the data from the adolescents' relationship example offer little evidence that the effects of the covariates change over time.

Competing-Risk Models

In the models we have considered so far, there is a single destination state from the origin state. In some applications, there may be more than one way

of (or reason for) exiting an origin state. Such reasons or destination states are referred to as *competing risks* (Chiang, 1991; David & Moeschberger, 1978). For example, in the analysis of mortality or death rates, one may want to distinguish different causes of death; in the analysis of partnership formation, one may transit from single state to either marriage or cohabitation (without formal marriage). The hazard in such cases is defined for single types of events, but now we have one for each competing risk. If there are *D* mutually exclusive destination states, then the hazard of event type *d* at time t_l is

$$h^{(d)}(t_l) = \Pr(\text{event of type } d \text{ at time } t_l \mid T \geq t_l). \quad (21)$$

The hazard that no event of any type occurs at t_l given survival to time period t_{l-1} is

$$h^{(0)}(t_l) = 1 - \sum_{d=1}^{D} h^{(d)}(t_l). \quad (22)$$

The survival function that the events occur after time t_l is the same as the probability that no event of any type occurs until and including time t_l is

$$S(t_l) = h^{(0)}(t_1) \times h^{(0)}(t_2) \times \ldots \times h^{(0)}(t_{l-1}). \quad (23)$$

The model that relates the hazards to the covariates when individuals may leave the origin state to different destination states is the competing-risk model. There are two approaches to model the hazards. One approach is to model the hazards of each competing risk separately using the discrete event time model, treating all other events as censored. This approach models the underlying risk of a particular event in the absence of all other risks. The other approach is modeling the hazards of the competing risks simultaneously using a multinomial logistic model.

For the multinomial logistic model, the person–period data set discussed earlier needs a minor change. A multinomial event indicating categorical variable (response variable) E_{ild} needs to be defined, indicating occurrence and type of event *d* at time period t_l for the *i*th person. The response categories of E_{il} are 0 (no event), 1, 2, . . ., *D*. The multiple records in the person–period data set for each person should be defined until one of the events or censoring occurs. The multinomial logistic model that contrasts event type d with no event for a person with covariates $X_1, X_2, \ldots, X_p$ is given by

$$Log_e \left(\frac{h_{X_p}^d(t_l)}{h_{X_p}^0(t_l)} \right) = \alpha_l^d + \sum_{k=1}^{p} \beta_k^d X_k. \qquad (24)$$

Comparison of this last model in Equation 24 with the model in Equation 12 shows that a separate set of time and covariate effects (α_l^d and β_k^d) are included for each type of event via the index d. Some of the covariates can be time varying and may need subscript l for such covariates in Equation 24. For the multinomial logistic model in Equation 24, we estimate D equations contrasting each of the competing risks with no event. Further contrasts to compare the competing risks among each other can then be obtained from those D equations. For example, for partnership formation, two contrasts (marriage with single, *no event*, cohabitation with single) can be obtained using the model in Equation 24. The remaining contrast, marriage with cohabitation, may be estimated from the other two contrasts. Using the modified person–period data set, a multinomial logistic model for discrete event time data in Equation 24 can be estimated using routines developed for standard multinomial logistic model in the commonly available software (e.g., SPSS, SAS, Stata).

Unobserved Heterogeneity

In the models discussed so far, variability in the hazard of event occurrence is explained using observed covariates and risk factors. However, even after controlling for these observed characteristics, some subjects will be more likely to experience the event than others as a result of unobserved subject-specific risk factors. This unobserved heterogeneity in the hazard is sometimes referred to as *frailty* (Hougaard, 1984, 1995). If there are subject-specific unobserved factors that affect the hazard, the estimated form of the hazard function at the population or group level will tend to be different from those at the subject level. For example, if the hazards of all subjects in a population are constant over time, the aggregate population hazard will be decreasing. This can be explained by what is called a selection effect—that is, high-risk subjects will tend to have the event first, leaving lower risk subjects in the population.

Therefore, as time goes by, the risk population is increasingly depleted of those subjects most likely to experience the event, leading to a decrease in the population hazard. Because of this selection, we may see a decrease in the population hazard even if individual hazards are constant (or even increasing). This selection effect not only affects the time dependence, but may, for example, also yield spurious time-covariate effects (Vermunt, 2002, 2009).

The common way to deal with unobserved heterogeneity is to include random effects (or subject-specific effects) in the models discussed so far. This involves the inclusion of a time-constant latent covariate in the model, and it requires an assumption about the distributional form of the latent variable. Mare (1994) and Vermunt (1997, 2002) presented discrete-time variants of such models. The amount of unobserved heterogeneity is determined by the variance of the latent variable, where the larger the variance the more unobserved heterogeneity. The interpretation of the regression parameters β will also change when random effects are included. In the models discussed so far without random effects, $\exp(\beta)$ is an odds ratio, and it compares the odds of an event for two randomly selected individuals with values one unit apart on covariate X, keeping the same values for other covariates in the model. In a model with random effects, $\exp(\beta)$ is an odds ratio only when the random effects are held constant, that is, if we are comparing two hypothetical individuals with the same random effect values. Using models with random effects makes sense when it can be expected that important time-constant risk factors are not included in the model. Failure to control for such unobserved factors may bias the estimates of the factors included in the model. Discrete-time models with random effects can be defined using software for multilevel logistic regression analysis. Routines for continuous-time modeling sometimes contain provisions for specifying models with unobserved heterogeneity (e.g., the Stata routines stcox and streg).

CONCLUSION

This chapter has given a gentle introduction to event history analysis for discrete event times. These methods were introduced to social and behavioral scientists by Allison (1982), Vermunt (1997, 2009), Willett and Singer (1993), Singer and Willett (2003), and Yamaguchi (1991), among others. These methods are still relatively unknown and not widely used in psychology, despite their appropriateness for many research questions. We have shown that with an appropriate restructuring of the data set, the software routines that are familiar to the applied researchers can be used for discrete event history analysis. That is, no specialized software is needed to perform a discrete event time analysis. The methods presented here are technically manageable and could also be used as an introduction to more advanced methods in continuous event time analysis, as, for example, described by Vermunt and Singer and Willett.

A logistic regression model is adopted to relate the hazard of event occurrence to covariates. With an appropriate data restructuring, both the censoring problem and the inclusion of time-varying covariates are managed. The discussion was confined to only right censoring. Left censoring is less common in practice and in general more difficult to deal with than right censoring. The method was extended for competing risks using multinomial logistic model. A more advanced technique to account for unobserved heterogeneity was discussed. Other more advanced topics that have not been discussed in this chapter include models for multivariate events, covariates containing measurement error, missing data on covariates, and recurrent events. Models for multivariate events consider distributions of two or more distinct event time variables and jointly model the time variables (Vermunt & Moors, 2005; Wei, Lin, & Weissfeld, 1989). The objective of simultaneous modeling is to take into account the fact that the occurrence of one life event might directly affect the hazard for another type of event. When the covariates or predictor variables are subject to measurement error, the estimates of regression coefficients and their corresponding confidence intervals may be biased and corrections are needed (Nakamura, 1992; Rosner, Spiegelman, & Willett, 1990; Vermunt, 1996). When a covariate is partially missing, excluding the subjects with partially missing covariate values

from the analysis leads to biased parameter estimates unless the missing mechanism is missing completely at random (Little & Rubin, 1987). *Recurrent event* refers to the situation in which subjects may experience the event of interest more than once, for example, repeated divorce or marriage, asthma attacks, child birth, employment, injury, and prison. Different techniques are suggested in literature for the analysis of recurrent event data. Lim, Liu, and Meltzer-Lange (2007) compared those methods using empirical data from a pediatric firearm victim's visit with data from the Department/Trauma Center at Children's Hospital of Wisconsin and all other hospitals in the Milwaukee metropolitan area between 1990 and 1995.

APPENDIX 13.1: SYNTAXES FOR THE CONVERSION OF PERSON-ORIENTED DATA SET TO PERSON-PERIOD DATA SET, ADOLESCENTS' RELATIONSHIP DATA

SPSS SYNTAX

```
*first open the data file 'relationships.sav' which can be obtained from one of the authors.
do repeat D = D12 to D24 /ptime = 12,13,14,15,16,17,18,19,20,21,22,23,24.
if (time_sleeping > ptime) D = 0.
if (time_sleeping = ptime) D = 1-censind1.
end repeat.
execute.
VARSTOCASES
/ID = id
/MAKE event FROM D12 D13 D14 D15 D16 D17 D18 D19 D20 D21 D22 D23 D24
/INDEX = period(13)
/KEEP = boy loweduc youthcen
/NULL = DROP.
COMPUTE period = period + 11.
EXECUTE.
*Making dummy variables for modeling
do repeat D = D12 to D24 /ptime = 12,13,14,15,16,17,18,19,20,21,22,23,24.
if (period > ptime) D = 0.
if (period = ptime) D = 1.
if (period < ptime) D = 0.
end repeat.
execute.
```

SAS SYNTAX

```
*Creating a person-period data set from a person-
    level data set;
*Assuming the person-level data set exists in drive C;
data relationships_pp1;
set 'c:\relationships';
do period = 12 to 24;
if (time_sleeping > period) then event = 0;
else if (time_sleeping = period) then event =
    1-censind1;
else if (time_sleeping < period) then delete;
output;
end;
keep id boy loweduc youthcen period event;
run;
proc print
data = relationships_pp1;
run;
data relationships_pp;
set relationships_pp1;
array AD[12:24] D12-D24;
do dummy = 12 to 24;
if (period eq dummy) then AD[dummy]=1;
else
AD[dummy]=0;
end;
drop dummy;
run;
proc print
data = relationships_pp;
run;
```

References

Allison, P. (1982). Discrete-time methods for the analysis of event histories. In S. Leinhardt (Ed.), *Sociological methodology* (pp. 61–98). San Francisco, CA: Jossey-Bass.

Blossfeld, p., & Rohwer, G. (1995). *Techniques of event history modeling: New approaches to causal analysis.* Mahwah, NJ: Erlbaum.

Chiang, C. L. (1991). Competing risks in mortality analysis. *Annual Review of Public Health, 12,* 281–307. doi:10.1146/annurev.pu.12.050191.001433

Collett, D. (2003). *Modelling survival data in medical studies* (2nd ed.). Boca Raton, FL: Chapman & Hall/CRC.

Cox, D. R. (1972). Regression models and life tables. *Journal of the Royal Statistical Society, Series B: Methodological, 34,* 187–220.

Cutler, S. J., & Ederer, F. (1958). Maximum utilisation of the life table method in analysing survival. *Journal of Chronic Diseases, 8,* 699–712. doi:10.1016/0021-9681(58)90126-7

D'Agostino, R. B., Lee, M. L., Belanger, A. J., Cupples, L. A., Anderson, K., & Kannel, W. B. (1990). Relation of pooled logistic regression to time dependent Cox regression analysis: The Framingham Heart Study. *Statistics in Medicine, 9,* 1501–1515. doi:10.1002/sim.4780091214

David, H. A., & Moeschberger, M. L. (1978). *The theory of competing risks.* London, England: Griffin.

Efron, B. (1988). Logistic regression, survival analysis, and the Kaplan-Meier curve. *Journal of the American Statistical Association, 83,* 414–425.

Fahrmeir, L., & Wagenpfeil, S. (1996). Smoothing hazard functions and time-varying effects in discrete duration and competing risks models. *Journal of the American Statistical Association, 91,* 1584–1594. doi:10.2307/2291584

Hougaard, P. (1984). Life table methods for heterogeneous populations: Distributions describing the heterogeneity. *Biometrika, 71,* 75–83. doi:10.1093/biomet/71.1.75

Hougaard, P. (1995). Frailty models for survival data. *Lifetime Data Analysis, 1,* 255–273. doi:10.1007/BF00985760

Kalbfleisch, J., & Prentice, R. (2002). *The statistical analysis of failure time data* (2nd ed.). Hoboken, NJ: Wiley.

Kaplan, E. L., & Meier, P. (1958). Nonparametric estimation from incomplete observations. *Journal of the American Statistical Association, 53,* 457–481. doi:10.2307/2281868

Lim, H. J., Liu, J., & Meltzer-Lange, M. (2007). Comparison of methods for analyzing recurrent event data: Application to emergency department visits of pediatric firearm victims. *Accident Analysis and Prevention, 39,* 290–299. doi:10.1016/j.aap.2006.07.009

Little, R. J. A., & Rubin, D. B. (1987). *Statistical analysis with missing data.* New York, NY: Wiley.

Mantel, M. H., & Hankey, B. F. (1978). A logistic regression analysis of response time data where the hazard function is time dependent. *Communications in Statistics Theory and Methods, 7,* 333–347. doi:10.1080/03610927808827627

Mare, R. D. (1994). Discrete-time bivariate hazards with unobserved heterogeneity: A partially observed contingency table approach. In P. V. Marsden (Ed.), *Sociological methodology* (pp. 341–383). Oxford, England: Basil Blackwell.

Merrell, M. (1947). Time-specific life tables contrasted with observed survivorship. *Biometrics, 3,* 129–136. doi:10.2307/3001948

Mould, R. F. (1976). Calculation of survival rates by the life table and other methods. *Clinical Radiology, 27,* 33–38. doi:10.1016/S0009-9260(76)80011-6

Myung, I. J. (2003). Tutorial on maximum likelihood estimation. *Journal of Mathematical Psychology, 47,* 90–100. doi:10.1016/S0022-2496(02)00028-7

Nakamura, T. (1992). Proportional hazards model with covariates subject to measurement error. *Biometrics, 48,* 829–838. doi:10.2307/2532348

Petersen, T. (1991). The statistical analysis of event histories. *Sociological Methods and Research, 19,* 270–323. doi:10.1177/0049124191019003002

Rao, C. R. (1973). *Linear statistical inference and its application* (2nd ed.). New York, NY: Wiley.

Rosner, B., Spiegelman, D., & Willett, W. C. (1990). Correction of logistic regression relative risk estimates and confidence intervals for measurement error: The case of multiple covariates measured with error. *American Journal of Epidemiology, 132,* 734–745.

SAS Institute. (2009). *Base SAS 9.2 procedures guide.* Cary, NC: Author.

Singer, J. D., & Willett, J. B. (1993). It's about time: Using discrete-time survival analysis to study duration and the timing of events. *Journal of Educational Statistics, 18,* 155–195. doi:10.2307/1165085

Singer, J. D., & Willett, J. B. (2003). *Applied longitudinal data analysis: methods for studying change and event occurrence.* New York, NY: Oxford University Press.

Thompson, W. A., Jr. (1977). On the treatment of grouped observations in life studies. *Biometrics, 33,* 463–470. doi:10.2307/2529360

Tuma, N. B., & Hannan, M. T. (1979). Approaches to the censoring problem in analysis of event histories. In K. F. Schuessler (Ed.), *Sociological methodology* (pp. 209–240). San Francisco, CA: Jossey-Bass.

Vermunt, J. K. (1996). *Log-linear event history analysis: A general approach with missing data, unobserved heterogeneity, and latent variables.* Tilburg, the Netherlands: Tilburg University Press.

Vermunt, J. K. (1997). *Advanced Quantitative Techniques in the Social Sciences: Vol. 8. Log-linear models for event histories.* London, England: Sage.

Vermunt, J. K. (2002). A general latent class approach to unobserved heterogeneity in the analysis of event history data. In J. Hagenaars & A. McCutcheon (Eds.), *Applied latent class analysis* (pp. 383–407). Cambridge, England: Cambridge University Press.

Vermunt, J. K. (2009). Event history analysis. In R. Millsap & A. Maydeu-Olivares (Eds.), *Handbook of quantitative methods in psychology* (pp. 658–674). London, England: Sage.

Vermunt, J. K., & Moors, G. B. D. (2005). Event history analysis. In B. Everitt & D. Howell (Eds.), *Encyclopedia of statistics in behavioral science* (pp. 568–575). Chichester, England: Wiley. doi:10.1002/0470013192.bsa204

Vinken, H. (1998). *Political values and youth centrism. Theoretical and empirical perspectives on the political value distinctiveness of Dutch youth centrists.* Tilburg, the Netherlands: Tilburg University Press.

Wei, L. J., Lin, D. Y., & Weissfeld, L. (1989). Regression analysis of multivariate incomplete failure time data by modeling marginal distributions. *Journal of the American Statistical Association, 84,* 1065–1073. doi:10.2307/2290084

Willett, J. B., & Singer, J. D. (1993). Investigating onset, cessation, relapse and recovery: Why you should, and how you can, use discrete-time survival analysis. *Journal of Consulting and Clinical Psychology, 61,* 952–965. doi:10.1037/0022-006X.61.6.952

Yamaguchi, K. (1991). *Event history analysis.* Newbury Park, CA: Sage.

## CHAPTER 14

LATENT STATE–TRAIT MODELS

Rolf Steyer, Christian Geiser, and Christiane Fiege

Latent state–trait models, which decompose observed variables into latent trait, latent state, and error components, have been developed in reaction to the person-situation debate in differential psychology (e.g., see Anastasi, 1983; Bowers, 1973; Endler & Magnusson, 1976; Epstein, 1979, 1980; Mischel, 1998). At about the same time, the distinction between states and traits became an issue (e.g., see Cattell, 1966, 1979; Cattell & Scheier, 1961; Nesselroade & Bartsch, 1977; Spielberger, 1972). Some researchers sought to assess states using items that ask for current mood states (How do you feel/think *right now*?) and to assess traits using items asking for traits (How do you feel/think, *in general*?; e.g., see Spielberger, 1972). Others sought to define and measure traits by aggregation of behavioral observations over representative samples of situations (e.g., Epstein, 1979, 1980), and still others tried to assess states and traits, representing them as latent variables in structural equation models (e.g., see Ormel & Schaufeli, 1991). Others (e.g., Hertzog & Nesselroade, 1987) suggested distinguishing states and traits by the size of their autocorrelations; they should be high for traits and low for states. But what is high and what is low? Hertzog and Nesselroade (1987) also suggested a more fundamental idea, writing, "Generally it is certainly the case that most psychological attributes will neither be, strictly speaking, traits or states. That is, attributes can have both trait and state components" (p. 95).

At about the same time, Steyer (1987, 1989) and his associates (e.g., see Majcen, Steyer, & Schwenkmezger, 1988; Steyer, Ferring, & Schmitt, 1992; Steyer, Majcen, Schwenkmezger, & Buchner, 1989; Steyer & Schmitt, 1990a, 1990b; Steyer, Schmitt, & Eid, 1999; Steyer, Schwenkmezger, & Auer, 1990) introduced the basic concepts of *latent state–trait theory* (LST theory) and developed *latent state–trait models* (LST models)—specific structural equation models in which the latent variables can be interpreted as reflecting latent-state or latent-trait components. In the late-1990s, *state change* (Steyer, Eid, & Schwenkmezger, 1997) and *trait change models* (Eid & Hoffmann, 1998; Steyer, Krambeer, & Hannöver, 2004) were introduced. Furthermore, recent research on multitrait–multimethod (MTMM) analysis has stimulated new ways of constructively defining and modeling method effects (e.g., Eid, 2000; Eid, Lischetzke, Nussbeck, & Trierweiler, 2003; Eid et al., 2008; Pohl, Steyer, & Kraus, 2008; Pohl & Steyer, 2010). These new approaches have been applied to model measure-specific (or indicator-specific) effects in LST models (Eid, Schneider, & Schwenkmezger, 1999) as well as to models with latent-state and trait change variables (Geiser, 2009; Geiser, Eid, Nussbeck, Courvoisier, & Cole, 2010a, 2010b; Vautier, Steyer, & Boomsma, 2008). Furthermore, LST models have been extended to *multiconstruct models* that simultaneously study the associations between the state and trait components pertaining to different psychological constructs (e.g.,

We thank Ginger Lockhart for helpful comments and for checking our use of the English language.

DOI: 10.1037/13621-014

Dumenci & Windle, 1998; Eid, Notz, Steyer, & Schwenkmezger, 1994; Steyer et al., 1990). Last but not least, LST models can also be used in modeling individual causal effects (e.g., see Steyer, 2005).

The organization of this chapter follows exactly these points. We start by defining the basic concepts of LST theory, present the assumptions defining various LST models, and show how to introduce latent-state and latent-trait change variables. We then discuss why the inclusion of method factors is often required in models of LST theory, and present different ways of constructively defining method factors in LST models. Finally, we discuss multiconstruct models as well as other recent extensions of the classic LST model.

BASIC CONCEPTS OF LATENT STATE–TRAIT THEORY

In LST theory, we do not simply assume that there is, for example, a latent variable that we label "trait factor" or "state residual factor." Instead, the latent variables are defined *constructively*, that is, on the basis of assumptions about well-defined concepts referring to the underlying *random experiment* (e.g., Steyer, 1988). Although involving some formalism, studying this random experiment is useful, because it helps us to come up with a clear definition of what the latent variables in LST models really are. This has the advantage that we know exactly what these variables mean, facilitating our interpretation of the results of specific models of LST theory.

In LST theory, we consider several observations Y_{it} of an attribute at time t. Two different observations are denoted by Y_{it} and Y_{jt}, $i \neq j$. We decompose each Y_{it} into three theoretical (latent) components, a *measurement error* component, a *trait* component, and a *state residual* component. The sum of the trait and the state residual components is the *latent-state* component.

The observations Y_{it} are considered to be random variables. Therefore, we also call them *observables*. Random variables always refer to a random experiment, which is the kind of empirical phenomenon with which the theory deals. The random experiment in LST theory is not an experiment in the classic sense (i.e., it does not involve an experimental manipulation of independent variables) but rather refers to making several observations of the same person that is possibly in a different situation at each time t of measurement. This is in line with the key idea of LST theory, according to which we never measure a person in a situational vacuum.

The random experiment considered in LST theory is as follows: We sample a person from a set Ω_U (*the population*) of persons, observe whatever is needed to determine the value of the observables Y_{i1} at Time 1 (e.g., answers to items of a questionnaire, behavior observations, or physiological measures) and repeat these observations at one or several other time points. We also assume that, at each time-point, there is a set Ω_{S_t} of situations, one of which will occur while the person is being assessed. Hence, the sample space, that is, the set of all possible outcomes of the random experiment has the following structure:

$$\Omega = \Omega_U \times \Omega_{S_1} \times \Omega_{O_1} \times \ldots \times \Omega_{S_t} \times \Omega_{O_t} \\ \times \ldots \times \Omega_{S_T} \times \Omega_{O_T}, \tag{1}$$

where Ω_{O_t} denotes the set of possible observations at time $t = 1, \ldots, T$ and $\times$ denotes the Cartesian product.

This structure of the sample space allows us to consider the following random variables:

Y_{it}: the observables, that is, the observations of an attribute at time t, which only depend on the elements of the set Ω_{O_t}, $t = 1, \ldots, T$. Because there are several observations of the same attribute at time t (e.g., several items or scales), the subscript i indicates the ith observation of the attribute.

U: the observational-unit variable (or *person variable* if the units are persons). The value u of U indicates which unit is sampled from the set Ω_U.

S_t: the situation variable pertaining to time t. The value s_t of S_t indicates the situation that realizes when the unit is assessed at time t.

As we will see later, it is not necessary that we observe the actual situations—the values of the situation variable S_t—in which the measurements are made. It is sufficient to assume that we always assess *a person-in-a-situation* (Anastasi, 1983).

Now we can define the latent-state variable

$$\tau_{it} = E(Y_{it} \mid U, S_t). \tag{2}$$

Its values $E(Y_{it} \mid U = u, S_t = s_t)$ are the conditional expectations of Y_{it} given the person u and the situation s_t in which the person is when Y_{it} is observed. In contrast, the latent-trait variable is defined by

$$\xi_{it} = E(Y_{it} \mid U). \tag{3}$$

Its values $E(Y_{it} \mid U = u)$ are the conditional expectations of Y_{it} given the person u. Furthermore, the measurement error variable is defined to be the residual

$$\varepsilon_{it} = Y_{it} - \tau_{it}. \tag{4}$$

Its values are the differences between the observed scores of Y_{it} and the latent-state scores $E(Y_{it} \mid U = u, S_t = s_t)$. Finally, the latent-state residual is the difference

$$\zeta_{it} = \tau_{it} - \xi_{it}. \tag{5}$$

Its values are the deviations of the latent-state scores from the latent-trait scores.

These are the four fundamental theoretical concepts of LST theory. These concepts are defined on the sole assumption that we consider a random experiment that can be structured by the type of sample space described in Equation 1 and that the observables Y_{it} have finite expectations. This guarantees that the conditional expectations and their residuals—and therefore also the latent-state and latent-trait variables—are well defined.

Furthermore, we can define the reliability coefficient as

$$Rel(Y_{it}) = Var(\tau_{it})/Var(Y_{it}), \tag{6}$$

which quantifies the degree to which the observables Y_{it} are error-free measures. In contrast, the *consistency coefficient*

$$Con(Y_{it}) = Var(\xi_{it})/Var(Y_{it}) \tag{7}$$

is a quantity describing the degree to which the latent trait ξ_{it} determines the observable Y_{it}. Finally, the *occasion specificity coefficient*

$$Spe(Y_{it}) = Var(\zeta_{it})/Var(Y_{it}) \tag{8}$$

represents the degree to which the situation and/or the interaction between person and situation determines the observable Y_{it}.

IMPLICATIONS OF THE DEFINITIONS OF LATENT STATES AND LATENT TRAITS

The definitions of latent-state and latent-trait variables—and the associated residuals, the measurement error variable, and the latent-state residual—imply a number of properties of these concepts (see Exhibit 14.1). These properties are special cases of the general properties of conditional expectations and their residuals (e.g., Steyer, Nagel, Partchev, & Mayer, in press). These properties cannot be tested empirically, in the same way that the statement *a bachelor is unmarried* cannot be tested empirically, because being unmarried is a logical implication of the concept of *bachelor*. The only thing that can be tested empirically is whether a particular man is a bachelor. Analogously, we cannot and need not empirically test whether a latent-state residual is correlated with a latent-trait variable or whether a measurement error variable is correlated with a latent-trait variable or with a latent-state variable pertaining to the same time-point t. These correlations are zero by definition of these theoretical concepts.

MODELS OF LATENT STATE–TRAIT THEORY

The theoretical concepts introduced thus far are well defined and do not rest on any restrictive assumptions that could be violated in an empirical

---

Exhibit 14.1

Properties of the Basic Concepts of Latent State–Trait Theory Implied by Their Definition

Decomposition of variables
  $Y_{it} = \tau_{it} + \varepsilon_{it}$
  $\tau_{it} = \xi_{it} + \zeta_{it}$
Decomposition of variances
  $Var(Y_{it}) = Var(\tau_{it}) + Var(\varepsilon_{it})$
  $Var(\tau_{it}) = Var(\xi_{it}) + Var(\zeta_{it})$
Other properties
  $E(\varepsilon_{it} \mid U, S_t) = E(\varepsilon_{it} \mid U) = E(\varepsilon_{it}) = 0$
  $E(\zeta_{it} \mid U) = E(\zeta_{it}) = 0$
  $Cov(\varepsilon_{it}, \zeta_{it}) = Cov(\varepsilon_{it}, \tau_{jt}) = Cov(\varepsilon_{it}, \xi_{js}) = Cov(\zeta_{it}, \xi_{js}) = 0$

application. This is true even though we do not know the expectations, variances, and covariances of the theoretical variables or the LST coefficients of reliability, consistency, and occasion specificity. Assumptions that could be violated in applications (e.g., about the homogeneity of trait variables pertaining to different observables) have to be introduced if we actually want to determine these parameters from other parameters that are empirically estimable. These assumptions define specific models of LST theory.

Single-Trait Model

The crudest model of LST theory is the single-trait model defined by two assumptions. The first one is

$$\tau_{it} = \lambda_{it0} + \lambda_{it1}\,\xi, \qquad \lambda_{it0}, \lambda_{it1} \in \mathbf{IR}, \qquad (9)$$

where λ_{it0} and λ_{it1} are real constants. This assumption means that all latent-state variables are linear functions of each other. It implies that all latent-state variables are perfectly correlated and may differ only with regard to their scale (i.e., their origin and units of measurement). The parameter λ_{it0} can be interpreted as an intercept (origin of measurement), and the parameter λ_{it1} as a slope coefficient (factor loading) that reflects the units of measurement. In sum, the first assumption suggests unidimensionality of all latent-state variables—irrespective of the measurement occasion (i.e., possible occasion- or situation-specific influences and person–situation interactions are ignored).

According to the second assumption, the measurement error variables are uncorrelated, that is,

$$Cov(\varepsilon_{it}, \varepsilon_{js}) = 0, \qquad \text{for } (i, t) \neq (j, s). \qquad (10)$$

This assumption implies that the latent-trait factor accounts for all of the covariation among the observed variables. Figure 14.1 displays the path diagram of the model for two observations at each of two occasions (time-points). According to this model, the latent-state and latent-trait components of an observable Y_{it} are identical, for all four observables considered. This means that there are neither situation effects nor interaction effects between person and situation. The only sources of variance in the observables are interindividual differences, which are represented by a unidimensional latent variable (ξ)

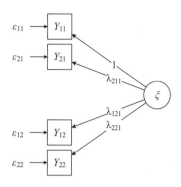

FIGURE 14.1. Single-trait model for two observed variables Y_{it} (i = variable, t = time-point) measured on two occasions of measurement. ξ = latent-trait factor; λ_{it1} = factor loading; ε_{it} = measurement error variable.

and measurement error. Unidimensionality means that we assume the different observations of the same attribute at each point of time to measure exactly the same latent trait (ξ), although perhaps on a different scale. These different scales are represented by the corresponding differences in the intercepts λ_{it0} and slope coefficients λ_{it1}. Finally, the model also implies that there is no change in the attribute over the time-points considered, neither change caused by situation and interaction effects nor change caused by a systematic change in the trait.

A technical issue that needs to be addressed in practical applications is that the scale of the latent-trait variable ξ is not uniquely determined per se, but needs to be fixed by the investigator. This can be done, for example, by setting $\lambda_{110} = 0$ and $\lambda_{111} = 1$. With these constraints, the latent trait ξ becomes identical to ξ_{11}, the latent-trait variable of Y_{11}, that is, $\xi = \xi_{11}$. An alternative option is to set $E(\xi) = 0$ and $Var(\xi) = 1$. With these constraints, the latent trait ξ is a linear function of any of the measure-specific latent-trait variables ξ_{it}. Either one of these options fixes the scale of the latent-trait factors.

As noted, the single-trait model is crude and simplistic because it assumes that the observables only depend on a common trait and measurement error. The model suggests that any changes in Y_{it} over time are just due to random measurement error or changes in the scale of Y_{it} (as reflected in different coefficients λ_{it0} and λ_{it1} over time). In none of the applications in different fields of psychology did we ever see an example in which the single-trait model showed an acceptable fit to actual data, and this includes the measurement of personality traits (Deinzer et al., 1995; Schmukle & Egloff, 2005), values (M. Schmitt, Schwartz, Steyer, & T. Schmitt, 1993), EEG measures (Hagemann, Hewig, Seifert, Naumann, & Bartussek, 2005; Hagemann & Naumann, 2009; Hagemann, Naumann, Thayer, & Bartussek, 2002), cerebral blood flow (Hermes et al., 2009), cortisol in saliva (Hellhammer et al., 2007; Kirschbaum et al., 1990) and, of course, mood states (e.g., Eid et al., 1994; Steyer et al., 1989).

Multistate Model

A much more realistic model is the multistate model defined by

$$\tau_{it} = \lambda_{it0} + \lambda_{it1}\, \tau_t, \qquad \lambda_{it0},\, \lambda_{it1} \in \mathbb{R}. \qquad (11)$$

This assumption means that all latent-state variables *that are measured on the same measurement occasion* are linear functions of each other. Hence, this assumption is less restrictive than the assumption made in the single-trait model, in which case we assumed *all* latent-state variables to be unidimensional (irrespective of the measurement occasion). Equation 11 implies that there is a common (occasion-specific) latent variable τ_t, which can be referred to as a *latent-state factor*. That is, the model also assumes homogeneity of the state variables, but only of those that are measured on the same occasion of measurement t.

The scales of the latent-state factors τ_t are uniquely determined by setting $\lambda_{1t0} = 0$ and $\lambda_{1t1} = 1$, or by $E(\tau_t) = 0$ and $Var(\tau_t) = 1$, for each $t = 1, \ldots, T$. With $\lambda_{1t0} = 0$ and $\lambda_{1t1} = 1$, the latent-state variable τ_t is identical to the measure-specific latent-state variable τ_{1t}, that is, $\tau_t = \tau_{1t}$. In contrast, with $E(\tau_t) = 0$ and $Var(\tau_t) = 1$, the latent-state variable τ_t is a linear function of any of the measure-specific latent-state variables τ_{it}. The second assumption is again the assumption of uncorrelated measurement errors (see Equation 10).

Figure 14.2 displays the path diagram of such a model for two observations at each of two occasions (time-points). According to this model, the latent-state components of an observable Y_{it} are identical

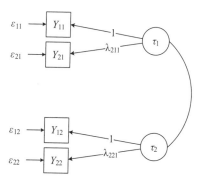

FIGURE 14.2. Multistate model for two observed variables Y_{it} (i = variable, t = time-point) measured on two occasions of measurement. τ_t = latent-state factor; λ_{it1} = factor loading; ε_{it} = measurement error variable.

within each occasion of measurement, at least in the sense that they are linear functions of each other.

In contrast to the single-trait model, the multistate model allows for situation effects or interaction between person and situation. Sources of variance in the observables are now interindividual differences, situation or interaction effects, and measurement errors. In this model we also assume that the two different observations of the same attribute at each point of time measure exactly the same latent-state variable τ_t, although perhaps on a different scale. Furthermore, both interindividual differences as well as situation and interaction effects may determine the latent-state variables τ_t. In this model, however, state and trait components are not separated. Nevertheless, we may consider the correlations between the latent-state variables pertaining to different time-points, the *latent-state stabilities*: The higher these correlations, the more likely it is that there are also stable individual differences over time.

Single-Trait/Multistate Model

To separate state and trait components, we have to introduce the trait component into the model as well. The *single-trait/multistate model* is the simplest kind of model in which this is achieved. It is defined by

$$\tau_{it} = \lambda_{it0} + \lambda_{it1}\, \tau_t, \qquad \lambda_{it0},\, \lambda_{it1} \in \mathbb{R} \qquad (12)$$

and

$$\xi_{it} = \gamma_{it0} + \gamma_{it1}\, \xi, \qquad \gamma_{it0},\, \gamma_{it1} \in \mathbb{R}, \qquad (13)$$

where γ_{it0} is an intercept and γ_{it1} is a slope coefficient (second order factor loading). These assumptions suggest that (a) as in the multistate model, all latent-state variables measured on the same occasion of measurement are unidimensional (so that we can introduce a common latent-state factor τ_t) and (b) trait variables are unidimensional as well (so that we can introduce a common trait factor ξ).

Assigning a scale to the latent-state factors τ_t is again achieved either by setting $\lambda_{1t0} = 0$ and $\lambda_{1t1} = 1$, or by setting $E(\tau_t) = 0$ and $Var(\tau_t) = 1$, for each $t = 1$, ..., T. Assigning a scale to the latent-trait factor ξ is achieved either by setting $\gamma_{110} = 0$ and $\gamma_{111} = 1$, or by setting $E(\xi) = 0$ and $Var(\xi) = 1$. Fixing the scales of the latent-state variables τ_t by setting $\lambda_{1t0} = 0$ and $\lambda_{1t1} = 1$ and the scale of the latent-trait variable ξ by setting $\gamma_{110} = 0$ and $\gamma_{111} = 1$ implies $\tau_t = \tau_{1t}$ and $\xi = \xi_{11}$. In contrast, with $E(\tau_t) = 0$, $Var(\tau_t) = 1$, $E(\xi) = 0$ and $Var(\xi) = 1$, the latent-state variable τ_t is a linear function of any of the measure-specific latent-state variables τ_{it}, and the latent-trait variable ξ is a linear function of any measure-specific latent-trait variable ξ_{it}. Again, it is assumed that the measurement error variables are uncorrelated (see Equation 10). Additionally, it is assumed that the latent-state residuals belonging to different occasions of measurement are uncorrelated, that is,

$$Cov(\zeta_{it}, \zeta_{js}) = 0, \text{ for } t \neq s. \qquad (14)$$

We can show algebraically that Equation 13 is equivalent to

$$\tau_t = \gamma_{t0} + \gamma_{t1} \xi + \zeta_t, \qquad \gamma_{t0}, \gamma_{t1} \in \mathbb{R}, \qquad (15)$$

which means that each latent-state factor can be additively decomposed into an intercept (γ_{t0}), a latent-trait component (ξ) that is weighted by a second-order factor loading (γ_{t1}), and a latent-state residual component (ζ_t). The assumptions of the single-trait–multistate model can be summarized by the path diagram displayed in Figure 14.3, again for two observations at each of two occasions (time-points). If we consider just two time-points, we either have to fix both coefficients γ_{11} and γ_{21} to 1 or fix the variance $Var(\xi) = 1$ with the additional constraint of setting the loadings equal: $\gamma_{11} = \gamma_{21}$. Otherwise, this part of the model would not be identified.

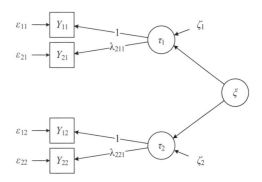

FIGURE 14.3.   Single-trait/multistate model for two observed variables Y_{it} (i = variable, t = time-point) measured on two occasions of measurement. τ_t = latent-state factor; ξ = latent-trait factor; ζ_t = latent-state residual; λ_{it1} = factor loading; ε_{it} = measurement error variable.

As in the multistate model, the latent-state components of an observable Y_{it} are identical within each occasion of measurement, at least in the sense that they are linear functions of each other. Additionally, in this model, we assume that the common latent-state variable τ_t can be decomposed into a trait component ξ that is invariant over all occasions of measurement and a latent-state residual ζ_t specific for occasion t. Assuming such a common latent trait ξ is equivalent to assuming that the measure-specific latent-trait components ξ_{it} are linear functions of each other.

Just as the multistate model, this model allows for situation effects or interaction between person and situation. It additionally decomposes the state components into a trait and a state residual. Sources of variance in the observables are now interindividual differences (explicitly represented by ξ), situation or interaction effects (explicitly represented by the components ζ_t), and measurement errors. Figure 14.3 shows that both, ξ and ζ_t, determine the latent-state variables τ_t. Just as in the multistate model, in this model, we also assume that the two different observations of the same attribute at each point of time measure exactly the same latent-state variable τ_t, again perhaps on a different scale. Hence, this model also allows for change in the attribute considered. This time, however, it is assumed that this change is due to situation or interaction effects but not to a systematic change in the trait components, at least not to change beyond what can be described by a deterministic linear function. For only two occasions of measurement, we have to assume that the coefficients γ_{t1} are identical. Otherwise, the variance of ξ (or the γ_{t1} coefficients) would not be identified. For three or more time-points, this constraint is not required.

Some Methodological Remarks

Note the way in which the latent variables have been constructed in all three classes of models. We started by describing a certain kind of random experiment, which is the *empirical phenomenon* we consider in LST theory. We showed how the sample space Ω is structured and introduced the *primitives of the theory*: the observables Y_{it}, the observational-unit variable U, and the situation variable S_t that indicates the situation in which the unit is when the observations Y_{it} are made. Then we used the conditional expectations of the observables Y_{it} given U and S_t to define the *fundamental concepts* of LST theory. Next, we introduced assumptions with regard to the relationships between these fundamental concepts. These assumptions imply the existence of certain latent variables, the *common latent-state variables* τ_t and the *common latent-trait variable* ξ. Hence, instead of drawing an egg and giving it a nice label, we *constructed* the latent variables as linear functions of the conditional expectations of the observables. Although we do not know the values of these latent variables, we know that they exist and that they are random variables referring to the same random experiment as the observables. Perhaps more important, knowing the observables Y_{it}, we also know the substantive meaning of their conditional expectations and the latent variables, which are linear functions of these conditional expectations. This constructive way of introducing latent variables can also be followed in more complex models. We start with introducing *latent-state change variables*.

Latent-State Change Models

Modeling change has been puzzling researchers for many decades (e.g., Collins & Horn, 1991; Collins & Sayer, 2001; Cronbach & Furby, 1970; Harris, 1963). In 1997, Steyer et al. showed how to introduce the difference between two latent-state variables as a single latent variable into a structural equation model by specifying the loadings in a particular way. In 1993, Raykov showed that latent

difference variables can also be introduced utilizing a trivial equation such as

$$\tau_2 = \tau_1 + (\tau_2 - \tau_1). \tag{16}$$

Using this equation, the path diagram of the multistate model presented in Figure 14.2 turns to the diagram presented in Figure 14.4.

For three occasions, we have the choice between the *baseline model* (see Figure 14.5a) and the *neighbor model* (Figure 14.5b; see also Steyer, Partchev, & Shanahan, 2000). In the baseline model, the latent-state change variables represent the latent-state change compared with the first occasion of measurement, whereas in the neighbor model, we consider the latent change variables with respect to adjacent time-points, that is, we consider change between Times 1 and 2 as well as change between Times 2 and 3.

A Linear Growth Curve Model

If we would like to formulate a model postulating linear change in the latent states between three occasions of measurement, the simplest way is to modify the multistate model as specified in Figure 14.5c. According to this model, the latent state at Occasion 2 is the sum of the latent-state variable at Time 1 plus the latent change variable between Occasions 1 and 2, that is,

$$\tau_2 = \tau_1 + (\tau_2 - \tau_1), \tag{17}$$

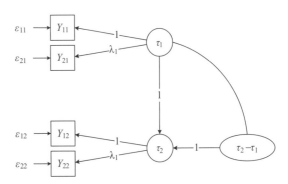

FIGURE 14.4. Latent-state change model for two observed variables Y_{it} (i = variable, t = time-point) measured on two occasions of measurement. τ_t = latent-state factor; $\tau_2 - \tau_1$ = latent-difference variable; λ_{it1} = factor loading; ε_{it} = measurement error variable. The factor loadings for each observed variable have to be constrained to be time-invariant.

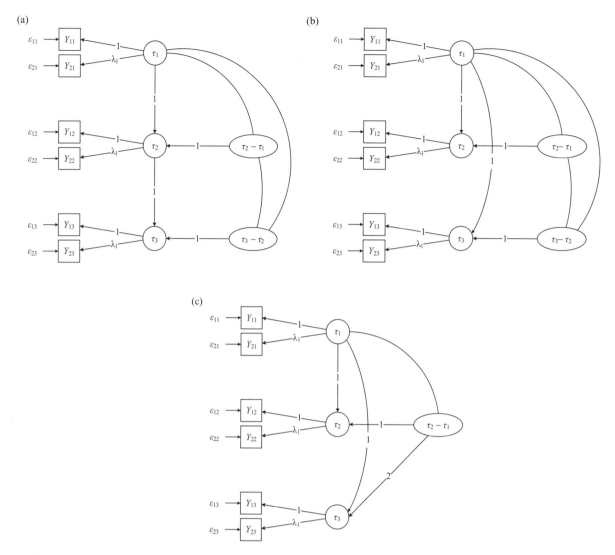

FIGURE 14.5. Latent-state change models for two observed variables Y_{it} (i = variable, t = time-point) measured on three occasions of measurement: (a) Baseline change model. (b) Neighbor change model. (c) Linear change model (linear growth curve model). τ_t = latent-state factor; $\tau_2 - \tau_1$ = latent-difference variable; λ_{it1} = factor loading; ε_{it} = measurement error variable. The factor loadings for each observed variable have to be constrained to be time-invariant.

whereas the latent state at Occasion 3 is the sum of the latent-state variable at Time 1 plus two times the latent change variable between Occasions 1 and 2, that is,

$$\tau_3 = \tau_1 + 2\,(\tau_2 - \tau_1). \tag{18}$$

Hence, in this model, we postulate a linear growth curve for each and every unit, because a value of the latent-state variable τ_t is the latent state of unit u at time t. Comparing this model with one of the change models depicted in Figures 14.5a and 14.5b allows testing the hypothesis of linear growth.

Of course, modeling quadratic and other growth curves is possible as well. Mayer, Steyer, and Partchev (in press) have presented a general way to construct these models.

Latent-Trait Change Models

The ideas outlined thus far can also be extended to modeling latent-trait change (e.g., Eid & Hoffmann, 1998). The goal of trait change models is to separate occasion-specific (state-residual) influences from trait change and measurement error. Trait change models generally require more than just two occasions of measurement. Otherwise, occasion-specific fluctuations cannot be separated from true trait change. In principle, we need at least two occasions for each latent-trait variable for which we want to assess trait change. If these design requirements are satisfied, we may introduce latent-trait change variables using the same principles as for the construction of the latent-state change models. Steyer, Krambeer, and Hannöver (2004) provided an example.

In addition, the approach described in Equations 17 and 18 can also be applied to the level of the latent-trait variables (rather than latent-state variables) to test latent growth curves on the level of latent-trait variables. In contrast to the latent-state growth curve model described in the preceding paragraphs, these models allow for a separation of the growth process from occasion-specific influences and are therefore more broadly applicable (Geiser, Keller, & Lockhart, 2011). These models have sometimes been referred to as *curve-of-factors models* (McArdle, 1988) or *second-order growth models* (e.g., Hancock, Kuo, & Lawrence, 2001; Sayer & Cumsille, 2001) because they model individual latent trajectories by means of second-order factors, that is, the growth curve components—as opposed to conventional growth curve models that employ only a single indicator per time-point. The advantage of second-order growth curve models is that—similar to classical LST models—they allow for a proper separation of systematic variance from measurement error variance, whereas in conventional (first-order) growth models, measurement error variance cannot be separated from systematic occasion-specific variance because there is only one single indicator per time-point.

METHODS FACTORS

The classical LST models may not always show a good fit in empirical applications. In principle, this can happen for several reasons. For example, if there are more than three occasions and if there is true trait change, then the single-trait–multistate model does not adequately represent the actual covariance structure of the observables. Another reason for a discrepancy between the covariance matrix implied by the model and the actual covariance matrix of the observables might be that the true-score variables of

the observables may not be exactly identical within time-points, even not in the sense that they are (perfect) linear functions of each other. In other words, each observable may contain a measure-specific component (sometimes also referred to as an *indicator-specific effect*) that is not shared with the other measures of the latent-state variable. Such a measure-specific component, for example, can be due to a specific response format, item wording, or rater effects (see Eid & Diener, 2006). In cross-sectional designs, this measure-specific component is not separable from random measurement error; however, as we consider longitudinal designs in which the same indicators are measured repeatedly, stable measure-specific variance and measurement error variance can be disentangled (see also Marsh & Grayson, 1994; Raffalovich & Bohrnstedt, 1987). The values of these measure-specific components represent the person-specific effects of using a particular measure over another one, or in other terms, the person-specific effects of using a particular *method* (of measurement) instead of another one. Hence, these components are also called *method effects*.

Different approaches are available to model person-specific method effects in longitudinal data. The simplest way is to allow for correlated error variables of the same indicator over time (e.g., Sörbom, 1975). In MTMM research, this is known as the *correlated uniqueness* (CU) *approach* to modeling method effects (Kenny, 1976; Marsh & Grayson, 1995). Although improving the fit of a model when method effects are present, the specification of correlated errors leaves these effects confounded with measurement error. This has the undesirable implication that a systematic source of variance is not explicitly modeled, which leads to an underestimation of

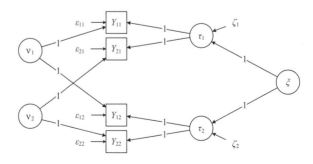

FIGURE 14.6. Single-trait/multistate model with *m* method factors (v_i).

the reliabilities of the observables in CU models. In more sophisticated LST measurement models, method effects are either modeled by defining additional latent variables (*method factors*) or by allowing for measure-specific latent-trait variables (e.g., Bonnefon, Vautier, & Eid, 2007; Eid et al., 1999).

Historically, orthogonal method factors for each of *m* indicators were introduced to model person-specific method effects (e.g., Steyer et al., 1992; see Figure 14.6), similar to a *correlated traits-uncorrelated methods* approach in MTMM research (Marsh & Grayson, 1995). Modeling one orthogonal method factor for each measure in LST models has the disadvantage that these method factors cannot be constructively defined (Eid, 1996). Furthermore, because method effects are assumed to be uncorrelated, the model may overfit the data and shared method effects between similar methods are not accounted for (Eid, 2000).

Method Factors Defined as Residuals

Recently, approaches that define a reference method and consider only *m* − 1 correlated method factors have gained popularity in MTMM research (Eid, 2000; Eid et al., 2003, 2008). This so-called *residual method factor approach* has also been applied to model method effects within the LST framework (Courvoisier, 2006; Courvoisier, Nussbeck, Eid, Geiser, & Cole, 2008; Eid et al., 1999; Geiser, 2009; Geiser et al., 2010a, 2010b).

Let us look at Eid's (2000) definition of a method effect in more detail. Using the index *r* to denote the reference method (or reference measure), we consider the regression $E(\tau_{it}|\tau_{rt})$, where $i \neq r$ and $E(\tau_{it}|\tau_{rt})$ denotes the conditional expectation (regression) of a true-score variable τ_{it} on the true-score variable τ_{rt} of the reference measure *r* at time *t*. The residuals $\tau_{it} - E(\tau_{it}|\tau_{rt})$ of this regression are the method variables (v_{it}), as they reflect that part of a nonreference true-score variable τ_{it} that cannot be predicted from the (reference) true-score variable τ_{rt}:

$$v_{it} = \tau_{it} - E(\tau_{it}|\tau_{rt}). \tag{19}$$

There is a separate method variable v_{it} for each indicator *i*, $i \neq r$. To actually separate method effects from random measurement error, we again need to introduce a homogeneity assumption. A reasonable

assumption is that all method variables pertaining to the same observable *i* differ only by a multiplicative constant κ_{its}:

$$v_{it} = \kappa_{its} v_{is}, \qquad \kappa_{its} \in \mathbb{R}. \tag{20}$$

This assumption implies the existence of a *common* method factor v_i for each nonreference measure as illustrated in Figure 14.7. Without loss of generality, we have selected the first measure as a reference in Figure 14.7, that is, *r* = 1; therefore, there is not a method factor for the first measure. The equations for this model are

$$Y_{it} = \begin{cases} \lambda_{rt0} + \lambda_{rt1}\tau_{rt} + \varepsilon_{rt}, & \text{for } i = r \\ \lambda_{it0} + \lambda_{it1}\tau_{rt} + \kappa_{it}v_i + \varepsilon_{it}, & \text{for } i \neq r, \end{cases} \tag{21}$$

where $\kappa_{it} \in \mathbb{R}$.

The definition of method factors as regression residuals with respect to a reference measure implies that there are *m* − 1 method factors v_i. Each of these method factors has the expectation (true mean) of zero and is uncorrelated with all state factors τ_{rt} pertaining to the same construct, but they may be correlated with other method factors v_j as well as with state factors pertaining to other constructs in multiconstruct LST models (see the section Multiconstruct Models). The correlations $Corr(v_i, v_j)$ between different method factors may be of interest if certain measures share a common method effect relative to the reference measure (e.g., two items may be more similar in wording relative to a third item). With only two measures and only two time-points, both loadings κ_{it} on the method factor have to be fixed to a nonzero value to achieve identification (e.g., $\kappa_{i1} = \kappa_{i2} = 1$). For an application of the residual method factor approach to LST models, see Eid et al. (1999).

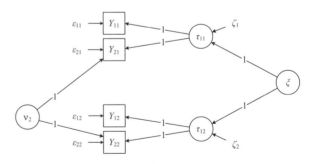

FIGURE 14.7. Single-trait/multistate model with residual method factor (v_2) according to Eid's (2000) *m* − 1 approach.

Method Factors Defined as Differences Between True-Score Variables

Suppose we have two observables that at each of two occasions of measurement measure the same latent-state variable. Then

$$\tau_{11} = \tau_{11} \qquad \text{and} \qquad \tau_{21} = \tau_{11} \qquad (22)$$

as well as

$$\tau_{12} = \tau_{12} \qquad \text{and} \qquad \tau_{22} = \tau_{12} \qquad (23)$$

will hold. In practice, however, this is very difficult to achieve. So what if we fail? Then, instead of Equations 22 and 23, the equations

$$\tau_{11} = \tau_{11} \qquad \text{and} \qquad \tau_{21} = \tau_{11} + (\tau_{21} - \tau_{11}) \quad (24)$$

as well as

$$\tau_{12} = \tau_{12} \qquad \text{and} \qquad \tau_{22} = \tau_{12} + (\tau_{22} - \tau_{12}) \quad (25)$$

still hold. In fact, these equations are tautological, that is, they are always true. The differences $\tau_{21} - \tau_{11}$ and $\tau_{22} - \tau_{12}$ between the two true-score variables at the two occasions are the systematic differences between the two observables at each of the two occasions. If the two observables are intended to measure the same latent state, then the differences

$$\delta_1 = \tau_{21} - \tau_{11} \qquad \text{and} \qquad \delta_2 = \tau_{22} - \tau_{12} \qquad (26)$$

exactly represent the individual effects of using Method 2 instead of Method 1 at time-points 1 and 2, respectively. Whereas δ_1 represents the method factor pertaining to Occasion 1, δ_2 is the method factor pertaining to Occasion 2 (see Pohl et al., 2008).

Why should these two method factors be different if exactly the same methods are applied at the two occasions of measurement? Hence, it is plausible to assume $\delta_1 = \delta_2$, which allows us to drop the index, that is,

$$\delta = \delta_1 = \delta_2, \qquad (27)$$

where δ represents the *method factor* assumed to be identical for both occasions of measurement. Note that τ_{11} is a constituting component of δ. Hence, it will correlate with δ, and the same applies to τ_{12}. The resulting model is represented in Figure 14.8.

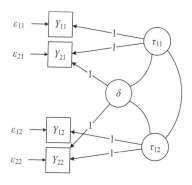

FIGURE 14.8. Multistate model with latent difference method factor (δ).

Method Factors for Common Latent-State Variables

Constructing method factors as latent difference variables in the way outlined in Equations 24 through 26 implies that the latent-state variables occurring in the path diagrams in Figures 14.7 and 14.8 are *specific* to the first measure. In fact, the latent-state variables presented in the path diagram are the true-score variable τ_{11} of the first observable Y_{11} at Occasion 1 and the true-score variable τ_{12} of the first observable Y_{12} at Occasion 2. If, however, we would like to have a *common latent-state variable* for both measures at each of the two time-points, we can define such a common latent-state variable by simply taking the averages

$$\eta_1 = (\tau_{11} + \tau_{21})/2 \qquad \text{and} \qquad \eta_2 = (\tau_{12} + \tau_{22})/2 \quad (28)$$

of the two true-score variables involved (for extensions allowing for different loadings, also see Pohl & Steyer, 2010). Now

$$\tau_{11} = \eta_1 + (\tau_{11} - \eta_1) \qquad \text{and} \qquad \tau_{21} = \eta_1 + (\tau_{21} - \eta_1) \quad (29)$$

as well as

$$\tau_{12} = \eta_2 + (\tau_{12} - \eta_2) \quad \text{and} \quad \tau_{22} = \eta_2 + (\tau_{22} - \eta_2) \quad (30)$$

trivially hold. Furthermore, some algebra shows that $\tau_{11} - \eta_1 = -(\tau_{21} - \eta_1)$ and $\tau_{12} - \eta_2 = -(\tau_{22} - \eta_2)$. The values of the difference variable $\tau_{11} - \eta_1$ are the deviations of the Measure 1–specific individual latent-state variables from the common latent-state variable at Occasion 1. Again, it is plausible to assume that the difference variables $\delta_1 = \tau_{11} - \eta_1$ and $\delta_2 = \tau_{12} - \eta_2$ are identical because the observables Y_{11} and Y_{12} are assessed with identical measurement

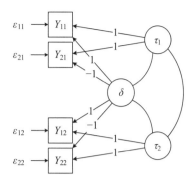

FIGURE 14.9. Multistate model with common latent-state factors using an effect parametrization for the method factor δ.

methods at the two occasions of measurement. Hence, if we assume

$$\delta = \tau_{11} - \eta_1 = \tau_{12} - \eta_2, \qquad (31)$$

the resulting model is represented in Figure 14.9.

In this model, the individual method effects are represented by an *effect parametrization* that compares the latent-state scores of Measures 1 and 2 with the average of the latent-state scores of the two measures. In contrast, in the model displayed in Figure 14.8, the individual method effects are represented by a *contrast parametrization* that compares the latent-state scores of Measure 2 with the latent-state scores of the first measure. Both parametrizations are equivalent to each other. Note, however, that not only the contents of the method factors are different between the two models. Instead, the content of the latent-state variables is different as well. In the effect parametrization, there is a *common latent-state variable* defined to be the average of the two measure-specific latent-state variables τ_{it}. In the contrast parametrization, there is a *specific latent-state variable*, the specific latent-state variables τ_{1t} pertaining to the first measure. Hence, we have the choice, but the choice has consequences for the substantive interpretation of both the method factors *and* the common latent-state variables.

The same is true for Eid's (2000) residual method factor approach, as the meaning of the state and method factors depends on the choice of the reference indicator in this approach. In general, researchers should select an approach that yields methods factors that are easily interpreted and

meaningful for the particular application at hand. Geiser, Eid, and Nussbeck (2008) as well as Geiser et al. (2010a) provided detailed guidelines as to the choice of a particular reference method in practical applications of the residual method factor approach.

THE LST MODEL WITH MEASURE-SPECIFIC TRAIT VARIABLES

Another way to account for method effects is to consider as many trait factors in an LST model as there are measures (as opposed to assuming only *one* general trait factor for all indicators). The trait factors in this model are measure-specific (e.g., Eid, 1996; see Figure 14.10). High correlations among the measure-specific trait factors indicate that the trait components of the observables are essentially homogeneous (i.e., that method effects are small), whereas moderate correlations suggest high method specificity (i.e., each observable may reflect a different facet of the construct).

The model with measure-specific trait factors has the advantage that no method factors are needed to model method effects and that each trait factor is clearly interpretable as the stable component of a specific observable. On the other hand, the model leaves method effects confounded with trait factors. Hence, in contrast to models with residual method factors, variance components caused by a reference trait cannot be separated from variance caused by a specific trait. We suggest that the LST model with measure-specific traits be used when researchers assume that each observable represents a distinct facet of a broadly defined construct. Conversely, models with method factors seem to be more

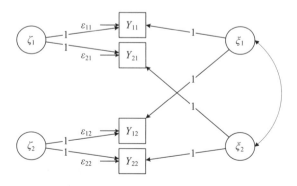

FIGURE 14.10. Latent state–trait model with indicator-specific trait variables ξ_i.

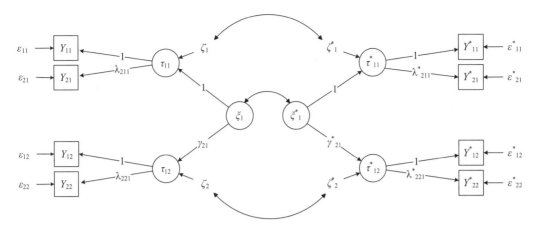

FIGURE 14.11. Multiconstruct latent state–trait model for two constructs.

suitable when theory suggests that the observables are indicators of a single underlying concept and differ only slightly (e.g., because of different item wording, etc.). For a recent application of the LST model with measure-specific trait variables see Bonnefon, Vautier, and Eid (2007).

These basic ideas can be generalized to more than two measures and more than two occasions of measurement as well as to models with unequal loadings of the observables on the latent variables (see Pohl & Steyer, 2010). Furthermore, method factors can also be combined with latent change variables and with models including latent-trait variables such as the single-trait/multistate model. Geiser and Lockhart (in press) discussed different approaches to account for method effects in LST analysis in detail. Extensions of LST models to models incorporating more than one construct[1] at a time are discussed in the next section.

Multiconstruct Models

In multiconstruct LST models, state and trait components of two or more constructs are considered simultaneously (see Figure 14.11). Multiconstruct LST models have been presented by Dumenci and Windle (1998), Eid et al. (1994), Steyer et al. (1990), Vautier (2004), and others. In these models, correlations between the trait components pertaining to different psychological variables indicate associations between the stable parts of these variables. Correlations between state residual components pertaining to the same measurement occasion indicate the degree to which the effects of a specific measurement occasion (or situation and person–situation interaction effects) generalize across different psychological variables. For example, Eid et al. found a correlation of .78 between the latent-trait variable pertaining to a mood-level scale and the latent-trait variable underlying repeatedly measured mood states. In addition, Eid et al. reported significant correlations between the state residual factors pertaining to different constructs on the same measurement occasion ($.32 \leq r \leq .45$) indicating a substantial amount of shared occasion-specific variance.

Schermelleh-Engel, Keith, Moosbrugger, and Hodapp (2004) extended multiconstruct LST models to hierarchical LST models. In these models, a general (third-order) trait factor is introduced to separate variance components caused by general and specific trait components (e.g., a general intelligence component as opposed to specific facets of intelligence). Although the hierarchical LST models proposed by Schermelleh-Engel et al. allowed for the estimation of interesting additional variance components, the third-order latent variables introduced in the models are not well defined and, as a consequence, their meaning is less clear than the meaning of the variables in the models presented in this chapter.

---

[1]We feel that there has not yet been a satisfactory suggestion as to how the term *construct* should be defined in psychology and what exactly it refers to. We use the term here nonetheless to refer to studies that attempt to study the relation between the trait and state components of different psychological variables (e.g., depression and anxiety).

Other Extensions of LST Models

LST models have been extended in a number of ways. Eid (1995, 1996; see also Eid & Hoffmann, 1998) has shown how LST models can be defined for ordered categorical (ordinal) outcomes. Tisak and Tisak (2000) have combined the idea of modeling latent-trait change through growth curve models with the idea of modeling occasion specificity through LST models and have presented a comprehensive framework for modeling variability and change in a single model. Cole, Martin, and Steiger (2005) have presented a so-called *trait–state occasion model* that features an autoregressive component on the level of the state residual variables. Courvoisier (2006; Courvoisier, Eid, & Nussbeck, 2007) extended the classical LST model to a mixture distribution model. Mixture distribution LST models allow identifying a priori unknown subgroups (latent classes) of individuals that differ, for example, in their *traitedness* or proneness to occasion-specific influences.

Another line of research has developed LST models for the case of a multimethod assessment (e.g., different raters assessing depression and anxiety of children on multiple time-points). Multimethod LST models (Courvoisier, 2006; Courvoisier et al., 2008; Scherpenzeel & Saris, 2007; Vautier, 2004) allow researchers to answer questions of stability versus occasion specificity simultaneously for different methods.

CONCLUSION

About 20 years ago, LST theory was introduced and the first LST models were applied to psychological data. As shown in this chapter, since then LST theory has seen numerous extensions that facilitate and broaden its applicability in psychological research. We see as one of the most important features of LST theory the fact that the underlying theoretical concepts of this theory are clearly defined, leading to a clear interpretation of the latent variables in LST models. The various extensions of basic LST theory presented in this chapter illustrate that the rigorous mathematical foundation and constructive definition of the latent variables do not attenuate but rather enhance the flexibility of the approach while at the same time allowing for a clear interpretation

of all theoretical concepts defined within this framework. Other latent variable models often suffer in their theoretical strength and empirical applicability if latent variables are not constructively defined but just assumed to be there—without explicating the random experiment that underlies the phenomenon under study and without specifying how the scores of the latent variables depend on the outcomes of the random experiment.

A good example is the so-called *correlated traits-correlated methods* (CTCM) model in MTMM research (e.g., Marsh & Grayson, 1995). In this model, each indicator is thought to be influenced by a latent trait, a latent method, and an error component. All trait factors can be intercorrelated as can be all methods factors, but trait and methods factors are assumed to be uncorrelated. The latent variables in the CTCM model cannot be constructively defined, and consequently, their meaning and interpretation remains dubious. Furthermore, the model lacks theoretical rigor, as it is not clear, for example, on which theoretical rationale the assumption of uncorrelated traits and methods is based.

One advantage of the constructive definition of latent variables is that we know exactly which correlations among latent variables are zero by definition. For example, in LST theory, trait variables and state residuals cannot be correlated by definition of these theoretical concepts (cf. Exhibit 14.1). Hence, the constructive definition of latent variables as functions of true-score variables makes clear which latent variables can be correlated in empirical applications and which cannot. Models in which latent variables or "factors" are not formally defined but simply "assumed to be" there may not allow for a clear interpretation of these variables and may obfuscate the question as to which correlations are admissible and which are not. We believe that in the future, other areas of latent variable research will greatly benefit from this way of defining latent variables constructively.

References

Anastasi, A. (1983). Traits, states, and situations: A comprehensive view. In H. Wainer & S. Messick (Eds.), *Principles of modern psychological measurement* (pp. 345–356). Hillsdale, NJ: Erlbaum.

Bonnefon, J.-F., Vautier, S., & Eid, M. (2007). Modeling individual differences in contrapositive reasoning with continuous latent state and trait variables. *Personality and Individual Differences, 42,* 1403–1413. doi:10.1016/j.paid.2006.10.017

Bowers, K. S. (1973). Situationism in psychology: An analysis and a critique. *Psychological Review, 80,* 307–336. doi:10.1037/h0035592

Cattell, R. B. (1966). The data box: Its ordering of total resources in terms of possible relational systems. In R. B. Cattell (Ed.), *Handbook of multivariate experimental psychology* (pp. 67–128). Chicago, IL: Rand McNally.

Cattell, R. B. (1979). *Personality and learning theory* (Vol. 1). Berlin, Germany: Springer.

Cattell, R. B., & Scheier, I. H. (1961). *The meaning and measurement of neuroticism and anxiety.* New York, NY: Ronald.

Cole, D. A., Martin, N. M., & Steiger, J. H. (2005). Empirical and conceptual problems with longitudinal trait-state models: Introducing a trait-state-occasion model. *Psychological Methods, 10,* 3–20. doi:10.1037/1082-989X.10.1.3

Collins, L. M., & Horn, J. L. (Eds.). (1991). *Best methods for the analysis of change: Recent advances, unanswered questions, future directions.* Washington, DC: American Psychological Association. doi:10.1037/10099-000

Collins, L. M., & Sayer, A. G. (Eds.). (2001). *New methods for the analysis of change.* Washington, DC: American Psychological Association. doi:10.1037/10409-000

Courvoisier, D. S. (2006). *Unfolding the constituents of psychological scores: Development and application of mixture and multitrait-multimethod LST models* (Unpublished doctoral dissertation). University of Geneva, Switzerland.

Courvoisier, D. S., Eid, M., & Nussbeck, F. W. (2007). Mixture distribution state–trait-models: Basic ideas and applications. *Psychological Methods, 12,* 80–104. doi:10.1037/1082-989X.12.1.80

Courvoisier, D. S., Nussbeck, F. W., Eid, M., Geiser, C., & Cole, D. A. (2008). Analyzing the convergent validity of states and traits: Development and application of multimethod latent state–trait models. *Psychological Assessment, 20,* 270–280. doi:10.1037/a0012812

Cronbach, L. J., & Furby, L. (1970). How should we measure "change"—or should we? *Psychological Bulletin, 74,* 68–80. doi:10.1037/h0029382

Deinzer, R., Steyer, R., Eid, M., Notz, P., Schwenkmezger, P., Ostendorf, F., & Neubauer, A. (1995). Situational effects in trait assessment: The FPI, NEOFFI and EPI questionnaires. *European Journal of Personality, 9,* 1–23. doi:10.1002/per.2410090102

Dumenci, L., & Windle, M. (1998). A multitrait-multioccasion generalization of the latent trait-state model: Description and application. *Structural Equation Modeling, 5,* 391–410. doi:10.1080/10705519809540114

Eid, M. (1995). *Modelle der Messung von Personen in Situationen* [Models for measuring persons in situations]. Weinheim, Germany: Psychologie Verlags Union.

Eid, M. (1996). Longitudinal confirmatory factor analysis for polytomous item responses: Model definition and model selection on the basis of stochastic measurement theory. *Methods of Psychological Research — Online, 1,* 65–85.

Eid, M. (2000). A multitrait-multimethod model with minimal assumptions. *Psychometrika, 65,* 241–261. doi:10.1007/BF02294377

Eid, M., & Diener, E. (Eds.). (2006). *Handbook of multimethod measurement in psychology.* Washington, DC: American Psychological Association. doi:10.1037/11383-000

Eid, M., & Hoffmann, L. (1998). Measuring variability and change with an item response model for polytomous variables. *Journal of Educational and Behavioral Statistics, 23,* 193–215.

Eid, M., Lischetzke, T., Nussbeck, F. W., & Trierweiler, L. (2003). Separating trait effects from trait-specific method effects in multitrait-multimethod analysis: A multiple indicator CTC(M-1) model. *Psychological Methods, 8,* 38–60. doi:10.1037/1082-989X.8.1.38

Eid, M., Notz, P., Steyer, R., & Schwenkmezger, P. (1994). Validating scales for the assessment of mood level and variability by latent state–trait analyses. *Personality and Individual Differences, 16,* 63–76. doi:10.1016/0191-8869(94)90111-2

Eid, M., Nussbeck, F. W., Geiser, C., Cole, D. A., Gollwitzer, M., & Lischetzke, T. (2008). Structural equation modeling of multitrait-multimethod data: Different models for different types of methods. *Psychological Methods, 13,* 230–253. doi:10.1037/a0013219

Eid, M., Schneider, C., & Schwenkmezger, P. (1999). Do you feel better or worse? The validity of perceived deviations of mood states from mood traits. *European Journal of Personality,13,* 283–306. doi:10.1002/(SICI)1099-0984(199907/08)13:4<283::AID-PER341>3.0.CO;2-0

Endler, N. S., & Magnusson, D. (Eds.). (1976). *Interactional psychology and personality.* New York, NY: Wiley.

Epstein, S. (1979). The stability of behavior: I. On predicting most of the people much of the time. *Journal of Personality and Social Psychology, 37,* 1097–1126. doi:10.1037/0022-3514.37.7.1097

Epstein, S. (1980). The stability of behavior: II. Implications for psychological research. *American Psychologist, 35,* 790–806. doi:10.1037/0003-066-X.35.9.790

Geiser, C. (2009). *Multitrait-multimethod-multioccasion modeling.* Munich, Germany: AVM.

Geiser, C., Eid, M., & Nussbeck, F. W. (2008). On the meaning of the latent variables in the CT-C(M-1) model: A comment on Maydeu-Olivares & Coffman (2006). *Psychological Methods, 13,* 49–57. doi:10.1037/1082-989X.13.1.49

Geiser, C., Eid, M., Nussbeck, F. W., Courvoisier, D. S., & Cole, D. A. (2010a). Analyzing true change in longitudinal multitrait-multimethod studies: Application of a multimethod change model to depression and anxiety in children. *Developmental Psychology, 46,* 29–45. doi:10.1037/a0017888

Geiser, C., Eid, M., Nussbeck, F. W., Courvoisier, D. S., & Cole, D. A. (2010b). Multitrait-multimethod change modeling. *Advances in Statistical Analysis, 94,* 185–201. doi:10.1007/s10182-010-0127-0

Geiser, C., Keller, B., & Lockhart, G. (2011). *First versus second order latent growth curve models: Some insights from latent state–trait theory.* Manuscript submitted for publication.

Geiser, C., & Lockhart, G. (in press). A comparison of four approaches to account for method effects in latent state–trait analyses. *Psychological Methods.*

Hagemann, D., Hewig, J., Seifert, J., Naumann, E., & Bartussek, D. (2005). The latent state–trait structure of resting EEG asymmetry: Replication and extension. *Psychophysiology, 42,* 740–752. doi:10.1111/j.1469-8986.2005.00367.x

Hagemann, D., & Naumann, E. (2009). States vs. traits: An integrated model for the test of Eysenck's arousal/arousability hypothesis. *Journal of Individual Differences, 30,* 87–99. doi:10.1027/1614-0001.30.2.87

Hagemann, D., Naumann, E., Thayer, J. F., & Bartussek, D. (2002). Does resting electroencephalograph asymmetry reflect a trait? An application of latent state–trait theory. *Journal of Personality and Social Psychology, 82,* 619–641. doi:10.1037/0022-3514.82.4.619

Hancock, G. R., Kuo, W., & Lawrence, F. R. (2001). An illustration of second-order latent growth models. *Structural Equation Modeling, 8,* 470–489. doi:10.1207/S15328007SEM0803_7

Harris, C. W. (Ed.). (1963). *Problems in measuring change.* Madison: University of Wisconsin Press.

Hellhammer, J., Fries, E., Schweisthal, O. W., Schlotz, W., Stone, A. A., & Hagemann, D. (2007). Several daily measurements are necessary to reliably assess the cortisol rise after awakening: State- and trait

components. *Psychoneuroendocrinology, 32,* 80–86. doi:10.1016/j.psyneuen.2006.10.005

Hermes, M., Hagemann, D., Britz, P., Lieser, S., Bertsch, K., Naumann, E., & Walter, C. (2009). Latent state–trait structure of cerebral blood flow in a resting state. *Biological Psychology, 80,* 196–202. doi:10.1016/j.biopsycho.2008.09.003

Hertzog, C., & Nesselroade, J. R. (1987). Beyond autoregressive models: Some implications of the trait-state distinction for the structural modeling of developmental change. *Child Development, 58,* 93–109. doi:10.2307/1130294

Kenny, D. A. (1976). An empirical application of confirmatory factor analysis to the multitrait–multimethod matrix. *Journal of Experimental Social Psychology, 12,* 247–252. doi:10.1016/0022-1031(76)90055-X

Kirschbaum, C., Steyer, R., Eid, M., Patalla, U., Schwenkmezger, P., & Hellhammer, D. H. (1990). Cortisol and behavior: 2. Application of a latent state–trait model to salivary cortisol. *Psychoneuroendocrinology, 15,* 297–307. doi:10.1016/0306-4530(90)90080-S

Majcen, A-M., Steyer, R., & Schwenkmezger, P. (1988). Konsistenz und spezifität bei eigenschafts- und zustandsangst [Consistency and specificity of trait anxiety and state anxiety]. *Zeitschrift für Differentielle und Diagnostische Psychologie, 9,* 105–120.

Marsh, H. W., & Grayson, D. (1994). Longitudinal confirmatory factor analysis: Common, time-specific, item-specific, and residual-error components of variance. *Structural Equation Modeling, 1,* 116–145. doi:10.1080/10705519409539968

Marsh, H. W., & Grayson, D. A. (1995). Latent variable models of multitrait-multimethod data. In R. H. Hoyle (Ed.), *Structural equation modeling. Concepts, issues, and applications* (pp. 177–198). Thousand Oaks, CA: Sage.

Mayer, A., Steyer, R., & Partchev, I. (in press). A general way to model growth curves and true intraindividual change. *Structural Equation Modeling.*

McArdle, J. J. (1988). Dynamic but structural equation modeling of repeated measures data. In R. B. Cattell & J. Nesselroade (Eds.), *Handbook of multivariate experimental psychology* (2nd ed., pp. 561–614). New York, NY: Plenum Press.

Mischel, W. (1998). *Personality and assessment.* New York, NY: Wiley.

Nesselroade, J. R., & Bartsch, T. W. (1977). Multivariate perspectives on the construct validity of the trait-state distinction. In R. B. Cattell & R. M. Dreger (Eds.), *Handbook of modern personality theory* (pp. 221–238). Washington, DC: Hemisphere.

Ormel, J., & Schaufeli, W. B. (1991). Stability and change in psychological distress and their relationship with self-esteem and locus of control: A dynamic equilibrium model. *Journal of Personality and Social Psychology, 60*, 288–299. doi:10.1037/0022-3514-.60.2.288

Pohl, S., & Steyer, R. (2010). Modeling common traits and method effects in multitrait-multimethod analysis. *Multivariate Behavioral Research,45*, 45–72. doi:10.1080/00273170903504729

Pohl, S., Steyer, R., & Kraus, K. (2008). Modelling method effects as individual causal effects. *Journal of the Royal Statistical Society, Series A (General),171*, 41–63.

Raffalovich, L. E., & Bohrnstedt, G. W. (1987). Common, specific, and error variance components of factor models: Estimation with longitudinal data. *Sociological Methods and Research, 15*, 385–405. doi:10.1177/0049124187015004003

Raykov, T. (1993). On estimating true change interrelationships with other variables. *Quality and Quantity, 27*, 353–370. doi:10.1007/BF01102498

Sayer, A. G., & Cumsille, P. E. (2001). Second-order latent growth models. In L. M. Collins & A. G. Sayer (Eds.), *New methods for the analysis of change* (pp. 179–200). Washington, DC: American Psychological Association. doi:10.1037/10409-006

Schermelleh-Engel, K., Keith, N., Moosbrugger, H., & Hodapp, V. (2004). Decomposing person and occasion-specific effects: An extension of latent state–trait theory to hierarchical LST models. *Psychological Methods, 9*, 198–219. doi:10.1037/1082-989X.9.2.198

Scherpenzeel, A., & Saris, W. E. (2007). Multitrait-multimethod models for longitudinal research. In K. van Montfort, A. Satorra, & H. Oud (Eds.), *Longitudinal models in the behavioral and related sciences* (pp. 381–401). Mahwah, NJ: Erlbaum.

Schmitt, M., Schwartz, S. H., Steyer, R., & Schmitt, T. (1993). Measurement models for the Schwartz Values Inventory. *European Journal of Psychological Assessment, 9*, 107–121.

Schmukle, S. C., & Egloff, B. (2005). A latent state–trait analysis of implicit and explicit personality measures. *European Journal of Psychological Assessment, 21*, 100–107. doi:10.1027/1015-5759.21.2.100

Sörbom, D. (1975). Detection of correlated errors in longitudinal data. *British Journal of Mathematical and Statistical Psychology, 28*, 138–151.

Spielberger, C. D. (1972). Anxiety as an emotional state. In C. D. Spielberger (Ed.), *Anxiety: Current trends in theory and research* (Vol. 1, pp. 23–49). New York, NY: Academic Press.

Steyer, R. (1987). Konsistenz und Spezifität: Definition zweier zentraler Begriffe der Differentiellen Psychologie und ein einfaches Modell zu ihrer Identifikation [Consistency and specificity: Definition of two central concepts of differential

psychology and a simple model for their identification]. *Zeitschrift für Differentielle und Diagnostische Psychologie, 8*, 245–258.

Steyer, R. (1988). *Experiment, Regression und Kausalität. die logische Struktur kausaler Regressionsmodelle* [Experiment, regression, and causality. The logical structure of causal regression models]. (Unpublished habilitation thesis). University of Trier, Trier, Germany.

Steyer, R. (1989). Models of classical psychometric test theory as stochastic measurement models: Representation, uniqueness, meaningfulness, identifiability, and testability. *Methodika, 3*, 25–60.

Steyer, R. (2005). Analyzing individual and average causal effects via structural equation models. *Methodology: European Journal of Research Methods for the Behavioral and Social Sciences, 1*, 39–54.

Steyer, R., Eid, M., & Schwenkmezger, P. (1997). Modeling true intraindividual change: True change as a latent variable. *Methods of Psychological Research–Online, 2*, 21–33.

Steyer, R., Ferring, D., & Schmitt, M. J. (1992). States and traits in psychological assessment. *European Journal of Psychological Assessment, 8*, 79–98.

Steyer, R., Krambeer, S., & Hannöver, W. (2004). Modeling latent trait-change. In K. Van Montfort, H. Oud, & A. Satorra (Eds.), *Recent developments on structural equation modeling: Theory and applications* (pp. 337–357). Amsterdam, the Netherlands: Kluwer Academic Press.

Steyer, R., Majcen, A.-M., Schwenkmezger, P., & Buchner, A. (1989). A latent state–trait anxiety model and its application to determine consistency and specificity coefficients. *Anxiety Research, 1*, 281–299.

Steyer, R., Nagel, W., Partchev, I., & Mayer, A. (in press). *Measure, probability and regression.* New York, NY: Springer.

Steyer, R., Partchev, I., & Shanahan, M. (2000). Modeling true intra-individual change in structural equation models: The case of poverty and children's psychosocial adjustment. In T. D. Little, K. U. Schnabel, & J. Baumert (Eds.), *Modeling longitudinal and multiple-group data: Practical issues, applied approaches, and specific examples* (pp. 109–126). Hillsdale, NJ: Erlbaum.

Steyer, R., & Schmitt, M. (1990a). The effects of aggregation across and within occasions on consistency, specificity, and reliability. *Methodika, 4*, 58–94.

Steyer, R., & Schmitt, M. J. (1990b). Latent state–trait models in attitude research. *Quality and Quantity, 24*, 427–445. doi:10.1007/BF00152014

Steyer, R., Schmitt, M., & Eid, M. (1999). Latent state–trait theory and research in personality and individual differences. *European Journal*

of Personality, 13, 389–408. doi:10.1002/
(SICI)1099-0984(199909/10)13:5<389::AID-
PER361>3.0.CO;2-A

Steyer, R., Schwenkmezger, P., & Auer, A. (1990). The
emotional and cognitive components of trait anxiety:
A latent state–trait model. *Personality and Individual
Differences, 11*, 125–134. doi:10.1016/0191-8869-
(90)90004-B

Tisak, J., & Tisak, M. S. (2000). Permanency and
ephemerality of psychological measures with application to organizational commitment. *Psychological

Methods, 5*, 175–198. doi:10.1037/1082-989-
X.5.2.175

Vautier, S. (2004). A longitudinal SEM approach to STAI
data: Two comprehensive multitrait-multistate
models. *Journal of Personality Assessment, 83*,
167–179. doi:10.1207/s15327752jpa8302_11

Vautier, S., Steyer, R., & Boomsma, A. (2008). The
true-change model with individual method effects:
Reliability issues. *British Journal of Mathematical
and Statistical Psychology, 61*, 379–399.
doi:10.1348/000711007X206826

## CHAPTER 15

LATENT VARIABLE MODELING OF CONTINUOUS GROWTH

David A. Cole and Jeffrey A. Ciesla

The goal of this chapter is to review a few types of structural equation models designed to estimate continuous growth in a targeted construct over time. We begin by describing the kinds of questions that such models can address, the data characteristics that are necessary for the application of these methods, and the broad assumptions that underlie these methods. The bulk of the chapter focuses on two general types of continuous growth models. The first is a single-measure, latent-growth approach in which latent trends are estimated from a time-series of data on a particular variable. The second method requires multiple measures of the same construct at multiple waves, and involves the extraction of a latent variable at each wave and then the extraction of latent trends in this latent variable over time. Finally, we note the development of new methods for assessing continuous change, providing references for the interested reader.

SETTING THE STAGE

Questions That These Models Address

Latent variable models of continuous growth can be used to address a wide range of questions. One set of questions focuses on the fundamental characterization of the growth trajectory. We have argued that understanding the longitudinal structure of our measures is as necessary for longitudinal research as understanding the factor structure of our measures is for cross-sectional research (Cole & Maxwell, 2009). These questions include the following:

- Is there an observable, nonzero trajectory of change over time?

- What is the shape of such change?
- When is change more or less rapid?
- On which dimensions of change are there reliable individual differences that might be predicted by other variables?
- How much time must elapse before change in the targeted construct can be detected?

Without reliable answers to these often overlooked questions, researchers run the expensive risk of launching longitudinal studies that attempt (a) to predict change in constructs over time intervals when the targeted construct does not actually change, (b) to find correlates of individual differences in change in variables on which reliable individual differences in change do not occur, (c) to discover correlates of linear change when actual change is nonlinear, and (d) to predict change over time intervals that are too brief or too long to capture change reliably.

A second set of questions pertains to correlates of change in the targeted construct. Change in the targeted variable can be variously conceptualized as a cause, a predictor, a correlate, or a consequence of another variable. This other variable has a temporal structure that may or may not mirror that of the target variable. This means that we must graduate from the simple question "what variables predict which outcomes?" to questions like

- Which dimensions of change in one set of variables are related to which dimensions of change or growth in the target variable?
- Over what time intervals or time frames does this relation exist?

DOI: 10.1037/13621-015
APA Handbook of Research Methods in Psychology: Vol. 3. Data Analysis and Research Publication, H. Cooper (Editor-in-Chief)

■ Is this relation equally strong for various subgroups of the targeted population?

Failure to address these more sophisticated questions can result in what Kimbal (1957) referred to as Type III error: "the error committed by giving the right answer to the wrong problem" (p. 134). Consequently, we run the risk of missing important relations that do exist and discovering apparent relations that do not.

Data Set Requirements

Latent variable models of growth require certain types of data. Clearly one needs to have repeated assessments of a given construct over time. Although the assessment schedule is often constant (e.g., monthly, annually), this is not a necessity; waves can be unevenly spaced. However, latent variable growth models require that the assessment schedule is the same for all participants. Other analytic procedures have been developed, such as hierarchical linear modeling, that can accommodate variable assessment schedules; however, such procedures have other limitations not inherent in latent variable models of growth (see Curran, 2003).

It is also important for the scaling of the outcome variable to be constant over time. Frequently this is ensured by the use of the same instrument at each wave. Unfortunately, this is not always possible. Sometimes researchers must utilize different measures of a construct at different waves, perhaps because change in participant ages requires the use of developmentally appropriate assessments. In some cases, standardized scores can be an effective way of handling shifts in measurement; however, too casual standardization can subtly generate serious problems to which the researcher must be alert.[1]

The number of waves necessary for latent variable models of growth depends on the shape of change that the researcher seeks to investigate. To investigate first-order or linear change, three waves are needed; second-order or quadratic

models require four waves. To achieve model identification of ith-order polynomials (e.g., cubic, quadratic), $i + 2$ waves of data are needed. With highly restrictive model constraints, it is possible to achieve model identification with one fewer wave (see Duncan, Duncan, & Strycker, 2006, p. 19), but this approach is not generally recommended.

As in most data analytic methods, one would ideally not have missing data. In longitudinal studies, however, various patterns of missing data are the norm. A wide range of methods exist for handling missing data in latent-growth models. Of these, multiple imputation methods and full information maximum likelihood (FIML) estimation have particular advantages (for a review, see Widaman, 2006). Some of these methods (e.g., FIML) are available in many of the commonly available statistical computer packages that enable latent-growth curve (LGC) analysis (e.g., for AMOS, see Arbuckle, 2006; for LISREL, see Jöreskog & Sörbom, 2003; for Mplus, see Muthén & Muthén, 2007).

Assumptions

A commonly overlooked assumption of LGC models is also the most basic: The specified growth trajectory should be reasonable for the phenomenon being studied over the window of time it is measured. Typically, this involves the assumption of continuous, noncyclical change during the study. However, extensions of LGC models have been developed to allow for discrete or cyclical change.

It is also important to be mindful of the influence of time and the spacing of measurements. First, results only pertain to the time frame covered by data collection. An adolescent boy may grow 3 inches per year over 3 years, but extrapolating this trajectory to conclude that he will exceed a height of 20 feet by retirement would be absurd. Furthermore, assessment intervals that are too short or too long can significantly influence observed trajectories. Exceedingly long intervals can obscure growth

---

[1] Three problems are particularly common. First, in some cases, changing the metric can change the nature or meaning of the variable. For example, the shift from raw-scores to scale-scores on intelligence quotient tests controls for expected age differences). Second, standardization of each time-specific variable relative to its own mean will completely detrend the data. At every time-point, the mean will become zero, masking real growth that might have been evident in the unstandardized variables. Third, to avoid this (second) problem, researchers sometime standardize a time series of variables relative to the mean and variance of a reference time-point. This procedure, however, rests on the potentially untenable assumption of homoskedasticity.

trends and hide complexities in the shape of change. Intervals that are too short can result in the failure to detect significant growth, or in the detection of small, uninteresting trends. An important related point pertains to the difference between modeling age versus wave. Often, the time that elapses between measurement occasions or waves of a study represents a relatively arbitrary duration. Nevertheless, estimates of growth will be calibrated against whatever temporal metric is used, be it arbitrary or not. Researchers interested in growth should give serious consideration to using age or time instead of wave or measurement to calibrate growth.

Time (or age) can be encoded in a wide variety of ways in LGC modeling. The most common method sets all loadings for the latent intercept at 1.0 and sets the loadings for latent growth at 0, 1, 2, 3, . . ., $t - 1$) for time-points 1 to t, respectively. Importantly, the intercept represents level of the dependent variable at the time-point with a latent-growth factor loading of zero. When the growth factor loading for Time 1 equals zero, the intercept represents the level of the dependent variable at baseline (i.e., at wave 1 of the study), and the latent slope variable represents change from that point. Alternative treatments of time may be useful for other research questions. For example, using a zero growth factor loading for the last wave of measurement (i.e., $1 - t$, . . ., -3, -2, -1, 0) allows the intercept to represent value of the dependent variable at the end of the study. Researchers can then use other variables to predict final rather than initial levels of the dependent variable.

Additionally, other treatments of time can be used to model nonlinear growth. Most common is the use of multiple latent-growth factors with higher order polynomials as their loadings, enabling the researcher to model growth as a function of an intercept and linear trend (0, 1, 2, 3, . . ., $t - 1$), a quadratic trend (0, 1, 4, 9, . . ., $t - 1^2$), and so on. Furthermore, researchers can allow for multiple linear trajectories or *splines*. For example, the first spline might have loadings of 0, 1, 2, 3, 4, 5 and a second factor might have loadings of 0, 0, 0, 1, 2. In such a model, the first linear factor estimates the general trend of linear growth in the study, whereas the second linear factor estimates change in growth

after Wave 3. A potential application of this model would be to test the hypothesis that the growth rate of drinking changes from early to late adolescence (when participants reach the legal drinking age).

Finally, researchers can also use freed-loading LGC, in which some the growth factor loadings are freely estimated (see Bollen & Curran, 2006, pp. 98–103). To set the metric of the latent-growth variable, one loading is set at 0 and another is set at 1. One example sets growth factor loadings at Times 1 through 6 to be 0, 1, *, *, *, *, where asterisks represent freely estimated loadings (Meredith & Tisak, 1990). In such a model, the factor loadings are interpreted relative to the change from Time 1 to Time 2. For example, an estimated Time 3 factor loading of 1.5 would imply that half as much growth occurred from Time 2 to 3 than from Time 1 to 2. Another useful method sets the final factor loading at 1 (0, *, *, *, *, 1), in which case each estimated loading represents the proportion of overall growth that has occurred since Time 1 (McArdle, 1988). Such approaches are a bit more exploratory, as the shape of the trajectory over time is not specified a priori.

As LGC models are typically estimated using maximum likelihood approximation and related techniques, multivariate normality of the outcome variable is also assumed. The outcome variable is also assumed to be measured on an interval or ratio scale. Specific extensions of LGC have been created for non-normal, noninterval outcomes (Duncan et al., 2006, pp. 165–178) and for zero-inflated count data (Liu & Powers, 2007) but will not be discussed here.

Single-Measure, Latent-Growth Modeling

Probably the most basic latent variable approach to continuous change is what we will refer to as a *single-measure, latent-growth model*. This approach starts with a single measure of a particular construct obtained at multiple time-points from a (relatively large) sample. In most forms of this approach, the elapsed time between any pair of waves is assumed to be the same for all participants; however, the elapsed time between one wave and the next need not be the same for all pairs of waves. That is, the waves can be unevenly spaced, as long as the spacing is the same for all participants. If complete data are available for all participants, such analyses can be conducted using only four kinds of information: an index of elapsed time (e.g., wave, age, months) as well as means, variances, and covariances (or means, standard deviations, and correlations).

In this section, we consider LGC models appropriate for testing several common types of hypotheses. We start with a relatively simple, intercept-only model (with waves that are equally spaced in time). We then proceed to test increasingly complex models in which more growth parameters are added. In the second model, we add and test growth parameters representing a linear growth trajectory. In the third model, we consider the case in which growth accelerates or decelerates over time. That is, we add and test parameters that represent a quadratic trajectory over time. We demonstrate the execution of all three analyses with an example data set.

Example.   For the relatively simple linear growth model, let us imagine that we have data from 300 cases on a random variable Y_i at each of five evenly space waves (where $i = 1$ to 5). Table 15.1 contains the means, standard deviations, and correlations for these variables. Table 15.1 also contains a sixth variable, TX, which we will save for analyses later in the chapter.

Although we are interested in linear growth, we test a series of nested or hierarchical models. We begin with the intercept-only model depicted in

Figure 15.1A. In this model, the variance of Y_i is partitioned into two parts: that attributable to a latent intercept random variable and that attributable to random error. As the factor loadings are all fixed at 1.0, the latent intercept can be conceptualized as the time-invariant factor that underlies Y_1 to Y_5. This model allows for individual differences in the latent intercept but does not allow for systematic change in Y over time. The model has seven free parameters to be estimated: the mean (M) and variance (V) of the latent intercept and the five error variances $V(e_i)$. All other means are fixed at zero, and all other path coefficients are fixed at unity. This model fits the data in Table 15.1 quite poorly, as indicated by a large and significant $\chi^2_{(13)} = 512.20$ ($p < .001$) and a very large value for the root-mean-square error of approximation (RMSEA) of 0.358 (90% confidence interval of 0.332–0.385). We

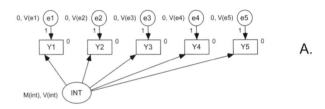

A.

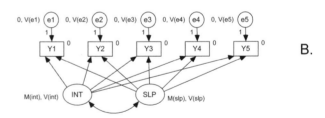

B.

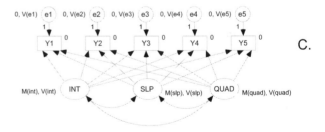

C.

FIGURE 15.1.   Three univariate latent-growth curve models. A. Intercept-only model (intercept [INT] loadings = 1). B. Linear model (INT loadings = 1; slope [SLP] loadings = 0, .25, .50, .75, 1.00). C. Quadratic (QUAD) model (INT loadings = 1; SLP loadings = 0, .25, .50, .75, 1.00; QUAD loadings = 0, .0625, .25, .5625, 1.0).

TABLE 15.1

Means, Standard Deviations, and Correlations for Five Waves of Data on Random Variable Y_i (Plus a Sixth Variable Called TX)

Variable	TX	Y_1	Y_2	Y_3	Y_4	Y_5
TX	1.000					
Y_1	0.019	1.000				
Y_2	0.125*	0.204***	1.000			
Y_3	−0.005	0.192***	0.202***	1.000		
Y_4	0.083	0.170**	0.225***	0.140*	1.000	
Y_5	0.092	0.233***	0.145*	0.284***	0.271***	1.000
M	0.473	6.933	7.607	8.452	9.133	9.737
SD	0.713	1.613	1.768	1.534	1.699	1.669

Note. N = 300.

*p < .05. **p < .01. *** p < .001.

concluded that an intercept-only model did not fit the data.

We followed this with the linear-growth model depicted in Figure 15.1B. This model contains three additional parameters: a mean and variance for a latent slope random variable and the covariance between the latent intercept and slope, *Cov(int, slp)*. This model appeared to fit the data well, as indicated by a nonsignificant $\chi^2_{(10)} = 10.28$ ($p > .40$) as well as large values for the comparative fit index (CFI = 0.997) and the incremental fit index (IFI = 0.997), and a small value for the RMSEA = 0.010 (90% confidence interval of 0.000 – 0.064). As the intercept-only model and the linear-growth model are hierarchically related, they can be statistically compared. The difference between the models was significant, $\Delta\chi^2_{(3)} = 501.92$ ($p < .001$), indicating that the linear model fit the data significantly better than did the intercept-only model.[2]

Before interpreting the linear model, however, it is wise to test an even higher order model to rule out at least some possibility of nonlinear growth, which (if ignored) could bias parameter estimates in the linear model. Here we tested the model in Figure 15.1C, containing a latent intercept, a latent slope, and a latent quadratic random variable. This model contains four new parameters: the mean and variance of the latent quadratic random variable and the covariances of the quadratic term with the intercept and slope. The factor loadings for the latent quadratic variable are fixed at values equal to the squares of the loadings for the latent linear variable (i.e., $0^2 = 0$, $.25^2 = .0625$, $.5^2 = .25$, $.75^2 = .5625$, $1^2 = 1$), thus forcing this latent variable to be the quadratic term. This model also fit the data well, as shown by a nonsignificant $\chi^2_{(6)} = 7.43$ ($p > .28$) as well as large values for the CFI = 0.99 and the IFI = 0.99, and a small value for the RMSEA = 0.028 (90% confidence interval of 0.000–0.084). However, the model did not represent a significantly better fit than did the linear model, $\Delta\chi^2_{(4)} = 2.85$ ($p > .50$).

Furthermore, the variance and mean of the latent quadratic variable were nonsignificant, suggesting that there was not a reliable quadratic trend in the data. Consequently, in the interest of parsimony, we elected to interpret the linear model.

Parameter estimates for the linear model appear in Table 15.2. The means of both the slope and the intercept were significantly different from zero. Interpretation of these parameters depends on the scaling of time. Here, we scaled Waves 1 to 5 to be 0, .25, .50, .75, and 1.0 (as shown in the loading of Y_i onto the latent slope variable). Because Wave 1 is encoded as zero in this analysis, the intercept represents the value of Y where time equals zero (Wave 1). Thus, our estimate of the intercept reveals that the expected value of Y at wave 1 (or time 0) is 6.95. We also observe this to be statistically significant, meaning that this expected value is significantly different from zero. The significant variance of the intercept (0.53) indicates that there are reliable individual differences in the Wave 1 values of Y. With respect to the slope, the estimate indicated that the value is equal to 2.84 and is statistically significant. This represents the expected change in the dependent variable for every one-unit change in time. Given our scaling of time, this is the expected change from Wave 1 to Wave 5. The significance of the mean slope value indicates that this is significantly different from zero. The variability of the slopes (0.337) is not significant, however. This suggests that although the scores on the dependent variable are increasing over time, there is no significant individual differences in this rate of change. Scores are significantly increasing, but they are increasing at roughly the same rate for all participants. Finally, we see that the covariation of the intercepts and slopes is –0.04, and is not significant. In general, a positive covariance would suggest that higher intercepts are associated with more positive slopes. Conversely, a negative covarianace reveals that higher intercepts are associated with smaller or even

---

[2]The chi-square tests the difference between the model-implied means and covariances and the observed means and covariances. Significant values imply that the model does not represent the data to some degree. It can be argued, however, that no model is completely right. Even when the degree of model misfit is small (and potentially tolerable), the chi-square becomes increasingly sensitive as sample sizes become larger, sometimes leading investigators to dismiss potentially acceptable models. As with any inferential statistic, one should examine the magnitude of the discrepancy before dismissing the model. Several indexes are often used for this purpose. The CFI and IFI provide indexes of relative fit, assessing whether the current model provides a superior fit to a null model, with values greater than 0.95 representing good fits. The RMSEA is especially useful as it has a known confidence interval. RMSEAs closer to zero (or at least less than 0.06) suggest a good fit. Other procedures are available for the assessment of model fit, and research continues to examine which are most appropriate for growth modeling (Wu, West, & Taylor, 2009).

TABLE 15.2

Parameter Estimates for Univariate Latent-Growth Model

Parameter	Estimate	*SE*	*t*	*p*
INT → Y_1	1.00	—	—	—
INT → Y_2	1.00	—	—	—
INT → Y_3	1.00	—	—	—
INT → Y_4	1.00	—	—	—
INT → Y_5	1.00	—	—	—
SLP → Y_1	0.00	—	—	—
SLP → Y_2	0.25	—	—	—
SLP → Y_3	0.50	—	—	—
SLP → Y_4	0.75	—	—	—
SLP → Y_5	1.00	—	—	—
M of INT	6.95	0.08	89.38	< .001
M of SLP	2.84	0.11	25.82	< .001
Var of INT	0.53	0.18	2.945	.003
Var of SLP	0.34	0.39	0.865	.387
Cov (INT, SLP)	−0.04	0.23	−0.178	.859

Note. INT = intercept; — = not applicable; SLP = slope; Var = variance; Cov = covariance.

negative slopes, a finding that may signify regression to the mean (see Campbell & Kenny, 1999).

Usually, researchers would like to see evidence of reliable variance in parameters (e.g., intercept or slope) before attempting to explain or predict individual differences in such parameters. On the basis of the current results, a researcher might legitimately seek predictors of individual differences in the intercept, but not the slope. Nevertheless, let us imagine that the researcher forged ahead despite these early results. For example, the researcher might be interested in whether the latent growth of Y differed for individuals receiving treatment as compared with those receiving placebo in a randomized treatment-control group design. For such a data set, simply add the *TX* variable in Table 15.1. *TX* is a dichotomous variable, on which 0s represent membership in the control group and 1s signify membership in the treatment group. Figure 15.2 depicts a model in which *TX* is added as a potential predictor of both the intercept and the slope of the latent grow of Y. This model fits the data well, with a $\chi^2_{(13)} = 14.78$ ($p > .32$) as well as large values for the CFI = 0.98 and the IFI = 0.98, and a small value for

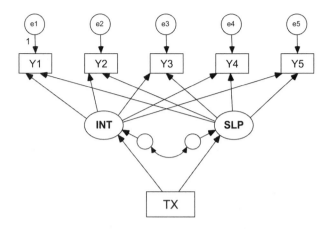

FIGURE 15.2. Univariate linear latent-growth curve model with *TX* as a predictor. Intercept (INI) loadings = 1; slope (SLP) loadings = 0, .25, .50, .75, and 1.00.

the RMSEA = 0.021 (90% confidence interval of 0.000 – 0.063). Examination of the model parameter estimates, however, reveals that the effect of *TX* on the intercept was 0.084 (*SE* = 0.109), and the effect of *TX* on the slope was 0.109 (*SE* = 0.155). Both were nonsignificant (*ps* > .40). Attempting to predict individual differences in slope in the absence of reliable variance in the latent-slope parameters would seem to be a fruitless endeavor.

Multivariate Latent-Growth Modeling

Even though the univariate growth models (like the ones discussed in the section Single-Measure, Latent-Growth Modeling) do extract latent-growth parameters, they are limited in that they represent the latent growth of the manifest variable. Manifest variable Y represents only one measure of the underlying construct. In the social sciences, most manifest variables are fallible, imperfect measures of the construct they were designed to measure. By obtaining multiple measures of the underlying construct at each wave of a longitudinal study, it may be possible (a) to extract a time-series of latent variables (one variable per wave) that represents the underlying construct of interest and (b) to model the growth of these latent variables, not just the growth of their fallible indicators.

In this section, we demonstrate the use of multivariate LGC modeling to test for evidence of a latent intercept, a latent slope, and a latent quadratic trend. We also demonstrate the utility of this method for revealing treatment differences in latent growth. As we will see, the multivariate approach can reveal trends and relations that may be missed by the univariate approach.

For this demonstration, we used the data in Table 15.3. As in the previous example, we have data at five waves. Unlike the previous example, however, we have three measures (not just one) of the underlying construct at each wave. We call these variables X_i, Y_i, and Z_i. In fact, Y_i is exactly the same variable that we used in the univariate example. (We have put the statistics for Y_i in boldface to highlight the fact that these are *exactly* the same values from Table 15.1 that we analyzed in the univariate LGC case.)

Here, we will focus on the strategy that Duncan et al. (2006, pp. 68–74) referred to as the *curve of factors* approach. (In the same book, they contrasted this approach with a *factor of curves* model, which we do not review in this chapter.) We walk through a series of models that we recommend and apply each of them to the data set contained in Table 15.3. This series contains four models: (a) a measurement model, (b) an intercept-only model, (c) a linear

model, and (d) a quadratic model. As will become evident, the linear model proves to be optimal. We contrast its results with those of the univariate LGC linear model from the section Single-Measure, Latent-Growth Modeling.

Measurement model. We begin with a measurement model. In this model, depicted in Figure 15.3A, we extract one latent variable (ξ_i) per wave from the three manifest variables (X_i, Y_i, Z_i) obtained at that wave. In this model, we place no constraints on the means, variances, or covariances of the latent variables. This model fit the data well, with $\chi^2_{(90)} = 102.95$ ($p > .16$), CFI = 0.99, IFI = 0.99, and RMSEA = 0.022 (90% confidence interval of 0.000 – 0.040). Standardized and unstandardized parameter estimates appear in Table 15.4. Using this model as a starting place, we can address several important issues.

1. Are the factor loadings reasonably large (and significantly different from zero)? In this case the answer is yes (see Table 15.4).
2. Many times, such simple measurement models will not fit longitudinal data. When measures X, Y,

TABLE 15.3

Means, Standard Deviations, and Correlations for Five Waves of Data on Random Variables X_I, Y_I, and Z_I (Plus TX)

Variable	TX	X₁	Y₁	Z₁	X₂	Y₂	Z₂	X₃	Y₃	Z₃	X₄	Y₄	Z₄	X₅	Y₅	Z₅
TX	1															
X₁	−.017	1														
Y₁	**.019**	.560	1													
Z₁	−.044	.776	.601	1												
X₂	.113	.308	.223	.365	1											
Y₂	**.125**	.306	**.204**	.379	.578	1										
Z₂	.124	.382	.278	.462	.832	.640	1									
X₃	.011	.248	.237	.253	.265	.221	.354	1								
Y₃	**−.005**	.249	**.192**	.281	.309	**.202**	.348	.508	1							
Z₃	−.052	.331	.271	.345	.369	.305	.431	.797	.586	1						
X₄	.017	.336	.222	.357	.327	.236	.374	.325	.329	.402	1					
Y₄	**.083**	.233	**.170**	.242	.318	**.225**	.367	.236	**.140**	.309	.552	1				
Z₄	.087	.378	.251	.373	.410	.318	.460	.347	.302	.451	.824	.609	1			
X₅	.188	.170	.197	.155	.365	.226	.364	.403	.258	.393	.430	.319	.461	1		
Y₅	**.092**	.205	**.233**	.233	.249	**.145**	.303	.351	**.284**	.354	.353	**.271**	.345	.564	1	
Z₅	.142	.255	.252	.269	.416	.226	.429	.436	.323	.450	.468	.402	.516	.825	.638	1
M	0.472	10.072	6.933	13.080	11.034	7.607	14.333	11.881	8.452	15.480	13.048	9.133	16.928	13.808	9.737	18.093
SD	0.713	1.639	1.613	1.870	1.775	1.768	1.981	1.623	1.534	1.848	1.694	1.699	1.955	1.858	1.669	2.121

Note. N = 300.

A.

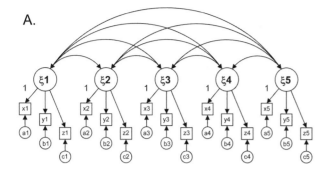

B.

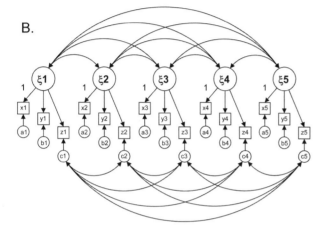

FIGURE 15.3. Measurement models (A) without correlated disturbances and (B) with correlated disturbances. Correlated disturbances are also included for the *X* variables and for the *Y* variables, but these are not shown to avoid the visual clutter.

and *Z* are repeated at each wave, the residual error variances at one wave are often correlated with their counterparts at subsequent waves. When such correlations exist, they must be modeled— usually by allowing carefully selected pairs of residuals to correlate (see LaGrange & Cole, 2008). Such a model is depicted in Figure 15.3B. Failure to allow for such correlated residuals in longitudinal designs can result in biased parameter estimates (Marsh, 1993). In the current case, however, the full and reduced models in Figure 15.3 were not significantly different, $\Delta\chi^2_{(30)} = 32.50$ ($p > .40$), so we proceeded with the more parsimonious measurement model (i.e., Figure 15.3A).

3. The good fit of this model also reveals that the expected values of the manifest variables (i.e., the manifest means) are proportionate to the latent variable means and reflect no evidence of measurement bias. In other words, $E(Y_i) = \lambda$

$E(\xi_i) + \tau$, where λ = the factor loading for Y_i and τ = bias of $Y_i = 0$.

4. In longitudinal designs, measurement invariance across waves is highly desirable. A key part of such invariance is that the factor loadings for *X*, *Y*, and *Z* at one wave are equivalent to their counterparts at other waves. Such equivalences provide some assurance that the latent variable does not change qualitatively over time. Examination of the factor loadings in Table 15.4 reveals a high degree of cross-wave consistency.

If a well-fitting (and theoretically justified) measurement model is found, it should be incorporated into the LGC model. If, however, a suitable measurement model cannot be constructed, proceeding with multivariate LGC will almost inevitably come to naught—because LGC models are more restrictive than the measurement model and therefore will typically provide worse fits to the data.

Growth model. We began with a multivariate intercept-only LGC model. This model provided a very poor fit to the data, as indicated by a large and significant $\chi^2_{(103)} = 1002.80$ ($p < .001$), a low CFI = 0.67, a low IFI = 0.67, and a large RMSEA = 0.171 (90% confidence interval of 0.161–0.181). Clearly, having only a latent intercept was insufficient to explain the observed means, the covariances, or both.

Next, we tested a model with both a latent intercept and a latent slope. This model is depicted in Figure 15.4a. This model fit the data well, with a $\chi^2_{(100)} = 114.99$ ($p > .14$), CFI = 0.99, IFI = 0.99, and RMSEA = 0.022 (90% confidence interval of 0.000–0.039). Adding the linear trend clearly improved the fit enormously.

To rule out the possibility of nonlinear growth, we tested a model with a latent intercept, slope, and quadratic term. This model appeared to fit the data well, with a $\chi^2_{(96)} = 113.56$ ($p > .14$), CFI = 0.99, IFI = 0.99, and RMSEA = 0.025 (90% confidence interval of 0.000–0.041). We noted two things, however. First, the fit was not significantly better than that for the linear model, $\Delta\chi^2_{(4)} = 1.43$ ($p > .50$). And second, out-of-range parameter estimates emerged. Specifically, the estimated variances of the latent slope and quadratic variables were negative.

TABLE 15.4

Measurement Model Parameter Estimates

Parameter	ξ_1	ξ_2	ξ_3	ξ_4	ξ_5
Unstandardized loadings					
X	1.00	1.00	1.00	1.00	1.00
Y	0.69	0.69	0.71	0.70	0.71
Z	1.30	1.30	1.30	1.30	1.31
Standardized loadings					
X	0.83	0.85	0.83	0.86	0.85
Y	0.60	0.61	0.62	0.61	0.66
Z	0.94	0.98	0.95	0.96	0.97
Correlations					
ξ_1	1.00				
ξ_2	0.49	1.00			
ξ_3	0.39	0.46	1.00		
ξ_4	0.43	0.49	0.49	1.00	
ξ_5	0.30	0.45	0.50	0.56	1.00
M	10.07	11.04	11.88	13.05	13.81
SD	1.36	1.50	1.35	1.45	1.57

TABLE 15.5

Structural Model Parameter Estimates for Two Latent-Growth Curve (LGC) Models

Parameter	Estimate	SE	t	p
LGC model with intercept and slope				
M (INT)	10.07	0.08	120.90	0.001
M (SLP)	3.80	0.11	33.30	0.001
Var (INT)	1.00	0.15	6.74	0.001
Var (SLP)	1.02	0.27	3.79	0.001
Cov (INT, SLP)	−0.28	0.16	−1.69	0.092
LGC model with *TX* predicting intercept and slope				
M (TX)	0.472	0.041	11.47	0.001
Var (TX)	0.507	0.041	12.23	0.001
β (TX → INT)	−0.03	0.105	−0.28	0.777
β (TX → SLP)	0.30	0.134	2.26	0.024
INT (INT)	10.09	0.097	104.06	.001
INT (SLP)	3.66	0.130	28.16	.001

Note. INT = intercept; SLP = slope; Var = variance; Cov = covariance.

Such problems can occur when a model is overparameterized.

For the sake of fit and parsimony, we elected to interpret the linear LGC model. Parameter estimates for the structural components of this model appear in the upper portion of Table 15.5. (The measure model parameters were essentially identical to those in Table 15.4.) Strong evidence emerged for the existence of both a latent intercept and slope, in that the means and variances for both latent-growth parameters were significantly greater than zero (all $ps < .001$). Furthermore, no out-of-range parameter estimates emerged.

With this justification, we tested our final model, in which we added TX as a predictor of the latent intercept and the latent slope (see lower panel of Figure 15.4). This model generated a marginally significant chi square, $\chi^2_{(113)} = 139.02$ ($p < .049$); however, all other goodness-of-fit indexes were excellent: CFI = 0.99, IFI = 0.99, and RMSEA = 0.028 (90% confidence interval of 0.002–0.042). There were no out-of-range parameter estimates. Consequently, we deemed this model to be a good fit and examined key parameter estimates (see lower portion of Table 15.5). The TX variable was not significantly related to

the latent intercept; however, TX was a significant predictor of the latent slope ($p < .02$). Given the 0,1 coding of TX, we see that the difference in slope between the control group ($TX = 0$) and the treatment group ($TX = 1$) was 0.30. Given that the standard deviation of the latent slope was 1.01, this represents an effect size of $d = 0.30$ (a small to medium effect, according to Cohen's [1977] criteria).

Comparing Univariate and Multivariate Approaches to LGC Analysis

Our univariate and multivariate results can be compared because variable Y, which was the focus of our univariate LGC, was embedded in the larger data set that was the focus of our multivariate analyses. As we will see, this comparison favors the multivariate approach in several ways. Some of the disadvantages of the univariate approach, however, are accentuated by our choice of variables. Although variable Y is not a bad variable, it was psychometrically weaker than X and Z (as seen by a close examination of their standardized factor loadings in Table 15.4). If the univariate approach were applied to a stronger variable, some of its disadvantages would diminish; however, other disadvantages would not.

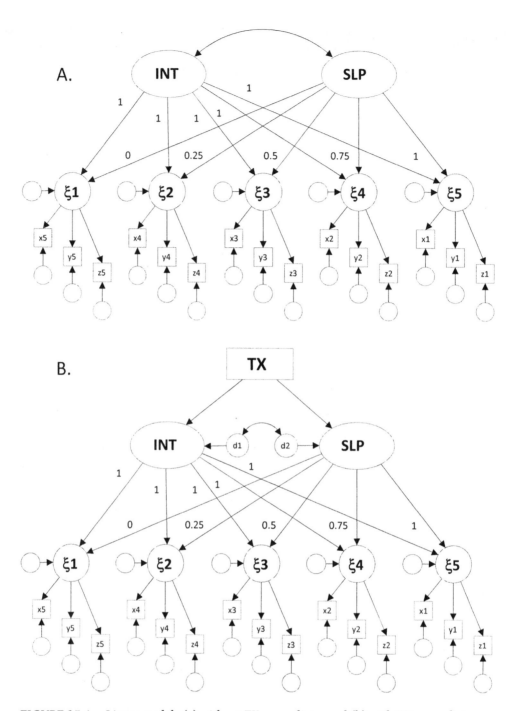

FIGURE 15.4. Linear models (a) without *TX* as predictor and (b) with *TX* as predictor.

The first disadvantage was one of reduced power. The univariate approach did not reveal that the latent slope had reliable variance, whereas the multivariate approach did. Faced with the univariate results, a prudent researcher might not attempt to explain individual differences in slope, assuming that it would be pointless to try to predict something that was not there. The multivariate approach, however, did uncover significant variance in the latent slope variable—a finding that might encourage further examination of the effect.

A second power-related concern also arose. *TX* differences in the slope were nonsignificant in the univariate approach but significant in the multivariate approach. The relatively small effect of TX on latent slope went undetected by the univariate approach; however, the enhanced power of the multivariate LGC resulted in a significant effect.

Such results are not guaranteed. This apparent power differential simply affects the likelihood of finding a significant effect when such an effect actually exists. Furthermore, if the variable selected for univariate analysis had been psychometrically stronger, the power differential would likely have been smaller.

Third, the multivariate approach to LGC analysis allowed us to test a variety of things that the univariate LGC approach either assumed to be true or simply ignored. In particular, the multivariate approach allowed us to

- examine the convergent validity of our measures of the underlying construct,
- test for evidence of additive measurement bias before engaging in LGC,
- test for measurement invariance across waves, and
- test for and (if necessary) model over-time correlated disturbances for repeated measures.

Failure to pass any of these tests would have provided warning signs for the researcher engaged in multivariate LGC analysis. The univariate method, however, provides no such opportunity. The researcher must assume that all of these potential problems do not exist. Furthermore, the researcher cannot construct models that allow for violations of these assumptions. When these problems do exist, two outcomes are possible. At best, the univariate model will simply fail to fit the data (or will generate intractable out-of-range parameter estimates that prevent further interpretation of the results). At worst, the researcher will fail to reject the model and proceed with the interpretation of parameter estimates that are most likely biased and misleading.

Multigroup LGC

Frequently, researchers are interested in examining trajectories in an outcome variable among two or more populations. One potential approach is to utilize dummy-coded exogenous variables as predictors of slopes and intercepts, as in the prior example. This method enables the investigator to test whether the observed group differences in growth parameters are statistically significant. Such methods might be used to test, for example, whether the emergence of

depressive symptoms during adolescence differs for girls versus boys. As parsimonious as this approach may be, a more flexible method is multigroup LGC analysis. In this approach, the growth parameters can be simultaneously, but separately, estimated for each group. This enables testing group differences not only on the mean slope and intercept but also on the variances and covariances of these parameters as well. Furthermore, researchers can examine whether exogenous predictors of the growth parameters differ from group to group. For example, are there gender differences in the degree to which age of pubertal onset predicts trajectory of depressive symptoms? Multigroup LGC models can be somewhat complex in implementation and interpretation. Fortunately, some excellent chapters have been dedicated to his topic (see Bollen & Curran, 2006, pp. 162–187; Duncan et al., 2006, pp. 81–92).

NEW DIRECTIONS

Latent Difference Score Analyses

Throughout this chapter, we have reviewed the LGC models in which functions of lines are used to characterize mean-level changes in measured variables. Intercepts, linear slopes, and higher order functions summarize individual growth. In some cases, however, the underlying latent change may not neatly map onto such functions. An alternative LGC approach that does not impose growth functions on the phenomenon of interest is called latent difference score (LDS) analysis (McArdle & Hagamami, 2001; McArdle & Nesselroade, 1994). In this approach, wave-to-wave differences in the outcome variable are explicitly modeled as separate parameters in a structural model. Following classical true score test theory, the manifest variable at each wave is first separated into a latent true score and a wave-specific error term. For every wave subsequent to the first, a latent difference score is created such that $\Delta y(t) = y(t) - y(t-1)$.

These latent difference scores can then be modeled in a number of different ways. One method for modeling these differences scores is what Hamagami and McArdle (2001) and McArdle and Hagamami (2001) referred to as the *dual-change score* model. Here, latent differences are allowed to vary as a function of a constant change score (α), and a proportionate change score (β), as expressed by $\Delta y(t) = \alpha + \beta * y(t-1)$. When α is nonzero, this reflects the addition of some constant at every wave, producing linear growth. When β is nonzero, this reflects the addition of some value that is proportionate to the score at the prior wave, producing nonlinear growth. The model is directly analogous to compound interest models in accounting.

Importantly, these change parameters can be allowed to vary from person to person. As such, interindividual variation in change is captured by some model parameters. Also, predictors of the change parameters can be included in the model, allowing researchers to ask such questions as, "Is gender related to wave-to-wave differences?" and "How many units of change are anticipated at each wave?"

Furthermore, the LDS model can be extended to the bivariate case so that the researcher can investigate change scores in two constructs simultaneously. This allows the researcher to examine whether wave-to-wave changes in one variable are associated with changes in another variable. For example, the α for variable X may be correlated with the α for variable Y, or the βs for these variables may be correlated. Wave-specific changes in the one variable can be used as predictors of subsequent changes in another variable. For example, "Is change in diet between ages 10 and 11 predictive of change in height from ages 11 to 12?"

The LDS model can be examined using most structural equation modeling packages. Equal wave spacing over time is critical to LDS modeling, although this is not a requirement of LGC. Despite this restriction and the complexities in its implementation, LDS modeling provides an important tool for researchers who are particularly interested in modeling how wave-to-wave change in one variable may be related to wave-to-wave changes in another.

Differential Structural Equation Modeling

Another recent innovation in the modeling of change is differential structural equation modeling (dSEM), developed by Boker and colleagues (Boker, 2001; Boker & Nesselroade, 2002). Boker noted that many phenomena in psychology and health are self-regulatory. That is, organisms often respond to stimuli with an effort to return the system to homeostasis. For example, when overheated the human body will attempt to cool itself, yet when cold the body will attempt to warm itself. Furthermore, regulatory systems often respond to external stimuli in a manner that is proportionate to the environmental challenge. A small challenge is met with a gradual and limited reaction, but an environmental crisis may necessitate a greater response.

Consider an experiment in which individuals are subjected to specific changes in room temperature, such that the temperature is raised to 100° Fahrenheit, and then lowered to 30°, only to then be raised back to 100°, and so on, for 10 full cycles before normal room temperature is restored. Furthermore, imagine that physiological markers of thermoregulation (e.g., blood vessel constriction and dilation, skin conductance) are measured among these individuals during the experiment. The researcher collects data from a large sample of individuals and seeks to model the dynamic physiological responses to thermoregulatory challenges. In this case, the predictor variable (room temperature) follows a cyclical, sinewave pattern. Accordingly, we may wish to examine whether physiological responses to changes in heat follow this same pattern. These patterns cannot be captured by more conventional LGC methods.

Using differential calculus, dSEM models three parameters of change for both the predictor and outcome variables: the current level, the rate of change (i.e., the first derivative of the outcome), and the acceleration of change (i.e., the second derivative of the outcome). As a result, we have repeated measures of six manifest variables in our example: current room temperature, rate of change, and acceleration of change in room temperature, and current physiology as well as its rate and acceleration of change. Via a series of model comparisons, one can address such questions as, are physiological thermoregulatory mechanisms most influenced by *current* temperature, *changes* in temperature, or *accelerations* in temperature change?

With dSEM, one can also study the effect of a system on itself over time. For example, in some systems, a cyclical pattern may slow over time and eventually reach stasis, rather like the slowing of a pendulum. Alternatively, a system may become dysregulated or demonstrate larger shifts over time. Changes such as these are modeled in dSEM by examining the direct influence of the first derivative (linear change) on the second derivative (acceleration). When this effect is negative, the cyclical changes decrease in magnitude and the system approaches homeostasis. When this is positive, the cyclical changes are growing in magnitude. When this path is zero, the cyclical change is unchanged. In our example, the investigator can examine whether, over the course of repeated temperature fluctuations, the body will slow in its regulatory responses. Finally, such models can be used to examine individual characteristics as predictors of these parameters. Using multiple groups, one can examine whether gender, medications, or obesity affect physiological changes caused by temperature variations.

At present, dSEM is not widely used in psychological research. One possible reason is that it is mathematically complex. A reason second is that most psychological theories anticipate linear (or at least noncyclical) relations. As psychological theories become more nuanced, dSEM may become a more widely used methodology.

Trait–State Models

A third recent development in the modeling of continuous change concerns the application of trait–state modeling (see Chapter 14 of this volume). Psychology has sometimes made a discrete distinction between trait-like and state-like constructs. Traits are thought to be highly stable across time and situations. In contrast, states have been conceptualized as constructs that show little stability or are highly reactive to situational demands. Such a strict distinction, however, may not pertain to most psychological constructs, which may actually contain varying degrees of both trait-like and state-like characteristics. Kenny and Zautra (2001) referred to this as a "continuum of traitness" in psychological measures.

Trait–state occasion (TSO) models (Ciesla, Cole, & Steiger, 2007; Cole, Martin, & Steiger, 2005) enable researchers to partition the variance of a given construct into that which is due to a time-invariant (or traitlike) construct and that which is due to a set of time-varying (or occasion) constructs.

Using this terminology, a person's state at any point in time reflects both kinds of influences. Only by examining repeated measures of a construct over time can the effects of trait and occasion factors be distinguished.

To describe how the TSO model accomplishes this goal, consider a researcher who collects two measures of anxiety annually from participants over a 4-year period. At each wave, a latent anxiety variable is extracted. The variance of these latent variables is then partitioned into two sources: a wave-specific occasion factor (O_t) and a time-invariant trait (T) factor. The occasion factors are part of an autoregressive submodel, allowing some degree of occasion factor stability from wave to wave.

This type of modeling allows the researcher to investigate potentially different correlates of both the trait and the occasion factors. For example, genetic factors may relate more strongly to the trait factor, whereas situational variables may better predict the wave-to-wave variations in the occasion factors. Cole, Nolen-Hoeksema, Girgus, and Paul (2006) utilized TSO modeling to investigate the association between depressive symptoms and stressful life events in a sample of adolescents. Disentangling the time-varying from the time-invariant components of depressive symptoms enabled cleaner identification of variables that predicted the time-varying components of depression.

CONCLUSION

This chapter has described multiple methods for modeling continuous growth and related forms of longitudinal change in a construct. Of these, LGC models are currently the most widely used in psychological research; however, the LDS, dSEM, and TSO models also provide useful tools in specific situations. None of the models presented in this chapter is inherently superior to the others. Each simply examines change in a particular way. Researchers who study growth should be aware of the various structural equation modeling options that are available. Deciding among these methods should be on the basis of one's understanding of the longitudinal structure of the construct under investigation.

References

Arbuckle, J. L. (2006). Amos (Version 7.0) [Computer program]. Chicago, IL: SPSS.

Boker, S. (2001). Differential structural equation modeling of intraindividual variability. In L. M. Collins & A. G. Sayer (Eds.), *New methods for the analysis of change* (pp. 5–27). Washington, DC: American Psychological Association. doi:10.1037/10409-001

Boker, S., & Nesselroade, J. R. (2002). A model for the intrinsic dynamics of intraindividual variability: Recovering the parameters of parameters of simulated oscillators in multi-wave panel data. *Multivariate Behavioral Research, 37,* 127–160. doi:10.1207/S15327906MBR3701_06

Bollen, K. A., & Curran, P. J. (2006). *Latent curve models: A structural equation perspective.* New York, NY: Wiley.

Campbell, D. T., & Kenny, D. A. (1999). *A primer on regression artifacts. Methodology in the social sciences.* New York, NY: Guilford Press.

Ciesla, J. A., Cole, D. A., & Steiger, J. H. (2007). Extending the trait-state-occasion model: How important is within-wave measurement equivalence? *Structural Equation Modeling, 14,* 77–97. doi:10.1207/s15328007sem1401_4

Cohen, J. (1977). *Statistical power analysis for the behavioral sciences.* Hillsdale, NJ: Erlbaum.

Cole, D. A., Martin, N. M., & Steiger, J. H. (2005). Empirical and conceptual problems with longitudinal trait-state models: Support for a trait-state-occasion model. *Psychological Methods, 10,* 3–20. doi:10.1037/1082-989X.10.1.3

Cole, D. A., & Maxwell, S. E. (2009). Statistical methods for risk-outcome research: Being sensitive to longitudinal structure. *Annual Review of Clinical Psychology, 5,* 71–96. doi:10.1146/annurev-clinpsy-060508-130357

Cole, D. A., Nolen-Hoeksema, S., Girgus, J., & Paul, G. (2006). Stress exposure and stress generation in child and adolescent depression: A latent state-trait-error approach to longitudinal analyses. *Journal of Abnormal Psychology, 115,* 40–51. doi:10.1037/0021-843X.115.1.40

Curran, P. J. (2003). Have multilevel models been structural equation models all along? *Multivariate Behavioral Research, 38,* 529–569. doi:10.1207/s15327906mbr3804_5

Duncan, T. E., Duncan, S. C., & Strycker, L. A. (2006). *An introduction to latent variable growth curve modeling: Concepts, issues, and applications* (2nd ed.). Mahwah, NJ: Erlbaum.

Hamagami, F., & McArdle, J. J. (2001). Advanced studies of individual differences linear dynamic models for longitudinal data analysis. In G. A. Marcoulides & R. E. Schumacker (Eds.), *New developments and techniques in structural equation modeling* (pp. 203–246). Mahwah, NJ: Erlbaum.

Jöreskog, K. G., & Sörbom, D. (2003). LISREL 8.7 for MAC OS 9 and X [Computer software]. Lincolnwood, IL: Scientific Software International.

Kenny, D. A., & Zautra, A. (2001). Trait–state models for longitudinal data. In L. M. Collins & A. G. Sayer (Eds.), *New methods for the analysis of change* (pp. 243–263). Washington, DC: American Psychological Association. doi:10.1037/10409-008

Kimbal, A. W. (1957). Errors of the third kind in statistical consulting. *Journal of the American Statistical Association, 52,* 133–142. doi:10.2307/2280840

LaGrange, B., & Cole, D. A. (2008). An expansion of the trait-state-occasion model: Accounting for shared method variance. *Structural Equation Modeling, 15,* 241–271. doi:10.1080/10705510801922381

Liu, H., & Powers, D. A. (2007). Growth curve models for zero-inflated count data: An application to smoking behavior. *Structural Equation Modeling, 14,* 247–279.

Marsh, H. W. (1993). Stability of individual differences in multiwave panel studies: Comparison of simplex models and one-factor models. *Journal of Educational Measurement, 30,* 157–183. doi:10.1111/j.1745-3984.1993.tb01072.x

McArdle, J. J. (1988). Dynamic but structural equation modeling of repeated measures data. In J. R. Nesselroade & R. B. Cattell (Eds.), *The handbook of multivariate experimental psychology* (2nd ed., pp. 561–614). New York, NY: Plenum Press.

McArdle, J. J., & Hagamami, F. (2001). Latent difference score structural models for linear dynamic analyses with incomplete longitudinal data. In L. M. Collins & A. G. Sayer (Eds.), *New methods for the analysis of change* (pp. 139–175). Washington, DC: American Psychological Association. doi:10.1037/10409-005

McArdle, J. J., & Nesselroade, J. R. (1994). Using multivariate data to structure developmental change. In S. H. Cohen & H. W. Reese (Eds.), *Life-span developmental psychology: Methodological contributions. The West Virginia University conferences on life-span developmental psychology* (pp. 223–267). Hillsdale, NJ: Erlbaum.

Meredith, W., & Tisak, J. (1990). Latent curve analysis. *Psychometrika, 55,* 107–122. doi:10.1007/BF02294746

Muthén, L. K., & Muthén, B. O. (2007). *Mplus user's guide* (5th ed.). Los Angeles, CA: Authors.

Widaman, K. F. (2006). Missing data: What to do with or without them. *Monographs of the Society for Research in Child Development, 71*(3), 42–64.

Wu, W., West, S. G., & Taylor, A. B. (2009). Evaluating model fit for growth curve models: Integration of fit indices from SEM and MLM frameworks. *Psychological Methods, 14,* 183–201. doi:10.1037/a0015858

## CHAPTER 16

DYNAMICAL SYSTEMS AND DIFFERENTIAL EQUATION MODELS OF CHANGE

Steven M. Boker

Theories that account for psychological change are generally concerned with how change comes about. That is to say, given that a person is in a particular state and in a particular context, in what manner would we expect the persons' state to change? The change so described could be a second-to-second change in emotional or cognitive state, it could be a longer term change in attitudes or behaviors over a period of days, or it could even be developmental changes that occur over a time span of years. The field of differential equations was developed to estimate meaningful parameters that describe physical systems undergoing change over time. These parameters describe characteristics of systems that have intuitive meaning resulting from our immersion in the physical world.

For instance, both people and tennis balls are described as being "resilient"; we say that resilient people "bounce back" from adversity. Does the resilience of a person involve a form of elasticity? Using differential equations, we can test whether the equations for the dynamics of elasticity are similar to the dynamics of resilient people. Dynamical systems theories allow the specification and testing of statistical models that parameterize the intuitive descriptions we commonly use for psychological phenomena. These models can be fit to data using standard statistical packages and give a better understanding of not just whether a variable's change follows a straight line or a line with a curve but also how that variable's change may evolve over time in a wide variety of contexts and starting states.

To test ideas from dynamical systems, one must master methods for fitting dynamical systems models to observed data from psychological processes. There are a variety of reasons for approaching data analysis in this manner. The logic was stated eloquently by Hotelling (1927) when he contrasted the use of curve fitting methods similar to growth curve modeling with the use of differential equation models:

> Although the customary method presents us with smooth, attractive curves to describe what has happened in the past and under known conditions, there must always be considerable hesitation about prolonging these curves into the future and the unknown. We have indeed, like Patrick Henry, no lamp to light our footsteps in the future save the past; but it does not follow that our future path is to be found as an analytic prolongation of some curve drawn among our old footprints. Rather, we require an analysis of causes, a study of the tendencies manifested repeatedly in the past upon the repeated occurrence of conditions, which we term essential, and in spite of the variation of other conditions that we consider nonessential. (p. 286)

Let us consider Hotelling's (1927) statement from the perspective of latent variable modeling. The level of some latent state may predict how that

Funding for this work was provided in part by National Institutes of Health Grant 1R21DA024304–01. Any opinions, findings, and conclusions or recommendations expressed in this material are those of the authors and do not necessarily reflect the views of the National Institutes of Health.

DOI: 10.1037/13621-016
APA Handbook of Research Methods in Psychology: Vol. 3. Data Analysis and Research Publication, H. Cooper (Editor-in-Chief)

state is likely to change in the immediate future. If so, there is some relationship between the latent variable and its derivatives with respect to time. In a very real sense, this relationship between level and change of the latent state is a characteristic of self-regulation for the latent state. In mathematical terms, the latent variable has intrinsic dynamics. Estimating the parameters that relate a variable to its time derivatives gives us a way to characterize how a within-individual process might regulate and respond to exogenous influences. In this way, we are able to describe and understand a whole family of possible trajectories that might occur given changes in a person's context.

A second reason why these models are appealing is that they can be constructed to test our *casual* use of physical analogies to describe *causal* processes. For instance, one might read an article that discusses "mood swings." The use of such a physical analogy in scientific writing is common—such analogies are easily understood by the reader in an intuitive way. The reader can be expected to have had the physical memory of sitting on a swing and directly feeling the changes in forces as the swing ascends and descends. Simultaneously the word *swing* conveys a sense of return, the "weightlessness" of an emotional high, and the "heavy burden" of an emotional low. By triggering such memories, physical analogies literally produce a feeling of visceral understanding.

But just because something is easily conveyed does not mean that it is a good analogy for the psychological process in question. Or, it might be that a given naive analogy is actually accurate in more ways than one might initially think. A swing implies momentum. Is there a concept equivalent to momentum that is implied by changes in mood? How do we test the implications of a physical analogy?

Because differential equations allow us to express physical analogies unambiguously, we can test the adequacy of the language we use in psychological descriptions. This is a powerful use of statistical modeling—there is the chance that the analysis of experimental data will change the words we use when we speak about psychological processes.

As another example, consider the word *resiliency* (Boker, Montpetit, Hunter, & Bergeman, 2010). A person is said to be resilient when he or she bounces back from an adverse life event. A physical object that is resilient will bounce back, and the equations for this phenomenon are given by Hooke's law of elasticity. The words we use to describe psychological regulation frequently imply physical analogies, and we can translate those analogies into differential equations that describe the physical properties that are invoked by the analogies.

To test a theory that is described by differential equations, one must have access to repeated observations data from a sample of individuals. Then, there are methods for estimating regression parameters that relate the derivatives to one another.

There are two main groups of methods. The first group of methods uses the integral form of the differential equation and includes estimation techniques such as Kalman filtering (e.g., Molenaar & Newell, 2003), the exact discrete method (Singer, 1993), and the approximate discrete method (Oud & Jansen, 2000).

This chapter focuses on the use of a second group of methods that fits the differential equations without taking an integral. These methods include generalized local linear approximation (GLLA; Boker, Deboeck, Edler, & Keel, 2010) and latent differential equations (LDE; Boker, Neale, & Rausch, 2004). GLLA estimates derivatives in a preprocessing step, whereas LDE estimates the regression parameters of interest as a structural model from the covariances of latent derivatives. Examples of specifying LDE models are given later in the chapter, but first a few introductory examples of differential equations are presented.

LINEAR DIFFERENTIAL EQUATIONS

To better understand how to choose a differential equation model for a given theory, it is instructive to consider some of the simple linear systems that are in use. These systems have been chosen as illustrative because in their integral form they become familiar regression models.

First-Order Differential Equations

A *first-order* differential equation is one in which the first derivative is the only derivative term to appear. One can think of a first derivative as an instantaneous estimate of a slope at a given moment in time. Suppose we have repeated measurements of a variable x. We will write the first derivative of x at time t as $\dot{x}(t)$.

A simple, and perhaps oversimplified, model for change is that the first derivative is a constant; thus change has a constant slope. This assumption is made in longitudinal analysis with linear regression when time is the predictor variable. The model can be written as the linear differential equation,

$$\dot{x}(t) = b_1, \tag{1}$$

where b_1 is a constant coefficient. This says that the rate of change of x is b_1 and does not depend on time. If we have an estimated value for b_1, we do not have a specific trajectory; instead, we have a family

of trajectories that look like the light gray lines in Figure 16.1a. A specific trajectory is defined if we choose an *initial condition*, that is to say a value for x at time $t = 0$. The dark line in Figure 16.1a plots the expected trajectory for $x(0) = -10$.

The specific integral of Equation 1 is

$$x(t) = b_0 + b_1 t. \tag{2}$$

Once the equation has been integrated, it gains a constant, b_0, that represents the initial conditions for the equation. This equation is familiar to anyone who has fit a univariate regression wherein b_0 is termed the intercept and b_1 the slope.

There are only two differences between Equations 1 and 2. The first is that the specific integral

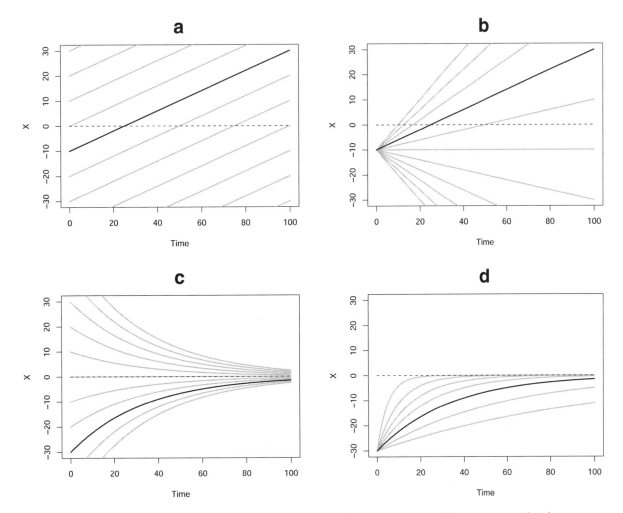

FIGURE 16.1. Trajectory plots of (a, b) Equation 1 and (b, c) Equation 3. Gray lines are examples drawn from the family of trajectories that fit each model. (a, c) Plot example trajectories with the same b_1 but with different values of b_0. (b, d) Plot example trajectories with the same b_0 but different values of b_1. For c and d, the horizontal dotted line at zero is the point equilibrium. The linear trajectories plotted in a and b do not have a point equilibrium except for the trivial example when the slope is zero.

form included an intercept term, which means it refers to a specific trajectory rather than a family of trajectories. The other difference is that if Equation 1 were fit as a regression, the residual term would refer to error in estimation of the slope, whereas in Equation 2, the residual term would refer to error in estimation of the score. There are specific integrals for all linear systems, so these systems can be fit statistically either in the integral or differential form depending on how the researcher wishes to formulate his or her questions.

Another popular model for change is the autoregression model for which scores at some time t are regressed on scores on a previous time $t - \Delta t$. The autoregression model is called a discrete time model because a discrete amount of time Δt elapses between observations. A fact that is generally ignored by those fitting autoregressive models is that the coefficients of the discrete time model are dependent on the choice of Δt. All too often, autoregression results sections state without justification that the assumption is made that $\Delta t = 1$. This problem is eliminated when the autoregressive model is written as a continuous time linear first-order differential equation in which the slope is proportional to the difference from equilibrium,

$$\dot{x}(t) = \zeta x(t). \tag{3}$$

Note that Δt does not appear in this equation, and so there is no dependency between the elapsed time between occasions of measurement and the coefficient ζ. Here we specify the first-order coefficient as the Greek letter zeta to distinguish the fact that it is a continuous-time parameter. Again, there is no intercept term b_0, so this system defines a family of curves as shown in the light gray lines in Figure 16.1c. This family of curves converges onto a single value, a *point equilibrium*, over the long run when $\zeta < 0$. For example, after participating in a learning-to-criterion study, participants might exhibit a forgetting curve that converged to a person-specific point equilibrium.

Equilibrium values are important when considering the correspondence between one's theory and a specific model. One should ask: "What is the expected long-run behavior of an individual?"; "Is the psychological process under study expected to be homeostatic?"; or "Is the process expected to cycle, such as, for example, sleep–wake cycles, hunger cycles, or seasonal affective disorder?" First-order processes never form a cyclic process. The simplest system that is cyclic is a second-order linear process.

Furthermore, one should note that the equilibrium for Equation 3 is equal to zero. That is to say, for ζ to be estimated without bias, the data must be centered around the equilibrium. Estimating the equilibrium to subtract its value from the data is a more difficult problem than is often assumed (for a discussion, see Boker & Bisconti, 2006). If the expected long-run equilibrium value of a process is known, one should subtract that value. If the equilibrium for each person in a sample can be estimated, then each individual's equilibrium values should be subtracted from their data. When equilibrium values are unknown, individuals' data are frequently centered about their respective means or about a linear trend. In the time-series literature, this is known as an instance of *prewhitening* a time-series. But one should not just blindly subtract the mean without giving consideration to whether there is something else one knows about the expected value of the equilibrium of the process in question.

The specific integral of Equation 3 is

$$x(t) = b_3 + e^{\ln(b_0) + \zeta t} \tag{4}$$
$$= b_3 + b_0 e^{\zeta t}, \tag{5}$$

where the asymptotic equilibrium is $\lim_{t \to \infty} x(t) = b_3$, b_0 is the intercept (value of the function at $t = 0$), and ζ describes the overall curvature of the exponential curve. Note that $x(t)$ is an exponential function of time, which is why the value of Δt must not be ignored if one chooses to fit a discrete time autoregressive model.

There are many uses of first-order linear differential equations. In particular, one may wish to test theories that include something akin to damping: how a regulatory process might return to equilibrium if it were displaced from its equilibrium by some exogenous influence. For instance, if one considers resilience to be long-term adaptation, the rate of adaptation could be modeled as a damping parameter (Boker, Montpetit, et al., 2010).

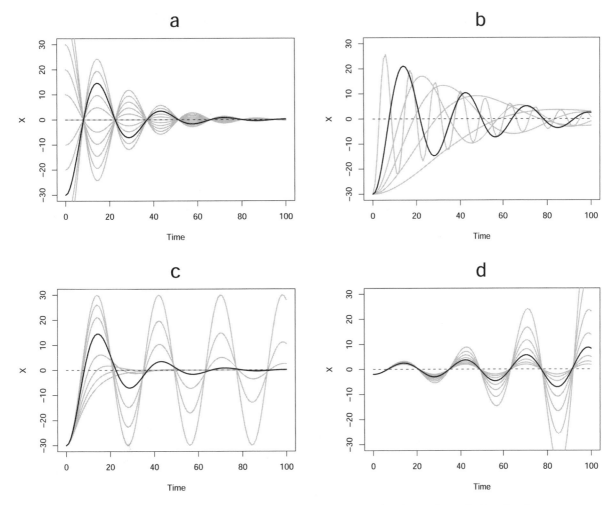

FIGURE 16.2. Trajectory plots of Equation 6. Gray lines are examples drawn from the family of trajectories that fit the model under different conditions. (a) Example trajectories with the same η and ζ but with different initial conditions for $x(0)$. (b) Example trajectories with the same initial conditions and ζ but different values of η. (c, d) Example trajectories with the same initial conditions and η but with (c) $\zeta < 0$ and (d) $\zeta > 0$. The horizontal dotted line at zero is the point equilibrium.

Linear Second-Order Differential Equations

Many psychological processes can be expected to show fluctuations about some equilibrium value. For instance, one might consider affect as having a trait-like component, an equilibrium value around which one's affect scores might fluctuate on a day-to-day basis. These fluctuations may exhibit an intrinsic dynamic. A simple model that allows cyclic fluctuation is a second-order linear differential equation with a damping term. This can be written as

$$\ddot{x}(t) = \eta x(t) + \zeta \dot{x}(t), \tag{6}$$

where x is the displacement from equilibrium and $\dot{x}(t)$ and $\ddot{x}(t)$ are the first and second derivatives, respectively. If the system oscillates, the parameter η is

related to the frequency of oscillation. One over the frequency is the wavelength—the elapsed time between successive peaks of the oscillation. When $\eta < 0$ and $(\eta + \zeta^2/4) < 0$, the equation is termed a damped linear oscillator and has a wavelength (interval of time between successive peaks) of $\lambda = 2\pi / \sqrt{-\left(\eta + \zeta^2/4\right)}$. In physics, the coefficient η is written as $\eta = -\omega^2$ so that η is constrained to be less than zero. Although this makes sense when thinking about pendulums or mass-spring systems, this constraint need not be imposed on psychological systems.

TIME DELAY EMBEDDING

To estimate dynamics from a time-series, one must capture the time-dependent part of the data. One of the most effective ways of capturing time dependence is called *time delay embedding* (Sauer, Yorke, & Casdagli, 1991; Takens, 1985; Whitney, 1936).

Suppose a time series X has been recorded for P repeated occasions on N individuals. If the original time series X is ordered by occasion j within individual i, then the series of all observations $x_{(i,j)}$ can be written as a vector of scores

$$X = \left\{ x_{(1,1)}, x_{(1,2)}, \cdots x_{(1,P)}, x_{(2,1)}, x_{(2,2)}, \cdots x_{(2,P)}, \right.$$
$$\left. \cdots, x_{(N,1)}, x_{(N,2)}, \cdots x_{(N,P)} \right\}. \quad (7)$$

If this vector is considered to be a data column and a participant ID column and occasion number column are prepended to each row, the resulting data are in what sometimes referred to as *tall format*. There are P rows in this data matrix belonging to each participant. To apply the LDE method, the data must first be converted into a format in which the time dependency is captured row by row: a time delay embedding of the data.

For N people, each of whom have been sampled P times, a five-dimensional time delay embedded matrix $X^{(5)}$ can be constructed as follows:

$$\mathbf{X}^{(5)} = \begin{bmatrix} x_{(1,1)} & x_{(1,2)} & x_{(1,3)} & x_{(1,4)} & x_{(1,5)} \\ x_{(1,2)} & x_{(1,3)} & x_{(1,4)} & x_{(1,5)} & x_{(1,6)} \\ \vdots & \vdots & \vdots & \vdots & \vdots \\ x_{(1,P-4)} & x_{(1,P-3)} & x_{(1,P-2)} & x_{(1,P-1)} & x_{(1,P)} \\ x_{(2,1)} & x_{(2,2)} & x_{(2,3)} & x_{(2,4)} & x_{(2,5)} \\ x_{(2,2)} & x_{(2,3)} & x_{(2,4)} & x_{(2,5)} & x_{(2,6)} \\ \vdots & \vdots & \vdots & \vdots & \vdots \\ x_{(2,P-4)} & x_{(2,P-3)} & x_{(2,P-2)} & x_{(2,P-1)} & x_{(2,P)} \\ \vdots & \vdots & \vdots & \vdots & \vdots \\ x_{(N,1)} & x_{(N,2)} & x_{(N,3)} & x_{(N,4)} & x_{(N,5)} \\ \vdots & \vdots & \vdots & \vdots & \vdots \\ x_{(N,P-4)} & x_{(N,P-3)} & x_{(N,P-2)} & x_{(N,P-1)} & x_{(N,P)} \end{bmatrix}. \quad (8)$$

This operation captures the time dependency in the data into the five columns of each row of the matrix so that these five columns can act as manifest variable indicators for latent variable derivatives (see Boker, Deboeck, et al., 2010, for R code). The covariance between these latent derivatives can then be used as a means to estimate the coefficients of differential equations (for effects of time delay

embedding on coefficient precision, see von Oertzen & Boker, 2010).

There is a choice to make in constructing the time delay embedded matrix: How many columns should be in the matrix? In practice, five is the minimum number of columns required to estimate a second-order differential equation while maintaining sufficient degrees of freedom for model stability. Also, when fitting a model that has a suspected oscillation, it is best to choose a number of columns such that the interval of time delay between the first column and the last column is between one quarter and one half the interval of time that elapses during one full cycle of the suspected oscillation. One may find that the total delay can be as long as three quarters of a cycle without the model breaking down, but a total delay longer than three quarters of a cycle approaches the Nyquist limit. Models estimated with total delay near or above the Nyquist limit of one full cycle are underidentified and will produce erratic and uninterpretable results.

SPECIFYING LDE MODELS

LDE models can be fit using many popular structural equation modeling (SEM) programs. Example OpenMx (Boker et al., 2011) scripts of the LDE models presented in this section can be found at http://openmx.psyc.virginia.edu.

First-Order Univariate LDE

A first-order LDE for Equation 3 can be specified as shown in the path diagram in Figure 16.3. The loading matrix L (Equation 9) contains fixed values such that F and $\dot{F}$ the latent intercept and slope of the variable x. The rows of L are centered around the middle row of L and thus the latent intercept is estimated at the time of measurement of the middle column of the time delay embedded matrix $\mathbf{X}^{(5)}$. The second column of L includes the value Δt, which is the interval of elapsed time between observations in the time series:

$$\mathbf{L} = \begin{bmatrix} 1 & -2\Delta t \\ 1 & -1\Delta t \\ 1 & 0 \\ 1 & 1\Delta t \\ 1 & 2\Delta t \end{bmatrix}. \quad (9)$$

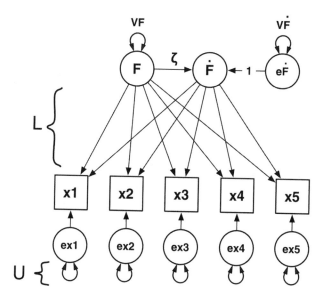

FIGURE 16.3. Univariate first-order latent differential equation path model. The loading matrix is represented by the fixed paths labeled L and the uniquenesses by U.

Now, using the reticular action model (RAM; McArdle & McDonald, 1984) SEM conventions, we can write the matrixes **A** and **S** to specify the regression coefficients, variance, and covariance relations among the latent derivatives as

$$\mathbf{A} = \begin{bmatrix} 0 & 0 \\ \zeta & 0 \end{bmatrix} \qquad (10)$$

$$\mathbf{S} = \begin{bmatrix} V_F & 0 \\ 0 & V_{\dot{F}} \end{bmatrix}. \qquad (11)$$

A diagonal matrix **U** is created to hold the residual variances of the time delay embedded matrix $\mathbf{X}^{(5)}$

$$\mathbf{L} = \begin{bmatrix} u_x & 0 & 0 & 0 & 0 \\ 0 & u_x & 0 & 0 & 0 \\ 0 & 0 & u_x & 0 & 0 \\ 0 & 0 & 0 & u_x & 0 \\ 0 & 0 & 0 & 0 & u_x \end{bmatrix}, \qquad (12)$$

which are all constrained to be equal to one another. Finally, the expected covariance matrix, **R**, of the time delay embedded matrix $\mathbf{X}^{(5)}$ can be written as

$$\mathbf{R} = \mathbf{L}(\mathbf{I} - \mathbf{A})^{-1}\mathbf{S}(\mathbf{I} - \mathbf{A})^{-1'}\mathbf{L}' + \mathbf{U}. \qquad (13)$$

This SEM model can now be fit to data using any of a variety of SEM packages. In practice, it is a good idea to place a lower bound near zero on the variance

term $V_{\dot{F}}$ in case the differential equation performs particularly well in explaining the variance of the first derivative. Doing so will ensure that the optimizer does not search for parameters that would result in negative residual variances.

Second-Order Univariate LDE

For processes that include oscillation, a second-order LDE may be specified as shown in Figure 16.4. This model is highly similar to the first-order LDE model in the previous section except that there is now a latent second derivative and the latent structural model has been altered to estimate Equation 6.

The fixed loading matrix L now has three columns. The first two columns are the same as in Equation 9, whereas the third column can be constructed from the second column in the following manner (Boker et al., 2004). Let the second column of L be denoted as the vector v. Then the third column of L is $v^2/2$ minus the mean of $v^2/2$. In the current example, the matrix L becomes

$$\mathbf{L} = \begin{bmatrix} 1 & -2\Delta t & 2\Delta t^2 \\ 1 & -1\Delta t & .5\Delta t^2 \\ 1 & 0 & 0 \\ 1 & 1\Delta t & .5\Delta t^2 \\ 1 & 2\Delta t & 2\Delta t^2 \end{bmatrix}. \qquad (14)$$

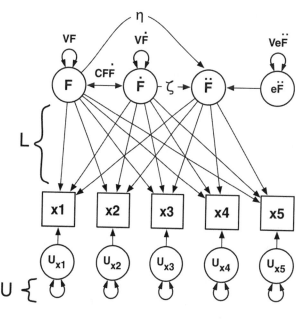

FIGURE 16.4. Univariate second-order latent differential equation path model. The loading matrix is represented by the fixed paths labeled L and the uniquenesses by U.

Another variant of this loading matrix can be calculated from the results of Deboeck (2010).

Again, the latent structure can be defined using the RAM convention as

$$\mathbf{A} = \begin{bmatrix} 0 & 0 & 0 \\ 0 & 0 & 0 \\ \eta & \zeta & 0 \end{bmatrix}, \text{ and} \qquad (15)$$

$$\mathbf{S} = \begin{bmatrix} V_F & C_{F\dot{F}} & 0 \\ C_{F\dot{F}} & V_{\dot{F}} & 0 \\ 0 & 0 & V_{\ddot{F}} \end{bmatrix}. \qquad (16)$$

If a diagonal matrix $\mathbf{U}$ is constructed as shown in Equation 12, then Equation 13 can again be used to calculate the expected covariance for the time delay embedded matrix $\mathbf{X}^{(5)}$.

In practice, it is recommended to first fit a saturated covariance-only model by setting the $\mathbf{A}$ matrix to all zeros and the $\mathbf{S}$ matrix to be all free parameters. Then, the total variance, $totalV_{\ddot{F}}$, of the second derivative can be estimated. If V_F is more than about 500 times larger than $totalV_{\ddot{F}}$, then SEM software may run into machine precision problems and not be able to give good estimates for the differential equation coefficients. In this case, it is recommended to standardize the indicator variable X before creating the time delay embedded matrix.

When writing an SEM program script to fit this model, it is a good idea to place a lower bound on $V_{\ddot{F}}$ so that the residual variance is constrained to be greater than zero. After running the saturated covariance-only model and the target differential equation model, a pseudo-R^2 can be calculated as $1 - (V_{\ddot{F}}/total\ V_{\ddot{F}})$.

Other Differential Equation Models

The LDE method is general in that there is no restriction on the differential equation specified between the latent derivatives. Third- and fourth-order differential equations can be created by adding more columns to the $\mathbf{L}$ matrix and using more columns in the time delay embedded matrix. Three other variants may be useful for psychological data: multivariate second-order LDEs, coupled second-order LDEs, and multilevel LDEs.

Multivariate Second-Order LDE

A multivariate generalization of the LDE model can be created by using more than one variable while time delay embedding and modifying the $\mathbf{L}$ matrix to both account for the multiple variables and to estimate the within-occasion factor loadings. For instance, a latent construct, such as positive affect, may be indicated by multiple subtests. The covariances between the estimated latent construct and its derivatives can be used to estimate the intrinsic dynamics of the factor as shown in Figure 16.5. Just as in cross-sectional between-persons designs, multivariate measurement is likely to result in a better, more reliable, and more meaningful construct than a univariate measure.

Coupled Second-Order LDE

When there are two processes of interest, a coupled model may be estimated. Examples of this type of system include coupling of disclosure and intimacy between married partners (Boker & Laurenceau, 2005), coupling between hormones and eating behavior in young women (Boker, Deboeck, et al., 2010), and coupling between negative affect and stress in older adults (Montpetit, Bergeman, Deboeck, Tiberio, & Boker, 2010). Although this type of model has often been fit using variants of local linear approximation, a better method involves an LDE model such as shown in Figure 16.6 (Boker & Laurenceau, 2007).

The model in Figure 16.6 is called *proportional asymmetric coupling* because the same proportion between the displacement and first derivative effects accounts for both the within-process intrinsic dynamic and between-processes coupling,

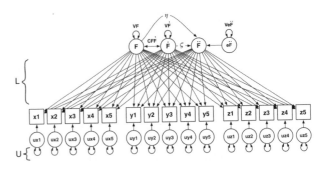

FIGURE 16.5. Multivariate linear second-order latent differential equation model with three indicator variables.

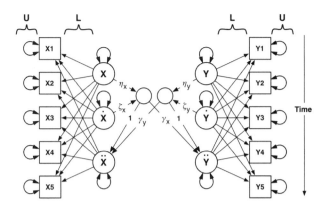

FIGURE 16.6. Coupled linear second-order latent differential equation model with one indicator variable per process and proportional asymmetric coupling.

$$\ddot{x}(t) = \eta_x x(t) + \zeta_x \dot{x}(t) + \gamma_y (\eta_y y(t) + \zeta_y \dot{y}(t)) + e_{\ddot{x}}(t)$$
$$\ddot{y}(t) = \eta_y y(t) + \zeta_y \dot{y}(t) + \gamma_x (\eta_x x(t) + \zeta_x \dot{x}(t)) + e_{\ddot{y}}(t),$$

$$(17)$$

where γ_y and γ_x are the proportional coupling coefficients. For instance, consider a husband and wife. Proportional coupling means that the same frequency and damping parameters that regulate the husband's behavior also influence the wife. Asymmetric coupling means that the effect of the husband on the wife is not necessary equal to the effect of the wife on the husband.

One note of caution when estimating coupled oscillator models: When $\eta_x = \eta_y$, the coupled oscillator model is empirically unidentified. Thus, if two processes have nearly the same intrinsic frequency, the coupling parameters γ_x and γ_y cannot be estimated. When this is the case, one may find that during the estimation procedure, the coupling parameters grow very large. If x and y have the same variance, it is unrealistic to expect a coupling parameter to be greater than one or less than negative one. In practice, constraining the coupling parameters $-0.8 < \gamma < 0.8$ can help a coupled model converge to realistic values.

Multilevel Second-Order LDE

It is often unrealistic to assume that the aggregate dynamic is a reasonable approximation of the within-person processes. In fact, it may be that no single person's dynamic resembles the dynamic of the aggregate (Molenaar, 2004). In such cases, a

multilevel model is an appropriate way to account for the within-person dynamics before estimating the mean and variance of the coefficients of the differential equation of interest. An empirical example of such a system is the process of grief in recent widows (Bisconti, Bergeman, & Boker, 2006) in which individual differences in initial conditions as well as dynamics were taken into account using a model for which indicators of social support were used as second-level predictors. For the widowhood data set, this multilevel model was written as

$$\ddot{x}_i(t) = \eta_i x_i(t) + \zeta_i \dot{x}_i(t) + e_i(t)$$
$$\eta_i = c_1 + y_i + z_i + w_i + u_{1i}$$
$$\zeta_i = c_2 + y_i + z_i + w_i + u_{2i}$$

$$(18)$$

where c_1 and c_2 were the mean values of η and ζ, respectively; y_i was perceived control; z_i was emotion-focused social support; w_i was problem-focused social support for widow i; and u_{1i} and u_{2i} were the residuals from the second-level model. Higher levels of emotion-focused coping were found to be related to greater values of damping (i.e., more negative values of ζ) and thus quicker damping of oscillations to equilibrium. In addition, greater values of perceived control were related to slower oscillations (i.e., values of η closer to zero).

DATA CONSIDERATIONS

First- and second-order linear differential equations have been explored extensively and can be fit reasonably in the context of either integral or differential form. To fit second-order differential equations, a sampling interval is needed that is no less than one sixth the estimated wavelength of the hypothesized cycle. For instance, weekly cycles would require sampling at least once a day. Without at least six samples per cycle, there are insufficient degrees of freedom in the data to uniquely determine all of the parameters, variances, and error terms. Higher order differential equations will require more samples per cycle—as degrees of freedom in the model increase, so too must the degrees of freedom in the data.

The absolute minimum number of samples per person required to fit a differential equation is the minimum number of samples per cycle. However, in that case, there are no degrees of freedom left to estimate individual differences in parameters, and thus the assumption must be made that all persons have the same regulatory process. When measurement instruments have high internal consistency, intensive longitudinal designs with as few as 20 samples per person can estimate individual differences in dynamic parameters. To the extent that instruments are poor measures of a latent process, however, greater numbers of observations per person will be required. Recent work suggests that when estimating first- and second-order processes using time delay embedding, adding observations within individuals has a greater effect on power than adding persons (von Oertzen & Boker, 2010).

CONCLUSION

Differential equation models hold great promise to estimate meaningful coefficients for psychological processes. How quickly does an emotional regulation system oscillate? How quickly do oscillations damp to equilibrium after a significant emotional shock? How do husbands and wives regulate their own and one another's need for intimacy and disclosure? Differential equation models can be constructed to test hypotheses about the language we use to describe psychological phenomena, language that is frequently drawn from physical analogy: *bouncing back*, emotional *swings*, absorbing *shocks*, interpersonal *friction*, cognitive *inertia*, the *force* of an argument. Not all such naive physical analogies will turn out to map onto the physical world. But when scientists use these words from dynamics to describe psychological phenomena, intuitive analogies are drawn and inferences are evoked that need to be tested. The resulting models fit Hotelling's (1927) desire for "an analysis of causes, a study of the tendencies manifested repeatedly in the past upon the repeated occurrence of conditions which we term essential, and in spite of the variation of other conditions which we consider non-essential" (p. 286).

References

Bisconti, T. L., Bergeman, C. S., & Boker, S. M. (2006). Social support as a predictor of variability: An examination of the adjustment trajectories of recent widows. *Psychology and Aging, 21*, 590–599. doi:10.1037/0882-7974.21.3.590

Boker, S. M., & Bisconti, T. L. (2006). Dynamical systems modeling in aging research. In C. S. Bergeman & S. M. Boker (Eds.), *Quantitative methodology in aging research* (pp. 185–229). Mahwah, NJ: Erlbaum.

Boker, S. M., Deboeck, P. R., Edler, C., & Keel, P. K. (2010). Generalized local linear approximation of derivatives from time series. In S.-M. Chow & C. E. Ferrar (Eds.), *Statistical methods for modeling human dynamics: An interdisciplinary dialogue* (pp. 161–178). Boca Raton, FL: Taylor & Francis.

Boker, S. M., & Laurenceau, J. P. (2005). Dynamical systems modeling: An application to the regulation of intimacy and disclosure in marriage. In T. A. Walls & J. L. Schafer (Eds.), *Models for intensive longitudinal data* (pp. 195–218). Oxford, England: Oxford University Press.

Boker, S. M., & Laurenceau, J. P. (2007). Coupled dynamics and mutually adaptive context. In T. D. Little, J. A. Bovaird, & N. A. Card (Eds.), *Modeling ecological and contextual effects in longitudinal studies of human development* (pp. 299–324). Mahwah, NJ: Erlbaum.

Boker, S. M., Montpetit, M. A., Hunter, M. D., & Bergeman, C. S. (2010). Modeling resilience with differential equations. In P. C. M. Molenaar & K. M. Newell (Eds.), *Individual pathways of change: Statistical models for analyzing learning and development* (pp. 183–206). Washington, DC: American Psychological Association. doi:10.1037/12140-011

Boker, S. M., Neale, M., Maes, H., Wilde, M., Spiegel, M., Brick, T., . . . Fox, J. (2011). OpenMx: An open-source extended structural equation modeling framework. *Psychometrika, 76*, 306–317. doi:10.1007/s11336-010-9200-6

Boker, S. M., Neale, M. C., & Rausch, J. (2004). Latent differential equation modeling with multivariate multi-occasion indicators. In K. van Montfort, H. Oud, & A. Satorra (Eds.), *Recent developments on structural equation models: Theory and applications* (pp. 151–174). Dordrecht, the Netherlands: Kluwer Academic.

Deboeck, P. R. (2010). Estimating dynamical systems: Derivative estimation hints from Sir Ronald A. Fisher. *Multivariate Behavioral Research, 45*, 725–745.

Hotelling, H. (1927). Differential equations subject to error, and population estimates. *Journal of the American Statistical Association, 22*, 283–314.

McArdle, J. J., & McDonald, R. P. (1984). Some algebraic properties of the reticular action model for moment structures. *British Journal of Mathematical and Statistical Psychology, 37*, 234–251.

Molenaar, P. C. M. (2004). A manifesto on psychology as idiographic science: Bringing the person back into scientific psychology, this time forever. *Measurement: Interdisciplinary Research and Perspectives*, *2*, 201–218.

Molenaar, P. C. M., & Newell, K. M. (2003). Direct fit of a theoretical model of phase transition in oscillatory finger motions. *British Journal of Mathematical and Statistical Psychology*, *56*, 199–214. doi:10.1348/000711003770480002

Montpetit, M. A., Bergeman, C. S., Deboeck, P. R., Tiberio, S. S., & Boker, S. M. (2010). Resilience-as-process: Negative affect, stress, and coupled dynamical systems. *Psychology and Aging*, *25*, 631–640. doi:10.1037/a0019268

Oud, J. H. L., & Jansen, R. A. R. G. (2000). Continuous time state space modeling of panel data by means of SEM. *Psychometrika*, *65*, 199–215. doi:10.1007/BF02294374

Sauer, T., Yorke, J., & Casdagli, M. (1991). Embedology. *Journal of Statistical Physics, 65* (3,4), 95–116.

Singer, H. (1993). Continuous-time dynamical systems with sampled data, errors of measurement and unobserved components. *Journal of Time Series Analysis, 14*, 527–545. doi:10.1111/j.1467-9892.1993.tb00162.x

Takens, F. (1985). Detecting strange attractors in turbulence. In A. Dold & B. Eckman (Eds.), *Lecture notes in mathematics 1125: Dynamical systems and bifurcations* (pp. 99–106). Berlin, Germany: Springer-Verlag.

von Oertzen, T., & Boker, S. M. (2010). Time delay embedding increases estimation precision of models of intraindividual variability. *Psychometrika, 75*, 158–175. doi:10.1007/s11336-009-9137-9

Whitney, H. (1936). Differentiable manifolds. *Annals of Mathematics, 37*, 645–680. doi:10.2307/1968482

## CHAPTER 17

A MULTIVARIATE GROWTH CURVE MODEL FOR THREE-LEVEL DATA

Patrick J. Curran, James S. McGinley, Daniel Serrano, and Chelsea Burfeind

One of the most vexing challenges that has faced the behavioral sciences over the past century has been how to optimally measure, summarize, and predict individual variability in stability and change over time. It has long been known that a multitude of advantages are associated with the collection and analysis of repeated measures data; indeed, longitudinal data have become nearly requisite in many disciplines within the behavioral sciences. The challenge of how to best empirically capture individual change cuts across every aspect of the empirical research endeavor, including study design, psychometric measurement, subject sampling, data analysis, and substantive interpretation. Although many textbooks have been devoted to each of these research dimensions, here we have the much more modest goal of exploring just one specific type of longitudinal data analytic method: the multivariate growth model.

Given our love of jargon in the social sciences, our field has coined a rather large number of terms to describe patterns of intraindividual change over time. These terms include (but are not limited to) *growth*, *curve*, *trajectory*, and *path*, among many others. Whether the term is *growth models*, *growth trajectories*, *growth curves*, *latent trajectories*, *developmental curves*, *latent curves*, *time paths*, or *latent developmental growth curve time path trajectories of growth*,[1] all tend to refer to the same thing. Namely, repeated measures are collected on a

sample of individuals followed over time, and models are designed to capture both the mean and variance components associated with patterns of stability and change over time.

There are two broad types of growth models: the structural equation model (SEM) and the multilevel linear model (MLM). Whereas the SEM approaches the repeated measures as observed indicators of an underlying latent-growth process (e.g., Bollen & Curran, 2006; McArdle, 1988; Meredith & Tisak, 1990), the MLM approaches these data as the hierarchical structuring of repeated measures nested within the individual (e.g., Bryk & Raudenbush, 1987; Raudenbush, 2001; Singer & Willett, 2003). A great deal of prior research has explored the similarities and dissimilarities of these two approaches, and the lines that demarcate the SEM and MLM are becoming increasingly blurred with the passing of each year (e.g., Bauer, 2003; Curran, 2003; Mehta & Neale, 2005; Newsom, 2002; Willett & Sayer, 1994). Suffice it to say that both methods are powerful and flexible approaches to the analysis of longitudinal data, the optimal choice of which depends strictly on the characteristics of the substantive question and the experimental design at hand (Raudenbush, 2001).

That said, here we focus exclusively on the growth model as estimated within the framework of the MLM, which stems directly from the substantive question on which we are currently working. As we

This research was partially funded by a grant from the Army Research Institute awarded to Patrick Sweeney; additional research team members included Kurt Dirks and Paul Lester. Sample computer code may be obtained from http://www.unc.edu/~curran

[1]OK, so we made up that last one.

DOI: 10.1037/13621-017
APA Handbook of Research Methods in Psychology: Vol. 3. Data Analysis and Research Publication, H. Cooper (Editor-in-Chief)

will describe in greater detail, we are interested in the longitudinal development of trust and integrity in cadets attending the U.S. Military Academy (USMA) at West Point. We quickly encounter, however, a significant challenge in applying existing multilevel growth models to our data. As we will describe in a moment, the three-level MLM is well developed for examining stability and change in a single outcome variable (e.g., trajectories of trust). Furthermore, the two-level model is well developed for examining stability and change in two or more outcome variables at once (e.g., trajectories of trust and trajectories of integrity). Our substantive research focus, however, is on the interrelations of growth in two dimensions of trust, yet the nesting of time within cadets and cadets within squads results in a three-level data structure. We must thus expand the standard three-level univariate growth model to allow for growth in two or more outcomes over time.

Although the two-level multivariate growth model has been well developed within the MLM (e.g., MacCallum, Kim, Malarkey, & Kiecolt-Glaser, 1997), we are unaware of any extensions of this model to allow for three levels of nesting. Our goal here is thus to review the current models available to estimate growth in two or more outcomes within the two-level MLM, to extend these models to allow for three levels of nesting, and to demonstrate this model using real data. Although by the end of our chapter we will find ourselves up to our eyeballs in equations, we make a concerted effort to retain a significant focus on the practical application of these techniques to real social science data in the face of the unavoidable yet necessary technical explication of the models.

We begin with a review of the univariate two-level growth model, and we consider predictors that do and do not change over time. We then draw on existing methods to extend this two-level model to include two or more outcomes at once. We take a step back and review the univariate three-level growth model, and we again consider predictors that do and do not change over time. We then generalize the multivariate methods for the two-level model for data characterized by three levels of nesting. Once defined, we demonstrate these methods using real empirical data drawn from the longitudinal study of

leadership and trust in a sample of cadets enrolled at the USMA at West Point. We conclude with potential limitations of our approach, and we offer recommendations for the use of these methods in practice.

TWO-LEVEL GROWTH MODELS

We begin our exploration of the unconditional growth model using a slightly modified version of notation used by Raudenbush and Bryk (2002, Equations 6.1 and 6.2). This notational scheme will allow us to easily expand the univariate two-level model to the more complex multivariate and three-level models that we present later.

Unconditional Two-Level Univariate Growth Model.

We can define the Level-1 equation for a two-level linear growth model as

$$y_{ti} = \pi_{0i} + \pi_{1i} time_{ti} + e_{ti}, \tag{1}$$

where y_{ti} is the measure of outcome y at time t ($t = 1, 2, \ldots, T$) for individual i ($i = 1, 2, \ldots, N$); π_{0i} and π_{1i} are the intercept and slope that define the linear trajectory unique to individual i; $time_{ti}$ is the numerical measure of time at assessment t for individual i; finally, e_{ti} is the time- and individual-specific residual. Time is often coded as $time_{ti} = t - 1$, so the intercept of the trajectory represents the initial assessment, although many other coding schemes are possible (e.g., Biesanz, Deeb-Sossa, Papadakis, Bollen, & Curran, 2004). Here we focus on a linear trajectory, but our developments directly expand to any functional form.

An important aspect of this model is that it is assumed that the individually varying parameters that define the growth trajectory (e.g., the intercept and slope) are themselves random variables. We can thus define Level-2 equations for these terms as

$$\begin{aligned} \pi_{0i} &= \beta_{00} + r_{0i} \\ \pi_{1i} &= \beta_{10} + r_{1i}, \end{aligned} \tag{2}$$

where β_{00} and β_{10} are the mean intercept and slope pooling over all individuals, and r_{0i} and r_{1i} are the deviation of each individual's trajectory parameters from their respective means.

The Level-1 and Level-2 expressions are primarily for pedagogical purposes, and the actual model of interest is the reduced form expression that results from the substitution of the Level-2 equations into the Level-1 equation. Substituting Equation 2 into Equation 1 results in

$$y_{ti} = \left(\beta_{00} + \beta_{10} time_{ti}\right) + \left(r_{0i} + r_{1i} time_{ti} + e_{ti}\right), \quad (3)$$

defined as in Equations 1 and 2. The first parenthetical term contains the fixed effects; these represent the mean intercept and mean linear slope pooling over all individuals. The second parenthetical term contains the individual deviations that constitute the random effects; the variance of these deviations represent the individual variability at both the Level-1 and Level-2 parts of the model. These random effects are an important component of any growth modeling application, but they are of particular interest to the models that we work to develop here. We will thus consider both the Level-1 and Level-2 deviations a bit more closely.

The Level-1 residuals (i.e., e_{ti}) are assumed to be multivariate normally distributed with a mean of zero and covariance matrix $\mathbf{R}$; more formally, this is expressed as $e_{ti} \sim MVN(\mathbf{0}, \mathbf{R})$ where $\mathbf{R}$ is the $T \times T$ covariance matrix and T is the total number of repeated observations. For example, for four repeated measures (i.e., $T = 4$) the Level-1 residual matrix is given as

$$\mathbf{R} = \begin{bmatrix} \sigma_1^2 & & & \\ 0 & \sigma_2^2 & & \\ 0 & 0 & \sigma_3^2 & \\ 0 & 0 & 0 & \sigma_4^2 \end{bmatrix}, \quad (4)$$

where a different residual variance is allowed at each time-point. The zeros in the off-diagonal elements reflect that there are no between-time residual covariances estimated. A number of alternative error structures are possible (e.g., the commonly used structure of equal variance over all time-points, or the allowance for correlated time-adjacent residuals, and so on), but we will primarily consider the heteroskedastic error structure for the models we examine here.

The Level-2 residuals are also assumed to be multivariate normally distributed with zero means and covariance matrix $\mathbf{T}$; more formally, this is given as $[u_{0i}, u_{1i}] \sim MVN(\mathbf{0}, \mathbf{T})$ where $\mathbf{T}$ is a $P \times P$ covariance matrix for which P is the total number of

random effects at Level 2. For example, for a linear growth model with a random intercept and slope (i.e., $P = 2$), the Level-2 covariance matrix is given as

$$\mathbf{T} = \begin{bmatrix} \tau_{00} & \\ \tau_{10} & \tau_{11} \end{bmatrix}, \quad (5)$$

where τ_{00} is the variance of the intercepts, τ_{11} is the variance of the slopes, and τ_{10} is the covariance between the intercepts and slopes. Larger Level-2 variance components imply greater individual variability in the starting point and rate of change over time. Recall that we are interested in the initial level and subsequent rate of change in self-reported trust of cadets at West Point. Significant variance components at Level 2 would imply that some cadets start higher versus lower in their initial reports of trust, and some cadets increase more rapidly versus less rapidly in the development of trust over time. In contrast, as these Level-2 random effects approach zero, this implies that cadets are becoming more and more similar to one another in terms of the values of the parameters that define their trajectories. At the extreme, if the variance components are equal to zero, then all cadets follow precisely the same trajectory; that is, each individual is characterized by the same initial level of trust and increase in trust at the same rate over time.

Importantly, larger random effects at Level 2 also suggest that one or more predictors could potentially be included to partially or wholly explain the individual variability in trajectory parameters (e.g., the intercepts and linear slopes). For example, say that the random effects suggested that cadets vary meaningfully in both their initial levels of trust and in their rates of change in trust over time. Then one or more time-specific or cadet-specific predictors could be included in the model to differentiate cadet-to-cadet variability in starting point and rate of change over time. This would allow us to build a more comprehensive model of possible determinants of developmental trajectories of trust, and it is to these conditional models we turn next.

Conditional Two-Level Univariate Growth Model: Time-Invariant Covariates

The prior models are sometimes called *unconditional* because there are no measured covariates used to predict the random parameters that define the growth trajectory.[2] We can easily expand the unconditional growth model to include one or more predictors at either Level 1, Level 2, or both. Predictors that are characteristics of the individual and thus do not change as a function of time are called time-invariant covariates (or TICs), and these are entered into the Level-2 equations. Examples of TICs might be biological sex, country of origin, ethnicity, or certain genetic characteristics. In some applications, the TIC might in principle change over time, but for empirical or substantive reasons, only the initial assessment is considered (e.g., Curran, Stice & Chassin, 1997). Because TICs only enter at Level 2, the Level-1 equation remains as defined in Equation 1. However, the Level-2 equation is expanded to include one or more person-specific measures that are constant over time.

For example, assuming a linear growth model defined at Level 1, a single person-specific TIC, denoted w_i, is included as

$$\pi_{0i} = \beta_{00} + \beta_{01}w_i + r_{0i} \qquad (6)$$
$$\pi_{1i} = \beta_{10} + \beta_{11}w_i + r_{1i},$$

where β_{01} and β_{11} capture the expected shift in the conditional means of the intercept and slope components associated with a one-unit shift in the TIC. For example, positive coefficients would reflect that higher values on the TIC are associated with higher initial values and steeper rates of change over time. Importantly, these shifts in the conditional means are independent of the passage of time, highlighted by the fact that the TICs are not subscripted by t to represent time. Thus, one might find that the developmental trajectories of trust in male cadets are defined by a different starting point and different rate of change relative to female cadets. These TICs could even be allowed to interact with one another—for example, the difference in trajectories of trust between male and female cadets could depend in part on the gender of the squad leader.

The inclusion of TICs is a powerful component of the MLM growth model. However, there may be important covariates we want to consider that are not constant over time. Instead, one or more covariates might take on a unique value at any given time-point, and treating these as invariant over time would be inappropriate (Curran & Bauer, 2011). This type of predictor can be included within the MLM as a time-varying covariate.

Conditional Two-Level Univariate Growth Model: Time-Varying Covariates

In contrast to the TICs that are assumed to be constant over time, time-varying covariates (or TVCs) can take on a unique value at any given point in time. For example, covariates such as peer influence, anxiety, delinquency, or substance use would be expected to change from time-point to time-point, and it is critical that these temporal fluctuations be incorporated into the model (e.g., Curran & Bauer, 2011; Curran, Lee, MacCallum, & Lane, in press). Because the value of the TVC is unique to a given individual and a given time-point, these covariates enter directly into the Level-1 equations.

For example, the Level-1 model with a single TVC, denoted z_{ti}, is given as

$$y_{ti} = \pi_{0i} + \pi_{1i}time_{ti} + \pi_{2i}z_{ti} + e_{ti}. \qquad (7)$$

Although π_{0i} and π_{1i} continue to represent the individual-specific intercept and slope components of the growth trajectory, these are now net the influence of the TVC (and vice versa). In other words, these are the parameters of the trajectory of the outcome controlling for the effects of the TVC. The impact of the TVC on the outcome is captured in π_{2i} which represents the shift in the mean of the outcome y at time t per one-unit shift in the TVC at the same time t. Importantly, whereas the TICs shift the conditional means of the trajectory parameters, the TVCs shift the conditional means of the outcome above and beyond the influence of the underlying growth trajectory. For example, the outcome of interest might be a cadet's trust, and the TVC is a measure of perceived integrity in that same individual; the TVC model would allow for the estimation of a developmental trajectory of trust, while simultaneously including the time-specific influence of

---

[2]This is a bit of a misnomer given that time is a predictor at Level 1, yet the term *unconditional* commonly implies no predictors in *addition* to the measure of time.

perceived integrity. Allowing integrity to vary in value over time is a marked improvement over using just the initial measure of integrity as a TIC because much additional time-specific information is incorporated into the model.

A particularly interesting aspect of the TVC model is that the magnitude of the effect of the TVC on the outcome can vary randomly across individuals. The inclusion of this random effect is not required and would be determined on the basis of substantive theory or empirical necessity. This can most clearly be seen in the Level-2 equations that correspond to the TVC model defined in Equation 7:

$$\pi_{0i} = \beta_{00} + r_{0i}$$
$$\pi_{1i} = \beta_{10} + r_{1i} \qquad (8)$$
$$\pi_{2i} = \beta_{20} + r_{2i},$$

where β_{00}, β_{10}, and β_{20} represent the mean of each random term, and the corresponding residuals represent the individually varying deviations around these means. Including the term r_{2i} allows for the magnitude of the relation between the TVC and the outcome to vary randomly over individuals; omitting this term implies that the magnitude of the TVC effects is constant for all individuals. These level-2 equations could easily be expanded to include one or more TICs to examine predictors of each random Level-1 effect, but we do not explore this further here (for further details, see Raudenbush & Bryk, 2002; Singer & Willett, 2003).

The TVC model offers a powerful and flexible method for examining individual variability in change over time as a function of one or more predictors that also vary as a function of time. One aspect of the TVC model that must be appreciated is that whereas an explicit growth process is estimated with respect to the outcome (i.e., y_{ti}), no such growth process is estimated with respect to the TVC (i.e., z_{ti}). In other words, although the TVC can take on unique values at any given time-point, it is not systematically related to the passage of time (e.g., Curran & Bauer, 2011). In many applications of the TVC model, this restriction is completely appropriate. One might be interested in examining trajectories of reading ability having controlled for the time-specific effects of days of instruction missed

(Raudenbush & Bryk, 2002, p. 179) or in examining trajectories of heavy alcohol use having controlled for the time-specific effects of a new marriage (Curran, Muthén, & Harford, 1998) or in a large variety of applications of daily diary studies (e.g., Bolger, Davis, & Rafaeli, 2003). In all of these examples, the TVC would not even be theoretically expected to change systematically over time. There are a variety of other examples in which the TVC is uniquely well suited to test the important questions of substantive interest.

Yet there are other situations in which substantive theory would not only predict that the TVC might take on different values over time, but that the TVC is itself developing systematically as a function of time. That is, the TVC may be expected to be characterized by a smoothed underlying trajectory that is defined by both fixed and random effects (Curran & Bauer, 2011). Our earlier hypothetical example considered the development of trust as the outcome and perceived integrity as the TVC. However, this strongly assumes that integrity is not developing systematically over time. Yet theory predicts that both trust and integrity codevelop systematically over time, and arbitrarily treating one of these constructs as a criterion and the other as a TVC would not correspond to our substantive theory. Furthermore, the core theoretical question of interest may not be related to how the *time-specific* value of the TVC is related to the *time-specific* value of the outcome (as is tested in the TVC model); instead, it may be how the parameters of the *trajectory* of the TVC relate to the parameters of the *trajectory* of the outcome. This is sometimes described as examining how two or more constructs "travel together" through time (e.g., McArdle, 1989). To test questions such as these, we must move to a multivariate growth model that allows for the simultaneous estimation of growth in both the outcome and the TVC.

Two-Level Multivariate Growth Model

Our goal is to define a model that allows for the estimation of growth processes in two or more constructs simultaneously. This is a distinct challenge given that the standard multilevel model is inherently univariate in that it is limited to a single criterion measure (e.g., Raudenbush & Bryk, 2002,

Equation 14.1). These univariate models have been expanded to the multivariate setting by Goldstein (1995), Goldstein et al. (1993), and MacCallum et al. (1997), among others; we draw on this collected body of work here.

The key to approaching this problem is to stack our multiple criterion variables into a newly created variable that is nominally univariate (i.e., there is just *one* variable), but this variable actually contains repeated assessments on two or more outcomes over time. This is sometimes called a *synthesized* variable (e.g., MacCallum et al., 1997). We will then incorporate a series of dummy variables as exogenous predictors that will give us full control of which specific outcomes we are referencing within different parts of the model. This will ultimately allow us to use our standard univariate multilevel modeling framework to fit what is in actuality a rather complex multivariate structure.

We begin by defining a simple linear growth model at Level 1, but we will add superscripts to all of the terms to identify to which outcome the term is associated. We use a linear trajectory here, but a variety of alternative functional forms could be used instead. Furthermore, a different form of growth could be used for each of the individual outcomes (e.g., linear in one outcome and quadratic in another). The general expression for $k = 1, 2, \ldots, K$ multivariate outcomes is

$$y_{ti}^{(k)} = \pi_{0i}^{(k)} + \pi_{1i}^{(k)} time_{ti}^{(k)} + e_{ti}^{(k)}. \tag{9}$$

So $y_{ti}^{(1)}$ would represent the outcome for the first construct (where $k = 1$; e.g., trust) and $y_{ti}^{(2)}$ would represent the outcome for the second construct (where $k = 2$; e.g., integrity), and so on. The level-2 equations are also modified to denote whether the term is associated with the first criterion measure ($k = 1$) or the second ($k = 2$):

$$\pi_{0i}^{(k)} = \beta_{00}^{(k)} + r_{0i}^{(k)}$$
$$\pi_{1i}^{(k)} = \beta_{10}^{(k)} + r_{1i}^{(k)}. \tag{10}$$

Compare this with Equation 2 to see the direct parallel between the Level-2 univariate and multivariate expressions. Finally, the reduced form expression is given as

$$y_{ti}^{(k)} = \left(\beta_{00}^{(k)} + \beta_{10}^{(k)} time_{ti}^{(k)}\right) + \left(r_{0i}^{(k)} + r_{1i}^{(k)} time_{ti}^{(k)} + e_{ti}^{(k)}\right). \tag{11}$$

We can combine these equations into a single multivariate expression in which there is a single synthesized criterion variable that we arbitrarily denote dv_{ti} to represent the dependent variable *dv* at time *t* for individual *i*. In other words, we manually create a new variable in the data set that stacks the multiple outcome variables into a single-column vector. Because multiple outcomes are now contained in a single variable, we must include additional information to distinguish which specific element belongs to which specific outcome. To do this, we create two or more new variables (denoted δ_k) that are simple binary dummy variables that represent which specific outcome is under consideration. There are *K* dummy variables, one each for $k = 1, 2, \ldots K$ outcomes. The dummy variable is $\delta_k = 1$ for construct *k*, and is equal to zero otherwise. (We will show a specific example of this in a moment.)

Finally, we can fit a single model to this new data structure in which a separate growth process is simultaneously fitted to each outcome *k*, the specific outcome of which is toggled in or out of the equation using an overall summation weighted by the dummy variables (e.g., MacCallum et al., 1997). More specifically, the general expression for the reduced-form model is

$$dv_{ti} = \sum_{k=1}^{K} \delta_k \left[\left(\beta_{00}^{(k)} + \beta_{10}^{(k)} time_{ti}^{(k)}\right) + \left(r_{0i}^{(k)} + r_{1i}^{(k)} time_{ti}^{(k)} + e_{ti}^{(k)}\right) \right]. \tag{12}$$

In words, Equation 12 defines the growth trajectory for each outcome of interest, and the dummy codes include or exclude the relevant values in the synthesized dependent variable through the overall summation.

To further explicate this, we can consider just the bivariate case in which $K = 2$. We define $k = 1$ to represent y_{ti} and $k = 2$ to represent z_{ti}, and we superscript with *y* and *z* to identify to which outcome each term belongs. For example, *y* might represent trust and *z* might represent integrity. In this case, Equation 12 simplifies to

$$dv_{ti} = \delta_y \left[\left(\beta_{00}^{(y)} + \beta_{10}^{(y)} time_{ti}^{(y)}\right) + \left(r_{0i}^{(y)} + r_{1i}^{(y)} time_{ti}^{(y)} + e_{ti}^{(y)}\right) \right]$$
$$+ \delta_z \left[\left(\beta_{00}^{(z)} + \beta_{10}^{(z)} time_{ti}^{(z)}\right) + \left(r_{0i}^{(z)} + r_{1i}^{(z)} time_{ti}^{(z)} + e_{ti}^{(z)}\right) \right]. \tag{13}$$

This expression highlights that this requires an atypical definition of the model relative to the standard two-level TVC growth model. To see this, we will first distribute the two binary variables and gather up our terms:

$$
\begin{aligned}
dv_{ti} =& \left(\beta_{00}^{(y)}\delta_y + \beta_{10}^{(y)}\delta_y time_{ti}^{(y)}\right) \\
&+ \left(r_{0i}^{(y)}\delta_y + r_{1i}^{(y)}\delta_y time_{ti}^{(y)} + e_{ti}^{(y)}\delta_y\right) \\
&+ \left(\beta_{00}^{(z)}\delta_z + \beta_{10}^{(z)}\delta_z time_{ti}^{(z)}\right) \\
&+ \left(r_{0i}^{(z)}\delta_z + r_{1i}^{(z)}\delta_z time_{ti}^{(z)} + e_{ti}^{(z)}\delta_z\right).
\end{aligned} \tag{14}
$$

There are two somewhat-odd things about this expression relative to the usual univariate growth model. First, there is no overall intercept term for this reduced-form model. Instead, the intercept for the first outcome (i.e., y_{ti}) is captured in the main effect of the first dummy variable (i.e., $\beta_{00}^{(y)}\delta_y$); similarly, the intercept for the second outcome (i.e., z_{ti}) is captured in the main effect of the second dummy variable (i.e., $\beta_{00}^{(z)}\delta_z$). Second, the linear slope for each outcome is captured in the interaction between each dummy variable and time. Specifically, the linear slope for the first outcome (i.e., y_{ti}) is captured in the interaction of the first dummy variable and time (i.e., $\beta_{10}^{(y)}\delta_y time_{ti}^{(y)}$); the linear slope for the second outcome (i.e., z_{ti}) is captured in the interaction of the second dummy variable and time (i.e., $\beta_{10}^{(z)}\delta_z time_{ti}^{(z)}$). Thus, the main effects of the dummy variables represent the outcome-specific intercepts, and the interactions between the dummy variables and time represent the outcome-specific slopes. See MacCallum et al. (1997) for an excellent description and demonstration of this model with three outcomes.

There are a number of advantages to this model expression, a key one of which is the inclusion of more complex error structures at both level 1 and level 2 than is possible within the univariate TVC growth model. The reason is that the covariance structure not only holds within each construct separately (e.g., within y_{ti} and within z_{ti}), but it also holds *across* construct. For example, a univariate growth model of trust examines covariance structures only within trust; and a univariate growth model of integrity examines covariance structures only within integrity. But a multivariate growth model of trust and integrity allows for the examination of covariance structures *between* trust and integrity both at the time-specific (i.e., Level-1) and trajectory-specific (i.e., Level-2) parts of the model. This can be critically important information to include, not only in terms of properly modeling the joint structure of the observed data but also in terms of fully evaluating the substantive research question of interest.

For example, consider the Level-1 covariance structure for the bivariate model of y_{ti} and z_{ti} (i.e., the model defined in Equation 14). The corresponding Level-1 covariance structure is

$$
\left[e_{1i}^{(y)}, e_{2i}^{(y)}, e_{3i}^{(y)}, e_{4i}^{(y)}, e_{1i}^{(z)}, e_{2i}^{(z)}, e_{3i}^{(z)}, e_{4i}^{(z)}\right] \sim MVN(0, \mathbf{R})
$$

with matrix elements

$$
\mathbf{R} = \left[\begin{array}{cccc|cccc}
\sigma_1^{2(y)} & & & & & & & \\
0 & \sigma_2^{2(y)} & & & & & & \\
0 & 0 & \sigma_3^{2(y)} & & & & & \\
0 & 0 & 0 & \sigma_4^{2(y)} & & & & \\
\hline
\sigma_{11}^{(z,y)} & 0 & 0 & 0 & \sigma_1^{2(z)} & & & \\
0 & \sigma_{22}^{(z,y)} & 0 & 0 & 0 & \sigma_2^{2(z)} & & \\
0 & 0 & \sigma_{33}^{(z,y)} & 0 & 0 & 0 & \sigma_3^{2(z)} & \\
0 & 0 & 0 & \sigma_{44}^{(z,y)} & 0 & 0 & 0 & \sigma_4^{2(z)}
\end{array}\right] \cdot \tag{15}
$$

The upper left quadrant represents the Level-1 residual covariance structure among the four repeated assessments of y_{ti}; this is equivalent to those of the univariate model shown in Equation 4. Similarly, the lower-right quadrant represents the Level-1 residual covariance structure among the four repeated assessments of z_{ti}. However, critically important information is contained in the lower left quadrant in the form of the within-time but across-construct residual covariance structure. For example, the element $\sigma_{11}^{(z,y)}$ represents the covariance between the Level-1 residuals of y_{ti} and z_{ti} at the first time-point (i.e., $t = 1$). This captures the part of trust at Time 1 that is unexplained by the trajectory of trust that covaries with the part of integrity at Time 1 that is unexplained by the trajectory of integrity. This provides a way to include potentially important covariances among the time-specific Level-1 residuals across the two or more multivariate outcomes, the omission of which could artificially inflate the variance components at Level 2.

The multivariate model also allows us to examine across-construct covariances among the Level-2 random effects. Again consider just two outcomes y_{ti} and z_{ti} where each is defined by a linear trajectory. The corresponding Level-2 covariance structure is $\left[r_{0i}^{(y)}, r_{1i}^{(y)}, r_{0i}^{(z)}, r_{1i}^{(z)} \right] \sim MVN\left(0, \mathbf{T} \right)$ with matrix elements

$$\mathbf{T} = \left[\begin{array}{cc|cc} \tau_{00}^{(y)} & & & \\ \tau_{10}^{(y)} & \tau_{11}^{(y)} & & \\ \hline \tau_{00}^{(z,y)} & \tau_{01}^{(z,y)} & \tau_{00}^{(z)} & \\ \tau_{10}^{(z,y)} & \tau_{11}^{(z,y)} & \tau_{10}^{(z)} & \tau_{11}^{(z)} \end{array} \right]. \tag{16}$$

The upper left and lower right quadrants represent the covariance structure of the growth parameters within outcome y_{ti} and outcome z_{ti}, respectively (as corresponds to the same elements for the univariate model presented in Equation 5). However, the lower left quadrant represents the covariance structure of the growth parameters *across* the two outcomes. More specifically, the covariance between the two random intercepts is $\tau_{00}^{(z,y)}$, between the two random slopes is $\tau_{11}^{(z,y)}$, between the intercept of z_{ti} and the slope of y_{ti} is $\tau_{01}^{(z,y)}$, and between the slope of z_{ti} and the intercept of y_{ti} is $\tau_{10}^{(z,y)}$.

These covariances (and their standardized correlation counterparts) can be extremely interesting. For example, a positive value for $\tau_{11}^{(z,y)}$ would imply that steeper rates of change on trust are associated with steeper rates of change on integrity (and vice versa), and this would be consistent with the notion that development in the two constructs is systematically related over time. Furthermore, a negative value for $\tau_{01}^{(z,y)}$ would imply that larger initial values of integrity are associated with less steep rates of change of trust over time (and vice versa), and this would be consistent with the notion that the initial values of integrity are systematically associated with the rates of change on trust. These across-construct covariances are often of key interest when attempting to understand how growth in one construct is related to growth in another construct. Furthermore, these covariances are only available via the multivariate growth model given that the standard multilevel model is limited to the estimation of trajectory parameters for one outcome at a time (e.g., as defined in Equation 7).

The Inclusion of One or More Predictors

Just as with the univariate model, the multivariate model can contain one or more predictors at either Level 1, Level 2, or both. Furthermore, interactions can be estimated within or across levels of analysis. In expectation of our later models, we focus on the inclusion of a single TIC, denoted w_i, entered at Level 2. For example, we are interested in the relation between the extent to which cadets view their fellow squad members as benevolent at the initial time period and how their trajectories of trust and integrity change over time. We will thus include a cadet-specific measure of perceived benevolence in fellow squad members at the initial time period with the goal of examining how initial perceived benevolence impacts the simultaneous unfolding of trust and integrity over time. The Level-1 equation remains as before (i.e., Equation 9), but the Level-2 equation is expanded to include the TIC:

$$\pi_{0i}^{(k)} = \beta_{00}^{(k)} + \beta_{01}^{(k)} w_i + r_{0i}^{(k)}$$
$$\pi_{1i}^{(k)} = \beta_{10}^{(k)} + \beta_{11}^{(k)} w_i + r_{1i}^{(k)}. \tag{17}$$

All of these terms are defined as before, but now the regression parameters linking the TIC to the random intercept and slope are unique to outcome k (e.g., $\beta_{01}^{(k)}$ and $\beta_{11}^{(k)}$).

The Level-2 equation is again substituted into the Level-1 equation to result in the reduced-form expression for the model. For example, for two outcomes denoted y and z, this expression is

$$dv_{ti} = \delta_y \left[\left(\beta_{00}^{(y)} + \beta_{10}^{(y)} time_{ti}^{(y)} + \beta_{01}^{(y)} w_i \right. \right.$$
$$\left. + \beta_{11}^{(y)} w_i time_{ti}^{(y)} \right) + \left(r_{0i}^{(y)} + r_{1i}^{(y)} time_{ti}^{(y)} + e_{ti}^{(y)} \right) \right]$$
$$+ \delta_z \left[\left(\beta_{00}^{(z)} + \beta_{10}^{(z)} time_{ti}^{(z)} + \beta_{01}^{(z)} w_i + \beta_{11}^{(z)} w_i time_{ti}^{(z)} \right) \right.$$
$$\left. + \left(r_{0i}^{(z)} + r_{1i}^{(z)} time_{ti}^{(z)} + e_{ti}^{(z)} \right) \right]. \tag{18}$$

Each bracketed term is multiplied by the dummy variable associated with that particular outcome (e.g., δ_y and δ_z). As such, the regression of the random intercept on the TIC is captured in the interaction between the dummy variable and the TIC (i.e., $\beta_{01}^{(y)} \delta_y w_i$ and $\beta_{01}^{(z)} \delta_z w_i$). Similarly, the regression of the random slope on the TIC is captured in the interaction between the dummy variable, time, and the TIC (i.e., $\beta_{11}^{(y)} \delta_y w_i time_{ti}$ and $\beta_{11}^{(z)} \delta_z w_i time_{ti}$). As with the univariate two-level model, the TIC shifts the conditional means of the random intercepts and slopes per unit shift in the TIC. In the multivariate model, however, these mean shifts affect all outcomes simultaneously.

Now that we have laid out the model equations, we find that a key practical challenge in fitting these models to real data is the need to restructure the data in a way that is not necessarily intuitive but that is needed to allow for proper model estimation. Despite the nonintuitiveness, a bit of careful thought shows that this can be accomplished in a straightforward manner; we demonstrate this in the next section.

Data Structure for the Two-Level Multivariate Growth Model

An example of the data structure for the standard organization for the univariate TVC model is

presented in the left panel of Figure 17.1. A sample data structure is given for four individuals where column i denotes the identification number of each person, column t denotes time-point, column y_{ti} denotes the criterion (e.g., trust), column z_{ti} denotes the TVC (e.g., integrity), and column w_i denotes a Level-2 TIC (e.g., benevolence). This is precisely how the data would be structured in the standard univariate growth model with one TVC and one TIC.

Compare this standard structure to that presented in the right panel of Figure 17.1 that is reformatted for the bivariate model. Note that these are *precisely* the same data as are shown in the left panel except for two key differences. First, the values on y_{ti} and z_{ti} are now strung out in a single column labeled dv_{ti}; this represents the newly synthesized criterion variable that we manually created and will be the

i	t	y_{ti}	z_{ti}	w_i		i	t	dv_{ti}	w_i	δ_y	δ_z
1	1	y_{11}	z_{11}	w_1		1	1	y_{11}	w_1	1	0
1	2	y_{21}	z_{21}	w_1		1	1	z_{11}	w_1	0	1
1	3	y_{31}	z_{31}	w_1		1	2	y_{21}	w_1	1	0
1	4	y_{41}	z_{41}	w_1		1	2	z_{21}	w_1	0	1
2	1	y_{12}	z_{12}	w_2		1	3	y_{31}	w_1	1	0
2	2	y_{22}	z_{22}	w_2		1	3	z_{31}	w_1	0	1
2	3	y_{32}	z_{32}	w_2		1	4	y_{41}	w_1	1	0
2	4	y_{42}	z_{42}	w_2		1	4	z_{41}	w_1	0	1
3	1	y_{13}	z_{13}	w_3		2	1	y_{12}	w_2	1	0
3	2	y_{23}	z_{23}	w_3		2	1	z_{12}	w_2	0	1
3	3	y_{33}	z_{33}	w_3		2	2	y_{22}	w_2	1	0
3	4	y_{43}	z_{43}	w_3		2	2	z_{22}	w_2	0	1
4	1	y_{14}	z_{14}	w_4		2	3	y_{32}	w_2	1	0
4	2	y_{24}	z_{24}	w_4		2	3	z_{32}	w_2	0	1
4	3	y_{34}	z_{34}	w_4		2	4	y_{42}	w_2	1	0
4	4	y_{44}	z_{44}	w_4		2	4	z_{42}	w_2	0	1
						3	1	y_{13}	w_3	1	0
						3	1	z_{13}	w_3	0	1
						3	2	y_{23}	w_3	1	0
						3	2	z_{23}	w_3	0	1
						3	3	y_{33}	w_3	1	0
						3	3	z_{33}	w_3	0	1
						3	4	y_{43}	w_3	1	0
						3	4	z_{43}	w_3	0	1
						4	1	y_{14}	w_4	1	0
						4	1	z_{14}	w_4	0	1
						4	2	y_{24}	w_4	1	0
						4	2	z_{24}	w_4	0	1
						4	3	y_{34}	w_4	1	0
						4	3	z_{34}	w_4	0	1
						4	4	y_{44}	w_4	1	0
						4	4	z_{44}	w_4	0	1

FIGURE 17.1. Standard data structure for a four-time-point two-level univariate growth model with one time-varying covariate (left panel) and the modified data structure for a four-time-point two-level bivariate growth model (right panel).

unit of analysis for the multivariate model. Second, the TIC remains constant across individuals but is now repeated for each outcome. Third, there are two new dummy variables, denoted δ_y and δ_z, each of which is equal to one when the corresponding element in dv_{ti} is from that construct, and zero otherwise. For example, in the first row of data $\delta_y = 1$ and $\delta_z = 0$ because the element of dv_{ti} is from outcome y_{ti}; similarly, in the second row of data $\delta_y = 0$ and $\delta_z = 1$ because the element of dv_{ti} is from outcome z_{ti}. This pattern repeats throughout the entire data matrix. The multivariate growth model can now be fitted directly to these newly structured data.[3]

THREE-LEVEL GROWTH MODELS

All of the models that we have explored thus far assume that the data structure is nested. That is, repeated measures are nested within individual, and this necessitates the two-level model. Importantly, this structure in turn implies that the individual subjects in the sample are mutually independent. In other words, it is strongly assumed that no two individuals are any more or less similar than any other two. This assumption is commonly met in practice, especially when subjects are obtained using some form of simple random sampling procedure, and subjects are not themselves nested in some higher structure (e.g., Raudenbush & Bryk, 2002).

However, there are many situations in which not only are the repeated measures nested within individuals but also individuals are in turn nested within groups. A common example is when repeated measures are nested within children, and children are in turn nested within classroom. In our case, we have repeated measures nested within cadet, and cadets are in turn nested within squads. Such a data structure would violate the assumptions of the two-level model because two cadets who are members of the same squad are likely to be more similar to one another than two cadets from different squads. A major strength of the multilevel model is the natural way that it may be expanded to many complex sampling designs, including three levels of nesting. But these models are understandably more complex, and

we must closely consider how the necessary expansions are possible in the multivariate case.

Three-Level Unconditional Univariate Growth Model

We will begin by moving back to the two-level univariate model and then extending it to allow for three levels of nesting. Our motivating example is time nested within cadet, and cadet is nested within squad. The Level-1 model becomes

$$y_{tij} = \pi_{0ij} + \pi_{1ij} time_{tij} + e_{tij}, \qquad (19)$$

where t and i continue to represent time and individual, respectively, but now j denotes group membership at level 3 ($j = 1, 2, \ldots, J$). More specifically, y_{tij} is the obtained measure on outcome y at time t for individual i nested in group j; π_{0ij} and π_{1ij} are the intercept and slope for individual i in group j; $time_{tij}$ is the numerical measure of time at time t for individual i in group j, and e_{tij} is the time-, individual-, and group-specific residual where $e_{tij} \sim MVN(0, \mathbf{R})$.

The Level-2 equations are

$$\begin{aligned} \pi_{0ij} &= \beta_{00j} + r_{0ij} \\ \pi_{1ij} &= \beta_{10j} + r_{1ij}, \end{aligned} \qquad (20)$$

where β_{00j} and β_{10j} are the group-specific intercept and slope of the linear trajectory. These terms are sometimes a bit tricky to think about at first. The group-specific intercept and slope (i.e., β_{00j} and β_{10j}) represent the mean of the intercepts and the mean of the slopes of the growth trajectories for all of the individuals nested within group j. For example, these might represent the mean initial value and mean rate of change in trust for all of the cadets who are nested within a given squad j. As such, the residuals r_{0ij} and r_{1ij} represent the deviation of each individual's intercept and slope around their group-specific mean values. That is, the residuals capture the variability of each cadet's trajectory of trust around their own squad-specific means trajectory of trust. More formally, this is given as $[r_{0ij}, r_{1ij}] \sim MVN(0, \mathbf{T}_\pi)$; we will explore the $\mathbf{T}_\pi$ covariance matrix of random effects more closely in a moment.

---

[3]A detailed example of this restructuring is available from Patrick J. Curran or from http://www.unc.edu/~curran

Finally, given the three-level structure of the data, the group-specific intercepts and slopes (e.g., β_{00j} and β_{10j}) themselves vary randomly across groups. The Level-3 equations are thus

$$\beta_{00j} = \gamma_{000} + u_{00j}$$
$$\beta_{10j} = \gamma_{100} + u_{10j}, \tag{21}$$

where γ_{000} and γ_{100} represent the grand mean intercept and slope pooling over all individuals and all groups, and the residual terms u_{00j} and u_{10j} capture the deviation of each group-specific value from the grand means, and $[u_{00j}, u_{10j}] \sim MVN(0, \mathbf{T}_\beta)$. The reduced form expression for the three-level univariate growth model is

$$y_{tij} = \left(\gamma_{000} + \gamma_{100} time_{tij}\right)$$
$$+ \left(u_{00j} + r_{0ij} + u_{10j} time_{tij} + r_{1ij} time_{tij} + e_{tij}\right). \tag{22}$$

See Raudenbush and Bryk (2002, Chapter 8) for an excellent description of the general three-level model as well as a discussion of studying individual change within groups.

A key characteristic of this model is the estimation of random components at both levels two and three, and the covariance structures of these random effects will be of specific interest in the models described in the section Three-Level Multivariate Growth Model. In the two-level model, the Level-2 covariance matrix was denoted $\mathbf{T}$. In the three-level model, however, there is a $\mathbf{T}$ matrix at Level 2 and at Level 3. This is why we must distinguish these $\mathbf{T}$ matrixes with the use of an additional subscript: $\mathbf{T}_\pi$ for Level 2 and $\mathbf{T}_\beta$ for Level 3. Let us first consider the covariance structure of the residuals at Level 2 captured in $\mathbf{T}_\pi$.

For a linear model defined at Level 1, the Level-2 covariance matrix takes the form

$$\mathbf{T}_\pi = \begin{bmatrix} \tau_{\pi_{00}} & \\ \tau_{\pi_{01}} & \tau_{\pi_{11}} \end{bmatrix}, \tag{23}$$

where $\tau_{\pi_{00}}$ represents the Level-2 variance of the intercepts, $\tau_{\pi_{11}}$ the variance of the slopes, and $\tau_{\pi_{01}}$ the covariance between the intercepts and slopes. These are sometimes challenging estimates to interpret given that they reside at the middle level of nesting. Specifically, these estimates represent the amount of variability among the individual-specific

trajectories within group (e.g., variability among trajectories of trust for each cadet sharing the same squad). Thus, larger values reflect greater person-to-person variability in the trajectories within group; similarly, smaller values reflect greater person-to-person similarity in the trajectories within group. At the extreme, if these variance components equal zero, then each person within the group is characterized by the same trajectory. For example, a larger value of $\tau_{\pi_{11}}$ would imply greater variability in rates of change in trust among cadets within the same squad. If $\tau_{\pi_{11}} = 0$ then every cadet within each squad is characterized by precisely the same developmental trajectory of trust over time. Although this implies that there is no cadet-to-cadet variability in the development of trust within squad, this does *not* imply that there is no meaningful squad-to-squad variability in the development of trust over time. To assess this, we must turn to the Level-3 covariance matrix of random effects.

The covariance matrix of random effects at the third level of analysis is denoted $\mathbf{T}_\beta$. For the linear model with full random effects defined in Equation 22), the elements of this matrix are

$$\mathbf{T}_\beta = \begin{bmatrix} \tau_{\beta_{00}} & \\ \tau_{\beta_{01}} & \tau_{\beta_{11}} \end{bmatrix}, \tag{24}$$

where $\tau_{\beta_{00}}$ represents the Level-3 variance of the intercepts, $\tau_{\beta_{11}}$ the variance of the slopes, and $\tau_{\beta_{01}}$ the covariance between the intercepts and slopes. In contrast to the Level-2 variance components that capture individual-level variability of the trajectory parameters *within* group (e.g., squad), $\mathbf{T}_\beta$ captures the group-to-group level variability of the trajectory parameters *between* group. For example, larger values of $\tau_{\beta_{00}}$ and $\tau_{\beta_{11}}$ would indicate greater squad-to-squad variability in intercepts and slopes; that is, some squads are characterized by higher versus lower starting points on the outcome variables and larger versus smaller rates of change over time. Alternatively, smaller values indicate less variability in the trajectory parameters across squad. For example, larger variance components would imply that there are potentially meaningful differences in the squad-level trajectories of trust over time across the set of squads; some squads might be defined by higher starting points and steeper rates of change, whereas others are not. At the extreme, values of zero reflect that all squads are governed by the same trajectory parameters; for example, all squads are defined by the same starting point of trust and same rate of change in trust over time. Indeed, in this extreme case, the three-level model simplifies to the two-level structure defined earlier given that there is no meaningful squad-to-squad variability.

To briefly summarize, the Level-1 variance components reflect the time-specific variations in trust around each cadet's trajectory of trust; the Level-2 variance components reflect the cadet-specific variations in the trajectories of trust around the mean trajectory of trust within each squad; and the Level-3 variance components reflect the squad-specific variations in the trajectories of trust around the grand mean trajectory of trust pooling over all cadets and all squads. This breakdown of the random effects is one of the most elegant aspects of the three-level model: The total variability observed in trust can be broken down into time-specific, cadet-specific, and squad-specific effects. And if meaningful random effects are identified at any level of analysis, one or more predictors can be included to attempt to explain these variations.

Three-Level Conditional Univariate Growth Model

Just as with the two-level model, covariates can be included at any level of analysis. In the three-level model, however, predictors can be time specific (i.e., Level-1 model), person specific (i.e., Level-2 model), or group specific (i.e., Level-3 model). Using our previous terminology, TVCs would thus appear at Level 1, and individual- and group-specific TICs would appear at Levels 2 and 3, respectively. Given our primary interest in change in two or more constructs over time, here we will focus just on the TVCs at Level 1; inclusion of TICs is a natural extension of the two-level model described earlier (e.g., Raudenbush & Bryk, 2002, pp. 241–245).

The Level-1 equation for a simple linear growth model with one TVC is defined as

$$y_{tij} = \pi_{0ij} + \pi_{1ij}time_{tij} + \pi_{2ij}z_{tij} + e_{tij}, \tag{25}$$

where z_{tij} is the time-, person-, and group-specific TVC, and π_{2ij} captures the relation between the TVC

and the outcome at time-point t. The magnitude of the relation between the TVC and the outcome can vary randomly over individual with corresponding Level-2 equations

$$\begin{aligned}\pi_{0ij} &= \beta_{00j} + r_{0ij}\\\pi_{1ij} &= \beta_{10j} + r_{1ij}\\\pi_{2ij} &= \beta_{20j} + r_{2ij}\end{aligned} \tag{26}$$

where β_{20j} represents the mean relation between the TVC and the outcome pooling over all individuals within group j. Finally, the magnitude of these within-group specific effects can itself vary over group, and this is captured in the Level-3 equations

$$\begin{aligned}\beta_{00j} &= \gamma_{000} + u_{00j}\\\beta_{10j} &= \gamma_{100} + u_{10j}\\\beta_{20j} &= \gamma_{200} + u_{20j}.\end{aligned} \tag{27}$$

The reduced form results from the substitution of Equation 27 into 26, and Equation 26 subsequently into Equation 25. Although tedious, it is interesting to see the full set of collected terms:

$$y_{tij} = \left(\gamma_{000} + \gamma_{100}time_{tij} + \gamma_{200}z_{tij}\right) + \left(u_{10j} + r_{0ij}\right)$$
$$time_{tij} + \left(u_{2ij} + r_{tij}\right)z_{tij} + \left(u_{00j} + r_{0ij} + e_{tij}\right). \tag{28}$$

This model is in the same form as its two-level counterpart with the key exception that an additional covariance matrix is allowed to capture between-group variability at the third level of nesting. We again assume, however, that although the TVC can take on a different numerical value at each time-point t, the TVC itself is assumed to not change systematically over time. Whether by theoretical rationale or empirical necessity, there are many situations in which we would like to expand the univariate three-level model to simultaneously capture growth in two or more constructs over time. Whereas the two-level multivariate model is well established in the literature (e.g., MacCallum et al., 1997), we are unaware of any prior presentation of the expansion of this model to three levels of nesting. It is to this that we now turn.

Three-Level Multivariate Growth Model

The expansion of the multivariate growth model from two to three levels of nesting is both intuitive and straightforward. Just as we expanded the univariate growth model to allow for individuals to be nested within group, we will expand the multivariate model in precisely the same way. Indeed, we will use the same dummy variable approach to combine the multiple outcomes into a single three-level model. The only difference here is that the reduced form expression is more complex because of the nesting of time within individual within group.

The general expression is

$$
dv_{tij} = \sum_{k=1}^{K} \delta_k \left[\left(\gamma_{000}^{(k)} + \gamma_{100}^{(k)} time_{tij}^{(k)} \right) + \left(u_{00j}^{(k)} + r_{0ij}^{(k)} \right. \right.
$$
$$
\left. \left. + u_{10j}^{(k)} time_{tij}^{(k)} + r_{1ij}^{(k)} time_{tij}^{(k)} + e_{tij}^{(k)} \right) \right] \tag{29}
$$

for $k = 1, 2, \ldots, K$ outcomes. There is no need to modify the notation for the dummy variables to include information about group membership because the dummy variables only demarcate to which outcome variable the numerical value belongs; this is not unique to time, person, or group. For the bivariate case, this simplifies to

$$
dv_{tij} = \delta_y \left[\left(\gamma_{000}^{(y)} + \gamma_{100}^{(y)} time_{tij}^{(y)} \right) + \left(u_{00j}^{(y)} + r_{0ij}^{(y)} \right. \right.
$$
$$
\left. \left. + u_{10j}^{(y)} time_{tij}^{(y)} + r_{1ij}^{(y)} time_{tij}^{(y)} + e_{tij}^{(y)} \right) \right]
$$
$$
+ \delta_z \left[\left(\gamma_{000}^{(z)} + \gamma_{100}^{(z)} time_{tij}^{(z)} \right) + \left(u_{00j}^{(z)} + r_{0ij}^{(z)} \right. \right.
$$
$$
\left. \left. + u_{10j}^{(z)} time_{tij}^{(z)} + r_{1ij}^{(z)} time_{tij}^{(z)} + e_{tij}^{(z)} \right) \right], \tag{30}
$$

where the first bracketed term captures the three-level growth process for outcome y_{tij} (e.g., trust) and the second bracketed term captures the three-level growth process for outcome z_{tij} (e.g., integrity). As before, these two growth processes need not be the same (e.g., the first could be linear and the second quadratic, and so on). As with the two-level multivariate expression, the definition of the model is atypical relative to the standard three-level growth model. The main effects of the two dummy codes are again the intercept of each construct, respectively, and the interaction between each dummy code and time are again the slope of each construct, respectively.

The key benefit stemming from this rather complex (yet intuitively appealing) model is the ability to explicitly incorporate various covariance structures among the residual terms at all three levels

both within and across constructs. The Level-1 covariance structure for this model is the same as that defined in Equation 15 for the two-level model. However, the covariance structures at Levels 2 and 3 can become quite interesting. Given space constraints and the similarity in the types of inferences that can be drawn, here we will focus primarily on the level-2 covariance structure as estimated both within and across the multivariate outcomes (i.e., $\mathbf{T}_\pi$). However, all of our descriptions would generalize naturally to the Level-3 covariance structure (i.e., $\mathbf{T}_\beta$). Furthermore, these generalizations offer unique insights into the relations among growth trajectories at the level of the group. Thus $\mathbf{T}_\pi$ estimates the random components of individual-level trajectories nested within groups, and $\mathbf{T}_\beta$ estimates the random components of group-level trajectories across groups. Only the three-level model provides this joint estimation of within- and between-group effects (the specific parameterization of which would depend on substantive theory and empirical necessity).

To remain concrete, we will continue to consider the three-level bivariate growth model defined in Equation 30. There is thus a linear trajectory estimated for both outcomes, and all trajectory parameters are allowed to vary both at Level 2 and Level 3. The joint covariance structure for the two growth processes at Level 2 is contained in the matrix $\mathbf{T}_\pi$. The specific elements of this matrix are

$$
\mathbf{T}_\pi = \left[\begin{array}{cc|cc}
\tau_{\pi_{00}}^{(y)} & & & \\
\tau_{\pi_{10}}^{(y)} & \tau_{\pi_{11}}^{(y)} & & \\
\hline
\tau_{\pi_{00}}^{(z,y)} & \tau_{\pi_{01}}^{(z,y)} & \tau_{\pi_{00}}^{(z)} & \\
\tau_{\pi_{10}}^{(z,y)} & \tau_{\pi_{11}}^{(z,y)} & \tau_{\pi_{10}}^{(z)} & \tau_{\pi_{11}}^{(z)}
\end{array} \right]. \tag{31}
$$

Note the substantial similarity to the Level-2 covariance matrix from the two-level bivariate growth model defined in Equation 16. The critical difference between the Level-2 covariance matrix $\mathbf{T}$ from the two-level model and the Level-2 covariance matrix $\mathbf{T}_\pi$ from the three-level model is that the latter explicitly accounts for the clustering of individuals within groups at the highest level of nesting. If we were to fix the Level-3 covariance matrix to zero (e.g., $T_\beta = 0$), then the three-level model would reduce to the two-level model and the Level-2 covariance matrices defined in Equations 16 and 31 would be equal (e.g., $T = T_\pi$).

The same pattern as was observed in the T matrix defined in Equation 16 holds here. Namely, the upper left and lower right quadrants represent the variance components of the trajectory parameters of the individuals nested within each group for outcome y and outcome z, respectively. Furthermore, the lower left quadrant represents the variance components across the two outcomes. For example, the element $\tau_{\pi_{00}}^{(z,y)}$ captures the covariance between the random intercepts on outcome z with the random intercepts on outcome y; this element assesses the extent of similarity in the starting points of the trajectories of z and y of individuals nested within group. Similarly, the element $\tau_{\pi_{11}}^{(z,y)}$ captures the covariance between the random slopes on outcome z with the random slopes on outcome y; this assesses the extent of similarity in the rates of change of the trajectories of z and y. Finally, the element $\tau_{\pi_{10}}^{(z,y)}$ captures the covariance between the random slopes on z and the random intercepts on y, and $\tau_{\pi_{01}}^{(z,y)}$ the covariance between the random intercepts on z with the random slopes on y. As with the two-level models, these covariances can be standardized into correlations for interpretation and effect size estimation.

These covariance estimates are often of key substantive interest when testing hypotheses regarding stability and change over time. As in the two-level bivariate growth model, the lower-left quadrant of the T_π matrix captures the similarity or dissimilarity in patterns of growth in the two outcomes over time. This can provide insight into a variety of interesting questions. For example, to what extent are the starting points of the trajectories of trust and integrity related? Is the rate of change in trust systematically related to the rate of change in integrity? Do individuals who report higher initial levels of trust also report steeper rates of change in integrity (and vice versa)? The key advantage of the three-level model is that these relations are estimated while properly allowing for the nesting of individuals within groups. Furthermore, similarly intriguing insights can be gained about group-level characteristics of

growth through the Level-3 variance components (i.e., T_β) that would not otherwise be accessible via the two-level model. For example, on average, do squads that are characterized by higher initial levels of trust tend to increase more steeply in integrity over time? These are just a few of the many advantages of the multivariate–multilevel growth models.

The Inclusion of One or More Predictors

One or more predictors can be included at any of the three levels of analyses. Furthermore, interactions can be estimated within one level, across two levels, or even across all three levels. Because the equations are direct extensions of those already defined, we do not repeat these here. For example, the inclusion of a single TIC at Level 2 follows the same structure as was defined in Equation 18 but with the addition of the necessary Level-3 error terms (for full details, see Raudenbush & Bryk, 2002, Chapter 8).

Data Structure for the Three-Level Multivariate Growth Model

The data structure required to fit the three-level bivariate growth model is a direct extension of that used for the two-level model. For example, the left panel in Figure 17.2 presents the standard data structure used to fit the three-level TVC model defined in Equation 22 to four individuals with the inclusion of a Level-2 TIC. There is more information here than was required for the two-level model given the need to simultaneously track group membership. Thus, column j denotes group, column i denotes individual, and column t denotes time. Subjects 1 and 2 are members of Group 1, and Subjects 3 and 4 are members of Group 2. Finally, y_{tij} is the observed outcome variable, z_{tij} is the TVC, and w_{ij} is the person-specific TIC. To combine the outcome and the TVC into a bivariate model, these must be restructured under a single column as the newly constructed (or synthesized) dependent variable.

These restructured data are shown in the right panel of Figure 17.2. Columns j, i, and t all remain as before, but there is a newly created column labeled dv_{tij}; this is the newly synthesized variable that is a stacked vector of y_{tij} and z_{tij}. The TIC w_{ij} is again repeated over both the outcome variables.

Finally, the binary variables denoted δ_y and δ_z again identify to which construct each element of the synthesized variable belongs. Note the significant similarities between the data structures presented in Figure 17.1 and Figure 17.2. The only meaningful difference is that Figure 17.1 implies that the four individuals are independent, whereas Figure 17.2 explicitly captures information about the group to which each individual belongs.[4]

We have now fully explicated the multivariate growth model for three levels of nesting, and we have described the data structure needed for estimation. We now turn to the application of these models to evaluate several research hypotheses about the development of trust and integrity over time using real empirical data drawn from a longitudinal study of military cadets.

EMPIRICAL EXAMPLE: THE LONGITUDINAL DEVELOPMENT OF TRUST IN MILITARY CADETS

The core constructs of trust, influence, and leadership have long been a critically important focus of past and ongoing military research. Despite the wealth of knowledge that has been gathered, little is known about how trust and influence codevelop over time (e.g., Sweeney, 2007; Sweeney, Dirks,

j	i	t	y_{tij}	z_{tij}	w_{ij}
1	1	1	y_{111}	z_{111}	w_{11}
1	1	2	y_{211}	z_{211}	w_{11}
1	1	3	y_{311}	z_{311}	w_{11}
1	1	4	y_{411}	z_{411}	w_{11}
1	2	1	y_{121}	z_{121}	w_{21}
1	2	2	y_{221}	z_{221}	w_{21}
1	2	3	y_{321}	z_{321}	w_{21}
1	2	4	y_{421}	z_{421}	w_{21}
2	3	1	y_{132}	z_{132}	w_{32}
2	3	2	y_{232}	z_{232}	w_{32}
2	3	3	y_{332}	z_{332}	w_{32}
2	3	4	y_{432}	z_{432}	w_{32}
2	4	1	y_{142}	z_{142}	w_{42}
2	4	2	y_{242}	z_{242}	w_{42}
2	4	3	y_{342}	z_{342}	w_{42}
2	4	4	y_{442}	z_{442}	w_{42}

j	i	t	dv_{tij}	w_{ij}	δ_y	δ_z
1	1	1	y_{111}	w_{11}	1	0
1	1	1	z_{111}	w_{11}	0	1
1	1	2	y_{211}	w_{11}	1	0
1	1	2	z_{211}	w_{11}	0	1
1	1	3	y_{311}	w_{11}	1	0
1	1	3	z_{311}	w_{11}	0	1
1	1	4	y_{411}	w_{11}	1	0
1	1	4	z_{411}	w_{11}	0	1
1	2	1	y_{121}	w_{21}	1	0
1	2	1	z_{121}	w_{21}	0	1
1	2	2	y_{221}	w_{21}	1	0
1	2	2	z_{221}	w_{21}	0	1
1	2	3	y_{321}	w_{21}	1	0
1	2	3	z_{321}	w_{21}	0	1
1	2	4	y_{421}	w_{21}	1	0
1	2	4	z_{421}	w_{21}	0	1
2	3	1	y_{132}	w_{32}	1	0
2	3	1	z_{132}	w_{32}	0	1
2	3	2	y_{232}	w_{32}	1	0
2	3	2	z_{232}	w_{32}	0	1
2	3	3	y_{332}	w_{32}	1	0
2	3	3	z_{332}	w_{32}	0	1
2	3	4	y_{432}	w_{32}	1	0
2	3	4	z_{432}	w_{32}	0	1
2	4	1	y_{142}	w_{42}	1	0
2	4	1	y_{142}	w_{42}	0	1
2	4	2	y_{242}	w_{42}	1	0
2	4	2	y_{242}	w_{42}	0	1
2	4	3	y_{342}	w_{42}	1	0
2	4	3	y_{342}	w_{42}	0	1
2	4	4	y_{442}	w_{42}	1	0
2	4	4	z_{442}	w_{42}	0	1

FIGURE 17.2. Standard data structure for a four-time-point three-level univariate growth model with one time-varying covariate (left panel) and the modified data structure for a four-time-point three-level bivariate growth model (right panel).

[4]Examples of how to reorder univariate data to a multivariate structure are available from Patrick J. Curran or from http://www.unc.edu/~curran

Curran, & Lester, 2010; Sweeney, Thompson, & Blanton, 2009). Gaining a better understanding of the etiological process that underlies the development of the determinants of trust and how trust subsequently affects influence is critical both from a theoretical and practical standpoint. Theoretically, a more rigorous study of these etiological processes would provide a greater and more nuanced understanding of the underlying developmental model; practically, understanding how leadership, trust, and influence develop, are maintained, and are potentially lost can directly inform how these important characteristics might be fostered and supported, particularly in a military training environment such as the USMA.

We focus on three specific dimensions that are related to trust and influence (Mayer & Davis, 1999): *trustworthiness*, *integrity*, and *benevolence*. All three constructs were assessed as each cadet's perception of their fellow squad members; there were 542 individual cadets, each nested within one of 131 squads. *Trustworthiness* represents the confidence or faithfulness a cadet holds in their fellow squad members; *integrity* represents the cadet's perception that fellow squad members adhere to ethical or moral principles; and *benevolence* represents the cadet's perception that fellow squad members care about the cadet's well-being. Our ultimate interest is in how these characteristics relate to influence (e.g., the ability of one individual to affect the behavior of another), but here we will specifically examine how trustworthiness and integrity codevelop over time and how initial levels of benevolence impact this developmental process.

Design

Data were obtained from 542 male and female cadets who attended the USMA at West Point. Cadets were assessed between one and four times throughout a single academic year (144 cadets were assessed once, 124 twice, 131 three times, and 136 four times) resulting in a total of 1,329 Person × Time observations. Although there was some subject attrition over time, these rates were modest and were addressed in the estimation of the multilevel models under the assumption that the data were missing at random (e.g., Allison, 2002). Although the structure of these data constitutes five levels of hierarchical nesting (repeated assessments nested within cadets; cadets nested within squads; squads nested within platoons; and platoons nested within companies) for purposes of demonstration, we focus here on the first three levels of nesting: time, cadet, and squad. More specifically, the 542 cadets were nested in 131 squads, which were nested in 39 platoons, which were nested in 10 companies. The mean number of cadets per squad was 4.08 with a range of 1 to 22. Although we are ignoring the nesting of squads in platoon, and platoons in company, preliminary analysis indicated that these fourth and fifth levels of nesting introduced only trivial dependence into the data (e.g., all intraclass correlations were less than .01).

Measures

We drew three measures from a much larger assessment battery given to each cadet at each time-point. We are interested in the cadets' report of *trust*, *integrity*, and *benevolence* of all of the other cadets that belong to their own squad[5] using items drawn from Mayer and Davis (1999). All three measures were assessed at all four time points; we considered the four repeated measures of trust and integrity and the initial assessment of benevolence that we used as a TIC. Further analysis might consider also growth in benevolence (e.g., a multivariate growth model with three outcomes), although we do not pursue these models here.

Trust was computed as the mean of four items, and integrity and benevolence as the mean of three items. All items were rated on a 7-point ordinal scale ranging from 1 (*strongly disagree*) to 7 (*strongly agree*). Reliability coefficients ranged from .89 to .92 across the four time-points for trust, from .89 to .93 for integrity, and was equal to .88 for the initial assessment of benevolence. Sample items for trust include "I feel secure in having my members of squad make decisions that critically affect me as a cadet" and "I would be willing to rely on my members of squad in a critical situation, such as combat." Sample items for integrity include "I like my members of

---

[5]That is, cadets reported on all of their fellow squad members as a group and not on each squad member individually.

squads' values" and "Sound principles seem to guide my members of squads' behavior." Finally, sample items for benevolence include "My members of squad are very concerned about my welfare" and "My members of squad will go out of their way to help me."

Summary Statistics

The mean reported levels of trust and integrity were both high at the first time-point and were generally increasing over time. On a scale ranging from one to seven, the sample means and standard deviations (*SD*) are as follows: for trust, Time 1 = 5.14 (*SD* = 1.22), Time 2 = 5.25 (*SD* = 1.13), Time 3 = 5.33 (*SD* = 1.14), and Time 4 = 5.54 (*SD* = 1.12); for integrity, Time 1 = 5.65 (*SD* = 0.87), Time 2 = 5.68 (*SD* = 0.88), Time 3 = 5.67 (*SD* = 0.98), and Time 4 = 5.85 (*SD* = 0.83); and for benevolence, at Time 1 = 5.40 (*SD* = 1.02). The within- and across-construct correlations between trust and integrity over time showed a general autoregressive pattern in which there were stronger correlations among observations taken closer in time compared with observations taken further apart in time. For example, the correlation between trust at Time 1 and trust at Time 2 was .51, at Times 1 and 3 was .46, and at Times 1 and 4 was .33. Trust and integrity also showed strong correlations both within and across time. For example, the correlation between trust at time 1 and integrity at Time 1 was .61, at Time 2 was .70, at Time 3 was .75, and at Time 4 was .76. Finally, the correlation between trust at Time 1 and integrity at Time 2 was .61, at Time 1 and Time 3 was .35, and at Time 1 and Time 4 was .31.

Results

We followed an analytic strategy that might be commonly used in practice: We estimated a total of four multilevel models: two univariate unconditional three-level growth models of trust and integrity independently, one unconditional three-level bivariate growth model of trust and integrity jointly, and one conditional three-level bivariate growth model of trust and integrity with benevolence as a TIC. We present each of these models in turn.

Univariate three-level growth model: Trust. We began by fitting a series of alternative functional

forms to the repeated measures of trust (e.g., intercept only, linear, quadratic), and standard likelihood ratio tests (LRTs) indicated that a linear trajectory was optimal. Furthermore, additional LRTs indicated that the optimal structure for the random effects was defined by homoskedastic residuals at Level 1, a random intercept and random slope at Level 2, and a random intercept at Level 3. This covariance structure allowed for variability among the repeated measures within each cadet (Level 1), variability in starting point and rate of change in trust across cadets within squad (Level 2), and variability in starting point across squads (Level 3). The grand mean intercept was 5.16 and mean slope was .11, and both were significantly different from zero (*p* < .001). This result indicated that there was a rather high initial level of cadet trust in their fellow squad members (5.16 on a 1-to-7 scale) and that trust increased linearly over the four time-points. Furthermore, there were significant variance components at all three levels of analysis, indicating potentially meaningful variability in time-specific levels of trust around each cadet's trajectory, cadet-specific trajectories around squad-specific mean trajectories, and squad-specific intercepts around the grand intercept. There was also a significant negative covariance between the intercept and slope, indicating that higher initial levels of trust were associated with less steep increases over time. All point estimates and standard errors for these random effects are presented in Table 17.1.

Univariate three-level growth model: Integrity. We followed the same model building strategy for the four repeated measures of integrity as we used for trust. The final model for integrity was defined and evaluated using the same structure as we used for trust. The optimal fitting model was defined by a linear trajectory with homoskedastic errors at Level 1, a random intercept and random slope at Level 2, and just a random intercept at Level 3. The mean intercept was 5.65 (*p* < .0001), and mean slope was .04 (*p* = .028) indicating that, as we saw with the trust outcome, there was a rather high initial level of perceived integrity among fellow squad members (5.65 on a 1-to-7 scale) and that integrity increased linearly over the four time points. Furthermore,

TABLE 17.1

Estimates, Standard Errors, and z Ratios for All Random Effects From the Three-Level Univariate Growth Model of Perceived Trust

Covariance parameter	Estimate	SE	z ratio	p value
Level 1 residual ($\hat{\sigma}^2$)	0.526	0.034	15.44	< .001
Level 2 intercept ($\hat{\tau}_{\pi_{00}}$)	0.870	0.103	8.47	< .001
Level 2 intercept-slope covariance ($\hat{\tau}_{\pi_{01}}$) / correlation	−0.151 / −.54	0.038	−4.00	< .001
Level 2 slope ($\hat{\tau}_{\pi_{11}}$)	0.089	0.019	4.59	< .001
Level 3 intercept ($\hat{\tau}_{\beta_{00}}$)	0.078	0.042	1.86	.031

TABLE 17.2

Estimates, Standard Errors, and z Ratios for All Random Effects From the Three-Level Univariate Growth Model of Perceived Integrity

Covariance parameter	Estimate	SE	z ratio	p value
Level 1 residual ($\hat{\sigma}^2$)	0.397	0.026	15.43	< .001
Level 2 intercept ($\hat{\tau}_{\pi_{00}}$)	0.393	0.059	6.61	< .001
Level 2 intercept-slope covariance ($\hat{\tau}_{\pi_{01}}$)/correlation	−0.292/−.30	0.021	−1.42	.16
Level 2 slope ($\hat{\tau}_{\pi_{11}}$)	0.025	0.011	2.19	.014
Level 3 intercept ($\hat{\tau}_{\beta_{00}}$)	0.037	0.026	1.46	.072

the Level-1 residual variance significantly differed from zero, as did the Level-2 random intercept and slope; however, the covariance between the intercept and slope was not significantly different from zero. Finally, the Level-3 random intercept was marginally significant (p = .072). The point estimates and standard errors for these random effects are presented in Table 17.2.

Bivariate three-level growth model: Trust and integrity. There were significant fixed effects defining a linear trajectory for both trust and integrity, and there were significant (and one marginally significant) random effects at all three levels of analysis. Each of the univariate models was estimated in isolation, however, and we do not yet know how trust and integrity are related over time. One option would be to use one measure as the outcome and

one as the TVC. Not only would the choice of which measure would be the outcome and which the TVC be arbitrary (because we are equally interested in both), but the standard TVC model would be inappropriate given the systematic growth in both constructs (e.g., Curran & Bauer, 2011).[6] We will thus use the multivariate techniques defined earlier to estimate a single bivariate model linking trust and integrity at the level of the trajectories while accounting for the nesting of cadet within squad (i.e., Equation 30).

The bivariate model was estimated consistent with Equation 30. Linear trajectories were estimated for both trust and integrity. Homoskedastic errors were estimated for both constructs at Level 1, and these residuals were allowed to covary within time and across construct (e.g., the residuals for trust and integrity covaried within Times 1, 2, 3, and 4, but

---

[6]It may seem equally arbitrary for us to then include the initial assessment of benevolence as a TIC and not consider systematic growth in this construct as well. However, our initial theoretical question relates to the initial status of benevolence on trajectories of trust and integrity, and this model would be logically extended to include the estimation of growth in all three constructs simultaneously in subsequent analysis.

TABLE 17.3

Fixed-Effects Estimates for Three-Level Bivariate Growth Model of Trust and Integrity With Benevolence as a Level-2 Time-Invariant Covariate

Coefficient	Estimate	SE	z ratio	p value
Trust intercept	5.124	0.041	126.09	< .001
Trust slope	0.096	0.026	3.69	.0002
Integrity intercept	5.660	0.037	151.42	< .001
Integrity slope	0.026	0.021	1.28	.199
Benevolence → trust intercept	0.894	0.039	22.88	< .001
Benevolence → trust slope	−0.195	0.025	−7.81	< .001
Benevolence → integrity intercept	0.523	0.036	14.66	< .001
Benevolence → integrity slope	−0.090	0.020	−4.56	< .001

Note. The first four rows represent the conditional means of the intercept and slope for trust and integrity, respectively; the second four rows represent the regression of the intercept and slope of trust and integrity on the Level-2 measure of benevolence.

they did not covary across time). Random intercepts and slopes were estimated at Level 2, and these were allowed to covary across construct (e.g., the intercepts and slopes for both trust and integrity freely covaried with one another). Finally, random intercepts were estimated at Level 3, and these two effects were allowed to covary across construct.

As expected, fixed effects and within-construct random effects estimates were similar to those obtained through the previous univariate growth models, and we do not report these again here. However, of primary interest in this model were the cross-construct correlations among the random effects. For cadets nested within squads (i.e., Level 2), the initial level of trust was significantly and positively correlated with the initial level of integrity ($r = .74, p < .001$); thus cadets reporting higher initial values on one construct tended to report higher initial values on the other. The slope of trust was significantly and positively correlated with the slope of integrity ($r = .78; p < .001$). This suggests that steeper increases in one construct were associated with steeper increases in the other construct, indicating that trust and integrity codevelop over time. Interestingly, there were nonsignificant covariances between the initial value of trust and change in

integrity and between the initial value of integrity and change in trust. This indicates that the starting point on one construct did not inform the subsequent rate of change in the other construct. Finally, the covariance between the initial status of trust and the initial status of integrity was nonsignificant at the level of the squad (i.e., Level 3), indicating that squad-specific means of the initial values of trust and integrity were not systematically related.

Bivariate three-level growth model: Benevolence as a TIC. Given that both trust and integrity show significant cadet-to-cadet variability in initial status and rate of change, we next introduced benevolence as a Level-2 TIC to help explain this variability.[7] As we described, the substantive question is whether initial levels of perceived benevolence predict later changes in both trust and integrity. Table 17.3 presents the fixed effects from this conditional three-level bivariate growth model. Benevolence was significantly and positively predictive of initial levels of both trust and integrity. This finding indicates that higher values of perceived benevolence at the initial time period were systematically related to higher values of both perceived trust and integrity. Interestingly, benevolence was significantly and

[7]The unconditional models were both based on a sample of $N = 542$ cadets. However, only $n = 344$ cadets reported on benevolence at the initial time period. The conditional model is thus based on the subsample of $n = 344$. To examine the potential impact of this reduction in sample size, we reestimated the conditional model using multiple imputation methods with 10 imputed data sets so that all 542 cadets were retained. The results for the pooled imputed analysis were nearly identical to that of the restricted sample.

negatively predictive of changes in both trust and integrity over time. This indicates that higher values of perceived benevolence at the initial time period were systematically related to less steep increases in both trust and integrity over time. Although this may initially seem like a paradoxical finding because of the negative relation, we must graphically probe this cross-level interaction to better understand the nature of this relation.

Following the strategies described in Curran, Bauer, and Willoughby (2006) and Preacher, Curran, and Bauer (2006), we probed the interaction between benevolence and change over time in trust and integrity and calculated the model-implied trajectories at plus and minus one standard deviation around the mean; these results are presented in Figures 17.3 and 17.4. Figure 17.3 shows that trust is significantly increasing over time, but only for those cadets who reported lower levels of initial benevolence; for those reporting higher benevolence, trust remains stably high (or slightly decreasing) across all four time-points. Figure 17.4 reports a similar pattern for integrity such that lower values of initial benevolence are associated with steeper increases in integrity over time. However, the magnitude of the relation between benevolence and change in integrity is smaller than is the relation between benevolence and change in trust. Further research is needed to better understand the nature of these rather complex relations.

Summary. Pooling over our set of results, we can draw several initial conclusions about the relations between cadet ratings of trust, integrity, and benevolence both within and across time. First, both trust and integrity were characterized by positive linear trajectories spanning the academic year at West Point. Second, there was significant variability in both the intercepts and the slopes of these trajectories among cadets nested within squad. This suggests that, within squads, some cadets are reporting higher versus lower initial levels of trust and integrity, and some are reporting steeper versus less steep changes over time. Third, the initial levels of both trust and integrity vary across squad as well. This finding indicates that the mean squad-level initial reports of each of these constructs varies from squad to squad. Thus some squads are characterized by higher overall initial levels of trust and integrity, whereas some squads are not.

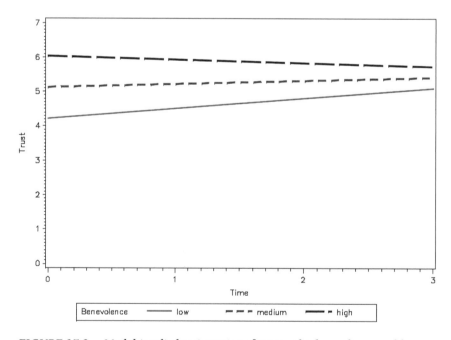

FIGURE 17.3.   Model-implied trajectories of trust at high, medium, and low levels of perceived benevolence.

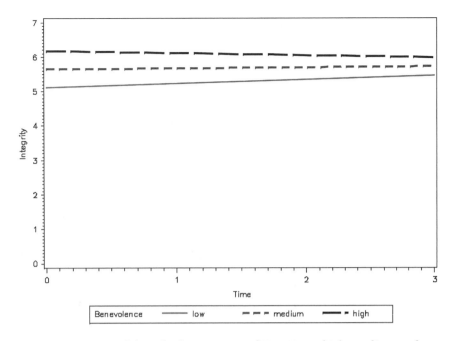

FIGURE 17.4. Model-implied trajectories of integrity at high, medium, and low levels of perceived benevolence.

Importantly, the bivariate model indicated that the trajectories of trust and integrity are systematically related to one another within and across time. In fact, the results showed strong correlations between both the initial levels and the rates of change over time between trust and integrity. This pattern of findings suggests that these two constructs codevelop across the span of the academic year. These across-construct relations could only be identified in the bivariate model in which change in each construct is estimated simultaneously. Interestingly, however, the initial level on one construct was not systematically related to the rate of change on the other. Finally, we considered benevolence as a Level-2 TIC and these results indicated significant relations between initial levels and rates of change for both trust and integrity. Probing of the cross-level interactions indicated that trust and integrity increased significantly more steeply for cadets who reported lower initial levels of perceived benevolence; for cadets reporting higher initial levels of benevolence, both trust and integrity remained high and stable, if not showing some slight decrease over time.

Again, we did not intend these analyses to be a rigorous test of our underlying theoretical model about the development of trust over time and the impact of this developmental process on later influence. Instead, we examined a specific subquestion relating to the unfolding of trust and integrity over time and the impact of initial benevolence on this process primarily to highlight the potential advantages and disadvantages of our proposed model. Ongoing work in our group is examining the broader theoretical questions of interest as well as potential further extensions of this modeling framework.

CONCLUSION

Our motivating substantive questions focused on the development of trust in cadets attending the USMA at West Point, and this analysis involved three levels of nesting: repeated measure nested within cadet, and cadet nested within squad. The multilevel growth-modeling framework was thus an ideal analytic method for testing our proposed hypotheses. Although prior work has proposed a multivariate–multilevel growth model for two levels of nesting, we are unaware of any prior attempts to extend this model to account for three levels of nesting. Explicating and demonstrating this three-level multivariate growth model has been our goal.

Although the equations necessary to define the multivariate three-level growth model are many, the underlying conceptual framework is both straightforward and elegant. Our goals were (a) to design a model to examine individual variability in trajectories of trust and integrity within each cadet, (b) to determine how these trajectories varied both within and between squads, (c) to estimate the degree of correspondence between the two trajectories over time, and (d) to test the extent to which benevolence influenced the parameters that defined the developmental trajectory within each cadet. Although a standard multilevel TVC model could be estimated to examine trust as the outcome and integrity as the TVC (or vice versa), whatever measure was defined as the TVC is assumed to not systematically vary with the passage of time. Yet there was clear evidence that both measures were increasing systematically over time, and thus arbitrarily treating one as the TVC would result in a misspecified model that did not evaluate the specific research hypotheses at hand.

More important, only the multivariate growth model allowed for the simultaneous estimation of growth in both trust and integrity, which in turn provides an explicit estimate of the covariance structure among the set of parameters that defines each of the trajectories. This analytic approach means that we can obtain estimates of the degree to which the initial levels of trust are related to changes in integrity, or the initial levels of integrity are related to changes in trust, or even the degree to which changes in trust are related to changes in integrity. The relation between changes in trust and changes in integrity was of primary substantive interest, and the multivariate growth model provides a means with which to directly and rigorously test our hypotheses.

The models we describe here could be extended in a number of interesting ways. We considered measures that were continuously and normally distributed, but these models can be estimated with such discrete outcomes as binary, ordinal, or count outcomes. We only considered simultaneous growth in two constructs, but this model could be extended to include three or even more outcomes (as was done by MacCallum et al., 1997, in the two-level framework). Although we used linear functions for both of our outcomes, these functional forms need not be the same; the functions can be mixes of linear, piecewise linear, or curvilinear trajectories over time. Finally, we only considered a single Level-2 time-invariant predictor; it is straightforward to include one or more predictors at any of the three levels of analysis as well as the inclusion of interactions within or across levels. Taken together, this approach offers a variety of significant strengths.

Despite these many strengths, there are of course associated limitations. First, although partially missing data can be included for each of the outcome measures, complete case data are required for the exogenous covariates (although multiple imputation methods can be used to circumvent this problem). Second, as with the traditional fixed effects regression model, all measured variables are assumed to be error free; any measurement error that exists attenuates the estimated regression coefficients relative to their population values. Third, the examination of the two outcome measures at the level of the trajectories is strictly a between-person comparison. In other words, the model-implied relations between trust and integrity are evaluated at the level of the cadet-specific trajectories. Additional analytic work would be needed to simultaneously obtain both between-person (i.e., at the level of the trajectory) and within-person (i.e., at the level of specific time assessments) components of the relation between the two outcomes (for further discussion, see Curran & Bauer, 2011; Curran et al., in press).

We have drawn on existing developments within the two-level multivariate–multilevel model and the three-level univariate–multilevel model to describe a general three-level growth model for two or more correlated outcomes. Because this model is embedded within the standard multilevel analytic framework, we can draw on all the strengths of this modeling tradition to provide a powerful and flexible method for testing a broad range of proposed hypotheses within the behavioral sciences. We have found these techniques to be highly applicable in our own work, and we hope that our discussion might be of some use to you in your own.

References

Allison, P. (2002). *Missing data* (Sage University Papers Series: Quantitative Applications in the Social Sciences, No. 07-136). Thousand Oaks, CA: Sage.

Bauer, D. J. (2003). Estimating multilevel linear models as structural equation models. *Journal of Educational and Behavioral Statistics, 28*, 135–167. doi:10.3102/10769986028002135

Biesanz, J. C., Deeb-Sossa, N., Papadakis, A., Bollen, K., & Curran, P. (2004). The role of coding time in estimating and interpreting growth curve models. *Psychological Methods, 9*, 30–52. doi:10.1037/1082-989X.9.1.30

Bolger, N., Davis, A., & Rafaeli, E. (2003). Diary methods: Capturing life as it is lived. *Annual Review of Psychology, 54*, 579–616. doi:10.1146/annurev.psych.54.101601.145030

Bollen, K. A., & Curran, P. J. (2006). *Latent curve models: A structural equation approach.* Hoboken, NJ: Wiley.

Bryk, A. S., & Raudenbush, S. W. (1987). Application of hierarchical linear models to assessing change. *Psychological Bulletin, 101*, 147–158. doi:10.1037/0033-2909.101.1.147

Curran, P. J. (2003). Have multilevel models been structural equation models all along? *Multivariate Behavioral Research, 38*, 529–569. doi:10.1207/s15327906mbr3804_5

Curran, P. J., & Bauer, D. J. (2011). The disaggregation of within-person and between-person effects in longitudinal models of change. *Annual Review of Psychology, 62*, 583–619.

Curran, P. J., Bauer, D. J., & Willoughby, M. T. (2006). Testing and probing interactions in hierarchical linear growth models. In C. S. Bergeman & S. M. Boker (Eds.), *The Notre Dame Series on Quantitative Methodology: Vol. 1. Methodological issues in aging research* (pp. 99–129). Mahwah, NJ: Erlbaum.

Curran, P. J., Lee, T.-H., MacCallum, R., & Lane, S. (in press). Disaggregating within-person and between-person effects in multilevel and structural equation growth models. In G. R. Hancock & J. R. Harring (Eds.), *Advances in longitudinal methods in the social and behavioral sciences.* Charlotte, NC: Information Age.

Curran, P. J., Muthén, B. O., & Harford, T. C. (1998). The influence of changes in marital status on developmental trajectories of alcohol use in young adults. *Journal of Studies on Alcohol, 59*, 647–658.

Curran, P. J., Stice, E., & Chassin, L. (1997). The relation between adolescent and peer alcohol use: A longitudinal random coefficients model. *Journal of Consulting and Clinical Psychology, 65*, 130–140. doi:10.1037/0022-006X.65.1.130

Goldstein, H. (1995). *Multilevel statistical models* (2nd ed.). New York, NY: Halsted.

Goldstein, H., Rasbash, J., Yang, M., Woodhouse, G., Pan, H., Nuttall, D., & Thomas, S. (1993). A multilevel analysis of school examination results. *Oxford Review of Education, 19*, 425–433. doi:10.1080/0305498930190401

MacCallum, R., Kim, C., Malarkey, W., & Kiecolt-Glaser, J. (1997). Studying multivariate change using multilevel models and latent curve models. *Multivariate Behavioral Research, 32*, 215–253. doi:10.1207/s15327906mbr3203_1

Mayer, R., & Davis, J. (1999). The effect of the performance appraisal system on trust for management: A field quasi-experiment. *Journal of Applied Psychology, 84*, 123–136. doi:10.1037/0021-9010.84.1.123

McArdle, J. J. (1988). Dynamic but structural equation modeling of repeated measures data. In J. R. Nesselroade & R. B. Cattell (Eds.), *Handbook of multivariate experimental psychology* (2nd ed., pp. 561–614). New York, NY: Plenum Press.

McArdle, J. J. (1989). Structural modeling experiments using multiple growth functions. In P. Ackerman, R. Kanfer, & R. Cudeck (Eds.), *Learning and individual differences: Abilities, motivation, and methodology* (pp. 71–117). Hillsdale, NJ: Erlbaum.

Mehta, P. D., & Neale, M. C. (2005). People are variables too: Multilevel structural equations modeling. *Psychological Methods, 10*, 259–284. doi:10.1037/1082-989X.10.3.259

Meredith, W., & Tisak, J. (1990). Latent curve analysis. *Psychometrika, 55*, 107–122. doi:10.1007/BF02294746

Newsom, J. (2002). A multilevel structural equation model for dyadic data. *Structural Equation Modeling, 9*, 431–447. doi:10.1207/S15328007SEM0903_7

Preacher, K. J., Curran, P. J., & Bauer, D. J. (2006). Computational tools for probing interactions in multiple linear regression, multilevel modeling, and latent curve analysis. *Journal of Educational and Behavioral Statistics, 31*, 437–448. doi:10.3102/10769986031004437

Raudenbush, S. W. (2001). Comparing personal trajectories and drawing causal inferences from longitudinal data. *Annual Review of Psychology, 52*, 501–525. doi:10.1146/annurev.psych.52.1.501

Raudenbush, S. W., & Bryk, A. S. (2002). *Hierarchical linear models: Applications and data analysis methods* (2nd ed.). Newbury Park, CA: Sage.

Singer, J., & Willett, J. (2003). *Applied longitudinal data analysis: Modeling change and event occurrence.* New York, NY: Oxford University Press.

Sweeney, P. J. (2007). Trust: The key to combat leadership. In D. Crandall (Ed.), *Leadership lessons from West Point* (pp. 252–277). San Francisco: Jossey-Bass.

Sweeney, P. J., Dirks, K. T., Curran, P. J., & Lester, P. B. (2010, January). *The trajectory of trust: How does trust develop and why?* Paper presented at the 5th EIASM Workshop on Trust Within and Between Organizations, Madrid, Spain.

Sweeney, P. J., Thompson, V. D., & Blanton, H. (2009). Trust and influence in combat: An interdependence model. *Journal of Applied Social Psychology, 39,* 235–264. doi:10.1111/j.1559-1816.2008.00437.x

Willett, J., & Sayer, A. (1994). Using covariance structure analysis to detect correlates and predictors of individual change over time. *Psychological Bulletin, 116,* 363–381. doi:10.1037/0033-2909.116.2.363

Multivariate Methods

## CHAPTER 18

EXPLORATORY FACTOR ANALYSIS AND CONFIRMATORY FACTOR ANALYSIS

Keith F. Widaman

Common factor analysis is arguably the most popular and useful method for identifying underlying dimensions that can account mathematically for behavior in a given domain. Spearman (1904, 1927) proposed novel calculations, applied first to test scores in the ability domain, that became known as *factor analysis*, and he used results of his analyses to argue for the existence of *g*, or general intelligence, the single ability dimension common to all tests of mental ability. Later, Thurstone (1931, 1935, 1938, 1947) generalized the common factor model to include multiple factors. After developing mathematical extensions of the model, Thurstone and his colleagues (e.g., Thurstone, 1938; Thurstone & Thurstone, 1941) identified and replicated seven or more dimensions of mental ability that became known as primary mental abilities. The most commonly accepted, current structure of the mental ability domain is often referred to as the Cattell–Horn–Carroll (or CHC) model, based on work by Cattell (1963, 1971), Horn (e.g., Horn & Hofer, 1992; Horn & Noll, 1997), and Carroll (1993). In the CHC model, three strata of factors are posited. At the lowest stratum, perhaps 30 or so primary abilities, such as verbal comprehension and numerical facility, can be identified. At the second stratum, eight or nine dimensions have been replicated, including factors for fluid intelligence (Gf), crystallized intelligence (Gc), and general speediness (Gs). At the third stratum, a single dimension has been posited—identified as general

intelligence, or *g*—although some dispute whether this dimension can be justified theoretically (e.g., Horn & McArdle, 2007; Horn & Noll, 1997).

Factor analysis has also been applied to behavioral phenomena in many other domains. One notable domain is that of personality. The most widely accepted taxonomy of dimensions in the personality domain is known as the Big Five (or the five-factor model), with dimensions of Extraversion, Agreeableness, Conscientiousness, Neuroticism, and Openness. Although one can trace the origins of the Big Five personality constructs to studies from the mid-1940s or even earlier (see Fiske, 1949; Thurstone, 1934), a consistent stream of research studies from the late 1950s to the present has offered convincing evidence that the Big Five dimensions can be recovered in data from many sources (e.g., self-reports, observer reports, reports by family members or friends) across an impressive number of cultures (Goldberg, 1993).

Factor analysis has been of central importance in evaluating empirical evidence, adjudicating conflicting conjectures, and developing usable dimensional taxonomies for mental abilities and personality as well as in many other domains. Thus, factor analysis is of foundational importance to many aspects of the research process. The goal of this chapter is to provide a general introduction to both exploratory factor analysis (EFA) and confirmatory factor analysis (CFA), noting the similarities and differences

This research was supported by National Institute of Child Health and Human Development Grants HD047573 and HD051746 (Rand D. Conger, Principal Investigator), National Institute of Mental Health Grant MH051361 (Rand D. Conger, Principal Investigator), and National Institute on Drug Abuse and National Institute on Alcohol Abuse and Alcoholism Grant DA017902 (Rand D. Conger, Richard W. Robins, and Keith F. Widaman, Joint Principal Investigators).

DOI: 10.1037/13621-018
APA Handbook of Research Methods in Psychology: Vol. 3. Data Analysis and Research Publication, H. Cooper (Editor-in-Chief)

between the methods. In addition to providing an introduction to the factor analysis model and various options for conducting analyses, several empirical applications will illustrate the use of factor analysis.

EXPLORATORY FACTOR ANALYSIS

EFA is a method for locating and characterizing the dimensions of individual difference in a domain of behavior or content without imposing an a priori structure on the dimensions. Indeed, Thurstone (1947) argued that factor analysis was of greatest use in initial explorations of a domain because a successful analysis would allow one to isolate the major dimensions of individual difference within the domain. Once the primary dimensions have been identified and replicated, later research can be designed to investigate the basis of individual differences on these dimensions.

Theoretical Orientation

The impetus for developing common factor analysis is a theoretical orientation that deserves mention. Beginning with Spearman (1904) and extended by Thurstone (1947), researchers have argued that scientific goals are furthered most by understanding the varied phenomena in a domain in terms of a smaller number of dimensions that can account for the phenomena in an economical fashion. But, economy of representation was not the only driving force or even the principal driving force. Instead, the method of factor analysis was considered the optimal way to isolate the underlying behavioral processes that generate the myriad forms of behavior that reflect a particular domain of content.

Key Equations

The fundamental equation of EFA is a data model that specifies the relations of latent factors to the manifest variables (MVs) in an analysis. This model is a linear model that represents MVs $Y_j (j = 1, \ldots, p)$ as additive, linear functions of one or more underlying unobserved factors or latent variables (LVs) $S_k (k = 1, \ldots, r)$, or

$$Y_{ji} = \tau_j + \lambda_{j1} S_{1i} + \lambda_{j2} S_{2i} + \ldots + \lambda_{jr} S_{ri} + \lambda_{j_u} S_{j_u i}, \quad (1)$$

where Y_{ji} is the score of individual i ($i = 1, \ldots, N$) on MV j, τ_j is the intercept (or mean) of MV j, λ_{jk} is the loading of MV j on LV k, S_{ki} is the score of individual i on LV k, λ_{j_u} is the loading of MV j on the jth unique factor, and $S_{j_u i}$ is the score of individual i on the jth unique factor.

The EFA model thus embodies the mathematical representation of p MVs in terms of, or as linear functions of, r common factors (with $r < p$) and p unique factors. The r common factors are identified as common factors because they have effects on more than a single MV. Thus, these factors represent sources of individual difference that have influences in common across two or more MVs. The variance in MV j that is explained mathematically by the common factors is termed the communality of variable j, which is typically represented as h_j^2.

In contrast, each of the p unique factors has an effect on a single MV, and each of the p MVs has its own unique factor. The variance of the unique factor for MV j is often represented as u_j^2. The unique variance for variable j can be conceived as the sum of two sources of variance: (a) specific variance, s_j^2, which is reliable variance in MV j that is linearly unrelated to the common factors; and (b) error variance, e_j^2, which is random measurement error.

Given the preceding partitioning and assuming that variance of MV j is standardized to 1.0, the communality of MV j is h_j^2, unique variance is u_j^2, and $h_j^2 + u_j^2 = 1$. But, reliable variance of MV j, or r_{jj}, can be represented as $r_{jj} = h_j^2 + s_j^2$. Thus, communality of MV j is a lower bound estimate of its reliability. Also, the EFA model can be seen as a generalization of the classical test theory decomposition of a MV into true and error components, a generalization that contains more than one true (i.e., common factor) score and a specific factor.

Equation 1 can be expressed in matrix form as

$$\mathbf{Y} = \boldsymbol{\tau} + \boldsymbol{\Lambda}\mathbf{S} + \boldsymbol{\Lambda}_u \mathbf{S}_u, \quad (2)$$

where $\mathbf{Y}$ is a ($p \times 1$) random vector (i.e., for a random observation), $\boldsymbol{\tau}$ is a ($p \times 1$) vector of intercepts, $\boldsymbol{\Lambda}$ is a ($p \times r$) matrix of loadings of the p MVs on the r common factors, $\mathbf{S}$ is an ($r \times 1$) random vector of common factor scores, $\boldsymbol{\Lambda}_u$ is a ($p \times p$) diagonal matrix of loadings of the p MVs on the p unique factors, and $\mathbf{S}_u$ is a ($p \times 1$) random vector of unique factor scores. Assuming that both common factor scores and unique factor scores have expected values of zero, unique factors are uncorrelated with common factor scores, and unique factors are mutually uncorrelated, one can postmultiply each side of Equation 2 by its transpose and take expectations, resulting in

$$E(Y) = \tau, \text{ and} \tag{3}$$
$$E(YY') = \Sigma_{YY} = \Lambda\Psi\Lambda' + \Theta, \tag{4}$$

where the mean structure of the MVs is simply τ, as shown in Equation 3. Furthermore, the covariance structure of the MVs is shown in Equation 4, where Σ_{YY} is the $(p \times p)$ population covariance matrix among the MVs, Ψ is the $(r \times r)$ matrix of covariances among common factors (i.e., LVs), Θ is the $(p \times p)$ matrix, usually diagonal, of covariances among unique factors, and other symbols were defined in Equation 2.

Obtaining a sample of observations and computing the sample matrix of covariances among MVs, S, enables one to estimate parameters in Equation 4, as

$$S \approx \hat{\Lambda}\hat{\Psi}\hat{\Lambda}' + \hat{\Theta} = \hat{\Sigma}, \tag{5}$$

where carets above matrices indicate the presence of parameter estimates in these matrices, and all symbols were defined in Equation 4. Equation 5 implies that the sample covariance matrix is approximated by the r-dimensional common factor solution, which in turn yields an estimate of the population covariances among MVs under the assumption that the model holds in the population.

EFA models are typically fit to matrices of correlations among MVs, rather than matrices of covariances. If D_s is a diagonal matrix of standard deviations of the MVs, then pre- and postmultiplying Equation 4 by the inverse of D_s yields

$$D_s^{-1}\Sigma_{YY}D_s^{-1} = D_s^{-1}\left(\Lambda\Psi\Lambda' + \Theta\right)D_s^{-1}$$
$$= D_s^{-1}\left(\Lambda\Psi\Lambda'\right)D_s^{-1} + D_s^{-1}\Theta D_s^{-1}, \text{so}$$
$$P_{YY} = \Lambda^*\Psi\Lambda^{*\prime} + \Theta^*, \tag{6}$$

where P_{YY} is the population correlation matrix among MVs, $\Lambda^*\left(= D_s^{-1}\Lambda\right)$ is the correlation-metric matrix of loadings of MVs on common factors, and $\Theta^*\left(= D_s^{-1}\Theta D_s^{-1}\right)$ is the population correlation-metric matrix of unique variances; other symbols

were defined in Equation 4. Thus, in correlation metric, three matrices—the matrix of covariances among MVs, the factor loading matrix, and the unique factor covariance matrix—are simply rescaled versions of their counterparts in covariance metric, and the matrix of correlations (or covariances) among LVs is unchanged.

In a sample of observations, computing the sample matrix of correlations among MVs, R, leads to a representation that is analogous to Equation 5, specifically

$$R \approx \hat{\Lambda}^*\hat{\Psi}\hat{\Lambda}^{*\prime} + \hat{\Theta}^* = \hat{P}, \tag{7}$$

where carets above matrices indicate the presence of parameter estimates in these matrices, and all symbols were defined in Equation 6. Equation 7 states that the sample correlation matrix R is approximated by the r-dimensional common factor solution $\hat{\Lambda}^*\hat{\Psi}\hat{\Lambda}^{*\prime} + \hat{\Theta}^*$, which in turn yields an estimate of the population correlations among MVs, $\hat{P}$, under the assumption that the model holds in the population.

Steps in Exploratory Factor Analysis
Selection of observations. Selection of observations (i.e., the selection of persons into a sample) is an underemphasized aspect of the conduct of EFA studies. Selection of observations involves at least two tasks: (a) the selection mechanism, or how observations are selected from the population for inclusion in a study, and (b) the number of observations to be included in the analysis.

In factor analytic studies, treatments are typically not evaluated, so random assignment of persons to treatments is not a major issue. Instead, the selection of observations from a population is a far more important matter. Differing points of view have been offered regarding the selection of observations (i.e., persons). For example, Guilford (1964) argued that samples of participants should be as homogeneous as possible, so that the influence of selection variables would be minimized. In contrast, Gorsuch (1988) opined that a researcher should attempt to obtain samples of participants who varied as much as possible on the dimensions that one expected to find in a factor analysis. A middle-ground position may be stated in the following way: (a) Define clearly the population from which observations (e.g., participants) were selected, (b) note clearly whether observations were randomly and representatively sampled from the population or whether some form of nonrandom selection occurred (e.g., obtaining a sample of convenience that may be unrepresentative on key dimensions), and (c) describe whether any participants either declined to participate or failed to complete the entire set of tests and were excluded from analyses because this may lead to unrepresentativeness of the final sample.

The second aspect of selection of observations—determining the minimum number of observations to include in an analysis—has had a spotty history. In early factor analytic studies (e.g., Spearman, 1904), little or no attention was paid to the number of observations. Later, experts in factor analysis often recommended that researchers follow a particular rule—such as obtaining at least five times the number of observations as MVs to be analyzed or having a sample size of at least 200 observations. However, MacCallum and colleagues (MacCallum, Widaman, Preacher, & Hong, 2001; MacCallum, Widaman, Zhang, & Hong, 1999) showed that simple rules of thumb for the number of observations could not be justified if the intent of a study was to recover the population factor structure. Instead, recovery of population factors was a complex function of the communality of variables, the number of indicators per factor, and sample size. With MVs having high communality and many indicators per factor, population factor loadings were recovered very well with an $N{:}p$ (or participant:MV) ratio of only 2:1 or 3:1. In contrast, if MVs had low communalities and a small number of indicators per factor were used, $N{:}p$ ratios of 15:1 or 20:1 were often required. In truly exploratory studies, no hard-and-fast rules for the proper sample size given the number of MVs can be generally recommended. Instead, larger sample sizes are better, and replication of factor patterns across samples provides greater assurance that an accurate factor structure has been obtained.

Selection of variables. The selection of MVs to be included in an EFA is a topic of more common discussion than the selection of observations, but it is a topic that deserves still greater attention (cf. Little, Lindenberger, & Nesselroade, 1999). In his

pioneering investigations, Thurstone (e.g., 1938) attempted to assemble batteries of MVs that would span a domain of content. When studying mental abilities, this meant including in a battery tests of widely varying content, encompassing as many kinds of content and mental operation as could be obtained. Although Thurstone had ambitious goals, hindsight reveals that his initial, rather large batteries of tests failed to include indicators for many factors that have subsequently been replicated. Still, as a general rule, careful consideration of the domain of content to be represented in the factor analysis should lead to attempts to ensure that all facets of the domain are reflected in MVs.

Common factor analysis was developed to analyze continuous MV scores as functions of continuous LV scores; test scores, which are sums of multiple item scores, often conform well to this approach. But, for more than 75 years, researchers have factor analyzed item scores, and several key issues arise in the context of item factor analysis. One issue is domain coverage. Factor analyzing an existing instrument can help a researcher revise a scale, including discarding items that appear not to reflect the major factors in the instrument or reformulating the dimensional structure of the instrument (see Floyd & Widaman, 1995). In such applications, an investigator may not be able to select the variables analyzed, as this selection is mandated by the aim of the research to evaluate the factor structure of an existing instrument. Experience with an existing scale, however, may lead a researcher to conclude that important aspects of the behavioral domain have, inadvertently or deliberately, been excluded from the existing instrument. In such cases, researchers can supplement an existing instrument with additional pertinent items to see whether this will result in a more adequate, theoretically compelling representation.

Other issues in item factor analysis are more mathematical or statistical, stemming from the fact that item scores are often binary (0 = *fail*, 1 = *pass*) or ordered–categorical in nature (e.g., falling on a 1–5 *agree–disagree* Likert scale). Artifactual *difficulty* factors can occur when analyzing binary data, a fact that has long been known (Ferguson, 1941; Guilford, 1941; Wherry & Gaylord, 1944). However, problems arising in analyses of Likert scale data have not been recognized in the substantive literature, in which standard factor analyses of item data have been conducted with impunity. More recently, many contributions have been made regarding proper ways to analyze binary and ordered–categorical variables (e.g., Bock, Gibbons, & Muraki, 1988; McDonald & Ahlawat, 1974; Millsap & Yun-Tein, 2004; B. O. Muthén, 1978, 1984; Wirth & Edwards, 2007). Details on these advanced methods are beyond the scope of this chapter, but researchers should be forewarned that standard factor analytic methods may yield biased results when applied to item-level data. For additional discussion, interested readers should consult the works cited as well as Volume 1, Chapters 32 and 35, this handbook.

Estimation. Estimation of parameters of the EFA model involves, principally, the estimation of loadings of MVs on the common factors (or LVs). This step in a factor analysis was often referred to as the extraction of factors. Referring to Equation 7, the estimation step involves the estimation of loadings in $\hat{\Lambda}^*$, typically under the restriction that the matrix of correlations among factors, $\hat{\Psi}$, is an identity matrix. In an identity matrix, all off-diagonal values are zero, so the extracted factors are orthogonal, which means they are mutually uncorrelated. The first factor explains the maximum amount of covariation among MVs, the second factor explains the maximum amount of remaining covariation among MVs while being orthogonal to the first factor, the third factor explains the maximum amount of remaining covariation among MVs while being orthogonal to the first two factors, and so on. After factors have been extracted and the number of factors has been determined, factors can be rotated, and the orthogonality constraint on factors can be relaxed. Rotation involves the transformation or spatial reorientation of the LVs so the mathematical description of the MVs is simplified.

For many years, noniterative methods of estimation were used, including, among others, centroid estimation and principal axes (PA) extraction (Harman, 1976; Thurstone, 1947). The PA method yields a least-squares fit of the factor model to the sample correlation matrix, so it is preferred over the centroid method, which is a hand-computational approximation to the PA solution. To extract the PA, one must estimate communality for each MV. Communality is the complement of unique variance (i.e., $h_j^2 = 1 - u_j^2$), so one can subtract a diagonal matrix of estimated uniquenesses from each side of Equation 7, giving $R - \hat{\Theta}^* \approx \hat{\Lambda}^* \hat{\Psi} \hat{\Lambda}^{*\prime}$. The matrix on the left of this equation, $R - \hat{\Theta}^*$, is called the *reduced correlation matrix* because the diagonal values of unity in R are reduced by estimates of unique variance. In effect, the matrix $R - \hat{\Theta}^*$ has communality estimates on its diagonal.

Several methods of communality estimation have been proposed. One of the most commonly used is the squared multiple correlation (SMC) of MV j with the remaining $(p - 1)$ MVs as predictors. Guttman (1956) proved that the SMC is a lower bound estimate of communality, and this theoretical property has been the primary basis for the use of the SMC as communality estimate. The highest correlation in the row (MAXR) was often used by Thurstone (e.g., 1947) as a communality estimate, however, and the MAXR appears often to provide a more accurate estimate of communality than does the SMC, which tends to have a negative bias. Widaman (1993) illustrated the negative bias in factor loadings and positive bias in factor correlations that result from use of SMCs that are underestimates of communality. The choice here, therefore, is between an estimator of communality (SMC) that has strong theoretical rationale, but is often negatively biased, versus an estimator (MAXR) that has a more informal rationale, but is often a more accurate estimator of communality; given this choice, I recommend the MAXR.

Once communalities have been estimated, factor loadings can be estimated from the reduced correlation matrix $R - \hat{\Theta}^*$. The PA solution is an eigenvector–eigenvalue decomposition or representation of $R - \hat{\Theta}^*$. An eigenvector is a unit-length vector that defines a directional vector in multidimensional space, and its associated eigenvalue represents variance on that dimension. Basically, $R - \hat{\Theta}^*$ is approximated by the eigensolution VD_lV', where V contains the first r eigenvectors of $R - \hat{\Theta}^*$, and D_l is a diagonal matrix containing the r largest eigenvalues. If we define $\hat{\Lambda}^* = VD_l^{1/2}$, then $R - \hat{\Theta}^* \approx \hat{\Lambda}^* \hat{\Lambda}^{*\prime}$. This method of extraction can be labeled *PA extraction of factors* using prior communality estimates. Once a set of factors has been estimated in this way, the investigator must decide on the number of factors. The PA solution obtained in this fashion yields a least squares fit to the correlation matrix conditional on the communality estimates employed. Different methods of communality estimation will result in different estimated factor loadings, although these differences typically are rather small.

With the advent of efficient computer algorithms over the past 3 decades or more, iterative methods of estimation have become more popular. Iterative methods employ a loss (or discrepancy) function. For example, the unweighted least-squares (ULS) discrepancy function is

$$F_{ULS} = \sum_{j} \sum_{k \leq j} \left(r_{jk} - \hat{\rho}_{jk} \right)^2, \qquad (8)$$

where r_{jk} is the observed correlation between MVs j and k, and $\hat{\rho}_{jk}$ is the reproduced correlation between MVs j and k. To use ULS estimation, one must first select a number of factors to retain, and ULS estimation then minimizes F_{ULS}, providing a least squares fit of an r-dimensional model to the data. Typically, researchers provide initial estimates of communality, such as SMC or MAXR estimates, but ULS simultaneously estimates parameters in the factor and unique variance matrices to minimize the discrepancy between observed and reproduced correlations among MVs. Indirectly, ULS iteratively estimates communality to obtain the closest fit, in the least squares sense, of an r-dimensional common factor solution to the observed correlations. Thus, ULS estimation provides a fit that is either comparable to or better than the fit of PA estimation using prior communality estimates because the latter method is conditional on the communality estimates employed. If the correlation matrix is well conditioned, and if a stringent iterative ULS stopping criterion is used, widely varying initial communality estimates—from unities to zero—have been found to converge to the same final solution (Widaman & Herringer, 1985).

Another commonly used iterative estimation method is the method of maximum likelihood (ML). Just as with ULS, ML estimation requires the selection of r, the number of common factors, to enable the estimation method to proceed. Under ML estimation, estimates of factor loadings and unique variances are obtained that maximize the likelihood of the observed data. ML estimation is based on the ML discrepancy function, which can be written as

$$F_{ML} = \ln|\mathbf{\Sigma}| - \ln|\mathbf{S}| + tr\left(\mathbf{S\Sigma}^{-1}\right) - p, \qquad (9)$$

where $\ln|\ |$ represents the natural log of the determinant of a matrix, the tr operator obtains the sum of the diagonal elements of a matrix, and all other symbols were defined in Equation 5. In an empirical application, the sample estimate of the population covariance matrix is substituted in Equation 9, yielding a sample ML discrepancy function of

$$\hat{F}_{ML} = \ln|\hat{\mathbf{\Sigma}}| - \ln|\mathbf{S}| + tr\left(\mathbf{S}\hat{\mathbf{\Sigma}}^{-1}\right) - p, \qquad (10)$$

where carets on symbols represent sample estimates of population values and symbols were defined in Equation 5.

If an ML solution in r factors reproduces the sample covariances (or correlations) among MVs well, $\hat{\mathbf{\Sigma}}$ will approximate S, and the ML discrepancy function will tend toward zero. The ML discrepancy function is bounded below by zero and will attain a value of zero only when $\hat{\mathbf{\Sigma}} = \mathbf{S}$. Thus, larger values of the ML discrepancy function indicate poorer fit of the factor model to the data. Jöreskog (1967) presented efficient algorithms for ML estimation of factor models, and ML estimation is widely available in EFA packages.

The major difference among the preceding methods of estimation is a choice between conditioning on particular communality estimates versus conditioning on the number of LVs. As mentioned, the (noniterative) PA solution yields a least squares fit of the EFA model to the data that is conditional on the prior estimates of communality used in the analysis. Conversely, iterative methods of estimation such as ULS and ML provide optimal fit of an EFA model to data that is conditional on the choice of a given number of factors. Because neither communality nor the correct number of factors is known with certainty, particularly when first investigating a domain, the optimal choice for estimating parameters in EFA is unclear. Rather than make a strong recommendation either way, I recommend that investigators try multiple methods of estimation to determine whether the choice makes a difference. Note that evidence has accumulated that ML estimation can miss small, but replicable, factors that PA and ULS estimation successfully identify (e.g., MacCallum & Tucker, 1991), and one cannot be sure that all factors in a domain are equally and fully represented when first investigating a domain. Thus, PA and ULS estimation are likely to be preferred to ML estimation in fully exploratory studies.

Other methods of estimation are available, including estimation via generalized least squares (GLS), alpha factor analysis, and canonical factor analysis (Harman, 1976; Mulaik, 2010). However, noniterative PA, ULS, and ML estimation are by far the most commonly used methods of estimation, and practicing scientists would have little need to move beyond these three methods.

Number of factors.   Selection of the number of factors to retain in an EFA is one of the most important steps in an EFA. Retaining an improper number of factors will have practical impacts, such as affecting factor loadings and correlations among rotated factors, and may have important theoretical effects as well, if the analysis is used to support arguments about the structure of a domain. Thus, the goal of the analyst is to identify the optimal number of factors in a given analysis. Three general methods have been proposed for selecting the number of factors to retain: mathematical rules, statistical tests, and rules of thumb.

The first category subsumes *mathematical rules* and is aligned most prominently with the three lower bounds discussed by Guttman (1954). The weakest lower bound corresponds to the number of dimensions with eigenvalues greater than 1.0 with unities on the main diagonal. The middle lower bound is the number of dimensions with eigenvalues greater than 0.0 with the square of the highest correlation in the row on the main diagonal. The strongest lower bound is the number of dimensions with eigenvalues greater than 0.0 with SMCs on the main diagonal. In deriving these bounds, Guttman assumed the presence of population data and that the *r*-dimensional solution fit the data perfectly in the population. Neither of these assumptions is likely to be true or approximately true in any

empirical application, reducing the likely utility of Guttman's bounds. Cliff (1988) provided a trenchant critique of the weakest lower bound, along with a demonstration of a failure to identify the correct number of factors. Furthermore, in Monte Carlo evaluations of tests for the number of factors, none of the Guttman bounds has performed well, with the weakest lower bound at times underestimating and at times overestimating the correct number of factors and the strongest lower bound frequently seriously overestimating the number of factors (e.g., Hakstian, Rogers, & Cattell, 1982; Tucker, Koopman, & Linn, 1969; Zwick & Velicer, 1982, 1986).

A second mathematical rule for determining the number of factors is the minimum average partial (MAP) correlation procedure proposed by Velicer (1976). Velicer argued that as one extracted principal components that accounted for common variance, the average partial correlation among MVs would decrease. One should observe this decrease in average partial correlations until the optimal number of dimensions for the data set was extracted. After this point, the remaining principal components represent more restricted amounts of variance, and the average off-diagonal partial correlation among MVs will rise again. The optimal number of dimensions to retain for a set of data is the solution with the smallest average partial correlation. The MAP test has performed well as an indicator of the correct number of factors in a number of Monte Carlo studies (e.g., Zwick & Velicer, 1986).

The second general approach to determining the number of factors includes *statistical tests*. The most commonly used statistical test is the likelihood ratio test statistic associated with ML estimation. The likelihood ratio test statistic is, essentially, a test of misfit of an *r*-dimensional factor solution to the matrix of covariances among MVs. Thus, a significant test statistic implies that the *r*-dimensional solution should be rejected in favor of an alternative with at least *r* + 1 factors. The statistical test is based on misfit of the factor model and sample size. Specifically, $(N-1)\hat{F}_{ML}$ is distributed as a chi-squared variate with degrees of freedom equal to $p(p + 1)/2 - k$, where *p* is the number of MVs and *k* is the number of parameter estimates in the *r*-factor model. Because r^2 constraints are required to identify an *r*-factor EFA model, the degrees of freedom for the test statistic are calculated as $((p - r)^2 - (p + r))/2$. A significant test statistic implies rejection of the hypothesis that an *r*-factor solution fits the data perfectly because of the presence of statistically significant levels of residual covariation unexplained by the model. Holding the ML fit function value constant, the ML test statistic is a direct function of sample size, so trivial levels of model misfit are increasingly likely to lead to rejection of a reasonable model as sample size increases. Statistical tests for the number of factors are available under other methods of estimation, including GLS and asymptotically distribution free estimation (Browne, 1984). Because these other methods of estimation are rarely used and because the testing sequence is similar to that for ML estimation, I will not provide more details here.

The third category of tests for the number of factors includes *rules of thumb*. During the first half of the 20th century, several reasonable rules of thumb were explored for ceasing the extraction of additional factors. For example, some investigators extracted factors until the residual correlations among variables had a distribution approximating that of population correlations of zero (cf. Thurstone, 1938). Or, researchers extracted factors until a certain percentage of the estimated common variance (e.g., at least 80% or at least 90%) was explained. Although these rules of thumb have some justification, they have been supplanted by other approaches over the past four or five decades.

One of the most commonly used rules of thumb is the scree test (Cattell, 1966). *Scree* is a geological term referring to the rock fragments, gravel, and silt that accumulate at the base of steep mountains as the result of erosion. Cattell adopted the name *scree* to describe a common pattern observed when plotting the eigenvalues for factors in the order in which they are extracted. Unrotated factors are in a conditionally variance-maximized orientation, such that each factor explains the greatest amount of remaining variance conditional on factors that have already been extracted. Thus, if one plots eigenvalues of factors in the order in which they were extracted, the first factor will explain the most variance, and succeeding factors will explain less and less variance.

Using the scree test, one looks for an elbow in the eigenvalue curve to retain the *r* common factors (or *mountains*) and the discard the $(p - r)$ remaining dimensions (or *scree*). The $(p - r)$ factors in the scree section of the plot thus represent fragmentary factors that explain too little variance to be useful.

A second rule of thumb, called *parallel analysis*, is based on the premise that factors extracted from real data should explain more variance than factors extracted from random data. This idea was first proposed by Horn (1965) for use with principal component analysis (PCA), a method discussed in the section Common Factor Analysis Versus Principal Component Analysis. Horn plotted PCA eigenvalues from real data on the same plot as corresponding PCA eigenvalues from a random data matrix with the same number of observations and MVs and argued that one should not retain a dimension from real data that explained less than the corresponding dimension from random data. Humphreys and Ilgen (1969) rapidly generalized this method to the EFA model and identified the method as parallel analysis. Humphreys and Montanelli (1975) evaluated the parallel analysis criterion in a number of classic data factor analytic data sets, verifying its ability to identify the correct number of factors. Then, Montanelli and Humphreys (1976) published results of a Monte Carlo study, including regression weights for predicting eigenvalues from random data that had been factor analyzed using PA extraction with SMCs as prior communality estimates. Thus, a researcher can extract factors from real data using the PA extraction with SMCs as prior communality estimates, use the Montanelli and Humphreys equations to obtain estimated random data eigenvalues, and plot the two sets of eigenvalues in a single plot to ensure that no factor from real data explains less variance than the corresponding factor from random data. A considerable number of publications during the past 20 years have investigated parallel analysis in the PCA context. Because PCA is not an EFA procedure, however, I stress here only the use of parallel analysis in an EFA context.

A third rule of thumb for the number of factors is derived from work by Tucker and Lewis (1973). To counter the tendency of the ML statistical test to suggest rejection of reasonable EFA models in the presence of trivial misfit if sample size is large, Tucker and Lewis developed an index they called a *reliability coefficient* for ML factor analysis. The Tucker–Lewis index (TLI) is computed as

$$\text{TLI} = \frac{\chi_0^2 \big/ df_0 - \chi_s^2 \big/ df_s}{\chi_0^2 \big/ df_0 - 1}, \tag{11}$$

where χ_0^2 and χ_s^2 represent the ML test statistic for a null (or zero-factor) model and a substantive model s, respectively, and df_0 and df_s are the degrees of freedom for the test statistics for the two models, respectively. When using ML estimation with a number of classic problems, Tucker and Lewis found that the ML test statistic often implied that the traditionally accepted number of factors would be rejected for a model with additional factors, whereas their reliability coefficient attained a value of approximately .95 or higher for the presumably correct number of factors. Tucker and Lewis then recommended that a value of the TLI of .95 or above be used to indicate that an EFA model provided close fit to a set of data, even if the ML test statistic implied the model in r factors was rejectable statistically. Bentler and Bonett (1980) argued for a more lenient criterion of .90 or above, but more recent research (e.g., Hu & Bentler, 1999) has restored .95 as a reasonable TLI value to attain to conclude that a model provides close fit to data.

A fourth useful rule of thumb is based on the root-mean-square error of approximation (RMSEA), first proposed by Steiger and Lind (1980). The RMSEA was formulated to reflect misfit of a model in the population. Any EFA model will fail to fit a correlation or covariance matrix for at least two reasons: sampling variability and misfit in the population. Sampling variability is a readily acknowledged source of model misfit. Thus, a model that fits perfectly in the population will have some misfit in any sample because of sampling variability, so the correct EFA model will not have a $\hat{F}_{\text{ML}} = 0$. Instead, because the expected value of the ML test statistic for the correct model for a set of data is equal to the df for the model, or $E\left[(N-1)\hat{F}_{\text{ML}}\right] = df$, the expected value of the ML fit function is $df/(N-1)$ for the correct model. But all structural models, including EFA

models, must be considered only approximations to reality (cf. MacCallum, Browne, & Cai, 2007) because of many replicable sources of variance, including nonlinearity of relations between factors and MVs and the presence of a multitude of minor factors of no theoretical importance. Because these perturbing influences represent misfit in the population, the expected value of the ML fit function for any empirical model is likely to deviate above $df/(N-1)$. The point estimate of the RMSEA, $\hat{\varepsilon}$, is calculated as

$$\hat{\varepsilon} = \sqrt{\frac{\max\left\{\left[\hat{F}_{\text{ML}} - df/(N-1)\right], 0\right\}}{df}} \tag{12}$$

(all symbols were defined in the preceding paragraphs). Browne and Cudeck (1993) stated that broad experience with the RMSEA demonstrated that values of .05 or less indicated close fit of a model to data, .05 to .08 indicated adequate fit, .08 to .10 indexed poor fit, and more than .10 indexed unacceptable fit.

One useful adjunct in using the RMSEA is that the sampling variability of $\hat{\varepsilon}$ is available, so an interval estimate of $\hat{\varepsilon}$ can be calculated. If the lower limit of the 90% confidence interval (CI) of the RMSEA includes .05, close fit of an EFA model to the data cannot be rejected at $\alpha = .05$. Furthermore, if the lower limit of the 90% CI includes zero, perfect model fit cannot be rejected.

Monte Carlo simulation studies and analyses of classic EFA data sets have supported the use of the scree and parallel analysis criteria as indicators of the correct number of factors (e.g., Zwick & Velicer, 1982, 1986). Less work has been performed on the TLI and RMSEA as "tests" for the number of factors, although the use of these indicators to assess close fit of an EFA model to data is appropriate. No single procedure for determining the number of factors to retain is always correct, and data examples can be constructed that will make a given test fail to function properly. As a result, the best advice is to use several methods to determine the number of factors, using the results of these tests along with interpretability of the resulting factors as the best way to arrive at an acceptable solution.

Rotation of factors. Once the number of factors is determined, factors typically must be rotated to an interpretable orientation. As noted, factors are initially extracted to meet a mathematical criterion of maximal variance explanation, but this is an arbitrary, if mathematical, criterion. Once extracted, factors can be rotated freely to an infinite number of alternative solutions in r-dimensional space and still provide an equally good mathematical description of the correlation matrix. Rotation involves the transformation or reorientation of the factors so the factors fall closer to clusters of vectors representing MVs, thereby simplifying the mathematical description of MVs. The mathematical criterion used to extract factors need not result in a scientifically meaningful representation of the data. For example, if the complexity of an MV is the number of LVs on which it loads at a nonzero level, most MVs have complexity r in the unrotated solution, with nonzero loadings on all factors. This solution fails to conform to the theoretical orientation of Thurstone (1947) regarding scientific use of factor analysis— that any behavioral phenomenon should, in general, be explained in terms of a small number of factors.

A second and equally important problem with an unrotated factor solution is the lack of invariance in this solution. If MVs are deleted from or added to an analysis, the loadings of MVs on unrotated factors will change, sometimes substantially. But Thurstone (1935, 1947) argued that any acceptable method of factor analysis should leave the factorial description of an MV unchanged if the MV were moved from one battery to another. Thus, to be an acceptable factor solution, the factorial description of a given MV must be invariant, rather than varying haphazardly as occurs in the matrix of extracted, or unrotated, factors.

Five criteria for simple structure were provided succinctly by Thurstone (1947). Among these criteria were that (a) each row of the factor matrix should have at least one zero, so the complexity of each MV should be no more than $(r - 1)$, and (b) each column of the factor matrix should have at least r zeroes. The zero loadings that Thurstone sought to achieve on a factor fall in the hyperplane for the factor, where the hyperplane is an $(r - 1)$ dimensional space that is orthogonal to the influence of the given factor. Loadings within the $\pm.10$ (or $\pm.20$) range are often described as falling in the

hyperplane, and these are usually treated as if they were essentially zero. The rules or criteria for simple structure outlined the appearance that a factor matrix should have, an appearance that was simpler to characterize than the pattern exhibited by the unrotated factor solution. Thurstone argued that rotation to simple structure would constitute a transformation of the unrotated factors to an orientation that would exhibit a simpler pattern of loadings than could be seen in the unrotated factor solution.

The nature of a simple structure solution should be appropriate for the data and the behavioral domain. Many researchers seem to think that all variables must have complexity of 1—exhibiting a nonzero loading on only one of the r factors—for simple structure to be attained. This is incorrect. Indeed, Thurstone (1947) presented a number of alternative simple structure patterns that had variables with complexity of 2 or 3 (i.e., with nonzero loadings on two or three factors, respectively), and his famous box problem (Thurstone, 1947, pp. 369–376) had at least two variables with nonzero loadings on all factors. The guiding principle underlying simple structure is that each MV should be as simple as possible in factorial description, given the behavioral phenomena under study.

Factor rotations can be either *orthogonal* or *oblique*. Orthogonal rotations involve rigid transformation of the factorial dimensions, retaining the 90-degree separation among all factors. Under orthogonal rotation, the matrix of correlations among rotated factors remains an identity matrix, with factor variances of unity and zero correlations among factors. With orthogonal rotation, the factor matrix is simplified as much as possible under the constraint that the correlations among factors remain maximally simple (i.e., uncorrelated). The alternative to orthogonal rotation is oblique rotations, discussed first by Tucker (1940). Under oblique rotation, the orthogonality constraint among factors is relaxed, and factors are allowed to correlate. The added complexity of allowing factors to correlate, however, is often justified by a much simpler matrix of factor loadings. In the ability domain, all MVs tend to be positively correlated. Orthogonal rotation will often lead to loadings by the MVs that define a factor in the .5 to .8 range, but the remaining loadings on a factor frequently fall outside the ±.10 hyperplane, often falling between .20 and .30. Although these loadings are too small for interpretation, they are not zero. Under oblique rotation, researchers can often obtain a rotated solution with the majority of nondefining loadings within the ±.10 or ±.15 hyperplane, loadings that are much closer to zero, although this simplicity is bought at the price of factors that correlate.

For many years, rotation of factors was done by hand, using methods of plotting points and time-consuming matrix multiplication to reorient the factors. With the availability of computers in the early 1950s, researchers developed mathematical criteria to embody Thurstone's criteria for simple structure, and algorithmic rotation via computer program is called analytic rotation. The most widely used orthogonal analytic rotation is varimax (Kaiser, 1958), a rotational criterion to maximize the variance of loadings simultaneously within rows and within columns of the factor-loading matrix. Crawford and Ferguson (1970) showed that the varimax rotation was a member of the orthomax family of rotations, a family of rotations that could be generated by varying a multiplier that changed the effect of simplicity of each factor on the rotational criterion. A multiplier of zero resulted in the quartimax criterion, which considered only row simplicity; a multiplier of unity led to the varimax criterion; a multiplier of 2 resulted in the equamax criterion, which gave more weight to column simplicity than did varimax, and so on.

Oblique analytic rotations were also heavily under development, and many researchers compared results of different rotations. In a set of major comparisons, Hakstian (1971) and Hakstian and Abell (1974) concluded that the Harris–Kaiser orthoblique (Harris & Kaiser, 1964) and promax (Hendrickson & White, 1964) rotations led to rotated solutions that more closely approximated the *accepted* solutions for classic factor analysis data sets than did other rotations. But, in recent years, many additional methods of oblique analytic rotation have been developed, and Browne (2001) provided the most up-to-date review of these procedures. These newer rotational criteria are not

available in the major statistical packages, but they can be used in CEFA (Browne, Cudeck, Tateneni, & Mels, 2010) and in some other packages (e.g., some are available in Mplus; see L. K. Muthén & Muthén, 1998–2010).

Researchers use results of rotated factor solutions in a number of ways. For example, they might use the rotated solution simply to identify the several subsets of variables that are loading highly on different factors. If used in this fashion, then precise and clean simple structure may not be the object of the analysis, and the rather crude result of an orthogonal rotation may be sufficient. However, if a researcher wished to use EFA with the goal of revising an instrument and ultimately engaging in CFA or structural equation modeling using the revised scale or battery, then oblique rotation of factors is the only meaningful approach to rotation that should be used.

Interpretation. Following rotation of factors, each factor in an analysis must be interpreted. In early applications of factor analysis (e.g., Thurstone, 1938), researchers often extracted and rotated more factors than were finally interpreted, leaving the uninterpreted factors in a limbo state with unknown utility or importance. This was an accepted practice at a time when the extraction and rotation of factors was a time-consuming, laborious process, sometimes taking months to complete. Today, extraction and rotation of factors can be done with tremendous speed, and the inclusion of extra, uninterpreted factors is rarely accepted. Rotation of the correct number of factors is the ideal, although this is a problematic goal in EFA given the exploratory nature of the analysis. Thus, a researcher might inadvertently underextract factors (i.e., extract too few factors) or overextract factors (i.e., extract too many factors). Research on under- and overextraction of factors indicates that underextraction does more harm to rotated solutions than does overextraction (see, e.g., Wood, Tataryn, & Gorsuch, 1996). Thus, if one were to err, erring on the side of too many factors will likely affect the factor solution negatively less than will extracting too few factors.

Interpretation of factors usually proceeds by considering what aspect the MVs that load highly on a factor have in common. If all variables that load highly on a factor involve giving speedy, correct answers to simple numeric problems (e.g., addition, subtraction, and so on), then the factor could be identified as *numerical facility*. This approach to interpretation involves primarily the pattern of loadings separately in each column of the factor matrix. But, just as important as attention to high loadings in a column, interpretation can at times be facilitated greatly by considering the factors that have hyperplanar loadings for a given MV. Factor loadings are regression weights for predicting MVs from factors, and an essentially zero, hyperplanar loading for an MV on a given factor implies that the factor has no effect on the MV if other factors are held constant. Attention to these facets of loading matrix may afford unique opportunity to interpret factors.

Factor scores.   As shown in Equation 1, the factor model represents MVs as weighted linear combinations of factor scores. The factor score matrix thus contains important information—the implied score for each individual on each factor. Because factors are true score variables, factor scores represent the true score for each person on each factor. Unfortunately, factor scores are not uniquely determined under the EFA model. Several methods for estimating factor scores have been proposed over the years, such as regression estimates and least squares estimates (see Harman, 1976; Tucker, 1971), and these yield different score estimates. That is, different methods of factor score estimation lead to different factor score estimates, a problem that has been identified as factor score indeterminacy.

The indeterminacy of factor scores was identified initially in the 1920s, but interest in the problem faded during the 1930s and 1940s as many of the key developments of multiple factor analysis were pursued. The 1970s saw a rebirth of interest in factor score indeterminacy, leading to a major controversy in the literature. The two sides in the controversy were aligned as follows: The pro-EFA position was that the EFA model was the preferred model, that indeterminacy of factor scores was a problem to be accommodated, and that the problem was minimized in well-researched domains in which a large number of MVs with high loadings could be

relied on to identify each factor. The contra-EFA position was that PCA was essentially the same as EFA, that PCA did not suffer from factor score indeterminacy because component scores could be computed directly, and that the conditions cited for lack of concern about factor scores—many MVs loading highly on factors—were rarely, if ever, met.

Interest in factor score indeterminacy has once again waned, but good historical accounts of the matter are available (e.g., Steiger, 1979, 1994). Several bases for the decline of interest can be identified. One reason for the decline of interest is the rise of CFA and structural equation modeling, which allow a researcher to investigate relations among factors without having to estimate factor scores. A second reason for the waning of interest may be concerns for robust estimation of factor scores. Fully accurate estimates of factor scores appear to work well in the sample on which the analysis was performed, but the matrices of factor scoring weights appear not to cross-validate well in new samples. However, robust factor weighting schemes—such as summing up standard scores on MVs that load highly on a factor—work almost as well as precise factor score weights in the derivation sample, but they seem to cross-validate much better in new samples. Still, the last word on the matter of factor score indeterminacy has almost certainly not been written, and continued interest in the problem will probably remain for some time.

An Empirical Example

To illustrate the methods of EFA discussed thus far, an empirical example is helpful. In 1961, Bechtoldt investigated whether the factor structure of a set of tests could be replicated across two random subsamples from a population. To do so, he used 17 of the 21 variables from the cross-validation sample ($N = 437$) in Thurstone and Thurstone (1941), discarding four variables that did not meet psychometric criteria for quality. Bechtoldt randomly divided the sample of participants into two subsamples, with Sample 1 consisting of 212 participants and Sample 2 of 213 participants. Correlations among a selected set of 12 tests from Bechtoldt (1961) are shown in Table 18.1, along with the means and standard deviations of variables for each sample. Correlations

							Variable					
Variable	**Sen**	**Voc**	**Com**	**FLet**	**FLW**	**Suff**	**LSer**	**Ped**	**LGrp**	**Flag**	**Fig**	**Card**
Sen		.828	.776	.439	.432	.447	.447	.541	.380	.117	.051	.151
Voc	.833		.779	.493	.464	.489	.432	.537	.358	.121	.077	.146
Com	.761	.772		.460	.425	.443	.401	.534	.359	.193	.180	.174
FLet	.402	.446	.394		.674	.590	.381	.350	.424	.178	.081	.158
FLW	.275	.358	.275	.627		.541	.402	.367	.446	.223	.192	.239
Suff	.374	.473	.426	.516	.480		.288	.320	.325	.118	.007	.114
LSer	.536	.507	.490	.404	.330	.327		.555	.598	.252	.203	.257
Ped	.567	.514	.512	.365	.275	.323	.671		.452	.085	.129	.151
LGrp	.468	.404	.430	.375	.317	.285	.622	.538		.270	.203	.293
Flag	.103	.109	.342	.176	.161	.079	.289	.277	.287		.593	.651
Fig	.019	.045	.227	.104	.138	.007	.160	.165	.181	.672		.684
Card	.077	.105	.294	.095	.049	.012	.200	.208	.207	.606	.728	
Sample 1												
M	13.420	27.030	31.970	36.650	11.080	9.070	12.400	16.100	13.320	25.080	22.700	26.450
SD	4.730	10.317	10.795	9.778	4.655	4.106	5.725	7.678	4.171	12.427	12.798	12.215
Sample 2												
M	13.750	26.710	31.890	36.180	10.850	8.460	12.460	16.450	13.350	24.440	22.010	24.850
SD	4.651	10.797	10.581	11.152	5.312	4.513	5.718	7.651	3.879	11.256	11.451	11.523

Note. Data from Bechtoldt (1961). Values are correlations from Sample 1 (*N* = 212) below the diagonal and from Sample 2 (*N* = 213) above the diagonal, with means and standard deviations as noted. Sen = sentences; Voc = vocabulary; Com = completion; FLet = first letters; FLW = four-letter words; Suff = suffixes; LSer = letter series; Ped = pedigrees; LGrp = letter grouping; Flag = flags; Fig = figures; Card = cards.

among MVs in Sample 1 are shown below the diagonal of Table 18.1, and those for Sample 2 are shown above the diagonal.

Selection of observations from the population and selection of MVs were beyond control in the current application. However, a reading of Thurstone and Thurstone (1941) leads one to infer that the sample was reasonably representative of school children in Chicago. The 12 MVs consisted of revised and improved versions of tests that had been used before by Thurstone and his colleagues, and thus they were probably an optimal selection. The 12 MVs consisted of (a) three tests for a verbal comprehension (V) factor—sentences, vocabulary, and completion—that require participants to extract meaning from text; (b) three tests for a word fluency (W) factor—first letters, four-letter words, and suffixes—that reflect fast access to or quick retrieval from long-term memory of words with particular structural features (e.g., words

beginning with *st*), regardless of the meaning of the words; (c) three tests for a reasoning (R) factor—letter series, pedigrees, and letter grouping—that require participants to infer the rule relating elements in a problem and then to provide the required next element or relation; and (d) three tests for a spatial (S) factor—flags, figures, and cards—that index speed in two-dimensional rotation and verification of figural stimuli. More detail regarding these tests is provided in Thurstone and Thurstone (1941).

Several tests for the number of factors were applied to the data from Sample 1, with results shown in Table 18.2. The first data column of Table 18.2 shows eigenvalues from PA extraction with unities on the diagonal, and three dimensions had eigenvalues more than 1.0. The second data column lists eigenvalues from PA extraction with SMCs on the diagonal, and five dimensions had positive eigenvalues. Therefore, Guttman's weakest lower

TABLE 18.2

Information for Deciding on the Number of Factors to Retain for Sample 1

Factor	Eigenvalues			MAP	Measures from maximum likelihood estimation				
	PCA	EFA	Random		χ^2	df	prob	TLI	RMSEA (CI)
1	5.01	4.61	0.48	.267	607.92	54	< .0001	.522	.221 (.205–.236)
2	2.21	1.80	0.35	.241	267.99	43	< .0001	.758	.158 (.140–.176)
3	1.24	0.77	0.28	.241	127.59	33	< .0001	.869	.117 (.096–.138)
4	0.92	0.50	0.22	.225	24.81	24	.41	.998	.014 (.000–.058)
5	0.52	0.01	0.15	.276	10.31	16	.85	1.016	.000 (.000–.036)
6	0.45	−0.03	0.08	.332					
7	0.39	−0.07		.376					
8	0.37	−0.08		.457					
9	0.31	−0.12		.546					
10	0.25	−0.14		.694					
11	0.19	−0.15							
12	0.15	−0.19							

Note. Data from Bechtoldt (1961). PCA = principal component analysis; EFA = exploratory common factor analysis, principal axes extraction, squared multiple correlations as communality estimates; Random = estimated random data values; MAP = minimum average partial correlation criterion; χ^2 = likelihood ratio chi-square; prob = probability level for likelihood ratio chi-square; TLI = Tucker–Lewis index; RMSEA (CI) = root-mean-square error of approximation (with its confidence interval [CI] in parentheses).

bound implies the presence of three dimensions, whereas the strongest lower bound implies five dimensions.

Eigenvalues from PA extraction with SMCs on the diagonal and estimated random data eigenvalues computed using the Montanelli and Humphreys (1976) equations, in the second and third data columns of Table 18.2, respectively, were plotted in Figure 18.1. As shown in Figure 18.1, four factors had relatively large eigenvalues, and the eigenvalues for the fifth and succeeding factors were very small. Moreover, the first four factors from real data had eigenvalues greater than those for the corresponding factors from random data, whereas the fifth and sixth random data factors had larger eigenvalues than corresponding factors for real data. Thus, the scree and parallel analysis criteria imply the presence of four factors. Furthermore, the values from the MAP criterion, shown in the fourth data column of Table 18.2, agree with the scree and parallel analysis criteria, as the average partial correlation was lowest for the four-factor solution.

The final three indicators of the number of factors were associated with ML estimation. As shown in Table 18.2, factor solutions with one, two, or

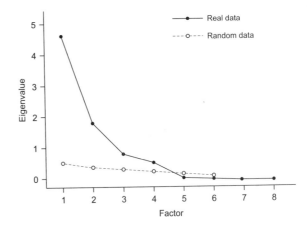

FIGURE 18.1. Plot of eigenvalues of the correlation matrix for Sample 1 from Bechtoldt (1961), compared with the plot of estimated eigenvalues from random data.

three common factors were associated with significant test statistics, implying rejection of these solutions. But, the solution with four common factors was not rejectable. In addition, the TLI and RMSEA were both in the unacceptable range for the solutions with one, two, or three common factors. But the TLI and RMSEA both had very acceptable values for the four-factor solution. In summary, most indicators for the number of factors converged on four factors as the optimal solution, and only the indicators that were based on Guttman's bounds failed to agree on this decision.

Two obliquely rotated four-factor solutions for the Sample 1 data are shown in Table 18.3. In the left half of Table 18.3, the solution obtained using SAS PROC FACTOR is shown, a solution using ML estimation and Harris–Kaiser orthoblique rotation with an exponent of zero. The three tests hypothesized to load highly on each factor did indeed load highly, with defining loadings ranging between .53 and .89 across factors. Of the 36 loadings that were expected to be small (nine loadings per factor), 30 of the 36 fell within the ±.10 hyperplane, and only two of the six loadings outside the ±.10 hyperplane were .20 or larger. This solution would be considered a very clean exploratory factor solution, and the largest deviation from expected values was the .25 loading of suffixes on V. Also note the relatively

high correlations among the first three factors and the low correlations of the S factor with the first three factors.

The rotated solution shown in the right half of Table 18.3 is an EFA performed using the Mplus program (L. K. Muthén & Muthén, 1998–2010), with ML estimation and geomin rotation. Loadings in this solution are very similar to those reported in the left half of the table. This solution has the additional information of the standard error (*SE*) for each parameter estimate (cf. Cudeck & O'Dell, 1994). The three large, defining loadings on each factor had *t* values of 7.5 or higher, as expected. But, this solution suggests that the .26 loading of comprehension on S (with *t* value of 5.2) is a substantially larger deviation from the expected hyperplanar loading than was the .25 loading of suffixes on V (with a *t* value less than 3.0). Because the loadings are of approximately the same magnitude,

TABLE 18.3

Rotated Four-Factor Exploratory Factor Analysis (EFA) Solutions for 12 Manifest Variables (MVs) in Sample 1

| | SAS PROC FACTOR | | | | | Mplus EFA | | | | |
| | Factor | | | | | Factor | | | | |
MV	V	W	R	S	h²	V	W	R	S	h²
Sentences	.84	−.05	.15	−.09	.84	**.83** (.05)	−.04 (.03)	*.16* (.06)	−.04 (.03)	.84
Vocabulary	.89	.11	−.03	−.04	.85	**.88** (.04)	*.12* (.05)	−.02 (.04)	.01 (.02)	.85
Completion	.82	.01	.01	.20	.77	**.81** (.04)	.01 (.03)	.01 (.04)	**.26** (.05)	.77
First letters	.08	.70	.08	.01	.62	.09 (.08)	**.70** (.07)	.08 (.08)	.01 (.04)	.62
FLW	−.06	.84	.00	.03	.67	−.05 (.03)	**.83** (.06)	.00 (.05)	.03 (.04)	.67
Suffixes	.25	.53	−.02	−.07	.44	*.25* (.09)	**.53** (.07)	−.02 (.07)	−.05 (.05)	.44
LSer	−.00	.02	.85	.00	.74	−.00 (.04)	.02 (.04)	**.86** (.06)	−.03 (.04)	.74
Pedigrees	.15	−.03	.68	.03	.61	.15 (.08)	−.03 (.04)	**.69** (.08)	.02 (.04)	.61
LGrp	−.00	.07	.67	.06	.52	−.00 (.06)	.07 (.07)	**.68** (.08)	.04 (.05)	.52
Flags	−.03	.04	.16	.72	.61	−.04 (.05)	.02 (.04)	.16 (.08)	**.72** (.04)	.61
Figures	−.02	.05	−.04	.89	.78	−.02 (.04)	.04 (.04)	−.05 (.06)	**.90** (.03)	.78
Cards	.08	−.08	.02	.81	.68	.08 (.06)	−.09 (.06)	.01 (.04)	**.82** (.03)	.68

Factor correlations										
V	1.00					1.00 (.00)				
W	.44	1.00				**.41** (.07)	1.00 (.00)			
R	.62	.47	1.00			**.60** (.06)	**.46** (.08)	1.00 (.00)		
S	.11	.12	.24	1.00		.07 (.08)	.13 (.08)	*.29* (.08)	1.00 (.00)	

Note. Tabled values are factor loadings or factor correlations, with standard errors in parentheses where appropriate. SAS details: ML estimation, Harris–Kaiser orthoblique rotation, with power = 0; Mplus details: ML estimation, Geomin rotation. Boldfaced loadings had *z* ratios greater than 5.0; italicized loadings had *z* ratios between 2.0 and 5.0. Data from Bechtoldt (1961), SAS, and Mplus Output. FLW = four-letter words; LSer = letter series; LGrp = letter grouping.

the additional information provided by the *SE* allows one to assess the importance of the deviation from zero of these loadings. The *SE*s for the factor correlations reveal that the first three factors—V, W, and R—are rather strongly and significantly correlated, with *t* values of 5.5 or higher, and that the fourth factor, S, is significantly related only to the R factor.

COMMON FACTOR ANALYSIS VERSUS PRINCIPAL COMPONENT ANALYSIS

One continuing issue in exploratory uses of methods to dimensionalize behavior is the choice between EFA and PCA. A single, seemingly minor difference exists between EFA and PCA: The EFA model was developed to account for off-diagonal covariation among MVs, necessitating the estimation of communalities so that diagonal elements of **R** would not overly influence the resulting factor matrices. In contrast, a PCA is conducted on the correlation matrix **R** with unities on the diagonal, so the PCA model is designed to account for maximal amounts of the total variance of MVs and only indirectly accounts for their off-diagonal covariation. Simply put, the matrix formulation for PCA that parallels Equation 7 is

$$\mathbf{R} = \mathbf{FF'} + \mathbf{GG'}, \tag{13}$$

where **F** is a $(p \times r)$ truncated solution containing the first r components, and **G** is a $(p \times [p-r])$ matrix of the $(p - r)$ discarded components.

Recall that an EFA solution involves a total of $(p + r)$ factors: r common factors and p unique factors. In contrast, a PCA involves representing mathematically the p MVs in terms of only p dimensions, r components in the **F** matrix in Equation 13, and $(p - r)$ components in the **G** matrix. The component space of **G** is orthogonal to the component space of **F**, so the r components in **F** can be rotated orthogonally or obliquely without concern for the discarded components in **G**. However, the residuals in **G** have a covariance structure represented by $\mathbf{GG'}$, and these residuals are not mutually uncorrelated as are the unique factors in **Θ** in the EFA model. Given the unknown and potentially haphazard nature of these residual covariances, PCA is not a statistical model

in the usual sense but rather is a data-reduction technique.

A central question is how closely the PCA matrix **F** in Equation 13 approximates the EFA matrix **Λ** in Equation 2. Some commentators argue that differences between EFA and PCA solutions are fairly minor and that PCA is an efficient approximation to EFA (e.g., Goldberg & Velicer, 2006; Thompson, 2004; Velicer & Jackson, 1990), implying that factor loading and component loading matrices are often very similar. The PCA model is not a common factor model, however, and should not be used to substitute for one. Among others, Widaman (1993, 2007) demonstrated the positive bias in loadings and negative bias in correlations among obliquely rotated dimensions that accompany the use of PCA relative to corresponding values from EFA. Furthermore, parameter estimates from EFA are expected to generalize to CFA (see the section Confirmatory Factor Analysis), whereas parameter estimates from PCA may find little generalization to CFA. The upshot of these concerns is that the use of PCA as an approximation to EFA should be strongly discouraged, and EFA methods should be used if the goal of a study is the representation of MVs as functions of LVs.

CONFIRMATORY FACTOR ANALYSIS

CFA arose in the 1960s with the development of efficient algorithms for estimating parameters in factor analysis models and the recognition that certain restrictions, such as fixing certain factor loadings to be precisely zero, were hypotheses that could be tested statistically. Early contributions to CFA by Jöreskog (e.g., 1969, 1971a, 1971b) were quickly followed by a spate of publications by researchers who understood the power of CFA to provide statistical tests of hypothesized factor structures.

The CFA approach is based on the same basic linear model as described for EFA, except that the model is usually formulated as a covariance, not correlation, structure (Cudeck, 1989). That is, MVs are modeled as linear combinations of the LVs, as shown in Equation 1. The major difference between EFA and CFA is the unrestricted estimation of parameters in EFA, allowing rotation to an infinite number of alternative orientations of the factors, versus the restricted estimation of parameters in CFA that typically yields an unrotatable solution. Theory and prior research are used to formulate the restrictions in a CFA model, and the resulting analytic machinery of CFA offers a surprisingly wide array of models to be investigated. Indeed, CFA can be seen as a restricted form of EFA, which implies a restricted set of options in CFA relative to EFA. Exploiting options for placement of fixed and free parameter estimates results in a general CFA model that affords far more flexibility than the standard EFA model, and the variety of models that can be investigated under CFA is far broader than under EFA.

Steps in Confirmatory Factor Analysis

Selection of observations. The key issues surrounding the selection of observations for CFA differ little from those for EFA, so discussion here can be brief. Random and representative selection of observations from a carefully delineated population is the optimal approach to sample selection. However, researchers are often keen to investigate whether factor solutions obtained in prior research, usually on European American or majority culture participants, will generalize to participants from other populations. In such investigations, the procedures for drawing the sample from the particular population must be carefully outlined to diminish the force of an alternative explanation in terms of unrepresentative sampling if an expected factor structure is not confirmed.

Selection of MVs. Ideally, variables used in a CFA will have been used in several earlier EFA studies so the psychometric properties and likely factor parameters for the tests are known. Furthermore, rather than ensuring that a domain of content is covered by the MVs in an analysis, investigators typically select a small set of the best indicators for each factor. So, rather than a widely varying selection of MVs, research is often based on a careful selection of the best indicators. If these indicators load highly on the LVs in a CFA, little concern regarding the results of analyses should arise.

Specification. Specification of a CFA model involves identification of the number of factors and

placement of fixed, free, and constrained model parameters. The fixing of any model parameter is a constraint that the parameter must take on a specified value. Two general kinds of constraints can be distinguished—minimally sufficient identification constraints, and overidentifying restrictions. Minimally sufficient identification (MSI) constraints are constraints that identify the scale of the LVs and identify all parameter estimates in the model. At least r^2 MSI constraints must be invoked to identify a factor model, where r is the number of factors. Because r^2 constraints are required to estimate parameters in a factor model, these are called MSI constraints. If only r^2 constraints are made, the resulting model will be equivalent to an EFA model; the associated CFA model will have the same chi square and degrees of freedom as an EFA model with the same number of factors. The CFA model will be fully rotatable factor model that is rotated to an a priori orientation, as will become clear when we consider Equation 14.

LVs have no natural scale, and certain MSI identification constraints set or fix the scale of the LVs. One common approach is to fix the variance of each LV to unity, by fixing or constraining diag (Ψ) = I. This approach provides LVs that have certain properties akin to z scores, with a mean of zero and a variance of 1. A second common identification constraint is to fix one factor loading per LV to unity, which then allows the variance of the LV to be estimated. Let us assume that the former approach—fixing LV variances to unity—is taken; this accounts for r of the MSI constraints. The remaining $r(r-1)$ MSI constraints are invoked by fixing certain factor loadings to zero. Consider the following CFA model matrices Λ, Ψ, and Θ:

$$\Lambda = \begin{bmatrix} \lambda_{11} & 0^* \\ \lambda_{21} & \lambda_{22} \\ \lambda_{31} & \lambda_{33} \\ 0^* & \lambda_{42} \\ \lambda_{51} & \lambda_{52} \\ \lambda_{61} & \lambda_{62} \end{bmatrix} \quad \Psi = \begin{bmatrix} 1^* & symm \\ \psi_{21} & 1^* \end{bmatrix} \quad \Theta = \text{diag} \begin{bmatrix} \theta_{11} \\ \theta_{22} \\ \theta_{33} \\ \theta_{44} \\ \theta_{55} \\ \theta_{66} \end{bmatrix}, \quad (14)$$

where the first three MVs (corresponding to the first three rows of Λ) are presumed to be indicators of the first LV, and the second three MVs are indicators for the second LV. Because two LVs are shown in these matrices, a total of $r^2 = 2^2 = 4$ MSI constraints must be made. Two of these MSI constraints are indicated by the asterisked values of 1 on the diagonal of $\mathbf{\Psi}$, and the remaining two MSI constraints are shown as the asterisked values of 0 in the two columns of $\mathbf{\Lambda}$. The placement of MSI constraints was determined in the following way, which can be generalized to models with any number of factors: (a) select a leading indicator for each factor, selecting the very best indicator of the factor on the basis of prior research, if such can be determined (here, MV1 is the leading indicator for the first LV, and MV4 is the leading indicator for LV2); (b) estimate the factor loading for the leading indicator on its factor, but fix at zero the factor loadings for the leading indicator on all other factors; (c) for the nonleading indicators of a factor, estimate all loadings for these variables on all other factors; (d) fix to one the variances of all LVs in $\mathbf{\Psi}$; (e) estimate all correlations among LVs; and (f) freely estimate diagonal values of $\mathbf{\Theta}$, which are variances of unique factors.

The model in Equation 14 has r^2 MSI constraints, so it is equivalent to an EFA model. The model is simply an EFA model estimated using CFA software and rotating the first LV right through the first MV and the second LV directly through the fourth MV. Because the first factor is colinear with the first MV, the first MV cannot load on any other factors, hence its fixed zero loadings on other factors. Similar constraints hold for the fourth MV.

Converting the CFA model in Equation 14 into a typical, restricted CFA model would involve constraining the four italicized factor loadings to be zero, but keeping the six boldfaced factor loadings estimated freely. This involves invoking the second type of constraint—overidentifying restrictions. Specifically, if the loadings of the second and third MVs on the second LV (i.e., λ_{22} and λ_{32}) and the loadings of the fifth and sixth MVs on the first LV (i.e., λ_{51} and λ_{61}) were fixed at zero, the resulting model would be a CFA model that is a restricted version of the model shown in Equation 14. The resulting CFA model would have four more *df* than the model shown in Equation 14 because four fewer parameter estimates were made.

Given the foregoing, one can see that a standard CFA model is a restricted factor model, or a restricted version of an EFA model. Typical CFA models are not confirmatory in a strong sense, meaning that a researcher does not test whether particular numerical values for certain model parameters can be confirmed or verified in a new sample. Instead, the typical CFA model involves obtaining best-fit estimates of all model parameters given a particular restricted pattern of fixed and free loadings. Adequate fit of a restricted CFA model thus *confirms*, or supports, the researcher's conjecture that a restricted form of factor model is consistent with the data. The restricted form of a CFA model means that it is no longer a freely rotatable solution, as any rotation would fail to retain the pattern of fixed zero loadings in the model. Furthermore, although not often performed, a researcher could test the fit of a CFA model against that of a freely rotatable EFA model with the same number of factors because the CFA model is nested within the EFA model. This test could be quite informative, providing a statistical test of the worsening of fit associated with the overidentifying restrictions in the CFA model.

Estimation. In CFA, parameters can be estimated using any of a number of methods of estimation. Available methods include ULS, ML, GLS, and a host of variants of these that provide test statistics and SEs that are robust to violations of normality assumptions (e.g., Browne, 1984; Satorra & Bentler, 1994; Savalei, 2010). Although myriad methods of estimation are available, the more esoteric methods are not frequently used. Instead, standard ML estimation is the method used in the vast majority of applications. Fortunately, ML estimation appears to be relatively robust to moderate or even fairly extensive violations of distributional assumptions, so its use in most studies is probably not a matter of major concern. If violation of assumptions is a concern, I recommend comparing results of ML estimation against those using a robust method of estimation. If important differences in results are obtained, then method of estimation is a matter of concern, and the researcher should justify the choice of method.

Evaluation.   Evaluation of the fit of a CFA model is typically done on at least two levels—the global fit of the overall CFA model, and a more detailed consideration of each parameter estimate. The global fit of the CFA model can be evaluated using statistical indexes or indexes of practical fit that are a function of the statistical indexes. In an earlier section on ML estimation in EFA, I discussed the use of the likelihood ratio chi-square test statistic; this test statistic is used in most CFA studies as a statistical indicator of model misfit. A significant test statistic is a statistical basis for rejection of the model tested. Because the test statistic is a direct function of sample size, trivial model misfit can lead to a significant test statistic if sample size is large, and important model misfit may not lead to a rejectable test statistic if sample size is small. In general, sample size should be 150 or larger to ensure adequate power of a model to reject a poorly fitting model, and the test statistic tends to become overly powerful when sample size exceeds 500. Thus, care must be taken in evaluating the ML test statistic.

Adjuncts to the statistical index of fit are found in practical fit indexes of global fit of a model to data. Several practical fit indexes were discussed in a preceding section, including the TLI and the RMSEA. Many additional practical fit indexes have been developed. One class of fit indexes is called information indexes, and these include the Akaike information criterion (AIC), the consistent AIC (or CAIC), and the Bayesian information criterion (BIC). These information criteria do not fall on a standardized metric; however, various models can be compared using these criteria. Thus, among several competing models, the model with the smallest (i.e., most negative) AIC is the optimally fitting model. Similar comparisons among models can be performed using the CAIC and the BIC. On the basis of simulation studies, the CAIC and BIC indexes appear to be better indicators of the correct model than does the AIC. Interested readers can consult Hu and Bentler (1999) for a comprehensive evaluation of different indicators of practical fit, particularly with regard to optimal cutoff points for different indexes, and Widaman and Thompson (2003) for a comparison of incremental fit indexes.

The second, more detailed level of model evaluation is conducted by considering each parameter estimate in a CFA model against its *SE*. A critical ratio (CR), distributed as an asymptotic z-ratio, can be formed by dividing a parameter estimate by its *SE* The tradition in the field is to deem any parameter with a CR of 2.0 or larger to be significant at the .05 level, and the *p* level for each CR is reported by most structural modeling programs. Thus, on a statistical basis, the evaluation of model parameters is highly structured.

Parameter estimates in a CFA model can also be evaluated with regard to their magnitude, supplementing a statistical evaluation with one that is based on practical importance. No hard-and-fast rules are available here, but simulation studies have often used .4, .6, and .8 standardized factor loadings to represent low, medium, and high levels of communality, respectively. Absent firmer bases, these values can be used to evaluate standardized factor loadings. Furthermore, Cohen (1988) used .10, .30, and .50 to indicate small, medium, and large correlations, so these values can be used when interpreting the magnitude of the correlations among factors.

Readjustment.   Readjustment of a CFA model consists of the respecification of fixed or free parameter estimates. Any respecification can be done on either of two grounds: (a) a priori and (b) empirical. A priori grounds for respecifying a model might be pursued to compare competing conjectures under different models for a given set of data. For example, in prior research, certain investigators may have found evidence that a three-factor structure underlies items on a given scale, whereas the developer of the scale sought to assess just two factors. Alternative CFA models could be formulated that were consistent with each of these competing schemes, and the relative fit of these alternate a priori models could be compared.

Researchers can also use empirical bases for model respecification, typically to improve model fit to the data. Most structural modeling programs report modification indexes, which estimate the change in chi square if a particular parameter were estimated rather than fixed in the current model. Experts on factor analysis differ with regard to their recommendations concerning modification indexes. Some experts advise never to base model respecification on modification indexes because of the capitalization on chance that can readily occur. Bolstering this position is Monte Carlo simulation work on specification searches, which has generally concluded that such searches rarely arrive at the model that generated the data (e.g., MacCallum, 1986). Other experts (e.g., Sörbom, 1989) see clear value in using modification indexes to aid model respecification, as these indexes reflect ways the data are informing the researcher of a need to account for particular patterns in data. If modification indexes are used to modify the specification of a model, most experts urge that these modifications should be cross-validated in an independent sample to verify their replicability.

Empirical Example

To exemplify the use of CFA, I reanalyzed the data from Sample 1 of Bechtoldt (1961). Specifically, I fit a model with a "perfect" restricted factor pattern, with the three tests for verbal comprehension loading on the first factor, the three word fluency tests loading on the second factor, the three tests for reasoning loading on the third factor, and the three spatial tests loading on the fourth factor. The resulting model had a significant ML test statistic, $\chi^2(48) = 106.51$, $p < .001$, suggesting rejection of the highly restricted model. Practical fit indexes included a TLI of .943 and an RMSEA of .076 (CI = .056–.095), which were of borderline acceptability. Furthermore, because this CFA model was nested within the four-factor EFA model presented earlier, the worsening of fit moving from the EFA model to the restricted CFA model could be tested. The resulting difference test was significant, $\Delta\chi^2(24) = 81.70$, $p < .001$.

Modification indexes suggested that freeing the loading of completion on the Spatial factor would improve model fit. Relaxing this factor loading constraint led to Model 2, which had a statistical test statistic that was of borderline significance, $\chi^2(47) = 71.28$, $p < .02$. Although this test statistic was significant at $\alpha = .05$, it was not rejectable at $\alpha = .01$. Moreover, the improvement in statistical fit associated with the one additional parameter estimate was

clearly significant, $\Delta\chi^2(1) = 35.23$, $p < .001$. The practical fit indexes of TLI = .976 and RMSEA = .049 (CI = .023–.072) suggested that this model fit the data closely. To avoid any further potential capitalization on chance, I ceased model fitting at this point.

The results of the CFA analysis are shown in Table 18.4, which reports standardized factor loadings and correlations among factors. The factor pattern had a highly constrained form, with leading loadings on each factor varying between .65 and .92 and having z-ratios above 10.0. The only deviation from a perfect pattern of loadings was the .26 (SE = .04) of completion on the spatial factor, a relatively small loading, but one that appeared to be required for the CFA model to fit the data closely. The correlations among factors in Table 18.4 tend to be slightly higher than corresponding values shown for EFA models in Table 18.3. The primary basis for this is the fact that a number of small, positive nonhyperplanar loadings were accommodated in the EFA solution in Table 18.3, but these loadings were fixed at zero in the CFA model in Table 18.4. To account for these small, but nonzero, contributions that are fixed to 0 in the CFA model required somewhat higher factor intercorrelations in the latter model.

Advanced Forms of CFA

To demonstrate the flexibility of the CFA approach to analyses, I will discuss several advanced forms of analysis. Because of space limitations, the presentation here necessarily will be brief, but I trust the reader will get a sense of the many interesting ideas that can be formulated and tested within the general CFA framework.

Multiple-group CFA. Multiple groups of participants can be identified by subsetting data as a function of person characteristics such as sex or ethnic status. A crucial scientific question quickly arises: Are factors identified in one group the same factors as those identified in other groups? This question has been studied under the rubric of factorial invariance.

Work on factorial invariance can be traced back over the past 60 years or more, with key contributions by Meredith (1964a, 1964b, 1993); Jöreskog (1971a); and Horn, McArdle, and Mason (1983),

TABLE 18.4

Confirmatory Factor Analysis for 12 Manifest Variables (MVs) in Sample 1

MV	Factor				h²
	V	W	R	S	
Sentences	**.91** (.02)	.0* (.00)	.0* (.00)	.0* (.00)	.84
Vocabulary	**.92** (.02)	.0* (.00)	.0* (.00)	.0* (.00)	.84
Completion	**.81** (.03)	.0* (.00)	.0* (.00)	**.26** (.04)	.76
First letters	.0* (.00)	**.83** (.04)	.0* (.00)	.0* (.00)	.69
Four-letter words	.0* (.00)	**.73** (.04)	.0* (.00)	.0* (.00)	.54
Suffixes	.0* (.00)	**.65** (.05)	.0* (.00)	.0* (.00)	.42
Letter series	.0* (.00)	.0* (.00)	**.85** (.03)	.0* (.00)	.71
Pedigrees	.0* (.00)	.0* (.00)	**.79** (.03)	.0* (.00)	.63
Letter grouping	.0* (.00)	.0* (.00)	**.72** (.04)	.0* (.00)	.51
Flags	.0* (.00)	.0* (.00)	.0* (.00)	**.77** (.04)	.60
Figures	.0* (.00)	.0* (.00)	.0* (.00)	**.87** (.03)	.76
Cards	.0* (.00)	.0* (.00)	.0* (.00)	**.82** (.03)	.67

	Factor correlations			
V	1.0* (.00)			
W	**.56** (.06)	1.0* (.00)		
R	**.69** (.05)	**.57** (.06)	1.0* (.00)	
S	.09 (.08)	.15 (.08)	*.31* (.07)	1.0* (.00)

Note: Tabled values are standardized factor loadings and factor correlations, with standard errors in parentheses. Boldfaced parameters had z ratios greater than 5.0; italicized parameters had z ratio between 2.0 and 5.0. Asterisked values fixed at reported values to identify model. Data from Bechtoldt (1961).

among others. To pursue factorial invariance, a model akin to Equations 3 and 4 can be written as

$$E\left(Y_g\right) = \boldsymbol{\tau}_g + \boldsymbol{\Lambda}_g \boldsymbol{\alpha}_g \qquad (15)$$

$$E\left(Y_g Y_g'\right) = \boldsymbol{\Sigma}_{YY_g} = \boldsymbol{\Lambda}_g \boldsymbol{\Psi}_g \boldsymbol{\Lambda}_g' + \boldsymbol{\Theta}_g, \qquad (16)$$

where the g subscript ($g = 1, \ldots, G$) is an indicator of group membership, α_g is a vector of mean differences on LVs for group g, and other symbols were defined in Equations 3 and 4. The g subscript on the matrices in Equations 15 and 16 indicates that different parameter estimates may be present for corresponding parameters across groups. But, the g subscript on a given matrix can be deleted if parameter estimates are constrained to numerical invariance across groups.

Widaman and Reise (1997) synthesized prior work and identified four levels of factorial invariance, which are (a) configural invariance, or invariance of the pattern of fixed and free factor loadings in $\boldsymbol{\Lambda}$; (b) weak factorial invariance, or invariance

of estimated loadings in $\boldsymbol{\Lambda}$; (c) strong factorial invariance, or invariance of estimated loadings in $\boldsymbol{\Lambda}$ and measurement intercepts in $\boldsymbol{\tau}$; (d) and strict factorial invariance, or invariance of estimated loadings in $\boldsymbol{\Lambda}$, measurement intercepts in $\boldsymbol{\tau}$, and unique factor variances in $\boldsymbol{\Theta}$. If strong or strict factorial invariance holds across groups, a researcher has putative evidence that the same factors have been found across groups. Given this, group differences in means and variances on the factors are open for study. Furthermore, if strict factorial invariance holds, all between-group differences in means and variances on MVs are a function of between-group differences on the latent variables. Thus, in a mathematical sense, the latent variables explain or represent group differences on MVs.

Factorial invariance and its implications have been matters of great interest. In addition to the preceding sources, interested readers should consult additional literature, including Browne and Arminger (1995), Cheung and Rensvold (1999),

Levy and Hancock (2007), Little (1997), McArdle (1996), McArdle and Cattell (1994), and Millsap and Meredith (2007).

The preceding approach to testing factorial invariance can be applied to the data from the two samples of participants contained in Table 18.1. First, I standardized the mean to zero and variance to one across groups for each MV, following procedures outlined by Jöreskog (1971a; input data sets available on request). I then fit a nonoverlapping simple structure solution in both groups, with the three key indicators of each factor having the only nonzero loadings on each factor. This model, Model 1, had generally adequate fit, with $\chi^2(96) = 179.86$, $p < .001$, and practical fit indexes of TLI = .959 and RMSEA = .064 (CI = .049–.078). However, the loading of the completion test on the S factor in Sample 1 and the loading of the pedigrees test on the V factor in Sample 2 had large modification indexes. After freeing both of these loadings in both samples, the resulting configural invariance model, termed Model 1a, had very close fit to the data, with $\chi^2(92) = 118.15$, $p = .03$, TLI = .987, and RMSEA = .037 (CI = .011–.055). Model 1a had significantly better fit than did Model 1, $\Delta\chi^2(4) = 61.71$, $p < .001$, and the practical fit indexes were much improved, supporting the addition of the two extra loadings in each sample.

Model 2 was the weak factorial invariance model, which was identical to Model 1a but enforced numerical invariance of factor loadings. The fit of Model 2 was very good, with $\chi^2(102) = 132.14$, $p = .02$, TLI = .986, and RMSEA = .037 (CI = .014–.054). Importantly, Model 2 showed a nonsignificant worsening of fit associated with the invariance constraint on factor loadings, $\Delta\chi^2(10) = 13.99$, ns, and practical fit indexes were essentially unchanged.

The next model, Model 3, was the strong factorial invariance model, which was identical to Model 2 except that invariance of measurement intercepts was invoked. The fit of Model 3 was also very good, with $\chi^2(110) = 138.60$, $p = .03$, TLI = .988, and RMSEA = .035 (CI = .010–.052). Compared with Model 2, Model 3 showed a nonsignificant worsening of fit associated with the invariance constraint on intercepts, $\Delta\chi^2(8) = 6.46$, ns, and practical fit indexes improved slightly.

The final model considered here, Model 4, was the strict factorial invariance model, which was identical to Model 3 except that invariance of unique variances was enforced. The fit of Model 4 was very good, with $\chi^2(122) = 145.70$, $p = .07$, TLI = .991, and RMSEA = .030 (CI = .000–.047). Supporting the invariance constraints on unique variances, the fit of Model 4 was not significantly worse than that of Model 3, $\Delta\chi^2(12) = 7.10$, ns, and practical fit indexes once again improved slightly.

Parameter estimates from Model 4 are shown in Table 18.5. The three primary indicators of each factor had large loadings, ranging between .62 and .91 and having CRs of 12 or higher. The two non-hypothesized loadings of completion on the S factor, $\lambda = .20$ ($SE = .03$), and pedigrees on the V factor, $\lambda = .25$ ($SE = .05$), had CRs of 4.68 and 5.93, respectively, and were significant at $p < .001$. Because all parameter estimates in τ, Λ, and Θ in the top half of Table 18.5 were invariant across samples, any differences across groups are captured by the moments (i.e., means, variances, covariances) of the latent variables. As shown in the bottom half of Table 18.5, factor means were fixed at zero in Sample 1 to identify the model; mean differences in Sample 2 showed small and nonsignificant variation from Sample 1 values. Factor variances were fixed at unity in Sample 1 to identify the model; estimated variances on factors in Sample 2 differed somewhat, but generally nonsignificantly from unity. Finally, both the factor covariances and their standardized values (i.e., correlations) appeared to vary little across samples. Thus, in the present application, parameter estimates in the three measurement matrices—τ, Λ, and Θ—demonstrated clear invariance across the two samples, and parameter estimates in the remaining two matrices—α and Ψ—also exhibited a high degree of similarity across samples. These results provide strong support for the claim that the same factors were identified in the two samples.

Longitudinal factor models. The issue of invariance of factors across groups can be generalized across the dimension of time. Here, the key scientific question concerns whether the latent factors identified at one point in time are the same as those

TABLE 18.5

Multiple-Group Confirmatory Factor Analysis for 12 Manifest Variables (MVs) in Samples 1 and 2

MV	τ	Factor				Θ
		V	**W**	**R**	**S**	
Sentences	−.01 (.07)	**.90** (.05)	.0* (.00)	.0* (.00)	.0* (.00)	**.17** (.02)
Vocabulary	−.01 (.07)	**.91** (.05)	.0* (.00)	.0* (.00)	.0* (.00)	**.16** (.02)
Completion	.00 (.07)	**.82** (.05)	.0* (.00)	.0* (.00)	**.20** (.03)	**.25** (.02)
First letters	.04 (.06)	.0* (.00)	**.75** (.05)	.0* (.00)	.0* (.00)	**.31** (.04)
Four-letter words	.03 (.06)	.0* (.00)	**.70** (.05)	.0* (.00)	.0* (.00)	**.40** (.04)
Suffixes	.03 (.06)	.0* (.00)	**.62** (.05)	.0* (.00)	.0* (.00)	**.54** (.04)
Letter series	−.01 (.07)	.0* (.00)	.0* (.00)	**.87** (.06)	.0* (.00)	**.29** (.04)
Pedigrees	−.01 (.06)	*.25* (.05)	.0* (.00)	**.56** (.06)	.0* (.00)	**.46** (.04)
Letter grouping	−.01 (.06)	.0* (.00)	.0* (.00)	**.75** (.06)	.0* (.00)	**.47** (.04)
Flags	.04 (.07)	.0* (.00)	.0* (.00)	.0* (.00)	**.81** (.06)	**.41** (.04)
Figures	.04 (.07)	.0* (.00)	.0* (.00)	.0* (.00)	**.89** (.06)	**.29** (.04)
Cards	.04 (.07)	.0* (.00)	.0* (.00)	.0* (.00)	**.88** (.06)	**.31** (.04)

Factor	Factor mean	Factor covariances			
		Sample 1			
V	.0* (.00)	1.0* (.00)	.56	.65	.11
W	.0* (.00)	**.56** (.06)	1.0* (.00)	.57	.15
R	.0* (.00)	**.65** (.05)	**.57** (.07)	1.0* (.00)	.32
S	.0* (.00)	.11 (.08)	.15 (.08)	*.32* (.07)	1.0* (.00)
		Sample 2			
V	.02 (.10)	**1.03** (.15)	.62	.57	.13
W	−.09 (.12)	**.76** (.13)	**1.44** (.24)	.59	.23
R	.02 (.11)	**.55** (.10)	**.67** (.12)	**.89** (.15)	.35
S	−.10 (.10)	.11 (.07)	*.24* (.09)	*.29* (.08)	**.77** (.12)

Note: Tabled values are parameter estimates, with standard errors in parentheses. Boldfaced parameters had z ratios greater than 5.0; italicized parameters had z ratios between 2.0 and 5.0. In factor covariance matrices, covariances are shown below the diagonal, correlations above the diagonal. Asterisked values fixed at reported values to identify model. Data from Bechtoldt (1961).

at other points in time. This is a crucial question because tracking growth over time requires the implicit assumption that one is assessing the same construct across time. Longitudinal CFA models can embody this assumption, especially if strong or strict factorial invariance holds across time.

The testing of levels of invariance—from configural invariance to strict factorial invariance—follows the same steps as outlined for multiple-group modeling. The one difference in longitudinal models is the need to allow covariances among unique factors for the same indicator across the multiple times of measurement. This is a reasonable a priori specification, as unique factors are hypothesized to consist of a combination of specific (i.e., reliable) variance and random error. The longitudinal stability of the specific portion of the unique factor is therefore the basis for such covariances among uniquenesses. Among the many sources that could be offered, the following provide accessible discussions of details: Ferrer, Balluerka, and Widaman (2008); Hancock, Kuo, and Lawrence (2001); McArdle (1988, 2007); Meredith and Horn (2001); Tisak and Meredith (1989); and Widaman, Ferrer, and Conger (2010).

Analyses of multitrait–multimethod data. In a seminal publication, Campbell and Fiske (1959) discussed convergent and discriminant validation using the multitrait–multimethod (MTMM) matrix. Convergent validation was shown if measures purportedly of the same construct had relatively high correlations with one another, and discriminant validation was supported if measures of different constructs had lower levels of correlation. Campbell and Fiske discussed four rules for interpreting trends in MTMM matrices. The most crucial rules dealt with particular comparisons among elements in an MTMM that provided evidence for convergent and discriminant validation of measures. Although the Campbell and Fiske rules are useful, nonindependence among comparisons made any statistical evaluation of evidence difficult.

With the advent of CFA, researchers quickly saw the utility of restricted factor models for evaluating trends in MTMM matrices. If t trait constructs are assessed using each of m methods, then the p MVs in an MTMM matrix consist of $(t \times m)$ MVs. The factor-loading matrix $\mathbf{\Lambda}$ can be structured as a matrix with $(p \times [t + m])$ factors. Each of the t trait factors would have m loadings, one from each of the methods of measurement; conversely, each of the m method factors would have t loadings, one from each of the traits assessed by that method. The matrix of covariances among factors $\mathbf{\Psi}$ could also be structured into a $([t + m] \times [t + m])$ matrix, with freely estimated correlations among the t trait factors, freely estimated correlations among the m method factors, and correlations between trait and method factors fixed at zero for identification. This model is often termed the *correlated trait–correlated method* (CT-CM) model.

One of the first to demonstrate the utility of CFA models for evaluating MTMM data was Jöreskog (1971b), who presented an analysis of one of the matrices contained in Campbell and Fiske (1959). To reconcile discrepancies in some prior work, Widaman (1985) offered a taxonomy of CFA models for MTMM data that cross-classified four trait structures with four method structures, yielding a set of 16 models that afforded interesting model comparisons. Widaman noted that trait factor loadings were direct and useful indicators of convergent validation,

as they reflect the alignment, or loading, of each of the MVs with their respective trait factors. In turn, method factor loadings are indicators of the degree to which an MV was imbued with the biasing influences of variance caused by method of measurement. Finally, the correlations among trait factors provide a useful index of discriminant validation, with correlations nearer zero providing stronger evidence of discriminant validation of trait constructs.

More recent work has concerned different options for representing method effects. Marsh (1989) reintroduced a variation of MTMM model specification in which shared method effects are represented by covariances among unique factors in the $\mathbf{\Theta}$ matrix, rather than as method factors. Later, Eid (2000) introduced a modified CT-CM model in which one method factor is left out of the model, an approach designed to improve the empirical identification of parameters in the CT-CM model and improve the likelihood of model convergence. A recent summary of multimethod approaches to research is contained in Eid and Diener (2006), and the chapter by Eid, Lischetzke, and Nussbeck (2006) in that volume is an up-to-date summary of different structural modeling approaches to evaluating MTMM data.

CONCLUSION

The first publication on factor analysis (Spearman, 1904) appeared more than a century ago, yet the use of factor analysis in all of its forms seems still to be on the ascendant. For the first half of the 20th century, factor analysis was limited in its application by the complexity of the calculations required. During the 1930s and 1940s, a considerable number of factor analytic studies were published, but these tended to be authored by a methodologically sophisticated elite in the field. With the advent of computers and efficient algorithms for estimating loadings and rotating factors in the 1950s and 1960s, factor analysis could routinely be used by practicing scientists to a wide array of domains. In addition to exploring new domains, researchers used EFA to explore the dimensionality of existing scales.

Experts on factor analysis have long had concerns about how users of the method used and, frequently, misused the method. Thurstone (1937) gave an early outline of certain misuses of factor analysis, and Guilford (1952) followed with his admonitions. Comrey (1978); Floyd and Widaman (1995); Fabrigar, Wegener, MacCallum, and Strahan (1999); and Reise, Waller, and Comrey (2000) provided further comments and suggestions. Factor analysis is a powerful method, but one that can be misused, whether consciously or not. Typical program package defaults—using principal components extraction, retaining components with eigenvalues greater than one, and rotating with varimax—will likely lead to a much poorer factor solution than using an EFA procedure with a more carefully considered set of options, such as those demonstrated in this chapter.

Many existing sources can provide additional information on the use of factor analysis. For EFA, the classic texts by Thurstone (1947) and Harman (1976) provided interesting and informative presentations of the multiple factor model; although obviously dated, much is to be learned about the general approach to factor analysis from these texts. Gorsuch (1983) has remained a good introductory guide to EFA, and Mulaik (2010) has provided a recent, state-of-the-art presentation of many advanced techniques in factor analysis. McDonald (1985) placed factor analytic procedures squarely within the psychometric tradition broadly construed, and later (McDonald, 1999) provided a unified treatment of classical and modern test theory, including the place of factor analysis in the context of psychological measurement. Finally, Brown (2006) and Jöreskog (2007) gave state-of-the-art presentations of CFA procedures, including many special cases. Armed with these sources, we can look forward to the next century of expanding use of factor analytic methods to explore and confirm patterns in behavioral data in increasingly precise fashion.

References

Bechtoldt, H. P. (1961). An empirical study of the factor analysis stability hypothesis. *Psychometrika, 26,* 405–432. doi:10.1007/BF02289771

Bentler, P. M., & Bonett, D. G. (1980). Significance tests and goodness of fit in the analysis of covariance structures. *Psychological Bulletin, 88,* 588–606. doi:10.1037/0033-2909.88.3.588

Bock, R. D., Gibbons, R., & Muraki, E. (1988). Full-information item factor analysis. *Applied Psychological Measurement, 12,* 261–280. doi:10.1177/014662168801200305

Brown, T. A. (2006). *Confirmatory factor analysis for applied research.* New York, NY: Guilford Press.

Browne, M. W. (1984). Asymptotically distribution-free methods for the analysis of covariance structures. *British Journal of Mathematical and Statistical Psychology, 37,* 62–83.

Browne, M. W. (2001). An overview of analytic rotation in exploratory factor analysis. *Multivariate Behavioral Research, 36,* 111–150. doi:10.1207/S15327906MBR3601_05

Browne, M. W., & Arminger, G. (1995). Specification and estimation of mean and covariance structure models. In G. Arminger, C. Clogg, & M. E. Sobel (Eds.), *Handbook of statistical modeling for the social and behavioral sciences* (pp. 185–249). New York, NY: Plenum Press.

Browne, M. W., & Cudeck, R. (1993). Alternative ways of assessing model fit. In K. A. Bollen & J. S. Long (Eds.), *Testing structural equation models* (pp. 136–162). Newbury Park, CA: Sage.

Browne, M. W., Cudeck, R., Tateneni, K., & Mels, G. (2010). *CEFA: Comprehensive exploratory factor analysis (Version 3.04)* [Computer software and manual]. Retrieved from http://faculty.psy.ohio-state.edu/browne

Campbell, D. T., & Fiske, D. W. (1959). Convergent and discriminant validation by the multitrait–multimethod matrix. *Psychological Bulletin, 56,* 81–105. doi:10.1037/h0046016

Carroll, J. B. (1993). *Human cognitive abilities: A survey of factor-analytic studies.* New York, NY: Cambridge University Press. doi:10.1017/CBO9780511571312

Cattell, R. B. (1963). Theory of fluid and crystallized intelligence: A critical experiment. *Journal of Educational Psychology, 54,* 1–22. doi:10.1037/h0046743

Cattell, R. B. (1966). The scree test for the number of factors. *Multivariate Behavioral Research, 1,* 245–276. doi:10.1207/s15327906mbr0102_10

Cattell, R. B. (1971). *Abilities: Their structure, growth, and action.* Boston, MA: Houghton Mifflin.

Cheung, G. W., & Rensvold, R. B. (1999). Testing factorial invariance across groups: A reconceptualization and proposed new method. *Journal of Management, 25,* 1–27. doi:10.1177/014920639902500101

Cliff, N. (1988). The eigenvalues-greater-than-one rule and the reliability of components. *Psychological Bulletin, 103,* 276–279. doi:10.1037/0033-2909.103.2.276

Cohen, J. (1988). *Statistical power analysis for the behavioral sciences* (2nd ed.). Hillsdale, NJ: Erlbaum.

Comrey, A. L. (1978). Common methodological problems in factor analytic studies. *Journal of Consulting and Clinical Psychology, 46*, 648–659. doi:10.1037/0022-006X.46.4.648

Crawford, C. B., & Ferguson, G. A. (1970). A general rotation criterion and its use in orthogonal rotation. *Psychometrika, 35*, 321–332. doi:10.1007/BF02310792

Cudeck, R. (1989). Analysis of covariance matrices using covariance structure models. *Psychological Bulletin, 105*, 317–327. doi:10.1037/0033-2909.105.2.317

Cudeck, R., & O'Dell, L. L. (1994). Applications of standard error estimates in unrestricted factor analysis: Significance tests for factor loadings and correlations. *Psychological Bulletin, 115*, 475–487. doi:10.1037/0033-2909.115.3.475

Eid, M. (2000). A multitrait–multimethod model with minimal assumptions. *Psychometrika, 65*, 241–261. doi:10.1007/BF02294377

Eid, M., & Diener, E. (Eds.). (2006). *Handbook of multimethod measurement in psychology*. Washington, DC: American Psychological Association. doi:10.1037/11383-000

Eid, M., Lischetzke, T., & Nussbeck, F. W. (2006). Structural equation models for multitrait–multimethod data. In M. Eid & E. Diener (Eds.), *Handbook of multimethod measurement in psychology* (pp. 283–299). Washington, DC: American Psychological Association. doi:10.1037/11383-020

Fabrigar, L. R., Wegener, D. T., MacCallum, R. C., & Strahan, E. J. (1999). Evaluating the use of exploratory factor analysis in psychological research. *Psychological Methods, 4*, 272–299. doi:10.1037/1082-989X.4.3.272

Ferguson, G. A. (1941). The factorial interpretation of test difficulty. *Psychometrika, 6*, 323–329. doi:10.1007/BF02288588

Ferrer, E., Balluerka, N., & Widaman, K. F. (2008). Factorial invariance and the specification of second-order growth models. *Methodology, 4*, 22–36.

Fiske, D. W. (1949). Consistency of the factorial structures of personality ratings from different sources. *Journal of Abnormal and Social Psychology, 44*, 329–344. doi:10.1037/h0057198

Floyd, F. J., & Widaman, K. F. (1995). Factor analysis in the development and refinement of clinical assessment instruments. *Psychological Assessment, 7*, 286–299. doi:10.1037/1040-3590.7.3.286

Goldberg, L. R. (1993). The structure of phenotypic personality traits. *American Psychologist, 48*, 26–34. doi:10.1037/0003-066X.48.1.26

Goldberg, L. R., & Velicer, W. F. (2006). Principles of exploratory factor analysis. In S. Strack (Ed.), *Differentiating normal and abnormal personality* (2nd ed., pp. 209–237). New York, NY: Springer.

Gorsuch, R. L. (1983). *Factor analysis* (2nd ed.). Hillsdale, NJ: Erlbaum.

Gorsuch, R. L. (1988). Exploratory factor analysis. In J. R. Nesselroade & R. B. Cattell (Eds.), *Handbook of multivariate experimental psychology* (2nd ed., pp. 231–258). New York, NY: Plenum Press.

Guilford, J. P. (1941). The difficulty of a test and its factor composition. *Psychometrika, 6*, 67–77. doi:10.1007/BF02292175

Guilford, J. P. (1952). When not to factor analyze. *Psychological Bulletin, 49*, 26–37. doi:10.1037/h0054935

Guilford, J. P. (1964). Zero correlations among tests of intellectual abilities. *Psychological Bulletin, 61*, 401–404. doi:10.1037/h0048576

Guttman, L. (1954). Some necessary conditions for common-factor analysis. *Psychometrika, 19*, 149–161. doi:10.1007/BF02289162

Guttman, L. (1956). "Best possible" systematic estimates of communality. *Psychometrika, 21*, 273–285. doi:10.1007/BF02289137

Hakstian, A. R. (1971). A comparative evaluation of several prominent methods of oblique factor transformation. *Psychometrika, 36*, 175–193. doi:10.1007/BF02291397

Hakstian, A. R., & Abell, R. A. (1974). A further comparison of oblique factor transformation methods. *Psychometrika, 39*, 429–444. doi:10.1007/BF02291667

Hakstian, A. R., Rogers, W. T., & Cattell, R. B. (1982). The behavior of number-of-factors rules with simulated data. *Multivariate Behavioral Research, 17*, 193–219. doi:10.1207/s15327906mbr1702_3

Hancock, G. R., Kuo, W-L., & Lawrence, F. R. (2001). An illustration of second-order latent growth models. *Structural Equation Modeling, 8*, 470–489. doi:10.1207/S15328007SEM0803_7

Harman, H. H. (1976). *Modern factor analysis* (3rd ed.). Chicago, IL: University of Chicago Press.

Harris, C. W., & Kaiser, H. F. (1964). Oblique factor solutions by orthogonal transformations. *Psychometrika, 29*, 347–362. doi:10.1007/BF02289601

Hendrickson, A. E., & White, P. O. (1964). Promax: A quick method for rotation to oblique simple structure. *British Journal of Statistical Psychology, 17*, 65–70.

Horn, J. L. (1965). A rationale and test for the number of factors in factor analysis. *Psychometrika, 30*, 179–185. doi:10.1007/BF02289447

Horn, J. L., & Hofer, S. M. (1992). Major abilities and development in the adult period. In R. J. Sternberg & C. A. Berg (Eds.), *Intellectual development* (pp. 44–99). New York, NY: Cambridge University Press.

Horn, J. L., & McArdle, J. J. (2007). Understanding human intelligence since Spearman. In R. Cudeck & R. C. MacCallum (Eds.), *Factor analysis at 100: Historical developments and future directions* (pp. 205–247). Mahwah, NJ: Erlbaum.

Horn, J. L., McArdle, J. J., & Mason, R. (1983). When is invariance not invariant: A practical scientist's look at the ethereal concept of factor invariance. *Southern Psychologist, 1*, 179–188.

Horn, J. L., & Noll, J. (1997). Human cognitive capabilities: Gf-Gc theory. In D. P. Flanagan, J. L. Genshaft, & P. L. Harrison (Eds.), *Contemporary intellectual assessment: Theories, tests, and issues* (pp. 53–91). New York, NY: Guilford Press.

Hu, L., & Bentler, P. M. (1999). Cutoff criteria for fit indexes in covariance structure analysis: Conventional criteria versus new alternatives. *Structural Equation Modeling, 6*, 1–55.

Humphreys, L. G., & Ilgen, D. R. (1969). Note on a criterion for the number of common factors. *Educational and Psychological Measurement, 29*, 571–578. doi:10.1177/001316446902900303

Humphreys, L. G., & Montanelli, R. G. (1975). An investigation of the parallel analysis criterion for determining the number of factors. *Multivariate Behavioral Research, 10*, 193–205. doi:10.1207/s15327906mbr1002_5

Jöreskog, K. G. (1967). Some contributions to maximum likelihood factor analysis. *Psychometrika, 32*, 443–482. doi:10.1007/BF02289658

Jöreskog, K. G. (1969). A general approach to confirmatory maximum likelihood factor analysis. *Psychometrika, 34*, 183–202. doi:10.1007/BF02289343

Jöreskog, K. G. (1971a). Simultaneous factor analysis in several populations. *Psychometrika, 36*, 409–426. doi:10.1007/BF02291366

Jöreskog, K. G. (1971b). Statistical analysis of sets of congeneric tests. *Psychometrika, 36*, 109–133. doi:10.1007/BF02291393

Jöreskog, K. G. (2007). Factor analysis models and its extensions. In R. Cudeck & R. C. MacCallum (Eds.), *Factor analysis at 100: Historical developments and future directions* (pp. 47–77). Mahwah, NJ: Erlbaum.

Kaiser, H. F. (1958). The varimax criterion for analytic rotation in factor analysis. *Psychometrika, 23*, 187–200. doi:10.1007/BF02289233

Levy, R., & Hancock, G. R. (2007). A framework of statistical tests for comparing mean and covariance structure models. *Multivariate Behavioral Research, 42*, 33–66.

Little, T. D. (1997). Mean and covariance structures (MACS) analyses of cross-cultural data: Practical and theoretical issues. *Multivariate Behavioral Research, 32*, 53–76. doi:10.1207/s15327906mbr3201_3

Little, T. D., Lindenberger, U., & Nesselroade, J. R. (1999). On selecting indicators for multivariate measurement and modeling with LVs: When "good" indicators are bad and "bad" indicators are good. *Psychological Methods, 4*, 192–211. doi:10.1037/1082-989X.4.2.192

MacCallum, R. (1986). Specification searches in covariance structure modeling. *Psychological Bulletin, 100*, 107–120. doi:10.1037/0033-2909.100.1.107

MacCallum, R. C., Browne, M. W., & Cai, L. (2007). Factor analysis models as approximations. In R. Cudeck & R. C. MacCallum (Eds.), *Factor analysis at 100: Historical developments and future directions* (pp. 153–175). Mahwah, NJ: Erlbaum.

MacCallum, R. C., & Tucker, L. R. (1991). Representing sources of error in the common-factor model: Implications for theory and practices. *Psychological Bulletin, 109*, 502–511. doi:10.1037/0033-2909.109.3.502

MacCallum, R. C., Widaman, K. F., Preacher, K. J., & Hong, S. (2001). Sample size in factor analysis: The role of model error. *Multivariate Behavioral Research, 36*, 611–637. doi:10.1207/S15327906MBR3604_06

MacCallum, R. C., Widaman, K. F., Zhang, S., & Hong, S. (1999). Sample size in factor analysis. *Psychological Methods, 4*, 84–99. doi:10.1037/1082-989X.4.1.84

Marsh, H. W. (1989). Confirmatory factor analyses of multitrait-multimethod data: Many problems and a few solutions. *Applied Psychological Measurement, 13*, 335–361. doi:10.1177/014662168901300402

McArdle, J. J. (1988). Dynamic but structural equation modeling of repeated measures data. In J. R. Nesselroade & R. B. Cattell (Eds.), *Handbook of multivariate experimental psychology* (2nd ed., pp. 561–614). New York, NY: Plenum.

McArdle, J. J. (1996). Current directions in structural factor analysis. *Current Directions in Psychological Science, 5*, 11–18. doi:10.1111/1467-8721.ep10772681

McArdle, J. J. (2007). Five steps in the structural factor analysis of longitudinal data. In R. Cudeck & R. C. MacCallum (Eds.), *Factor analysis at 100: Historical developments and future directions* (pp. 99–130). Mahwah, NJ: Erlbaum.

McArdle, J. J., & Cattell, R. B. (1994). Structural equation models of factorial invariance in parallel proportional profiles and oblique confactor problems. *Multivariate Behavioral Research, 29*, 63–113. doi:10.1207/s15327906mbr2901_3

McDonald, R. P. (1985). *Factor analysis and related methods*. Hillsdale, NJ: Erlbaum.

McDonald, R. P. (1999). *Test theory*. Mahwah, NJ: Erlbaum.

McDonald, R. P., & Ahlawat, K. S. (1974). Difficulty factors in binary data. *British Journal of Mathematical and Statistical Psychology, 27*, 82–99.

Meredith, W. (1964a). Notes on factorial invariance. *Psychometrika, 29*, 177–185. doi:10.1007/BF02289699

Meredith, W. (1964b). Rotation to achieve factorial invariance. *Psychometrika, 29*, 187–206. doi:10.1007/BF02289700

Meredith, W. (1993). Measurement invariance, factor analysis and factorial invariance. *Psychometrika, 58*, 525–543. doi:10.1007/BF02294825

Meredith, W., & Horn, J. (2001). The role of factorial invariance in modeling growth and change. In L. M. Collins & A. G. Sayer (Eds.), *New methods for the analysis of change* (pp. 203–240). Washington, DC: American Psychological Association. doi:10.1037/10409-007

Millsap, R. E., & Meredith, W. (2007). Factorial invariance: Historical perspectives and new problems. In R. Cudeck & R. C. MacCallum (Eds.), *Factor analysis at 100: Historical perspectives and future directions* (pp. 131–152). Mahwah, NJ: Erlbaum.

Millsap, R. E., & Yun-Tein, J. (2004). Assessing factorial invariance in ordered-categorical measures. *Multivariate Behavioral Research, 39*, 479–515. doi:10.1207/S15327906MBR3903_4

Montanelli, R. G., & Humphreys, L. G. (1976). Latent roots of random data correlation matrices with squared multiple correlations on the diagonal: A Monte Carlo study. *Psychometrika, 41*, 341–348. doi:10.1007/BF02293559

Mulaik, S. A. (2010). *Foundations of factor analysis* (2nd ed.). New York, NY: Chapman & Hall.

Muthén, B. O. (1978). Contributions to factor analysis of dichotomous variables. *Psychometrika, 43*, 551–560. doi:10.1007/BF02293813

Muthén, B. O. (1984). A general structural equation model with dichotomous, ordered categorical, and continuous latent variable indicators. *Psychometrika, 49*, 115–132. doi:10.1007/BF02294210

Muthén, L. K., & Muthén, B. O. (1998–2010). *Mplus user's guide* (6th ed.) [Computer software]. Los Angeles, CA: Muthén & Muthén.

Reise, S. P., Waller, N. G., & Comrey, A. L. (2000). Factor analysis and scale revision. *Psychological Assessment, 12*, 287–297. doi:10.1037/1040-3590.12.3.287

Satorra, A., & Bentler, P. M. (1994). Corrections to test statistics and standard errors in covariance structure analysis. In A. von Eye & C. C. Clogg (Eds.), *LVs analysis: Applications for developmental research* (pp. 399–419). Thousand Oaks, CA: Sage.

Savalei, V. (2010). Small sample statistics for incomplete nonnormal data: Extensions of complete data formulae and a Monte Carlo comparison. *Structural Equation Modeling, 17*, 241–264. doi:10.1080/10705511003659375

Sörbom, D. (1989). Model modification. *Psychometrika, 54*, 371–384. doi:10.1007/BF02294623

Spearman, C. (1904). "General intelligence," objectively determined and measured. *American Journal of Psychology, 15*, 201–293. doi:10.2307/1412107

Spearman, C. (1927). *The abilities of man*. Oxford, England: Macmillan.

Steiger, J. H. (1979). Factor indeterminacy in the 1930s and 1970s: Some interesting parallels. *Psychometrika, 44*, 157–167. doi:10.1007/BF02293967

Steiger, J. H. (1994). Factor analysis in the 1980's and the 1990's: Some old debates and some new developments. In I. Borg & P. P. Mohler (Eds.), *Trends and perspectives in empirical social research* (pp. 201–224). Berlin, Germany: Walter de Gruyter.

Steiger, J. H., & Lind, J. C. (1980, May). *Statistically based tests for the number of common factors*. Paper presented at the annual meeting of the Psychometric Society, Iowa City.

Thompson, B. (2004). *Exploratory and confirmatory factor analysis: Understanding concepts and applications*. Washington, DC: American Psychological Association. doi:10.1037/10694-000

Thurstone, L. L. (1931). Multiple factor analysis. *Psychological Review, 38*, 406–427. doi:10.1037/h0069792

Thurstone, L. L. (1934). The vectors of mind. *Psychological Review, 41*, 1–32. doi:10.1037/h0075959

Thurstone, L. L. (1935). *The vectors of mind*. Chicago, IL: University of Chicago Press.

Thurstone, L. L. (1937). Current misuse of the factorial methods. *Psychometrika, 2*, 73–76. doi:10.1007/BF02288060

Thurstone, L. L. (1938). Primary mental abilities. *Psychometric Monographs*, No. 1.

Thurstone, L. L. (1947). *Multiple factor analysis*. Chicago, IL: University of Chicago Press.

Thurstone, L. L., & Thurstone, T. G. (1941). Factorial studies of intelligence. *Psychometric Monographs*, No. 2.

Tisak, J., & Meredith, W. (1989). Exploratory longitudinal factor analysis in multiple populations. *Psychometrika, 54*, 261–281. doi:10.1007/BF02294520

Tucker, L. R. (1940). The role of correlated factors in factor analysis. *Psychometrika, 5*, 141–152. doi:10.1007/BF02287872

Tucker, L. R. (1971). Relations of factor score estimates to their use. *Psychometrika, 36*, 427–436. doi:10.1007/BF02291367

Tucker, L. R., Koopman, R. F., & Linn, R. L. (1969). Evaluation of factor analytic research procedures by means of simulated correlation matrices. *Psychometrika, 34*, 421–459. doi:10.1007/BF02290601

Tucker, L. R., & Lewis, C. (1973). A reliability coefficient for maximum likelihood factor analysis. *Psychometrika, 38*, 1–10. doi:10.1007/BF02291170

Velicer, W. F. (1976). Determining the number of components from the matrix of partial correlations. *Psychometrika, 41*, 321–327. doi:10.1007/BF02293557

Velicer, W. F., & Jackson, D. N. (1990). Component analysis versus common factor analysis: Some issues in selecting an appropriate procedure. *Multivariate Behavioral Research, 25*, 1–28. doi:10.1207/s15327906mbr2501_1

Wherry, R. J., & Gaylord, R. H. (1944). Factor pattern of test items and tests as a function of the correlation coefficient: Content, difficulty, and constant error factors. *Psychometrika, 9*, 237–244. doi:10.1007/BF02288734

Widaman, K. F. (1985). Hierarchically nested covariance structure models for multitrait–multimethod data. *Applied Psychological Measurement, 9*, 1–26. doi:10.1177/014662168500900101

Widaman, K. F. (1993). Common factor analysis versus principal component analysis: Differential bias in representing model parameters? *Multivariate Behavioral Research, 28*, 263–311. doi:10.1207/s15327906mbr2803_1

Widaman, K. F. (2007). Common factors versus components: Principals and principles, errors and misconceptions. In R. Cudeck & R. C. MacCallum (Eds.), *Factor analysis at 100: Historical developments and future directions* (pp. 177–203). Mahwah, NJ: Erlbaum.

Widaman, K. F., Ferrer, E., & Conger, R. D. (2010). Factorial invariance within longitudinal structural equation models: Measuring the same construct across time. *Child Development Perspectives, 4*, 10–18. doi:10.1111/j.1750-8606.2009.00110.x

Widaman, K. F., & Herringer, L. W. (1985). Iterative least squares estimates of communality: Initial estimate need not affect stabilized value. *Psychometrika, 50*, 469–477. doi:10.1007/BF02296264

Widaman, K. F., & Reise, S. P. (1997). Exploring the measurement invariance of psychological instruments: Applications in the substance use domain. In K. J. Bryant, M. Windle, & S. G. West (Eds.), *The science of prevention: Methodological advances from alcohol and substance abuse research* (pp. 281–324). Washington, DC: American Psychological Association. doi:10.1037/10222-009

Widaman, K. F., & Thompson, J. S. (2003). On specifying the null model for incremental fit indices in structural equation modeling. *Psychological Methods, 8*, 16–37. doi:10.1037/1082-989X.8.1.16

Wirth, R. J., & Edwards, M. C. (2007). Item factor analysis: Current approaches and future directions. *Psychological Methods, 12*, 58–79. doi:10.1037/1082-989X.12.1.58

Wood, J. M., Tataryn, D. J., & Gorsuch, R. L. (1996). Effects of under- and overextraction on principal axis factor analysis with varimax rotation. *Psychological Methods, 1*, 354–365. doi:10.1037/1082-989-X.1.4.354

Zwick, W. R., & Velicer, W. F. (1982). Factors influencing four rules for determining the number of components to retain. *Multivariate Behavioral Research, 17*, 253–269. doi:10.1207/s15327906mbr1702_5

Zwick, W. R., & Velicer, W. F. (1986). Comparison of five rules for determining the number of components to retain. *Psychological Bulletin, 99*, 432–442. doi:10.1037/0033-2909.99.3.432

## CHAPTER 19

LATENT CLASS AND LATENT PROFILE MODELS

Brian P. Flaherty and Cara J. Kiff

Psychology's concern with unobservable constructs has necessitated the development of appropriate research design and analytic techniques. Spearman's initial interest in IQ and ability differences (Spearman, 1904) led to his introduction and then the subsequent development of factor analysis (Thurstone, 1935). These continuous latent variable models have a long history in psychometrics (Cudeck & MacCallum, 2007). Factor analysis models (see Chapter 18 of this volume) have coevolved with psychometrics, leading to sophisticated current-day measurement approaches (such as item response models; see Embretson & Reise, 2000; Volume 1, Chapter 36, this handbook). As a discipline, psychology readily adopted factor models, leading to their frequent and sometimes automatic use. For example, stage and typological theories—for example Piaget's theory of cognitive development (Piaget, 1960), Kohlberg's theory of moral development (Kohlberg, 1963), and Baumrind's parenting styles (Baumrind, 1967)—have typically been analyzed with continuous variable approaches, even though a categorical approach arguably better represents these categorical constructs.

Outside of psychology, scaling people along a continuum has not always been a primary interest. Taxonomy research in biology seeks to hierarchically organize data, and cluster analysis approaches developed accordingly (Blashfield & Aldenderfer, 1988). *Cluster analysis* refers broadly to a class of approaches that group observations in terms of similarity. In sociology, many researchers wanted to categorize individuals, leading to Lazarsfeld's initial development of latent class models (Lazarsfeld & Henry, 1968). Latent profile models were introduced in psychology (Gibson, 1959), but until relatively recently have seen limited use. Latent class and latent profile models both model subgroups in a population, but they differ by the scale of the data. Latent class models were originally developed for categorical responses, whereas latent profile models were used with continuous variables.

Unlike the development of factor analysis and psychometrics in psychology, these other analytic approaches have not tended to also be connected to advances in measurement. Many cluster analysis techniques are algorithmic (i.e., rule-based) approaches, lacking a statistical basis for a measurement model, such as probability distributions of the data and accompanying statistical tests. In contrast, latent class and latent profile models are statistical models, primarily employed as descriptive, data-partitioning tools. They are not typically treated as a model for a latent construct deserving serious consideration of measurement. In addition to introducing and discussing latent class and latent profile analysis, this chapter highlights the use of these models as measurement models useful in psychological and other research.

This work was supported by National Institutes of Health Grant R37DA18673 and a grant from the American Legacy Foundation.

DOI: 10.1037/13621-019
APA Handbook of Research Methods in Psychology: Vol. 3. Data Analysis and Research Publication, H. Cooper (Editor-in-Chief)

CONCEPTUAL OVERVIEW

Researchers commonly choose latent class and latent profile models when they expect different types of people or observations in a study. Rather than assume homogeneity—that is, a single set of distributions and associations hold for an entire population—distributions and associations may differ on the basis of unobservable subgroup membership. As a result, these models readily accommodate heterogeneous data. If a population does contain subgroups with different distributions and patterns of association and if these subgroups are ignored, then the analytic model is misspecified. In this case, it is unlikely that the sample averaged estimates are very meaningful or accurately reflect associations among phenomena of interest (Flaherty, 2010). Applications of latent class and latent profile models include temperament types in young children (Sanson et al., 2009; Stern, Arcus, Kagan, Rubin, & Snidman, 1995), children's disruptive behavior problems (Degnan, Calkins, Keane, & Hill-Soderlund, 2008), adolescent socialization (Cumsille, Darling, Flaherty, & Martínez, 2006), and patterns of substance use (Flaherty, 2002; O'Connor & Colder, 2005).

We review and discuss these two models as well as rationale for their use. Then we illustrate these models with parallel analyses of nicotine-dependence data. The same data are analyzed with both models. These data are treated as continuous for the latent profile analysis and dichotomized for latent class analysis with binary items. Binary data are not necessary for latent class analysis, but they simplify the presentation and interpretation. The intent of analyzing the same data with both latent class and latent profile models is to emphasize similarities and differences between the models as well as provide a platform for considering measurement of categorical latent variables. No argument is made for which model is better for this particular data or construct.

LATENT CLASS MODELS

A primary goal of latent class models is to partition a heterogeneous population into homogeneous subgroups, that is, the latent classes or latent profiles.

Just as relative position on a latent factor is expected to predict how someone answers a set of items, latent class or profile membership is expected to predict item responses. Viewed from the item level, we treat the items in a depression scale as indirect indicators of a latent depression factor. Similarly, the items in a latent class or profile analysis may be thought of as indicators of an unobservable class membership.

To aid discussion, we will use LC to abbreviate latent class, LCA for latent class analysis, LP for latent profile, LPA for latent profile analysis, and LC/LP and LCA/LPA to refer to both models at the same time. Until recently, the LC model referred to a categorical data model, with categorical items and latent variables. LPA refers to a similar categorical latent variable model but with continuous items. Now, however, LC is often used to refer to any model including an unmeasured categorical variable. For this chapter, we use LCA and LPA as originally described.

In the standard LC model, the items are nominal level and may have more than two response categories. There are two types of estimates in the LC model: LC proportions and conditional response probabilities. The LC proportions are the percent of the sample expected to be members of specific LCs. The conditional response probabilities are the estimates linking items to the latent variable. Specifically, they are the probabilities that members of a particular class endorse a specific item response. Table 19.1 contains fabricated LC estimates to illustrate the model.

In this example, there are two classes and three binary items intended to measure nicotine dependence. The columns of Table 19.1 correspond to the items and the rows are the LCs. The probability of a yes response is given in the table. The probability of a no response is simply $1 - P(Y \mid LC)$ with binary data. This notation, $P(Y \mid LC)$, is shorthand meaning the probability of a yes response to an item given membership in a particular LC.

Table 19.1 contains examples of good and poor items. The first column is a good item for measuring members of each class. People in the first class (LC 1) have a 0.2 probability of replying yes to this item, meaning that a no response is a likely characteristic of people in Class 1. Conversely, people in LC 2

TABLE 19.1

Latent Class (LC) Model Illustration

LC	When you haven't had a cigarette for a while, you feel you need to have one to feel better	Compared to when you started smoking, you now need to smoke more in order to feel the effects	You smoke the same number of cigarettes every day
1 (30%)	0.2	0.5	0.9
2 (70%)	0.9	0.9	0.9

Note. The probability of a yes or true response is shown.

have a 0.9 probability of replying yes. This item provides relatively clear information about a defining characteristic of members of each class. The next two items are not equally good class indicators. The second clearly measures LC 2 well, but provides no information about people in LC 1. That is, the second item contains the same information as a fair coin-flip for people in LC 1. This does not mean one would necessarily throw out Item 2. Item 2 could be a salient, theoretically important measure of LC 2, and it could be useful for that reason. Item 3 does not help us distinguish the classes. Item responses are equally likely for members of both classes. The value of this item is also not clear. If there were more classes in the population, it could be good at distinguishing other classes from the two shown in Table 19.1. For measuring only the two classes in Table 19.1, however, it does not help distinguish these classes.

Response probabilities are used to interpret the classes. The first class does not endorse craving (Item 1), is mixed on nicotine tolerance (Item 2), and endorses continuity of smoking (Item 3). So, LC 1 smokes similarly over days but does not experience cravings between cigarettes. Perhaps they are very light smokers and not (or minimally) nicotine dependent. The LC proportions are given in parentheses in the first column. LC 1 includes 30% of the sample. Members of LC 2 are likely to endorse all the items positively and could be labeled nicotine dependent.

Notice that good estimates are near 1.0 (e.g., $P(Y)$ for LC 2 across items and $P(N)$ for LC 1 for item 1). The closer endorsement probabilities are to 1.0, the more highly linked that characteristic is to class membership. This is analogous to factor analysis when the loadings are near an absolute value of 1.0. In Table 19.1, members of LC 2 have a probability of 0.9 of replying yes to Item 1 and 10% are expected to reply no. One way to interpret this 10% is as measurement error. It can also be interpreted as true variability of the presence of the characteristic in question. Often in applied problems it is probably both.

The individual parameter estimates provide the basis for interpreting the classes and for evaluating the measurement characteristics of the items (Clogg & Manning, 1996; Flaherty, 2002). However, the actual data of an LCA are response pattern frequencies. A response pattern is a set of responses to all the measured items. In the three-item example, YYY is one example of a response pattern. With three binary items, there are a total of eight response patterns (2^3) and accompanying response pattern frequencies. Highlighting the pattern orientation of LCA, one can calculate class membership probabilities for each response pattern (referred to as item–set reliabilities).

Each of the eight possible response patterns has an associated probability of LC membership in this example. For example, respondents providing the response pattern YYY will have a high probability of membership in LC 2 (e.g., 0.93) and a correspondingly low probability of LC 1 membership (e.g., 1 – .93 or .07). Response patterns that are less expected or less clearly linked to a LC will typically have weaker class membership probabilities. For example, the response pattern NYN would probably have class membership probabilities much closer to 50/50. In terms of reliability, that response pattern is much less so. (For more detail, including the equations explaining reliability in LCA and an empirical illustration, see Flaherty, 2002.)

LCA is a nonparametric procedure and has relatively few assumptions. First, it is assumed that the LCs are mutually exclusive and exhaustive, meaning that every entity in a population is a member of one and only one LC. Furthermore, it is assumed the members of a class are homogeneous, that is, the conditional response probabilities describe everyone in the class equally well. Third, conditional independence is assumed, meaning that item responses are statistically independent after we know a person's LC membership. This is a common assumption of most simple measurement models and implies that class membership is responsible for item covariation.

From Table 19.1, we can also illustrate the number of estimates in a given LC model. Let C denote the number of classes in a given model. The number of estimated LC proportions is $C - 1$. This is because any one LC proportion can be calculated by subtracting the sum of the rest from 1.0. The conditional response probabilities also sum to 1 for every item–LC combination. As described in the previous paragraph, for binary data, if the $P(Y \mid LC)$ is 0.9, then $P(N \mid LC)$ is 0.1. If there were four response categories, only three response probabilities would be estimated. Therefore, if R denotes the number of response categories for an item, the number of response probabilities estimated is $C(R - 1)$ for that item. For the total number of estimates, this is simply the sum across all the items. The number of response categories can vary across items in any given analysis.

An important step in LCA applications involves assessing the empirical identification of a given model. Is a set of estimates best and unique? LC models are typically estimated with iterative computer algorithms, and these algorithms often require starting values. This would not be interesting, except that the likelihood function for LC models is often multimodal. This means that there are multiple solutions to the likelihood function, referred to as local maxima. Running only one set of start values to completion leads to one set of estimates, but one cannot be sure if these are the best set of estimates for the current data. Therefore, one should run many sets of random start values to assess empirical identification. Ideally, many or most sets of random start values converge to the same, best fitting solution. In this case, it is likely the model is clearly identified. However, one can obtain two or more sets of estimates that fit the data nearly equally well yet have different substantive conclusions. In this case, there is no statistical basis to prefer one

model over another, and either a simpler model should be fit or more data should be obtained. Model simplifications include fitting fewer classes and parameter restrictions (discussed in the section Additional Topics; also see Flaherty, 2002; Formann, 1985).

Using LC models is a model-fitting exercise akin to that used in confirmatory factor analysis (CFA) and structural equation modeling (SEM; Bollen & Long, 1993). One is not proposing a straw-person null hypothesis and hoping to reject it. In LCA, the model being fit is the model of scientific interest and, therefore, the researcher typically wants to retain it.

LC models are contingency table models, like log-linear models (Bishop, Fienberg, & Holland, 1975; Hagenaars, 1998). In LCA, the proposed model and estimates are used to reproduce the contingency table formed by cross-tabulating all the measured items (i.e., the response patterns). When the data are not sparse (defined later in this section), categorical data fit statistics, such as Pearson's X^2 or the likelihood ratio statistic (G^2) can be used to assess the absolute fit of the model to the data. That is, does the model fit the data well enough such that random sampling variation is a plausible explanation for any discrepancies between expected values and the data? If the null hypothesis is true (i.e., the model we are fitting is the population model), then the distribution of either of these fit statistics is centered on the degrees of freedom (df). The df are equal to the number of cells in the full contingency table – number of estimates – 1.

Just as in CFA and SEM, an overidentified model has at least one df. If we fit a two-class model to four binary items, then the df equals six ($2^4 - 9 - 1$). When data are not sparse, the p value of the statistic can be found by checking its probability against a chi-square distribution with the model's df. A nonsignificant test statistic means that one should retain the model.

Sparse data occur when there are many cells with zero or few observations (Agresti & Yang, 1987; Collins, Fidler, Wugalter, & Long, 1993). When data are sparse, the chi-square distribution is not distributed with the nominal degrees of freedom. The mean of the distribution is different but unknown. Therefore, when data are sparse, a

Pearson's X^2 or G^2 statistic that appears nonsignificant may indeed be significant. For this reason, many users have stopped reporting these values. However, it is somewhat similar to the use of the chi-square statistic in CFA and SEM. That statistic is not used alone to make decisions about model fit, but it is always reported. The same should be done with LC models because the statistics can still be useful. For example, if data are sparse and the G^2 statistic is significant, then it is very likely that the model does not fit.

Thus far, we have discussed absolute fit statistics. The primary other model selection tools are relative fit indexes, such as information criteria. The two most popular information criteria are Akaike's information criteria (AIC; Akaike, 1987) and Bayesian information criteria (BIC; also referred to as *Schwarz information criteria*; Schwarz, 1978). These are penalized fit measures that attempt to balance model fit with parsimony. These values do not reflect model fit to the data, but rather they reflect which one model of several is best. Lower values reflect better model fit and one simply finds the lowest AIC or BIC among the set to see which model is preferred. Ideally, absolute and relative fit measures point to the same final model (see Burnham & Anderson, 2004, for a good discussion of AIC and BIC).

The interpretability of a final model is also critical. If a set of estimates makes no sense, what use are they? For example, if several classes in a solution had essentially similar response probabilities, then there are no interesting differences among the classes (e.g., similar to item 3 in Table 19.1). Alternatively, if an LC proportion is very small, one must decide whether it reflects noise in the data or a substantively interesting group (e.g., a rare subgroup). Essentially, one should scrutinize one's results to ensure that they are substantively meaningful. On the other hand, surprises may also reveal interesting, unanticipated aspects of phenomena under study.

Although this presentation has introduced many aspects of LC models, it has still been limited. More thorough presentations can be obtained from the citations provided as well as from McCutcheon (1987), Clogg (1995), Goodman (1974), and Bartholomew (1987). These are presented in order of the authors' opinions about their accessibility to a general psychology audience. Furthermore, both LCA and LPA are types of statistical mixture models (McLachlan & Peel, 2000), so relevant literature may be found with that term as well.

LATENT PROFILE MODELS

LCA and LPA are similar models and much of the LCA discussion applies to LPA too. The difference is the scale of the data and resulting changes. LPA was adapted from LCA for quantitative or metric items by Gibson (1959). Rather than conditional response probabilities linking classes and items, conditional means link the profiles and items. Furthermore, residual variances are estimated for the items. Typically, this variance is pooled across the profiles, yielding only one residual variance per item. Thus an important assumption of LPA is that the items are assumed to be normally distributed, conditional on profile membership. The specific normal distribution is specified by the profile item mean and pooled residual variance. LP proportions are interpreted just as in the LCA case. Table 19.2 contains fabricated estimates to illustrate an LPA.

As with the previous example, there are two profiles and three items. Now, however, the items are continuous measures of nicotine dependence (as *z*-scores). To interpret the LPs, profile means are

TABLE 19.2

Latent Profile (LP) Model Illustration

LP	When you haven't had a cigarette for a while, you feel you need to have one to feel better	Compared to when you started smoking, you now need to smoke more in order to feel the effects	You smoke the same number of cigarettes every day
1 (30%)	-0.50	-0.05	0.10
2 (70%)	0.80	1.20	0.05
Residual variance	0.40	0.60	0.94

Note. Profile means and a residual variance for each item are shown, in standardized scale. Higher scores represent higher dependence.

compared with the overall sample mean as well as across profiles. Item 1 again differentiates the profiles because the profile means are quite different. This result is also reflected in the smaller residual variance for Item 1. Item 2 again does a good job measuring LP 2 but not so much for LP 1. The conditional mean for LP 1 is nearly zero, so it is not different from the population mean. Item 3 has almost the same means for both profiles. Item 2 does help us distinguish the profiles, whereas Item 3 does not. Items with a wider range of profile means will have lower residual variance. This is an assessment of how well items are measuring the profiles.

Because there are no restrictions among means in an LPA, the number of estimates in the model is straightforward to compute. As with LCA, there are $C - 1$ LP proportions, where C denotes the number profiles. If there are q items, then $C \times q$ conditional means and q residual variances are estimated. Unlike LCA, there are no absolute fit statistics for LPA. Therefore, model fit tends to be evaluated with AIC and BIC solely.

Most LCA and LPA analyses are exploratory, so often researchers run a sequence of models with increasing numbers of classes or profiles and then choose the best model of that set. However, this can be challenging. First, AIC, BIC, and other fit statistics often disagree. Second, it is possible that all of the models being assessed with AIC or BIC do not fit the data well. Relative comparisons always point to one model as the best, but it could be the best of several bad choices. Better, generally accepted model selection criteria for both LCA and LPA are needed. Ultimately, the best model should be chosen on the basis of a combination of model fit and estimates, researcher hypotheses and expectations, and the interpretability of the solution (Edwards, 1992; Hu & Bentler, 1995; Marsh, Hau, & Wen, 2004).

EMPIRICAL ILLUSTRATION

Nicotine dependence has been conceptualized as both a binary state (addicted or not) and as a continuum (degree of dependence). Consequently, Goedeker and Tiffany (2008) performed a taxometric analysis (Waller & Meehl, 1998) to examine nicotine dependence and concluded that it may be a

little of both. However, a limitation of standard taxometric analysis is that only two groups are compared with a continuum. Following up the categorical view of nicotine dependence, we use data from the Nicotine Dependence Syndrome Scales (NDSS; Shiffman, Waters, & Hickcox, 2004) to illustrate the use of LCA and LPA. The decision of what representation best suits the construct is beyond the scope of this chapter.

Sample and Procedures

Data are from the 2004 National Survey of Drug Use and Health (U.S. Department of Health and Human Services, 2004) a national survey of U.S. households focused on substance use, abuse, and associated factors. These data are publicly available allowing readers to replicate this work. For this illustration, we limited the sample to Caucasian adults (18 or older) who indicated smoking daily in the past 30 days. The sample was nearly equally split by gender (49.5% male). Nearly 52% of the sample was between 18 and 25. The total sample size was 5,926.

Measures

Items were selected from the 23-item NDSS, which contains five subscales: Drive, Priority, Continuity, Stereotypy, and Tolerance. For each item, participants reported the degree to which the item was true for them on a 5-point Likert scale (ranging from 1 = *not at all true* to 5 = *extremely true*). To form the variables to use in our analysis, we combined the subscale items. Three items measured tolerance, the degree individuals have increased their smoking as a result of decreased sensitivity to nicotine. Continuity, composed of three items, is the degree individuals were smoking consistently across the day. Stereotypy (three items) reflects the rigidity of an individual's smoking. The Priority subscale (three items) taps the importance and value placed on smoking. The four-item Drive subscale assesses the avoidance of withdrawal symptoms. Because this scale included more items, and to include an example of multiple indicators, the drive items were split into two sets. Drive 1 reflects irritability or craving experienced when not smoking. Drive 2 captures the sense of control one feels over his or her cigarette smoking.

Data Preparation

An LPA was run on the six standardized composite scores corresponding to the NDSS subscales. For the LCA, we created binary indicators of dependence. Participants received a 0 (no) if they did not endorse any of the dependence items within one of the subscales. Participants received a 1 (yes) for the subscale if they endorsed any level of dependence on any of the corresponding items. For example, to be given a 0 for the binary stereotypy indicator, a participant must have replied that none of the three stereotypy items were at all true.

Data Analyses

LCA and LPA models were estimated with Mplus Version 5.21 (L. K. Muthén & Muthén, 1998–2009). We ran 1,000 sets of random start values to assess model identification and used full information maximum likelihood (FIML; Schafer & Graham, 2002) estimation to retain cases with some missing data. For LCA, we fit unrestricted models with two through six classes, using both the absolute and relative fit measures discussed earlier. For LPA, we started by fitting two to seven profiles, but ultimately fit up to 10 profiles to reach a point at which AIC or BIC indicated a preferred model.

LCA Results

Table 19.3 presents the fit information for models with two to five LCs. The six-class model failed to converge. Table 19.3 is a perfect example of how different fit indexes suggest different conclusions. Each points to a different conclusion: BIC indicates the two-class model, the G^2 statistic points to three

classes, and AIC points to four classes. In this situation, interpretation and substantive expectations can (and should) play a significant role in model selection. For the following reasons, we have chosen the four-class model. The three-class model includes a very small LC (<1%), and the two-class model does not fit the data as reflected by the large G^2. The fourth class is also small (<2%), but because the sample size is so large, it translates to almost 100 people. Furthermore, because these are exploratory analysis with no theoretical guidance about the class structure, the richer solution may be more compelling (Flaherty, 2009). Finally, pedagogically, the four-class solution better highlights features of the model.

Figure 19.1 contains plots of the four classes. Notably, LC 1 and LC 3 are the very small classes. Members of LC 1 are most likely to report no to all the items, except for the two drive items. Here their response probabilities are nearly split 50/50. Perhaps this is a class of relatively new smokers who have not developed other symptoms. LC 3, including 1.6% of the sample, have a high probability of endorsing continuity, stereotypy, and tolerance, but they are split again on the drive items and are unlikely to endorse priority. These cigarette smokers appear to be smoking over time and contexts and have experienced tolerance. Yet, for them craving and control of smoking are mixed. LC 4 are the dependent smokers, but notice that the response probabilities for priority are not a strong as for the other items. Members of LC 2 tend to endorse most of the dependence items, except for priority and tolerance.

With the items in this binary format, priority looks like the weakest item across classes. Additionally, continuity and stereotypy are largely parallel and only really distinguish LC 1 from the other classes. The drive and tolerance items have the most variability in response probabilities across the classes. It is also nice to see that the two drive items largely do appear to function as redundant, parallel indicators.

TABLE 19.3

Latent Class Model Fit Statistics and Indicators

Classes	G^2	df	p	AIC	BIC
2	95.7	49	< 0.001	17,312.6	17,339.5
3	43.0	42	0.43	17,271.9	17,405.7
4	24.5	35	0.91	17,267.4	17,448.0
5	17.3	28	0.94	17,274.1	17,501.5

Note. The six-class model failed to converge. AIC = Akaike's information criteria; BIC = Bayesian information criteria.

LPA Results

Table 19.4 presents the model fit information for unrestricted LP models ranging from two and 10 profiles. A minimum AIC or BIC was not reached. The lowest value of each occurs for the 10-profile

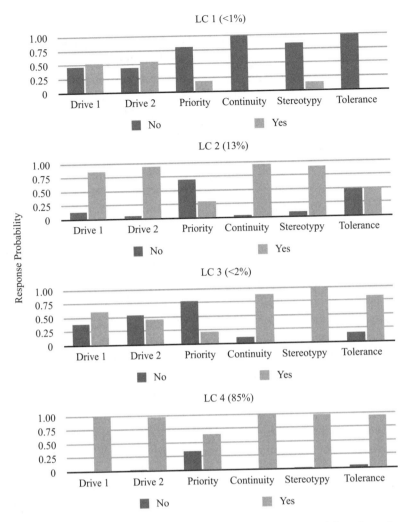

FIGURE 19.1. Four-class model (latent class [LC] analysis) based on six nicotine-dependence indicators from the Nicotine Dependence Syndrome Scale. LC proportions are shown in parenthesis above each barplot.

model, and presumably, both would have continued decreasing further. Additionally, the 10-class model is not composed of a couple of large profiles and several tiny ones, but rather, the sample is increasingly split into moderately sized profiles and a few small profiles. It is likely that models with more profiles would have continued to be preferred statistically until the profile proportions became very small, or perhaps the relative fit measures would indicate that a preferred model had been found. Were this for a substantively oriented paper, we would need a rationale to select a specific model. For the purpose of this chapter, we present the five-profile solution. Too many profiles would be unnecessarily complex, and a moderate number of profiles and classes facilitates comparing LCA and LPA.

TABLE 19.4

Latent Profile Model Fit Indicators

Profiles	Number of estimates	AIC value	BIC value
2	19	97,224.478	97,351.530
3	26	95,263.590	95,437.450
4	33	94,528.605	94,749.274
5	40	94,028.905	94,296.383
6	47	93,465.085	93,779.371
7	54	93,105.039	93,466.134
8	61	92,937.963	93,345.866
9	68	92,500.540	92,955.252
10	75	92,415.683	92,917.203

Note. Akaike's information criteria (AIC) and Bayesian information criteria (BIC) both indicated more profiles were needed to fit the data. For ease of presentation and for a more concise comparison with the latent class analysis model, the five-profile solution was selected.

Figure 19.2 contains the conditional means of the six standardized indicators for the five nicotine-dependence profiles. In Figure 19.2, a conditional mean near 0 denotes a profile mean near the sample average. The most noticeable feature in Figure 19.2 is a very high mean priority score for members of Profile 5 (approximately 2.8 standard deviations). Members of Profile 5 also tend to have mean dependence scores around 0.75, with the exception of stereotypy. For members of this class, smoking priority is very high, relative to the sample and drive, continuity and tolerance are above average. Profiles 1 and 2 are the largest profiles. Profile 1 is characterized by lower than average scores on all the nicotine-dependence indicators, implying that 36% of the sample has relatively low dependence symptoms. Profile 2 (37%) is characterized by higher than average craving (drive 1) and lower than average priority. Profile 3 is characterized by the highest average drive and tolerance scores. Members of this profile also have relatively high priority scores, but continuity and stereotypy are not as high. This profile represents about 11% of the sample. Last, Profile 4 has a pattern of high priority with slightly below average scores on the other items. Profiles 3 and 5 have the highest dependence levels overall, but together they account for only approximately 16% of the sample.

The residual variances for the six items measuring the NDSS subscales indicated mixed measurement quality. Priority had the lowest residual variance at 0.18, reflecting the range in priority means across the profiles. However, the model did not do nearly as well with any of the other items. The next lowest residual variance was .50 for Drive 1. Stereotypy had the largest residual variance, 0.97, following the similar conditional means across the profiles.

MODEL COMPARISON

We started with the same data to emphasize similarities and differences between the models and to highlight how each may be thought of as a measurement model. This comparison works for illustrating model selection, interpretation, and some assessment of measurement quality. Different data go into each analysis and the models carve the sample up differently.

The LCA includes one large, one moderate, and two small classes. People highly likely to endorse each item, except priority, characterize the largest class. This class is closest to a prototypical dependent class. Members of the moderately sized class, LC 2, are likely to endorse three of the five dependence symptoms, but not tolerance or priority. The fact that this class represents approximately 770 people

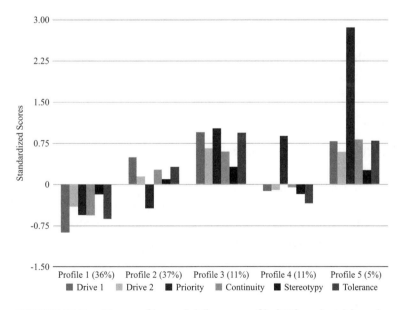

FIGURE 19.2. Five-profile model (latent profile [LP] analysis) based on six nicotine-dependence indicators from the Nicotine Dependence Syndrome Scale. LP proportions are shown in parenthesis along the *x*-axis. Plotted values are standard scores.

suggests it may be a subgroup worth further consideration. LC 1 and LC 3 could represent random variation, relatively new smokers who met the inclusion criteria or people with unusual dependence characteristics. Recall that the sample was relatively homogeneous: U.S. White adult daily smokers.

LPA results look quite different. LP 1 and LP 2, the largest, are characterized by below-average nicotine-dependence symptoms (Profile 1) or somewhat above average (Profile 2), with below average priority. Two of the other three profiles have above average dependence scores, and Profile 4 is characterized by high mean priority.

Substantively, these results are not comparable because a final LPA model was not identified. However, psychometrically, we can consider the models and the data features each reproduces. In our case, the LCA data are modeling presence and absence combinations of nicotine dependence. The LCA is explaining portions of the six-way contingency table with the identified classes. The LPA is similarly explaining areas and patterns of covariance among the five-category Likert items. Comparing the reported results, the variability in the priority indicator largely drives the LPA solutions we saw. In contrast, when coded as presence or absence, priority was the weakest LCA indicator. Furthermore, stereotypy and the two drive items looked quite good in the LCA, whereas this was not true in the LPA. These comparisons highlight the fact that our measurement interacts with our models, and we need to think seriously about both.

ADDITIONAL TOPICS

This chapter has introduced LCA and LPA, underscoring their use as measurement models. Some associated topics are introduced or expanded here.

Model Testing and Selection

Many issues fall under this broad heading, including parameter restrictions, model selection, diagnostics, hypothesis testing, and confirmatory modeling. Two drive items were used to highlight the idea of parallel items in these analyses. With parallel items, one would likely want to constrain the item estimates to be equal across two or more classes to test or enforce

the assumed parallelism. The ability to impose restrictions of various sorts leads to confirmatory modeling. Formann (1985, 1989) and Hoijtink (2001) discussed types of parameter restrictions, and Flaherty (2002) provided a measurement-oriented LCA example. Lanza, Collins, Schafer, and Flaherty (2005) presented a Bayesian approach to multiparameter hypothesis testing in LCA and corresponding longitudinal models. Parameter restrictions are more commonly used in LCA, typically to reduce the size of the model to improve estimation. Theoretically motivated uses of parameter restrictions in LCA are less common than unrestricted, exploratory analyses. As these models are applied in more theoretically meaningful ways, use of restrictions should increase. We are unaware of the use of parameter restrictions in LPA, although such could be developed.

Model selection and some accompanying issues were briefly touched on in this chapter, but as the empirical illustrations successfully demonstrate, model selection can be a challenge with these models. Given a set of plausible models, such as when determining the appropriate number of classes or profiles in an exploratory analysis, it is imperative to make the best choice. The difficulty in choosing the number of classes or profiles statistically arises from data sparseness and because nested model tests do not necessarily work for choosing the numbers of classes (for a readable yet thorough discussion of why the statistic fails, see Aitkin & Rubin, 1985).

To circumvent these statistical challenges, many approaches and recommendations have been put forth: bootstrapping (Efron & Tibshirani, 1993; Nylund, Asparouhov, & Muthén, 2007), likelihood ratio test *p* value adjustment (Lo, Mendell, & Rubin, 2001), entropy (Celeux & Soromenho, 1996), Bayesian posterior predictive check distributions (Rubin & Stern, 1994), Bayes's factors (Hoijtink, 2001), and cross-validation (Collins, Graham, Long, & Hansen, 1994). Although all of these approaches have strengths, none have yet been identified as the best way to select LC and LP models.

Covariates

Covariate models (Dayton & Macready, 1988) have been developed to explore constructs and characteristics associated with likely class membership. In these models, logistic regression models (Hosmer & Lemeshow, 1989) predict class or profile membership as a function of covariates. That is, the LC or LP membership becomes the response. Thorough presentations as well as illustrative examples can be found in Chung, Flaherty, and Schafer (2006) and Reboussin, Song, Shrestha, Lohman, and Wolfson (2006). Others have extended these models to allow covariates to predict item responses as well as LC membership (Pfeffermann, Skinner, & Humphreys, 1998). Covariates predicting class membership should have only a minimal impact on the interpretation of the classes, but when covariates predict measurement parameters, class interpretations can change substantially.

Other and Mixed Indicators

LCA/LPA are each based on nominal categorical and continuous measured items, respectively. Comparable models for ordinal data have also been developed (Rost, 1988, and references therein). When one has data with only one scale of measured variable, these models are sufficient. However, sometimes one has items with different scales. Reducing the scale of all the items to the lowest common scale (e.g., nominal) potentially removes important information from the analysis. To avoid this, LC models for mixed items have been developed, with one example being nominal and continuous indicators (Flaherty, 2003; Moustaki, 1996). Our understanding of how these models perform in empirical data is less developed than in the case of a single item type.

Longitudinal Models

Thus far, our discussion has only involved cross-sectional models. However, longitudinal LC models allow for the study of change over time among class memberships. Latent Markov models (van de Pol & Langeheine, 1990) were originally developed for a single, repeatedly measured variable, whereas latent transition models (Collins & Wugalter, 1992) had multiple indicators. In addition to the measurement estimates linking items to classes, these models also estimate transition probabilities among the classes between assessment points. Transition probabilities quantify change and stability of the classes over

time. For example, suppose someone was a member of a class of nondependent smokers at Time 1. At Time 2, how likely is it that that the nondependent smoker changed to a dependent smoker? What is the probability a Time 1 nondependent smoker is still a nondependent smoker at Time 2? These longitudinal LC models are flexible models of change and are different from continuous models of change, such as growth curve models (Rogosa, Brandt, & Zimowski, 1982).

CONCLUSION

This chapter has focused on two categorical latent variable models: the LC and LP models. In addition to introducing these models, we emphasized their use as measurement models. In this regard, these models can be viewed in the broader class of latent variable measurement models, including factor and structural equation models. Furthermore, LCA and LPA are two simple mixture models, sharing many similarities with newer models, such as mixture regression models (DeSarbo & Cron, 1988), growth mixture models (B. O. Muthén & Shedden, 1999), and factor mixture models (Lubke & Muthén, 2005).

The empirical example was chosen to highlight differences in the models and, secondarily, differences in the results. However, the NDSS scale was based on a factor analytic view of nicotine dependence. As such, this instrument may not be ideal for identifying different subgroups of nicotine-dependent smokers. Perhaps items specifically designed to differentiate important groups are required. Our conceptualization of the construct drives our measurement of it, but our measurement may limit the adequacy with which we model it.

These models are large sample procedures and are often more difficult to estimate than standard factor analytic models. As such, some considerations and precautions may be offered. Sample size requirements are difficult to make because they depend on factors such as class separation (i.e., the *distance* between the class in multivariate space) and measurement quality. A large sample combined with poor measurement may lead to difficulty identifying meaningful classes. On the other hand, if you have very clear response associations with class membership, then a much smaller sample may still yield meaningful classes. All this said, the authors' sense is that 300 is an absolute minimum sample size without other information (e.g., very strong parameter restrictions or prior information incorporated via a Bayesian approach).

Establishing that one's results are identified is another important issue when using these models. To that end, one should run many sets of random start values, on the order of thousands not dozens. Furthermore, many software packages will run some number of start values for a limited number of iterations (e.g., 20) and then run the best solution to completion. There is no guarantee, however, that the solution that looks best after 20 iterations is the best overall. One also does not know whether there are one or more other models with different interpretations but nearly equal fit. For that reason, we recommend running many sets of start values to completion and determining identification status on those results.

There are multiple software options to fit these models. Free programs include Proc LCA and Proc LTA (available from http://methodology.psu.edu) for LCA (and longitudinal models) as well as several packages for R, including poLCA and mclust, among others. Commercial programs include Mplus and LatentGold, and others are available as well.

Ideally this chapter has provided a foundation from which you can work toward incorporating these models in your own work and with serious consideration of these models as measurement models. Expanding psychological research beyond dimensions to qualitatively different subgroups could prove invaluable to our understanding of behavior.

References

Agresti, A., & Yang, M. (1987). An empirical investigation of some effects of sparseness in contingency tables. *Computational Statistics and Data Analysis, 5*, 9–21. doi:10.1016/0167-9473(87)90003-X

Aitkin, M., & Rubin, D. B. (1985). Estimation and hypothesis testing in finite mixture models. *Journal of the Royal Statistical Society, Series B (Methodological), 47*, 67–75.

Akaike, H. (1987). Factor analysis and AIC. *Psychometrika, 52*, 317–332. doi:10.1007/BF02294359

Bartholomew, D. J. (1987). *Latent variable models and factor analysis.* New York, NY: Oxford University Press.

Baumrind, D. (1967). Child care practices anteceding three patterns of preschool behavior. *Genetic Psychology Monographs, 75*, 43–88.

Bishop, Y. M. M., Fienberg, S. E., & Holland, P. W. (1975). *Discrete multivariate analysis: Theory and practice.* Cambridge, MA: MIT Press.

Blashfield, R. K., & Aldenderfer, M. S. (1988). The methods and problems of cluster analysis. In J. Nesselroade & R. Cattell (Eds.), *Handbook of multivariate experimental psychology* (pp. 447–473). New York, NY: Plenum Press.

Bollen, K. A., & Long, J. S. (1993). *Testing structural equation models.* Newbury Park, CA: Sage.

Burnham, K. P., & Anderson, D. R. (2004). Multimodel inference: Understanding AIC and BIC in model selection. *Sociological Methods and Research, 33*, 261–304. doi:10.1177/0049124104268644

Celeux, G., & Soromenho, G. (1996). An entropy criterion for assessing the number of clusters in a mixture model. *Journal of Classification, 13*, 195–212. doi:10.1007/BF01246098

Chung, H., Flaherty, B. P., & Schafer, J. L. (2006). Latent class logistic regression: Application to marijuana use and attitudes among high school seniors. *Journal of the Royal Statistical Society, Series A (General), 169*, 723–743.

Clogg, C. C. (1995). Latent class models. In G. Arminger, C. C. Clogg, & M. E. Sobel (Eds.), *Handbook of statistical modeling for the social and behavioral sciences* (pp. 311–359). New York, NY: Plenum Press.

Clogg, C. C., & Manning, W. D. (1996). Assessing reliability of categorical measurements using latent class models. In A. von Eye & C. C. Clogg (Eds.), *Categorical variables in developmental research: Methods of analysis* (pp. 169–182). San Diego, CA: Academic Press. doi:10.1016/B978-012724965-0/50011-0

Collins, L. M., Fidler, P. L., Wugalter, S. E., & Long, J. D. (1993). Goodness-of-fit testing for latent class models. *Multivariate Behavioral Research, 28*, 375–389. doi:10.1207/s15327906mbr2803_4

Collins, L. M., Graham, J. W., Long, J. D., & Hansen, W. B. (1994). Crossvalidition of latent class models of early substance use onset. *Multivariate Behavioral Research, 29*, 165–183. doi:10.1207/s15327906mbr2902_3

Collins, L. M., & Wugalter, S. E. (1992). Latent class models for stage-sequential dynamic latent-variables. *Multivariate Behavioral Research, 27*, 131–157. doi:10.1207/s15327906mbr2701_8

Cudeck, R., & MacCallum, R. C. (Eds.). (2007). *Factor analysis at 100: Historical developments and future directions.* London, England: Psychology Press.

Cumsille, P., Darling, N., Flaherty, B. P., & Martínez, M. L. (2006). Chilean adolescents' beliefs about the legitimacy of parental authority: Individual and age-related differences. *International Journal of Behavioral Development, 30*, 97–106. doi:10.1177/0165025406063554

Dayton, C. M., & Macready, G. B. (1988). Concomitant-variable latent-class models. *Journal of the American Statistical Association, 83*, 173–178. doi:10.2307/2288938

Degnan, K. A., Calkins, S. D., Keane, S. P., & Hill-Soderlund, A. L. (2008). Profiles of disruptive behavior across early childhood: Contributions of frustration reactivity, physiological regulation, and maternal behavior. *Child Development, 79*, 1357–1376. doi:10.1111/j.1467-8624.2008.01193.x

DeSarbo, W. S., & Cron, W. L. (1988). A maximum likelihood methodology for clusterwise linear regression. *Journal of Classification, 5*, 249–282. doi:10.1007/BF01897167

Edwards, A. W. F. (1992). *Likelihood.* Baltimore, MD: Johns Hopkins University Press.

Efron, B., & Tibshirani, R. J. (1993). *An introduction to the bootstrap.* Boca Raton, FL: Chapman & Hall/CRC.

Embretson, S. E., & Reise, S. P. (2000). *Item response theory for psychologists.* Mahwah, NJ: Erlbaum.

Flaherty, B. P. (2002). Assessing reliability of categorical substance use measures with latent class analysis. *Drug and Alcohol Dependence, 68*, S7–S20. doi:10.1016/S0376-8716(02)00210-7

Flaherty, B. P. (2003). *Continuous and categorical indicator latent class models* (Unpublished doctoral dissertation). Pennsylvania State University, University Park.

Flaherty, B. P. (2009, July). *Model selection in exploratory latent class and mixture models: What's to be preferred?* Paper presented at the 16th International Meeting of the Psychometric Society, Cambridge, England.

Flaherty, B. P. (2010). Latent class and mixture models' potential contributions to understanding connections between menthol and other cigarette smoking characteristics. *Addiction, 105*(Suppl. 1), 11–12.

Formann, A. K. (1985). Constrained latent class models: Theory and applications. *British Journal of Mathematical and Statistical Psychology, 38*, 87–111.

Formann, A. K. (1989). Constrained latent class models: Some further applications. *British Journal of Mathematical and Statistical Psychology, 42*, 37–54.

Gibson, W. A. (1959). Three multivariate models: Factor analysis, latent structure analysis, and latent profile analysis. *Psychometrika, 24*, 229–252. doi:10.1007/BF02289845

Goedeker, K. C., & Tiffany, S. T. (2008). On the nature of nicotine addiction: A taxometric analysis. *Journal of Abnormal Psychology, 117*, 896–909. doi:10.1037/a0013296

Goodman, L. A. (1974). Exploratory latent structure analysis using both identifiable and unidentifiable models. *Biometrika, 61*, 215–231. doi:10.1093/biomet/61.2.215

Hagenaars, J. A. (1998). Categorical causal modeling: Latent class analysis and directed log-linear models with latent variables. *Sociological Methods and Research, 26*, 436–486. doi:10.1177/0049124198026004002

Hoijtink, H. (2001). Confirmatory latent class analysis: Model selection using Bayes factors and (pseudo) likelihood ratio statistics. *Multivariate Behavioral Research, 36*, 563–588. doi:10.1207/S15327906MBR3604_04

Hosmer, D. W., & Lemeshow, S. (1989). *Applied logistic regression.* New York, NY: Wiley.

Hu, L., & Bentler, P. M. (1995). Evaluating model fit. In R. H. Hoyle (Ed.), *Structural equation modeling: Concepts, issues, and applications* (pp. 76–99). Thousand Oaks, CA: Sage.

Kohlberg, L. (1963). The development of children's orientation toward a moral order. *Vita Humana, 6*, 11–33.

Lanza, S. T., Collins, L. M., Schafer, J. L., & Flaherty, B. P. (2005). Using data augmentation to obtain standard errors and conduct hypothesis tests in latent class and latent transition analysis. *Psychological Methods, 10*, 84–100. doi:10.1037/1082-989X.10.1.84

Lazarsfeld, P. F., & Henry, N. W. (1968). *Latent structure analysis.* Boston, MA: Houghton Mifflin.

Lo, Y., Mendell, N. R., & Rubin, D. B. (2001). Testing the number of components in a normal mixture. *Biometrika, 88*, 767–778. doi:10.1093/biomet/88.3.767

Lubke, G. H., & Muthén, B. (2005). Investigating population heterogeneity with factor mixture models. *Psychological Methods, 10*, 21–39. doi:10.1037/1082-989X.10.1.21

Marsh, H. W., Hau, K., & Wen, Z. (2004). In search of golden rules: Comment on hypothesis-testing approaches to setting cutoff values for fit indexes and dangers in overgeneralizing Hu and Bentler's (1999) findings. *Structural Equation Modeling, 11*, 320–341. doi:10.1207/s15328007sem1103_2

McCutcheon, A. L. (1987). *Latent class analysis.* Thousand Oaks, CA: Sage.

McLachlan, G., & Peel, D. (2000). *Finite mixture models.* New York, NY: Wiley.

Moustaki, I. (1996). A latent trait and latent class model for mixed observed variables. *British Journal of Mathematical and Statistical Psychology, 49*, 313–334.

Muthén, B. O., & Shedden, K. (1999). Finite mixture modeling with mixture outcomes using the EM algorithm. *Biometrics, 55,* 463–469. doi:10.1111/j.0006-341X.1999.00463.x

Muthén, L. K., & Muthén, B. O. (1998–2009). *Mplus user's guide* (5th ed.). Los Angeles, CA: Muthén & Muthén.

Nylund, K. L., Asparouhov, T., & Muthén, B. O. (2007). Deciding on the number of classes in latent class analysis and growth mixture modeling: A Monte Carlo simulation study. *Structural Equation Modeling, 14,* 535–569.

O'Connor, R. M., & Colder, C. R. (2005). Predicting alcohol patterns in first-year college students through motivational systems and reasons for drinking. *Psychology of Addictive Behaviors, 19,* 10–20. doi:10.1037/0893-164X.19.1.10

Pfeffermann, D., Skinner, C., & Humphreys, K. (1998). The estimation of gross flows in the presence of measurement error using auxiliary variables. *Journal of the Royal Statistical Society, Series A (General), 161,* 13–32.

Piaget, J. (1960). The general problems of the psychobiological development of the child. In J. M. Tanner & B. Inhelder (Eds.), *Discussions on child development* (Vol. 4, pp. 2–27). New York, NY: International Universities Press.

Reboussin, B. A., Song, E. Y., Shrestha, A., Lohman, K. K., & Wolfson, M. (2006). A latent class analysis of underage problem drinking: Evidence from a community sample of 16–20 year olds. *Drug and Alcohol Dependence, 83,* 199–209. doi:10.1016/j.drugalcdep.2005.11.013

Rogosa, D., Brandt, D., & Zimowski, M. (1982). A growth curve approach to the measurement of change. *Psychological Bulletin, 92,* 726–748. doi:10.1037/0033-2909.92.3.726

Rost, J. (1988). Rating-scale analysis with latent class models. *Psychometrika, 53,* 327–348. doi:10.1007/BF02294216

Rubin, D. B., & Stern, H. S. (1994). Testing in latent class models using a posterior predictive check distribution. In A. von Eye & C. C. Clogg (Eds.), *Latent variables analysis: Applications for developmental research* (pp. 420–438). Thousand Oaks, CA: Sage.

Sanson, A., Letcher, P., Smart, D., Prior, M., Toumbourou, J. W., & Oberklaid, F. (2009). Associations between early childhood temperament clusters and later psychosocial adjustment. *Merrill-Palmer Quarterly, 55,* 26–54. doi:10.1353/mpq.0.0015

Schafer, J. L., & Graham, J. W. (2002). Missing data: Our view of the state of the art. *Psychological Methods, 7,* 147–177. doi:10.1037/1082-989X.7.2.147

Schwarz, G. (1978). Estimating the dimension of a model. *Annals of Statistics, 6,* 461–464. doi:10.1214/aos/1176344136

Shiffman, S., Waters, A., & Hickcox, M. (2004). The nicotine dependence syndrome scale: A multidimensional measure of nicotine dependence. *Nicotine and Tobacco Research, 6,* 327–348. doi:10.1080/1462220042000202481

Spearman, C. (1904). "General intelligence," objectively determined and measured. *American Journal of Psychology, 15,* 201–292. doi:10.2307/1412107

Stern, H. S., Arcus, D., Kagan, J., Rubin, D. B., & Snidman, N. (1995). Using mixture models in temperament research. *International Journal of Behavioral Development, 18,* 407–423.

Thurstone, L. L. (1935). *The vectors of mind; multiple-factor analysis for the isolation of primary traits.* Chicago, IL: University of Chicago Press. doi:10.1037/10018-000

U.S. Department of Health and Human Services, Substance Abuse and Mental Health Services Administration, Office of Applied Studies. (2004). *National Survey on Drug Use and Health, 2004* [Computer file] (Publication No. ICPSR04373-v1). Ann Arbor, MI: Interuniversity Consortium for Political and Social Research. doi:10.3886/ICPSR04373

van de Pol, F., & Langeheine, R. (1990). Mixed Markov latent class models. *Sociological Methodology, 20,* 213–247. doi:10.2307/271087

Waller, N. G., & Meehl, P. E. (1998). *Multivariate taxometric procedures: Distinguishing types from continua.* Thousand Oaks, CA: Sage.

## CHAPTER 20

EXPLORATORY DATA MINING USING CART IN THE BEHAVIORAL SCIENCES

John J. McArdle

The term *exploratory* is considered by many as less than an approach to data analysis and more a confession of guilt—a dishonest act has been performed with one's data. These considerations become obvious when we immediately recoil at exploratory methods, or when immediate rejections occur when one proposes research exploration in a research grant, or when one tries to publish new results found by exploration. We in the field of psychology need to face up to the fact that there is currently an extreme preference for confirmatory and a priori testing of well-formulated research hypotheses in psychological research. One radical interpretation of this preference is that we simply do not yet trust one another.

Unfortunately, as many researchers know, quite the opposite approach is closer to our standard. That is, it can be said that exploratory analyses predominate our actual research activities. To be more extreme, we can assert there is actually no such thing as a true confirmatory analysis of data, nor should there be. Either way, we can try to be clearer about this problem. We need better responses when well-meaning students and colleagues ask, "Is it okay to do procedure X?" I assume they are asking, "Is there a well-known probability basis for procedure X and will I be able to publish it?" Fear of rejection is strong among many good researchers, probably because rewards do not always follow risks, and one side effect is that rejection leaves scientific creativity only to the bold and to people who are not constrained by their research setting. As I

will imply at several times here, the only requirement for a useful data analysis is that we remain honest (see McArdle, 2010b).

The traditional use of the simple independent groups *t* test should have provided our first clue that something was wrong about the standard "confirmatory" mantras. For example, we know it is fine to calculate the classic test of the mean difference between two groups and calculate the probability of equality or significance of the mean difference under the typical assumptions (i.e., random sampling of persons, random assignment to groups, equal variance within cells). But we also know it is not appropriate to achieve significance by (a) using another variable when the first fails, (b) getting data on more people until the difference is significant, (c) using various transformations of the data until we achieve significance, (d) tossing out outliers until we achieve significance, (e) examining the difference in the variance instead of the means, or (f) accepting a significant difference in the opposite direction than we originally thought. Do you know of anyone who has done any of these things? I do. Actually, I assume we all do them all the time. In my view, the problem is not with us but with the way we are taught to revere the apparent objectivity of the *t*-test approach. It is bound to be even more complex when we use this *t*-test procedure repeatedly in hopes of isolating multivariate relationships.

For similar reasons, the one-way analysis of variance (ANOVA) should have been our next clue to

I thank the National Institute on Aging (Grant AG-07137-20) and the American Psychological Association Science Directorate for funds to support this ongoing research. I also thank my many colleagues for pointing out where the CART approach can be useful and where it can fail.

DOI: 10.1037/13621-020
APA Handbook of Research Methods in Psychology: Vol. 3. Data Analysis and Research Publication, H. Cooper (Editor-in-Chief)

the overall dilemma. When we have three or more groups and perform a one-way ANOVA, we can consider the resulting F ratio as an indicator of any group difference. In practice, we can calculate the optimal contrast weights assigned to the groups to create an optimal linear combination of the three groups—credit for this clarification is due to Scheffé (1959). The F is an indicator of the t^2 value that would be obtained if we had, on an a priori basis, used this new linear contrast. As a corrective, we typically evaluate this F value on the basis of the number of groups ($df = G - 1$), but we often struggle with the appropriate use of planned contrasts or with optimal post hoc testing strategies. And when the results are not significant, we start to worry about the rigid model assumptions (like equal variances) and we try transformations and outliers, typically, until we find a significant result.

A lot of well-known work is based on linear regression analysis (LRA), and these are the techniques I focus on in this chapter. We typically substitute LRA for controlled manipulations, when random assignment to groups (RAG; following Fisher, 1936) is not possible for practical or ethical reasons. There are many good reasons to think LRA is a good substitute for RAG because all we need is to include is the proper variables in the equation to estimate the independent effects of each one "controlling" for all others. There are also many good reasons to think that LRA is a poor substitute for RAG, including the lack of inclusion of the proper X variables, the unreliability of Y and Xs, and the often-arbitrary choice of Y as a focal outcome. It is really surprising that so many social and economic impacts are simply indicated by B-weights from relatively extensive regression equations with little attention paid to the underlying model assumptions. If we did pay attention to every detail, we would never get anywhere. Nevertheless, little attention is paid to the obviously key feature of replication or even cross-validation.

For the more advanced researcher, we do not miss the next fairly obvious exploratory clues in our procedures. In the context of principal components (PC) analysis, we define the first component by a process in which the variable weights are chosen so the resulting variable has maximum variance. In

canonical correlations (CC) analysis, we choose both the Set 1 composite weights and the Set 2 composite weights so that the resulting correlations of the composites are as high as possible. Of course, CC analysis can be algebraically derived from a PC analysis of the PCs. In the subset of CC known as T^2, we choose the dependent variable (DV) weights to maximize the resulting t value. In the subset of CC known as multivariate analysis of variance (MANOVA), we create the composite of the DVs to maximize Scheffé's contrast among the groups. Although all this optimization sounds perfectly straightforward, because the weights are not chosen on an a priori basis, this could be taken to mean that this aspect of our classical techniques is actually quite an exploration. The test statistic requires degrees of freedom (dfs) that attempt to take into account all possible weights.

Several scientists have come to view the process of research as partly confirmatory and partly exploratory, including Tukey (1962, 1977), who was considered by many as a radical—the main message was "plot the data and take a good look at it." Another more subtle message was "confirmatory analysis should be done first, and when it fails, as it so often does, then do a good exploratory analysis." The overviews by Cattell (1966) and Box (1976) pointed to a similar theme. The general message was that an "inductive–deductive spiral" is an essential process in a good science (after Cattell, 1966, p. 1). Cooley and Lohnes (1962, 1971, 1985) showed how multivariate techniques also generally require this approach. The problem is that our standard statistical methods seemed to lag behind this interesting formulation (also see Hoaglin, 1982; Velleman & Hoaglin, 1981).

The literature in common factor analysis (e.g., McDonald, 1985) has tried to come to grips with such problems, but confusion is still apparent. It seems that Tucker and Lewis (1973) tried to distinguish between what they termed *exploratory* and *confirmatory* factor analysis, and these labels seem to have stuck. Specifically, Tucker suggested that common factor models with enough restrictions could not be rotated any further and retain the same goodness of fit, whereas exploratory models were *just identified* and could be rotated further without change in the common factor space or goodness of fit (see McArdle & Cattell, 1994). This suggestion leads to a whole range of possible labels on the basis of the kinds of identification conditions, and this *hybrid* mixture of exploration and confirmation seems reasonable (see Jöreskog & Sörbom, 1979). Nevertheless, it is rare to find anyone advocating a priori known weights for the fixed effects in these models, the true confirmatory models, or even a large number of equality constraints (i.e., as in the Rasch model; see McDonald, 1999).

These kinds of restrictions would be truly confirmatory. Instead, many parameters are allowed to be estimated from the data, and only the pattern of nonzero parameters is actually examined. Further confusion abounds in more recent model fitting exercises in which some researchers think it is reasonable to add *correlated errors* on the basis of the model fits and still retain probability testing with countable *dfs* (e.g., Brown, 2006). This inferential language is considered disingenuous for almost any model (see Meredith & Horn, 2001). Furthermore, modification indices are one-parameter-at-a-time respecifications that are highly exploratory and have already been found to lead to undesirable results (see MacCallum, Roznowski, & Necowitz, 1992).

The literature on *item response theory* (IRT; see McDonald, 1999) seems to be a bit less confusing. In the most common form of IRT applications, a highly restricted model of item functioning may be chosen (i.e., a Rasch model), and items that do not meet these desirable criteria are simply eliminated from the scale. This approach makes it clear that the IRT development of a measure could be simply phrased as a technical engineering task instead of a scientific endeavor—we are not trying to find a model for the data, but we are in search of data that fit the model. This is not intended to denigrate IRT approaches. Although there are now many perceived benefits of this IRT approach, it might be best thought of as a partial exploration with a noble goal in mind (i.e., the creation of a good scale of measurement).

When we want to describe the relationships between an outcome variable and several input variables, we can choose among many methods. The typical multiple regression prediction offers many alternative techniques (e.g., confirmatory, hierarchical, stepwise, best subsets). These represent classical ways to accomplish the basic analytic goals of dealing with multiple predictors (see Fox, 1997; Keith, 2006). One alternative method for the same problem is termed *classification and regression trees* (CART), which is a relatively newer form of data analysis that is computer-assisted and based on machine learning. It has been formally developed over the past 3 decades (see Berk, 2009; Brieman, Friedman, Olshen, & Stone, 1984). Some new CART methods and examples will be described in some detail in this chapter.

Let me now assume the motives of most researchers are based on honest ethics and that we do not report everything we do because of a lack of available techniques or knowledge. Next, let us consider having new tools in our toolbox and pulling out the right one when needed. The most widely known of the exploratory data mining (EDM) techniques is CART. Most current versions of CART started with the early work of Morgan and Sonquist (1963), later elaborated on by Brieman et al. (1984), and more recent informative papers include Brieman (2001) and Strobl, Malley, and Tutz (2009) and the excellent book by Berk (2009). At the end of this chapter, a variety of other multivariate methods are considered (e.g., Neural Nets and others).

A BRIEF HISTORY OF CART

The historical view of CART started around 1959 when Belson suggested that person matching could be considered as prediction and could be created by a binary search strategy (see Fielding & O'Muircheartaigh, 1977). Other researchers have had a lot to say about this as well (Fisher, 1936; Lazersfeld, 1955). In the decade from 1960 to 1970, the stimulus and tools of the most current version of CART were created in the early *automatic interaction detector* (AID) programs advocated and used by John Sonquist and John Morgan at the Institute for Social Research (University of Michigan). The work reported by Sonquist (1970) is instructive. In his own words,

> This investigation had its origin in what, in retrospect, was a rather remarkable

conversation between Professor James Morgan, the author, and several others, in which the topic was whether a computer could ever replace the research analyst himself, as well as replacing many of his statistical clerks. Discarding as irrelevant whether or not the computer could "think," we explored the question whether or not it might simply be programmed to make some of the decisions ordinarily made by the scientist in the course of handling a typical analysis problem, as well as doing computations.... This required examining decision points, alternative courses of action, and the logic for choosing one rather than the other; then formalizing the decision procedure and programming it, but with the capacity to handle many variables instead of only a few. (pp. iii–iv)

The application of such an approach can be explained using the result presented in Figure 20.1 (from Sonquist & Morgan, 1964, p. 66). Here the investigators examined a real data set of N = 2,980 non-farm-working individuals in a survey. The regression model can be fitted to either continuous or categorical outcomes, and the binary outcome case is easy to describe, so we deal with this first. In one example, the original researchers were interested in the many precursors of one binary outcome item, "Do you own a home?" They found 54% of the people responded "yes." They realized this binary outcome could be predicted from at least nine *independent* variables in many different ways, including many forms of multiple LRA (i.e., stepwise, logistic, stepwise logistic), but this approach could include many possible nonlinear terms and interactions. So, instead, what they did that was somewhat revolutionary. They first looked at each variable in their data set (nine possible predictors) at every possible cutpoint or split on each variable to see which variable, at which cut, led to the highest prediction accuracy with the outcome criterion—in this case, they formed a 2 × 2 table with the biggest chi-square value. It is fairly obvious that this approach to data analysis is an exploration, and they used a fast computer to do this work. But the authors suggested that this is exactly what a good scientist would do.

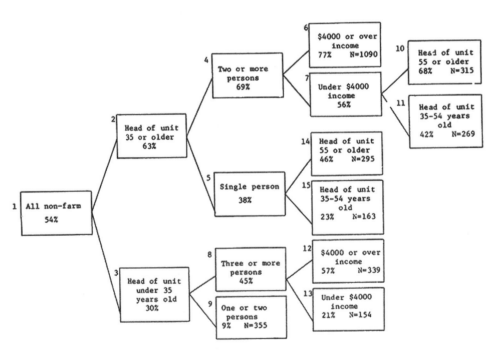

FIGURE 20.1. An initial CART using a binary outcome. From *The Detection of Interaction Effects* (p. 66), by J. Sonquist and J. N. Morgan, 1964, Ann Arbor, MI: Institute for Social Research. Copyright 1964 The University of Michigan. Permission granted by the Institute for Social Research.

In these data, the first variable entering the tree was one that distinguished the homeowners: *Head of the Household Age* > 35. This split the data into two sets of people: n_1 = 2,132 (72%), of whom 63% had a home, and n_2 = 848 (18%), of whom only 30% had a home. That is, this variable (*Age*) split at this point (*Age* = 35 years) created the maximum distance in the outcome proportion (from 54% to 63% and 30%). As an aside, Morgan and Sonquist (1963) did not suggest that we evaluate the probability of the statistical test because they knew this selection of age in the model was not an a priori selection. Following the use of "protected test" logic, however, they could have required this first selection to meet a minimum standard of probability before going on (i.e., if this one were not significant, then no other one would be either). They did not.

The next radical move that they made was to split up or partition the data at this particular variable (*Age*) at this particular cutpoint (35 years) and redo the search procedure. That is, for the "under 35 years of age" group, they repeated the process and recursively predicted the outcome using all nine variables again (including the possibility of another *Age* split). Within this upper age group they found the next best variable was the question, "How many people are living with you?" and the answer "two or more persons" was at 69%, whereas the answer "single person" was at 38%. They then used the same search procedure in the group of persons under 35 years of age and found the best split on the same variable but at different cutpoints. The answer "three or more persons" included 45% homeowners, whereas "one or two persons" included only 9% homeowners. This recursive partitioning was repeated in all subgroups until it was no longer useful in making an accurate prediction (for details, see next section). This last split is interesting because Sonquist and Morgan (1964) reported that no other variable could be found to usefully split the 9% group, and thus that group became the first *terminal node* (with the ninth node n_9 = 355, or 12% of the sample). For purposes of later prediction, every member of this group was assigned an expected probability of 9% homeowner.

To describe these optimal variables and splits Sonquist and Morgan (1964) drew the first classification tree (copied here as Figure 20.1). This tree-like diagram starts out with a box representing scores on the dependent variable for all persons on one variable (termed the *root node*) followed by additional boxes for variables and cutscores that represent the optimal way to split up the data. The diagram has a set of seven terminal nodes, suggesting that no further splits were useful, so all persons in these boxes are taken to be similar on the outcome (only later reinterpreted as an expected probability).

This computer-intensive approach was studied in great detail by Sonquist (1970), and this treatment is worthwhile reading today. He attributed a lot of the stimulus for this approach to earlier work by others. But there are 15 diagrams of trees in this report, so it is clearly focused on this CART-type approach with little appeal to prior theory. Later, Morgan and Sonquist used the chi-square (CHIAD) and theta (THIAD) indexes to define the splits and created popular programs in which, again, it seemed as if they were trying to automatically mimic scientists at work. A large number of other scientists joined in these efforts (e.g., Ritschard, 2007), but CART did not yet seem popular to mainstream scientists.

From 1980 to 1990 the Berkeley/Stanford Statistics Department revived the AID work and used the term CART. In fact, Brieman et al. (1984) developed several proofs of these earlier concepts and developed an original CART program. At the same time, Friedman (1991) developed a slightly advanced version of the model including linear combinations on the basis of multivariate adaptive splines (MARS). (MARS is actually a univariate technique with multiple predictors, and we return to this issue in the last section of this chapter.) From 1990 to 2000 there still seemed to be much resistance to CART/MARS in most any form, but there are the seeds of growth in respectability among many statisticians (and many publications). However, from 2001 to 2009, the work of Brieman et al. (1984) caught on rapidly, and there was a massive growth of alternative CART/MARS package programs and applications. These were most popular in business research, but also in molecular genetics research, and in 2009 even the American Psychological Association (APA) sponsored its first CART conference (at the University of Southern California, sponsored by the APA Science

Directorate). Since very little had changed about CART in the 40 years since it was originally defined by Morgan and Sonquist (1963), something must have changed about the needs of the scientists themselves: It seems we were no longer morally opposed to using computer search strategies (also see Leamer, 1978; Miller, 1990).

SELECTED CART APPLICATIONS IN THE BEHAVIORAL SCIENCES

There are many applications of the CART techniques to formal scientific classification problems (e.g., Put et al., 2003; Sephton, 2001; Vayssières, Plant, & Allen-Diaz, 2000). In addition to the original AID models reported by Sonquist (1970), most of the contemporary applications use some form of CART. A few selected substantive examples are as follows:

1. Temkin, Holubkov, Machamer, Winn, and Dikmen (1995) on problems following head trauma.
2. Seroczynski, Cole, and Maxwell (1997) on different pathways to childhood depression.
3. Monahan et al. (2001) on mental health and violence (see also Steadman et al., 1998, 2000).
4. Sullivan, Kovalenko, York, Prescott, and Kendler (2003) on reasons for survey fatigue in twins.
5. Dierker, Avenevoli, Goldberg, and Glantz (2004) on adolescent smoking.
6. Rovlias and Kotsou (2004) on severe head injury.
7. Granger, Lackner, Kulas, and Russell (2003) on low back pain.
8. Gruenewald, Mroczek, Ryff, and Singer (2008) on affect in later life.
9. Weber, Vinterbo, and Ohno-Machado (2004) on genetics and diagnosis.
10. McArdle (2010a) on adaptive testing, longitudinal attrition, and Internet usage.

A few common features of these CART analyses are as follows: (a) They are admittedly *explorations* of available data. (b) In most of these analyses, the outcomes are considered to be so important to understand that it does not really matter how we create the forecasts. (c) Some of the analyses have a totally unknown structure, and experimental control is not a formal consideration, but we still need a good forecast. (d) CART is only one of many statistical tools that could have been used. The biggest question, then, seems to be, "Do you have any similar research problems?" Our answer is usually yes!

In the next section, several key methodological features of CART are described. Then results from one simple example are presented to illustrate specific features of CART applied to real problems. I focus on the methodology of CART to highlight some special features.

METHODS OF CART

Some of the popularity of CART comes from its topographic trees and Cartesian subplots (e.g., Figure 20.1). CART programs are now widely available and very easy to use and interpret, and these are discussed later. Figure 20.1 from Sonquist and Morgan (1964) appears to be the first of its kind for a binary application and is worth considering in some detail. Before doing so, let me state that CART is based on the utterly simple ideas that we can deal with a multivariate prediction or classification by (a) using only parts of the database at any time (partition), and (b) doing some procedure over and over again in subsets (i.e., recursively). In steps:

0. We define one DV (binary or continuous) and a set (many, p) of independent variables (IVs).
1. We search for the best predictor of the DV among *all* IVs, considering *all ordered splits* of IVs (i.e., we can split on the value of 1 vs. all others, or 1 + 2 vs. all others, or 1 + 2 + 3 vs. all others, etc.).
2. We split (partition) the data into two subsets of data according to the optimal splitting rule developed in Step 1.
3. We reapply the search strategy on each subset of the data.
4. We do this splitting of the data over and over again (recursively) until a final split is not warranted or a *stopping criterion* has been reached.
5. We recognize that this approach clearly would not be possible without modern-day computers.

KEY TECHNICAL ISSUES FOR CART APPLICATIONS

There are many technical questions about computer search strategies, and not all of these questions are answered in this section. But some of these questions are essential to our understanding of any results, so a few technical issues are described now.

One common question is, "How is the best split found?" As stated, for any subpartition of the data, CART is designed to examines *all* predictors $X(j)$ at *all* possible cutpoints $C(k)$ with respect to the criterion Y. For example, the first split of all variables possible in Figure 20.1 was $C(Head\ of\ Unit\ Age) = 35$—this was empirically defined as the best way to split these data to yield the biggest discrepancy in home ownership. Instead of 54% total homeownerships (in 1959), we now have splits with 63% and 30%. Because we needed to search every variable at every cutpoint, optimal computer routines are needed to make this a feasible and relatively rapid search. The cutpoint $C(k)$ on variable $X(j)$ that maximizes the association with scores on Y (either by discrimination or similarity) is chosen as a splitting variable. To accomplish this, with continuous outcomes, we simply find the cutpoint with the highest resulting *t*-value among all other splits. Interestingly, this approach is similar to what Fisher (1936) suggested to find optimal but unknown classifications. With binary outcomes, the optimal cutpoint is typically defined as an index of the resulting classification tables using some index of *impurity* or *diversity*, such as the Gini index, rather than using another index of similarity (i.e., the phi or tetrachoric index), but it also is possible to choose some statistical test (such as chi-square in CHIAD). This simple ordered choice of a cutpoint also makes CART quite resistant to highly skewed distributions and even extreme scores or outliers. Of course, this could be a big benefit for data analyses. That is, because we are simply looking at each variable in a rank-order form, the sensitivity of standard methods to non-normal distributions and extreme scores simply does not matter. Unfortunately, in the same sense, this selection of variables and cutpoints can be rather arbitrary for a specific data set, and replication may not follow. In any case, all the data are used to define the first split, and then the same testing procedure is applied recursively.

There are many alternative ways to defining the best splits. Given a specific data partition (D_j), we can define the best split in several ways. This is always based on (a) the relationship of the outcome variable $(Y|D_j)$ in some subset of data, and (b) a *search* through every possible subset of the predictor variable $X(j)$. For any split on X at a cutpoint $C(k)$ where $p(k) =$ the proportion of data split one way, we can define the following four measures: (a) Bayes Error $= Max\{XC(j)\} = Min\{p(k), 1 - p(k)\}$, (b) Gini Index $= Max\{XC(j)\} = \{p(k) * 1 - p(k)\}$, (c) Cross-Entropy $= Max\{XC(j)\} = -p(k)\ log(pk) - [1 - p(k)\ log(1 - p(k)]$, or (d) Chi-Square/$Max\{$Chi-Square$\}$. These indexes range between 0 and 1, and the Gini is typically used. Most informatively, however, it does not seem to matter which specific cutpoint index is chosen (see Hastie, Tibshirani, & Freidman, 2001).

How do we create a "recursive stopping rule"? In every data set, the splitting can go on as long as the dependent scores differ within a node. But it will not be feasible to continue to create splits of the data because the sample sizes become too small to consider or no new variable can be found. Among several choices, we can define a limit on the number of data in the node or base it on the increment in overall accuracy found. Second, Brieman (2001) suggested that a full tree should be created and that this should be "pruned" back to the point at which these conditions are found. Third, Hothorn, Hornik, and Zeileis (2006) suggested those $X(j)$ with more values had more possible splits, so he created a permutation test with Bonferroni correction for unbiased results. In any case, the desired relationship between *model prediction* and *model complexity* needs to be considered in detail (see Berk, 2009; Hastie et al., 2001).

The next question, after a tree is formed, is, "How can we tell the importance of each variable?" There are many ways to define the variable importance (VI) to a specific CART result (for details, see Ishwaran, 2007). One obvious way that is not discussed in great detail in the literature is simple and classical—remove that variable and see how much loss of fit occurs—either by decrease in R^2 or increase in misclassification error E^2. Another way is to consider the numerical amount of data that has been split by a single variable—the percentage of the data split by any score. We can judge that one variable is the most informative splitter and the rest is a ratio of this one (as done in CART PRO 6.0 by Steinberg,

2006). Alternative indexes of VI each summarize the key information, and it may lead to model comparison and future uses of CART. Of course, the VI may be altered quite a bit by the introduction of highly correlated variables (as in ordinary least squares [OLS]). Somewhat surprisingly, colinearity will not be a problem because CART is designed to select the best one of a set of correlated variables.

We should not forget the importance of utilities. Any formal decision split in a tree is based on a combination of *objective* data and *subjective* utilities defined by the researchers. In the simple two-choice (2 × 2) case, the exact value of the utility numbers does not matter, just their ratio across the actual outcomes. Practically speaking, simply weight all benefits = 0 and then the relative costs can define the needed utility ratio of weighed false positives (WFP) over weighted false negatives (WFN). Another way to consider this issue is that the data for one group simply need to be weighted in terms of this ratio (WFP/WFN) to deal with this decision analysis. But either way, the maximum cutoff is established at the same point for all indexes but differs because of this weighting. Ignoring this weighting gives the usual decision tree, which assumes that costs are one to one, and this is rarely intentional (see Hastie & Dawes, 2010).

STATISTICAL TESTING ISSUES IN CART

One reasonable criticism of exploratory methods is that they take advantage of chance occurrences in the data, and we are not likely to produce replicable results (e.g., Browne & Cudeck, 1984). Furthermore, as stated, CART is usually done without standard statistical tests of probability, largely because it is difficult to define a full basis against which to judge the probability of any specific result. To ensure repeatability, however, it is not unusual for CART users to explore one or more cross-validation strategies. For example, it is common to use a *learn, then test* paradigm. For this paradigm, generally about half of the data are used to develop a model (train), and the other half are used to evaluate the model predictions (test). Another common treatment is to use a general form of *internal cross-validation*. In these cases, a random sample of

individuals is drawn without replacement for the training sample, this is repeated T (~10) times, and splits that are consistently obtained are reported. Finally, we can also use *bootstrap cross-validation*, in which a random sample is drawn with replacement for the training sample, this is repeated T (~2N) times, and splits that are consistently obtained are reported. Incidentally, bootstraps also can provide empirical estimates of the $SE\{\text{cutoff}\}$ (see Berk, 2009; Strobl, Malley, & Tutz, 2009).

CART performance has been shown to improve using aggregations of data and models—for example, random forests, boosting, and similar ensemble approaches (see Strobl, Malley, & Tutz, 2009). The technique known as Random Forests (Brieman, 2001) can be considered as a repeated random sampling of the predictor variables, whereas the technique known as Boosting (Berk, 2009) can be considered as a repeated weighting of the largest residuals, and the method known as Ensembles (Strobl, Malley, & Tutz, 2009) can be considered as combinations of each of these and several other approaches. Of course, these are computer-intensive strategies that would not be possible without current computer power.

CART users are limited by a key fact—the key predictors must be measured and included in the data set—if key outcomes or predictors are not measured, CART surely will be biased and unrepeatable. Thus, CART is sensitive to random noise in data, such as measurement error, so we cannot count on CART to find best solutions with bad data. As usual, there is no substitute for good measurement. It would also be good if there were an overall objective function to be minimized, and then CART would have a simple way of measuring prediction accuracy (ACC) compared with model complexity (as in the root-mean-square error of approximation [RMSEA], BIC, AIC, etc.). In real applications, the number of parameters used is hard to define in advance of the model fitted, and there is no simple way around this problem (e.g., see Berk, 2009).

AVAILABLE CART COMPUTER PROGRAMS

There are already many computer programs that can be used to carry out these calculations, and some of these are simply smoothing techniques, including commonly used nonlinear transformations, Box–Cox powers of the DV, transforms of the joint relationships (e.g., lowess tranforms of the relationships), and curve-fitting programs that are based on exhaustive searchers (e.g., T2CURVE, T3CURVE, etc.). Other computer programs offer relatively advanced search techniques, including best subsets regression, a commonly used regression technique for examining all possible (integer) combination of predictor variables.

The explicit CART techniques can be found in many different computer packages, including the following:

- **R-Code.** Contains many state-of-the-art algorithms covering many different topics that are general and freely available (e.g., Party, RPART, RATTLE, TrajMINR, MASS).
- **XLMINER.** A very popular and inexpensive suite of programs built around on EXCEL structures (also see XLFIT, TABU, and RTREE).
- **SAS Enterprise, SPSS Clementine, SYSTAT Trees.** Features added exploratory data-mining suites for well-known packages of programs with broad and general use.
- *CART-PRO* **Classification and Regression Tree.** A search approach for categorical outcomes. This approach supposedly yields optimal discrimination using successive search techniques (but watch out when analyses ignore utility theory).
- *MARS* **(Multivariate Adaptive Splines).** Offers newer regression techniques for examining all possible functions of predictor variables using linearity with cutpoints.
- **TREENET.** Implements random forests using the CART-PRO approach.
- **SAS NLMIXED and PLS, WinBUGS, and Latent GOLD.** SEM-based programs marketed as SEM rather than CART.

A reasonable question that is often asked is, "Do these CART programs produce different results than each other? The answer is, "Yes, sometimes substantially." But this is not because the data are read in different formats, and it is not because of computational inaccuracies, as was the case of some regression programs (see Beaton, Rubin, & Barone, 1976). Instead, differences in resulting trees are partly due to the use of different options for split criteria and partly due to

different stopping rules. All is not lost, however, because the availability of different user options imply that the resulting tree may not be unique; it may not even seem to be the same for the same data even for very simple problems. The first variable (at the root node) may be different, and the cutpoints may be different too, and then the second variables might differ, and so on. Perhaps we should take solace in the fact that what is more likely to remain similar across different programs is the VI and the predicted outcome (Yhat) for each person. And, although not formally stated, the use of alternative CART programs to examine the range of possible results, could by itself be considered a benefit of ensemble calculations (see Strobl, Malley, & Tutz, 2009). But this certainly means that CART results require detailed explanations before they can be useful.

A SIMPLE EXAMPLE—USING CART TO PREDICT CORONARY HEART DISEASE (CHD) FROM AGE

In this section, we discuss one simple example of CART analyses to illustrate the benefits and limitations. The first example is taken from Hosmer and Lemeshow (2000, pp. 2–4). In this example $N = 100$ people were examined at a hospital for the presence of CHD. Among many variables also measured was the age of the person (in years) at the time of the medical evaluation. The question raised by Hosmer and Lemeshow was, "Is age predictive of CHD?"

One answer to this question was provided by logistic regression, for which the binary variable CHD was predicted. The logistic regression of CHD on age was a significant predictor, with a prediction equation of $ln(P_n/1 - P_n) = -5.03 - 0.12\ Age_n$ (see the R-code for this example in Appendix 20.1). This finding can be interpreted as a significantly increasing risk of 1.00 to 1.12 per year of age (with a confidence interval of 1.07 to 1.17). This analysis also gives a pseudo-explained variance of $PR^2 = 0.25$ with a maximum of $PR^2 = 0.32$. By turning the logistic model expectations (and CI) into expected probabilities for each value of age, we can draw the expected value plot of Figure 20.2a. Here, it is now fairly obvious that the predicted probability of CHD for any person increases with age (in log-linear fashion).

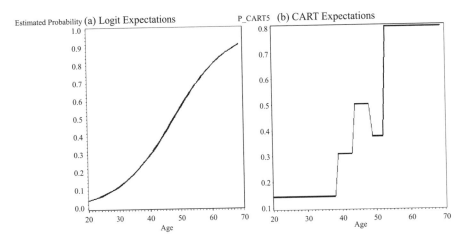

FIGURE 20.2. Age plots of (a) logit model probabilities and (b) CART model probabilities.

The expected result of the alternative CART is presented in Figure 20.2b. Here the value of the optimal prediction is given by five linked horizontal lines over age. Each of these lines represents the expected value of one terminal node defined as a specific age range. This is an empirical plot of the best predictions from the data, and it is not linear. That is, up to about age 38 years, the CHD risk is about 15%, but risk increases to about 30% for ages 40 to 44 years, and then increases again to 50% for ages 45 to 49 years. Most informative, the risk decreases to about 40% for a specific subset of ages 50 to 52 years, before it increases again to 80% for those 53 years and older. Although the expectations largely increase, this analysis shows that this is not always the case with CART.

This simple one-predictor illustration shows the potential for nonlinearity within a single variable for any $Y \leftarrow X$ relationship with CART. The fact that CART expectations are different than logistic expectations is a question well studied (e.g., Lemon, Roy, Clark, Friedmann, & Rakowski, 2003). The substantive question that is commonly raised is, "Is there something special about the act of becoming 50 that makes a person enough aware of the risk to prevent it?" This is a clear hypothesis that is generated from this result and one that may be studied further, but it is certainly not an explicit a priori intention of the CART analysis.

The previous discussion has not focused on the interpretation of the tree structure, but the tree of Figure 20.2b is presented in Figure 20.3a. This was initially defined by using the XLMINER program

with four categorical splits at ages 52.5 (splitting below 53 from 53 and above), at 58.5, at 39.5, at 33.5, and at 29.5. The built-in stopping rules suggest we stop at eight terminal nodes, and the unweighted decision accuracy of this tree is 78%, with a $PR^2 = 0.27$. This prediction accuracy is typically greater than the logistic explained variance, but only at specific cutpoints, so this is not easily compared with the PR^2 (see Lemon et al., 2003; Penny & Chesney, 2006) for this complexity of the model search (i.e., eight groups).

To examine this in further detail, the same data and model was refit using the PARTY program in R-code (Strobl, Hothorn, & Zeileis, 2009; see Appendix 20.1). With PARTY, the stopping criteria suggested that only the first two splits were significant by the built-in permutation rules, as seen in Figure 20.3b, and the unweighted decision accuracy of this tree is 75%, but with a $PR^2 = 0.28$.

Finally, a subset of the same data (i.e., the 43 persons originally thought of as being at risk) were are reanalyzed using CART-PRO (6.0; Steinberg, 2006), using the built-in algorithm with a 10-fold cross-validation to create only one split—at age 33—and the unweighted decision accuracy of this tree is 75% (see Figure 20.3c). Thus, using these alternative stopping rules, a model of substantially less complexity is actually needed. In sum, the three different CART programs are doing similar calculations, but they give slightly different results for even this simple one-predictor model.

This does not end our analysis, because most programs allow sampling weights or other forms of

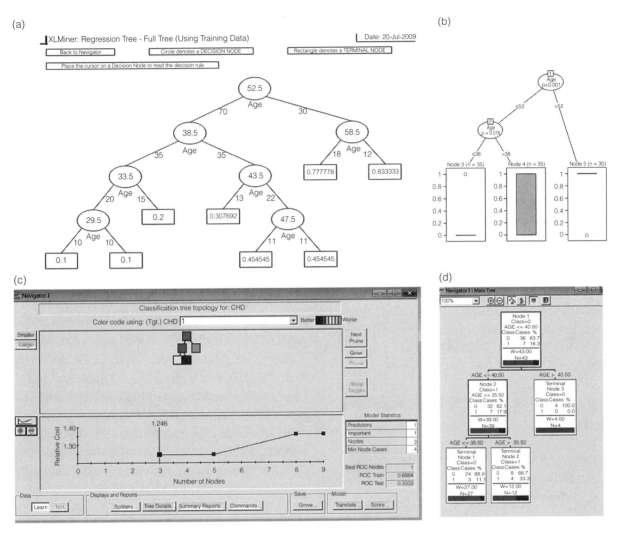

FIGURE 20.3. (a) CART result from XLMINER. (b) CART Result from PARTY. (c) Initial output from CART PRO. (d) CART result from CART PRO.

weighting, such as the inclusion of utility structures, and we can examine a few of these here. For example, suppose we add the additional restriction that the mistakes are not of equal magnitude in this classification, and the false negatives (FN) are much worse that the false positives (FP).

For example, in cases in which we do not want to miss anyone using a simple age cutoff, possibly because this is a first-stage screening, we would redo the analysis using FN:FP weights of, say, 2:1, and the result is a new cross-validated decision rule based at an age cutoff of 32 years. This yields a weighted accuracy of 71%. If the opposite approach were taken and we did not want to say someone had CHD when they did not, we would reverse the FN:FP utility weights to be 1:2, and the resulting cross-validated CART would still have a cutoff at age

52 years. This analysis makes it clear that any sampling weights, such as the utilities of the mistakes, are an integral part of any decision rule, and they can alter the point of optimal splits or the variable. This is true of regression models also, but utility analysis is not highlighted as much as it could be in that modeling context.

The examples used here were designed to illustrate a range of CART applications. In the first example, the simplest possible relationship between CHD and age was explored, comparing logistic expectations and CART classification, and several technical issues were raised. In all cases, CART analyses could be used directly to create optimal contrasts in future analyses, or we might say it was useful as a baseline against which to judge the success of any previous analysis.

CART SUCCESSES AND FAILURES

When do we expect CART to be most helpful? It may be most helpful in the context of a lot of real applications, but especially when we have little information and are not sure what to do next. Similarly, CART is useful when there are many interactions, and we do not know which ones are crucial. Of course, this happens most when the model assumptions are not met because of nonlinearity or outliers or combinations. That is, CART may be most helpful when data suggest a variable ordering or scaling that the researcher would not have predicted.

When do we expect CART to be least helpful? A lot of the time we can pick up on unnecessary artifacts or chance events in the data that are unlikely to replicate. This can occur when the model is linear and additive, and all assumptions are met. This is also true when there are limited (specific) hypotheses we want to test, including those formed on the basis of interactions. Most interesting, when the initial split is incorrect, the rest of the splits cannot recover from the original mishap. Also, if you cannot buy into the idea that it is important to maximize some goodness of fit and minimize error, then this approach would not be recommended.

For these reasons, CART is both easy and hard to use. The easy parts come because CART is an automated stepwise procedure that considers most nonlinearity and all interactions. CART does not need assistance with scaling and scoring and variable redundancy is allowed (we put all IVs in). CART does a lot of numerical searching, but it is very fast. The hard parts come when we realize that we need to know the key outcome variable well, and we need to judge how many nodes should be used. Of course, we have other hard questions to answer, such as, "Is this sample of persons an adequate representation of the population?" Furthermore, CART handles missing data but not by direct imputation (Brieman et al., 1984; Horton & Kleinman, 2007; Steinberg & Colla, 1999).

MULTIVARIATE EXTENSIONS USING A CART APPROACH

As stated earlier, the approaches termed CART and MARS handle one outcome variable at a time, so these are not strictly multivariate techniques (see Cattell, 1966). There is a great deal of similarity in this approach as well as in the prior literature in exploratory factor analysis (see Browne, 2001; Horn, 1965; Yates, 1987) and canonical analysis (Cliff & Krus, 1976; Liang, Krus, & Webb, 1995). We also isolated a CART-like approach for the analysis of multivariate repeated measures (Zhang, 2004), and these measures are based on a generic likelihood splitting that could be considered for any multiple outcome model (e.g., a latent variable path model).

Although the prior SEMs have been considered informative, there is much more to be considered when dealing with multivariate data. For example, one key idea in the current literature is that we may want to consider heterogeneous groups of participants (see Tucker & Lewis, 1973). Many recent papers deal with what is now termed *growth-mixture modeling* (e.g., Grimm & McArdle, 2007; McLachlan & Peel, 2005; Muthén & Asparouhov, 2009; Nagin & Land, 1993). However, an entirely different way of viewing this problem has been created by CART approaches. This approach seems to have been initiated by Segal (1992); Zhang (1997, 1999, 2004; Zhang & Singer, 1999); and Abdolell, LeBlanc, Stephens and Harrison (2002), but these early works both follow the basic logic of survival CART (S-CART; Gordon & Olshen, 1985; Su & Tsai, 2005). The key idea is that we can use multiple measured variables to split the data into subgroups of persons with common patterns of longitudinal scores. It is interesting that the same form of observed-variable pattern-split model forms the basis of both survival CART analysis (Su & Tsai, 2005; Ture, Tokatli, & Kurt, 2009) and event history CART analysis (McVicar & Anyadike-Danes, 2002; Ritschard, 2007).

This leads to the creation of a more general structural equation model CART (SEM-CART). The key idea is that we have some kind of SEM for a set of data, either a path model, or a factor model, or a growth model, or some combination of each. If we fit the SEM to a group of participants, we end up with parameter estimates and a scalar from of an individual likelihood (e.g., $L_n^2\{\mu[t], \Sigma[t]\} = K + \{Y[t]_n - \mu[t]\} \Sigma[t]^{-1} \{Y[t]_n - \mu[t]\}'$), where the individual's scores ($Y[t]$) are compared with a population mean

($\mu[t]$) and the population covariance ($\Sigma[t]$) is defined by a model (and K is a constant). It follows that the total misfit for any model is the sum of these likelihoods (*Overall $L^2 = \Sigma\, L^2_n$*). Indeed, isolating each person's misfit can be a useful way to examine influential observations (see McArdle, 1997).

Now we can explore the possibility of splitting the people into groups defined by an observed independent splitting variable (X) into subsets *a* and *b*. From this split we can form a new likelihood for each person as being in one of two data splits (*For $X = s$, $L^2_{ns}\{\mu[t]_s$, $\Sigma[t]_s\} = K +\{Y[t]_{ns} - \mu[t]_s\}\, \Sigma s^{-1}\, \{Y[t]_{ns} - \mu[t]_s\}$'*). The total misfit for this joint model is the weighted sum of these likelihoods (*Split $L^2 = \Sigma\, L^2_{na} + \Sigma\, L^2_{nb}$*), so the effectiveness of the split of data is defined by the likelihood difference (*Gain $L^2 = Split\, L^2 - Overall\, L^2$*). Of course, this is very similar to a multiple groups structural equation model, but the splitting on the basis of a measured input variable on the whole outcome vector is done automatically. Several new programs can be used to calculate this form of recursive partitioning on the likelihood, and these are continuing to grow.

Of course, this new type of SEM-CART analysis is not needed at the confirmatory or testing stage of research, but this analysis is almost always needed near the end of a research enterprise when we are evaluating the single-group assumption. This could be correct for almost any substantive hypothesis, so it is always wise to check the results of any exploratory SEM-CART analysis against a more rigid multiple group hypothesis.

CONCLUSION

This brings us directly back to the early work by Sonquist (1970), who showed how the principles of CART (then embodied in AID) could be useful when dealing with nonadditive and nonlinear relations and, importantly, how these techniques would not be misleading in situations in which they were not needed. It is also fair to say that the current status of CART has increased dramatically over the past few decades, probably because of the interest among professional statisticians (e.g., Brieman, 2001; Brieman et al., 1984).

But it also seems there is much left to be done to deal effectively with the simultaneous analysis of multiple inputs and multiple outcomes, and this is typical empirical situation, so there is a need to improve multivariate versions of CART and similar techniques (e.g., Marcoulides & Dresner, 2004). Also, work needs to be done to decrease the skepticism and understand limitations and strengths of the approach in psychology. As this work is being carried out, a CART-based simultaneous approach to multivariate structural analysis (SEM-CART) can and should be compared with other popular confirmatory techniques (e.g., LISREL; Jöreskog & Sörbom, 1979; McArdle, 2009) and exploratory techniques (e.g., Jöreskog & Wold, 1982; Marcoulides, Chin, & Saunders, 2009). Virtually any SEM-CART-type approach will open new avenues to understand complex data and, given our current state of multivariate prediction, such improvements are obviously needed.

APPENDIX 20.1 R-CODE SCRIPT FOR CHD DATA USING LOGISTIC REGRESSION AND CART CLASSIFICATIONS

```
# REG2_CHD.R
# Compare predicted values from
regression and regression trees

setwd("Data")
CHD_HL <- read.table("chd_hl.dat",
   header = FALSE)
names(CHD_HL) <-
   c("GROUP","YEARSAGE","CHD")
attach(CHD_HL)

# Simple Linear Regression

REG1 <- lm(CHD ~ YEARSAGE)
summary(REG1)
plot(REG1, which = 2)
YHAT.REG1 <- predict(REG1)
PRED.REG1 <- cor(YHAT.REG1, CHD)**2
PRED.REG1

# Simple Logistic Regression

REG2 <- glm(CHD ~ YEARSAGE, family =
   binomial())
summary(REG2)
exp(REG2$coefficients)
plot(REG2, which = 2)
```

417

John J. McArdle

```
x <- predict(REG2)
YHAT.REG2 <- exp(x)/(1 + exp(x))
plot(YHAT.REG2, YEARSAGE)
table(YHAT.REG2, CHD)
PRED.REG2 <- cor(YHAT.REG2, CHD)**2
PRED.REG2

# Newer Regression Tree 2

library(party)
CART2 <- ctree(CHD ~ YEARSAGE)
plot(CART2)
YHAT.CART2 <- predict(CART2)
table(YHAT.CART2, CHD)
plot(YHAT.CART2, CHD)
plot(YHAT.REG2, YHAT.CART2)
PRED.CART2 <- cor(YHAT.CART2,
   CHD)**2
PRED.CART2
```

References

Abdolell, M., LeBlanc, D. Stephens, & Harrison, R. V. (2002). Binary partitioning for continuous longitudinal data: Categorizing a prognostic variable. *Statistics in Medicine, 21,* 3395–3409. doi:10.1002/sim.1266

Beaton, A. E., Rubin, D. B., & Barone, J. L. (1976). The acceptability of regression solutions: Another look at computational accuracy. *Journal of the American Statistical Association, 71,* 158–168.

Belson, W. A. (1959). Matching and prediction on the principle of biological classification. *Applied Statistics, 8,* 65–75. doi:10.2307/2985543

Berk, R. A. (2009). *Statistical learning from a regression perspective.* New York, NY: Springer.

Box, G. E. P. (1976). Science and statistics. *Journal of the American Statistical Association, 71,* 791–799. doi:10.2307/2286841

Brieman, L. (2001). Statistical modeling: The two cultures. *Statistical Science, 16,* 199–231. doi:10.1214/ss/1009213726

Brieman, L., Friedman, J., Olshen, R., & Stone, C. (1984). *Classification and regression trees.* Pacific Grove, CA: Wadsworth & Brooks/Cole.

Brown, T. A. (2006). *Confirmatory factor analysis for applied research.* New York, NY: Guilford Press.

Browne, M. B. (2001). An overview of analytic rotation in exploratory factor analysis. *Multivariate Behavioral Research, 36,* 111–150. doi:10.1207/S15327906MBR3601_05

Browne, M. W., & Cudeck, R. (1984). Single sample cross-validation indices for covariance structures.

British Journal of Mathematical and Statistical Psychology, 37, 62–83.

Cattell, R. B. (1966). Psychological theory and scientific method. In R. B. Cattell (Ed.), *Handbook of multivariate experimental psychology* (pp. 1–18). Chicago: Rand McNally.

Cliff, N., & Krus, D. J. (1976). Interpretation of canonical variate analysis: Rotated vs. unrotated solutions. *Psychometrika, 41,* 35–42. doi:10.1007/BF02291696

Cooley, J., & Lohnes, P. (1962, 1971, 1985). *Mutivariate data analysis.* Boston, MA: Duxbury Press.

Dierker, L. C., Avenevoli, S., Goldberg, A., & Glantz, M. (2004). Defining subgroups of adolescents at risk for experimental and regular smoking. *Prevention Science, 5,* 169–183. doi:10.1023/B:PREV.0000037640.66607.6b

Fielding, A., & O'Muircheartaigh, C. A. (1977). Binary segmentation in survey analysis with particular reference to AID. *The Statistician, 26,* 17–28. doi:10.2307/2988216

Fisher, R. A. (1936). The use of multiple measurements in taxonomic problems. *Annals of Eugenics, 7,* 179–188. doi:10.1111/j.1469-1809.1936.tb02137.x

Fox, J. (1997). *Applied regression analysis, linear models, and related methods.* Thousand Oaks, CA: Sage.

Gordon, L., & Olshen, R. (1985). Tree-structured survival analysis. *Cancer Treatment Reports, 69,* 1065–1069.

Granger, C. V., Lackner, J. M., Kulas, M., & Russell, C. F. (2003). Outpatients with low back pain: An analysis of the rate per day of pain improvement that may be expected and factors affecting improvement. *American Journal of Physical Medicine and Rehabilitation, 82,* 253–260. doi:10.1097/01.PHM.0000057224.20987.2A

Grimm, K. J., & McArdle, J. J. (2007). A dynamic structural analysis of the potential impacts of major context shifts on lifespan cognitive development. In T. D. Little, J. A. Bovaird, & N. A. Card (Eds.), *Modeling contextual effects in longitudinal studies* (pp. 363–386). Mahwah, NJ: Erlbaum.

Gruenewald, T. L., Mroczek, D. K., Ryff, C. D., & Singer, B. H. (2008). Diverse pathways to positive and negative affect in adulthood and later life: An integrative approach using recursive partitioning. *Developmental Psychology, 44,* 330–343. doi:10.1037/0012-1649-.44.2.330

Hastie, R., & Dawes, R. (2010). *Rational choice in an uncertain world: The psychology of judgment and decision making* (2nd ed.). Los Angeles, CA: Sage.

Hastie, T., Tibshirani, R., & Freidman, J. (2001). *The elements of statistical learning: Data mining, inference, and prediction.* New York, NY: Springer.

Hoaglin, D. C. (1982). Exploratory data analysis. In S. Kotz, N. L. Johnson, & C. B. Read (Eds.), *Encyclopedia of statistical sciences* (Vol. 2, pp. 579–583). New York, NY: Wiley.

Horn, J. L. (1965). An empirical comparison of methods for estimating factor scores. *Educational and Psychological Measurement, 25,* 313–322.

Horton, N. J., & Kleinman, K. (2007). Much ado about nothing: A comparison of missing data methods and software to fit incomplete data regression. *Journal of the American Statistical Association, 61,* 79–90. doi:10.1198/000313007X172556

Hosmer, D. W., & Lemeshow, S. (2000). *Applied logistic regression.* New York, NY: Wiley. doi:10.1002/0471722146

Hothorn, T., Hornik, K., & Zeileis, A. (2006). Unbiased recursive partitioning: A conditional inference framework. *Journal of Computational and Graphical Statistics, 15,* 651–674. doi:10.1198/106186006X133933

Ishwaran, H. (2007). Variable importance in binary regression trees and forests. *Electronic Journal of Statistics, 1,* 519–537. doi:10.1214/07-EJS039

Jöreskog, K. G., & Sörbom, D. (1979). *Advances in factor analysis and structural equation models.* Cambridge, MA: Abt.

Jöreskog, K. G., & Wold, H. (1982). The ML and PLS techniques for modeling with latent variables: Historical and comparative aspects. In H. Wold & K. Jöreskog (Eds.), *Systems under indirect observation: Causality, structure, prediction* (Vol. 1, pp. 263–270). Amsterdam, the Netherlands: North-Holland.

Keith, T. Z. (2006). *Multiple regression analysis and beyond.* Boston, MA: Allyn & Bacon.

Lazersfeld, P. F. (1955). The interpretation of statistical relations as a research operation. In P. F. Lazersfeld & M. Rosenberg (Eds.), *The language of social research* (pp. 101–112). Glencoe, IL: Free Press.

Leamer, E. E. (1978). *Specification searches: Ad hoc inferences with nonexperimental data.* New York, NY: Wiley.

Lemon, S. C., Roy, J., Clark, M. A., Friedmann, P. D., & Rakowski, W. (2003). Classification and regression tree analysis in public health: Methodological review and comparison with logistic regression. *Annals of Behavioral Medicine, 26,* 172–181. doi:10.1207/S15324796ABM2603_02

Liang, K. H., Krus, D. J., & Webb, J. M. (1995). K-fold cross-validation in canonical analysis. *Multivariate Behavioral Research, 30,* 539–545. doi:10.1207/s15327906mbr3004_4

MacCallum, R. C., Roznowski, M., & Necowitz, L. B. (1992). Model modifications in covariance structure analysis: The problem of capitalization

on chance. *Psychological Bulletin, 111,* 490–504. doi:10.1037/0033-2909.111.3.490

Marcoulides, G. A., Chin, W. W., & Saunders, C. (2009). A critical look at partial least squares modeling. *Management Information Systems Quarterly, 33,* 171–175.

Marcoulides, G. A., & Dresner, Z. (2004). Tabu search variable selection with resource constraints. *Communications in Statistics, 33,* 355–362.

McArdle, J. J. (1997). Modeling longitudinal data by latent growth curve methods. In G. Marcoulides (Ed.), *Modern methods for business research* (pp. 359–406). Mahwah, NJ: Erlbaum.

McArdle, J. J. (2009). Latent variable modeling of longitudinal data. *Annual Review of Psychology, 60,* 577–605. doi:10.1146/annurev.psych.60.110707.163612

McArdle, J. J. (2010a). Adaptive testing of the Number Series test using standard approaches and a new classification and regression tree approach. *Woodcock–Munoz Research Foundation Journal, 1,* 1–33.

McArdle, J. J. (2010b). Some ethical issues in factor analysis. In A. T. Panter & S. K. Sterba (Eds.), *Handbook of ethics in quantitative methodology* (pp. 313–340). New York, NY: Taylor & Francis.

McArdle, J. J., & Cattell, R. B. (1994). Structural equation models of factorial invariance in parallel proportional profiles and oblique confactor problems. *Multivariate Behavioral Research, 29,* 63–113. doi:10.1207/s15327906mbr2901_3

McDonald, R. P. (1985). *Factor analysis and related methods.* Hillsdale, NJ: Erlbaum.

McDonald, R. P. (1999). *Test theory.* Mahwah, NJ: Erlbaum.

McLachlan, G., & Peel, D. (2005). *Finite mixture models.* New York, NY: Wiley.

McVicar, D., & Anyadike-Danes, M. (2002). Predicting successful and unsuccessful transitions from school to work by using sequence methods. *Journal of the Royal Statistical Society. Series A (General), 165*(Pt. 2), 317–334.

Meredith, W., & Horn, J. L. (2001). The role of factorial invariance in modeling growth and change. In A. G. Sayer & L. Collins (Eds.), *New methods for the analysis of change* (pp. 204–230). Washington, DC: American Psychological Association.

Miller, A. J. (1990). *Subset selection in regression.* London, England: Chapman & Hall.

Monahan, J., Steadman, H. J., Silver, E., Appelbaum, P. S., Robbins, P. C., Mulvey, E. P., … Banks, S. (2001). *Rethinking risk assessment: The MacArthur study of mental disorder and violence.* Oxford, England: Oxford University Press.

Morgan, J. N., & Sonquist, J. A. (1963). Problems in the analysis of survey data: And a proposal. *Journal of* the *American Statistical Association, 58*, 415–434. doi:10.2307/2283276

Muthén, B., & Asparouhov, T. (2009). Multilevel regression mixture analysis. *Journal of the Royal Statistical Society, Series A: Statistics in Society, 172*, 639–657. doi:10.1111/j.1467-985X.2009.00589.x

Nagin, D. S., & Land, K. C. (1993). Age, criminal careers, and population heterogeneity: Specification and estimation of a nonparametric, mixed Poisson model. *Criminology, 31*, 327–362. doi:10.1111/j.1745-9125.1993.tb01133.x

Penny, K., & Chesney, T. (2006). A comparison of data mining methods and logistic regression to determine factors associated with death following injury. In S. Zani, A. Cerioli, M. Riani, & M. Vichi (Eds.), *Data analysis, classification and the forward search* (pp. 417–423). Heidelberg, Germany: Springer-Verlag. doi:10.1007/3-540-35978-8_46

Put, R., Perrin, C., Questier, F., Coomans, D., Massart, D. L., & Vander Heyden, Y. (2003). Classification and regression tree analysis for molecular descriptor selection and retention prediction in chromatographic quantitative structure-retention relationship studies. *Journal of Chromatography A, 988*, 261–276. doi:10.1016/S0021-9673(03)00004-9

Riley, M. W. (1964). Sources and types of sociological data. In R. E. Faris (Ed.), *Handbook of modern sociology* (pp. 978–1026). Chicago, IL: Rand-McNally.

Ritschard, G. (2007). *CHAID* (Unpublished manuscript). Department of Econometrics, University of Geneva. Geneva, Switzerland.

Rovlias, A., & Kotsou, S. (2004). Classification and regression tree for prediction of outcome after severe head injury using simple clinical and laboratory variables. *Journal of Neurotrauma, 21*, 886–893. doi:10.1089/0897715041526249

Scheffé, H. (1959). *The analysis of variance.* New York, NY: Wiley.

Segal, M. R. (1992). Tree-structured methods for longitudinal data. *Journal of the American Statistical Association, 87*, 407–417. doi:10.2307/2290271

Sephton, P. (2001). Forecasting recessions: Can we do better on MARS? *Federal Reserve Bank of St Louis Review, 83*, 39–49.

Seroczynski, A. D., Cole, D. A., & Maxwell, S. E. (1997). Cumulative and compensatory effects of competence and incompetence on depressive symptoms in children. *Journal of Abnormal Psychology, 106*, 586–597. doi:10.1037/0021-843X.106.4.586

Sonquist, J. (1970). *Multivariate model building.* Ann Arbor, MI: Institute for Social Research.

Sonquist, J., & Morgan, J. N. (1964). *The detection of interaction effects.* Ann Arbor, MI: Institute for Social Research.

Steadman, H. J., Mulvey, E., Monahan, J., Robbins, P., Appelbaum, P., Grisso, T., … Silver, E. (1998). Violence by people discharged from acute psychiatric inpatient facilities and by others in the same neighborhoods. *Archives of General Psychiatry, 55*, 393–401. doi:10.1001/archpsyc.55.5.393

Steadman, H. J., Silver, E., Monohan, J., Applebaum, P. S., Robbins, P. C., Mulvey, E. P., … Banks, S. (2000). A classification tree approach to the development of actuarial violence risk assessment tools. *Law and Human Behavior, 24*, 83–100. doi:10.1023/A:1005478820425

Steinberg, D. (2006). CART PRO 6.0 [Computer software]. San Diego, CA: Salford Systems.

Steinberg, D., & Colla, P. (1999). *MARS: An introduction.* San Diego, CA: Salford Systems.

Strobl, C., Hothorn, T., & Zeileis, A. (2009). Party on! A new, conditional variable importance measure for random forests available in the party package. *The R Journal, 1*, 14–17.

Strobl, C., Malley, J., & Tutz, G. (2009). An introduction to recursive partitioning: Rationale, application and characteristics of classification and regression trees, bagging and random forests. *Psychological Methods, 14*, 323–348. doi:10.1037/a0016973

Su, X., & Tsai, C. (2005). Tree-augmented Cox proportional hazards models. *Biostatistics, 6*, 486–499. doi:10.1093/biostatistics/kxi024

Sullivan, P. F., Kovalenko, P., York, T. P., Prescott, C. A., & Kendler, K. S. (2003). Fatigue in a community sample of twins. *Psychological Medicine, 33*, 263–281. doi:10.1017/S0033291702007031

Temkin, N. R., Holubkov, R., Machamer, J. E., Winn, H. R., & Dikmen, S. S. (1995). Classification and regression trees (CART) for prediction of function at 1 year following head trauma. *Journal of Neurosurgery, 82*, 764–771. doi:10.3171/jns.1995.82.5.0764

Tucker, L. R., & Lewis, C. (1973). The reliability coefficient for maximum likelihood factor analysis. *Psychometrika, 38*, 1–10. doi:10.1007/BF02291170

Tukey, J. W. (1962). The future of data analysis. *Annals of Mathematical Statistics, 33*, 1–67. doi:10.1214/aoms/1177704711

Tukey, J. W. (1977). *Exploratory data analysis.* Reading, MA: Addison-Wesley.

Ture, M., Tokatli, F., & Kurt, I. (2009). Using Kaplan-Meier analysis together with decision tree methods (C&RT, CHAID, QUEST, C4.5 and ID3) in determining recurrence-free survival of breast cancer patients. *Expert Systems with Applications, 36*, 2017–2026. doi:10.1016/j.eswa.2007.12.002

Vayssières, M. P., Plant, R. E., & Allen-Diaz, B. H. (2000). Classification trees: An alternative non-parametric approach for predicting species distributions. *Journal of Vegetation Science, 11*, 679–694. doi:10.2307/3236575

Velleman, P. F., & Hoaglin, D. C. (1981). *Applications, basics, and computing of exploratory data analysis.* Boston, MA: Duxbury Press.

Weber, G., Vinterbo, S., & Ohno-Machado, L. (2004). Multivariate selection of genetic markers in diagnostic classification. *Artificial Intelligence in Medicine, 31*, 155–167. doi:10.1016/j.artmed.2004.01.011

Yates, A. (1987). *Multivariate exploratory data analysis.* Albany, NY: State University Press.

Zhang, H., & Singer, B. (1999). *Recursive partitioning in the health sciences.* New York, NY: Springer.

Zhang, H. P. (1997). Multivariate adaptive splines for longitudinal data. *Journal of Computational and Graphical Statistics, 6*, 74–91. doi:10.2307/1390725

Zhang, H. P. (1999). Analysis of infant growth curves using multivariate adaptive splines. *Biometrics, 55*, 452–459. doi:10.1111/j.0006-341X.1999.00452.x

Zhang, H. P. (2004). Multivariate adaptive splines in the analysis of longitudinal and growth curve data. *Statistical Methods in Medical Research, 13*, 63–82. doi:10.1191/0962280204sm353ra

Dyadic and Social Network Data

USING THE SOCIAL RELATIONS MODEL TO UNDERSTAND INTERPERSONAL PERCEPTION AND BEHAVIOR

P. Niels Christensen and Deborah A. Kashy

Many psychological phenomena are inherently tied to an interpersonal context. In developmental psychology, both peer and family interactions play critical roles in a child's development. In group psychotherapy, a group member's well-being may depend on her own attributes as well as the attributes of the other group members. Likewise, being an effective leader may depend on the leader's skills as well as the strengths and weaknesses of the individuals being led. In each of these examples a person's outcomes are, at least to some degree, dependent on others. Given this naturally occurring interdependence, studies of interpersonal phenomena require that researchers learn methods designed to examine individual behavior within the social context. In this chapter, we introduce the social relations model (SRM; Kenny, 1994) as one such methodological approach.

Developed by Kenny and his colleagues (Kenny, 1994; Warner, Kenny, & Stoto, 1979), the SRM provides a general framework from which interpersonal behavior can be studied. The most basic assumption of the SRM is that a person's behavior with a particular partner may reflect aspects of the larger group to which the two individuals belong, aspects of the individual emitting the behavior, aspects of the partner, and qualities unique to the two individuals' relationship with one another. For example, a daughter's conflict with her mother may reflect family-level norms (e.g., everyone in the family is contentious, and so conflict is common), qualities of the daughter (e.g., she may be low in trait agreeableness, and so she fights with all family members),

qualities of the mother (e.g., she makes heavy demands from everyone in the family, so everyone fights with her), and unique attributes of the mother–daughter relationship (their similarity to one another makes them highly competitive).

As is perhaps clear from the complexity of this initial example, the SRM provides a means to examine interpersonal behavior that is multiply determined. We begin this chapter by defining the components of the model, including the data structures typically used to extract the model components. Next, examples of previous SRM research are provided to illustrate the types of questions that can be asked using the model. Third, we outline methodological issues central to SRM research, including procedural and measurement considerations. The chapter concludes with a brief introduction to a few issues involved in analyzing SRM data, and readers are referred to other sources for more specific guidance in this area.

THE SRM COMPONENTS

Consider as an example a study of self-disclosure in roommate relationships. In the study, we include residents living in 20 four-person dormitory suites, and we measure how much each person discloses to each of his or her other roommates. One observation we obtain is that Pat discloses a great deal of personal information to her roommate Sue. Why might this occur? It might be that Pat, Sue, and their other two roommates are all very close friends and everyone shares information with one another, and so

DOI: 10.1037/13621-021
APA Handbook of Research Methods in Psychology: Vol. 3. Data Analysis and Research Publication, H. Cooper (Editor-in-Chief)

Pat's particular behavior with Sue might simply reflect a group-level norm. However, Pat's behavior with Sue might also be driven by something about Pat—she might be the kind of person who talks to anyone and everyone. Alternatively, Sue might be a sympathetic listener who tends to elicit self-disclosure from everyone, and so Pat's behavior with Sue could reflect something about Sue. Finally, it might be that Pat's level of disclosure to Sue is uniquely high, higher than Pat typically discloses to others, higher than others typically disclose to Sue, and higher than their group-level norm. This unique element of Pat's disclosure to Sue might occur if Pat and Sue are especially close friends.

This example highlights the fact that interpersonal behavior between two individuals within a group can reflect group-level, individual-level, and dyad-level effects (see Table 21.1). The *group effect* measures the average level of the behavior across all group members. In the example, it might be that some groups of roommates experience significant interpersonal conflict and therefore no one in the suite discloses much to any of their roommates, whereas other groups (like Pat and Sue's) become quite close. The two individual-level factors that might contribute to the particular behavior within a dyad are called actor effects and partner effects. *Actor effects* refers to the degree to which a person's behavior toward others is consistent across all partners. In our example, Pat would have a strong actor effect if she discloses a great deal to all of her roommates. *Partner effects* refers to the degree to which everyone who interacts with a person behaves in the same way with that person. If Sue has a tendency to elicit self-disclosure from everyone in her suite, then she would have a strong partner effect.

The labels *actor effects* and *partner effects* are typically used in reference to behaviors (e.g., self-disclosure, smiling, touching). The SRM, however, is often used to study interpersonal perception, and in this domain, actor and partner effects are typically described as *perceiver effects* and *target effects*, respectively. For instance, if we also measure Pat's perception of Sue's warmth, Pat's perceiver effect would be her tendency to see all of her roommates as warm. Likewise, Sue's target effect would measure the degree to which everyone in the suite thinks that Sue is warm. To summarize, actor or perceiver effects describe causes due to the person *performing* the action or perception. Partner or target effects describe causes due to the *recipient* of the action or perception.

Finally, as we have noted, Pat's behavior with Sue might also be unique to their specific relationship. This is the dyad-level effect, which is termed the *relationship effect* in the SRM. The relationship effect indicates whether the behavior (or perception) might be due to aspects of the dyad that go beyond the group-level and individual-level components. So

---

TABLE 21.1

Social Relations Model Components for Rating Measures and Behavioral Measures

Score	=	Group mean	+	Pat's actor effect	+	Sue's partner effect	+	Pat's relationship effect with Sue
				Behavioral measure				
Pat's level of self-disclosure with Sue	=	Group mean for self-disclosure	+	Pat's tendency to self-disclose to all partners	+	Sue's tendency to elicit self-disclosure from all partners	+	Pat's unique amount of self-disclosure to Sue

Score	=	Group mean	+	Pat's perceiver effect	+	Sue's target effect	+	Pat's relationship effect with Sue
				Rating measure				
Pat's rating of Sue's warmth	=	Group mean for ratings of warmth	+	Pat's tendency to see all partners as warm	+	Sue's tendency to be seen by all partners as warm	+	Pat's unique perception of Sue's warmth

even if Pat self-discloses to all of her roommates (a strong actor effect) and Sue elicits self-disclosure from all of her roommates (a strong partner effect), we might still find *especially* strong self-disclosure from Pat to Sue.

Data Structures for the SRM

The fundamental data requirement for an SRM analysis is that each person must be paired with (i.e., interact with or rate) multiple partners. It is these multiple interactions that allow the SRM to separate the group-, individual-, and dyad-level effects. Here, we describe the two types of data structures that have most often been used in SRM research: round-robin designs and block designs.

Round-robin designs. As shown in Table 21.2, in round-robin data structures, every member of the group interacts with or rates every other individual in the group; the key requirement is that each dyadic combination provides an outcome score from both members. Consider a suite of four male roommates in our fictitious study: Andy (A), Bob (B), Chuck (C), and Dave (D). In a typical round-robin design, we have observations of Andy's disclosure to Bob (AB), Andy's disclosure to Chuck (AC), and so on. Moreover, we would also measure Bob's and Chuck's

disclosures to Andy (BA and CA). In this way, each dyad actually generates two scores.

The diagonal of a round-robin design would be self-data (i.e., Andy's rating of himself), although such measures are optional. For behavioral measures, self-data are relatively rare, but for rating data, researchers often collect self-reports for many of the rated variables. Because self-ratings can differ in systematic ways from ratings of others (e.g., they may be subject to self-enhancement biases), these scores are typically not included in the estimation of the basic SRM parameters. Instead, they are treated as individual-level covariates that may relate to the actor and partner effects (discussed in greater detail in the section Types of Research Questions). It is possible, however, to collect "dyadic" self-ratings. For example, one might want to investigate whether self-perceptions of competence vary across interaction partners (i.e., Do I feel more competent when I'm around Andy vs. when I am with Bob?). For such analyses, self-perceptions would be measured across partners and treated like any other dyadic rating (for an example, see Christensen, Stein, & Means-Christensen, 2003).

Block designs. The block design is actually a family of designs, including the full block, half block, and asymmetric block. In the *full-block design*, a group is

---

TABLE 21.2

Common Data Structures That Can Be Analyzed Using the Social Relations Model

Round robin		Partners (targets)			
		Andy (A)	Bob (B)	Chuck (C)	Dave (D)
	Andy (A)		AB	AC	AD
Actors (perceivers)	Bob (B)	BA		BC	BD
	Chuck (C)	CA	CB		CD
	Dave (D)	DA	DB	DC	

Full block		Partners (targets)							
		Andy (A)	Bob (B)	Chuck (C)	Dave (D)	Ed (E)	Frank (F)	George (G)	Hal (H)
	Andy (A)					AE	AF	AG	AH
	Bob (B)					BE	BF	BG	BH
	Chuck (C)					CE	CF	CG	CH
Actors (perceivers)	Dave (D)					DE	DF	DG	DH
	Ed (E)	EA	EB	EC	ED				
	Frank (F)	FA	FB	FC	FD				
	George (G)	GA	GB	GC	GD				
	Hal (H)	HA	HB	HC	HD				

broken into two subgroups and individuals interact with only those in the other subgroup. So if the group includes eight individuals, A through H, persons A, B, C, and D interact with or rate persons E, F, G, and H. Thus, as indicated in Table 21.2, the full-block design results in two sets of observations: the upper right section and the lower left section. As was true in the round-robin design, in the full-block design, each dyad produces two scores (e.g., A with E and E with A).

Sometimes data are collected from only one half of the block design, such that A, B, C, and D rate E, F, G, and H, but not vice versa. This is called a *half-block design*. Kwan, Gosling, and John (2008) made use of the half-block approach to study anthropomorphism in the perception of dogs. In this case, multiple human judges rated multiple dogs and their owners, but not vice versa. Finally, the *asymmetric-block* design is similar to the full-block design with the exception that persons A through D can be distinguished from persons E through H on a meaningful variable. For example, in a study of reciprocal liking in speed dating (Eastwick, Finkel, Mochon, & Ariely, 2007), subgroups of men interacted with subgroups of women. In the *asymmetric block*, separate SRM parameter estimates are computed for the subgroups (e.g., men's perceptions of women and women's perceptions of men).

Finally, the round-robin and block designs can be combined. This approach was taken in Boldry and Kashy (1999) in a study of intergroup perception. Members of high- and low-status groups rated every member of their own group *and* every member of the other group. This approach resulted in two round-robins for the *within*-group data: one for high-status groups and another for low-status groups. In addition, the study included an asymmetric block design for the *between*-group data (i.e., high-status group members rated members of the low-status group, and low-status group members rated members of the high-status group). Combining these different SRM designs permitted the researchers to test hypotheses about in-group bias and out-group homogeneity.

The SRM Variances

An important focus of a basic SRM study is on estimating the degree to which a particular behavior or rating reflects group-level, individual-level, and dyad-level effects. To address this question, SRM analyses estimate the amount of variance in dyadic scores that is due to these different effects, and so the SRM is often described as a variance decomposition model. To illustrate the variance decomposition, Table 21.3 presents fictitious data from a single half-block design in which eight perceivers rate the physical attractiveness of seven targets. The final column in the top panel of the table shows the average ratings made by each perceiver, and the bottom row shows the average ratings received by each target.

The *perceiver (actor) variance* measures whether there is variation from perceiver to perceiver in their average ratings of the targets' attractiveness. Thus, this variance is based on the row main effect. In studies of interpersonal perception, the perceiver variance is often considered a measure of the degree of *assimilation*. For the attractiveness example, perceiver variance suggests that some perceivers tend to rate all of the targets as high in attractiveness (e.g., Perceiver G), and other perceivers tend to rate all of the targets as low (e.g., Perceiver F). For behavioral variables, actor variance could be considered an indicator of trait-like behavioral tendencies because it represents consistency across partners. For example, significant actor variance might suggest that some individuals are consistently high disclosers and others are consistently low disclosers.

The *target (partner) variance* measures the degree to which some individuals are consistently seen by others as high in attractiveness (e.g., Target 2), whereas others are seen by everyone as low in attractiveness (e.g., Target 6). Therefore, the estimate of target variance is based on the *variability among the column means* after averaging across perceivers. In interpersonal data, the target variance measures *consensus* (the degree to which all individuals agree that some targets are high on a trait whereas other targets are low on the trait). With behavioral measures, the partner variance assesses whether individuals vary in the degree to which they elicit similar behavior from others. For self-disclosure, some individuals might elicit a great deal of self-disclosure, whereas other individuals are rarely the recipient of self-disclosure.

TABLE 21.3

The Social Relations Model Variances

Perceiver	Target 1	Target 2	Target 3	Target 4	Target 5	Target 6	Target 7	Perceiver *M*
A	5	6	5	6	5	4	7	5.428
B	3	5	4	7	3	3	6	4.428
C	4	7	6	6	4	4	4	5.000
D	4	8	6	8	8	4	5	6.142
E	3	7	5	7	4	2	6	4.857
F	3	6	4	5	3	2	5	4.000
G	6	8	7	7	6	5	8	6.714
H	5	6	5	5	4	4	6	5.000
Target *M*	4.125	6.625	5.525	6.375	4.625	3.500	5.875	5.196

Source of variation	E(MS)	Estimated MS
Perceiver	$\sigma_e^2 + \sigma_{PT}^2 + t\sigma_P^2$	5.467
Target	$\sigma_e^2 + \sigma_{PT}^2 + p\sigma_T^2$	10.994
Perceiver × Target	$\sigma_e^2 + \sigma_{PT}^2$	0.776

Note. In the expected mean square (E(MS)), $t = 7$, the number of targets; $p = 8$, the number of perceivers. The estimated mean squares (MSs) are from a mixed model analysis of variance treating Target as a within-subjects factor and Perceiver as a between-subjects factor. Equating the E(MS) to the estimated values provides estimates of the perceiver variance, $\sigma_P^2 = .670$, target variance, $\sigma_T^2 = 1.277$, and relationship (plus error) variance $\sigma_e^2 + \sigma_{PT}^2 = .776$.

The *relationship variance* measures the degree to which dyadic scores vary depending on the specific individuals in the dyad, after partialing out variance caused by those individuals' perceiver and target effects. That is, the relationship variance is the *variability in the cells*, after the row marginal means and the column marginal means have been removed. For example, in Table 21.3, Perceiver B's rating of Target 7 is a 6, which is a high value relative to this perceivers other ratings, and it is high relative to other perceivers' ratings of Target 7. Relationship variance might be especially likely for ratings of romantic attraction. In such an example, people are attracted to specific others beyond any perceiver and target effects.

The bottom section of Table 21.3 presents the expected mean squares (E(MS)) for the half-block design. These formulas show that observed variation in the row means, which is the estimated mean square (MS) for the effect of Perceiver in analysis of variance (ANOVA) terms, reflects three sources of variance: error variance (σ_e^2), variance caused by the perceiver by target interaction—which is relationship variance (σ_{PT}^2), and perceiver variance (σ_P^2). The variance in the column means, which is the estimated mean square for the effect of Target in

ANOVA terms, is similarly composed of error variance (σ_e^2), relationship variance (σ_{PT}^2), and target variance (σ_T^2). With this single half-block design, we can actually use ANOVA to estimate the mean squares, and then with simple algebra, solve for these values. The one constraint is that with only one rating per cell (i.e., perceivers only rate target attractiveness once), true relationship variance cannot be separated from error variance. Finally, note that although these calculations can be relatively simple in a half-block design, in other SRM designs, these calculations are more complex and are generally conducted using one of the programs written by David Kenny: SOREMO for round robin designs or BLOCKO for block designs (Kenny, 1996a, 1996b).

Developing an SRM Study: Types of Research Questions

The SRM can address a variety of research questions; we offer only select examples here (for an extensive list of SRM articles and chapters, see Kenny, 2008). Some important research questions can be addressed by simply examining the amount of actor, partner, or relationship variance. For example, theories of leadership might be informed by asking the basic question: "Do people agree on who is a good leader?" A review of SRM studies on leadership revealed that target variance is typically more than twice as large as perceiver variance (Livi, Kenny, Albright, & Pierro, 2008). This finding suggests that there is consensus about who is a good leader: Perceptions of leadership are more a function of the person being rated than the person making the rating. Conversely, other research suggests that ratings of agreeableness among unacquainted college students have more perceiver variance than target variance (Graziano & Tobin, 2002). This result suggests that people assimilate their ratings of agreeableness for new acquaintances: Some individuals see new acquaintances as agreeable, but others tend to see new acquaintances as disagreeable.

More complex research questions examine associations between individual-level (i.e., actor or partner) effects or between dyad-level (i.e., relationship) effects across variables. For example, actor–actor correlations can investigate whether a person's behavior on one variable is related to his or her behavior on another variable. Similarly, partner–partner correlations indicate whether a person's ability to elicit one type of response is related to eliciting another response. Examples of these correlations can be found the Schrodt, Soliz, and Braithwaite (2008) study on communication within stepfamilies. They found evidence that stepparents—but not the biological parents or children—who talk more with their family also report more relational satisfaction across all members of their family (actor–actor correlation). In contrast, the children demonstrated a partner–partner correlation: Children with whom other family members reported greater relationship satisfaction tended to elicit more talking from those family members.

Correlating the SRM effects with each other can also test for reciprocity (i.e., If I see others a particular way, do they see me the same way?). Reciprocity in the SRM can be examined two ways: generalized and dyadic. *Generalized reciprocity* is the correlation between actor and partner effects, which determines whether a general response to others elicits a similar response from most others. So if I generally report liking others (strong actor effect), do most other people report liking me (strong partner effect)?

Dyadic reciprocity is the correlation between individuals' relationship effects. This tests the more specific question, "If I particularly like you, do you particularly like me?" Interestingly, these two approaches to reciprocity can yield different patterns of results. In the Eastwick et al. (2007) study of speed dating, reciprocity correlations for romantic interest were positive at the dyadic level but negative at the generalized level. This suggests that if Andy particularly likes Ellen, Ellen is likely to feel especially positive about Andy. However, if Andy reports high romantic interest for all women (e.g., Ellen, Frances, Ginger, and Holly), those women are *less* likely to be interested in him.

Other research questions can be based on correlations between the actor or partner effects and individual differences (e.g., self-ratings or personality data). For example, one could correlate self-perceptions with target effects to investigate *self-accuracy* or *self–other agreement*. Such correlations estimate whether seeing oneself in a particular way is related to how a person is actually seen by others. Using this approach, researchers have demonstrated that, in general, people are rather accurate in their self-perceptions of status in small groups (Anderson, Srivastava, Beer, Spataro, & Chatman, 2006). Self-perceptions can also be used to predict perceiver effects, which provides an estimate of *assumed similarity*. For example, does seeing oneself as likeable mean that one will see others as likeable too? Mahaffey and Marcus (2006) measured assumed similarity in sex offenders and found that those with more psychopathy also believed that other offenders had higher psychopathy.

Christensen and Kashy (1998) provided an example of correlating personality variables with the SRM individual-level effects. Specifically, trait loneliness was used to predict how participants perceived the other members of their group and how they were perceived by other members of the group. This approach allowed us to demonstrate that lonelier participants viewed others somewhat more positively (small, positive correlations between loneliness and perceiver effects), whereas the lonely were generally not seen differently by the group members (no correlations between loneliness and target effects). The one exception for target effects was that the lonely were seen as somewhat more friendly.

Finally, experimental manipulations can be included in SRM studies. Such manipulations can occur either within or between groups. Within-group manipulations would be treated as individual-difference variables and could be used to predict actor or partner effects. By using a between-group manipulation, researchers can evaluate whether the variance or the relationships among the SRM components are different across groups. Details about experimental manipulations in SRM studies are included in the section Experimental Manipulations.

Developing an SRM Study: Procedure Considerations

Several issues related to conducting an SRM study are outlined in this section. Across all of these decisions, one practical issue pervades: Participants and researchers must be able to identify the actor–perceiver and partner–target of each piece of dyadic data. In studies of acquainted individuals (e.g., roommates), this is usually easy for the participants. In such cases, the participants can write the target's name on each rating sheet (although even this can be problematic when group members share the same first name). In studies of unacquainted individuals, researchers typically provide a name tag for each participant to reduce confusion. In such cases, the name tags are often labeled with letters (A, B, C, etc.) for round-robin designs, or letters and numbers (A, B, C, etc., and 1, 2, 3, etc.) for block designs. If coded nametags are used, the researcher can also prelabel a series of rating sheets for each dyadic combination (e.g., A→B, B→A, C→D). Although it is somewhat time-consuming to label all the possible combinations, it makes the data collection much more organized. Researchers then need only ensure that the right participant gets the right rating sheet for the right interaction.

Video-recording behavioral data adds another layer of complexity to the identification of actors and partners in the data. This issue is addressed in greater detail in the section on measuring behavioral data.

Number of participants per group. In a social relations analysis, the variances for the three central components, actor, partner, and relationship, are estimated for each group, and then these variances are pooled across groups. Therefore, statistical power is a joint function of the size of the groups and number of groups, although group size has a stronger effect on power (for details about power in SRM research, see Lashley & Kenny, 1998). Group size is important because larger groups generate more precise estimates of the SRM variances and, in turn, more power for statistical tests. Indeed, a single large group can have more power than several smaller groups. Also, power is lower in block designs than round-robin designs with the same group size because fewer pieces of data are collected in block designs (i.e., not everyone is rating or interacting with everyone else). Thus, number of groups needed depends on the group size, the design, and the size of the effects the researchers are seeking to detect. For example, one might need only two 12-person groups to reach .80 power for larger effects in a round-robin design, whereas more than a 1,000 four-person groups would be needed with a small effect in an asymmetric block design (Lashley & Kenny, 1998). In sum, from a purely statistical standpoint, larger groups and round-robin designs will have more power, whereas smaller groups and block designs will have less statistical power.

Despite the statistical benefits of larger groups, they are not always practical because of participant fatigue. For example, consider a study of self-disclosure among previously unacquainted students. Using a round-robin design, the researcher has each participant interact with each other participant for 10 min. If there were 10 students in the group, each participant would have 90 min of interactions. This time burden would be even more exhausting if the participants were required to complete questionnaires following each interaction.

Given the statistical benefits and practical limitations of large groups, researchers need to balance the burden they are placing on the participants against the number of groups that they will need to include. Studies that include simple and easy tasks for participants (e.g., ratings of physical attractiveness at zero acquaintance) can benefit from having a larger group. As participant burden increases, researchers will need to use more, smaller groups to achieve sufficient power.

The minimum group size (round-robin design) or subgroup size (block design) is three participants. This minimum is only possible for round-robin studies, however, if the researcher can assume that no dyadic reciprocity exists. For some research contexts, such as a study of interpersonal perception with unacquainted group members, it may be reasonable to expect that the unique way person A sees B has no relation to B's unique perception of A. However, some variables, such as liking, and some research contexts, such as studies of well-acquainted individuals, make such a restriction untenable. In these cases, researchers should plan to include groups of four or more participants.

In most round-robin designs, there are a minimum of four participants in each group. The maximum number of participants in a group or subgroup is theoretically unlimited, although practical constraints will typically limit this size. Note that the software designed for analyzing SRM data limit group size to 25 in round-robin designs and subgroup size to 20 in block designs.

Timing of the interactions.   Dyadic interactions among unacquainted participants can occur *simultaneously* in the presence of the entire group or *sequentially* in a series of one-on-one interactions. Using the simultaneous approach, Andy, Bob, Chuck, and Dave would be seated in the same room and asked to interact with each other. In an example of simultaneous interactions, Christensen and Kashy (1998) had four undergraduates participate in each session. After completing measures of loneliness, the individuals were seated around a table to work together on a problem-solving task. In this case, the task was merely a tool to get the participants to interact with one another. Following the task, each participant provided perception ratings about each other participant (i.e., a round-robin design). This approach allowed us to evaluate whether the lonely people were seen differently by others, which was tested by the correlation between each participants' loneliness scores and their target effects on the perception ratings.

Alternatively, a sequential procedure would have Andy and Bob interact in one location while Chuck and Dave interact in another. After the first set of interactions, half of the partners switch locations so that A and C interact while B and D interact, and so on. The sequential approach was used to study dyadic negotiations in four- and five-person groups (Elfenbein, Cuhran, Eisenkraft, Shirako, & Baccaro, 2008). Within each group, the students engaged in a series of negotiation tasks with each other member of their group (round-robin design). By using the SRM to investigate dyadic negotiations, they were able to identify individual differences associated with successful bargaining outcomes.

The simultaneous approach has the benefit of efficiency, but it might limit the expression of partner-specific responses (behavioral data) or the discrimination among the different partners (rating data). These problems would be expected to increase with the size of the group. Conversely, the sequential approach is potentially more time-consuming, but participants need only attend to one partner at a time. Decisions about which approach to use are often determined by the variables to be measured. Some behavioral data (e.g., smiling at specific others) would be difficult for experimenters to record for many participants simultaneously, especially in a large group. Similarly, complex rating data (e.g., assessments of each member's personality along multiple dimensions) will be challenging for participants if they do not have enough information to distinguish among the group members. In both cases, one would find mostly actor variance and little partner variance: If participants cannot make clear distinctions among the other group members, their behavior and perceptions will be driven by their own attributes. That is, they will report (dis)liking everyone in the group or they will (in)frequently smile at everyone in the group. Other types of data are more amenable to collection in large groups. For example, Lönnqvist, Leikas, Verkasalo, and Paunonen (2008) had cadets rate the performance of every other member of their platoon in round-robin fashion. Even though the platoons ranged in size from 14 to 21 cadets, the round-robin design could be used because the cadets were familiar with each other and the ratings were relatively simple.

Researchers who are deciding between a sequential or simultaneous approach must also consider practical issues related to space. Simultaneous interactions usually can be conducted in one large room.

However, having interactions in sequence typically requires multiple, adjoining lab rooms where each dyad can be seated. In a round-robin study with a group size of four participants, a researcher could conduct the study with as few as two rooms. Andy would interact with Bob in one room while Chuck interacts with Dave in the other room. After the first interaction, Bob and Dave switch rooms for the second interaction, then Chuck and Dave switch rooms for the final interaction. If one were conducting a block design with four participants in each subgroup, four rooms would now be required (A with E, B with F, C with G, and D with H). Finally, researchers must also consider whether participants will need privacy while completing ratings of their interaction partners. If so, one would need as many spaces as there are participants in the group.

Data from previously acquainted participants (e.g., roommates, teammates) likely represent the combination of simultaneous and sequential approaches. In the case of a suite of roommates, these participants have typically interacted as a group and as dyads. In naturally existing groups, the amount of previous contact between individuals is likely to vary from dyad to dyad. In such cases, researchers might measure familiarity as a covariate or include it as a variable of interest (e.g., Are differences in dyadic familiarity correlated with relationship effects in liking?).

Roles. Thus far in our discussion, we have treated individuals within groups as indistinguishable or interchangeable (e.g., four roommates, five unacquainted individuals). However the SRM can also be used when groups are composed of individuals who fall into particular roles within the group. Although this type of design can also be used when group members are randomly assigned to roles within the group, the most common type of study that uses an SRM with roles design is a study of family members. The key idea is that within a family (or other group), each individual can be distinguished by their family role (e.g., mother, father, older child, younger child). The SRM then uses dyadic data on the basis of each pairing of roles to estimate separate actor and partner effects for each role and separate relationship effects for each combination of roles.

For example, Ackerman, Kashy, Donnellan, and Conger (2011) examined positive interpersonal behavior in family conflict resolution interactions with four-person families. Families were videotaped while trying to resolve a difficult family problem, and then coders rated how warm and supportive each person was with every other family member. Thus, in this research, 12 data points were coded in each interaction (Mother's support of Father or MF, Mother's support of Older child or MO, Mother's support of Younger child or MY as well as FM, FO, FY, OM, OF, OY, and YM, YF, and YO).

The SRM for families then partitions the variance in these ratings into a family mean effect, actor effects for each role, partner effects for each role, and relationship effects for each dyadic combination of roles. In the example, the family effect simply refers to the average level of positive behavior in a particular family, and the presence of family variance indicates that some families exhibit higher levels of supportive communication than others. The father's actor effect would measure his general tendency to engage in warm and supportive interactions with all of his family members. The mother's partner effect would measure whether all family members elicit warm and supportive behavior from the mother. Finally, the father–mother relationship effect would measure the tendency for the father to behave in a unique fashion with the mother, perhaps exhibiting less positive behavior with her than with other family members.

The SRM for families estimates the actor, partner, and relationship variances for each role or combination of roles. The variance in the mother–actor effects measures the degree to which some mothers tend to be generally supportive toward family members, whereas other mothers are not. There may be little actor variance for mothers if they are all supportive (perhaps there is something implicit in the role that demands mothers communicate in such a fashion). If there were a great deal of actor variance for fathers, it would indicate that some fathers are highly supportive but others are not; that is, fathers' supportive communication may be more of an individual difference rather than a characteristic that is inherent in the father role.

Briefly, in the Ackerman et al. (2011) study, results suggested that there is a strong family-level component to positive interpersonal behavior. Beyond this, there was substantial actor variance for each role, suggesting that individual differences are a key determinant of warmth and supportive behavior in families (i.e., some people are warm to all family members but others are not). Finally, there was evidence of relationship variance—especially for mothers' and fathers' communication with one another.

Experimental manipulations. As noted, experimental manipulations can either be within-group or between-groups. *Within-group* manipulations could occur at the individual or dyad level. Individual-level manipulations could be treated like measured individual difference variables and used to predict actor–perceiver effects or partner–target effects. In a hypothetical study on self-disclosure, half the participants could be given bogus information that their interaction partner is especially friendly. Each individual's expectation would then be treated as a dummy-coded individual difference variable. Alternatively, if each group member is assigned to a condition, an SRM with roles approach could be taken, treating the manipulation as the *role* variable.

Dyad-level manipulations within groups could be designed to influence sets of interaction partners in different ways. For example, Back, Schmukle, and Egloff (2008) randomly assigned students to different seats on the first day of a class and, a year later, the students indicated their strength of friendship with each other student. In this way, the researchers were manipulating the distance between members of each dyad rather than manipulating the experience of individuals. This approach allowed the researchers to demonstrate that physical proximity predicted dyadic friendship intensity beyond perceiver and target effects.

Between-group manipulations could occur in either a round-robin or block design. In a round-robin design, each group would be assigned to one level of the independent variable. When analyzing the data, SRM effects and variances are generated separately for the groups at each level of the independent variable and then compared across groups. In a similar approach, Albright, Cohen, Malloy,

Christ, and Bromgard (2004) had some students participate as *conversants*, whereas other students were *observers* of the conversations. Because the conversants interacted with and rated each other, their data were analyzed as a round-robin design. The observer data was analyzed as a half-block design because they rated, but were not rated by, the conversants. The researchers then compared consensus in ratings across the two types of participant groups.

In a block design, each subgroup could be assigned to one level of the independent variable. If so, an asymmetric-block design would be used to compare results across the subgroups. Because these designs use two subgroups, the independent variable would generally be limited to two levels. Unlike the round-robin example, data from both subgroups in an asymmetric-block design would be analyzed together

Although we discuss examples of experimental design, the same principles apply to quasi-experimental or measured differences between groups. The Boldry and Kashy (1999) study of intergroup bias compared high-status and low-status groups, with status as a measured variable (year in school). To test some of their hypotheses, the researchers ran separate round-robin analyses for high-status group members rating one another and for low-status group members rating one another. They also analyzed the high-status individuals' ratings of the low-status group members and vice versa. A key hypothesis that was tested using this approach was whether there was greater target variance for in-group ratings relative to out-group ratings.

Developing an SRM Study: Measurement Considerations

As noted in the section on developing research questions, there are few limits to the type of questions that can be addressed with the SRM. The researcher must measure some dyadic variable, and the participants must make multiple ratings. These requirements can be met in different ways.

Measuring perception data. One consideration is the timing of the measures. In the *variable fastest moving* approach, participants rate several characteristics for each target at once. After making all of the ratings for one target, participants then make the same ratings for the next target. It is also possible to collect data with the *person fastest moving*. With this strategy, the participants rate all targets on one variable, then all targets on a second variable, and so on.

Although the variable fastest moving is more common, researchers should reflect on the implications of each approach. The benefit of the variable-fastest moving approach is that participants can focus on their assessments or memories of a single target. This is especially helpful when participants have sequential interactions with targets and can make ratings immediately after each dyadic interaction while the experience is fresh in their minds. Yet problems can arise if participants rely on heuristics about the target's personality. If so, "central characteristics" (e.g., warmth, physical attractiveness) have the potential to bias other ratings of that target (Asch, 1946). In this way target–target correlations might be inflated because of the method of data collection.

Conversely, the person fastest moving approach can make it easier for participants to contrast among targets on a given variable and, in turn, avoid reliance on target heuristics. This approach is most practical when participants are involved in a simultaneous interaction. The person fastest moving approach might be challenging for participants, however, if they have to constantly switch between memories or schemas for different targets. This effort could result in greater participant fatigue, which could have two practical consequences. Some fatigued participants might begin to respond haphazardly, increasing overall error variance. Other fatigued participants might begin relying on a response set (i.e., not discriminating among targets), which would inflate perceiver variance.

Measuring behavior data. Behavior data are challenging in an SRM study because multiple participants must be coded or recorded simultaneously. Although it is possible for researchers to code participant behaviors in situ, they will often want a video record of the participants' actions. The number of cameras required will depend of the type of

behaviors the researcher wants to study. Macrolevel behaviors (e.g., leaning forward, proportion of time talking) can be recorded for two participants using a single camera that captures them in profile. Coding smaller behaviors (e.g., smiling, eye gaze), however, will often require a separate camera facing each participant. If so, the number of participants in each group will be limited by the number of cameras unless the researchers stagger the interactions, which would require more participant time.

Measuring behavioral data is more feasible in studies that use sequential interactions than in studies using simultaneous interactions. The main limitation of simultaneous interactions is that one cannot determine the target of most behaviors. That is, if one is smiling, talking, or leaning forward in a group, to whom is the person directing the behavior? It is possible to identify the specific targets on occasion, but these behaviors are often directed toward the group as a whole. If so, the behaviors are no longer dyadic and, therefore, not appropriate for an SRM analysis. These behaviors could, however, be included as individual differences variables and predicted by other SRM data. For example, a researcher might conduct a simultaneous interaction of four participants and measure how much each person spoke to the group. The researcher could also collect round-robin ratings of liking within the group, which would allow a test of whether talking time predicts being liked by the group (i.e., correlating individual differences in talking with target variance in liking).

Regardless of the study set-up, researchers must have a system to clearly identify the actor and partner captured by each camera. If a single camera is used to record both members of a dyad, name tags might be sufficient if they are clearly visible to the camera. Tracking data becomes more complicated, however, when each dyad member is captured by a single camera. In this situation, the actor is identified, but the partner will be unseen. In such a case, the researcher must have a clear plan to identify the partner of each interaction. One solution is for the experimenter to record him- or herself on each camera before each interaction. The experimenter would state the identifying information for that actor and partner (e.g., "This is group number 23, person B being recorded while interacting with person C").

After the SRM Study: Analysis Considerations

Data from an SRM study are typically analyzed using one of two specialized statistical programs that Kenny has made available on his website (Kenny, 1996a, 1996b). Round-robin designs are analyzed using the SOREMO program and block designs are analyzed using BLOCKO. These programs generate estimates of the variances, correlations among the SRM effects, and correlations between the SRM effects and individual difference data. Kashy and Kenny (2000) provided an introduction to using SOREMO and interpreting the output from this program.

The programs can also output the SRM effect estimates for further analysis in other statistics programs to test more complex hypotheses. For example, Christensen et al. (2003) evaluated whether the relationship between social anxiety and metaperceptions was mediated by self-perceptions (i.e., Is the reason I think you don't like me that I don't like myself?). To do so, SRM effects were generated by SOREMO and then outputted to a file that could be read by a standard statistical package (e.g., SPSS). The social anxiety data were incorporated into the file and regression analyses were conducted.

When conducting subsequent analyses of the SRM effects that were generated by SOREMO or BLOCKO, researchers should ensure that any SRM effect of interest has sufficient variance. The SRM software provides tests of the variance for each component, although tests for relationship variance require multiple measures (either two or more indicators of the construct or two or more measures over time) to separate the relationship variance from error variance (see Kenny, 1994). If a measure has nonsignificant variance on one of the SRM effects, researchers should use caution when correlating that effect with other variables in subsequent analyses.

CONCLUSION

In the 30 years since the first publication of an SRM analysis, Kenny's model has proven to be a useful tool for studying dyadic phenomena in many fields of psychology. Although most widely utilized in social psychology, the SRM has been used to address wide-ranging research questions about development (e.g., Buist, Reitz, & Dekovic, 2008), intrafamily communication (Schrodt et al., 2008), decision making (Bagozzi, Ascione, & Mannebach, 2005), team performance (Greguras, Robie, Born, & Koenigs, 2007), psychopathology (Mahaffey & Marcus, 2006), and cooperative learning (Horn, Collier, Oxford, Bond, & Dansereau, 1998). The SRM has even been used to examine interactions between pairs of fish (Dunlap, 2002). To date, more than 200 articles, chapters, and dissertations have included the model to provide a more refined understanding of dyadic behaviors and perceptions. We hope this chapter will entice even more scientists to consider an SRM approach for their own research questions.

References

Ackerman, R. A., Kashy, D. A., Donnellan, M. B., & Conger, R. D. (2011). Positive engagement in family interactions: A social relations perspective. *Journal of Family Psychology, 25*, 719–730. doi:10.1037/a0025288

Albright, L., Cohen, A. I., Malloy, T. E., Christ, T., & Bromgard, G. (2004). Judgments of communicative intent in conversation. *Journal of Experimental Social Psychology, 40*, 290–302. doi:10.1016/j.jesp.2003.06.004

Anderson, C., Srivastava, S., Beer, J. S., Spataro, S. E., & Chatman, J. A. (2006). Knowing your place: Self-perception of status in face-to-face groups. *Journal of Personality and Social Psychology, 91*, 1094–1110. doi:10.1037/0022-3514.91.6.1094

Asch, S. E. (1946). Forming impressions of personality. *Journal of Abnormal and Social Psychology, 41*, 258–290. doi:10.1037/h0055756

Back, M. D., Schmukle, S. C., & Egloff, B. (2008). Becoming friends by chance. *Psychological Science, 19*, 439–440. doi:10.1111/j.1467-9280.2008.02106.x

Bagozzi, R. P., Ascione, F. J., & Mannebach, M. A. (2005). Inter-role relationships in hospital-based pharmacy and therapeutics committee decision making. *Journal of Health Psychology, 10*, 45–64. doi:10.1177/1359105305045347

Boldry, J. G., & Kashy, D. A. (1999). Intergroup perception in naturally occurring groups of differential status: A social relations perspective. *Journal of Personality and Social Psychology, 77*, 1200–1212. doi:10.1037/0022-3514.77.6.1200

Buist, K. L., Reitz, E., & Dekovic, M. (2008). Attachment stability and change during adolescence: A longitudinal application of the social relations model. *Journal of Social and Personal Relationships, 25*, 429–444. doi:10.1177/0265407508090867

Christensen, P. N., & Kashy, D. A. (1998). Perceptions of and by lonely people in initial social interaction. *Personality and Social Psychology Bulletin, 24*, 322–329. doi:10.1177/0146167298243009

Christensen, P. N., Stein, M. B., & Means-Christensen, A. J. (2003). Social anxiety and interpersonal perception: A social relations model analysis. *Behaviour Research and Therapy, 41*, 1355–1371. doi:10.1016/S0005-7967(03)00064-0

Dunlap, K. D. (2002). Hormonal and body size correlates of electrocommunication behavior during dyadic interactions in a weakly electric fish, *Apteronotus leptorhynchus. Hormones and Behavior, 41*, 187–194. doi:10.1006/hbeh.2001.1744

Eastwick, P. W., Finkel, E. J., Mochon, D., & Ariely, D. (2007). Selective versus unselective romantic desire: Not all reciprocity is created equal. *Psychological Science, 18*, 317–319. doi:10.1111/j.1467-9280.2007.01897.x

Elfenbein, H. A., Cuhran, J. R., Eisenkraft, N., Shirako, A., & Baccaro, L. (2008). Are some negotiators better than others? Individual differences in bargaining outcomes. *Journal of Research in Personality, 42*, 1463–1475. doi:10.1016/j.jrp.2008.06.010

Graziano, W. G., & Tobin, R. M. (2002). Agreeableness: Dimension of personality or social desirability artifact? *Journal of Personality, 70*, 695–728. doi:10.1111/1467-6494.05021

Greguras, G. J., Robie, C., Born, M. P., & Koenigs, R. J. (2007). A social relations analysis of team performance ratings. *International Journal of Selection and Assessment, 15*, 434–448. doi:10.1111/j.1468-2389.2007.00402.x

Horn, E. M., Collier, W. G., Oxford, J. A., Bond, C. F., & Dansereau, D. F. (1998). Individual differences in dyadic cooperative learning. *Journal of Educational Psychology, 90*, 153–161. doi:10.1037/0022-0663.90.1.153

Kashy, D. A., & Kenny, D. A. (2000). The analysis of data from dyads and groups. In H. T. Reis & C. M. Judd (Eds.), *Handbook of research methods in social and personality psychology* (pp. 451–477). Cambridge, England: Cambridge University Press.

Kenny, D. A. (1994). *Interpersonal perception: A social relations analysis.* New York, NY: Guilford Press.

Kenny, D. A. (1996a). BLOCKO [Computer software]. Retrieved from http://davidakenny.net/srm/srmp.htm

Kenny, D. A. (1996b). SOREMO [Computer software]. Retrieved from http://davidakenny.net/srm/srmp.htm

Kenny, D. A. (2008). *SRM references.* Retrieved from http://davidakenny.net/srm/srm.htm

Kwan, V. S. Y., Gosling, S. D., & John, O. P. (2008). Anthropomorphism as a special case of social perception: A cross-species social relations model analysis of humans and dogs. *Social Cognition, 26*, 129–142. doi:10.1521/soco.2008.26.2.129

Lashley, B. R., & Kenny, D. A. (1998). Power estimation in social relations analysis. *Psychological Methods, 3*, 328–338. doi:10.1037/1082-989X.3.3.328

Livi, S., Kenny, D. A., Albright, L., & Pierro, A. (2008). A social relations analysis of leadership. *Leadership Quarterly, 19*, 235–248. doi:10.1016/j.leaqua.2008.01.003

Lönnqvist, J., Leikas, A., Verkasalo, M., & Paunonen, S. V. (2008). Does self-enhancement have implications for adjustment? *Basic and Applied Social Psychology, 30*, 377–386. doi:10.1080/01973530802502374

Mahaffey, K. J., & Marcus, D. K. (2006). Interpersonal perception of psychopathy: A social relations analysis. *Journal of Social and Clinical Psychology, 25*, 53–74. doi:10.1521/jscp.2006.25.1.53

Schrodt, P., Soliz, J., & Braithwaite, D. O. (2008). A social relations analysis model of everyday talk and relational satisfaction in stepfamilies. *Communication Monographs, 75*, 190–217. doi:10.1080/03637750802023163

Warner, R. M., Kenny, D. A., & Stoto, M. (1979). A new round robin analysis of variance for social interaction data. *Journal of Personality and Social Psychology, 37*, 1742–1757. doi:10.1037/0022-3514.37.10.1742

## CHAPTER 22

DYADIC DATA ANALYSIS

Richard Gonzalez and Dale Griffin

The study of interdependence contributes to a rich understanding of social life. Does a husband's depression influence his wife's depression? Does his depression influence her marital satisfaction? What is the similarity of the husband and wife's depression within a couple and does that similarity predict other variables such as marital satisfaction? What predicts the degree of similarity in depression between husband and wife? Research questions such as these involve data that span two individuals, so we say the data are *interdependent*. Such research questions frequently include multiple variables and sometimes involve longitudinal data. What makes these research questions psychologically interesting is that they focus on interpersonal processes. Of course, if one wants to study interpersonal processes, then it would be useful to collect data and use analytic procedures that permit the assessment and testing of interpersonal processes.

The analysis of interdependent data presents special issues because the covariance across individuals needs to be addressed in the analyses. Failure to account for these interpersonal correlations can introduce bias into an analysis but, more important, consideration of these interpersonal correlations allows one to assess interesting interpersonal psychological processes. The violation of independence is the ugly pebble that can be transformed into the pearl of interdependence. In this chapter, we illustrate a few analytic techniques that go beyond "fixing" data for independence violations to providing rich models that permit the researcher to assess psychological processes of interdependence.

Interdependence is not treated as a nuisance that needs to be corrected but rather as one of the key psychological parameters to model. We view this chapter as introductory, focusing on the special case of dyads, and review a few of the analysis techniques that are currently available.

The analysis of dyadic data can become detailed in that there are many issues that need to be addressed in the analysis, such as whether dyad members are exchangeable or distinguishable, whether dyadic data are cross-sectional or longitudinal, whether one wants to frame the analysis as a multilevel model or a structural equation model (SEM), whether one takes a latent variable approach to individual and dyadic variance or whether one's theoretical model focuses more on direct relations across people and across variables on observed data, whether data are normally distributed or categorical, and so on. As with any data analysis exercise, these different design features and priorities yield many combinations that are too numerous to review in a short introductory chapter. We refer the reader to a comprehensive treatment by Kenny, Kashy and Cook (2006), which covers many of these different combinations, and the edited volume by Card, Selig, and Little (2008).

Our goal for this chapter is to highlight some simple concepts so researchers can develop an intuition and an appreciation for the procedures that are possible when one includes both individuals from a dyad in the same analyses. We discuss some of our favorite issues surrounding dyadic analyses and review a handful of the available data analytic

DOI: 10.1037/13621-022
APA Handbook of Research Methods in Psychology: Vol. 3. Data Analysis and Research Publication, H. Cooper (Editor-in-Chief)

techniques, taking a more intuitive and basic approach rather than presenting a general framework in which the designs are special cases.

STUDY OF INTERDEPENDENCE VERSUS VIOLATION OF INDEPENDENCE

We initially became interested in dyadic data analysis because as social psychologists we wanted to study dyadic processes but recognized that the analytic techniques available at the time were too limiting. It seemed strange to us that researchers who studied dating couples, for example, collected data from only one individual in the couple. This practice occurred partly because it was a way to bypass the violation of independence. One automatically has independent data when only one member of each couple is represented in the data set. Can a researcher who is interested in studying dating couples make claims about the couple from data from only one person? Rather than go down the road of "one-hand clapping" philosophical-type arguments, we decided instead to work on analytic procedures that allowed the study of the couple.

A study that assesses only one dating partner from each dyad gathers information about the relationship, as indexed by that single subject. One can learn about the husband's marital satisfaction or the wife's satisfaction but not how each dyad member influences the other's marital satisfaction. A study that assesses both members of the couple can examine how one person influences another, can examine the similarity or dissimilarity of the couple members, can examine whether the degree of similarity predicts some other variable, and so on. The potential for testing richer psychological questions increases dramatically when the researcher collects data from both individuals. One can now study the dyad in a deeper way.

The analysis of dyadic data has gone through an identity crisis over the past two decades. In the early days, methodologists warned about the dangers of failing to properly account for dependency in data when observations are made on both members of a dyad. The basic idea was that when members of the same dyad are analyzed together, their data are dependent on each other in much the same way that

two observations in a two-time-point repeated measures design are related to each other. We understand well what happens to statistical inference if we ignore temporal dependence in a repeated measures analysis, and the early literature on dyadic data analysis focused on the analogous effects of ignoring nonindependence in dyadic research (e.g., Kenny, 1990; Kenny & Judd, 1986). This early literature made use of the intraclass correlation (ICC) as a tool to model the effects of violating independence. The ICC can be used to show how classic analysis of variance (ANOVA) and regression designs go awry in the presence of nonindependent data, such as how parameters are biased or when *p* values become either too liberal or too conservative.

Concern about the violation of independence seems to be a small piece of the larger puzzle. If one wants to study couples, then interdependence comes with the territory. Interdependence is part of the phenomenon, not a statistical flaw in one's data. The problem of violating independence is not with the data or the research question, but it is merely a symptom that one is using an inappropriate analytic technique for the research question. A researcher of dyadic processes should not have to adjust their interdependent data, or their interdependent research question, to conform to a statistical model of independence. Instead, the statistical tools should allow the researcher to model interdependence directly in much the same way that a researcher has tools for analyzing data that are temporally dependent. The tools should provide ways to assess and measure interdependence, and should provide ways to test theories of interdependence. In short, statistical techniques should facilitate the goals of the researcher, not provide roadblocks that get in the way of testing theory and understanding process.

Fortunately, the field of dyadic data analysis has moved away from primarily being concerned about the bias introduced through violations of the independence assumption. The current focus is on developing methods that facilitate the testing of research questions about interdependence. We next turn to a general introduction to types of association in data, which will provide a grounding for understanding dyadic data analysis.

TEMPORAL, INTERPERSONAL, AND MULTIVARIATE CORRELATIONS

There are three common types of associations that occur in psychological data. One type is temporal association. For example, data from the same participant are collected multiple times. We do not treat those observations as independent because we want to capture the temporal association, and in many cases, the temporal association is the key focal point. We do not merely use repeated measures or longitudinal designs because they provide more statistical power; we use repeated measurements because they provide unique information about change processes. A second type of association is due to interrelations among multiple variables. Such associations across variables are what multiple regression and SEMs assess. What is the relation between marital satisfaction and depression? We use multivariate techniques to study the association between variables. The third type of association is interpersonal association as seen in dyadic designs. Observations may have interpersonal associations because they come from the same members of a social unit, such as the two members of a dyad, or students in the same classroom. We use dyadic techniques because we are interested in studying interpersonal processes.

These three kinds of associations between observations are not mutually exclusive, with one, two, or all three possibly occurring in the same study. For example, if there is a single dependent variable for each member of the dyad, then the observations are correlated by virtue of the interpersonal relations. If those same observations are also repeated for each dyad member, now there are associations both interpersonally and temporally in the data. If the dyad members are each measured once but on different variables, then both multivariate and interpersonal associations exist in the data. If both dyad members are observed repeatedly over time across several variables, then the observations exhibit associations temporally, interpersonally, and across variables. Analyses should account for all types of associations present in the data set.

Fortunately, there is a single basic idea that captures all three types of associations. Various models such as repeated measures analyses, multilevel analyses, and SEM provide similar ways of capturing the associations that occur between observations. A relatively easy way to conceptualize these associations is through the covariance matrix between all observations lumping people, time, and variables. We begin with a simple description and build up the elements. Suppose we have 20 individuals measured once on a single variable and we want to estimate the mean across the 20 individuals. We can model the data as $Y_i = \mu + \varepsilon_i$ (i.e., a constant intercept for all 20 participants, which in this case will be the mean μ, and an error term ε). The usual assumption is that the error terms are independent and identically distributed. In other words, these 20 error terms are modeled as a 20×20 covariance matrix with a special structure. The diagonal contains a constant number, which is the variance of the residuals (the "identically distributed" part yields the same error variance across all observations). The off-diagonal terms are all zero because the residuals are assumed to be independent. This model imposes a theoretical covariance structure on the observations Y (also a 20×20 covariance matrix) such that any two observations are independent and there is a common variance across all observations.

It may seem like overkill to explain so much detail for the simple model of the mean of 20 observations, but this is the basic structure we need to illustrate the three types of association. The different types of association impose structure on the covariance matrix of observations, and it is helpful to take this view to gain insight into the issues surrounding interdependent data.

Now we turn to the case of temporal association by considering two observations for the same person, that is, the 20 individuals are measured twice so there are a total of 40 observations. The model for comparing the difference between the mean at each time becomes $Y_{ti} = \mu + \beta_t + \alpha_i + \varepsilon_{ti}$ with grand mean μ, a time fixed effects factor β, a subject main effect treated as a random effect factor α, and error term ε. This results in 40 error terms, which can be placed in a 40×40 covariance matrix.[1] The random effect terms α introduce a covariance across the

---

[1] In this introductory chapter, we take liberties with notation. For example, we frequently switch between two subscripts t and i to denote time (e.g., 1 or 2) and person (e.g., 1 to 20), and a single subscript i to denote time and person (e.g., 1 to 40). We also do not carefully distinguish population and sample parameters.

40 observations: Two observations from the same person, that is, two observations having the same α, are now associated relative to other observations even though the residuals remain independent. So, in the 40×40 covariance matrix of observations Person 1's Time 1 and Time 2 scores have a nonzero entry, Person 2's Time 1 and Time 2 scores have the same nonzero entry, and so on. We typically assume homogeneity of covariance, so each of the nonzero entries in the off-diagonal are constrained to be equal.

This framework can be extended to dyads. Suppose the 40 observations came from 20 heterosexual dating couples. A covariance is introduced between two members of the same dyad (interpersonal association) in just the same way as a covariance is introduced by two observations from the same person (temporal association). Similarly, the covariance between individuals from different dyads is zero, just as the covariance between observations of two different people in the case of repeated measurement is zero.

Standard methods for analysis of dyadic data automatically take proper account of the temporal, interpersonal, and multivariate associations across observations. For example, a multilevel modeling approach to dyadic data takes the information supplied by the user that two individuals are nested in the same dyad and internally constructs a covariance matrix that has the proper structure. Likewise, other approaches to dyadic data analysis, such as SEM, also establish a covariance matrix with the proper structure. It is for this reason that different approaches can be used to analyze dyadic data—the key feature is how the analytic approach structures the covariance between observations. Different analytic frameworks like multilevel models and SEMs merely become the user interface by which the user can communicate the proper structure of the covariance matrix.

In the remaining sections of this chapter, we build on this basic intuition that design features in dyadic data require particular analytic elements. Readers familiar with multilevel modeling will recognize that we treat individuals as nested within dyads. Readers familiar with SEMs will recognize that we create latent variables to model shared dyadic variance. Dyadic data analysis can be discussed in terms of either multilevel models or SEMs. We switch back and forth between both representations freely because both offer unique insights into dyadic data analysis and some problems are easier to specify in one representation than the other. The covariance representation presents a common language to discuss these different analytic strategies. We first present the simple case of a single dependent variable collected from dyad members, and then we explore other design features involving temporal and multivariate elements.

THE BASIC INTERDEPENDENT MODEL: A SINGLE DEPENDENT VARIABLE, TWO PEOPLE

A key distinction is whether dyad members are distinguishable or exchangeable (e.g., Griffin & Gonzalez, 1995). Dyad members are distinguishable when the individuals can be identified on the basis of a theoretically meaningful variable such as gender in the case of heterosexual dating couples. Dyad members are exchangeable when the individuals cannot be distinguished on the basis of a theoretically meaningful variable, such as in the case of homosexual dating couples. In this chapter we mostly focus on the distinguishable case. For details on the exchangeable case, see Griffin and Gonzalez (1995) and Kenny et al. (2006).

Interdependence between interval scaled data in the context of linear models is captured by the ICC. The basic intuition for the ICC is that it is the percentage of variance associated with between couple variance. One standard formulation takes the variance associated with a dyad-level parameter and normalizes it by the sum of that dyad-level variance plus the variance of the individual-level error term. In the context of the general linear model, the underlying structural model for an observation Y for the jth person in the ith dyad is

$$Y_{ij} = \mu + \beta_j + \alpha_i + \varepsilon_{ij}, \tag{1}$$

where the μ is the fixed effect constant, β_j is the fixed effect term for the jth subject in a dyad (such as husband and wife), α_i is a random effect for dyad that is assumed to be normally distributed with mean zero and variance, σ_α^2 and the usual error term ε with variance σ_ε^2. Note the similarity of this model and the model for the two-time repeated measures presented earlier in the chapter. There are slightly different estimation formulas for the ICC depending on whether one uses maximum likelihood or restricted maximum likelihood (the latter accounts for degrees of freedom as in an ANOVA) estimation, but the basic logic is similar. The ICC becomes the ratio

$$\frac{\sigma_\alpha^2}{\sigma_\alpha^2 + \sigma_\varepsilon^2}. \qquad (2)$$

Some people like to represent this framework in the context of a multilevel model with the first level representing data at the individual level and the second level representing dyads. This model is written in two parts:

$$Y_{ij} = \gamma_i + \beta_j + \varepsilon_{ij} \text{ and} \qquad (3)$$
$$\gamma_i = \mu + \alpha_i, \qquad (4)$$

where β is a fixed effect term that estimates, say, the difference between the two distinguishable dyad members, γ is a random effect dyad term, and the ε is the usual error term. If one substitutes Equation 4 into Equation 3, then the result is the same as Equation 1. The two approaches are the same.

A third way to conceptualize the ICC is as an SEM with two indicators, one latent factor, and a specific set of restrictions. If one sets the variance of the latent factor to one, the two indicator paths to the observed variables equal to each other, and the error variances equal to each other, then the indicator paths are equal to the square root of the ICC (see Figure 22.1). The rationale for equating the two indicator paths is because the interpretation of the latent variable is one of *shared variance* in which both individuals (regardless of whether they are exchangeable or distinguishable) contribute equally. This is a different parameterization and interpretation than the usual latent factor in which indicators can have different path estimates and so can relate differentially to the latent variable.

Thus, there are several ways to conceptualize the logic of interdependence as indexed by the ICC, and they all lead to the same result. One can model the intraclass as a linear mixed model, as a multilevel model, or as an SEM. The results will be the same as

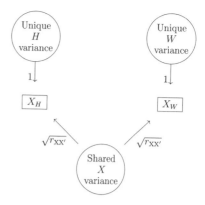

FIGURE 22.1. Illustration of the structural equations approach to estimating the intraclass correlation between husband (X_H) and wife (X_W) data.

long as the same estimation procedure is used (such as maximum likelihood) and the proper constraints on the parameters are imposed throughout. All three approaches impose the identical structure on the relevant covariance matrix. There really is no conceptual reason to favor one statistical framework over the other when it comes to dyadic data analysis. It is not necessary to limit oneself to using, say, multilevel modeling programs when one has nested data of the type seen in dyadic research. We find that other considerations, such as the ability to relax some constraints or the ability to handle missing data in sensible ways, turn out to be important in choosing one statistics package or modeling framework over another. For example, it may be easier to test some constraints, such as the equality of error variance across individuals, or to generalize the model to allow for differential error variance in one approach rather than another. The interdependence issue present in dyadic data analysis does not by itself force an analyst into one specific type of statistical representation.

Throughout this chapter, we focus on a normally distributed interval scale data. Given that we operate in the context of a linear mixed model (i.e., a general linear model with random effects), it is relatively straightforward to test these models within the generalized linear mixed model (GLMM). This generalization includes extensions to regression models on various distributions such as the binomial, the negative binomial, and the Poisson. These extensions may turn out to be relatively straightforward for simple models, but as we introduce more complicated multivariate dyadic models, the GLMM approach needs to be studied more carefully given that some distributions impose some challenging restrictions on some parameters, for example, the definition of the ICC in the context of binomial data is tricky because the usual GLMM logit link function imposes a constraint on the error variance (e.g., Snijders & Bosker, 1999). The generalization of dyadic models to nonnormal distributions remains an open area of research.

A MULTIVARIATE INTERDEPENDENT MODEL: TWO DEPENDENT VARIABLES, TWO PEOPLE

Latent Variable Model

Our discussion of the ICC so far has focused on one variable (Figure 22.1). We extend this framework to the case of two variables observed on each member of the dyad (Figure 22.2). For instance, we collect data on depression and marital satisfaction for each member of the couple. In addition to two ICCs, one for each variable X (depression) and Y (satisfaction), the model adds two new terms that span the two variables. One term is the dyad-level covariance, which is interpreted as the covariance between two latent variables, or the dyadic relation between

dyadic depression and dyadic satisfaction. In the context of dyadic data analysis, the latent variable estimated under the constraints shown in Figure 22.2 represents the shared variance between husband and wife within each respective variable. So the covariance is the covariance between the shared variance on depression and the shared variance on marital satisfaction. The dyad correlation is not equivalent to the correlation between the dyad means (Griffin & Gonzalez, 1995). The individual-level covariance is the covariance between the individual factor variance on each variable. That is, the husband and wife each have error variance remaining after accounting for the shared dyadic variance on each variable. The individual-level covariance represents the covariance across those individual-level error terms (e.g., the covariance between the husband's individual error term on depression and his individual error term on marital satisfaction). When couple members are distinguishable, it is possible to test the assumption of equal individual-level covariances by allowing the two terms to be freely estimated and comparing the free model to the constrained model using the likelihood ratio test (i.e., Gonzalez & Griffin, 2001).

The model depicted in Figure 22.2 can be equivalently estimated in the context of a multilevel model. Unfortunately, the description of the multivariate

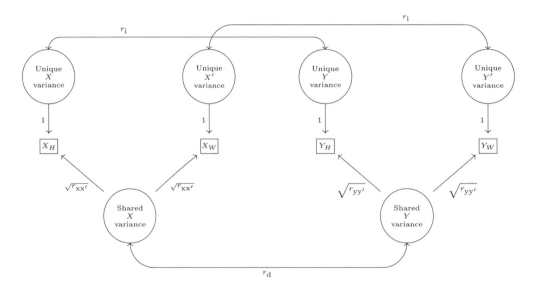

FIGURE 22.2. Illustration of the structural equations approach to estimating the intraclass correlation between husband and wife on two variables X and Y, the dyad level correlation r_d and the individual level correlation r_i.

model is not straightforward because multilevel models are typically expressed for a single variable with a single residual term ε at level 1. But we need separate error terms for each of the two variables. As we show later in this section, to fit the multilevel model to the multivariate example in Figure 22.2, it is necessary to express the multilevel model in a way that allows for different residual variances for each variable. We present one method to model multiple variables in the multilevel model using a switching regression technique.

The variables are represented in a single long column of data, which we denote **Y**. That is, we have a single column of data that includes the husband's depression, the wife's depression, the husband's marital satisfaction, and the wife's marital satisfaction. So, if there are 20 dyads, there are a total of 80 observations because each dyad member contributes two scores. It may seem strange to place data from different people and different variables into the same column, but by using proper codes, we can account for data associated with different variables and different people. The approach constructs the appropriate 80×80 covariance matrix for the 80 observations. One way to account for the dependence of multiple variables is to use the repeated measures option common in most multilevel model programs (e.g., depression and marital satisfaction would be treated as a repeated measures with an unconstrained covariance matrix, including heterogeneous variances, because we would not necessarily require that the variance for depression equal the variance for marital satisfaction). Then, the dyadic part of the analyses is implemented in a two-level model. This approach is described in Kenny et al. (2006).

An equivalent way to represent this multivariate framework in a multilevel model involves a *switching regression* approach, and we briefly review it here because it illuminates key points about the multivariate dyadic latent model (see Gonzalez & Griffin, 2001). First, place all observations from both partners and from both variables into a single long column **Y**. Second, create two columns of dummy codes. One dummy code D1 assigns a one to all depression scores and a zero for all marital satisfaction scores. The other dummy code D2 assigns a

zero to all depression scores and a one to all marital satisfaction scores. The dummy codes perfectly partition the long column of observations into depression data and into marital satisfaction data. The first-level equation is written as follows and does not include an error variance at Level 1 (this can be easily implemented in the MLWin multilevel modeling program) nor an intercept:

$$\mathbf{Y} = \beta_d D1 + \beta_s D2. \qquad (5)$$

These two βs from Level 1 are modeled as random effects. The error terms for each variable can be modeled separately for each variable because they will be attached to different βs at the second level. We omitted the intercept and the error term at this first level to estimate them separately for each variable at the higher level.

The second level of regression equations are as follows:

$$\beta_d = \text{intercept}_d + v_{dg} + u_{di} \text{ and} \qquad (6)$$

$$\beta_s = \text{intercept}_s + v_{sg} + u_{si}, \qquad (7)$$

where v and u are random effects that code group and individual terms (respectively), each equation has its own fixed effect intercept term, the subscripts d, s, g, and i refer to depression, satisfaction, group, and individual, respectively. The random effect v assesses group-level variance, and the random effect u assesses individual-level variance. In short, the switching regression (Level 1) isolates the two variables depression and marital satisfaction, and the next two levels capture the dyadic structure. This is implemented as a three-level model as far as the statistical program is concerned, but some researchers would call this a two-level model given that there is no error variance in the first level with the switching regression (Equation 5).

Now comes the important part of this particular formulation, which provides some new intuition. We formulate a covariance structure on each of the random effects v (group level) and u (individual level). Let the two group-level vs be bivariate normally distributed with covariance matrix

$$\Omega_v = \begin{bmatrix} \sigma_{vd}^2 & \\ \sigma_{vds} & \sigma_{vs}^2 \end{bmatrix}, \qquad (8)$$

where d and s denote depression and satisfaction, respectively. This means that the random effect v associated with depression has variance σ^2_{vd}, random effect v associated with satisfaction has variance σ^2_{vs}, and the two have covariance σ_{vds}. Similarly, an analogous covariance is formulated on the two individual-level us

$$\Omega_u = \begin{bmatrix} \sigma^2_{ud} & \\ \sigma_{uds} & \sigma^2_{us} \end{bmatrix}. \tag{9}$$

This covariance matrix gives the variances and covariance between depression and satisfaction at the individual level. In this formulation, we require equality of all individual-level correlations (i.e., referring to Figure 22.2, this particular multilevel model implementation forces the two individual-level correlations for husband and wife to be identical).

These two covariance matrixes contain information about group-level and individual-level variance for each variable and information about group-level and individual-level covariance between the two variables. They provide all the information necessary to compute the terms in the latent group model as well as each of the two ICCs. Using the terms in those two covariance matrixes, we have

intraclass correlation for depression: $\dfrac{\sigma^2_{vd}}{\sigma^2_{vd} + \sigma^2_{ud}}$,

intraclass correlation for satisfaction: $\dfrac{\sigma^2_{vs}}{\sigma^2_{vs} + \sigma^2_{us}}$,

individual level correlation between

depression and satisfaction: $\dfrac{\sigma_{uds}}{\sqrt{\sigma^2_{ud}\sigma^2_{us}}}$, and

dyad level correlation between

depression and satisfaction: $\dfrac{\sigma_{vds}}{\sqrt{\sigma^2_{vd}\sigma^2_{vs}}}$.

The two intraclass definitions are identical to what we presented in a previous section. The form of the individual- and dyad-level correlations is the usual correlation (a covariance divided by the square root of a product of variances). The individual-level correlation uses terms from the individual-level covariance matrix u and the group-level correlation uses terms from the group-level covariance matrix v. Thus, these two covariance matrixes yield the ICCs,

the variances of the individual- and group-level latent variables, and the individual- and group-level correlations, and the matrixes are identical to the SEM represented in Figure 22.2. This framework sets up the same structure on the 80 × 80 covariance matrix as the SEM in Figure 22.2.

The basic dyadic structure for the two variable latent model can be extended to more variables and to more complicated models. For example, one can take the two-variable model described in Figure 22.2 and use those variables (depression and marital satisfaction) to predict a third variable, say, parenting quality. The prediction can be modeled at both the individual level and the dyad level so that the prediction of parenting quality can occur at two levels. Does the shared variance of depression (dyad level) predict parental quality? Does the shared variance of marital satisfaction predict parental quality? Does the individual-level variance of the husband's depression predict his individual-level variance of parenting?

The take-home message of this type of modeling is that the variance and covariance is partitioned into individual-level and dyad-level terms. Once the partition is performed, many research questions can be tested at each level. It is in this way that the analysis of dyadic data goes beyond "correcting" data for violations of independence and instead directly modeling the interdependence. We can see how partitioning the analysis into separate individual-level and dyad-level covariance matrixes provides useful terms, such as ICCs, to illuminate the study of interpersonal processes.

Actor–Partner Model

A different representation of the latent variable model in Figure 22.2 is the *actor–partner model* (APM) depicted in Figure 22.3. The difference between the two models is how the interdependence is modeled—the latent variable model uses latent variables, whereas the APM uses observed variables directly. Is the wife's marital satisfaction predicted by both the husband's and the wife's depression? In this research question, there are no latent variables representing dyadic- and individual-level variance. Instead, we have two actor paths (a and d) that represent an individual's influence of depression on the same individual's score of marital satisfaction. There are two cross-person cross-variable paths (b and c)

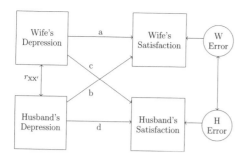

FIGURE 22.3. Actor–partner model for depression and marital satisfaction.

that represent the effect of wife's depression on husband's marital satisfaction and the effect of husband's depression on wife's satisfaction. The two exogenous predictors (depression from each couple member) are correlated and the residuals associated with satisfaction as the dependent variable are correlated. The model fits from the latent variable model in Figure 22.2 and the APM in Figure 22.3 are equivalent under some special restrictions. When two equality constraints are placed on the path coefficients ($a = d$ and $b = c$), the two residual variances are constrained to be equal, and the variances of the two predictors (depression) are constrained to be equal, then the models yield identical measures of fit. Of course, it is possible to generalize the models in different ways, and this is what makes each of them differentially useful as models. In general, a good use of the latent variable model formulation is when one wants to partition individual- and dyad-level variance; a good use of the APM is when one wants to examine interrelations of individuals (in particular, how one couple member's data predicts the other member's data). Research questions involving similarity of dyad members are naturally tested with the latent variable model, whereas research questions of interpersonal influence are naturally tested with the APM (Gonzalez & Griffin, 2001). In some literatures the APM is known as a *seemingly unrelated regression* (SUR).

THE LONGITUDINAL INTERDEPENDENT MODEL: A SINGLE VARIABLE, TWO TRAJECTORIES, TWO PEOPLE

There has been much progress on longitudinal data analysis, such as latent growth curve analysis (e.g.,

Singer, 1998). We can combine advances from latent growth modeling with those in dyadic models. Within our framework, these hybrid designs produce data with both temporal and interpersonal association. For simplicity in exposition, we assume a relatively simple example in which the investigator has three time-points, and each member of the couple provides depression data at each of those three time-points. There are at least two ways one can approach the modeling of this situation. One is to focus on the latent growth curve to model a curve for each person. This places priority on the temporal association. To deal with the interpersonal association, or interdependence, one could allow covariances across key terms in the latent growth curve. Suppose we fit both a random intercept and a random slope to the three waves of depression data with separate trajectories for the wife and for the husband. To model the interdependence attributable to couples, we estimate additional covariances between the husband and wife's random effect intercept, a covariance between the husband and wife's random effect slope, and cross-covariances spanning one person's intercept with the other's slope. The model assesses, for instance, the relation between latent parameters of the growth model, the intercept and slope, across dyad members.

A second way to model these data is to take the latent variable dyadic model as primary and apply it three times, once for each time-point. So there are three V-style diagrams as in Figure 22.1, one for each time the depression variable is assessed. This portion of the model accounts for the interpersonal association. To account for temporal association, one can estimate covariance terms across individual- and dyadic-level variances, or instead of covariances, one could estimate an autoregressive model having regression paths across time predicting the individual- and dyad-level variances. This model can be used to assess the stability of the dyadic- and individual-level variances.

These two model frameworks differ in their priority. The first model places priority on the trajectories over time and addresses interdependence over the parameters of the trajectory. The second model places priority on the interdependence between dyad members and addresses temporal association over the interdependence parameters. Both models can yield identical model fits depending on how they are parameterized and the nature of constraints that are imposed. That is, they both can imply the same covariance structure on the observations by properly accounting for both temporal and interpersonal association in the observations. They can also be relaxed and generalized in different ways and so can be used to test different models with different psychological implications. Both of these frameworks can be specified in the context of multilevel models. For an example of a longitudinal design in the multilevel framework for couple research using a single dependent variable, see Barnett, Raudenbush, Brennan, Pleck, and Marshall (1995). We prefer to conceptualize latent growth models in the context of SEM because it is sometimes easier to generalize the temporal part of the model, such as being able to specify unconstrained error variances at each time. But we recognize that both the multilevel and structural equation modeling approaches to latent growth modeling have their merits and can be identical depending on how the constraints are imposed within each framework.

A LONGITUDINAL, MULTIVARIATE INTERDEPENDENT MODEL: TWO DEPENDENT VARIABLES, TWO TRAJECTORIES, TWO PEOPLE

This design contains all three types of association: temporal, multivariate, and interpersonal. It arises when the research design measures couples on multiple variables such as depression and marital satisfaction over multiple time-points. For example, husband and wife dyad pairs are assessed on both depression and marital satisfaction at each of three time-points. We describe one way to model these three associations simultaneously. Conceptually, we can estimate the latent group model (i.e., the model depicted in Figure 22.2) separately at each time. But rather than estimating three separate submodels (one for Time 1, a second for Time 2, and a third for Time 3), it is appropriate to estimate the entire model simultaneously (i.e., the latent group model at all three times together). This simultaneous

model permits, among other things, the estimation of stability of the latent variable terms. This can be accomplished either by estimating covariances between all time i latent variables and all time $i + 1$ latent variables or by estimating regression paths between two adjacent time-points for different terms in the multivariate interdependent model. There is a sense that this representation gives priority to interdependence, then models the cross-variable association and the temporal association.

Other frameworks are possible too, such as placing priority on the temporal part and estimating trajectories for each person on each variable. Once the latent trajectories are estimated, then the multivariate and interpersonal associations are added across the relevant trajectory parameters. One can also perform additional analyses (such as moderation and mediation) to gain a deeper understanding of the contributors to the different elements of this general model, such as examining the predictors of group-level stability or individual-level stability, or examining interesting combinations such as cross-variable individual-level stability, for example, examining the correlation between the error for husbands' depression at Time 1 with the error of husbands' marital satisfaction at Time 2. This model can also be implemented in a multilevel framework.

STRUCTURAL EQUATION MODELING, MULTILEVEL MODELS, AND GENERALIZATIONS

Our general formulation of temporal, multivariate, and interpersonal association has been useful for organizing many of the dyadic models that have been discussed in the literature. We see that different implementations, such as in an SEM approach or in a multilevel modeling approach, offer advantages and disadvantages. Sometimes it is easier to work with an SEM program such as when dyads are distinguishable, there are multiple variables, or one wants to test mediation and moderation. Sometimes a multilevel model approach is easier to implement, such as when dyads are exchangeable, there are missing data, or one is primarily concerned with partitioning dyad and individual random effect variance. Some generalizations or tests of constraints are easier within one framework than another, but many features can be implemented with either approach. For example, exchangeable and distinguishable dyads can be modeled with either multilevel models or with SEMs (e.g., Woody & Sadler, 2005).

The analysis of the latent dyad model can be conducted even when some groups have data from only one member (e.g., Snijders & Bosker, 1999). Multilevel techniques permit *units* of unequal sizes. So, if the unit is the individual with, say, four time-points, then one way to handle missing data would be to treat the missingness as something that yields unequal-size units. The general multilevel framework can thus handle missing observations in a longitudinal design as well as groups of unequal sizes (as would be encountered, for example, in research in which a family is the unit of analysis and families vary in size); for a complete discussion, see Raudenbush and Bryk (2002).

We view the close connection to both structural equation and multilevel modeling frameworks as a plus rather than a negative, as providing insight rather than a source of confusion. As new methods become available in either framework, the dyadic researcher can easily switch back and forth to take advantage of new developments. For example, recent advances in growth mixture modeling techniques for simultaneously estimating trajectories and identifying different classes of individuals exhibiting different trajectory patterns could be extended to dyadic research.

SOFTWARE IMPLEMENTATIONS

The dyadic researcher has a broad array of software choices. Major statistical programs (such as SPSS, SAS, R, and Stata) can run the procedures described in this chapter. The user must be mindful of the particular defaults in any statistical program they use. Researchers preferring an SEM framework can use any SEM program, including EQS, LISREL, AMOS, and Mplus. Those who prefer a multilevel modeling approach can use programs such as HLM, MLWin, and Mplus. Again, careful attention to defaults in any statistical program one uses is important.

Some statistical programs such as Mplus and SAS NLMIXED make estimating and testing general models relatively easy. We welcome such flexible software. At the same time, we caution researchers that as new procedures are created by mixing and matching diverse elements (such as a dyadic longitudinal growth mixture model on binary data), it becomes even more important to understand the statistical underpinnings of one's model. It is common to see strange behavior in such novel hybrid models, such as negative error variances. The researcher should seek methodological advice when exploring new modeling territory. It is not advisable to use quick fixes, such as setting a negative error variance to zero, or setting a particular equality constraint, merely because that makes the program converge or run without error. Rather, when a new hybrid model produces strange output, it is best to consult a methodologist.

We recommend that the dyadic researcher maintain an open mind when choosing among different statistical packages. There is probably no single statistics package, or framework, that will serve all research needs. The dyadic researcher will also need to be flexible in setting up the data in different ways for different analyses. Sometimes dyadic analyses can be done in wide format, such that each row represents a couple, and data from both members of the couple appear on the same row of the data matrix (as when using an SEM framework). Other times analyses are easier in long format, such that each row represents a person, so data from a couple spans two rows in the data matrix, as when using a multilevel framework. Each of those two data formats requires careful use of couple codes; data for distinguishable individuals is coded by individual codes in the long format but automatically by columns in the wide format. Sometimes data need to be entered twice, in the sense that one column contains data from Harry and Sally (separate rows), whereas a second column contains the same data for the same variable but in reverse order (i.e., Sally and Harry). This type of data entry can be used for the pairwise approach to dyadic data analysis (Griffin & Gonzalez, 1995) and in the APM (Kenny et al., 2006), and it directly provides maximum likelihood estimates in the case of no missing data.

CONCLUSION

Dyadic designs provide researchers an exciting route to study interpersonal processes. The inclusion of both individuals from the dyad in the data set provides the opportunity to study interdependence. Interdependence is not a problem with the data but is a limitation of the standard statistical techniques psychologists tend to use. By framing interdependence in the language of associations, we showed that it is possible to discuss temporal, interpersonal, and multivariate associations together. The richness of dyadic data analysis is such that sometimes it is longitudinal, sometimes multivariate, and sometimes both. So it is necessary to take into account three sources of association that may be present in a dyadic design. We hope this chapter has convinced the reader that it is no longer necessary to avoid analyzing interdependent data that violate the independence assumption and has inspired the reader to study dyadic processes.

References

Barnett, R. C., Raudenbush, S. W., Brennan, R. T., Pleck, J. H., & Marshall, N. L. (1995). Change in job and marital experiences and change in psychological distress: A longitudinal study of dual-earner couples. *Journal of Personality and Social Psychology, 69,* 839–850. doi:10.1037/0022-3514.69.5.839

Card, N., Selig, J., & Little, T. (2008). *Modeling dyadic and interdependent data in the developmental and behavioral sciences.* New York, NY: Routledge.

Gonzalez, R., & Griffin, D. (2001). A statistical framework for modeling homogeneity and interdependence in groups. In M. Clark & G. Fletcher (Eds.), *Handbook of Social Psychology: Vol. 2. Interpersonal processes* (pp. 505–534). Malden, MA: Blackwell.

Griffin, D., & Gonzalez, R. (1995). The correlational analysis of dyad-level data: Models for the exchangeable case. *Psychological Bulletin, 118,* 430–439. doi:10.1037/0033-2909.118.3.430

Kenny, D. A. (1990). Design issues in dyadic research. In C. Hendrick & M. S. Clark (Eds.), *Review of Personality and Social Psychology: Vol. 11. Research methods in personality and social psychology* (pp. 164–184). Newbury Park, CA: Sage.

Kenny, D. A., & Judd, C. M. (1986). Consequences of violating the independence assumption in the analysis of variance. *Psychological Bulletin, 99,* 422–431. doi:10.1037/0033-2909.99.3.422

Kenny, D. A., Kashy, D. A., & Cook, W. L. (2006). *Dyadic data analysis.* New York, NY: Guilford Press.

Raudenbush, S., & Bryk, A. (2002). *Hierarchical linear models: Applications and data analysis methods* (2nd ed.). Thousand Oaks, CA: Sage.

Singer, J. (1998). Using SAS PROC MIXED to fit multilevel models, hierarchical models and individual growth models. *Journal of Educational and Behavioral Statistics, 23,* 323–355.

Snijders, T., & Bosker, R. (1999). *Multilevel analysis: An introduction to basic and advanced multilevel modeling.* Thousand Oaks, CA: Sage.

Woody, E., & Sadler, P. (2005). Structural equation models for interchangeable dyads: Being the same makes a difference. *Psychological Methods, 10,* 139–158. doi:10.1037/1082-989X.10.2.139

## CHAPTER 23

SOCIAL NETWORK RESEARCH: THE FOUNDATION OF NETWORK SCIENCE

Stanley Wasserman and Garry Robins

A *social network* is a system of *social actors* and a *set of relationships* among them. In its simplest form, a network has one type of social actor, typically, but not necessarily, individuals, with one type of social relationship. The type of social relationship(s) define the social connections or relational ties among the actors.

For instance, a study may examine online texting behavior among a classroom of school students. Here the actors are the students and the ties are the text communication links among them. As only one type of actor is to be studied in this little example, it is a *unipartite* or *one-mode* network; as there is only one type of relational tie examined, it is also a *univariate* or single relational network.

There is a very long history of the intersection between network science and psychology. Psychology, particularly social psychology, and social network research are both centrally concerned with human sociality, specifically human-to-human interactions. Social network perspectives are increasingly seen as relevant in a variety of behavioral science disciplines: for example, organizational psychology, social support in clinical and community psychology, health-related behaviors, school- and classroom-based research in educational psychology, team structures in sports psychology, online Internet behaviors (e.g., cyber-bullying). The network paradigm has made a large impact on behavioral science over the past decade.

Our basic premise in this chapter is that every social actor is embedded in (possibly) a wide variety of networks that provide connections of different types to other social actors. Social actors do not operate as isolated *social atoms* independently of one another. The network perspective enables a precise formulation of how a system of actors may be interdependent. So a social network, properly, is not just the property of one actor; furthermore, it is a misnomer to talk of "the social network of a person" as if a network belonged to an individual.

A network is a very multidimensional thing. There are multiple types of social ties connecting multiple individuals in a variety of ways, or as the definition states: *a set of relationships*. The different types of relational ties (e.g., friendship, cooperation, antagonism, communication, authority) serve different functions and may operate in different ways. Here, we will not only review prominent network research methods, but we will describe psychological theories that have generated many of them.

Network Science has exploded as a discipline over the past 15 years (Watts, 2004). There are new books, research from physics, computer science, engineering, biology, bioinformatics, animal behavior, education, and so forth.

Much of the material defined and discussed here can be found in more complete network science compendia; we refer the interested reader to

We are very grateful to Jen Miller for her comments and additions to this chapter and to Eric Quebbeman for editorial assistance. Research was sponsored by the Army Research Laboratory and was accomplished under Cooperative Agreement No. W911NF-09-2-0053. The views and conclusions contained in this document are those of the authors and should not be interpreted as representing the official policies, either expressed or implied, of the Army Research Laboratory or the U.S. government. The U.S. government is authorized to reproduce and distribute reprints for government purposes notwithstanding any copyright notation hereon.

DOI: 10.1037/13621-023
APA Handbook of Research Methods in Psychology: Vol. 3. Data Analysis and Research Publication, H. Cooper (Editor-in-Chief)

Wasserman and Faust (1994); Carrington, Scott, and Wasserman (2005); Jackson (2008); and Kolaczyk (2009) for lengthier and more detailed discussions on network methods. Network theory is well described in Monge and Contractor (2003).

NETWORKS IN BEHAVIORAL SCIENCE RESEARCH

A social network approach is relevant when researchers are interested in problems relating to social systems. In much of social psychology, the focus is on individual social cognition: that is, responses by individuals to social situations. When, however, the interest lies more in how a set of individuals form a social system, an individualized account will be incomplete (for a discussion, see Robins & Kashima, 2008). A network conceptualization permits an understanding of how individuals may be interdependent in various ways. This is obviously important in many research areas (possible examples abound: the structure of sporting teams, communication patterns within organizations, the spread of contagious diseases and of rumors, alliances among politicians, trade among countries, bullying among schoolchildren). When complex interdependence is a key consideration, then traditional statistical methods that rely on assumptions of independent observations are certainly inadequate. Accordingly, social network methods for dealing with interconnections among a set of individuals have been developed.

Social network analysis now has a long tradition in social and behavioral science research, going back to the 1920s. The founding of the journal *Sociometry* by (perhaps) the first quantitative network researcher Jacob Moreno was an important start in developing and popularizing network methodology (see Moreno & Jennings, 1938). After the 1940s, as described in Freeman's (2004) history of network analysis and Kirke's (2007) review of networks and behavioral science, advances were made in a number of research areas, including sociology, anthropology, organizational science, and social psychology. Of course, mathematicians, and more recently statisticians, have a long tradition in graph theory and greatly influenced these developments. Another

dramatic surge occurred in the mid-1990s as first physicists, then biologists, and more recently, computer scientists saw the relevance of networks within their own disciplines. Much has changed since Kirke's (2007) review; here, in the 21st century, with a new understanding and appreciation for interconnectedness and globalization, along with the growth of the Internet and social media, network methods seem an increasingly natural way to research many aspects of modern society and the individuals within it.

Networks as Explanatory/Predictors

Much of the early work in network analysis focused on the network as the primary unit of analysis—which actors are most prominent, which actors are cohesively linked to others, which are balanced structurally, which are equivalent to others, and so forth (these concepts will be discussed in this chapter). But networks now, to a large extent, are being viewed as explanatory factors, as predictors of particular behaviors. Interest in network theory and methods has boomed over the past decade, no doubt due to the fact that researchers are beginning to think about relational variables, linking subjects or respondents to other individuals, as explanatory.

Our focus here is on behavioral science; so, for example, it is theoretically interesting to ask such questions as

- "Am I happy because my best friends are usually happy?"
- "Will it be hard for me to quit smoking because everyone in my family smokes?"
- "How are overweight people affected by their overweight friends?"
- "If a subject has a hereditary tendency toward diabetes, can the probability of acquiring the disease be lessened if the family and friends of the subject have good eating habits?"

Such questions put attention on particular actor behaviors and can be answered by studying whether there are interactions between the people an actor is tied to and the behaviors of those individuals. The network lingo labels a particular actor *ego*, and the people ego is relationally tied to *alters*. The theoretical idea here is *social influence*—how actor behaviors are influenced by the behavioral aspects of the alters relationally tied to the actor as ego.

Networks as Responses/Outcomes

It is less common in behavioral science to have network variables as outcomes in psychological research, but it is of major interest in other domains in which the *structure* of the social system is an important research question. Questions such as

- What is the structure of communication within an organization?
- What is the structure of kinship in an anthropological study?
- What is the structure of particular social hierarchies or social movements in sociology?
- What is the structure of various forms of institutional governance or alliances among leaders in political science?

are answered by focusing primarily on the relational measurements. When studying the network as a response or an outcome variable, the research enquiry centers on how best to describe the network and on what social processes might explain how the network came into being.

A very good example comes from health psychology, in which one can study whether certain health behaviors (e.g., smoking or marijuana usage) among adolescents arise through social influence within school classrooms. We may observe an association between network ties and smoking, where we might find that smoking tends to occur within sets of friends. But before we can conclude that smoking arises from social influence, we must exclude the possibility that smokers come together as friends because they share the activity of smoking. In other words, we must understand the processes that could lead to the formation of the network; so that the issue of network as outcome (the structure) cannot be divorced from the issue of network as explanatory. This is a "which came first: the chicken or the egg" thing. Which behavior is the antecedent of the other?

BASIC NETWORK CONCEPTS

What makes a network a *social network*? Some researchers would say that if the actors are people,

the network is social. Natural scientists prefer to think of network science as a field that subsumes the study of social networks. There appears to be no hard and fast rule in the literature. We might state that only *social* networks are *self-organizing*—social ties between network actors have the ability to be created or dissolved by the actors. A social network therefore differs from certain other types of network, such as a railway, a system of air routes, a hard-wired computer network, or a network of protein-protein interactions in that there is an element of randomness to the value (or presence or absence) of a tie between any two social actors. With social networks, it is natural to talk about the probability that a tie occurs or the probability a tie takes on a large value. Such probabilities may properly be viewed as functions of the actors involved.

Network science, as an academic discipline, has exploded since 1995. Physicists, biologists, computer scientists, and engineers now feel comfortable conducting and are excited about network research. We think of social network analysis, methods, and theory as the central components of network science. Networks were first studied quantitatively by behavioral scientists. Without question, psychological research has had an important impact on the discipline by proposing theories, such as structural balance, transitivity, reciprocity, and social influence, that have been measured, recorded, and then analyzed over the past 80 years using a variety of sophisticated methods.

A social network can conveniently be represented as a *graph*, a mathematical object that has a set N of *nodes* (sometimes called *vertices*), representing actors, and a set L of *edges* (undirected) or *arcs* (directed). A *network visualization* depicts such a graph, with the nodes as points, the edges as lines, and the arcs as arrows. Network visualizations, in conjunction with other analytic approaches, can be useful in understanding the regularities and idiosyncrasies within social systems.

Actors and Relational Ties

A *relational tie*, which is represented mathematically as an edge or an arc, is a property of two actors. It is the basic unit in network science. The *relational content* of the tie is the type of relationship under study and being measured. From Wasserman and Faust (1994), but updated to take into account the many new applications of networks, a small typology of behavioral relations follows:

- Individual evaluations: friendship, liking, respect, social support, and so forth
- Transactions or transfer of material resources: lending or borrowing; buying or selling
- Transfer of nonmaterial resources: sending/receiving information
- Interactions, particularly communication: phone calls, e-mail, Facebook friends, texts, Tweets
- Formal roles: authority, power
- Kinship: marriage, descent

The relational content(s) studied by a researcher depends on the research question and associated theory about relevant social processes. A decision about the types of network ties appropriate to a particular research question needs to be made with care: No off-the-shelf network scales are suitable for all situations (although there are some general measurement approaches that we discuss in subsequent sections).

A tie can be *directed* if it flows from the first actor to the second (e.g., one actor might admire another) but not necessarily from the second to the first, or it can be *undirected* if neither of the two actors are distinguished (e.g., the two actors might simply live near each other). This is clearly a measurement aspect of the tie itself. It is best to decide before collecting data whether a tie should be measured as directed or undirected. Sometimes this is not a simple decision. For instance, friendship is commonly considered a *symmetric* relationship (many people argue that unless a friendship is mutual it is not a real friendship). If a researcher takes this position, then a friendship tie is conceptually undirected. Yet social network researchers often treat friendship as directed and find that unreciprocated friendship choices (*asymmetric* dyads) can provide important empirical information. Asymmetric friendship dyads are actually quite common in empirical data. If directed relational data are collected, then undirected relations can still be extracted. In the friendship example, it might make sense to study directed friendship ties to see how the asymmetric ties (*I like you* but *you don't like me*) differ from the mutual

dyads (*I like you* and *you like me*). If there are substantial differences, then the mutual ties might be considered as stronger, mutual friendship dyads, rather than simple and weaker asymmetric dyads.

Relational ties may change over time. This is a natural consequence of a self-organizing social system in which the actors are not necessarily constrained to operate with the same set of ties forever. Relational ties can come into existence and dissolve—friendships, acquaintances, business partnerships, and so forth come and go over time. Usually, data are gathered cross-sectionally, at one point in time. If the relation is truly longitudinal, changing over time, then data can be collected on the same set of nodes at multiple time-points in a panel design, or even as a continuous record (e.g., when Senator A coauthors a bill with Senator B during a particular session of the U.S. Congress). A relational tie may be present because of a durable legal or organizational arrangement (e.g., a contract, a marriage, or the formal hierarchy prescribed by the board of a company), but it may occur simply because it entails some form of social commitment or pattern of behavior that is psychologically present for some subset of the actors contained in a *group* (which could be quite large) of social actors.

A relational tie is usually presumed to have the following measurement qualities: A tie has some reasonable duration and is not marked by necessary immediacy, and it is quantifiable (i.e., can be recorded as a particular relational variable). Relational ties do not necessary have to be dichotomous or binary. One can measure valued ties, which can be observed at various strengths. A good example of valued friendship ties comes right from sociological theory, in which *weak* friendship ties have been theorized to be as important as *strong* friendship ties, particularly with respect to information flows (Granovetter, 1973).

Sometimes a network contains more than one set of actors, and interest centers on relational ties from actors in one set of actors in the other. The number of sets of actors is referred to as the *mode* of the network; studying friendship ties between managers (first set) and workers (second set) in a large factory produces a univariate two-mode network. If we were interested in how teachers regulate the texting behavior among students, we might study how the teachers (first set) discipline the students (second set) when students text during class.

When considering a social network, it is important to realize that it is not just the presence of ties that define the network but also their absence. This point sometimes escapes newcomers to network analysis (even in data collection, a researcher must understand what counts as an absent tie). If everyone is connected to everyone else (defined as a *complete network*), there is not much of interest to be said from a network perspective. Accordingly, a basic network measure is that of *density*, the proportion of observed ties to possible ties. For an undirected network with g actors, the density is $2L/g(g-1)$; for a directed network, it is $L/g(g-1)$. A complete network has density one, and an *empty network* (a network with no ties) has density zero. Because not all ties are present in a network, the ties that are observed may tend to be arranged in particular patterns of interest. These may reflect simple human social processes that are a basis for network self-organization. A simple process is that of reciprocity in which ties tend to be reciprocated in directed networks, so that the presence of a tie from node i to j tends to be accompanied by a tie from j to i. (By "tend to be," we mean that the pattern occurs more frequently than would be expected by chance.) In many human social situations (e.g., friendship, exchange of favors, cooperation), reciprocity is an important and common occurrence.

Another important pattern relates to triangles in a graph. Humans tend to operate not just in pairs but in small groups, and the simplest notion of a group can be represented by a *triangle* (a complete subgraph on three nodes). The sociologist Simmel (1908) was the first theorist to distinguish between the social circumstances of a *triad* of individuals (i.e., three individuals and the relationships among them) as opposed to a *dyad* (i.e., a pair of individuals and the relationship between them). This basic idea is an important feature of network theory and analysis. The formation of triangles (sometimes called nodal *transitivity* or *clustering*) is often seen as a process of network closure, whereby a two path among three actors (i.e., a network path involving two network ties, from actor i to actor j and from j to k) is closed by the addition of a direct tie from i

to k. Network closure can be interpreted in many ways: the formation of a small group, the introduction of two individuals by a third, and so on. Empirically it is a common feature in many human social networks.

There are times when researchers are interested in examining how nodes are indirectly connected with one another. These include graph features such as walks, paths, and geodesics.

In a network, nodes are often not adjacent or even connected at all to other nodes. Researchers are often interested in how resources such as information can travel or flow from node to node. To capture how information can travel to specific nodes, the shortest path between nodes, or the *geodesic*, is often considered. The geodesic distance is the length of the geodesic (the number of relational ties in the path). Although there are often many paths between nodes, the key element in the geodesic distance is the shortest path between two nodes. If there are no paths between the nodes, then the distance is considered infinite, and we say that the nodes are not connected or not reachable from each other.

Geodesics have many uses, for example, studying coauthorship networks in academia. The *Erdös number*, named after Paul Erdös, who heavily influenced discrete mathematics, and particularly graph theory, is a good example. The number is calculated based on how far removed an author is in terms of coauthorship from the very prolific Erdös. It is the geodesic distance in this coauthorship network from an individual to Erdös. The average Erdös number among mathematical researchers is 4.7; the maximum number is 15 (Newman, 2003).

The *degree* of a particular node is how many relational ties are incident with the node. For an undirected graph, the degree of a node can range from 0 to $g-1$. If a node has a degree of zero, the node is properly termed an isolate. In directed networks, degrees can be divided into outdegree and indegree when considering the directionality of ties. *Outdegree* is the number of ties from one node to the other nodes, and *indegree* is the number of ties to one node from other nodes.

There are many techniques to find subgroups within a network or *community structure*. A clique is defined as a complete subgraph containing three or more actors. With a directed relation, all dyads in a clique are mutual. Additional methods have been developed to include some of the concerns raised with cliques. Researchers have used other methods to find cohesive subgroups, such as reachability, path distance, diameter, and nodal degree.

Attributes of Actors

Actors in social networks are often treated as if they only express or receive relational ties (possibly at various strengths). Of course, in a complex social system, individuals have a range of personal qualities, capabilities, and purposes that can affect social behaviors. These individual actor-level variables need to be studied, quantified, and then analyzed to obtain a complete and (hopefully) accurate representation of a social system A social network is more than just a collection of relational ties. In network parlance, individual-level variables are referred to as *actor attributes*.

In terms of a network visualization, relational ties are drawn with different colors or types of lines, whereas attribute variables may be represented as different colors for the nodes (to represent categorical variables) or different-size nodes (if attributes are continuous). There may be many different types of actor attributes relevant to a network study, including standard demographic variables, and also important psychological variables, including attitudes and behaviors. Robins (2009) discussed the different types of attribute variables. Consideration of individual attributes naturally leads into a discussion of network processes, as often the interest in network-based research is to understand processes that may affect individual attributes within a social system. And one of the most recent uses of the social network paradigm is the in-depth study of social influence processes in social systems; for example, can one predict or model body-mass index (BMI) and tendencies toward illness (such as diabetes) as a function of the BMI of one's friends? Do tendencies toward obesity influence, through social processes, one's own tendencies?

NETWORK THEORETICAL CONCEPTS

In this section, we present and discuss some of the network processes that are relevant to understanding human social systems. There are a number of important theoretical arguments and concepts that are specific to social network theory. We briefly discuss several of these concepts, noting that this collection is neither complete nor comprehensive.

Strong and Weak Ties

Granovetter (1973) introduced an important distinction between strong and weak network ties. He argued that strong network ties tended to exhibit network closure and form into cliquelike structures, whereas this tendency did not apply to weak ties. In that case, weak ties would provide the means of connectivity between cliques of strong ties, representing an important place in an individual's structural autonomy. If only strong ties were available to an individual, redundant information would be passed through these ties. Weak ties afford new opportunities to acquire new information and resources.

Structural Holes

Burt (1992) argued that the *holes* in a structure were crucial—that is, the *places* in a network where ties are absent. In other words, focus attention on the less dense regions of the networks. Although not a new idea, Burt argued that individuals who could provide such connectivity by occupying structural holes were network entrepreneurs or network brokers and could gain personal advantage from their structural position. Researchers have known for years that the sparse areas of a network can be just as important as the dense regions, but Burt was able to give some new theoretical reasons why analysts should look more carefully at where ties are not. Individuals who fill the structural holes are dependent on different factors, such as the timing, access, and referral of information. For example, by accessing the information that other individuals do not have access to, an *information overload* may occur. Individuals may need to filter out unnecessary information that is present by *filling* the structural hole. The ability to fill structural holes obviously gives an advantage of additional opportunities from other individuals.

Small-World Networks

The well-known social psychologist Milgram (1967) conducted an empirical study in social network connectivity well ahead of his time. He sought to determine the average path length between two individuals in the United States in the mid-1960s. He sent individuals letters asking them to locate a person, unknown to them, of a particular type by only using people they already knew. Each respondent was asked to name a person who might know the unknown, target person. The people named by the respondent were then asked the same question, and so on. This experiment, referred to as the *small-world* paradigm, generated a set of *paths* or chains of letters from acquaintance to acquaintance trying to locate the targets. The majority of Milgram's chains did not complete (a fact often neglected today when describing this work), but for those that did, the median number of intermediaries was five, the mean was 5.8, giving an approximate average path length of six. This result has since become famously known as *six degrees of separation*, accompanied by the claim that any two people on the planet are connected by a path of only six steps or less. Hence, the world is *small*.

This rather dramatic claim ignores the fact that Milgram's (1967) result was about the average path over just the completed paths, not the maximum, and it ignored the many incomplete paths. Nevertheless, interest in small-world networks has been revived considerably over the past 10 years with the work of Duncan Watts (1999, 2003). Watts and Strogatz (1998) argued that a small-world network was exemplified by the combination of short average geodesics, high clustering, and low density—all expected features of many large-scale social networks. It is not intuitive how these three properties could coexist, but Watts showed that adding a small amount of random connections to highly structured, *long-path* networks provided network *shortcuts* that would dramatically reduce average geodesic distance and yet retain relatively high levels of network clustering.

Degree Distributions

Social networks typically have positively skewed degree distributions. In other words, many actors have small degrees, but a few can have very large values. Usually there is considerable variation in the network activity of actors, so that in directed networks, for instance, some actors may be highly popular (indegree) and/or highly active (sometimes referred to as expansive–outdegree). There may even be outliers with particularly large values in the degree distribution. In the literature, such actors are termed *hubs* and are quite important in studying whether a network has small-world characteristics.

Interest in degree distributions is quite old and can be found in the research of Moreno and Jennings (1938). Barabasi and Albert (1999) proposed an inverse power law degree distribution for networks with highly skewed degree distributions; networks that can be fit with this single parameter distribution are said to be *scale free*. Whether a given social network exhibits a scale-free degree distribution is a matter of empirical study and should not be taken for granted. A good statistician would evaluate the fit of such a distribution with an appropriate test statistic.

Social Selection

Social selection arises when actors choose others on the basis of their attributes. Pairs of individuals may form a tie because of their individual qualities. Such processes are labeled *social selection*. A common process is *homophily*, whereby individuals form a relationship because they have the same or similar attributes—that is, "birds of a feather flock together." "I'm like you; you are like me, so let's hook up" is social selection in action. Homophily can be divided into status homophily, ties that are formed on the basis of informal status, or value homophily, ties formed on the basis of values or beliefs (Lazarsfeld & Merton, 1954). Status homophily includes measures such as age, sex, and race, whereas value homophily is predominately based on personal principles. Another mechanism for homophily is largely based on geography; individuals are more likely to interact with other individuals who close.

Homophily may lead to triangles when three individuals, who share the same attribute, each form relational ties. Accordingly, the presence of triangles in the network is not in itself evidence for a homophily or a network closure process because such structural features may arise from a variety of theoretical causes.

The term *generalized selection* was first used by Robins (2009) to describe the situation in which an actor may select not just network partners but particular network positions. For instance, in line with Burt's (1992) argument, network brokers seek to occupy structural holes to gain advantage. The motivation is not about choosing a particular partner as much as getting a particular position.

Social Influence

Actors may be influenced by their network partners, so that attitudes or behaviors may diffuse across a network. Certain attributes such as knowledge (information), behaviors, or attitudes may become diffused across the network through processes of *social influence*. Analogously, certain diseases spread through social connections, so social influence in network parlance is sometimes called *contagion* or *diffusion*. Individual actors (or egos) can learn from their alters and may seek to copy or mimic these alters: *We are friends, so I want to be like you* is social influence in action. Twenty-first-century marketing strategies utilize social influence heavily; word-of-mouth marketing (also referred to as buzz or viral marketing) makes extensive use of the assumption that the interaction of consumers and users of a product or service amplifies the original marketing message.

Individuals may be influenced not so much because of the direct effect of network partners but rather by the social position that they occupy. For instance, individuals may change certain attributes in response to occupying a particular social role (Burt, 1987; White, Boorman, & Breiger, 1976). Such theories can be labeled *generalized influence*.

Structural Balance

Because of basic aspects of human sociality, particular types of relational ties tend to occur in certain patterns. These processes tend to occur irrespective of individual attributes or of external factors exogenous to the networks. Such endogenous processes operating on and among the network ties are sometimes referred to as *network self-organization*. As noted, the most basic form of network self-organization is *reciprocity*. For directed relational ties measuring positive affect, and for simple exchange, there are often strong tendencies for reciprocation of ties, so that the presence of a tie from person i to person j encourages the presence of a tie from j to i. Another common self-organizing process is the tendency toward triangulation, whereby in many networks, a two-path among a triple of actors (i.e., ties i–j and j–k) *closes* to form a triangle (i.e., the tie i–k occurs). Triangles will usually occur together in the denser regions of the network, and this feature may reflect the fact that humans tend to operate in small groups rather than as isolates or as isolated dyads. Triangles may also form when an actor is introduced by a network partner to a new network partner.

The presence of triangles in a network may be the result of what are called balance processes. Heider's (1946) balance theory is well known in social psychology. The theory argues that individuals seek balanced relationships with others in regard to third objects. So, for instance, if John likes Mary and both like opera, this is seen as a balanced situation, whereas if Mary hates opera, then the situation is unbalanced. Heider argued that individuals would change unbalanced situations, for example, John might cease to like Mary or change his attitude toward opera (or perhaps Mary will come to like opera through Johns influence). Cartwright and Harary (1956) extended this idea to structural balance in which the object was in fact a third person. In that case, a two-path (John likes Mary and John likes Oliver, but Mary does not) was regarded as unbalanced with pressures to revert to a balanced situation (e.g., John ceases to like one of Mary or Oliver, or Mary comes to like Oliver). This notion of structural balance provided a social mechanism that explained the presence of triangles in human social networks.

Structural Equivalence

Loosely speaking, *structural equivalence* refers to the extent to which two actors are connected to the same others—that is, they act identically and are viewed as identical in the social system. It may be the case that structurally equivalent actors are similar in other ways as well, such as in attitudes, behaviors or performance.

Structurally equivalent actors are often said to occupy the same role in the social system.

By categorizing nodes into a small number of classes of approximately structurally equivalent actors, a blockmodel of the network can be produced (White et al., 1976). A blockmodel simplifies the network by collapsing the nodes into their structural equivalence classes with ties represented as the density (or possibly some dichotomized form of density) within and between the classes. A complex network may then be presented as a small number of roles (equivalence classes) with ties between them (blocks). Doreian, Batagelj, and Ferligoj (2005) provided some recent generalizations.

Coevolution of Networks and Attributes

Although networks are often measured as static entities, the self-organizing perspective implies that they are dynamic entities that evolve over time. This does not preclude important conclusions being drawn from cross-sectional network data, but it does imply that processes such as social selection and social influence may occur simultaneously in a network. Hence, it is possible that across time both network structure and actor attributes might evolve together in ways that are mutually reinforcing.

DATA-COLLECTION AND MEASUREMENT ISSUES

Complete Network Studies

Complete or whole networks take a global view of social structure, including information on all actors in the population, and all existing ties among these actors. Data collection of these networks begins from a list of included nodes and includes data on the presence or absence of relations between every pair of nodes. There are many, many examples of such networks. For instance, Padgett's Florentine families included data on several relations for all 16 actors in a set of families. These data were taken from a much larger study in Padgett and Ansell (1993), which contained archival data on eight types of relations among elite Florentine families in the 15th century to show how some of the families, particularly the Medicis, used economic ties to secure political support from geographically neighboring families, and used marriage and friendship ties with more distant families to build and maintain the family's status.

For complete network studies, network data may be collected on the basis of documentary or electronic records, but for unipartite networks, actors are commonly asked to respond to a survey. In that case, actors are presented with one or more name generator items for which they are asked to identify other individuals with whom they have a relationship consistent with the name generator. For instance, in a study of workplace structure, respondents might be presented with a name generator item such as: "In this organization, with whom do you work closely to ensure that you complete your work-based tasks?" Respondents might then provide names using simple recall, or if the organization is small enough, they might be given a list of people in the organization and asked to tick of those consistent with the name generator. The name generator item then measures network ties with that particular content.

Egocentered Network Studies

Egocentered network data focus on the network surrounding one actor, commonly known as *ego*. Relational ties are usually measured if they involve the ego as well as, perhaps, ties among the *alters* (those actors directly connected to ego). What results from such studies are isolated personal networks centered at a number of (usually sampled) ego respondents.

Such studies are much cheaper and quicker to conduct than complete network studies, and can be done in conjunction with larger-scale studies of associations among a variety of psychological variables (such as the effects of network ties and socioeconomic status on loneliness in teenaged children).

Egocentered network data can certainly include multiple relations—for example, different types of support (emotional, financial) flowing between egos and their alters. Good examples of such studies can be found in the work of Wellman (see Wellman, 1979; Wellman & Wortley, 1990). Typically, the respondents are treated as the units of analysis and the egocentered networks are either analyzed directly or a quantified into a few measures to be used as explanatory variables.

Network Boundary

Which actors belong in the set of actors in a complete network study? This basic question defines the network boundary (Laumann, Marsden, & Prensky, 1983) and involves important research decisions. Sometimes a boundary can be specified because all people within the boundary are known (e.g., all members in a work team, all students in a school); but there are occasions in which the boundary is imprecise because the membership is uncertain (e.g., key individuals involved in the development of health policy, sex workers in a city who are HIV-positive.) A clear boundary means that all possible ties are known and can potentially be measured. When boundaries are not clear, some form of snowball sampling may be useful. For instance, to identify individuals involved in major decisions about health policy, it might be helpful to start with known key players and ask them to specify others who they know are involved. Then the newly identified actors can also be interviewed in another wave of sampling, until eventually no new actors are mentioned.

Other Measurement Considerations

For a complete unipartite network study, having decided on a network boundary, a number of important considerations need to be determined by the researcher. The types of questions that need to be addressed include the following:

- What are the types of relationships to be studied? What are appropriate name generators?
- What are the individual-level factors that will be measured (i.e., the actor attributes)?
- Are there tie covariates that need to be considered? These are covariates relating to pairs of actors that might help explain the presence of network ties (e.g., in an organizational study, the formal hierarchy; in an environmental study, geographic distances between individuals).
- Will the study be conducted cross-sectionally, or perhaps longitudinally to examine the coevolution of attributes and structure?

Bipartite Networks

Yet a social system does not comprise simply one type of actor. For instance, individuals may be associated with organizations, and the system could include both as actors. A bipartite network is a representation of associations, whereby individuals are associated with particular groups. In such a network, there are two types of actors, with a relational tie present to represent association. So in a bipartite network, there are ties between nodes of different types but not among nodes of the same type. Similarly, when there are three types of nodes, we will have tripartite networks or, more generally, k-partite networks.

Multivariate Networks

A social system is based not just on one type of relationship. As Robins and Pattison (2005) observed, human relationships are complex and multifaceted, and relationships between two people can take many forms and serve many different purposes. It is often an error to conflate different types of relational ties into the one relationship for the purposes of understanding networks. What is often important in understanding social systems is the manner in which different types of relational ties associate or disassociate with one another. For instance, positive and negative ties (i.e., ties relating to cooperation and ties relating to antagonisms, respectively) can obviously produce different outcomes for a dyadic relationship, and the way in which they are structured across a social system may have implications for how that system operates. A system in which all negative ties are between two groups of individuals is more likely to produce intergroup conflict than a system in which negative ties are dispersed more homogeneously among positive ties. It can also be useful to distinguish between ties that involve some level of positive affect or trust, such as friendship and trust, and ties that are more instrumental, such as information exchange or work collaboration.

Longitudinal Networks: Coevolution of Structure and Attributes

Social systems are never stagnant and exhibit ongoing change across time as relationships come in and out of existence. In this sense, social systems are stochastic and do not evolve to some optimal point at which they settle into a fixed structure. This is not to say that the systems are random or that they are not stable; rather, they may operate quite systematically across time according to their own internal logics whereby ties change on the basis of certain stochastic rules. Overall global structures may be reasonably stable and consistent across time even when underpinning local structures exhibit change as ties appear and disappear.

Hence, it is often desirable to observe networks across time in a panel study, together with measures of attributes. This enables the study of coevolution of ties and attributes. Selection and influence are two processes that involve both network ties and individual attributes, but the sequencing of events differs. In selection, the presence of individuals with similar attributes leads to a network tie; in influence, the presence of a network tie leads to changes of attributes toward similarity. There is no reason to suppose that both processes may not proceed in parallel, along with network self-organizing processes. The network then may exhibit ongoing change through stable processes, as both network ties and individual attributes evolve across time in ways that are possibly linked; in other words, we may see the coevolution of network structure and attributes (Snijders, Steglich, & Schweinberger, 2007).

Other Network Measurements

Sometimes network studies are small scale, based on workplaces or schools with well-defined boundaries, in circumstances in which individuals are in reasonable proximity. In these circumstances, geographic distances may not be an immediate concern. Some network studies on the other hand involve virtual systems, such as the Internet or electronic communications, in which geographic distance may be largely or completely irrelevant. Typically, these types of network studies do not incorporate the geographic distance between individuals or their specific locations. In social systems more generally, however, individuals are distributed across geographic space in ways that may be important to the formation or maintenance of network ties or that may have independent effects on the spread of information, behaviors, and even diseases. Geospatial variables may be an important element when the geography is not homogeneous, so that people in different places experience different environmental or economic circumstances. The simultaneous examination of networks and geospatial effects is a

relatively new development in social network research and one that is of potentially major importance for environmental issues.

STRUCTURAL ANALYSIS AND ANALYTIC TECHNIQUES

Data Representation

The most common ways to represent network data are as an edge list or an adjacency matrix. In both cases, actors in the network are given an identification (ID) number. An edge list simply lists the pairs of IDs for those actors between whom there is a tie. It is often more useful analytically to represent the same information in matrix form, where the rows and columns are the ID numbers and the matrix cells contain a one (or possibly a value) to indicate a tie from the row actor to the column actor. In an adjacency matrix, it is usual to have zeroes on the diagonal, so that self-ties are not permitted.

Several software packages can undertake network analytic techniques and create network visualizations. Two of the most prominent are *UCINET* and *Pajek*.

Centrality

Centrality is an indicator of how important an actor is in the network. The most common measures used to assess centrality include degree, betweeness, and closeness; prestige is an analogue to centrality but focuses on choices received (which differ from choices made when a relation is directed). Degree centrality is simply the normalized degree of each node in the network. Betweeness centrality, first used by Freeman, measures the extent that a node falls on the shortest path between two other nodes and is typically averaged across all the possible pairs in the network (Wasserman & Faust, 1994, Chapter 5). This measure relates to ideas of information flow throughout the network; individuals with a higher betweeness scores can potentially block or assist information transfer. Closeness centrality measures how directly or indirectly connected a node is to all the nodes in the network. This measure relates to how efficiently information can spread through a network even when individuals are not connected to one another. As mentioned, prestige is based on directed relationships; actors that have large indegrees or are chosen by actors with large prestige are more prestigious than other actors.

Dyads and Triads

Pairs of nodes are a focus in the study of reciprocity or mutuality. Threesomes of nodes, and their incidental ties, are of interest in the study of transitivity.

For a directed relation, there are only three types of dyads: dyads with no ties between the pair of nodes (a null dyad), dyads with one tie (asymmetric), and dyads with two ties (mutual). The counts of null, asymmetric, and mutual dyads for a network are often referred to as the *dyad census*, and this is a simple, yet basic way to describe a network. Similarly, there are a limited number of *patterns* for triads in a network (for a full description, see Wasserman & Faust, 1994, Chapter 6); counts of these different types of triads are referred to as the *triad census*.

Another useful triadic index is the clustering coefficient that identifies the extent of network closure. It is the proportion of complete triangles compared with the number of two-paths that could have been closed into triangles (for a discussion of how this index compares with a more traditional index of transitivity, see Wasserman, 2010).

Roles and Positions

We mentioned earlier the determination of blockmodels based on structurally equivalent nodes. Other definitions of equivalence can be used (see Wasserman & Faust, 1994, Chapter 10). Finding sets of exactly equivalent nodes is difficult, if not impossible. Accordingly, a number of algorithms have been developed to find approximately equivalent classes of nodes. In essence these, different approaches provide various clusterings of nodes on the basis of the adjacency matrix. Many of these techniques are provided in *UCINET*; more recent ideas populate *Pajek*.

Cohesive Subgroups and Connectivity

Often researchers wish to identify cohesive subgroups of actors—subgroups of nodes with greater density of ties among the nodes than in the graph as a whole. We mentioned such identification earlier in the section Basic Network Concepts in which we presented the concept of a clique. Cliques are generated via a stringent definition of a cohesive subset; hence, there have been a number of longstanding generalizations in graph theory, including *n*-cliques, *n*-clans, *k*-cores, *LS*-sets, and lambda sets, all of which are discussed in Wasserman and Faust (1994, Chapter 7). All of these can be applied to empirical data using *UCINET*.

An issue with many of these subgroup definitions and resulting algorithms is that they allow overlapping memberships, so, for instance, an actor may belong to many cliques. This makes good theoretical sense because in social systems group membership may indeed overlap. For analytic purposes, however, researchers often wish to have disjoint–nonoverlapping subsets of nodes to enable simple comparisons between them, including comparisons on the basis of actor attributes (e.g., Do actors in some subgroups have higher performance than others?). Accordingly, it may be more convenient to use methods that partition the nodes, such as equivalence and blockmodeling techniques, or the growing number of algorithms designed to detect *community structure* (Newman & Girvan, 2004; see also Kolaczyk, 2009, Chapter 4). *UCINET* can be used to study the connectivity of the network by examining geodesic distributions and other measures of graph reachability and distance.

STATISTICAL MODELS

We begin with a graph (or a directed graph), a single set of nodes $\mathcal{N}$, and a set of lines or arcs $\mathcal{L}$. It is common to use this mathematical concept to represent a *network*. We use the notation of Wasserman and Faust (1994, especially Chapters 13 and 15). There are extensions of these ideas to a wide range of networks, including multiple relations, affiliation relations, valued relations, and social influence and selection situations, all of which can be found in Carrington, Scott, and Wasserman (2005).

The statistical modeling of social networks is advancing quite quickly. The many exciting new developments include, for instance, longitudinal models for the coevolution of networks and behavior (Snijders et al., 2007) and latent space models for social networks (Hoff, Raftery, & Handcock, 2002).

Background

An area of rapid growth in network analysis has been the development and use of new statistical models for social networks. A recent, comprehensive review of this research can be found in Kolaczyk (2009). In this chapter, we concentrate on two statistical models that we consider to be of interest to psychological researchers: the exponential family of random graph models for cross-sectional network data (known as p^*) and stochastic actor-oriented models for longitudinal network data. Both models permit inferences about the structure of an empirical social network, including associations between individual attributes and network tie variables. Using these models, statistical inferences can be made about such research questions as the following:

- Do relationships of trust among humans tend to be reciprocated or are they hierarchical?
- Are shared job attitudes associated with work collaboration?
- Does common drinking behavior among adolescents lead to friendship, or do adolescent binge drinkers learn their drinking behavior from their friends?

Network statistical models often have some important differences from the standard statistical approaches typically used by psychological researchers. Usually, psychologists rely on general linear model techniques that have an assumption of independence of observations. Independence is useful technically because it enables simple likelihood functions and relatively straightforward estimation from empirical data. Networks, however, imply *dependence* among observations. For instance, in the spread of HIV, whether an individual is HIV-positive is not independent of others but crucially depends on the HIV status of sexual partners. So, individuals within a network cannot be assumed to be independent of one another.

Less obviously, network ties cannot necessarily be assumed to be independent of each other. If the research interest is to understand network structure (e.g., the patterns of sexual relationships that might

affect HIV spread), then we cannot suppose that social ties come into being or disappear without taking into account other social ties. An individual's possible sexual relationships are not necessarily independent of each other: For instance, a monogamous individual's sexual relationship precludes other relationships forming. To make the point more generally, a network-based social system implies dependence among possible ties; otherwise there is no systemic element to it. With dependence, however, then various patterns of ties become possible in a systematic way. Accordingly, one of the issues facing the development of network statistical models has been how to formulate models that express dependence among network tie variables.

An Exponential Family of Random Graph Distributions

Statistical models for social networks have at their basis a probability distribution of graphs. Early work on distributions for graphs was quite limiting, forcing researchers to adopt assumptions of independence among tie variables (see Wasserman & Faust, 1994, Chapters 13–16). As noted, it is hard to accept the standard assumption common in much of the literature, especially in physics, of complete independence and then to adopt the misnamed and overly simplistic *random graph* (Erdös–Renyi) distribution as a basis for empirical modeling. The random graph distribution, often referred to as a *Bernoulli graph*, assumes no dependencies at all among the random components of a graph.

The breakthrough in statistical modeling of networks was first made by Frank and Strauss (1986), who proposed what they termed a Markov random graph model. This model had explicit dependence among tie variables that permitted parameters for the presence of network ties, stars, and triangles in the graph. Further developments, especially commentary on estimation of distribution parameters, were given by Strauss and Ikeda (1990). In the 1990s, Wasserman and Pattison (1996) elaborated the model, describing a more general family of distributions. Pattison and Wasserman (1999); Robins, Pattison, and Wasserman (1999); and Anderson, Crouch, and Wasserman (1999) further developed this family of models, showing how a Markov parametric assumption gives just one, of many, possible sets of parameters. This family, with its variety and extensions, became known as p^* or exponential-family random graph models (ERGM). The parameters (which are determined by the hypothesized dependence structure) reflect structural concerns, which are assumed to be governing the probabilistic nature of the underlying social or behavioral process.

The p^* label (first used by Wasserman & Pattison, 1996) derives from the research on statistical modeling commenced by Holland and Leinhardt (1981) with their dyadic independence p_1 model.

Statistical theory.   A network is a set $\mathcal{N} = \{1, 2, \ldots, g\}$ of g actors and a collection of r relations that specify how these actors are related to each other. We let χ denote a particular relation defined on the actors (here, we let $r = 1$). As defined by Wasserman and Faust (1994, Chapter 3), a network can also contain a collection of attribute characteristics, measured on the actors. A binary relation can be represented by a set of ordered pairs recording the presence or absence of relational ties between pairs of actors. This binary relation can be represented by a $g \times g$ matrix X, with elements

$$X_{ij} = \begin{cases} 1 \text{ if } (i, j) \in \chi, \\ 0 \text{ otherwise.} \end{cases} \tag{1}$$

We assume throughout that X and its elements are random variables, so that any observed single relational network can be regarded as a realization $\mathbf{x} = [x_{ij}]$ of X. Typically, these variables are assumed to be interdependent, given the interactive nature of the social processes that generate and sustain a network. Much of the work over the past decade has been on explicit hypotheses underlying different types of dependencies among the $\{X_{ij}\}$.

In fact, one of the new ideas for network analysis, utilized by the p^* family of models is a *dependence graph*, a device that allows one to consider which elements of X are independent. Wasserman and Robins (2005) discussed such graphs at length. A dependence graph is also the starting point for the Hammersley–Clifford theorem, which posits a general probability distribution for network random variables using the postulated dependence graph. The exact form of the dependence graph depends on

the nature of the substantive hypotheses about the network under study. The full description of dependence graphs is beyond the scope of this chapter, but further details can be found in Robins and Pattison (2005).

The Hammersley–Clifford theorem (for a summary, see Wasserman & Robins, 2005) establishes that a probability model for X depends only on the cliques of the dependence graph D. In particular, application of the Hammersley–Clifford theorem yields a characterization of $Pr(\mathbf{X} = \mathbf{x})$ in the form of an exponential family of distributions,

$$Pr(\boldsymbol{X} = \boldsymbol{x}) = \left(\frac{1}{\kappa}\right) \exp\left(\sum_{A \subseteq \mathcal{D}} \lambda_A \prod_{(i,j) \in A} x_{ij}\right), \tag{2}$$

where

- $\kappa = \sum_{\mathbf{x}} \exp\left\{\sum_{A \subseteq \mathcal{D}} \lambda_A \prod_{(i,j) \in A} x_{ij}\right\}$ is a normalizing quantity;
- $\mathcal{D}$ is the dependence graph for X; the summation is over all subsets A of nodes of $\mathcal{D}$;
- $\prod_{(i,j) \in A} x_{ij}$ is the sufficient statistic corresponding to the parameter λ_A; and
- $\lambda_A = 0$ whenever the subgraph induced by the nodes in A is not a clique of $\mathcal{D}$.

Different dependence assumptions result in different types of configurations. Frank and Strauss (1986) first showed that configurations for Markov dependence were edges, stars of various types (a single node with arcs going in or out), and triangles or triads. The model in effect supposes that the observed network is built up from combinations of these various configurations, and the parameters express the presence (or absence) of the configurations in the observed network. For instance, a strongly positive triangle parameter is evidence for more triangulation in the network, implying that networks with large numbers of triangles have larger probabilities of arising.

There are a variety of dependence graphs well known in the literature. One general and simple member of the p^* family is the Bernoulli graph in which ties are assumed to be independent of each other. For directed networks, dyadic independence assumptions propose that there is dependence only within but not between dyads: Holland and Leinhardt's (1981) p_1 is an example. Markov dependence as introduced by Frank and Strauss (1986) assumes that ties involving the same actor are dependent: precisely X_{ij} and X_{kl} are conditionally independent if and only if $\{i, j\} \cap \{k, l\} = \emptyset$. Because of the similarity to the dependence inherent in a Markov spatial process, such a random graph was labeled *Markov* by Frank and Strauss (1986).

One can also formulate dependence graphs when data on attribute variables measured on the nodes are available. If the attribute variables are taken as fixed, with network ties varying depending on the attributes, then models for social selection arise (Robins, Elliott, & Pattison, 2001). If, on the other hand, the network is assumed fixed, with the distribution of attributes dependent on the pattern of network ties, the outcomes are models for social influence (Robins, Pattison, & Elliott, 2001).

Parameters.   Limiting the number of parameters is wise—one can either postulate a simple dependence graph or make assumptions about the parameters. The usual assumption is *homogeneity*, in which parameters for isomorphic *configurations* of nodes are equated.

Even with homogeneity imposed, models may not be identifiable. Typically, parameters for higher order configurations (e.g., higher order stars or triads) are set to zero (equivalent to setting higher order interactions to zero in general linear models).

As mentioned, Markov random graph models were indeed a breakthrough in moving toward more realistic dependence assumptions. But recently it has been shown that Markov dependence is often inadequate in handling typical social network data. Frequently, parameters arising from Markov dependence assumptions are consistent with either complete or sparse networks, which are unhelpful in modeling realistic data. Several authors have provided technical demonstrations of this problem (Handcock, 2002; Park & Newman, 2004; Robins, Pattison, & Woolcock, 2005; Robins, Snijders, Wang, Handcock, & Pattison, 2007; Snijders, 2002; Snijders, Pattison, Robins, & Handcock, 2006).

Snijders et al. (2006) proposed a method of combining counts of all the Markov star parameters into one statistic, with geometrically decreasing weights on the higher order star counts so that they did not dominate the calculation. The resulting parameter is termed a *geometrically weighted degree parameter* or an *alternating k-star parameter* (the term alternating comes from alternating signs in the calculation of the statistic.) Various versions of this new degree-based parameter have been proposed (see Hunter, 2007, who shows the linkages between them), but whatever the precise form of the parameter, it permits greater heterogeneity in the degree distribution. As a result, it is more capable of modeling high-degree nodes than a small number of low-order Markov star parameters. Such parameters appear to greatly increase the *fittability* of models. In addition, the introduction of *k-triangles*, configurations with k separate triangles sharing one edge, the base of the k-triangle, has helped model-fitting immensely. These configurations also introduce a new distribution of graph features (alongside the degree distribution and the geodesic distribution): the *edgewise shared partner distribution*. A summary of these more recent developments can be found in Robins, Snijders, et al. (2007). For further elaborations, see Hunter and Handcock (2006).

The introduction of k-triangles is based on a new dependence assumption, termed *social circuit dependence* (Robins, Snijders, et al., 2007; Snijders et al., 2006). Two tie variables are assumed to be conditionally dependent if when observed they would form a four-cycle. This assumption supposes that dependence emerges from the observed data, so it is somewhat different from previous assumptions. It makes theoretical sense, however, that in a social system the presence of certain network ties would affect the contingencies among other possible network ties.

Simulation, Estimation, and Goodness of Fit

It is relatively straightforward to simulate p^* models and estimate parameters, using long-established statistical approaches such as the Metropolis algorithm (Snijders, 2002) implementation of a Markov chain Monte Carlo. As first noted by Anderson et al. (1999), if the model is not degenerate, the algorithm will "burn-in" to a stationary distribution of graphs reflecting the parameter values in the model. It is then possible to sample a number of graphs from this distribution and look at typical features of them, for instance, the density, the geodesic distribution, the frequencies of various triads, and so on (Robins, Pattison, et al., 2007). In other words, although the model is based on certain configurations, the graphs from the distribution typically will exhibit certain other features of interest that can be investigated.

These models are especially appealing not only because they are readily simulated but also because the parameters can be estimated from available data. In the past, p^* models were fitted using pseudo-likelihood estimation on the basis of logistic regression procedures (for a review, see Anderson et al., 1999; Strauss & Ikeda, 1990). Although pseudo-likelihood can provide information about the data, especially in terms of identifying major effects (Robins, Snijders, et al., 2007), when close to degeneracy or when dependency is strong, the precise pseudo-likelihood parameter estimates are likely to be misleading.

A more reliable way to fit the models is through Markov chain Monte Carlo Maximum Likelihood Estimation (MCMCMLE). There are various algorithms possible to do this (see Hunter & Handcock, 2006; Snijders, 2002). Although the technical details are complicated, the underlying conceptual basis is straightforward. MCMCMLE is based on simulation (hence, the MCMC part of the acronym). A distribution of graphs is simulated from an initial guess at parameter estimates. A sample from the resulting graph distribution is compared with the observed graph to see how well the observed graph is reproduced by the modeled configurations. If it is not well reproduced, the parameter estimates are appropriately adjusted. If the model is well behaved, this procedure usually results in increasingly refined parameter estimates, until finally the procedure stops under some criterion. We do note one large difference between Markov models and models containing parameters from the new specifications: The new specifications are more likely to be well behaved and result in convergent parameter estimates.

Once estimates have been obtained, the model can be simulated and assessed. The assessment is accomplished by comparing a statistic calculated from the observed graph to the distribution of the statistic generated by the model. This can be seen as a (rather demanding) goodness-of-fit diagnostic for

the model. It is also an approach that permits judgments about how well competing models might represent the network (Hunter, Goodreau, & Handcock, 2008).

Currently, three programs are publicly available for the simulation, estimation, and goodness of fit of p^* models:

- the *stocnet* suite of programs from the University of Groningen http://stat.gamma.rug.nl/stocnet/ (especially *SIENA*)
- the *statnet* program from the University of Washington http://csde.washington.edu/statnet
- the *pnet* program from the University of Melbourne http://www.sna.unimelb.edu.au

Longitudinal Models

When data have been collected in longitudinal panel designs with appropriately selected actor attribute and network tie variables, the possible coevolution of network structure and attributes can be examined. Because of the longitudinal data, social influence and social selection effects can be differentiated using stochastic actor-oriented models (SAOM) for network evolution (Snijders et al., 2007). The models are based on Markov chains of latent changes in attributes given the network structure, and latent changes in network ties given the attributes, using simulation procedures. Parameter estimates are adjusted to compare with the observed panel data, so that the estimates produce the most likely series of changes consistent with the effects in the model and the panel data. The final parameter estimates in effect relate to those series of changes that are probabilistically most likely within this simulation. The models are actor oriented in the sense that each actor is assumed to wish to change the social environment to a more optimal form: Such a change occurs in attributes or in structure, contingent on the structure and other attributes in the actor's local social network. For instance, in a study of the social effects of obesity, there might be a parameter for an actor to change their eating habits based on the habits of their friends and to change their friendships to those who share their eating habits. With both these parameters in the model, it is possible to distinguish whether people choose friends with similar eating behaviors or adapt their eating behaviors to conform to those of their friends (or indeed both).

We do not provide full detail of SAOMs in this review chapter. Interested readers should consult Snijders, van de Bunt, and Steglich (2010) who provide a tutorial-style article that explains recent developments. When longitudinal network data are available, these models should be increasingly of interest to psychological researchers. For instance, Selfhout et al. (2010) used an SAOM to determine how the personality traits of adolescents affected the development of social relationships within schools. There has already been extensive work on the coevolution of social structure among school children and health behaviors, such as smoking and drinking, with a focus on identifying both selection and influence effects (e.g., Mercken, Snijders, Steglich, Vartiainen, & de Vries, 2010). These examples illustrate the potential for psychological research to benefit from application of SAOMs in the right contexts.

CONCLUSION

Network theoretical and analytic approaches have reached a new level of sophistication in recent years, accompanied by a rapid growth of interest in adopting these approaches in social science research generally. Of course, much psychological research focuses on individuals but there are often situations in which the social environment—and more generally, the social system—affects individual responses. In these circumstances, to treat individuals as isolated social atoms, a necessary assumption for the application of standard statistical analysis, is to risk poor inference. Network methods should be part of the theoretical and analytic arsenal available to psychological researchers in such domains.

References

Anderson, C. J., Crouch, B., & Wasserman, S. (1999). A *p** primer: Logit models for social networks. *Social Networks, 21*, 37–66.

Barabasi, A.-L. & Albert, R. (1999). Emergence of scaling in random networks. *Science, 286*, 509–512. doi:10.1126/science.286.5439.509

Burt, R. S. (1992). *Structural holes: The social structure of competition.* Cambridge, MA: Harvard University Press.

Burt, R. S. (1987). Social contagion and innovation, Cohesion versus structural equivalence. *American Journal of Sociology, 92*, 1287–1335.

Carrington, P. J., Scott, J., & Wasserman, S. (Eds.). (2005). *Models and methods in social network analysis.* New York, NY: Cambridge University Press.

Cartwright, D., & Harary, F. (1956). Structural balance: A generalization of Heider's theory. *Psychological Review, 63*, 277–293.

Doreian, P., Batagelj, V., & Ferligoj, A. (2005). *Generalized blockmodeling.* New York, NY: Cambridge University Press.

Freeman, L. C. (2004). *The development of social network analysis: A study in the sociology of science.* Vancouver, British Columbia, Canada: Empirical Press.

Frank, O., & Strauss, D. (1986). Markov graphs. *Journal of the American Statistical Association, 81*, 832–842.

Granovetter, M. S. (1973). The strength of weak ties. *American Journal of Sociology, 78*, 1360–1380.

Handcock, M. S. (2002). Statistical models for social networks: Degeneracy and inference. In R. Breiger, K. Carley, & P. Pattison (Eds.), *Dynamic social network modeling and analysis* (pp. 229–240). Washington, DC: National Academies Press.

Heider, F. (1946). Attitudes and cognitive organization. *Journal of Psychology, 21*, 107–112.

Hoff, P., Raftery, A., & Handcock, M. (2002). Latent space approaches to social network analysis. *Journal of the American Statistical Association, 97*, 1090–1098.

Holland, P. W., & Leinhardt, S. (1981). An exponential family of probability distributions for directed graphs. *Journal of the American Statistical Association, 76*, 33–65.

Hunter, D. R. (2007). Curved exponential family models for social networks. *Social Networks, 29*, 216–230.

Hunter, D., Goodreau, S., & Handcock, M. (2008). Goodness of fit of social network models. *Journal of the American Statistical Association, 103*, 248–258.

Hunter, D., & Handcock, M. (2006). Inference in curved exponential family models for networks. *Journal of Computational and Graphical Statistics, 15*, 565–583.

Jackson, M. O. (2008). *Social and economic networks.* Princeton, NJ: Princeton University Press.

Kirke, D. M. (2007). Social network analysis and psychological research. *Irish Journal of Psychology, 28*, 53–61.

Kolaczyk, E. D. (2009). *Statistical analysis of network data: Methods and model.* New York, NY: Springer.

Laumann, E. O., Marsden, P. V., & Prensky, D. (1983). The boundary-specification problem in network analysis. In R. Burt & M. Minor (Eds.), *Applied network analysis* (pp. 18–34). Beverly Hills, CA: Sage.

Lazarsfeld, P. F., & Merton, R. K. (1954). Friendship as a social process: A substantive and methodological analysis. In M. Berger, T. Abel, & C. H. Page (Eds.), *Freedom and control in modern society* (pp. 18–66). Princeton, NJ: Van Nostrand.

Mercken, L., Snijders, T. A. B., Steglich, C., Vartiainen E., & de Vries, H. (2010). Dynamics of adolescent friendship networks and smoking behavior. *Social Networks, 32*, 72–81.

Milgram, S. (1967). The small world problem. *Psychology Today, 22*, 61–67.

Monge, P. R., & Contractor, N. (2003). *Theories of communication networks.* New York, NY: Oxford University Press.

Moreno, J. L., & Jennings, H. H. (1938). Statistics of social configurations. *Sociometry, 1*, 342–374.

Newman, M. E. (2003). The structure and function of complex networks. *SIAM Review, 45*, 167–256.

Newman, M. E., & Girvan, M. (2004). Finding and evaluating community structure in networks. *Physical Review E, 69*, 026113. doi:10.1103/PhysRevE.69.026113

Padgett, J. F., & Ansell, C. K. (1993). Robust action and the rise of the Medici, 1400–1434. *American Journal of Sociology, 98*, 1259–1319.

Park, J., & Newman, M. (2004). Solution of the 2-star model of a network. *Physical Review E, 70*, 066146. doi:10.1103/PhysRevE.70.066146

Pattison, P. E., & Wasserman, S. (1999). Logit models and logistic regressions for social networks: II. Multivariate relations. *British Journal of Mathematical and Statistical Psychology, 52*, 169–193.

Robins, G. (2009). Understanding individual behaviors within covert networks: The interplay of individual qualities, psychological predispositions, and network effects. *Trends in Organized Crime, 12*, 166–187.

Robins, G. L., Elliott, P., & Pattison, P. E. (2001). Network models for social selection processes. *Social Networks, 23*, 1–30.

Robins, G., & Kashima, Y. (2008). Social psychology and social networks. *Asian Journal of Social Psychology, 11*, 1–12.

Robins, G. L., & Pattison, P. (2005). Interdependencies and social processes: Generalized dependence structures. In P. Carrington, J. Scott, & S. Wasserman (Eds.), *Models and methods in social network analysis* (pp. 192–214). New York, NY: Cambridge University Press.

Robins, G. L., Pattison, P. E., & Elliott, P. (2001). Network models for social influence processes. *Psychometrika, 66*, 161–189.

Robins, G., Pattison, P., Kalish, Y., & Lusher, D. (2007). An introduction to exponential random graph ($p*$) models for social networks. *Social Networks, 29*, 173–191.

Robins, G. L., Pattison, P. E., & Wasserman, S. (1999). Logit models and logistic regressions for social networks, III. Valued relations. *Psychometrika, 64*, 371–394.

Robins, G. L., Pattison, P. E., & Woolcock, J. (2005). Social networks and small worlds. *American Journal of Sociology, 110*, 894–936.

Robins, G. L., Snijders, T. A. B., Wang, P., Handcock, M., & Pattison, P. E. (2007). Recent developments in exponential random graph ($p*$) models for social networks. *Social Networks, 29*, 192–215.

Selfhout, M., Burk, W., Branje, S., Denissen, J., van Aken, M., & Meeus, W. (2010). Emerging late adolescent friendship networks and Big Five personality traits: A social network approach. *Journal of Personality, 78*, 509–538.

Simmel, G. (1908). Soziologie, Untersuchungen uber die Formen der Vergesellschaftung. In K. H. Wolff (Ed. & Trans.), *The sociology of Georg Simmel.* New York, NY: Free Press.

Snijders, T. A. B. (2002). Markov chain Monte Carlo estimation of exponential random graph models. *Journal of Social Structure, 3*, 2.

Snijders, T. A. B., Pattison, P. E., Robins, G. L., & Handcock, M. S. (2006). New specifications for exponential random graph models. *Sociological Methodology, 36*, 99–153.

Snijders, T. A. B., Steglich, C. E. G., & Schweinberger, M. (2007). Modeling the co-evolution of networks and behavior. In K. van Montfort, H. Oud, & A. Satorra (Eds.), *Longitudinal models in the behavioral and related sciences* (pp. 41–71). New York, NY: Erlbaum.

Snijders, T. A. B., van de Bunt, G. G., & Steglich, C. E. G. (2010). Introduction to stochastic actor-based models for network dynamics. *Social Networks, 32*, 44–60.

Strauss, D., & Ikeda, M. (1990). Pseudolikelihood estimation for social networks. *Journal of the American Statistical Association, 85*, 204–212.

Wasserman, S. (2010). Mr. Holland's networks: A brief review of the importance of statistical studies of local subgraphs or one small tune in a large opus. In *Festschrift upon the retirement of Paul Holland.* Princeton, NJ: Educational Testing Service.

Wasserman, S., & Faust, K. (1994). *Social network analysis: Methods and applications.* New York, NY: Cambridge University Press.

Wasserman, S., & Pattison, P. E. (1996). Logit models and logistic regressions for social networks: I. An introduction to Markov random graphs and *p**. *Psychometrika, 61*, 401–425.

Wasserman, S., & Robins, G. L. (2005). An introduction to random graphs, dependence graphs, and *p**. In P. J. Carrington, J. Scott, & S. Wasserman (Eds.), *Models and methods in social network analysis* (pp. 148–161). New York, NY: Cambridge University Press.

Watts, D. J. (1999). *Small worlds: The dynamics of networks between order and randomness*. Princeton, NJ: Princeton University Press.

Watts, D. J. (2003). *Six degrees: The science of a connected age*. New York, NY: W.W. Norton.

Watts, D. J. (2004). The "new" science of networks. *Annual Review of Sociology, 30*, 243–270.

Watts, D. J., & Strogatz, S. H. (1998). Collective dynamics of "small-world" networks. *Nature, 393*, 440–442.

Wellman, B. (1979). The community question: The intimate networks of East Yorkers. *American Journal of Sociology, 84*, 1201–1231.

Wellman, B., & Wortley, S. (1990). Different strokes from different folks: Community ties and social support. *American Journal of Sociology, 96*, 558–588.

White, H. C., Boorman, S. A., & Breiger, R. L. (1976). Social structure from multiple networks: I. Blockmodels of roles and positions. *American Journal of Sociology, 87*, 517–547.

Using Data Collected by Others

## CHAPTER 24

SECONDARY ANALYSIS AND ARCHIVAL RESEARCH: USING DATA COLLECTED BY OTHERS

David W. Stewart

There are very few genuinely new research questions. Whatever the topic, it is likely that someone or some organization has collected some relevant information. In some cases, this information might provide an immediate and direct answer to a current research question. More often, the existing information will provide an important starting point for additional research. Information about a large array of topics is available from numerous sources. Published academic research and government information in the form of reports or raw data addresses a wide range of topics in economics, demography, health care, geography, social behavior, and media use, among others. In addition, there is a vast array of documents and data that has been archived for historical and record-keeping purposes. These documents include meeting minutes of government bodies and other organizations, permits obtained from and contracts filed with government entities, voting records, court proceedings, tax records, and a host of other information. There also exists a large and diverse commercial industry devoted to gathering information for specific purposes. This industry consists of survey research firms, media research agencies, consulting firms, think tanks, professional associations, and similar organizations.

Research that makes use of these many preexisting sources of information is known as *secondary analysis*, or, in the case of information that has been archived for historical or legal reasons, *archival research*. The reason for the name *secondary analysis* is because the analysis of the information is for a purpose other than that for which the data were originally collected.

In contrast to *primary research*, in which a researcher collects information directly relevant to and for the purpose of answering a specific research question, secondary analysis focuses on the use of information that was collected for some other purpose to answer specific questions. The sources of such preexisting information are known as *secondary sources* to contrast them with data collected primarily for a specific purpose, or primary research.

Secondary research can also be divided into custom research and syndicated research. Custom research involves secondary analysis that is conducted for one or more specific organizations, and circulation of this research is generally limited to the sponsoring organization. On the other hand, some research providers use secondary research, primary research, or both to create data and reports that are available to whomever is willing to pay for the report. This latter type of research is called *syndicated research*. Many organizations offer syndicated research reports or data ranging from government agencies like the Census Bureau to commercial organizations that charge a substantial fee for access to the information that they provide. The issues that arise in using and evaluating custom secondary research and syndicated secondary research are similar, but it is important to recognize that some secondary analysis begins with the results of secondary analyses of others.

SECONDARY ANALYSIS

Secondary analysis involves the use of sources of data and other information collected by others and

DOI: 10.1037/13621-024
APA Handbook of Research Methods in Psychology: Vol. 3. Data Analysis and Research Publication, H. Cooper (Editor-in-Chief)

473

archived in some form. Secondary information offers relatively quick and inexpensive answers to many questions. Such information may take a variety of forms. It may be little more than a copy of a published report. In some cases, it may involve a repackaging or reanalysis of data. For example, a number of commercial research providers obtain government data, such as that obtained by the Census Bureau, and develop specialized reports, create convenient data access capabilities, or combine data from multiple sources into a single source. Such repackaged research is often sold as syndicated research because it is made available to multiple users. Other syndicated data providers may obtain information from nongovernment sources. For example, several commercial research providers obtain electronic scanner information from retailers and package it to provide reports on the sales, prices, and other features of retail products for retailers and manufacturers.

In contrast to research providers who offer only secondary research, in which data and information are obtained from other sources, a significant segment of this industry consists of organizations that collect their own information and make it available, often at a price, to other organizations. For example, some commercial research providers collect information about product awareness and preference and customer satisfaction for entire industries and sell reports of this research to other organizations. Although these firms are engaged in primary research, the users of the information to whom they provide are engaged in secondary analysis. Similarly, some organizations offer reports of large-scale tracking studies of media usage habits, lifestyles, and eating habits and health-related behavior. Such research would be considered primary research by the provider but represents secondary research to users because they did not materially participate in the design and analysis of the research.

Like most research tools and methods, secondary analysis has both advantages and disadvantages. Secondary research and analysis generally offers a faster and less expensive means for obtaining information than would be the case if a researcher were to undertake primary research. Because data and reports are already available, they can be obtained

within days, hours, and, in the age of the Internet, often minutes. Because the cost of data collection and reporting has been covered, or, in the case of syndicated research, can be shared by all of the organizations that might be interested, secondary research tends to be less expensive than comparable data obtained through primary research. On the other hand, secondary research may not provide the specific information required for a given purpose and it may not be as timely as data that are obtained in response to an immediate question.

Secondary analysis can also provide a useful starting point for additional research by suggesting problem formulations, research hypotheses, and research methods. Secondary analysis can increase the efficiency of research expenditures by identifying significant gaps in knowledge. Secondary analysis may also provide a useful tool for making comparisons. New data may be compared with existing data to examine differences or trends. It may provide a basis for determining whether new information is representative of a population, as in the case of sampling. Comparison of the demographic characteristics of a sample to those of a larger population, as specified by the Bureau of the Census, may reveal how representative the sample is of the larger population.

On the other hand, there are significant disadvantages associated with secondary analysis, at least for some purposes. The underlying data may not address the research question of interest. Even if the data do address the research question of interest in a general way, the way in which the data were collected, the manner in which variables were defined, or the sample from which the data were obtained may not be appropriate for the research question. If data collection, variable definition, and the sample are appropriate, the passage of time may make the data less relevant for an immediate research question.

THE COMPLEMENTARITY OF SECONDARY AND PRIMARY RESEARCH

In most research situations, primary and secondary research are used in a complementary fashion, rather than as substitutes for one another. Research efforts generally begin with a question or set of objectives. These objectives are met and the research question is answered through the acquisition of information. The source of the information—whether it is secondary source or primary research—is really not important as long as the information is trustworthy and answers the question at hand. In fact, it will be less expensive and time-consuming to use secondary sources. Frequently, however, at least some of the questions at hand have not been answered by prior research; answering these questions requires primary research. In these cases, secondary research helps define the agenda for subsequent primary research by suggesting which questions require answers that have not been obtained in previous research. Secondary data may identify the means by which the primary research should be carried out: (a) questions that should be addressed, (b) measurement instruments such as questionnaires and measurement scales, and (c) relevant respondents.

SOURCES OF SECONDARY RESEARCH AND DATA

There are many sources of secondary data and reports. Online searches using Google, Bing, or other search engines often reveal many relevant sources. There are also specialized online vendors that provide access to and search capabilities for locating secondary sources relevant to particular research questions. An example of such a commercial vendor is Proquest (http://www.proquest.com/en-US), which allows researchers to search nearly 3,000 worldwide business periodicals that cover business and economic conditions; management techniques; theory and practice of business; as well as advertising, marketing, economics, human resources, finance, taxation, and computers, among other topics. Such sites typically require a subscription or charge users per search.

In contrast, there are websites that provide access to social science research, including research papers not yet published, that do not charge for a search or charge a nominal fee. One example of the latter is the Social Science Research Network (SSRN) electronic library, which is composed of a number of specialized research networks in the social sciences.

Topics covered by networks include accounting, economics, financial economics, legal scholarship, and management (including negotiation and marketing). The SSRN eLibrary consists of an abstract database containing abstracts of scholarly working papers and forthcoming papers, and an electronic paper collection of downloadable full-text documents in portable document format (PDF). Access to the database and collection is free; some services may require registration or fees (http://papers.ssrn.com/sol3/DisplayAbstractSearch.cfm). Barker, Barker, and Pinard (2010) provided a useful and highly accessible introduction to the use of the Internet as a tool for finding information as well as the limitations and cautions that go hand in hand with an open and largely unregulated medium like the Internet.

There are a number of "metasites" online that provide a large array of links to other sites. Some of these sites are accessible without cost and others require a subscription or fee. These sites differ with respect to their focus, scope, and attention to the quality of information available in the linked sites. There are, in fact, many such sites. Exhibit 24.1 provides a list of some of the more representative broad-based metasites.

Government Sources of Information

Some of the most reliable and comprehensive sources of secondary data are government sources. Much of the data provided by the U.S. government is collected by the Census Bureau, which employs elaborate quality controls. Although best known for its work on the population census, which occurs every 10 years, the Census Bureau conducts a wide array of other censuses and surveys. It is also the primary collector of data for many other government agencies, such as the Bureau of Labor Statistics. Exhibit 24.2 provides a list of some of the more general government sources of information and data and associated webpages.

One of the larger sectors of the U.S. economy and an area of significant research activity in the social sciences and other fields is health and human services. The U.S. government as well as many other state and local governments and commercial organizations collect and disseminate an enormous

---

Exhibit 24.1
Representative Metasites for Finding Secondary Sources in the Social Sciences

- **Data and Information Services Center** (http://www.disc.wisc.edu): Provides links to more than 700 searchable online data sources, including government and nongovernment sources. This site is maintained by the University of Wisconsin–Madison. Online links are related to economics, demographics, politics, education, health, education, history, sociology, and geography, among others. Includes both United States and international sources.
- **Econdata.Net** (http://www.econdata.net): This site, which is sponsored by the U.S. Economic Development Administration, is designed to be a first stop for researchers who need demographic, social, and economic information at the state and substate level.
- **Intute** (http://www.intute.ac.uk): A catalog of thousands of searchable websites in the social sciences and other disciplines. Hosted by a consortium of universities in the United Kingdom, this site is an outstanding source of high-quality international information. This site includes links to sources related to agriculture, business and management, communications, the creative and performing arts, education, law, medicine, engineering, and the physical sciences as well as the social sciences.
- **Lexis-Nexis** (http://www.lexisnexis.com): Like Proquest, Lexis-Nexis is a commercial database for which a subscription is required. Lexis-Nexis provides links to legal literature, including judicial decisions as well as information relevant to for business and market analyses, selected academic literature and government reports, and data sets related to demographic and economic variables.
- **Population Reference Bureau** (http://www.prb.org): This website provides summaries of information, including charts, maps, rankings and graphs for a wide array of demographic, social, health, economic, environmental, and family structure data for the United States and the world. This site also includes teaching resources, including lesson plans and teaching guides, for use in designing course modules using such data.

Exhibit 24.2
General Sources of Government Data

- **U.S. Census Bureau** (http://www.census.gov): This general website for the Census Bureau provides links to reports, data summaries, and raw data for all of the censuses conducted by the Bureau, including the decennial census and the several economic censuses. The site also provides links to the American Community Survey, an ongoing survey that provides annual data about a wide array of population characteristics, and to the Population Estimates Program, which provides estimates of population statistics between censuses.
- **FedStats** (http://www.fedstats.gov): A well-organized source of statistical information available from more than 100 U.S. government agency sites. Includes links to information on agricultural production, health care, industries, crime and judicial data, education, energy, labor force, housing, poverty, children, aging populations, and tax returns, among others.
- **USA.gov** (http://www.usa.gov/Topics/Reference_Shelf/Data.shtml): A website provided by the U.S. Department of Commerce. It is designed to be a single point of access to information about business, trade, and economics from across federal government agencies.
- **EDGAR** (http://www.sec.gov/edgar.shtml): Maintained by the Securities and Exchange Commission, this website is a repository for the filing of annual and quarterly reports by all publicly traded corporations in the United States. It is a good source of information about individual companies.
- **United Nations Statistics Division** (http://unstats.un.org/unsd/default.htm): The United Nations serves as a repository for social, economic, population, energy, crime environment, geographic, and health care data from countries around the world. It also provides an online gateway to statistics relevant to its member nations (http://data.un.org).

---

amount of information and data regarding health and disease, health-related behaviors, quality of life, and human development. Exhibit 24.3 provides a brief description of several online sources of secondary data related to heath and human services.

Commercial and Nonprofit Information Providers

In the 21st-century information-driven economy, there is a huge commercial industry involved in the collection, analysis, and reporting of information for various purposes. Much of the data are of high quality and are used by businesses and policy makers for decision making. However, such data also can and have been used to address important basic research questions and to test theories. Although much of this type of data is available only for a fee, commercial providers often have programs for providing access to their data to academic researchers and students. In addition, various nonprofit centers maintain data sources and will often provide access to the data for no or a modest cost. Exhibit 24.4 offers a brief description of five different commercial and nonprofit providers of secondary data.

Exhibit 24.3
Selected Online Sources of Health and Human Services Information

---

- **National Center for Health Statistics** (http://www.cdc.gov/nchs): The National Center for Health Statistics' website, operated by the Centers for Disease Control and Prevention, provides a deep and diverse portal for information about health and health care. Health statistics provided on this site include information related to the health status of the population, experiences with the health care system, enumeration of health problems, the impact of health policies, and trends in health care delivery systems.

- **World Health Organization** (http://www.who.int/research/en): The most comprehensive guide to world health. This website includes worldwide national statistics for 70 core indicators on mortality, morbidity, risk factors, service coverage, and health systems; data on chronic diseases and their risk factors for all World Health Organization member states; standardized data and statistics for infectious diseases at country, regional, and global levels; and links to local and region information of member nations.

- **National Center for Educational Statistics** (http://nces.ed.gov): The National Center for Education Statistics is the U.S. agency with primary responsibility for collecting and analyzing data related to education. This website includes information on a wide array of education issues including reports and raw data.

- **Child Trends Databank** (http://www.childtrendsdatabank.org): The Child Trends website is maintained by a nonprofit research organization dedicated to providing research and data to inform decision making that affects children.

- **Department of Health and Human Services Gateway to Data and Statistics** (http://www.hhs.gov): Designed to complement other U.S. government data resources, this website provides links to academic research, government reports, and databases related to health, poverty, special populations, and family and community services.

Exhibit 24.4
Representative Commercial and Nonprofit Sources of Secondary Information

---

- **Easy Analytic Software, Inc.** (http://www.easidemographics.com/index.asp): A commercial data provider that organizes demographic data by geography and life-stage cluster. Information includes data from Mediamark Research, which includes comprehensive demographic, lifestyle, product usage, and media exposure, to all forms of advertising media collected from a single sample of more than 26,000 households.

- **Roper Center for Public Opinion Research** (http://www.ropercenter.uconn.edu): The Roper Center, housed at the University of Connecticut, is one of the largest archives of social science data, with particular emphasis on data from public opinion surveys. Data date from the 1930s, when survey research was in its infancy, to the present. Most of the data are related to the United States, but more than 50 nations are represented in the archives.

- **The Economist Intelligence Unit** (http://www.eiu.com/index.asp?rf=0): The Economist Intelligence Unit provides a constant flow of information, data, analysis, and forecasts related to social, economic, demographic, and political variables on more than 200 countries and six key industries.

- **A. C. Nielsen** (http://www.nielsen.com): Nielsen is one of the largest providers of data on product purchase and use, retail sales, media use, online and mobile telephone use, and other information about consumer behavior. Data and reports are available for much of the world. The site offers Nielsen Scholastic Services, which provides programs, data, curriculum materials, and other resources for faculty members and students.

- **IMS** (http://www.imshealth.com/portal/site/imshealth): IMS is one of the largest commercial providers of information about health care and health care products. IMS provides worldwide data on the sale and prescription of pharmaceutical products and medical devices, disease and treatment patterns, and industry trends.

The listings of various secondary data sources in Exhibits 24.1 through 24.4 are by no means comprehensive. Rather, they are intended to provide examples of more general information sources. There are other general sources as well, and a huge number of highly specialized sources. Whatever the topic, there is likely to be a secondary source of information that can be used as a first point of analysis for a research question. Whatever the source of the data and the type of analysis to be undertaken, however, it is important to carefully evaluate the integrity and reliability of the data before proceeding with an analysis.

EVALUATING SECONDARY SOURCES

Not all information obtained is equally reliable or valid. Information must be evaluated carefully and weighted according to its credibility and how recent it was obtained. Fortunately, the same questions that arise in the evaluation of secondary sources also arise in the context of primary research. The only difference is that these questions must be addressed retrospectively in the case of secondary research, whereas they should be addressed prospectively in the case of primary research. It is also important to recognize that information may simultaneously be valid for drawing some conclusions and invalid for drawing other conclusions. Research is not uniformly valid or invalid; rather, it is only valid or invalid with respect to specific questions.

When evaluating secondary source information six questions must be answered: (a) Why was the study or data collection effort undertaken? (b) Who obtained the information? (c) What information or data were actually collected? (d) During what time period was the information or data collected? (e) By what method(s) was the information or data obtained? (f) How consistent is the information or data with that found in other sources? In answering these basic questions other, more specific questions will arise. These more specific questions include the source(s) of the data, measures used, the time of data collection, and the appropriateness of analyses and conclusions. Use of these six generic questions can provide a means for assessing the validity of research for any given purpose.

Why Was the Study or Data Collection Effort Undertaken?

Information is rarely collected without some intent. The intent of a particular data-collection effort significantly influences the data collected and findings produced by any analysis. Data collected to further the interests of a particular group or organization are especially suspect. For example, the results of survey reported by a lobbyist organization seeking support for a particular policy position is likely to be less objective than results of research carried out by a neutral third party. Unfortunately, it is not always easy to determine when vested interests have influenced the design of prior research. Even when researchers are more neutral, it is possible for biases and frames of reference to influence research outcomes. The degree of precision, the types of classifications or categories used, and the method by which data are collected and reported are often dictated by the intent of the study. Thus, in evaluating research,

a researcher conducting a secondary analysis must always ask whether the purpose of the study was to reach a predetermined conclusion or whether the primary researcher was potentially influenced by a strong point of view.

Even when data are not collected for purposes of advocating or supporting a particular position, the purpose of a study may confound the interpretation of the data. Consider the following example. The best-known measure of price movements in the United States is the Consumer Price Index (CPI) calculated monthly by the U.S. Bureau of Labor Statistics. This index is based on the prices of about 80,000 items of consumption in more than 200 categories. The price of each item contributing to the index is calculated by surveying urban wage earners and clerical workers in some base year and computing the average price paid for each item (Greenlees & McClelland, 2008). The index represents an average for a representative family of four (father, mother, and two children under the age of 18) living in an urban but not a rural area (Johnson et al., 2001). Thus, although the index is a useful point of reference for making comparisons over time, it is not representative of the expenditures of most families. It is only a rough index of what is happening to purchasing power and is not often useful for specific decisions for which a high degree of precision is required or for which expenditure patterns are different from those used to define the index.

The purpose of the original data-collection effort also has an influence on its credibility. Some data are collected to product quick-and-dirty results intended only to provide direction for decision making or rough approximations. Such results may be perfectly appropriate in the context in which the data were collected but may lack the precision or reliability required by other research questions.

Who Obtained the Information?

Information from certain sources may be more credible than information from others. This arises not just from the biases that may be at work but also from differences in technical competence, resources, and quality. Some organizations have developed reputations for high quality control work and for the integrity of their data. Others have reputations for poor work. Generally, those sources of high integrity will provide sufficient information about how the information was obtained to enable a review of the technical adequacy of the data. Learning about the reputations of various sources of information requires investigating their previous work. Contacting clients and others who have used information supplied by the organization will also provide some indication of the reputation of an organization. One might also examine the training and expertise present in an organization supplying the information.

As noted, it is also worthwhile determining whether the organization that sponsored or conducted the research had a vested interest in any particular outcome. For example, an organization that reports a study of its own effectiveness might have a vested interest in accentuating the positive. A rather sizable industry exists to produce what is often called *advocacy research*. Such research is not designed to produce unbiased answers to questions. Rather, the research is conducted to provide support for a particular conclusion or position. Although such research may still yield insights, it must be interpreted with caution.

What Information or Data Was Actually Collected?

In the early 1950s, a congressional committee published an estimate of the annual "take" from gambling in the United States. The figure, $20 billion, was actually picked at random. One committee member was quoted as saying, "We had no real idea of the money spent. The California Crime Commission said $14 billion. Virgil Peterson of Chicago said $30 billion. We picked $20 billion as the balance of the two" (Singer, 1971). This is an example of information entered into the public record that had no empirical basis. No data were collected at all; only a couple of opinions were sought and averaged. *Mythical numbers* are more common than one would wish. These mythical numbers, estimates derived from pure guesswork, represent the extreme case, but they emphasize the need for asking what information was actually collected in the primary research effort.

There are frequently big differences in the frequencies with which individuals actually engage in a behavior, as measured by actual observation and counting and self-reported frequencies (Gosling, John, Robins, & Craik, 1998). This is not just because people want to look better to others by overreporting socially desirable behaviors and underweighting undesirable behavior, although that certainly happens. It is also the case that the limitations of human memory and selective attention biases distort self-report behavior (Schwarz & Vaughn, 2002). This does not mean that self-reported data are never useful. Indeed, there are many behaviors that are not easily observed by others, and such information as perceptions, preferences, opinions, and attitudes are accessible only by the person that holds them. This handbook includes several chapters on self-report and observational data that elaborate on the relative advantages and disadvantages of such data (see Volume 1, Chapters 12–16, this handbook; Chapter 21 of this volume).

The context in which data are collected may also influence the results. Consider a study of consumer preferences that found 60% of all consumers preferred Brand A. Such a finding is impressive until one learns that brands B and C, the major competitors of A, were not included on the list from which consumers were to select a product. Voter preferences may appear very different depending on how the question is asked (e.g., "Do you prefer candidate A to candidate B?" vs. "Do you approve of candidate A?"). Relative judgments often produce different results from absolute judgments and relative judgments may differ depending on the point of comparison. There are many contexts in which relative judgments are the most useful because they better mirror behaviors of interest. This is especially true in the context of voting behavior and product choices for which someone might select the "lesser of evils."

Many of the things researchers wish to measure cannot be observed directly. In such circumstances, it may be possible to obtain an estimate indirectly, by using a surrogate measure that is observable and assumed to be related to the more interesting phenomenon. The critical assumption of such indirect measurement techniques is that there is a relationship between the observable measure and the unobservable event of interest. Even when this

479

assumption is correct, however, the relationship may be decidedly less than perfect. Consider studies of the success of graduates of corporate training programs. Success is difficult to measure because it involves a variety of dimensions and can be measured at many different points in time.

One organization may report results using turnover during the year following completion of the training program. A second organization may use rapidity of advancement within the organization and salary increases over a 3-year period. Still another organization may use ratings of success by supervisors after 6 months on the job. In each case, the data may be used to relate completion of the training program to success on the job. Yet the relationship reported may vary widely from one study to another. The differences in the findings are attributable to the data that were actually collected not what these data were interpreted to mean. Knowing what information was actually obtained is often useful for reconciling conflicting results.

Even when direct measurement is possible, the ways in which data are defined and classified may confound the interpretations made. Categorizations and classifications may vary widely, and their relevance and meaning for a particular purpose must always be investigated. For example, what is a family? Is a single, self-supporting person living alone a family? Are unmarried cohabitants a family? For some purposes and in some studies, the answer is likely to be yes, whereas in other cases, the answer is likely to be no. Apparent inconsistencies across studies often have more to do with the operational definition of terms than the actual differences in the underlying phenomena. Such problems hinder the effective comparison of results across studies and therefore affect the generalizabilty of conclusions that can be drawn from secondary analysis.

During What Time Period Was the Information or Data Collected?

In a study of the perception of the price of long-distance telephone calls, it was found that consumers were very much aware of the price of long-distance calls and very sensitive to even small rate hikes. The results of the study might be interpreted as an indication that consumers are very price sensitive. The study, however, was carried out while an intense, highly publicized debate over a telephone price hike was raging, a debate that included several prominent politicians involved in a political campaign. It is likely that the results of the study would have been different had the study been carried out when there was less publicity about telephone rates.

Time is an important factor to be considered when evaluating information. As in the telephone rates example, factors present at the time of information collection may influence the results obtained. Time may also influence the definition of measures. For example, in the context of retailing activity, when is a sale made? Does the sale occur upon the placement of an order, receipt of the order, time of shipment, time of delivery, date of billing, date of payment, or the date payment is actually recorded? Are returned items, which can account for 20% of all sales in some product categories, included or excluded in the measurement of sales? Different accounting systems place emphasis on different points in time and produce differences in information. Shifts in the point of time when measurements are taken may have pronounced effects on the results obtained.

Time may also make information obsolete. Technological changes may change perceptions; lifestyles may change. Sooner or later, most data become obsolete and of interest only for historical purposes. How quickly data become obsolete depends on the type of data, the purpose for which they are used, and changes in the environment over time. The user of secondary information should always know when data were collected, however, particularly because there may be a time lag between data collection and the availability of results.

By What Method(s) Was the Information or Data Obtained?

The quality of any research cannot be evaluated without knowledge of the methodology employed when collecting the data. This is no less true of secondary data. Information about the size and nature of samples, response rates, experimental procedures, validation efforts, questionnaires, interview guides or protocols, and analytic methods should be available in sufficient detail to allow a knowledgeable critique of the data collection procedure. For example, it has become fashionable for many periodicals to publish questionnaires for readers to complete and return. The responses are then complied and reported in the publication. Although these surveys may make entertaining reading, it is not clear to whom the results apply. How are readers of particular publications different from the general population? One would certainly expect very different responses on certain topics from readers of *Playboy* and readers of the *Christian Science Monitor*. It is not even reasonable to generalize such results to all readers of the magazine; the people who elect to respond may differ from those who did not. Many organizations report results of surveys of their customers or clients. Such surveys may be quite useful, but indicate nothing about individuals or organizations that are not customers or clients.

If observations of behavior or activity are reported, who did the observation and under what circumstances? Are the data based solely on human observation or is there a written or electronic record? How representative were the circumstances under which the observations occurred? Was there potential for the very act of observation to influence the outcomes? For example, in evaluating classroom-teaching performance, were the teacher and students aware that the observation was occurring? Did the teacher have prior notice of the observation, which might have provided an opportunity for preparation that might not otherwise be typical?

The question of sampling and sample design— that is, how people are selected for participation in a survey—is a critical issue for the evaluation of survey data because it deals with the question of the generalizability of results. It is also important to determine who responded and the response rate. A survey with a response rate of 80% is certainly more credible than one with a 5% response rate, all else being equal. Given that a result was obtained in a particular study, can that result be considered representative of some larger population? What is the nature of that population? All too frequently in examining secondary data it is impossible to identify that larger population. A description of the sampling procedure is always necessary when evaluating the usefulness of data. For example, suppose that it was

reported by an independent research firm that 60% of subjects given a choice between a charter school and a traditional public school selected the charter school. This result is impressive for the charter school but becomes questionable if it were determined that all of those sampled lived in an area with a high number of students enrolled in the charter school.

How Consistent Is the Information or Data With That Found in Other Sources?

When information obtained from multiple independent sources is consistent, confidence in that information is increased. Whether evaluating data obtained from secondary sources or the results of primary research efforts, the best strategy is to determine the extent to which the information is consistent with information obtained from other sources. Ideally, two or more independent sources should arrive at the same or similar conclusions. When disagreement among sources does exist, it is helpful to identify reasons for such differences and to determine which source is more credible. This is not always easy, even with relatively complete information. Nevertheless, careful analysis of the secondary sources may reveal reasons for the inconsistency that lead to greater insights. For example, different measures may have been employed or data may have been obtained at different points in time. On the other hand, when radically different results are reported and little basis for evaluating the information-collection procedure is found, it is appropriate to be skeptical of all of the data.

ARCHIVAL DATA

To this point, this chapter has largely focused on the reanalysis of data or research reports originally collected for purposes of research. The original research that gave rise to the data or research report may have had a different purpose than that of the intended secondary analysis, but the process that gave rise to it included a research design that when adequately described provides a basis for evaluating the integrity, relevance, and generalizability of the underlying data and reported results. There are many other sources of secondary information, however, that do not originate in a formal research process. Government, corporate, and church records; reports and filings; personal correspondence; medical treatment records; minutes of meetings; court records; and genealogical records are all examples of written documents that may be archived and used for secondary analysis. Archives may also include photographs, video and audio recordings, oral histories, maps, furniture, architectural drawings, and land surveys, among others. Indeed, almost any artifact can become the basis for archival research.

Although it might seem that archival research is most useful for conducting historical analysis, and a great deal of archival research is of a historical nature, archival data also lend themselves to other types of secondary analyses. For example, a robust stream of research on the economics and sociology of organizational relationships rests on the secondary analysis of legal contracts (MacNeil, 1978). Tax records, which are collected for government record keeping and legal purposes, have been used in a secondary analyses to evaluate the effects of different tax policies over time and across different political units on such things as philanthropic giving, entrepreneurial activity, and investment in research and development by corporations. The spectrum of research topics that has been addressed by secondary analysis is broad and limited only by the imagination and creativity of researchers.

The secondary analysis of archival records and artifacts brings special problems, however. Because the underlying data or artifact was not created by a formal research process, there is a need to understand the reasons for its existence as well as why it was saved or survived. The context in which the underlying data were created also is important to understanding its meaning. Authenticating the archival artifact can be a challenge, especially for such things as personal correspondence, written accounts of events, and even visual media such as photographs.

ANALYTIC TECHNIQUES

Secondary analysis can take many forms. Generally the primary determinants of the analysis are the research question itself and the characteristics of the underlying data. Identifying information relevant to a particular research question is only the first step in secondary analysis. In an age of instant access to information, it is easy to become overwhelmed by information. Finding order and meaning in a plethora of information is often difficult, particularly when there are inconsistencies, omissions, and differences in methods among various sources. A common problem faced by researchers employing secondary analysis is that of combining the findings and conclusions of several sources of information. The synthesis of information is an important skill and was long criticized for its lack of objectivity (Glass, 1977).

Secondary analysis can range from simple descriptive reporting of results, to new analyses of underlying data, to efforts to combine different sources of information to construct an answer to a new research question, to efforts to integrate a body of literature to reconcile contradictions and draw conclusions about the presence or absence (and strength) of specific effects or variables. A number of authors have addressed specific approaches to the analysis of secondary sources (e.g., Bulmer, Sturgis, & Allum, 2009; Smith, 2008; Stewart & Kamins, 1993). The most common approaches to secondary analysis are (a) descriptive analysis, (b) interpretive analysis, (c) comparative analysis, (d) verification, (e) reanalysis of data, and (f) integration through analysis of research design and setting (*meta-analysis*).

Descriptive analysis involves describing the attributes, findings, and conclusions of past research. There is little effort to integrate or interpret the underlying data beyond reporting what was found and perhaps counting or otherwise summarizing various results. For example, a review of surveys of schools undertaken by different researchers that provides the numbers of students with particular special education needs and the number and types of programs offered to such students would be an example of a descriptive analysis.

In contrast, *interpretive analysis* seeks to go beyond the data or particular set of findings to develop a larger meaning of the underlying data. For example, in the analysis of a survey of schools, the secondary analyst might go beyond mere description to related program availability to classroom success and draw conclusions about the relative efficacy of program types. Interpretive analysis is especially common in archival research in which there is a need to place a particular artifact or set of artifacts within a social, cultural, or economic context. Interpretive research often seeks to identify a larger meaning of an artifact by identifying its social or cultural significance and origins.

Comparative analysis focuses on the identification of similarities and differences across sources and data-collection efforts. Comparisons may involve analyses of differences over time or among social groups or regions. In such cases, comparative analysis may be combined with primary research in a replication or restudy of the original research to follow up the original sample or to make comparisons with additional groups, settings, or circumstances. An example of comparative analysis is found in Di Gropello (2006), who used secondary data to analyze the effects of decentralization of school management in Central America and compare centralized management systems with decentralized management systems. Key conclusions of this analysis, which was sponsored by the World Bank, were that decentralized, school-based management models produce greater community involvement and greater effort on the part of teachers while still producing learning outcomes as high as in traditional schools despite being located primarily in the poorest and more isolated areas.

Verification is similar to comparative analysis but with the more limited objective of substantiating prior results. The prior results provide the point of comparison to which new data are applied. For example, in examining the efficacy of a particular treatment for a psychological disorder, secondary analysis of medical records may demonstrate that efficacy is similar to what had previously been demonstrated in more controlled clinical research.

Among the more common types of secondary analysis is *reanalysis* of the underlying data. Such reanalysis might take the form of applying different analytic tools or adding new variables obtained from other sources. More often, reanalysis involves asking new questions of the data that are different from the questions that gave rise to the original data-collection

effort. This involves approaching the data in ways that were not originally intended by using the data to investigate a different research question, theme, or topic. Generally, the more in-depth the material, and the more information that exists about the underlying data and how it was obtained, the greater the likelihood that the data's utility for addressing new questions can be evaluated. For example, data originally obtained for purposes of understanding access to health care among lower socioeconomic families might be used in secondary analysis to examine the impact of health access and health problems on the educational achievement of children in these families. This analysis might involve the use of data with respect to educational performance obtained in the original study or the combination of data from the health care study with other secondary data related to educational performance.

Finally, in the context of long-term streams of carefully designed research, it is often possible to use differences in the research designs of different studies to examine the relative influence of variables that contribute to the obtained outcomes of results. Such meta-analyses involve the statistical analysis of differences and similarities in both the design and results of different studies to identify the degree to which different effects and different design parameters (such a sample and type of measure) explain the pattern of results obtained across studies. There is a rich literature on the technical details of conducting meta-analysis (e.g., Borenstein, Hedges, Higgins, & Rothstein, 2009; Cooper, 2008). The chapters in this handbook on meta-synthesis and meta-analysis also provide a useful introduction and more technical information about performing such informative analyses (see Volume 2, Chapter 2, this handbook; Chapter 25 of this volume).

Ultimately, the type of secondary analysis that a researcher carries out must be dictated by the research question. In many applied contexts a simple descriptive analysis may be sufficient. In other situations, the research question may require integration across studies and sources but not at highly quantified and specific level. Secondary analysis that focuses on the testing and development of theory may require the quantitative precision of meta-analysis.

CONCLUSION

Secondary analysis and archival research are common in both academic research in the social sciences and in applied research designed to address practical policy and business question. The prudent user of such information will know what information is relevant for a given situation and will select an appropriate source of information. Even when information appears appropriate for answering a particular business question, it is important to evaluate the validity of the information by asking six generic questions: (a) Why was the study or data collection effort undertaken? (b) Who obtained the information? (c) What information or data were actually collected? (d) During what time period was the information or data collected? (e) By what methods(s) was the information or data obtained? and (f) How consistent is the information or data with that found in other sources? Answers to these questions will indicate whether information is reliable and appropriate and will also establish the limits of the information and the degree to which additional information may be required to answer the pending research question.

References

Barker, D. I., Barker, M., & Pinard, K. T. (2010). *Internet research—Illustrated* (5th ed.). Florence, KY: Course Technology.

Borenstein, M., Hedges, L. V., Higgins, J. P. T., & Rothstein, H. R. (2009). *Introduction to meta-analysis.* New York, NY: Wiley. doi:10.1002/9780470743386

Bulmer, M. I., Sturgis, P., & Allum, N. (2009). *The secondary analysis of survey data.* London, England: Sage.

Cooper, H. M. (2008). *Research synthesis and meta-Analysis: A step-by-step approach* (4th ed.). Thousand Oaks, CA: Sage.

Di Gropello, E. (2006). *A comparative analysis of school-based management in Central America* (World Bank Working Paper No. 72). Washington, DC: World Bank.

Glass, G. V. (1977). *Integrating findings: The meta-analysis of research.* Beverly Hills, CA: Sage.

Gosling, S. D., John, O. E., Robins, R. W., & Craik, K. H. (1998). Do people know how they behave? Self-reported act frequencies compared with on-line codings by observers. *Journal of Personality and Social Psychology, 74*, 1337–1349. doi:10.1037/0022-3514.74.5.1337

Greenlees, J. S., & McClelland, R. B. (2008). Addressing misconceptions about the consumer price index. *Monthly Labor Review, 131*, 3–19.

Johnson, D. S., Rogers, J. M., & Tan, L. (2001). A century of family budgets in the United States. *Monthly Labor Review, 124*, 28–45.

MacNeil, I. R. (1978). Contracts: Adjustment of long-term economic relations under classical, neoclassical, and relational contract law. *Northwestern University Law Review, 72*, 854–905.

Schwarz, N., & Vaughn, L. A. (2002). The availability heuristic revisited: Ease of recall and content of recall as distinct sources of information. In T. Gilovich, D. Griffin, & D. Kahneman (Eds.), *Heuristics and biases: The psychology of intuitive judgment* (pp. 103–119). New York, NY: Cambridge University Press.

Singer, M. (1971). The vitality of mythical numbers. *Public Interest, 23*, 3–9.

Smith, E. (2008). *Using secondary data in educational and social research.* Maidenhead, England: Open University Press.

Stewart, D. W., & Kamins, M. A. (1993). *Secondary research: Information sources and methods.* Thousand Oaks, CA: Sage.

## CHAPTER 25

META-ANALYSIS

Jeffrey C. Valentine

Meta-analysis (literally, *after* or *beyond* analysis) is a statistical technique for combining the results of multiple studies. In this chapter, I provide a context for thinking about the logic of meta-analysis and show how it is often a better approach to determining what a collection of studies says about a relationship, especially when conducted in conjunction with a research synthesis. I will demonstrate how to carry out a meta-analysis, using techniques that are analogous to the analysis of variance (ANOVA) and multiple regression procedures with which many readers will already be familiar. I will also discuss several important methodological and statistical considerations, including the choice of error model in meta-analysis, options for handling violations of the assumption of statistical independence, moderator tests, and publication bias. All of these issues have been described in greater detail in Cooper, Hedges, and Valentine (2009).

To set the stage for the discussion that follows, imagine that you are interested in the effects of programs that pair an adult (called a *mentor*) with a child (called a *mentee*) for the purpose of providing the mentee with an extrafamilial adult relationship in hopes of fostering positive development. Many studies have been conducted on the effectiveness of such interventions. How should you use the available studies to help you answer the question of whether mentoring is an effective intervention?

METHODS USED TO UNDERSTAND WHAT STUDIES SAY ABOUT A RELATIONSHIP

Let me begin with the observation that the decision to synthesize a group of studies is an important one that needs careful consideration. That is, there is no reason to ask what a group of studies reveal about a relationship unless those studies are similar at a useful level of abstraction.[1] Determining this is not easy. As Hume (1739/1740) argued about identity in general, whether a group of studies are "the same" or "different" will depend on one's perspective. If we focus on relatively abstract characteristics, such as whether the studies all employed mentoring, and whether mentoring meant more or less the same thing across studies, then we are more likely to see synthesis of those studies as a valid activity. If we focus on concrete operational details, such as the average amount of time mentors and mentees met per month, we may be more likely to see the programs as different because studies will likely vary quite a bit along these dimensions. This implies that there is often no single correct answer to the question of whether it makes sense to synthesize a group of studies.

As much as judgment will always play a role in determining whether a synthesis is sensible, two strategies might be helpful. First, given sufficient understanding of the theoretical concerns relevant to a particular intervention, one strategy would be to use this as a basis for determining whether critical

[1]See Valentine et al. (2011) for an elaboration of this argument.

DOI: 10.1037/13621-025
APA Handbook of Research Methods in Psychology: Vol. 3. Data Analysis and Research Publication, H. Cooper (Editor-in-Chief)

program elements are consistent across studies. For example, I defined *mentoring* as an adult–child extra-familial relationship that is meant to foster positive development. If the studies all employ this definition (and therefore do not, e.g., include interventions in which peers mentored other peers) and are similar in other critical ways, then this might be an argument in favor of synthesizing the studies.

An alternative view was given by Glass (2000), who argued that the question of identity is actually empirical as opposed to logical. As long as studies seem to belong to the same general class of interventions, Glass argued that they are effectively "the same" if their effects on the dependent variable are the same. An even stronger version of this view is that one might consider programs to be "the same" if they are believed to (or in fact do) affect mediating variables in a similar way. If so, then it might make sense to consider the studies sufficiently conceptually similar that they support a synthesis (despite any other differences in the characteristics of the studies). Ultimately, because reasonable people can disagree about whether studies should be synthesized, it is critical that synthesists specify in detail (and preferably before data collection) the conditions under which studies will be synthesized. If one accepts the logic of this view it is still necessary to determine *how* studies should be synthesized.

In fact, scholars have used several different strategies to make inferences about what a research literature suggests regarding a relationship. Too often in the history of the clinical and social sciences, the strategies used have lacked explicit standards of proof and precision in both process and outcome (e.g., Johnson & Eagly, 2000; Rosenthal, 1984). For example, reviewers do not always declare in advance, or even after the fact for that matter, what pattern of results across studies will be used to accept or reject a hypothesis. The lack of openness in process runs counter to the usual scientific standards of transparency (which serve in part to support replication efforts). It also suggests that the conclusions drawn by reviewers could be the product of their own experiences, preferences, and cognitive algebra.

Two additional (and related) strategies have been employed to make inferences about what a research literature suggests regarding a relationship. In the first of these, an intervention is said to "work" if there are at least two good studies demonstrating that the intervention is more effective than some alternative. For example, Kirby (2001) reviewed studies of interventions targeting teen pregnancy rates and labeled the interventions as having "strong evidence of success" if, among other characteristics, the interventions had been found to be effective in at least two studies conducted by independent research teams. Similarly, the Collaborative for Academic, Social, and Emotional Learning (2003) assigned the highest ratings of effectiveness to interventions that demonstrated positive results in at least two studies. Such lists of effective programs are quite common.

A second strategy, more common in formal literature reviews than in the creation of lists of effective programs, is to use a method called a vote count. To conduct a vote count, the scholar gathers a set of studies that pertain to the research question and then determines what each study says about that relationship. In its most typical form, this determination is made on the basis of the statistical significance of the results. So, if Study A finds a statistically significant effect favoring the intervention, the synthesist casts a vote *for* the intervention. If Study B finds a statistically significant effect favoring the comparison condition, the synthesist casts a vote *against* the intervention. If Study C did not find a statistically significant difference between conditions, the synthesist casts an *undecided* vote. This process continues until the synthesist has polled all of the studies, at which point the category with the most votes *wins*.

Both of these strategies share similar strengths and drawbacks. In terms of the strengths of these approaches, both are relatively easy to implement and, at least on the surface, are intuitively appealing. On reflection however, their drawbacks are both obvious and disqualifying. Among other problems, the approach of labeling an intervention as *effective* if two studies have demonstrated effectiveness ignores the question of the number of times the intervention has been investigated. It is an entirely different thing if an intervention has been found to be effective in both of two studies that have been conducted, or if an intervention that has been found to be effective in two of the 40 studies that have been conducted.

Vote counting overcomes this problem by examining all of the evidence that the synthesist has collected (I explore a somewhat different question, whether the studies that the synthesist has are a biased set, later in the paper). Because studies typically do not have high statistical power, however, vote counting is an approach with an unacceptably high error rate (specifically, by failing to detect real intervention effects when they exist). In fact, Hedges and Olkin (1985) demonstrated the counterintuitive result that in many situations common in social research (i.e., interventions with moderate effects investigated in studies with moderate statistical power), vote counting on the basis of statistical significance can actually have *less* statistical power the *more* studies are available. In addition, the vote counting strategy does not differentially weight studies on the basis of sample size. This is a problem because a study with 100 participants and a study with 1,000 participants are given equal weight, even though the larger study provides the more precise and reliable estimate of the effect. Furthermore, the effect size of the studies reviewed is not considered. A study showing small negative effects is given the same weight as a study showing large positive ones; this is true of the at-least-two-studies approach as well. For these reasons, neither analytic approach is considered a credible analytic strategy for drawing inferences (Cooper & Dorr, 1995).

These strategies are also based on a misunderstanding (or, at least, a misuse) of the probability values arising from tests of statistical significance. When conducting a test of statistical significance for a relationship, the probability value is the chance of observing a relationship at least as large as the one observed, given a true null hypothesis (Cohen, 1994). The relationship between the probability values in one study and the likelihood of successful replication in even an exactly replicated second study is therefore not straightforward. If a study rejects the null hypothesis at $p = .05$, for example, that does not mean that an exact replication has a 95% chance of rejecting the null hypothesis (if the population and sample effect sizes are very similar, the probability is actually closer to 50%; see Greenwald, Gonzalez, Harris, &

Guthrie, 1996; Valentine, Pigott, & Rothstein, 2010).

As an alternative to these two strategies, the synthesist could carry out a *research synthesis* (also known as a *systematic review*), which is a form of research that involves a systematic approach to the identification, collection, coding, and evaluation of studies thought to be relevant to a research question; often, research syntheses culminate in a meta-analysis of the available evidence. In a research synthesis, the synthesists usually set out to collect all the research they believe addresses their research question and then use predetermined protocols to guide their work. These rules, for example, guide decisions regarding the strategies that are used to search for studies, the criteria for including studies in the review, and the operational definitions of study characteristics. They may also choose to use meta-analysis to synthesize the results of the studies that are found to meet inclusion criteria. Critically, the probability values from the studies that meet inclusion criteria are not of primary interest. Rather, the meta-analyst examines effect sizes.

EFFECT SIZE

An *effect size* is a measure of the strength of the relationship between two variables. Chapter 6 of this volume provides the computational details for the most common effect size metrics. Briefly, effect sizes can be unstandardized or standardized. Examples of unstandardized effect sizes include the finding that the average participant in the mentoring condition gained 0.25 more points in grade point average (GPA) than did controls, or that the average number of days of school attended was the same across intervention and control group.

Standardized effect sizes are used to express study results in a metric that is not directly tied to the original scale in which the outcome was measured. Most readers are familiar with the correlation coefficient (or *r*); it is a standardized effect size. Another standardized effect size is the standardized mean difference (also known as Cohen's *d*, the *d*-index, or simply *d*), which expresses differences between two means in terms of standard deviation units (often, the posttest standard deviation pooled across both groups).[2] An example would be to say that a mentoring intervention was associated with a *d*-index of + 0.25, which suggests an increase of 0.25 standard deviation units for the average child who received mentoring relative to the average child who did not receive mentoring. Finally, the odds ratio and its relatives (e.g., the risk ratio) are effect sizes that are used with two dichotomous variables (e.g., received mentoring vs. not; graduated from high school vs. not). The odds ratio expresses the odds of an event (e.g., graduating) in one group relative to the odds of the event in a second group.

THE BENEFITS OF META-ANALYSIS

I defined meta-analysis as a statistical technique for combining the results of multiple studies. Meta-analysis is conducted using open standards of proof, and is approached with the same structure and rigor as is data analysis in primary studies. It also effectively addresses several of the limitations of other inferential techniques. Specifically, meta-analysis takes into account all of the research that the synthesist has located that addresses the research question and uses statistical techniques analogous to ANOVA and multiple regression to summarize the results of the studies. To illustrate how a meta-analysis unfolds, assume that you have decided to conduct a research synthesis of studies that examine the effectiveness of mentoring interventions and that you plan to conduct a meta-analysis because you are persuaded about the limitations of other synthesis techniques. Therefore, you have (a) operationally defined the characteristics of studies that will be required for inclusion in your synthesis, (b) carried out an exhaustive search for relevant studies, and (c) carefully coded important characteristics of those studies (e.g., information about study design; sample characteristics). Your next step is to statistically summarize the results of the studies.

FIXED EFFECT META-ANALYSIS

One weakness of the vote count procedure is that all studies, regardless of their sample sizes, are assigned equal weight. This is problematic because we know

that studies with larger samples provide better estimates (i.e., have smaller standard errors) than those with small samples. In addition, the very idea that studies estimate the population parameter with varying degrees of precision presents a challenge for the statistical summary of the data. Techniques like ANOVA and multiple regression are based in part on the assumption that the residual variance associated with every observation is the same (the homoskedasticity assumption). The residual variance of an effect size is related inversely to the sample size with which the effect is estimated. Therefore, a collection of studies with varying sample sizes (which is almost always the case) will violate the assumption of homoskedasticity. Meta-analysis addresses the problems presented by studies with different sample sizes by weighting effect sizes. More specifically, studies are weighted in a way that gives relatively more influence to effect sizes that come from relatively larger sample sizes. These weights are then used to create a weighted mean effect size and confidence interval for the set of studies. The logic here is the same as the logic underlying weighted means in general. For example, assume you are interested in finding the average grades earned by students in a particular school. You survey one class of 15 and find a GPA of 3.5, and another class of 30 and find a GPA of 2.5. If you were to take the straight mean of the two classes, you would conclude that the average student has a GPA of 3.0. It is clear, however, that this strategy ignores the fact that your estimates are based on different sample sizes, and the resulting mean is different from the mean that could have been computed from the original student-level data.

A weighted mean overcomes this problem. The formula for computing a weighted mean is

$$\bar{Y} = \frac{\Sigma w_i Y_i}{\Sigma w_i}, \tag{1}$$

where $\bar{Y}$ is the weighted mean, w_i is the weight for each observation i, and Y_i is the mean for each observation i. To complete the example,

$$GPA = \frac{\Sigma w_i Y_i}{\Sigma w_i} = \frac{(15 \times 3.5) + (30 \times 2.5)}{15 + 30}$$
$$= \frac{52.5 + 75}{45} = 2.833. \tag{2}$$

---

[2]Hedges (1982) demonstrated that *d* is biased in small samples and suggested a correction to remove this bias. The resulting effect size is sometimes referred to as *g* or as Hedges's *g*.

Note that 2.833 is the same answer that would be obtained if the mean had been computed from the student-level data instead of the classroom-level data.

The formula for computing a weighted mean effect size in meta-analysis will now seem very familiar:

$$\overline{ES} = \frac{\Sigma w_i ES_i}{\Sigma w_i}, \tag{3}$$

where $\overline{ES}$ is the weighted mean effect size, w_i is the weight for study i, and ES_i is the effect size for each study i.

Computing Weights

In meta-analysis, the most common weighting scheme is known as the *inverse-variance* method, in which the weight given to a study is dependent on the variance of its effect size estimate. The variance of an effect size is computed as one over the square of its standard error. Given that larger studies have smaller standard errors, they will be given proportionally more weight in a meta-analysis.

The formulas for the variances of the common effect size metrics are given in Chapter 6 of this volume. Computing weights is then straightforward. Expressed generically, the weight for an effect size can be defined as

$$w = \frac{1}{v}, \tag{4}$$

where w is the study weight and v is the effect size variance. However, the variance (and hence the weight) are computed differently for different effect sizes. For the standardized mean difference (d), the weight is computed as

$$w = \frac{2n_1 n_2 (n_1 + n_2)}{2(n_1 + n_2)^2 + n_1 n_2 d^2}, \tag{5}$$

where n_1 and n_2 are the sample sizes for groups 1 and 2, and d is the standardized mean difference effect size for the study.

For the correlation coefficient, for statistical reasons these are transformed (to Fisher's z) for meta-analysis using the formula

$$z = .5 \times \ln\left(\frac{1 + r}{1 - r}\right). \tag{6}$$

Calculators for this statistic are available on the Internet, and in the appendixes of many statistical text books. The weight for a Fisher z-transformed correlation is simply $n - 3$, where n is the number of pairs of scores. For ease of interpretation, Fisher's z can be transformed back to a simple correlation.

The odds ratio also needs to be transformed before meta-analysis. Specifically, odds ratios are transformed to (natural) logged odds ratios. Almost any hand calculator will carry out this transformation, and calculators are also available on the Internet. The weight for a logged odds ratio is

$$w = \frac{abcd}{ab(c + d) + cd(a + b)}, \tag{7}$$

where a, b, c, and d correspond with the number of events in cells a, b, c, and d respectively (for a discussion of how to assign events to cells, see Chapter 6 of this volume). Like Fisher's z, logged odds ratios are transformed back to odds ratios (again by exponentiation).

It is worthwhile to examine the weights for each of these metrics a bit more closely. All of them depend on the sample sizes on which the effect sizes are based. In fact, with the exception of the standardized mean difference, the only variable that contributes to the computation of the weight is sample size (the standardized mean difference weight includes d^2 in the denominator, which has the effect of decreasing the weight given to a study with a large effect size relative to a study of the same size with a smaller effect size). As such, conceptually it is sufficiently accurate to think of meta-analysis as weighting effect sizes by (some function of) sample size.

Weighted Mean Effect Size

Once weights have been computed, a weighted mean effect size can be computed using Equation 3. Assume that your literature search yielded five studies on mentoring that met your inclusion criteria and measured well-being as an outcome. These studies are given in Table 25.1, along with their effect sizes (expressed in terms of the standardized mean difference) and sample sizes. The first step in the meta-analysis is to compute weights. An extended example showing how to do this is given in Table 25.1. The next step is to compute the

TABLE 25.1

Data and Computation of Weights for Mentoring Studies Examining Well-Being as an Outcome

1	2	3	4	5	6	7	8	9	10	11	12
						Numerator of d (Col.			Denominator of d (Col. 8 +	Weight (Col. 7 ÷	Training to
Study	d_i	n_1	n_2	$2n_1n_2$	$n_1 + n_2$	5 × Col. 6)	$2(n_1 + n_2)^2$	$n_1n_2d^2$	Col. 9)	Col. 10)	mentors?
Gibson	.45	123	124	30,504	247	7,534,488	122,018	3088.53	125,106.53	60.22	Yes
Cepeda	.30	72	75	10,800	147	1,587,600	43,218	486.0	43,704	36.33	Yes
Brock	.25	22	15	660	37	24,420	2,738	20.625	2,758.625	8.85	Yes
Javier	.30	69	69	9,522	138	1,314,036	38,088	428.49	38,516.49	34.12	No
Flood	−.15	88	91	16,016	179	2,866,864	64,082	180.18	64,262.18	44.61	No

Note. d_i is the standardized mean difference effect size for study i; n_1 and n_2 are the sample sizes for Groups 1 and 2, respectively. Col. = column.

overall mean effect size, as shown in Table 25.2. Using Equation 3 and the data in Table 25.2, the overall mean effect size is computed as

$$\overline{ES} = \frac{\Sigma w_i ES_i}{\Sigma w_i} = \frac{43.76}{184.13} = +0.238. \qquad (8)$$

Finally, it is always a good idea to surround a sample mean with a confidence interval. Like any other confidence interval, the confidence interval around a weighted mean effect size is based on a standard error and some critical test value. In meta-analysis, the large sample z-distribution is used for the critical test value, meaning that if a 95% confidence interval is desired then the critical value is 1.96 (and if a 90% confidence interval is desired, the critical value is 1.645). The standard error for a mean effect size can be expressed as

$$SE_{\overline{ES}} = \sqrt{\frac{1}{\Sigma w_i}}. \qquad (9)$$

Here, the standard error is equal to .074 (i.e., the square root of the inverse of 183.14). The 95% confidence interval can be expressed as

$$95\%CI = 1.96(SE_{\overline{ES}}). \qquad (10)$$

In our data

$$95\%CI = 1.96(.074) = .145. \qquad (11)$$

Therefore, our weighted mean standardized mean difference effect is + 0.238, and the 95% confidence interval runs from a low value of + 0.092 to a

high value of + 0.382. Because the 95% confidence does not contain the value of zero, we know that this mean effect size is statistically significant at our chosen Type I error rate level (i.e., α = .05). A direct test of the null hypothesis significance test can be carried out using the z-distribution

$$z = \frac{|\overline{ES}|}{SE_{\overline{ES}}}. \qquad (12)$$

Here, $0.24 \div 0.074 = 3.20$, $p < .001$. Probabilities for z can be found using online calculators and in many statistical textbooks.

It is important to examine Equation 9 to highlight the fact that the confidence interval for a weighted mean effect size is based on the standard error of the effect size, which itself is the square root of the inverse of the sum of the weights for the individual studies that contribute to the weighted mean. Because the weights are very closely tied to sample size, this means that the confidence interval is a function of sample size. I return to this point again when discussing random effects meta-analysis.

Testing Homogeneity

In addition to the mean weighted effect size and its confidence interval, meta-analysts are also interested in testing the variation among the effect size estimates. To do so, they carry out a homogeneity test. This test addresses the question of whether the individual study effect sizes are estimating the same

TABLE 25.2

Meta-Analysis for Five Mentoring Studies

Study	ES_i	w_i	$w_i \times ES_i$	$\overline{ES}$	$w_i(ES_i - \overline{ES})^2$	Training?
Gibson	.45	60.22	27.101	.238	2.716	Yes
Cepeda	.30	36.33	10.898	.238	0.141	Yes
Brock	.25	8.85	2.213	.238	0.001	Yes
Javier	.30	34.12	10.235	.238	0.133	No
Flood	−.15	44.61	−6.692	.238	6.703	No
		$\Sigma = 184.13$	$\Sigma = 43.755$		$\Sigma = 9.69 = Q$	

Note. ES_i is the effect size (in this case, a standardized mean difference) for each study i, w_i is the weight for each study i, $\overline{ES}$ is the overall weighted average effect size, and Q is the total homogeneity statistic (see Equation 13). The sums in the columns labeled w_i and $w_i \times ES_i$ are used to compute the overall weighted average effect size (see Equation 3).

population parameter. An important consideration is that we do not expect a series of studies to yield exactly the same effect sizes even if the studies are exact replicates of one another. The reason for this is random sampling error. The question is whether sampling error alone is sufficient to explain the extent of the observed differences in effect sizes across the studies.

To carry out this test, we compute a statistic known as Q:

$$Q = \Sigma w_i(ES_i - \overline{ES})^2, \qquad (13)$$

where w_i is the weight for study i, ES_i is the effect size for study i, and $\overline{E}$ is the overall average effect size. Note that Q is simply a weighted sum of squares. The Q statistic is approximately distributed as a chi square and is evaluated against the critical value of χ^2 at $k - 1$ degrees of freedom, where k is the number of studies. The computation of Q for the five mentoring studies that measure well-being as an outcome is presented in Table 25.2. As can be seen, $Q = 9.69$. The critical value of χ^2 at 4 degrees of freedom and a Type I error rate of .05 is 9.49, so we can reject the null hypothesis that the studies are all estimating the same population parameter.

Quantifying Heterogeneity

Like all tests of statistical significance, the homogeneity test tells us whether some observed pattern in the data (in this case, the heterogeneity in effect size estimates) is relatively likely or unlikely given some

null hypothesis. As such, it does not quantify how much variability there is among the study effects. The statistic I^2 can serve as a measure of this inconsistency. I^2 is independent of both the number of studies in the analysis and of the underlying scale. It can be computed as

$$I^2 = \left(\frac{Q - k - 1}{Q}\right) \times 100\%, \qquad (14)$$

where k is the number of studies in the analysis and Q is defined as in Equation 13. Like the related τ^2, discussed in the next section, I^2 can yield negative values, but by convention is set to zero when this happens. For our set of five studies, $I^2 = 58.7\%$. This result suggests that approximately 59% of the variability in effect sizes is due to variability in the population of studies rather than sampling error. This variability is relative. That is, as Borenstein, Hedges, Higgins, and Rothstein (2009) point out, if effects are measured precisely, I^2 can be quite large even if all effects are distributed over a very small range. Conversely, if effects are measured imprecisely, I^2 can be small even if the effects are distributed over a very large range.

RANDOM EFFECTS META-ANALYSIS

So far the discussion of meta-analysis has been based on a particular model, known as the *fixed effect* approach. In this model, studies are assumed to be estimating a single underlying population parameter (i.e., the null hypothesis is that the studies are all estimating a single population value of zero) and any variation in observed effects across studies is presumed to be a function of random sampling error (an assumption that can be evaluated using the homogeneity test). One important implication of this choice is that the confidence intervals around a weighted mean effect size are essentially only a function of the sample size of the underlying studies: The larger the total sample size, the narrower the confidence interval.

An alternative to the fixed effect model is known as the *random effects* model. Here, studies are not presumed to be estimating the same population parameter but instead are presumed to be drawn from a population of effect sizes (i.e., the null hypothesis is that the studies are drawn from a distribution of effect sizes that have a mean of zero). Another way to conceptualize this difference is to think about the null hypotheses for the two models. In both the fixed and random effects models, the mean population effect is zero, but in the random effects case, the mean of a distribution is being estimated, rather than one single value (Borenstein et al., 2009). Later I will discuss ways that meta-analysts choose between the fixed and random effects approaches.

Random effects meta-analysis proceeds like fixed effects meta-analysis, with the exception of the computation of study weights. Using this model, the weights (and, hence, the overall weighted mean effect size and its confidence interval) are based not only on the total sample size but also on information about the extent to which the effect size estimates vary between studies (known as the between-studies variance component, or τ^2). One relatively simple method for estimating τ^2 is known as the method of moments, and is given by

$$\tau^2 = \frac{Q - k - 1}{\Sigma w_i - (\Sigma w_i^2 / \Sigma w_i)}, \qquad (15)$$

where Q is defined as in Equation 13, k is defined as in Equation 14, and w_i is the fixed effect weight for study i (as given for the standardized mean difference effect size using Equation 5). Like I^2, by convention τ^2 is set to zero if it yields a negative value. For our example set of studies, τ^2 is .041. Random effects weights are computed using a modification of

the fixed effect weight. Specifically, the value of τ^2 is added to the fixed effect weight to arrive at the new random effects weights. Equation 4 can be rewritten to provide a generic expression of the random effects weight

$$w^* = \frac{1}{v + \tau^2}, \qquad (16)$$

where w^* is the random effects weight, v is the effect size variance, and τ^2 is the between-studies variance component as defined in Equation 15. For example, the random effects weight for Gibson's study in our example could be found by first taking the inverse of its fixed effect weight (the weight was 60.22, so the inverse of that weight is .0167). Next, add the between-studies variance component to this quantity; here, this yields .0167 + .041 = .0577. Finally, take the inverse of this quantity to find the random effects weight. Doing so for Gibson's study yields a random effects weight of 17.33. Compare this with the fixed effects weight of 60.22. As long as τ^2 is greater than zero, random effects weights will always be less extreme than their fixed effect counterparts. Because computation of the random effects weight involves adding a constant to the fixed effects weight, the rank ordering of the weights will not change (i.e., the study with the greatest fixed effect weight will also have the greatest random effects weight), but the relative magnitude will change.

Random effects weights are used in place of the fixed effect weights in meta-analysis, but otherwise the process is the same as described for the fixed effect case. For this example, the overall random effects weighted effect size is +0.23, with a 95% confidence interval from −0.01 to +0.47. So, the overall average effect size did not differ much between the two models. However, the standard error for the random effects estimate is about 64% larger (0.121 vs. 0.074) than its fixed effect counterpart. This suggests another important lesson: Random effects confidence intervals will never be smaller and will often be larger than their fixed effect counterparts (the only time the confidence intervals will have identical width in the two models is when the between-studies variance component is exactly zero). As such, statistical power can be higher in the random effects model, though such cases are unusual. If τ^2 is greater than zero, then statistical power will almost always be lower in the random effects model relative to the fixed effects model (for demonstrations of power computations for the overall weighted mean effect size, see Hedges & Pigott, 2001; Valentine et al., 2010).

CHOOSING BETWEEN FIXED AND RANDOM EFFECTS MODELS

The choice between fixed and random effects models can have important implications for the inferences that are drawn from a meta-analysis. As such, meta-analysts need to think carefully about which model to employ. It is fairly common to base the choice of model on the results of the statistical test of homogeneity. Specifically, if this test does not reject the null hypothesis, then the fixed effect model is adopted. If the test does result in the rejection of the null hypothesis of homogeneity, then the synthesists adopt the random effects model. This is a problematic approach.

One issue is that like any other statistical test, tests of homogeneity are not always conducted with high statistical power (for demonstrations of power computations for the homogeneity test, see Hedges & Pigott, 2001; Valentine et al., 2010). Low statistical power can mislead the synthesist into thinking that a set of studies share a common population effect, when in fact they do not. In these cases, adopting the fixed effect model can lead to an increased Type I error rate.

Another consideration relevant to the choice of error model concerns the assumptions underlying each model. I mentioned that the fixed effect model can be thought of as assuming that each study is estimating the same population parameter. This means that a series of exactly replicated studies should yield effect size estimates that vary only as a function of sampling error. If studies are not exact replicates, the fixed effect model is still justifiable if the synthesist can identify and account for all of the relevant covariates (because in this case the residuals of the effect sizes would all be the same). The random effects model assumes that studies are drawn from a population of studies that share a common mean effect. So, for example, if studies are

not exact replicates of one another and the synthesist is not confident that all relevant covariates can be identified and accounted for—probably a relatively common situation—then the random effects model would seem to be justified.

In addition, Hedges and Vevea (1998) suggested that the fixed effect model allows for inferences that generalize to studies that are very much like the ones included in the analysis, whereas the random effects model allows for generalizations to a broader range of studies, specifically, the population of studies from which the observed studies were sampled. Usually (although not always) synthesists are interested in generalizing beyond the observed studies. As such, this is an argument in favor of the random effects model.

The choice between error models is best made conceptually, rather than empirically. The strong assumptions and limited range of generalization associated with the fixed effect model are significant limitations that often favor adoption of the random effects model. In addition, the random effects model has the benefit of reducing to the fixed effect model if the assumptions of that model are exactly met, so in a sense there is no penalty for being wrong if the random effects model is chosen (the same is not true of the fixed effect model).

DEPENDENT EFFECT SIZES

Like all statistics that are based on the general linear model, the statistics used in meta-analysis are based on the assumption of statistical independence. In meta-analysis, dependence can arise from many common situations. For example, studies can take multiple measures of the same outcome (e.g., well-being as measured by two different self-report instruments). Studies can measure the outcome at multiple points in time (e.g., at 6 months into the mentoring program and again 6 months later). Studies can employ a single treatment group with multiple comparison groups (e.g., a wait-list control group and another control group that receives a placebo) or multiple treatment groups with a single comparison group (e.g., one group of children received intensive mentoring while another group of children receives less intensive mentoring).

The meta-analyst must decide how to handle these situations because ignoring them can lead to inflated Type I error rates. Sophisticated statistical techniques have been developed to address the problem (see Gleser & Olkin, 2009). These are rarely used, however, in part because the data needed to employ them are usually not available in studies. As such, the meta-analyst is usually left with a few options, none of which are perfect.

One option is to choose only one effect size to represent the study. This can be done using a random process or an intentional one. For the latter, the meta-analyst will usually choose the effect size that maximizes comparability with the other studies in the analysis (Lipsey & Wilson, 2001). For example, assume that a mentoring study measured the outcome at posttest and at a 12-month follow-up, and that this study is the only study that included a follow-up. One strategy would be to drop the 12-month effect size from the meta-analytic database, thereby maximizing the comparability of the effects in the analysis. Both the random and the intentional strategies are unbiased if carried out in this way (the intentional strategy would not be unbiased if, say, the meta-analyst examined the effect sizes and dropped the smallest one). However, they both result in a loss of information.

Another strategy is to average effect sizes. For example, assume that a study has two measures of well-being. Rather than choosing one, a defensible option might be to compute an effect size for both measures and report the mean effect size as the study's overall effect size. This strategy has the benefit of retaining all of the available information and also takes advantage of a fundamental principle in psychological measurement (specifically, that given multiple measures of a construct, some combination of all measures is likely to be a better representation of the underlying construct than any single measure). In general, it is probably sensible to start with this approach and only not use effect sizes as a last resort. For example, it may or may not be sensible to average effects for a more intensive and a less intensive version of the intervention. If it is not, dropping one effect size might be the best option.

ANALYSIS OF MODERATOR EFFECTS IN META-ANALYSIS

A moderator variable is one that affects the direction or strength of the relation between the independent variable and the dependent variable (see Chapter 5 of this volume). In meta-analysis, moderator variables can explain some of the heterogeneity between studies and thus contribute to a greater understanding of the phenomenon being studied. For example, assume that three of our five studies on how mentoring affects well-being provided training to mentors, whereas the other two did not. A moderator test allows us to assess whether study effects vary as a function of whether training was provided.

Generally, moderator analysis in meta-analysis is analogous to common statistical procedures that are based on the general linear model (multiple regression and ANOVA). Moderators in meta-analysis can be categorical (e.g., whether training was provided to mentors) or continuous (e.g., average number of hours of mentor–mentee contact per month), and multiple predictors can be accommodated given a sufficient number of studies. For the sake of simplicity, the next example employs a categorical moderator, but it is important to keep in mind that moderator analysis in meta-analysis is not limited to categorical variables.

As with the meta-analysis of the overall weighted mean effect size, meta-analysts need to make a choice regarding whether to use the fixed or the random effects model. Again, the main issue is whether the studies are believed to be estimating the same population parameter. If so, then identified covariates should explain all of the variability in observed effect sizes that goes beyond what would be expected given sampling error alone. In most real-world contexts, this seems unlikely, and as such the random effects model is probably generally more appropriate for moderator analyses (just like the overall analysis). A complication is that the statistic τ^2 is computed separately for each subgroup; these can be pooled to form a single estimate of τ^2 for the analysis. Alternatively, the separate values of τ^2 computed for each subgroup can be applied only to their respective subgroups. For the sake of presentational simplicity, I will use the fixed effect approach to demonstrate how subgroup analysis works in meta-analysis. It is probably the case, however, that the random effects model is generally the better option.

In our example, in three studies mentors were provided with training, whereas in two studies they were not. The question is whether mentor training seems to matter—that is, whether studies in which mentors were trained yield the same effects as studies in which mentors were not trained. Categorical moderators are tested using techniques that are analogous to ANOVA. One way to think about this analysis is that we are partitioning the variance of the observed effect sizes into that which is explained by the grouping variable (training) and that which remains unexplained (i.e., error). On the basis of Equation 13, (and shown in Table 25.2), we know that the total homogeneity statistic, Q, is 9.69. Next, we use Equation 13 to compute Q *within* each group; these values are summed together to create the statistic Q_{within} (i.e., the within-group homogeneity). For the data in Table 25.3, the relevant within-group sum of squares is 0.68 for the training group of studies, and 3.92 for the no training studies, so Q_{within} = 0.68 + 3.92 = 4.60. We next need to compute the weighted sum of squares for the *group* means, Q_{bet}. Because we have already partitioned the total homogeneity statistic into one of its two parts, this second quantity can be found via subtraction:

$$Q_{bet} = Q - Q_{within}. \tag{17}$$

Here, Q_{bet} = 9.69 – 4.60 = 5.09. Like Q, Q_{bet} is evaluated against a χ^2 distribution with j – 1 degrees of

freedom, where j is the number of levels for the moderator variable (i.e., the number of groups). Because Q_{bet} exceeds the critical value for the χ^2 distribution at 1 degree of freedom (3.84), we can reject the null hypothesis that the group means are equal.

We can also quantify the extent to which training matters. The most obvious way to do this is to compare the group means. The studies that employed training yielded an average effect size of d = 0.38, whereas those that did not yielded an average effect size of d = 0.05. Thus, the average difference is d_{diff} = .33. To compute a 95% confidence interval for this estimate, we need to first compute the standard error for the difference, using the formula

$$SE_{diff} = \sqrt{v_1 + v_2}, \tag{18}$$

where v_1 and v_2 are the variances for the mean effect size in the training and no-training groups. Recall that the variance for a mean effect size is simply the inverse of the sum of the weights for the studies that contributed to that effect size (see Equation 9). Here, the variance for the training group is .009 and the variance for the no-training group is .013, so the standard error for the difference between the means is the square root of .022, or .148. To compute the 95% confidence interval for the difference, the standard error for the difference is multiplied by the critical value 1.96, so the confidence interval around the mean is .148 × 1.96 or .29. Therefore, the plausible range for the difference in effects estimated in

TABLE 25.3

Computation of the Moderator Test for Mentor Training

Study	ES_i	Training?	w_i	$\overline{ES}_j$	$w_i(ES_i - \overline{ES}_j)^2$
Gibson	.45	Yes	60.22	.382	0.278
Cepeda	.30	Yes	36.33	.382	0.253
Brock	.25	Yes	8.85	.382	0.154
			Σ = 105.4		Σ = 0.685
Javier	.30	No	34.12	.045	2.219
Flood	–.15	No	44.61	.045	1.696
			Σ = 78.73		Σ = 3.915

Note. ES_i is the effect size (in this case, a standardized mean difference) for each study i, w_i is the weight for each study i, and $\overline{ES}_j$ is the overall weighted average effect size for group j. The sums in the column labeled w_i were used to compute the variance for the overall weighted average effect size for each group j, whereas the sums in the column labeled $w_i(ES_i - \overline{ES}_j)^2$ are the within-group homogeneity statistics (Q_{within}).

studies that trained mentors compared with those that did not runs from a low of .04 standard deviation units to a high of .62 standard deviation units.

It is also of interest to examine the Q_{within} statistics for each group, which provide an indication of the extent to which effect sizes are homogeneous within groups. Just like with the overall homogeneity analysis, Q_{within} is evaluated against a χ^2 distribution with $k - 1$ degrees of freedom. If effects appear to be heterogeneous even after accounting for the grouping variable, it suggests that other factors might be influencing effect sizes. Note that in our example, the training group studies yielded effects that appear to be homogeneous, $Q(2) = 0.685$, $p > .70$, whereas the no-training group studies yielded effects that appear heterogeneous, $Q(1) = 3.92$, $p < .05$.

In our example set of studies, providing training to mentors seems to be associated with larger effects. This finding probably makes sense from a practical standpoint and perhaps from theoretical perspectives as well. However, meta-analysts need to be careful not to overinterpret moderator analyses. The language I used in describing this finding ("seems to be associated") reflects this caution. Like all inferential tests, moderator analyses in meta-analysis are conducted with varying degrees of statistical power, and as such a failure to reject the null hypothesis does not necessarily mean that the putative moderator variable is not associated with the outcomes under study. Just as important, a finding that a variable does appear to moderate a relationship should not be interpreted as providing strong evidence of moderation. Two related considerations are most essential, and these stem from the same source. Specifically, it is important to recognize that studies were not randomly assigned to different levels of the moderator variable (e.g., to provide training to mentors or not to provide this training). This means that comparisons of the effects arising from studies employing different levels of moderator variables are correlational. That is, even if all of the studies randomly assigned youth to either receive or not to receive a mentor, mentors were never randomly assigned to receive training or not, and thus an analysis of the effects of training is correlational. Furthermore, it is often difficult to disentangle confounding of multiple predictors. Studies in

which training was provided to mentors might differ from those that do not in other important ways, and neither ANOVA nor regression-based approaches to testing moderators are likely to fully address the confounding. It is important to treat moderator tests as promising directions for future research, rather than as strong findings on which policy or practice decisions should be made.

PUBLICATION BIAS

Publication bias refers to the well-known tendency for studies lacking statistically significant results to be less likely to be published in peer-reviewed journals. This happens because authors are less likely to submit, and editors and reviewers are less likely to accept for publication, papers that lack statistically significant results for their primary outcomes (for a review, see Dickersin, 2005). Fundamentally, this process means that small studies with large effects are more likely to be published than small studies with small effects. Because published studies are easier to find than unpublished studies, this can create a bias against the null hypothesis in the meta-analytic database. The task of the meta-analyst is to determine whether publication bias might be present in the set of studies included in the review, and if so, how extensive the problem might be.

Unfortunately, for statistical or practical reasons, there are currently no very good tests for publication bias. As described in the volume by Rothstein, Sutton, and Borenstein (2005), existing methods can have low statistical power in many common analytic situations or rest on assumptions that are difficult for the analyst to make. In addition, all methods are based on the assumption that a negative relationship between sample size and effect size (i.e., as sample size increases, effect size decreases) is evidence of publication bias. This may not be the case. For example, assume that in mentoring interventions the quality of mentoring decreases with study size (i.e., mentoring in larger studies tends to be implemented with less fidelity than mentoring in smaller studies), and implementation fidelity is positively related to effect size (i.e., better implemented mentoring produces larger effects). In this case, there will be a negative relationship between sample size and effect size. Tests of publication bias will tend to detect this as an indicator of publication bias, when in fact in this case it is indicative of another process.

These problems highlight the critical need for meta-analyses to be based on a thorough search of literature. Keeping this in mind, meta-analysts have employed several different strategies to investigate the plausibility (and potential severity of) publication bias. The simplest strategy is to carry out a moderator test comparing the effects from published studies with those from unpublished studies. If the effects from published versus unpublished studies are similar, then this is a reasonable argument that publication bias is not having a major impact on the results. Recall, however, that univariate moderator tests can suffer from low statistical power, and even more seriously, cannot untangle the effects of potentially confounding third variables. As such, meta-analysts with sufficient data should consider using meta-regression to help address confounding and should focus more on the magnitude of the differences between effects from published versus unpublished studies, and less on the statistical significance of those differences.

Funnel plots are another common method used for detecting publication bias. In a funnel plot, study effect sizes are given on the *x*-axis, whereas the standard error (preferably, but sample size and variance are also used) is plotted on the *y*-axis. Note that in Figure 25.1, the *y*-axis is arranged such that the standard error ranges from small to large moving from the top to the bottom of the graph. When structured in this way, larger studies are represented at the top of the graph, and as you move down the *y*-axis, the studies become smaller. Because we expect more consistency between large studies than small studies (i.e., larger studies have smaller standard errors and should therefore group more tightly than smaller studies), the funnel plot should look like an inverted funnel when the studies are graphed. The meta-analyst can examine the plot for gaps, and if these exist, it might suggest a publication bias problem. Unfortunately, this method is fairly subjective and in practice often involves a judgment for which no clear answer is present. Beyond these general guidelines, there are few specific rules that can help reduce the ambiguity. This subjectivity is problematic for a number of reasons, not the least of which is that judgments of ambiguous stimuli are the ones most likely to reflect the biases and predispositions of the judge (for a review, see Gilovich, 1991). In addition, the funnel plot

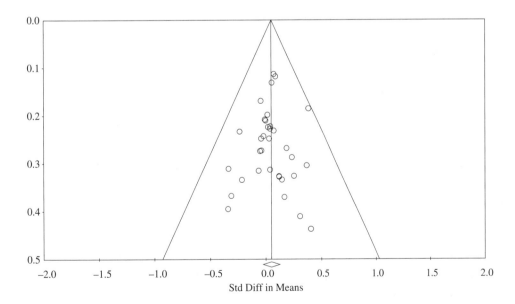

FIGURE 25.1. Funnel plot of effect size by standard error. Stand diff in means refers to the standardized mean difference effect size *d*. From "The Effects of Attrition on Baseline Comparability in Randomized Experiments in Education: A Meta-Analysis," by J. C. Valentine and C. M. McHugh, 2007, *Psychological Methods, 12*, p. 278. Copyright 2007 by the American Psychological Association.

method works best when there is a relatively large number of studies, and many meta-analyses simply will not have enough studies to produce a plot that can be interpreted with a high degree of confidence. Figure 25.1 is actually relatively clear in this regard. That is, there appear to be no significant gaps in the plot, and the studies (more or less) behave as expected in that those toward the top of the plot (with smaller standard errors) group together more than those toward the bottom of the plot.

A statistical technique is available that builds on the logic of the funnel plot and (imperfectly) addresses some of these concerns. *Trim and fill* (Duval & Tweedie, 2000) is a statistical algorithm that iteratively removes (trims) the extreme small studies until the plot is symmetric. The procedure then (a) replaces the trimmed studies and imputes a mirror image for each (this is the *fill* part of the analysis), (b) computes a new weighted mean effect size on the basis of only the studies that survived the trimming procedure, and (c) computes a new confidence interval for that mean effect size on the basis of the full distribution of observed and imputed effects. Like visual inspection of the funnel plot, the trim and fill procedure requires a relatively large number of studies before it has a reasonable chance of working well. However, it does remove the subjectivity of the judgment (or perhaps stated better, the subjectivity is operationalized in terms of the assumptions underlying the model rather than remaining a cognitive process that is not observable by others).

If the effects from published versus unpublished studies do seem to vary, then the analyst still has to determine how extensive the problem of publication bias might be. This can be hard to determine from visual inspection of the funnel plot. A moderator test comparing the results of published and unpublished studies does better in this regard, as does the trim and fill procedure. Given the limitations of these techniques, however, meta-analysts should be careful about concluding that publication bias is not present or important even if that is the result that follows from their application. Until we have more information from a variety of disciplines about how publication bias operates, the safest way to minimize publication bias is to undertake a vigorous search for literature.

CONCLUSION

In this chapter, I have presented the computational details for conducting a basic meta-analysis. Although some issues in meta-analysis can be relatively complex mathematically, most involve straight-forward extensions of statistical procedures with which many scholars are already familiar. Indeed, the computations in this chapter involve nothing more than basic algebra and can be implemented using virtually any spreadsheet software application. My hope is that the chapter clearly communicates not only the technical considerations important to conducting a meta-analysis but also the important conceptual issues, such as whether it makes sense to synthesize a group of studies that are not direct replicates of one another but instead vary from one another along multiple dimensions, why it is important to give larger studies more weight in an analysis, and why meta-analysis is a better synthesis technique than its alternatives.

References

Borenstein, M., Hedges, L. V., Higgins, J. P. T., & Rothstein, H. R. (2009). *Introduction to meta-analysis.* Chichester, England: Wiley. doi:10.1002/97804 70743386

Cohen, J. (1994). The Earth is round ($p < .05$). *American Psychologist, 49,* 997–1003. doi:10.1037/0003-066X. 49.12.997

Collaborative for Academic, Social, and Emotional Learning. (2003). *Safe and sound: An educational leader's guide to evidence-based social and emotional learning (SEL) programs.* Chicago, IL: Author.

Cooper, H., & Dorr, N. (1995). Race comparisons on need for achievement: A meta-analytic alternative to Graham's narrative review. *Review of Educational Research, 65,* 483–508.

Cooper, H., Hedges, L. V., & Valentine, J. C. (Eds.). (2009). *The handbook of research synthesis and meta-analysis* (2nd ed.). New York, NY: Russell Sage Foundation.

Dickersin, K. (2005). Publication bias: Recognizing the problem, understanding its origins and scope, and preventing harm. In H. R. Rothstein, A. J. Sutton, & M. Borenstein (Eds.), *Publication bias in meta-analysis: Prevention, assessment and adjustments* (pp. 11–33). Chichester, England: Wiley.

Duval, S., & Tweedie, R. (2000). Trim and fill: A simple funnel-plot-based method of testing and adjusting for publication bias in meta-analysis. *Biometrics, 56,* 455–463. doi:10.1111/j.0006-341X.2000.00455.x

Gilovich, T. (1991). *How we know what isn't so: The fallibility of human reason in everyday life.* New York, NY: Free Press.

Glass, G. V. (2000). *Meta-analysis at 25.* Retrieved from http://glass.ed.asu.edu/gene/papers/meta25.html

Gleser, L. J., & Olkin, I. (2009). Stochastically dependent effect sizes. In H. Cooper, L. V. Hedges, & J. C. Valentine (Eds.), *The handbook of research synthesis and meta-analysis* (2nd ed., pp. 357–376). New York, NY: Russell Sage Foundation.

Greenwald, A. G., Gonzalez, R., Harris, R. J., & Guthrie, D. (1996). Effect sizes and *p* values: What should be reported and what should be replicated? *Psychophysiology, 33,* 175–183. doi:10.1111/j.1469-8986.1996.tb02121.x

Hedges, L. V. (1982). Estimation and testing for differences in effect size: A comment on Hsu. *Psychological Bulletin, 91,* 691–693. doi:10.1037/0033-2909.91.3.691

Hedges, L. V., & Olkin, I. (1985). *Statistical methods for meta-analysis.* Orlando, FL: Academic Press.

Hedges, L. V., & Pigott, T. D. (2001). The power of statistical tests in meta-analysis. *Psychological Methods, 6,* 203–217. doi:10.1037/1082-989X.6.3.203

Hedges, L. V., & Vevea, J. L. (1998). Fixed and random effects models in meta-analysis. *Psychological Methods, 3,* 486–504. doi:10.1037/1082-989X.3.4.486

Hume, D. (1739/1740). *A treatise of human nature: Being an attempt to introduce the experimental method of reasoning into moral subjects.* Retrieved from http://www.gutenberg.org/etext/4705

Johnson, B. T., & Eagly, A. H. (2000). Quantitative synthesis of social psychological research. In H. T. Reis & C. M. Judd (Eds.), *Handbook of research methods in social and personality psychology* (pp. 496–528). New York, NY: Cambridge University Press.

Kirby, D. (2001). *Emerging answers: Research findings on programs to reduce teen pregnancy.* Washington, DC: National Campaign to Prevent Teen Pregnancy.

Lipsey, M. W., & Wilson, D. B. (2001). *Practical meta-analysis.* Thousand Oaks, CA: Sage.

Rosenthal, R. (1984). *Meta-analytic procedures for social research.* Beverly Hills, CA: Sage.

Rothstein, H. R., Sutton, A. J., & Borenstein, M. (Eds.). (2005). *Publication bias in meta-analysis: Prevention, assessment, and adjustment.* Chichester, England: Wiley. doi:10.1002/0470870168

Valentine, J. C., Biglan, A., Boruch, R. F., Castro, F. G., Collins, L. M., Flay, B. R., . . . Schinke, S. P. (2011). Replication in prevention science. *Prevention Science, 12,* 103–117. doi:10.1007/S1112101102176

Valentine, J. C., & McHugh, C. M. (2007). The effects of attrition on baseline comparability in randomized experiments in education: A meta-analysis. *Psychological Methods, 12,* 268–282. doi:10.1037/1082-989X.12.3.268

Valentine, J. C., Pigott, T. D., & Rothstein, H. R. (2010). How many studies do you need? A primer on statistical power for meta-analysis. *Journal of Educational and Behavioral Statistics, 35,* 215–247. doi:10.3102/1076998609346961

## Part II

PUBLISHING AND
THE PUBLICATION PROCESS

## CHAPTER 26

PREPARING A MANUSCRIPT FOR PUBLICATION

Karin Sternberg and Robert J. Sternberg

You often hear researchers say that the fun for them is to conduct the research but that they do not find much satisfaction in writing up the results of their research. Fact is, however, that writing about your research belongs just as much to the research process as planning and conducting your research. Only by writing up your results and giving your peers and the public access to your work can discourse take place that will ultimately bring forward not only your own research, but also the entire field. Science is by definition public, so that until research is written up, it is not fully part of the scientific process.

Although your research questions and designs may vary, there are some general rules and guidelines you can follow when writing up your results. This chapter outlines the process of preparing your manuscript for publication. We first consider how best to structure a literature review. Then we have a look at the components of an experimental research paper. Next we consider grammar and style issues when writing a paper. We then discuss the importance of proofreading and revising your manuscript. Finally, we go through some guidelines that can help you decide on an appropriate outlet for your work. If you are interested in learning more about these topics, we recommend you consult *The Psychologist's Companion* (Sternberg & Sternberg, 2010) on which this chapter is, in part, based.

WRITING A LITERATURE REVIEW

When you reach the point at which you write your literature review, most of the work has already been done. You have defined the problem you want to work on; you have located and retrieved the relevant information and worked your way through it; you have made sense of the information and drawn your conclusions. But how do you structure your literature review in the best possible way to communicate your results to your readers and to maximize the chances of getting your review published?

First of all, you have to be clear about what the goals of your literature review are and how best to achieve them. The sixth edition of the *Publication Manual of the American Psychological Association* (APA, 2010, p. 10; henceforth, *Publication Manual*) states that literature reviews have four different goals:

1. defining and clarifying problems;
2. informing the reader about a subject by summarizing and evaluating studies;
3. identifying inconsistencies, gaps, contradictions, and relationships in the literature; and
4. suggesting future steps and approaches in order to solve the issues identified.

Depending on what the aim of your review is, you can strive to (a) generate new knowledge, (b) test theories, (c) integrate theories, (d) develop a new theory, or (e) integrate existing knowledge.

This chapter is based in part on *The Psychologist's Companion* (5th ed.), by R. J. Sternberg and K. Sternberg, 2010, New York, NY: Cambridge University Press.

DOI: 10.1037/13621-026
APA Handbook of Research Methods in Psychology: Vol. 3. Data Analysis and Research Publication, H. Cooper (Editor-in-Chief)

How to Organize the Outline

Outlines can be organized in many ways. Many decisions regarding organization are unique to each particular situation. Generally, the organization of your paper should be logical and straightforward; you should lead your reader from one point you make to the next, and so on. Do not organize your paper around individual studies but rather around models or viewpoints. Five principles of organization are common to all outlines and the papers that evolve from them:

1. The organization should include a beginning, a middle, and an end, in which you say what you're going to say, say it, and say what you've said. Readers always need a sense of direction and purpose for your paper. When readers begin a paper, they need some general statements that tell them what the paper is about and how it is organized; without this orientation, they may become lost almost as soon as they start the paper. When readers complete the main part of the paper, they need a summary of the main ideas, and whatever final comments you want to supply; without this review, readers may not realize what you consider to be your main points and what conclusions you draw.

2. Once you decide upon a principle of organization, stick with it. Beginning writers often change their way of organizing papers midstream, usually without first informing readers that the change is about to take place. Change in midstream confuses readers. If you must change your organizational principle, be sure to let the reader know. But avoid the change if possible.

    Suppose you write a paper comparing two personality tests. You can structure the paper in a way so that you first discuss the content of the tests, then the administration, and then the scoring methods (thematic presentation). Or you can present each test after the other, first going over the content, administration, and scoring method of Test A, and then going over the same topics for Test B (outline by test). Whatever you decide to do, however, do not mix these two approaches unless it is unavoidable.

3. Organize your writing thematically. Thematic organization enhances the clarity of a paper. In

our example, the three themes were content, administration, and scoring. The reader would complete a paper on the basis of this outline with a clear idea of how the Stanford–Binet and Wechsler Intelligence Tests differ in these three respects.

The organization by test is not confusing, but it is inferior to the thematic organization. In thematic organization, readers can compare the two tests on each theme as they read through the main part of the paper, gradually developing a perspective on how the tests differ. In the organization by test, readers are unable to begin comparing the tests until they are halfway through the main part of the paper. By this time, readers may have forgotten the characteristics of the first test because they had no motivation to remember them. In reading the section of the paper on the Stanford–Binet, they probably will have to refer to the section on the Wechsler to draw a comparison. If readers are unwilling to spend the time or effort doing what the writer should have done, they may never understand the comparison altogether.

The same principle would apply if, say, one wished to compare the viewpoints of Sigmund Freud and Konrad Lorenz on aggression toward oneself, aggression toward others, and aggression toward objects. The preferred way to organize the paper would be by the successive themes of aggression toward self, others, and objects, not by the successive authors, Freud and Lorenz.

There are two exceptions to this principle. The first exception arises when there are no well-developed themes in the literature you plan to review. Each theorist, for example, may deal with a different set of issues. The second exception arises when your focus is genuinely on the objects of comparison rather than on the themes along which they are compared. In a book presenting theories of personality, for example, the author's emphasis might be on the individual perspective of each theorist, rather than on the themes dealt with in their theories.

4. Organize your outline hierarchically. Beginning writers tend to overuse coordination of ideas and to underuse subordination of ideas. If a paper contains a large number of "main" ideas, the

reader will have some difficulty understanding the ideas and more difficulty remembering them. When you find yourself with a large number of "main" ideas, try to subordinate some of them. You will then communicate the same number of ideas at the same time that you increase the effectiveness with which you communicate them. In our example, you would use the topic "content" as one level, and then have subordinate levels that discuss the content of the Stanford–Binet and the Wechsler. You would not want to present the content twice at the same level, once as "Content of the Stanford–Binet" and once as "Content of the Wechsler." Make use of subordination whenever you can to present your ideas more clearly.

5. Organize for your audience. In arranging your outline, it is essential that you keep your audience in mind. The level of description for each topic in the outline should be appropriate for the target audience; the level of description that is adequate for one audience may be inadequate for another. A brief introduction may be sufficient for a professional seeking a one-paragraph description of salient differences between the Stanford–Binet and the Wechsler, but it probably will be insufficient for a layperson unfamiliar with personality tests. Such a person requires more orientation to the topic of the exposition. An expanded introduction is therefore appropriate and could include topics such as the purpose and general characteristics of intelligence tests as well as a short overview of the differences among intelligence tests in general, and the Stanford–Binet and the Wechsler in particular. The general reader will then be able to follow the remainder of the exposition.

The Purpose of Outlines

Writers often wonder whether outlines are worth the time and trouble. Using outlines has three advantages that more than offset the extra work they require:

1. Outlines help you organize your writing. In writing the actual paper, organization will be just one of many concerns you have. Because there are so many different things to keep track of in writing the paper, and because your capacity to keep track of many things at once is limited, organization will receive only limited attention. Because organization of a paper is so important, however, it pays to insert a step before writing the paper in which you can devote your full attention to organizing the paper.

2. Outlines prevent omission of relevant topics. In doing your research or in compiling your topic notes, you may have inadvertently omitted a topic that you intended or should have thought to include in your paper. Omissions are much easier for the author to spot in an outline than in a paper. They are also much easier to correct before writing of the paper has begun.

3. Outlines prevent inclusion of irrelevant topics. Authors sometimes find that a topic that had seemed relevant to the paper in the early stages of research no longer seems relevant when the research is being organized. Irrelevant material shows itself in an obvious way during preparation of an outline because the material seems to have no place. By discovering irrelevancies during preparation of the outline, authors can discard them so that later they do not distract them in writing the paper.

Writing Your Review

In writing your literature review, you should keep several points in mind (see also Eisenberg, 2000):

1. Have a message. Authors of literature reviews are at particular risk to write long and elaborate papers in which their readers get lost. You have reviewed a large amount of literature that can be confusing at times, so it is all the more important that you provide your readers with a thread throughout your paper and a clear message they can take away from reading your work.

2. Have sufficient breadth of review. How many publications you include in your review depends on your topic and the goal you want to achieve by writing your paper. Generally, you should discuss a good part of the empirical literature and make sure that different methodological approaches are being considered. You do not have to discuss every study in detail, however. Just make sure that the literature that you do include is in fact relevant to your endeavor.

3. Be accurate. Always pay attention that you do not misrepresent the results of studies you include in your literature review. It is fine to disagree with the author's interpretation of results, however.

4. Include a critique. It is important to include in your literature review a critique of methods, conclusions, and strengths and weaknesses of the works you reviewed. You should do this not study by study, however, but rather evaluate entire bodies of work. Remember to be fair and not to be unduly harsh toward other people's work. You should review the work of others with the same respect with which you would want your work to be reviewed.

5. Have an end. The ending of your literature review should not only summarize findings, but also draw new conclusions, point out new explanations, or suggest further steps for the exploration of the problem.

Evaluating Your Literature Review and Getting Feedback

Once you are finished writing your review, revisit and evaluate it using the same (or similar) criteria to those you used to evaluate the papers and books you read:

1. Validity. Are your arguments consistent with the literature you reviewed? Have you explained inconsistencies? Have you properly substantiated each of your arguments?

2. Internal consistency. Are your arguments consistent with each other? Are they consistent with your general point of view?

3. Presuppositions. Have you made clear to the reader what you presuppose? Are your presuppositions reasonable ones that the reader is likely to accept? Has the impact of your presuppositions upon your conclusions been discussed?

4. Implications. Have you discussed the implications of your arguments? Are these implications realistic? Do these implications strengthen or weaken your arguments?

5. Importance. Have you emphasized your important arguments and conclusions, and subordinated the less important ones? Have you explained why you view certain arguments and conclusions as important and others as less so?

By using these five criteria to evaluate your literature review, you will improve its quality. Later, we will consider in more detail criteria for evaluating the quality of all psychology papers.

If you plan to submit your literature review to a journal and have to decide on where to submit it, you may want to read some literature reviews that have been published in the journal(s) you are considering to determine whether your paper is a good fit to the journal. Generally, the probability of a paper getting accepted is highest when you develop new knowledge or a new theory, or when you integrate several theories (instead of just reviewing and summarizing the literature on a particular topic; Eisenberg, 2000). Frequently, the best literature reviews do not merely summarize literature, but also create new knowledge by placing the literature into a new framework or at least seeing the literature in a new way.

WRITING AN EXPERIMENTAL RESEARCH PAPER

Experimental research papers differ in presentation quite substantially from literature reviews. In this section, we will look at the different parts of a manuscript describing an experiment. If you are interested in a more detailed overview, we recommend the *Guide to Publishing in Psychology Journals* (Sternberg, 2000). Authors of experimental research papers are expected to comply with the Journal Article Reporting Standards described in the *Publication Manual* (APA, 2010, pp. 21–23) as well as the appendix tables and flowchart (also see the Introduction to Volume 1 in this handbook).

We suggest that you write an outline before writing the paper, just as you would if you were writing a literature review. A standard format for the outline looks like this:

Title
Author's Name and Affiliation
Author Notes
Abstract
I. Introduction
II. Method

Title

The title should inform the reader simply and concisely what the topic of the paper is. It is important that the title be self-explanatory. Readers will come across the title in other papers that refer to your paper and in PsycINFO, and they may have to decide on the basis of the title alone whether they want to read your paper. Therefore, you may want to catch the attention of your potential readers with the title. The title should include keywords, for example, the theoretical issue to which the paper is addressed, the dependent variable(s), and the independent variable(s). Keywords are important because the title will be stored in information-retrieval networks that rely on such words to determine the relevance of your study to someone else's research interests. For the same reason, it is important to avoid irrelevant and misleading words because such words spuriously may lead an investigator uninterested in your topic to your paper. Try not to use abbreviations. The title should not exceed 12 to 15 words in length.

When submitting a paper to a journal, you will also be asked to provide a running title. The running title will be displayed at the top of the page. When readers open a journal in the middle of an article, they still will be able to determine what article they are looking at by means of the running title. As for the regular title, focus on keywords when you formulate your running title.

Author's Name and Institutional Affiliation

Write your name as you wish it to be recognized professionally. Thus, you might choose John Jones,
John J. Jones, John James Jones, J. Jones, J. J. Jones, or J. James Jones. A first name, middle initial, and last name is the most commonly used form of presentation. Omit titles, such as BA, MA, PhD, Lover of Mankind, and so on. Underneath your name, write your institutional affiliation: Podunk College, Frink University, and so forth. If you have changed your affiliation since you did the research, list the old affiliation under your name and the new affiliation in a footnote. A dual affiliation is listed under your name only if both institutions contributed financially to the study. If you are unaffiliated with any institution, list your city and state. If there is more than one author, you may wish to discuss the order of appearance of names as soon as possible with your collaborators.

To the extent possible, always list your name in the same form in all articles. Although you may know that Melvin Fritzelbank and Melvin Z. Fritzelbank are the same person, electronic databases will not and likely will view Melvin and Melvin Z. as two separate persons.

Abstract

The abstract summarizes your paper. Its length depends on your target journal, but generally ranges between 150 and 250 words. The abstract, like the title, should be self-explanatory and self-contained because it is also used for indexing by information-retrieval networks. The abstract should include, if possible, (a) the major hypotheses; (b) a summary of the method, including a description of the materials, apparatus, participants, design, and procedure; (c) a synopsis of the main results; and (d) the conclusions drawn from the results. Do not include in the abstract any information that is not included in the body of the paper. Because you will not know until you are done with the outline what information you will include, you are well advised to defer writing the abstract until after you have otherwise completed the outline, or even the paper itself.

Remember that most people will read your abstract only if your title interests them, and will read your article only if your abstract interests them. It is therefore essential that the abstract interest your reader. You can interest the reader by showing that the problem is an important one, that your hypotheses about the problem are insightful ones, and that you will test these hypotheses in a convincing way. The *Publication Manual* (APA, 2010) states that abstracts should be (a) accurate, (b) self-contained, (c) concise and specific, (d) non-evaluative, and (e) coherent and readable.

Introduction

The introduction orients the reader to the research. In the paper, it does not receive a heading because its function is obvious. The task of your opening paragraph is to appeal to readers and to animate them to read on. There are several ways in which you can achieve this function (Kendall, Silk, & Chu, 2000):

- Ask a *rhetorical question* that inspires readers to consider what they think about a certain issue.
- Mention an *everyday experience* that readers can relate to and that makes the relevance of your topic apparent.
- Use an *analogy* or *metaphor* to address general principles.
- Mention an *interesting fact* that captures the interest of the reader.
- Give some *historical facts* to place the problem in context.
- Point out the *lack of previous research* to highlight the importance of your work.

After the opening paragraph, with which you elicit the readers' interest, your introduction should answer four basic questions:

1. What previous research led up to your research?
2. What does your research add to this previous research?
3. Why is the addition made by your research important or interesting?
4. How is the addition made?

The introduction usually contains a brief review of the literature most pertinent to your research. A lengthy literature review is inappropriate, except sometimes for theses and course assignments. Focus on the integration of the literature rather than summarizing many single studies. If a voluminous literature exists on the topic, cite a literature review to which the reader can refer for further information if it is wanted. Assume in your review, however, that readers are familiar with the general area of research. The readers' main interest is in what you have to contribute. They are interested in the previous literature only as it relates directly to your contribution.

Once you have told readers what is already known, you must relate what still needs to be known, that is, what you intend to find out. Tell readers not only what you intend to contribute but also what the nature of the contribution is. Does your research resolve an issue that has been unresolved in the past? Or does it deal with an issue that others have not thought about? Or does it attempt to correct an artifact in previous investigations? This information will give readers a good idea of what you view as the purpose of your study.

Next, you should show readers that the contribution is a potentially interesting or important one. Why have people paid attention to this particular issue? Or why is the new issue one to which people should pay attention? Or does an artifact in previous experimental research really undermine conclusions that previous investigators have drawn? Remember that a major purpose of the introduction is to interest readers in your paper and that your explanation of why your study is potentially important can motivate readers either to continue the article or to toss it aside.

Finally, you should tell readers how you intend to make your contribution. Sketch your experimental design, leaving a detailed description for the design section later in the paper. Show how your design relates to the theoretical issues you address. It is important to convince your readers at this point that your experiment actually does test the hypothesis you want to investigate.

Many APA journals limit the length of the introduction to five to nine manuscript pages. As a rule of thumb, keep in mind that the longer your Results section is, the longer your introduction section can be (Kendall, Silk, & Chu, 2000). That said, journal space is a valuable commodity, and you should keep your article as short as possible while still telling the full story of the research.

Method

The Method section tells the reader how the experiment was conducted. You should include just enough information so that the reader could replicate your study. If you include less information, other investigators will be unable to verify your results. If you include more information, you risk boring and possibly losing the reader in needless detail. When you are uncertain as to whether a piece of information is essential, it is better to err in the direction of including too much rather than too little.

The section describing method is usually divided into a number of subsections. Although use of these subsections is optional, it usually simplifies and clarifies the presentation for the reader. The subsections most often used are *materials, apparatus, participants, design,* and *procedure,* although not necessarily in that order. If there is no apparatus, you do not need the section. Use the order that best conveys the methods used in your particular experiment.

Materials. You should describe in this subsection the stimulus material used in the experiment. Sufficient detail should be given so that the reader could generate the same or equivalent stimuli. If the stimuli are unconventional, you might reproduce examples in a table or figure.

Apparatus. The apparatus used in the experiment should be described in this subsection. Present a general description of the apparatus, including any details that might affect the outcome of the experiment. If the apparatus is a standard piece of manufactured equipment, the name and model number will substitute for most details because the reader can then learn the details from the manufacturer. If the apparatus is unusual, you might want to photograph it and present it as a figure. This entire subsection can be omitted if no special apparatus is used. If you merely use a standard computer for stimulus presentation, you do not need to have a section to describe the computer.

Participants. You should describe in this subsection (a) the total number of participants, (b) the number of participants receiving each treatment, (c) the population from which the participants were drawn, (d) how participants were selected, and (e) the circumstances under which the participants participated (e.g., for pay, for course credit, as a favor

to the experimenter). In describing the sample in your study, include any details that might affect the outcome of the experiment—sex, ethnic or socially defined racial groups, age, education, and so on. The nature of the experiment will determine what other attributes of the participants might be relevant. The term *subject* can be used for nonhuman organisms or when referring to people in the abstract. For example, use the term when describing designs, such as a between-subjects design.

Design. This subsection should include a description of the following

- Type of design. Did you use an experimental, quasi-experimental, or correlational design? You should also give information on the number of factors and their levels, and whether a between-subjects, within-subjects, or mixed design was used. In *between-subjects designs*, every participant is assigned to just one condition, whereas in *within-subject designs*, each person participates in more than one condition. *Mixed designs* have at least one between-subjects and one within-subject variable. If you employ a within-subject design, the order in which participants are subjected to the conditions can influence the results; therefore you need to mention if you counterbalanced and, if so, how you counterbalanced for order effects (see also Reis, 2000).
- Independent variable(s).Which independent variables were used and what were their values?
- Dependent variable(s). On which variables did you measure the effect(s) of the independent variable(s)?
- The way in which participants were assigned to groups.

The design section is sometimes omitted, with the relevant information divided among the other sections. We prefer to include this section because it provides the reader with a compact overview of how the experiment was put together. If you are interested in a more detailed treatise on how to write the design section, we suggest you consult Reis's chapter "Writing Effectively About Design" in Sternberg (2000).

Procedure. This subsection should describe what happened to the participants in the study sessions from the time they entered the study to the time they completed it. A chronological account is usually best. Paraphrase directions to participants, unless they were unconventional, in which case you might want to present them verbatim. Because you assume that your readers have a general knowledge of the relevant literature, you can also assume that they are familiar with standard testing procedures. Therefore, describe such procedures more generally, always being sure to include any details that plausibly might affect the outcome of the experiment.

Results

The order in which results are reported is of critical importance. Authors often report first those results that are of most interest or relevance to the hypotheses being tested. Less interesting or relevant results are reported later. You may wish to report first a general conclusion or interpretation, followed by some descriptive statistics that support your assertion, followed only at the end by the inferential statistics that buttress the conclusion. This style of presentation often makes for more interesting reading than does a mélange of facts and statistics, followed by an obscurely placed conclusion that the bored reader may never even reach, having given up on your article pages before. Results should not be reported in the order in which the data analyses were conducted but rather in a way that makes sense to the story you want to tell.

This section should include (a) *descriptive statistics*, which summarize the data in a readily comprehensible form, and (b) *inferential statistics*, which test the likelihood of the obtained results, were chance alone operating. Techniques you used for data analysis should be reported with sufficient clarity that someone else could replicate them on the basis of your description. If you had the choice of which statistical methods to employ, give a rationale for what you did. If you plan to present a large number of results, divide this section into subsections. The particular subsections used will depend on the nature of the experiment.

It is expected that authors will provide effect sizes as well as significance values. The field is divided regarding the value of conventional significance testing, but it nevertheless is the most commonly used basis for reporting results. The *Publication Manual* (APA, 2010) recommends that confidence intervals also be reported when describing results of research.

As in the previous sections, you should make an effort to report the right amount of information, neither underreporting nor overreporting your results. And as in the previous sections, it is usually better to report a result if you are uncertain whether to include it. The criteria you should follow are to report (a) all data that are directly relevant to your hypotheses and (b) other data that may be peripheral to your hypotheses but that are of particular interest in their own right. Do not present data for individual participants unless (a) you used an $N = 1$ (single-subject) design, (b) the individual data show trends that are masked in the group data, or (c) your hypotheses are relevant to each individual's data rather than to the group data.

It is often convenient to summarize your data in the form of one or more tables or figures. In planning tables and figures, keep in mind that (a) you should not repeat in the text information that is contained in tables and figures, and (b) tables and figures should be largely self-explanatory, although you should certainly discuss them in the text. Two more considerations are relevant, but only if you plan to submit a paper to a journal: (a) Large numbers of tables and figures are discouraged (because they are expensive to reproduce in journals), and (b) one or two sentences often can summarize data that initially seem to require a table or figure.

In deciding between presentation of data in a table versus a figure, you face a trade-off. On the one hand, figures tend to give the reader a better global sense of the data; on the other hand, tables convey information to the reader more precisely. In general, tables are preferred, but your own judgment of what best conveys your message should be the arbiter of how the data are presented.

In reporting tests of statistical significance, include (a) the name of the test, (b) the value of the test statistic, (c) the degrees of freedom (if relevant), and (d) the significance level of the test. Readers should also be informed whether the test is directional and what the direction of the effect was. Assume that your reader is knowledgeable about basic statistics but describe briefly the assumptions and theory underlying unconventional tests, giving if possible a reference to which the reader can refer. Editors generally also require you to indicate the power of the significance test. They typically also want you to report the strength of the effect you obtained.

Discussion

This section should include

1. an explanation of how well your data fit your original hypotheses;
2. how your data fit in with the existing body of literature;
3. a statement of your conclusions; and
4. a discussion of theoretical and, if relevant, practical implications of the results.

It is appropriate to include in the discussion a consideration of why the findings are important, why the topic itself and the problem under it are important, why you chose the level of analysis you did, and how, if at all, the findings can be applied.

You may open the discussion with a paragraph that summarizes the purpose of your study, your hypotheses, and your most important findings. Then continue with a general statement of how well the data fit your hypotheses. If the data fit your hypotheses, your task is straightforward. If the data do not fit your hypotheses, then you can approach the data from either of two angles. One angle is an acceptance of the data as uninterpretable; the other angle is an interpretation of the data as fitting hypotheses different from those you originally suggested. In either case, you should be as clear in describing lack of fit as you are in describing fit. Typically, authors reconceptualize papers that originally were designed to show one thing but end up showing another, writing up the paper in a way differently from that originally planned.

If your data are uninterpretable or only partially interpretable, say so. Convoluted explanations of unexpected data are easily recognized as rationalizations of failures. If you have good reason to believe that some aspect of your experiment was responsible for the uninterpretable results, say so briefly and let matters stand there. Do not, however, waste space listing possible reasons for the uninterpretable results: Such lists can go on forever and are boring to read. They also usually are inconclusive.

As a guideline, use about one paragraph or more for each main point in your discussion. Ensure that you do not merely reiterate results but also integrate them somehow (Calfee, 2000).

If your data are unexpected but interpretable, it is permissible to interpret them in light of new, reformulated hypotheses. You must make clear, however, that your explanation is post hoc and speculative. There is a fine line between reformulation of hypotheses and empty rationalization, so you must convince your reader that your post hoc explanation provides a compelling account of the data.

Afterward, comment on how your data fit into the existing literature. Where do your results differ, and where do they fit right in? What do the discrepancies and parallels suggest?

After you have discussed the fit of your data to the original hypotheses as well as existing literature, and any new hypotheses you might have, a concise statement of your conclusions should be presented. Because the conclusions are the major message of your paper, you should phrase them with great care, thereby ensuring that the reader will interpret them as you intended.

Finally, you should discuss theoretical and possibly practical implications of the results. Consider internal and external validity in your discussion. If you have drawn conclusions different from your original hypotheses, you might suggest ways in which these conclusions could be verified in future research. Do not merely say, however, that future research will be needed to clarify the issues without giving the reader any inkling of what form this research might take. Every reader knows that more research can be done on any topic. What the reader wants to learn from you is what direction this research should take.

An Alternative: Results and Discussion

The Results and Discussion sections are sometimes combined into one section called Results and Discussion, especially when each section is relatively short. We recommend this combination even when the individual sections are not short. The problem with a

Results section standing by itself is that it is difficult to follow and makes for dry reading. The reader is confronted with masses of statistics without being told what the statistics mean or why they are important. Meaningful discussion is deferred until later.

Reconsider our previous discussion of thematic versus nonthematic organization. In the present context, one's choices are outlined in Exhibit 26.1. In the nonthematic organization (the format on the left), the reader will almost certainly have to refer to the results from the discussion, unless the results are represented in the Discussion section, an undesirable redundancy. Readers are unlikely to remember all the results from the Results section if they have been presented in an unmotivated fashion with no interpretation to make them meaningful.

In the thematic organization (the format on the right), there is no need for backward page turning. The results are discussed as they are presented, so that readers can understand why they are important when they are presented. They do not have to wait until later to discover why the author bothered to present those particular results and not others. Consequently, readers can form a more integrated and coherent representation of the author's results–discussion package.

If the thematic organization on the right is easier to follow than the nonthematic organization on the left, why has the organization on the left been the more widely used? We suspect it is because of a tacit fear that in a joint presentation of results and

discussion, the discussion will somehow contaminate the results: Combining the sections will result in a blurring of the distinction between objective and subjective information. This argument, although understandable, is weak. Even a slightly skilled writer can interweave data and discussion of the data in a way that makes clear the distinction between the two. A writer can, of course, be dishonest and try to pass off his opinions as facts. But such a writer can distort his data regardless of the way in which the paper is organized.

Regardless of which organization one chooses, related results may be presented and discussed in clusters to increase the meaningfulness of the presentation. For example, Results A and B might be clustered together as outlined in Exhibit 26.2.

References

The reference section provides a complete list of the sources you cite in your paper. The format of references is discussed in detail in the *Publication Manual* (APA, 2010). Be sure your references are accurate. Incorrect citations are a disservice to readers and show sloppy scholarship.

Appendix

An appendix is rarely used in psychological papers, although it is valuable in certain cases. It is appropriate for (a) computer programs designed explicitly for your research, unavailable elsewhere, and possibly valuable to others; (b) unpublished tests; (c) mathematical proofs that are relevant to your paper

---

Exhibit 26.1
Ways to Organize Results and Discussion

NONTHEMATIC ORGANIZATION	**THEMATIC ORGANIZATION**
III. Results	III. Results and Discussion
A. Presentation of Result A	A. Result A
B. Presentation of Result B	1. Presentation
C. Presentation of Result C	2. Discussion
IV. Discussion	B. Result B
A. Discussion of Result A	1. Presentation
B. Discussion of Result B	2. Discussion
C. Discussion of Result C	C. Result C
	1. Presentation
	2. Discussion

Exhibit 26.2
Clustered Presentation of Results and Discussion

NONTHEMATIC ORGANIZATION	**THEMATIC ORGANIZATION**
III. Results	III. Results and Discussion
A. Presentation of Result Cluster (A, B)	A. Result Cluster (A, B)
B. Presentation of Result C	1. Presentation
IV. Discussion	2. Discussion
A. Discussion of Result Cluster (A,B)	B. Result C
B. Discussion of Result C	1. Presentation
	2. Discussion

---

but would distract the reader if included in the text; (d) lists of stimulus materials, if the materials are unusual or particularly important to your conclusions; and (e) other supplemental materials (APA, 2010). An appendix should be included only if it is especially enlightening or helpful in enabling others to replicate your study. Sometimes multiple appendixes are used. In this case, label each appendix with a capital letter (e.g., Appendix A, Appendix B). If you have only one appendix, name it Appendix. Multiple tables per appendix must be labeled with the capital letter of the appendix and a number (A1, A2, A3, B1, B2, etc.). Even if you have only one appendix (which in this case would just be named Appendix), you still have to label your tables in the appendix A1, A2, and so forth to indicate that these tables are located in the appendix.

Order of Sections

Once you are ready to write your paper in final form, you should order the sections in the following way:

1. Title page (including your name and affiliation)
2. Author identification notes
3. Abstract
4. Text
5. References
6. Footnotes
7. Tables (one table per page)
8. Figures with figure captions (one figure per page)

This ordering is to facilitate editing and printing. It is not the order in which the various parts will appear in the paper. Pages should be numbered consecutively using Arabic numerals, beginning with the title page and ending with the figure captions. If your figures will be submitted in hard copy, they should be numbered on the back with their respective figure numbers. Place page numbers in the upper right corner of each page. Immediately above the page number, write the first few words of your title or the whole title if the title is short. This way, the pages can be returned to a manuscript in case they are temporarily misplaced.

Once you have finished ordering and numbering your pages, the paper is complete. Once you have proofread it, you are ready to hand it in or send it off.

ON QUALITATIVE RESEARCH

Qualitative research papers generally have to meet the same requirements as experimental research papers. Their abstracts need to have the same core elements outlined in the previous section, they have to justify the sample size and constitution, data collection and analyses have to be described in detail, and so forth. The criteria for the evaluation of qualitative research papers therefore are similar to the ones for experimental research as well.

There are a few particularities of qualitative research that one should be aware of, however. Data analyses in qualitative research typically are not as straightforward as in quantitative research, mainly because data collection and analysis are more entangled with each other. The researcher has to be aware of her relationship with the subjects. Social position and demographic factors of the individuals collecting and providing the data as well as gender relations are of great importance and can influence the data as well as their interpretation.

It is also more difficult to determine when one has sufficient data for analysis. As a general guideline, data analysis is completed when new cases do not result in any more information.

Finally, special effort has to be made so that the data analysis is transparent and replicable. The units containing data should be enumerated, the interpretation of the data should be broken down into steps, and the rules for interpretation of data should be made explicit. These processes ensure that anybody can reconstruct the process of data analysis and interpretation.

Students and even experienced researchers sometimes get into a debate whether quantitative research is better than qualitative research, or vice versa. Our view is that quantitative and qualitative research are complementary: Each can teach us things that the other does not, and hence there is much value in using them together.

AMERICAN PSYCHOLOGICAL ASSOCIATION GUIDELINES FOR PSYCHOLOGY PAPERS

When you prepare a manuscript, it is not enough to ensure that the content is valuable and well thought through. Your intention in writing is to communicate your findings to your audience, and you can do this efficiently only if your readers are able to understand you. Therefore, do not neglect language and style issues.

You may want to pay attention to frequently misused words. Dowling (2008) provided an extensive overview of misused words, and Garner (2003) provided a complete dictionary of American usage. Psychological dictionaries and encyclopedias like the *APA Concise Dictionary of Psychology* (APA, 2009) provide extensive lists of psychological terms.

The *Publication Manual* (APA, 2010) provides a good overview of grammar and style issues, addressing such issues as tone and reduction of bias in writing as well as grammar and usage guidelines. The *Publication Manual* furthermore gives precise guidelines as to how to prepare your paper for submission with respect to data presentation, punctuation, capitalization, crediting sources, and much more; if you plan to publish your work, you cannot afford to be without this manual. Not only do APA journals adhere to the APA style guidelines, but there are many other journals that use the *Publication Manual* as well. Journals of the British Psychological Society (BPS) adopted the APA style as of October 2001. Publications of the BPS other than journal articles follow the *Style Guide* that can be found online by entering the search words "BPS style" in a search engine. Many other non-APA journals will accept papers prepared in accordance with APA guidelines as well, even though there are minor differences in style. Always consult the guidelines of the journal to which you plan to submit your paper to ensure that you are adhering to their style regulations.

PROOFREADING AND REVISING

It is a common misperception that once you have written your first draft, you are done. Good writers do not submit their first draft. Indeed, a good part of the work on your manuscript only starts once the first draft has been written. Do not get into the bad habit of thinking that the draft is the final version. Advisors, editors, reviewers, and others are likely to make you do at least one, and probably more, revisions before your paper ever sees the light of day.

General Tips

Following are some general tips for successful proofreading and revising:

- Get some distance.
- Rethink.
- Do not fix what you think is good.
- Make structural changes first.
- Check for typos and orthographic errors.
- Write for your likely referees and readers.
- Try to think of your work in terms of explaining it to a layperson.
- Check for fit to journal guidelines and subject matter.
- Read your paper at least once while imagining yourself to be a critical reviewer or, even better, ask a colleague to do the same.
- Cite likely referees (who conceivably merit citation).
- Make sure all cited works are in your references.

Get some distance. When you have worked on your paper for a long time, you get so involved in it that it is hardly possible to see it in an objective way. You do not read sentences carefully anymore because you have read them so many times that you feel like you know already what comes next; and maybe you are just bored by reading your paper for the 10th time. Just put it away for a while. Ideally, let it rest for a few days or weeks, or if you are in a rush, try to not look at it for at least a day or so. A fresh perspective will be very helpful in revising your chapter, aiding you in finding incongruities and passages that are difficult to comprehend, and seeing other shortcomings that might have eluded you so far.

Rethink. When you look at a paragraph, think about its intention. And then try to think about what you are saying in a different way. Are there other ways to put it? Are there parts of the picture that have been left out so far, or have you taken sides without being justified? Once you have reconsidered what you have written, you are ready to reformulate problematic sentences or paragraphs and add or delete information that you have reevaluated.

Do not fix what you think is good. In the heat of the battle, it is easy to keep revising and making changes until your paper looks very different from your first draft. Be cautious and selective in revision. Do not revise things just for the sake of revising them—have a reason for changing them.

Make structural changes first. Before you start working on the details, reconsider the big picture.

What is the message of your paper? Does it come across clearly? Does your paper contain a lot of redundancy that you could eliminate? Does the organization of your paper follow logical principles? Evaluate these aspects of your paper first and make those changes before concentrating on details.

Check for typos and orthographic errors. As the editor of the journal *Psychological Bulletin*, the second author of the current chapter found that the single most annoying flaw in a submitted paper is a slew of typographical errors. Why? Because they are the easiest thing for the author to correct. It is not the editor's or the reviewers' job to do your proofreading for you. Always proofread. It is the one thing you most easily can do to improve the impression you make. If you do not proofread, some reviewers and editors will simply tell you to do it. But others will not be so congenial, and you may have problems changing that first impression. (No mater hwat, you loose if U don't prufreed!) Spell-check features associated with word processors help, but they are no substitute for proofreading, as shown in the preceding sentence. A spellchecker would pick up the first spelling error (*hwat*) because it is not an English word, but it would not detect the other spelling error (*loose*), which is an English word.

Write for your likely referees and readers. Expert article writers do not just write articles. They write for an audience. They decide on likely journals before they put pen to paper (or fingers to computer keys).

You can get a good idea of the types of articles a given journal publishes simply by reading the journal's mission statement (usually near the front or back of the journal and often online) and by looking at recent past issues. But there is a more informal kind of knowledge you need to acquire either through your own experience or from the experience of others.

Many characteristics of journals go beyond mission statements. Some journals seem to emphasize methodological rigor above all else. One reads them and has the feeling that the study could be infinitely trivial but nevertheless published as long as it was methodologically sound. Other journals seem to emphasize articles that are interesting but flakey: The ideas are provocative, but the evidence for them is slim. Still other journals seem more concerned about length than about anything else. These journals will not publish relatively longer articles, no matter how good those articles may be. One journal to which we have submitted seems to care more that the article is in standard APA article format than about what is said in this or any other format. These kinds of characteristics tend to come and go as the editorships of journals change, but often the "culture" of a given journal endures beyond any single editorial board.

It thus behooves you to find out as much as you can about the kinds of issues that are important to the editor and referees of a given journal. You can save yourself a lot of lost time by seeking journals that publish the kind of article you have written and by avoiding journals that do not publish this kind of article.

Try to think of your work in terms of explaining it to a layperson. If you feel stuck with the organization and formulation of your paper, try to think about ways to convey your message to a layperson. This rethinking will help you to reflect on your subject in a different way. It will facilitate finding simpler words and ways to explain what you are talking about.

Check for fit to journal guidelines and subject matter. One of the single most common causes of outright rejection is the submission of papers that even a casual review would reveal to be inappropriate for that journal. For example, people sent the second author of this chapter, as editor, empirical studies of substantive psychological phenomena, despite the fact that *Psychological Bulletin* never accepts articles of this type. They wasted their own time and his. We also returned papers that departed substantially from APA writing guidelines (e.g., were single-spaced or used notes in place of references). You can save yourself and others a major headache by checking the submission guidelines, usually printed in each issue of the journal, to ensure that your paper fits its intended home. (You have probably guessed by now that this very chapter was rejected from *Physical Sciences Ideas of the Century*.)

Read your paper at least once while imagining yourself to be a critical reviewer or, even better,

ask a colleague to do the same. We tend to be enamored of our own work. We often do not see the flaws that would be obvious if the same paper had someone else's name on it. So try reading your paper with the same devastating analytical acuity you would use if you wished to demolish the work of your most loathsome enemy. Ask a colleague to do the same. In this way, you will be able to anticipate and perhaps eliminate some reviewer criticisms—use of faulty logic, for example. If your logic is faulty, your paper suffers; of course, perfect logic does not guarantee a perfect paper or even a good one.

Cite likely referees (who conceivably merit citation). It is impossible to anticipate everyone who might referee an article. Nor can one cite every potential reviewer. But it is important to cite likely referees who have made a serious contribution to work in the field that the article covers. And if the editor has sent the article to a particular reviewer, the editor, at least, considers the individual to be one of the more active contributors to the field the article covers. Thus, this suggestion is not a cynical one: The likely referees are the same people who are likely to be the major contributors to the field.

Make sure all cited works are in your references. Always ensure that the works and sources you are citing in your paper are listed in the reference list.

HOW TO DECIDE UPON A JOURNAL AND SUBMIT YOUR WORK

In many cases, authors decide where they are going to submit their work before they even have written it up. This is because journals have different restrictions with regard to the topics on which they publish papers, what the maximum length of these papers is, who reads the papers, and so forth. Eight considerations, described in the following paragraphs, should enter your decision.

Quality
Journals vary widely in quality. Some journals publish papers that do little more than fill up journal space; other journals publish only outstanding

contributions to the literature. Better journals generally have higher rejection rates for submitted papers, so the probability of a paper's being accepted in such journals is lower.

One way to evaluate quality is to look at the impact factor of the journal. Later in this section, under the section Journal Citation Reports, we describe how you can determine the journal's *impact factor*, or the extent to which papers in the journal are cited by authors in the field.

Content
All journals limit by content the kinds of papers they accept. Journal editors use either or both of two criteria in deciding on the appropriateness of a paper's content. The first criterion is substantive focus. What is the topic of research? The journal may accept, for example, only developmental, or cognitive, or applied papers. The second criterion is methodological focus. How was the research done? The journal may accept, for example, only experimental, or theoretical, or review papers.

Readership
Journals vary in (a) who reads them and in (b) how many people read them. Readership depends in turn on the quality and content of each journal and, to a lesser extent, upon the cost of the journal. Journals publish annual statements of their circulation, so that the extent of the readership can be determined by looking through recent back issues of a journal for the annual statement. The composition of the readership can be inferred by assessing quality and content and by examining the kinds of papers in which articles from the journal are cited.

Length Restrictions
Most journals have implicit restrictions on length of submitted papers, and some journals have explicit restrictions. If the journal's editorial statement (carried in every issue of most journals) does not make any statement about length, an examination of several recent issues of the journal will indicate the range in length acceptable to the journal editor.

Publication Lag

The length of time between acceptance of an article and publication of the article is the *publication lag*. Journals vary in publication lags from as little as 1 month to as much as 18 months or more. In submitting an article, the author should decide how long he is willing to wait for the article to be published, keeping in mind that there will be an additional lag from the time the paper is submitted to the time the paper is either accepted or rejected.

Cost of Submission

Most journals do not charge authors for publication. Some journals do charge, however, so that publication of even a short article can cost an author several hundred dollars. The journal's editorial statement will indicate what costs, if any, are involved. The author must decide before submitting an article to such a journal whether she is willing and able to meet the costs of publication.

Authorship Restrictions

A small number of journals restrict in some way their potential contributors. Submission may be by invitation only, or it may be limited to individuals belonging to or sponsored by members of some organization. The journal's editorial statement will indicate whether any such restrictions apply.

Journal Citation Reports

A good way to compare and evaluate journals is to have a look at the Journal Citation Reports (JCR) published by the ISI (formerly the Institute for Scientific Information). Of particular importance to social scientists is the Social Science Citation Index (SSCI), which contains statistics about hundreds of journals that can be accessed through the ISI Web of Knowledge database. The JCR gives you a variety of statistics about the journals. Here are some that might be of particular importance to you:

- *Total cites*. This number indicates the total number of citations to a particular journal in a given year.
- *Impact factor*. The impact factor is the average number of citations to articles of a given journal published during the previous 2 years. For example, the impact factor for the year 2008 of the *Journal for Psychology in the Himalayas* gives you the average number of citations in 2008 to articles that were published in 2006 and 2007 in that journal. So the impact factor is calculated by dividing the number of citations in the report year (in this case, 2008) by the total number of articles that were published in the preceding 2 years. Note that *all* citations in journals ISI monitors count, including the ones in different journals. However, ISI does not monitor all journals, so citations in some journals will not be counted simply because they are not included in the database.

- *5-year journal impact factor*. The 5-year impact factor does essentially the same thing as the impact factor; however, it indicates the average number of times in the particular JCR year that articles from the journal were cited that were published by that journal during the past 5 years.
- *Immediacy index*. The immediacy index indicates how often an article is cited in the year it is published. It is computed by dividing the number of citations to articles published in 1 year by the total number of articles published in that year. Note that articles published earlier in the year will have an advantage in the immediacy index, as they will have had more opportunity to be cited. Also, articles from journals that publish more frequently during the year will have an advantage because there is more opportunity for articles in frequently publishing journals to appear earlier in the year.
- *Articles*. This is the total number of articles that were published in a given year by the journal.

When you look at the JCR for different journals, do remember that prestigious, high-impact journals are not always the best choice for your article. The other seven points made, like content and readership of the journal, play a role as well. A journal that is highly rated in the JCR but that does not publish on the topic of your study will, in all likelihood, not publish your article. You should also consider that the more prestigious a journal, the higher the rejection rates typically are. Some journals have rejection rates of 90% or more, so you may end up wasting valuable time trying to get your paper published before it gets out of date.

In general, then, you need to weigh many factors in deciding to what journal to submit a paper. The decision is important but it can be extremely difficult. For example, if you are trying to get a job or receive tenure, articles will count little on your vita if they are not at least in press. Articles *in preparation* or *in progress* or *under editorial consideration* often count little, if at all. If you aim too high in submitting a paper to a journal, you may find that it does not have a publisher when you need it to count on your vita. If you aim too low, you may find that the paper has an acceptance or even is published, but it is weighted less because it has not been published in a first-rate journal. Thus, an important part of the process in writing is targeting a journal at the right level—aiming neither too high nor too low. You might want to seek advice from people with more experience in the field as to what they believe is a reasonable journal to which to submit your paper.

Submitting Your Paper

Once you have decided on a journal, you should make certain that your paper meets the editorial requirements of the journal. In most cases, this means that the paper conforms to the APA guidelines outlined in the *Publication Manual* (APA, 2010). If your paper conforms to these (or other) guidelines, you are ready to send it out. Most (but certainly not all) journals now have an electronic submission portal where you can submit your manuscript. If you submit a paper version, you will generally be required to submit several copies of the paper, with the exact number depending on the journal.

You may not simultaneously submit what is essentially the same paper to two different journals, even if the papers differ in minor respects. You should therefore send the paper initially to your first choice for publication, keeping in mind a second and possibly a third choice in case your paper is rejected.

When you send the manuscript, include a cover letter indicating

- your intention to submit the manuscript;
- the title of the manuscript;
- the length of the manuscript and the number of tables and figures in the manuscript;

- requests for masked review (i.e., review that does not identify you to reviewers), if you wish it and the journal offers this option;
- information regarding any previous presentations of the data (such as in scientific talks);
- information regarding any closely related manuscripts, such as ones that report portions of the data;
- suggestions for potential reviewers or persons who should not review the manuscript (optional);
- notice of any possible conflicts of interest;
- verification that human or animal subjects have been treated in accordance with APA guidelines; and
- any permissions that may be needed for reproduction of copyrighted material.

You may also be asked to confirm that the paper has not simultaneously been submitted elsewhere. Additionally, be sure to indicate in the notes to the paper sources of financial support you received for the research described in the paper and for preparation of the paper. A sample cover letter to your editor appears in Exhibit 26.3. Once you have submitted

---

Exhibit 26.3
Sample Cover Letter

Dear Dr. Knowitall,

Attached please find my submission entitled "Do I Like It or Do I Not: The Impact of Personal Preferences on Personal Preferences." The manuscript is 27 pages long and includes one table.

I wish to request masked review and I have deleted all references in the manuscript that contain my name.

Parts of the data in this paper have been previously presented at the Annual Convention of Preferential Psychology in Adversity, OH, in May 2009.

When conducting the research, I followed informed consent procedures as well as APA ethical standards. The article is original and not submitted elsewhere

Thank you very much in advance for considering my paper.

Sincerely,

Like A. Roni
Department of Psychology
University of Likeridge
144 Chooseitall Way
Favortown, MN 11222
222-333-4444 (voice)
222-333-5555 (fax)
LikeARoni@likeridge.edu

---

your paper to a journal, the publication process starts. This process is explained in detail in Chapter 27 of this volume.

References

American Psychological Association. (2010). *Publication manual of the American Psychological Association* (6th ed.). Washington, DC: Author.

American Psychological Association. (2009). *APA concise dictionary of psychology*. Washington, DC: Author.

Calfee, R. (2000). What does it all mean: The discussion. In R. J. Sternberg (Ed.), *Guide to publishing in psychology journals* (pp. 133–145). New York, NY: Cambridge University Press.

Dowling, D. (2008). *The wrong word dictionary*. Victoria, British Columbia, Canada: Castle Books.

Eisenberg, N. (2000). Writing a literature review. In R. J. Sternberg (Ed.), *Guide to publishing in psychology journals* (pp. 17–27). New York, NY: Cambridge University Press.

Garner, B. A. (2003). *Garner's modern American usage*. New York, NY: Oxford University Press.

Kendall, P. C., Silk, J. S., & Chu, B. C. (2000). Introducing your research report: Writing the introduction. In R. J. Sternberg (Ed.), *Guide to publishing in psychology journals* (pp. 41–57). New York, NY: Cambridge University Press.

Reis, H. T. (2000). Writing effectively about design. In R. J. Sternberg (Ed.), *Guide to publishing in psychology journals* (pp. 81–97). New York, NY: Cambridge University Press.

Sternberg, R. J. (Ed.). (2000). *Guide to publishing in psychology journals*. New York, NY: Cambridge University Press.

Sternberg, R. J., & Sternberg, K. (2010). *The psychologist's companion* (5th ed.). New York, NY: Cambridge University Press.

## CHAPTER 27

HOW TO PUBLISH YOUR MANUSCRIPT

Gary R. VandenBos

Authors and editors have more in common than many authors think. Authors want to get their research published in the most highly regarded scientific journal possible, and editors want to publish the highest quality research they can possibly obtain for their journal. Authors need to do the best job possible drafting an interesting, theoretically important, scientifically sound, logically compelling, and verbally effective manuscript. Using the feedback from the peer review process and other input, the editor will select the best manuscripts from among those submitted to the journal to further develop, refine, and enhance by providing editorial guidance on how to best shape and craft the manuscript to reach the goal of effectively and efficiently communicating its key findings to the reader. This is the author–editor partnership in successful scholarly communication.

The basic process of preparing a manuscript should be enjoyable. And it can be, if you have a good model for how to approach the task. It is a creative challenge. Good science reporting is similar to all narrative writing; it involves telling a story. The story you are telling involves your research interests and your research project, so you know it very well. No one is more knowledgeable and better prepared to tell the story of your research project than you. And, fortunately, there is a model for the storytelling. All good stories have a beginning, a middle, and an end. In the case of scientific writing, the beginning is the introduction (which closes with the hypotheses or research questions), the middle is the methods and then the results, and the end is the discussion and conclusions and implications.

This chapter describes the publication process related to the writing, reviewing, and revising of scientific journal articles. Topics covered include preparing to submit, selecting a journal, the submission process, what happens during the review process, the basic review criteria, and editorial appeals. Additional topics covered include determining authorship credit, conflict of interest, and plagiarism and self-plagiarism.

ARE YOU READY TO SUBMIT?

Before you submit a manuscript to a journal, you need to determine whether your manuscript is ready for submission. The first self-check of your manuscript involves simply looking at the pieces and thinking about how they compare with what is published in most journals. How long is your manuscript? Most psychology journals that publish empirical research typically consider manuscripts with between 18 and 28 pages of text, four to six pages of references, and one to three tables or figures—with an overall total number of pages being between 30 and 38. For more medically oriented journals, there may be a specific word limit of 2,000 words or 3,000 words. Most European and Asian journals use word counts, usually between 5,000 and 7,000 words, rather than an overall number of pages. Is your manuscript too long or too short? If it is a little too long, can you justify the additional length, and is the editor likely to agree? If the total length of your manuscript exceeds 50 double-spaced, 12-point type pages in length, it is probably

DOI: 10.1037/13621-027
APA Handbook of Research Methods in Psychology: Vol. 3. Data Analysis and Research Publication, H. Cooper (Editor-in-Chief)

just too long, and you should be considering how to cut or condense it before submitting it.

The relative length of the sections within your manuscript should be examined. If your manuscript overall is 24 pages long, then one might guess that you have six pages of introduction, six pages of methods, six pages of results, and six pages of discussion. How do the relative sizes of each of your sections compare with each other? Are one or two sections too short—and, hence, lacking in detail? Are one or two sections far too long in comparison with the others, such that they should be cut back in length? For those publishing studies using qualitative methods, the Methods section would likely be no more than one page, with the Results section about 10 to 12 pages.

Another self-check process involves consideration of how many times you have read and revised your manuscript and how much presubmission editorial feedback you have gotten from others. Few psychologists can write final draft copy off the top of their heads, even if working from a detailed outline. In general, you should do a first draft of your manuscript and later rewrite or edit it at least three to four times. The initial writing will generally take the most time and be the slowest process, whereas later editing and rewrite passes through the manuscript might be done in an hour or two (but done multiple times, thinking about and considering different aspects of the manuscript and its content during a different pass). In addition to your self-editing, have you gotten sufficient editorial feedback from trusted but demanding colleagues? Getting some presubmission feedback will improve your manuscript and increase the likelihood that you receive a *revise-and-resubmit* editorial decision from the editors. Presubmission feedback will provide you with an independent double-check on whether you have been as clear as you thought you were being, whether you forgot to mention some important details, and whether your presentation is logical and convincing. Always get presubmission feedback from two to three colleagues and further revise your manuscript before formal submission to a journal.

A final self-check is to proofread your manuscript. Are there typos? If so, fix the typos. Using a spell-checking program is simple and easy. Use it. However, spell-check programs only check for the most common

spelling errors and other grammar and style matters. Using them is not a substitute for a final proofreading of the manuscript by yourself or someone else. As one reads, it often becomes apparent that some terms used are not quite the right or best terms to capture what you are trying to communicate. Change them to better ones. You should also check for consistency of language. Once you name a test, a process, or a variable, be sure you keep using that same term consistently. Do not use alternative phrasing or synonyms because that adds an extra burden for the reviewer and reader in understanding your writing and research.

SELECTING A JOURNAL

Once your manuscript is ready to be submitted to a journal, you need to decide where you are going to submit it. One way to identify an appropriate journal is to create a list of journals that published the background research that led to your project. Use your reference list to create a list of journals from which you have cited research, noting the frequency of citations from each relevant journal. The journal from which you have cited the most articles may very well be the most appropriate journal to which you should submit your manuscript because it has published work that you value.

A second way to identify potential journals to which to submit your manuscript is to ask more experienced colleagues who are familiar with your work. Which journals do they see as being the most appropriate for your manuscript? In what order would they list the journals in terms of their quality, reputation, and impact? In general, you want to submit your manuscript to the highest quality journal that is appropriate for your research and its quality level, so you have to make a quality assessment of your manuscript and make a quality-match determination between your manuscript and the potential journals.

A third way of selecting a journal is to consider its *impact* as reflected by how often articles published in it are cited by other researchers. The *Journal Citation Reports* published by the ISI (formally the Institute for Scientific Research, Research/Web of Science/Thompson) is an aid for determining the rank order and the importance of a journal's standing in the field, both in terms of immediate impact and long-term impact. A journal with a higher impact factor may not necessarily be a better publishing outlet than another journal with a somewhat lower impact rating. You should consider where each is on a continuum ranging from broad–general journals to specific–niche journals. Which journal has the readership audience you most wish to reach? The best audience for your manuscript may be a psychology journal or it might be better suited to an interdisciplinary journal or a medical or nursing journal. You may also want to consider journals published in other English-speaking countries outside North America, such as Australia, New Zealand, South Africa, and the United Kingdom. All have active national psychological, medical, and nursing associations that publish well-respected, medium- to high-impact factor journals.

Before you submit to a given journal, be sure to examine a physical copy of the journal or visit the journal's website. You should read the editorial coverage domain of the journal as it appears in a recent copy of the journal or on the website. You should examine the table of contents of several issues to get a sense of how this editorial coverage statement actually manifests itself in the form of the articles published. If you do not regularly read articles in the journal, you should read some manuscripts in the journal to see whether they are similar to yours in terms of types of questions asked, literature review, and methods utilized. You should also read the journal's instructions to authors because this provides you with the specific information about that journal's expectations about manuscript preparation and style used. Do they use regular narrative abstracts or structured abstracts? Do they use American Psychological Association (APA) style, the *Chicago Manual of Style*, or some other style? Are there specific supplemental documents they want you to provide at the time of submission, such as an approval letter from your institutional review board (IRB) or a statement about the ethical treatment of subjects? Where, and how, do they want you to submit your manuscript?

You might also consider how fast or slow a journal is in terms of the editorial handling of manuscripts and in terms of publishing them after acceptance. This may be more important early in your career, particularly if you have a tenure decision coming up in 12 months. You might also weigh the speed of a journal's publishing process against the importance of the project you are reporting. If it is a good study but not groundbreaking, you may just want to get it in print soon with as few rewrites as possible. If your manuscript is a major contribution, you will want to submit it to a high-impact, slow-processing journal, even though it will take longer, because of the added prestige of having a publication in that journal.

Manuscripts submitted to journals that are outside the editorial coverage domain, that are significantly lower in methodological quality and sophistication than that published in the journal, or that are written in a style that is significantly different in the length and depth of analysis are likely to be rejected without formal peer review. It makes no sense to waste your time and a journal's time by submitting a manuscript to a journal that never publishes work similar to yours. This is why it is important for the author to consider the *match* or *fit* of his or her manuscript to the content regularly appearing in a journal to which the author is considering as a possible publishing outlet.

SUBMITTING YOUR MANUSCRIPT

Once you have selected a journal to which you want to submit, double-check the website for the journal or printed copies of the journal. Double-check the editorial requirements and whether there are any atypical submission procedures. Submissions are now normally made via an electronic submission portal. There may or may not be forms or checklists for you to complete as part of the submission process. And address the letter to the current editor who is handling submissions—and not to the person who was the editor 5 or 10 years ago.

Your submission should be accompanied by a cover letter in which you cover the issues required in the journal's instructions to authors or the APA *Publication Manual* (APA, 2010b). The most common information needed is the following:

1. the title of the manuscript you are submitting, its total length, and the number of tables and figures (with appendixes and supplemental material attached);

2. a statement that the manuscript is an original work that has not been previously published and is not under review by any other journals;

3. a statement that the research was conducted with the approval of an IRB and in accordance with APA guidelines or other relevant guidelines;

4. information on previous presentations of the data at conferences or closely related manuscripts;

5. a statement of any conflict of interest or other declarations about which it is important to inform the editor (and possibly the readers); and

6. any other statements or information that a specific journal requires (e.g., masked vs. open review, copyright transfer permission, etc.).

Most of the time there is no expectation that the author will suggest possible reviewers. This is particularly true for authors early in their careers. However, you can suggest potential reviewers if you wish because the editor is free to use none, some, or all of them. Clearly, if you suggest reviewers, they need to be individuals with whom you have no current or recent connection, so that there is no conflict of interest issue. You should make a clear statement about this in your letter. It is more common that authors mention reviewers whom the author would prefer the editor not to use because of previous run-ins or a hostile exchange that the author believes would prevent the reviewer from providing an objective review. The editor is free to honor or ignore such a request but would be aware of the reviewer's potential bias against the author.

MEANING OF *UNDER REVIEW*

A manuscript should only be submitted to one scholarly journal at a time. While it is under review at that journal, you should not submit it to another journal. It is *under review* at the journal you submitted it to until such time as you receive a letter from the editor accepting or rejecting it—or you formally write the editor and withdraw it. A manuscript for which you have received a revise-and-resubmit letter is still under review with the journal to which you submitted it, unless you formally withdraw it. After a manuscript has been rejected by the journal

to which you submitted it (or you have withdrawn it), you are free to further revise the manuscript and submit it to another journal.

When you submit a manuscript to a journal, you should receive an acknowledgment of the receipt of the manuscript, either immediately with an automated computer response or within several days after you have submitted it. If you submit a manuscript and have not received an acknowledgment within 2 weeks after it was scheduled to reach the editorial office, you should write the editor or manuscript coordinator to confirm receipt or determine whether something went wrong in the transmittal process. Once you know that your manuscript has been received, the waiting begins.

WHAT HAPPENS AFTER YOU SUBMIT YOUR MANUSCRIPT?

First, there will be some administrative handling. Someone will move the manuscript from the submission portal into the manuscript tracking system. Then the editor of the journal will read the manuscript and make a decision as to whether it is appropriate for the journal and whether it appears to have sufficient scientific merit to warrant a formal peer review. If the answer to either of these is no, you will receive a quick *reject, without review* editorial action letter. Journals vary in the extent to which they use a *reject, without review* function, with the frequency of its use varying from 0% to 35% across journals in psychology.

If the editor decides that your manuscript should receive a formal peer review, it will be assigned to an action editor, who might be the editor or one of the associate editors. The action editor will then read the manuscript and assign potential reviewers from whom reviews will be requested. The review requests will go out, the reviewers will read your manuscript, and the reviewers will complete and return their reviews to the journal. The action editor will then read the review, reread your manuscript, and start the final editorial decision-making process.

It takes most journals 7 to 10 days to do the administration, complete the initial read, assign the reviewer, and make review requests to the potential reviewer. Journals differ in the length of time that they give reviewers to complete reviews. For most journals this ranges from 10 days to 2 months, with the most typical being 30 days. After the review process is complete, the editor or action editor will need to read the reviews, reread your manuscript, reflect on the package of information, and then write an editorial action letter to you.

In psychology, the general expectation is that 95% of the time all of this will occur within 90 days after submission (and with a goal that a simple majority of manuscripts will complete the review process within 60 days). Of course, there are certain times of the year when slowdowns in review completion occur (e.g., holidays, summer vacation), and in some cases, problems emerge in obtaining qualified reviewers to review a given manuscript. If you have not received an editorial action letter within 90 days after submission, it is reasonable for you to write the editor or the manuscript coordinator to ask about the status of the processing of your manuscript and when they estimate an editorial decision will be made.

WHAT ARE SOME OF THE REVIEW CRITERIA?

Manuscripts are reviewed simultaneously at several levels. The overall assessment is whether a manuscript represents quality research reported in a quality writing manner. The importance of the topic and the newness of the information play a role. The logic and thoroughness of the presentation, and the integrity of the theoretical presentation, play a role. The suitability and execution of appropriate methodological and statistical procedures play a role.

Initial overarching nonsubstantive questions include whether the content and methods are an appropriate match with the journal, whether the manuscript is prepared in a manner that reasonably approaches the style used by the journal, and whether the length of the manuscript and number of figures and tables are consistent with what is typical in the journal. A quick examination of the format of the reference list, the use of a regular abstract or a structured abstract, how references are cited in the text, and the level of the headers will let the editor know whether the author has read the journal's instructions

to authors on manuscript preparation. Few editors will reject a manuscript because of a few small variations from desired style format expectations, but large and extensive deviations in style will cause comprehension problems for reviewers and readers—and the editor may reject such manuscripts without review.

Each of the common sections of the manuscript (e.g., introduction, methods, results, limitations, and discussion) are likely to be examined as individual components as well. The introduction will be assessed in terms of whether it is a well-integrated and systematic review of the theory and research—and builds to a thoughtful justification for the research. Does the coverage of the literature focus on what is essential to know to understand the research questions, methodology used, and issues to be discussed? The introduction should "foreshadow" the rest of the manuscript, such that no new topic or concept suddenly appears later in the manuscript. The introduction should also not include ideas, topics, theories, and citations that, although interesting, are not directly relevant to and later utilized in the manuscript.

The Method section will receive considerable and intense examination. Does it clearly and completely describe all of the methods, measures, and procedures used in the research? Could another researcher use the methods as described and actually replicate the research in exactly the same manner as originally done? The expectations of the specificity of methodological detail has increased in recent years, after guidelines were developed and released by the Consolidated Standards of Reporting Trials (CONSORT: Transparent Reporting of Trials, 2007) and Transparent Reporting of Evaluations With Nonexperimental Designs (TREND; Des Jarlais, Lyles, Crepaz, & the TREND Group, 2004). The Journal Article Reporting Standards (JARS; APA Publications and Communications Board Working Group on Journal Article Reporting Standards, 2008) in psychology and the Meta-Analysis Reporting Standards (MARS) reporting guidelines were also recently released (see APA, 2010b, p. 22).

Increasingly important is information on the population from which subjects were recruited, recruitment and selection procedures and criteria, and inclusion and exclusion factors leading to the final sample of subjects. Was the population sampled from the entire community, students in a given course, or patients at a clinic? How were potential subjects identified and approached, and who made the approach? What factors singled them out as possible research participants, and what factors resulted in not further considering someone? What participation rate was initially achieved, and what dropout rates occurred at various steps as tests and meetings occurred? The major demographics and other factors related to the final sample should be carefully described—and contrasted with the same factors in the overall population from which they were obtained. The reviewer will assess such information because it is essential for the reader to understand to whom the results might generalize as well as important to other researchers in terms of their ability to potentially replicate the study and findings.

The measures and details of measurement are carefully considered. Are they appropriate to the research questions and likely to generate data relevant to the questions asked? Each measure used in a study should be named or otherwise identified and described. What does it claim to measure, how is it scored, and has a sample item been presented? Is there a statement about reliability and validity? The same parallel construction, covering the same aspects in the same order, should be used in describing each measure for ease of quick comprehension by the reviewer and reader. The exact methods, order, and procedures of data acquisition should be adequately described.

The details of the experimental manipulation or intervention will be closely examined. Can the reviewer fully and clearly understand what actually was done? Who did what with or to whom? How was it done? Did it occur one time or repeatedly? Does it appear to be credible in terms of being likely to generate the effect expected? Could others replicate it?

Consideration of the statistical analysis is also key to the assessment of a report of a research project. Do the statistical procedures utilized fit the data, and are they appropriate to address the research questions? Is there evidence that they were utilized in a competent manner? Are there other statistical methods that would be more appropriate, and if so, has the author explained the rationale for not using them?

The examination of the presentation of the results; description of the limitations of the research; and discussion of the results in relation to the existing literature, future research, and potential application will follow in order. Are the most relevant data presented in tables, figures, and text? Are the data in the tables and figures consistent with the data and interpretations given in the text of the manuscript? Do the interpretations of the results and the discussion of the results occur in an orderly manner, consistent with the order of the research questions and consistent with the theories and research presented in the introduction? Are the limitations of the data, methods of collection or analysis, and so forth mentioned and considered in a meaningful manner?

Citations are evaluated in terms of whether they are systematic, representative, and selective—but not exhaustively comprehensive. Are there too many or too few? Is there a good balance between classic historical references, major reviews, and current empirical research? Do the citations appear in a flowing and nonintrusive manner, without *citation lumps* (repeated strings of five to seven references at a time) or repeated use of the same citations more than once in a single paragraph? Does the selection of citations demonstrate an understanding of the research area, do the chosen citations capture the state of the research, and do the citations contribute to creating an integrated and coherent narrative?

HOW DOES THE EDITOR USE THE REVIEW?

The editor is the actual decision maker regarding accepting or rejecting a given manuscript. Reviewers provide content expertise and technical advice to help inform the editor about the strengths and weaknesses of a manuscript under editorial consideration. Journals and editors vary in terms of whether they ask for an accept or reject recommendation from reviewers. Some journals and editors do seek such a recommendation, and some do not. Even when recommendations of editorial decisions are allowed, however, editors do not function as mere "vote counters". Editors may, and do, reject manuscripts that all reviewers felt could be published. Likewise, editors may, and do, accept manuscripts or seek revisions of manuscripts for which all of the reviewers recommended rejection. Editors evaluate the review commentaries as well as the manuscript.

Editors use a variety of approaches in selecting or assigning reviewers. Some editors may simply select the first three experts who come to mind in relation to the research topic. Other editors may consider who would most love or hate a given manuscript and select someone from each camp, plus someone the editor believes will be more neutral. Still others might select reviewers from a pool of authors who have recently published in the journal on the same or a related topic or select a reviewer from among those who have recently volunteered to review for the journal. But in most cases, the editor selects reviewers whose expertise, ideas, and biases are known to the editor.

The editor reads the review commentary on a given manuscript knowing the identity and background of the reviewer. The editor considers whether the reviewer commented on what the editor expected the reviewer to comment on, or on something else. Did the reviewer say what he or she always says in reviews, or are there remarks unique to the current manuscript? The editor judges which criticisms are absolute problems, relative problems, and fixable problems. The editor evaluates the review commentary to determine what evaluative information it provides from the actual in-depth evaluation of the manuscript under consideration. When making an editorial decision, 30, 40, or more individual comments and criticisms are considered and weighted.

WHAT ARE THE POSSIBLE EDITORIAL OUTCOMES?

There are only three functional editorial outcomes to a submission—a manuscript is rejected (or withdrawn), a manuscript is accepted (although this rarely occurs upon first submission), or you are given an opportunity to revise and resubmit your manuscript. Although there are probably 20 different labels or phrases that are used by different journals to convey subtle differences within these actions, the possible editorial outcomes boil down, functionally, to these three outcomes.

If you have been provided the opportunity to revise and resubmit your manuscript from the journal to which you submitted it, do so. Read the editorial action letter and the review commentaries when you initially receive them and then put them aside for a few days to give yourself time to absorb and reflect on the feedback. Look for a time in your schedule when you will have 2 to 3 hours to reread all the feedback as well as write yourself some notes on what you want to revise and how. Try to do this initial rereading and planning within 2 weeks after the receipt of the editorial action letter. It is important that you are active in making your revisions within a reasonable time frame because as most journals expect the typical revision to be returned within 45 to 60 days of receipt of the opportunity to revise and resubmit. If you need additional time beyond the length of time stated by the action editor in the decision letter, you should write the action editor, explain why you need more time, and propose a specific date by which you will resubmit your revision.

Undertaking the revision of a manuscript in response to review commentary is a challenge. The revisions suggested by different reviewers may be inconsistent with each other, making it impossible to do everything the reviewers recommend. And you may have no interest in making some of the suggested changes. In most cases, in the editorial action letter the editor will have signaled to you which issues he or she believes are most essential to address, although the editor will also expect you to be responsive to editorial feedback from the reviewers that the editor did not summarize or highlight.

But remember that the manuscript is your manuscript, and it will have your name on it when published, so you need to see the merits of making any specific suggested editorial change. Reviewers' comments are ideas and suggestions meant to help you improve your manuscript. Reviewers' comments are not orders or directives. The concerns of the editor carry greater weight, but even the editor's comments are not absolute orders.

Editors typically expect the author to be responsive to the editorial feedback, but how that responsiveness is done includes a range of options. You might make a suggested change, or you might add words or sentences to your text to better describe your point. You might add more arguments to your presentation or summarize and document additional information and citations from the literature. You might conduct additional or different statistical analyses, or you might run another set of subjects and add another study to your manuscript. Or, you might just acknowledge an issue you did not address or acknowledge a limitation of your study. And in some situations, you may make no change in your manuscript around a particular point in the editorial feedback—and explain in your resubmission cover memo to the editor why you did nothing and your rationale for that. The editor will judge whether what you did or did not do is within the acceptable range of responsive actions.

Your revisions are likely to be done piecemeal and at different points in your manuscript. After you have made revisions in response to specific editorial suggestions, you should put your revision aside for a few days and come back to it again—that is, at the global level. You need to do another overarching edit of the manuscript as a total manuscript and scientific communication vehicle. Do you need to add, drop, or edit the transition material between paragraphs or sections of the manuscript? Should you reorder any topics in light of the edits made? Have you introduced duplicative material during editing? Before resubmitting, you need to do a final shaping and polishing edit of your revision.

RESUBMISSIONS: REVIEWED AGAIN OR NOT?

Journals and editors vary in terms of whether or not a first revision (and a later revision) will go through another full external peer review cycle. First revisions are more likely to receive a full rereview than are second or third versions. The greater the number of changes and the extent of the changes, the greater the likelihood that the editor will want reviewer input on your revision. The greater the reputation and prestige of a journal, the greater is the likelihood that revisions will undergo another full round of reviews. Often, in the earlier editorial action letter, the editor will state or hint at whether a full rereview will occur (or whether the editor alone will assess the adequacy of the editorial changes).

Journals and editors also vary in how they evaluate revisions. Some editors will do a full rereview of a revision without regard to its status as a revision. In this case, new reviewers (or a mix of old and new reviewers) may be used—and the reviewers might not be given a copy of your revision cover memo describing the editorial changes you have made. Other editors may do a narrow and specific rereview of your revision—using only reviewers who have seen your earlier manuscript, giving them a copy of your resubmission cover memo describing how you have responded to the earlier editorial concerns and feedback, and asking for the reviewer assessment of the adequacy of your editorial changes and the resulting revised manuscript (and whether it is now ready for publication).

The editorial outcomes of a revision are the same as those for an initial submission: reject, accept, or further revise (and resubmit again). Being invited to revise and resubmit is not a guarantee of eventual acceptance of your manuscript. In some cases, revision is needed to fully, accurately, and adequately evaluate the quality of your research and the resulting manuscript. Thus, after revision, your manuscript may be rejected. It is also the case that the editor may request further revisions. Generally, being invited to do a second revision is a good sign, and it typically means that you are now in a stage of shaping and crafting the manuscript to best meet the needs, interests, and focus of the journal and its readers. When asking for a second revision, the editor will make a clearer statement of how close to making a final decision the editor is or the editor's best guess about the final editorial outcome. Although a manuscript can be rejected after two or three revisions, the probability of that occurring decreases.

APPEALING AN EDITORIAL DECISION

Most journals and publishers allow for the possibility of appealing an editorial decision. Editorial appeals are most effective when they occur close to the level of the original decision, are handled among colleagues, and are communicated about in a cordial and collegial manner.

The editorial appeal should be made only if it is absolutely obvious that a blatant and critical mistake was the core element in the editorial decision. The procedural error should be blatant and obvious, not subjective or inferred. It should be so clear that it only takes a few lines (not several pages) to identify, and everyone hearing the summary of the problem would immediately agree. This rarely occurs in scholarly publishing, however, and subtle nuances, complex interrelationships, and thoughtful reflection are generally involved.

One should never impulsively make an editorial appeal after a manuscript is rejected. When you receive a rejection letter, you will be disappointed and possibly upset. This is understandable because considerable effort went into creating the manuscript. As one reads the review commentaries accompanying the rejection letter, intense affect may be triggered as one comment or another is read and you are shocked that the reviewer could have misunderstood the manuscript so badly or been so apparently ill-informed about relevant research or theory. It is not wise to write an appeal letter while you are actively upset. Put the material aside and come back to it after a few days (and repeat as needed).

The APA editorial appeal process is a hierarchical one. The first level of appeal is to the action editor who made the editorial decision. Such an appeal is based on the substance of the article and the review commentaries. It should be written in a thoughtful and nonaccusatory manner, and it should request that the deciding editor reconsider the editorial decision in light of the points articulated in the letter of appeal. The requested outcome should usually be an opportunity to revise and resubmit. The second level of appeal within the APA system is to the editor of the journal. This appeal is also primarily a substantive appeal, although some procedural factors may appear at this level. The third level of appeal is to the APA chief editorial advisor (CEA), and an appeal at this level is somewhat more oriented toward policy and procedure than substance. The CEA has no decision-making power or authority but rather represents a neutral party who is available to independently consider the situation and offer her or his observations to all parties. The CEA handles about 40 to 50 appeals per year across APA journals. The fourth level of appeal is to the APA Publications and Communications (P&C) Board. Appeals at this level are strictly limited to issues of policy and procedure. They are rare, occurring once every 2 to 4 years.

As noted, editorial appeals are rare. Other than the occasional appeal for the opportunity to revise and resubmit, editorial appeals are generally unproductive for both the author and the editor. Much affect may be expressed, but whether it achieves a cathartic release is questionable. Rather than wasting one's time on an editorial appeal, that time is better spent on revising and resubmitting the manuscript to another journal. Rarely is it essential to publish a given manuscript in a given journal. There are many journals in psychology, and you can readily revise and resubmit your manuscript to another journal. Appealing an editorial decision above the level of a journal editor should be a rare event that might occur once in an individual's career but probably not at all.

PLAGIARISM, SELF-PLAGIARISM, AND DUPLICATIVE PUBLICATION

Plagiarism is the presentation of the ideas, data, and written words of others as if they were your own. Plagiarism is a violation of APA's (2010a) *Ethical Principles of Psychologists and Code of Conduct* (APA Ethics Code), and it is a violation of general scholarly and academic standards (and often can be a legal violation of copyright law). When authors repeat the words of others, quotation marks should be used and the page number given for where the exact quoted material appears in the cited reference. When paraphrasing the words of another author, a citation to the source of that paraphrasing should be given at each instance of paraphrasing. In addition, an author can acknowledge the source of an idea or research design through the language used within the text of a manuscript (e.g., "This project was conceptualized after reading the 2007 exploratory study by Smith and Jones.").

Self-plagiarism is the presentation of one's earlier work or data as if it were a new scholarly contribution. This is most critical when the manuscript includes data, as compared with literature reviews of research issues and trends in findings. Of course, when an author has developed a theory or is publishing on a program of research or a longitudinal study, some republishing of identical words is undoubtedly necessary—even required. The methodology of a longitudinal study does not change, and there are only a few ways to concisely describe a theory—but best practices suggest that in the majority of cases the author should include a citation to the his or her earlier work at the point at which the reproduced words occur in the new manuscript. This should be further highlighted within the text of a manuscript (e.g., "As I have described previously . . . "). Reproduction of one's own exact words or paraphrased words is most likely to occur in the Method section and next most likely to occur as a small portion of the introduction.

Given that scholarly literature is readily available in electronic format, there is rarely a need to present the same research data and analysis to different scholarly audiences as if it were an initial report of new research. Rather, when writing for a new audience, previously published research should clearly be presented as a summary of previous research. When data from a previously published archival research article are republished in another publication (review article or book chapter), it is critical that the republished nature of the data be completely obvious to any reader. To achieve this, three or four features are essential. If the data appear in a table or figure, the legend should include a citation to the original published source. In the text of the article, the author should clearly describe the data as previously published (e.g., "In an earlier study, we found . . . "), and a citation to the original source should occur in that sentence or at the end of it. Additionally, a citation to the earlier publication should appear in the reference list. If the amount of republished data and reproduced words is large, an author footnote should also include a statement about the present article being "based on an earlier publication" or as "drawing heavily on material originally published in" another work.

A closely related topic is *piecemeal* or fragmented publication, which occurs when a single data-collection activity occurs but the results using different measures are reported in separate articles, as if they were independent projects. This is not a good practice because it can lead to the impression that more research has been conducted than is the case, and it can cause confusion and lead meta-analysts to double count a particular study. It can also result in some data never being published

(e.g., the relationship between the variables that were separately reported). Authors should, to the maximum extent possible, include all of the data from a single project in one article. When multiple articles are needed to report all aspects of a research project, each article should include clear mention and description in the text of the article about its relationship to the other articles (and include citations to those articles). It is also the responsibility of submitting authors to inform the editor of a journal of any articles, manuscripts, or conference presentations that are closely related to the submitted manuscript (and provide copies as needed).

CONFLICT OF INTEREST AND APPROPRIATE ACKNOWLEDGMENT

The topic of conflict of interest is often misunderstood. The reaction of some to the question, "Do you have a conflict of interest around this?" is the same as, say, "You are unethical" or "You have done something wrong." That is not the case. There are many kinds of conflict of interests, and what is most critical is publicly acknowledging conflict or the perception of conflict. In terms of conflict of interest involved in scientific publishing, the issue is whether, and to what extent, the author's methodology, statistical analyses, and interpretation of findings could have been influenced, positively or negatively, by economic, personal, or professional factors of which the reader might not normally be aware. The best protection for the author (and the science) is to publicly acknowledge any possible conflict. Potential conflict should be acknowledged in the author footnote of a manuscript, and if the author believes the conflict might be viewed as particularly strong by some parties, the author might note the conflict or perceived potential conflict in the submission cover letter to the editor. If one's manuscript is accepted for publication, the journal may require the author to sign a formal conflict-of-interest disclosure form.

Most typically conflict of interest is conceptualized in financial terms, but it is actually broader than that. Nonetheless, if one has a financial interest in products, services, tests, or training programs utilized or researched in an article, this is generally viewed as significant and should be disclosed. Holding the copyright to a test, holding a patent for a device or drug, or receiving royalties on any of these should be acknowledged. Being the owner of a center that trains individuals in a specific intervention or receiving extra consulting fees for teaching in such a program should be acknowledged. The above circumstances tend to generate or be perceived as generating a positive bias. The opposite is also possible, and it should be acknowledged when relevant. Consultation fees, forensic testimony fees, and technical advising fees related to tests, software, products, services, model programs, diagnoses, and so forth should also be considered for disclosure, as should membership on advisory councils, technical panels, or boards of directors. In contrast, holding stock in a mutual fund or large retirement fund is not significant enough to warrant disclosure. How direct or close the relation is between one's own interests and the object or entity in question is a relevant dimension. Holding 10% of the stock in a small company selling six products (one of which is utilized in a research project) is more direct and significant than personally holding 1,000 shares of stock in a multinational company with annual sales of $20 billion dollars that has a small unit within it that manufactures a device used in your research project.

The author's personal assessment of the significance of a possible conflict of interest may be easily different from that of the editor—or the eventual reader. Thus, it is important that the author not prejudge the significance and make the decision not to disclose (because of the self-judged minor nature of the conflict). Rather, the safest course of action is for the author to include the potential conflict-of-interest information and disclose it, draw the editor's attention to it, and ask whether it is significant enough to warrant that it be included. The editor can then make the decision in light of the journal's policy and the value to the reader. Many readers would prefer to know the facts of any perceived conflict of interest so that they can judge for themselves whether, or to what degree (and how), the interpretation of the findings might have been influenced by such factors.

Obviously, reviewers and editors also have potential conflicts of interest. Ethical standards, professional expectations for avoiding the most serious conflicted situations, and procedural safeguards exist to address these issues, but these topics are not the core of this chapter and are not discussed here. However, one particular challenge does exist in scholarly publishing that is somewhat different from other situations in which conflict of interest may arise. Editors of a given journal are selected because of their expertise in the content area of the journal. As such, they hold theoretical beliefs, advocate particular types of statistical analyses, and possibly have created specific tests or software. The editor search committee generally considers such factors before selecting a given editor, and one of the factors that they explore is whether there is evidence that the editorial candidate has supported the publication of manuscripts that run counter to the candidate's personal views and opinions in the past. It is generally believed that it is better to have an editor who is knowledgeable about a research area but might have some conflicts than to have an editor who knows nothing about a content area but has no conflicts of interests.

PUBLICATION OR AUTHORSHIP CREDIT (AND RESPONSIBILITY)

As noted in the APA *Publication Manual* (APA, 2010b), "Authorship is reserved for persons who make a substantial contribution to and who accept the responsibility for a published work" (p. 18). And, the APA Ethics Code states that "individuals should only take authorship credit for work they have actually performed or to which they have substantially contributed" (Standard 8.12a), and "principal authorship and the order of authorship credit should accurately reflect the relative contributions of the persons involved" (Standard 8.12b).

To warrant authorship credit, an individual should contribute to the research and the reporting of it in one or more of several ways. Research activities generally viewed as representing significant scientific contributions include conceptually formulating the research question and research hypotheses, creating the experimental design of the research project, conceptualizing and performing the statistical analyses, interpreting the results and noting the limitations of the results, and making a substantial contribution to the writing and editing of the manuscript. As described in the APA *Publication Manual* (APA, 2010b), lesser contributions, which alone do not constitute sufficient contributions to warrant authorship credit, include designing and building apparatus, general advising on statistical analyses, collecting or entering data, modifying or structuring a computer program, recruiting participants or obtaining animals, and conducting routine observations or diagnoses. However, performing some combination of these tasks might rise to the level of warranting authorship credit. Contributions on a level lower than authorship should be acknowledged in the author footnote, and it is the author's responsibility to secure the permission of individuals to be mentioned in an author footnote to be so acknowledged. And, finally, at least in the field of American psychology, so-called honorary authorship credits for being the head of an institution or laboratory are not given if the individual has not actively contributed to the specific research project being reported in a given publication.

It is generally recommended that when a group is developing the ideas and design of a research project, they should discuss and document their initial thinking on the order of authorship on the basis of their expected relative contributions. This discussion should include assigning the tasks of data collection and management, initial and in-depth statistical analyses, and initial drafting of the manuscript or specific portions of it. This initial discussion and planning of the project and its eventual publication should also include a discussion of how the group will address changes in the work that finally occurs and how they will factor that into any changes in the authorship order of the submitted manuscript (including the dropping of planned authors and the possible addition of new authors). It is important for a research group to document such a discussion earlier on in a project because plans do change in light of changes in events in the lives of the individuals who make up the research team.

The basic principle in determining authorship order is the relative contribution of each party. The first author should be the principal contributor to the project and its publication (overall and across all of the possible tasks and roles). Each successive author listed should have made a corresponding lesser contribution to the research and publication. These are the core principles of authorship order within the field of psychology, but these principles can vary in other disciplines. And, in the field of psychology, relative status (e.g., full professor vs. assistant professor, faculty member vs. student, department chair vs. regular faculty member, laboratory chief vs. regular laboratory researcher) should not play a role in determining the order of authorship, although some variation does occur in other disciplines. If the contribution of two authors is viewed as equal, this information can be noted and described in the author footnote. The research involvement and contribution of students, at varying levels, in relationship to authorship credit and authorship order can be complex and needs special attention and consideration, so as to neither give too much or too little credit to their contribution. The APA *Publication Manual* (APA, 2010b, p. 19) provides guidance on such matters.

References

American Psychological Association. (2010a). *Ethical principles of psychologists and code of conduct (2002, Amended June 1, 2010)*. Retrieved from http://www.apa.org/ethics/code/index.aspx

American Psychological Association. (2010b). *Publication manual of the American Psychological Association* (6th ed.). Washington, DC: Author.

American Psychological Association Publications and Communications Board Working Group on Journal Article Reporting Standards. (2008). Reporting standards for research in psychology: Why do we need them? What might they be? *American Psychologist, 63,* 839–851.

CONSORT: Transparent Reporting of Trials. (2007). *Consolidated standards of reporting trials.* Retrieved from http://www.consort-statement.org

Des Jarlais, D. C., Lyles, C., Crepaz, N., & the TREND Group. (2004). Improving the reporting quality of nonrandomized evaluations of behavioral and public health interventions: The TREND statement. *American Journal of Public Health, 94,* 361–366. Retrieved from http://www.cdc.gov/trendstatement and http://www.cdc.gov/trendstatement/docs/AJPH_Mar2004_Trendstatement.pdf

Index

Volume numbers are printed in boldface type, followed by a colon and the relevant page numbers.

Alphabetization strategies, question order experiments, 1: 245

Alpha coefficient, Cronbach's, 1: 357, 359–361, 377, 629, 651–653

Alpha-frequency TMS, 1: 594

Alpha power, 1: 511–513

Alpha value correction, fMRI studies, 1: 552–553

ALT (autoregressive latent trajectory), 1: 279

Alternate types, in CA, 2: 107–108

Alternating current stimulation, transcranial, 1: 613, 614

Alternating k-star parameter, Markov random graph models, 3: 465

Alternating treatments design (ATD), 2: 604–605

Alternative distributions, 1: 187–188

Alternative fit indexes, 2: 351, 352–353; 3: 258–259

Alternative forms, in repeated measures designs, 3: 250

Alternative hypothesis, group comparison approach, 2: 590

Alternative models approach, SEM, 2: 338, 356–357

Alters, social network research, 3: 452–453, 458, 459

Altman, D. G., 1: 200

Altshuler, D., 2: 693

Amazon Mechanical Turk, 2: 304

Ambient noise, in psychophysiological research, 1: 463–464

Ambiguity
    in projective tests, 1: 330, 332
    research questions generating, 1: 122
    of word *projective*, 1: 330–331

Ambivalence, and question order effects, 1: 242

Amedi, A., 1: 596

Amended versions, NIH grant applications, 1: 154–155

American Psychological Association (APA). *See also* Ethics Code, APA
    editorial appeal process, 3: 529
    literature searches, 1: 140
    publication guidelines, 3: 503, 508, 513–514
    research with nonhuman animals, 1: 81
    Task Force on External Funding, 1: 69

American Statistical Association, 1: 135

Amodio, D. M., 1: 512

AMOS software, 2: 349

Amplification of meaning, 1: 19–20

Amplifiers
    in combined EEG and fMRI, 1: 587
    concurrent TMS–EEG, 1: 595
    EMG, 1: 477

Amplitude, peak value when quantifying ERP components, 1: 540, 542

Amplitude domain, EMG signal, 1: 478–479

Amygdala, 1: 466

Anacona, I., 1: 282

Analgesics, in animal research, 1: 79

Analogies, to describe causal processes, 3: 324

Analyse-It Software, 1: 735

Analysis. *See also* Automated computer analyses of verbal content; Data analysis; Statistical analysis
    in causal models, 1: 42–44
    of interviews, 1: 272
    levels of, in cross-cultural research, 1: 91, 93
    narrative methods, 2: 89–92
    recording skeletomotor activity, 1: 478
    status of in qualitative research, 1: 9

Analysis model, MI, 3: 29, 34–35, 39, 44

Analysis of covariance (ANCOVA), 1: 497; 2: 494–498, 514–515, 518

Analysis of variance (ANOVA), 3: 163–179
    analyzing mean differences, 3: 165–167, 168–172
    asserting equivalence between groups, 3: 178–179
    cell means approach, 3: 168–172
    comparing group means with, 3: 67
    controlling family-wise error rates, 3: 176–177
    displays of means, 3: 125–128
    and EDA, 3: 62–66, 69
    in ERP research, 1: 543
    factorial, 1: 177; 3: 62, 169–170, 172
    hormone assays, 1: 497
    indexes of effect size, 3: 178
    interactions, 3: 101, 120–128, 177–178
    Internet-based research, 2: 306
    interrater reliability, 1: 649–651
    issues in application of, 3: 172–179
    model-based analysis, 3: 163–165, 167–168
    moderator analysis for meta-analysis, 3: 495–496
    one-way, 3: 405–406
    outliers, 3: 174–175

overview, 3: 163

power of, and outlier RTs, 1: 434–435

robust alternatives to, 3: 175–176

violations of homogeneity of variance and normality, 3: 173–174

Analytical approaches
    mathematical psychology, 2: 375
    visual research, 2: 197–199

Analytical integration, 2: 417

Analytic generalizations, case study methods, 2: 148–149

Analytic rotation, EFA, 3: 371

Analytic units, observational sessions as, 1: 207–208

Analyze-as-treated estimate, RD designs, 2: 521

Anastasi, A., 1: 127

Anatomical modularity, 2: 636

Anatomy and physiology, 1: 465, 471–472

Ancestors, in PCM, 1: 30, 31

Ancestry, in genetic research, 2: 673

Ancestry approach to literature searches, 1: 142

Anchoring graphic displays of data, 3: 80–82

ANCOVA (analysis of covariance), 1: 497; 2: 494–498, 514–515, 518

Andrich, D., 1: 717

Anesthetics, in animal research, 1: 79

Anger, and frontal alpha power asymmetry, 1: 512–514

Angoff, W. H., 1: 379

Angoff method, 1: 389

Animal and Plant Health Inspection Service (APHIS), USDA, 1: 79

Animal Care Annual Report of Activities, USDA, 1: 79

Animal research, 1: 75–81; 2: 556–557

Animal rights, 1: 76

Animal welfare, 1: 76–78

Animal Welfare Act Regulations (AWARs), 1: 81

Animal Welfare Assurances, 1: 77

Annotating graphic displays of data, 3: 82

Announcements, NIH, 1: 146, 148

Annual protocol reviews, by IACUCs, 1: 79

Anode-cathode electrode montage, tDCS, 1: 611, 613

Anomalous words, fixating on in reading, 1: 420

Anonymity
    in visual research, 2: 202
    and web surveys, 2: 295